Financial Accounting Fundamentals

7th edition

John J. Wild
University of Wisconsin at Madison

McGraw Hill Education

To my students and family, especially Kimberly, Jonathan, Stephanie, and Trevor.

FINANCIAL ACCOUNTING FUNDAMENTALS, SEVENTH EDITION

Published by McGraw-Hill Education, 2 Penn Plaza, New York, NY 10121. Copyright ©2019 by McGraw-Hill Education. All rights reserved. Printed in the United States of America. Previous editions ©2018, 2016, and 2013. No part of this publication may be reproduced or distributed in any form or by any means, or stored in a database or retrieval system, without the prior written consent of McGraw-Hill Education, including, but not limited to, in any network or other electronic storage or transmission, or broadcast for distance learning.

Some ancillaries, including electronic and print components, may not be available to customers outside the United States.

This book is printed on acid-free paper.

1 2 3 4 5 6 7 8 9 LWI 21 20 19 18

ISBN 978-1-260-24786-2 (bound edition)
MHID 1-260-24786-4 (bound edition)
ISBN 978-1-260-48286-7 (loose-leaf edition)
MHID 1-260-48286-3 (loose-leaf edition)

Executive Portfolio Manager: *Steve Schuetz*
Product Developers: *Michael McCormick, Christina Sanders*
Marketing Manager: *Michelle Williams*
Content Project Managers: *Lori Koetters, Brian Nacik*
Buyer: *Sandy Ludovissy*
Design: *Debra Kubiak*
Content Licensing Specialist: *Melissa Homer*
Cover Image: *Runner: ©Maridav/Shutterstock; Statistics icons: ©A-spring/Shutterstock;*
  Background image: ©Vector work/Shutterstock
Compositor: *Aptara®, Inc.*

All credits appearing on page or at the end of the book are considered to be an extension of the copyright page.

Library of Congress Control Number: 2018959693

The Internet addresses listed in the text were accurate at the time of publication. The inclusion of a website does not indicate an endorsement by the authors or McGraw-Hill Education, and McGraw-Hill Education does not guarantee the accuracy of the information presented at these sites.

About the Author

Courtesy of John J. Wild

JOHN J. WILD is a distinguished professor of accounting at the University of Wisconsin at Madison. He previously held appointments at Michigan State University and the University of Manchester in England. He received his BBA, MS, and PhD from the University of Wisconsin.

John teaches accounting courses at both the undergraduate and graduate levels. He has received numerous teaching honors, including the Mabel W. Chipman Excellence-in-Teaching Award and the departmental Excellence-in-Teaching Award, and he is a two-time recipient of the Teaching Excellence Award from business graduates at the University of Wisconsin. He also received the Beta Alpha Psi and Roland F. Salmonson Excellence-in-Teaching Award from Michigan State University. John has received several research honors, is a past KPMG Peat Marwick National Fellow, and is a recipient of fellowships from the American Accounting Association and the Ernst and Young Foundation.

John is an active member of the American Accounting Association and its sections. He has served on several committees of these organizations, including the Outstanding Accounting Educator Award, Wildman Award, National Program Advisory, Publications, and Research Committees. John is author of *Financial Accounting, Managerial Accounting, Fundamental Accounting Principles,* and *College Accounting,* all published by McGraw-Hill Education.

John's research articles on accounting and analysis appear in *The Accounting Review; Journal of Accounting Research; Journal of Accounting and Economics; Contemporary Accounting Research; Journal of Accounting, Auditing and Finance; Journal of Accounting and Public Policy; Accounting Horizons;* and other journals. He is past associate editor of *Contemporary Accounting Research* and has served on several editorial boards including *The Accounting Review* and the *Journal of Accounting and Public Policy.*

In his leisure time, John enjoys hiking, sports, boating, travel, people, and spending time with family and friends.

Author Letter   Using Learning Science and Data Analytics

We use data to make decisions and maximize performance. Like the runner on the cover who uses data to track her progress, we used student performance data to identify content areas that can be made more direct, concise, and systematic.

Learning science reveals that students do not read large chunks of text, so we streamlined this edition to present it in a more focused, succinct, blocked format to improve student learning and retention. Our new edition delivers the same content in 96 fewer pages. Visual aids and numerous videos offer additional learning aids. New summary Cheat Sheets conclude each chapter to visually reinforce key concepts and procedures.

Our new edition has over 1,000 videos to engage students and improve outcomes:

- **Concept Overview Videos**—cover each chapter's learning objectives with multimedia presentations that include Knowledge Checks to engage students and assess comprehension.
- **Need-to-Know Demos**—walk-through demonstrations of key procedures and analysis to ensure success with assignments and tests.
- **Guided Examples (Hints)**—step-by-step walk-through of assignments that mimic Quick Studies, Exercises, and General Ledger.

Difference Makers in Teaching . . .

Learning Science

Learning analytics show that students learn better when material is broken into "blocks" of content. Each chapter opens with a visual preview. Learning objective numbers highlight the location of related content. Each "block" of content concludes with a Need-to-Know (NTK) to aid and reinforce student learning. Visual aids and concise, bullet-point discussions further help students learn.

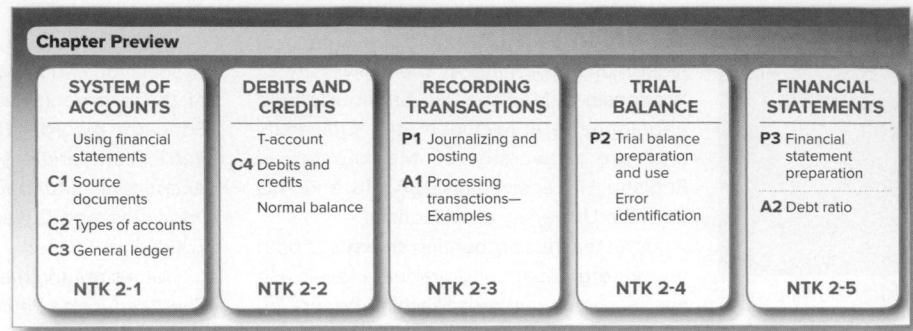

Chapter Preview

SYSTEM OF ACCOUNTS	DEBITS AND CREDITS	RECORDING TRANSACTIONS	TRIAL BALANCE	FINANCIAL STATEMENTS
Using financial statements	T-account	**P1** Journalizing and posting	**P2** Trial balance preparation and use	**P3** Financial statement preparation
C1 Source documents	**C4** Debits and credits	**A1** Processing transactions—Examples	Error identification	**A2** Debt ratio
C2 Types of accounts	Normal balance			
C3 General ledger				
NTK 2-1	NTK 2-2	NTK 2-3	NTK 2-4	NTK 2-5

Sales Discounts, Returns, and Allowances—Adjusting Entries Revenue recognition rules require sales to be reported at the amount expected to be received. This means that period-end adjusting entries are commonly made for

- Expected sales discounts.
- Expected returns and allowances (revenue side).
- Expected returns and allowances (cost side).

These three adjustments produce three new accounts: Allowance for Sales Discounts, Sales Refund Payable, and Inventory Returns Estimated. Appendix 4B covers these accounts and the adjusting entries.

New Revenue Recognition

- Wild uses the popular gross method for merchandising transactions (net method is covered in an appendix). The gross method is widely used in practice and best for student success.
- Adjusting entries for new revenue recognition rules are included in an appendix. Assignments are clearly marked and separated. Wild is GAAP compliant.

Up-to-Date

This book reflects changes in accounting for revenue recognition, investments, leases, and extraordinary items. It is important that students learn GAAP accounting.

Less Is More

Wild has markedly fewer pages than competing books covering the same material.
- The text is to the point and uses visuals to aid student learning.
- Bullet-point discussions and active writing aid learning.
- The 7th edition has 96 fewer pages than the 6th edition—a 10% reduction!

Visual Learning

- Learning analytics tell us today's students do not read large blocks of text. Wild has adapted to student needs by having informative visual aids throughout. Many visuals and exhibits are new to this edition.

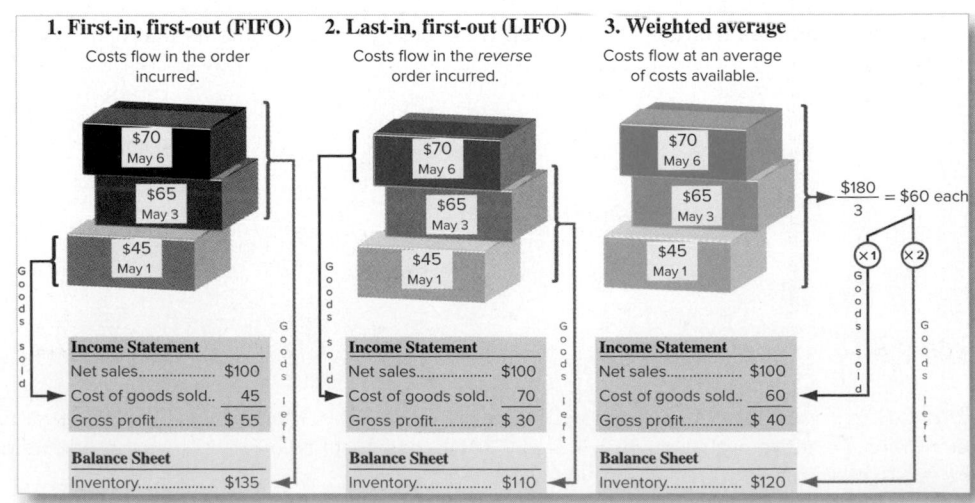

Videos

- A growing number of students now learn accounting online. **Wild offers over 1,000** videos designed to increase student engagement and improve outcomes.
- Hundreds of hint videos or Guided Examples provide a narrated, animated, step-by-step walk-through of select exercises similar to those assigned. These short presentations, which can be turned on or off by instructors, provide reinforcement when students need it most. (Exercise PowerPoints are available for instructors.)
- Concept Overview Videos cover each chapter's learning objectives with narrated, animated presentations that frequently assess comprehension.

Three adjusting entries:

Expected sales discounts.

Expected sales returns & allowances (revenue).

Expected sales returns & allowances (cost).

Need-to-Know Demos

Need-to-Know demonstrations are located at key junctures in each chapter. These demonstrations pose questions about the material just presented—content that students "need to know" to learn accounting. Accompanying solutions walk students through key procedures and analysis necessary to be successful with homework and test materials.

Need-to-Know demonstrations are supplemented with narrated, animated, step-by-step walk-through videos led by an instructor and available via **Connect**.

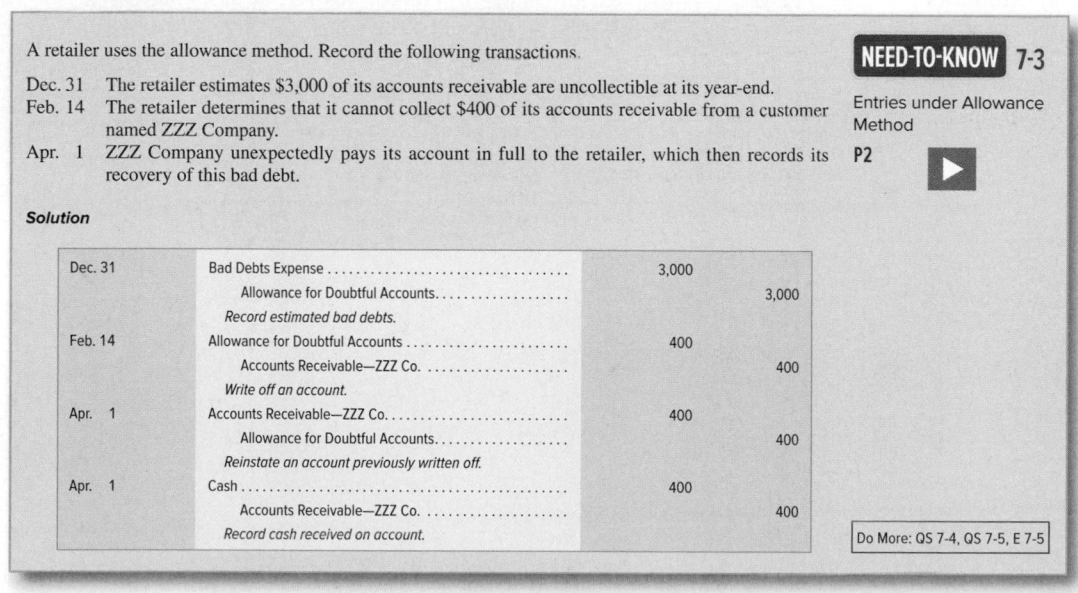

A retailer uses the allowance method. Record the following transactions.

NEED-TO-KNOW 7-3

Dec. 31   The retailer estimates $3,000 of its accounts receivable are uncollectible at its year-end.

Feb. 14   The retailer determines that it cannot collect $400 of its accounts receivable from a customer named ZZZ Company.

Entries under Allowance Method

Apr. 1   ZZZ Company unexpectedly pays its account in full to the retailer, which then records its recovery of this bad debt.

P2

Solution

Dec. 31	Bad Debts Expense	3,000	
	Allowance for Doubtful Accounts.		3,000
	Record estimated bad debts.		
Feb. 14	Allowance for Doubtful Accounts	400	
	Accounts Receivable—ZZZ Co.		400
	Write off an account.		
Apr. 1	Accounts Receivable—ZZZ Co.	400	
	Allowance for Doubtful Accounts.		400
	Reinstate an account previously written off.		
Apr. 1	Cash	400	
	Accounts Receivable—ZZZ Co.		400
	Record cash received on account.		

Do More: QS 7-4, QS 7-5, E 7-5

Comprehensive Need-to-Know   Comprehensive Need-to-Knows are problems that draw on material from the entire chapter. They include a complete solution, allowing students to review the entire problem-solving process and achieve success.

Difference Makers in Teaching . . .

Driving Decisions

Whether we prepare, analyze, or apply accounting information, one skill remains essential: decision making. To help develop good decision-making habits and to show the relevance of accounting, we use a learning framework.

- **Decision Insight** provides context for business decisions.
- **Decision Ethics** and **Decision Maker** are role-playing scenarios that show the relevance of accounting.
- **Decision Analysis** provides key tools to assess company performance.

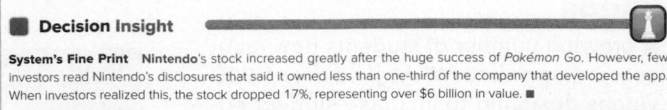

■ Decision Insight ━━━━━━━━━━━━━━━━━━━

System's Fine Print   Nintendo's stock increased greatly after the huge success of *Pokémon Go*. However, few investors read Nintendo's disclosures that said it owned less than one-third of the company that developed the app. When investors realized this, the stock dropped 17%, representing over $6 billion in value. ■

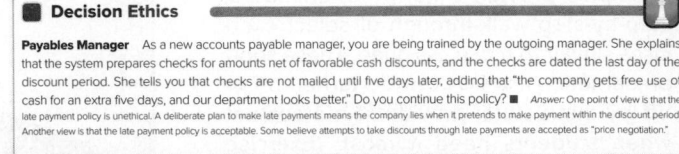

■ Decision Ethics ━━━━━━━━━━━━━━━━━━━

Payables Manager   As a new accounts payable manager, you are being trained by the outgoing manager. She explains that the system prepares checks for amounts net of favorable cash discounts, and the checks are dated the last day of the discount period. She tells you that checks are not mailed until five days later, adding that "the company gets free use of cash for an extra five days, and our department looks better." Do you continue this policy? ■   *Answer:* One point of view is that the late payment policy is unethical. A deliberate plan to make late payments means the company lies when it pretends to make payment within the discount period. Another view is that the late payment policy is acceptable. Some believe attempts to take discounts through late payments are accepted as "price negotiation."

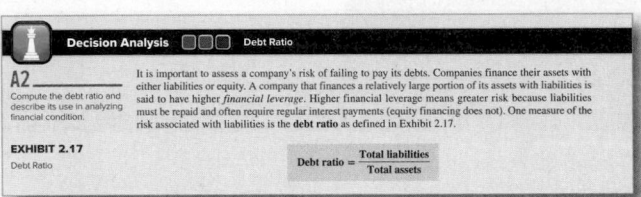

Decision Analysis ☐☐☐   **Debt Ratio**

A2
Compute the debt ratio and describe its use in analyzing financial condition.

It is important to assess a company's risk of failing to pay its debts. Companies finance their assets with either liabilities or equity. A company that finances a relatively large portion of its assets with liabilities is said to have higher *financial leverage*. Higher financial leverage means greater risk because liabilities must be repaid and often require regular interest payments (equity financing does not). One measure of the risk associated with liabilities is the **debt ratio** as defined in Exhibit 2.17.

EXHIBIT 2.17
Debt Ratio

$$\text{Debt ratio} = \frac{\text{Total liabilities}}{\text{Total assets}}$$

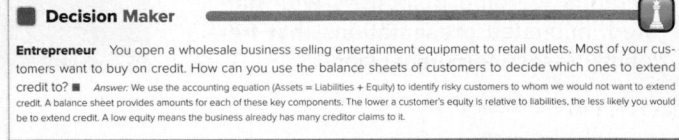

■ Decision Maker ━━━━━━━━━━━━━━━━━━━

Entrepreneur   You open a wholesale business selling entertainment equipment to retail outlets. Most of your customers want to buy on credit. How can you use the balance sheets of customers to decide which ones to extend credit to? ■   *Answer:* We use the accounting equation (Assets = Liabilities + Equity) to identify risky customers to whom we would not want to extend credit. A balance sheet provides amounts for each of these key components. The lower a customer's equity is relative to liabilities, the less likely you would be to extend credit. A low equity means the business already has many creditor claims to it.

Accounting Analytics

New to this edition, Accounting Analysis assignments have students evaluate the most current financial statements from Apple, Google, and Samsung. Students compute key metrics and compare performance between companies and industry.

These assignments are auto-gradable in Connect and are included after Problem Set B in the text.

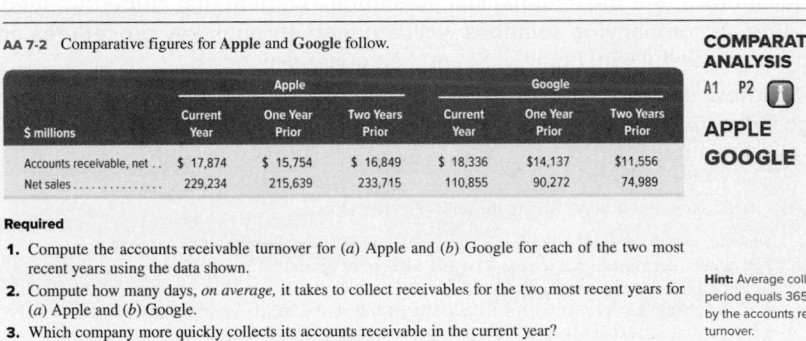

AA 7-2   Comparative figures for **Apple** and **Google** follow.

COMPARATIVE ANALYSIS

A1   P2

APPLE
GOOGLE

$ millions	Apple			Google		
	Current Year	One Year Prior	Two Years Prior	Current Year	One Year Prior	Two Years Prior
Accounts receivable, net ..	$ 17,874	$ 15,754	$ 16,849	$ 18,336	$14,137	$11,556
Net sales	229,234	215,639	233,715	110,855	90,272	74,989

Required

1. Compute the accounts receivable turnover for (*a*) Apple and (*b*) Google for each of the two most recent years using the data shown.
2. Compute how many days, *on average*, it takes to collect receivables for the two most recent years for (*a*) Apple and (*b*) Google.
3. Which company more quickly collects its accounts receivable in the current year?

Hint: Average collection period equals 365 divided by the accounts receivable turnover.

Cheat Sheets

New to this edition, Cheat Sheets are provided at the end of each chapter. Cheat Sheets are roughly one page in length and include key procedures, concepts, journal entries, and formulas.

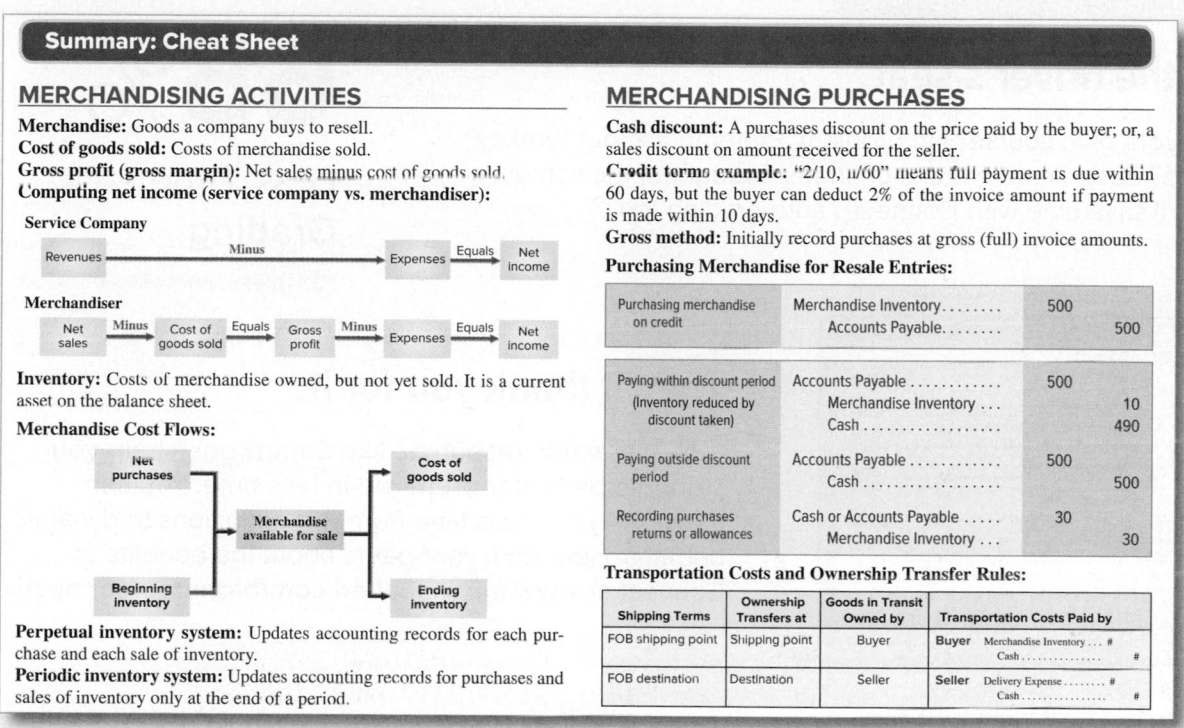

Summary: Cheat Sheet

MERCHANDISING ACTIVITIES

Merchandise: Goods a company buys to resell.
Cost of goods sold: Costs of merchandise sold.
Gross profit (gross margin): Net sales minus cost of goods sold.
Computing net income (service company vs. merchandiser):

Service Company

Revenues → Minus → Expenses → Equals → Net income

Merchandiser

Net sales → Minus → Cost of goods sold → Equals → Gross profit → Minus → Expenses → Equals → Net income

Inventory: Costs of merchandise owned, but not yet sold. It is a current asset on the balance sheet.

Merchandise Cost Flows:

Net purchases → Merchandise available for sale → Cost of goods sold
Beginning inventory → Merchandise available for sale → Ending inventory

Perpetual inventory system: Updates accounting records for each purchase and each sale of inventory.
Periodic inventory system: Updates accounting records for purchases and sales of inventory only at the end of a period.

MERCHANDISING PURCHASES

Cash discount: A purchases discount on the price paid by the buyer; or, a sales discount on amount received for the seller.
Credit terms example: "2/10, n/60" means full payment is due within 60 days, but the buyer can deduct 2% of the invoice amount if payment is made within 10 days.
Gross method: Initially record purchases at gross (full) invoice amounts.

Purchasing Merchandise for Resale Entries:

| Purchasing merchandise on credit | Merchandise Inventory........ | 500 | |
| | Accounts Payable........ | | 500 |

Paying within discount period (Inventory reduced by discount taken)	Accounts Payable	500	
	Merchandise Inventory ...		10
	Cash		490
Paying outside discount period	Accounts Payable	500	
	Cash		500
Recording purchases returns or allowances	Cash or Accounts Payable	30	
	Merchandise Inventory ...		30

Transportation Costs and Ownership Transfer Rules:

Shipping Terms	Ownership Transfers at	Goods in Transit Owned by	Transportation Costs Paid by		
FOB shipping point	Shipping point	Buyer	Buyer	Merchandise Inventory ... #	
				Cash	#
FOB destination	Destination	Seller	Seller	Delivery Expense .... #	
				Cash	#

Keep It Real

Research shows that students learn best when using current data from real companies. Wild uses the most current data from real companies for assignments, examples, and analysis in the text. See Chapter 13 for use of real data.

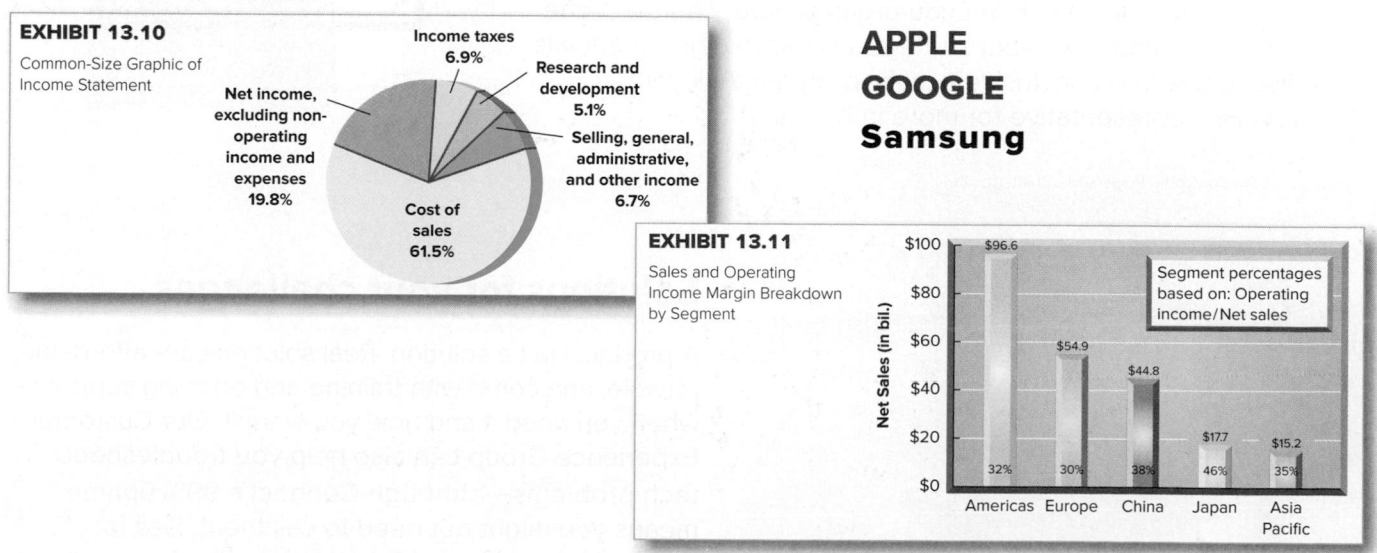

EXHIBIT 13.10

Common-Size Graphic of Income Statement

Income taxes 6.9%
Research and development 5.1%
Net income, excluding non-operating income and expenses 19.8%
Selling, general, administrative, and other income 6.7%
Cost of sales 61.5%

APPLE
GOOGLE
Samsung

EXHIBIT 13.11

Sales and Operating Income Margin Breakdown by Segment

Segment percentages based on: Operating income/Net sales

Net Sales (in bil.)

$100 — Americas $96.6, 32%
$80 — Europe $54.9, 30%
$60 —
$40 — China $44.8, 38%
$20 — Japan $17.7, 46%; Asia Pacific $15.2, 35%
$0 —

Americas   Europe   China   Japan   Asia Pacific

Students—study more efficiently, retain more and achieve better outcomes. Instructors—focus on what you love—teaching.

SUCCESSFUL SEMESTERS INCLUDE CONNECT

FOR INSTRUCTORS

You're in the driver's seat.

Want to build your own course? No problem. Prefer to use our turnkey, prebuilt course? Easy. Want to make changes throughout the semester? Sure. And you'll save time with Connect's auto-grading too.

65%
Less Time Grading

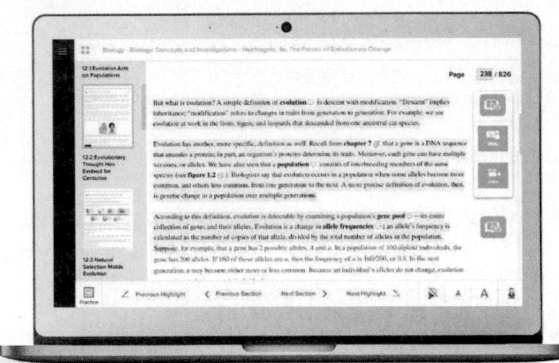

They'll thank you for it.

Adaptive study resources like SmartBook® help your students be better prepared in less time. You can transform your class time from dull definitions to dynamic debates. Hear from your peers about the benefits of Connect at **www.mheducation.com/highered/connect**

Make it simple, make it affordable.

Connect makes it easy with seamless integration using any of the major Learning Management Systems—Blackboard®, Canvas, and D2L, among others—to let you organize your course in one convenient location. Give your students access to digital materials at a discount with our inclusive access program. Ask your McGraw-Hill representative for more information.

©Hill Street Studios/Tobin Rogers/Blend Images LLC

Solutions for your challenges.

A product isn't a solution. Real solutions are affordable, reliable, and come with training and ongoing support when you need it and how you want it. Our Customer Experience Group can also help you troubleshoot tech problems—although Connect's 99% uptime means you might not need to call them. See for yourself at **status.mheducation.com**

FOR STUDENTS

Effective, efficient studying.

Connect helps you be more productive with your study time and get better grades using tools like SmartBook, which highlights key concepts and creates a personalized study plan. Connect sets you up for success, so you walk into class with confidence and walk out with better grades.

> **"** I really liked this app—it made it easy to study when you don't have your textbook in front of you.**"**
>
> - Jordan Cunningham,
> Eastern Washington University

Study anytime, anywhere.

Download the free ReadAnywhere app and access your online eBook when it's convenient, even if you're offline. And since the app automatically syncs with your eBook in Connect, all of your notes are available every time you open it. Find out more at **www.mheducation.com/readanywhere**

No surprises.

The Connect Calendar and Reports tools keep you on track with the work you need to get done and your assignment scores. Life gets busy; Connect tools help you keep learning through it all.

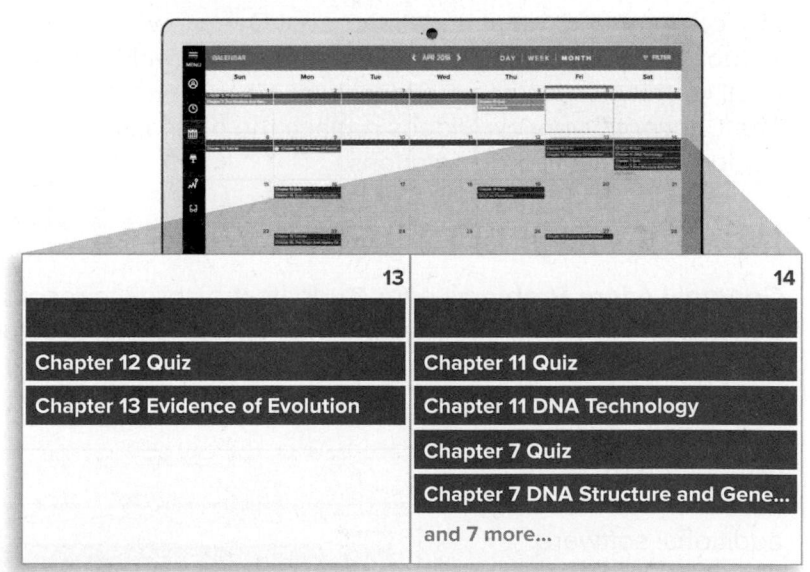

13	14
Chapter 12 Quiz	Chapter 11 Quiz
Chapter 13 Evidence of Evolution	Chapter 11 DNA Technology
	Chapter 7 Quiz
	Chapter 7 DNA Structure and Gene...
	and 7 more...

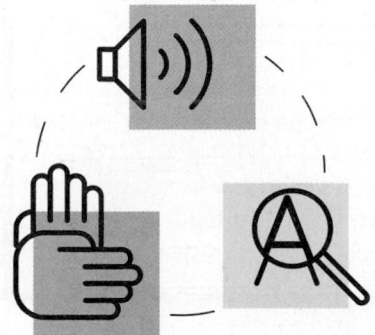

Learning for everyone.

McGraw-Hill works directly with Accessibility Services Departments and faculty to meet the learning needs of all students. Please contact your Accessibility Services office and ask them to email accessibility@mheducation.com, or visit **www.mheducation.com/accessibility** for more information.

SUPERIOR ASSIGNMENTS

Connect helps students learn more efficiently by providing feedback and practice material when they need it, where they need it. Connect grades homework automatically and gives immediate feedback.

- Wild has auto-gradable and algorithmic assignments; most focus on one learning objective and are targeted at introductory students.
- 90% of Wild's Quick Study, Exercise, and Problem Set A assignments are available in Connect with algorithmic options.
- Over 150 assignments new to this edition—all available in Connect with algorithmic options. Nearly all are Quick Studies (brief exercises) and Exercises.

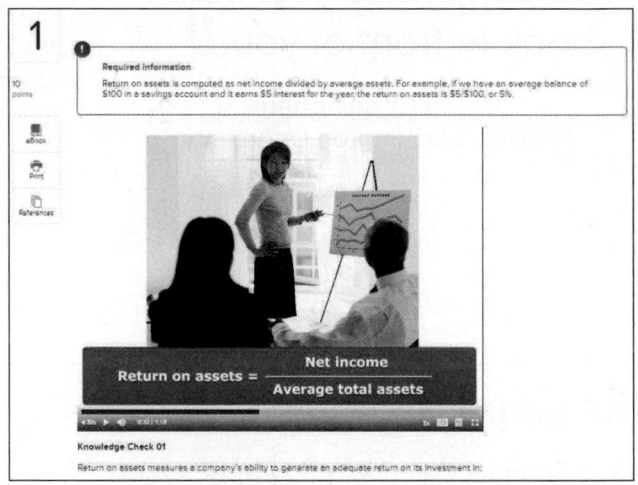

NEW! Concept Overview Videos

Concept Overview Videos teach each chapter's learning objectives through an engaging multimedia presentation. These learning tools enhance the text through video, audio, and checkpoint questions that can be graded—ensuring students complete and comprehend the material. Concept Overview Videos harness the power of technology to appeal to all learning styles and are ideal in all class formats. The Concept Overview Videos replace the previous edition's Interactive Presentations.

General Ledger Problems

General Ledger Problems offer students the ability to record financial transactions and see how these transactions flow into financial statements. Easy minimal-scroll navigation, instant "Check My Work" feedback, and fully integrated hyperlinking across tabs show how inputted data affect each stage of the accounting process. General Ledger Problems expose students to general ledger software similar to that in practice, without the expense and hassle of downloading additional software. Algorithmic versions are available. **All are auto-gradable.**

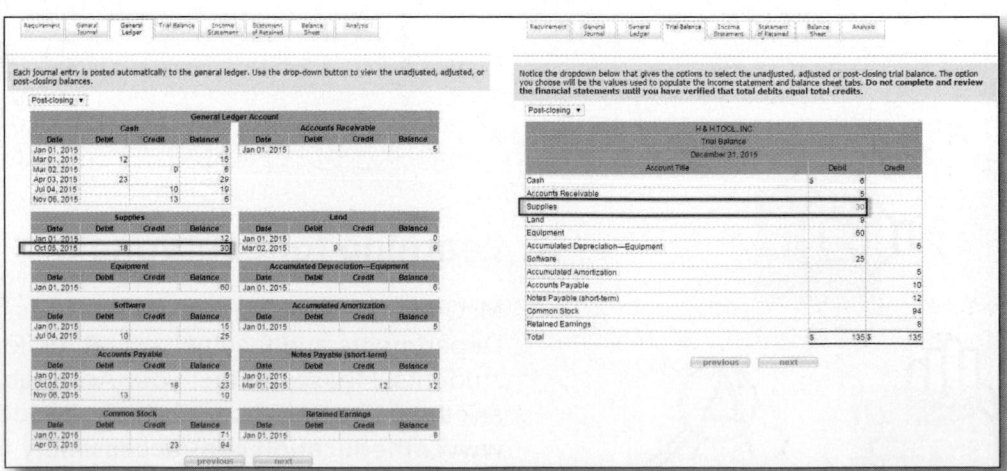

NEW! Applying Excel

Applying Excel enables students to work select chapter problems or examples in Excel. These problems are assignable in Connect and give students instant feedback as they work through the problems in Excel. Accompanying Excel videos teach students how to use Excel and the primary functions needed to complete the assignment. Short assessments can be assigned to test student comprehension of key Excel skills.

Excel Simulations

Simulated Excel Questions, assignable within Connect, allow students to practice their Excel skills—such as basic formulas and formatting—within the context of accounting. These questions feature animated, narrated Help and Show Me tutorials (when enabled), as well as automatic feedback and grading for both students and professors. These questions differ from Applying Excel in that students work in a simulated version of Excel. *Downloading the Excel application is **not** required to complete Simulated Excel Questions.*

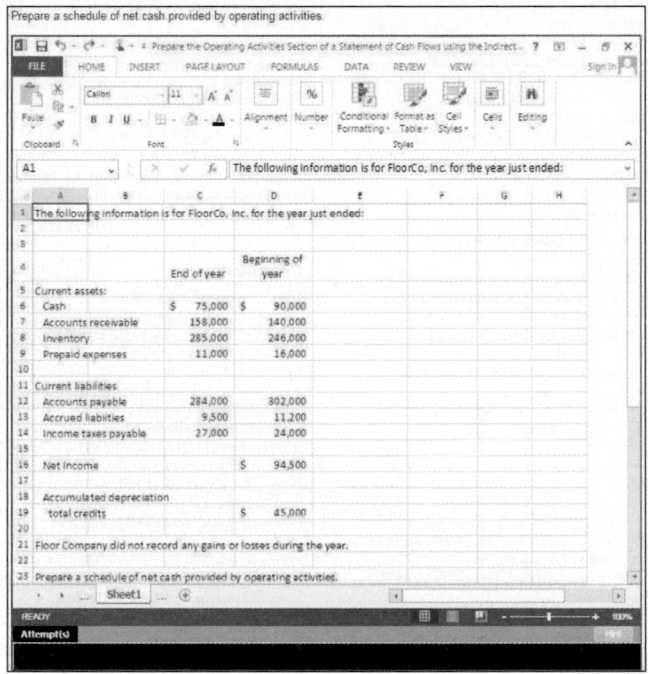

Guided Examples

The **Guided Examples** (*Hints*) in Connect provide a narrated, animated, step-by-step walk-through of most Quick Studies, Exercises, and General Ledger Problems similar to those assigned. These short presentations can be turned on or off by instructors and provide reinforcement when students need it most.

Exercise Presentations

Animated PowerPoints, created from text assignments, enable instructors to be fully prepared for in-class demonstrations. Instructors also can use these with Tegrity (in Connect) to record online lectures.

Content Revisions Enhance Learning

Instructors and students guided this edition's revisions. Revisions include

- New **Cheat Sheets** at each chapter-end visually reinforce key chapter concepts.
- More concise text covering the same content. New 7th edition has 96 fewer pages than 6th edition.
- Over 150 new assignments—all available in Connect with algorithmic options.
- Gross method is used for merchandising transactions, reflecting practice—adjusting entries for new revenue recognition rules are set in an appendix.
- Revised Investments appendix for the new standard.

- New **Accounting Analysis** assignments—all available in Connect— using real-world data from **Apple**, **Google**, and **Samsung**.
- Many new and revised **General Ledger** and **Excel** assignments.
- New assignments that focus on financial statement preparation.
- Updated videos for each learning objective in new **Concept Overview Video** format.
- Many new **Need-to-Know (NTK)** demos and accompanying videos to reinforce learning.

Chapter 1

Updated opener—**Apple** and entrepreneurial assignment.
Updated salary info for accountants.
Revised business entity section along with adding LLC.
Updated section on FASB objectives and accounting constraints.
New layout for introducing the expanded accounting equation.
New layout for introducing financial statements.
Updated **Apple** numbers for NTK 1-5.
New Cheat Sheet reinforces chapter content.
Updated return on assets analysis using **Nike** and **Under Armour**.
Added a new Exercise assignment and Quick Study assignment.
Added new analysis assignments: Company Analysis, Comparative Analysis, and Global Analysis.

Chapter 2

NEW opener—**Fitbit** and entrepreneurial assignment.
New visual for process to get from transactions to financial statements.
New layout on four types of accounts that determine equity.
Improved presentation of "Double-Entry System" section.
Updated **Apple** data for NTK 2-4.
Updated debt ratio analysis using **Costco** and **Walmart**.
New Cheat Sheet reinforces chapter content.
Added four new Quick Studies.
Added three new Exercises.
Added new analysis assignments: Company Analysis, Comparative Analysis, and Global Analysis.

Chapter 3

NEW opener—**Snapchat** and entrepreneurial assignment.
Revised learning objectives and chapter preview—each type of adjusting entry is assigned its own learning objective.
Updated "Recognizing Revenues and Expenses" section.
New streamlined "Framework for Adjustments" section.
Enhanced Exhibit 3.12 on summary of adjustments.
Enhanced Exhibit 3.19 on steps of accounting cycle with images.

Streamlined section on classified balance sheet.
Updated profit margin analysis using **Visa** and **Mastercard**.
Updated current ratio analysis using **Costco** and **Walmart**.
Improved layouts for Exhibits 3A.1 through 3A.5.
New Cheat Sheet reinforces chapter content.
Added three new Quick Studies.
Added two new Exercises.
Added new analysis assignments: Company Analysis, Comparative Analysis, and Global Analysis.

Chapter 4

NEW opener—**Build-A-Bear** and entrepreneurial assignment.
Updated introduction for servicers vs. merchandisers using **Liberty Tax** and **Nordstrom**.
Revised NTK 4-1 covers basics of merchandising.
Reorganized "Purchases" section to aid learning.
New Decision Insight on growing number of returns for businesses.
Enhanced entries on payment of purchases within discount period vs. after discount period.
Improved discussion of entries for sales with discounts vs. sales without discounts.
Color-coded Exhibit 4.12 highlights different merchandising transactions.
Updated acid-test ratio and gross margin analysis using **Nike** and **Under Armour**.
Appendix 4B explains adjusting entries for future sales discounts, returns, and allowances.
Appendix 4C covers the net method.
Appendix 4D moved to online only.
New Cheat Sheet reinforces chapter content.
Added three new Quick Studies.
Added four new Exercises.
Added new analysis assignments: Company Analysis, Comparative Analysis, and Global Analysis.

Chapter 5

NEW opener—**Shake Shack** and entrepreneurial assignment.
New Ethical Risk on the alleged fraud of **Homex**.
Simplified introduction to inventory costing.

Shortened explanation for specific identification.
Enhanced layout to explain effects of inventory errors across years.
Updated inventory turnover and days' sales in inventory analysis using **Costco** and **Walmart**.
Added colored arrow lines to Exhibits 5A.3 and 5A.4 to show cost flows from purchases to sales.
New Cheat Sheet reinforces chapter content.
Added one new Quick Study.
Added two new Exercises.
Added new analysis assignments: Company Analysis, Comparative Analysis, and Global Analysis.

Chapter 6

NEW opener—**Care.com** and entrepreneurial assignment.
New COSO framework to guide internal control, including COSO cube.
New discussion of internal control failure at **Amazon** that cost customers $150 million.
Simplified bank statement for learning.
Revised "Bank Reconciliation" section to separate bank balance adjustments and book balance adjustments.
New summary image on adjustments for bank balance and for book balance.
Removed collection expenses and NSF fees—most are immaterial and covered in advanced courses.
Updated days' sales uncollected analysis using **Starbucks** and **Jack in the Box**.
New Cheat Sheet reinforces chapter content.
Added three new Quick Studies.
Added eight new Exercises.
Added new analysis assignments: Company Analysis, Comparative Analysis, and Global Analysis.

Chapter 7

NEW opener—**Facebook** and entrepreneurial assignment.
Updated company data in Exhibit 7.1.
Streamlined direct write-off method.
Enhanced Exhibit 7.6 showing allowances set aside for future bad debts along with journal entries.
New calendar graphic added as learning aid with Exhibit 7.12.
New Excel demo to compute maturity dates.

Updated accounts receivable analysis using **Visa** and **Mastercard**.
New Cheat Sheet reinforces chapter content.
Added five new Quick Studies.
Added one new Exercise.
Added new analysis assignments: Company Analysis, Comparative Analysis, and Global Analysis.

Chapter 8

NEW opener—**New Glarus Brewery** and entrepreneurial assignment.
Updated company data in Exhibit 8.1.
Added entry with Exhibit 8.3 and Exhibit 8.4.
Simplified "Partial-Year Depreciation" section.
Added margin table to Exhibit 8.14 as a learning aid.
New Decision Insight box on extraordinary repairs to **SpaceX**'s reusable orbital rocket.
New simple introduction to finance leases and operating leases for the new standard.
Updated asset turnover analysis using **Starbucks** and **Jack in the Box**.
Simplified Appendix 8A by postponing exchanges without commercial substance to advanced courses.
New Cheat Sheet reinforces chapter content.
Added two new Quick Studies.
Added one new Exercise.
Added two new Problems.
Added new analysis assignments: Company Analysis, Comparative Analysis, and Global Analysis.

Chapter 9

NEW opener—**Pandora** and entrepreneurial assignment.
Updated data in Exhibit 9.2.
Streamlined "Short-Term Notes Payable" section.
Simplified explanation of FICA taxes.
Updated payroll tax rates and explanations.
Revised NTK 9-4.
New W-4 form added to Appendix 9A.
New Cheat Sheet reinforces chapter content.
Added two new Quick Studies.
Added four new Exercises.
Added new analysis assignments: Company Analysis, Comparative Analysis, and Global Analysis.

Chapter 10

NEW opener—**e.l.f. Cosmetics** and entrepreneurial assignment.
Updated **IBM** bond quote data.
Simplified numbers in Exhibit 10.7.
Simplified Exhibit 10.10 on premium bonds.
Simplified numbers in Exhibit 10.11.
Bond pricing moved to Appendix 10A.
Simplified Exhibit 10.12 for teaching the note amortization schedule.
Updated debt-to-equity analysis using **Nike** and **Under Armour**.
New Excel computations for bond pricing in Appendix 10A.
Simplified numbers in Exhibits 10B.1 and 10B.2.
Revised Appendix 10C for new standard on finance leases and operating leases.
New Cheat Sheet reinforces chapter content.
Added five new Quick Studies.
Added four new Exercises.
Added four new Problems.
Added new analysis assignments: Company Analysis, Comparative Analysis, and Global Analysis.

Chapter 11

NEW opener—**Yelp** and entrepreneurial assignment.
New Decision Insight on bots investing in stocks based on erroneous news.

New **AT&T** stock quote explanation.
New graphic visually depicting cash dividend dates.
New table summarizing differences between small stock dividends, large stock dividends, and stock splits.
Updated **Apple** statement of equity in Exhibit 11.10.
Updated PE ratio and dividend yield using **Amazon**, **Altria**, **Visa**, and **Mastercard**.
Simplified book value per share explanation and computations.
New Cheat Sheet reinforces chapter content.
Added six new Quick Studies.
Added four new Exercises
Added new analysis assignments: Company Analysis, Comparative Analysis, and Global Analysis.

Chapter 12

NEW opener—**Vera Bradley** and entrepreneurial assignment.
Slightly revised infographics on cash flows from operating, investing, and financing.
Streamlined sections on analyzing the cash account and noncash accounts.
New presentation to aid learning of indirect adjustments to income.
Simplified T-accounts to reconstruct cash flows.
New box on **Tesla**'s cash outflows and growing market value.

Simplified reconstruction entries to help compute cash flows.
Updated cash flow on total assets analysis using **Nike** and **Under Armour**.
New Cheat Sheet reinforces chapter content.
Added ten new Quick Studies.
Added four new Exercises.
Added new analysis assignments: Company Analysis, Comparative Analysis, and Global Analysis.

Chapter 13

Updated opener—**Morgan Stanley** and entrepreneurial assignment.
Updated data for all analyses of **Apple** using horizontal, vertical, and ratio analysis.
Updated comparative analysis using **Google** and **Samsung**.
Streamlined section on ratio analysis.
Streamlined the "Analysis Reporting" section.
Shortened Appendix 13A.
New Cheat Sheet reinforces chapter content.
Added eight new Quick Studies.
Added two new Exercises.
Added new analysis assignments: Company Analysis, Comparative Analysis, and Global Analysis.

Appendix A

New financial statements for **Apple**, **Google**, and **Samsung**.

Appendix B

New Decision Maker on postponed retail pricing.
Continued Excel demos for PV and FV of lump sums.
Continued Excel demos for PV and FV of annuities.

Appendix C

New learning objective P4 for new category of stock investments.
Revised and simplified Exhibit C.2 for new standard on investments.
Reorganized text to first explain debt securities and then stock securities.
Revised trading and available-for-sale securities to cover only debt securities given the new standard.
New section on stock investments with insignificant influence.
New Exhibit C.6 to describe accounting for equity securities by ownership level.
Updated component-returns analysis using **Costco** and **Walmart**.
New Cheat Sheet reinforces chapter content.
Added three new Quick Studies.
Added four new Exercises.
Added two new Problems.
Added new analysis assignments: Company Analysis, Comparative Analysis, and Global Analysis.

Acknowledgments

John J. Wild and McGraw-Hill Education recognize the following instructors for their valuable feedback and involvement in the development of *Financial Accounting Fundamentals*. We are thankful for their suggestions, counsel, and encouragement.

Darlene Adkins, University of Tennessee–Martin

Peter Aghimien, Indiana University South Bend

Janice Akao, Butler Community College

Nathan Akins, Chattahoochee Technical College

John Alpers, Tennessee Wesleyan University

Sekhar Anantharaman, Indiana University of Pennsylvania

Karen Andrews, Lewis-Clark State College

Chandra D. Arthur, Cuyahoga Community College

Steven Ault, Montana State University

Victoria Badura, Metropolitan Community College

Felicia Baldwin, City College of Chicago

Reb Beatty, Anne Arundel Community College

Robert Beebe, Morrisville State College

George Henry Bernard, Seminole State College of Florida

Cynthia Bird, Tidewater Community College, Virginia Beach

Pascal Bizarro, Bowling Green State University

Amy Bohrer, Tidewater Community College, Virginia Beach

John Bosco, North Shore Community College

Nicholas Bosco, Suffolk County Community College

Jerold K. Braun, Daytona State College

Doug Brown, Forsyth Technical Community College

Tracy L. Bundy, University of Louisiana at Lafayette

Marci Butterfield, University of Utah

Ann Capion, Scott Community College

Amy Cardillo, Metropolitan State University of Denver

Anne Cardozo, Broward College

Crystal Carlson-Myer, Indian River State College

Julie Chasse, Des Moines Area Community College

Patricia Chow, Grossmont College

Maria Coclin, Community College of Rhode Island

Michael Cohen, Lewis-Clark State College

Jerilyn Collins, Herzing University

Scott Collins, Penn State University, University Park

William Conner, Tidewater Community College

Erin Cornelsen, University of South Dakota

Mariah Dar, John Tyler Community College

Nichole Dauenhauer, Lakeland Community College

Donna DeMilia, Grand Canyon University

Tiffany DeRoy, University of South Alabama

Susan Dickey, Motlow State Community College

Erin Dischler, Milwaukee Area Technical College–West Allis

Holly Dixon, State College of Florida

Vicky Dominguez, College of Southern Nevada

David Doyon, Southern New Hampshire University

Chester Drake, Central Texas College

Christopher Eller, Appalachian State University

Cynthia Elliott, Southwest Tennessee Community College–Macon

Kim Everett, East Carolina University

Corinne Frad, Eastern Iowa Community College

Krystal Gabel, Southeast Community College

Harry Gallatin, Indiana State University

Rena Galloway, State Fair Community College

Rick Gaumer, University of Wisconsin–Green Bay

Tammy Gerszewski, University of North Dakota

Pradeep Ghimire, Rappahannock Community College

Marc Giullian, Montana State University, Bozeman

Nelson Gomez, Miami Dade College–Kendall

Robert Goodwin, University of Tampa

Steve G. Green, U.S. Air Force Academy

Darryl Greene, Muskegon Community College

Lisa Hadley, Southwest Tennessee Community College–Macon

Penny Hahn, KCTCS Henderson Community College

Yoon Han, Bemidji State University

Becky Hancock, El Paso Community College

Amie Haun, University of Tennessee–Chattanooga

Michelle Hays, Kalamazoo Valley Community College

Rhonda Henderson, Olive Harvey College

Lora Hines, John A. Logan College

Rob Hochschild, Ivy Tech Community College of Indiana–South Bend

John Hoover, Volunteer State Community College

Roberta Humphrey, Southeast Missouri State University

Carley Hunzeker, Metro Community College, Elkhorn

Kay Jackson, Tarrant County College South

Elizabeth Jennison, Saddleback College

Mary Jepperson, Saint John's University

Vicki Jobst, Benedictine University

Odessa Jordan, Calhoun Community College

Susan Juckett, Victoria College

Amanda Kaari, Central Georgia Technical College

Ramadevi Kannan, Owens Community College

Jan Klaus, University of North Texas

Aaron P. Knape, The University of New Orleans

Cedric Knott, Henry Ford Community College

Robin Knowles, Texas A&M International University

Kimberly Kochanny, Central Piedmont Community College

Sergey Komissarov, University of Wisconsin–La Crosse

Stephanie Lareau Kroeger, Ocean County College

Joseph Krupka, Lander University

Tara Laken, Joliet Junior College

Suzanne Lay, Colorado Mesa University

Brian Lazarus, Baltimore City Community College

Kevin Leifer, Long Island University, CW Post Campus

Harold Levine, Los Angeles Valley College

Yuebing Liu, University of Tampa

Philip Lee Little, Coastal Carolina University

Delores Loedel, Miracosta College

Rebecca Lohmann, Southeast Missouri State University

Ming Lu, Santa Monica Community College

Annette C. Maddox, Georgia Highlands College

Natasha Maddox, KCTCS Maysville Community and Technical College

Rich Mandau, Piedmont Technical College

Robert Maxwell, College of the Canyons

Karen McCarron, Georgia Gwinnett College

Michael McDonald, College of Southern Nevada

Gwendolyn McFadden-Wade, North Carolina A&T University

Allison McLeod, University of North Texas

Kate McNeil, Johnson County Community College

Jane Medling, Saddleback College

Heidi H. Meier, Cleveland State University

Tammy Metzke, Milwaukee Area Technical College

Jeanine Metzler, Northampton Community College

Michelle Meyer, Joliet Junior College

Pam Meyer, University of Louisiana at Lafayette

Deanne Michaelson, Pellissippi State Community College

Susan Miller, County College of Morris

Carmen Morgan, Oregon Tech

Karen Satterfield Mozingo, Pitt Community College

Haris Mujahid, South Seattle College

Andrea Murowski, Brookdale Community College

Jaclynn Myers, Sinclair Community College

Micki Nickla, Ivy Tech Community College of Indiana–Gary

Dan O'Brien, Madison College–Truax

Jamie O'Brien, South Dakota State University

Grace Odediran, Union County College

Ashley Parker, Grand Canyon University

Pamela Parker, NOVA Community College Alexandria

Margaret Parrish, John Tyler Community College

Reed Peoples, Austin Community College

Rachel Pernia, Essex County College

Brandis Phillips, North Carolina A&T University

Debbie Porter, Tidewater Community College–Virginia Beach

M. Jeff Quinlan, Madison Area Technical College

James E. Racic, Lakeland Community College

Ronald de Ramon, Rockland Community College

Robert J. Rankin, Texas A&M University–Commerce

Robert Rebman, Benedictine University

Jenny Resnick, Santa Monica Community College

DeAnn Ricketts, York Technical College

Renee Rigoni, Monroe Community College

Kevin Rosenberg, Southeastern Community College

David Rosser, University of Texas at Arlington

Michael J. Rusek, Eastern Gateway Community College

Alfredo Salas, El Paso Community College

Carolyn Satz, Tidewater Community College–Chesapeake

Kathy Saxton, Bryant & Stratton College

Wilson Seda, Lehman College–CUNY

Perry Sellers, Lonestar College–North Harris

James Shimko, Ferris State University

Philip Slater, Forsyth Technical Community College

Clayton Smith, Columbia College Chicago

Patricia Smith, DePaul University

Jane Stam, Onondaga Community College

Natalie Strouse, Notre Dame College

Erica Teague-Friend, Gwinnett Technical College

Louis Terrero, Lehman College

Geoff Tickell, Indiana University of Pennsylvania

Judith A. Toland, Bucks County Community College

Debra Touhey, Ocean County College

Jim Ulmer, Angelina College

Bob Urell, Irvine Valley College

Kevin Veneskey, Ivy Tech Community College

Teresa Walker, North Carolina A&T University

Terri Walsh, Seminole State College of Florida

Eric Weinstein, Suffolk County Community College, Brentwood

Andy Welchel, Greenville Technical College

Joe Welker, College of Western Idaho

Jean Wells, Howard University

Denise White, Austin Community College

Jonathan M. Wild, Oklahoma State University

Kenneth Wise, Wilkes Community College

Shondra Woessner, Holyoke Community College

Mindy Wolfe, Arizona State University

Jan Workman, East Carolina University

Lori Zaher, Bucks County Community College

Jessie Zetnick, Texas Woman's University

Laurence Zuckerman, Fulton-Montgomery Community College

Many talented educators and professionals have worked hard to create the materials for this product, and for their efforts, we're grateful. **We extend a special thank you to our contributing and technology supplement authors,** who have worked so diligently to support this product.

Contributing Author, Connect Content, General Ledger Problems, and **Exercise PowerPoints:** Kathleen O'Donnell, *Onondaga Community College*

Text and Supplements Accuracy Checkers: Dave Krug, *Johnson County Community College;* Mark McCarthy, *East Carolina University;* Kate McNeil, *Johnson County Community College;* Wanda Wong, *Chabot College;* and Beth Kobylarz

Test Bank Authors and Accuracy Checkers: Melodi Bunting, *Madison College;* Brian Schmoldt, *Madison College;* M. Jeff Quinlan, *Madison College;* and Teri Zuccaro, *Clarke University*

LearnSmart Author, Concept Overview Videos, PowerPoint Presentations, and **Instructor Resource Manual:** April Mohr, *Jefferson Community and Technical College, SW*

Special recognition extends to the entire team at McGraw-Hill Education: Tim Vertovec, Steve Schuetz, Natalie King, Michelle Williams, Julie Wolfe, Michele Janicek, Christina Sanders, Michael McCormick, Lori Koetters, Xin Lin, Kevin Moran, Debra Kubiak, Brian Nacik, Missy Homer, Sandy Ludovissy, and Daryl Horrocks. We could not have published this new edition without your efforts.

John J. Wild

Brief Contents

Contents

Design elements: Lightbulb: ©Chuhail/Getty Images; Blue globe: ©nidwlw/Getty Images and ©Dizzle52/Getty Images; Chess piece: ©Andrei Simonenko/Getty Images and ©Dizzle52/Getty Images; Mouse: ©Siede Preis/Getty Images; Global View globe: ©McGraw-Hill Education and ©Dizzle52/Getty Images; Sustainability: ©McGraw-Hill Education and ©Dizzle52/Getty Images

Financial Accounting Fundamentals

1 Accounting in Business

Chapter Preview

ACCOUNTING USES

C1 Purpose of accounting

C2 Accounting information users

Opportunities in accounting

NTK 1-1

ETHICS AND ACCOUNTING

C3 Ethics

C4 Generally accepted accounting principles

Conceptual framework

NTK 1-2

TRANSACTION ANALYSIS

A1 Accounting equation and its components

Expanded accounting equation

P1 Transaction analysis—Illustrated

NTK 1-3, 1-4

FINANCIAL STATEMENTS

P2 Income statement

Statement of retained earnings

Balance sheet

Statement of cash flows

A2 Financial analysis

NTK 1-5

Chapter Preview is organized by *"blocks"* of key content and learning objectives followed by *Need-to-Know (NTK)* guided video examples

Learning Objectives are classified as conceptual, analytical, or procedural

Learning Objectives

CONCEPTUAL

C1 Explain the purpose and importance of accounting.

C2 Identify users and uses of, and opportunities in, accounting.

C3 Explain why ethics are crucial to accounting.

C4 Explain generally accepted accounting principles and define and apply several accounting principles.

C5 *Appendix 1B*—Identify and describe the three major activities of organizations.

ANALYTICAL

A1 Define and interpret the accounting equation and each of its components.

A2 Compute and interpret return on assets.

A3 *Appendix 1A*—Explain the relation between return and risk.

PROCEDURAL

P1 Analyze business transactions using the accounting equation.

P2 Identify and prepare basic financial statements and explain how they interrelate.

Big Apple

"We ran the business . . . with just a few hundred bucks"—**STEVE WOZNIAK**

CUPERTINO, CA—"When I designed the Apple stuff," says Steve Wozniak, "I never thought in my life I would have enough money to fly to Hawaii or make a down payment on a house." But some dreams do come true. Woz, along with Steve Jobs and Ron Wayne, founded **Apple** (**Apple.com**) when Woz was 25 and Jobs was 21.

The young entrepreneurs faced challenges, including how to read and interpret accounting data. They also needed to finance the company, which they did by selling Woz's HP calculator and Jobs's Volkswagen van. The $1,300 raised helped them purchase the equipment Woz used to build the first Apple computer.

In setting up their company, the owners chose between a partnership and a corporation. They decided on a partnership that included Ron as a third partner with 10% ownership. Days later, Ron withdrew when he considered the unlimited liability of a partnership. He sold his 10% share to Woz and Jobs for $800. Within nine months, Woz and Jobs converted Apple to a corporation.

As Apple grew, Woz and Jobs had to learn more accounting, along with details of preparing and interpreting financial statements. Important questions involving transaction analysis and financial reporting arose, and the owners took care to do things

©Miguel Medina/AFP/Getty Images

right. "Everything we did," asserts Woz, "we were setting the tone for the world."

Woz and Jobs focused their accounting system to provide information for Apple's business decisions. Today, Woz believes that Apple is key to the language of technology, just as accounting is the language of business. In retrospect, Woz says, "Every dream I have ever had in life has come true ten times over."

Sources: *Apple website,* January 2019; *Woz.org,* January 2019; *Apple 2016 Sustainability Report,* April 2016; *Greenbiz,* October 2014; *iWoz: From Computer Geek to Cult Icon,* W.W. Norton & Co., 2006; *Founders at Work,* Apress, 2007

IMPORTANCE OF ACCOUNTING

Why is accounting so popular on campus? Why are there so many openings for accounting jobs? Why is accounting so important to companies? The answer is that we live in an information age in which accounting information impacts us all.

C1
Explain the purpose and importance of accounting.

Accounting is an information and measurement system that identifies, records, and communicates an organization's business activities. Exhibit 1.1 shows these accounting functions.

Identifying	Recording	Communicating
Select transactions and events	Input, measure, and log	Prepare, analyze, and interpret
Examples are **Apple**'s sale of iPhones and **TicketMaster**'s receipt of ticket money.	Examples are dated logs of transactions measured in dollars.	Examples are reports that we analyze and interpret.

EXHIBIT 1.1

Accounting Functions

Our most common contact with accounting is through credit checks, checking accounts, tax forms, and payroll. These experiences focus on **recordkeeping,** or **bookkeeping,** which is the recording of transactions and events. This is just one part of accounting. Accounting also includes analysis and interpretation of information.

Technology plays a major role in accounting. Technology reduces the time, effort, and cost of recordkeeping while improving accuracy. As technology makes more information available, the demand for accounting knowledge increases. Consulting, planning, and other financial services are closely linked to accounting.

Users of Accounting Information

C2

Identify users and uses of, and opportunities in, accounting.

Accounting is called the *language of business* because it communicates data that help people make better decisions. People using accounting information are divided into two groups: *external users* and *internal users*. **Financial accounting** focuses on the needs of external users, and **managerial accounting** focuses on the needs of internal users.

External Users   **External users** of accounting information do *not* directly run the organization and have limited access to its accounting information. These users get accounting information from general-purpose financial statements. Following is a partial list of external users and decisions they make with accounting information.

- *Lenders* (creditors) loan money or other resources to an organization. Banks, savings and loans, and mortgage companies are lenders. Lenders use information to assess if an organization will repay its loans.
- *Shareholders* (*investors*) are the owners of a corporation. They use accounting reports to decide whether to buy, hold, or sell stock.
- *Boards of directors* oversee organizations. Directors use accounting information to evaluate the performance of executive management.
- *External* (independent) *auditors* examine financial statements to verify that they are prepared according to generally accepted accounting principles.
- *Nonmanagerial* and *nonexecutive employees* and *labor unions* use external information to bargain for better wages.
- *Regulators* have legal authority over certain activities of organizations. For example, the Internal Revenue Service (IRS) requires accounting reports for computing taxes.
- *Voters* and *government officials* use information to evaluate government performance.
- *Contributors* to nonprofits use information to evaluate the use and impact of donations.
- *Suppliers* use information to analyze a customer before extending credit.
- *Customers* use financial reports to assess the stability of potential suppliers.

Internal Users   **Internal users** of accounting information directly manage the organization. Internal reports are designed for the unique needs of managerial or executive employees, such as the chief executive officer (CEO). Following is a partial list of internal users and decisions they make with accounting information.

- *Purchasing managers* need to know what, when, and how much to purchase.
- *Human resource managers* need information about employees' payroll, benefits, and performance.
- *Production managers* use information to monitor costs and ensure quality.
- *Distribution managers* need reports for timely and accurate delivery of products and services.
- *Marketing managers* use reports to target consumers, set prices, and monitor consumer needs.
- *Service managers* use reports to provide better service to customers.
- *Research and development managers* use information on projected costs and revenues of innovations.

Opportunities in Accounting

Accounting has four areas of opportunities: financial, managerial, taxation, and accounting-related. Exhibit 1.2 lists selected opportunities in each area.

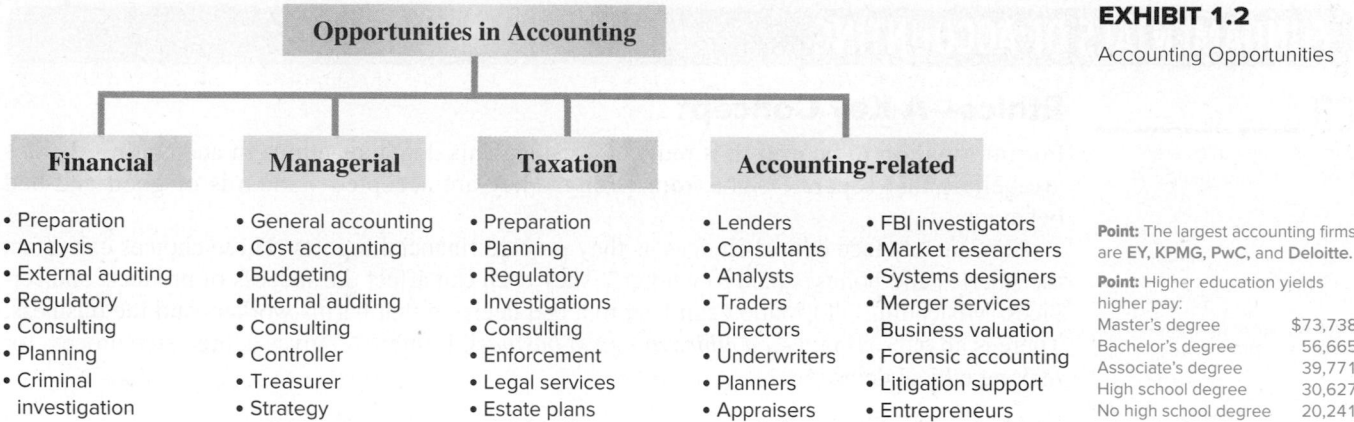

EXHIBIT 1.2
Accounting Opportunities

Opportunities in Accounting			
Financial	**Managerial**	**Taxation**	**Accounting-related**

- Preparation
- Analysis
- External auditing
- Regulatory
- Consulting
- Planning
- Criminal investigation

- General accounting
- Cost accounting
- Budgeting
- Internal auditing
- Consulting
- Controller
- Treasurer
- Strategy

- Preparation
- Planning
- Regulatory
- Investigations
- Consulting
- Enforcement
- Legal services
- Estate plans

- Lenders
- Consultants
- Analysts
- Traders
- Directors
- Underwriters
- Planners
- Appraisers

- FBI investigators
- Market researchers
- Systems designers
- Merger services
- Business valuation
- Forensic accounting
- Litigation support
- Entrepreneurs

Point: The largest accounting firms are **EY, KPMG, PwC,** and **Deloitte.**

Point: Higher education yields higher pay:

Master's degree	$73,738
Bachelor's degree	56,665
Associate's degree	39,771
High school degree	30,627
No high school degree	20,241

Exhibit 1.3 shows that the majority of opportunities are in *private accounting,* which are employees working for businesses. *Public accounting* involves accounting services such as auditing and taxation. Opportunities also exist in government and not-for-profit agencies, including business regulation and law enforcement.

Accounting specialists are highly regarded, and their professional standing is often denoted by a certificate. Certified public accountants (CPAs) must meet education and experience requirements, pass an exam, and be ethical. Many accounting specialists hold certificates in addition to or instead of the CPA. Two of the most common are the certificate in management accounting (CMA) and the certified internal auditor (CIA). Employers also look for specialists with designations such as certified bookkeeper (CB), certified payroll professional (CPP), certified fraud examiner (CFE), and certified forensic accountant (CrFA).

Accounting specialists are in demand. Exhibit 1.4 reports average annual salaries for several accounting positions. Salaries vary based on location, company size, and other factors.

EXHIBIT 1.3
Accounting Jobs by Area

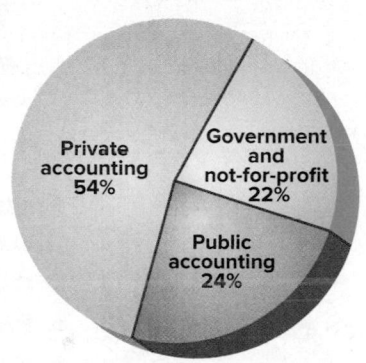

EXHIBIT 1.4
Accounting Salaries

Public Accounting	Salary
Partner	$245,000
Manager (6–8 years)	112,000
Senior (3–5 years)	90,000
Junior (0–2 years)	62,500

Private Accounting	Salary
CFO	$290,000
Controller/Treasurer	180,000
Manager (6–8 years)	98,500
Senior (3–5 years)	81,500
Junior (0–2 years)	58,000

Recordkeeping	Salary
Full-charge bookkeeper	$60,500
Accounts manager	58,000
Payroll manager	59,500
Accounting clerk (0–2 years)	39,500

NEED-TO-KNOWs highlight key procedures and concepts in learning accounting; instructional audio/video recordings accompany each one

Identify the following users of accounting information as either an (a) external or (b) internal user.

1. ___ Regulator
2. ___ CEO
3. ___ Shareholder
4. ___ Marketing manager
5. ___ Executive employee
6. ___ External auditor
7. ___ Production manager
8. ___ Nonexecutive employee
9. ___ Bank lender

NEED-TO-KNOW 1-1

Accounting Users

C1 C2

Solution

1. a 2. b 3. a 4. b 5. b 6. a 7. b 8. a 9. a.

Do More: QS 1-1, QS 1-2, E 1-1, E 1-2, E 1-3

FUNDAMENTALS OF ACCOUNTING

C3

Explain why ethics are crucial to accounting.

Point: A *Code of Conduct* is available at **AICPA.org**.

Ethics—A Key Concept

For information to be useful, it must be trusted. This demands ethics in accounting. **Ethics** are beliefs that separate right from wrong. They are accepted standards of good and bad behavior.

Accountants face ethical choices as they prepare financial reports. These choices can affect the salaries and bonuses paid to workers. They even can affect the success of products and services. Misleading information can lead to a bad decision that harms workers and the business. There is an old saying: *Good ethics are good business.* Exhibit 1.5 gives a three-step process for making ethical decisions.

EXHIBIT 1.5

Ethical Decision Making

1. Identify ethical concerns	2. Analyze options	3. Make ethical decision

Use ethics to recognize an ethical concern.	Consider all consequences.	Choose best option after weighing all consequences.

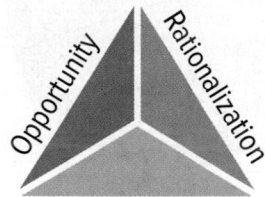

Pressure

Fraud Triangle: Ethics under Attack
The fraud triangle shows that *three* factors push a person to commit fraud.

- **Opportunity**. A person must be able to commit fraud with a low risk of getting caught.
- **Pressure**, or incentive. A person must feel pressure or have incentive to commit fraud.
- **Rationalization**, or attitude. A person justifies fraud or does not see its criminal nature.

The key to stopping fraud is to focus on prevention. It is less expensive and more effective to prevent fraud from happening than it is to detect it.

To help prevent fraud, companies set up internal controls. **Internal controls** are procedures to protect assets, ensure reliable accounting, promote efficiency, and uphold company policies. Examples are good records, physical controls (locks), and independent reviews.

Point: SOX requires a business that sells stock to disclose a code of ethics for its executives.

Point: An audit examines whether financial statements are prepared using GAAP.

Enforcing Ethics
In response to major accounting scandals, like those at **Enron** and **WorldCom**, Congress passed the **Sarbanes-Oxley Act,** also called *SOX,* to help stop financial abuses. SOX requires documentation and verification of internal controls and emphasizes effective internal controls. Management must issue a report stating that internal controls are effective. **Auditors** verify the effectiveness of internal controls. Ignoring SOX can lead to penalties and criminal prosecution of executives. CEOs and CFOs who knowingly sign off on bogus accounting reports risk millions of dollars in fines and years in prison.

Dodd-Frank Wall Street Reform and Consumer Protection Act, or *Dodd-Frank,* has two important provisions.

- *Clawback* Mandates recovery (clawback) of excessive pay.
- *Whistleblower* SEC pays whistleblowers 10% to 30% of sanctions exceeding $1 million.

Ethical Risk boxes highlight ethical issues from practice

Ethical Risk

Ethics Pay   The $100 million mark in total payments made by the SEC to whistleblowers was recently surpassed. Since the SEC began awarding whistleblowers a percentage of money from sanctions, over 14,000 tips have been reported. Many of the tips come from accountants. ∎

Generally Accepted Accounting Principles

Financial accounting is governed by concepts and rules known as **generally accepted accounting principles (GAAP)**. GAAP wants information to have *relevance* and *faithful representation*. Relevant information affects decisions of users. Faithful representation means information accurately reflects the business results.

The **Financial Accounting Standards Board (FASB)** is given the task of setting GAAP from the **Securities and Exchange Commission (SEC)**. The SEC is a U.S. government agency that oversees proper use of GAAP by companies that sell stock and debt to the public.

International Standards Our global economy demands comparability in accounting reports. The **International Accounting Standards Board (IASB)** issues **International Financial Reporting Standards (IFRS)** that identify preferred accounting practices. These standards are similar to, but sometimes different from, U.S. GAAP. The FASB and IASB are working to reduce differences between U.S. GAAP and IFRS.

C4
Explain generally accepted accounting principles and define and apply several accounting principles.

Point: CPAs who audit financial statements must disclose if they do not comply with GAAP.

Conceptual Framework

The FASB **conceptual framework** in Exhibit 1.6 consists of the following.

- **Objectives**—to provide information useful to investors, creditors, and others.
- **Qualitative characteristics**—to require information that has *relevance* and *faithful representation*.
- **Elements**—to define items in financial statements.
- **Recognition and measurement**—to set criteria for an item to be recognized as an element; and how to measure it.

EXHIBIT 1.6
Conceptual Framework

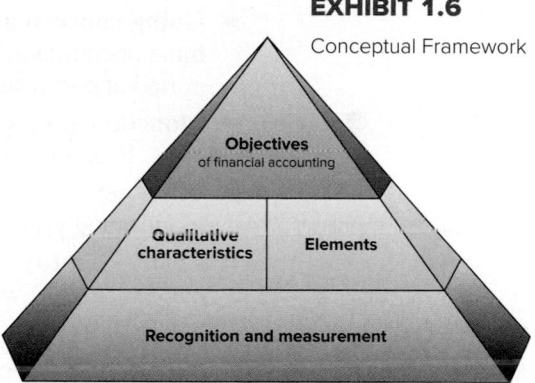

Principles, Assumptions, and Constraint There are two types of accounting principles (and assumptions). *General principles* are the assumptions, concepts, and guidelines for preparing financial statements; these are shown in purple font in Exhibit 1.7, along with key assumptions in red font. *Specific principles* are detailed rules used in reporting business transactions and events; they are described as we encounter them.

Accounting Principles There are four general principles.

- **Measurement principle (cost principle)** Accounting information is based on actual cost. Cost is measured on a cash or equal-to-cash basis. This means if cash is given for a service, its cost is measured by the cash paid. If something besides cash is exchanged (such as a car traded for a truck), cost is measured as the cash value of what is given up or received. Information based on cost is considered objective. *Objectivity* means that information is supported by independent, unbiased evidence. Later chapters cover adjustments to market and introduce *fair value*.
- **Revenue recognition principle** Revenue is recognized (1) when goods or services are provided to customers and (2) at the amount expected to be received from the customer. Revenue (sales) is the amount received from selling products and services. The amount received is usually in cash, but it also can be a customer's promise to pay at a future date, called credit sales. (To *recognize* means to record it.)

EXHIBIT 1.7
Building Blocks for GAAP

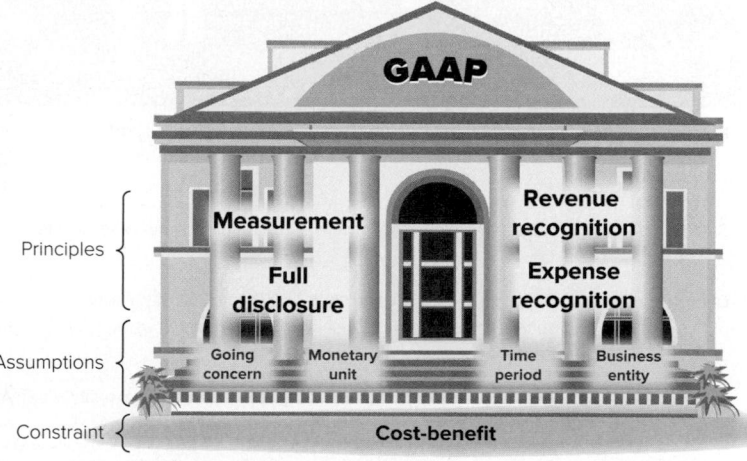

Point: A company pays $500 for equipment. The cost principle requires it be recorded at $500. It makes no difference if the owner thinks this equipment is worth $700.

Example: A lawn service bills a customer $800 on June 1 for two months of mowing (June and July). The customer pays the bill on July 1. When is revenue recorded? *Answer:* It is recorded over time as it is earned; record $400 revenue for June and $400 for July.

- **Expense recognition principle (matching principle)** A company records the expenses it incurred to generate the revenue reported. An example is rent costs of office space.
- **Full disclosure principle** A company reports the details behind financial statements that would impact users' decisions. Those disclosures are often in footnotes to the statements.

©Shane Roper/CSM/REX/Shutterstock

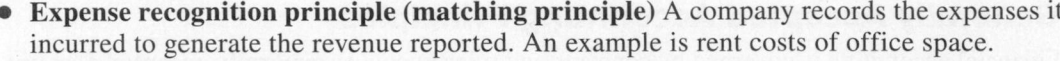

Decision Insight

Measurement and Recognition   Revenues for the **Seattle Seahawks**, **Atlanta Falcons**, **Green Bay Packers**, and other professional football teams include ticket sales, television broadcasts, concessions, and advertising. Revenues from ticket sales are earned when the NFL team plays each game. Advance ticket sales are not revenues; instead, they are a liability until the NFL team plays the game for which the ticket was sold. At that point, the liability is removed and revenues are reported. ■

Accounting Assumptions   There are four accounting assumptions.

- **Going-concern assumption** Accounting information presumes that the business will continue operating instead of being closed or sold. This means, for example, that property is reported at cost instead of liquidation value.
- **Monetary unit assumption** Transactions and events are expressed in monetary, or money, units. Examples of monetary units are the U.S. dollar and the Mexican peso.
- **Time period assumption** The life of a company can be divided into time periods, such as months and years, and useful reports can be prepared for those periods.
- **Business entity assumption** A business is accounted for separately from other business entities and its owner. Exhibit 1.8 describes four common business entities.

EXHIBIT 1.8

Attributes of Businesses

	Sole Proprietorship	Partnership	Corporation	Limited Liability Company (LLC)
Number of owners	1 owner; easy to set up.	2 or more, called *partners;* easy to set up.	1 or more, called *stockholders;* can get many investors by selling **stock** or **shares** of corporate ownership.*	1 or more, called *members.*
Business taxation	No additional business income tax.	No additional business income tax.	Additional corporate income tax.	No additional business income tax.
Owner liability	Unlimited liability. Owner is personally liable for proprietorship debts.	Unlimited liability. Partners are jointly liable for partnership debts.	Limited liability. Owners, called **stockholders (or shareholders)**, are not liable for corporate acts and debts.	Limited liability. Owners, called **members**, are not personally liable for LLC debts.
Legal entity	*Not* a separate legal entity.	*Not* a separate legal entity.	A separate entity with the same rights and responsibilities as a person.	A separate entity with the same rights and responsibilities as a person.
Business life	Business ends with owner death or choice.	Business ends with a partner death or choice.	Indefinite.	Indefinite.

*When a corporation issues only one class of stock, it is called **common stock** (or *capital stock*).

Accounting Constraint   The **cost-benefit constraint,** or **cost constraint,** says that information disclosed by an entity must have benefits to the user that are greater than the costs of providing it. *Materiality,* or the ability of information to influence decisions, is also sometimes mentioned as a constraint. *Conservatism* and *industry practices* are sometimes listed as well.

Decision Ethics boxes are role-playing exercises that stress ethics in accounting

 **Decision Ethics**

Entrepreneur You and a friend develop a new design for ice skates that improves speed. You plan to form a business to manufacture and sell the skates. You and your friend want to minimize taxes, but your big concern is potential lawsuits from customers who might be injured on these skates. What form of organization do you set up? ■ *Answer:* You should probably form an LLC. An LLC helps protect *personal* property from lawsuits directed at the business. Also, an LLC is not subject to an additional business income tax. You also must examine the ethical and social aspects of starting a business where injuries are expected.

Point: Double taxation means that (1) the corporation income is taxed and (2) any dividends to owners are taxed as part of the owners' personal income.

Part 1: Identify each of the following terms/phrases as either an accounting (a) principle, (b) assumption, or (c) constraint.

NEED-TO-KNOW 1-2

Accounting Guidance

C3 C4 ▶

1. ___ Cost-benefit
2. ___ Measurement
3. ___ Business entity
4. ___ Going-concern
5. ___ Full disclosure
6. ___ Time period
7. ___ Expense recognition
8. ___ Revenue recognition

Solution

1. c **2.** a **3.** b **4.** b **5.** a **6.** b **7.** a **8.** a

Part 2: Complete the following table with either a *yes* or a *no* regarding the attributes of a partnership, corporation, and LLC.

Attribute Present	Partnership	Corporation	LLC
Business taxed	a. ___	e. ___	i. ___
Limited liability	b. ___	f. ___	j. ___
Legal entity	c. ___	g. ___	k. ___
Unlimited life	d. ___	h. ___	l. ___

Solution

a. no **b.** no **c.** no **d.** no **e.** yes **f.** yes **g.** yes **h.** yes **i.** no **j.** yes **k.** yes **l.** yes

Do More: QS 1-3, QS 1-4, QS 1-5, QS 1-6, E 1-4, E 1-5, E 1-6, E 1-7

BUSINESS TRANSACTIONS AND ACCOUNTING

Accounting shows two basic aspects of a company: what it owns and what it owes. *Assets* are resources a company owns or controls. The claims on a company's assets—what it owes—are separated into owner (equity) and nonowner (liability) claims. Together, liabilities and equity are the source of funds to acquire assets.

A1_____

Define and interpret the accounting equation and each of its components.

Assets Assets are resources a company owns or controls. These resources are expected to yield future benefits. Examples are web servers for an online services company, musical instruments for a rock band, and land for a vegetable grower. Assets include cash, supplies, equipment, land, and accounts receivable. A *receivable* is an asset that promises a future inflow of resources. A company that provides a service or product on credit has an account receivable from that customer.

Point: "On credit" and "on account" mean cash is paid at a future date.

Liabilities Liabilities are creditors' claims on assets. These claims are obligations to provide assets, products, or services to others. A *payable* is a liability that promises a future outflow of resources. Examples are wages payable to workers, accounts payable to suppliers, notes (loans) payable to banks, and taxes payable.

Equity Equity is the owner's claim on assets and is equal to assets minus liabilities. Equity is also called *net assets* or *residual equity*.

Accounting Equation

The relation of assets, liabilities, and equity is shown in the following **accounting equation.** The accounting equation applies to all transactions and events, to all companies and organizations, and to all points in time.

Point: This equation can be rearranged. Example: Assets − Liabilities = Equity

$$\text{Assets} = \text{Liabilities} + \text{Equity}$$

We can break down equity to get the **expanded accounting equation.**

$$\text{Assets} = \text{Liabilities} + \overbrace{\text{Contributed Capital} + \text{Retained Earnings}}^{\text{Equity}}$$
$$= \text{Liabilities} + \text{Common Stock} - \text{Dividends} + \text{Revenues} - \text{Expenses}$$

We see that equity increases from **owner investments,** called *stock issuances,* and from revenues. It decreases from dividends and from expenses. Equity consists of four parts.

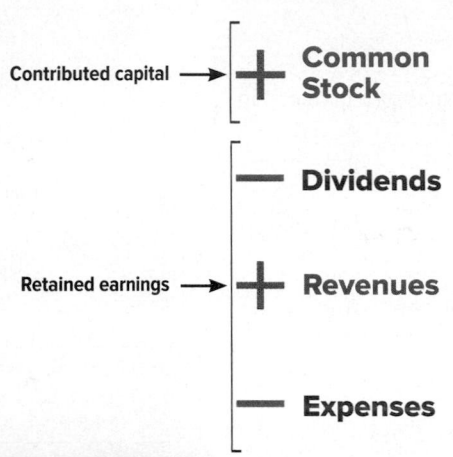

Contributed capital ⟶ **+ Common Stock**

Common stock reflects inflows of cash and other net assets from stockholders in exchange for stock (stock is part of contributed capital and covered in later chapters).

— Dividends

Dividends are outflows of cash and other assets to stockholders that reduce equity.

Retained earnings ⟶ **+ Revenues**

Revenues increase equity (via net income) from sales of products and services to customers; examples are sales of products, consulting services provided, facilities rented to others, and commissions from services.

— Expenses

Expenses decrease equity (via net income) from costs of providing products and services to customers; examples are costs of employee time, use of supplies, advertising, utilities, and insurance fees.

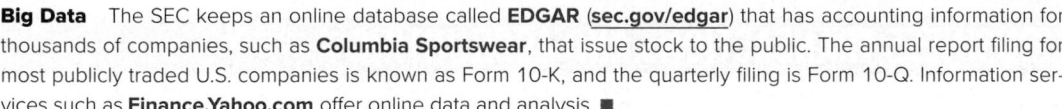
■ **Decision Insight**

Big Data The SEC keeps an online database called **EDGAR** (**sec.gov/edgar**) that has accounting information for thousands of companies, such as **Columbia Sportswear**, that issue stock to the public. The annual report filing for most publicly traded U.S. companies is known as Form 10-K, and the quarterly filing is Form 10-Q. Information services such as **Finance.Yahoo.com** offer online data and analysis. ■

©Greg Epperson/Shutterstock

NEED-TO-KNOW **1-3**

Accounting Equation

A1

Part 1: Use the *accounting equation* to compute the missing financial statement amounts.

Company	Assets	Liabilities	Equity
Bose	$150	$ 30	$ (a)
Vogue	$ (b)	$100	$300

Solution

a. $120   **b.** $400

Part 2: Use the *expanded accounting equation* to compute the missing financial statement amounts.

Company	Assets	Liabilities	Common Stock	Dividends	Revenues	Expenses
Tesla	$200	$ 80	$100	$5	$ (a)	$40
YouTube	$400	$160	$220	$ (b)	$ 120	$90

Do More: QS 1-7, QS 1-8, E 1-8, E 1-9

Solution

a. $65   **b.** $10

Transaction Analysis

Business activities are described in terms of transactions and events. **External transactions** are exchanges of value between two entities, which cause changes in the accounting equation. An example is the sale of the *AppleCare Protection Plan* by **Apple**. **Internal transactions** are exchanges within an entity, which may or may not affect the accounting equation. An example is **Target**'s use of its supplies, which are reported as expenses when used. **Events** are happenings that affect the accounting equation *and* are reliably measured. They include business events such as changes in the market value of certain assets and liabilities and natural events such as fires that destroy assets and create losses.

This section uses the accounting equation to analyze 11 transactions and events of FastForward, a start-up consulting (service) business, in its first month of operations. Remember that after each transaction and event, assets *always* equal liabilities plus equity.

P1

Analyze business transactions using the accounting equation.

Transaction 1: Investment by Owner   On December 1, Chas Taylor forms a consulting business named FastForward and set up as a corporation. FastForward evaluates the performance of footwear and accessories. Taylor owns and manages the business, which will publish online reviews and consult with clubs, athletes, and others who purchase **Nike** and **Adidas** products. ← ***Real company names are in bold magenta***

Taylor invests $30,000 cash in the new company and deposits the cash in a bank account opened under the name of FastForward. After this transaction, cash (an asset) and stockholders' equity each equals $30,000. Equity is increased by the owner's investment (stock issuance), which is included in the column titled Common Stock. The effect of this transaction on FastForward is shown in the accounting equation as follows (we label the equity entries).

	Assets	=	Liabilities	+	Equity
	Cash	=			Common Stock
(1)	+$30,000	=			+$30,000 Owner investment

Transaction 2: Purchase Supplies for Cash   FastForward uses $2,500 of its cash to buy supplies of Nike and Adidas footwear for performance testing over the next few months. This transaction is an exchange of cash, an asset, for another kind of asset, supplies. It simply changes the form of assets from cash to supplies. The decrease in cash is exactly equal to the increase in supplies. The supplies of footwear are assets because of the expected future benefits from the test results of their performance.

	Assets			=	Liabilities	+	Equity
	Cash	+	Supplies	=			Common Stock
Old Bal.	$30,000			=			$30,000
(2)	−2,500	+	$2,500				
New Bal.	$27,500	+	$ 2,500	=			$30,000

$30,000 $30,000

Transaction 3: Purchase Equipment for Cash   FastForward spends $26,000 to acquire equipment for testing footwear. Like Transaction 2, Transaction 3 is an exchange of one asset, cash, for another asset, equipment. The equipment is an asset because of its expected future benefits from testing footwear. This purchase changes the makeup of assets but does not change the asset total. The accounting equation remains in balance.

	Assets					=	Liabilities	+	Equity
	Cash	+	Supplies	+	Equipment	=			Common Stock
Old Bal.	$27,500	+	$2,500			=			$30,000
(3)	−26,000			+	$26,000				
New Bal.	$ 1,500	+	$2,500	+	$ 26,000	=			$30,000

$30,000 $30,000

Transaction 4: Purchase Supplies on Credit

Taylor decides more supplies of footwear and accessories are needed. These additional supplies cost $7,100, but FastForward has only $1,500 in cash. Taylor arranges to purchase them on credit from CalTech Supply Company. Thus, FastForward acquires supplies in exchange for a promise to pay for them later. This purchase increases assets by $7,100 in supplies, and liabilities (called *accounts payable* to CalTech Supply) increase by the same amount.

	Cash	+	Supplies	+	Equipment	=	Accounts Payable	+	Common Stock
									Assets = Liabilities + Equity
Old Bal.	$1,500	+	$2,500	+	$26,000	=			$30,000
(4)		+	7,100				+$7,100		
New Bal.	$1,500	+	$9,600	+	$26,000	=	$7,100	+	$30,000
			$37,100					$37,100	

Transaction 5: Provide Services for Cash

FastForward plans to earn revenues by selling online ad space and consulting with clients about footwear and accessories. It earns net income only if its revenues are greater than its expenses. In its first job, FastForward provides consulting services and immediately collects $4,200 cash. The accounting equation reflects this increase in cash of $4,200 and in equity of $4,200. This increase in equity is shown in the far right column under Revenues because the cash received is earned by providing consulting services.

	Cash	+	Supplies	+	Equipment	=	Accounts Payable	+	Common Stock	+	Revenues
Old Bal.	$1,500	+	$9,600	+	$26,000	=	$7,100	+	$30,000		
(5)	+4,200									+	$4,200 Consulting
New Bal.	$5,700	+	$9,600	+	$26,000	=	$7,100	+	$30,000	+	$4,200
			$41,300						$41,300		

Transactions 6 and 7: Payment of Expenses in Cash

FastForward pays $1,000 to rent its facilities. Paying this amount allows FastForward to occupy the space for the month of December. The rental payment is shown in the following accounting equation as Transaction 6. FastForward also pays the biweekly $700 salary of the company's only employee. This is shown in the accounting equation as Transaction 7. Both Transactions 6 and 7 are December expenses for FastForward. The costs of both rent and salary are expenses, not assets, because their benefits are used in December (they have no future benefits after December). The accounting equation shows that both transactions reduce cash and equity. The far right column shows these decreases as Expenses.

Increases in expenses yield decreases in equity.

	Cash	+	Supplies	+	Equipment	=	Accounts Payable	+	Common Stock	+	Revenues	−	Expenses
Old Bal.	$5,700	+	$9,600	+	$26,000	=	$7,100	+	$30,000	+	$4,200		
(6)	−1,000											−	$1,000 Rent
Bal.	4,700	+	9,600	+	26,000	=	7,100	+	30,000	+	4,200	−	1,000
(7)	− 700											−	700 Salaries
New Bal.	$4,000	+	$9,600	+	$26,000	=	$7,100	+	$30,000	+	$4,200	−	$1,700
			$39,600							$39,600			

Transaction 8: Provide Services and Facilities for Credit
FastForward provides consulting services of $1,600 and rents its test facilities for an additional $300 to Adidas on credit. Adidas is billed for the $1,900 total. This transaction creates a new asset, called *accounts receivable,* from Adidas. Accounts receivable is increased instead of cash because the payment has not yet been received. Equity is increased from the two revenue components shown in the Revenues column of the accounting equation.

Point: Transaction 8, like 5, records revenue when work is performed, not necessarily when cash is received.

	Assets				=	Liabilities	+		Equity		
	Cash	+ Accounts Receivable	+ Supplies	+ Equipment	=	Accounts Payable	+	Common Stock	+ Revenues	− Expenses	
Old Bal.	$4,000		+ $9,600	+ $26,000	=	$7,100	+	$30,000	+ $4,200	− $1,700	
(8)		+ $1,900							+ 1,600 Consulting		
									+ 300 Rental		
New Bal.	$4,000	+ $ 1,900	+ $9,600	+ $26,000	=	$7,100	+	$30,000	+ $6,100	− $1,700	
		$41,500							$41,500		

Transaction 9: Receipt of Cash from Accounts Receivable
The client in Transaction 8 (Adidas) pays $1,900 to FastForward 10 days after it is billed for consulting services. This Transaction 9 does not change the total amount of assets and does not affect liabilities or equity. It converts the receivable (an asset) to cash (another asset). It does not create new revenue. Revenue was recognized when FastForward performed the services in Transaction 8, not when the cash is collected.

Point: Transaction 9 involved no added client work, so no added revenue is recorded.

Point: Receipt of cash is not always a revenue.

	Assets				=	Liabilities	+		Equity	
	Cash	+ Accounts Receivable	+ Supplies	+ Equipment	=	Accounts Payable	+	Common Stock	+ Revenues	− Expenses
Old Bal.	$4,000	+ $1,900	+ $9,600	+ $26,000	=	$7,100	+	$30,000	+ $6,100	− $1,700
(9)	+1,900	− 1,900								
New Bal.	$5,900	+ $ 0	+ $9,600	+ $26,000	=	$7,100	+	$30,000	+ $6,100	− $1,700
		$41,500							$41,500	

Transaction 10: Payment of Accounts Payable
FastForward pays CalTech Supply $900 cash as partial payment for its earlier $7,100 purchase of supplies (Transaction 4), leaving $6,200 unpaid. This transaction decreases FastForward's cash by $900 and decreases its liability to CalTech Supply by $900. Equity does not change. This event does not create an expense even though cash flows out of FastForward (instead the expense is recorded when FastForward uses these supplies).

	Assets				=	Liabilities	+		Equity	
	Cash	+ Accounts Receivable	+ Supplies	+ Equipment	=	Accounts Payable	+	Common Stock	+ Revenues	− Expenses
Old Bal.	$5,900	+ $ 0	+ $9,600	+ $26,000	=	$7,100	+	$30,000	+ $6,100	− $1,700
(10)	−900					−900				
New Bal.	$5,000	+ $ 0	+ $9,600	+ $26,000	=	$6,200	+	$30,000	+ $6,100	− $1,700
		$40,600							$40,600	

Transaction 11: Payment of Cash Dividend   FastForward declares and pays a
$200 cash dividend to its owner (the sole shareholder). Dividends (decreases in equity) are not reported as expenses because they do not help earn revenue. Because dividends are not expenses, they are not used in computing net income.

Increases in dividends yield decreases in equity.

	Assets				=	Liabilities	+			Equity			
	Cash	+ Accounts Receivable	+ Supplies	+ Equipment	=	Accounts Payable	+ Common Stock	–	Dividends	+ Revenues	– Expenses
Old Bal.	$5,000	+ $ 0	+ $9,600	+ $26,000	=	$6,200	+ $30,000			+ $6,100	– $1,700
(11)	– 200								– $200 Dividends		
New Bal.	$4,800	+ $ 0	+ $9,600	+ $26,000	=	$6,200	+ $30,000	–	$200	+ $6,100	– $1,700
			$40,400						$40,400		

EXHIBIT 1.9

Summary of Transactions Using the Accounting Equation

Summary of Transactions

Exhibit 1.9 shows the effects of these 11 transactions of FastForward using the accounting equation. Assets equal liabilities plus equity after each transaction.

	Assets				=	Liabilities	+		Equity		
	Cash	+ Accounts Receivable	+ Supplies	+ Equipment	=	Accounts Payable	+ Common Stock	– Dividends	+ Revenues	– Expenses
(1)	$30,000				=		$30,000			
(2)	– 2,500		+ $2,500							
Bal.	27,500		+ 2,500		=		30,000			
(3)	–26,000			+ $26,000						
Bal.	1,500		+ 2,500	+ 26,000	=		30,000			
(4)			+ 7,100		=	+$7,100				
Bal.	1,500		+ 9,600	+ 26,000	=	7,100	+ 30,000			
(5)	+ 4,200								+ $4,200	
Bal.	5,700		+ 9,600	+ 26,000	=	7,100	+ 30,000		+ 4,200	
(6)	– 1,000									– $1,000
Bal.	4,700		+ 9,600	+ 26,000	=	7,100	+ 30,000		+ 4,200	– 1,000
(7)	– 700									– 700
Bal.	4,000		+ 9,600	+ 26,000	=	7,100	+ 30,000		+ 4,200	– 1,700
(8)		+ $1,900							+ 1,600	
									+ 300	
Bal.	4,000	+ 1,900	+ 9,600	+ 26,000	=	7,100	+ 30,000		6,100	– 1,700
(9)	+ 1,900	– 1,900								
Bal.	5,900	+ 0	+ 9,600	+ 26,000	=	7,100	+ 30,000		+ 6,100	– 1,700
(10)	– 900					– 900				
Bal.	5,000	+ 0	+ 9,600	+ 26,000	=	6,200	+ 30,000		+ 6,100	– 1,700
(11)	– 200							– $200		
Bal.	$ 4,800	+ $ 0	+ $9,600	+ $26,000	=	$ 6,200	+ $ 30,000	– $ 200	+ $6,100	– $ 1,700

NEED-TO-KNOW 1-4

Transaction Analysis

P1

Do More: QS 1-10, QS 1-11, E 1-10, E 1-11, E 1-13

Assume Tata Company began operations on January 1 and completed the following transactions during its first month of operations. Arrange the following asset, liability, and equity titles in a table like Exhibit 1.9: Cash; Accounts Receivable; Equipment; Accounts Payable; Common Stock; Dividends; Revenues; and Expenses.

Jan. 1   Jamsetji Tata invested $4,000 cash in Tata Company in exchange for its common stock.
      5   The company purchased $2,000 of equipment on credit.
     14   The company provided $540 of services for a client on credit.
     21   The company paid $250 cash for an employee's salary.

Solution

	Assets					=	Liabilities	+			Equity				
	Cash	+	Accounts Receivable	+	Equipment	=	Accounts Payable	+	Common Stock	−	Dividends	+	Revenues	−	Expenses
Jan. 1	$4,000					=			$4,000						
Jan. 5				+	$2,000		+$2,000								
Bal.	4,000			+	2,000	=	2,000	+	4,000						
Jan. 14		+	$540									+	$540		
Bal.	4,000	+	540	+	2,000	=	2,000	+	4,000			+	540		
Jan. 21	−250													−	$250
Bal.	3,750	+	540	+	2,000	=	2,000	+	4,000			+	540	−	250

$6,290 $6,290

COMMUNICATING WITH USERS

Financial statements are prepared in the order below using the 11 transactions of FastForward. (These statements are *unadjusted*—we explain this in Chapters 2 and 3.) The four financial statements and their purposes follow.

P2

Identify and prepare basic financial statements and explain how they interrelate.

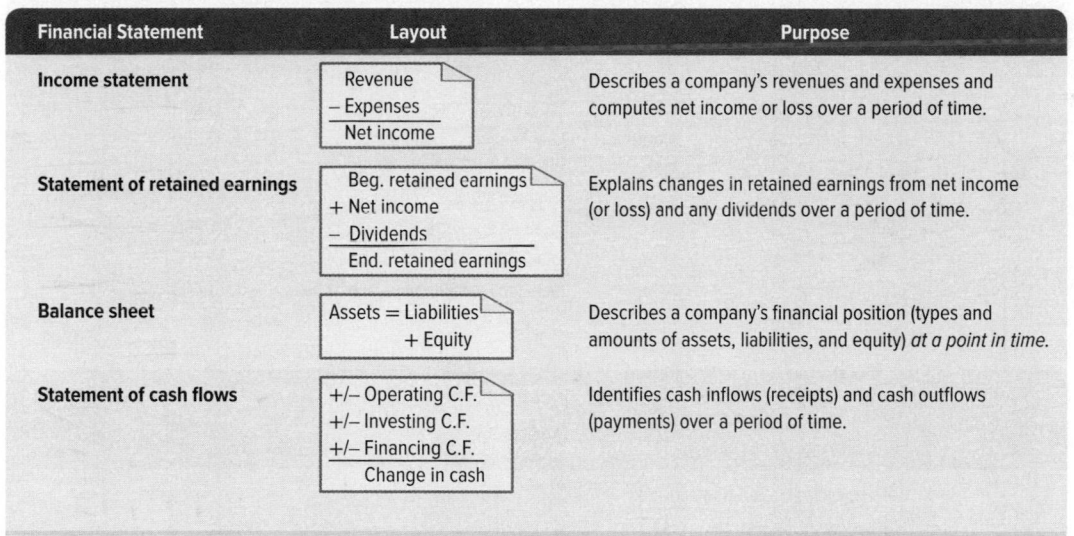

Financial Statement	Layout	Purpose
Income statement	Revenue − Expenses Net income	Describes a company's revenues and expenses and computes net income or loss over a period of time.
Statement of retained earnings	Beg. retained earnings + Net income − Dividends End. retained earnings	Explains changes in retained earnings from net income (or loss) and any dividends over a period of time.
Balance sheet	Assets = Liabilities + Equity	Describes a company's financial position (types and amounts of assets, liabilities, and equity) *at a point in time*.
Statement of cash flows	+/− Operating C.F. +/− Investing C.F. +/− Financing C.F. Change in cash	Identifies cash inflows (receipts) and cash outflows (payments) over a period of time.

Income Statement

FastForward's income statement for December is shown at the top of Exhibit 1.10. Information about revenues and expenses is taken from the Equity columns of Exhibit 1.9. Revenues are reported first on the income statement. They include consulting revenues of $5,800 from Transactions 5 and 8 and rental revenue of $300 from Transaction 8. Expenses are reported after revenues. Rent and salary expenses are from Transactions 6 and 7. Expenses are the costs to generate the revenues reported. **Net income** occurs when revenues exceed expenses. A **net loss** occurs when expenses exceed revenues. Net income (or loss) is shown at the bottom of the statement and is the amount reported in December. Stockholders' investments and dividends are *not* part of income.

*Key **terms** are in bold and defined again in the glossary*

Point: Net income is sometimes called *earnings* or *profit*.

EXHIBIT 1.10

Financial Statements and
Their Links

FASTFORWARD
Income Statement
For Month Ended December 31, 2019

Revenues		
Consulting revenue ($4,200 + $1,600)	$ 5,800	
Rental revenue	300	
Total revenues		$ 6,100
Expenses		
Rent expense	1,000	
Salaries expense	700	
Total expenses		1,700
Net income		$ 4,400

FASTFORWARD
Statement of Retained Earnings
For Month Ended December 31, 2019

Retained earnings, December 1, 2019		$ 0
Plus: Net income		4,400
		4,400
Less: Dividends		200
Retained earnings, December 31, 2019		$ 4,200

FASTFORWARD
Balance Sheet
December 31, 2019

Assets		Liabilities	
Cash	$ 4,800	Accounts payable	$ 6,200
Supplies	9,600	Total liabilities	6,200
Equipment	26,000	**Equity**	
		Common stock	30,000
		Retained earnings	4,200
		Total equity	34,200
Total assets	$40,400	Total liabilities and equity	$ 40,400

FASTFORWARD
Statement of Cash Flows
For Month Ended December 31, 2019

Cash flows from operating activities		
Cash received from clients ($4,200 + $1,900)	$ 6,100	
Cash paid for expenses ($2,500 + $900 + $1,000 + $700)	(5,100)	
Net cash provided by operating activities		$ 1,000
Cash flows from investing activities		
Cash paid for equipment	(26,000)	
Net cash used by investing activities		(26,000)
Cash flows from financing activities		
Cash investments from shareholders	30,000	
Cash dividends to shareholders	(200)	
Net cash provided by financing activities		29,800
Net increase in cash		$ 4,800
Cash balance, December 1, 2019		0
Cash balance, December 31, 2019		$ 4,800

Statement of Retained Earnings

The statement of retained earnings reports how retained earnings changes over the reporting period. This statement shows beginning retained earnings, events that increase it (net income), and events that decrease it (dividends and net loss). Ending retained earnings is computed in this statement and is carried over and reported on the balance sheet. FastForward's statement of retained earnings is the second report in Exhibit 1.10. The beginning balance is measured as of the start of business on December 1. It is zero because FastForward did not exist before then. An existing business reports a beginning balance equal to the prior period's ending balance (such as from November 30). FastForward's statement shows the $4,400 of net income for the period, which links the income statement to the statement of retained earnings (see line ①). The statement also reports the $200 cash dividend and FastForward's end-of-period retained earnings balance.

©Pavel1964/Shutterstock

Balance Sheet

FastForward's balance sheet is the third report in Exhibit 1.10. This statement shows FastForward's financial position at the end of business day on December 31. The left side of the balance sheet lists FastForward's assets: cash, supplies, and equipment. The upper right side of the balance sheet shows that FastForward owes $6,200 to creditors. Any other liabilities (such as a bank loan) would be listed here. The equity balance is $34,200. Line ② shows the link between the ending balance of the statement of retained earnings and the retained earnings balance on the balance sheet. (This presentation of the balance sheet is called the *account form:* assets on the left and liabilities and equity on the right. Another presentation is the *report form:* assets on top, followed by liabilities and then equity at the bottom. Both are acceptable.) As always, the accounting equation balances: Assets of $40,400 = Liabilities of $6,200 + Equity of $34,200.

Statement of Cash Flows

FastForward's statement of cash flows is the final report in Exhibit 1.10. The first section reports cash flows from *operating activities*. It shows the $6,100 cash received from clients and the $5,100 cash paid for supplies, rent, and employee salaries. Outflows are in parentheses to denote subtraction. Net cash provided by operating activities for December is $1,000. The second section reports *investing activities,* which involve buying and selling assets such as land and equipment that are held for *long-term use* (typically more than one year). The only investing activity is the $26,000 purchase of equipment. The third section shows cash flows from *financing activities,* which include *long-term* borrowing and repaying of cash from lenders and the cash investments from, and dividends to, stockholders. FastForward reports $30,000 from the owner's initial investment and a $200 cash dividend. The net cash effect of all financing transactions is a $29,800 cash inflow. The final part of the statement shows an increased cash balance of $4,800. The ending balance is also $4,800 as it started with no cash—see line ③.

Point: Payment for supplies is an operating activity because supplies are expected to be used up in short-term operations (typically less than one year).

Point: Investing activities refer to long-term asset investments by the company, *not* to owner investments.

Prepare the (a) income statement, (b) statement of retained earnings, and (c) balance sheet for **Apple** using the following *condensed* data from its fiscal year ended September 30, 2017 ($ in millions).

NEED-TO-KNOW 1-5

Financial Statements

P2

APPLE

Accounts payable	$ 49,049	Revenues	$229,234
Other liabilities	192,223	Investments and other assets	303,373
Cost of sales	141,048	Land and equipment (net)	33,783
Cash	20,289	Selling, general, and other expenses	39,835
Common stock	35,867	Accounts receivable	17,874
Retained earnings, Sep. 24, 2016	96,998	Net income	48,351
Dividends	47,169	Retained earnings, Sep. 30, 2017	98,180

Solution ($ in millions)

APPLE
Income Statement
For Fiscal Year Ended September 30, 2017

Revenues	$229,234
Expenses	
Cost of sales....................................	$141,048
Selling, general, and other expenses	39,835
Total expenses	180,883
Net income	**$ 48,351**

APPLE
Statement of Retained Earnings
For Fiscal Year Ended September 30, 2017

Retained earnings, Sep. 24, 2016...........................	$ 96,998
Plus: Net income..	48,351
	145,349
Less: Dividends	47,169
Retained earnings, Sep. 30, 2017...........................	$ 98,180

APPLE
Balance Sheet
September 30, 2017

Assets		**Liabilities**	
Cash	$ 20,289	Accounts payable....................	$ 49,049
Accounts receivable.....................	17,874	Other liabilities......................	192,223
Land and equipment (net)	33,783	Total liabilities.......................	241,272
Investments and other assets	303,373	**Equity**	
		Common stock......................	35,867
		Retained earnings	98,180
		Total equity........................	134,047
Total assets...........................	$375,319	Total liabilities and equity	$375,319

Do More: QS 1-12, QS 1-13, QS 1-14, E 1-15, E 1-16, E 1-17

Decision Analysis (a section at the end of each chapter) covers ratios for decision making using real company data. Instructors can skip this section and cover all ratios in Chapter 13

 Decision Analysis    **Return on Assets**

A2

Compute and interpret return on assets.

We organize financial statement analysis into four areas: (1) liquidity and efficiency, (2) solvency, (3) profitability, and (4) market prospects—Chapter 13 has a ratio listing with definitions and groupings by area. When analyzing ratios, we use a company's prior-year ratios and competitor ratios to identify good, bad, or average performance.

This chapter presents a profitability measure: return on assets. Return on assets is useful in evaluating management, analyzing and forecasting profits, and planning activities. **Return on assets (ROA),** also called *return on investment* (*ROI*), is defined in Exhibit 1.11.

EXHIBIT 1.11

Return on Assets

$$\text{Return on assets} = \frac{\text{Net income}}{\text{Average total assets}}$$

Net income is from the annual income statement, and average total assets is computed by adding the beginning and ending amounts for that same period and dividing by 2. **Nike** reports total net income of $4,240 million for the current year. At the beginning of the current year its total assets are $21,396 million, and at the end of the current year they total $23,259 million. Nike's return on assets for the current year is:

$$\text{Return on assets} = \frac{\$4,240 \text{ million}}{(\$21,396 \text{ million} + \$23,259 \text{ million})/2} = 19.0\%$$

Is a 19.0% return on assets good or bad for Nike? To help answer this question, we compare (benchmark) Nike's return with its prior performance and the return of its competitor, **Under Armour** (see Exhibit 1.12). Nike shows a stable pattern of good returns that reflects effective use of assets. Nike has outperformed Under Armour in each of the last three years. Its management performed well based on Nike's return on assets.

Return on Assets	Current Year	1 Year Ago	2 Years Ago
Nike...................	19.0%	17.5%	16.3%
Under Armour..........	7.9	9.4	11.4

EXHIBIT 1.12

Nike and Under Armour Returns

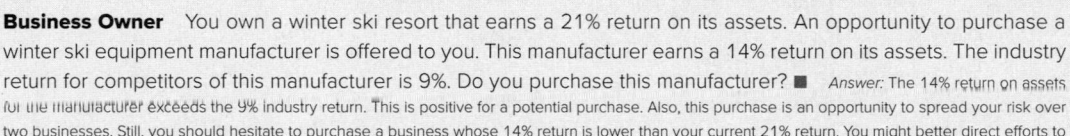

Decision Analysis ends with a role-playing scenario to show the usefulness of ratios

■ **Decision Maker**

Business Owner   You own a winter ski resort that earns a 21% return on its assets. An opportunity to purchase a winter ski equipment manufacturer is offered to you. This manufacturer earns a 14% return on its assets. The industry return for competitors of this manufacturer is 9%. Do you purchase this manufacturer? ■   *Answer:* The 14% return on assets for the manufacturer exceeds the 9% industry return. This is positive for a potential purchase. Also, this purchase is an opportunity to spread your risk over two businesses. Still, you should hesitate to purchase a business whose 14% return is lower than your current 21% return. You might better direct efforts to increase investment in your resort if it can earn more than the 14% alternative.

Comprehensive Need-to-Know is a review of key chapter content; the Planning the Solution section offers strategies in solving it

After several months of planning, Jasmine Worthy started a haircutting business called Expressions. The following events occurred during its first month of business.

NEED-TO-KNOW 1-6

COMPREHENSIVE

Transaction Analysis, Statement Preparation, and Return on Assets

a. Aug. 1 Worthy invested $3,000 cash and $15,000 of equipment in Expressions in exchange for its common stock.
b. 2 Expressions paid $600 cash for furniture for the shop.
c. 3 Expressions paid $500 cash to rent space in a strip mall for August.
d. 4 Purchased $1,200 of equipment on credit for the shop (recorded as accounts payable).
e. 15 Expressions opened for business on August 5. Cash received from haircutting services in the first week and a half of business (ended August 15) was $825.
f. 16 Expressions provided $100 of haircutting services on credit.
g. 17 Expressions received a $100 check for services previously rendered on credit.
h. 18 Expressions paid $125 cash to an assistant for hours worked for the grand opening.
i. 31 Cash received from services provided during the second half of August was $930.
j. 31 Expressions paid $400 cash toward the accounts payable entered into on August 4.
k. 31 Expressions paid a $900 cash dividend to Worthy (sole shareholder).

Required

1. Arrange the following asset, liability, and equity titles in a table similar to the one in Exhibit 1.9: Cash; Accounts Receivable; Furniture; Store Equipment; Accounts Payable; Common Stock; Dividends; Revenues; and Expenses. Show the effects of each transaction using the accounting equation.
2. Prepare an income statement for August.
3. Prepare a statement of retained earnings for August.
4. Prepare a balance sheet as of August 31.
5. Prepare a statement of cash flows for August.
6. Determine the return on assets ratio for August.

PLANNING THE SOLUTION

- Set up a table like Exhibit 1.9 with the appropriate columns for accounts.
- Analyze each transaction and show its effects as increases or decreases in the appropriate columns. Be sure the accounting equation remains in balance after each transaction.
- Prepare the income statement, and identify revenues and expenses. List those items on the statement, compute the difference, and label the result as *net income* or *net loss*.
- Use information in the Equity columns to prepare the statement of retained earnings.
- Use information in the last row of the transactions table to prepare the balance sheet.
- Prepare the statement of cash flows; include all events listed in the Cash column of the transactions table. Classify each cash flow as operating, investing, or financing.
- Calculate return on assets by dividing net income by average assets.

SOLUTION

1.

	Cash	+	Accounts Receivable	+	Furniture	+	Store Equipment	=	Accounts Payable	+	Common Stock	−	Dividends	+	Revenues	−	Expenses
a.	$3,000						$15,000				$18,000						
b.	− 600			+	$600												
Bal.	2,400			+	600	+	15,000	=			18,000						
c.	− 500															−	$500
Bal.	1,900			+	600	+	15,000	=			18,000					−	500
d.						+	1,200		+$1,200								
Bal.	1,900			+	600	+	16,200	=	1,200	+	18,000					−	500
e.	+ 825													+	$ 825		
Bal.	2,725			+	600	+	16,200	=	1,200	+	18,000			+	825	−	500
f.		+	$100											+	100		
Bal.	2,725	+	100	+	600	+	16,200	=	1,200	+	18,000			+	925	−	500
g.	+ 100	−	100														
Bal.	2,825	+	0	+	600	+	16,200	=	1,200	+	18,000			+	925	−	500
h.	− 125															−	125
Bal.	2,700	+	0	+	600	+	16,200	=	1,200	+	18,000			+	925	−	625
i.	+ 930													+	930		
Bal.	3,630	+	0	+	600	+	16,200	=	1,200	+	18,000			+	1,855	−	625
j.	− 400								− 400								
Bal.	3,230	+	0	+	600	+	16,200	=	800	+	18,000			+	1,855	−	625
k.	− 900											−	$900				
Bal.	$ 2,330	+	0	+	$ 600	+	$ 16,200	=	$ 800	+	$ 18,000	−	$ 900	+	$1,855	−	$625

2.

EXPRESSIONS
Income Statement
For Month Ended August 31

Revenues		
Haircutting services revenue		$ 1,855
Expenses		
Rent expense	$ 500	
Wages expense	125	
Total expenses		625
Net income		$ 1,230

3.

EXPRESSIONS
Statement of Retained Earnings
For Month Ended August 31

Retained earnings, August 1*.............	$ 0
Plus: Net income	1,230
	1,230
Less: Dividends	900
Retained earnings, August 31	$ 330

*If Expressions had existed before August 1, the beginning retained earnings balance would equal the prior period's ending balance.

[continued on next page]

4.

EXPRESSIONS			
Balance Sheet			
August 31			

Assets		**Liabilities**	
Cash.....................	$ 2,330	Accounts payable	$ 800
Furniture	600	**Equity**	
Store equipment	16,200	Common stock	18,000
		Retained earnings	330
		Total equity........................	18,330
Total assets	$19,130	Total liabilities and equity	$19,130

5.

EXPRESSIONS
Statement of Cash Flows
For Month Ended August 31

Cash flows from operating activities		
Cash received from customers...........................	$1,855	
Cash paid for expenditures ($500 + $125 + $400)..........	(1,025)	
Net cash provided by operating activities		$ 830
Cash flows from investing activities		
Cash paid for furniture		(600)
Cash flows from financing activities		
Cash investments from shareholders.....................	3,000	
Cash dividends to shareholders.........................	(900)	
Net cash provided by financing activities		2,100
Net increase in cash		$2,330
Cash balance, August 1		0
Cash balance, August 31		$2,330

6. Return on assets $= \dfrac{\text{Net income}}{\text{Average assets}} = \dfrac{\$1,230}{(\$18,000^* + \$19,130)/2} = \dfrac{\$1,230}{\$18,565} = \underline{\underline{6.63\%}}$

*Uses the initial $18,000 investment as the beginning balance for the *start-up period only*.

Return and Risk

1A

A3

Explain the relation between return and risk.

This appendix covers return and risk analysis.

Net income is often linked to **return.** Return on assets (ROA) is stated in ratio form as income divided by assets invested. For example, banks report return from a savings account in the form of an interest return such as 2%. We also could invest in a company's stock, or even start our own business. How do we decide among these options? The answer depends on our trade-off between return and risk.

Risk is the uncertainty about the return we will earn. All business investments involve risk, but some investments involve more risk than others. The lower the risk of an investment, the lower is our expected return. The reason that savings accounts pay such a low return is the low risk of not being repaid with interest (the government guarantees most savings accounts). If we buy a share of eBay or any other company, we might get a large return. However, we have no guarantee of any return; there is even the risk of loss.

Exhibit 1A.1 shows recent returns for 10-year bonds with different risks. *Bonds* are written promises by organizations to repay amounts loaned with interest. U.S. Treasury bonds have a low expected return, but they also have low risk because they are backed by the U.S. government. High-risk corporate bonds have a much larger potential return but have much higher risk.

The trade-off between return and risk is a normal part of business. Higher risk implies higher, but riskier, expected returns. To help us make better decisions, we use accounting information to assess both return and risk.

EXHIBIT 1A.1

Average Returns for Bonds with Different Risks

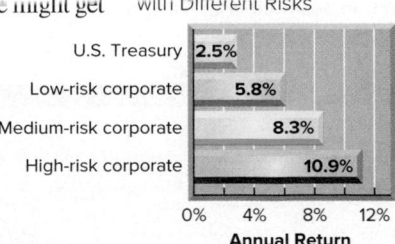

APPENDIX

1B

Business Activities

C5

Identify and describe the three major activities of organizations.

Point: Investing (assets) and financing (liabilities plus equity) totals are *always* equal.

EXHIBIT 1B.1

Activities of Organizations

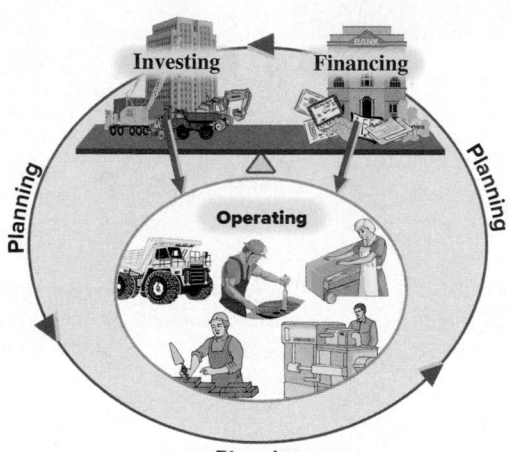

This appendix explains how the accounting equation is linked to business activities. There are three major types of business activities: financing, investing, and operating. Each of these requires planning. *Planning* is defining an organization's ideas, goals, and actions.

Financing   *Financing activities* provide the resources organizations use to pay for assets such as land, buildings, and equipment. The two sources of financing are owner and nonowner. *Owner financing* refers to resources contributed by the owner along with any income the owner leaves in the organization. *Nonowner* (or *creditor*) *financing* refers to resources loaned by creditors (lenders).

Investing   *Investing activities* are the acquiring and disposing of assets that an organization uses to buy and sell its products or services. Some organizations require land and factories to operate. Others need only an office. Invested amounts are referred to as *assets*. Creditor and owner financing hold claims on assets. Creditors' claims are called *liabilities,* and the owner's claim is called *equity*. This yields the *accounting equation:* Assets = Liabilities + Equity.

Operating   *Operating activities* involve using resources to research, develop, purchase, produce, distribute, and market products and services. Sales and revenues are the inflow of assets from selling products and services. Costs and expenses are the outflow of assets to support operating activities.

Exhibit 1B.1 summarizes business activities. Planning is part of each activity and gives them meaning and focus. Investing (assets) and financing (liabilities and equity) are opposite each other because they always are equal. Operating activities are below to show that they are the result of investing and financing.

Summary: Cheat Sheet

ACCOUNTING USES

External users: Do not directly run the organization and have limited access to its accounting information. Examples are lenders, shareholders, boards of directors, external auditors, nonexecutive employees, labor unions, regulators, voters, donors, suppliers, and customers.
Internal users: Directly manage organization operations. Examples are the CEO and other executives, research and development managers, purchasing managers, production managers, and other managerial-level employees.
Private accounting: Accounting employees working for businesses.
Public accounting: Offering audit, tax, and accounting services to others.

ETHICS AND ACCOUNTING

Fraud triangle: Factors that push a person to commit fraud.
- **Opportunity:** Must be able to commit fraud with a low risk of getting caught.
- **Pressure,** or incentive: Must feel pressure or have incentive to commit fraud.
- **Rationalization,** or attitude: Justifies fraud or does not see its criminal nature.

Common business entities:

	Sole Proprietorship	Partnership
Number of owners	1 owner; easy to set up.	2 or more, called *partners;* easy to set up.
Business taxation	No additional business income tax.	No additional business income tax.
Owner liability	Unlimited liability. Owner is personally liable for proprietorship debts.	Unlimited liability. Partners are jointly liable for partnership debts.
Legal entity	*Not* a separate legal entity.	*Not* a separate legal entity.
Business life	Business ends with owner death or choice.	Business ends with a partner death or choice.

	Corporation	Limited Liability Company (LLC)
Number of owners	1 or more, called *stockholders;* can get many investors by selling **stock** or **shares** of corporate ownership.	1 or more, called *members*.
Business taxation	Additional corporate income tax.	No additional business income tax.
Owner liability	Limited liability. Owners, called **stockholders** (or **shareholders**), are not liable for corporate acts and debts.	Limited liability. Owners, called **members**, are not personally liable for LLC debts.
Legal entity	A separate entity with the same rights and responsibilities as a person.	A separate entity with the same rights and responsibilities as a person.
Business life	Indefinite.	Indefinite.

SYSTEM OF ACCOUNTS

Assets: Resources a company owns or controls that are expected to yield future benefits.
Liabilities: Creditors' claims on assets. These are obligations to provide assets, products, or services to others.
Equity: Shareholders' claim on assets. It consists of:

+ Common Stock   **Common stock** reflects inflows of cash and other net assets from stockholders in exchange for stock.

− Dividends   **Dividends** are outflows of cash and other assets to stockholders that reduce equity.

+ Revenues   **Revenues** increase equity (via net income) from sales of products and services to customers; examples are sales of products, consulting services provided, facilities rented to others, and commissions from services.

− Expenses   **Expenses** decrease equity (via net income) from costs of providing products and services to customers; examples are costs of employee time, use of supplies, advertising, utilities, and insurance fees.

TRANSACTION ANALYSIS

Accounting equation: Applies to all transactions and events, to all companies and organizations, and to all points in time.

$$\text{Assets} = \text{Liabilities} + \text{Equity}$$

Summary of transactions:

	Cash	+ Accounts Receivable	+ Supplies	+ Equipment	= Accounts Payable	+ Common Stock	− Dividends	+ Revenues	− Expenses
(1)	$30,000				=	$30,000			
(2)	− 2,500		+ $2,500						
Bal.	27,500		+ 2,500		=	30,000			
(3)	−26,000			+ $26,000					
Bal.	1,500		+ 2,500	+ 26,000	=	30,000			
(4)			+ 7,100		= +$7,100				
Bal.	1,500		+ 9,600	+ 26,000	= 7,100	+ 30,000			
(5)	+ 4,200							+ $4,200	
Bal.	5,700		+ 9,600	+ 26,000	= 7,100	+ 30,000		+ 4,200	
(6)	− 1,000								− $1,000
Bal.	4,700		+ 9,600	+ 26,000	= 7,100	+ 30,000		+ 4,200	− 1,000
(7)	− 700								700
Bal.	4,000		+ 9,600	+ 26,000	= 7,100	+ 30,000		+ 4,200	− 1,700
(8)		+ $1,900						+ 1,600	
								+ 300	
Bal.	4,000	+ 1,900	+ 9,600	+ 26,000	= 7,100	+ 30,000		6,100	− 1,700
(9)	+ 1,900	− 1,900							
Bal.	5,900	+ 0	+ 9,600	+ 26,000	= 7,100	+ 30,000		+ 6,100	− 1,700
(10)	− 900				− 900				
Bal.	5,000	+ 0	+ 9,600	+ 26,000	= 6,200	+ 30,000		+ 6,100	− 1,700
(11)	− 200						− $200		
Bal.	$ 4,800	+ $ 0	+ $9,600	+ $ 26,000	= $ 6,200	+ $ 30,000	− $ 200	+ $6,100	− $ 1,700

←*A list of key terms concludes each chapter (a complete glossary is also available)*

Transaction 1: Investment by owner
Transaction 2: Purchase supplies for cash
Transaction 3: Purchase equipment for cash
Transaction 4: Purchase supplies on credit
Transaction 5: Provide services for cash
Transactions 6 and 7: Payment of expenses in cash
Transaction 8: Provide services and facilities for credit
Transaction 9: Receipt of cash from accounts receivable
Transaction 10: Payment of accounts payable
Transaction 11: Payment of cash dividends

FINANCIAL STATEMENTS

Financial Statement	Layout	Purpose
Income statement	Revenue − Expenses / Net income	Describes a company's revenues and expenses and computes net income or loss over a period of time.
Statement of retained earnings	Beg. retained earnings + Net income / Dividends / End. retained earnings	Explains changes in retained earnings from net income (or loss) and any dividends over a period of time.
Balance sheet	Assets = Liabilities + Equity	Describes a company's financial position (types and amounts of assets, liabilities, and equity) at a point in time.
Statement of cash flows	+/− Operating C.F. / +/− Investing C.F. / +/− Financing C.F. / Change in cash	Identifies cash inflows (receipts) and cash outflows (payments) over a period of time.

Key Terms

Accounting (3)
Accounting equation (10)
Assets (9)
Audit (6)
Auditors (6)
Balance sheet (15)
Bookkeeping (3)
Business entity assumption (8)
Common stock (8, 10)
Conceptual framework (7)
Contributed capital (10)
Corporation (8)
Cost-benefit constraint (8)
Cost constraint (8)
Cost principle (7)
Dividends (10)
Dodd-Frank Wall Street Reform and Consumer Protection Act (6)
Double taxation (9)
Equity (9)
Ethics (6)
Events (11)
Expanded accounting equation (10)
Expense recognition principle (8)

Expenses (10)
External transactions (11)
External users (4)
Financial accounting (4)
Financial Accounting Standards Board (FASB) (7)
Full disclosure principle (8)
Generally accepted accounting principles (GAAP) (7)
Going-concern assumption (8)
Income statement (15)
Internal controls (6)
Internal transactions (11)
Internal users (4)
International Accounting Standards Board (IASB) (7)
International Financial Reporting Standards (IFRS) (7)
Liabilities (9)
Limited liability company (LLC) (8)
Managerial accounting (4)
Matching principle (8)
Measurement principle (7)
Members (8)

Monetary unit assumption (8)
Net income (15)
Net loss (15)
Owner investments (10)
Partnership (8)
Proprietorship (8)
Recordkeeping (3)
Retained earnings (10)
Return (21)
Return on assets (ROA) (18)
Revenue recognition principle (7)
Revenues (10)
Risk (21)
Sarbanes-Oxley Act (SOX) (6)
Securities and Exchange Commission (SEC) (7)
Shareholders (8)
Shares (8)
Sole proprietorship (8)
Statement of cash flows (15)
Statement of retained earnings (15)
Stock (8)
Stockholders (8)
Time period assumption (8)

Multiple Choice Quiz

1. A building is offered for sale at $500,000 but is currently assessed at $400,000. The purchaser of the building believes the building is worth $475,000, but ultimately purchases the building for $450,000. The purchaser records the building at:

a. $50,000.   **c.** $450,000.   **e.** $500,000.
b. $400,000.   **d.** $475,000.

2. On December 30 of the current year, **KPMG** signs a $150,000 contract to provide accounting services to one of its clients in *the next year*. KPMG has a December 31 year-end. Which accounting principle or assumption requires KPMG to record the accounting services revenue from this client in *the next year* and not in the current year?

 a. Business entity assumption

 b. Revenue recognition principle

 c. Monetary unit assumption

 d. Cost principle

 e. Going-concern assumption

3. If the assets of a company increase by $100,000 during the year and its liabilities increase by $35,000 during the same year, then the change in equity of the company during the year must have been:

 a. An increase of $135,000.   **d.** An increase of $65,000.

 b. A decrease of $135,000.   **e.** An increase of $100,000.

 c. A decrease of $65,000.

4. **Brunswick** borrows $50,000 cash from Third National Bank. How does this transaction affect the accounting equation for Brunswick?

 a. Assets increase by $50,000; liabilities increase by $50,000; no effect on equity.

 b. Assets increase by $50,000; no effect on liabilities; equity increases by $50,000.

 c. Assets increase by $50,000; liabilities decrease by $50,000; no effect on equity.

 d. No effect on assets; liabilities increase by $50,000; equity increases by $50,000.

 e. No effect on assets; liabilities increase by $50,000; equity decreases by $50,000.

5. **Geek Squad** performs services for a customer and bills the customer for $500. How would Geek Squad record this transaction?

 a. Accounts receivable increase by $500; revenues increase by $500.

 b. Cash increases by $500; revenues increase by $500.

 c. Accounts receivable increase by $500; revenues decrease by $500.

 d. Accounts receivable increase by $500; accounts payable increase by $500.

 e. Accounts payable increase by $500; revenues increase by $500.

ANSWERS TO MULTIPLE CHOICE QUIZ

1. c; $450,000 is the actual cost incurred.

2. b; revenue is recorded when services are provided.

3. d;

Assets	=	Liabilities	+	Equity
+$100,000	=	+$35,000	+	?

Change in equity = $100,000 − $35,000 = $65,000

4. a

5. a

---

^{A(B)} *Superscript letter A or B denotes assignments based on Appendix 1A or 1B.*

[I] Icon denotes assignments that involve decision making.

Discussion Questions

1. What is the purpose of accounting in society?

2. Technology is increasingly used to process accounting data. Why then must we study and understand accounting?

3. [I] Identify four kinds of external users and describe how they use accounting information.

4. [I] What are at least three questions business owners and managers might be able to answer by looking at accounting information?

5. Identify three actual businesses that offer services and three actual businesses that offer products.

6. [I] Describe the internal role of accounting for organizations.

7. Identify three types of services typically offered by accounting professionals.

8. [I] What type of accounting information might be useful to the marketing managers of a business?

9. Why is accounting described as a service activity?

10. What are some accounting-related professions?

11. How do ethics rules affect auditors' choice of clients?

12. What work do tax accounting professionals perform in addition to preparing tax returns?

13. What does the concept of *objectivity* imply for information reported in financial statements?

14. A business reports its own office stationery on the balance sheet at its $400 cost, although it cannot be sold for more than $10 as scrap paper. Which accounting principle and/or assumption justifies this treatment?

15. Why is the revenue recognition principle needed? What does it demand?

16. Describe the four basic forms of business organization and their key attributes.

17. Define (*a*) *assets,* (*b*) *liabilities,* (*c*) *equity,* and (*d*) *net assets.*

18. What events or transactions change equity?

19. Identify the two main categories of accounting principles.

20. What do accountants mean by the term *revenue*?

21. Define *net income* and explain its computation.

22. Identify the four basic financial statements of a business.

23. 🕐 What information is reported in an income statement?

24. Give two examples of expenses a business might incur.

25. What is the purpose of the statement of retained earnings?

26. 🕐 What information is reported in a balance sheet?

27. The statement of cash flows reports on what major activities?

28. 🕐 Define and explain return on assets.

29.ᴬ 🕐 Define return and risk. Discuss the trade-off between them.

30.ᴮ Describe the three major business activities in organizations.

31.ᴮ Explain why investing (assets) and financing (liabilities and equity) totals are always equal.

32. Refer to **Google**'s financial statements in Appendix A near the end of the text. To what level of significance are dollar amounts rounded? What time period does its income statement cover?   **GOOGLE**

33. 🕐 Access the SEC EDGAR database (**SEC.gov**) and retrieve **Apple**'s 2017 10-K (filed November 3, 2017). Identify its auditor. What responsibility does its independent auditor claim regarding Apple's financial statements?   **APPLE**

Connect reproduces assignments online, in static or algorithmic mode, which allows instructors to monitor, promote, and assess student learning. It can be used for practice, homework, or exams

connect

Quick Study exercises offer a brief check of key points.

QUICK STUDY

Choose the term or phrase below that best completes each statement.

a. Accounting   **c.** Recording   **e.** Governmental   **g.** Language of business

b. Identifying   **d.** Communicating   **f.** Technology   **h.** Recordkeeping (bookkeeping)

1. _____ reduces the time, effort, and cost of recordkeeping while improving clerical accuracy.

2. _____ requires that we input, measure, and log transactions and events.

3. _____ is the recording of transactions and events, either manually or electronically.

QS 1-1
Understanding accounting
C1

Identify the following users as either external users (E) or internal users (I).

_____ **a.** Customers   _____ **e.** Managers   _____ **i.** Controllers

_____ **b.** Suppliers   _____ **f.** District attorney   _____ **j.** FBI and IRS

_____ **c.** External auditors _____ **g.** Shareholders   _____ **k.** Consumer group

_____ **d.** Business press   _____ **h.** Lenders   _____ **l.** Directors

QS 1-2
Identifying accounting users
C2

The fraud triangle asserts that the following *three* factors must exist for a person to commit fraud.

A. Opportunity   **B.** Pressure   **C.** Rationalization

Identify the fraud risk factor (A, B, or C) in each of the following situations.

_____ **1.** The business has no cameras or security devices at its warehouse.

_____ **2.** Managers are expected to grow business or be fired.

_____ **3.** A worker sees other employees regularly take inventory for personal use.

_____ **4.** No one matches the cash in the register to receipts when shifts end.

_____ **5.** Officers are told to show rising income or risk layoffs.

_____ **6.** A worker feels that fellow employees are not honest.

QS 1-3
Identifying ethical risks
C3

This icon highlights ethics-related assignments

Identify each of the following terms or phrases as an accounting (*a*) principle, (*b*) assumption, or (*c*) constraint.

_____ **1.** Full disclosure   _____ **3.** Going-concern

_____ **2.** Time period   _____ **4.** Revenue recognition

QS 1-4
Identifying principles, assumptions, and constraints   C4

Complete the following table with either a *yes* or *no* regarding the attributes of a proprietorship, partnership, corporation, and limited liability company (LLC).

QS 1-5
Identifying attributes of businesses
C4

Attribute Present	Proprietorship	Partnership	Corporation	LLC
1. Business taxed	___	___	___	___
2. Limited liability	___	___	___	___
3. Legal entity	___	___	___	___

QS 1-6

Identifying accounting
principles and assumptions

C4

Identify the letter for the principle or assumption from *A* through *F* in the blank space next to each numbered situation that it best explains or justifies.

A. General accounting principle   **D.** Revenue recognition principle

B. Measurement (cost) principle   **E.** Expense recognition (matching) principle

C. Business entity assumption   **F.** Going-concern assumption

_____ **1.** In December of this year, Chavez Landscaping received a customer's order and cash prepayment to install sod at a house that would not be ready for installation until March of *next year.* Chavez should record the revenue from the customer order in March of *next year,* not in December of this year.

_____ **2.** If $51,000 cash is paid to buy land, the land is reported on the buyer's balance sheet at $51,000.

_____ **3.** Mike Derr owns both Sailing Passions and Dockside Digs. In preparing financial statements for Dockside Digs, Mike makes sure that the expense transactions of Sailing Passions are kept separate from Dockside Digs's transactions and financial statements.

QS 1-7

Applying the accounting
equation   A1

a. Total assets of Charter Company equal $700,000 and its equity is $420,000. What is the amount of its liabilities?

b. Total assets of Martin Marine equal $500,000 and its liabilities and equity amounts are equal to each other. What is the amount of its liabilities? What is the amount of its equity?

This icon highlights assignments that enhance decision-making skills

QS 1-8

Applying the accounting
equation

A1

1. Use the accounting equation to compute the missing financial statement amounts (*a*), (*b*), and (*c*).

	A	B	C	D
1	**Company**	**Assets** =	**Liabilities** +	**Equity**
2	1	$ 75,000	$ _(a)_	$ 40,000
3	2	_(b)_	25,000	70,000
4	3	85,000	20,000	_(c)_

2. Use the expanded accounting equation to compute the missing financial statement amounts (*a*) and (*b*).

	A	B	C	D	E	F	G
1				**Common**			
2	**Company**	**Assets**	**Liabilities**	**Stock**	**Dividends**	**Revenues**	**Expenses**
3	1	$ 40,000	$ 16,000	$ 20,000	$ 0	_(a)_	$ 8,000
4	2	$ 80,000	$ 32,000	$ 44,000	_(b)_	$ 24,000	$ 18,000

QS 1-9

Identifying and computing
assets, liabilities, and equity

A1 **GOOGLE**

Use **Google**'s December 31, 2017, financial statements, in Appendix A near the end of the text, to answer the following.

a. Identify the amounts (in $ millions) of its 2017 (1) assets, (2) liabilities, and (3) equity.

b. Using amounts from part *a*, verify that Assets = Liabilities + Equity.

QS 1-10

Identifying effects of
transactions using
accounting equation—
Revenues and Expenses

P1

Create the following table similar to the one in Exhibit 1.9.

Assets			=	Liabilities	+	Equity						
Cash	+	Accounts Receivable	=	Accounts Payable	+	Common Stock	−	Dividends	+	Revenues	−	Expenses

Then use additions and subtractions to show the dollar effects of each transaction on individual items of the accounting equation (identify each revenue and expense type, such as commissions revenue or rent expense).

a. The company completed consulting work for a client and immediately collected $5,500 cash earned.

b. The company completed commission work for a client and sent a bill for $4,000 to be received within 30 days.

c. The company paid an assistant $1,400 cash as wages for the period.

d. The company collected $1,000 cash as a partial payment for the amount owed by the client in transaction *b*.

e. The company paid $700 cash for this period's cleaning services.

Create the following table similar to the one in Exhibit 1.9.

Assets	=	Liabilities	+			Equity			
Cash + Supplies + Equipment + Land	=	Accounts Payable	+	Common Stock	−	Dividends	+	Revenues	− Expenses

QS 1-11
Identifying effects of transactions using accounting equation—Assets and Liabilities
P1

Then use additions and subtractions to show the dollar effects of each transaction on individual items of the accounting equation.

a. The owner invested $15,000 cash in the company in exchange for its common stock.

b. The company purchased supplies for $500 cash.

c. The owner invested $10,000 of equipment in the company in exchange for more common stock.

d. The company purchased $200 of additional supplies on credit.

e. The company purchased land for $9,000 cash.

Indicate in which financial statement each item would most likely appear: income statement (I), balance sheet (B), or statement of cash flows (CF).

_____ **a.** Assets

_____ **b.** Cash from operating activities

_____ **c.** Equipment

_____ **d.** Expenses

_____ **e.** Liabilities

_____ **f.** Net decrease (or increase) in cash

_____ **g.** Revenues

_____ **h.** Total liabilities and equity

QS 1-12
Identifying items with financial statements
P2

Classify each of the following items as revenues (R), expenses (EX), or dividends (D).

_____ **1.** Cost of sales

_____ **2.** Service revenue

_____ **3.** Wages expense

_____ **4.** Cash dividends

_____ **5.** Rent expense

_____ **6.** Rental revenue

_____ **7.** Insurance expense

_____ **8.** Consulting revenue

QS 1-13
Identifying income and equity accounts
P2

Classify each of the following items as assets (A), liabilities (L), or equity (EQ).

_____ **1.** Land

_____ **2.** Common stock

_____ **3.** Equipment

_____ **4.** Accounts payable

_____ **5.** Accounts receivable

_____ **6.** Supplies

QS 1-14
Identifying assets, liabilities, and equity   **P2**

On December 31, Hawkin's records show the following accounts. Use this information to prepare a December income statement for Hawkin.

Equipment	$3,000	Accounts receivable	$ 600	Wages expense	$8,000
Cash	2,400	Services revenue	16,000	Utilities expense	700
Rent expense	1,500	Accounts payable	6,000		

QS 1-15
Preparing an income statement
P2

In a recent year's financial statements, **Home Depot** reported the following results. Compute and interpret Home Depot's return on assets (assume competitors average an 11.0% return on assets).

Sales	$95 billion	Net income	$8 billion	Average total assets	$42 billion

QS 1-16
Computing and interpreting return on assets
A2

Use **Samsung**'s December 31, 2017, financial statements in Appendix A near the end of the text to answer the following.

a. Identify the amounts (in millions of Korean won) of Samsung's 2017 (1) assets, (2) liabilities, and (3) equity.

b. Using amounts from part *a*, verify that Assets = Liabilities + Equity.

QS 1-17
Identifying and computing assets, liabilities, and equity
A1
Samsung

Most **Exercises** and **Quick Study** assignments are supported with Guided Examples ("Hints") in Connect using different numbers; an instructor can choose whether to make them available to students

■ connect

EXERCISES

Exercise 1-1
Classifying activities reflected in the accounting system **C1**

Classify the following activities as part of the identifying (I), recording (R), or communicating (C) aspects of accounting.

_____ **1.** Analyzing and interpreting reports.   _____ **5.** Preparing financial statements.
_____ **2.** Presenting financial information.   _____ **6.** Acquiring knowledge of revenue transactions.
_____ **3.** Keeping a log of service costs.   _____ **7.** Observing transactions and events.
_____ **4.** Measuring the costs of a product.   _____ **8.** Registering cash sales of products sold.

Exercise 1-2
Identifying accounting users and uses

C2

Part A. Identify the following questions as most likely to be asked by an internal (I) or an external (E) user of accounting information.

_____ **1.** Which inventory items are out of stock?
_____ **2.** Should we make a five-year loan to that business?
_____ **3.** What are the costs of our product's ingredients?
_____ **4.** Should we buy, hold, or sell a company's stock?
_____ **5.** Should we spend additional money for redesign of our product?
_____ **6.** Which firm reports the highest sales and income?
_____ **7.** What are the costs of our service to customers?

Part B. Identify the following users as either an internal (I) or an external (E) user.

_____ **1.** Research and development executive   _____ **5.** Distribution manager
_____ **2.** Human resources executive   _____ **6.** Creditor
_____ **3.** Politician   _____ **7.** Production supervisor
_____ **4.** Shareholder   _____ **8.** Purchasing manager

Exercise 1-3
Describing accounting responsibilities

C2

Many accounting professionals work in one of the following three areas.

A. Financial accounting   **B.** Managerial accounting   **C.** Tax accounting

Identify the area of accounting that is most involved in each of the following responsibilities.

_____ **1.** Internal auditing   _____ **5.** Enforcing tax laws
_____ **2.** External auditing   _____ **6.** Planning transactions to minimize taxes
_____ **3.** Cost accounting   _____ **7.** Preparing external financial statements
_____ **4.** Budgeting   _____ **8.** Analyzing external financial reports

Exercise 1-4
Learning the language of business

C1   C2   C3

Match each of the numbered descriptions *1* through *5* with the term or phrase it best reflects. Indicate your answer by writing the letter *A* through *H* for the term or phrase in the blank provided.

A. Audit   **C.** Ethics   **E.** SEC   **G.** Net income
B. GAAP   **D.** FASB   **F.** Public accountants   **H.** IASB

_____ **1.** An assessment of whether financial statements follow GAAP.
_____ **2.** Amount a business earns in excess of all expenses and costs associated with its sales and revenues.
_____ **3.** A group that sets accounting principles in the United States.
_____ **4.** Accounting professionals who provide services to many clients.
_____ **5.** Principles that determine whether an action is right or wrong.

Exercise 1-5
Identifying ethical terminology

C3

Match each of the numbered descriptions *1* through *7* with the term or phrase it best reflects. Indicate your answer by writing the letter *A* through *G* for the term or phrase in the blank provided.

A. Ethics   **D.** Internal controls   **F.** Audit
B. Fraud triangle   **E.** Sarbanes-Oxley Act   **G.** Dodd-Frank Act
C. Prevention

_____ **1.** Requires the SEC to pay whistleblowers.
_____ **2.** Examines whether financial statements are prepared using GAAP; it does not ensure absolute accuracy of the statements.

_____ **3.** Requires documentation and verification of internal controls and increases emphasis on internal control effectiveness.

_____ **4.** Procedures set up to protect company property and equipment, ensure reliable accounting, promote efficiency, and encourage adherence to policies.

_____ **5.** A less expensive and more effective means to stop fraud.

_____ **6.** Three factors push a person to commit fraud: opportunity, pressure, and rationalization.

_____ **7.** Beliefs that distinguish right from wrong.

The following describe several different business organizations. Determine whether each description best refers to a sole proprietorship (SP), partnership (P), corporation (C), or limited liability company (LLC).

_____ **a.** Micah and Nancy own Financial Services, which pays a business income tax. Micah and Nancy do not have personal responsibility for the debts of Financial Services.

_____ **b.** Riley and Kay own Speedy Packages, a courier service. Both are personally liable for the debts of the business.

_____ **c.** IBC Services does not have separate legal existence apart from the one person who owns It.

_____ **d.** Trent Company is owned by Trent Malone, who is personally liable for the company's debts.

_____ **e.** Ownership of Zander Company is divided into 1,000 shares of stock. The company pays a business income tax.

_____ **f.** Physio Products does not pay income taxes and has one owner. The owner has unlimited liability for business debt.

_____ **g.** AJ Company pays a business income tax and has two owners.

_____ **h.** Jeffy Auto is a separate legal entity from its owner, but it does not pay a business income tax.

Exercise 1-6
Distinguishing business organizations
C4

Enter the letter A through H for the principle or assumption in the blank space next to each numbered description that it best reflects.

A. General accounting principle

B. Measurement (cost) principle

C. Business entity assumption

D. Revenue recognition principle

E. Specific accounting principle

F. Expense recognition (matching) principle

G. Going-concern assumption

H. Full disclosure principle

_____ **1.** A company reports details behind financial statements that would impact users' decisions.

_____ **2.** Financial statements reflect the assumption that the business continues operating.

_____ **3.** A company records the expenses incurred to generate the revenues reported.

_____ **4.** Concepts, assumptions, and guidelines for preparing financial statements.

_____ **5.** Each business is accounted for separately from its owner or owners.

_____ **6.** Revenue is recorded when products and services are delivered.

_____ **7.** Detailed rules used in reporting events and transactions.

_____ **8.** Information is based on actual costs incurred in transactions.

Exercise 1-7
Identifying accounting principles and assumptions
C4

Determine the missing amount from each of the separate situations a, b, and c below.

Exercise 1-8
Using the accounting equation
A1

	A		B		C
1	**Assets**	**=**	**Liabilities**	**+**	**Equity**
2	$ *(a)*		$ 20,000		$ 45,000
3	100,000		34,000		*(b)*
4	154,000		*(c)*		40,000

Answer the following questions. *Hint:* Use the accounting equation.

a. At the beginning of the year, Addison Company's assets are $300,000 and its equity is $100,000. During the year, assets increase $80,000 and liabilities increase $50,000. What is the equity at year-end?

b. Office Store Co. has assets equal to $123,000 and liabilities equal to $47,000 at year-end. What is the equity for Office Store Co. at year-end?

c. At the beginning of the year, Quaker Company's liabilities equal $70,000. During the year, assets increase by $60,000, and at year-end assets equal $190,000. Liabilities decrease $5,000 during the year. What are the beginning and ending amounts of equity?

Exercise 1-9
Using the accounting equation
A1

Check (c) Beg. equity, $60,000

Exercise 1-10

Analysis using the accounting equation

P1

Zen began a new consulting firm on January 5. Following is a financial summary, including balances, for each of the company's first five transactions (using the accounting equation form).

	Assets					=	Liabilities	+		Equity	
Transaction	Cash	+	Accounts Receivable	+	Office Supplies	+	Office Furniture	=	Accounts Payable	+	Common Stock	+	Revenues
___ 1.	$40,000	+	$ 0	+	$ 0	+	$ 0	=	$ 0	+	$40,000	+	$ 0
___ 2.	38,000	+	0	+	3,000	+	0	=	1,000	+	40,000	+	0
___ 3.	30,000	+	0	+	3,000	+	8,000	=	1,000	+	40,000	+	0
___ 4.	30,000	+	6,000	+	3,000	+	8,000	=	1,000	+	40,000	+	6,000
___ 5.	31,000	+	6,000	+	3,000	+	8,000	=	1,000	+	40,000	+	7,000

Identify the explanation from *a* through *j* below that best describes each transaction *1* through *5* above and enter it in the blank space in front of each numbered transaction.

a. The company purchased office furniture for $8,000 cash.

b. The company received $40,000 cash from a bank loan.

c. The owner invested $1,000 cash in the business in exchange for its common stock.

d. The owner invested $40,000 cash in the business in exchange for its common stock.

e. The company purchased office supplies for $3,000 by paying $2,000 cash and putting $1,000 on credit.

f. The company billed a customer $6,000 for services provided.

g. The company purchased office furniture worth $8,000 on credit.

h. The company provided services for $1,000 cash.

i. The company sold office supplies for $3,000 and received $2,000 cash and $1,000 on credit.

j. The company provided services for $6,000 cash.

Exercise 1-11

Identifying effects of transactions on the accounting equation

P1

The following table shows the effects of transactions *1* through *5* on the assets, liabilities, and equity of Mulan's Boutique.

	Assets							=	Liabilities	+		Equity	
	Cash	+	Accounts Receivable	+	Office Supplies	+	Land	=	Accounts Payable	+	Common Stock	+	Revenues
	$ 21,000	+	$ 0	+	$3,000	+	$19,000	=	$ 0	+	$43,000	+	$ 0
___ 1.	− 4,000					+	4,000						
___ 2.				+	1,000				+1,000				
___ 3.		+	1,900									+	1,900
___ 4.	− 1,000								− 1,000				
___ 5.	+ 1,900	−	1,900										
	$ 17,900	+	$ 0	+	$4,000	+	$23,000	=	$ 0	+	$43,000	+	$1,900

Identify the explanation from *a* through *j* below that best describes each transaction *1* through *5* and enter it in the blank space in front of each numbered transaction.

a. The company purchased $1,000 of office supplies on credit.

b. The company collected $1,900 cash from an account receivable.

c. The company sold land for $4,000 cash.

d. The company paid $1,000 cash in dividends to shareholders.

e. The company purchased office supplies for $1,000 cash.

f. The company purchased land for $4,000 cash.

g. The company billed a client $1,900 for services provided.

h. The company paid $1,000 cash toward an account payable.

i. The owner invested $1,900 cash in the business in exchange for its common stock.

j. The company sold office supplies for $1,900 on credit.

For each transaction *a* through *f*, identify its impact on the accounting equation (select from *1* through *5* below).

_____ **a.** The company pays cash toward an account payable.

_____ **b.** The company purchases equipment on credit.

_____ **c.** The owner invests cash in the business in exchange for its common stock.

_____ **d.** The company pays cash dividends to shareholders.

_____ **e.** The company purchases supplies for cash.

_____ **f.** The company provides services for cash.

1. Decreases an asset and decreases equity.

2. Increases an asset and increases a liability.

3. Decreases an asset and decreases a liability.

4. Increases an asset and decreases an asset.

5. Increases an asset and increases equity.

Exercise 1-12
Identifying effects of
transactions on the
accounting equation

P1

Ming Chen began a professional practice on June 1 and plans to prepare financial statements at the end of each month. During June, Ming Chen (the owner) completed these transactions.

a. Owner invested $60,000 cash in the company along with equipment that had a $15,000 market value in exchange for its common stock.

b. The company paid $1,500 cash for rent of office space for the month.

c. The company purchased $10,000 of additional equipment on credit (payment due within 30 days).

d. The company completed work for a client and immediately collected the $2,500 cash earned.

e. The company completed work for a client and sent a bill for $8,000 to be received within 30 days.

f. The company purchased additional equipment for $6,000 cash.

g. The company paid an assistant $3,000 cash as wages for the month.

h. The company collected $5,000 cash as a partial payment for the amount owed by the client in transaction *e*.

i. The company paid $10,000 cash to settle the liability created in transaction *c*.

j. The company paid $1,000 cash in dividends to the owner (sole shareholder).

Exercise 1-13
Identifying effects of
transactions using the
accounting equation

P1

Required

Create the following table similar to the one in Exhibit 1.9.

Assets			=	Liabilities	+	Equity				
Cash +	Accounts Receivable	+ Equipment	=	Accounts Payable	+ Common Stock	– Dividends	+ Revenues	– Expenses

Then use additions and subtractions to show the dollar effects of the transactions on individual items of the accounting equation. Show new balances after each transaction.

Check   Ending balances:
Cash, $46,000; Expenses,
$4,500

Swiss Group reports net income of $40,000 for 2019. At the beginning of 2019, Swiss Group had $200,000 in assets. By the end of 2019, assets had grown to $300,000. What is Swiss Group's 2019 return on assets? How would you assess its performance if competitors average an 11% return on assets?

Exercise 1-14
Analyzing return on assets

A2

On October 1, Ebony Ernst organized Ernst Consulting; on October 3, the owner contributed $84,000 in assets in exchange for its common stock to launch the business. On October 31, the company's records show the following items and amounts. Use this information to prepare an October income statement for the business.

Exercise 1-15
Preparing an income
statement

P2

Cash..........................	$11,360	Cash dividends	$ 2,000
Accounts receivable............	14,000	Consulting revenue...................	14,000
Office supplies	3,250	Rent expense........................	3,550
Land.........................	46,000	Salaries expense.....................	7,000
Office equipment	18,000	Telephone expense...................	760
Accounts payable..............	8,500	Miscellaneous expenses..............	580
Common stock	84,000		

Check   Net income, $2,110

Use the information in Exercise 1-15 to prepare an October statement of retained earnings for Ernst Consulting.

Exercise 1-16
Preparing a statement of
retained earnings   **P2**

Exercise 1-17

Preparing a balance
sheet   **P2**

Use the information in Exercise 1-15 to prepare an October 31 balance sheet for Ernst Consulting. *Hint:*
The solution to Exercise 1-16 can help.

Exercise 1-18

Preparing a statement of
cash flows

P2

Check Net increase in cash,
$11,360

Use the information in Exercise 1-15 to prepare an October 31 statement of cash flows for Ernst
Consulting. Assume the following additional information.

a. The owner's initial investment consists of $38,000 cash and $46,000 in land in exchange for its common
   stock.

b. The company's $18,000 equipment purchase is paid in cash.

c. The accounts payable balance of $8,500 consists of the $3,250 office supplies purchase and $5,250 in
   employee salaries yet to be paid.

d. The company's rent, telephone, and miscellaneous expenses are paid in cash.

e. No cash has been collected on the $14,000 consulting fees earned.

Exercise 1-19

Identifying sections of the
statement of cash flows

P2

Indicate the section (O, I, or F) where transactions *1* through *8* would appear on the statement of cash flows.

O. Cash flows from operating activity   **F.** Cash flows from financing activity

I. Cash flows from investing activity

_____ **1.** Cash purchase of equipment   _____ **5.** Cash paid on account payable to supplier

_____ **2.** Cash paid for dividends   _____ **6.** Cash received from clients

_____ **3.** Cash paid for advertising   _____ **7.** Cash paid for rent

_____ **4.** Cash paid for wages   _____ **8.** Cash investment from shareholders

---

Exercise 1-20

Preparing an income
statement for a company

P2

Ford Motor Company, one of the world's largest automakers, reports the following income statement
accounts for the year ended December 31 ($ in millions). Use this information to prepare Ford's income
statement for the year ended December 31.

Selling and administrative costs	$ 12,196	Revenues.	$151,800
Cost of sales	126,584	Other expenses.	8,413

Exercise 1-21ᴮ

Identifying business
activities

C5

Match each transaction *a* through *e* to one of the following activities of an organization: financing activity
(F), investing activity (I), or operating activity (O).

_____ **a.** An owner contributes cash to the business in exchange for its common stock.

_____ **b.** An organization borrows money from a bank.

_____ **c.** An organization advertises a new product.

_____ **d.** An organization sells some of its land.

_____ **e.** An organization purchases equipment.

Exercise 1-22

Preparing an income
statement for a company

P2

BMW Group, one of Europe's largest manufacturers, reports the following income statement accounts
for the year ended December 31 (euros in millions). Use this information to prepare BMW's income statement for the year ended December 31.

Revenues.	€75,350	Selling and administrative costs	€6,139
Cost of sales	60,946	Other expenses	4,988

Exercise 1-23

Using the accounting
equation

A1

*This icon highlights
sustainability-related
assignments*

Answer the following questions. *Hint:* Use the accounting equation.

a. On January 1, Lumia Company's liabilities are $60,000 and its equity is $40,000. On January 3, Lumia
   purchases and installs solar panel assets costing $10,000. For the panels, Lumia pays $4,000 cash and
   promises to pay the remaining $6,000 in six months. What is the total of Lumia's assets after the solar
   panel purchase?

b. On March 1, ABX Company's assets are $100,000 and its liabilities are $30,000. On March 5, ABX is
   fined $15,000 for failing emission standards. ABX immediately pays the fine in cash. After the fine is
   paid, what is the amount of equity for ABX?

c. On August 1, Lola Company's assets are $30,000 and its liabilities are $10,000. On August 4, Lola
   issues a sustainability report following SASB guidelines. Investors react positively to this report. On
   August 5, a new investor contributes $3,000 cash and $7,000 in equipment in exchange for ownership
   in Lola. After the investment, what is the amount of equity for Lola?

Problem Set B, *located at the end of **Problem Set A,** is provided for each problem to reinforce the learning process*

■ connect

Identify how each of the following separate transactions *1* through *10* affects financial statements. For increases, place a "+" *and* the dollar amount in the column or columns. For decreases, place a "−" *and* the dollar amount in the column or columns. Some cells may contain both an increase (+) and a decrease (−) along with dollar amounts. The first transaction is completed as an example.

PROBLEM SET A

Problem 1-1A
Identifying effects of transactions on financial statements

A1   P1

Required

a. For the balance sheet, identify how each transaction affects total assets, total liabilities, and total equity. For the income statement, identify how each transaction affects net income.

b. For the statement of cash flows, identify how each transaction affects cash flows from operating activities, cash flows from investing activities, and cash flows from financing activities.

		a.				b.		
		Balance Sheet			Income Statement	Statement of Cash Flows		
	Transaction	Total Assets	Total Liab.	Total Equity	Net Income	Operating Activities	Investing Activities	Financing Activities
1	Owner invests $900 cash in business in exchange for stock	+900		+900				+900
2	Receives $700 cash for services provided							
3	Pays $500 cash for employee wages							
4	Buys $100 of equipment on credit							
5	Purchases $200 of supplies on credit							
6	Buys equipment for $300 cash							
7	Pays $200 on accounts payable							
8	Provides $400 services on credit							
9	Pays $50 cash in dividends							
10	Collects $400 cash on accounts receivable							

The following financial statement information is from five separate companies.

Problem 1-2A
Computing missing information using accounting knowledge

A1   P1

	Company A	Company B	Company C	Company D	Company E
December 31, 2018					
Assets	$55,000	$34,000	$24,000	$60,000	$119,000
Liabilities	24,500	21,500	9,000	40,000	?
December 31, 2019					
Assets	58,000	40,000	?	85,000	113,000
Liabilities	?	26,500	29,000	24,000	70,000
During year 2019					
Stock issuances	6,000	1,400	9,750	?	6,500
Net income (loss)	8,500	?	8,000	14,000	20,000
Cash dividends	3,500	2,000	5,875	0	11,000

Required

1. Answer the following questions about Company A.
  a. What is the amount of equity on December 31, 2018?
  b. What is the amount of equity on December 31, 2019?
  c. What is the amount of liabilities on December 31, 2019?
2. Answer the following questions about Company B.
  a. What is the amount of equity on December 31, 2018?
  b. What is the amount of equity on December 31, 2019?
  c. What is net income for year 2019?

[continued on next page]

Check (1*b*) $41,500

(2*c*) $1,600

(3) $55,875

3. Compute the amount of assets for Company C on December 31, 2019.

4. Compute the amount of stock issuances for Company D during year 2019.

5. Compute the amount of liabilities for Company E on December 31, 2018.

Problem 1-3A
Preparing an income statement
P2

As of December 31, 2019, Armani Company's financial records show the following items and amounts.

Cash.	$10,000	Retained earnings, Dec. 31, 2019.	$ 5,000
Accounts receivable	9,000	Dividends	13,000
Supplies.	7,000	Consulting revenue	33,000
Equipment.	4,000	Rental revenue	22,000
Accounts payable	11,000	Salaries expense.	20,000
Common stock	14,000	Rent expense	12,000
Retained earnings, Dec. 31, 2018.	3,000	Selling and administrative expenses.	8,000

Required

Check   Net income, $15,000   Prepare the 2019 year-end income statement for Armani Company.

Problem 1-4A
Preparing a statement of retained earnings   **P2**

Use the information in Problem 1-3A to prepare a year-end statement of retained earnings for Armani Company.

Problem 1-5A
Preparing a balance sheet
P2

Use the information in Problem 1-3A to prepare a year-end balance sheet for Armani Company.

Problem 1-6A
Preparing a statement of cash flows
P2

Following is selected financial information of Kia Company for the year ended December 31, 2019.

Cash used by investing activities.	$(2,000)	Cash from operating activities.	$6,000
Net increase in cash.	1,200	Cash, December 31, 2018.	2,300
Cash used by financing activities.	(2,800)		

Required

Check   Cash balance, Dec. 31, 2019, $3,500   Prepare the 2019 year-end statement of cash flows for Kia Company.

Problem 1-7A
Analyzing transactions and preparing financial statements
P1   P2

Gabi Gram started The Gram Co., a new business that began operations on May 1. The Gram Co. completed the following transactions during its first month of operations.

May 1   G. Gram invested $40,000 cash in the company in exchange for its common stock.

     1   The company rented a furnished office and paid $2,200 cash for May's rent.

     3   The company purchased $1,890 of office equipment on credit.

     5   The company paid $750 cash for this month's cleaning services.

     8   The company provided consulting services for a client and immediately collected $5,400 cash.

    12   The company provided $2,500 of consulting services for a client on credit.

    15   The company paid $750 cash for an assistant's salary for the first half of this month.

    20   The company received $2,500 cash payment for the services provided on May 12.

    22   The company provided $3,200 of consulting services on credit.

    25   The company received $3,200 cash payment for the services provided on May 22.

    26   The company paid $1,890 cash for the office equipment purchased on May 3.

    27   The company purchased $80 of office equipment on credit.

    28   The company paid $750 cash for an assistant's salary for the second half of this month.

    30   The company paid $300 cash for this month's telephone bill.

    30   The company paid $280 cash for this month's utilities.

    31   The company paid $1,400 cash in dividends to the owner (sole shareholder).

Required

1. Create the following table similar to the one in Exhibit 1.9.

	Assets			=	Liabilities	+		Equity				
Date	Cash	+	Accounts Receivable	+	Office Equipment	=	Accounts Payable	+	Common Stock	–	Dividends	+	Revenues	–	Expenses

Enter the effects of each transaction on the accounts of the accounting equation by recording dollar increases and decreases in the appropriate columns. Do not determine new account balances after each transaction. Determine the final total for each account and verify that the equation is in balance.

2. Prepare the income statement and the statement of retained earnings for the month of May, and the balance sheet as of May 31.

3. Prepare the statement of cash flows for the month of May.

Lita Lopez started Biz Consulting, a new business, and completed the following transactions during its first year of operations.

Problem 1-8A
Analyzing effects of transactions
A1   P1

a. Lita Lopez invested $70,000 cash and office equipment valued at $10,000 in the company in exchange for its common stock.
b. The company purchased an office suite for $40,000 cash.
c. The company purchased office equipment for $15,000 cash.
d. The company purchased $1,200 of office supplies and $1,700 of office equipment on credit.
e. The company paid a local newspaper $500 cash for printing an announcement of the office's opening.
f. The company completed a financial plan for a client and billed that client $2,800 for the service.
g. The company designed a financial plan for another client and immediately collected a $4,000 cash fee.
h. The company paid $3,275 cash in dividends to the owner (sole shareholder).
i. The company received $1,800 cash as partial payment from the client described in transaction f.
j. The company made a partial payment of $700 cash on the equipment purchased in transaction d.
k. The company paid $1,800 cash for the office secretary's wages for this period.

Required

1. Create the following table similar to the one in Exhibit 1.9.

Assets								=	Liabilities	+	Equity				
Cash	+	Accounts Receivable	+	Office Supplies	+	Office Equipment	+	Office Suite	=	Accounts Payable	+	Common Stock	–	Dividends	+	Revenues	–	Expenses

Use additions and subtractions within the table to show the dollar effects of each transaction on individual items of the accounting equation. Show new balances after each transaction.

2. Determine the company's net income.

Sanyu Sony started a new business and completed these transactions during December.

Problem 1-9A
Analyzing transactions and preparing financial statements
C4   P1   P2

Dec. 1 Sanyu Sony transferred $65,000 cash from a personal savings account to a checking account in the name of Sony Electric in exchange for its common stock.
2 The company rented office space and paid $1,000 cash for the December rent.
3 The company purchased $13,000 of electrical equipment by paying $4,800 cash and agreeing to pay the $8,200 balance in 30 days.
5 The company purchased office supplies by paying $800 cash.
6 The company completed electrical work and immediately collected $1,200 cash for these services.
8 The company purchased $2,530 of office equipment on credit.
15 The company completed electrical work on credit in the amount of $5,000.
18 The company purchased $350 of office supplies on credit.
20 The company paid $2,530 cash for the office equipment purchased on December 8.
24 The company billed a client $900 for electrical work completed; the balance is due in 30 days.
28 The company received $5,000 cash for the work completed on December 15.
29 The company paid the assistant's salary of $1,400 cash for this month.
30 The company paid $540 cash for this month's utility bill.
31 The company paid $950 cash in dividends to the owner (sole shareholder).

Required

1. Create the following table similar to the one in Exhibit 1.9.

			Assets							=	Liabilities	+				Equity				
Date	Cash	+	Accounts Receivable	+	Office Supplies	+	Office Equipment	+	Electrical Equipment	=	Accounts Payable	+	Common Stock	−	Dividends	+	Revenues	−	Expenses

Use additions and subtractions within the table to show the dollar effects of each transaction on individual items of the accounting equation. Show new balances after each transaction.

2. Prepare the income statement and the statement of retained earnings for the current month, and the balance sheet as of the end of the month.

3. Prepare the statement of cash flows for the current month.

Analysis Component

4. Assume that the owner investment transaction on December 1 was $49,000 cash instead of $65,000 and that Sony Electric obtained another $16,000 in cash by borrowing it from a bank. Compute the dollar effect of this change on the month-end amounts for (*a*) total assets, (*b*) total liabilities, and (*c*) total equity.

Problem 1-10A
Determining expenses, liabilities, equity, and return on assets

A1 A2

Kyzera manufactures, markets, and sells cellular telephones. The average total assets for Kyzera is $250,000. In its most recent year, Kyzera reported net income of $65,000 on revenues of $475,000.

Required

1. What is Kyzera's return on assets?

2. Does return on assets seem satisfactory for Kyzera given that its competitors average a 12% return on assets?

3. What are total expenses for Kyzera in its most recent year?

4. What is the average total amount of liabilities plus equity for Kyzera?

Problem 1-11A
Computing and interpreting return on assets

A2

Coca-Cola and PepsiCo both produce and market beverages that are direct competitors. Key financial figures for these businesses for a recent year follow.

Key Figures ($ millions)	Coca-Cola	PepsiCo
Sales	$46,542	$66,504
Net income	8,634	6,462
Average assets	76,448	70,518

Required

1. Compute return on assets for (*a*) Coca-Cola and (*b*) PepsiCo.

2. Which company is more successful in its total amount of sales to consumers?

3. Which company is more successful in returning net income from its assets invested?

Analysis Component

4. Write a one-paragraph memorandum explaining which company you would invest your money in and why. (Limit your explanation to the information provided.)

Problem 1-12A[A]
Identifying risk and return

A3

All business decisions involve aspects of risk and return. Rank order the following investment activities from *1* through *4*, where "1" is most risky and "4" is least risky.

    _____ **a.** Lowest-risk corporate bond   _____ **c.** Company stock in a start-up

    _____ **b.** Medium-risk corporate bond   _____ **d.** U.S. government Treasury bond

---

Problem 1-13A[B]
Describing business activities

C5

A start-up company often engages in the following transactions during its first year of operations. Classify those transactions in one of the three major categories of an organization's business activities.

F. Financing   **I.** Investing   **O.** Operating

    _____ **1.** Shareholders investing in business   _____ **5.** Purchasing equipment

    _____ **2.** Purchasing a building   _____ **6.** Selling and distributing products

    _____ **3.** Purchasing land   _____ **7.** Paying for advertising

    _____ **4.** Borrowing cash from a bank   _____ **8.** Paying employee wages

An organization undertakes various activities in pursuit of business success. Identify an organization's three major business activities, and describe each activity.

Problem 1-14A[B]

Describing business activities   C5

Identify how each of the following separate transactions *1* through *10* affects financial statements. For increases, place a "+" *and* the dollar amount in the column or columns. For decreases, place a "−" *and* the dollar amount in the column or columns. Some cells may contain both an increase (+) and a decrease (−) along with dollar amounts. The first transaction is completed as an example.

PROBLEM SET B

Problem 1-1B

Identifying effects of transactions on financial statements

Required

a. For the balance sheet, identify how each transaction affects total assets, total liabilities, and total equity. For the income statement, identify how each transaction affects net income.

b. For the statement of cash flows, identify how each transaction affects cash flows from operating activities, cash flows from investing activities, and cash flows from financing activities.

A1   P1

| | | a. | | | | b. | | |
| | | Balance Sheet | | | Income Statement | Statement of Cash Flows | | |
	Transaction	Total Assets	Total Liab.	Total Equity	Net Income	Operating Activities	Investing Activities	Financing Activities
1	Owner invests $800 cash in business in exchange for stock	+800		+800				+800
2	Purchases $100 of supplies on credit							
3	Buys equipment for $400 cash							
4	Provides services for $900 cash							
5	Pays $400 cash for rent incurred							
6	Buys $200 of equipment on credit							
7	Pays $300 cash for wages incurred							
8	Pays $50 cash in dividends							
9	Provides $600 services on credit							
10	Collects $600 cash on accounts receivable							

The following financial statement information is from five separate companies.

Problem 1-2B

Computing missing information using accounting knowledge

A1   P1

	Company V	Company W	Company X	Company Y	Company Z
December 31, 2018					
Assets	$54,000	$ 80,000	$141,500	$92,500	$144,000
Liabilities	25,000	60,000	68,500	51,500	?
December 31, 2019					
Assets	59,000	100,000	186,500	?	170,000
Liabilities	36,000	?	65,800	42,000	42,000
During year 2019					
Stock issuances	5,000	20,000	?	48,100	60,000
Net income (or loss)	?	40,000	18,500	24,000	32,000
Cash dividends	5,500	2,000	0	20,000	8,000

Required

1. Answer the following questions about Company V.

    a. What is the amount of equity on December 31, 2018?

    b. What is the amount of equity on December 31, 2019?

    c. What is the net income or loss for the year 2019?

[continued on next page]

Check   (1*b*) $23,000

2. Answer the following questions about Company W.

   a. What is the amount of equity on December 31, 2018?

   b. What is the amount of equity on December 31, 2019?

(2c) $22,000   **c.** What is the amount of liabilities on December 31, 2019?

3. Compute the amount of stock issuances for Company X during 2019.

(4) $135,100   **4.** Compute the amount of assets for Company Y on December 31, 2019.

5. Compute the amount of liabilities for Company Z on December 31, 2018.

Problem 1-3B

Preparing an income statement

P2

As of December 31, 2019, Audi Company's financial records show the following items and amounts.

Cash.	$2,000	Retained earnings, Dec. 31, 2019.	$1,300
Accounts receivable	1,800	Dividends	2,600
Supplies.	1,200	Consulting revenue	6,600
Equipment.	1,000	Rental revenue	4,400
Accounts payable	3,600	Salaries expense.	4,000
Common stock	1,100	Rent expense	2,400
Retained earnings, Dec. 31, 2018.	900	Selling and administrative expenses.	1,600

Required

Check   Net income, $3,000

Prepare the 2019 year-end income statement for Audi Company.

Problem 1-4B

Preparing a statement of retained earnings   **P2**

Use the information in Problem 1-3B to prepare a year-end statement of retained earnings for Audi Company.

Problem 1-5B

Preparing a balance sheet   **P2**

Use the information in Problem 1-3B to prepare a year-end balance sheet for Audi Company.

Problem 1-6B

Preparing a statement of cash flows

P2

Selected financial information of Banji Company for the year ended December 31, 2019, follows.

Cash from investing activities	$1,600	Cash used by operating activities	$(3,000)
Net increase in cash.	400	Cash, December 31, 2018.	1,300
Cash from financing activities	1,800		

Required

Prepare the 2019 year-end statement of cash flows for Banji Company.

Problem 1-7B

Analyzing transactions and preparing financial statements

P1   P2

Nina Niko launched a new business, Niko's Maintenance Co., that began operations on June 1. The following transactions were completed by the company during that first month.

June 1   Nina Niko invested $130,000 cash in the company in exchange for its common stock.
  2   The company rented a furnished office and paid $6,000 cash for June's rent.
  4   The company purchased $2,400 of equipment on credit.
  6   The company paid $1,150 cash for this month's advertising of the opening of the business.
  8   The company completed maintenance services for a customer and immediately collected $850 cash.
  14   The company completed $7,500 of maintenance services for City Center on credit.
  16   The company paid $800 cash for an assistant's salary for the first half of the month.
  20   The company received $7,500 cash payment for services completed for City Center on June 14.
  21   The company completed $7,900 of maintenance services for Paula's Beauty Shop on credit.
  24   The company completed $675 of maintenance services for Build-It Coop on credit.
  25   The company received $7,900 cash payment from Paula's Beauty Shop for the work completed on June 21.
  26   The company made payment of $2,400 cash for equipment purchased on June 4.
  28   The company paid $800 cash for an assistant's salary for the second half of this month.
  29   The company paid $4,000 cash in dividends to the owner (sole shareholder).
  30   The company paid $150 cash for this month's telephone bill.
  30   The company paid $890 cash for this month's utilities.

Required

1. Create the following table similar to the one in Exhibit 1.9.

	Assets			=	Liabilities	+		Equity			
Date	Cash +	Accounts Receivable	+ Equipment	=	Accounts Payable	+	Common Stock	– Dividends	+	Revenues	– Expenses

Enter the effects of each transaction on the accounts of the accounting equation by recording dollar increases and decreases in the appropriate columns. Do not determine new account balances after each transaction. Determine the final total for each account and verify that the equation is in balance.

2. Prepare the income statement and the statement of retained earnings for the month of June, and the balance sheet as of June 30.

3. Prepare the statement of cash flows for the month of June.

Check (1) Ending balances: Cash, $130,060; Expenses, $9,790

(2) Net income, $7,135; Total assets, $133,135

Neva Nadal started a new business, Nadal Computing, and completed the following transactions during its first year of operations.

a. Neva Nadal invested $90,000 cash and office equipment valued at $10,000 in the company in exchange for its common stock.

b. The company purchased an office suite for $50,000 cash.

c. The company purchased office equipment for $25,000 cash.

d. The company purchased $1,200 of office supplies and $1,700 of office equipment on credit.

e. The company paid a local newspaper $750 cash for printing an announcement of the office's opening.

f. The company completed a financial plan for a client and billed that client $2,800 for the service.

g. The company designed a financial plan for another client and immediately collected a $4,000 cash fee.

h. The company paid $11,500 cash in dividends to the owner (sole shareholder).

i. The company received $1,800 cash from the client described in transaction *f*.

j. The company made a payment of $700 cash on the equipment purchased in transaction *d*.

k. The company paid $2,500 cash for the office secretary's wages.

Problem 1-8B
Analyzing effects of transactions

A1   P1

Required

1. Create the following table similar to the one in Exhibit 1.9.

Check (1) Ending balances: Cash, $5,350; Expenses, $3,250; Accounts Payable, $2,200

	Assets					=	Liabilities	+		Equity			
Cash +	Accounts Receivable	+ Office Supplies	+ Office Equipment	+ Office Suite	=	Accounts Payable	+	Common Stock	– Dividends	+	Revenues	– Expenses

Use additions and subtractions within the table to show the dollar effects of each transaction on individual items of the accounting equation. Show new balances after each transaction.

2. Determine the company's net income.

(2) Net income, $3,550

Rivera Roofing Company, owned by Reyna Rivera, began operations in July and completed these transactions during that first month of operations.

July 1   Reyna Rivera invested $80,000 cash in the company in exchange for its common stock.
     2   The company rented office space and paid $700 cash for the July rent.
     3   The company purchased roofing equipment for $5,000 by paying $1,000 cash and agreeing to pay the $4,000 balance in 30 days.
     6   The company purchased office supplies for $600 cash.
     8   The company completed work for a customer and immediately collected $7,600 cash for the work.
    10   The company purchased $2,300 of office equipment on credit.
    15   The company completed work for a customer on credit in the amount of $8,200.
    17   The company purchased $3,100 of office supplies on credit.
    23   The company paid $2,300 cash for the office equipment purchased on July 10.
    25   The company billed a customer $5,000 for work completed; the balance is due in 30 days.
    28   The company received $8,200 cash for the work completed on July 15.
    30   The company paid an assistant's salary of $1,560 cash for this month.
    31   The company paid $295 cash for this month's utility bill.
    31   The company paid $1,800 cash in dividends to the owner (sole shareholder).

Problem 1-9B
Analyzing transactions and preparing financial statements

C4   P1   P2

Required

1. Create the following table similar to the one in Exhibit 1.9.

	Assets				=	Liabilities	+			Equity			
Date Cash +	Accounts Receivable	+	Office Supplies	+ Office Equipment	+ Roofing Equipment	=	Accounts Payable	+	Common Stock	− Dividends	+	Revenues	− Expenses

Use additions and subtractions within the table to show the dollar effects of each transaction on individual items of the accounting equation. Show new balances after each transaction.

2. Prepare the income statement and the statement of retained earnings for the month of July, and the balance sheet as of July 31.

3. Prepare the statement of cash flows for the month of July.

Analysis Component

4. Assume that the $5,000 purchase of roofing equipment on July 3 was financed from an owner investment of another $5,000 cash in the business in exchange for more common stock (instead of the purchase conditions described in the transaction above). Compute the dollar effect of this change on the month-end amounts for (*a*) total assets, (*b*) total liabilities, and (*c*) total equity.

Problem 1-10B

Determining expenses, liabilities, equity, and return on assets

A1   A2

Ski-Doo Company manufactures, markets, and sells snowmobiles and snowmobile equipment and accessories. The average total assets for Ski-Doo is $3,000,000. In its most recent year, Ski-Doo reported net income of $201,000 on revenues of $1,400,000.

Required

1. What is Ski-Doo Company's return on assets?

2. Does return on assets seem satisfactory for Ski-Doo given that its competitors average a 9.5% return on assets?

3. What are the total expenses for Ski-Doo Company in its most recent year?

4. What is the average total amount of liabilities plus equity for Ski-Doo Company?

Problem 1-11B

Computing and interpreting return on assets

A2

AT&T and **Verizon** produce and market telecommunications products and are competitors. Key financial figures for these businesses for a recent year follow.

Key Figures ($ millions)	AT&T	Verizon
Sales	$126,723	$110,875
Net income	4,184	10,198
Average assets	269,868	225,233

Required

1. Compute return on assets for (*a*) AT&T and (*b*) Verizon.

2. Which company is more successful in the total amount of sales to consumers?

3. Which company is more successful in returning net income from its assets invested?

Analysis Component

4. Write a one-paragraph memorandum explaining which company you would invest your money in and why. (Limit your explanation to the information provided.)

Problem 1-12B[A]

Identifying risk and return

A3

All business decisions involve aspects of risk and return. Rank order the following investment activities from *1* through *4*, where "1" reflects the highest expected return and "4" the lowest expected return.

_____ **a.** Low-risk corporate bond   _____ **c.** Money stored in a fireproof vault

_____ **b.** Stock of a successful company   _____ **d.** U.S. Treasury bond

---

Problem 1-13B[B]

Describing business activities

C5

A start-up company often engages in the following activities during its first year of operations. Classify each of the following activities into one of the three major activities of an organization.

F. Financing   **I.** Investing   **O.** Operating

_____ **1.** Providing client services   _____ **5.** Supervising workers

_____ **2.** Obtaining a bank loan   _____ **6.** Shareholders investing in business

_____ **3.** Purchasing machinery   _____ **7.** Renting office space

_____ **4.** Research for its products   _____ **8.** Paying utilities expenses

Identify in outline format the three major business activities of an organization. For each of these activities, identify at least two specific transactions or events normally undertaken by the business's owners or its managers.

Problem 1-14B[B]
Describing business
activities   C5

Serial Problem starts here and continues throughout the text

SP 1   On October 1, 2019, Santana Rey launched a computer services company, **Business Solutions**, that is organized as a corporation and provides consulting services, computer system installations, and custom program development.

SERIAL PROBLEM
Business Solutions
C4   P1

©Alexander Image/Shutterstock

Required

Create a table like the one in Exhibit 1.9 using the following headings for columns: Cash; Accounts Receivable; Computer Supplies; Computer System; Office Equipment; Accounts Payable; Common Stock; Dividends; Revenues; and Expenses. Then use additions and subtractions within the table to show the dollar effects for each of the following October transactions for Business Solutions on the individual items of the accounting equation. Show new balances after each transaction

Oct. 1   S. Rey invested $45,000 cash, a $20,000 computer system, and $8,000 of office equipment in the company in exchange for its common stock.
3   The company purchased $1,420 of computer supplies on credit from Harris Office Products.
6   The company billed Easy Leasing $4,800 for services performed in installing a new web server.
8   The company paid $1,420 cash for the computer supplies purchased from Harris Office Products on October 3.
10   The company hired Lyn Addie as a part-time assistant for $125 per day, as needed.
12   The company billed Easy Leasing another $1,400 for services performed.
15   The company received $4,800 cash from Easy Leasing as partial payment toward its account.
17   The company paid $805 cash to repair computer equipment damaged when moving it.
20   The company paid $1,728 cash for advertisements published in the local newspaper.
22   The company received $1,400 cash from Easy Leasing toward its account.
28   The company billed IFM Company $5,208 for services performed.
31   The company paid $875 cash for Lyn Addie's wages for seven days of work this month.
31   The company paid $3,600 cash in dividends to the owner (sole shareholder).

Check Ending balances:
Cash, $42,772; Revenues,
$11,408; Expenses, $3,408

Accounting professionals apply many technology tools to aid them in their everyday tasks and decision making. The **General Ledger** tool in Connect automates several of the procedural steps in the accounting cycle so the accounting professional can focus on the impacts of each transaction on the full set of financial statements. Chapter 2 is the first chapter to use this tool in helping students see the advantages of technology and, in particular, the power of the General Ledger tool in accounting practice, including financial analysis and "what-if" scenarios.

**GENERAL
LEDGER
PROBLEM**

Accounting Analysis (AA) is a section aimed to refine company analysis, comparative analysis, and global analysis skills; Accounting Analysis assignments are available in Connect.

Accounting Analysis

AA 1-1   Key financial figures for **Apple**'s two most recent fiscal years follow.

$ millions	Current Year	Prior Year
Liabilities + Equity	$375,319	$321,686
Net income	48,351	45,687
Revenues	229,234	215,639

**COMPANY
ANALYSIS**
A1   A2
APPLE

Required

1. What is the total amount of assets invested in Apple in the current year?
2. What is Apple's return on assets for the current year?
3. How much are total expenses for Apple for the current year?
4. Is Apple's current-year return on assets better or worse than competitors' average of 10% return?

COMPARATIVE ANALYSIS

A1   A2

APPLE

GOOGLE

AA 1-2   Key comparative figures ($ millions) for both **Apple** and **Google** follow.

Key Figures	Apple		Google	
	Current Year	Prior Year	Current Year	Prior Year
Liabilities + Equity	$375,319	$321,686	$197,295	$167,497
Net income	48,351	45,687	12,662	19,478
Revenues.	229,234	215,639	110,855	90,272

Note: Reference to **Google** throughout the text refers to **Alphabet Inc.**, as Google is a wholly owned subsidiary of Alphabet.

Required

1. What is the total amount of assets invested for the current year in (*a*) Apple and (*b*) Google?
2. What is the current-year return on assets for (*a*) Apple and (*b*) Google?
3. How much are current-year expenses for (*a*) Apple and (*b*) Google?
4. Is the current-year return on assets better than the 10% return of competitors for (*a*) Apple and (*b*) Google?
5. Relying only on return on assets, would we invest in Google or Apple?

GLOBAL ANALYSIS

A1   A2

Samsung

APPLE

GOOGLE

AA 1-3   **Samsung** is a leading global manufacturer that competes with **Apple** and **Google**. Key financial figures for Samsung follow.

Korean Won & USD in millions	Samsung*		Apple	Google
	Current Year	Prior Year	Current Year	Current Year
Average assets	₩281,963,207	₩252,176,923	$348,503	$182,396
Net income	42,186,747	22,726,092	48,351	12,662
Revenues.	239,575,376	201,866,745	229,234	110,855

*Figures prepared in accordance with International Financial Reporting Standards as adopted by the Republic of Korea.

Required

1. What is the return on assets for Samsung in the (*a*) current year and (*b*) prior year?
2. Does Samsung's return on assets exhibit a favorable or unfavorable change?
3. Is Samsung's current-year return on assets better or worse than that for (*a*) Apple and (*b*) Google?

Beyond the Numbers (BTN) is a special problem section aimed to refine communication, conceptual, analysis, and research skills. It includes many activities helpful in developing an active learning environment.

Beyond the Numbers

ETHICS CHALLENGE

C3   C4

BTN 1-1   Tana Thorne works in a public accounting firm and hopes to eventually be a partner. The management of Allnet Company invites Thorne to prepare a bid to audit Allnet's financial statements. In discussing the audit fee, Allnet's management suggests a fee range in which the amount depends on the reported profit of Allnet. The higher its profit, the higher will be the audit fee paid to Thorne's firm.

Required

1. Identify the parties potentially affected by this audit and the fee plan proposed.
2. What are the ethical factors in this situation? Explain.
3. Would you recommend that Thorne accept this audit fee arrangement? Why or why not?
4. Describe some ethical considerations guiding your recommendation.

COMMUNICATING IN PRACTICE

C2   C4

APPLE

BTN 1-2   Refer to this chapter's opening feature about **Apple**. Assume that the owners, sometime during their first five years of business, desire to expand their computer product services to meet business demand regarding computing services. They eventually decide to meet with their banker to discuss a loan to allow Apple to expand and offer computing services.

Required

1. Prepare a half-page report outlining the information you would request from the owners if you were the loan officer.
2. Indicate whether the information you request and your loan decision are affected by the form of business organization for Apple.

BTN 1-3   Visit the EDGAR database at <u>SEC.gov</u>. Access the Form 10-K report of **Rocky Mountain Chocolate Factory** (ticker: RMCF) filed on May 23, 2017, covering its 2017 fiscal year.

Required

1. Item 6 of the 10-K report provides comparative financial highlights of RMCF for the years 2013–2017. Describe the revenue trend for RMCF over this five-year period.
2. Has RMCF been profitable (see net income) over this five-year period? Support your answer.

TAKING IT TO THE NET

A2

BTN 1-4   Teamwork is important in today's business world. Successful teams schedule convenient meetings, maintain regular communications, and cooperate with and support their members. This assignment aims to establish support/learning teams, initiate discussions, and set meeting times.

Required

1. Form teams and open a team discussion to determine a regular time and place for your team to meet between each scheduled class meeting. Notify your instructor via a memorandum or e-mail message as to when and where your team will hold regularly scheduled meetings.
2. Develop a list of telephone numbers, LinkedIn pages, and/or e-mail addresses of your teammates.

TEAMWORK IN ACTION

C1

BTN 1-5   Refer to this chapter's opening feature about **Apple**. Assume that the owners decide to open a new company with an innovative mobile app devoted to microblogging for accountants and those learning accounting. This new company will be called **AccountApp**.

Required

1. AccountApp obtains a $500,000 loan and the two owners contribute $250,000 in total from their own savings in exchange for ownership of the new company.
   a. What is the new company's total amount of liabilities plus equity?
   b. What is the new company's total amount of assets?
2. If the new company earns $80,250 in net income in the first year of operation, compute its return on assets (assume average assets equal $750,000). Assess its performance if competitors average a 10% return.

ENTREPRENEURIAL DECISION

A1   A2

APPLE

Check   (2) 10.7%

BTN 1-6   You are to interview a local business owner. (This can be a friend or relative.) Opening lines of communication with members of the business community can provide personal benefits of business networking. If you do not know the owner, you should call ahead to introduce yourself and explain your position as a student and your assignment requirements. You should request a 30-minute appointment for a face-to-face or phone interview to discuss the form of organization and operations of the business. Be prepared to make a good impression.

Required

1. Identify and describe the main operating activities and the form of organization for this business.
2. Determine and explain why the owner(s) chose this particular form of organization.
3. Identify any special advantages and/or disadvantages the owner(s) experiences in operating with this form of business organization.

HITTING THE ROAD

C4

---

2 Accounting for Business Transactions

Learning Objectives

CONCEPTUAL

C1 Explain the steps in processing transactions and the role of source documents.

C2 Describe an account and its use in recording transactions.

C3 Describe a ledger and a chart of accounts.

C4 Define *debits* and *credits* and explain double-entry accounting.

ANALYTICAL

A1 Analyze the impact of transactions on accounts and financial statements.

A2 Compute the debt ratio and describe its use in analyzing financial condition.

PROCEDURAL

P1 Record transactions in a journal and post entries to a ledger.

P2 Prepare and explain the use of a trial balance.

P3 Prepare financial statements from business transactions.

Have a Fit

"I'm always confident"—**JAMES PARK**

SAN FRANCISCO—James Park and Eric Friedman created a wooden box with a circuit board inside. James recalls that to fix an antenna, he "literally took a piece of foam and put it on the circuit board." Their device could be used to track fitness activity, such as steps taken. The device James and Eric built would later be known as a **Fitbit (Fitbit.com)**.

As Fitbit grew, the co-founders struggled to track sales and expenses. "It was pretty challenging," recalls James. "I would just try to use the weekend to see if I could catch up." James and Eric knew that having reliable accounting data would help "manage the ups and downs of running a company."

To address this concern, the co-founders took action. They set up recordkeeping processes, transaction analysis, control procedures, and financial statement reporting. "You need to see the data," insists James.

With accounting data, James says he "can uncover insights that weren't possible or very practical before . . . and enable the discovery of new insights and trends."

©Daniel Boczarski/Stringer/Fitbit/Getty Images

Eric offers the following advice to aspiring entrepreneurs unsure of how to unlock the potential of accounting data: "Get your hands dirty and do it yourself. You learn more that way."

Sources: *Fitbit website,* January 2019; *Wareable.com,* September 2016; *Business Wire,* November 2015; *Fortune,* July 2015; *Marketing Land,* March 2015; *Fast Company,* March 2014

BASIS OF FINANCIAL STATEMENTS

Business transactions and events are the starting points of financial statements. The process to go from transactions and events to financial statements includes the following.

- Identify each transaction and event from source documents.
- Analyze each transaction and event using the accounting equation.
- Record relevant transactions and events in a journal.
- Post journal information to ledger accounts.
- Prepare and analyze the trial balance and financial statements.

C1 _____

Explain the steps in processing transactions and the role of source documents.

| Transaction occurs with source documents | Transactions analyzed with accounting equation | Transactions recorded and posted | Transactions reported in financial statements |

Source Documents

Source documents identify and describe transactions and events entering the accounting system. They can be in hard copy or electronic form. Examples are sales receipts, checks, purchase orders, bills from suppliers, payroll records, and bank statements. For example, cash registers record each sale on a tape or electronic file. This record is a source document for recording sales in the accounting system. Source documents are objective and reliable evidence about transactions and events and their amounts.

Point: Accounting records also are called *accounting books* or *the books.*

The "Account" Underlying Financial Statements

An **account** is a record of increases and decreases in a specific asset, liability, equity, revenue, or expense. The **general ledger,** or simply **ledger,** is a record of all accounts used by a company. The ledger is often in electronic form. While most companies' ledgers have similar accounts, a company often uses one or more unique accounts to match its type of operations. An ***unclassified balance sheet*** broadly groups accounts into assets, liabilities, and equity. Exhibit 2.1 shows common asset, liability, and equity accounts.

C2 _____

Describe an account and its use in recording transactions.

Asset Accounts   Assets are resources owned or controlled by a company. Resources have expected future benefits. Most accounting systems include (at a minimum) separate accounts for the assets described here.

Cash   A *Cash* account shows a company's cash balance. All increases and decreases in cash are recorded in the Cash account. It includes money and any funds that a bank accepts for deposit (coins, checks, money orders, and checking account balances).

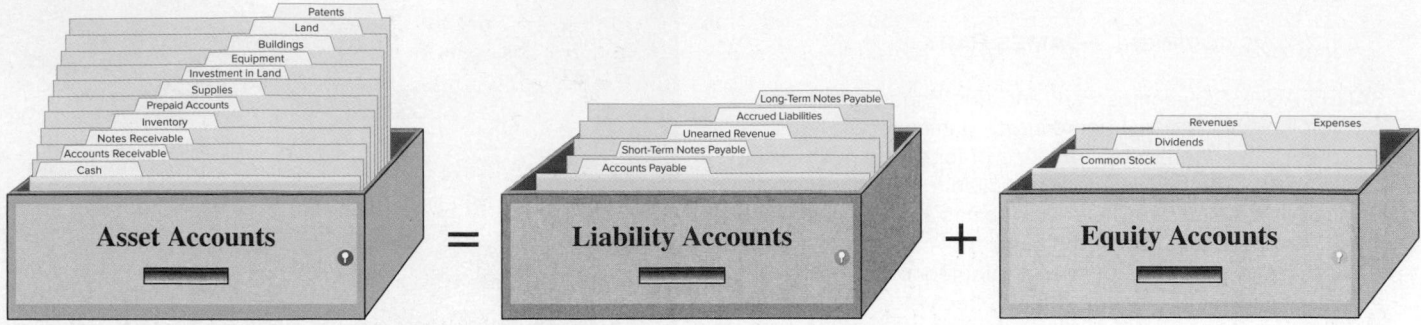

EXHIBIT 2.1

Accounts Organized by the
Accounting Equation

Point: Customers and others who
owe a company are **debtors**.

Point: A note receivable is different than an account receivable
because it comes from a *formal
contract called a promissory note*.
A note receivable usually requires
interest, whereas an account
receivable does not.

Point: At the beginning of the
term, a prepaid college parking
pass is an asset that allows a student to park on campus. Benefits
of the parking pass expire as the
term progresses. At term-end,
prepaid parking (asset) equals
zero as it has been entirely
recorded as parking expense.

Accounts Receivable   *Accounts receivable* are held by a seller and are promises of payment from customers to sellers. Accounts receivable are increased by *credit sales* or *sales on account* (or *on credit*). They are decreased by customer payments. We record all increases and decreases in receivables in the Accounts Receivable account. When there are multiple customers, separate records are kept for each, titled Accounts Receivable—'Customer Name'.

Note Receivable   A *note receivable,* or promissory note, is a written promise of another en-tity to pay a specific sum of money on a specified future date to the holder of the note; the holder has an asset recorded in a Note (or Notes) Receivable account.

Prepaid Accounts   *Prepaid accounts* (or *prepaid expenses*) are assets from prepayments of future expenses (expenses expected to be incurred in future accounting periods). When the ex-penses are later incurred, the amounts in prepaid accounts are transferred to expense accounts. Common examples of prepaid accounts are prepaid insurance, prepaid rent, and prepaid ser-vices. Prepaid accounts expire with the passage of time (such as with rent) or through use (such as with prepaid meal plans). When financial statements are prepared, (1) all expired and used prepaid accounts are recorded as expenses and (2) all unexpired and unused prepaid accounts are recorded as assets (reflecting future benefits). Chapter 3 covers prepaid accounts in detail.

Supplies Accounts   *Supplies* are assets until they are used. When they are used up, their costs are reported as expenses. Unused supplies are recorded in a Supplies asset account. Supplies often are grouped by purpose—for example, office supplies and store supplies. *Office supplies* include paper and pens. *Store supplies* include packaging and cleaning materials.

Equipment Accounts   *Equipment* is an asset. When equipment is used and wears down, its cost is gradually reported as an expense (called *depreciation*). Equipment often is grouped by its purpose—for example, office equipment and store equipment. *Office equipment* includes com-puters and desks. The *Store Equipment* account includes counters and cash registers.

Point: Some assets are called
intangible because they do
not have physical existence.
Coca-Cola reports billions in
intangible assets.

Buildings Accounts   *Buildings* such as stores, offices, warehouses, and factories are assets because they provide expected future benefits. When a building is used and wears down, its cost is reported as an expense (called *depreciation*). When several buildings are owned, separate ac-counts are sometimes kept for each of them.

Land   The cost of *land* is recorded in a Land account. The cost of buildings located on the land is separately recorded in building accounts.

©Rob Kim/Getty Images

■ Decision Insight

Women Entrepreneurs   Sara Blakely (in photo), the billionaire entrepreneur/owner of **SPANX**, has promised to do-nate half of her wealth to charity. The Center for Women's Business Research reports the following for women-owned businesses.

- They total more than 11 million and employ nearly 20 million workers.
- They generate $2.5 trillion in annual sales and tend to embrace technology.
- They are philanthropic—70% of owners volunteer at least once per month. ■

Liability Accounts   Liabilities are obligations to transfer assets or provide products or services to others. They are claims (by creditors) against assets. **Creditors** are individuals and organizations that have rights to receive payments from a company. Common liability accounts are described here.

Accounts Payable   *Accounts payable* are promises to pay later. Payables can come from purchases of merchandise-for-resale, supplies, equipment, and services. We record all increases and decreases in payables in the Accounts Payable account. When there are multiple suppliers, separate records are kept for each, titled Accounts Payable—'Supplier Name'.

Point: Accounts payable also are called *trade payables*.

Note Payable   A *note payable* is a written promissory note to pay a future amount. It is recorded as either a short-term note payable or a long-term note payable, depending on when it must be repaid. We explain short- and long-term classification in the next two chapters.

Point: A note payable is different than an account payable because it comes from a *formal contract called a promissory note* and requires interest.

Unearned Revenue Accounts   **Unearned revenue** is a liability that is settled in the future when a company delivers its products or services. When customers pay in advance for products or services (before revenue is earned), the seller records this receipt as unearned revenue. Examples of unearned revenue include magazine subscriptions collected in advance by a publisher, rent collected in advance by a landlord, and season ticket sales by sports teams. The seller would record these in liability accounts such as Unearned Subscriptions and Unearned Rent. When products and services are later delivered, the earned portion of the unearned revenue is transferred to revenue accounts such as Subscription Fees Revenue and Rent Revenue.[1]

Point: Two words that almost always identify liability accounts: "payable," meaning liabilities that must be paid, and "unearned," meaning liabilities that must be fulfilled.

Accrued Liabilities   *Accrued liabilities* are amounts owed that are not yet paid. Examples are wages payable, taxes payable, and interest payable. These often are recorded in separate liability accounts by the same title. If they are not a large amount, one or more ledger accounts can be added and reported as a single amount on the balance sheet. (Financial statements often report totals of several ledger accounts.)

 Decision Insight

Unearned Revenue   The **Dallas Cowboys**, **Atlanta Falcons**, **New England Patriots**, and most NFL teams have over $100 million in advance ticket sales in *Unearned Revenue*. When a team plays its home games, it settles this liability to its ticket holders and then transfers the amount earned to *Ticket Revenue*. Teams in other major sports such as the National Women's Soccer League and the Women's National Basketball Association also have unearned revenue. ■

©Mike Zarrilli/Getty Images

Equity Accounts   The owner's claim on a company's assets is called *equity, stockholders' equity,* or *shareholders' equity.* Equity is the owner's *residual interest* in the assets of a business after subtracting liabilities. Equity is impacted by four types of accounts.

$$\text{Equity} = \text{Common stock} - \text{Dividends} + \text{Revenues} - \text{Expenses}$$

We show this in Exhibit 2.2 by expanding the accounting equation. We also organize assets and liabilities into subgroups that have similar attributes. An important subgroup for both assets and liabilities is the *current* items. Current items are expected to be either collected or owed within the next year. The next chapter explains this. At this point, know that a ***classified balance sheet*** groups accounts into classifications (such as land and buildings into Plant Assets) *and* it reports current assets before noncurrent assets and current liabilities before noncurrent liabilities.

---

[1]In practice, account titles vary. Subscription Fees Revenue is sometimes called Subscription Fees, Subscription Fees Earned, or Earned Subscription Fees. Rent Revenue is sometimes called Rent Earned, Rental Revenue, or Earned Rent Revenue. Titles can differ even within the same industry. Product sales are called *net sales* at **Apple**, *revenues* at **Google**, and *revenue* at **Samsung**. *Revenues* or *fees* is commonly used with service businesses, and *net sales* or *sales* is used with product businesses.

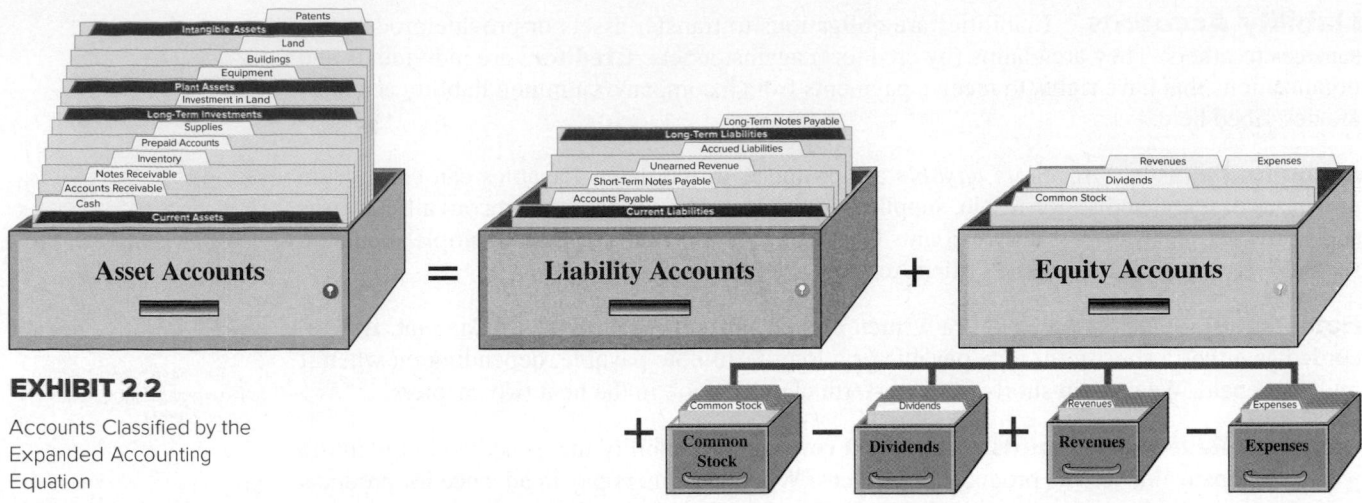

EXHIBIT 2.2

Accounts Classified by the Expanded Accounting Equation

Owner Investments   When an owner invests in a company, it increases both assets and equity. The increase to equity is recorded in the account titled **Common Stock**. Owner investments are not revenues of the business.

Point: Dividends account can be viewed as a *contra equity* account because it reduces the normal balance of equity.

Owner Distributions   When a corporation distributes assets to its owners, it decreases both company assets and total equity. The decrease to equity is recorded in an account titled **Dividends**. Dividends are not expenses of the business; they are simply the opposite of owner investments.

Revenue Accounts   Amounts received from sales of products and services to customers are recorded in revenue accounts, which increase equity. Examples of revenue accounts are Sales, Commissions Earned, Professional Fees Earned, Rent Revenue, and Interest Revenue. **Revenues always increase equity.**

Expense Accounts   Amounts used for costs of providing products and services are recorded in expense accounts, which decrease equity. Examples of expense accounts are Advertising Expense, Salaries Expense, Rent Expense, Utilities Expense, and Insurance Expense. **Expenses always decrease equity.** A variety of revenues and expenses are in the *chart of accounts* at the end of this book. (Different companies use different account titles to describe the same thing. For example, some use Interest Revenue instead of Interest Earned.)

■ Decision Insight

Sporting Accounts   The **Cleveland Cavaliers**, **Boston Celtics**, **Golden State Warriors**, and other NBA teams have revenue accounts that include Ticket Sales, Broadcast Fees, and Advertising Revenues. Expense accounts include Player Salaries, NBA Franchise Costs, and Promotional Costs. ■

C3_____   Ledger and Chart of Accounts

Describe a ledger and a chart of accounts.

EXHIBIT 2.3

Typical Chart of Accounts for a Smaller Business

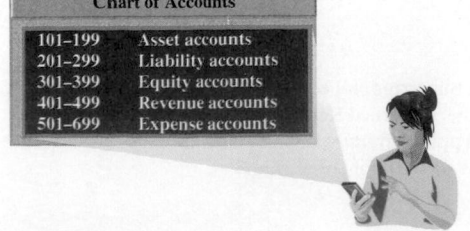

The collection of all accounts and their balances is called a *ledger* (or *general ledger*). A company's size and diversity of operations affect the number of accounts needed. A small company can have as few as 20 accounts; a large company can require thousands. The **chart of accounts** is a list of all ledger accounts and has an identification number assigned to each account. Exhibit 2.3 shows a common numbering system of accounts for a smaller business.

These account numbers have a three-digit code that is useful in recordkeeping. In this example, the first digit of asset accounts is a 1, the first digit of liability accounts is a 2, and so on. The second and third digits relate to the accounts' subcategories. Exhibit 2.4 shows a partial chart of accounts for FastForward.

EXHIBIT 2.4

Partial Chart of Accounts for FastForward

Chart of Accounts					
Assets	**Liabilities**	**Equity**			

Assets	**Liabilities**	**Equity**					
101 Cash	201 Accounts payable		**Revenues**		**Expenses**	
106 Accounts receivable	236 Unearned consulting	307 Common stock	403 Consulting revenue	622 Salaries expense	
126 Supplies	revenue	318 Retained earnings	406 Rental revenue	637 Insurance expense	
128 Prepaid insurance		319 Dividends		640 Rent expense	
167 Equipment				652 Supplies expense	
				690 Utilities expense	

Classify each of the following accounts as either an asset (A), liability (L), or equity (EQ) account.

____ **1.** Prepaid Rent   ____ **5.** Accounts Receivable   ____ **9.** Land

____ **2.** Common Stock   ____ **6.** Equipment   ____ **10.** Prepaid Insurance

____ **3.** Note Receivable   ____ **7.** Interest Payable   ____ **11.** Wages Payable

____ **4.** Accounts Payable   ____ **8.** Unearned Revenue   ____ **12.** Rent Payable

Solution

1. A   **2.** EQ   **3.** A   **4.** L   **5.** A   **6.** A   **7.** L   **8.** L   **9.** A   **10.** A   **11.** L   **12.** L

NEED-TO-KNOW 2-1

Classifying Accounts

C1 C2 C3

▶

Do More: QS 2-2, QS 2-3

DOUBLE-ENTRY ACCOUNTING

Debits and Credits

A **T-account** represents a ledger account and is used to show the effects of transactions. Its name comes from its shape like the letter **T**. The layout of a T-account is shown in Exhibit 2.5.

The left side of an account is called the **debit** side, or *Dr.* The right side is called the **credit** side, or *Cr.* To enter amounts on the left side of an account is to *debit* the account. To enter amounts on the right side is to *credit* the account. The term *debit* or *credit,* by itself, does not mean increase or decrease. Whether a debit or a credit is an increase or decrease depends on the account.

Account Title	
(Left side)	(Right side)
Debit	**Credit**

The difference between total debits and total credits for an account, including any beginning balance, is the **account balance.** When total debits exceed total credits, the account has a *debit balance*. It has a *credit balance* when total credits exceed total debits. When total debits equal total credits, the account has a *zero balance*.

Double-Entry System

Double-entry accounting demands the accounting equation remain in balance, which means that for each transaction:

- **At least two accounts are involved, with at least one debit and one credit.**
- **Total amount debited must equal total amount credited.**

This means total debits must equal total credits for all entries, and total debit account balances in the ledger must equal total credit account balances. The system for recording debits and credits follows the accounting equation—see Exhibit 2.6.

C4

Define *debits* and *credits* and explain double-entry accounting.

EXHIBIT 2.5

The T-Account

Point: *Dr.* and *Cr.* come from 18th-century English where terms *debitor* and *creditor* were used instead of *debit* and *credit. Dr.* and *Cr.* use the first and last letters of these terms, just as we still do for Saint (St.) and Doctor (Dr.).

"Total debits equal total credits for each entry."

EXHIBIT 2.6

Debits and Credits in the
Accounting Equation

Point: *Debit* and *credit* are
accounting directions for left
and right.

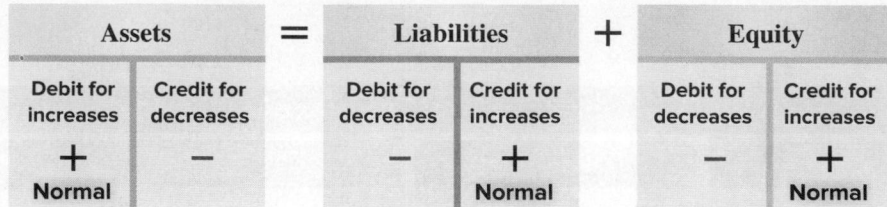

Point: Assets are on the left-hand
side of the equation and thus increase on the left. Liabilities and
equity are on the right-hand side
of the equation and thus increase
on the right.

Net increases or decreases on one side have equal net effects on the other side.   For example, a net increase in assets must include an equal net increase on the liabilities and equity side.
Some transactions affect only one side of the equation, such as acquiring a land asset by giving
up a cash asset, but their net effect on this one side is zero.

**The left side is the *normal balance* side for assets; the right side is the *normal balance* side for
liabilities and equity.**   This matches their layout in the accounting equation, where assets are on
the left side and liabilities and equity are on the right.

**Equity increases from revenues and owner investments (stock issuances), and it decreases
from expenses and dividends.**   We see this by expanding the accounting equation to include
debits and credits in double-entry form, as shown in Exhibit 2.7.

EXHIBIT 2.7

Debit and Credit Effects for
Component Accounts

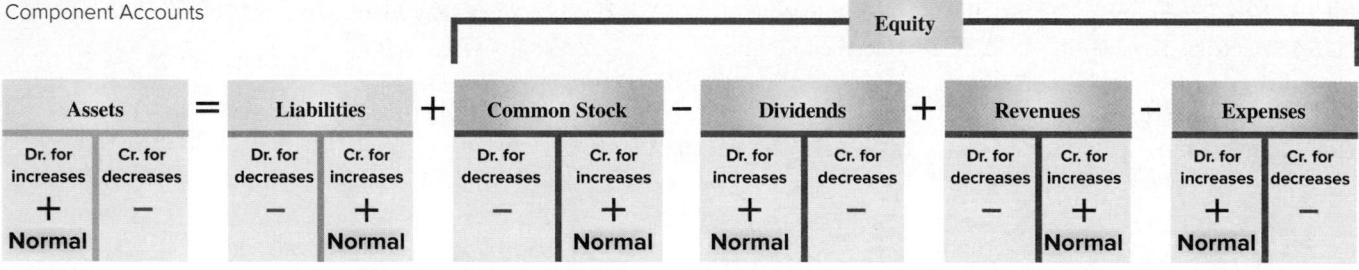

**Increases (credits) to common stock and revenues *increase* equity; increases (debits) to
dividends and expenses *decrease* equity.**   The normal balance of each account is the side
where *increases* are recorded.

Point: DrEAD means debit (**Dr**)
is the normal balance side for
Expense, **A**sset, and **D**ividend
accounts; credit the others.

     The T-account for FastForward's Cash account, reflecting its first 11 transactions (from
Exhibit 1.9), is shown in Exhibit 2.8. The total increases (debits) in its Cash account are $36,100,
and the total decreases (credits) are $31,300. Total debits exceed total credits by $4,800, resulting in its ending debit balance of $4,800.

EXHIBIT 2.8

Computing the Balance for
a T-Account

Point: The ending balance is on
the side with the larger dollar
amount. Also, a plus (+) and
minus (−) are *not* used in a
T-account.

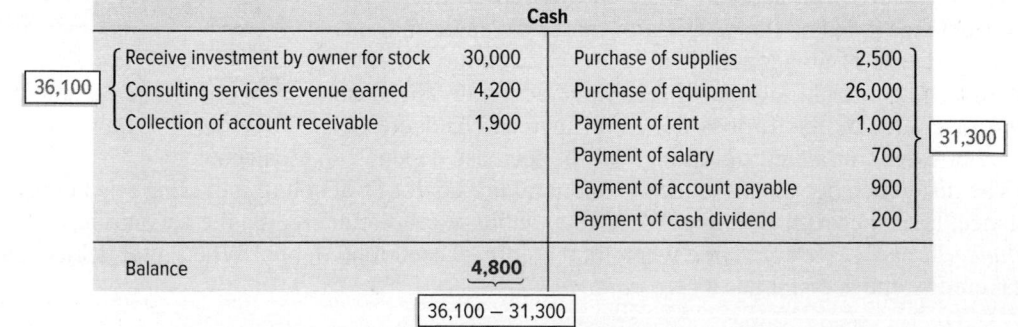

Do More: QS 2-4, QS 2-5,
QS 2-7, E 2-4

NEED-TO-KNOW 2-2

Normal Account Balance

C4

Identify the normal balance (debit [Dr] or credit [Cr]) for each of the following accounts.

____ **1.** Prepaid Rent	____ **5.** Accounts Receivable	____ **9.** Land
____ **2.** Common Stock	____ **6.** Equipment	____ **10.** Prepaid Insurance
____ **3.** Note Receivable	____ **7.** Interest Payable	____ **11.** Dividends
____ **4.** Accounts Payable	____ **8.** Unearned Revenue	____ **12.** Utilities Expense

Solution

1. Dr.   **2.** Cr.   **3.** Dr.   **4.** Cr.   **5.** Dr.   **6.** Dr.   **7.** Cr.   **8.** Cr.   **9.** Dr.   **10.** Dr.   **11.** Dr.   **12.** Dr.

ANALYZING AND PROCESSING TRANSACTIONS

This section explains the analyzing, recording, and posting of transactions.

Journalizing and Posting Transactions

The four steps of processing transactions are shown in Exhibit 2.9. Steps 1 and 2—transaction analysis and the accounting equation—already were covered. This section focuses on steps 3 and 4. Step 3 is to record each transaction chronologically in a journal. A **journal** is a complete record of each transaction in one place. It also shows debits and credits for each transaction. Recording transactions in a journal is called **journalizing.** Step 4 is to transfer (or *post*) entries from the journal to the ledger. Transferring journal entry information to the ledger is called **posting.**

P1

Record transactions in a journal and post entries to a ledger.

EXHIBIT 2.9

Steps in Processing Transactions

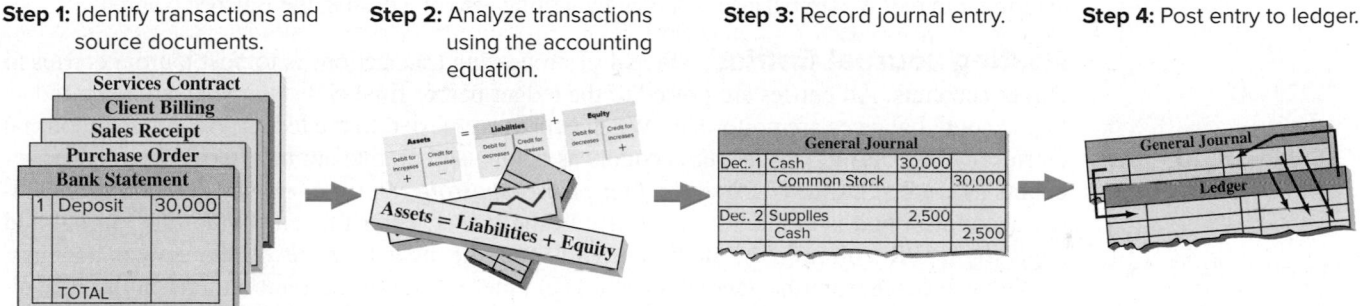

Step 1: Identify transactions and source documents.

Step 2: Analyze transactions using the accounting equation.

Step 3: Record journal entry.

Step 4: Post entry to ledger.

Journalizing Transactions   Journalizing transactions requires an understanding of a journal. While companies can use various journals, every company uses a **general journal.** It can be used to record any transaction. Exhibit 2.10 shows how the first two transactions of FastForward are recorded in a general journal.

To record entries in a general journal, apply these steps; refer to Exhibit 2.10.

(a) Date the transaction: Enter the year at the top of the first column and the month and day on the first line of each journal entry.

(b) Enter titles of accounts debited and then enter amounts in the Debit column on the same line. Account titles are taken from the chart of accounts and are aligned with the left margin of the Account Titles and Explanation column.

(c) Enter titles of accounts credited and then enter amounts in the Credit column on the same line. Account titles are from the chart of accounts and are indented from the left margin of the Account Titles and Explanation column to separate them from debited accounts.

(d) Enter a brief explanation of the transaction on the line below the entry (it often references a source document). This explanation is indented about half as far as the credited account titles to avoid confusing it with accounts, and it is italicized.

General Journal

Date	Account Titles and Explanation	PR	Debit	Credit
2019 (a)				
Dec. 1	(b) Cash		30,000	
	(c) Common Stock			30,000
	Receive investment by owner. (d)			
Dec. 2	Supplies		2,500	
	Cash			2,500
	Purchase supplies for cash.			

EXHIBIT 2.10

Partial General Journal for FastForward

Point: There are no exact rules for a journal entry explanation—it should be short yet describe why an entry is made.

A blank line is left between each journal entry for clarity. When a transaction is first recorded, the **posting reference (PR) column** is left blank (in a manual system). Later, when posting entries to the ledger, the identification numbers of the individual ledger accounts are entered in the PR column.

Balance Column Account   T-accounts are simple and show how the accounting process works. However, actual accounting systems need more structure and therefore use a different formatting of T-accounts, called **balance column accounts,** shown in Exhibit 2.11.

General Ledger					
Cash					**Account No. 101**
Date	Explanation	PR	Debit	Credit	Balance
2019					
Dec. 1		G1	30,000		30,000
Dec. 2		G1		2,500	27,500
Dec. 3		G1		26,000	1,500
Dec. 10		G1	4,200		5,700

EXHIBIT 2.11

Cash Account in Balance
Column Format

Point: Explanations are included in
ledger accounts only for unusual
transactions or events.

The balance column account format is similar to a T-account in having columns for debits and credits. It is different in including transaction date and explanation columns. It also has a column with the balance of the account after each entry is recorded. FastForward's Cash account in Exhibit 2.11 is debited on December 1 for the $30,000 owner investment, yielding a $30,000 debit balance. The account is credited on December 2 for $2,500, yielding a $27,500 debit balance. On December 3, it is credited for $26,000, and its debit balance is reduced to $1,500. The Cash account is debited for $4,200 on December 10, and its debit balance increases to $5,700; and so on.

The heading of the Balance column does not show whether it is a debit or credit balance. Instead, an account is assumed to have a *normal balance*. Unusual events can sometimes temporarily create an abnormal balance. An *abnormal balance* is a balance on the side where decreases are recorded. For example, a customer might mistakenly overpay a bill. This gives that customer's account receivable an abnormal (credit) balance. An abnormal balance often is identified by setting it in brackets or entering it in red. A zero balance is shown by writing zero or a dash in the Balance column.

Posting Journal Entries   Step 4 of processing transactions is to post journal entries to ledger accounts. All entries are posted to the ledger before financial statements are prepared so that account balances are up-to-date. When entries are posted to the ledger, the debits in journal entries are transferred into ledger accounts as debits, and credits are transferred into ledger accounts as credits. Exhibit 2.12 shows *four parts to **posting** a journal entry.* Ⓐ Identify the ledger account(s) that is debited in the entry. In the ledger, enter the entry date, the journal and page in its PR column, the debit amount, and the new balance of the ledger account. (*G* shows it came from the general journal.) Ⓑ Enter the ledger account number in the PR column of the journal. Parts Ⓒ and Ⓓ repeat the first two steps for credit entries and amounts. The posting process creates a link between the ledger and the journal entry. This link is a useful cross-reference for tracing an amount from one record to another.

Point: Posting is automatic with
accounting software.

Point: The fundamental concepts
of a manual system are identical
to those of a computerized
information system.

EXHIBIT 2.12

Posting an Entry to the
Ledger

Key:
Ⓐ Identify debit account in ledger: enter date,
   journal page, amount, and balance (red line).
Ⓑ Enter the debit account number from the
   ledger in the PR column of the journal (blue line).
Ⓒ Identify credit account in ledger: enter date,
   journal page, amount, and balance (gold line).
Ⓓ Enter the credit account number from the
   ledger in the PR column of the journal (green line).

Processing Transactions—An Example

A1_____

Analyze the impact of
transactions on accounts
and financial statements.

We use FastForward to show how double-entry accounting is used in analyzing and processing transactions. Analysis of each transaction follows the four steps of Exhibit 2.9.

Step 1 Identify the transaction and any source documents.

Step 2 Analyze the transaction using the accounting equation.

Step 3 Record the transaction in journal entry form applying double-entry accounting.

Step 4 Post the entry (for simplicity, we use T-accounts to represent ledger accounts).

Study each transaction before moving to the next. The first 11 transactions are from Chapter 1, and we analyze five additional December transactions of FastForward (numbered 12 through 16).

Point: In Need-to-Know 2-5, we show how to use balance column accounts for the ledger.

1. Receive Investment by Owner

1 IDENTIFY FastForward receives $30,000 cash from Chas Taylor in exchange for common stock.

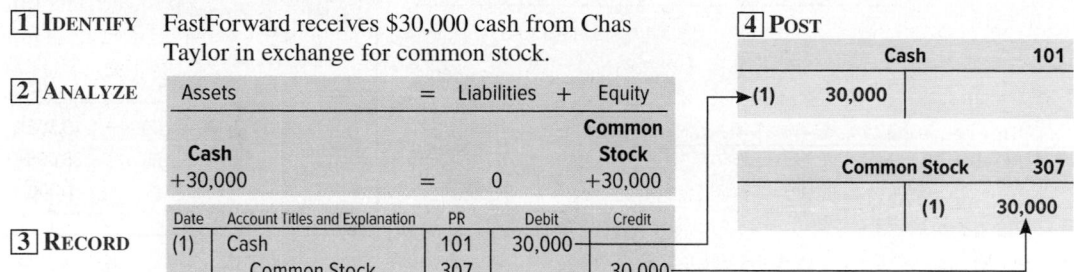

2 ANALYZE

Assets	=	Liabilities	+	Equity
Cash				**Common Stock**
+30,000	=	0		+30,000

3 RECORD

Date	Account Titles and Explanation	PR	Debit	Credit
(1)	Cash	101	30,000	
	Common Stock	307		30,000

4 POST

Cash		101
(1)	30,000	

Common Stock		307
	(1)	30,000

2. Purchase Supplies for Cash

1 IDENTIFY FastForward pays $2,500 cash for supplies.

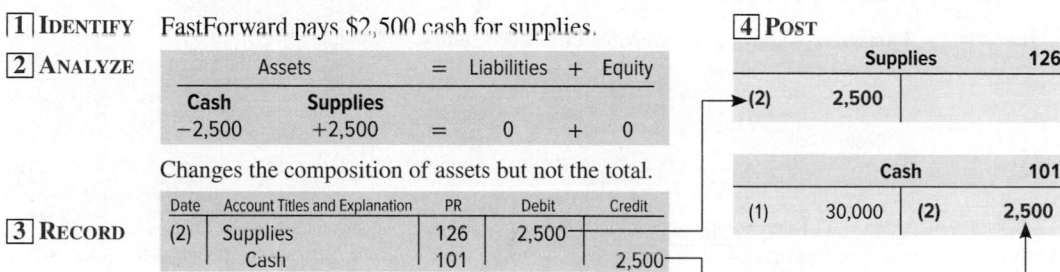

2 ANALYZE

Assets		=	Liabilities	+	Equity
Cash	**Supplies**				
−2,500	+2,500	=	0	+	0

Changes the composition of assets but not the total.

3 RECORD

Date	Account Titles and Explanation	PR	Debit	Credit
(2)	Supplies	126	2,500	
	Cash	101		2,500

4 POST

Supplies		126
(2)	2,500	

Cash			101
(1)	30,000	(2)	2,500

3. Purchase Equipment for Cash

1 IDENTIFY FastForward pays $26,000 cash for equipment.

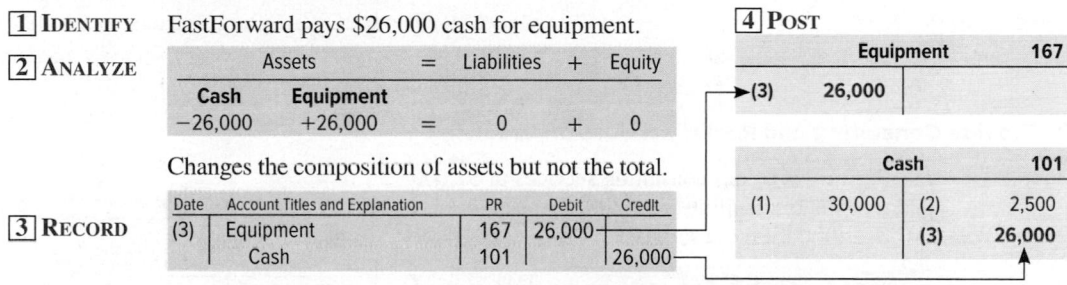

2 ANALYZE

Assets		=	Liabilities	+	Equity
Cash	**Equipment**				
−26,000	+26,000	=	0	+	0

Changes the composition of assets but not the total.

3 RECORD

Date	Account Titles and Explanation	PR	Debit	Credit
(3)	Equipment	167	26,000	
	Cash	101		26,000

4 POST

Equipment		167
(3)	26,000	

Cash			101
(1)	30,000	(2)	2,500
		(3)	26,000

4. Purchase Supplies on Credit

1 IDENTIFY FastForward purchases $7,100 of supplies on credit from a supplier.

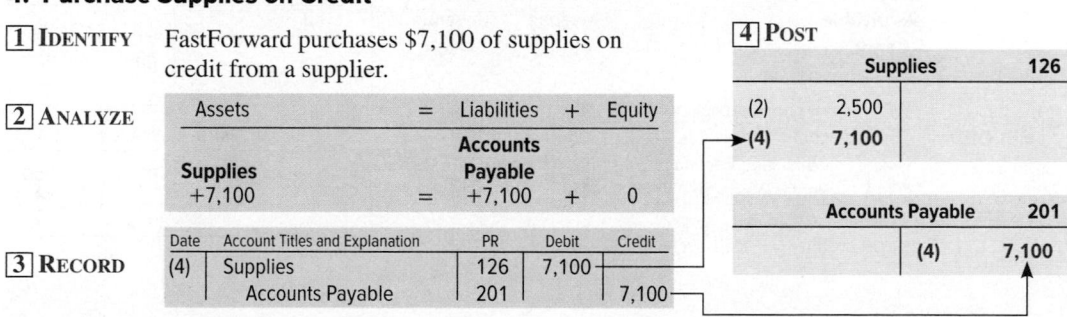

2 ANALYZE

Assets	=	Liabilities	+	Equity
Supplies		**Accounts Payable**		
+7,100	=	+7,100	+	0

3 RECORD

Date	Account Titles and Explanation	PR	Debit	Credit
(4)	Supplies	126	7,100	
	Accounts Payable	201		7,100

4 POST

Supplies		126
(2)	2,500	
(4)	7,100	

Accounts Payable		201
	(4)	7,100

5. Provide Services for Cash

1 IDENTIFY FastForward provides consulting services and immediately collects $4,200 cash.

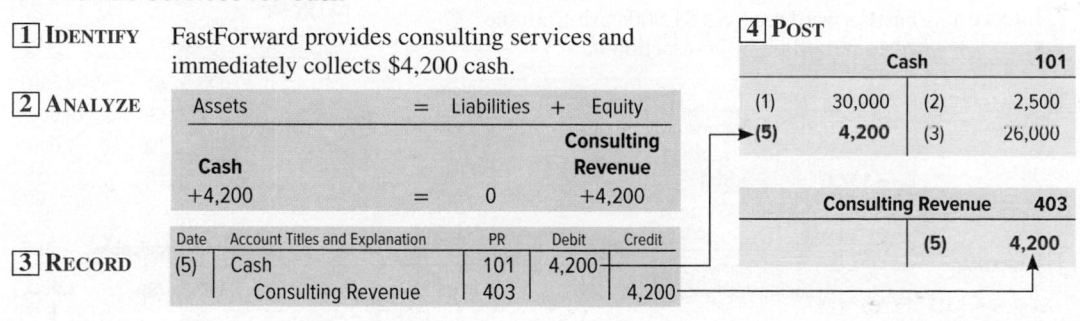

2 ANALYZE

Assets	=	Liabilities	+	Equity
Cash				**Consulting Revenue**
+4,200	=	0		+4,200

3 RECORD

Date	Account Titles and Explanation	PR	Debit	Credit
(5)	Cash	101	4,200	
	Consulting Revenue	403		4,200

4 POST

Cash			101
(1)	30,000	(2)	2,500
(5)	4,200	(3)	26,000

Consulting Revenue		403
	(5)	4,200

©Adie Bush/Getty Images

6. Payment of Expense in Cash

1 IDENTIFY   FastForward pays $1,000 cash for December rent.

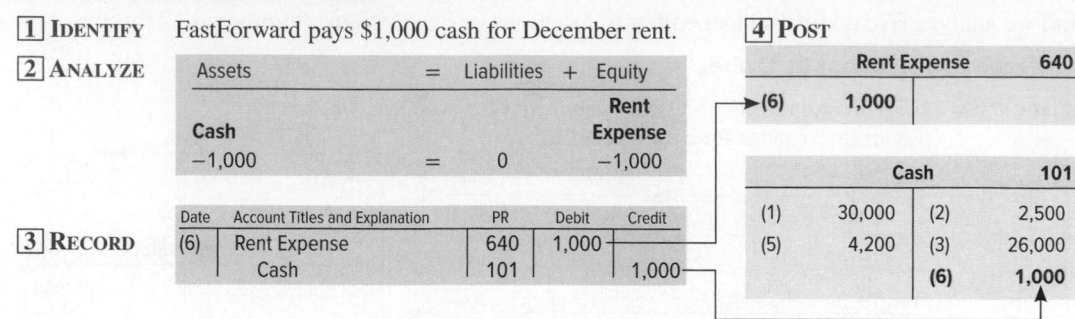

2 ANALYZE

Assets	=	Liabilities	+	Equity
Cash				**Rent Expense**
−1,000	=	0		−1,000

3 RECORD

Date	Account Titles and Explanation	PR	Debit	Credit
(6)	Rent Expense	640	1,000	
	Cash	101		1,000

4 POST

Rent Expense		640
►(6)	1,000	

Cash			101
(1)	30,000	(2)	2,500
(5)	4,200	(3)	26,000
		(6)	1,000

---

7. Payment of Expense in Cash

Point: *Salary* usually refers to compensation of a fixed amount for a given time period. *Wages* is compensation based on time worked.

1 IDENTIFY   FastForward pays $700 cash for employee salary.

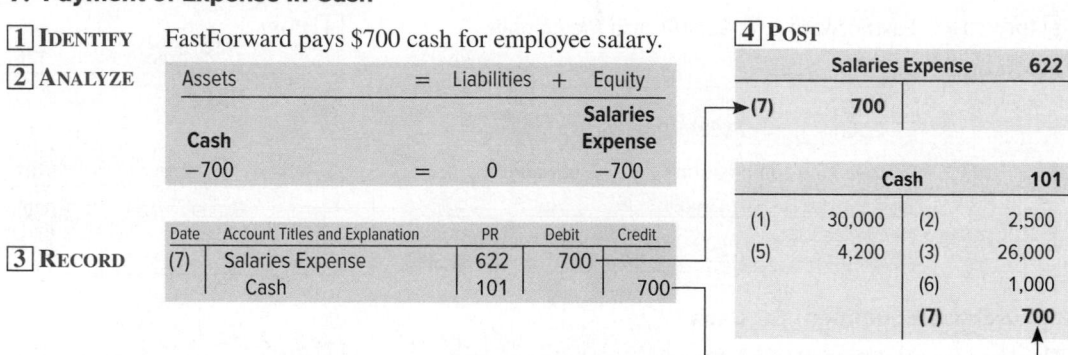

2 ANALYZE

Assets	=	Liabilities	+	Equity
Cash				**Salaries Expense**
−700	=	0		−700

3 RECORD

Date	Account Titles and Explanation	PR	Debit	Credit
(7)	Salaries Expense	622	700	
	Cash	101		700

4 POST

Salaries Expense		622
►(7)	700	

Cash			101
(1)	30,000	(2)	2,500
(5)	4,200	(3)	26,000
		(6)	1,000
		(7)	700

---

8. Provide Consulting and Rental Services on Credit

Point: The *revenue recognition principle* requires revenue to be recognized when the company provides products and services to a customer. This is not necessarily the same time that the customer pays.

1 IDENTIFY   FastForward provides consulting services of $1,600 and rents its test facilities for $300. The customer is billed $1,900 for these services.

2 ANALYZE

Assets	=	Liabilities	+	Equity	
Accounts Receivable				**Consulting Revenue**	**Rental Revenue**
+1,900	=	0		+1,600	+300

Point: Transaction 8 is a **compound journal entry,** which is an entry that affects three or more accounts. The rule that total debits equal total credits continues.

3 RECORD

Date	Account Titles and Explanation	PR	Debit	Credit
(8)	Accounts Receivable	106	1,900	
	Consulting Revenue	403		1,600
	Rental Revenue	406		300

4 POST

Accounts Receivable		106
►(8)	1,900	

Consulting Revenue			403
		(5)	4,200
		(8)	1,600

Rental Revenue			406
		(8)	300

---

9. Receipt of Cash on Account

1 IDENTIFY   FastForward receives $1,900 cash from the customer billed in Transaction 8.

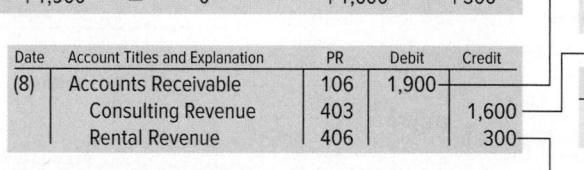

2 ANALYZE

Assets		=	Liabilities	+	Equity
Cash	**Accounts Receivable**				
+1,900	−1,900	=	0	+	0

3 RECORD

Date	Account Titles and Explanation	PR	Debit	Credit
(9)	Cash	101	1,900	
	Accounts Receivable	106		1,900

4 POST

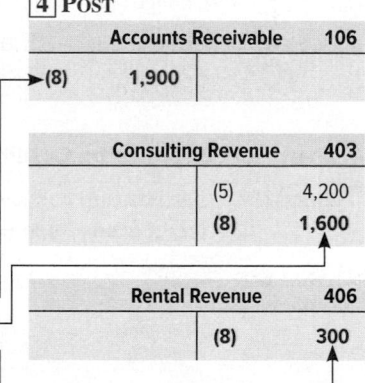

Cash			101
(1)	30,000	(2)	2,500
(5)	4,200	(3)	26,000
►(9)	1,900	(6)	1,000
		(7)	700

Accounts Receivable			106
(8)	1,900	(9)	1,900

10. Partial Payment of Accounts Payable

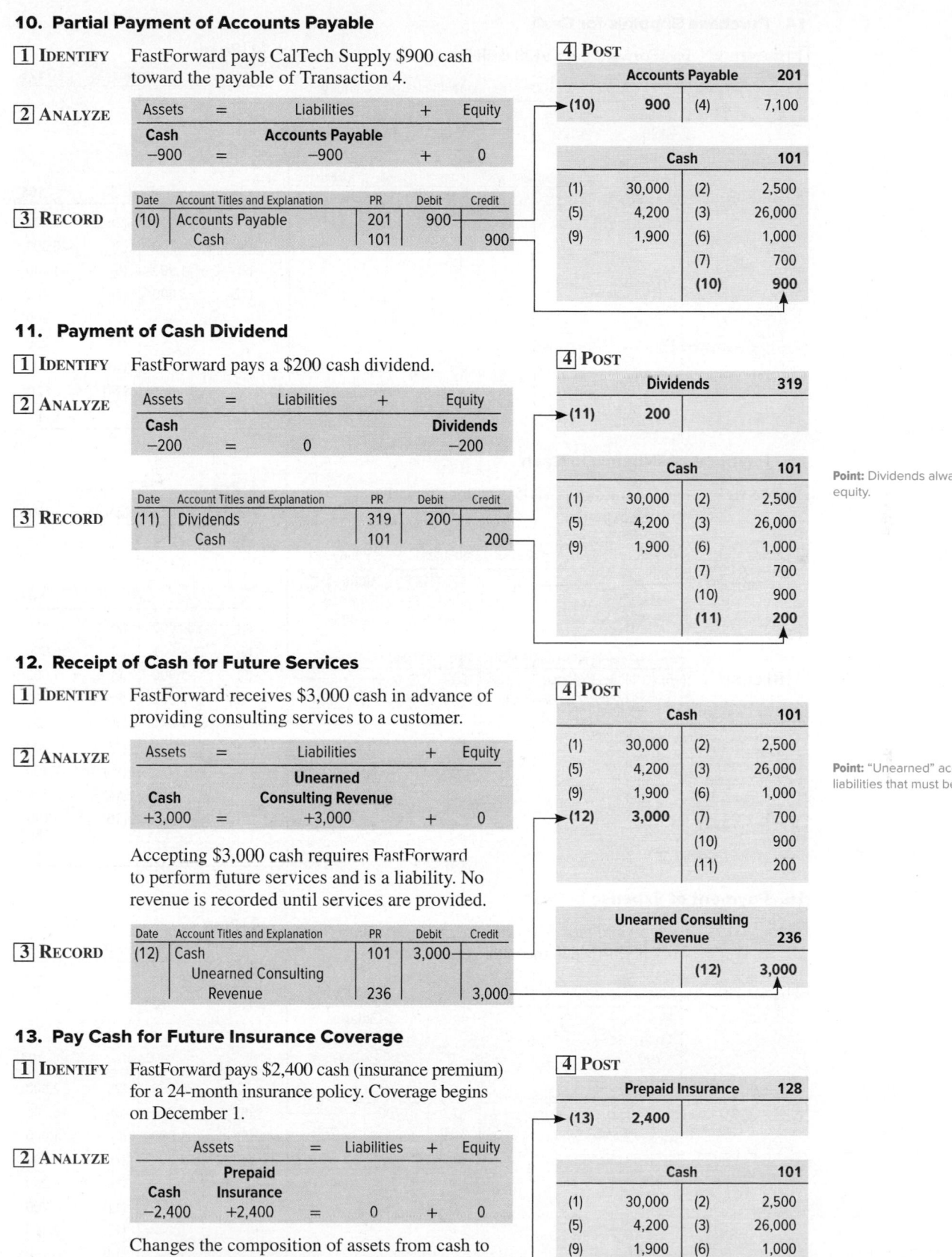

1 IDENTIFY   FastForward pays CalTech Supply $900 cash toward the payable of Transaction 4.

2 ANALYZE

Assets	=	Liabilities	+	Equity
Cash		**Accounts Payable**		
−900	=	−900	+	0

3 RECORD

Date	Account Titles and Explanation	PR	Debit	Credit
(10)	Accounts Payable	201	900	
	Cash	101		900

4 POST

Accounts Payable			201
►(10)	900	(4)	7,100

Cash			101
(1)	30,000	(2)	2,500
(5)	4,200	(3)	26,000
(9)	1,900	(6)	1,000
		(7)	700
		(10)	**900**

11. Payment of Cash Dividend

1 IDENTIFY   FastForward pays a $200 cash dividend.

2 ANALYZE

Assets	=	Liabilities	+	Equity
Cash				**Dividends**
−200	=	0		−200

3 RECORD

Date	Account Titles and Explanation	PR	Debit	Credit
(11)	Dividends	319	200	
	Cash	101		200

4 POST

Dividends			319
►(11)	200		

Cash			101
(1)	30,000	(2)	2,500
(5)	4,200	(3)	26,000
(9)	1,900	(6)	1,000
		(7)	700
		(10)	900
		(11)	**200**

Point: Dividends always decrease equity.

12. Receipt of Cash for Future Services

1 IDENTIFY   FastForward receives $3,000 cash in advance of providing consulting services to a customer.

2 ANALYZE

Assets	=	Liabilities	+	Equity
		Unearned		
Cash		**Consulting Revenue**		
+3,000	=	+3,000	+	0

Accepting $3,000 cash requires FastForward to perform future services and is a liability. No revenue is recorded until services are provided.

3 RECORD

Date	Account Titles and Explanation	PR	Debit	Credit
(12)	Cash	101	3,000	
	Unearned Consulting			
	Revenue	236		3,000

4 POST

Cash			101
(1)	30,000	(2)	2,500
(5)	4,200	(3)	26,000
(9)	1,900	(6)	1,000
►(12)	3,000	(7)	700
		(10)	900
		(11)	200

Unearned Consulting Revenue			236
		(12)	**3,000**

Point: "Unearned" accounts are liabilities that must be fulfilled.

13. Pay Cash for Future Insurance Coverage

1 IDENTIFY   FastForward pays $2,400 cash (insurance premium) for a 24-month insurance policy. Coverage begins on December 1.

2 ANALYZE

	Assets	=	Liabilities	+	Equity
	Prepaid				
Cash	**Insurance**				
−2,400	+2,400	=	0	+	0

Changes the composition of assets from cash to prepaid insurance. Expense is recorded as insurance coverage expires.

3 RECORD

Date	Account Titles and Explanation	PR	Debit	Credit
(13)	Prepaid Insurance	128	2,400	
	Cash	101		2,400

4 POST

Prepaid Insurance			128
►(13)	2,400		

Cash			101
(1)	30,000	(2)	2,500
(5)	4,200	(3)	26,000
(9)	1,900	(6)	1,000
(12)	3,000	(7)	700
		(10)	900
		(11)	200
		(13)	**2,400**

14. Purchase Supplies for Cash

1 IDENTIFY   FastForward pays $120 cash for supplies.

2 ANALYZE

Assets		=	Liabilities	+	Equity
Cash	Supplies				
−120	+120	=	0	+	0

3 RECORD

Date	Account Titles and Explanation	PR	Debit	Credit
(14)	Supplies	126	120	
	Cash	101		120

4 POST

Supplies		126
(2)	2,500	
(4)	7,100	
▶(14)	120	

Cash		101
(1)	30,000	(2)	2,500
(5)	4,200	(3)	26,000
(9)	1,900	(6)	1,000
(12)	3,000	(7)	700
		(10)	900
		(11)	200
		(13)	2,400
		(14)	**120**

Point: Luca Pacioli, a 15th-century monk and famous mathematician, was the first to devise double-entry accounting.

15. Payment of Expense in Cash

1 IDENTIFY   FastForward pays $305 cash for December utilities expense.

2 ANALYZE

Assets	=	Liabilities	+	Equity
				Utilities
Cash				Expense
−305	=	0		−305

3 RECORD

Date	Account Titles and Explanation	PR	Debit	Credit
(15)	Utilities Expense	690	305	
	Cash	101		305

4 POST

Utilities Expense		690
▶(15)	305	

Cash		101
(1)	30,000	(2)	2,500
(5)	4,200	(3)	26,000
(9)	1,900	(6)	1,000
(12)	3,000	(7)	700
		(10)	900
		(11)	200
		(13)	2,400
		(14)	120
		(15)	**305**

16. Payment of Expense in Cash

1 IDENTIFY   FastForward pays $700 cash in employee salary for work performed in the latter part of December.

2 ANALYZE

Assets	=	Liabilities	+	Equity
				Salaries
Cash				Expense
−700	=	0		−700

3 RECORD

Date	Account Titles and Explanation	PR	Debit	Credit
(16)	Salaries Expense	622	700	
	Cash	101		700

4 POST

Salaries Expense		622
(7)	700	
▶(16)	700	

Cash		101
(1)	30,000	(2)	2,500
(5)	4,200	(3)	26,000
(9)	1,900	(6)	1,000
(12)	3,000	(7)	700
		(10)	900
		(11)	200
		(13)	2,400
		(14)	120
		(15)	305
		(16)	**700**

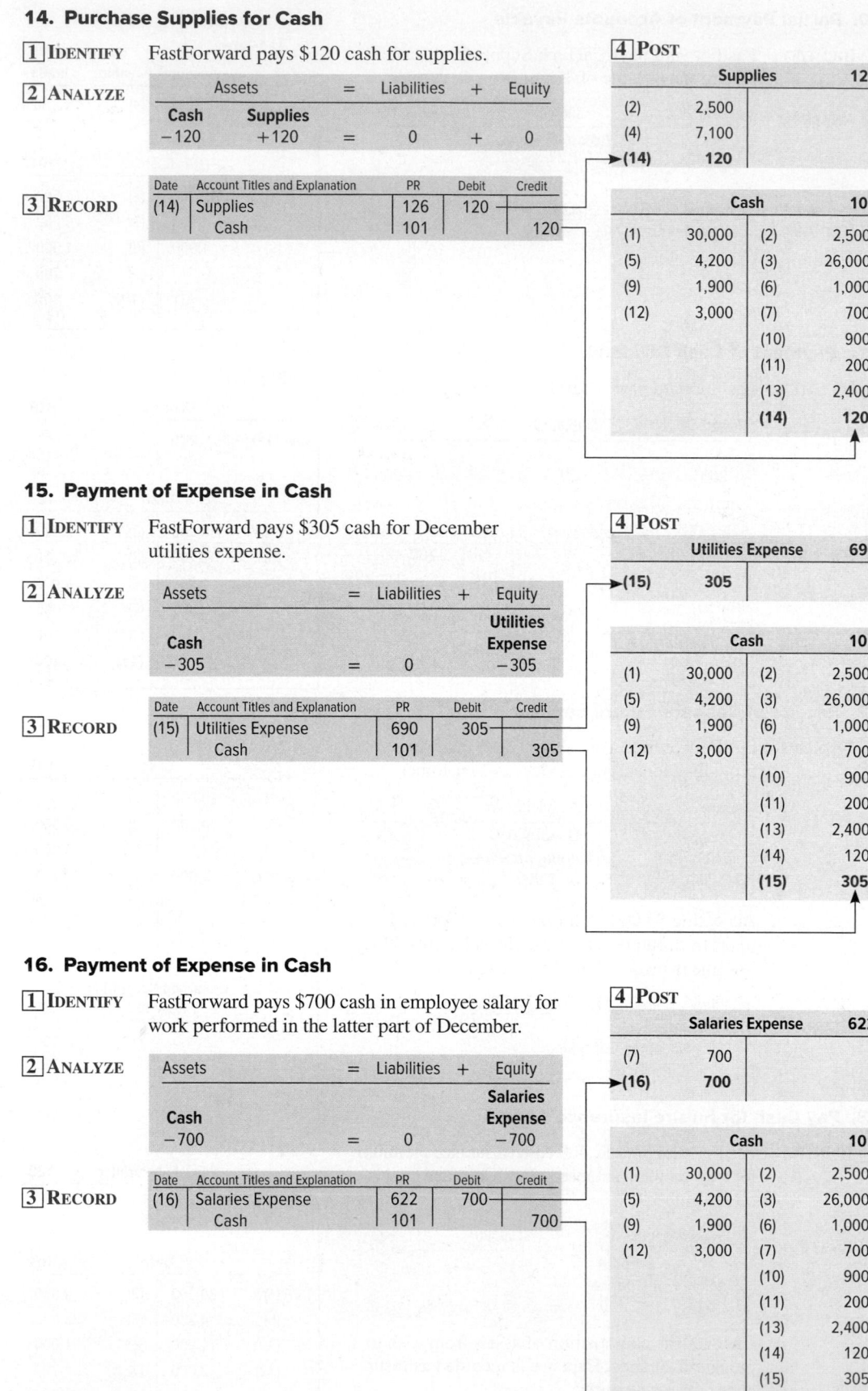

Summarizing Transactions in a Ledger

Exhibit 2.13 shows the ledger accounts (in T-account form) of FastForward after all 16 transactions are recorded and posted and the balances computed. The accounts are grouped into three columns following the accounting equation: assets, liabilities, and equity.

- Totals for the three columns obey the accounting equation:
  Assets equal **$42,395** ($4,275 + $0 + $9,720 + $2,400 + $26,000).
  Liabilities equal **$9,200** ($6,200 + $3,000).
  Equity equals **$33,195** ($30,000 − $200 + $5,800 + $300 − $1,400 − $1,000 − $305).
  The accounting equation: $42,395 = $9,200 + $33,195.
- Common stock, dividends, revenue, and expense accounts reflect transactions that change equity.
- Revenue and expense account balances are reported in the income statement.

Debit and Credit Rules

Accounts	Increase (normal bal.)	Decrease
Asset	Debit	Credit
Liability..........	Credit	Debit
Common Stock	Credit	Debit
Dividends.........	Debit	Credit
Revenue	Credit	Debit
Expense	Debit	Credit

EXHIBIT 2.13

*FAST*forward

Ledger for FastForward (in T-Account Form)

General Ledger

Assets = Liabilities + Equity

Cash 101

(1)	30,000	(2)	2,500
(5)	4,200	(3)	26,000
(9)	1,900	(6)	1,000
(12)	3,000	(7)	700
		(10)	900
		(11)	200
		(13)	2,400
		(14)	120
		(15)	305
		(16)	700
Balance	4,275		

Accounts Receivable 106

(8)	1,900	(9)	1,900
Balance	0		

Supplies 126

(2)	2,500	
(4)	7,100	
(14)	120	
Balance	9,720	

Prepaid Insurance 128

(13)	2,400	

Equipment 167

(3)	26,000	

Accounts Payable 201

(10)	900	(4)	7,100
		Balance	6,200

Unearned Consulting Revenue 236

		(12)	3,000

Common Stock 307

	(1)	30,000

Dividends 319

(11)	200	

Consulting Revenue 403

		(5)	4,200
		(8)	1,600
		Balance	5,800

Rental Revenue 406

	(8)	300

Salaries Expense 622

(7)	700	
(16)	700	
Balance	1,400	

Rent Expense 640

(6)	1,000	

Utilities Expense 690

(15)	305	

Accounts in this white area are on the income statement.

$42,395 = $9,200 + $33,195

NEED-TO-KNOW 2-3

Recording Transactions

P1   A1

Assume Tata Company began operations on January 1 and completed the following transactions during its first month of operations. For each transaction, (a) analyze the transaction using the accounting equation, (b) record the transaction in journal entry form, and (c) post the entry using T-accounts to represent ledger accounts. Tata Company has the following (partial) chart of accounts—account numbers in parentheses: Cash (101); Accounts Receivable (106); Equipment (167); Accounts Payable (201); Common Stock (307); Dividends (319); Services Revenue (403); and Wages Expense (601).

Jan. 1   Jamsetji Tata invested $4,000 cash in the Tata Company in exchange for common stock.
      5   Tata Company purchased $2,000 of equipment on credit.
     14   Tata Company provided $540 of services for a client on credit.

Solution

Jan. 1 Receive Investment by Owner

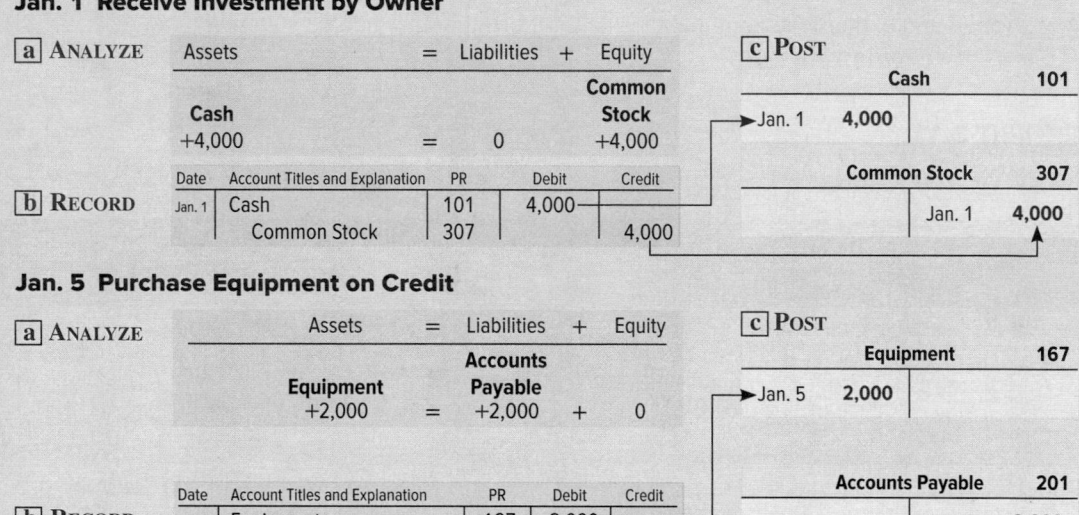

Jan. 5 Purchase Equipment on Credit

Jan. 14 Provide Services on Credit

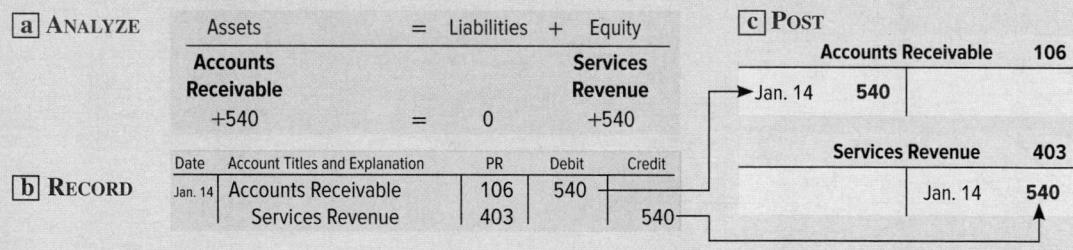

Do More: QS 2-6, E 2-7, E 2-9, E 2-11, E 2-12

TRIAL BALANCE

P2

Prepare and explain the use of a trial balance.

A **trial balance** is a list of all ledger accounts and their balances at a point in time. Exhibit 2.14 shows the trial balance for FastForward after its 16 entries are posted to the ledger. (This is an *unadjusted* trial balance. Chapter 3 explains adjustments.)

Preparing a Trial Balance

Preparing a trial balance has three steps.

1. List each account title and its amount (from the ledger) in the trial balance. If an account has a zero balance, list it with a zero in its normal balance column (or omit it).
2. Compute the total of debit balances and the total of credit balances.
3. Verify (*prove*) total debit balances equal total credit balances.

The total of debit balances equals the total of credit balances for the trial balance in Exhibit 2.14. Equality of these two totals does not guarantee that no errors were made. For example, the column totals will be equal when a debit or credit of a correct amount is made to a wrong account. Another error not identified with a trial balance is when equal debits and credits of an incorrect amount are entered.

Searching for Errors
If the trial balance does not balance (when its columns are not equal), the error(s) must be found and corrected. An efficient way to search for an error is to check the journalizing, posting, and trial balance preparation in *reverse order*. Step 1 is to verify that the trial balance columns are correctly added. If step 1 does not find the error, step 2 is to verify that account balances are accurately entered from the ledger. Step 3 is to see whether a debit (or credit) balance is mistakenly listed in the trial balance as a credit (or debit). A clue to this error is when the difference between total debits and total credits equals twice the amount of the incorrect account balance. Step 4 is to recompute each account balance in the ledger. Step 5 is to verify that each journal entry is properly posted. Step 6 is to verify that the original journal entry has equal debits and credits. At this point, the errors should be uncovered.

EXHIBIT 2.14

Trial Balance (Unadjusted)

FASTForward

FASTFORWARD Trial Balance December 31, 2019		
	Debit	Credit
Cash.	$ 4,275	
Accounts receivable	0	
Supplies.	9,720	
Prepaid insurance.	2,400	
Equipment.	26,000	
Accounts payable		$ 6,200
Unearned consulting revenue . . .		3,000
Common stock		30,000
Dividends	200	
Consulting revenue		5,800
Rental revenue		300
Salaries expense.	1,400	
Rent expense	1,000	
Utilities expense.	305	
Totals.	$45,300	$45,300

Point: A trial balance is *not* a financial statement but a tool for checking equality of debits and credits in the ledger.

Example: If a credit to Unearned Revenue was incorrectly posted to the Revenue ledger account, would the ledger still balance? *Answer:* The ledger would balance, but liabilities would be understated, equity would be overstated, and income would be overstated.

Ethical Risk

Accounting Quality   Recording valid and accurate transactions enhances the quality of financial statements. Roughly 30% of employees in IT report observing misconduct such as falsifying accounting data. They also report increased incidences of such misconduct in recent years. Source: KPMG. ■

Financial Statements Prepared from Trial Balance

Financial Statements across Time
How financial statements are linked in time is shown in Exhibit 2.15. A balance sheet reports an organization's financial position at a *point in time*. The income statement, statement of retained earnings, and statement of cash flows report financial performance over a *period of time*. The three statements in the middle column of Exhibit 2.15 explain how financial position changes from the beginning to the end of a reporting period.

A one-year (annual) reporting period is common, as are semiannual, quarterly, and monthly periods. The one-year reporting period is called the *accounting,* or *fiscal, year*. Businesses whose accounting year begins on January 1 and ends on December 31 are called *calendar-year* companies.

P3

Prepare financial statements from business transactions.

EXHIBIT 2.15

Links between Financial Statements across Time

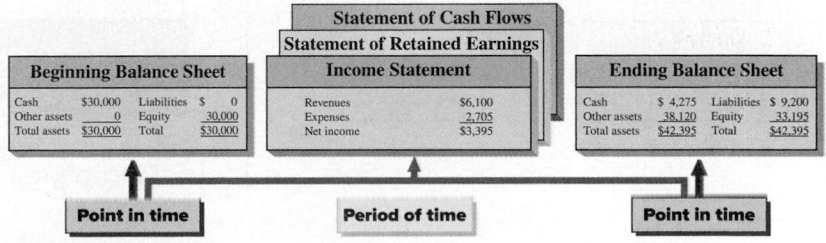

Financial Statement Preparation
This section shows how to prepare *financial statements* from the trial balance. (These are *unadjusted statements*. Chapter 3 explains adjustments.) We prepare these statements in the following order.

❶ Income Statement   An income statement reports revenues earned minus expenses incurred over a period of time. FastForward's income statement for December is shown at the top right side of Exhibit 2.16. Information about revenues and expenses is taken from the trial balance on the left side. Net income of $3,395 is the *bottom line* for the income statement. Owner investments and dividends are *not* part of income.

Point: An income statement also is called an *earnings statement,* a *statement of operations,* or a *P&L* (profit and loss) *statement.* A balance sheet also is called a *statement of financial position.*

❷ Statement of Retained Earnings   The statement of retained earnings reports how retained earnings changes over the reporting period. FastForward's statement of retained earnings is the second report in Exhibit 2.16. It shows the $3,395 of net income, the $200 dividend, and the $3,195 end-of-period balance. (The beginning balance in the statement of retained earnings is rarely zero, except in the first period of operations. The beginning balance in January 2020 is $3,195, which is December 2019's ending balance.)

Point: Revenues and expenses are not reported in detail in the statement of retained earnings. Instead, their effects are reflected through net income.

❸ Balance Sheet   The balance sheet reports the financial position of a company at a point in time. FastForward's balance sheet is the third report in Exhibit 2.16. This statement shows financial condition at the close of business on December 31. The left side of the balance

EXHIBIT 2.16

Financial Statements Prepared from Trial Balance

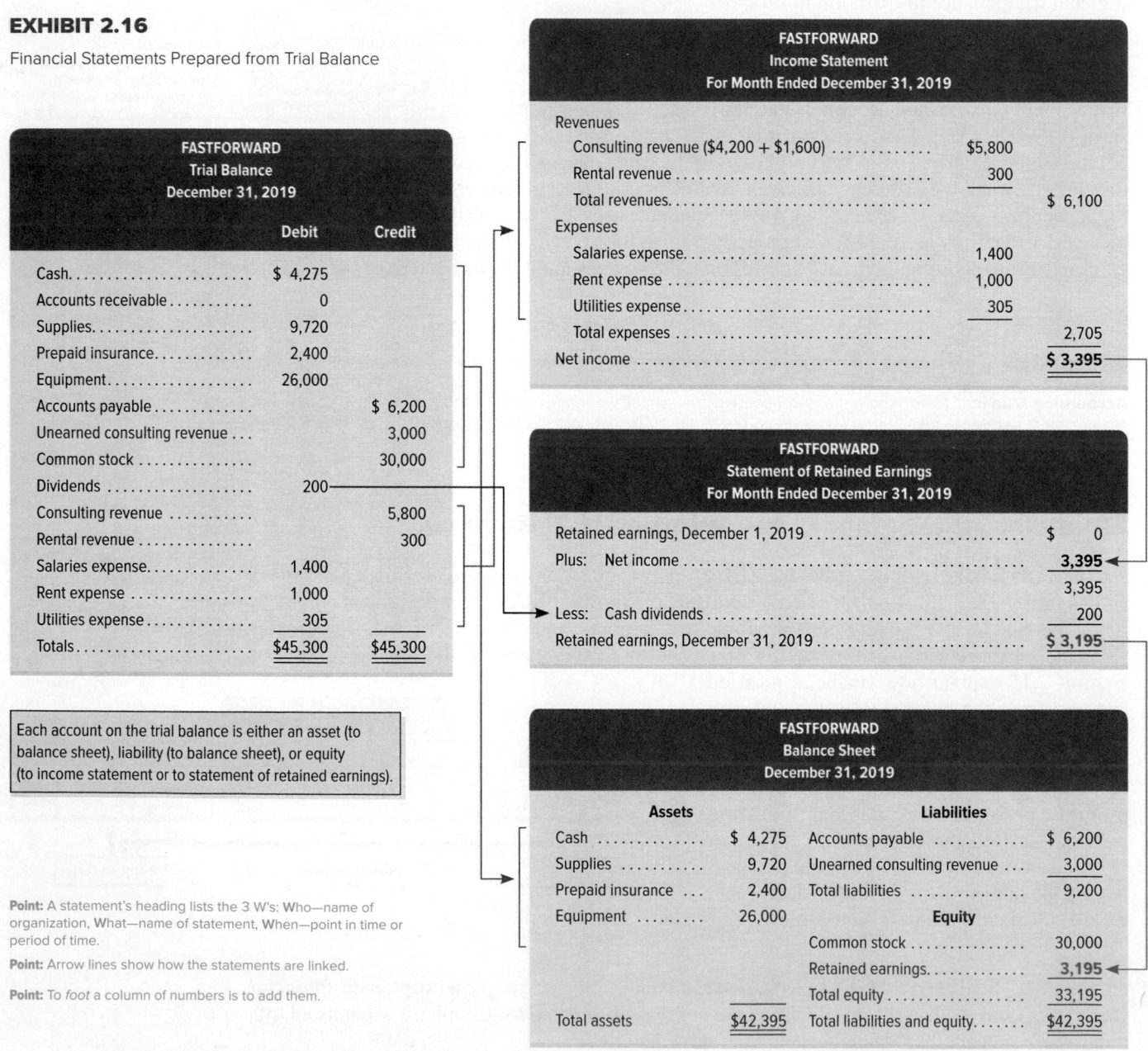

FASTFORWARD
Trial Balance
December 31, 2019

	Debit	Credit
Cash.	$ 4,275	
Accounts receivable	0	
Supplies.	9,720	
Prepaid insurance.	2,400	
Equipment.	26,000	
Accounts payable		$ 6,200
Unearned consulting revenue . . .		3,000
Common stock		30,000
Dividends	200	
Consulting revenue		5,800
Rental revenue		300
Salaries expense.	1,400	
Rent expense	1,000	
Utilities expense	305	
Totals.	$45,300	$45,300

Each account on the trial balance is either an asset (to balance sheet), liability (to balance sheet), or equity (to income statement or to statement of retained earnings).

FASTFORWARD
Income Statement
For Month Ended December 31, 2019

Revenues		
Consulting revenue ($4,200 + $1,600)	$5,800	
Rental revenue	300	
Total revenues.		$ 6,100
Expenses		
Salaries expense.	1,400	
Rent expense	1,000	
Utilities expense	305	
Total expenses		2,705
Net income		$ 3,395

FASTFORWARD
Statement of Retained Earnings
For Month Ended December 31, 2019

Retained earnings, December 1, 2019	$ 0
Plus: Net income	3,395
	3,395
Less: Cash dividends	200
Retained earnings, December 31, 2019	$ 3,195

Point: A statement's heading lists the 3 W's: Who—name of organization, What—name of statement, When—point in time or period of time.

Point: Arrow lines show how the statements are linked.

Point: To *foot* a column of numbers is to add them.

FASTFORWARD
Balance Sheet
December 31, 2019

Assets		Liabilities	
Cash	$ 4,275	Accounts payable	$ 6,200
Supplies	9,720	Unearned consulting revenue . . .	3,000
Prepaid insurance . . .	2,400	Total liabilities	9,200
Equipment	26,000	**Equity**	
		Common stock	30,000
		Retained earnings.	3,195
		Total equity	33,195
Total assets	$42,395	Total liabilities and equity.	$42,395

sheet lists its assets: cash, supplies, prepaid insurance, and equipment. The liabilities section of the balance sheet shows that it owes $6,200 to creditors and $3,000 in services to customers who paid in advance. The equity section shows an ending balance of $33,195. Note the link between the ending balance of the statement of retained earnings and the retained earnings balance. (This presentation of the balance sheet is called the *account form:* assets on the left and liabilities and equity on the right. Another presentation is the *report form:* assets on top, followed by liabilities and then equity. Either presentation is acceptable.)

Presentation Issues   Dollar signs are not used in journals and ledgers. They do appear in financial statements and other reports such as trial balances. We usually put dollar signs beside only the first and last numbers in a column. **Apple**'s financial statements in Appendix A show this. Companies commonly round amounts in reports to the nearest dollar, or even to a higher level. Apple, like many large companies, rounds its financial statement amounts to the nearest million. This decision is based on the impact of rounding for users' decisions.

Decision Maker

Entrepreneur   You open a wholesale business selling entertainment equipment to retail outlets. Most of your customers want to buy on credit. How can you use the balance sheets of customers to decide which ones to extend credit to? ■   *Answer:* We use the accounting equation (Assets = Liabilities + Equity) to identify risky customers to whom we would not want to extend credit. A balance sheet provides amounts for each of these key components. The lower a customer's equity is relative to liabilities, the less likely you would be to extend credit. A low equity means the business already has many creditor claims to it.

©REDPIXEL.PL/Shutterstock

Prepare a trial balance for **Apple** using the following condensed data from its recent fiscal year ended September 30 ($ in millions).

NEED-TO-KNOW 2-4

Preparing Trial Balance

P2

APPLE

Common stock	$ 35,867	Dividends	$ 47,169
Accounts payable	49,049	Investments and other assets	303,373
Other liabilities	192,223	Land and equipment	33,783
Cost of sales (and other expenses)	141,048	Selling and other expense	39,835
Cash	20,289	Accounts receivable	17,874
Revenues	229,234	Retained earnings, beginning fiscal year	96,998

Solution ($ in millions)

APPLE Trial Balance September 30	Debit	Credit
Cash	$ 20,289	
Accounts receivable	17,874	
Land and equipment	33,783	
Investments and other assets	303,373	
Accounts payable		$ 49,049
Other liabilities		192,223
Common stock		35,867
Retained earnings, beginning fiscal year		96,998
Dividends	47,169	
Revenues		229,234
Cost of sales (and other expenses)	141,048	
Selling and other expense	39,835	
Totals	$603,371	$603,371

Do More: E 2-8, E 2-10

Decision Analysis    **Debt Ratio**

A2

Compute the debt ratio and describe its use in analyzing financial condition.

It is important to assess a company's risk of failing to pay its debts. Companies finance their assets with either liabilities or equity. A company that finances a relatively large portion of its assets with liabilities is said to have higher *financial leverage*. Higher financial leverage means greater risk because liabilities must be repaid and often require regular interest payments (equity financing does not). One measure of the risk associated with liabilities is the **debt ratio** as defined in Exhibit 2.17.

EXHIBIT 2.17

Debt Ratio

$$\text{Debt ratio} = \frac{\text{Total liabilities}}{\text{Total assets}}$$

Costco's total liabilities, total assets, and debt ratio for the past three years are shown in Exhibit 2.18. Costco's debt ratio ranges from a low of 0.63 to a high of 0.70. Its ratio exceeds Walmart's in each of the last three years, suggesting a higher than average risk from financial leverage. So, is financial leverage good or bad for Costco? The answer: If Costco is making more money with this debt than it is paying the lenders, then it is successfully borrowing money to make more money. A company's use of debt can turn unprofitable quickly if its return from that money drops below the rate it is paying lenders.

EXHIBIT 2.18

Computation and Analysis of Debt Ratio

Company	($ millions)	Current Year	1 Year Ago	2 Years Ago
Costco	Total liabilities.........................	$25,268	$20,831	$22,174
	Total assets...........................	$36,347	$33,163	$33,017
	Debt ratio...........................	**0.70**	**0.63**	**0.67**
Walmart	Debt ratio	0.59	0.58	0.58

 Decision Maker

Investor   You consider buying stock in **Converse**. As part of your analysis, you compute the company's debt ratio for 2017, 2018, and 2019 as 0.35, 0.74, and 0.94, respectively. Based on the debt ratio, is Converse a low-risk investment? Has the risk of buying Converse stock changed over this period? (The industry debt ratio averages 0.40.) ■   *Answer:* The debt ratio suggests that Converse's stock is of higher risk than normal and that this risk is rising. The average industry ratio of 0.40 supports this conclusion. The 2019 debt ratio for Converse is twice the industry norm. Also, a debt ratio approaching 1.0 indicates little to no equity.

NEED-TO-KNOW 2-5

COMPREHENSIVE

Journalizing and Posting Transactions, Statement Preparation, and Debt Ratio

This problem extends Need-to-Know 1-6 from Chapter 1: Jasmine Worthy started a haircutting business called Expressions. The following events occurred during its first month.

Aug. 1   Worthy invested $3,000 cash and $15,000 of equipment in Expressions in exchange for common stock.
  2   Expressions paid $600 cash for furniture for the shop.
  3   Expressions paid $500 cash to rent space in a strip mall for August.
  4   Expressions purchased $1,200 of equipment on credit for the shop (recorded as accounts payable).
  15   Expressions opened for business on August 5. Cash received from haircutting services in the first week and a half of business (ended August 15) was $825.
  16   Expressions provided $100 of haircutting services on account.
  17   Expressions received a $100 check for services previously rendered on account.
  18   Expressions paid $125 to an assistant for hours worked for the grand opening.
  31   Cash received from services provided during the second half of August was $930.
  31   Expressions paid $400 cash toward the account payable entered into on August 4.
  31   Expressions paid a $900 cash dividend to Worthy (sole shareholder).

Required

1. Open the following ledger accounts in balance column format (account numbers are in parentheses): Cash (101); Accounts Receivable (102); Furniture (161); Store Equipment (165); Accounts Payable (201); Common Stock (307); Dividends (319); Haircutting Services Revenue (403); Wages Expense (623); and Rent Expense (640). Prepare general journal entries for the transactions.

2. Post the journal entries from part 1 to the ledger accounts.

3. Prepare a trial balance as of August 31.

4. Prepare an income statement for August.

5. Prepare a statement of retained earnings for August.

6. Prepare a balance sheet as of August 31.

7. Determine the debt ratio as of August 31.

Extended Analysis

8. In the coming months, Expressions will have a greater variety of business transactions. Identify which accounts are debited and which are credited for the following transactions. *Hint:* We must use some accounts not opened in part 1.

a. Purchase supplies with cash.

b. Pay cash for future insurance coverage.

c. Receive cash for services to be provided in the future.

d. Purchase supplies on account.

PLANNING THE SOLUTION

- Analyze each transaction and use the debit and credit rules to prepare a journal entry for each.
- Post each debit and each credit from journal entries to their ledger accounts and cross-reference each amount in the posting reference (PR) columns of the journal and ledger.
- Calculate each account balance and list the accounts with their balances on a trial balance.
- Verify that total debits in the trial balance equal total credits.
- To prepare the income statement, identify revenues and expenses. List those items on the statement, compute the difference, and label the result as *net income* or *net loss*.
- Use information in the ledger to prepare the statement of retained earnings.
- Use information in the ledger to prepare the balance sheet.
- Calculate the debt ratio by dividing total liabilities by total assets.
- Analyze the future transactions to identify the accounts affected and apply debit and credit rules.

SOLUTION

1. General journal entries.

Date	Account Titles and Explanation	PR	Debit	Credit
Aug. 1	Cash	101	3,000	
	Store Equipment.....	165	15,000	
	Common Stock	307		18,000
	Owner's investment in exchange for stock.			
2	Furniture.....	161	600	
	Cash.....	101		600
	Purchased furniture for cash.			
3	Rent Expense	640	500	
	Cash.....	101		500
	Paid rent for August.			
4	Store Equipment.....	165	1,200	
	Accounts Payable	201		1,200
	Purchased additional equipment on credit.			
15	Cash	101	825	
	Haircutting Services Revenue.....	403		825
	Cash receipts from first half of August.			

[continued on next page]

[continued from previous page]

16	Accounts Receivable	. . . .	102	100	
		Haircutting Services Revenue	403		100
		Record revenue for services provided on account.			
17	Cash	. . . .	101	100	
		Accounts Receivable	102		100
		Record cash received as payment on account.			
18	Wages Expense	. . . .	623	125	
		Cash	101		125
		Paid wages to assistant.			
31	Cash	. . . .	101	930	
		Haircutting Services Revenue	403		930
		Cash receipts from second half of August.			
31	Accounts Payable	201	400	
		Cash	101		400
		Paid cash toward accounts payable.			
31	Dividends	. . . .	319	900	
		Cash	101		900
		Paid a cash dividend.			

2. Post journal entries from part 1 to the ledger accounts (in balance column format).

General Ledger

Cash   Account No. 101

Date	PR	Debit	Credit	Balance
Aug. 1	G1	3,000		3,000
2	G1		600	2,400
3	G1		500	1,900
15	G1	825		2,725
17	G1	100		2,825
18	G1		125	2,700
31	G1	930		3,630
31	G1		400	3,230
31	G1		900	2,330

Accounts Receivable   Account No. 102

Date	PR	Debit	Credit	Balance
Aug. 16	G1	100		100
17	G1		100	0

Furniture   Account No. 161

Date	PR	Debit	Credit	Balance
Aug. 2	G1	600		600

Store Equipment   Account No. 165

Date	PR	Debit	Credit	Balance
Aug. 1	G1	15,000		15,000
4	G1	1,200		16,200

Accounts Payable   Account No. 201

Date	PR	Debit	Credit	Balance
Aug. 4	G1		1,200	1,200
31	G1	400		800

Common Stock   Account No. 307

Date	PR	Debit	Credit	Balance
Aug. 1	G1		18,000	18,000

Dividends   Account No. 319

Date	PR	Debit	Credit	Balance
Aug. 31	G1	900		900

Haircutting Services Revenue   Account No. 403

Date	PR	Debit	Credit	Balance
Aug. 15	G1		825	825
16	G1		100	925
31	G1		930	1,855

Wages Expense   Account No. 623

Date	PR	Debit	Credit	Balance
Aug. 18	G1	125		125

Rent Expense   Account No. 640

Date	PR	Debit	Credit	Balance
Aug. 3	G1	500		500

3. Prepare a trial balance from the ledger—see how it feeds the financial statements.

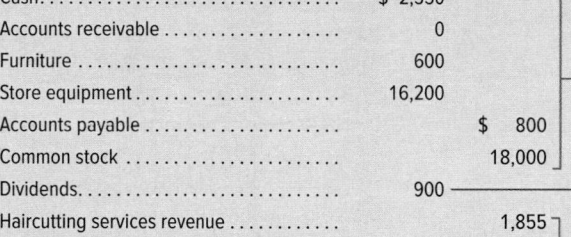

EXPRESSIONS
Trial Balance
August 31

	Debit	Credit
Cash................................	$ 2,330	
Accounts receivable	0	
Furniture	600	
Store equipment......................	16,200	
Accounts payable		$ 800
Common stock		18,000
Dividends............................	900	
Haircutting services revenue		1,855
Wages expense.......................	125	
Rent expense	500	
Totals	$20,655	$20,655

4.

EXPRESSIONS
Income Statement
For Month Ended August 31

Revenues		
Haircutting services revenue		$1,855
Operating expenses		
Rent expense	$500	
Wages expense.......................	125	
Total operating expenses..............		625
Net income		$1,230

5.

EXPRESSIONS
Statement of Retained Earnings
For Month Ended August 31

Retained earnings, August 1		$ 0
Plus: Net income		1,230
		1,230
Less: Cash dividends.......................		900
Retained earnings, August 31		$ 330

6.

EXPRESSIONS
Balance Sheet
August 31

Assets		Liabilities	
Cash	$ 2,330	Accounts payable	$ 800
Furniture	600	**Equity**	
Store equipment...........	16,200	Common stock	18,000
		Retained earnings	330
		Total equity.......................	18,330
Total assets	$19,130	Total liabilities and equity	$19,130

7. Debt ratio $= \dfrac{\text{Total liabilities}}{\text{Total assets}} = \dfrac{\$800}{\$19,130} = \underline{\underline{\mathbf{4.18\%}}}$

8a. Supplies *debited*
    Cash *credited*

8c. Cash *debited*
    Unearned Services Revenue *credited*

8b. Prepaid Insurance *debited*
    Cash *credited*

8d. Supplies *debited*
    Accounts Payable *credited*

Summary: Cheat Sheet

SYSTEM OF ACCOUNTS

Asset Accounts

Cash: A company's cash balance.

Accounts receivable: Held by a seller; promises of payment from customers to sellers. Accounts receivable are increased by credit sales; often phrased as sales *on account* or *on credit*.

Note receivable: Held by a lender; a borrower's written promise to pay the lender a specific sum of money on a specified future date.

Prepaid accounts (or expenses): Assets that arise from prepayment of future expenses. Examples are prepaid insurance and prepaid rent.

More assets: Supplies, equipment, buildings, and land.

Liability Accounts

Accounts payable: Held by a buyer; a buyer's promise to pay a seller later for goods or services received. More generally, payables arise from purchases of merchandise for resale, supplies, services, and other items.

Note payable: Held by a borrower; a written promissory note to pay a future amount at a future date.

Unearned revenue: A liability to be settled in the future when a company delivers its products or services. When a customer pays in advance for products or services (before revenue is earned), the seller records this receipt as unearned revenue.

Accrued liabilities: Amounts owed that are not yet paid. Examples are wages payable, taxes payable, and interest payable.

Equity Accounts

Common stock: When an owner invests in a company in exchange for stock, the company increases both assets and equity.

Dividends: When a company pays dividends, it decreases both company assets and total equity.

Revenue: Amounts received from sales of products and services to customers. Revenue increases equity.

Expenses: Costs of providing products and services. Expenses decrease equity.

DEBITS AND CREDITS

The left side of an account is called the **debit** side, or Dr.
The right side is called the **credit** side, or Cr.

Double-entry accounting transaction rules:
- At least two accounts are involved, with at least one debit and one credit.
- Total amount debited must equal total amount credited.

Debits and credits in accounting equation:

Assets	=	Liabilities	+	Common Stock	−	Dividends	+	Revenues	−	Expenses
Dr. for increases / Cr. for decreases		Dr. for decreases / Cr. for increases		Dr. for decreases / Cr. for increases		Dr. for increases / Cr. for decreases		Dr. for decreases / Cr. for increases		Dr. for increases / Cr. for decreases
+ / − Normal		− / + Normal		− / + Normal		+ / − Normal		− / + Normal		+ / − Normal

Net increases or decreases on one side have equal net effects on the other side.
Left side is the normal balance side for assets.
Right side is the normal balance side for liabilities and equity.

RECORDING TRANSACTIONS

Receive owner investment for stock:

Date	Account Titles and Explanation	PR	Debit	Credit
(1)	Cash	101	30,000	
	Common Stock	307		30,000

Purchase supplies for cash:

Date	Account Titles and Explanation	PR	Debit	Credit
(2)	Supplies	126	2,500	
	Cash	101		2,500

Purchase equipment for cash:

Date	Account Titles and Explanation	PR	Debit	Credit
(3)	Equipment	167	26,000	
	Cash	101		26,000

Purchase supplies on credit:

Date	Account Titles and Explanation	PR	Debit	Credit
(4)	Supplies	126	7,100	
	Accounts Payable	201		7,100

Provide services for cash:

Date	Account Titles and Explanation	PR	Debit	Credit
(5)	Cash	101	4,200	
	Consulting Revenue	403		4,200

Payment of expenses in cash:

Date	Account Titles and Explanation	PR	Debit	Credit
(6)	Rent Expense	640	1,000	
	Cash	101		1,000

Date	Account Titles and Explanation	PR	Debit	Credit
(7)	Salaries Expense	622	700	
	Cash	101		700

Date	Account Titles and Explanation	PR	Debit	Credit
(15)	Utilities Expense	690	305	
	Cash	101		305

Provide consulting and rental services on credit:

Date	Account Titles and Explanation	PR	Debit	Credit
(8)	Accounts Receivable	106	1,900	
	Consulting Revenue	403		1,600
	Rental Revenue	406		300

Receipt of cash on account:

Date	Account Titles and Explanation	PR	Debit	Credit
(9)	Cash	101	1,900	
	Accounts Receivable	106		1,900

Partial payment of accounts payable:

Date	Account Titles and Explanation	PR	Debit	Credit
(10)	Accounts Payable	201	900	
	Cash	101		900

Payment of cash dividend:

Date	Account Titles and Explanation	PR	Debit	Credit
(11)	Dividends	319	200	
	Cash	101		200

Receipt of cash for future services:

Date	Account Titles and Explanation	PR	Debit	Credit
(12)	Cash	101	3,000	
	Unearned Consulting Revenue	236		3,000

Pay cash for future insurance coverage:

Date	Account Titles and Explanation	PR	Debit	Credit
(13)	Prepaid Insurance	128	2,400	
	Cash	101		2,400

FINANCIAL STATEMENTS

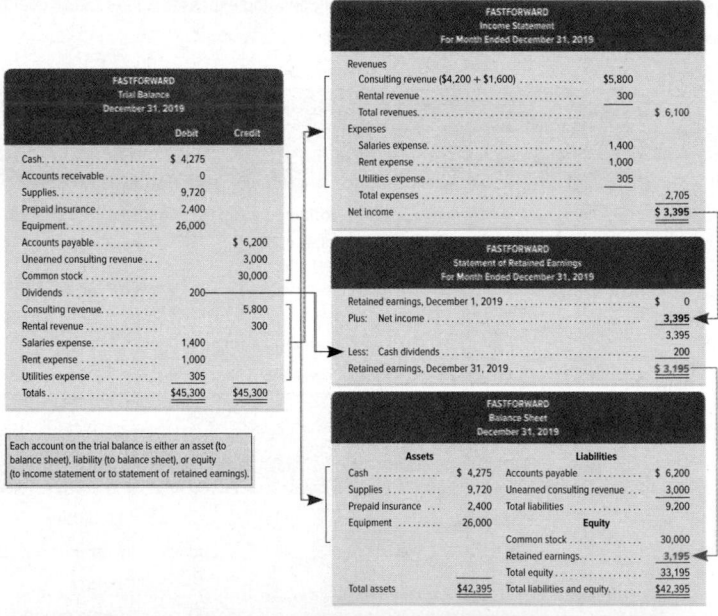

FASTFORWARD
Trial Balance
December 31, 2019

	Debit	Credit
Cash	$ 4,275	
Accounts receivable	0	
Supplies	9,720	
Prepaid insurance	2,400	
Equipment	26,000	
Accounts payable		$ 6,200
Unearned consulting revenue		3,000
Common stock		30,000
Dividends	200	
Consulting revenue		5,800
Rental revenue		300
Salaries expense	1,400	
Rent expense	1,000	
Utilities expense	305	
Totals	$45,300	$45,300

Each account on the trial balance is either an asset (to balance sheet), liability (to balance sheet), or equity (to income statement or to statement of retained earnings).

FASTFORWARD
Income Statement
For Month Ended December 31, 2019

Revenues		
Consulting revenue ($4,200 + $1,600)	$5,800	
Rental revenue	300	
Total revenues		$ 6,100
Expenses		
Salaries expense	1,400	
Rent expense	1,000	
Utilities expense	305	
Total expenses		2,705
Net income		$ 3,395

FASTFORWARD
Statement of Retained Earnings
For Month Ended December 31, 2019

Retained earnings, December 1, 2019		$ 0
Plus: Net income		3,395
		3,395
Less: Cash dividends		200
Retained earnings, December 31, 2019		$ 3,195

FASTFORWARD
Balance Sheet
December 31, 2019

Assets		Liabilities	
Cash	$ 4,275	Accounts payable	$ 6,200
Supplies	9,720	Unearned consulting revenue	3,000
Prepaid insurance	2,400	Total liabilities	9,200
Equipment	26,000		
		Equity	
		Common stock	30,000
		Retained earnings	3,195
		Total equity	33,195
Total assets	$42,395	Total liabilities and equity	$42,395

Key Terms

Multiple Choice Quiz

1. Amalia Company received its utility bill for the current period of $700 and immediately paid it. Its journal entry to record this transaction includes a
   a. Credit to Utility Expense for $700.
   b. Debit to Utility Expense for $700.
   c. Debit to Accounts Payable for $700.
   d. Debit to Cash for $700.
   e. Credit to Accounts Receivable for $700.

2. On May 1, Mattingly Lawn Service collected $2,500 cash from a customer in advance of five months of lawn service. Mattingly's journal entry to record this transaction includes a
   a. Credit to Unearned Lawn Service Fees for $2,500.
   b. Debit to Lawn Service Fees Earned for $2,500.
   c. Credit to Cash for $2,500.
   d. Debit to Unearned Lawn Service Fees for $2,500.
   e. Credit to Accounts Payable for $2,500.

3. Liang Shue contributed $250,000 cash and land worth $500,000 to open his new business, Shue Consulting. Which of the following journal entries does Shue Consulting make to record this transaction?
   a. Cash Assets   750,000
        Common Stock   750,000
   b. Common Stock   750,000
        Assets.   750,000

   c. Cash   250,000
      Land   500,000
        Common Stock   750,000
   d. Common Stock   750,000
        Cash   250,000
        Land   500,000

4. A trial balance prepared at year-end shows total credits exceed total debits by $765. This discrepancy could have been caused by
   a. An error in the general journal where a $765 increase in Accounts Payable was recorded as a $765 decrease in Accounts Payable.
   b. The ledger balance for Accounts Payable of $7,650 being entered in the trial balance as $765.
   c. A general journal error where a $765 increase in Accounts Receivable was recorded as a $765 increase in Cash.
   d. The ledger balance of $850 in Accounts Receivable was entered in the trial balance as $85.
   e. An error in recording a $765 increase in Cash as a credit.

5. Bonaventure Company has total assets of $1,000,000, liabilities of $400,000, and equity of $600,000. What is its debt ratio (rounded to a whole percent)?
   a. 250%   c. 67%   e. 40%
   b. 167%   d. 150%

ANSWERS TO MULTIPLE CHOICE QUIZ

1. b; debit Utility Expense for $700, and credit Cash for $700.
2. a; debit Cash for $2,500 and credit Unearned Lawn Service Fees for $2,500.
3. c; debit Cash for $250,000, debit Land for $500,000, and credit Common Stock for $750,000.
4. d
5. e; Debt ratio = $400,000/$1,000,000 = 40%

🔲 Icon denotes assignments that involve decision making.

Discussion Questions

1. Provide the names of two (a) asset accounts, (b) liability accounts, and (c) equity accounts.
2. What is the difference between a note payable and an account payable?
3. 🔲 Discuss the steps in processing business transactions.
4. What kinds of transactions can be recorded in a general journal?
5. Are debits or credits typically listed first in general journal entries? Are the debits or the credits indented?
6. Should a transaction be recorded first in a journal or the ledger? Why?
7. If assets are valuable resources and asset accounts have debit balances, why do expense accounts also have debit balances?
8. 🔲 Why does the recordkeeper prepare a trial balance?
9. If an incorrect amount is journalized and posted to the accounts, how should the error be corrected?
10. Identify the four financial statements of a business.
11. 🔲 What information is reported in a balance sheet?
12. 🔲 What information is reported in an income statement?
13. 🔲 Why does the user of an income statement need to know the time period that it covers?
14. Define (a) assets, (b) liabilities, and (c) equity.
15. Which financial statement is sometimes called the statement of financial position?
16. 🔲 Review the **Apple** balance sheet in Appendix A. Identify three accounts on its balance sheet that carry debit balances and three accounts on its balance sheet that carry credit balances.   **APPLE**

17. Review the **Google** balance sheet in Appendix A. Identify an asset with the **GOOGLE** word *receivable* in its account title and a liability with the word *payable* in its account title.

18. Review the **Samsung** balance sheet in Appendix A. Identify three current liabilities and three noncurrent liabilities in its balance sheet. **Samsung**

Mc Graw Hill connect

QUICK STUDY

QS 2-1

Identifying source documents **C1**

Identify the items from the following list that are likely to serve as source documents.
- **a.** Sales receipt
- **b.** Trial balance
- **c.** Balance sheet
- **d.** Prepaid insurance account
- **e.** Invoice from supplier
- **f.** Company revenue account
- **g.** Income statement
- **h.** Bank statement
- **i.** Telephone bill

QS 2-2

Identifying financial statement accounts **C2**

Classify each of the following accounts as an asset (A), liability (L), or equity (EQ) account.
- **a.** Cash
- **b.** Prepaid Rent
- **c.** Office Supplies
- **d.** Prepaid Insurance
- **e.** Office Equipment
- **f.** Common Stock
- **g.** Accounts Payable
- **h.** Unearned Rent Revenue
- **i.** Dividends

QS 2-3

Reading a chart of accounts **C3**

A chart of accounts is a list of all ledger accounts and an identification number for each. One example of a chart of accounts is near the end of the book on pages CA and CA-1. Using that chart, identify the following accounts as either an asset (A), liability (L), equity (EQ), revenue (R), or expense (E) account, along with its identification number.
- **a.** Advertising Expense
- **b.** Rent Revenue
- **c.** Rent Receivable
- **d.** Machinery
- **e.** Accounts Payable
- **f.** Furniture
- **g.** Notes Payable
- **h.** Common Stock
- **i.** Utilities Expense

QS 2-4

Identifying normal balance **C4**

Identify the normal balance (debit or credit) for each of the following accounts.
- **a.** Fees Earned (Revenues)
- **b.** Office Supplies
- **c.** Dividends
- **d.** Wages Expense
- **e.** Accounts Receivable
- **f.** Prepaid Rent
- **g.** Wages Payable
- **h.** Building
- **i.** Common Stock

QS 2-5

Linking debit or credit with normal balance **C4**

Indicate whether a debit or credit *decreases* the normal balance of each of the following accounts.
- **a.** Interest Payable
- **b.** Service Revenue
- **c.** Salaries Expense
- **d.** Accounts Receivable
- **e.** Common Stock
- **f.** Prepaid Insurance
- **g.** Buildings
- **h.** Interest Revenue
- **i.** Dividends
- **j.** Unearned Revenue
- **k.** Accounts Payable
- **l.** Land

QS 2-6

Analyzing transactions and preparing journal entries **P1**

For each transaction, (1) analyze the transaction using the accounting equation, (2) record the transaction in journal entry form, and (3) post the entry using T-accounts to represent ledger accounts. Use the following (partial) chart of accounts—account numbers in parentheses: Cash (101); Accounts Receivable (106); Office Supplies (124); Trucks (153); Equipment (167); Accounts Payable (201); Unearned Landscaping Revenue (236); Common Stock (307); Dividends (319); Landscaping Revenue (403); Wages Expense (601), and Landscaping Expense (696).

- **a.** On May 15, DeShawn Tyler opens a landscaping company called Elegant Lawns by investing $7,000 in cash along with equipment having a $3,000 value in exchange for common stock.
- **b.** On May 21, Elegant Lawns purchases office supplies on credit for $500.
- **c.** On May 25, Elegant Lawns receives $4,000 cash for performing landscaping services.
- **d.** On May 30, Elegant Lawns receives $1,000 cash in advance of providing landscaping services to a customer.

QS 2-7

Analyzing debit or credit by account **A1**

Identify whether a debit or credit results in the indicated change for each of the following accounts.
- **a.** To increase Land
- **b.** To decrease Cash
- **c.** To increase Fees Earned (Revenues)
- **d.** To increase Salaries Expense
- **e.** To decrease Unearned Revenue
- **f.** To decrease Prepaid Rent
- **g.** To increase Notes Payable
- **h.** To decrease Accounts Receivable
- **i.** To increase Common Stock
- **j.** To increase Store Equipment

A trial balance has total debits of $20,000 and total credits of $24,500. Which one of the following errors would create this imbalance? Explain.

a. A $2,250 debit to Utilities Expense in a journal entry was incorrectly posted to the ledger as a $2,250 credit, leaving the Utilities Expense account with a $3,000 debit balance.

b. A $4,500 debit to Salaries Expense in a journal entry was incorrectly posted to the ledger as a $4,500 credit, leaving the Salaries Expense account with a $750 debit balance.

c. A $2,250 credit to Consulting Fees Earned (Revenues) in a journal entry was incorrectly posted to the ledger as a $2,250 debit, leaving the Consulting Fees Earned account with a $6,300 credit balance.

d. A $2,250 debit posting to Accounts Receivable was posted mistakenly to Land.

e. A $4,500 debit posting to Equipment was posted mistakenly to Cash.

f. An entry debiting Cash and crediting Accounts Payable for $4,500 was mistakenly not posted.

QS 2-8
Identifying a posting error
P2

Indicate the financial statement on which each of the following items appears. Use *I* for income statement, *E* for statement of retained earnings, and *B* for balance sheet.

a. Services Revenue
b. Interest Payable
c. Accounts Receivable
d. Salaries Expense
e. Equipment
f. Prepaid Insurance
g. Buildings
h. Rental Revenue
i. Dividends
j. Office Supplies
k. Interest Expense
l. Insurance Expense

QS 2-9
Classifying accounts in financial statements
P3

Determine the ending balance of each of the following T-accounts.

QS 2-10
Computing T-account balance
C4

a.

Cash	
100	50
300	60
20	

b.

Accounts Payable	
2,000	8,000
2,700	

c.

Supplies	
10,000	3,800
1,100	

d.

Accounts Receivable	
600	150
	150
	150
	100

e.

Wages Payable	
	700
700	

f.

Cash	
11,000	4,500
800	6,000
100	1,300

Prepare general journal entries for the following transactions of Green Energy Company. Use the following (partial) chart of accounts: Cash; Accounts Receivable; Supplies; Accounts Payable; Consulting Revenue; and Utilities Expense.

May 1   The company billed a customer $2,000 in consulting revenue for sustainable proposals.
3   The company purchased $300 of energy-efficient supplies on credit.
9   The company collected $500 cash as partial payment of the May 1 consulting revenue.
20   The company paid $300 cash toward the payable for energy-efficient supplies.
31   The company paid $100 cash for May's renewable energy utilities.

QS 2-11
Preparing journal entries
P1

Liu Zhang operates Lawson Consulting, which began operations on June 1. On June 30, the company's records show the following selected accounts and amounts for the month of June. Prepare a June income statement for the business.

Cash	$5,000	Accounts payable	$ 3,000	Service revenue	$12,000
Accounts receivable	4,500	Common stock	10,500	Rent expense	2,000
Equipment	6,500	Dividends	1,500	Wages expense	6,000

QS 2-12
Preparing an income statement
P3

Use the information in QS 2-12 to prepare a June statement of retained earnings for Lawson Consulting. The Retained Earnings account balance at June 1 was $0. *Hint:* Net income for June is $4,000.

QS 2-13
Preparing a statement of retained earnings   **P3**

QS 2-14 Preparing a balance sheet **P3**	Use the information in QS 2-12 and QS 2-13 to prepare a June 30 balance sheet for Lawson Consulting. *Hint:* The ending Retained Earnings account balance as of June 30 is $2,500.
QS 2-15 Computing and using the debt ratio **A2**	In a recent year's financial statements, **Home Depot** reported the following: Total liabilities = $38,633 million and Total assets = $42,966 million. Compute and interpret Home Depot's debt ratio (assume competitors average a 60.0% debt ratio).

connect

EXERCISES

Exercise 2-1
Steps in analyzing and
recording transactions **C1**

Order the following steps in the accounting process that focus on analyzing and recording transactions.
_____ **a.** Prepare and analyze the trial balance.
_____ **b.** Analyze each transaction from source documents.
_____ **c.** Record relevant transactions in a journal.
_____ **d.** Post journal information to ledger accounts.

Exercise 2-2
Identifying and classifying
accounts
C2

Enter the number for the item that best completes each of the descriptions below.
1. Asset   **2.** Equity   **3.** Account   **4.** Liability   **5.** Three
a. Balance sheet accounts are arranged into _____ general categories.
b. Common Stock and Dividends are examples of _____ accounts.
c. Accounts Payable and Note Payable are examples of _____ accounts.
d. Accounts Receivable, Prepaid Accounts, Supplies, and Land are examples of _____ accounts.
e. A(n) _____ is a record of increases and decreases in a specific asset, liability, equity, revenue, or expense item.

Exercise 2-3
Identifying a ledger and
chart of accounts
C3

Enter the number for the item that best completes each of the descriptions below.
1. Chart   **2.** General ledger   **3.** Journal   **4.** Account   **5.** Source document
a. A(n) _____ of accounts is a list of all accounts a company uses, not including account balances.
b. The _____ is a record containing all accounts used by a company, including account balances.
c. A(n) _____ describes transactions entering an accounting system, such as a purchase order.
d. Increases and decreases in a specific asset, liability, equity, revenue, or expense are recorded in a(n) _____.
e. A(n) _____ has a complete record of every transaction recorded.

Exercise 2-4
Identifying type and normal
balances of accounts
C4

For each of the following, (1) identify the type of account as an asset, liability, equity, revenue, or expense; (2) identify the normal balance of the account; and (3) enter *debit* (*Dr.*) or *credit* (*Cr.*) to identify the kind of entry that would increase the account balance.

a. Land	**e.** Accounts Receivable	**i.** Fees Earned
b. Cash	**f.** Dividends	**j.** Equipment
c. Legal Expense	**g.** License Fee Revenue	**k.** Notes Payable
d. Prepaid Insurance	**h.** Unearned Revenue	**l.** Common Stock

Exercise 2-5
Analyzing effects of a
compound entry
A1

Groro Co. bills a client $62,000 for services provided and agrees to accept the following three items in full payment: (1) $10,000 cash, (2) equipment worth $80,000, and (3) to assume responsibility for a $28,000 note payable related to the equipment. For this transaction, (*a*) analyze the transaction using the accounting equation, (*b*) record the transaction in journal entry form, and (*c*) post the entry using T-accounts to represent ledger accounts. Use the following (partial) chart of accounts—account numbers in parentheses: Cash (101); Supplies (124); Equipment (167); Accounts Payable (201); Note Payable (245); Common Stock (307); and Revenue (404).

Exercise 2-6
Analyzing account entries
and balances
A1

Use the information in each of the following separate cases to calculate the unknown amount.
a. Corentine Co. had $152,000 of accounts payable on September 30 and $132,500 on October 31. Total purchases on account during October were $281,000. Determine how much cash was paid on accounts payable during October.
b. On September 30, Valerian Co. had a $102,500 balance in Accounts Receivable. During October, the company collected $102,890 from its credit customers. The October 31 balance in Accounts Receivable was $89,000. Determine the amount of sales on account that occurred in October.

[continued on next page]

c. During October, Alameda Company had $102,500 of cash receipts and $103,150 of cash disbursements. The October 31 Cash balance was $18,600. Determine how much cash the company had at the close of business on September 30.

Prepare general journal entries for the following transactions of a new company called Pose-for-Pics. Use the following (partial) chart of accounts: Cash; Office Supplies; Prepaid Insurance; Photography Equipment; Common Stock; Photography Fees Earned; and Utilities Expense.

Aug. 1   Madison Harris, the owner, invested $6,500 cash and $33,500 of photography equipment in the company in exchange for common stock.
     2   The company paid $2,100 cash for an insurance policy covering the next 24 months.
     5   The company purchased office supplies for $880 cash.
    20   The company received $3,331 cash in photography fees earned.
    31   The company paid $675 cash for August utilities.

Exercise 2-7
Preparing general journal entries
P1

Use the information in Exercise 2-7 to prepare a trial balance for Pose-for-Pics. Begin by opening these T-accounts: Cash; Office Supplies; Prepaid Insurance; Photography Equipment; Common Stock; Photography Fees Earned; and Utilities Expense. Then, (1) post the general journal entries to these T-accounts (which will serve as the ledger) and (2) prepare the August 31 trial balance.

Exercise 2-8
Preparing T-accounts (ledger) and a trial balance   **P2**

Prepare general journal entries to record the transactions below for Spade Company by using the following accounts: Cash; Accounts Receivable; Office Supplies; Office Equipment; Accounts Payable; Common Stock; Dividends; Fees Earned; and Rent Expense. Use the letters beside each transaction to identify entries. After recording the transactions, post them to T-accounts, which serve as the general ledger for this assignment. Determine the ending balance of each T-account.

a. Kacy Spade, owner, invested $100,750 cash in the company in exchange for common stock.
b. The company purchased office supplies for $1,250 cash.
c. The company purchased $10,050 of office equipment on credit.
d. The company received $15,500 cash as fees for services provided to a customer.
e. The company paid $10,050 cash to settle the payable for the office equipment purchased in transaction c.
f. The company billed a customer $2,700 as fees for services provided.
g. The company paid $1,225 cash for the monthly rent.
h. The company collected $1,125 cash as partial payment for the account receivable created in transaction f.
i. The company paid a $10,000 cash dividend to the owner (sole shareholder).

Exercise 2-9
Recording effects of transactions in T-accounts
A1

Check   Cash ending balance, $94,850

After recording the transactions of Exercise 2-9 in T-accounts and calculating the balance of each account, prepare a trial balance. Use May 31 as its report date.

Exercise 2-10
Preparing a trial balance   **P2**

---

1. Prepare general journal entries for the following transactions of Valdez Services.
   a. The company paid $2,000 cash for payment on a 6-month-old account payable for office supplies.
   b. The company paid $1,200 cash for the just completed two-week salary of the receptionist.
   c. The company paid $39,000 cash for equipment purchased.
   d. The company paid $800 cash for this month's utilities.
   e. The company paid a $4,500 cash dividend to the owner (sole shareholder)
2. Transactions a, c, and e did not result in an expense. Match each transaction (a, c, and e) with one of the following reasons for not recording an expense.

   _____ This transaction is a distribution of cash to the owner. Even though equity decreased, that decrease did not occur in the process of providing goods or services to customers.
   _____ This transaction decreased cash in settlement of a previously existing liability (equity did not change). Supplies expense is recorded when assets are used, not necessarily when cash is paid.
   _____ This transaction involves the purchase of an asset. The form of the company's assets changed, but total assets did not (and neither did equity).

Exercise 2-11
Analyzing and journalizing transactions involving cash payments
P1

Exercise 2-12

Analyzing and journalizing transactions involving receipt of cash

P1

1. Prepare general journal entries for the following transactions of Valdez Services.
   a. Brina Valdez invested $20,000 cash in the company in exchange for common stock.
   b. The company provided services to a client and immediately received $900 cash.
   c. The company received $10,000 cash from a client in payment for services to be provided next year.
   d. The company received $3,500 cash from a client in partial payment of accounts receivable.
   e. The company borrowed $5,000 cash from the bank by signing a note payable.

2. Transactions *a, c, d,* and *e* did not yield revenue. Match each transaction (*a, c, d,* and *e*) with one of the following reasons for not recording revenue.

_____ This transaction changed the form of an asset from a receivable to cash. Total assets were not increased (revenue was recognized when the services were originally provided).

_____ This transaction brought in cash (increased assets), and it also increased a liability by the same amount (represented by the signing of a note to repay the amount).

_____ This transaction brought in cash, but this is an owner investment.

_____ This transaction brought in cash, but it created a liability to provide services to the client in the next year.

Exercise 2-13

Entering transactions into T-accounts

A1

Fill in each of the following T-accounts for Belle Co.'s seven transactions listed here. The T-accounts represent Belle Co.'s general ledger. Code each entry with transaction number *1* through *7* (in order) for reference.

1. D. Belle created a new business and invested $6,000 cash, $7,600 of equipment, and $12,000 in web servers in exchange for common stock.
2. The company paid $4,800 cash in advance for prepaid insurance coverage.
3. The company purchased $900 of supplies on account.
4. The company paid $800 cash for selling expenses.
5. The company received $4,500 cash for services provided.
6. The company paid $900 cash toward accounts payable.
7. The company paid $3,400 cash for equipment.

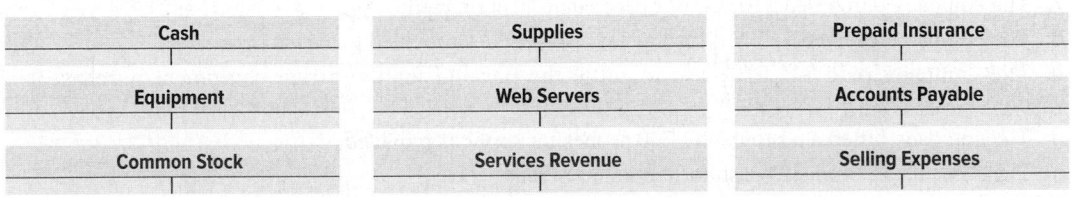

Cash	Supplies	Prepaid Insurance
Equipment	Web Servers	Accounts Payable
Common Stock	Services Revenue	Selling Expenses

Exercise 2-14

Preparing general journal entries **P1**

Use information from Exercise 2-13 to prepare the general journal entries for Belle Co.'s first seven transactions.

Exercise 2-15

Computing net income

A1

A corporation had the following assets and liabilities at the beginning and end of this year.

	Assets	Liabilities
Beginning of the year.............	$ 60,000	$20,000
End of the year	105,000	36,000

Determine net income or net loss for the business during the year for each of the following *separate* cases.
   a. Owner made no investments in the business, and no dividends were paid during the year.
   b. Owner made no investments in the business, but dividends were $1,250 cash per month.
   c. No dividends were paid during the year, but the owner did invest an additional $55,000 cash in exchange for common stock.
   d. Dividends were $1,250 cash per month, and the owner invested an additional $35,000 cash in exchange for common stock.

Exercise 2-16

Preparing an income statement **C3   P3**

Carmen Camry operates a consulting firm called Help Today, which began operations on August 1. On August 31, the company's business records show the following selected accounts and amounts for the month of August. Use this information to prepare an August income statement for the business.

Cash	$25,360	Accounts payable..........	$ 10,500	Salaries expense	$5,600
Accounts receivable......	22,360	Common stock	102,000	Telephone expense	860
Office supplies	5,250	Dividends	6,000	Miscellaneous expenses	520
Land	44,000	Consulting fees earned	27,000		
Office equipment	20,000	Rent expense	9,550		

Check Net income, $10,470

Use the information in Exercise 2-16 to prepare an August statement of retained earnings for Help Today. The Retained Earnings account balance at August 1 was $0. *Hint:* Net income for August is $10,470.

Exercise 2-17
Preparing a statement of retained earnings **P3**

Use the information in Exercise 2-16 to prepare an August 31 balance sheet for Help Today. *Hint:* The ending Retained Earnings account balance as of August 31 is $4,470.

Exercise 2-18
Preparing a balance sheet **P3**

Compute the missing amount for each of the following separate companies in columns B through E.

Exercise 2-19
Analyzing changes in a company's equity

P3

	A	B	C	D	E
1		CBS	ABC	CNN	NBC
2	Equity, beginning of year	$ 0	$ 0	$ 0	$ 0
3	Owner investments during the year	110,000	?	87,000	210,000
4	Dividends during the year	?	(47,000)	(10,000)	(55,000)
5	Net income (loss) for the year	22,000	90,000	(4,000)	?
6	Equity, end of year	104,000	85,000	?	110,000

Posting errors are identified in the following table. In column (1), enter the amount of the difference between the two trial balance columns (debit and credit) due to the error. In column (2), identify the trial balance column (debit or credit) with the larger amount if they are not equal. In column (3), identify the account(s) affected by the error. In column (4), indicate the amount by which the account(s) in column (3) is under- or overstated. Item (a) is completed as an example.

Exercise 2-20
Identifying effects of posting errors on the trial balance **A1   P2**

	Description of Posting Error	(1) Difference between Debit and Credit Columns	(2) Column with the Larger Total	(3) Identify Account(s) Incorrectly Stated	(4) Amount That Account(s) Is Over- or Understated
a.	$3,600 debit to Rent Expense is posted as a $1,340 debit.	$2,260	Credit	Rent Expense	Rent Expense understated $2,260
b.	$6,500 credit to Cash is posted twice as two credits to Cash.				
c.	$10,900 debit to the Dividends account is debited to Common Stock.				
d.	$2,050 debit to Prepaid Insurance is posted as a debit to Insurance Expense.				
e.	$38,000 debit to Machinery is posted as a debit to Accounts Payable.				
f.	$5,850 credit to Services Revenue is posted as a $585 credit.				
g.	$1,390 debit to Store Supplies is not posted.				

You are told the column totals in a trial balance are not equal. After careful analysis, you discover only one error. Specifically, a correctly journalized credit purchase of an automobile for $18,950 is posted from the journal to the ledger with an $18,950 debit to Automobiles and another $18,950 debit to Accounts Payable. The Automobiles account has a debit balance of $37,100 on the trial balance. (1) Answer each of the following questions and (2) compute the dollar amount of any misstatement for parts *a* through *d*.

Exercise 2-21
Analyzing a trial balance error

P1   P2

a. Is the Debit column total of the trial balance overstated, understated, or correctly stated?

b. Is the Credit column total of the trial balance overstated, understated, or correctly stated?

c. Is the Automobiles account balance overstated, understated, or correctly stated in the trial balance?

d. Is the Accounts Payable account balance overstated, understated, or correctly stated in the trial balance?

e. If the Debit column total of the trial balance is $200,000 before correcting the error, what is the total of the Credit column before correction?

Exercise 2-22

Calculating and interpreting the debt ratio

A2

Company	Expenses	Total Assets	Net Income	Total Liabilities
DreamWorks	$22,000	$ 40,000	$19,000	$ 30,000
Pixar	67,000	150,000	27,000	147,000
Universal	12,000	68,000	5,000	17,000

a. Compute the debt ratio for each of the three companies.

b. Which company has the most financial leverage?

Exercise 2-23

Preparing journal entries

P1

Prepare general journal entries for the following transactions of Sustain Company. Use the following (partial) chart of accounts: Cash; Prepaid Insurance; Accounts Receivable; Furniture; Accounts Payable; Unearned Revenue; Fees Earned; and Common Stock.

June 1   T. James, owner, invested $11,000 cash in Sustain Company in exchange for common stock.
      2   The company purchased $4,000 of furniture made from reclaimed wood on credit.
      3   The company paid $600 cash for a 12-month insurance policy on the reclaimed furniture.
      4   The company billed a customer $3,000 in fees earned from preparing a sustainability report.
     12   The company paid $4,000 cash toward the payable from the June 2 furniture purchase.
     20   The company collected $3,000 cash for fees billed on June 4.
     21   T. James invested an additional $10,000 cash in Sustain Company in exchange for common stock.
     30   The company received $5,000 cash in advance of providing sustainability services to a customer.

PROBLEM SET A

Karla Tanner opened a web consulting business called Linkworks and completed the following transactions in its first month of operations.

Problem 2-1A

Preparing and posting journal entries; preparing a trial balance

C3   C4   A1   P1   P2

Apr. 1   Tanner invested $80,000 cash along with office equipment valued at $26,000 in the company in exchange for common stock.
      2   The company prepaid $9,000 cash for 12 months' rent for office space. *Hint:* Debit Prepaid Rent for $9,000.
      3   The company made credit purchases for $8,000 in office equipment and $3,600 in office supplies. Payment is due within 10 days.
      6   The company completed services for a client and immediately received $4,000 cash.
      9   The company completed a $6,000 project for a client, who must pay within 30 days.
     13   The company paid $11,600 cash to settle the account payable created on April 3.
     19   The company paid $2,400 cash for the premium on a 12-month insurance policy. *Hint:* Debit Prepaid Insurance for $2,400.
     22   The company received $4,400 cash as partial payment for the work completed on April 9.
     25   The company completed work for another client for $2,890 on credit.
     28   The company paid a $5,500 cash dividend.
     29   The company purchased $600 of additional office supplies on credit.
     30   The company paid $435 cash for this month's utility bill.

Required

1. Prepare general journal entries to record these transactions (use account titles listed in part 2).

Check   (2) Ending balances: Cash, $59,465; Accounts Receivable, $4,490; Accounts Payable, $600

(3) Total debits, $119,490

2. Open the following ledger accounts—their account numbers are in parentheses (use the balance column format): Cash (101); Accounts Receivable (106); Office Supplies (124); Prepaid Insurance (128); Prepaid Rent (131); Office Equipment (163); Accounts Payable (201); Common Stock (307); Dividends (319); Services Revenue (403); and Utilities Expense (690). Post journal entries from part 1 to the ledger accounts and enter the balance after each posting.

3. Prepare a trial balance as of April 30.

Problem 2-2A

Preparing and posting journal entries; preparing a trial balance

C3   C4   A1   P1   P2

Aracel Engineering completed the following transactions in the month of June.

a. Jenna Aracel, the owner, invested $100,000 cash, office equipment with a value of $5,000, and $60,000 of drafting equipment to launch the company in exchange for common stock.

b. The company purchased land worth $49,000 for an office by paying $6,300 cash and signing a long-term note payable for $42,700.

c. The company purchased a portable building with $55,000 cash and moved it onto the land acquired in *b*.

d. The company paid $3,000 cash for the premium on an 18-month insurance policy.

e. The company completed and delivered a set of plans for a client and collected $6,200 cash.

f. The company purchased $20,000 of additional drafting equipment by paying $9,500 cash and signing a long-term note payable for $10,500.

g. The company completed $14,000 of engineering services for a client. This amount is to be received in 30 days.

h. The company purchased $1,150 of additional office equipment on credit.

i. The company completed engineering services for $22,000 on credit.

j. The company received a bill for rent of equipment that was used on a recently completed job. The $1,333 rent cost must be paid within 30 days.

k. The company collected $7,000 cash in partial payment from the client described in transaction *g*.

l. The company paid $1,200 cash for wages to a drafting assistant.

m. The company paid $1,150 cash to settle the account payable created in transaction *h*.

n. The company paid $925 cash for minor maintenance of its drafting equipment.

o. The company paid a $9,480 cash dividend.

p. The company paid $1,200 cash for wages to a drafting assistant.

q. The company paid $2,500 cash for advertisements on the web during June.

Required

1. Prepare general journal entries to record these transactions (use the account titles listed in part 2).

2. Open the following ledger accounts—their account numbers are in parentheses (use the balance column format): Cash (101); Accounts Receivable (106); Prepaid Insurance (108); Office Equipment (163); Drafting Equipment (164); Building (170); Land (172); Accounts Payable (201); Notes Payable (250); Common Stock (307); Dividends (319); Engineering Fees Earned (402); Wages Expense (601); Equipment Rental Expense (602); Advertising Expense (603); and Repairs Expense (604). Post the journal entries from part 1 to the accounts and enter the balance after each posting.

3. Prepare a trial balance as of the end of June.

Check (2) Ending balances: Cash, $22,945; Accounts Receivable, $29,000; Accounts Payable, $1,333

(3) Trial balance totals, $261,733

Problem 2-3A
Preparing and posting journal entries; preparing a trial balance

C3 C4 A1 P1 P2

Denzel Brooks opened a web consulting business called Venture Consultants and completed the following transactions in March.

Mar. 1   Brooks invested $150,000 cash along with $22,000 in office equipment in the company in exchange for common stock.

2   The company prepaid $6,000 cash for six months' rent for an office. *Hint:* Debit Prepaid Rent for $6,000.

3   The company made credit purchases of office equipment for $3,000 and office supplies for $1,200. Payment is due within 10 days.

6   The company completed services for a client and immediately received $4,000 cash.

9   The company completed a $7,500 project for a client, who must pay within 30 days.

12   The company paid $4,200 cash to settle the account payable created on March 3.

19   The company paid $5,000 cash for the premium on a 12-month insurance policy. *Hint:* Debit Prepaid Insurance for $5,000.

22   The company received $3,500 cash as partial payment for the work completed on March 9.

25   The company completed work for another client for $3,820 on credit.

29   The company paid a $5,100 cash dividend.

30   The company purchased $600 of additional office supplies on credit.

31   The company paid $500 cash for this month's utility bill.

Required

1. Prepare general journal entries to record these transactions (use the account titles listed in part 2).

2. Open the following ledger accounts—their account numbers are in parentheses (use the balance column format): Cash (101); Accounts Receivable (106); Office Supplies (124); Prepaid Insurance (128); Prepaid Rent (131); Office Equipment (163); Accounts Payable (201); Common Stock (307); Dividends (319); Services Revenue (403); and Utilities Expense (690). Post the journal entries from part 1 to the ledger accounts and enter the balance after each posting.

3. Prepare a trial balance as of the end of March.

Check (2) Ending balances: Cash, $136,700; Accounts Receivable, $7,820; Accounts Payable, $600

(3) Total debits, $187,920

Problem 2-4A
Recording transactions; posting to ledger; preparing a trial balance

C3 A1 P1 P2

Business transactions completed by Hannah Venedict during the month of September are as follows.

a. Venedict invested $60,000 cash along with office equipment valued at $25,000 in a new business named HV Consulting in exchange for common stock.

b. The company purchased land valued at $40,000 and a building valued at $160,000. The purchase is paid with $30,000 cash and a long-term note payable for $170,000.

c. The company purchased $2,000 of office supplies on credit.

[continued on next page]

[continued from previous page]

d. Venedict invested her personal automobile in the company in exchange for more common stock. The automobile has a value of $16,500 and is to be used exclusively in the business.

e. The company purchased $5,600 of additional office equipment on credit.

f. The company paid $1,800 cash salary to an assistant.

g. The company provided services to a client and collected $8,000 cash.

h. The company paid $635 cash for this month's utilities.

i. The company paid $2,000 cash to settle the account payable created in transaction c.

j. The company purchased $20,300 of new office equipment by paying $20,300 cash.

k. The company completed $6,250 of services for a client, who must pay within 30 days.

l. The company paid $1,800 cash salary to an assistant.

m. The company received $4,000 cash in partial payment on the receivable created in transaction k.

n. The company paid a $2,800 cash dividend.

Required

1. Prepare general journal entries to record these transactions (use account titles listed in part 2).

Check (2) Ending balances: Cash, $12,665; Office Equipment, $50,900

2. Open the following ledger accounts—their account numbers are in parentheses (use the balance column format): Cash (101); Accounts Receivable (106); Office Supplies (108); Office Equipment (163); Automobiles (164); Building (170); Land (172); Accounts Payable (201); Notes Payable (250); Common Stock (307); Dividends (319); Fees Earned (402); Salaries Expense (601); and Utilities Expense (602). Post the journal entries from part 1 to the ledger accounts and enter the balance after each posting.

(3) Trial balance totals, $291,350

3. Prepare a trial balance as of the end of September.

Problem 2-5A
Computing net income from equity analysis, preparing a balance sheet, and computing the debt ratio

C2   A1   A2   P3

The accounting records of Nettle Distribution show the following assets and liabilities as of December 31, 2018 and 2019.

December 31	2018	2019	December 31	2018	2019
Cash	$ 64,300	$ 15,640	Building.....................	$ 0	$80,000
Accounts receivable...........	26,240	19,100	Land	0	60,000
Office supplies	3,160	1,960	Accounts payable.............	3,500	33,500
Office equipment	44,000	44,000	Note payable	0	40,000
Trucks	148,000	157,000			

Required

1. Prepare balance sheets for the business as of December 31, 2018 and 2019. *Hint:* Report only total equity on the balance sheet and remember that total equity equals the difference between assets and liabilities.

Check (2) Net income, $6,000

2. Compute net income for 2019 by comparing total equity amounts for these two years and using the following information: During 2019, the owner invested $35,000 additional cash in the business (in exchange for common stock) and the company paid a $19,000 cash dividend.

(3) Debt ratio, 19.5%

3. Compute the 2019 year-end debt ratio (in percent and rounded to one decimal).

Problem 2-6A
Analyzing account balances and reconstructing transactions

C1   C3   A1   P2

Yi Min started an engineering firm called Min Engineering. He began operations and completed seven transactions in May, which included his initial investment of $18,000 cash. After those seven transactions, the ledger included the following accounts with normal balances.

Cash	$37,600	Office equipment	$12,900	Dividends	$ 3,370
Office supplies	890	Accounts payable.......	12,900	Engineering fees earned	36,000
Prepaid insurance.......	4,600	Common stock	18,000	Rent expense	7,540

Required

Check (1) Trial balance totals, $66,900

(2) Ending Cash balance, $37,600

1. Prepare a trial balance for this business as of the end of May.

2. The following seven transactions produced the account balances shown above.

a. Y. Min invested $18,000 cash in the business in exchange for common stock.

b. Paid $7,540 cash for monthly rent expense for May.

c. Paid $4,600 cash in advance for the annual insurance premium beginning the next period.

d. Purchased office supplies for $890 cash.

e. Purchased $12,900 of office equipment on credit (with accounts payable).

f. Received $36,000 cash for engineering services provided in May.

g. The company paid a $3,370 cash dividend.

Prepare a Cash T-account, enter the cash effects (if any) of each transaction, and compute the ending Cash balance. Code each entry in the T-account with one of the transaction codes *a* through *g*.

Angela Lopez owns and manages a consulting firm called Metrix, which began operations on March 1. On March 31, Metrix shows the following selected accounts and amounts for the month of March.

Problem 2-7A
Preparing an income statement, statement of retained earnings, and balance sheet

P3

Equipment............	$ 4,000	Accounts receivable........	$ 3,500	Prepaid insurance.......	$1,000
Salaries expense	3,000	Common stock	11,600	Accounts payable.......	1,300
Consulting revenue	12,000	Dividends	2,000	Note receivable	2,500
Cash	8,000	Office supplies	1,500	Rent expense	2,000
Utilities expense	200	Rental revenue	500	Unearned revenue	300
Note payable	2,400	Advertising expense........	400		

Required

1. Prepare a March income statement for the business.

2. Prepare a March statement of retained earnings. The Retained Earnings account balance at March 1 was $0, and the owner invested $11,600 cash in the company on March 2 in exchange for common stock.

3. Prepare a March 31 balance sheet. *Hint:* Use the Retained Earnings account balance calculated in part 2.

Humble Management Services opened for business and completed these transactions in September.

PROBLEM SET B

Problem 2-1B
Preparing and posting journal entries; preparing a trial balance

C3   C4   A1   P1   P2

Sep. 1   Henry Humble, the owner, invested $38,000 cash along with office equipment valued at $15,000 in the company in exchange for common stock.

2   The company prepaid $9,000 cash for 12 months' rent for office space. *Hint:* Debit Prepaid Rent for $9,000.

4   The company made credit purchases for $8,000 in office equipment and $2,400 in office supplies. Payment is due within 10 days.

8   The company completed work for a client and immediately received $3,280 cash.

12   The company completed a $15,400 project for a client, who must pay within 30 days.

13   The company paid $10,400 cash to settle the payable created on September 4.

19   The company paid $1,900 cash for the premium on an 18-month insurance policy. *Hint:* Debit Prepaid Insurance for $1,900.

22   The company received $7,700 cash as partial payment for the work completed on September 12.

24   The company completed work for another client for $2,100 on credit.

28   The company paid a $5,300 cash dividend.

29   The company purchased $550 of additional office supplies on credit.

30   The company paid $860 cash for this month's utility bill.

Required

1. Prepare general journal entries to record these transactions (use account titles listed in part 2).

2. Open the following ledger accounts—their account numbers are in parentheses (use the balance column format): Cash (101); Accounts Receivable (106); Office Supplies (124); Prepaid Insurance (128); Prepaid Rent (131); Office Equipment (163); Accounts Payable (201); Common Stock (307); Dividends (319); Services Revenue (401); and Utilities Expense (690). Post journal entries from part 1 to the ledger accounts and enter the balance after each posting.

3. Prepare a trial balance as of the end of September.

Check   (2) Ending balances: Cash, $21,520; Accounts Receivable, $9,800; Accounts Payable, $550

(3) Total debits, $74,330

At the beginning of April, Bernadette Grechus launched a custom computer solutions company called Softworks. The company had the following transactions during April.

Problem 2-2B
Preparing and posting journal entries; preparing a trial balance

C3   C4   A1   P1   P2

a. Bernadette Grechus invested $65,000 cash, office equipment with a value of $5,750, and $30,000 of computer equipment in the company in exchange for common stock.

b. The company purchased land worth $22,000 for an office by paying $5,000 cash and signing a long-term note payable for $17,000.

[continued on next page]

[continued from previous page]

c. The company purchased a portable building with $34,500 cash and moved it onto the land acquired in *b*.

d. The company paid $5,000 cash for the premium on a two-year insurance policy.

e. The company provided services to a client and immediately collected $4,600 cash.

f. The company purchased $4,500 of additional computer equipment by paying $800 cash and signing a long-term note payable for $3,700.

g. The company completed $4,250 of services for a client. This amount is to be received within 30 days.

h. The company purchased $950 of additional office equipment on credit.

i. The company completed client services for $10,200 on credit.

j. The company received a bill for rent of a computer testing device that was used on a recently completed job. The $580 rent cost must be paid within 30 days.

k. The company collected $5,100 cash in partial payment from the client described in transaction *i*.

l. The company paid $1,800 cash for wages to an assistant.

m. The company paid $950 cash to settle the payable created in transaction *h*.

n. The company paid $608 cash for minor maintenance of the company's computer equipment.

o. The company paid a $6,230 cash dividend.

p. The company paid $1,800 cash for wages to an assistant.

q. The company paid $750 cash for advertisements on the web during April.

Required

1. Prepare general journal entries to record these transactions (use account titles listed in part 2).

Check (2) Ending balances: Cash, $17,262; Accounts Receivable, $9,350; Accounts Payable, $580

2. Open the following ledger accounts—their account numbers are in parentheses (use the balance column format): Cash (101); Accounts Receivable (106); Prepaid Insurance (108); Office Equipment (163); Computer Equipment (164); Building (170); Land (172); Accounts Payable (201); Notes Payable (250); Common Stock (307); Dividends (319); Fees Earned (402); Wages Expense (601); Computer Rental Expense (602); Advertising Expense (603); and Repairs Expense (604). Post the journal entries from part 1 to the accounts and enter the balance after each posting.

(3) Trial balance totals, $141,080

3. Prepare a trial balance as of the end of April.

Problem 2-3B

Preparing and posting journal entries; preparing a trial balance

C3 C4 A1 P1 P2

Zucker Management Services opened for business and completed these transactions in November.

Nov. 1 Matt Zucker, the owner, invested $30,000 cash along with $15,000 of office equipment in the company in exchange for common stock.
2 The company prepaid $4,500 cash for six months' rent for an office. *Hint:* Debit Prepaid Rent for $4,500.
4 The company made credit purchases of office equipment for $2,500 and of office supplies for $600. Payment is due within 10 days.
8 The company completed work for a client and immediately received $3,400 cash.
12 The company completed a $10,200 project for a client, who must pay within 30 days.
13 The company paid $3,100 cash to settle the payable created on November 4.
19 The company paid $1,800 cash for the premium on a 24-month insurance policy.
22 The company received $5,200 cash as partial payment for the work completed on November 12.
24 The company completed work for another client for $1,750 on credit.
28 The company paid a $5,300 cash dividend.
29 The company purchased $249 of additional office supplies on credit.
30 The company paid $831 cash for this month's utility bill.

Required

1. Prepare general journal entries to record these transactions (use account titles listed in part 2).

Check (2) Ending balances: Cash, $23,069; Accounts Receivable, $6,750; Accounts Payable, $249

2. Open the following ledger accounts—their account numbers are in parentheses (use the balance column format): Cash (101); Accounts Receivable (106); Office Supplies (124); Prepaid Insurance (128); Prepaid Rent (131); Office Equipment (163); Accounts Payable (201); Common Stock (307); Dividends (319); Services Revenue (403); and Utilities Expense (690). Post the journal entries from part 1 to the ledger accounts and enter the balance after each posting.

(3) Total debits, $60,599

3. Prepare a trial balance as of the end of November.

Nuncio Consulting completed the following transactions during June.

a. Armand Nuncio, the owner, invested $35,000 cash along with office equipment valued at $11,000 in the new company in exchange for common stock.

b. The company purchased land valued at $7,500 and a building valued at $40,000. The purchase is paid with $15,000 cash and a long-term note payable for $32,500.

c. The company purchased $500 of office supplies on credit.

d. A. Nuncio invested his personal automobile in the company in exchange for more common stock. The automobile has a value of $8,000 and is to be used exclusively in the business.

e. The company purchased $1,200 of additional office equipment on credit.

f. The company paid $1,000 cash salary to an assistant.

g. The company provided services to a client and collected $3,200 cash.

h. The company paid $540 cash for this month's utilities.

i. The company paid $500 cash to settle the payable created in transaction *c*.

j. The company purchased $3,400 of new office equipment by paying $3,400 cash.

k. The company completed $4,200 of services for a client, who must pay within 30 days.

l. The company paid $1,000 cash salary to an assistant.

m. The company received $2,200 cash in partial payment on the receivable created in transaction *k*.

n. The company paid a $1,100 cash dividend.

Required

1. Prepare general journal entries to record these transactions (use account titles listed in part 2).

2. Open the following ledger accounts—their account numbers are in parentheses (use the balance column format): Cash (101); Accounts Receivable (106); Office Supplies (108); Office Equipment (163); Automobiles (164); Building (170); Land (172); Accounts Payable (201); Notes Payable (250); Common Stock (307); Dividends (319); Fees Earned (402); Salaries Expense (601); and Utilities Expense (602). Post the journal entries from part 1 to the ledger accounts and enter the balance after each posting.

3. Prepare a trial balance as of the end of June.

Problem 2-4B
Recording transactions; posting to ledger; preparing a trial balance
C3 A1 P1 P2

Check (2) Ending balances: Cash, $17,860; Office Equipment, $15,600

(3) Trial balance totals, $95,100

The accounting records of Tama Co. show the following assets and liabilities as of December 31, 2018 and 2019.

December 31	2018	2019	December 31	2018	2019
Cash	$30,000	$ 5,000	Building	$ 0	$250,000
Accounts receivable	35,000	25,000	Land	0	50,000
Office supplies	8,000	13,500	Accounts payable	4,000	12,000
Office equipment	40,000	40,000	Note payable	0	250,000
Machinery	28,000	28,500			

Problem 2-5B
Computing net income from equity analysis, preparing a balance sheet, and computing the debt ratio
C2 A1 A2 P3

Required

1. Prepare balance sheets for the business as of December 31, 2018 and 2019. *Hint:* Report only total equity on the balance sheet and remember that total equity equals the difference between assets and liabilities.

2. Compute net income for 2019 by comparing total equity amounts for these two years and using the following information: During 2019, the owner invested $5,000 additional cash in the business (in exchange for common stock) and the company paid a $3,000 cash dividend.

3. Compute the December 31, 2019, debt ratio (in percent and rounded to one decimal).

Check (2) Net income, $11,000

(3) Debt ratio, 63.6%

Roshaun Gould started a web consulting firm called Gould Solutions. He began operations and completed seven transactions in April that resulted in the following accounts, which all have normal balances.

Cash	$20,000	Office equipment	$12,250	Dividends	$ 5,200
Office supplies	750	Accounts payable	12,250	Consulting fees earned	20,400
Prepaid rent	1,800	Common stock	15,000	Miscellaneous expenses	7,650

Problem 2-6B
Analyzing account balances and reconstructing transactions
C1 C3 A1 P2

Required

1. Prepare a trial balance for this business as of the end of April.

2. The following seven transactions produced the account balances shown above.

    a. Gould invested $15,000 cash in the business in exchange for common stock.

    b. Paid $1,800 cash in advance for next month's rent expense.

    c. Paid $7,650 cash for miscellaneous expenses.

    d. Purchased office supplies for $750 cash.

    e. Purchased $12,250 of office equipment on credit (with accounts payable).

    f. Received $20,400 cash for consulting services provided in April.

    g. The company paid a $5,200 cash dividend.

Prepare a Cash T-account, enter the cash effects (if any) of each transaction, and compute the ending Cash balance. Code each entry in the T-account with one of the transaction codes *a* through *g*.

Problem 2-7B

Preparing an income
statement, statement of
retained earnings, and
balance sheet

P3

Victoria Rivera owns and manages a consulting firm called Prisek, which began operations on July 1. On July 31, the company's records show the following selected accounts and amounts for the month of July.

Equipment............	$12,000	Accounts receivable.......	$10,500	Prepaid insurance.......	$3,000
Salaries expense	9,000	Common stock	34,800	Accounts payable.......	3,900
Consulting revenue	36,000	Dividends	6,000	Note receivable	7,500
Cash	24,000	Office supplies	4,500	Rent expense	6,000
Utilities expense........	600	Rental revenue	1,500	Unearned revenue	900
Note payable	7,200	Advertising expense........	1,200		

Required

1. Prepare a July income statement for the business.

2. Prepare a July statement of retained earnings. The Retained Earnings account balance at July 1 was $0, and the owner invested $34,800 cash in the company on July 2 in exchange for common stock.

3. Prepare a July 31 balance sheet. *Hint:* Use the Retained Earnings account balance calculated in part 2.

SERIAL PROBLEM

Business Solutions

A1 P1 P2

©Alexander Image/Shutterstock

This serial problem started in Chapter 1 and continues through most of the chapters. If the Chapter 1 segment was not completed, the problem can begin at this point.

SP 2 On October 1, 2019, Santana Rey launched a computer services company called **Business Solutions**, which provides consulting services, computer system installations, and custom program development. Rey adopts the calendar year for reporting purposes and expects to prepare the company's first set of financial statements on December 31, 2019. The company's initial chart of accounts follows.

Account	No.	Account	No.
Cash..........................	101	Common Stock........................	307
Accounts Receivable	106	Dividends	319
Computer Supplies..............	126	Computer Services Revenue	403
Prepaid Insurance................	128	Wages Expense	623
Prepaid Rent....................	131	Advertising Expense....................	655
Office Equipment	163	Mileage Expense	676
Computer Equipment............	167	Miscellaneous Expenses	677
Accounts Payable...............	201	Repairs Expense—Computer.............	684

Required

1. Prepare journal entries to record each of the following transactions for Business Solutions.

Oct. 1   S. Rey invested $45,000 cash, a $20,000 computer system, and $8,000 of office equipment in the company in exchange for common stock.

     2   The company paid $3,300 cash for four months' rent. *Hint:* Debit Prepaid Rent for $3,300.

     3   The company purchased $1,420 of computer supplies on credit from Harris Office Products.

     5   The company paid $2,220 cash for one year's premium on a property and liability insurance policy. *Hint:* Debit Prepaid Insurance for $2,220.

     6   The company billed Easy Leasing $4,800 for services performed in installing a new web server.

8   The company paid $1,420 cash for the computer supplies purchased from Harris Office Products on October 3.

10   The company hired Lyn Addie as a part-time assistant.

12   The company billed Easy Leasing another $1,400 for services performed.

15   The company received $4,800 cash from Easy Leasing as partial payment on its account.

17   The company paid $805 cash to repair computer equipment that was damaged when moving it.

20   The company paid $1,728 cash for advertisements published in the local newspaper.

22   The company received $1,400 cash from Easy Leasing on its account.

28   The company billed IFM Company $5,208 for services performed.

31   The company paid $875 cash for Lyn Addie's wages for seven days' work.

31   The company paid a $3,600 cash dividend.

Nov. 1   The company reimbursed S. Rey in cash for business automobile mileage allowance (Rey logged 1,000 miles at $0.32 per mile).

2   The company received $4,633 cash from Liu Corporation for computer services performed.

5   The company purchased computer supplies for $1,125 cash from Harris Office Products.

8   The company billed Gomez Co. $5,668 for services performed.

13   The company agreed to perform future services for Alex's Engineering Co. No work has yet been performed.

18   The company received $2,208 cash from IFM Company as partial payment of the October 28 bill.

22   The company paid $250 cash for miscellaneous expenses. *Hint:* Debit Miscellaneous Expenses for $250.

24   The company completed work and sent a bill for $3,950 to Alex's Engineering Co.

25   The company sent another bill to IFM Company for the past-due amount of $3,000.

28   The company reimbursed S. Rey in cash for business automobile mileage (1,200 miles at $0.32 per mile).

30   The company paid $1,750 cash for Lyn Addie's wages for 14 days' work.

30   The company paid a $2,000 cash dividend.

2. Open ledger accounts (in balance column format) and post the journal entries from part 1 to them.

3. Prepare a trial balance as of the end of November.

Check   (2) Cash, Nov. 30 bal., $38,264
(3) Trial bal. totals, $98,659

Using transactions from the following assignments along with the **General Ledger** tool, prepare journal entries for each transaction and identify the financial statement impact of each entry. The financial statements are automatically generated based on the journal entries recorded.

GENERAL LEDGER PROBLEM

GL 2-1   Transactions from the FastForward illustration in this chapter

GL 2-2   Based on Exercise 2-9

GL 2-3   Based on Exercise 2-12

GL 2-4   Based on Problem 2-1A

Using transactions from the following assignments, record journal entries, create financial statements, and assess the impact of each transaction on financial statements.

GL 2-5   Based on Problem 2-2A   **GL 2-7**   Based on Problem 2-4A

GL 2-6   Based on Problem 2-3A   **GL 2-8**   Based on the Serial Problem SP 2

Accounting Analysis

AA 2-1   Refer to **Apple**'s financial statements in Appendix A for the following questions.

Required

1. What amount of total liabilities does Apple report for each of the fiscal years ended (*a*) September 30, 2017, and (*b*) September 24, 2016?

2. What amount of total assets does it report for each of the fiscal years ended (*a*) September 30, 2017, and (*b*) September 24, 2016?

3. Compute its debt ratio for each of the fiscal years ended (*a*) September 30, 2017, and (*b*) September 24, 2016. (Report ratio in percent and round it to one decimal.)

4. In which fiscal year did it employ more financial leverage: September 30, 2017, or September 24, 2016? Explain.

COMPANY ANALYSIS

A1   A2

APPLE

**COMPARATIVE
ANALYSIS**

A1   A2

APPLE

GOOGLE

AA 2-2   Key comparative figures for **Apple** and **Google** follow.

$ millions	Apple Current Year	Apple Prior Year	Google Current Year	Google Prior Year
Total liabilities	$241,272	$193,437	$ 44,793	$ 28,461
Total assets	375,319	321,686	197,295	167,497

1. What is the debt ratio for Apple in the current year and for the prior year?
2. What is the debt ratio for Google in the current year and for the prior year?
3. Which of the two companies has the higher degree of financial leverage in the current year?

GLOBAL ANALYSIS

A2

APPLE

GOOGLE

Samsung

AA 2-3   Key comparative figures for **Apple**, **Google**, and **Samsung** follow.

In millions	Samsung Current Year	Samsung Prior Year	Apple Current Year	Google Current Year
Total liabilities	₩ 87,260,662	₩ 69,211,291	$241,272	$ 44,793
Total assets	301,752,090	262,174,324	375,319	197,295

Required

1. Compute Samsung's debt ratio for the current year and prior year.
2. Is Samsung on a trend toward increased or decreased financial leverage?
3. Looking at the current-year debt ratio, is Samsung a more risky or less risky investment than (*a*) Apple and (*b*) Google?

Beyond the Numbers

**ETHICS
CHALLENGE**

C1

BTN 2-1   Assume that you are a cashier and your manager requires that you immediately enter each sale when it occurs. Recently, lunch hour traffic has increased and the assistant manager asks you to avoid delays by taking customers' cash and making change without entering sales. The assistant manager says she will add up cash and enter sales after lunch. She says that, in this way, customers will be happy and the register record will always match the cash amount when the manager arrives at three o'clock.

   The advantages to the process proposed by the assistant manager include improved customer service, fewer delays, and less work for you. The disadvantage is that the assistant manager could steal cash by simply recording less sales than the cash received and then pocketing the excess cash. You decide to reject her suggestion without the manager's approval and to confront her on the ethics of her suggestion.

Required

Propose and evaluate two other courses of action you might consider, and explain why.

**COMMUNICATING
IN PRACTICE**

C1   C2   A1   P3

BTN 2-2   Lila Corentine is an aspiring entrepreneur and your friend. She is having difficulty understanding the purposes of financial statements and how they fit together across time.

Required

Write a one-page memorandum to Corentine explaining the purposes of the four financial statements and how they are linked across time.

**TAKING IT TO
THE NET**

A1

BTN 2-3   Access EDGAR online (**SEC.gov**) and locate the 2016 10-K report of **Amazon.com** (ticker: AMZN) filed on February 10, 2017. Review its financial statements reported for years ended 2016, 2015, and 2014 to answer the following questions.

Required

1. What are the amounts of Amazon's net income or net loss reported for each of these three years?
2. Do Amazon's operating activities provide cash or use cash for each of these three years? *Hint:* See the statement of cash flows.
3. If Amazon has 2016 net income of $2,371 million and 2016 operating cash flows of $16,443 million, how is it possible that its cash balance at December 31, 2016, increases by only $3,444 million relative to its balance at December 31, 2015?

BTN 2-4 The expanded accounting equation consists of assets, liabilities, common stock, dividends, revenues, and expenses. It can be used to reveal insights into changes in a company's financial position.

TEAMWORK IN ACTION

C1 C2 C4 A1

Required

1. Form *learning teams* of six (or more) members. Each team member must select one of the six components, and each team must have at least one expert on each component: (*a*) assets, (*b*) liabilities, (*c*) common stock, (*d*) dividends, (*e*) revenues, and (*f*) expenses.

2. Form *expert teams* of individuals who selected the same component in part 1. Expert teams are to draft a report that each expert will present to his or her learning team addressing the following:

   a. Identify for its component the (i) increase and decrease side of the account and (ii) normal balance side of the account.

   b. Describe a transaction, with amounts, that increases its component.

   c. Using the transaction and amounts in (*b*), verify the equality of the accounting equation and then explain any effects on the income statement and statement of cash flows.

   d. Describe a transaction, with amounts, that decreases its component.

   e. Using the transaction and amounts in (*d*), verify the equality of the accounting equation and then explain any effects on the income statement and statement of cash flows.

3. Each expert should return to his/her learning team. In rotation, each member presents his/her expert team's report to the learning team. Team discussion is encouraged.

BTN 2-5 Assume that James Park and Eric Friedman of **Fitbit** plan on expanding their business to accommodate more product lines. They are considering financing expansion in one of two ways: (1) contributing more of their own funds to the business or (2) borrowing the funds from a bank.

ENTREPRENEURIAL DECISION

A1 A2 P3

Required

Identify at least two issues that James and Eric should consider when trying to decide on the method for financing their expansion.

BTN 2-6 Angel Martin is a young entrepreneur who operates Martin Music Services, offering singing lessons and instruction on musical instruments. Martin wishes to expand but needs a $30,000 loan. The bank requests that Martin prepare a balance sheet and key financial ratios. Martin has not kept formal records but is able to provide the following accounts and their amounts as of December 31.

ENTREPRENEURIAL DECISION

A1 A2 P3

Cash	$ 3,600	Accounts receivable	$ 9,600	Prepaid insurance	$ 1,500
Prepaid rent	9,400	Store supplies	6,600	Equipment	50,000
Accounts payable	2,200	Unearned lesson fees	15,600	Total equity*	62,900
Annual net income	40,000				

*The total equity amount reflects all owner investments, dividends, revenues, and expenses as of December 31.

Required

1. Prepare a balance sheet as of December 31 for Martin Music Services. (Report only the total equity amount on the balance sheet.)

2. Compute Martin's debt ratio and its return on assets (the latter ratio is defined in Chapter 1). Assume average assets equal its ending balance.

3. Do you believe the prospects of a $30,000 bank loan are good? Why or why not?

BTN 2-7 Obtain a recent copy of the most prominent newspaper distributed in your area. Research the classified section and prepare a report answering the following questions (attach relevant printouts to your report). Alternatively, you may want to search the web for the required information. One suitable website is **CareerOneStop** (**CareerOneStop.org**). For documentation, print copies of websites accessed.

HITTING THE ROAD

C1

1. Identify the number of listings for accounting positions and the various accounting job titles.

2. Identify the number of listings for other job titles, with examples, that require or prefer accounting knowledge/experience but are not specifically accounting positions.

3. Specify the salary range for the accounting and accounting-related positions if provided.

4. Indicate the job that appeals most to you, the reason for its appeal, and its requirements.

---

3 Adjusting Accounts for Financial Statements

Chapter Preview

DEFERRAL OF EXPENSE	DEFERRAL OF REVENUE	ACCRUED EXPENSE	ACCRUED REVENUE	REPORTING	CLASSIFICATION AND ANALYSIS
C1 Timing Accrual vs. cash 3-Step process **P1** Framework Examples	**P2** Framework Examples	**P3** Framework Examples	**P4** Framework Examples Summary	**P5** Adjusted trial balance **P6** Financial statements **P7** Closing process **P8** Post-closing trial balance	**C2** Accounting cycle **C3** Classified balance sheet **A1** Profit margin **A2** Current ratio
NTK 3-1	NTK 3-2	NTK 3-3	NTK 3-4	NTK 3-5, 6	NTK 3-7

Learning Objectives

CONCEPTUAL

C1 Explain the importance of periodic reporting and the role of accrual accounting.

C2 Identify steps in the accounting cycle.

C3 Explain and prepare a classified balance sheet.

ANALYTICAL

A1 Compute profit margin and describe its use in analyzing company performance.

A2 Compute the current ratio and describe what it reveals about a company's financial condition.

PROCEDURAL

P1 Prepare adjusting entries for deferral of expenses.

P2 Prepare adjusting entries for deferral of revenues.

P3 Prepare adjusting entries for accrued expenses.

P4 Prepare adjusting entries for accrued revenues.

P5 Explain and prepare an adjusted trial balance.

P6 Prepare financial statements from an adjusted trial balance.

P7 Describe and prepare closing entries.

P8 Explain and prepare a post-closing trial balance.

P9 *Appendix 3A*—Explain the alternatives in accounting for prepaids.

P10 *Appendix 3B*—Prepare a work sheet and explain its usefulness.

P11 *Appendix 3C*—Prepare reversing entries and explain their purpose.

Snap!

©J. Emilio Flores/Corbis/Getty Images

"Creativity creates value"—Evan Spiegel

VENICE, CA—Evan Spiegel met his future co-founder Bobby Murphy in college. "We weren't cool," recalls Bobby, "so we tried to build things to be cool!" One of their cool projects was an app that could send messages that disappeared after a few seconds. This app would later be called **Snapchat** (**Snapchat.com**).

The first headquarters of Snapchat was the home of Evan's dad. However, within a matter of months, their app had over a million users.

As Snapchat grew, Evan and Bobby knew an effective accounting system was key to attracting investors. "One of the things I did underestimate," admits Evan, "was how much more important communication becomes [when seeking investors]."

Investors wanted to know revenues, costs, assets, and liabilities for Snapchat. "You really need to explain . . . how your business works," insists Evan.

To communicate "the Snap story," the entrepreneurs learned how to defer and accrue revenues and expenses and to prepare financial statements for investors. This included learning the accounting cycle. With accounting reports in hand, Evan and Bobby were able to secure additional financing. Exclaims Evan: "That was the greatest feeling of all time!"

Sources: *Snapchat website*, January 2019; *Vanity Fair*, October 2017; *LA Times*, March 2017; *Forbes*, January 2014

TIMING AND REPORTING

The Accounting Period

The value of information is linked to its timeliness. Useful information must reach decision makers frequently. To provide timely information, accounting systems prepare reports at regular intervals. The **time period assumption** presumes that an organization's activities can be divided into specific time periods such as a month, a three-month quarter, a six-month interval, or a year. Exhibit 3.1 shows various **accounting,** or *reporting,* **periods.** Most organizations use a year as their primary accounting period. Reports covering a one-year period are known as **annual financial statements.** Many organizations also prepare **interim financial statements** covering one, three, or six months of activity.

C1

Explain the importance of periodic reporting and the role of accrual accounting.

"Apple announces annual income of . . ."

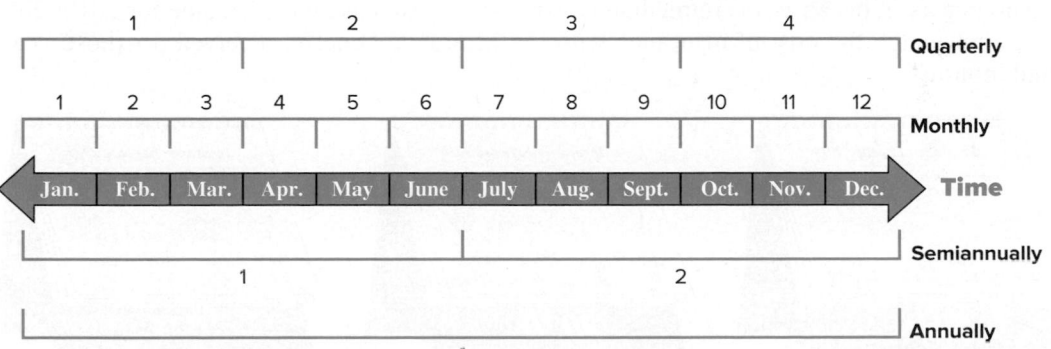

EXHIBIT 3.1

Accounting Periods

The annual reporting period is not always a calendar year ending on December 31. An organization can use a **fiscal year** consisting of any 12 consecutive months or 52 weeks. For example, **Gap**'s fiscal year consistently ends the final week of January or the first week of February each year.

©Vixit/Shutterstock

Companies with little seasonal variation in sales often use the calendar year as their fiscal year. **Facebook** uses calendar-year reporting. Companies that have seasonal variations in sales often use a **natural business year** end, which is when sales are at their lowest level for the year. The natural business year for retailers such as **Target** and **Dick's Sporting Goods** ends around January 31, after the holidays.

Accrual Basis versus Cash Basis

After external transactions and events are recorded, several accounts require adjustments before their balances appear in financial statements. This is needed because internal transactions and events are not yet recorded.

- **Accrual basis accounting** records revenues when services and products are delivered and records expenses when incurred (matched with revenues).
- **Cash basis accounting** records revenues when cash is received and records expenses when cash is paid. Cash basis income is cash receipts minus cash payments.

Most agree that accrual accounting better reflects business performance than cash basis accounting. Accrual accounting also increases the *comparability* of financial statements from period to period.

Accrual Basis   To compare these two systems, let's consider FastForward's Prepaid Insurance account. FastForward paid $2,400 for 24 months of insurance coverage that began on December 1, 2019. Accrual accounting requires that $100 of insurance expense be reported each month, from December 2019 through November 2021. (This means expenses are $100 in 2019, $1,200 in 2020, and $1,100 in 2021.) Exhibit 3.2 shows this allocation of insurance cost across the three years. Any unexpired premium is reported as a Prepaid Insurance asset on the accrual basis balance sheet.

EXHIBIT 3.2

Accrual Accounting for Allocating Prepaid Insurance to Expense

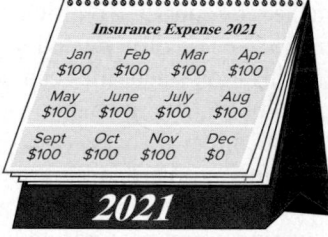

Point: Annual income statements for Exhibit 3.2 follow:

Accrual Basis	2019	2020	2021
Revenues.......	$ #	$ #	$ #
Insurance exp.	$100	$1,200	$1,100

EXHIBIT 3.3

Cash Accounting for Allocating Prepaid Insurance to Expense

Cash Basis   A *cash basis* income statement for December 2019 reports insurance expense of $2,400, as shown in Exhibit 3.3. The cash basis income statements for years 2020 and 2021 report no insurance expense. The cash basis balance sheet never reports a prepaid insurance asset because it is immediately expensed. Also, cash basis income for 2019–2021 does not match the cost of insurance with the insurance benefits received for those years and months.

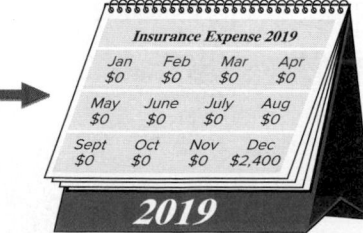

Point: Annual income statements for Exhibit 3.3 follow:

Cash Basis	2019	2020	2021
Revenues.......	$ #	$#	$#
Insurance exp.	$2,400	$0	$0

Recognizing Revenues and Expenses

We divide a company's activities into time periods, but not all activities are complete when financial statements are prepared. Thus, adjustments are required to get proper account balances.

We use two principles in the adjusting process: revenue recognition and expense recognition.

- **Revenue recognition principle** requires that revenue be recorded when goods or services are provided to customers and at an amount expected to be received from customers. Adjustments ensure revenue is recognized (reported) in the time period when those services and products are provided.

- **Expense recognition** (or matching) **principle** requires that expenses be recorded in the same accounting period as the revenues that are recognized as a result of those expenses.

Point: Recording revenue early overstates current-period income; recording it late understates current-period income.

Point: Recording expense early understates current-period income; recording it late overstates current-period income.

Ethical Risk

Clawbacks from Accounting Fraud   Former executives at **Saba Software**, a cloud-based talent management system, were charged with accounting fraud by the SEC for falsifying revenue to boost income. This alleged overstatement of income led to a payback of millions of dollars to the company by the former CEO and former CFO. See SEC release 2015–28. ∎

©Marco Marchi/Getty Images

Framework for Adjustments

Four types of adjustments exist for transactions and events that extend over more than one period.

⟨ **Deferral of expense** ⟩   ⟨ **Deferral of revenue** ⟩   ⟨ **Accrued expense** ⟩   ⟨ **Accrued revenue** ⟩

Adjustments are made using a 3-step process, as shown in Exhibit 3.4.

Step 1:   Determine what the current account balance *equals*.

Step 2:   Determine what the current account balance *should equal*.

Step 3:   Record an adjusting entry to get from step 1 to step 2.

EXHIBIT 3.4

Three-Step Process for Adjusting Entries

Each **adjusting entry** made at the end of an accounting period reflects a transaction or event that is not yet recorded. An adjusting entry affects one or more income statement accounts *and* one or more balance sheet accounts (but never the Cash account).

DEFERRAL OF EXPENSE

Prepaid expenses, or *deferred expenses,* are assets *paid for* in advance of receiving their benefits. When these assets are used, those advance payments become expenses.

Framework   Adjusting entries for prepaid expenses increase expenses and decrease assets, as shown in the T-accounts of Exhibit 3.5. This adjustment shows the using up of prepaid expenses. To demonstrate accounting for prepaid expenses, we look at prepaid insurance, supplies, and depreciation. In each case we decrease an asset (balance sheet) account and increase an expense (income statement) account.

P1

Prepare adjusting entries for deferral of expenses.

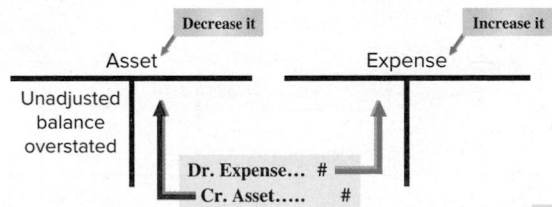

EXHIBIT 3.5

Adjusting for Prepaid Expenses (decrease an asset and record an expense)

Prepaid Insurance

Prepaid insurance expires with time. We use our three-step process.

Step 1:   We determine that the current balance of FastForward's prepaid insurance is equal to its $2,400 payment for 24 months of insurance benefits that began on December 1, 2019.

Step 2:   As time passes, the benefits of the insurance gradually expire and a portion of the Prepaid Insurance asset becomes expense. For instance, one month's insurance coverage expires by December 31, 2019. This expense is $100, or 1/24 of $2,400, which leaves $2,300.

Insurance

Dec. 1   Pay insurance premium and record asset
Prepaid Insurance....... 2,400
  Cash........................   2,400

Two-Year Insurance Policy
Total cost is $2,400
Monthly cost is $100

Dec. 31   Coverage expires and record expense

Step 3:   The adjusting entry to record this expense and reduce the asset, along with T-account postings, follows.

Assets = Liabilities + Equity
−100   −100

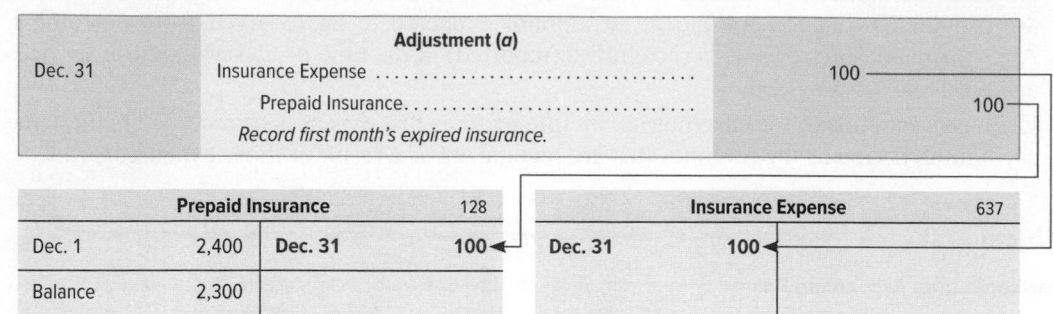

	Adjustment (a)		
Dec. 31	Insurance Expense	100	
	Prepaid Insurance...............................		100
	Record first month's expired insurance.		

Prepaid Insurance			128		Insurance Expense			637
Dec. 1	2,400	Dec. 31	100	Dec. 31	100			
Balance	2,300							

Explanation   After adjusting and posting, the $100 balance in Insurance Expense and the $2,300 balance in Prepaid Insurance are ready for reporting in financial statements. *Not* making the adjustment on or before December 31 would

- Understate expenses by $100 for the December income statement.
- Overstate prepaid insurance (assets) by $100 in the December 31 balance sheet.

The following highlights the adjustment for prepaid insurance.

Before Adjustment	Adjustment	After Adjustment
Prepaid Insurance = $2,400	**Deduct $100 from Prepaid Insurance** **Add $100 to Insurance Expense**	**Prepaid Insurance = $2,300**
Reports $2,400 policy for 24 months' coverage.	Record current month's $100 insurance expense and $100 reduction in prepaid.	Reports $2,300 in coverage for remaining 23 months.

Supplies

We count supplies at period-end and make an adjusting entry.

Supplies

Dec. 2,6,26   Purchase supplies
and record asset

Dec. 31   Physical count
Dec. 31   Record expense

Step 1:   FastForward purchased $9,720 of supplies in December, some of which were used during that same month. When financial statements are prepared at December 31, the cost of supplies used during December is expensed.

Step 2:   When FastForward computes (physically counts) its remaining unused supplies at December 31, it finds $8,670 of supplies remaining of the $9,720 total supplies. The $1,050 difference between these two amounts is December's supplies expense.

Step 3:   The adjusting entry to record this expense and reduce the Supplies asset account, along with T-account postings, follows.

Assets = Liabilities + Equity
−1,050   −1,050

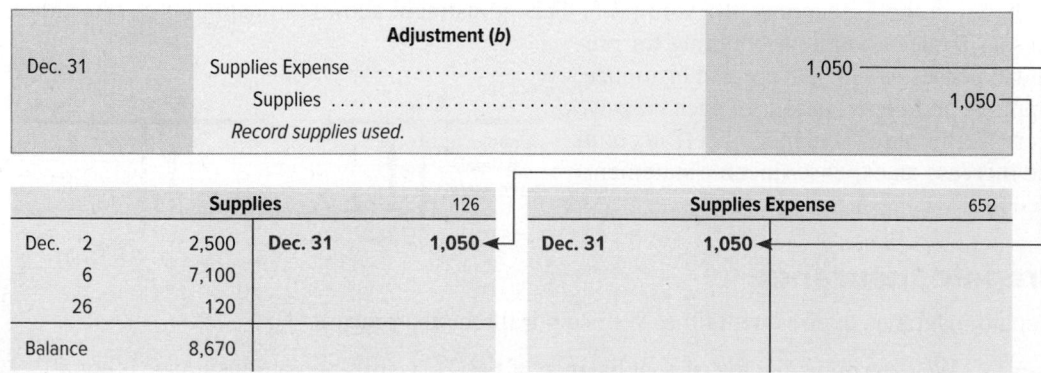

	Adjustment (b)		
Dec. 31	Supplies Expense	1,050	
	Supplies		1,050
	Record supplies used.		

Supplies			126		Supplies Expense			652
Dec. 2	2,500	Dec. 31	1,050	Dec. 31	1,050			
6	7,100							
26	120							
Balance	8,670							

Explanation   The balance of the Supplies account is $8,670 after posting—equaling the cost of the remaining supplies. *Not* making the adjustment on or before December 31 would

- Understate expenses by $1,050 for the December income statement.
- Overstate supplies by $1,050 in the December 31 balance sheet.

The following highlights the adjustment for supplies.

Before Adjustment	Adjustment	After Adjustment
Supplies = $9,720	Deduct $1,050 from Supplies Add $1,050 to Supplies Expense	Supplies = $8,670
Reports $9,720 in supplies.	Record $1,050 in supplies used and $1,050 as supplies expense.	Reports $8,670 in supplies.

Other Prepaid Expenses

Other prepaid expenses, such as Prepaid Rent and Prepaid Advertising, are accounted for exactly as insurance and supplies are.

Some prepaid expenses are both paid for *and* fully used up within a single period. One example is when a company pays monthly rent on the first day of each month. In this case, we record the cash paid with a debit to Rent Expense instead of an asset account.

Decision Maker

Investor A publisher signs an Olympic skier to write a book. The company pays the skier $500,000 to sign plus future book royalties. A note to the company's financial statements says that "prepaid expenses include $500,000 in author signing fees to be matched against future expected sales." How does this affect your analysis? ■ *Answer:* Prepaid expenses are assets paid for in advance of receiving their benefits–they are expensed as they are used up. As an investor, you are concerned about the risk of future book sales. The riskier the likelihood of future book sales is, the more likely your analysis is to treat the $500,000, or a portion of it, as an expense, not a prepaid expense (asset).

©Don Hammond/Design Pics

Depreciation

A special category of prepaid expenses is **plant assets,** which are long-term tangible assets used to produce and sell products and services. Plant assets provide benefits for more than one period. Examples of plant assets are buildings, machines, vehicles, and fixtures. All plant assets (excluding land) eventually wear out or become less useful. The costs of plant assets are gradually reported as expenses in the income statement over the assets' useful lives (benefit periods). **Depreciation** is the allocation of the costs of these assets over their expected useful lives. Depreciation expense is recorded with an adjusting entry similar to that for other prepaid expenses.

Point: Plant assets are also called *Plant & Equipment* or *Property, Plant & Equipment (PP&E).*

Point: Depreciation does not necessarily measure decline in market value.

Point: An asset's expected value at the end of its useful life is called *salvage value.*

Step 1: FastForward purchased equipment for $26,000 in early December to use in earning revenue. This equipment's cost must be depreciated.

Step 2: The equipment is expected to have a useful life (benefit period) of five years and to be worth about $8,000 at the end of five years. This means the *net* cost of this equipment over its useful life is $18,000 ($26,000 − $8,000). FastForward depreciates it using **straight-line depreciation,** which allocates equal amounts of the asset's net cost to depreciation during its useful life. Dividing the $18,000 net cost by the 60 months (5 years) in the asset's useful life gives a monthly cost of $300 ($18,000/60).

Step 3: The adjusting entry to record monthly depreciation expense, along with T-account postings, follows.

Depreciation
Dec. 3 Purchase equipment and record asset
    Equipment............ 26,000
      Cash................   26,000

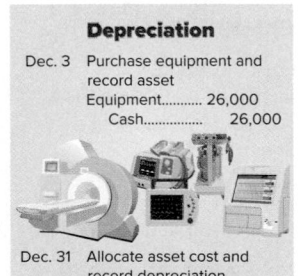

Dec. 31 Allocate asset cost and record depreciation

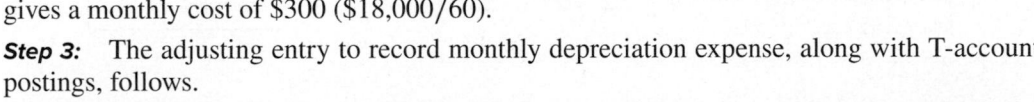

Dec. 31	Adjustment (c)		
	Depreciation Expense	300	
	Accumulated Depreciation—Equipment		300
	Record monthly equipment depreciation.		

Assets = Liabilities + Equity
−300   −300

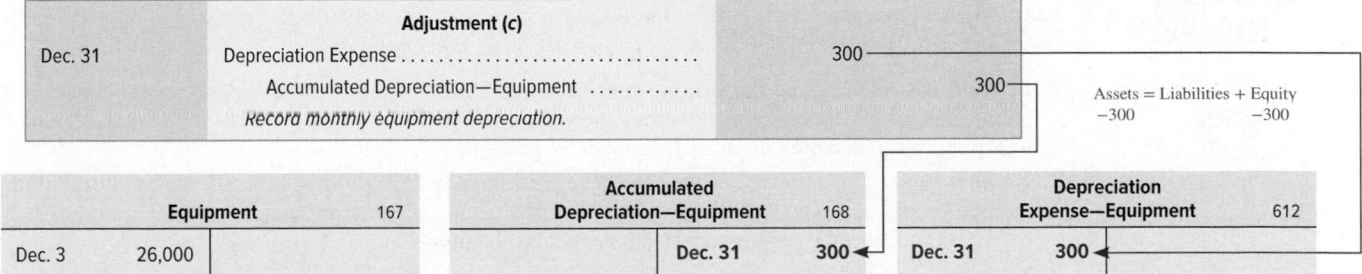

Equipment	167		Accumulated Depreciation—Equipment	168		Depreciation Expense—Equipment	612
Dec. 3 26,000			Dec. 31 300			Dec. 31 300	

Explanation After posting the adjustment, the Equipment account ($26,000) minus its Accumulated Depreciation ($300) account equals the $25,700 net cost. The $300 balance in the

Depreciation Expense account is reported in the December income statement. *Not* making the adjustment at December 31 would

- Understate expenses by $300 for the December income statement.
- Overstate assets by $300 in the December 31 balance sheet.

The following highlights the adjustment for depreciation.

Before Adjustment	Adjustment	After Adjustment
Equipment, net = $26,000	Deduct $300 from Equipment, net Add $300 to Depreciation Expense	Equipment, net = $25,700
Reports $26,000 in equipment.	Record $300 in depreciation and $300 as accumulated depreciation.	Reports $25,700 in equipment, net of accumulated depreciation.

Point: Accumulated Depreciation has a normal credit balance; it decreases the asset's reported value.

Accumulated Depreciation is a separate contra account. A **contra account** is an account linked with another account, it has an opposite normal balance, and it is reported as a subtraction from that other account's balance. FastForward's contra account of Accumulated Depreciation—Equipment is subtracted from the Equipment account in the balance sheet.

The Accumulated Depreciation contra account includes total depreciation expense for all prior periods for which the asset was used. To demonstrate, on February 28, 2020, after three months of adjusting entries, the Equipment and Accumulated Depreciation accounts appear as in Exhibit 3.6. The $900 balance in the Accumulated Depreciation account is subtracted from its related $26,000 asset cost. The difference ($25,100) between these two balances is called **book value,** or *net amount,* which is the asset's costs minus its accumulated depreciation.

Point: The net cost of equipment is also called *depreciable basis.*

EXHIBIT 3.6

Accounts after Three Months of Depreciation Adjustments

Equipment		167
Dec. 3	26,000	

Accumulated Depreciation—Equipment		168
	Dec. 31	300
	Jan. 31	300
	Feb. 28	300
	Balance	**900**

These account balances are reported in the assets section of the February 28 balance sheet in Exhibit 3.7. This presentation shows the full cost of assets and accumulated depreciation.

EXHIBIT 3.7

Equipment and Accumulated Depreciation on February 28 Balance Sheet

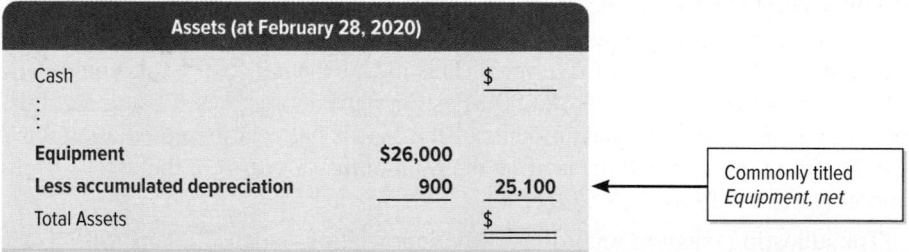

Assets (at February 28, 2020)		
Cash		$ ____
⋮		
Equipment	$26,000	
Less accumulated depreciation	900	25,100
Total Assets		$ ____

Commonly titled
Equipment, net

For each separate case below, follow the three-step process for adjusting the prepaid asset account at December 31. *Assume no other adjusting entries are made during the year.*

1. **Prepaid Insurance.** The Prepaid Insurance account has a $5,000 debit balance to start the year, and no insurance payments were made during the year. A review of insurance policies shows that $1,000 of unexpired insurance remains at its December 31 year-end.

2. **Prepaid Rent.** On October 1 of the current year, the company prepaid $12,000 for one year of rent for facilities being occupied from that day forward. The company debited Prepaid Rent and credited Cash for $12,000. December 31 year-end statements must be prepared.

3. **Supplies.** The Supplies account has a $1,000 debit balance to start the year. Supplies of $2,000 were purchased during the current year and debited to the Supplies account. A December 31 physical count shows $500 of supplies remaining.

4. Accumulated Depreciation. The company has only one fixed asset (equipment) that it purchased at the start of this year. That asset had cost $38,000, had an estimated life of 10 years, and is expected to be valued at $8,000 at the end of the 10-year life. December 31 year-end statements must be prepared.

Solution

1. Step 1: Prepaid Insurance equals $5,000 (before adjustment)

Step 2: Prepaid Insurance should equal $1,000 (the unexpired part)

Step 3: Adjusting entry to get from step 1 to step 2

Dec. 31	Insurance Expense..	4,000	
	Prepaid Insurance..		4,000
	Record expired insurance coverage ($5,000 – $1,000).		

2. Step 1: Prepaid Rent equals $12,000 (before adjustment)

Step 2: Prepaid Rent should equal $9,000 (the unexpired part)*

Step 3: Adjusting entry to get from step 1 to step 2

Dec. 31	Rent Expense...	3,000	
	Prepaid Rent..		3,000
	*Record expired prepaid rent. *$12,000 – $3,000 = $9,000,*		
	where $3,000 is from: ($12,000/12 months) × 3 months		

3. Step 1: Supplies equal $3,000 (from $1,000 + $2,000; before adjustment)

Step 2: Supplies should equal $500 (what's left)

Step 3: Adjusting entry to get from step 1 to step 2*

Dec. 31	Supplies Expense...	2,500	
	Supplies...		2,500
	*Record supplies used. *$1,000 + $2,000 purchased –*		
	*$ **2,500** supplies used = $500 remaining*		

4. Step 1: Accumulated Depreciation equals $0 (before adjustment)

Step 2: Accumulated Depreciation should equal $3,000 (after current-period depreciation of $3,000)*

Step 3: Adjusting entry to get from step 1 to step 2

Dec. 31	Depreciation Expense—Equipment.....................................	3,000	
	Accumulated Depreciation—Equipment............................		3,000
	*Record depreciation for period. *($38,000 – $8,000)/10 years*		

> Do More: QS 3-5, QS 3-6, QS 3-7, QS 3-8, QS 3-9

DEFERRAL OF REVENUE

Unearned revenue is cash received in advance of providing products and services. Unearned revenues, or *deferred revenues,* are liabilities. When cash is accepted, an obligation to provide products or services is accepted.

P2

Prepare adjusting entries for deferral of revenues.

Framework   As products or services are provided, the liability decreases and the unearned revenues become *earned* revenues. Adjusting entries for unearned revenue decrease the unearned revenue (balance sheet) account and increase the revenue (income statement) account, as shown in Exhibit 3.8.

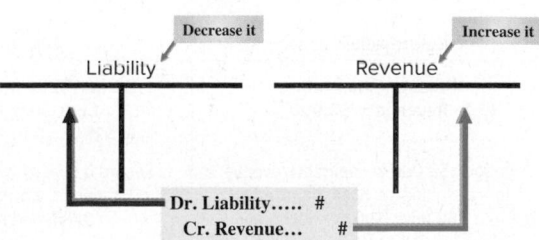

EXHIBIT 3.8

Adjusting for Unearned Revenues (decrease a liability and record revenue)

Point: To *defer* is to postpone. We postpone reporting amounts received as revenues until the product or service is provided.

Unearned revenues are common in sporting and concert events. When the **Boston Celtics** receive cash from advance ticket sales, they record it in an unearned revenue account called *Deferred Game Revenues*. The Celtics record revenue as games are played.

Unearned Consulting Revenue

FastForward has unearned revenues. The company agreed on December 26 to provide consulting services to a client for 60 days for a fixed fee of $3,000.

> ***Step 1:***   On December 26, the client paid the 60-day fee in advance, covering the period December 27 to February 24. The entry to record the cash received in advance is

Assets = Liabilities + Equity
+3,000   +3,000

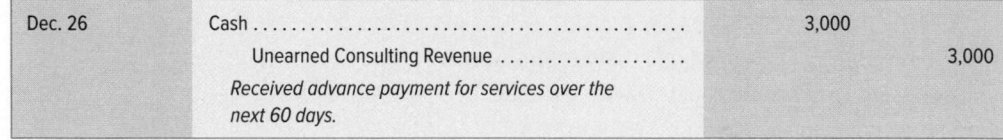

Dec. 26	Cash	3,000	
	Unearned Consulting Revenue		3,000
	Received advance payment for services over the next 60 days.		

Unearned Revenues

Dec. 26   Cash received in advance and record liability

Thanks for cash in advance. I'll work now through Feb. 24

Dec. 31   Provided 5 days of services and record revenue

This advance payment increases cash and creates a liability to do consulting work over the next 60 days (5 days this year and 55 days next year).

Step 2:   As time passes, FastForward earns this payment through consulting. By December 31, it has provided five days' service and earned 5/60 of the $3,000 unearned revenue. This amounts to $250 ($3,000 × 5/60). The *revenue recognition principle* requires that $250 of unearned revenue be reported as revenue on the December income statement.

Step 3:   The adjusting entry to reduce the liability account and recognize earned revenue, along with T-account postings, follows.

Assets = Liabilities + Equity
          −250   +250

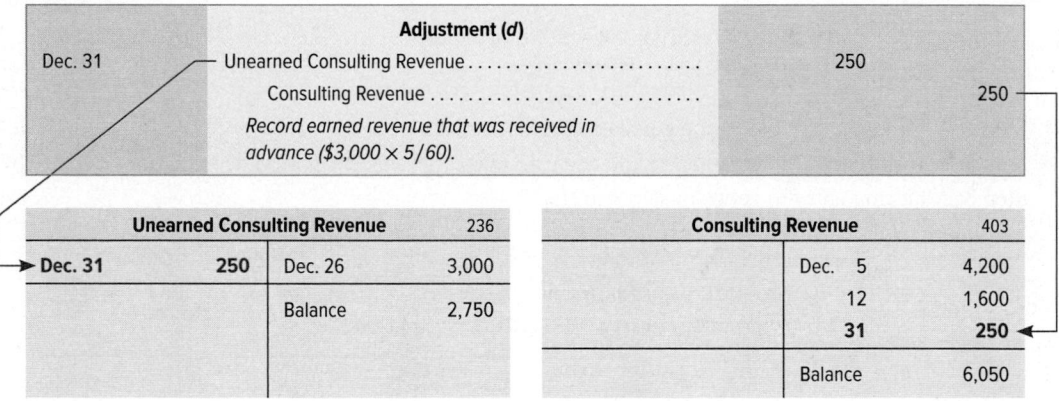

Adjustment (d)

Dec. 31	Unearned Consulting Revenue	250	
	Consulting Revenue		250
	Record earned revenue that was received in advance ($3,000 × 5/60).		

Unearned Consulting Revenue		236
Dec. 31	**250**	Dec. 26 3,000
		Balance 2,750

Consulting Revenue		403
		Dec. 5 4,200
		12 1,600
		31 250
		Balance 6,050

Explanation   The adjusting entry transfers $250 from unearned revenue (a liability account) to a revenue account. *Not* making the adjustment

- Understates revenue by $250 in the December income statement.
- Overstates unearned revenue by $250 on the December 31 balance sheet.

The following highlights the adjustment for unearned revenue.

Before Adjustment	Adjustment	After Adjustment
Unearned Consulting Revenue = $3,000	**Deduct $250 from Unearned Consulting Revenue** **Add $250 to Consulting Revenue**	**Unearned Consulting Revenue = $2,750**
Reports $3,000 in unearned revenue for consulting services promised for 60 days ($50 per day).	Record 5 days of earned consulting revenue, which is 5/60 of unearned amount.	Reports $2,750 in unearned revenue for consulting services owed over next 55 days (55 days × $50 = $2,750).

For each separate case below, follow the three-step process for adjusting the unearned revenue liability account at December 31. *Assume no other adjusting entries are made during the year.*

a. Unearned Rent Revenue. The company collected $24,000 rent in advance on September 1, debiting Cash and crediting Unearned Rent Revenue. The tenant was paying 12 months' rent in advance and moved in on September 1.

Unearned Revenues

P2

b. Unearned Services Revenue. The company charges $100 per month to spray a house for insects. A customer paid $600 on November 1 in advance for six treatments, which was recorded with a debit to Cash and a credit to Unearned Services Revenue. At year-end, the company has applied two treatments for the customer.

Solution

a. Step 1: Unearned Rent Revenue equals $24,000 (before adjustment)

Step 2: Unearned Rent Revenue should equal $16,000 (current-period earned revenue is $8,000*)

Step 3: Adjusting entry to get from step 1 to step 2

Dec. 31	Unearned Rent Revenue	8,000	
	Rent Revenue		8,000
	Record earned portion of rent received in advance.		
	*($24,000/12 months) × 4 months' rental usage		

b. Step 1: Unearned Services Revenue equals $600 (before adjustment)

Step 2: Unearned Services Revenue should equal $400 (current-period earned revenue is $200*)

Step 3: Adjusting entry to get from step 1 to step 2

Dec. 31	Unearned Services Revenue........................	200	
	Services Revenue		200
	Record earned portion of revenue received in advance.		
	*$100 × 2 treatments = Services revenue		

Do More: QS 3-10, QS 3-11

ACCRUED EXPENSE

Accrued expenses are costs that are incurred in a period that are both unpaid and unrecorded. Accrued expenses are reported on the income statement for the period when incurred.

P3 _____

Prepare adjusting entries for accrued expenses.

Framework   Adjusting entries for recording accrued expenses increase the expense (income statement) account and increase a liability (balance sheet) account, as shown in Exhibit 3.9. This adjustment recognizes expenses incurred in a period but not yet paid. Common examples of accrued expenses are salaries, interest, rent, and taxes. We use salaries and interest to show how to adjust accounts for accrued expenses.

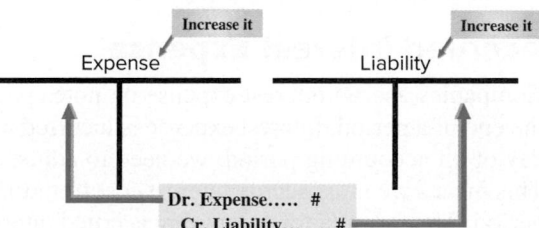

EXHIBIT 3.9

Adjusting for Accrued Expenses (increase a liability and record an expense)

Point: Accrued expenses are also called *accrued liabilities.*

Accrued Salaries Expense

FastForward's employee earns $70 per day, or $350 for a five-day workweek beginning on Monday and ending on Friday.

Step 1:   Its employee is paid every two weeks on Friday. On December 12 and 26, the wages are paid, recorded in the journal, and posted to the ledger.

Step 2:   The calendar in Exhibit 3.10 shows three working days after the December 26 payday (29, 30, and 31). This means the employee has earned three days' salary by the close of business on Wednesday, December 31, yet this salary cost has not been paid or recorded. FastForward must report the added expense and liability for unpaid salary from December 29, 30, and 31.

EXHIBIT 3.10

Salary Accrual and Paydays

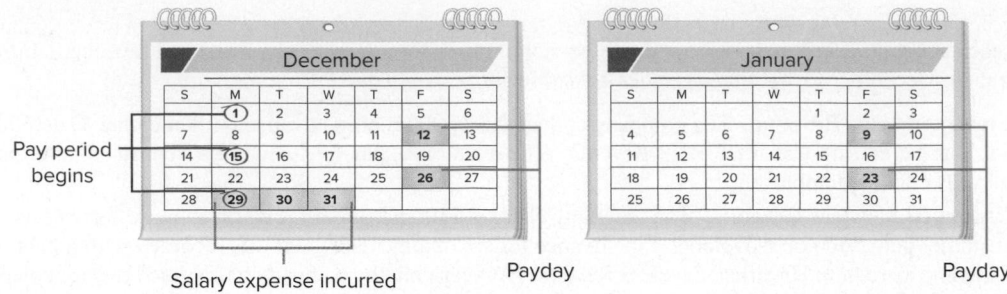

Pay period begins

Salary expense incurred   Payday   Payday

Step 3:   The adjusting entry for accrued salaries, along with T-account postings, follows.

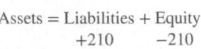
Assets = Liabilities + Equity
      +210   −210

Adjustment (e)		
Dec. 31 Salaries Expense	210	
Salaries Payable		210
Record three days' accrued salary (3 × $70).		

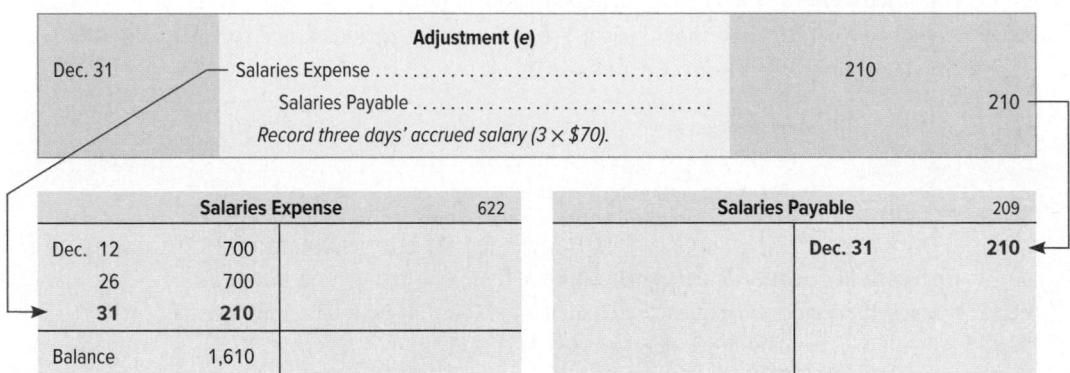

Salaries Expense		622
Dec. 12	700	
26	700	
31	210	
Balance	1,610	

Salaries Payable		209
	Dec. 31	210

Explanation   Salaries expense of $1,610 is reported on the December income statement, and $210 of salaries payable (liability) is reported in the balance sheet. *Not* making the adjustment

* Understates salaries expense by $210 in the December income statement.
* Understates salaries payable by $210 on the December 31 balance sheet.

The following highlights the adjustment for salaries incurred.

Before Adjustment	Adjustment	After Adjustment
Salaries Payable = $0	**Add $210 to Salaries Payable** **Add $210 to Salaries Expense**	**Salaries Payable = $210**
Reports $0 from employee salaries incurred but not yet paid in cash.	Record 3 days' salaries owed, but not yet paid, at $70 per day.	Reports $210 salaries payable to employee but not yet paid.

Accrued Interest Expense

©Plus One Pix/Alamy Stock Photo

Point: Interest computations use a 360-day year, called the *bankers' rule*.

Companies accrue interest expense on notes payable (loans) and other long-term liabilities at the end of a period. Interest expense is incurred as time passes. Unless interest is paid on the last day of an accounting period, we need to adjust for interest expense incurred but not yet paid. This means we must accrue interest cost from the most recent payment date up to the end of the period. The formula for computing accrued interest is

Principal amount owed × Annual interest rate × Fraction of year since last payment

If a company has a $6,000 loan from a bank at 5% annual interest, then 30 days' accrued interest expense is $25—computed as $6,000 × 0.05 × 30/360. The adjusting entry debits Interest Expense for $25 and credits Interest Payable for $25.

Future Cash Payment of Accrued Expenses

Accrued expenses at the end of one accounting period result in *cash payment* in a *future period(s)*. Recall that FastForward recorded accrued salaries of $210. On January 9, the first payday of the next period, the following entry settles the accrued liability (salaries payable) and records salaries expense for seven days of work in January.

Jan. 9	Salaries Payable (3 days at $70 per day)	210	
	Salaries Expense (7 days at $70 per day)	490	
	Cash		700
	Paid two weeks' salary including three days accrued.		

Assets = Liabilities + Equity
−700   −210   −490

The $210 debit is the payment of the liability for the three days' salary accrued on December 31. The $490 debit records the salary for January's first seven working days (including the New Year's Day holiday) as an expense of the new accounting period. The $700 credit records the total amount of cash paid to the employee.

For each separate case below, follow the three-step process for adjusting the accrued expense account at December 31. *Assume no other adjusting entries are made during the year.*

a. Salaries Payable. At year-end, salaries expense of $5,000 has been incurred by the company but is not yet paid to employees.

b. Interest Payable. At its December 31 year-end, the company holds a mortgage payable that has incurred $1,000 in annual interest that is neither recorded nor paid. The company intends to pay the interest on January 3 of the next year.

NEED-TO-KNOW 3-3

Accrued Expenses

P3

Solution

a. Step 1: Salaries Payable equals $0 (before adjustment)

Step 2: Salaries Payable should equal $5,000 (not yet recorded)

Step 3: Adjusting entry to get from step 1 to step 2

Dec. 31	Salaries Expense	5,000	
	Salaries Payable		5,000
	Record employee salaries earned but not yet paid.		

b. Step 1: Interest Payable equals $0 (before adjustment)

Step 2: Interest Payable should equal $1,000 (not yet recorded)

Step 3: Adjusting entry to get from step 1 to step 2

Dec. 31	Interest Expense	1,000	
	Interest Payable		1,000
	Record interest incurred but not yet paid.		

Do More: QS 3-12, QS 3-13

ACCRUED REVENUE

Accrued revenues are revenues earned in a period that are both unrecorded and not yet received in cash (or other assets). An example is a technician who bills customers after the job is done. If one-third of a job is complete by the end of a period, then the technician must record one-third of the expected billing as revenue in that period—even though there is no billing or collection.

Framework   The adjusting entries for accrued revenues increase a revenue (income statement) account and increase an asset (balance sheet) account, as shown in Exhibit 3.11. Accrued revenues usually come from services, products, interest, and rent. We use service fees and interest to show how to adjust for accrued revenues.

P4 _____

Prepare adjusting entries for accrued revenues.

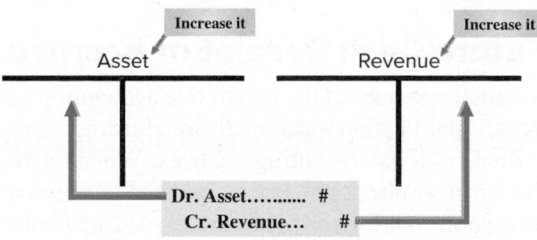

EXHIBIT 3.11

Adjusting for Accrued Revenues (increase an asset and record revenue)

Point: Accrued revenues are also called *accrued assets.*

Accrued Services Revenue

Accrued revenues are recorded when adjusting entries are made at the end of the accounting period. These accrued revenues are earned but unrecorded because either the buyer has not yet paid or the seller has not yet billed the buyer. FastForward provides an example.

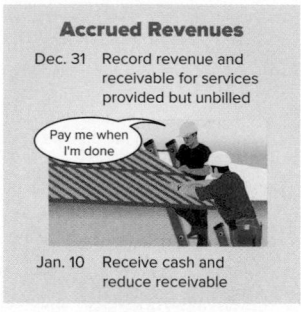

Accrued Revenues

Dec. 31   Record revenue and receivable for services provided but unbilled

Pay me when I'm done

Jan. 10   Receive cash and reduce receivable

Step 1:   In the second week of December, FastForward agreed to provide 30 days of consulting services to a fitness club for a fixed fee of $2,700 (or $90 per day). FastForward will provide services from December 12 through January 10, or 30 days of service. The club agrees to pay FastForward $2,700 on January 10 when the service is complete.

Step 2:   At December 31, 20 days of services have already been provided. Because the contracted services have not yet been entirely provided, FastForward has neither billed the club nor recorded the services already provided. Still, FastForward has earned two-thirds of the 30-day fee, or $1,800 ($2,700 × 20/30). The *revenue recognition principle* requires FastForward to report the $1,800 on the December income statement. The balance sheet reports that the club owes FastForward $1,800.

Step 3:   The adjusting entry for accrued services, along with T-account postings, follows.

Assets = Liabilities + Equity
+1,800   +1,800

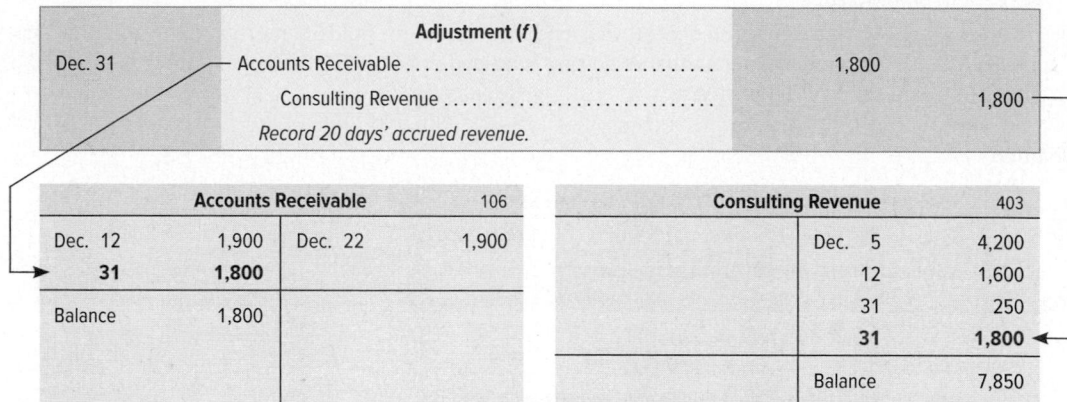

	Adjustment (*f*)	
Dec. 31	Accounts Receivable	1,800
	Consulting Revenue	1,800
	Record 20 days' accrued revenue.	

Accounts Receivable			106
Dec. 12	1,900	Dec. 22	1,900
31	**1,800**		
Balance	1,800		

Consulting Revenue		403
	Dec. 5	4,200
	12	1,600
	31	250
	31	**1,800**
	Balance	7,850

Example: What is the adjusting entry if the 30-day consulting period began on December 22? *Answer:* One-third of the fee is earned:
Accounts Receivable 900
  Consulting Revenue   900

Explanation   Accounts receivable are reported on the balance sheet at $1,800, and the $7,850 total of consulting revenue is reported on the income statement. *Not* making the adjustment

- Understates consulting revenue by $1,800 in the December income statement.
- Understates accounts receivable by $1,800 on the December 31 balance sheet.

The following highlights the adjustment for accrued revenue.

Before Adjustment	**Adjustment**	**After Adjustment**
Accounts Receivable = $0	Add $1,800 to Accounts Receivable Add $1,800 to Consulting Revenue	Accounts Receivable = $1,800
Reports $0 from revenue earned but not yet received in cash.	Record 20 days of earned revenue, which is 20/30 of total contract.	Reports $1,800 in accounts receivable from services provided.

Accrued Interest Revenue

If a company is holding notes receivable that produce interest revenue, we must adjust the accounts to record any earned and yet uncollected interest revenue. The adjusting entry is similar to the one for accruing services revenue. Specifically, debit Interest Receivable (asset) and credit Interest Revenue.

Future Cash Receipt of Accrued Revenues

Accrued revenues at the end of one accounting period result in *cash receipts* in a *future period(s)*. Recall that FastForward made an adjusting entry for $1,800 to record 20 days' accrued revenue earned from its consulting contract. When FastForward receives $2,700 cash on January 10 for the entire contract amount, it makes the following entry to remove the accrued asset (accounts receivable) and record revenue earned in January. The $2,700 debit is the cash received. The $1,800 credit is the removal of the receivable, and the $900 credit is revenue earned in January.

Jan. 10	Cash	2,700	
	Accounts Receivable (20 days at $90 per day)		1,800
	Consulting Revenue (10 days at $90 per day)		900
	Received cash for accrued asset and recorded earned		
	consulting revenue for January.		

Assets = Liabilities + Equity
+2,700   +900
−1,800

 Decision Maker

Loan Officer   The owner of a home theater store applies for a business loan. The store's financial statements reveal large increases in current-year revenues and income. Increases are due to a promotion that let consumers buy now and pay nothing until January 1 of next year. The store recorded these sales as accrued revenue. Does your analysis raise any concerns? ■   *Answer: While increased revenues and income are fine, your concern is with collectibility of these promotional sales. If the store sold products to customers with poor records of paying bills, then collectibility of these sales is low. Your analysis must assess this possibility and estimate losses.*

©Yin Yang/Getty Images

For each separate case below, follow the three-step process for adjusting the accrued revenue account at December 31. *Assume no other adjusting entries are made during the year.*

a. **Accounts Receivable.** At year-end, the company has completed services of $1,000 for a client, but the client has not yet been billed for those services.

b. **Interest Receivable.**   At year-end, the company has earned, but not yet recorded, $500 of interest earned from its investments in government bonds.

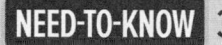 NEED-TO-KNOW **3-4**

Accrued Revenues

P4

Solution

a. Step 1: Accounts Receivable equals $0 (before adjustment)

Step 2: Accounts Receivable should equal $1,000 (not yet recorded)

Step 3: Adjusting entry to get from step 1 to step 2

Dec. 31	Accounts Receivable	1,000	
	Services Revenue		1,000
	Record services revenue earned but not yet received.		

b. Step 1: Interest Receivable equals $0 (before adjustment)

Step 2: Interest Receivable should equal $500 (not yet recorded)

Step 3: Adjusting entry to get from step 1 to step 2

Dec. 31	Interest Receivable	500	
	Interest Revenue		500
	Record interest earned but not yet received.		

Do More: QS 3-3, QS 3-14

Links to Financial Statements

Exhibit 3.12 summarizes the four adjustments. Each adjusting entry affects one or more income statement (revenue or expense) accounts *and* one or more balance sheet (asset or liability) accounts, but never the Cash account.

EXHIBIT 3.12

Summary of Adjustments and Financial Statement Links

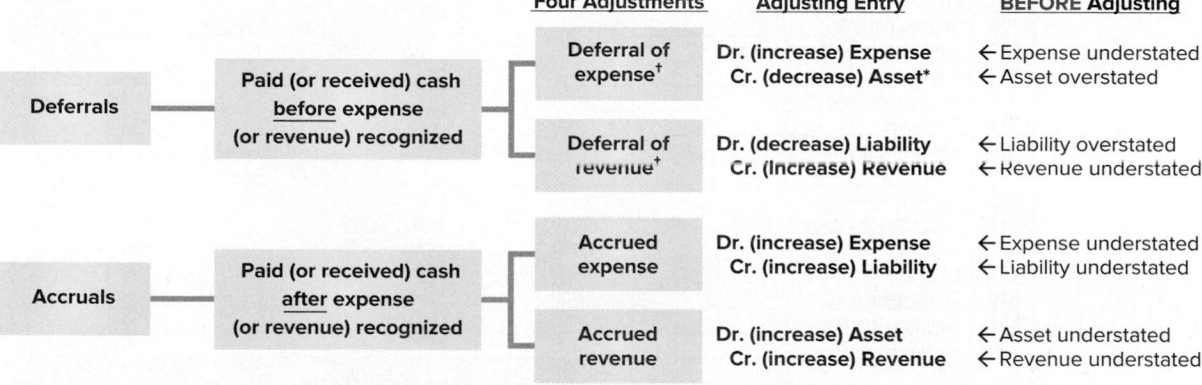

		Four Adjustments	Adjusting Entry	BEFORE Adjusting
Deferrals	**Paid (or received) cash before expense (or revenue) recognized**	Deferral of expense†	Dr. (increase) Expense Cr. (decrease) Asset*	← Expense understated ← Asset overstated
		Deferral of revenue†	Dr. (decrease) Liability Cr. (increase) Revenue	← Liability overstated ← Revenue understated
Accruals	**Paid (or received) cash after expense (or revenue) recognized**	Accrued expense	Dr. (increase) Expense Cr. (increase) Liability	← Expense understated ← Liability understated
		Accrued revenue	Dr. (increase) Asset Cr. (increase) Revenue	← Asset understated ← Revenue understated

*For depreciation, the credit is to Accumulated Depreciation (contra asset).
†Exhibit assumes that deferred expenses are initially recorded as assets and that deferred revenues are initially recorded as liabilities.

Information for some adjustments is not available until after the period-end. This means that some adjusting and closing entries are recorded later than, but dated as of, the last day of the period. One example is a company that receives a December utility bill on January 10. When it receives the bill, the company records the expense and the payable as of December 31. The income statement and balance sheet include these adjustments even though amounts were not known at period-end.

■ Decision Ethics

Financial Officer   At year-end, the president instructs you, the financial officer, not to record accrued expenses until next year because they will not be paid until then. The president also directs you to record in current-year sales a recent purchase order from a customer that requires merchandise to be delivered two weeks after the year-end. Your company would report a net income instead of a net loss if you follow these instructions. What do you do? ■   *Answer:* Omitting accrued expenses and recognizing revenue early mislead financial statement users. One action is to explain to the president what is required. If the president persists, you might talk to lawyers and any auditors involved.

TRIAL BALANCE AND FINANCIAL STATEMENTS

P5

Explain and prepare an adjusted trial balance.

Adjusted Trial Balance

An **unadjusted trial balance** is a list of accounts and balances *before* adjustments are recorded. An **adjusted trial balance** is a list of accounts and balances *after* adjusting entries have been recorded and posted to the ledger.

Exhibit 3.13 shows both the unadjusted and the adjusted trial balances for FastForward at December 31, 2019. The order of accounts in the trial balance usually matches the order in the chart of accounts. Several new accounts usually arise from adjusting entries.

Each adjustment (see middle columns) has a letter that links it to an adjusting entry explained earlier. Each amount in the Adjusted Trial Balance columns is computed by taking that account's amount from the Unadjusted Trial Balance columns and adding or subtracting any adjustment(s). To demonstrate, Supplies has a $9,720 Dr. balance in the unadjusted columns. Subtracting the $1,050 Cr. amount shown in the Adjustments columns equals an adjusted $8,670 Dr. balance for Supplies. An account can have more than one adjustment, such as for Consulting Revenue. Also, some accounts might not require adjustment for this period, such as Accounts Payable.

EXHIBIT 3.13

Unadjusted and Adjusted Trial Balances

*FAST*forward

FASTFORWARD
Trial Balances
December 31, 2019

Acct. No.	Account Title	Unadjusted Trial Balance Dr.	Unadjusted Trial Balance Cr.	Adjustments Dr.	Adjustments Cr.	Adjusted Trial Balance Dr.	Adjusted Trial Balance Cr.
101	Cash	$ 4,275				$ 4,275	
106	Accounts receivable	0		(f) $1,800		1,800	
126	Supplies	9,720			(b) $1,050	8,670	
128	Prepaid insurance	2,400			(a) 100	2,300	
167	Equipment	26,000				26,000	
168	Accumulated depreciation—Equip.		$ 0		(c) 300		$ 300
201	Accounts payable		6,200				6,200
209	Salaries payable		0		(e) 210		210
236	Unearned consulting revenue		3,000	(d) 250			2,750
307	Common stock		30,000				30,000
318	Retained earnings		0				0
319	Dividends	200				200	
403	Consulting revenue		5,800		(d) 250		7,850
					(f) 1,800		
406	Rental revenue		300				300
612	Depreciation expense—Equip.	0		(c) 300		300	
622	Salaries expense	1,400		(e) 210		1,610	
637	Insurance expense	0		(a) 100		100	
640	Rent expense	1,000				1,000	
652	Supplies expense	0		(b) 1,050		1,050	
690	Utilities expense	305				305	
	Totals	$45,300	$45,300	$3,710	$3,710	$47,610	$47,610

Preparing Financial Statements

We can prepare financial statements directly from information in the *adjusted* trial balance. Exhibit 3.14 shows how revenue and expense balances are transferred from the adjusted trial balance to the income statement (red lines). The net income and dividends amounts are then used to prepare the statement of retained earnings (black lines). Asset and liability balances are

P6

Prepare financial statements from an adjusted trial balance.

EXHIBIT 3.14

Preparing Financial Statements (Adjusted Trial Balance from Exhibit 3.13)

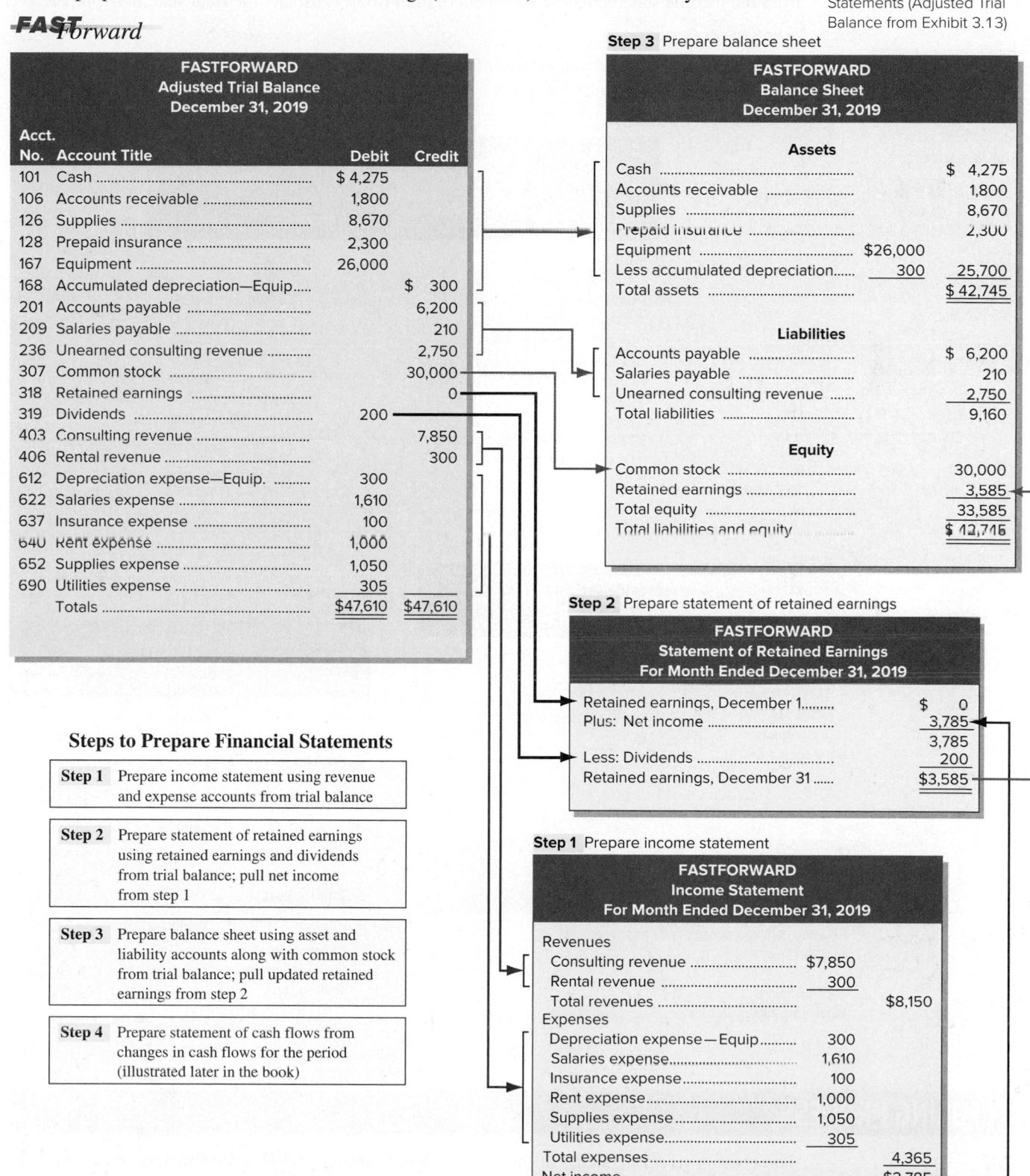

Steps to Prepare Financial Statements

Step 1	Prepare income statement using revenue and expense accounts from trial balance
Step 2	Prepare statement of retained earnings using retained earnings and dividends from trial balance; pull net income from step 1
Step 3	Prepare balance sheet using asset and liability accounts along with common stock from trial balance; pull updated retained earnings from step 2
Step 4	Prepare statement of cash flows from changes in cash flows for the period (illustrated later in the book)

then transferred to the balance sheet (blue lines). The ending retained earnings is computed in the statement of retained earnings and transferred to the balance sheet (green line).

We prepare financial statements in the following order: (1) income statement, (2) statement of retained earnings, and (3) balance sheet. This order makes sense because the balance sheet uses information from the statement of retained earnings, which in turn uses information from the income statement. The statement of cash flows is usually the final statement prepared.

Point: Each trial balance amount is used in only *one* financial statement.

NEED-TO-KNOW 3-5

Preparing Financial Statements from a Trial Balance

P6

Use the following adjusted trial balance of Magic Company to prepare its December 31 year-end (1) income statement, (2) statement of retained earnings, and (3) balance sheet (unclassified). The Retained Earnings account balance was $45,000 on December 31 of the *prior year*.

MAGIC COMPANY
Adjusted Trial Balance
December 31

Account Title	Debit	Credit
Cash	$ 13,000	
Accounts receivable	17,000	
Land	85,000	
Accounts payable		$ 12,000
Long-term notes payable		33,000
Common stock		30,000
Retained earnings		45,000
Dividends	20,000	
Fees earned		79,000
Salaries expense	56,000	
Office supplies expense	8,000	
Totals	$199,000	$199,000

Solution

Step 1

MAGIC COMPANY
Income Statement
For Year Ended December 31

Fees earned		$79,000
Expenses		
Salaries expense	$56,000	
Office supplies expense	8,000	
Total expenses		64,000
Net income		$15,000

Step 2

MAGIC COMPANY
Statement of Retained Earnings
For Year Ended December 31

Retained earnings, December 31 prior year-end	$45,000
Add: Net income	15,000
	60,000
Less: Dividends	20,000
Retained earnings, December 31 current year-end	$40,000

Do More: QS 3-22, E 3-8, P 3-4

Step 3

MAGIC COMPANY
Balance Sheet
December 31

Assets

Cash	$ 13,000
Accounts receivable	17,000
Land	85,000
Total assets	$115,000

Liabilities

Accounts payable	$ 12,000
Long-term notes payable	33,000
Total liabilities	45,000

Equity

Common stock	30,000
Retained earnings	40,000
Total equity	70,000
Total liabilities and equity	$115,000

CLOSING PROCESS

P7

Describe and prepare closing entries.

The **closing process** occurs at the end of an accounting period *after* financial statements are completed. In the closing process we (1) identify accounts for closing, (2) record and post the closing entries, and (3) prepare a post-closing trial balance. The closing process has two purposes. First, it resets revenue, expense, and dividends account balances to zero at the end of each period (which updates the Retained Earnings account for inclusion on the balance sheet). This is done so that these accounts can properly measure income and dividends for the next period. Second, it helps summarize a period's revenues and expenses. This section explains the closing process.

Temporary and Permanent Accounts

Temporary accounts relate to one accounting period. They include all income statement accounts, the dividends account, and the **Income Summary** account. They are temporary because the accounts are opened at the beginning of a period, used to record transactions and events for that period, and then closed at the end of the period. **The closing process applies only to temporary accounts.**

Temporary Accounts (closed at period-end)	Permanent Accounts (not closed at period-end)
Revenues	Assets
Expenses	Liabilities
Dividends	Common Stock
Income Summary	Retained Earnings

Permanent accounts report on activities related to one or more future accounting periods. They include asset, liability, and equity accounts (all balance sheet accounts). **Permanent accounts are not closed each period and carry their ending balance into future periods.**

Recording Closing Entries

Closing entries transfer the end-of-period balances in revenue, expense, and dividends accounts to the permanent Retained Earnings account. Closing entries are necessary at the end of each period after financial statements are prepared because

- Revenue, expense, and dividends accounts must begin each period with zero balances.
- Retained Earnings must reflect prior periods' revenues, expenses, and dividends.

An income statement reports revenues and expenses for a *specific accounting period*. Dividends are also for a specific accounting period. Because revenue, expense, and dividends accounts record information separately for each period, they must start each period with zero balances.

Exhibit 3.15 uses the adjusted account balances of FastForward (from the Adjusted Trial Balance columns of Exhibit 3.14 or from the left side of Exhibit 3.16) to show the four steps to close its temporary accounts.

① ② To close revenue and expense accounts, we transfer their balances to Income Summary. **Income Summary is a temporary account only used for the closing process** that contains a credit for total revenues (and gains) and a debit for total expenses (and losses).

Point: If **Apple** did not make closing entries, prior-year revenue from iPhone sales would be included with current-year revenue.

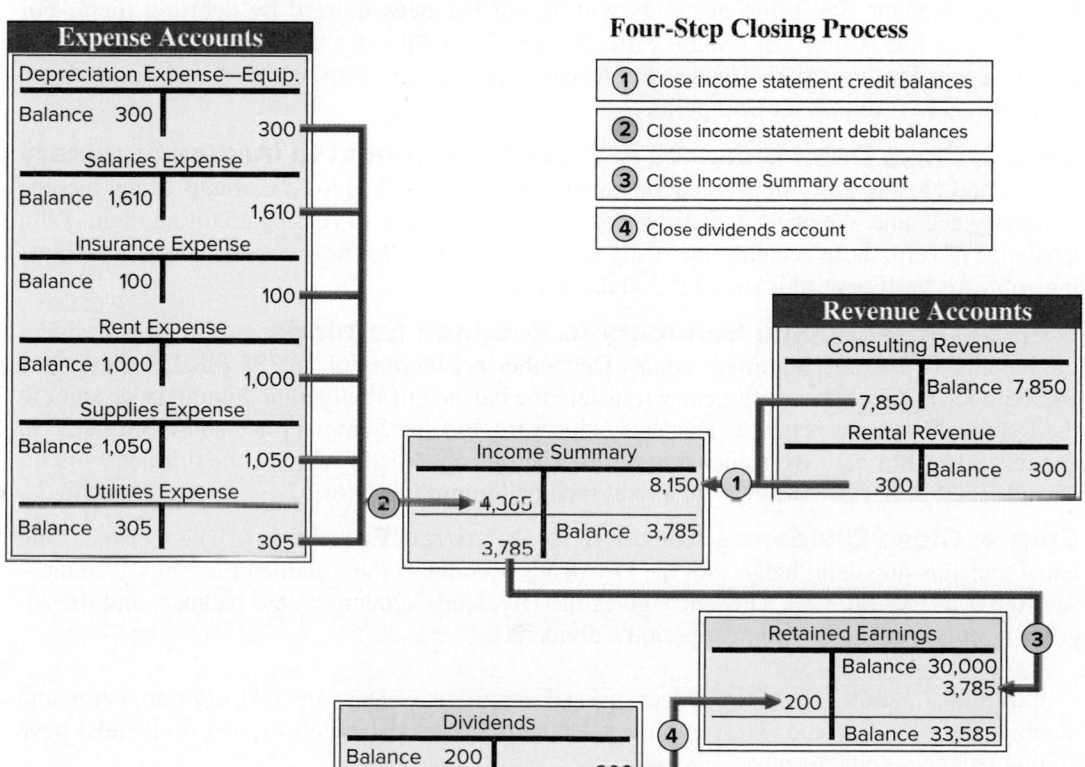

Four-Step Closing Process

① Close income statement credit balances
② Close income statement debit balances
③ Close Income Summary account
④ Close dividends account

EXHIBIT 3.15

Four-Step Closing Process

Point: Retained Earnings is the only *permanent account* in Exhibit 3.15—meaning it is not closed, but it does have Income Summary closed to it.

③ The Income Summary balance, which equals net income or net loss, is transferred to the Retained Earnings account.

④ The Dividends account balance is transferred to the Retained Earnings account. After closing entries are posted, the revenue, expense, dividends, and Income Summary accounts have zero balances and are said to be *closed* or *cleared*.

Exhibit 3.16 shows the four closing journal entries to apply the closing process of Exhibit 3.15.

EXHIBIT 3.16

Preparing Closing Entries

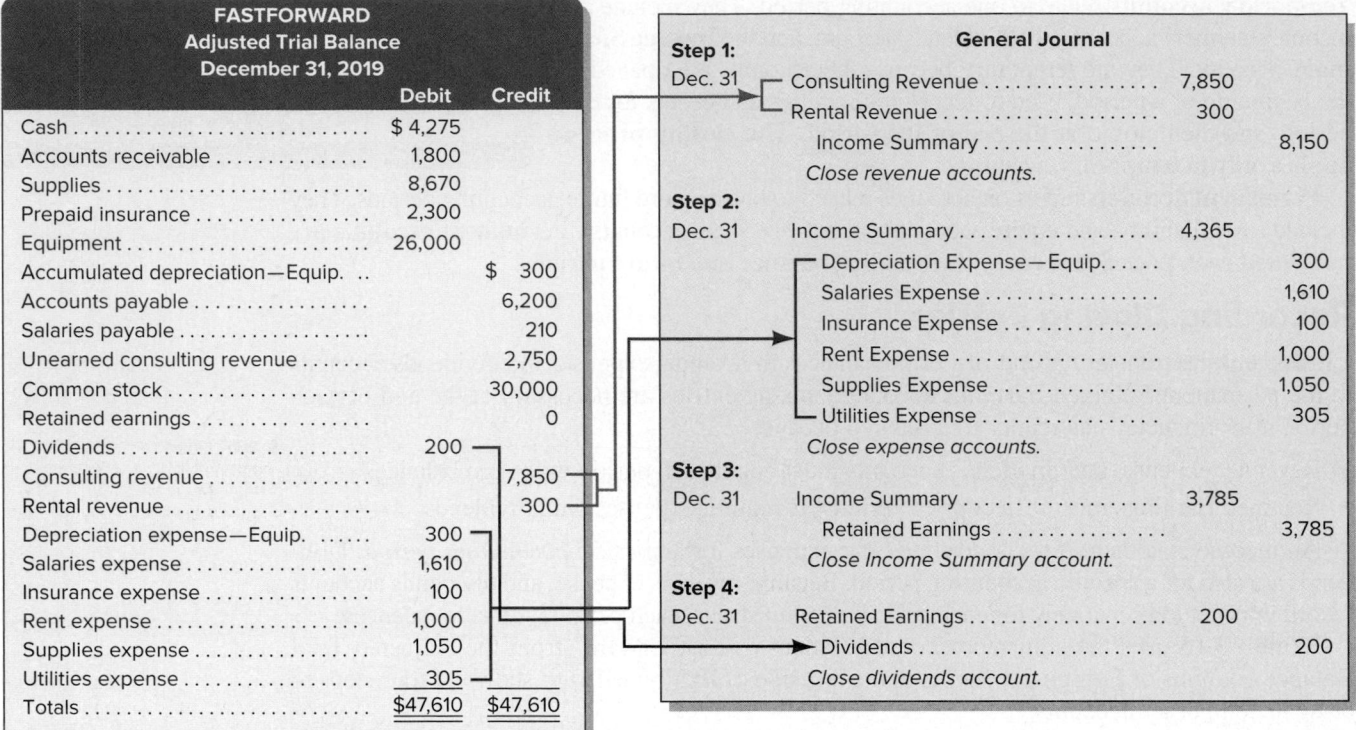

Step 1: Close Credit Balances in Revenue Accounts to Income Summary
The first closing entry transfers credit balances in revenue (and gain) accounts to the Income Summary account. We bring accounts with credit balances to zero by debiting them. For FastForward, this is step 1 in Exhibit 3.16. The $8,150 credit entry to Income Summary equals total revenues for the period. This leaves revenue accounts with zero balances, and they are now ready to record revenues for next period.

Step 2: Close Debit Balances in Expense Accounts to Income Summary
The second closing entry transfers debit balances in expense (and loss) accounts to the Income Summary account. We bring expense accounts' debit balances to zero by crediting them. With a balance of zero, these accounts are ready to record expenses for next period. This second closing entry for FastForward is step 2 in Exhibit 3.16.

Step 3: Close Income Summary to Retained Earnings   After steps 1 and 2, the balance of Income Summary equals December net income of $3,785 ($8,150 credit less $4,365 debit). The third closing entry transfers the balance of the Income Summary account to the Retained Earnings account. This entry closes the Income Summary account—see step 3 in Exhibit 3.16. (If a net loss occurred because expenses exceeded revenues, the third entry is reversed: debit Retained Earnings and credit Income Summary.)

Step 4: Close Dividends Account to Retained Earnings   The fourth closing entry transfers any debit balance in the Dividends account to the Retained Earnings account—see step 4 in Exhibit 3.16. This entry gives the Dividends account a zero balance, and the account is now ready to record next period's dividends.

Exhibit 3.17 shows the entire ledger of FastForward as of December 31 *after* adjusting and closing entries are posted. The temporary accounts (revenues, expenses, and dividends) have ending balances equal to zero.

EXHIBIT 3.17

General Ledger after the Closing Process for FastForward

Asset Accounts

Cash — Acct. No. 101

Date	Explan.	PR	Debit	Credit	Balance
2019					
Dec. 1	(1)	G1	30,000		30,000
2	(2)	G1		2,500	27,500
3	(3)	G1		26,000	1,500
5	(5)	G1	4,200		5,700
6	(13)	G1		2,400	3,300
12	(6)	G1		1,000	2,300
12	(7)	G1		700	1,600
22	(9)	G1	1,900		3,500
24	(10)	G1		900	2,600
24	(11)	G1		200	2,400
26	(12)	G1	3,000		5,400
26	(14)	G1		120	5,280
26	(15)	G1		305	4,975
26	(16)	G1		700	**4,275**

Accounts Receivable — Acct. No. 106

Date	Explan.	PR	Debit	Credit	Balance
2019					
Dec. 12	(8)	G1	1,900		1,900
22	(9)	G1		1,900	0
31	Adj.(f)	G1	1,800		**1,800**

Supplies — Acct. No. 126

Date	Explan.	PR	Debit	Credit	Balance
2019					
Dec. 2	(2)	G1	2,500		2,500
6	(4)	G1	7,100		9,600
26	(14)	G1	120		9,720
31	Adj.(b)	G1		1,050	**8,670**

Prepaid Insurance — Acct. No. 128

Date	Explan.	PR	Debit	Credit	Balance
2019					
Dec. 6	(13)	G1	2,400		2,400
31	Adj.(a)	G1		100	**2,300**

Equipment — Acct. No. 167

Date	Explan.	PR	Debit	Credit	Balance
2019					
Dec. 3	(3)	G1	26,000		**26,000**

Accumulated Depreciation—Equipment — Acct. No. 168

Date	Explan.	PR	Debit	Credit	Balance
2019					
Dec. 31	Adj.(c)	G1		300	300

Liability and Equity Accounts

Accounts Payable — Acct. No. 201

Date	Explan.	PR	Debit	Credit	Balance
2019					
Dec. 6	(4)	G1		7,100	7,100
24	(10)	G1	900		**6,200**

Salaries Payable — Acct. No. 209

Date	Explan.	PR	Debit	Credit	Balance
2019					
Dec. 31	Adj.(e)	G1		210	210

Unearned Consulting Revenue — Acct. No. 236

Date	Explan.	PR	Debit	Credit	Balance
2019					
Dec. 26	(12)	G1		3,000	3,000
31	Adj.(d)	G1	250		2,750

Common Stock — Acct. No. 307

Date	Explan.	PR	Debit	Credit	Balance
2019					
Dec. 1	(1)	G1		30,000	30,000

Retained Earnings — Acct. No. 318

Date	Explan.	PR	Debit	Credit	Balance
2019					
Dec. 31	Clos.(3)	G1		3,785	3,785
31	Clos.(4)	G1	200		3,585

Dividends — Acct. No. 319

Date	Explan.	PR	Debit	Credit	Balance
2019					
Dec. 24	(11)	G1	200		200
31	Clos.(4)	G1		200	0

Revenue and Expense Accounts (Including Income Summary)

Consulting Revenue — Acct. No. 403

Date	Explan.	PR	Debit	Credit	Balance
2019					
Dec. 5	(5)	G1		4,200	4,200
12	(8)	G1		1,600	5,800
31	Adj.(d)	G1		250	6,050
31	Adj.(f)	G1		1,800	7,850
31	Clos.(1)	G1	7,850		0

Rental Revenue — Acct. No. 406

Date	Explan.	PR	Debit	Credit	Balance
2019					
Dec. 12	(8)	G1		300	**300**
31	Clos.(1)	G1	300		0

Depreciation Expense—Equipment — Acct. No. 612

Date	Explan.	PR	Debit	Credit	Balance
2019					
Dec. 31	Adj.(c)	G1	300		300
31	Clos.(2)	G1		300	0

Salaries Expense — Acct. No. 622

Date	Explan.	PR	Debit	Credit	Balance
2019					
Dec. 12	(7)	G1	700		700
26	(16)	G1	700		1,400
31	Adj.(e)	G1	210		1,610
31	Clos.(2)	G1		1,610	0

Insurance Expense — Acct. No. 637

Date	Explan.	PR	Debit	Credit	Balance
2019					
Dec. 31	Adj.(a)	G1	100		100
31	Clos.(2)	G1		100	0

Rent Expense — Acct. No. 640

Date	Explan.	PR	Debit	Credit	Balance
2019					
Dec. 12	(6)	G1	1,000		**1,000**
31	Clos.(2)	G1		1,000	0

Supplies Expense — Acct. No. 652

Date	Explan.	PR	Debit	Credit	Balance
2019					
Dec. 31	Adj.(b)	G1	1,050		1,050
31	Clos.(2)	G1		1,050	0

Utilities Expense — Acct. No. 690

Date	Explan.	PR	Debit	Credit	Balance
2019					
Dec. 26	(15)	G1	305		**305**
31	Clos.(2)	G1		305	0

Income Summary — Acct. No. 901

Date	Explan.	PR	Debit	Credit	Balance
2019					
Dec. 31	Clos.(1)	G1		8,150	8,150
31	Clos.(2)	G1	4,365		3,785
31	Clos.(3)	G1	3,785		0

Post-Closing Trial Balance

P8 _____

Explain and prepare a post-closing trial balance.

A **post-closing trial balance** is a list of permanent accounts and their balances after all closing entries. It lists the balances for all accounts not closed. A post-closing trial balance verifies that (1) total debits equal total credits for permanent accounts and (2) all temporary accounts have zero balances. FastForward's post-closing trial balance is in Exhibit 3.18 and often is the last step in the accounting process.

EXHIBIT 3.18

Post-Closing Trial Balance

Point: Only balance sheet (permanent) accounts are on a post-closing trial balance.

FASTFORWARD Post-Closing Trial Balance December 31, 2019	Debit	Credit
Cash	$ 4,275	
Accounts receivable	1,800	
Supplies	8,670	
Prepaid insurance	2,300	
Equipment	26,000	
Accumulated depreciation—Equipment		$ 300
Accounts payable		6,200
Salaries payable		210
Unearned consulting revenue		2,750
Common stock		30,000
Retained earnings		3,585
Totals	$43,045	$43,045

©IM_photo/Shutterstock

Decision Maker

Staff Accountant　A friend shows you the post-closing trial balance she is working on. You review the statement and see a line item for rent expense. How do you know that an error exists? ■ *Answer:* This error is apparent in a post-closing trial balance because Rent Expense is a temporary account. Post-closing trial balances only contain permanent accounts.

NEED-TO-KNOW 3-6

Closing Entries

P7

Do More: QS 3-18, E 3-9, E 3-10

Use the adjusted trial balance solution for Magic Company from Need-to-Know 3-5 to prepare its closing entries—the accounts are also listed here for convenience.

Cash	$13,000 Dr.	Retained earnings	$45,000 Cr.
Accounts receivable	17,000 Dr.	Dividends	20,000 Dr.
Land	85,000 Dr.	Fees earned	79,000 Cr.
Accounts payable	12,000 Cr.	Salaries expense	56,000 Dr.
Long-term notes payable	33,000 Cr.	Office supplies expense	8,000 Dr.
Common stock	30,000 Cr.		

Solution

Dec. 31	Fees Earned	79,000	
	Income Summary		79,000
	Close revenue account.		
Dec. 31	Income Summary	64,000	
	Salaries Expense		56,000
	Office Supplies Expense		8,000
	Close expense accounts.		

Dec. 31	Income Summary	15,000	
	Retained Earnings		15,000
	Close Income Summary.		
Dec. 31	Retained Earnings	20,000	
	Dividends		20,000
	Close Dividends account.		

ACCOUNTING CYCLE

C2 _____

Identify steps in the accounting cycle.

The **accounting cycle** is the steps in preparing financial statements. It is called a *cycle* because the steps are repeated each reporting period. Exhibit 3.19 shows the 10 steps in the cycle. Steps 1 through 3 occur regularly as a company enters into transactions. Steps 4 through 9 are done at the end of a period. *Reversing entries* in step 10 are optional and are explained in Appendix 3C.

EXHIBIT 3.19

Steps in the Accounting Cycle*

1. Analyze transactions

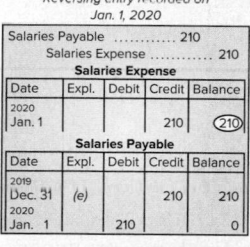

	Assets			= Liabilities	+ Equity
	Cash +	Supplies +	Equipment =	Accounts Payable	+ Common Stock
Old Bal.	$1,500 +	$2,500 +	$26,000 =		$30,000
(4)	+	7,100		+$7,100	
New Bal.	$1,500 +	$9,600 +	$26,000 =	$7,100 +	$30,000

2. Journalize

Date	Account Titles and Explanation	PR	Debit	Credit
(4)	Supplies	126	7,100	
	Accounts Payable	201		7,100

3. Post

General Ledger

Supplies	126		Accounts Payable	201
(2) 2,500				(4) 7,100
(4) 7,100				

10. Reverse and post (optional)

Reversing entry recorded on Jan. 1, 2020

Salaries Payable 210
   Salaries Expense 210

Salaries Expense

Date	Expl.	Debit	Credit	Balance
2020 Jan. 1			210	(210)

Salaries Payable

Date	Expl.	Debit	Credit	Balance
2019 Dec. 31	(e)		210	210
2020 Jan. 1		210		0

Accounting Cycle

4. Prepare unadjusted trial balance

FASTFORWARD
Trial Balance
December 31, 2019

	Debit	Credit
Cash	$ 4,275	
Accounts receivable	0	
Supplies	9,720	
Prepaid insurance	2,400	
Equipment	26,000	
Accounts payable		$6,200
Unearned consulting revenue		3,000

5. Adjust and post accounts

Adjustment (b)

Dec. 31 — Supplies Expense 1,050
             Supplies 1,050
          Record supplies used.

Supplies Expense	652		Supplies		126
Dec. 31 1,050			Dec. 2 2,500	Dec. 31	1,050
			6 7,100		
			26 120		
			Balance 8,670		

9. Prepare post-closing trial balance

FASTFORWARD
Post-Closing Trial Balance
December 31, 2019

	Debit	Credit
Cash	$ 4,275	
Accounts receivable	1,800	
Supplies	8,670	
Prepaid insurance	2,300	
Equipment	26,000	
Accumulated depreciation—Equipment		$ 300
Accounts payable		6,200

8. Close accounts

Step 1:	General Journal		
Dec. 31	Consulting Revenue	7,850	
	Rental Revenue	300	
	Income Summary		8,150
	Close revenue accounts.		
Step 2:			
Dec. 31	Income Summary	4,365	
	Depreciation Expense—Equip.		300
	Salaries Expense		1,610
	Insurance Expense		100
	Rent Expense		1,000
	Supplies Expense		1,050
	Utilities Expense		305
	Close expense accounts.		

7. Prepare financial statements

FASTFORWARD
Statement of Retained Earnings
For Month Ended December 31, 2019

Retained earnings, December 1 ...
Plus ...

FASTFORWARD
Income Statement
For Month Ended December 31, 2019

Revenues
  Consulting revenue $7,850

FASTFORWARD
Balance Sheet
December 31, 2019

Assets

Cash	$ 4,275
Accounts receivable	1,800
Supplies	8,670
Prepaid insurance	2,300

6. Prepare adjusted trial balance

FASTFORWARD
Trial Balances
December 31, 2019

Acct. No.	Account Title	Unadjusted Trial Balance		Adjustments		Adjusted Trial Balance	
		Dr.	Cr.	Dr.	Cr.	Dr.	Cr.
101	Cash	$ 4,275				$ 4,275	
106	Accounts receivable	0		(f) $1,800		1,800	
126	Supplies	9,720			(b) $1,050	8,670	
128	Prepaid insurance	2,400			(a) 100	2,300	
167	Equipment	26,000				26,000	
168	Accumulated depreciation—Equip.		$ 0		(c) 300		$ 300
201	Accounts payable		6,200				6,200
209	Salaries payable		0		(e) 210		210

Explanations

1. Analyze transactions	Analyze transactions to prepare for journalizing.
2. Journalize	Record accounts, including debits and credits, in a journal.
3. Post	Transfer debits and credits from the journal to the ledger.
4. Prepare unadjusted trial balance	Summarize unadjusted ledger accounts and amounts.
5. Adjust and post	Record adjustments to bring account balances up to date; journalize and post adjustments.
6. Prepare adjusted trial balance	Summarize adjusted ledger accounts and amounts.
7. Prepare financial statements	Use adjusted trial balance to prepare financial statements.
8. Close accounts	Journalize and post entries to close temporary accounts.
9. Prepare post-closing trial balance	Test clerical accuracy of the closing procedures.
10. Reverse and post (optional step)	Reverse certain adjustments in the next period—optional step; see Appendix 3C.

* Steps 4, 6, and 9 can be done on a work sheet. A work sheet is useful in planning adjustments, but adjustments (step 5) must always be journalized and posted. Steps 3, 4, 6, and 9 are automatic with a computerized system.

CLASSIFIED BALANCE SHEET

This section describes a classified balance sheet. An **unclassified balance sheet** broadly groups accounts into assets, liabilities, and equity. One example is FastForward's balance sheet in Exhibit 3.14. A **classified balance sheet** organizes assets and liabilities into subgroups.

C3

Explain and prepare a classified balance sheet.

Classification Structure

A classified balance sheet typically contains the categories in Exhibit 3.20 (there is no required layout). An important classification is the separation between current and noncurrent for both

EXHIBIT 3.20

Typical Categories in a Classified Balance Sheet

Assets	Liabilities and Equity
Current assets	Current liabilities
Noncurrent assets	Noncurrent liabilities
Long-term investments	Equity
Plant assets	
Intangible assets	

assets and liabilities. Current items are expected to come due (either collected or owed) within one year or the company's operating cycle, whichever is longer. The **operating cycle** is the time span from when *cash is used* to acquire goods and services until *cash is received* from the sale of goods and services. Most operating cycles are less than one year, which means most companies use a one-year period to classify current and noncurrent items. To make it easy, assume an operating cycle of one year, unless we say otherwise.

A balance sheet lists current assets before noncurrent assets and current liabilities before noncurrent liabilities. Current assets and current liabilities are listed in order of how quickly they will be converted to, or paid in, cash.

Classification Categories

©Sean Sullivan/Getty Images

Point: Current is also called *short-term,* and noncurrent is also called *long-term.*

EXHIBIT 3.21

Example of a Classified Balance Sheet

The balance sheet for Snowboarding Components in Exhibit 3.21 shows the typical categories. Its assets are classified as either current or noncurrent. Its noncurrent assets include three main categories: long-term investments, plant assets, and intangible assets. Its liabilities are classified as either current or long-term. Not all companies use the same categories. **Jarden**, a producer of snowboards, reported a balance sheet with five asset classes: current assets; property, plant, and equipment; goodwill; intangibles; and other assets.

Current Assets   Current assets are cash and other resources that are expected to be sold, collected, or used within one year or the company's operating cycle, whichever is longer. Examples are cash, short-term investments, accounts receivable, short-term notes receivable, goods for sale (called *merchandise* or *inventory*), and prepaid expenses.

Long-Term Investments   **Long-term** (or *noncurrent*) **investments** include notes receivable and investments in stocks and bonds when they are expected to be held for more than the longer of one year or the operating cycle. Land held for future expansion is a long-term investment because it is *not* used in operations.

SNOWBOARDING COMPONENTS Balance Sheet January 31, 2019					
Assets			**Liabilities**		
Current assets			**Current liabilities**		
Cash..................................	$ 6,500		Accounts payable	$15,300	
Short-term investments	2,100		Wages payable	3,200	
Accounts receivable, net	4,400		Notes payable (due within one year)	3,000	
Merchandise inventory..................	27,500		Current portion of long-term liabilities........	7,500	
Prepaid expenses......................	2,400		Total current liabilities.....................		$ 29,000
Total current assets.....................		$ 42,900			
Long-term investments			**Long-term liabilities** (net of current portion).....		150,000
Notes receivable (due in three years)	1,500		Total liabilities..............................		179,000
Investments in stocks and bonds..........	18,000				
Land held for future expansion	48,000				
Total long-term investments..............		67,500			
Plant assets			**Equity**		
Equipment and buildings	203,200		Common stock.............................		50,000
Less accumulated depreciation	53,000		Retained earnings		114,800
Equipment and buildings, net		150,200	Total equity.................................		164,800
Land......................................		73,200			
Total plant assets		223,400			
Intangible assets		10,000			
Total assets		$343,800	Total liabilities and equity		$343,800

Plant Assets   Plant assets are tangible assets that are both *long-lived* and *used to produce or sell products and services*. Examples are equipment, machinery, buildings, and land that are used to produce or sell products and services.

Point: Plant assets are also called *fixed assets; property, plant and equipment (PP&E);* or *long-lived assets.*

Intangible Assets   **Intangible assets** are long-term assets that benefit business operations but lack physical form. Examples are patents, trademarks, copyrights, franchises, and goodwill. Their value comes from the privileges or rights granted to or held by the owner.

Current Liabilities   **Current liabilities** are liabilities due to be paid or settled within one year or the operating cycle, whichever is longer. They usually are settled by paying out cash. Current liabilities include accounts payable, notes payable, wages payable, taxes payable, interest payable, and unearned revenues. Also, any portion of a long-term liability due to be paid within one year or the operating cycle, whichever is longer, is a current liability. Unearned revenues are current liabilities when products or services are to be provided within one year or the operating cycle, whichever is longer.

Long-Term Liabilities   **Long-term liabilities** are liabilities *not* due within one year or the operating cycle, whichever is longer. Notes payable, mortgages payable, bonds payable, and lease obligations are common long-term liabilities. If a company has both short- and long-term items in each of these categories, they are commonly separated into two accounts in the ledger.

©Johannes Simon/Getty Images

Equity   Equity is the owner's claim on assets. For a corporation, this claim is reported in the equity section as common stock and retained earnings.

Point: Only assets and liabilities (not equity) are classified as current or noncurrent.

Use the following account balances for Magic Company from Need-To-Know 3-5 to prepare its classified balance sheet as of December 31.

NEED-TO-KNOW 3-7

Classified Balance Sheet

C3

Cash.	$13,000 Dr.	Retained earnings	$40,000 Cr.
Accounts receivable	17,000 Dr.	Dividends	20,000 Dr.
Land.	85,000 Dr.	Fees earned	79,000 Cr.
Accounts payable	12,000 Cr.	Salaries expense	56,000 Dr.
Long-term notes payable	33,000 Cr.	Office supplies expense	8,000 Dr.
Common stock	30,000 Cr.		

Solution

MAGIC COMPANY
Balance Sheet
December 31

Assets		Liabilities	
Current assets		Current liabilities	
Cash	$ 13,000	Accounts payable	$ 12,000
Accounts receivable	17,000	Total current liabilities	12,000
Total current assets	30,000	Long-term notes payable	33,000
Plant assets		Total liabilities	45,000
Land	85,000	**Equity**	
Total plant assets	85,000	Common stock	30,000
		Retained earnings	40,000
		Total equity	70,000
Total assets	$115,000	Total liabilities and equity	$115,000

Do More: QS 3-21, QS 3-23, E 3-12, P 3-7

Decision Analysis Profit Margin and Current Ratio

Profit Margin

A useful measure of a company's operating results is the ratio of its net income to net sales. This ratio is called **profit margin,** or *return on sales,* and is computed as in Exhibit 3.22. This ratio shows the percent of profit in each dollar of sales.

EXHIBIT 3.22

Profit Margin

A1
Compute profit margin and describe its use in analyzing company performance.

$$\text{Profit margin} = \frac{\text{Net income}}{\text{Net sales}}$$

Visa's profit margins are shown in Exhibit 3.23. Visa's profit margin is superior to **Mastercard**'s in each of the last three years. For Mastercard to improve its profit margin, it must either reduce expenses or increase revenues at a relatively greater amount than expenses.

EXHIBIT 3.23

Computation and Analysis using Profit Margin

Company	Figure ($ millions)	Current Year	1 Year Ago	2 Years Ago
Visa	Net income	$ 6,699	$ 5,991	$ 6,328
	Net sales	$18,358	$15,082	$13,880
	Profit margin	**36%**	**40%**	**46%**
Mastercard	Profit margin	31%	38%	39%

■ Decision Maker

CFO   Your health care equipment company consistently reports a 9% profit margin, which is similar to that of competitors. The treasurer argues that profit margin can be increased to 20% if the company cuts marketing expenses. Do you cut those expenses? ■   *Answer:* Cutting those expenses increases profit margin in the short run. However, over the long run, cutting such expenses can hurt current and future sales. You must explain that the company can cut the "fat" (expenses that do not create sales) but should be careful if cutting those that create sales.

Current Ratio

A2
Compute the current ratio and describe what it reveals about a company's financial condition.

An important use of financial statements is to help assess a company's ability to pay its debts in the near future. Such analysis affects decisions by suppliers when allowing a company to buy on credit. It also affects decisions by creditors when lending money to a company, including loan terms such as interest rate and due date. The **current ratio** is one measure of a company's ability to pay its short-term obligations. It is defined in Exhibit 3.24.

EXHIBIT 3.24

Current Ratio

$$\text{Current ratio} = \frac{\text{Current assets}}{\text{Current liabilities}}$$

Costco's current ratio for each of the last three years is in Exhibit 3.25. A current ratio of over 1.0 means that current obligations can be covered with current assets. For the recent two years, Costco's current ratio was slightly below 1.0. This means Costco could face challenges in covering current liabilities. Although Costco has a better ratio than **Walmart** in each of the last three years, management must continue to monitor current assets and liabilities.

EXHIBIT 3.25

Computation and Analysis using Current Ratio

Company	Figure ($ millions)	Current Year	1 Year Ago	2 Years Ago
Costco	Current assets..............	$17,317	$15,218	$16,779
	Current liabilities	$17,495	$15,575	$16,539
	Current ratio	**0.99**	**0.98**	**1.01**
Walmart	Current ratio	0.86	0.93	0.97

■ Decision Maker

Analyst   You are analyzing a dirt bike company's ability to meet upcoming loan payments. You compute its current ratio as 1.2. You find that a major portion of accounts receivable is due from one client who has not made any payments in the past 12 months. Removing this receivable from current assets lowers the current ratio to 0.7. What do you conclude? ■   *Answer:* A current ratio of 1.2 suggests that current assets are sufficient to cover current liabilities. Removing the past-due receivable reduces the current ratio to 0.7. You conclude that the company will have difficulty meeting its loan payments.

NEED-TO-KNOW 3-8

COMPREHENSIVE 1

Preparing Year-End
Accounting Adjustments

The following information relates to Fanning's Electronics on December 31, 2019. The company, which uses the calendar year as its annual reporting period, initially records prepaid and unearned items in balance sheet accounts (assets and liabilities, respectively).

a. The company's weekly payroll is $8,750, paid each Friday for a five-day workweek. Assume December 31, 2019, falls on a Monday, but the employees will not be paid their wages until Friday, January 4, 2020.

b. Eighteen months earlier, on July 1, 2018, the company purchased equipment that cost $20,000. Its useful life is predicted to be five years, at which time the equipment is expected to be worthless (zero salvage value).

c. On October 1, 2019, the company agreed to work on a new housing development. The company is paid $120,000 on October 1 in advance of future installation of similar alarm systems in 24 new homes. That amount was credited to the Unearned Services Revenue account. Between October 1 and December 31, work on 20 homes was completed.

d. On September 1, 2019, the company purchased a 12-month insurance policy for $1,800. The transaction was recorded with an $1,800 debit to Prepaid Insurance.

e. On December 29, 2019, the company completed a $7,000 service that has not been billed or recorded as of December 31, 2019.

Required

1. Prepare any necessary adjusting entries on December 31, 2019, in relation to transactions and events *a* through *e*.

2. Prepare T-accounts for the accounts affected by adjusting entries, and post the adjusting entries. Determine the adjusted balances for the Unearned Revenue and the Prepaid Insurance accounts.

3. Complete the following table and determine the amounts and effects of your adjusting entries on the year 2019 income statement and the December 31, 2019, balance sheet. Use up (down) arrows to indicate an increase (decrease) in the Effect columns.

Entry	Amount in the Entry	Effect on Net Income	Effect on Total Assets	Effect on Total Liabilities	Effect on Total Equity

PLANNING THE SOLUTION

- Analyze each situation to determine which accounts need to be updated with an adjustment.
- Calculate the amount of each adjustment and prepare the necessary journal entries.
- Show the amount of each adjustment in the designated accounts, determine the adjusted balance, and identify the balance sheet classification of the account.
- Determine each entry's effect on net income for the year and on total assets, total liabilities, and total equity at the end of the year.

SOLUTION

1. Adjusting journal entries.

(a) Dec. 31	Wages Expense	1,750	
	Wages Payable		1,750
	Accrue wages for last day of year ($8,750 × 1/5).		
(b) Dec. 31	Depreciation Expense—Equipment	4,000	
	Accumulated Depreciation—Equipment		4,000
	Record depreciation expense for year ($20,000/5 years = $4,000 per year).		
(c) Dec. 31	Unearned Services Revenue	100,000	
	Services Revenue		100,000
	Record revenue earned ($120,000 × 20/24).		
(d) Dec. 31	Insurance Expense	600	
	Prepaid Insurance		600
	Adjust for expired portion of insurance ($1,800 × 4/12).		
(e) Dec. 31	Accounts Receivable	7,000	
	Services Revenue		7,000
	Record services revenue earned.		

2. T-accounts for adjusting journal entries *a* through *e*.

Accounts Receivable			Wages Payable			Wages Expense		
(e)	7,000				(a)	1,750	(a)	1,750	

Prepaid Insurance			Unearned Services Revenue			Insurance Expense		
Unadj. Bal.	1,800				Unadj. Bal.	120,000	(d)	600	
		(d)	600	(c)	100,000				
Adj. Bal.	1,200				Adj. Bal.	20,000			

Accumulated Depreciation—Equipment			Services Revenue			Depreciation Expense—Equipment		
		(b)	4,000			(c)	100,000	(b)	4,000	
						(e)	7,000			
						Adj. Bal.	107,000			

3. Financial statement effects of adjusting journal entries.

Entry	Amount in the Entry	Effect on Net Income	Effect on Total Assets	Effect on Total Liabilities	Effect on Total Equity
a	$ 1,750	$ 1,750 ↓	No effect	$ 1,750 ↑	$ 1,750 ↓
b	4,000	4,000 ↓	$4,000 ↓	No effect	4,000 ↓
c	100,000	100,000 ↑	No effect	$100,000 ↓	100,000 ↑
d	600	600 ↓	$ 600 ↓	No effect	600 ↓
e	7,000	7,000 ↑	$7,000 ↑	No effect	7,000 ↑

NEED-TO-KNOW **3-9**

COMPREHENSIVE 2

Preparing Financial Statements from Adjusted Account Balances

Use the following year-end adjusted trial balance to answer questions 1–3.

CHOI COMPANY
Adjusted Trial Balance
December 31

	Debit	Credit
Cash	$ 3,050	
Accounts receivable	400	
Prepaid insurance	910	
Equipment	217,200	
Accumulated depreciation—Equipment		$ 29,100
Interest payable		4,480
Unearned rent		460
Long-term notes payable		150,000
Common stock..		10,000
Retained earnings		30,340
Dividends	21,000	
Rent earned		57,500
Wages expense	25,000	
Utilities expense	1,900	
Insurance expense	3,450	
Depreciation expense—Equipment	5,970	
Interest expense	3,000	
Totals	$281,880	$281,880

1. Prepare the annual income statement from the adjusted trial balance of Choi Company.

Answer:

CHOI COMPANY Income Statement For Year Ended December 31		
Revenues		
Rent earned		$57,500
Expenses		
Wages expense	$25,000	
Utilities expense	1,900	
Insurance expense	3,450	
Depreciation expense—Equipment	5,970	
Interest expense	3,000	
Total expenses		39,320
Net income		$18,180

2. Prepare a statement of retained earnings from the adjusted trial balance of Choi Company.

Answer:

CHOI COMPANY Statement of Retained Earnings For Year Ended December 31	
Retained earnings, December 31 prior year-end	$30,340
Plus: Net income	18,180
	48,520
Less: Dividends	21,000
Retained earnings, December 31 current year-end	$27,520

3. Prepare a balance sheet (unclassified) from the adjusted trial balance of Choi Company.

Answer:

CHOI COMPANY Balance Sheet December 31		
Assets		
Cash		$ 3,050
Accounts receivable		400
Prepaid insurance		910
Equipment	$217,200	
Less accumulated depreciation............	29,100	188,100
Total assets		$192,460
Liabilities		
Interest payable		$ 4,480
Unearned rent		460
Long-term notes payable		150,000
Total liabilities		154,940
Equity		
Common stock		10,000
Retained earnings......................		27,520
Total equity		37,520
Total liabilities and equity................		$192,460

Alternative Accounting for Prepayments 3A

This appendix explains alternative accounting for deferred expenses and deferred revenues.

RECORDING PREPAYMENT OF EXPENSES IN EXPENSE ACCOUNTS

An alternative method is to record *all* prepaid expenses with debits to expense accounts. If any prepaids remain unused or unexpired at the end of an accounting period, then adjusting entries transfer the cost of the unused portions from expense accounts to prepaid expense (asset) accounts. The financial statements are identical under either method, but the adjusting entries are different. To demonstrate the differences between these two methods, let's look at FastForward's cash payment on December 1 for 24 months of insurance coverage beginning on December 1. FastForward recorded that payment with a debit to an asset account, but it could have recorded a debit to an expense account. These alternatives are shown in Exhibit 3A.1.

Payment Recorded as Asset		
Dec. 1	Prepaid Insurance 2,400	
	Cash..............	2,400

Payment Recorded as Expense		
Dec. 1	Insurance Expense 2,400	
	Cash	2,400

EXHIBIT 3A.1

Alternative Initial Entries for Prepaid Expenses

At the end of its accounting period on December 31, insurance protection for one month has expired. This means $100 ($2,400/24) of insurance coverage expired and is an expense for December. The adjusting entry depends on how the original payment was recorded. This is shown in Exhibit 3A.2.

EXHIBIT 3A.2

Adjusting Entry for Prepaid Expenses for the Two Alternatives

Payment Recorded as Asset			Payment Recorded as Expense		
Dec. 31	Insurance Expense	100	Dec. 31	Prepaid Insurance	2,300
	Prepaid Insurance	100		Insurance Expense ..	2,300

When these entries are posted, we see in Exhibit 3A.3 that the two methods give identical results.

EXHIBIT 3A.3

Account Balances under Two Alternatives for Recording Prepaid Expenses

Payment Recorded as Asset				Payment Recorded as Expense			
Prepaid Insurance			128	**Prepaid Insurance**			128
Dec. 1	2,400	Dec. 31	100	Dec. 31	2,300		
Balance	2,300						

Insurance Expense			637	**Insurance Expense**			637
Dec. 31	100			Dec. 1	2,400	Dec. 31	2,300
				Balance	100		

RECORDING PREPAYMENT OF REVENUES IN REVENUE ACCOUNTS

An alternative method is to record *all* unearned revenues with credits to revenue accounts. If any revenues are unearned at the end of an accounting period, then adjusting entries transfer the unearned portions from revenue accounts to unearned revenue (liability) accounts. The adjusting entries are different for these two alternatives, but the financial statements are identical. To demonstrate the differences between these two methods, let's look at FastForward's December 26 receipt of $3,000 for consulting services covering the period December 27 to February 24. FastForward recorded this transaction with a credit to a liability account. The alternative is to record it with a credit to a revenue account, as shown in Exhibit 3A.4.

EXHIBIT 3A.4

Alternative Initial Entries for Unearned Revenues

Receipt Recorded as Liability			Receipt Recorded as Revenue		
Dec. 26	Cash	3,000	Dec. 26	Cash	3,000
	Unearned Consulting Revenue ...	3,000		Consulting Revenue ..	3,000

By the end of its accounting period on December 31, FastForward has earned $250 of this revenue. This means $250 of the liability has been satisfied. Depending on how the initial receipt is recorded, the adjusting entry is as shown in Exhibit 3A.5.

EXHIBIT 3A.5

Adjusting Entry for Unearned Revenues for the Two Alternatives

Receipt Recorded as Liability			Receipt Recorded as Revenue		
Dec. 31	Unearned Consulting Revenue .	250	Dec. 31	Consulting Revenue	2,750
	Consulting Revenue	250		Unearned Consulting Revenue ..	2,750

After adjusting entries are posted, the two alternatives give identical results, as shown in Exhibit 3A.6.

EXHIBIT 3A.6

Account Balances under Two Alternatives for Recording Unearned Revenues

Receipt Recorded as Liability				Receipt Recorded as Revenue			
Unearned Consulting Revenue			236	**Unearned Consulting Revenue**			236
Dec. 31	250	Dec. 26	3,000			Dec. 31	2,750
		Balance	2,750				

Consulting Revenue			403	**Consulting Revenue**			403
		Dec. 31	250	Dec. 31	2,750	Dec. 26	3,000
						Balance	250

Work Sheet as a Tool

3B

Benefits of a Work Sheet (Spreadsheet)
A **work sheet** is a document that is used internally by companies to help with adjusting and closing accounts and with preparing financial statements. It is an internal accounting aid and is not a substitute for journals, ledgers, or financial statements. A work sheet

P10

Prepare a work sheet and explain its usefulness.

- Helps in preparing financial statements.
- Reduces the risk of errors when working with many accounts and adjustments.
- Links accounts and adjustments to financial statements.
- Shows the effects of proposed or "what-if" transactions.

Use of a Work Sheet
When a work sheet is used to prepare financial statements, it is constructed at the end of a period before the adjusting process. The complete work sheet includes a list of the accounts, their balances and adjustments, and their sorting into financial statement columns. It provides two columns each for the unadjusted trial balance, the adjustments, the adjusted trial balance, the income statement, and the balance sheet. To describe and interpret the work sheet, we use the information from FastForward. Preparing the work sheet has five steps.

FAST*forward*

1 **Step 1. Enter Unadjusted Trial Balance**

Refer to Exhibit 3B.1—green section. The first step in preparing a work sheet is to list the title of every account and its account number that appears on its financial statements. This includes all accounts in the ledger plus any new ones from adjusting entries. The unadjusted balance for each account is then entered in the correct Debit or Credit column of the Unadjusted Trial Balance columns. The totals of these two columns must be equal. The light green section of Exhibit 3B.1 shows FastForward's work sheet after completing this first step (dark green rows show accounts that arise because of the adjustments). Sometimes an account can require more than one adjustment, such as for Consulting Revenue. The additional adjustment can be added to a blank line below (as in Exhibit 3B.1), squeezed on one line, or combined into one adjustment amount.

2 **Step 2. Enter Adjustments**

Exhibit 3B.1—yellow section. The second step is to enter adjustments in the Adjustments columns. The adjustments shown are the same ones shown in Exhibit 3.13. An identifying letter links the debit and credit of each adjustment. This is called *keying* the adjustments. After preparing a work sheet, **adjustments must still be entered in the journal and posted to the ledger.** The Adjustments columns provide the information for adjusting entries in the journal.

3 **Step 3. Prepare Adjusted Trial Balance**

Exhibit 3B.1—blue section. The adjusted trial balance is prepared by combining the adjustments with the unadjusted balances for each account. As an example, the Prepaid Insurance account has a $2,400 debit balance in the Unadjusted Trial Balance columns. This $2,400 debit is combined with the $100 credit in the Adjustments columns to give Prepaid Insurance a $2,300 debit in the Adjusted Trial Balance columns. The totals of the Adjusted Trial Balance columns confirm debits and credits are equal.

4 **Step 4. Sort Adjusted Trial Balance Amounts to Financial Statements**

Exhibit 3B.1—orange section. This step involves sorting account balances from the adjusted trial balance to their proper financial statement columns. Expenses go to the Income Statement Debit column and revenues to the Income Statement Credit column. Assets and dividends go to the Balance Sheet Debit column. Liabilities, retained earnings, and common stock go to the Balance Sheet Credit column.

5 **Step 5. Total Statement Columns, Compute Income or Loss, and Balance Columns**

Exhibit 3B.1—purple section. Each financial statement column (from step 4) is totaled. The difference between the Debit and Credit column totals of the Income Statement columns is net income or net loss. This occurs because revenues are entered in the Credit column and expenses in the Debit column. If the Credit total exceeds the Debit total, there is net income. If the Debit total exceeds the Credit total, there is a net loss. For FastForward, the Credit total exceeds the Debit total, giving a $3,785 net income.

EXHIBIT 3B.1

Work Sheet with Five-Step Process for Completion

FAST*forward*

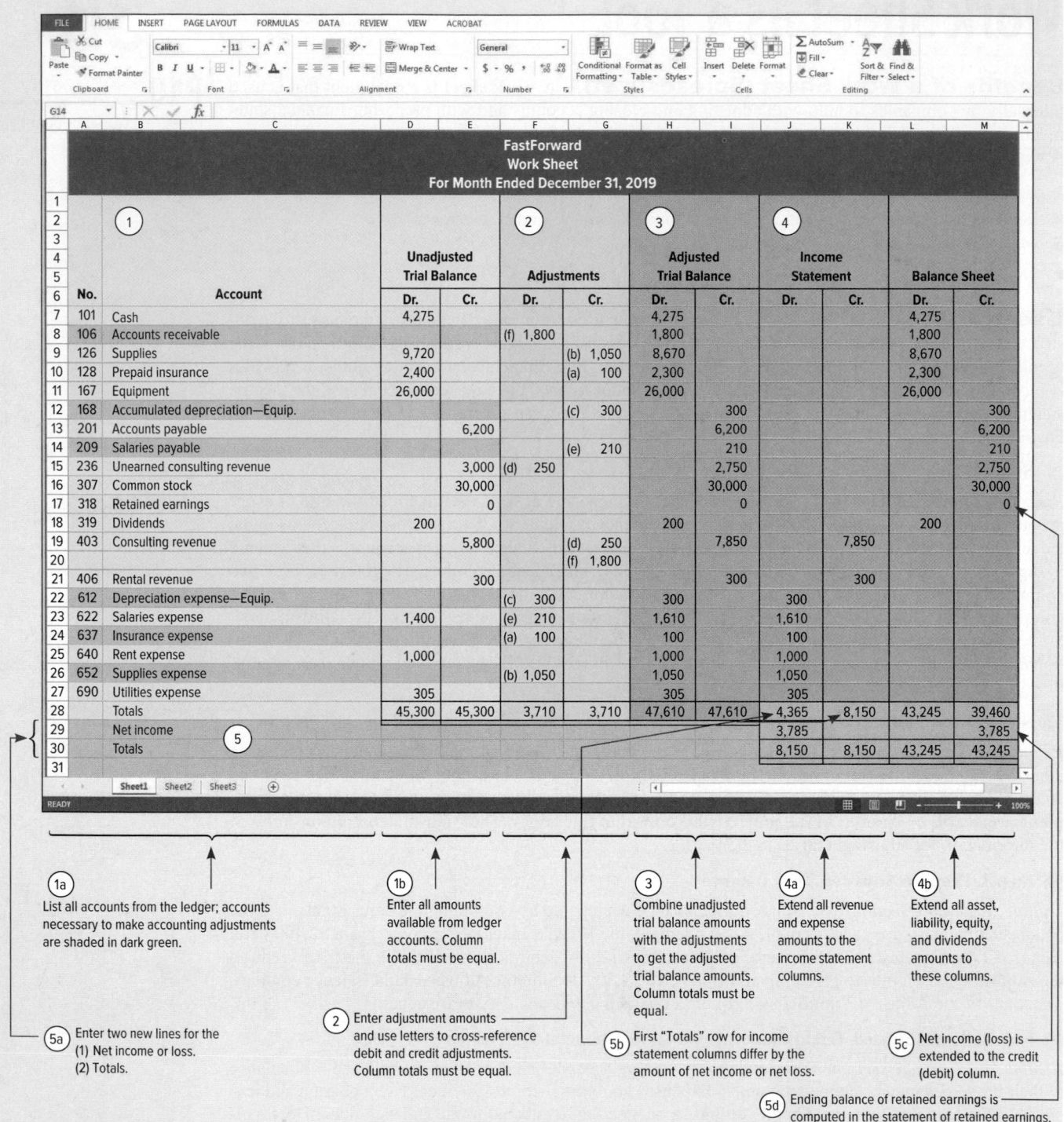

FastForward
Work Sheet
For Month Ended December 31, 2019

No.	Account	Unadjusted Trial Balance Dr.	Cr.	Adjustments Dr.	Cr.	Adjusted Trial Balance Dr.	Cr.	Income Statement Dr.	Cr.	Balance Sheet Dr.	Cr.
101	Cash	4,275				4,275				4,275	
106	Accounts receivable			(f) 1,800		1,800				1,800	
126	Supplies	9,720			(b) 1,050	8,670				8,670	
128	Prepaid insurance	2,400			(a) 100	2,300				2,300	
167	Equipment	26,000				26,000				26,000	
168	Accumulated depreciation—Equip.				(c) 300		300				300
201	Accounts payable		6,200				6,200				6,200
209	Salaries payable				(e) 210		210				210
236	Unearned consulting revenue		3,000	(d) 250			2,750				2,750
307	Common stock		30,000				30,000				30,000
318	Retained earnings		0				0				0
319	Dividends	200				200				200	
403	Consulting revenue		5,800		(d) 250		7,850		7,850		
					(f) 1,800						
406	Rental revenue		300				300		300		
612	Depreciation expense—Equip.			(c) 300		300		300			
622	Salaries expense	1,400		(e) 210		1,610		1,610			
637	Insurance expense			(a) 100		100		100			
640	Rent expense	1,000				1,000		1,000			
652	Supplies expense			(b) 1,050		1,050		1,050			
690	Utilities expense	305				305		305			
	Totals	45,300	45,300	3,710	3,710	47,610	47,610	4,365	8,150	43,245	39,460
	Net income							3,785			3,785
	Totals							8,150	8,150	43,245	43,245

1a List all accounts from the ledger; accounts necessary to make accounting adjustments are shaded in dark green.

1b Enter all amounts available from ledger accounts. Column totals must be equal.

3 Combine unadjusted trial balance amounts with the adjustments to get the adjusted trial balance amounts. Column totals must be equal.

4a Extend all revenue and expense amounts to the income statement columns.

4b Extend all asset, liability, equity, and dividends amounts to these columns.

5a Enter two new lines for the
(1) Net income or loss.
(2) Totals.

2 Enter adjustment amounts and use letters to cross-reference debit and credit adjustments. Column totals must be equal.

5b First "Totals" row for income statement columns differ by the amount of net income or net loss.

5c Net income (loss) is extended to the credit (debit) column.

5d Ending balance of retained earnings is computed in the statement of retained earnings.

A work sheet organizes information used to prepare adjusting entries, financial statements, and closing entries.

The net income from the Income Statement columns is then entered in the Balance Sheet Credit column. Adding net income to the last Credit column means that it is to be added to retained earnings. If a loss occurs, it is added to the Debit column. This means that it is to be subtracted from retained earnings. **The ending balance of retained earnings does not appear in the last two columns as a single amount, but it is computed in the statement of retained earnings** using these account balances. When net income or net loss is added to the proper Balance Sheet column, the totals of the last two columns must balance. If they do not, one or more errors have occurred.

Work Sheet Applications and Analysis A work sheet does not substitute for financial statements. It is a tool we use to help prepare financial statements. FastForward's financial statements are shown in Exhibit 3.14. Its income statement amounts are taken from the Income Statement columns of the work sheet. Amounts for its balance sheet and its statement of retained earnings are taken from the Balance Sheet columns of the work sheet.

Work sheets are also useful in analyzing the effects of proposed, or what-if, transactions. This is done by entering financial statement amounts in the Unadjusted (what-if) columns. Proposed transactions are then entered in the Adjustments columns. We then compute "adjusted" amounts from these proposed transactions. The extended amounts in the financial statement columns produce **pro forma financial statements** because they show the statements *as if* the proposed transactions had occurred.

APPENDIX

Reversing Entries

3C

P11
Prepare reversing entries and explain their purpose.

Reversing entries are optional. They are recorded in response to accrued assets and accrued liabilities that were created by adjusting entries at the end of a reporting period. Reversing entries simplify recordkeeping. Exhibit 3C.1 shows an example of FastForward's reversing entries. The top of the exhibit shows the adjusting entry FastForward recorded on December 31 for its employee's earned but unpaid salary. The entry recorded three days' salary of $210, which increased December's total salary expense to $1,610. The entry also recognized a liability of $210. The expense is reported on December's income statement. The expense account is then closed. The ledger on January 1, 2020, shows a $210 liability and a zero balance in the Salaries Expense account. At this point, the choice is made between using or not using reversing entries.

Accounting *without* Reversing Entries The path down the left side of Exhibit 3C.1 is described in the chapter. To summarize, when the next payday occurs on January 9, we record payment with a compound entry that debits both the expense and liability accounts and credits Cash. Posting that entry creates a $490 balance in the expense account and reduces the liability account balance to zero because the payable has been settled.

Accounting *with* Reversing Entries The right side of Exhibit 3C.1 shows reversing entries. A reversing entry is the exact opposite of an adjusting entry. For FastForward, the Salaries Payable liability account is debited for $210, meaning that this account now has a zero balance after the entry is posted on January 1. The Salaries Payable account temporarily understates the liability, but this is not a problem because financial statements are not prepared before the liability is settled on January 9. The credit to the Salaries Expense account is unusual because it gives the account an *abnormal credit balance*. We highlight an abnormal balance by circling it. Because of the reversing entry, the January 9 entry to record payment debits the Salaries Expense account and credits Cash for the full $700 paid. It is the same as all other entries made to record 10 days' salary for the employee. We see that after the payment entry is posted, the Salaries Expense account has a $490 balance that reflects seven days' salary of $70 per day (see the lower right side of Exhibit 3C.1). The zero balance in the Salaries Payable account is now correct. The lower section of Exhibit 3C.1 shows that the expense and liability accounts have exactly the same balances whether reversing entries are used or not.

Point: Adjusting entries that create new asset or liability accounts likely require reversing.

EXHIBIT 3C.1

Reversing Entries for an
Accrued Expense

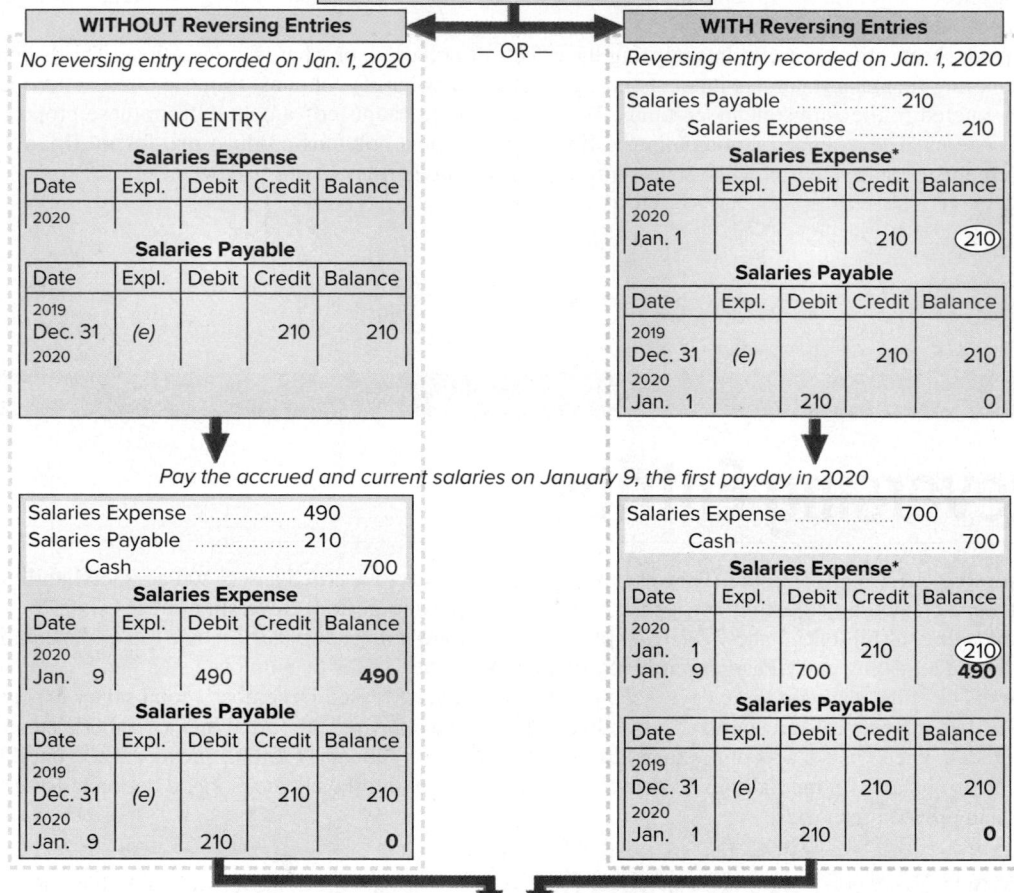

Accrue salaries expense on December 31, 2019

| Salaries Expense | | 210 | | |
| Salaries Payable | | | 210 | |

Salaries Expense

Date	Expl.	Debit	Credit	Balance
2019				
Dec. 12	(7)	700		700
26	(16)	700		1,400
31	(e)	210		1,610

Salaries Payable

Date	Expl.	Debit	Credit	Balance
2019				
Dec. 31	(e)		210	210

WITHOUT Reversing Entries

No reversing entry recorded on Jan. 1, 2020

— OR —

NO ENTRY

Salaries Expense

Date	Expl.	Debit	Credit	Balance
2020				

Salaries Payable

Date	Expl.	Debit	Credit	Balance
2019				
Dec. 31	(e)		210	210
2020				

WITH Reversing Entries

Reversing entry recorded on Jan. 1, 2020

| Salaries Payable | | 210 | | |
| Salaries Expense | | | 210 | |

Salaries Expense*

Date	Expl.	Debit	Credit	Balance
2020				
Jan. 1			210	(210)

Salaries Payable

Date	Expl.	Debit	Credit	Balance
2019				
Dec. 31	(e)		210	210
2020				
Jan. 1		210		0

Pay the accrued and current salaries on January 9, the first payday in 2020

Salaries Expense		490		
Salaries Payable		210		
Cash			700	

Salaries Expense

Date	Expl.	Debit	Credit	Balance
2020				
Jan. 9		490		**490**

Salaries Payable

Date	Expl.	Debit	Credit	Balance
2019				
Dec. 31	(e)		210	210
2020				
Jan. 9		210		0

| Salaries Expense | | 700 | | |
| Cash | | | 700 | |

Salaries Expense*

Date	Expl.	Debit	Credit	Balance
2020				
Jan. 1			210	(210)
Jan. 9		700		**490**

Salaries Payable

Date	Expl.	Debit	Credit	Balance
2019				
Dec. 31	(e)		210	210
2020				
Jan. 1		210		**0**

Under both approaches, the expense and liability accounts have
identical balances after the cash payment on January 9.

| Salaries Expense | | $490 |
| Salaries Payable | | $ 0 |

*Circled numbers in the *Balance* column indicate abnormal balances.

Summary: Cheat Sheet

DEFERRAL OF EXPENSE

Prepaid expenses: Assets paid for in advance of receiving their benefits.
When these assets are used, the advance payments become expenses.

Prepaid insurance expires:

| Insurance Expense | 100 | |
| Prepaid Insurance | | 100 |

Supplies are used up:

| Supplies Expense | 1,050 | |
| Supplies | | 1,050 |

Accumulated depreciation: A separate contra account. A **contra account**
is an account linked with another account. It has an opposite normal balance and is a subtraction from that other account's balance.

Depreciation of assets:

| Depreciation Expense | 300 | |
| Accumulated Depreciation—Equipment | | 300 |

DEFERRAL OF REVENUE

Unearned revenue: Cash received in advance of providing products and services. When cash is accepted, the company has a liability to provide products or services.

Record unearned revenue (cash received in advance):

Cash	3,000	
Unearned Consulting Revenue..............		3,000

Reduce unearned revenue (products or services are provided):

Unearned Consulting Revenue	250	
Consulting Revenue		250

ACCRUED EXPENSE

Accrued expenses: Costs incurred in a period that are both unpaid and unrecorded. They are reported on the income statement for the period when incurred.

Salaries expense owed but not yet paid:

Salaries Expense	210	
Salaries Payable		210

Accrued interest formula:

Principal amount owed × Annual interest rate × Fraction of year since last payment

Payment of accrued expenses:

Salaries Payable (3 days at $70 per day)	210	
Salaries Expense (7 days at $70 per day)	490	
Cash		700

ACCRUED REVENUE

Accrued revenues: Revenues earned in a period that are both unrecorded and not yet received in cash.

Revenue earned but not received in cash:

Accounts Receivable	1,800	
Consulting Revenue		1,800

Receipt of accrued revenue:

Cash	2,700	
Accounts Receivable (20 days at $90 per day) ...		1,800
Consulting Revenue (10 days at $90 per day) ...		900

REPORTING AND ANALYSIS

Unadjusted trial balance: A list of ledger accounts and balances *before* adjustments are recorded.

Adjusted trial balance: A list of accounts and balances *after* adjusting entries have been recorded and posted to the ledger.

Preparing financial statements from adjusted trial balance:

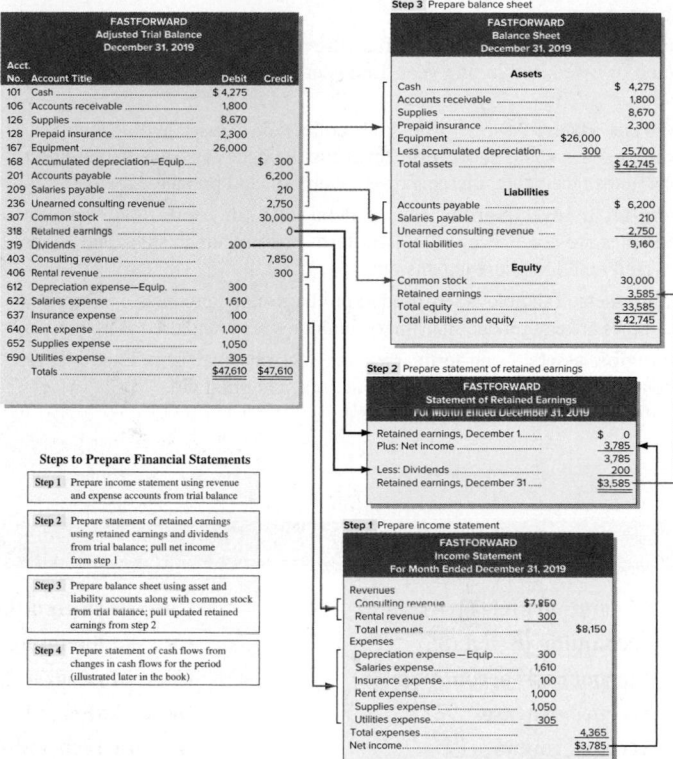

Steps to Prepare Financial Statements

Step 1 Prepare income statement using revenue and expense accounts from trial balance

Step 2 Prepare statement of retained earnings using retained earnings and dividends from trial balance; pull net income from step 1

Step 3 Prepare balance sheet using asset and liability accounts along with common stock from trial balance; pull updated retained earnings from step 2

Step 4 Prepare statement of cash flows from changes in cash flows for the period (illustrated later in the book)

CLOSING PROCESS

Closing process: Occurs at period-end after financial statements have been prepared. Resets revenue, expense, and dividends balances to zero.

Temporary accounts: Closed at period-end. They consist of revenue, expense, dividends, and Income Summary.

Permanent accounts: *Not* closed at period-end. They consist of asset, liability, common stock, and retained earnings (all balance sheet accounts).

Income Summary: A temporary account only used for the closing process that has a credit for total revenues and a debit for total expenses.

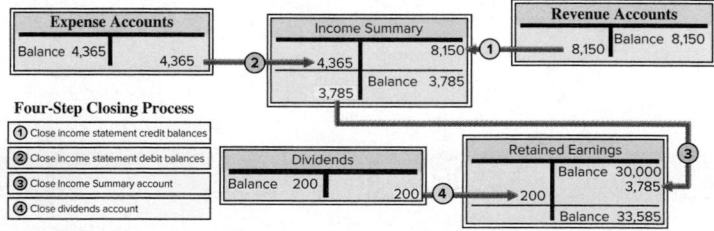

Closing Process Journal Entries by Step

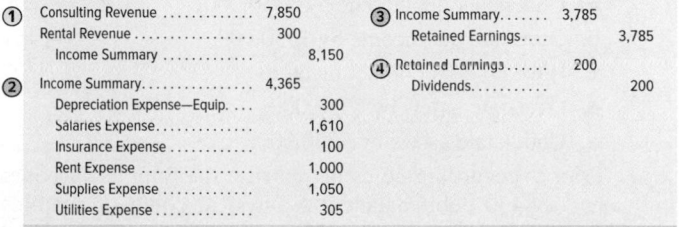

Post-closing trial balance: A list of permanent accounts (assets, liabilities, equity) and their balances after all closing entries.

CLASSIFIED BALANCE SHEET

Classified balance sheet: Organizes assets and liabilities into meaningful subgroups.

Current vs. long-term classification: Current items are to be collected or owed within one year. Long-term items are expected after one year.

Current assets: Assets to be sold, collected, or used within one year. Examples are cash, short-term investments, accounts receivable, short-term notes receivable, merchandise, inventory, and prepaid expenses.

Long-term investments: Assets to be held for more than one year. Examples are notes receivable, long-term investments in stock and bonds, and land held for future expansion.

Plant assets: Tangible assets used to produce or sell products and services. Examples are equipment, machinery, buildings, and land used in operations.

Intangible assets: Long-term assets that lack physical form. Examples are patents, trademarks, copyrights, franchises, and goodwill.

Current liabilities: Liabilities to be paid or settled within one year. Examples are accounts payable, wages payable, taxes payable, interest payable, unearned revenues, and current portions of notes or long-term debt.

Long-term liabilities: Liabilities not due within one year. Examples are notes payable, mortgages payable, bonds payable, and lease obligations.

Equity: The owner's claim on assets. For a corporation, this is common stock and retained earnings.

Common Layout of Classified Balance Sheet

Assets	Liabilities and Equity
Current assets	Current liabilities
Noncurrent assets	Noncurrent liabilities
Long-term investments	
Plant assets	Equity
Intangible assets	

Key Terms

Accounting cycle (104)
Accounting period (85)
Accrual basis accounting (86)
Accrued expenses (93)
Accrued revenues (95)
Accumulated depreciation (90)
Adjusted trial balance (98)
Adjusting entry (87)
Annual financial statements (85)
Book value (90)
Cash basis accounting (86)
Classified balance sheet (105)
Closing entries (101)
Closing process (100)
Contra account (90)

Current assets (106)
Current liabilities (107)
Current ratio (108)
Depreciation (89)
Expense recognition (or matching) principle (87)
Fiscal year (85)
Income Summary (101)
Intangible assets (107)
Interim financial statements (85)
Long-term investments (106)
Long-term liabilities (107)
Natural business year (86)
Operating cycle (106)
Permanent accounts (101)

Plant assets (89)
Post-closing trial balance (104)
Prepaid expenses (87)
Pro forma financial statements (115)
Profit margin (108)
Revenue recognition principle (87)
Reversing entries (115)
Straight-line depreciation (89)
Temporary accounts (101)
Time period assumption (85)
Unadjusted trial balance (98)
Unclassified balance sheet (105)
Unearned revenue (91)
Work sheet (113)

Multiple Choice Quiz

1. A company forgot to record accrued and unpaid employee wages of $350,000 at period-end. This oversight would
   a. Understate net income by $350,000.
   b. Overstate net income by $350,000.
   c. Have no effect on net income.
   d. Overstate assets by $350,000.
   e. Understate assets by $350,000.

2. Prior to recording adjusting entries, the Supplies account has a $450 debit balance. A physical count of supplies shows $125 of unused supplies still available. The required adjusting entry is

   a. Debit Supplies $125; credit Supplies Expense $125.
   b. Debit Supplies $325; credit Supplies Expense $325.
   c. Debit Supplies Expense $325; credit Supplies $325.
   d. Debit Supplies Expense $325; credit Supplies $125.
   e. Debit Supplies Expense $125; credit Supplies $125.

3. On May 1 of the current year, a two-year insurance policy was purchased for $24,000 with coverage to begin immediately. What is the amount of insurance expense that appears on the company's income statement for the current year ended December 31?

   a. $4,000   **c.** $12,000   **e.** $24,000
   b. $8,000   **d.** $20,000

4. On November 1, Stockton Co. receives $3,600 cash from Hans Co. for consulting services to be provided evenly over the period November 1 to April 30—at which time Stockton credits $3,600 to Unearned Consulting Fees. The adjusting entry on December 31 (Stockton's year-end) would include a

   a. Debit to Unearned Consulting Fees for $1,200.
   b. Debit to Unearned Consulting Fees for $2,400.
   c. Credit to Consulting Fees Earned for $2,400.
   d. Debit to Consulting Fees Earned for $1,200.
   e. Credit to Cash for $3,600.

5. The following information is available for a company before closing the accounts. After all of the closing entries are made, what will be the balance in the Retained Earnings account?

Total revenues ..	$300,000	Retained earnings ...	$100,000
Total expenses ..	195,000	Dividends	45,000

   a. $360,000   **d.** $150,000
   b. $250,000   **e.** $60,000
   c. $160,000

ANSWERS TO MULTIPLE CHOICE QUIZ

1. b; the forgotten adjusting entry is: *dr.* Wages Expense, *cr.* Wages Payable.

2. c; Supplies used = $450 − $125 = $325

3. b; Insurance expense = $24,000 × (8/24) = $8,000; adjusting entry is: *dr.* Insurance Expense for $8,000, *cr.* Prepaid Insurance for $8,000.

4. a; Consulting fees earned = $3,600 × (2/6) = $1,200; adjusting entry is: *dr.* Unearned Consulting Fees for $1,200, *cr.* Consulting Fees Earned for $1,200.

5. c; $100,000 + $300,000 − $195,000 − $45,000

$^{A(B,C)}$ *Superscript letter A, B, or C denotes assignments based on Appendix 3A, 3B, or 3C.*

[I] Icon denotes assignments that involve decision making.

Discussion Questions

1. What is the difference between the cash basis and the accrual basis of accounting?

2. [I] Why is the accrual basis of accounting generally preferred over the cash basis?

3. What type of business is most likely to select a fiscal year that corresponds to its natural business year instead of the calendar year?

4. What is a prepaid expense and where is it reported in the financial statements?

5. [I] What contra account is used when recording and reporting the effects of depreciation? Why is it used?

6. What is an accrued revenue? Give an example.

7. What are the steps in recording closing entries?

8. What is the purpose of the Income Summary account?

9. [I] Explain whether an error has occurred if a post-closing trial balance includes a Depreciation Expense account.

10. What is a company's operating cycle?

11. What classes of assets and liabilities are shown on a typical classified balance sheet?

12. How is unearned revenue classified on the balance sheet?

13.^{A} If a company initially records prepaid expenses with debits to expense accounts, what type of account is debited in the adjusting entries for those prepaid expenses?

14.^{C} If a company recorded accrued salaries expense of $500 at the end of its fiscal year, what reversing entry could be made? When would it be made?

15. [I] Refer to **Apple**'s most recent balance sheet in Appendix A. What five main noncurrent asset categories are used on its classified balance sheet? **APPLE**

16. [I] Refer to **Google**'s most recent balance sheet in Appendix A. Identify the six accounts listed as current liabilities. **GOOGLE**

17. [I] Review **Google**'s balance sheet in Appendix A. Identify the amount for property and equipment. What adjusting entry is necessary (no numbers required) for this account when preparing financial statements? **GOOGLE**

18. [I] Refer to **Samsung**'s financial statements in Appendix A. What journal entry was likely recorded as of December 31, 2017, to close its Income Summary account? **Samsung**

---

connect

Choose from the following list of terms and phrases to best complete the statements below.

a. Fiscal year   **c.** Accrual basis accounting   **e.** Cash basis accounting
b. Timeliness   **d.** Annual financial statements   **f.** Time period assumption

1. _____ presumes that an organization's activities can be divided into specific time periods.

2. Financial reports covering a one-year period are known as _____.

3. A(n) _____ consists of any 12 consecutive months.

4. _____ records revenues when services are provided and records expenses when incurred.

5. The value of information is often linked to its _____.

QUICK STUDY

QS 3-1
Periodic reporting

C1

QS 3-2

Computing accrual and cash income

C1

In its first year of operations, Roma Company reports the following.

• Earned revenues of $45,000 ($37,000 cash received from customers).
• Incurred expenses of $25,500 ($20,250 cash paid toward them).
• Prepaid $6,750 cash for costs that will not be expensed until next year.

Compute Roma's first-year net income under the cash basis *and* the accrual basis of accounting.

QS 3-3

Identifying accounting adjustments

P1   P2   P3   P4

Classify the following adjusting entries as involving prepaid expenses (PE), unearned revenues (UR), accrued expenses (AE), or accrued revenues (AR).

_____ **a.** To record revenue earned that was previously received as cash in advance.

_____ **b.** To record wages expense incurred but not yet paid (nor recorded).

_____ **c.** To record revenue earned but not yet billed (nor recorded).

_____ **d.** To record expiration of prepaid insurance.

_____ **e.** To record annual depreciation expense.

QS 3-4

Concepts of adjusting entries

P1   P2   P3   P4

During the year, a company recorded prepayments of expenses in asset accounts and cash receipts of unearned revenues in liability accounts. At the end of its annual accounting period, the company must make three adjusting entries.

(1) Accrue salaries expense. . . . .   Dr. ___ Cr. ___

(2) Adjust the Unearned Services Revenue account to recognize earned revenue. . . . . . .   Dr. ___ Cr. ___

(3) Record services revenue earned for which cash will be received the following period. . .   Dr. ___ Cr. ___

For each of the adjusting entries (1), (2), and (3), indicate the account to be debited and the account to be credited—from *a* through *i* below.

a. Prepaid Insurance	**d.** Unearned Services Revenue	**g.** Accounts Receivable
b. Cash	**e.** Salaries Expense	**h.** Accounts Payable
c. Salaries Payable	**f.** Services Revenue	**i.** Depreciation Expense

---

QS 3-5

Prepaid (deferred) expenses adjustments

P1

For each separate case below, follow the three-step process for adjusting the prepaid asset account at December 31. Step 1: Determine what the current account balance equals. Step 2: Determine what the current account balance should equal. Step 3: Record the December 31 adjusting entry to get from step 1 to step 2. *Assume no other adjusting entries are made during the year.*

a. Prepaid Insurance. The Prepaid Insurance account has a $4,700 debit balance to start the year. A review of insurance policies shows that $900 of unexpired insurance remains at year-end.

b. Prepaid Insurance. The Prepaid Insurance account has a $5,890 debit balance at the start of the year. A review of insurance policies shows $1,040 of insurance has expired by year-end.

c. Prepaid Rent. On September 1 of the current year, the company prepaid $24,000 for two years of rent for facilities being occupied that day. The company debited Prepaid Rent and credited Cash for $24,000.

QS 3-6

Prepaid (deferred) expenses adjustments

P1

For each separate case below, follow the three-step process for adjusting the Supplies asset account at December 31. Step 1: Determine what the current account balance equals. Step 2: Determine what the current account balance should equal. Step 3: Record the December 31 adjusting entry to get from step 1 to step 2. *Assume no other adjusting entries are made during the year.*

a. Supplies. The Supplies account has a $300 debit balance to start the year. No supplies were purchased during the current year. A December 31 physical count shows $110 of supplies remaining.

b. Supplies. The Supplies account has an $800 debit balance to start the year. Supplies of $2,100 were purchased during the current year and debited to the Supplies account. A December 31 physical count shows $650 of supplies remaining.

c. Supplies. The Supplies account has a $4,000 debit balance to start the year. During the current year, supplies of $9,400 were purchased and debited to the Supplies account. The inventory of supplies available at December 31 totaled $2,660.

QS 3-7

Adjusting prepaid (deferred) expenses

P1

For each separate case, record the necessary adjusting entry.

a. On July 1, Lopez Company paid $1,200 for six months of insurance coverage. No adjustments have been made to the Prepaid Insurance account, and it is now December 31. Prepare the year-end adjusting entry to reflect expiration of the insurance as of December 31.

b. Zim Company has a Supplies account balance of $5,000 at the beginning of the year. During the year, it purchases $2,000 of supplies. As of December 31, a physical count of supplies shows $800 of supplies available. Prepare the adjusting journal entry to correctly report the balance of the Supplies account and the Supplies Expense account as of December 31.

For each separate case below, follow the three-step process for adjusting the Accumulated Depreciation account at December 31. Step 1: Determine what the current account balance equals. Step 2: Determine what the current account balance should equal. Step 3: Record the December 31 adjusting entry to get from step 1 to step 2. *Assume no other adjusting entries are made during the year.*

a. Accumulated Depreciation. The Krug Company's Accumulated Depreciation account has a $13,500 balance to start the year. A review of depreciation schedules reveals that $14,600 of depreciation expense must be recorded for the year.

b. Accumulated Depreciation. The company has only one fixed asset (truck) that it purchased at the start of this year. That asset had cost $44,000, had an estimated life of five years, and is expected to have zero value at the end of the five years.

c. Accumulated Depreciation. The company has only one fixed asset (equipment) that it purchased at the start of this year. That asset had cost $32,000, had an estimated life of seven years, and is expected to be valued at $4,000 at the end of the seven years.

QS 3-8
Accumulated depreciation adjustments
P1

For each separate case, record an adjusting entry (if necessary).

a. Barga Company purchases $20,000 of equipment on January 1. The equipment is expected to last five years and be worth $2,000 at the end of that time. Prepare the entry to record one year's depreciation expense of $3,600 for the equipment as of December 31.

b. Welch Company purchases $10,000 of land on January 1. The land is expected to last forever. What depreciation adjustment, if any, should be made with respect to the Land account as of December 31?

QS 3-9
Adjusting for depreciation
P1

For each separate case below, follow the three-step process for adjusting the unearned revenue liability account at December 31. Step 1: Determine what the current account balance equals. Step 2: Determine what the current account balance should equal. Step 3: Record the December 31 adjusting entry to get from step 1 to step 2. *Assume no other adjusting entries are made during the year.*

a. Unearned Rent Revenue. The Krug Company collected $6,000 rent in advance on November 1, debiting Cash and crediting Unearned Rent Revenue. The tenant was paying 12 months' rent in advance and occupancy began November 1.

b. Unearned Services Revenue. The company charges $75 per insect treatment. A customer paid $300 on October 1 in advance for four treatments, which was recorded with a debit to Cash and a credit to Unearned Services Revenue. At year-end, the company has applied three treatments for the customer.

c. Unearned Rent Revenue. On September 1, a client paid the company $24,000 cash for six months of rent in advance (the client leased a building and took occupancy immediately). The company recorded the cash as Unearned Rent Revenue.

QS 3-10
Unearned (deferred) revenues adjustments
P2

For each separate case, record the necessary adjusting entry.

a. Tao Co. receives $10,000 cash in advance for four months of evenly planned legal services beginning on October 1. Tao records it by debiting Cash and crediting Unearned Revenue both for $10,000. It is now December 31, and Tao has provided legal services as planned. What adjusting entry should Tao make to account for the work performed from October 1 through December 31?

b. Caden started a new publication called *Contest News*. Its subscribers pay $24 to receive 12 monthly issues. With every new subscriber, Caden debits Cash and credits Unearned Subscription Revenue for the amounts received. The company has 100 new subscribers as of July 1. It sends *Contest News* to each of these subscribers every month from July through December. Assuming no changes in subscribers, prepare the year-end journal entry that Caden must make as of December 31 to adjust the Subscription Revenue account and the Unearned Subscription Revenue account.

QS 3-11
Adjusting for unearned (deferred) revenues
P2

For each separate case below, follow the three-step process for adjusting the accrued expense account at December 31. Step 1: Determine what the current account balance equals. Step 2: Determine what the current account balance should equal. Step 3: Record the December 31 adjusting entry to get from step 1 to step 2. *Assume no other adjusting entries are made during the year.*

a. Salaries Payable. At year-end, salaries expense of $15,500 has been incurred by the company but is not yet paid to employees.

QS 3-12
Accrued expenses adjustments
P3

[continued on next page]

b. Interest Payable. At its December 31 year-end, the company owes $250 of interest on a line-of-credit loan. That interest will not be paid until sometime in January of the next year.

c. Interest Payable. At its December 31 year-end, the company holds a mortgage payable that has incurred $875 in annual interest that is neither recorded nor paid. The company intends to pay the interest on January 7 of the next year.

QS 3-13

Accruing salaries

P3

Molly Mocha employs one college student every summer in her coffee shop. The student works the five weekdays and is paid on the following Monday. (For example, a student who works Monday through Friday, June 1 through June 5, is paid for that work on Monday, June 8.) The coffee shop adjusts its books *monthly*, if needed, to show salaries earned but unpaid at month-end. The student works the last week of July, which is Monday, July 28, through Friday, August 1. If the student earns $100 per day, what adjusting entry must the coffee shop make on July 31 to correctly record accrued salaries expense for July?

QS 3-14

Accrued revenues adjustments

P4

For each separate case below, follow the three-step process for adjusting the accrued revenue account at December 31. Step 1: Determine what the current account balance equals. Step 2: Determine what the current account balance should equal. Step 3: Record the December 31 adjusting entry to get from step 1 to step 2. *Assume no other adjusting entries are made during the year.*

a. Accounts Receivable. At year-end, the L. Cole Company has completed services of $19,000 for a client, but the client has not yet been billed for those services.

b. Interest Receivable. At year-end, the company has earned, but not yet recorded, $390 of interest earned from its investments in government bonds.

c. Accounts Receivable. A painting company bills customers when jobs are complete. The work for one job is now complete. The customer has not yet been billed for the $1,300 of work.

QS 3-15

Recording and analyzing adjusting entries

P1   P2   P3   P4

Adjusting entries affect at least one balance sheet account and at least one income statement account. For the entries below, identify the account to be debited and the account to be credited from the following accounts: Cash; Accounts Receivable; Prepaid Insurance; Equipment; Accumulated Depreciation; Wages Payable; Unearned Revenue; Revenue; Wages Expense; Insurance Expense; and Depreciation Expense. Indicate which of the accounts is the income statement account and which is the balance sheet account.

a. Entry to record revenue earned that was previously received as cash in advance.

b. Entry to record wage expenses incurred but not yet paid (nor recorded).

c. Entry to record revenue earned but not yet billed (nor recorded).

d. Entry to record expiration of prepaid insurance.

e. Entry to record annual depreciation expense.

QS 3-16

Determining effects of adjusting entries

P1   P3

In making adjusting entries at the end of its accounting period, Chao Consulting mistakenly forgot to record:

1. $3,200 of insurance coverage that had expired (this $3,200 cost had been initially debited to the Prepaid Insurance account).

2. $2,000 of accrued salaries expense.

As a result of these two oversights, the financial statements for the reporting period will [choose one]:

a. Understate assets by $3,200.   **c.** Understate net income by $2,000.

b. Understate expenses by $5,200.   **d.** Overstate liabilities by $2,000.

QS 3-17

Preparing an adjusted trial balance

P5

Following are unadjusted balances along with year-end adjustments for Quinlan Company. Complete the adjusted trial balance by entering the adjusted balance for each of the following accounts.

No.	Account Title	Unadjusted Trial Balance		Adjustments		Adjusted Trial Balance	
		Dr.	Cr.	Dr.	Cr.	Dr.	Cr.
101	Cash	$8,000					
106	Accounts receivable	2,000		$4,000			
126	Supplies	4,500			$2,500		
209	Salaries payable		$ 0		400		
307	Common stock		3,000				
318	Retained earnings		6,000				
403	Consulting revenue		11,000		4,000		
622	Salaries expense	5,500		400			
652	Supplies expense	0		2,500			

QS 3-18

Preparing closing entries from the ledger   **P7**

The ledger of Mai Company includes the following accounts with normal balances as of December 31: Common Stock $9,000; Dividends $800; Services Revenue $13,000; Wages Expense $8,400; and Rent Expense $1,600. Prepare its December 31 closing entries.

Identify which of the following accounts would be included in a post-closing trial balance.

_____ **a.** Accounts Receivable   _____ **c.** Goodwill   _____ **e.** Income Tax Expense

_____ **b.** Salaries Expense   _____ **d.** Land   _____ **f.** Salaries Payable

QS 3-19

Identifying post-closing accounts   **P8**

List the following steps of the accounting cycle in their proper order.

_____ **a.** Posting the journal entries.

_____ **b.** Journalizing and posting adjusting entries.

_____ **c.** Preparing the adjusted trial balance.

_____ **d.** Journalizing and posting closing entries.

_____ **e.** Analyzing transactions and events.

_____ **f.** Preparing the financial statements.

_____ **g.** Preparing the unadjusted trial balance.

_____ **h.** Journalizing transactions and events.

_____ **i.** Preparing the post-closing trial balance.

QS 3-20

Identifying the accounting cycle

C2

The following are common categories on a classified balance sheet.

A. Current assets   **C.** Plant assets   **E.** Current liabilities

B. Long-term investments   **D.** Intangible assets   **F.** Long-term liabilities

For each of the following items, select the letter that identifies the balance sheet category where the item typically would best appear.

_____ **1.** Land held for future expansion

_____ **2.** Notes payable (due in five years)

_____ **3.** Accounts receivable

_____ **4.** Trademarks

_____ **5.** Accounts payable

_____ **6.** Store equipment

_____ **7.** Wages payable

_____ **8.** Cash

QS 3-21

Classifying balance sheet items

C3

Use the following adjusted trial balance of Sierra Company to prepare its (1) income statement and (2) statement of retained earnings for the year ended December 31. The Retained Earnings account balance was $5,500 on December 31 of the *prior year*.

QS 3-22

Preparing financial statements

P6

Adjusted Trial Balance	Debit	Credit
Cash	$ 5,000	
Prepaid insurance	500	
Notes receivable (due in 5 years)	4,000	
Buildings	20,000	
Accumulated depreciation—Buildings		$12,000
Accounts payable		2,500
Notes payable (due in 3 years)		3,000
Common stock		5,000
Retained earnings		5,500
Dividends	1,000	
Consulting revenue		9,500
Wages expense	3,500	
Depreciation expense—Buildings	2,000	
Insurance expense	1,500	
Totals	$37,500	$37,500

Use the information in the adjusted trial balance reported in QS 3-22 to prepare Sierra Company's *classified* balance sheet as of December 31.

QS 3-23

Preparing a classified balance sheet   **C3**

Damita Company reported net income of $48,025 and net sales of $425,000 for the current year. Calculate the company's profit margin and interpret the result. Assume that its competitors earn an average profit margin of 15%.

QS 3-24

Analyzing profit margin

A1

Compute Chavez Company's current ratio using the following information.

QS 3-25

Identifying current accounts and computing the current ratio

A2

Accounts receivable............	$18,000	Long-term notes payable..............	$21,000
Accounts payable..............	11,000	Office supplies	2,800
Buildings.....................	45,000	Prepaid insurance....................	3,560
Cash.........................	7,000	Unearned services revenue	3,000

QS 3-26ᴬ
Preparing adjusting entries
P9

Garcia Company had the following selected transactions during the year. (A partial chart of accounts follows: Cash; Accounts Receivable; Prepaid Insurance; Wages Payable; Unearned Revenue; Revenue; Wages Expense; Insurance Expense; Depreciation Expense.)

Jan. 1   The company paid $6,000 cash for 12 months of insurance coverage beginning immediately.
Aug. 1   The company received $2,400 cash in advance for 6 months of contracted services beginning on August 1 and ending on January 31.
Dec. 31   The company prepared any necessary year-end adjusting entries related to insurance coverage and services performed.

a. Record journal entries for these transactions assuming Garcia follows the usual practice of recording a prepayment of an expense in an asset account *and* recording a prepayment of revenue received in a liability account.

b. Record journal entries for these transactions assuming Garcia follows the alternative practice of recording a prepayment of an expense in an expense account *and* recording a prepayment of revenue received in a revenue account.

QS 3-27ᴮ
Extending accounts in a
work sheet **P10**

The Adjusted Trial Balance columns of a 10-column work sheet for Planta Company follow. Complete the work sheet by extending the account balances into the appropriate financial statement columns and by entering the amount of net income for the reporting period.

No.	Account Title	Unadjusted Trial Balance		Adjustments		Adjusted Trial Balance		Income Statement		Balance Sheet	
		Dr.	Cr.	Dr.	Cr.	Dr.	Cr.	Dr.	Cr.	Dr.	Cr.
101	Cash					$ 7,000					
106	Accounts receivable					27,200					
153	Trucks					42,000					
154	Accumulated depreciation—Trucks						$ 17,500				
183	Land					32,000					
201	Accounts payable						15,000				
209	Salaries payable						4,200				
233	Unearned fees						3,600				
307	Common stock						20,000				
318	Retained earnings						45,500				
319	Dividends					15,400					
401	Plumbing fees earned						84,000				
611	Depreciation expense—Trucks					6,500					
622	Salaries expense					38,000					
640	Rent expense					13,000					
677	Miscellaneous expenses					8,700					
	Totals					$189,800	$189,800				
	Net income										
	Totals										

Check Net income, $17,800

QS 3-28ᶜ
Reversing entries
P11

On December 31, Yates Co. prepared an adjusting entry for $12,000 of earned but unrecorded consulting revenue. On January 16, Yates received $26,700 cash as payment in full for consulting work it provided that began on December 18 and ended on January 16. The company uses reversing entries.

a. Prepare the December 31 adjusting entry.   **c.** Prepare the January 16 cash receipt entry.

b. Prepare the January 1 reversing entry.

connect

EXERCISES

Exercise 3-1
Preparing adjusting entries
P1   P2   P3

Prepare adjusting journal entries for the year ended (date of) December 31 for each of these separate situations. Entries can draw from the following partial chart of accounts: Cash; Accounts Receivable; Supplies; Prepaid Insurance; Prepaid Rent; Equipment; Accumulated Depreciation—Equipment; Wages Payable; Unearned Revenue; Revenue; Wages Expense; Supplies Expense; Insurance Expense; Rent Expense; and Depreciation Expense—Equipment.

a. Depreciation on the company's equipment for the year is computed to be $18,000.

b. The Prepaid Insurance account had a $6,000 debit balance at December 31 before adjusting for the costs of any expired coverage. An analysis of the company's insurance policies showed that $1,100 of unexpired insurance coverage remains.

Check (c) Dr. Supplies
Expense, $3,880

c. The Supplies account had a $700 debit balance at the beginning of the year; and $3,480 of supplies were purchased during the year. The December 31 physical count showed $300 of supplies available.

d. Two-thirds of the work related to $15,000 of cash received in advance was performed this period.

e. The Prepaid Rent account had a $6,800 debit balance at December 31 before adjusting for the costs of expired prepaid rent. An analysis of the rental agreement showed that $5,800 of prepaid rent had expired.

f. Wage expenses of $3,200 have been incurred but are not paid as of December 31.

(e) Dr. Rent Expense, $5,800

Pablo Management has five employees, each of whom earns $250 per day. They are paid on Fridays for work completed Monday through Friday of the same week. Near year-end, the five employees worked Monday, December 31, and Wednesday through Friday, January 2, 3, and 4. New Year's Day (January 1) was an unpaid holiday.

a. Prepare the year-end adjusting entry for wages expense.

b. Prepare the journal entry to record payment of the employees' wages on Friday, January 4.

Exercise 3-2
Adjusting and paying accrued wages
P3

The following three *separate* situations require adjusting journal entries to prepare financial statements as of April 30. For each situation, present both:

• The April 30 adjusting entry.

• The subsequent entry during May to record payment of the accrued expenses.

Entries can draw from the following partial chart of accounts: Cash; Accounts Receivable; Salaries Payable; Interest Payable; Legal Services Payable; Unearned Revenue; Revenue; Salaries Expense; Interest Expense; Legal Services Expense; and Depreciation Expense.

a. On April 1, the company hired an attorney for a flat monthly fee of $3,500. Payment for April legal services was made by the company on May 12.

b. As of April 30, $3,000 of interest expense has accrued on a note payable. The full interest payment of $9,000 on the note is due on May 20.

c. Total weekly salaries expense for all employees is $10,000. This amount is paid at the end of the day on Friday of each five-day workweek. April 30 falls on a Tuesday, which means that the employees had worked two days since the last payday. The next payday is May 3.

Exercise 3-3
Adjusting and paying accrued expenses
P3

Check (b) May 20, Dr. Interest Expense, $6,000

For each of the following separate cases, prepare adjusting entries required of financial statements for the year ended (date of) December 31. Entries can draw from the following partial chart of accounts: Cash; Interest Receivable; Supplies; Prepaid Insurance; Equipment; Accumulated Depreciation—Equipment; Wages Payable; Interest Payable; Unearned Revenue; Interest Revenue; Wages Expense; Supplies Expense; Insurance Expense; Interest Expense; and Depreciation Expense—Equipment.

a. Wages of $8,000 are earned by workers but not paid as of December 31.

b. Depreciation on the company's equipment for the year is $18,000.

c. The Supplies account had a $240 debit balance at the beginning of the year. During the year, $5,200 of supplies are purchased. A physical count of supplies at December 31 shows $440 of supplies available.

d. The Prepaid Insurance account had a $4,000 balance at the beginning of the year. An analysis of insurance policies shows that $1,200 of unexpired insurance benefits remain at December 31.

e. The company has earned (but not recorded) $1,050 of interest revenue for the year ended December 31. The interest payment will be received 10 days after the year-end on January 10.

f. The company has a bank loan and has incurred (but not recorded) interest expense of $2,500 for the year ended December 31. The company will pay the interest five days after the year-end on January 5.

Exercise 3-4
Preparing adjusting entries
P1   P3   P4

Check (d) Dr. Insurance Expense, $2,800

(e) Cr. Interest Revenue, $1,050

Prepare year-end adjusting journal entries for M&R Company as of December 31 for each of the following separate cases. Entries can draw from the following partial chart of accounts: Cash; Accounts Receivable; Interest Receivable; Equipment; Wages Payable; Salary Payable; Interest Payable; Lawn Services Payable; Unearned Revenue; Revenue; Interest Revenue; Wages Expense; Salary Expense; Supplies Expense; Lawn Services Expense; and Interest Expense.

a. M&R Company provided $2,000 in services to customers in December, which are not yet recorded. Those customers are expected to pay the company in January following the company's year-end.

b. Wage expenses of $1,000 have been incurred but are not paid as of December 31.

c. M&R Company has a $5,000 bank loan and has incurred (but not recorded) 8% interest expense of $400 for the year ended December 31. The company will pay the $400 interest in cash on January 2 following the company's year-end.

d. M&R Company hired a firm that provided lawn services during December for $500. M&R will pay for December lawn services on January 15 following the company's year-end.

e. M&R Company has earned $200 in interest revenue from investments for the year ended December 31. The interest revenue will be received on January 15 following the company's year-end.

f. Salary expenses of $900 have been earned by supervisors but not paid as of December 31.

Exercise 3-5
Preparing adjusting entries—accrued revenues and expenses
P3   P4

Exercise 3-6

Preparing adjusting entries

P1   P2   P3   P4

For each of the following separate cases, prepare the required December 31 year-end adjusting entries. Entries can draw from this partial chart of accounts: Interest Receivable; Prepaid Insurance; Accumulated Depreciation—Equipment; Wages Payable; Unearned Revenue; Consulting Revenue; Interest Revenue; Wages Expense; Insurance Expense; Interest Expense; and Depreciation Expense—Equipment.

a. Depreciation on the company's wind turbine equipment for the year is $5,000.

b. The Prepaid Insurance account for the solar panels had a $2,000 debit balance at December 31 before adjusting for the costs of any expired coverage. Analysis of prepaid insurance shows that $600 of unexpired insurance coverage remains at year-end.

c. The company received $3,000 cash in advance for sustainability consulting work. As of December 31, one-third of the sustainability consulting work had been performed.

d. As of December 31, $1,200 in wages expense for the organic produce workers has been incurred but not yet paid.

e. As of December 31, the company has earned, but not yet recorded, $400 of interest revenue from investments in socially responsible bonds. The interest revenue is expected to be received on January 12.

Exercise 3-7

Analyzing and preparing adjusting entries

P5

Following are two income statements for Alexis Co. for the year ended December 31. The left number column is prepared before adjusting entries are recorded, and the right column is prepared after adjusting entries. Analyze the statements and prepare the seven adjusting entries *a* through *g* that likely were recorded. *Hint:* The entry for *a* refers to fees that have been earned but not yet billed. None of the entries involve cash.

Income Statements For Year Ended December 31			
	Unadjusted	**Adjustments**	**Adjusted**
Revenues			
Fees earned	$18,000	a.	$25,000
Commissions earned	36,500		36,500
Total revenues	54,500		61,500
Expenses			
Depreciation expense—Computers	0	b.	1,600
Depreciation expense—Office furniture	0	c.	1,850
Salaries expense	13,500	d.	15,750
Insurance expense	0	e.	1,400
Rent expense	3,800		3,800
Office supplies expense	0	f.	580
Advertising expense	2,500		2,500
Utilities expense	1,245	g.	1,335
Total expenses	21,045		28,815
Net income	$33,455		$32,685

Exercise 3-8

Preparing financial statements from a trial balance

P6

Following are the accounts and balances (in random order) from the adjusted trial balance of Stark Company. Prepare the (1) income statement and (2) statement of retained earnings for the year ended December 31 and (3) balance sheet at December 31. The Retained Earnings account balance was $14,800 on December 31 of the *prior year*.

Notes payable.........................	$11,000	Accumulated depreciation—Buildings............	$15,000
Prepaid insurance	2,500	Accounts receivable	4,000
Interest expense	500	Utilities expense	1,300
Accounts payable	1,500	Interest payable	100
Wages payable	400	Unearned revenue	800
Cash	10,000	Supplies expense	200
Wages expense	7,500	Buildings	40,000
Insurance expense	1,800	Dividends	3,000
Common stock	10,000	Depreciation expense—Buildings	2,000
Retained earnings	14,800	Supplies......................................	800
Services revenue	20,000		

Following are **Nintendo**'s revenue and expense accounts for a recent March 31 fiscal year-end (yen in millions). Prepare the company's closing entries for (1) its revenues and (2) its expenses.

Exercise 3-9
Preparing closing entries

P7

| Net sales............................. | ¥504,459 | Advertising expense .... | ¥ 46,636 |
| Cost of sales........................ | 283,494 | Other expense, net .... | 157,811 |

The following adjusted trial balance contains the accounts and year-end balances of Cruz Company as of December 31. (1) Prepare the December 31 closing entries for Cruz Company. Assume the account number for Income Summary is 901. (2) Prepare the December 31 post-closing trial balance for Cruz Company. *Note:* The Retained Earnings account balance was $37,600 on December 31 of the *prior year.*

Exercise 3-10
Preparing closing entries and a post-closing trial balance

P7   P8

No.	Account Title	Debit	Credit
101	Cash..	$19,000	
126	Supplies....................................	13,000	
128	Prepaid insurance...........................	3,000	
167	Equipment...................................	24,000	
168	Accumulated depreciation—Equipment		$ 7,500
307	Common stock		10,000
318	Retained earnings...........................		37,600
319	Dividends...................................	7,000	
404	Services revenue		44,000
612	Depreciation expense—Equipment	3,000	
622	Salaries expense............................	22,000	
637	Insurance expense	2,500	
640	Rent expense	3,400	
652	Supplies expense	2,200	
	Totals......................................	$99,100	$99,100

Use the following adjusted year-end trial balance at December 31 of Wilson Trucking Company to prepare the (1) income statement and (2) statement of retained earnings for the year ended December 31. The Retained Earnings account balance was $155,000 at December 31 of the *prior year.*

Exercise 3-11
Preparing financial statements   **P6**

Account Title	Debit	Credit
Cash..	$ 8,000	
Accounts receivable.........................	17,500	
Office supplies	3,000	
Trucks	172,000	
Accumulated depreciation—Trucks..............		$ 36,000
Land.......................................	85,000	
Accounts payable...........................		12,000
Interest payable		4,000
Long-term notes payable.....................		58,000
Common stock		15,000
Retained earnings..........................		155,000
Dividends	20,000	
Trucking fees earned		130,000
Depreciation expense—Trucks	23,500	
Salaries expense...........................	61,000	
Office supplies expense.....................	8,000	
Repairs expense—Trucks.....................	12,000	
Totals.....................................	$410,000	$410,000

Exercise 3-12

Preparing a classified
balance sheet   **C3**

Use the information in the adjusted trial balance reported in Exercise 3-11 to prepare Wilson Trucking Company's *classified* balance sheet as of December 31.

Exercise 3-13

Computing and interpreting
profit margin

A1

Use the following information to compute profit margin for each separate company a through e. Which of the five companies is the most profitable according to the profit margin ratio? Interpret the profit margin ratio for company c.

	Net Income	Net Sales		Net Income	Net Sales
a.	$ 4,361	$ 44,500	d.	$65,646	$1,458,800
b.	97,706	398,800	e.	80,132	435,500
c.	111,281	257,000			

Exercise 3-14

Computing and analyzing
the current ratio

A2

Calculate the current ratio for each of the following companies (round the ratio to two decimals). Identify the company with the strongest liquidity position. (These companies are competitors in the same industry.)

	Current Assets	Current Liabilities
Edison	$ 79,040	$ 32,000
MAXT	104,880	76,000
Chatter	45,080	49,000
TRU	85,680	81,600
Gleeson	61,000	100,000

Exercise 3-15^A

Adjusting for prepaids
recorded as expenses and
unearned revenues
recorded as revenues

P9

Ricardo Construction began operations on December 1. In setting up its accounting procedures, the company decided to debit expense accounts when it prepays its expenses and to credit revenue accounts when customers pay for services in advance. Prepare journal entries for items a through d and the adjusting entries as of its December 31 period-end for items e through g. Entries can draw from the following partial chart of accounts: Cash; Accounts Receivable; Interest Receivable; Supplies; Prepaid Insurance; Unearned Remodeling Fees; Remodeling Fees Earned; Supplies Expense; Insurance Expense; and Interest Expense.

a. Supplies are purchased on December 1 for $2,000 cash.

b. The company prepaid its insurance premiums for $1,540 cash on December 2.

c. On December 15, the company receives an advance payment of $13,000 cash from a customer for remodeling work.

d. On December 28, the company receives $3,700 cash from another customer for remodeling work to be performed in January.

e. A physical count on December 31 indicates that the company has $1,840 of supplies available.

Check   (f) Cr. Insurance
Expense, $1,200

f. An analysis of insurance policies in effect on December 31 shows that $340 of insurance coverage had expired.

(g) Dr. Remodeling Fees
Earned, $11,130

g. As of December 31, only one remodeling project has been worked on and completed. The $5,570 fee for this project had been received in advance and recorded as remodeling fees earned.

Exercise 3-16^B

Preparing unadjusted and
adjusted trial balances,
including the adjustments

P10

The following data are taken from the unadjusted trial balance of the Westcott Company at December 31. Each account carries a normal balance. Set up a 10-column work sheet to answer the requirements.

Accounts Payable....................	$ 6	Prepaid Insurance......	$18	Retained Earnings............	$32
Accounts Receivable	12	Revenue..............	75	Dividends...................	6
Accumulated Depreciation—Equip.......	15	Salaries Expense.......	18	Unearned Revenue	12
Cash	21	Supplies..............	24	Utilities Expense	12
Equipment	39	Common Stock	10		

1. Enter the accounts in proper order and enter their balances in the correct Debit or Credit column of the Unadjusted Trial Balance columns of the 10-column work sheet.

[continued on next page]

2. Use the following adjustment information to complete the Adjustments columns of the work sheet from part 1.

  a. Depreciation on equipment, $3   **d.** Supplies available at December 31, $15

  b. Accrued salaries, $6   **e.** Expired insurance, $15

  c. The $12 of unearned revenue has been earned

3. Extend the balances in the Adjusted Trial Balance columns of the work sheet to the proper financial statement columns. Compute totals for those columns, including net income.

The following two events occurred for Trey Co. on October 31, the end of its fiscal year.

a. Trey rents a building from its owner for $2,800 per month. By a prearrangement, the company delayed paying October's rent until November 5. On this date, the company paid the rent for both October and November.

b. Trey rents space in a building it owns to a tenant for $850 per month. By prearrangement, the tenant delayed paying the October rent until November 8. On this date, the tenant paid the rent for both October and November.

Exercise 3-17^C
Preparing reversing entries

P11

Required

1. Prepare adjusting entries that the company must record for these events as of October 31.

2. Assuming Trey does *not* use reversing entries, prepare journal entries to record Trey's payment of rent on November 5 and the collection of the tenant's rent on November 8.

3. Assuming that the company uses reversing entries, prepare reversing entries on November 1 and the journal entries to record Trey's payment of rent on November 5 and the collection of the tenant's rent on November 8.

---

connect

For journal entries *1* through *12*, enter the letter of the explanation that most closely describes it in the space beside each entry. You can use letters more than once.

A. To record receipt of unearned revenue.
B. To record this period's earning of prior unearned revenue.
C. To record payment of an accrued expense.
D. To record receipt of an accrued revenue.
E. To record an accrued expense.
F. To record an accrued revenue.
G. To record this period's use of a prepaid expense.
H. To record payment of a prepaid expense.
I. To record this period's depreciation expense.

PROBLEM SET A

Problem 3-1A
Identifying adjusting entries with explanations

P1 P2 P3 P4

___ 1.	Interest Expense	1,000	
	Interest Payable		1,000
___ 2.	Depreciation Expense	4,000	
	Accumulated Depreciation		4,000
___ 3.	Unearned Professional Fees	3,000	
	Professional Fees Earned		3,000
___ 4.	Insurance Expense	4,200	
	Prepaid Insurance		4,200
___ 5.	Salaries Payable	1,400	
	Cash		1,400
___ 6.	Prepaid Rent	4,500	
	Cash		4,500

___ 7.	Salaries Expense	6,000	
	Salaries Payable		6,000
___ 8.	Interest Receivable	5,000	
	Interest Revenue		5,000
___ 9.	Cash	9,000	
	Accounts Receivable (from consulting)		9,000
___ 10.	Cash	7,500	
	Unearned Professional Fees		7,500
___ 11.	Cash	2,000	
	Interest Receivable		2,000
___ 12.	Rent Expense	2,000	
	Prepaid Rent		2,000

Arnez Company's annual accounting period ends on December 31, 2019. The following information concerns the adjusting entries to be recorded as of that date. Entries can draw from the following partial chart of accounts: Cash; Rent Receivable; Office Supplies; Prepaid Insurance; Building; Accumulated Depreciation—Building; Salaries Payable; Unearned Rent; Rent Earned; Salaries Expense; Office Supplies Expense; Insurance Expense; and Depreciation Expense—Building.

Problem 3-2A
Preparing adjusting and subsequent journal entries

P1 P2 P3 P4

[continued on next page]

a. The Office Supplies account started the year with a $4,000 balance. During 2019, the company purchased supplies for $13,400, which was added to the Office Supplies account. The inventory of supplies available at December 31, 2019, totaled $2,554.

b. An analysis of the company's insurance policies provided the following facts. The total premium for each policy was paid in full (for all months) at the purchase date, and the Prepaid Insurance account was debited for the full cost. (Year-end adjusting entries for Prepaid Insurance were properly recorded in all prior years.)

Policy	Date of Purchase	Months of Coverage	Cost
A	April 1, 2017	24	$14,400
B	April 1, 2018	36	12,960
C	August 1, 2019	12	2,400

c. The company has 15 employees, who earn a total of $1,960 in salaries each working day. They are paid each Monday for their work in the five-day workweek ending on the previous Friday. Assume that December 31, 2019, is a Tuesday, and all 15 employees worked the first two days of that week. Because New Year's Day is a paid holiday, they will be paid salaries for five full days on Monday, January 6, 2020.

d. The company purchased a building on January 1, 2019. It cost $960,000 and is expected to have a $45,000 salvage value at the end of its predicted 30-year life. Annual depreciation is $30,500.

e. Since the company is not large enough to occupy the entire building it owns, it rented space to a tenant at $3,000 per month, starting on November 1, 2019. The rent was paid on time on November 1, and the amount received was credited to the Rent Earned account. However, the tenant has not paid the December rent. The company has worked out an agreement with the tenant, who has promised to pay both December and January rent in full on January 15. The tenant has agreed not to fall behind again.

f. On November 1, the company rented space to another tenant for $2,800 per month. The tenant paid five months' rent in advance on that date. The payment was recorded with a credit to the Unearned Rent account.

Check (1b) Dr. Insurance Expense, $7,120
(1d) Dr. Depreciation Expense, $30,500

Required

1. Use the information to prepare adjusting entries as of December 31, 2019.
2. Prepare journal entries to record the first subsequent cash transaction in 2020 for parts c and e.

Problem 3-3A
Preparing adjusting entries, adjusted trial balance, and financial statements

P1 P2 P3 P4 P5 P6

Wells Technical Institute (WTI), a school owned by Tristana Wells, provides training to individuals who pay tuition directly to the school. WTI also offers training to groups in off-site locations. Its unadjusted trial balance as of December 31 follows, along with descriptions of items a through h that require adjusting entries on December 31.

Additional Information

a. An analysis of WTI's insurance policies shows that $2,400 of coverage has expired.
b. An inventory count shows that teaching supplies costing $2,800 are available at year-end.
c. Annual depreciation on the equipment is $13,200.
d. Annual depreciation on the professional library is $7,200.
e. On September 1, WTI agreed to do five courses for a client for $2,500 each. Two courses will start immediately and finish before the end of the year. Three courses will not begin until next year. The client paid $12,500 cash in advance for all five courses on September 1, and WTI credited Unearned Training Fees.
f. On October 15, WTI agreed to teach a four-month class (beginning immediately) for an executive with payment due at the end of the class. At December 31, $7,500 of the tuition has been earned by WTI.
g. WTI's two employees are paid weekly. As of the end of the year, two days' salaries have accrued at the rate of $100 per day for each employee.
h. The balance in the Prepaid Rent account represents rent for December.

WELLS TECHNICAL INSTITUTE Unadjusted Trial Balance December 31	Debit	Credit
Cash	$ 34,000	
Accounts receivable	0	
Teaching supplies	8,000	
Prepaid insurance	12,000	
Prepaid rent	3,000	
Professional library	35,000	
Accumulated depreciation—Professional library		$ 10,000
Equipment	80,000	
Accumulated depreciation—Equipment		15,000
Accounts payable		26,000
Salaries payable		0
Unearned training fees		12,500
Common stock		10,000
Retained earnings		80,000
Dividends	50,000	
Tuition fees earned		123,900
Training fees earned		40,000
Depreciation expense—Professional library	0	
Depreciation expense—Equipment	0	
Salaries expense	50,000	
Insurance expense	0	
Rent expense	33,000	
Teaching supplies expense	0	
Advertising expense	6,000	
Utilities expense	6,400	
Totals	$317,400	$317,400

Required

1. Prepare T-accounts (representing the ledger) with balances from the unadjusted trial balance.
2. Prepare the necessary adjusting journal entries for items *a* through *h* and post them to the T-accounts. Assume that adjusting entries are made only at year-end.
3. Update balances in the T-accounts for the adjusting entries and prepare an adjusted trial balance.
4. Prepare Wells Technical Institute's income statement and statement of retained earnings for the year and prepare its balance sheet as of December 31. The Retained Earnings account balance was $80,000 on December 31 of the *prior year.*

Check   (2e) Cr. Training Fees Earned, $5,000
(2f) Cr. Tuition Fees Earned, $7,500
(3) Adj. trial balance totals, $345,700
(4) Net income, $49,600

The adjusted trial balance for Chiara Company as of December 31 follows.

Problem 3-4A
Preparing financial statements from the adjusted trial balance
P6

	Debit	Credit
Cash	$ 30,000	
Accounts receivable	52,000	
Interest receivable	18,000	
Notes receivable (due in 90 days)	168,000	
Office supplies	16,000	
Automobiles	168,000	
Accumulated depreciation—Automobiles		$ 50,000
Equipment	138,000	
Accumulated depreciation—Equipment		18,000
Land	78,000	
Accounts payable		96,000
Interest payable		20,000
Salaries payable		19,000
Unearned fees		30,000
Long-term notes payable		138,000
Common stock		20,000
Retained earnings..................................		235,800
Dividends	46,000	

[continued on next page]

[continued from previous page]

Fees earned		484,000
Interest earned		24,000
Depreciation expense—Automobiles	26,000	
Depreciation expense—Equipment	18,000	
Salaries expense	188,000	
Wages expense	40,000	
Interest expense	32,000	
Office supplies expense	34,000	
Advertising expense	58,000	
Repairs expense—Automobiles	24,800	
Totals	$1,134,800	$1,134,800

Required

Check   Total assets, $600,000

Use the information in the adjusted trial balance to prepare (a) the income statement for the year ended December 31; (b) the statement of retained earnings for the year ended December 31 [*Note:* Retained Earnings at December 31 of the *prior year* was $235,800]; and (c) the balance sheet as of December 31.

Problem 3-5A
Applying the accounting cycle

P1 P2 P3 P4 P5 P6 P7 P8

On April 1, Jiro Nozomi created a new travel agency, Adventure Travel. The following transactions occurred during the company's first month.

Apr.	1	Nozomi invested $30,000 cash and computer equipment worth $20,000 in the company in exchange for common stock.
	2	The company rented furnished office space by paying $1,800 cash for the first month's (April) rent.
	3	The company purchased $1,000 of office supplies for cash.
	10	The company paid $2,400 cash for the premium on a 12-month insurance policy. Coverage begins on April 11.
	14	The company paid $1,600 cash for two weeks' salaries earned by employees.
	24	The company collected $8,000 cash for commissions earned.
	28	The company paid $1,600 cash for two weeks' salaries earned by employees.
	29	The company paid $350 cash for minor repairs to the company's computer.
	30	The company paid $750 cash for this month's telephone bill.
	30	The company paid $1,500 cash in dividends.

The company's chart of accounts follows.

101	Cash	307	Common Stock	640	Rent Expense
106	Accounts Receivable	318	Retained Earnings	650	Office Supplies Expense
124	Office Supplies	319	Dividends	684	Repairs Expense
128	Prepaid Insurance	405	Commissions Earned	688	Telephone Expense
167	Computer Equipment	612	Depreciation Expense—Computer Equip.	901	Income Summary
168	Accumulated Depreciation—Computer Equip.	622	Salaries Expense		
209	Salaries Payable	637	Insurance Expense		

Required

1. Use the balance column format to set up each ledger account listed in its chart of accounts.
2. Prepare journal entries to record the transactions for April and post them to the ledger accounts. The company records prepaid and unearned items in balance sheet accounts.

Check   (3) Unadj. trial balance totals, $58,000

(4a) Dr. Insurance Expense, $133

3. Prepare an unadjusted trial balance as of April 30.
4. Use the following information to journalize and post adjusting entries for the month:
   a. Prepaid insurance of $133 has expired this month.
   b. At the end of the month, $600 of office supplies are still available.
   c. This month's depreciation on the computer equipment is $500.
   d. Employees earned $420 of unpaid and unrecorded salaries as of month-end.
   e. The company earned $1,750 of commissions that are not yet billed at month-end.

(5) Net income, $2,197; Total assets, $51,117

(7) P-C trial balance totals, $51,617

5. Prepare the adjusted trial balance as of April 30. Prepare the income statement and the statement of retained earnings for the month of April and the balance sheet at April 30.
6. Prepare journal entries to close the temporary accounts and post these entries to the ledger.
7. Prepare a post-closing trial balance.

The adjusted trial balance for Tybalt Construction as of December 31, 2019, follows. O. Tybalt invested $5,000 cash in the business in exchange for common stock during year 2019. The December 31, 2018, credit balance of the Retained Earnings account was $121,400.

Problem 3-6A

Preparing closing entries and financial statements

P6   P7

No.	Account Title	Debit	Credit
	Adjusted Trial Balance		
	December 31, 2019		
101	Cash	$ 5,000	
104	Short-term investments	23,000	
126	Supplies	8,100	
128	Prepaid insurance	7,000	
167	Equipment....................................	40,000	
168	Accumulated depreciation—Equipment		$ 20,000
173	Building......................................	150,000	
174	Accumulated depreciation—Building		50,000
183	Land	55,000	
201	Accounts payable..............................		16,500
203	Interest payable		2,500
208	Rent payable..................................		3,500
210	Wages payable................................		2,500
213	Property taxes payable		900
233	Unearned professional fees......................		7,500
244	Current portion of long-term note payable..........		7,000
251	Long-term notes payable........................		60,000
307	Common stock		5,000
318	Retained earnings		121,400
319	Dividends	13,000	
401	Professional fees earned........................		97,000
406	Rent earned		14,000
407	Dividends earned..............................		2,000
409	Interest earned................................		2,100
606	Depreciation expense—Building..................	11,000	
612	Depreciation expense—Equipment................	6,000	
623	Wages expense	32,000	
633	Interest expense...............................	5,100	
637	Insurance expense	10,000	
640	Rent expense	13,400	
652	Supplies expense..............................	7,400	
682	Postage expense	4,200	
683	Property taxes expense	5,000	
684	Repairs expense...............................	8,900	
688	Telephone expense	3,200	
690	Utilities expense...............................	4,600	
	Totals......................................	$411,900	$411,900

Required

1. Prepare the income statement and the statement of retained earnings for calendar-year 2019 and the classified balance sheet at December 31, 2019.

2. Prepare the necessary closing entries at December 31, 2019.

Check (1) Total assets (12/31/2019), $218,100; Net income, $4,300

In the blank space beside each numbered balance sheet item, enter the letter of its balance sheet classification. If the item should not appear on the balance sheet, enter a Z in the blank.

A. Current assets

B. Long-term investments

C. Plant assets

D. Intangible assets

E. Current liabilities

F. Long-term liabilities

G. Equity

Problem 3-7A

Determining balance sheet classifications

C3

_____ **1.** Long-term investment in stock

_____ **2.** Depreciation expense—Building

_____ **3.** Prepaid rent (2 months of rent)

_____ **4.** Interest receivable

_____ **5.** Taxes payable (due in 5 weeks)

_____ **6.** Automobiles

_____ **7.** Notes payable (due in 3 years)

_____ **8.** Accounts payable

_____ **9.** Cash

_____ **10.** Common stock

_____ **11.** Unearned services revenue

_____ **12.** Accumulated depreciation—Trucks

_____ **13.** Prepaid insurance (expires in 5 months)

_____ **14.** Buildings

_____ **15.** Store supplies

_____ **16.** Office equipment

_____ **17.** Land (used in operations)

_____ **18.** Repairs expense

_____ **19.** Office supplies

_____ **20.** Current portion of long-term note payable

PROBLEM SET B

Problem 3-1B

Identifying adjusting entries
with explanations

P1   P2   P3   P4

For each of the following journal entries *1* through *12*, enter the letter of the explanation that most closely describes it in the space beside each entry. You can use letters more than once.

A. To record payment of a prepaid expense.

B. To record this period's use of a prepaid expense.

C. To record this period's depreciation expense.

D. To record receipt of unearned revenue.

E. To record this period's earning of prior unearned revenue.

F. To record an accrued expense.

G. To record payment of an accrued expense.

H. To record an accrued revenue.

I. To record receipt of accrued revenue.

____	1. Interest Receivable	3,500	
	Interest Revenue		3,500
____	2. Salaries Payable	9,000	
	Cash		9,000
____	3. Depreciation Expense	8,000	
	Accumulated Depreciation . .		8,000
____	4. Cash	9,000	
	Unearned Professional Fees .		9,000
____	5. Insurance Expense	4,000	
	Prepaid Insurance		4,000
____	6. Interest Expense	5,000	
	Interest Payable		5,000

____	7. Cash	1,500	
	Accounts Receivable (from services)		1,500
____	8. Salaries Expense	7,000	
	Salaries Payable		7,000
____	9. Cash	1,000	
	Interest Receivable		1,000
____	10. Prepaid Rent	3,000	
	Cash		3,000
____	11. Rent Expense	7,500	
	Prepaid Rent		7,500
____	12. Unearned Professional Fees	6,000	
	Professional Fees Earned		6,000

Problem 3-2B

Preparing adjusting and
subsequent journal entries

P1   P2   P3   P4

Natsu Company's annual accounting period ends on October 31, 2019. The following information concerns the adjusting entries that need to be recorded as of that date. Entries can draw from the following partial chart of accounts: Cash; Rent Receivable; Office Supplies; Prepaid Insurance; Building; Accumulated Depreciation—Building; Salaries Payable; Unearned Rent; Rent Earned; Salaries Expense; Office Supplies Expense; Insurance Expense; and Depreciation Expense—Building.

a. The Office Supplies account started the fiscal year with a $600 balance. During the fiscal year, the company purchased supplies for $4,570, which was added to the Office Supplies account. The supplies available at October 31, 2019, totaled $800.

b. An analysis of the company's insurance policies provided the following facts. The total premium for each policy was paid in full (for all months) at the purchase date, and the Prepaid Insurance account was debited for the full cost. (Year-end adjusting entries for Prepaid Insurance were properly recorded in all prior fiscal years.)

Policy	Date of Purchase	Months of Coverage	Cost
A	April 1, 2018	24	$6,000
B	April 1, 2019	36	7,200
C	August 1, 2019	12	1,320

c. The company has four employees, who earn a total of $1,000 for each workday. They are paid each Monday for their work in the five-day workweek ending on the previous Friday. Assume that October 31, 2019, is a Monday, and all four employees worked the first day of that week. They will be paid salaries for five full days on Monday, November 7, 2019.

d. The company purchased a building on November 1, 2016, that cost $175,000 and is expected to have a $40,000 salvage value at the end of its predicted 25-year life. Annual depreciation is $5,400.

e. Because the company does not occupy the entire building it owns, it rented space to a tenant at $1,000 per month, starting on September 1, 2019. The rent was paid on time on September 1, and the amount received was credited to the Rent Earned account. However, the October rent has not been paid. The company has worked out an agreement with the tenant, who has promised to pay both October and November rent in full on November 15. The tenant has agreed not to fall behind again.

f. On September 1, the company rented space to another tenant for $725 per month. The tenant paid five months' rent in advance on that date. The payment was recorded with a credit to the Unearned Rent account.

Check   (1*b*) Dr. Insurance
Expense, $4,730
(1*d*) Dr. Depreciation
Expense, $5,400

Required

1. Use the information to prepare adjusting entries as of October 31, 2019.

2. Prepare journal entries to record the first subsequent cash transaction in November 2019 for parts *c* and *e*.

Following is the unadjusted trial balance for Alonzo Institute as of December 31. The Institute provides one-on-one training to individuals who pay tuition directly to the business and offers extension training to groups in off-site locations. Shown after the trial balance are items *a* through *h* that require adjusting entries as of December 31.

Problem 3-3B
Preparing adjusting entries, adjusted trial balance, and financial statements

P1 P2 P3 P4 P5 P6

ALONZO INSTITUTE Unadjusted Trial Balance December 31	Debit	Credit
Cash	$ 60,000	
Accounts receivable	0	
Teaching supplies	70,000	
Prepaid insurance	19,000	
Prepaid rent	3,800	
Professional library	12,000	
Accumulated depreciation—Professional library		$ 2,500
Equipment	40,000	
Accumulated depreciation—Equipment		20,000
Accounts payable		11,200
Salaries payable		0
Unearned training fees		28,600
Common stock		11,000
Retained earnings		60,500
Dividends	20,000	
Tuition fees earned		129,200
Training fees earned		68,000
Depreciation expense—Professional library	0	
Depreciation expense—Equipment	0	
Salaries expense	44,200	
Insurance expense	0	
Rent expense	29,600	
Teaching supplies expense	0	
Advertising expense	19,000	
Utilities expense	13,400	
Totals	$331,000	$331,000

Additional Information

a. An analysis of the Institute's insurance policies shows that $9,500 of coverage has expired.

b. An inventory count shows that teaching supplies costing $20,000 are available at year-end.

c. Annual depreciation on the equipment is $5,000.

d. Annual depreciation on the professional library is $2,400.

e. On November 1, the Institute agreed to do a special two-month course (starting immediately) for a client. The contract calls for a $14,300 monthly fee, and the client paid the two months' fees in advance. When the cash was received, the Unearned Training Fees account was credited.

f. On October 15, the Institute agreed to teach a four-month class (beginning immediately) to an executive with payment due at the end of the class. At December 31, $5,750 of the tuition has been earned by the Institute.

g. The Institute's only employee is paid weekly. As of the end of the year, three days' salaries have accrued at the rate of $150 per day.

h. The balance in the Prepaid Rent account represents rent for December.

Required

1. Prepare T-accounts (representing the ledger) with balances from the unadjusted trial balance.

2. Prepare the necessary adjusting journal entries for items *a* through *h*, and post them to the T-accounts. Assume that adjusting entries are made only at year-end.

3. Update balances in the T-accounts for the adjusting entries and prepare an adjusted trial balance.

4. Prepare the company's income statement and statement of retained earnings for the year, and prepare its balance sheet as of December 31. The Retained Earnings account balance was $60,500 on December 31 of the *prior year*.

Check (2e) Cr. Training Fees Earned, $28,600
(2f) Cr. Tuition Fees Earned, $5,750
(3) Adj. trial balance totals, $344,600
(4) Net income, $54,200

Problem 3-4B

Preparing financial
statements from adjusted
trial balance

P6

The adjusted trial balance for Speedy Courier as of December 31 follows.

	Debit	Credit
Cash	$ 58,000	
Accounts receivable	120,000	
Interest receivable	7,000	
Notes receivable (due in 90 days)	210,000	
Office supplies	22,000	
Trucks	134,000	
Accumulated depreciation—Trucks		$ 58,000
Equipment	270,000	
Accumulated depreciation—Equipment		200,000
Land	100,000	
Accounts payable		134,000
Interest payable		20,000
Salaries payable		28,000
Unearned delivery fees		120,000
Long-term notes payable		200,000
Common stock		15,000
Retained earnings		110,000
Dividends	50,000	
Delivery fees earned		611,800
Interest earned		34,000
Depreciation expense—Trucks	29,000	
Depreciation expense—Equipment	48,000	
Salaries expense	74,000	
Wages expense	300,000	
Interest expense	15,000	
Office supplies expense	31,000	
Advertising expense	27,200	
Repairs expense—Trucks	35,600	
Totals	$1,530,800	$1,530,800

Required

Check Total assets,
$663,000

Use the information in the adjusted trial balance to prepare (a) the income statement for the year ended December 31; (b) the statement of retained earnings for the year ended December 31 [*Note:* Retained Earnings at Dec. 31 of the *prior year* was $110,000]; and (c) the balance sheet as of December 31.

Problem 3-5B

Applying the accounting
cycle

P1 P2 P3 P4 P5 P6 P7 P8

On July 1, Lula Plume created a new self-storage business, Safe Storage Co. The following transactions occurred during the company's first month.

July	1	Plume invested $30,000 cash and buildings worth $150,000 in the company in exchange for common stock.
	2	The company rented equipment by paying $2,000 cash for the first month's (July) rent.
	5	The company purchased $2,400 of office supplies for cash.
	10	The company paid $7,200 cash for the premium on a 12-month insurance policy. Coverage begins on July 11.
	14	The company paid an employee $1,000 cash for two weeks' salary earned.
	24	The company collected $9,800 cash for storage fees from customers.
	28	The company paid $1,000 cash for two weeks' salary earned by an employee.
	29	The company paid $950 cash for minor repairs to a leaking roof.
	30	The company paid $400 cash for this month's telephone bill.
	31	The company paid $2,000 cash in dividends.

The company's chart of accounts follows.

101	Cash	307	Common Stock	640	Rent Expense
106	Accounts Receivable	318	Retained Earnings	650	Office Supplies Expense
124	Office Supplies	319	Dividends	684	Repairs Expense
128	Prepaid Insurance	401	Storage Fees Earned	688	Telephone Expense
173	Buildings	606	Depreciation Expense—Buildings	901	Income Summary
174	Accumulated Depreciation—Buildings	622	Salaries Expense		
209	Salaries Payable	637	Insurance Expense		

Required

1. Use the balance column format to set up each ledger account listed in its chart of accounts.

2. Prepare journal entries to record the transactions for July and post them to the ledger accounts. Record prepaid and unearned items in balance sheet accounts.

3. Prepare an unadjusted trial balance as of July 31.

4. Use the following information to journalize and post adjusting entries for the month:

   a. Prepaid insurance of $400 has expired this month.

   b. At the end of the month, $1,525 of office supplies are still available.

   c. This month's depreciation on the buildings is $1,500.

   d. An employee earned $100 of unpaid and unrecorded salary as of month-end.

   e. The company earned $1,150 of storage fees that are not yet billed at month-end.

5. Prepare the adjusted trial balance as of July 31. Prepare the income statement and the statement of retained earnings for the month of July and the balance sheet at July 31.

6. Prepare journal entries to close the temporary accounts and post these entries to the ledger.

7. Prepare a post-closing trial balance.

Check (3) Unadj. trial balance totals, $189,800

(4a) Dr. Insurance Expense, $400

(5) Net income, $2,725; Total assets, $180,825

(7) P-C trial balance totals, $182,325

The adjusted trial balance for Anara Co. as of December 31, 2019, follows. P. Anara invested $40,000 cash in the business in exchange for common stock during year 2019. The December 31, 2018, credit balance of the Retained Earnings account was $52,800.

Problem 3-6B
Preparing closing entries and financial statements

P6 P7

	Adjusted Trial Balance December 31, 2019		
No.	**Account Title**	**Debit**	**Credit**
101	Cash	$ 7,400	
104	Short-term investments	11,200	
126	Supplies	4,600	
128	Prepaid insurance	1,000	
167	Equipment	24,000	
168	Accumulated depreciation—Equipment		$ 4,000
173	Building	100,000	
174	Accumulated depreciation—Building		10,000
183	Land	30,500	
201	Accounts payable		3,500
203	Interest payable		1,750
208	Rent payable		400
210	Wages payable		1,280
213	Property taxes payable		3,330
233	Unearned professional fees		750
244	Current portion of long-term notes payable		8,400
251	Long-term notes payable		31,600
307	Common stock		40,000
318	Retained earnings		52,800
319	Dividends	8,000	
401	Professional fees earned		59,600
406	Rent earned		4,500
407	Dividends earned		1,000
409	Interest earned		1,320
606	Depreciation expense—Building	2,000	
612	Depreciation expense—Equipment	1,000	
623	Wages expense	18,500	
633	Interest expense	1,550	
637	Insurance expense	1,525	
640	Rent expense	3,600	
652	Supplies expense	1,000	
682	Postage expense	410	
683	Property taxes expense	4,825	
684	Repairs expense	679	
688	Telephone expense	521	
690	Utilities expense	1,920	
	Totals	$224,230	$224,230

Required

1. Prepare the income statement and the statement of retained earnings for calendar-year 2019 and the classified balance sheet at December 31, 2019.

2. Prepare the necessary closing entries at December 31, 2019.

Problem 3-7B

Determining balance sheet classifications

C3

In the blank space beside each numbered balance sheet item, enter the letter of its balance sheet classification. If the item should not appear on the balance sheet, enter a *Z* in the blank.

A. Current assets   **D.** Intangible assets   **F.** Long-term liabilities

B. Long-term investments   **E.** Current liabilities   **G.** Equity

C. Plant assets

_____ **1.** Commissions earned   _____ **11.** Rent receivable

_____ **2.** Interest receivable   _____ **12.** Salaries payable

_____ **3.** Long-term investment in stock   _____ **13.** Income taxes payable

_____ **4.** Prepaid insurance (4 months of rent)   (due in 11 weeks)

_____ **5.** Machinery   _____ **14.** Common stock

_____ **6.** Notes payable (due in 15 years)   _____ **15.** Office supplies

_____ **7.** Copyrights   _____ **16.** Interest payable

_____ **8.** Current portion of long-term   _____ **17.** Rent revenue

       note payable   _____ **18.** Notes receivable (due in 120 days)

_____ **9.** Accumulated depreciation—Trucks   _____ **19.** Land (used in operations)

_____ **10.** Office equipment   _____ **20.** Depreciation expense—Trucks

---

SERIAL PROBLEM

Business Solutions

P1 P2 P3 P4 P5 P6 P7 P8

©Alexander Image/Shutterstock

This serial problem began in Chapter 1 and continues through most of the book. If previous chapter segments were not completed, the serial problem can begin at this point.

SP 3   After the success of the company's first two months, Santana Rey continues to operate **Business Solutions**. (Transactions for the first two months are described in the Chapter 2 serial problem.) The November 30, 2019, unadjusted trial balance of Business Solutions (reflecting its transactions for October and November of 2019) follows.

No.	Account Title	Debit	Credit
101	Cash	$38,264	
106	Accounts receivable.............................	12,618	
126	Computer supplies	2,545	
128	Prepaid insurance................................	2,220	
131	Prepaid rent	3,300	
163	Office equipment	8,000	
164	Accumulated depreciation—Office equipment..................		$ 0
167	Computer equipment	20,000	
168	Accumulated depreciation—Computer equipment		0
201	Accounts payable		0
210	Wages payable		0
236	Unearned computer services revenue		0
307	Common stock		73,000
318	Retained earnings...............................		0
319	Dividends	5,600	
403	Computer services revenue		25,659
612	Depreciation expense—Office equipment	0	
613	Depreciation expense—Computer equipment	0	
623	Wages expense	2,625	
637	Insurance expense	0	
640	Rent expense	0	
652	Computer supplies expense	0	
655	Advertising expense.............................	1,728	
676	Mileage expense	704	
677	Miscellaneous expenses	250	
684	Repairs expense—Computer	805	
	Totals	$98,659	$98,659

Business Solutions had the following transactions and events in December 2019.

Dec. 2   Paid $1,025 cash to Hillside Mall for Business Solutions's share of mall advertising costs.
3   Paid $500 cash for minor repairs to the company's computer.
4   Received $3,950 cash from Alex's Engineering Co. for the receivable from November.
10   Paid cash to Lyn Addie for six days of work at the rate of $125 per day.
14   Notified by Alex's Engineering Co. that Business Solutions's bid of $7,000 on a proposed project has been accepted. Alex's paid a $1,500 cash advance to Business Solutions.
15   Purchased $1,100 of computer supplies on credit from Harris Office Products.
16   Sent a reminder to Gomez Co. to pay the fee for services recorded on November 8.
20   Completed a project for Liu Corporation and received $5,625 cash.
22–26   Took the week off for the holidays.
28   Received $3,000 cash from Gomez Co. on its receivable.
29   Reimbursed S. Rey for business automobile mileage (600 miles at $0.32 per mile).
31   The company paid $1,500 cash in dividends.

The following additional facts are collected for use in making adjusting entries prior to preparing financial statements for the company's first three months.

a. The December 31 inventory count of computer supplies shows $580 still available.

b. Three months have expired since the 12-month insurance premium was paid in advance.

c. As of December 31, Lyn Addie has not been paid for four days of work at $125 per day.

d. The computer system, acquired on October 1, is expected to have a four-year life with no salvage value.

e. The office equipment, acquired on October 1, is expected to have a five-year life with no salvage value.

f. Three of the four months' prepaid rent have expired.

Required

1. Prepare journal entries to record each of the December transactions and events for Business Solutions. Post those entries to the accounts in the ledger.

2. Prepare adjusting entries to reflect *a* through *f*. Post those entries to the accounts in the ledger.

3. Prepare an adjusted trial balance as of December 31, 2019.

4. Prepare an income statement for the three months ended December 31, 2019.

5. Prepare a statement of retained earnings for the three months ended December 31, 2019.

6. Prepare a balance sheet as of December 31, 2019.

7. Record and post the necessary closing entries as of December 31, 2019.

8. Prepare a post-closing trial balance as of December 31, 2019.

Check   (3) Adjusted trial balance totals, $109,034

(6) Total assets, $83,460

(8) Post-closing trial balance totals, $85,110

The **General Ledger** tool in Connect allows students to immediately see the financial statements as of a specific date. Each of the following questions begins with an unadjusted trial balance. Using transactions from the following assignment, prepare the necessary adjustments and determine the impact each adjustment has on net income. The financial statements are automatically populated.

GENERAL

GL LEDGER PROBLEM

GL 3-1   Based on the FastForward illustration in this chapter

Using transactions from the following assignments, prepare the necessary adjustments, create the financial statements, and determine the impact each adjustment has on net income.

GL 3-2   Based on Problem 3-3A

GL 3-3   Extension of Problem 2-1A

GL 3-4   Extension of Problem 2-2A

GL 3-5   Based on Serial Problem SP 3

Accounting Analysis

AA 3-1   Use **Apple**'s financial statements in Appendix A to answer the following.

1. Compute Apple's profit margin for fiscal years ended (*a*) September 30, 2017, and (*b*) September 24, 2016.

2. Is the change in Apple's profit margin favorable or unfavorable?

3. In 2017, did Apple's profit margin outperform or underperform the industry (assumed) average of 12%?

4. For the fiscal year ended September 30, 2017, what is the balance of its Income Summary account before it is closed?

COMPANY ANALYSIS

A1   P7

APPLE

**COMPARATIVE
ANALYSIS**

A1   A2

APPLE

GOOGLE

AA 3-2   Key figures for the recent two years of both **Apple** and **Google** follow.

$ millions	Apple		Google	
	Current Year	Prior Year	Current Year	Prior Year
Net income..................	$ 48,351	$ 45,687	$ 12,662	$ 19,478
Net sales	229,234	215,639	110,855	90,272
Current assets	128,645	106,869	124,308	105,408
Current liabilities	100,814	79,006	24,183	16,756

Required

1. Compute profit margins for (*a*) Apple and (*b*) Google for the two years of data reported above.
2. In the current year, which company is more successful on the basis of profit margin?
3. Compute current ratios for (*a*) Apple and (*b*) Google for the two years reported above.
4. In the current year, which company has the better ability to pay short-term obligations according to the current ratio?

GLOBAL ANALYSIS

A1

Samsung

APPLE

GOOGLE

AA 3-3   Key comparative figures for **Samsung, Apple,** and **Google** follow.

In millions	Samsung	Apple	Google
Net income	₩ 42,186,747	$ 48,351	$ 12,662
Net sales	239,575,376	229,234	110,855

Required

1. Compute profit margin for Samsung, Apple, and Google.
2. Which company has the highest profit margin?

Beyond the Numbers

**ETHICS
CHALLENGE**

P4   P6

BTN 3-1   On January 20, 2019, Tamira Nelson, the accountant for Picton Enterprises, is feeling pressure to complete the annual financial statements. The company president has said he needs up-to-date financial statements to share with the bank on January 21 at a dinner meeting that has been called to discuss Picton's obtaining loan financing for a special building project. Tamira knows that she will not be able to gather all the needed information in the next 24 hours to prepare the entire set of adjusting entries. Those entries must be posted before the financial statements accurately portray the company's performance and financial position for the fiscal period ended December 31, 2018. Tamira ultimately decides to estimate several expense accruals at the last minute. When deciding on estimates for the expenses, she uses low estimates because she does not want to make the financial statements look worse than they are. Tamira finishes the financial statements before the deadline and gives them to the president without mentioning that several account balances are estimates that she provided.

Required

1. Identify several courses of action that Tamira could have taken instead of the one she took.
2. If you were in Tamira's situation, what would you have done? Briefly justify your response.

**COMMUNICATING
IN PRACTICE**

P7   P8

BTN 3-2   One of your classmates states that a company's books should be ongoing and therefore not closed until that business is terminated. Write a half-page memo to this classmate explaining the concept of the closing process by drawing analogies between (1) a scoreboard for an athletic event and the revenue and expense accounts of a business or (2) a sports team's record book and the retained earnings account. *Hint:* Think about what would happen if the scoreboard were not cleared before the start of a new game.

BTN 3-3 Access EDGAR online (<u>SEC.gov</u>) and locate the 10-K report of **The Gap, Inc.** (ticker: GPS), filed on March 20, 2017. Review its financial statements reported for the year ended January 28, 2017, to answer the following questions.

TAKING IT TO THE NET

A1

Required

1. What are Gap's main brands?
2. When is Gap's fiscal year-end?
3. What is Gap's net sales for the period ended January 28, 2017?
4. What is Gap's net income for the period ended January 28, 2017?
5. Compute Gap's profit margin for the year ended January 28, 2017.
6. Do you believe Gap's decision to use a year-end of late January or early February relates to its natural business year? Explain.

BTN 3-4 Four types of adjustments are described in the chapter: (1) prepaid expenses, (2) unearned revenues, (3) accrued expenses, and (4) accrued revenues.

TEAMWORK IN ACTION

P1 P2 P3 P4

Required

1. Form *learning teams* of four (or more) members. Each team member must select one of the four adjustments as an area of expertise (each team must have at least one expert in each area).
2. Form *expert teams* from the individuals who have selected the same area of expertise. Expert teams are to discuss and write a report that each expert will present to his or her learning team addressing the following:
   a. Description of the adjustment and why it's necessary.
   b. Example of a transaction or event, with dates and amounts, that requires adjustment.
   c. Adjusting entry(ies) for the example in requirement *b*.
   d. Status of the affected account(s) before and after the adjustment in requirement *c*.
   e. Effects on financial statements of not making the adjustment.
3. Each expert should return to his or her learning team. In rotation, each member should present his or her expert team's report to the learning team. Team discussion is encouraged.

BTN 3-5 Review this chapter's opening feature involving Evan and Bobby and **Snapchat**.

ENTREPRENEURIAL DECISION

C3 P7

1. Explain how a classified balance sheet can help Evan and Bobby know what bills are due when and whether they have the resources to pay those bills.
2. Why is it important for Evan and Bobby to match costs and revenues in a specific time period? How do closing entries help them in this regard?
3. What objectives are met when Evan and Bobby apply closing procedures each fiscal year-end?

BTN 3-6 Select a company that you can visit in person or interview on the telephone. Call ahead to the company to arrange a time when you can interview an employee (preferably an accountant) who helps prepare the annual financial statements. Inquire about the following aspects of its *accounting cycle:*

HITTING THE ROAD

C1 C2

1. Does the company prepare interim financial statements? What time period(s) is used for interim statements?
2. Does the company use the cash or accrual basis of accounting?
3. Does the company use a work sheet in preparing financial statements? Why or why not?
4. Does the company use a spreadsheet program? If so, which software program is used?
5. How long does it take after the end of its reporting period to complete annual statements?

---

4 Accounting for Merchandising Operations

Chapter Preview

MERCHANDISING ACTIVITIES

C1 Income and inventory for merchandisers

C2 Operating cycle

Inventory cost flows

NTK 4-1

MERCHANDISING PURCHASES

P1 Accounting for:

Purchases discounts

Purchases returns and allowances

Transportation costs

NTK 4-2

MERCHANDISING SALES

P2 Accounting for:

Sales of merchandise

Sales discounts

Sales returns and allowances

NTK 4-3

MERCHANDISER REPORTING

P3 Adjusting and closing

P4 Multiple-step and single-step income statements

A1 Acid-test analysis

A2 Gross margin analysis

NTK 4-4, 4-5

Learning Objectives

CONCEPTUAL

C1 Describe merchandising activities and identify income components for a merchandising company.

C2 Identify and explain the inventory asset and cost flows of a merchandising company.

ANALYTICAL

A1 Compute the acid-test ratio and explain its use to assess liquidity.

A2 Compute the gross margin ratio and explain its use to assess profitability.

PROCEDURAL

P1 Analyze and record transactions for merchandise purchases using a perpetual system.

P2 Analyze and record transactions for merchandise sales using a perpetual system.

P3 Prepare adjustments and close accounts for a merchandising company.

P4 Define and prepare multiple-step and single-step income statements.

P5 *Appendix 4A*—Record and compare merchandising transactions using both periodic and perpetual inventory systems.

P6 *Appendix 4B*—Prepare adjustments for discounts, returns, and allowances per revenue recognition rules.

P7 *Appendix 4C*—Record and compare merchandising transactions using the gross method and net method.

Bear Up

"Understand what matters"—**MAXINE CLARK**

ST. LOUIS—"When I graduated from college," explains Maxine Clark, "I felt the retail world had lost its spark. I wanted to be more creative." Maxine was determined to start a business that would be different. Then she went shopping with the young daughter of a friend. "When we couldn't find anything new, Katie picked up a Beanie Baby and said we could make one," recalls Maxine. "Her words gave me the idea to create a company that would allow people to create their own customized stuffed animals." **Build-A-Bear Workshop** (**BuildaBear.com**) was born!

"I did some research and began putting together a plan," says Maxine. The Build-A-Bear Workshops were an instant success.

As her company grew, Maxine says accounting data on her merchandising operations fell short. "We can't give up!" was her view. In response, Maxine set up an accounting system to measure, track, summarize, and report on merchandising transactions, especially purchases.

Maxine computerized the accounting system, prepared monthly financial statements per store, developed annual budgets, and tracked all bank accounts and payables.

Build-A-Bear's successful use of accounting data has made Maxine a self-made woman. She insists, however, it is not about

©Monty Brinton/CBS/Getty Images

the financial rewards. "We're a family business," explains Maxine. "It's important to set an example for children by being a company that does good things and cares about the well-being of others."

Sources: *Build-A-Bear website,* January 2019; *Fortune,* March 2012; *LEADERS,* April 2011; *CSRwire,* August 2008

MERCHANDISING ACTIVITIES

Previous chapters covered accounting for service companies. A merchandising company's activities differ from those of a service company. **Merchandise** refers to products, also called *goods,* that a company buys to resell. A **merchandiser** earns net income by buying and selling merchandise. Merchandisers are wholesalers or retailers. A **wholesaler** buys products from manufacturers and sells them to retailers. A **retailer** buys products from manufacturers or wholesalers and sells them to consumers.

C1

Describe merchandising activities and identify income components for a merchandising company.

Reporting Income for a Merchandiser

Net income for a merchandiser equals revenues from selling merchandise minus both the cost of merchandise sold and other expenses—see Exhibit 4.1. Revenue from selling merchandise is called *sales,* and the expense of buying and preparing merchandise is called **cost of goods sold.** (Some service companies use the term *sales* instead of revenues; cost of goods sold is also called *cost of sales.*)

Point: SuperValu and SYSCO are wholesalers. Target and Walmart are retailers.

Service Company

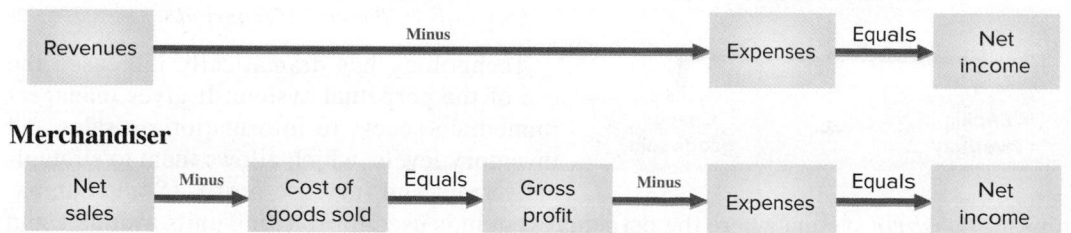

EXHIBIT 4.1

Computing Income for a Merchandising Company versus a Service Company

The income statements for a service company, **Liberty Tax**, and for a merchandiser, **Nordstrom**, are in Exhibit 4.2. We see that the merchandiser, Nordstrom, reports cost of goods sold, which is not reported by the service company. The merchandiser also reports **gross profit,** or **gross margin,** which is net sales minus cost of goods sold.

EXHIBIT 4.2

Income Statement for a Service Company and a Merchandising Company

Service Company	
LIBERTY TAX Income Statement ($ millions)	
Revenues.	$174
Expenses.	162
Net income	$ 12

Merchandising Company	
NORDSTROM INC. Income Statement ($ millions)	
Net sales	$14,757
Cost of goods sold	9,440
Gross profit	5,317
Expenses.	4,963
Net income	$ 354

C2

Identify and explain the inventory asset and cost flows of a merchandising company.

Reporting Inventory for a Merchandiser

A merchandiser's balance sheet has a current asset called *merchandise inventory,* an item not on a service company's balance sheet. **Merchandise inventory,** or simply **inventory,** refers to products that a company owns and intends to sell. Inventory cost includes the cost to buy the goods, ship them to the store, and make them ready for sale.

EXHIBIT 4.3

Merchandiser's Operating Cycle

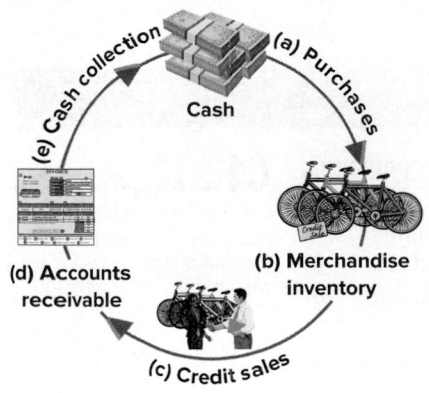

Operating Cycle for a Merchandiser

Exhibit 4.3 shows an operating cycle for a merchandiser with credit sales. The cycle moves from (*a*) cash purchases of merchandise to (*b*) inventory for sale to (*c*) credit sales to (*d*) accounts receivable to (*e*) receipt of cash. The length of an operating cycle differs across the types of businesses. Department stores often have operating cycles of two to five months. Operating cycles for grocery stores are usually from two to eight weeks. Companies try to keep their operating cycles short because assets tied up in inventory and receivables are not productive. Cash sales shorten operating cycles.

Inventory Systems

Exhibit 4.4 shows that a company's merchandise available for sale consists of what it begins with (beginning inventory) and what it purchases (net purchases). The merchandise available for sale is either sold (cost of goods sold) or kept for future sales (ending inventory).

Companies account for inventory in one of two ways: *perpetual system* or *periodic system.*

- **Perpetual inventory system** updates accounting records for *each* purchase and *each* sale of inventory.
- **Periodic inventory system** updates accounting records for purchases and sales of inventory *only at the end of a period.*

Technology has dramatically increased the use of the perpetual system. It gives managers immediate access to information on sales and inventory levels, which allows them to strategically react and increase profit. (Some compa-nies use a *hybrid* system where the perpetual system is used for tracking units available and the periodic system is used to compute cost of sales.)

EXHIBIT 4.4

Merchandiser's Cost Flow for a Single Time Period

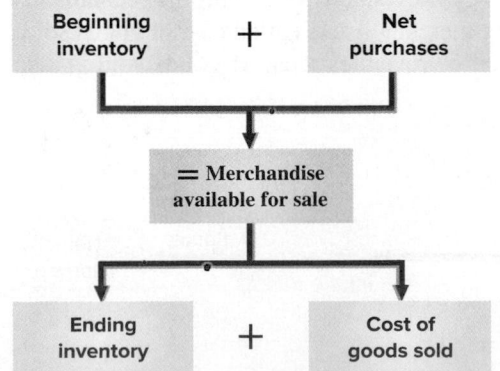

Merchandise Inventory		
Beg. inventory	#	
Net purchases	#	
Merchandise avail. for sale	#	
		COGS #
End. inventory	#	

Point: Merchandise avail. for sale: MAS = EI + COGS, which can be rewritten as MAS − EI = COGS, or MAS − COGS = EI.

Use the following information (in random order) from a merchandising company and from a service company to complete the requirements. *Hint:* Not all information may be necessary for the solutions.

SaveCo Merchandiser			
Supplies.............	$ 10	Expenses.......	$ 20
Beginning inventory...	100	Net purchases ...	80
Ending inventory......	50	Net sales	190

Hi-Tech Services			
Expenses.....	$170	Prepaid rent........	$25
Revenues.....	200	Accounts payable ...	35
Cash........	10	Supplies..........	65

NEED-TO-KNOW **4-1**

Merchandise Accounts and Computations

C1 **C2**

1. For the merchandiser only, compute (a) goods available for sale, (b) cost of goods sold, and (c) gross profit.

2. Compute net income for each company.

Solution

1. a. Computation of goods available for sale (SaveCo).

b. Computation of cost of goods sold (SaveCo).

c. Computation of gross profit (SaveCo).

Beginning inventory..........	$100
Plus: Net purchases..........	80
Goods available for sale	$180

Beginning inventory..........	$100
Plus: Net purchases..........	80
Goods available for sale	180
Less: Ending inventory........	50
Cost of goods sold...........	$130

Net sales.................	$190
Less: Cost of goods	
sold (from part b).........	130
Gross profit...............	$ 60

2. Computation of net income for each company.

SaveCo Merchandiser	
Net sales....................................	$190
Less: Cost of goods sold (from part 1b)..........	130
Gross profit.................................	60
Less: Expenses.............................	20
Net income.................................	$ 40

Hi-Tech Services	
Revenues......................	$200
Less: Expenses.................	170
Net income....................	$ 30

Do More: QS 4-3, E 4-1, E 4-2

ACCOUNTING FOR MERCHANDISE PURCHASES

This section explains how we record purchases under different purchase terms.

Purchases <u>without</u> Cash Discounts

Z-Mart records a $500 cash purchase of merchandise on November 2 as follows.

Nov. 2	Merchandise Inventory.............................	500	
	Cash..		500
	Purchased goods for cash.		

If these goods are instead *purchased on credit,* and no discounts are offered for early payment, Z-Mart makes the same entry except that Accounts Payable is credited instead of Cash.

⬛ **Decision Insight** ━━━━━━━━━━━━━━━━━━━━━━━━

Trade Discounts   When a manufacturer or wholesaler prepares a catalog of items for sale, each item has a **list price**, or *catalog price.* However, an item's *selling price* equals list price minus a percent called a **trade discount.** A wholesaler buying in large quantities gets a larger discount than a retailer buying in small quantities. A buyer records the net amount of list price minus trade discount. If a supplier of Z-Mart lists an item at $625 and gives Z-Mart a 20% trade discount, Z-Mart's purchase price is $500, computed as $625 − (20% × $625). ⬛

Purchases <u>with</u> Cash Discounts

The purchase of goods on credit requires credit terms. **Credit terms** include the amounts and timing of payments from a buyer to a seller. To demonstrate, when sellers require payment within 10 days after the end of the month (**EOM**) of the invoice date, credit terms are "n/10

P1_____

Analyze and record transactions for merchandise purchases using a perpetual system.

Assets = Liabilities + Equity
+500
−500

Point: Costs recorded in Merchandise Inventory are called *inventoriable costs.*

Point: Trade discounts are not journalized; purchases are recorded based on the invoice amount.

EOM." When sellers require payment within 30 days after the invoice date, credit terms are "n/30," meaning *net 30 days*.

Credit Terms   Exhibit 4.5 explains credit terms. The amount of time allowed before full payment is due is the **credit period.** Sellers can grant a **cash discount** to encourage buyers to pay earlier. A buyer views a cash discount as a **purchases discount.** A seller views a cash discount as a **sales discount.** Any cash discounts are described on the invoice. For example, credit terms of "2/10, n/60" mean that full payment is due within a 60-day credit period, but the buyer can deduct 2% of the invoice amount if payment is made within 10 days of the invoice date. This reduced payment is only for the **discount period.**

EXHIBIT 4.5

Credit Terms

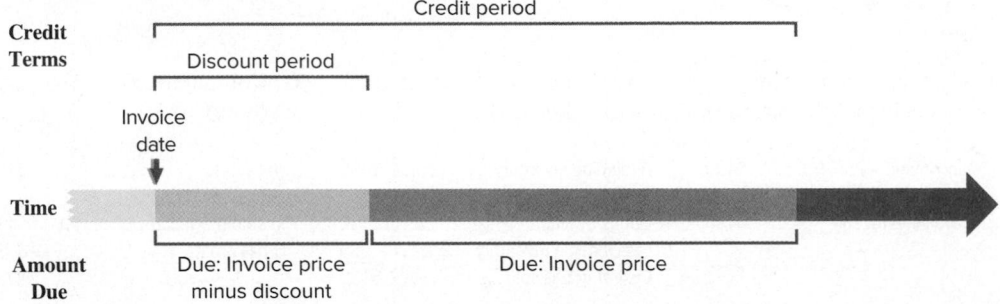

Invoice   On November 2, Z-Mart purchases $500 of merchandise **on credit** with terms of 2/10, n/30. The invoice for this purchase is shown in Exhibit 4.6. This is a purchase invoice for Z-Mart (buyer) and a sales invoice for Trex (seller). The amount recorded for merchandise inventory includes its purchase cost, shipping fees, taxes, and any other costs necessary to make it ready for sale.

EXHIBIT 4.6

Invoice

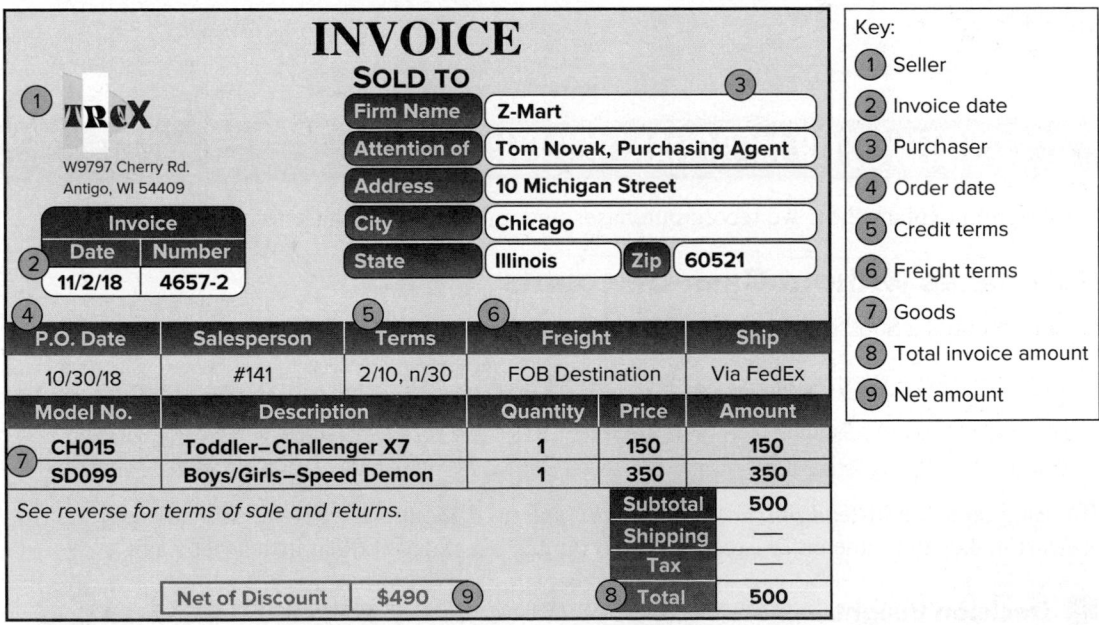

Point: The invoice date sets the discount and credit periods.

Gross Method   Z-Mart purchases $500 of merchandise on credit terms of 2/10, n/30. The November 2 invoice offers a 2% discount if paid within 10 days; if not, Z-Mart must pay the full amount within 30 days. The buyer has two options.

- Pay within discount period (Nov. 2 through Nov. 12):   Due = $490.
    or
- Pay after discount period (Nov. 13 through Dec. 2):   Due = $500.

The $490 equals the $500 invoice minus $10 discount (computed as $500 × 2%).

On the purchase date, we do not know if payment will occur within the discount period. The **gross method** records the purchase at its *gross* (full) invoice amount. For Z-Mart, the purchase of $500 of merchandise with terms of 2/10, n/30 is recorded at $500. *The gross method is used here because it is (1) used more in practice, (2) easier to apply, and (3) less costly.*

Purchases on Credit   Z-Mart's entry to record the November 2 purchase of $500 of merchandise on credit follows. (For recording, it can help to add the name to the payable, such as Accounts Payable—Trex.)

(*a*) Nov. 2	Merchandise Inventory	500	
	Accounts Payable		500
	Purchased goods, terms 2/10, n/30.		

Assets = Liabilities + Equity
+500   +500

Point: Appendix 4A repeats journal entries *a* through *g* using the periodic system.

Payment within Discount Period   Good cash management means that invoices are not paid until the last day of the discount or credit period. This is because the buyer can use that money until payment is required. If Z-Mart pays the amount due on (or before) November 12, the entry is

(*b1*) Nov. 12	Accounts Payable.	500	
	Merchandise Inventory.		10
	Cash*.		490
	*Paid for goods within discount period. *$500 × (100% − 2%)*		

Assets = Liabilities + Equity
−490   −500
− 10

The Merchandise Inventory account equals the $490 net cost of purchases after these entries, and the Accounts Payable account has a zero balance.

Accounts Payable					Merchandise Inventory					Cash		
		Nov. 2	500		Nov. 2	500						
Nov. 12	500						Nov. 12	10		Nov. 12	**490**	
		Bal.	**0**		Bal.	**490**						

Payment after Discount Period   If the invoice is paid *after* November 12, the discount is lost. If Z-Mart pays the gross (full) amount due on December 2 (the n/30 due date), the entry is

(*b2*) Dec. 2	Accounts Payable.	500	
	Cash.		500
	Paid for goods outside discount period.		

Assets = Liabilities + Equity
−500   −500

Purchases <u>with</u> Returns and Allowances

Purchases returns are merchandise a buyer purchases but then returns. *Purchases allowances* refer to a seller granting a price reduction (allowance) to a buyer of defective or unacceptable merchandise.

Point: When a buyer returns or takes an allowance on merchandise, the buyer issues a **debit memorandum.** This informs the seller of a debit made to the seller's account payable in the buyer's records.

Purchases Allowances   On November 5, Z-Mart (buyer) agrees to a $30 allowance from Trex for defective merchandise (assume allowance is $30 whether paid within the discount period or not). Z-Mart's entry to update Merchandise Inventory and record the allowance follows. Z-Mart's allowance for defective merchandise reduces its account payable to the seller. If cash is refunded, Cash is debited instead of Accounts Payable.

(*c1*) Nov. 5	Accounts Payable.	30	
	Merchandise Inventory.		30
	Allowance for defective goods.		

Assets = Liabilities + Equity
−30   −30

Purchases Returns   Returns of inventory are recorded at the amount charged for that inventory. On June 1, Z-Mart purchases $250 of merchandise with terms 2/10, n/60—see entries below. On June 3, Z-Mart returns $50 of those goods. When Z-Mart pays on June 11, it takes the 2% discount only on the $200 remaining balance ($250 − $50). When goods are returned, a buyer takes a discount on only the remaining balance. This means the discount is $4 (computed as $200 × 2%) and the cash payment is $196 (computed as $200 − $4).

June 1	Merchandise Inventory	250	
	Accounts Payable		250
	Purchased goods, terms 2/10, n/60.		
(c2) June 3	Accounts Payable.................................	50	
	Merchandise Inventory...........................		50
	Returned goods to seller.		
June 11	Accounts Payable.................................	200	
	Merchandise Inventory...........................		4
	Cash...		196
	Paid for $200 of goods less $4 discount.		

These T-accounts show the final $196 in inventory, the zero balance in Accounts Payable, and the $196 cash payment.

Accounts Payable			
		Jun. 1	250
Jun. 3	50		
Jun. 11	200		
		Bal.	0

Merchandise Inventory			
Jun. 1	250		
		Jun. 3	50
		Jun. 11	4
Bal.	**196**		

Cash			
		Jun. 11	**196**

Decision Insight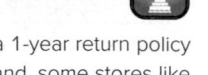

What's Your Policy? Return policies are a competitive advantage for businesses. **REI** offers a 1-year return policy on nearly every product it sells. **Amazon** picks up returned items at your door. On the other hand, some stores like **Best Buy** allow only 14 days to return products. ∎

Purchases and Transportation Costs

The buyer and seller must agree on who is responsible for paying freight (shipping) costs and who has the risk of loss during transit. This is the same as asking at what point ownership transfers from the seller to the buyer. The point of transfer is called the **FOB** (*free on board*) point.
  Exhibit 4.7 covers two alternative points of transfer.

1. *FOB shipping point* means the buyer accepts ownership when the goods depart the seller's place of business. The buyer pays shipping costs and has the risk of loss in transit. The goods are part of the buyer's inventory when they are in transit because ownership has transferred to the buyer. **1-800-Flowers.com**, a floral merchandiser, uses FOB shipping point.

2. *FOB destination* means ownership of goods transfers to the buyer when the goods arrive at the buyer's place of business. The seller pays shipping charges and has the risk of loss in transit. The seller does not record revenue until the goods arrive at the destination.

EXHIBIT 4.7

Ownership Transfer and Transportation Costs

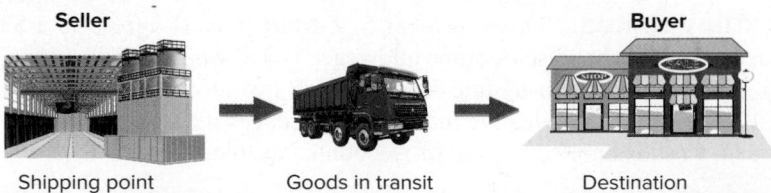

Seller — Shipping point   Goods in transit   Buyer — Destination

Shipping Terms	Ownership Transfers at	Goods in Transit Owned by	Transportation Costs Paid by		
FOB shipping point	Shipping point	Buyer	**Buyer**	Merchandise Inventory ... #	
				Cash	#
FOB destination	Destination	Seller	**Seller**	Delivery Expense .... #	
				Cash	#

©Michael DeYoung/Blend Images

When a buyer is responsible for paying transportation costs, the payment is made to a carrier or directly to the seller. The cost principle requires that transportation costs of a buyer (often called *transportation-in* or *freight-in*) be part of the cost of merchandise inventory. Z-Mart's entry to record a $75 freight charge from **UPS** for merchandise purchased FOB shipping point is

(*d*) Nov. 24	Merchandise Inventory	75	
	Cash...		75
	Paid freight costs on goods.		

Point: If we place an order online and receive free shipping, we have terms FOB destination.

Assets = Liabilities + Equity
+75
−75

When a seller is responsible for paying shipping costs, it records these costs in a Delivery Expense account. Delivery expense, also called *transportation-out* or *freight-out,* is reported as a selling expense in the seller's income statement.

Point: INcoming freight costs are charged to INventory. When inventory EXits, freight costs are charged to EXpense.

Itemized Costs of Purchases

In summary, purchases are recorded as debits to Merchandise Inventory (or Inventory). Purchases discounts, returns, and allowances are credited to (subtracted from) Merchandise Inventory. Transportation-in is debited (added) to Merchandise Inventory. Z-Mart's itemized costs of merchandise purchases for the year are in Exhibit 4.8.

The accounting system described here does not provide separate records (accounts) for total purchases, total purchases discounts, total purchases returns and allowances, and total transportation-in. Many companies collect this information in supplementary records to evaluate these costs. **Supplementary records,** or *supplemental records,* refer to information outside the usual ledger accounts.

Itemized Costs of Merchandise Purchases	
Invoice cost of merchandise purchases	$ 235,800
Less: Purchases discounts received	(4,200)
Purchases returns and allowances.........	(1,500)
Add: Costs of transportation-in	2,300
Total net cost of merchandise purchases	$232,400

EXHIBIT 4.8

Itemized Costs of Merchandise Purchases

Point: Some companies have separate accounts for purchases discounts, returns and allowances, and transportation-in. These accounts are then transferred to Merchandise Inventory at period-end. This is a *hybrid system* of perpetual and periodic. That is, Merchandise Inventory is updated on a perpetual basis but only for purchases and cost of goods sold.

■ Decision Ethics

Payables Manager As a new accounts payable manager, you are being trained by the outgoing manager. She explains that the system prepares checks for amounts net of favorable cash discounts, and the checks are dated the last day of the discount period. She tells you that checks are not mailed until five days later, adding that "the company gets free use of cash for an extra five days, and our department looks better." Do you continue this policy? ■ *Answer:* One point of view is that the late payment policy is unethical. A deliberate plan to make late payments means the company lies when it pretends to make payment within the discount period. Another view is that the late payment policy is acceptable. Some believe attempts to take discounts through late payments are accepted as "price negotiation."

Prepare journal entries to record each of the following purchases transactions of a merchandising company. Assume a perpetual inventory system using the gross method for recording purchases.

Oct. 1 Purchased $1,000 of goods. Terms of the sale are 4/10, n/30, and FOB shipping point; the invoice is dated October 1.
   3 Paid $30 cash for freight charges from UPS for the October 1 purchase.
   7 Returned $50 of the $1,000 of goods from the October 1 purchase and received full credit.
   11 Paid the amount due from the October 1 purchase (less the return on October 7).
   31 *Assume the October 11 payment was never made.* Instead, payment of the amount due, less the return on October 7, occurred on October 31.

Merchandise Purchases

P1

Solution

Oct. 1	Merchandise Inventory	1,000	
	Accounts Payable................................		1,000
	Purchased goods, terms 4/10, n/30.		
Oct. 3	Merchandise Inventory	30	
	Cash...		30
	Paid freight on purchases FOB shipping point.		

[continued on next page]

[continued from previous page]

Oct. 7	Accounts Payable.	50	
	Merchandise Inventory.		50
	Returned goods.		
Oct. 11	Accounts Payable.	950	
	Merchandise Inventory*		38
	Cash†		912
	Paid for goods within discount period.		
	$950 × 4% †$950 − ($950 × 4%)		
Oct. 31	Accounts Payable†	950	
	Cash.		950
	Paid for goods outside discount period. †*$1,000 − $50*		

Do More: QS 4-5, QS 4-6, QS 4-7, E 4-3, E 4-5

ACCOUNTING FOR MERCHANDISE SALES

P2

Analyze and record transactions for merchandise sales using a perpetual system.

Merchandising companies must account for sales, sales discounts, sales returns and allowances, and cost of goods sold. Z-Mart has these items in its gross profit computation—see Exhibit 4.9. This shows that customers paid $314,700 for merchandise that cost Z-Mart $230,400, yielding a gross profit of $84,300.

EXHIBIT 4.9

Gross Profit Computation

Computation of Gross Profit	
Net sales (net of discounts, returns, and allowances)	$314,700
Cost of goods sold	230,400
Gross profit	**$ 84,300**

The perpetual accounting system requires that **each sales transaction for a merchandiser, whether for cash or on credit, has** *two entries:* **one for revenue and one for cost.**

1. **Revenue received (and asset increased) from the customer.**
2. **Cost of goods sold incurred (and asset decreased) to the customer.**

Sales <u>without</u> Cash Discounts

Revenue Side: Inflow of Assets   Z-Mart sold $1,000 of merchandise on credit terms n/60 on November 12. The revenue part of this transaction is recorded as follows. This entry shows an increase in Z-Mart's assets in the form of accounts receivable. It also shows the increase in revenue (Sales). If the sale is for cash, debit Cash instead of Accounts Receivable.

Assets = Liabilities + Equity
+1,000   +1,000

Nov. 12	Accounts Receivable	1,000	
	Sales		1,000
	Sold goods on credit.		

Point: Gross profit on Nov. 12 sale:

Net sales	$1,000
Cost of goods sold.	300
Gross profit	$ 700

Cost Side: Outflow of Assets   The cost side of each sale requires that Merchandise Inventory decrease by that item's cost. The cost of the merchandise Z-Mart sold on November 12 is $300, and the entry to record the cost part of this transaction follows.

Assets = Liabilities + Equity
−300   −300

Nov. 12	Cost of Goods Sold	300	
	Merchandise Inventory.		300
	Record cost of Nov. 12 sale.		

Decision Insight

Future Demands   Large merchandising companies, such as **Amazon**, bombard suppliers with demands. These include discounts for bar coding and technology support systems and fines for shipping errors. Merchandisers' goals are to reduce inventories, shorten lead times, and eliminate errors. Colleges offer programs in supply chain management and logistics to train future employees to help merchandisers meet such goals. ∎

©Polaris/Newscom

Sales with Cash Discounts

Offering discounts on credit sales benefits a seller through earlier cash receipts and reduced collection efforts. We use the *gross method,* which records sales at the full amount and records sales discounts if, and when, they are taken. The gross method requires a period-end adjusting entry to estimate future sales discounts. (The **net method** records sales at the net amount, which assumes all discounts are taken. This method requires an adjusting entry to estimate future discounts lost. See Appendix 4C.)

Sales on Credit   Z-Mart makes a credit sale for $1,000 on November 12 with terms of 2/10, n/45 (cost of the merchandise sold is $300). The entries to record this sale follow.

Nov. 12	Accounts Receivable	1,000	
	Sales		1,000
	Sold goods, terms 2/10, n/45.		
Nov. 12	Cost of Goods Sold	300	
	Merchandise Inventory		300
	Record cost of Nov. 12 sale.		

Assets = Liabilities + Equity
+1,000   +1,000

Assets = Liabilities + Equity
−300   −300

Buyer Pays within Discount Period   One option is for the buyer to pay $980 within the 10-day discount period ending November 22. The $20 sales discount is computed as $1,000 × 2%. If the customer pays on (or before) November 22, Z-Mart records the cash receipt as follows. **Sales Discounts** is a **contra revenue account,** meaning the Sales Discounts account is subtracted from the Sales account when computing net sales. The Sales Discounts account has a *normal debit balance* because it is subtracted from Sales, which has a normal credit balance.

Point: Net sales is the amount received from the customer.

Sales.	$1,000
Sales discounts	(20)
Net sales	$ 980

Nov. 22	Cash*	980	
	Sales Discounts	20	
	Accounts Receivable.		1,000
	Received payment on Nov. 12 sale less discount.		
	*$1,000 − ($1,000 × 2%)		

Assets = Liabilities + Equity
+ 980   −20
−1,000

Buyer Pays after Discount Period   The customer's second option is to wait 45 days until December 27 (or at least until after the discount period) and then pay $1,000. Z-Mart records that cash receipt as

Dec. 27	Cash	1,000	
	Accounts Receivable.		1,000
	Received payment on Nov. 12 sale after discount period.		

Assets = Liabilities + Equity
+1,000
−1,000

Sales with Returns and Allowances

If a customer is unhappy with a purchase, many sellers allow the customer to either return the merchandise for a full refund (*sales return*) or keep the merchandise along with a partial refund (*sales allowance*). Most sellers can reliably estimate returns and allowances (abbreviated *R&A*).

Buyer Returns Goods—Revenue Side   When a buyer returns goods, it impacts the seller's revenue *and* cost sides. When a return occurs, the seller debits **Sales Returns and**

Allowances, a **contra revenue account** to Sales. Assume that a customer returns merchandise on November 26 that sold for $15 and cost $9; the revenue-side returns entry is

Assets = Liabilities + Equity
−15   −15

(e1) Nov. 26	Sales Returns and Allowances	15	
	Cash..		15
	Goods returned from Nov. 12 sale.		

Buyer Returns Goods—Cost Side

When a return occurs, the seller must reduce the cost of sales. Continuing the example where the returned items sold for $15 and cost $9, the cost-side entry depends on whether the goods are defective.

Returned Goods Not Defective.   If the merchandise returned is not defective and can be resold, there is a cost-side entry. The seller adds the cost of the returned goods back to inventory and reduces cost of goods sold as follows. This entry reverses the cost-side entry of November 12 for only $9 of goods returned.

Assets = Liabilities + Equity
+9   +9

(e2) Nov. 26	Merchandise Inventory	9	
	Cost of Goods Sold.............................		9
	Returned goods are added back to inventory.		

Returned Goods Are Defective.   If the merchandise returned is defective, the returned inventory is recorded at its estimated value, not its cost. The following entry assumes the returned goods costing $9 are defective and are worth $2.

Assets = Liabilities + Equity
+2   −7
                      +9

Nov. 26	Merchandise Inventory	2	
	Loss from Defective Merchandise......................	7	
	Cost of Goods Sold.............................		9
	Returned defective goods to inventory and record loss.		

Buyer Granted Allowances

If a buyer is not satisfied with the goods, the seller might offer a price reduction for the buyer to keep the goods. There is no cost-side entry in this case as the inventory is not returned. On the revenue side, the seller debits Sales Returns and Allowances and credits Cash or Accounts Receivable depending on what's agreed. Assume that $40 of merchandise previously sold is defective. The seller gives a price reduction and credits the buyer's accounts receivable for $10. The seller records this allowance as follows.

Assets = Liabilities + Equity
−10   −10

(f) Nov. 24	Sales Returns and Allowances	10	
	Accounts Receivable............................		10
	Sales allowance granted.		

Point: When a seller accepts returns or grants an allowance, the seller issues a **credit memorandum.** This informs the buyer of a credit made to the buyer's account in the seller's records.

If the seller has already collected cash for the sale, the seller could give the price reduction in cash. For example, instead of crediting the buyer's Accounts Receivable in the entry above, the seller can credit Cash for $10.

NEED-TO-KNOW 4-3

Merchandise Sales

P2

Prepare journal entries to record each of the following sales transactions of a merchandising company. Assume a perpetual inventory system and use of the gross method (beginning inventory equals $9,000).

June   1   Sold 50 units of merchandise to a customer for $150 per unit under credit terms of 2/10, n/30, FOB shipping point, and the invoice is dated June 1. The 50 units of merchandise had cost $100 per unit.

   7   The customer returns 2 units purchased on June 1 because those units did not fit its needs. The seller restores those units to its inventory (as they are not defective) and credits Accounts Receivable from the customer.

   11   The seller receives the balance due from the June 1 sale to the customer less returns and allowances.

   14   The customer discovers that 10 units have minor damage but keeps them because the seller sends a $50 cash payment allowance to compensate.

Solution

June	1	Accounts Receivable...............................	7,500	
		Sales..		7,500
		Sold goods. 50 units × $150		
June	1	Cost of Goods Sold...............................	5,000	
		Merchandise Inventory...........................		5,000
		Cost of sale. 50 units × $100		
June	7	Sales Returns and Allowances......................	300	
		Accounts Receivable............................		300
		Returns accepted. 2 units × $150		
June	7	Merchandise Inventory............................	200	
		Cost of Goods Sold.............................		200
		Returns added to inventory. 2 units × $100		
June	11	Cash..	7,056	
		Sales Discounts*...............................	144	
		Accounts Receivable...........................		7,200
		Received payment. *($7,500 − $300) × 2%		
June	14	Sales Returns and Allowances......................	50	
		Cash...		50
		Recorded allowance on goods.		

> **Do More:** QS 4-8, E 4-4,
> E 4-6, E 4-7

ADJUSTING AND CLOSING FOR MERCHANDISERS

Exhibit 4.10 shows the flow of merchandising costs during a period and where these costs are reported at period-end. Specifically, beginning inventory plus the net cost of purchases is the merchandise available for sale. As inventory is sold, its cost is recorded in cost of goods sold on the income statement; what remains is ending inventory on the balance sheet. A period's ending inventory is the next period's beginning inventory.

EXHIBIT 4.10

Merchandising Cost Flow in the Accounting Cycle

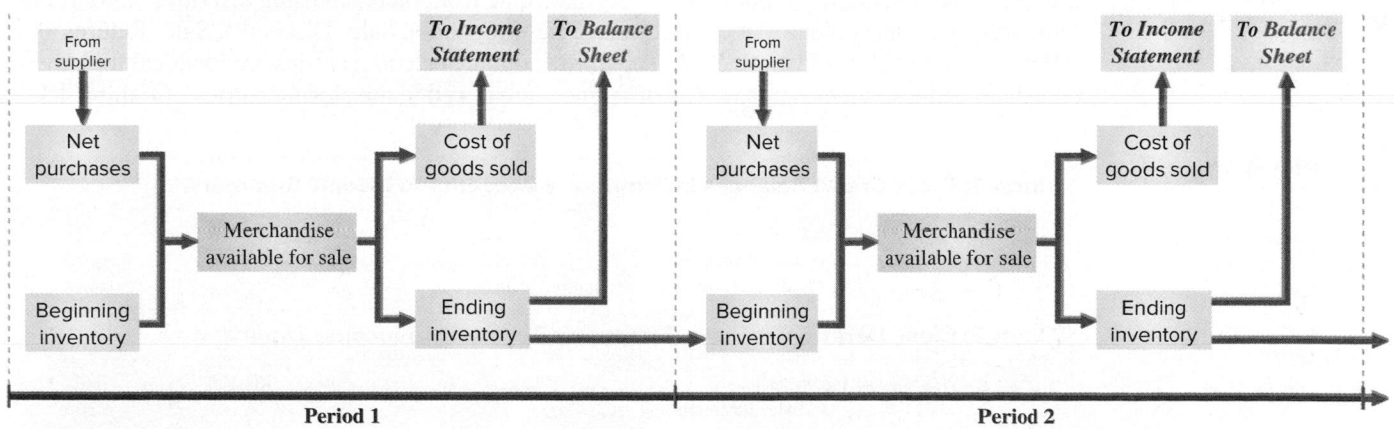

Adjusting Entries for Merchandisers

Each of the steps in the accounting cycle described in the prior chapter applies to a merchandiser. We expand upon three steps of the accounting cycle for a merchandiser—adjustments, statement preparation, and closing.

Inventory Shrinkage—Adjusting Entry   A merchandiser using a *perpetual* inventory system makes an adjustment to Merchandise Inventory for any loss of merchandise, including theft and deterioration. **Shrinkage** is the loss of inventory, and it is computed by comparing a physical count of inventory with recorded amounts.

P3 _____

Prepare adjustments and close accounts for a merchandising company.

Z-Mart's Merchandise Inventory account at the end of the year has a balance of $21,250, but a physical count shows only $21,000 of inventory exists. The adjusting entry to record this $250 shrinkage is

Assets = Liabilities + Equity
−250   −250

Dec. 31	Cost of Goods Sold	250	
	Merchandise Inventory...........................		250
	Adjust for $250 shrinkage.		

Sales Discounts, Returns, and Allowances—Adjusting Entries   Revenue recognition rules require sales to be reported at the amount expected to be received. This means that period-end adjusting entries are commonly made for

- Expected sales discounts.
- Expected returns and allowances (revenue side).
- Expected returns and allowances (cost side).

These three adjustments produce three new accounts: Allowance for Sales Discounts, Sales Refund Payable, and Inventory Returns Estimated. Appendix 4B covers these accounts and the adjusting entries.

Preparing Financial Statements

The financial statements of a merchandiser are similar to those for a service company described in prior chapters. The income statement mainly differs by the addition of *cost of goods sold* and *gross profit*. Net sales is affected by discounts, returns and allowances, and some additional expenses such as delivery expense and loss from defective merchandise. The balance sheet differs by the addition of *merchandise inventory* as part of current assets. (Appendix 4B explains *inventory returns estimated* as part of current assets and *sales refund payable* as part of current liabilities.) The statement of retained earnings is unchanged.

Closing Entries for Merchandisers

Closing entries are similar for service companies and merchandising companies. The difference is that we close some new temporary accounts that come from merchandising activities. Z-Mart has temporary accounts unique to merchandisers: Sales (of goods), Sales Discounts, Sales Returns and Allowances, and Cost of Goods Sold. The third and fourth closing entries are identical for a merchandiser and a service company. The differences are in **red** in the closing entries of Exhibit 4.11.

EXHIBIT 4.11

Closing Entries for a Merchandiser

Step 1: Close Credit Balances in Temporary Accounts to Income Summary.

Dec. 31	Sales	**321,000**	
	Income Summary		321,000
	Close credit balances in temporary accounts.		

Step 2: Close Debit Balances in Temporary Accounts to Income Summary.

Dec. 31	Income Summary....................................	308,100	
	Sales Discounts................................		**4,300**
	Sales Returns and Allowances		**2,000**
	Cost of Goods Sold		**230,400**
	Depreciation Expense...........................		3,700
	Salaries Expense		43,800
	Insurance Expense		600
	Rent Expense		9,000
	Supplies Expense		3,000
	Advertising Expense		11,300
	Close debit balances in temporary accounts.		

Step 3: Close Income Summary.

| Dec. 31 | Income Summary...... | 12,900 | |
| | Retained Earnings.. | | 12,900 |

Step 4: Close Dividends.

| Dec. 31 | Retained Earnings .... | 4,000 | |
| | Dividends............ | | 4,000 |

Sales, having a normal credit balance, is debited in step 1. Sales Discounts, Sales Returns and Allowances, and Cost of Goods Sold, having normal debit balances, are credited in step 2.

Summary of Merchandising Entries

Exhibit 4.12 summarizes the adjusting and closing entries of a merchandiser (using a perpetual inventory system).

	Merchandising Transactions	Merchandising Entries	Dr.	Cr.
Purchases	Purchasing merchandise for resale.	Merchandise Inventory . . . . Cash or Accounts Payable	#	#
	Paying freight costs on purchases; FOB shipping point.	Merchandise Inventory . . . . Cash	#	#
	Paying within discount period.	Accounts Payable . . . . Merchandise Inventory. . . . . Cash	#	# #
	Paying outside discount period.	Accounts Payable . . . . Cash	#	#
	Recording purchases returns or allowances.	Cash or Accounts Payable. . . . . Merchandise Inventory.	#	#
Sales	Selling merchandise.	Cash or Accounts Receivable . . . . Sales	#	#
		Cost of Goods Sold . . . . Merchandise Inventory.	#	#
	Receiving payment within discount period.	Cash. . . . . Sales Discounts . . . . Accounts Receivable	# #	#
	Receiving payment outside discount period.	Cash. . . . . Accounts Receivable	#	#
	Receiving sales returns of nondefective inventory.	Sales Returns and Allowances . . . . Cash or Accounts Receivable	#	#
		Merchandise Inventory . . . . Cost of Goods Sold	#	#
	Recognizing sales allowances.	Sales Returns and Allowances . . . . Cash or Accounts Receivable	#	#
	Paying freight costs on sales; FOB destination.	Delivery Expense. . . . . Cash	#	#

	Merchandising Events	Adjusting and Closing Entries		
Adjusting	Adjustment for shrinkage (occurs when recorded amount larger than physical inventory).	Cost of Goods Sold . . . . Merchandise Inventory.	#	#
	Period-end adjustment for expected sales discounts.*	Sales Discounts . . . . Allowance for Sales Discounts.	#	#
	Period-end adjustment for expected returns—both revenue side and cost side.*	Sales Returns and Allowances . . . . Sales Refund Payable. . . . . Inventory Returns Estimated. . . . . Cost of Goods Sold	# #￼	# #
Closing	Closing temporary accounts with credit balances.	Sales . . . . Income Summary	#	#
	Closing temporary accounts with debit balances.	Income Summary . . . . Sales Returns and Allowances. . . . . Sales Discounts . . . . Cost of Goods Sold . . . . Delivery Expense . . . . "Other Expenses"	#	# # # # #

EXHIBIT 4.12

Summary of Key Merchandising Entries (using perpetual system and gross method)

Merchandise Inventory	
Beginning inventory	
Purchases	Pur. returns
Freight-in (FOB shp pt)	Pur. allowances
	Pur. discounts
	Shrinkage
Goods avail. for sale	
Customer returns	COGS
Ending inventory	

*Period-end adjustments depend on unadjusted balances, which can reverse the debit and credit in the adjusting entries shown; these three entries are covered in Appendix 4B.

NEED-TO-KNOW 4-4

Recording Shrinkage
and Closing Entries

P3

A merchandising company's ledger on May 31, its fiscal year-end, includes the following accounts that have normal balances (it uses the perpetual inventory system). A physical count of its May 31 year-end inventory reveals that the cost of the merchandise inventory still available is $656. (a) Prepare the entry to record any inventory shrinkage. (b) Prepare the four closing entries as of May 31.

Merchandise inventory .... $ 756	Sales $4,300	Depreciation expense......... $400
Common stock........... 1,000	Sales discounts 50	Salaries expense............. 600
Retained earnings 1,300	Other operating expenses 300	Sales returns and allowances... 250
Dividends 150	Cost of goods sold 2,100	

Solution

a.

May 31	Cost of Goods Sold	100	
	Merchandise Inventory...........................		100
	Adjust for shrinkage ($756 — $656).		

b.

May 31	Sales...	4,300	
	Income Summary		4,300
	Close temporary accounts with credit balances.		
May 31	Income Summary....................................	3,800	
	Sales Discounts................................		50
	Sales Returns and Allowances.....................		250
	Cost of Goods Sold*		2,200
	Depreciation Expense...........................		400
	Salaries Expense...............................		600
	Other Operating Expenses.......................		300
	Close temporary accounts with debit balances.		
	*$2,100 (Unadj. bal.) + $100 (Shrinkage)		
May 31	Income Summary....................................	500	
	Retained Earnings..............................		500
	Close Income Summary account.		
May 31	Retained Earnings	150	
	Dividends		150
	Close Dividends account.		

Do More: QS 4-9, QS 4-10,
E 4-10, E 4-12, P 4-4

MORE ON FINANCIAL STATEMENT FORMATS

P4

Define and prepare
multiple-step and single-
step income statements.

This section covers two income statement formats: multiple-step and single-step. The classified balance sheet of a merchandiser also is covered.

Multiple-Step Income Statement

A **multiple-step income statement** details net sales and expenses and reports subtotals for various types of items. Exhibit 4.13 shows a multiple-step income statement. The statement has three main parts: (1) *gross profit,* which is net sales minus cost of goods sold; (2) *income from operations,* which is gross profit minus operating expenses; and (3) *net income,* which is income from operations plus or minus nonoperating items.

Operating expenses are separated into two sections. **Selling expenses** are the expenses of advertising merchandise, making sales, and delivering goods to customers. **General and administrative expenses** support a company's overall operations and include expenses related to accounting, human resources, and finance. Expenses are allocated between sections when they contribute to more than one. Z-Mart allocates rent expense of $9,000 from its store building between two sections: $8,100 to selling expense and $900 to general and administrative expenses.

Nonoperating activities consist of other expenses, revenues, losses, and gains that are unrelated to a company's operations. *Other revenues and gains* commonly include interest revenue, dividend revenue, rent revenue, and gains from asset disposals. *Other expenses and losses* commonly include interest expense, losses from asset disposals, and casualty losses. When there are no reportable nonoperating activities, its income from operations is simply labeled *net income.*

Example: Sometimes interest revenue and interest expense are netted and reported on the income statement as *Interest, net.*

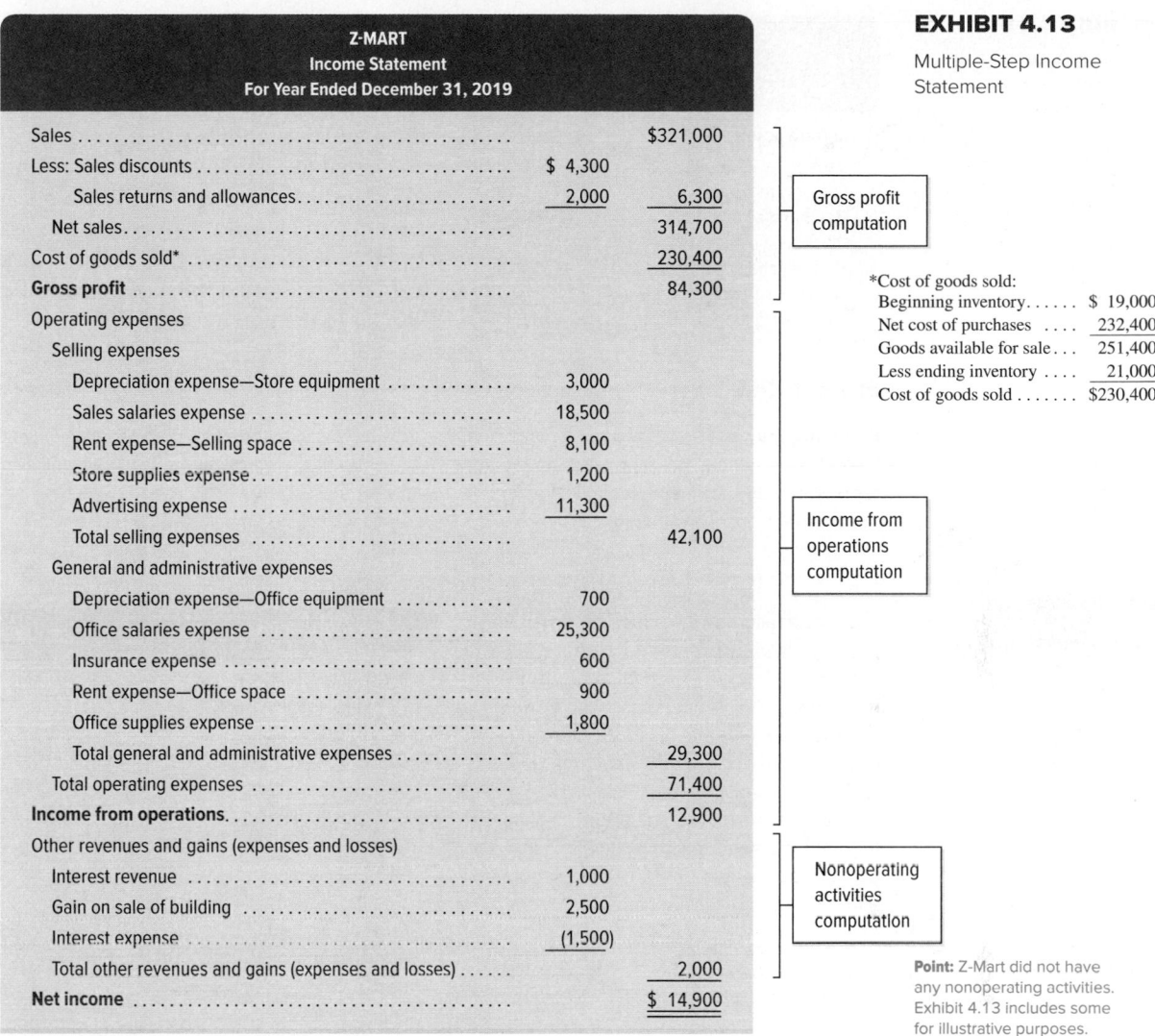

EXHIBIT 4.13

Multiple-Step Income Statement

Z-MART Income Statement For Year Ended December 31, 2019		
Sales		$321,000
Less: Sales discounts	$ 4,300	
Sales returns and allowances......................	2,000	6,300
Net sales...		314,700
Cost of goods sold*		230,400
Gross profit		84,300
Operating expenses		
Selling expenses		
Depreciation expense—Store equipment	3,000	
Sales salaries expense	18,500	
Rent expense—Selling space	8,100	
Store supplies expense..........................	1,200	
Advertising expense	11,300	
Total selling expenses		42,100
General and administrative expenses		
Depreciation expense—Office equipment	700	
Office salaries expense	25,300	
Insurance expense	600	
Rent expense—Office space	900	
Office supplies expense	1,800	
Total general and administrative expenses.............		29,300
Total operating expenses		71,400
Income from operations.............................		12,900
Other revenues and gains (expenses and losses)		
Interest revenue	1,000	
Gain on sale of building	2,500	
Interest expense	(1,500)	
Total other revenues and gains (expenses and losses)		2,000
Net income		$ 14,900

Gross profit computation

*Cost of goods sold:
Beginning inventory...... $ 19,000
Net cost of purchases 232,400
Goods available for sale... 251,400
Less ending inventory 21,000
Cost of goods sold $230,400

Income from operations computation

Nonoperating activities computation

Point: Z-Mart did not have any nonoperating activities. Exhibit 4.13 includes some for illustrative purposes.

Single-Step Income Statement

A **single-step income statement** is shown in Exhibit 4.14. It lists cost of goods sold as another expense and shows only one subtotal for total expenses. Expenses are grouped into few, if any, categories. Many companies use formats that combine features of both single- and multiple-step statements. Management chooses the format that best informs users.

EXHIBIT 4.14

Single-Step Income Statement

Z-MART Income Statement For Year Ended December 31, 2019		
Revenues		
Net sales.....................................		$314,700
Interest revenue..............................		1,000
Gain on sale of building		2,500
Total revenues		318,200
Expenses		
Cost of goods sold............................	$230,400	
Selling expenses	42,100	
General and administrative expenses	29,300	
Interest expense	1,500	
Total expenses		303,300
Net income		$ 14,900

Point: Net income is identical under the single-step and multiple-step formats.

EXHIBIT 4.15

Classified Balance Sheet
(partial) of a Merchandiser

Z-MART
Balance Sheet (partial)
December 31, 2019

Current assets	
Cash	$ 8,200
Accounts receivable.............	11,200
Merchandise inventory	**21,000**
Office supplies	550
Store supplies..................	250
Prepaid insurance..............	300
Total current assets	$41,500

Classified Balance Sheet

The classified balance sheet reports merchandise inventory as a current asset, usually after accounts receivable, according to how quickly they can be converted to cash. Inventory is converted less quickly to cash than accounts receivable because inventory first must be sold before cash can be received. Exhibit 4.15 shows the current asset section of Z-Mart's classified balance sheet (other sections are similar to the previous chapter).

Ethical Risk

Shenanigans Accurate invoices are important to both sellers and buyers. Merchandisers use invoices to make sure they receive full payment for products provided. To achieve this, controls are set up. Still, failures occur. A survey reports that 30% of employees in sales and marketing witnessed false or misleading invoices sent to customers. Another 29% observed employees violating contract terms with customers (KPMG). ∎

NEED-TO-KNOW 4-5

Multiple- and Single-Step Income Statements

P4

Taret's adjusted trial balance on April 30, its fiscal year-end, is shown here (accounts in random order). (a) Prepare a multiple-step income statement that begins with gross sales and includes separate categories for net sales, cost of goods sold, selling expenses, and general and administrative expenses. (b) Prepare a single-step income statement that begins with net sales and includes these expense categories: cost of goods sold, selling expenses, and general and administrative expenses.

Adjusted Trial Balance	Debit	Credit
Merchandise inventory....................	$ 800	
Other (noninventory) assets...............	2,600	
Total liabilities.........................		$ 500
Common stock		400
Retained earnings.......................		1,700
Dividends	300	
Sales		9,500
Sales discounts.........................	260	
Sales returns and allowances	240	
Cost of goods sold	6,500	
Sales salaries expense...................	450	
Rent expense—Selling space.............	400	
Store supplies expense	30	
Advertising expense	20	
Office salaries expense	420	
Rent expense—Office space	72	
Office supplies expense	8	
Totals.................................	$12,100	$12,100

Solution

a. Multiple-step income statement.

TARET
Income Statement
For Year Ended April 30

Sales..........................		$9,500
Less: Sales discounts	$260	
Sales returns and allowances....................	240	500
Net sales		9,000
Cost of goods sold		6,500
Gross profit		2,500
Operating expenses		
Selling expenses		
Sales salaries expense.........................	450	
Rent expense—Selling space.....................	400	
Store supplies expense	30	
Advertising expense...........................	20	
Total selling expenses		900
General and administrative expenses		
Office salaries expense	420	
Rent expense—Office space	72	
Office supplies expense	8	
Total general and administrative expenses		500
Total operating expenses		1,400
Net income.......................................		$1,100

b. Single-step income statement.

TARET
Income Statement
For Year Ended April 30

Net sales		$9,000
Expenses		
Cost of goods sold	$6,500	
Selling expenses............................	900	
General and administrative expenses...........	500	
Total expenses		7,900
Net income......................................		$1,100

Do More: QS 4-11, E 4-11, E 4-15, P 4-3

Acid-Test and Gross Margin Ratios   **Decision Analysis**

Acid-Test Ratio

One measure of a merchandiser's ability to pay its current liabilities (referred to as its *liquidity*) is the acid-test ratio. The **acid-test ratio,** also called *quick ratio,* is defined as *quick assets* (cash, short-term investments, and current receivables) divided by current liabilities—see Exhibit 4.16. It differs from the current ratio by excluding less liquid current assets such as inventory and prepaid expenses that take longer to be converted to cash.

$$\text{Acid-test ratio} = \frac{\text{Cash and cash equivalents} + \text{Short-term investments} + \text{Current receivables}}{\text{Current liabilities}}$$

A1

Compute the acid-test ratio and explain its use to assess liquidity.

EXHIBIT 4.16

Acid-Test (Quick) Ratio

Exhibit 4.17 shows both the acid-test and current ratios of **Nike** and **Under Armour** for three recent years. Nike's acid-test ratio implies that it has enough quick assets to cover current liabilities. It is also on par with its competitor, Under Armour. Nike's current ratio suggests it has more than enough current assets to cover current liabilities. Analysts might argue that Nike could invest some current assets in more productive assets. An acid-test ratio less than 1.0 means that current liabilities exceed quick assets. A rule of thumb is that the acid-test ratio should have a value near, or higher than, 1.0. Less than 1.0 raises liquidity concerns unless a company can get enough cash from sales or if liabilities are not due until late in the next period.

EXHIBIT 4.17

Acid-Test and Current Ratios for two competitors

Company	$ millions	Current Year	1 Year Ago	2 Years Ago
Nike	Total quick assets	$ 9,856	$ 8,698	$ 9,282
	Total current assets	$16,061	$15,025	$15,587
	Total current liabilities	$ 5,474	$ 5,358	$ 6,332
	Acid-test ratio	1.8	1.6	1.5
	Current ratio	2.9	2.8	2.5
Under Armour	Acid-test ratio	0.9	1.3	1.2
	Current ratio	2.2	2.9	3.1

■ Decision Maker

Supplier   A retailer requests to purchase supplies on credit from your company. You have no prior experience with this retailer. The retailer's current ratio is 2.1, its acid-test ratio is 0.5, and inventory makes up most of its current assets. Do you extend credit? ■ *Answer:* A current ratio of 2.1 suggests sufficient current assets to cover current liabilities. An acid-test ratio of 0.5 suggests, however, that quick assets can cover only about one-half of current liabilities. The retailer depends on money from sales of inventory to pay current liabilities. If sales decline, the likelihood that this retailer will default on its payments increases. You probably do not extend credit.

Point: Successful use of a just-in-time inventory system can narrow the gap between the acid-test ratio and the current ratio.

Gross Margin Ratio

Without enough gross profit, a merchandiser can fail. The gross margin ratio helps understand this link. It differs from the profit margin ratio in that it excludes all costs except cost of goods sold. The **gross margin ratio** (or *gross profit ratio*) is defined as *gross margin* (net sales minus cost of goods sold) divided by net sales—see Exhibit 4.18.

$$\text{Gross margin ratio} = \frac{\text{Net sales} - \text{Cost of goods sold}}{\text{Net sales}}$$

A2

Compute the gross margin ratio and explain its use to assess profitability.

EXHIBIT 4.18

Gross Margin Ratio

Exhibit 4.19 shows the gross margin ratio of **Nike** for three recent years. For Nike, each $1 of sales in the current year yielded about 44.6¢ in gross margin to cover all expenses and still produce a net income. This 44.6¢ margin is down from 46.2¢ in the prior year. This decrease is unfavorable.

EXHIBIT 4.19

Nike's Gross Margin Ratio

$ millions	Current Year	1 Year Ago	2 Years Ago
Gross margin	$15,312	$14,971	$14,067
Net sales	$34,350	$32,376	$30,601
Gross margin ratio	44.6%	46.2%	46.0%

Decision Maker

Financial Officer   Your company has a 36% gross margin ratio and a 17% net profit margin ratio. Industry averages are 44% for gross margin and 16% for net profit margin. Do these comparative results concern you? ■   *Answer:* Your company's net profit margin is about equal to the industry average. However, gross margin shows that your company is paying far more in cost of goods sold or receiving far less in sales price than competitors. You should try to find the problem with cost of goods sold, sales, or both.

NEED-TO-KNOW 4-6

COMPREHENSIVE 1

Single- and Multiple-Step Income Statements, Closing Entries, and Analysis Using Acid-Test and Gross Margin

Use the following adjusted trial balance and additional information to complete the requirements.

KC ANTIQUES Adjusted Trial Balance December 31		
	Debit	Credit
Cash.	$ 7,000	
Accounts receivable	13,000	
Merchandise inventory (ending)	60,000	
Store supplies	1,500	
Equipment	45,600	
Accumulated depreciation—Equipment		$ 16,600
Accounts payable		9,000
Salaries payable		2,000
Common stock		20,000
Retained earnings.		59,000
Dividends	10,000	
Sales		343,250
Sales discounts.	5,000	
Sales returns and allowances	6,000	
Cost of goods sold	159,900	
Depreciation expense—Store equipment	4,100	
Depreciation expense—Office equipment	1,600	
Sales salaries expense	30,000	
Office salaries expense	34,000	
Insurance expense	11,000	
Rent expense—Selling space.	16,800	
Rent expense—Office space	7,200	
Store supplies expense	5,750	
Advertising expense	31,400	
Totals	$449,850	$449,850

KC Antiques's *supplementary records* for the year reveal the following itemized costs for merchandising activities.

Invoice cost of merchandise purchases	$150,000	Purchases returns and allowances	$2,700
Purchases discounts received	2,500	Cost of transportation-in	5,000

Required

1. Use the supplementary records to compute the total cost of merchandise purchases for the year.
2. Prepare a multiple-step income statement for the year. (Beginning inventory was $70,100.)
3. Prepare a single-step income statement for the year.
4. Prepare closing entries for KC Antiques at December 31.
5. Compute the acid-test ratio and the gross margin ratio. Explain the meaning of each ratio and interpret them for KC Antiques.

PLANNING THE SOLUTION

- Compute the total cost of merchandise purchases for the year.
- To prepare the multiple-step statement, first compute net sales. Then, to compute cost of goods sold, add the net cost of merchandise purchases for the year to beginning inventory and subtract the cost of ending inventory. Subtract cost of goods sold from net sales to get gross profit. Then classify expenses as selling expenses or general and administrative expenses.
- To prepare the single-step income statement, begin with net sales. Then list and subtract the expenses.
- The first closing entry debits all temporary accounts with credit balances and opens the Income Summary account. The second closing entry credits all temporary accounts with debit balances. The third entry closes the Income Summary account to the Retained Earnings account, and the fourth entry closes the Dividends account to the Retained Earnings account.
- Identify the quick assets on the adjusted trial balance. Compute the acid-test ratio by dividing quick assets by current liabilities. Compute the gross margin ratio by dividing gross profit by net sales.

SOLUTION

1.

Invoice cost of merchandise purchases	$150,000
Less: Purchases discounts received	2,500
Purchases returns and allowances	2,700
Add: Cost of transportation-in	5,000
Total cost of merchandise purchases	$149,800

2. Multiple-step income statement.

KC ANTIQUES
Income Statement
For Year Ended December 31

Sales		$343,250
Less: Sales discounts	$ 5,000	
Sales returns and allowances	6,000	11,000
Net sales		332,250
Cost of goods sold*		159,900
Gross profit		172,350
Expenses		
Selling expenses		
Depreciation expense—Store equipment	4,100	
Sales salaries expense	30,000	
Rent expense—Selling space	16,800	
Store supplies expense	5,750	
Advertising expense	31,400	
Total selling expenses		88,050
General and administrative expenses		
Depreciation expense—Office equipment	1,600	
Office salaries expense	34,000	
Insurance expense	11,000	
Rent expense—Office space	7,200	
Total general and administrative expenses		53,800
Total operating expenses		141,850
Net income		$ 30,500

3. Single-step income statement.

KC ANTIQUES
Income Statement
For Year Ended December 31

Net sales		$332,250
Expenses		
Cost of goods sold	$159,900	
Selling expenses	88,050	
General and administrative expenses	53,800	
Total expenses		301,750
Net income		$ 30,500

Tax expense for a corporation appears immediately before Net income in its own category.

*Cost of goods sold also can be directly computed:

Beginning merchandise inventory	$ 70,100
Total cost of merchandise purchases (from part 1)	149,800
Goods available for sale	219,900
Ending merchandise inventory	60,000
Cost of goods sold	$159,900

4.

Dec. 31	Sales	343,250	
	Income Summary		343,250
	Close credit balances in temporary accounts.		
Dec. 31	Income Summary	312,750	
	Sales Discounts		5,000
	Sales Returns and Allowances		6,000
	Cost of Goods Sold		159,900
	Depreciation Expense—Store Equipment		4,100
	Depreciation Expense—Office Equipment		1,600
	Sales Salaries Expense		30,000
	Office Salaries Expense		34,000
	Insurance Expense		11,000
	Rent Expense—Selling Space		16,800
	Rent Expense—Office Space		7,200
	Store Supplies Expense		5,750
	Advertising Expense		31,400
	Close debit balances in temporary accounts.		
Dec. 31	Income Summary	30,500	
	Retained Earnings		30,500
	Close Income Summary account.		
Dec. 31	Retained Earnings	10,000	
	Dividends		10,000
	Close Dividends account.		

5. Acid-test ratio = (Cash and equivalents + Short-term investments + Current receivables)/ Current liabilities

$$= \text{(Cash + Accounts receivable)}/\text{(Accounts payable + Salaries payable)}$$

$$= (\$7{,}000 + \$13{,}000)/(\$9{,}000 + \$2{,}000) = \$20{,}000/\$11{,}000 = \underline{1.82}$$

Gross margin ratio = Gross profit/Net sales = $172{,}350/$332{,}250 = \underline{0.52}$ (or 52%)

KC Antiques has a healthy acid-test ratio of 1.82. This means it has $1.82 in liquid assets to satisfy each $1.00 in current liabilities. The gross margin of 0.52 shows that KC Antiques spends 48¢ ($1.00 − $0.52) of every dollar of net sales on the costs of acquiring the merchandise it sells. This leaves 52¢ of every dollar of net sales to cover other expenses incurred in the business and to provide a net profit.

NEED-TO-KNOW 4-7

COMPREHENSIVE 2

Recording Merchandising Transactions—Both Seller and Buyer

Prepare journal entries for the following transactions for both the seller (BMX) and buyer (Sanuk).

May 4 BMX sold $1,500 of merchandise on account to Sanuk, terms FOB shipping point, n/45, invoice dated May 4. The cost of the merchandise was $900.
6 Sanuk paid transportation charges of $30 on the May 4 purchase from BMX.
8 BMX sold $1,000 of merchandise on account to Sanuk, terms FOB destination, n/15, invoice dated May 8. The cost of the merchandise was $700. This sale permitted returns for 30 days.
10 BMX paid transportation costs of $50 for delivery of merchandise sold to Sanuk on May 8.
16 BMX issued Sanuk a $200 credit memorandum for merchandise returned. The merchandise was purchased by Sanuk on account on May 8. The cost of the merchandise returned was $140.
18 BMX received payment from Sanuk for the May 8 purchase.
21 BMX sold $2,400 of merchandise on account to Sanuk, terms FOB shipping point, 2/10, n/EOM. The cost of the merchandise was $1,440. This sale permitted returns for 90 days.
31 BMX received payment from Sanuk for the May 21 purchase, less discount.

Solution

	BMX (Seller)		
May 4	Accounts Receivable—Sanuk	1,500	
	Sales		1,500
	Cost of Goods Sold	900	
	Merchandise Inventory		900
6	No entry.		
8	Accounts Receivable—Sanuk	1,000	
	Sales		1,000
	Cost of Goods Sold	700	
	Merchandise Inventory		700
10	Delivery Expense	50	
	Cash		50
16	Sales Returns & Allowances	200	
	Accounts Receivable—Sanuk		200
	Merchandise Inventory	140	
	Cost of Goods Sold		140
18	Cash	800	
	Accounts Receivable—Sanuk		800
21	Accounts Receivable—Sanuk	2,400	
	Sales		2,400
	Cost of Goods Sold	1,440	
	Merchandise Inventory		1,440
31	Cash	2,352	
	Sales Discounts	48	
	Accounts Receivable—Sanuk		2,400

Sanuk (Buyer)		
Merchandise Inventory	1,500	
Accounts Payable—BMX		1,500
Merchandise Inventory	30	
Cash		30
Merchandise Inventory	1,000	
Accounts Payable—BMX		1,000
No entry.		
Accounts Payable—BMX	200	
Merchandise Inventory		200
Accounts Payable—BMX	800	
Cash		800
Merchandise Inventory	2,400	
Accounts Payable—BMX		2,400
Accounts Payable—BMX	2,400	
Merchandise Inventory		48
Cash		2,352

Periodic Inventory System

4A

A periodic inventory system requires updating the inventory account only at the *end of a period*. During the period, the Merchandise Inventory balance remains unchanged and cost of merchandise is recorded in a temporary *Purchases* account. When a company sells merchandise, it records revenue **but not the cost of the goods sold.** At the end of the period, it takes a *physical count of inventory* to get ending inventory. The cost of goods sold is then computed as cost of merchandise available for sale minus ending inventory.

Recording Merchandise Purchases Under a periodic system, the purchases, purchases returns and allowances, purchases discounts, and transportation-in transactions are recorded in separate temporary accounts. At period-end, each of these temporary accounts is closed, which updates the Merchandise Inventory account. To demonstrate, journal entries under the periodic inventory system are shown for the most common transactions (codes *a* through *d* link these transactions to those in the chapter). For comparison, perpetual system journal entries are shown to the right of each periodic entry. Differences are highlighted.

P5

Record and compare merchandising transactions using both periodic and perpetual inventory systems.

Credit Purchases with Cash Discounts The periodic system uses a temporary **Purchases** account that accumulates the cost of all purchase transactions during each period. The Purchases account has a normal debit balance, as it increases the cost of merchandise available for sale. Z-Mart's November 2 entry to record the purchase of merchandise for $500 on credit with terms of 2/10, n/30 is

(a)

Periodic		
Purchases	500	
Accounts Payable		500

Perpetual		
Merchandise Inventory	500	
Accounts Payable		500

Payment of Purchases The periodic system uses a temporary **Purchases Discounts** account that accumulates discounts taken during the period. If payment for transaction *a* is made *within the discount period,* the entry is

(b1)

Periodic				Perpetual		
Accounts Payable	500			Accounts Payable	500	
Purchases Discounts*.....		10		Merchandise Inventory*.......		10
Cash		490		Cash		490
*$500 × 2%				*$500 × 2%		

If payment for transaction *a* is made *after the discount period expires,* the entry is

(b2)

Periodic			Perpetual	
Accounts Payable	500		Accounts Payable	500
Cash		500	Cash	500

Purchases Allowances The buyer and seller agree to a $30 purchases allowance for defective goods (whether paid within the discount period or not). In the periodic system, the temporary **Purchases Returns and Allowances** account accumulates the cost of all returns and allowances during a period. The buyer records the $30 allowance as

Point: Purchases Discounts and Purchases Returns and Allowances are contra purchases accounts *and* have normal credit balances, as they both decrease the cost of merchandise available for sale.

(c1)

Periodic			Perpetual	
Accounts Payable	30		Accounts Payable	30
Purchases Returns and Allowances		30	Merchandise Inventory	30

Purchases Returns The buyer returns $50 of merchandise within the discount period. The entry is

(c2)

Periodic			Perpetual	
Accounts Payable	50		Accounts Payable	50
Purchases Returns and Allowances		50	Merchandise Inventory	50

Transportation-In The buyer paid a $75 freight charge to transport goods with terms FOB destination. In the periodic system, this cost is recorded in a temporary **Transportation-In** account, which has a normal debit balance as it increases the cost of merchandise available for sale.

(d)

Periodic			Perpetual	
Transportation-In	75		Merchandise Inventory	75
Cash..................		75	Cash	75

Recording Merchandise *Sales*

Journal entries under the periodic system are shown for the most common transactions (codes *e* through *h* link these transactions to those in the chapter). Perpetual system entries are shown to the right of each periodic entry. Differences are highlighted.

Credit Sales and Receipt of Payments Both the periodic and perpetual systems record sales entries similarly, using the gross method. The same holds for entries related to payment of receivables from sales both during and after the discount period. However, under the periodic system, the cost of goods sold is *not* recorded at the time of each sale (whereas it is under the perpetual system). The entry to record $1,000 in credit sales (costing $300) is

Periodic			Perpetual		
Accounts Receivable..........	1,000		Accounts Receivable..............	1,000	
Sales.................		1,000	Sales......................		1,000
			Cost of Goods Sold	300	
No cost-side entry			Merchandise Inventory		300

Returns Received by Seller A customer returned merchandise for a cash refund. The goods sell for $15 and cost $9. (*Recall:* The periodic system records only the revenue effect, not the cost effect, for sales transactions.) The entry for the seller to take back the return is

	Periodic				Perpetual	
(e1)	Sales Returns and Allowances	15		Sales Returns and Allowances......	15	
	Cash		15	Cash.....................		15
(e2)				Merchandise Inventory	9	
	No entry			Cost of Goods Sold		9

Allowances Granted by Seller The seller gives a price reduction and credits the buyer's accounts receivable for $10. The entry is identical under the periodic and perpetual systems. The seller records this allowance as

	Periodic				Perpetual	
(f)	Sales Returns and Allowances	10		Sales Returns and Allowances......	10	
	Accounts Receivable		10	Accounts Receivable.........		10

Recording Adjusting Entries

Shrinkage—Adjusting Entry Adjusting (and closing) entries for the two systems are in Exhibit 4A.1. The $250 shrinkage is only recorded under the perpetual system—see entry *z* in Exhibit 4A.1. Shrinkage in cost of goods is unknown using a periodic system because inventory is not continually updated and therefore cannot be compared to the physical count.

	Periodic Adjusting Entries				Perpetual Adjusting Entries	
(z)	None			Cost of Goods Sold	250	
				Merchandise Inventory		250
(g)	Sales Discounts................	50		Sales Discounts	50	
	Allowance for Sales Discounts		50	Allowance for Sales Discounts ..		50
(h1)	Sales Returns and Allowances	900		Sales Returns and Allowances......	900	
	Sales Refund Payable.......		900	Sales Refund Payable		900
(h2)	Inventory Returns Estimated......	300		Inventory Returns Estimated	300	
	Purchases................		300	Cost of Goods Sold		300

Entries in gray are covered in Appendix 4B.   Entries in gray are covered in Appendix 4B.

EXHIBIT 4A.1

Comparison of Adjusting and Closing Entries— Periodic and Perpetual

	Periodic Closing Entries				Perpetual Closing Entries	
(1)	Sales	321,000		Sales	321,000	
	Merchandise Inventory (ending)	**21,000**				
	Purchases Discounts	**4,200**				
	Purchases Returns and Allowances	**1,500**				
	Income Summary		347,700	Income Summary		321,000
(2)	Income Summary	334,800		Income Summary	308,100	
	Sales Discounts		4,300	Sales Discounts		4,300
	Sales Returns and Allowances		2,000	Sales Returns and Allowances ..		2,000
	Merch. Inven. (beginning)...		**19,000**			
	Purchases		**235,800**	Cost of Goods Sold		230,400
	Transportation-In		**2,300**			
	Depreciation Expense		3,700	Depreciation Expense		3,700
	Salaries Expense		43,800	Salaries Expense		43,800
	Insurance Expense		600	Insurance Expense		600
	Rent Expense		9,000	Rent Expense		9,000
	Supplies Expense		3,000	Supplies Expense		3,000
	Advertising Expense		11,300	Advertising Expense		11,300
(3)	Income Summary	12,900		Income Summary	12,900	
	Retained Earnings		12,900	Retained Earnings..........		12,900
(4)	Retained Earnings	4,000		Retained Earnings	4,000	
	Dividends		4,000	Dividends.................		4,000

Expected Sales Discounts—Adjusting Entry   Both the periodic and perpetual methods make a period-end adjusting entry under the gross method to estimate the $50 sales discounts arising from current-period sales that are likely to be taken in future periods. Z-Mart made the period-end adjusting entry *g* in Exhibit 4A.1 for expected sales discounts.

Expected Returns and Allowances—Adjusting Entry   Both the periodic and perpetual inventory systems estimate returns and allowances arising from current-period sales that will occur in future periods. The adjusting entry for both systems is identical for the sales side, but slightly different for the cost side. The period-end entries *h1* and *h2* in Exhibit 4A.1 are used to record the updates to expected sales refunds of $900 and the cost side of $300. Under both systems, the seller sets up a **Sales Refund Payable** account, which is a current liability reflecting the amount expected to be refunded to customers, and an **Inventory Returns Estimated** account, which is a current asset reflecting the inventory estimated to be returned.

Recording Closing Entries
Periodic and perpetual inventory systems have slight differences in closing entries. The period-end Merchandise Inventory balance (unadjusted) is $19,000 under the periodic system. Because the periodic system does not update the Merchandise Inventory balance during the period, the $19,000 amount is the beginning inventory. A physical count of inventory taken at the end of the period reveals $21,000 of merchandise available. The adjusting and closing entries for the two systems are in Exhibit 4A.1. Recording the periodic inventory balance is a two-step process. The ending inventory balance of $21,000 is entered by debiting the inventory account in the first closing entry. The beginning inventory balance of $19,000 is deleted by crediting the inventory account in the second closing entry.[1]

By updating Merchandise Inventory and closing Purchases, Purchases Discounts, Purchases Returns and Allowances, and Transportation-In, the periodic system transfers the cost of sales amount to Income Summary. Review the periodic side of Exhibit 4A.1 and see that the **red** items affect Income Summary as follows.

Credit to Income Summary in the first closing entry includes amounts from	
Merchandise inventory (ending)	$ 21,000
Purchases discounts	4,200
Purchases returns and allowances	1,500
Debit to Income Summary in the second closing entry includes amounts from	
Merchandise inventory (beginning)	(19,000)
Purchases	(235,800)
Transportation-in	(2,300)
Net effect on Income Summary (net debit = cost of goods sold)	**$(230,400)**

This $230,400 effect on Income Summary is the cost of goods sold amount (which is equal to cost of goods sold reported in a perpetual inventory system). The periodic system transfers cost of goods sold to the Income Summary account but without using a Cost of Goods Sold account. Also, the periodic system does not separately measure shrinkage. Instead, it computes cost of goods available for sale, subtracts the cost of ending inventory, and defines the difference as cost of goods sold, which includes shrinkage.

Calculation of Cost of Goods Sold	
Beginning inventory	$ 19,000
Net cost of purchases.	232,400
Cost of goods available for sale	251,400
Less ending inventory	21,000
Cost of goods sold	$230,400

Preparing Financial Statements
The financial statements of a merchandiser using the periodic system are similar to those for a service company described in prior chapters. The income statement mainly differs by the inclusion of *cost of goods sold* and *gross profit*—of course, net sales is affected by discounts, returns, and allowances. The cost of goods sold section under the periodic system follows. The balance sheet mainly differs by the inclusion of *merchandise inventory,* inventory returns estimated, allowance for sales discounts, and sales refund payable. *Visit the Additional Student Resource section of the Connect ebook to view sample chart of accounts for periodic and perpetual systems.*

---

[1]This approach is called the *closing entry method.* An alternative approach, referred to as the *adjusting entry method,* would not make any entries to Merchandise Inventory in the closing entries of Exhibit 4A.1, but instead would make two adjusting entries. Using Z-Mart data, the two adjusting entries would be (1) Dr. Income Summary and Cr. Merchandise Inventory for $19,000 each and (2) Dr. Merchandise Inventory and Cr. Income Summary for $21,000 each. The first entry removes the beginning balance of Merchandise Inventory, and the second entry records the actual ending balance.

Adjusting Entries under New Revenue Recognition Rules

4B

Expected Sales Discounts—Adjusting Entry New revenue recognition rules require sales to be reported at the amount expected to be received. This means that a period-end adjusting entry is made to estimate sales discounts for current-period sales that are expected to be taken in future periods. To demonstrate, assume Z-Mart has the following unadjusted balances.

P6

Prepare adjustments for discounts, returns, and allowances per revenue recognition rules.

Accounts Receivable.........	$11,250	Allowance for Sales Discounts	$0

Of the $11,250 of receivables, $2,500 of them are within the 2% discount period for which we expect buyers to take $50 in future-period discounts (computed as $2,500 × 2%) arising from this period's sales. The adjusting entry for the $50 update to Allowance for Sales Discounts is

(g) Dec. 31	Sales Discounts	50	
	Allowance for Sales Discounts.....................		50
	Adjustment for future discounts.		

Assets = Liabilities + Equity
−50   −50

Allow. for Sales Discounts

	Beg. bal.	0
	Req. adj.	50
	Est. bal.	50

Allowance for Sales Discounts is a **contra asset account** and is reported on the balance sheet as a reduction to the Accounts Receivable asset account. The Allowance for Sales Discounts account has a *normal credit balance* because it reduces Accounts Receivable, which has a normal debit balance. This adjusting entry results in both accounts receivable and sales being reported at expected amounts.*

Balance Sheet—partial	
Accounts receivable	$11,250
Less allowance for sales discounts	50
Accounts receivable, net	$11,200

Income Statement—partial	
Sales	$321,000
Less sales discounts, returns & allowances	6,300
Net sales.................................	$314,700

***Next Period Adjustment** The Allowance for Sales Discounts balance remains unchanged during a period except for the period-end adjusting entry. At next period end, assume that Z-Mart computes an $80 balance for the Allowance for Sales Discounts. Using our three-step adjusting process we get:

Step 1: Current bal. is $50 credit in Allowance for Sales Discounts.
Step 2: Current bal. should be $80 credit in Allowance for Sales Discounts.
Step 3: Record entry to get from step 1 to step 2.　　Sales Discounts 30
　　　　　　　　　　　　　　　　　　　　　　　Allowance for Sales Discounts..... 　　30

Expected Returns and Allowances—Adjusting Entries To avoid overstatement of
sales and cost of sales, sellers estimate sales returns and allowances in the period of the sale. Estimating returns and allowances requires companies to maintain the following two balance sheet accounts that are set up with adjusting entries. Two adjusting entries are made: one for the revenue side *and* one for the cost side.

Current Asset→Inventory Returns Estimated	**Current Liability**→Sales Refund Payable

Revenue Side for Expected R&A When returns and allowances are expected, a seller sets up a **Sales Refund Payable** account, which is **a current liability showing the amount expected to be refunded to customers.** Assume that on December 31 the company estimates future sales refunds to be $1,200. Assume also that the *unadjusted balance* in Sales Refund Payable is a $300 credit. The adjusting entry for the $900 update to Sales Refund Payable follows. The Sales Refund Payable account is updated only during the adjusting entry process. Its balance remains unchanged during the period when actual returns and allowances are recorded.

(h1) Dec. 31	Sales Returns and Allowances	900	
	Sales Refund Payable		900
	*Expected refund of sales.**		

Assets = Liabilities + Equity
　　　　　　　+900　　　−900

Sales Refund Payable

	Beg. bal.	300
	Req. adj.	900
	Est. bal.	1,200

*This entry uses our three-step adjusting process:
Step 1: Current bal. is $300 credit for Sales Refund Payable.
Step 2: Current bal. should be $1,200 credit for Sales Refund Payable.
Step 3: Record entry to get from step 1 to step 2.

Cost Side for Expected R&A   On the cost side, some inventory is expected to be returned, which means that cost of goods sold recorded at the time of sale is overstated due to expected returns. A seller sets up an **Inventory Returns Estimated** account, which is **a current asset showing the inventory estimated to be returned.** Extending the example above, assume that the company estimates future inventory returns to be $500 (which is the cost side of the $1,200 expected returns and allowances above). Assume also that the (beginning) *unadjusted balance* in Inventory Returns Estimated is a $200 debit. The adjusting entry for the $300 update to expected returns follows. The Inventory Returns Estimated account is updated only during the adjusting entry process. Its balance remains unchanged during the period when actual returns and allowances are recorded.

Point: If estimates of returns and allowances prove too high or too low, we adjust future estimates accordingly.

Assets = Liabilities + Equity
+300   +300

Inventory Returns Est.		
Beg. bal.	200	
Req. adj.	300	
Est. bal.	500	

(h2) Dec. 31	Inventory Returns Estimated	300	
	Cost of Goods Sold.		300
	Expected return of inventory. *		

*This entry uses our three-step adjusting process:
Step 1: Current bal. <u>is</u> $200 debit for Inventory Returns Estimated.
Step 2: Current bal. <u>should be</u> $500 debit for Inventory Returns Estimated.
Step 3: Record entry to get from step 1 to step 2.

NEED-TO-KNOW 4-8

Estimating Discounts, Returns, and Allowances

P6

At the current year-end, a company shows the following unadjusted balances for selected accounts.

Allowance for Sales Discounts.	$ 75 credit	Sales Discounts	$1,850 debit
Sales Refund Payable.	800 credit	Sales Returns and Allowances	4,825 debit
Inventory Returns Estimated	450 debit	Cost of Goods Sold	9,875 debit

a. After an analysis of future sales discounts, the company estimates that the Allowance for Sales Discounts account should have a $275 credit balance. Prepare the current year-end adjusting journal entry for future sales discounts.

b. After an analysis of future sales returns and allowances, the company estimates that the Sales Refund Payable account should have an $870 credit balance (revenue side).

c. After an analysis of future inventory returns, the company estimates that the Inventory Returns Estimated account should have a $500 debit balance (cost side).

Solution

Dec. 31	Sales Discounts	200	
	Allowance for Sales Discounts.		200
	Adjustment for future discounts. $275 Cr. − $75 Cr.		
Dec. 31	Sales Returns and Allowances	70	
	Sales Refund Payable.		70
	Adjustment for future sales refund. $870 Cr. − $800 Cr.		
Dec. 31	Inventory Returns Estimated.	50	
	Cost of Goods Sold.		50
	Adjustment for future inventory returns. $500 Dr. − $450 Dr.		

Do More: QS 4-19, QS 4-20, E 4-20, E 4-21, E 4-22

4C   Net Method for Merchandising

P7

Record and compare merchandising transactions using the gross method and net method.

The **net method** records an invoice at its *net* amount (net of any cash discount). The **gross method,** covered earlier in the chapter, initially records an invoice at its gross (full) amount. This appendix records merchandising transactions using the net method. Differences with the gross method are highlighted.

   When invoices are recorded at *net* amounts, any cash discounts are deducted from the balance of the Merchandise Inventory account when initially recorded. **This assumes that all cash discounts will be taken.** If any discounts are later lost, they are recorded in a **Discounts Lost** expense account reported on the income statement.

Perpetual Inventory System

PURCHASES—Perpetual   A company purchases merchandise on November 2 at a $500 invoice price ($490 net) with terms of 2/10, n/30. Its November 2 entries under the gross and net methods are

Gross Method—Perpetual		Net Method—Perpetual	
Merchandise Inventory	500	Merchandise Inventory	490
Accounts Payable	500	Accounts Payable	490

If the invoice is paid on (or before) November 12 within the discount period, it records

Gross Method—Perpetual		Net Method—Perpetual	
Accounts Payable	500	Accounts Payable	490
Merchandise Inventory . . .	10		
Cash	490	Cash	490

If the invoice is paid *after the discount period,* it records

Gross Method—Perpetual		Net Method—Perpetual	
Accounts Payable	500	Accounts Payable	490
		Discounts Lost*	10
Cash	500	Cash	500

*For simplicity, we record Discounts Lost on the *payment date.*

SALES—Perpetual   A company sells merchandise on November 2 at a $500 invoice price ($490 net) with terms of 2/10, n/30. The goods cost $200. Its November 2 entries are

Gross Method—Perpetual		Net Method—Perpetual	
Accounts Receivable	500	Accounts Receivable	490
Sales	500	Sales	490

Gross Method—Perpetual		Net Method—Perpetual	
Cost of Goods Sold	200	Cost of Goods Sold	200
Merchandise Inventory . . .	200	Merchandise Inventory	200

If cash is received on (or before) November 12 within the discount period, it records

Gross Method—Perpetual		Net Method—Perpetual	
Cash	490	Cash	490
Sales Discounts	10		
Accounts Receivable	500	Accounts Receivable	490

If cash is received *after the discount period,* it records

Gross Method—Perpetual		Net Method—Perpetual	
Cash	500	Cash	500
		Interest Revenue	10
Accounts Receivable	500	Accounts Receivable	490

Periodic Inventory System

PURCHASES—Periodic   Under the periodic system, the balance of the Merchandise Inventory account remains unchanged during the period and is updated at period-end. During the period, three accounts are used to record purchases of inventory: Purchases; Purchases Discounts; and Purchases Returns and Allowances. *The entries below are identical to the perpetual system except that Merchandise Inventory is substituted for each of the three purchases accounts.*

To demonstrate, we apply the periodic system to purchases transactions. On November 2, a buyer purchases goods ($500 gross; $490 net) with terms of 2/10, n/30. Its November 2 entries under the gross and net methods are

Gross Method—Periodic		Net Method—Periodic	
Purchases	500	Purchases	490
Accounts Payable	500	Accounts Payable	490

If the invoice is paid on (or before) November 12 within the discount period, it records

Gross Method—Periodic		
Accounts Payable	500	
Purchases Discounts		10
Cash		490

Net Method—Periodic		
Accounts Payable	490	
Cash		490

If the invoice is paid *after the discount period,* it records

Gross Method—Periodic		
Accounts Payable	500	
Cash		500

Net Method—Periodic		
Accounts Payable	490	
Discounts Lost	10	
Cash		500

SALES—Periodic   For sales transactions, the **perpetual and periodic entries are identical except that under the periodic system the cost-side entries are *not* made at the time of each sale nor for any subsequent returns.** Instead, the cost of goods sold is computed at period-end based on a physical count of inventory. This entry is shown in Exhibit 4A.1.

APPENDIX

4D   Work Sheet—Perpetual System

This appendix along with assignments is available online.

Summary: Cheat Sheet

MERCHANDISING ACTIVITIES

Merchandise: Goods a company buys to resell.
Cost of goods sold: Costs of merchandise sold.
Gross profit (gross margin): Net sales minus cost of goods sold.
Computing net income (service company vs. merchandiser):

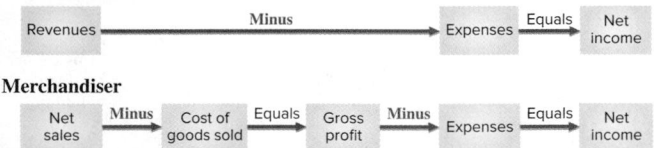

Inventory: Costs of merchandise owned, but not yet sold. It is a current asset on the balance sheet.

Merchandise Cost Flows:

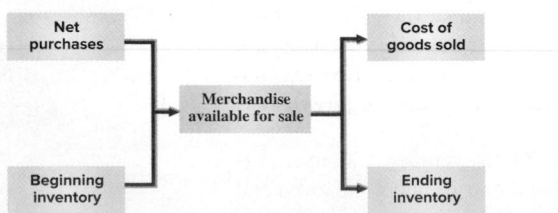

Perpetual inventory system: Updates accounting records for each purchase and each sale of inventory.
Periodic inventory system: Updates accounting records for purchases and sales of inventory only at the end of a period.

MERCHANDISING PURCHASES

Cash discount: A purchases discount on the price paid by the buyer; or, a sales discount on amount received for the seller.
Credit terms example: "2/10, n/60" means full payment is due within 60 days, but the buyer can deduct 2% of the invoice amount if payment is made within 10 days.
Gross method: Initially record purchases at gross (full) invoice amounts.

Purchasing Merchandise for Resale Entries:

Purchasing merchandise on credit	Merchandise Inventory	500	
	Accounts Payable		500

Paying within discount period (Inventory reduced by discount taken)	Accounts Payable	500	
	Merchandise Inventory . . .		10
	Cash		490
Paying outside discount period	Accounts Payable	500	
	Cash		500
Recording purchases returns or allowances	Cash or Accounts Payable	30	
	Merchandise Inventory . . .		30

Transportation Costs and Ownership Transfer Rules:

Shipping Terms	Ownership Transfers at	Goods in Transit Owned by	Transportation Costs Paid by	
FOB shipping point	Shipping point	Buyer	**Buyer** Merchandise Inventory . . . #	
			Cash	#
FOB destination	Destination	Seller	**Seller** Delivery Expense . . . . #	
			Cash	#

MERCHANDISING SALES

Selling merchandise on credit	Accounts Receivable..........	1,000	
	Sales....................		1,000
	Cost of Goods Sold...........	300	
	Merchandise Inventory		300
Receiving payment within discount period	Cash......................	980	
	Sales Discounts.............	20	
	Accounts Receivable		1,000

Receiving payment outside discount period	Cash......................	1,000	
	Accounts Receivable		1,000

Sales Discounts: A contra revenue account, meaning Sales Discounts is subtracted from Sales when computing net sales.

Customer Merchandise Returns Entries:

Receiving sales returns of nondefective inventory	Sales Returns and Allowances..	15	
	Cash or Accounts Receivable		15
	Merchandise Inventory........	9	
	Cost of Goods Sold........		9

If goods are defective, Inventory is debited for estimated value. A loss is recorded for the difference between cost of merchandise and estimated value.

Receiving sales returns of defective inventory	Merchandise Inventory	2	
	Loss from Defective Merchandise...	7	
	Cost of Goods Sold		9

Sales allowance: A price reduction agreed to with the buyer if they are unsatisfied with the goods.

Recognizing sales allowances	Sales Returns and Allowances..	10	
	Cash or Accounts Receivable		10

MERCHANDISER REPORTING

Inventory shrinkage: An adjusting entry to account for the loss of inventory due to theft or deterioration. It is computed by comparing a physical count of inventory with recorded amounts.

Adjustment for shrinkage (occurs when recorded amount larger than physical inventory)	Cost of Goods Sold..............	250	
	Merchandise Inventory		250

Closing Entries: Differences between merchandisers and service companies in red.

Step 1: Close Credit Balances in Temporary Accounts to Income Summary	Sales........................	321,000	
	Income Summary.............		321,000

Step 2: Close Debit Balances in Temporary Accounts to Income Summary	Income Summary	308,100	
	Sales Discounts		4,300
	Sales Returns and Allowances..		2,000
	Cost of Goods Sold...........		230,400
	Other Expenses		71,400

Steps 3 and 4: Same entries as those for service companies.

Multiple-step income statement: Three parts: (1) gross profit; (2) income from operations, which is gross profit minus operating expenses; and (3) net income, which is income from operations plus or minus nonoperating items.

Operating expenses: Separated into selling expenses and general & administrative expenses.

Selling expenses: Expenses of advertising merchandise, making sales, and delivering goods to customers.

General & administrative expenses: Expenses that support a company's overall operations, including accounting and human resources.

Nonoperating activities: Consist of expenses, revenues, losses, and gains that are unrelated to a company's main operations.

Multiple-Step Income Statement Example

Sales...			$321,000
Less: Sales discounts................................	$4,300		
Sales returns and allowances....................	2,000		6,300
Net sales.......................................			314,700
Cost of goods sold			230,400
Gross profit			84,300
Operating Expenses			
Selling expenses[†]			
General and administrative expenses[†]			
Total operating expenses			71,400
Income from operations			12,900
Total other revenues and gains (expenses and losses)			2,000
Net income			$ 14,900

[†]Must list all individual expenses and amounts—see Exhibit 4.13 (not done here for brevity).

Single-Step Income Statement Example

Revenues	
Total revenues*	$318,200
Expenses	
Total expenses*	303,300
Net income	$ 14,900

*Must list all individual items and amounts—see Exhibit 4.14 (not done here for brevity).

Key Terms

Acid-test ratio (159)

Allowance for Sales Discounts (167)

Cash discount (146)

Cost of goods sold (143)

Credit memorandum (152)

Credit period (146)

Credit terms (145)

Debit memorandum (147)

Discount period (146)

Discounts Lost (168)

EOM (145)

FOB (148)

General and administrative expenses (156)

Gross margin (144)

Gross margin ratio (159)

Gross method (147, 168)

Gross profit (144)

Inventory (144)

Inventory Returns Estimated (166)

List price (145)

Merchandise (143)

Merchandise inventory (144)

Merchandiser (143)

Multiple-step income statement (156)

Net method (151, 168)

Periodic inventory system (144)

Perpetual inventory system (144)

Purchases discount (146)
Retailer (143)
Sales discount (146)
Sales Refund Payable (166)

Sales Returns and Allowances (151)
Selling expenses (156)
Shrinkage (153)
Single-step income statement (157)

Supplementary records (149)
Trade discount (145)
Wholesaler (143)

Multiple Choice Quiz

1. A company has $550,000 in net sales and $193,000 in gross profit. This means its cost of goods sold equals
   a. $743,000.
   b. $550,000.
   c. $357,000.
   d. $193,000.
   e. $(193,000).

2. A company purchased $4,500 of merchandise on May 1 with terms of 2/10, n/30. On May 6, it returned $250 of that merchandise. On May 8, it paid the balance owed for merchandise, taking any discount it is entitled to. The cash paid on May 8 is
   a. $4,500.
   b. $4,250.
   c. $4,160.
   d. $4,165.
   e. $4,410.

3. A company has cash sales of $75,000, credit sales of $320,000, sales returns and allowances of $13,700, and sales discounts of $6,000. Its net sales equal
   a. $395,000.
   b. $375,300.
   c. $300,300.
   d. $339,700.
   e. $414,700.

4. A company's quick assets are $37,500, its current assets are $80,000, and its current liabilities are $50,000. Its acid-test ratio equals
   a. 1.600.
   b. 0.750.
   c. 0.625.
   d. 1.333.
   e. 0.469.

5. A company's net sales are $675,000, its cost of goods sold is $459,000, and its net income is $74,250. Its gross margin ratio equals
   a. 32%.
   b. 68%.
   c. 47%.
   d. 11%.
   e. 34%.

ANSWERS TO MULTIPLE CHOICE QUIZ

1. c; Gross profit = $550,000 − $193,000 = $357,000
2. d; ($4,500 − $250) × (100% − 2%) = $4,165
3. b; Net sales = $75,000 + $320,000 − $13,700 − $6,000 = $375,300
4. b; Acid-test ratio = $37,500/$50,000 = 0.75
5. a; Gross margin ratio = ($675,000 − $459,000)/$675,000 = 32%

$^{A(B,C)}$ Superscript letter A, B, or C denotes assignments based on Appendix 4A, 4B, or 4C.

[i] Icon denotes assignments that involve decision making.

Discussion Questions

1. What items appear in financial statements of merchandising companies but not in the statements of service companies?

2. In comparing the accounts of a merchandising company with those of a service company, what additional accounts would the merchandising company likely use, assuming it employs a perpetual inventory system?

3. [i] Explain how a business can earn a positive gross profit on its sales and still have a net loss.

4. [i] Why do companies offer a cash discount?

5. How does a company that uses a perpetual inventory system determine the amount of inventory shrinkage?

6. Distinguish between cash discounts and trade discounts for purchases. Is the amount of a trade discount on purchased merchandise recorded in the accounts?

7. What is the difference between a sales discount and a purchases discount?

8. [i] Why would a company's manager be concerned about the quantity of its purchases returns if its suppliers allow unlimited returns?

9. Does the sender (maker) of a debit memorandum record a debit or a credit in the recipient's account? What entry (debit or credit) does the recipient record?

10. What is the difference between the single-step and multiple-step income statement formats?

11. [i] Refer to **Apple**'s balance sheet and income statement in Appendix A. What does the company title its inventory account? Does the company present a detailed calculation of its cost of goods sold? **APPLE**

12. Refer to **Google**'s income statement in Appendix A. What title does it use for cost of goods sold? **GOOGLE**

13. Refer to **Samsung**'s income statement in Appendix A. What does Samsung title its cost of goods sold account? **Samsung**

14. Refer to **Samsung**'s income statement in Appendix A. Does its income statement report a gross profit figure? If yes, what is the amount? **Samsung**

15. [i] Buyers negotiate purchase contracts with suppliers. What type of shipping terms should a buyer attempt to negotiate to minimize freight-in costs?

≡ connect

Enter the letter for each term in the blank space beside the definition that it most closely matches.

A. Sales discount   **D.** FOB destination   **G.** Merchandise inventory

B. Credit period   **E.** FOB shipping point   **H.** Purchases discount

C. Discount period   **F.** Gross profit

QS 4-1

Applying merchandising terms

C1   P1

_____ **1.** Goods a company owns and expects to sell to its customers.

_____ **2.** Time period that can pass before a customer's full payment is due.

_____ **3.** Seller's description of a cash discount granted to buyers in return for early payment.

_____ **4.** Ownership of goods is transferred when the seller delivers goods to the carrier.

_____ **5.** Purchaser's description of a cash discount received from a supplier of goods.

_____ **6.** Difference between net sales and the cost of goods sold.

_____ **7.** Time period in which a cash discount is available.

_____ **8.** Ownership of goods is transferred when delivered to the buyer's place of business.

Costs of $5,000 were incurred to acquire goods and make them ready for sale. The goods were shipped to the buyer (FOB shipping point) for a cost of $200. Additional necessary costs of $400 were incurred to acquire the goods. No other incentives or discounts were available. What is the buyer's total cost of merchandise inventory?

QS 4-2

Identifying inventory costs

C2

a. $5,000   **b.** $5,200   **c.** $5,400   **d.** $5,600

Use the following information (in random order) from a merchandising company and from a service company. *Hint:* Not all information may be necessary for the solutions.

a. For the merchandiser only, compute (1) goods available for sale, (2) cost of goods sold, and (3) gross profit.

b. Compute net income for each company.

QS 4-3

Merchandise accounts and computations

C2

Kleiner Merchandising Company			
Accumulated depreciation...	$ 700	Expenses........	$1,450
Beginning inventory........	5,000	Net purchases....	3,900
Ending inventory...........	1,700	Net sales........	9,500

Krug Service Company			
Expenses...........	$12,500	Prepaid rent	$ 800
Revenues...........	14,000	Accounts payable	200
Cash...............	700	Equipment	1,300

Compute the amount to be paid for each of the four separate invoices assuming that all invoices are paid *within* the discount period.

QS 4-4

Computing net invoice amounts

P1

Merchandise (gross)	Terms	Merchandise (gross)	Terms
a. $5,000	2/10, n/60	**c.** $75,000	1/10, n/30
b. $20,000	1/15, EOM	**d.** $10,000	3/15, n/45

Prepare journal entries to record each of the following transactions of a merchandising company. The company uses a perpetual inventory system and the gross method.

QS 4-5

Recording purchases, returns, and discounts taken

P1

Nov. 5   Purchased 600 units of product at a cost of $10 per unit. Terms of the sale are 2/10, n/60; the invoice is dated November 5.

7   Returned 25 defective units from the November 5 purchase and received full credit.

15   Paid the amount due from the November 5 purchase, minus the return on November 7.

Prepare journal entries to record each of the following transactions. The company records purchases using the gross method and a perpetual inventory system.

QS 4-6

Recording purchases and discounts taken

P1

Aug. 1   Purchased merchandise with an invoice price of $60,000 and credit terms of 3/10, n/30.

11   Paid supplier the amount owed from the August 1 purchase.

Prepare journal entries to record each of the following transactions. The company records purchases using the gross method and a perpetual inventory system.

QS 4-7

Recording purchases and discounts missed

P1

Sep. 15   Purchased merchandise with an invoice price of $35,000 and credit terms of 2/5, n/15.

29   Paid supplier the amount owed on the September 15 purchase.

QS 4-8

Recording sales, returns, and discounts taken

P2

Prepare journal entries to record each of the following sales transactions of a merchandising company. The company uses a perpetual inventory system and the gross method.

Apr. 1   Sold merchandise for $3,000, with credit terms n/30; invoice dated April 1. The cost of the merchandise is $1,800.

     4   The customer in the April 1 sale returned $300 of merchandise for full credit. The merchandise, which had cost $180, is returned to inventory.

     8   Sold merchandise for $1,000, with credit terms of 1/10, n/30; invoice dated April 8. Cost of the merchandise is $700.

    11   Received payment for the amount due from the April 1 sale less the return on April 4.

QS 4-9

Accounting for shrinkage— perpetual system

P3

Nix'It Company's ledger on July 31, its fiscal year-end, includes the following selected accounts that have normal balances (Nix'It uses the perpetual inventory system).

Merchandise inventory	$ 37,800	Sales returns and allowances	$ 6,500
Retained earnings	115,300	Cost of goods sold	105,000
Dividends	7,000	Depreciation expense	10,300
Sales	160,200	Salaries expense	32,500
Sales discounts	4,700	Miscellaneous expenses	5,000

A physical count of its July 31 year-end inventory discloses that the cost of the merchandise inventory still available is $35,900. Prepare the entry to record any inventory shrinkage.

QS 4-10

Closing entries   **P3**

Refer to QS 4-9 and prepare journal entries to close the balances in temporary revenue and expense accounts. Remember to consider the entry for shrinkage from QS 4-9.

QS 4-11

Multiple-step income statement

P4

For each item below, indicate whether the statement describes a multiple-step income statement or a single-step income statement.

a. Multiple-step income statement   **b.** Single-step income statement

_____ **1.** Commonly reports detailed computations of net sales and other costs and expenses.

_____ **2.** Statement limited to two main categories (revenues and expenses).

_____ **3.** Reports gross profit on a separate line.

_____ **4.** Separates income from operations from the other revenues and gains.

QS 4-12

Preparing a multiple-step income statement

P4

Save-the-Earth Co. reports the following income statement accounts for the year ended December 31. Prepare a multiple-step income statement that includes separate categories for net sales, cost of goods sold, selling expenses, and general and administrative expenses. Categorize the following accounts as selling expenses: Sales Staff Salaries and Advertising Expense. Categorize the remaining expenses as general and administrative.

Sales discounts	$ 750	Office supplies expense	$ 500
Office salaries expense	2,000	Cost of goods sold	9,000
Rent expense—Office space	1,500	Sales	20,000
Advertising expense	500	Insurance expense	1,000
Sales returns and allowances	250	Sales staff salaries	2,500

QS 4-13

Preparing a classified balance sheet for a merchandiser

P4

Clear Water Co. reports the following balance sheet accounts as of December 31. Prepare a classified balance sheet.

Buildings	$25,000	Notes payable (due in 7 years)	$30,000
Accounts receivable	2,000	Office supplies	1,000
Land	11,000	Common stock	10,000
Merchandise inventory	7,000	Retained earnings	6,000
Accounts payable	5,000	Wages payable	3,000
Cash	8,000		

Use the following information on current assets and current liabilities to compute and interpret the acid-test ratio. Explain what the acid-test ratio of a company measures.

Cash	$1,490	Prepaid expenses	$ 700
Accounts receivable	2,800	Accounts payable	5,750
Inventory	6,000	Other current liabilities	850

QS 4-14
Computing and interpreting acid-test ratio

A1

Compute net sales, gross profit, and the gross margin ratio for each of the four separate companies. Interpret the gross margin ratio for Carrier.

	Carrier	Lennox	Trane	York
Sales	$150,000	$550,000	$38,700	$255,700
Sales discounts	5,000	17,500	600	4,800
Sales returns and allowances	20,000	6,000	5,100	900
Cost of goods sold	79,750	329,589	24,453	126,500

QS 4-15
Computing and analyzing gross margin ratio

A2

Identify whether each description best applies to a periodic or a perpetual inventory system.

_____ **a.** Updates the inventory account only at period-end.

_____ **b.** Requires an adjusting entry to record inventory shrinkage.

_____ **c.** Returns immediately affect the account balance of Merchandise Inventory.

_____ **d.** Records cost of goods sold each time a sales transaction occurs.

_____ **e.** Provides more timely information to managers.

QS 4-16ᴬ
Contrasting periodic and perpetual systems

P5

Refer to QS 4-5 and prepare journal entries to record each of the merchandising transactions assuming that the company records purchases using the *gross* method and a *periodic* inventory system.

QS 4-17ᴬ
Recording purchases, returns, and discounts—periodic & gross methods **P5**

Refer to QS 4-8 and prepare journal entries to record each of the merchandising transactions assuming that the company records purchases using the *gross* method and a *periodic* inventory system.

QS 4-18ᴬ
Recording sales, returns, and discounts—periodic & gross methods **P5**

ProBuilder has the following June 30 fiscal-year-end unadjusted balances: Allowance for Sales Discounts, $0; and Accounts Receivable, $10,000. Of the $10,000 of receivables, $2,000 are within a 3% discount period, meaning that it expects buyers to take $60 in future discounts arising from this period's sales.

a. Prepare the June 30 fiscal-year-end adjusting journal entry for future sales discounts.

b. Assume the same facts above *and* that there is a $10 fiscal-year-end unadjusted credit balance in the Allowance for Sales Discounts. Prepare the June 30 fiscal-year-end adjusting journal entry for future sales discounts.

QS 4-19ᴮ
Recording estimates of future discounts

P6

ProBuilder reports merchandise sales of $50,000 and cost of merchandise sales of $20,000 in its first year of operations ending June 30. It makes fiscal-year-end adjusting entries for estimated future returns and allowances equal to 2% of sales, or $1,000, and 2% of cost of sales, or $400.

a. Prepare the June 30 fiscal-year-end adjusting journal entry for future returns and allowances related to sales.

b. Prepare the June 30 fiscal-year-end adjusting journal entry for future returns and allowances related to cost of sales.

QS 4-20ᴮ
Recording estimates of future returns

P6

Refer to QS 4-5 and prepare journal entries to record each of the merchandising transactions assuming that the company records purchases using the *net* method and a *perpetual* inventory system.

QS 4-21ᶜ
Recording purchases, returns, and discounts—net & perpetual methods **P7**

Refer to QS 4-8 and prepare journal entries to record each of the merchandising transactions assuming that the company records purchases using the *net* method and a *perpetual* inventory system.

QS 4-22ᶜ
Recording sales, returns, and discounts—net & perpetual methods **P7**

QS 4-23
Sales transactions

P2

Prepare journal entries to record each of the following sales transactions of EcoMart Merchandising. EcoMart uses a *perpetual* inventory system and the *gross* method.

Oct. 1   Sold fair trade merchandise for $1,500, with credit terms n/30, invoice dated October 1. The cost of the merchandise is $900.

     6   The customer in the October 1 sale returned $150 of fair trade merchandise for full credit. The merchandise, which had cost $90, is returned to inventory.

     9   Sold recycled leather merchandise for $700, with credit terms of 1/10, n/30, invoice dated October 9. Cost of the merchandise is $450.

    11   Received payment for the amount due from the October 1 sale less the return on October 6.

EXERCISES

Fill in the blanks in the following separate income statements *a* through *e*. Identify any negative amount by putting it in parentheses.

Exercise 4-1
Computing revenues, expenses, and income

C1   C2

	a	b	c	d	e
Sales	$62,000	$43,500	$46,000	$?	$25,600
Cost of goods sold					
Merchandise inventory (beginning)...............	8,000	17,050	7,500	8,000	4,560
Total cost of merchandise purchases	38,000	?	?	32,000	6,600
Merchandise inventory (ending)	?	(3,000)	(9,000)	(6,600)	?
Cost of goods sold	34,050	16,000	?	?	7,000
Gross profit......................................	?	?	3,750	45,600	?
Expenses	10,000	10,650	12,150	3,600	6,000
Net income (loss)	$?	$16,850	$ (8,400)	$42,000	$?

Exercise 4-2
Operating cycle for merchandiser

C2

The operating cycle of a merchandiser with credit sales includes the following five activities. Starting with merchandise acquisition, identify the chronological order of these five activities.

_____ **a.** Prepare merchandise for sale.   _____ **d.** Purchase merchandise.

_____ **b.** Collect cash from customers on account.   _____ **e.** Monitor and service accounts receivable.

_____ **c.** Make credit sales to customers.

Exercise 4-3
Recording purchases, purchases returns, and purchases allowances

P1

Prepare journal entries to record the following transactions for a retail store. The company uses a perpetual inventory system and the gross method.

Apr. 2   Purchased $4,600 of merchandise from Lyon Company with credit terms of 2/15, n/60, invoice dated April 2, and FOB shipping point.

     3   Paid $300 cash for shipping charges on the April 2 purchase.

     4   Returned to Lyon Company unacceptable merchandise that had an invoice price of $600.

    17   Sent a check to Lyon Company for the April 2 purchase, net of the discount and the returned merchandise.

    18   Purchased $8,500 of merchandise from Frist Corp. with credit terms of 1/10, n/30, invoice dated April 18, and FOB destination.

    21   After negotiations over scuffed merchandise, received from Frist a $500 allowance toward the $8,500 owed on the April 18 purchase.

Check Apr. 28, Cr. Cash, $7,920

    28   Sent check to Frist paying for the April 18 purchase, net of the allowance and the discount.

Exercise 4-4
Recording sales, sales returns, and sales allowances

P2

Allied Merchandisers was organized on May 1. Macy Co. is a major customer (buyer) of Allied (seller) products. Prepare journal entries to record the following transactions for Allied assuming it uses a perpetual inventory system and the gross method.

May 3   Allied made its first and only purchase of inventory for the period on May 3 for 2,000 units at a price of $10 cash per unit (for a total cost of $20,000).

     5   Allied sold 1,500 of the units in inventory for $14 per unit (invoice total: $21,000) to Macy Co. under credit terms 2/10, n/60. The goods cost Allied $15,000.

     7   Macy returns 125 units because they did not fit the customer's needs (invoice amount: $1,750). Allied restores the units, which cost $1,250, to its inventory.

     8   Macy discovers that 200 units are scuffed but are still of use and, therefore, keeps the units. Allied gives a price reduction (allowance) and credits Macy's accounts receivable for $300 to compensate for the damage.

    15   Allied receives payment from Macy for the amount owed on the May 5 purchase; payment is net of returns, allowances, and any cash discount.

Refer to Exercise 4-4 and prepare journal entries for Macy Co. to record each of the May transactions. Macy is a retailer that uses the gross method and a perpetual inventory system; it purchases these units for resale.

Exercise 4-5
Recording purchases, purchases returns, and purchases allowances   **P1**

Santa Fe Retailing purchased merchandise "as is" (with no returns) from Mesa Wholesalers with credit terms of 3/10, n/60 and an invoice price of $24,000. The merchandise had cost Mesa $16,000. Assume that both buyer and seller use a perpetual inventory system and the gross method.
1. Prepare entries that the *buyer* records for the (*a*) purchase, (*b*) cash payment *within* the discount period, and (*c*) cash payment *after* the discount period.
2. Prepare entries that the *seller* records for the (*a*) sale, (*b*) cash collection *within* the discount period, and (*c*) cash collection *after* the discount period.

Exercise 4-6
Recording sales, purchases, and cash discounts—buyer *and* seller

P1   P2

Sydney Retailing (buyer) and Troy Wholesalers (seller) enter into the following transactions. Both Sydney and Troy use a perpetual inventory system and the gross method.

May 11   Sydney accepts delivery of $40,000 of merchandise it purchases for resale from Troy: invoice dated May 11, terms 3/10, n/90, FOB shipping point. The goods cost Troy $30,000. Sydney pays $345 cash to Express Shipping for delivery charges on the merchandise.
   12   Sydney returns $1,400 of the $40,000 of goods to Troy, who receives them the same day and restores them to its inventory. The returned goods had cost Troy $1,050.
   20   Sydney pays Troy for the amount owed. Troy receives the cash immediately.

1. Prepare journal entries that Sydney Retailing (buyer) records for these three transactions.
2. Prepare journal entries that Troy Wholesalers (seller) records for these three transactions.

Exercise 4-7
Recording sales, purchases, shipping, and returns—buyer *and* seller

P1   P2

Check   (1) May 20, Cr. Cash, $37,442

The following summarizes Tesla's merchandising activities for the year. Set up T-accounts for Merchandise Inventory and for Cost of Goods Sold. Enter each line item into one of the two T-accounts and compute the T-account balances.

Cost of merchandise sold to customers	$196,000
Merchandise inventory, beginning-year	25,000
Cost of merchandise purchases, gross amount	192,500
Shrinkage on merchandise as of year-end	800
Cost of transportation-in for merchandise purchases	2,900
Cost of merchandise returned by customers and restored to inventory	2,100
Discounts received from suppliers on merchandise purchases	1,700
Returns to and allowances from suppliers on merchandise purchases	4,000

Exercise 4-8
Inventory and cost of sales transactions in T-accounts

P1   P2

Check   Ending Merch. Inventory, $20,000

Prepare journal entries for the following merchandising transactions of Dollar Store assuming it uses a perpetual inventory system and the gross method.

Nov. 1   Dollar Store purchases merchandise for $1,500 on terms of 2/5, n/30, FOB shipping point, invoice dated November 1.
   5   Dollar Store pays cash for the November 1 purchase.
   7   Dollar Store discovers and returns $200 of defective merchandise purchased on November 1, and paid for on November 5, for a cash refund.
   10   Dollar Store pays $90 cash for transportation costs for the November 1 purchase.
   13   Dollar Store sells merchandise for $1,600 with terms n/30. The cost of the merchandise is $800.
   16   Merchandise is returned to the Dollar Store from the November 13 transaction. The returned items are priced at $160 and cost $80; the items were not damaged and were returned to inventory.

Exercise 4-9
Recording purchases, sales, returns, and shipping

P1   P2

The following list includes selected permanent accounts and all of the temporary accounts from the December 31 unadjusted trial balance of Emiko Co., a business owned by Kumi Emiko. Use these account balances along with the additional information to journalize (*a*) adjusting entries and (*b*) closing entries. Emiko Co. uses a perpetual inventory system.

Exercise 4-10
Preparing adjusting and closing entries for a merchandiser

P3

	Debit	Credit		Debit	Credit
Merchandise inventory	$30,000		Cost of goods sold	$212,000	
Prepaid selling expenses	5,600		Sales salaries expense	48,000	
Dividends	33,000		Utilities expense	15,000	
Sales		$529,000	Selling expenses	36,000	
Sales returns and allowances	17,500		Administrative expenses	105,000	
Sales discounts	5,000				

[continued on next page]

Additional Information

Accrued and unpaid sales salaries amount to $1,700. Prepaid selling expenses of $3,000 have expired. A physical count of year-end merchandise inventory is taken to determine shrinkage and shows $28,700 of goods still available.

Exercise 4-11

Computing net sales for multiple-step income statement

P4

A company reports the following sales-related information. Compute and prepare the net sales portion only of this company's multiple-step income statement.

Sales, gross	$200,000	Sales returns and allowances.	$16,000
Sales discounts	4,000	Sales salaries expense	10,000

Exercise 4-12

Impacts of inventory error on key accounts

P3

A retailer completed a physical count of ending merchandise inventory. When counting inventory, employees did not include $3,000 of incoming goods shipped by a supplier on December 31 under FOB shipping point. These goods had been recorded in Merchandise Inventory, but *they were not included in the physical count because they were in transit*. This means shrinkage was incorrectly overstated by $3,000.

Compute the amount of overstatement or understatement for each of the following amounts for this period.

a. Ending inventory   **b.** Total assets   **c.** Net income   **d.** Total equity

---

Exercise 4-13

Physical count error and profits   **A2**

Refer to the information in Exercise 4-12 and indicate whether the failure to include in-transit inventory as part of the physical count results in an overstatement, understatement, or no effect on the following ratios.

a. Gross margin ratio   **b.** Profit margin ratio   **c.** Acid-test ratio   **d.** Current ratio

---

Exercise 4-14

Computing and analyzing acid-test and current ratios

A1

Compute the current ratio and acid-test ratio for each of the following separate cases. (Round ratios to two decimals.) Which company is in the best position to meet short-term obligations? Explain.

	Camaro	GTO	Torino
Cash.	$2,000	$ 110	$1,000
Short-term investments	50	0	580
Current receivables	350	470	700
Inventory.	2,600	2,420	4,230
Prepaid expenses.	200	500	900
Total current assets	$5,200	$3,500	$7,410
Current liabilities.	$2,000	$1,000	$3,800

Exercise 4-15

Preparing a multiple-step income statement

P4

Fit-for-Life Foods reports the following income statement accounts for the year ended December 31. Prepare a multiple-step income statement that includes separate categories for net sales; cost of goods sold; selling expenses; general and administrative expenses; and other revenues, gains, expenses, and losses. Categorize the following accounts as selling expenses: Sales Staff Wages, Rent Expense—Selling Space, TV Advertising Expense, and Sales Commission Expense. Categorize the remaining expenses as general and administrative.

Gain on sale of equipment.	$ 6,250	Depreciation expense—Office copier.	$ 500
Office supplies expense.	700	Sales discounts	16,000
Insurance expense	1,300	Sales returns and allowances.	4,000
Sales	220,000	TV advertising expense.	2,000
Office salaries expense	32,500	Interest revenue	750
Rent expense—Selling space.	10,000	Cost of goods sold.	90,000
Sales staff wages	23,000	Sales commission expense.	13,000

Exercise 4-16

Preparing a classified balance sheet for a merchandiser

P4

Adams Co. reports the following balance sheet accounts as of December 31. Prepare a classified balance sheet.

Salaries payable	$ 6,000	Retained earnings	$50,000
Buildings	55,000	Notes payable (due in 9 years)	30,000
Prepaid rent	7,000	Office supplies.	2,000
Merchandise inventory.	14,000	Land.	22,000
Accounts payable	10,000	Accumulated depreciation—Building	5,000
Prepaid insurance.	3,000	Mortgages payable (due in 5 years)	12,000
Accounts receivable	4,000	Cash	16,000
Common stock	10,000		

Refer to Exercise 4-3 and prepare journal entries to record each of the merchandising transactions assuming that the buyer uses the *periodic inventory system* and the *gross method*.

Exercise 4-17ᴬ
Recording purchases, returns, and allowances—periodic **P5**

Refer to Exercise 4-6 and prepare journal entries to record each of the merchandising transactions assuming that the *periodic inventory system* and the *gross method* are used by both the buyer and the seller.

Exercise 4-18ᴬ
Recording sales, purchases, and discounts: buyer and seller—periodic **P5**

Refer to Exercise 4-7 and prepare journal entries to record each of the merchandising transactions assuming that the *periodic inventory system* and the *gross method* are used by both the buyer and the seller.

Exercise 4-19ᴬ
Recording sales, purchases, shipping, and returns: buyer and seller—periodic **P5**

Med Labs has the following December 31 year-end unadjusted balances: Allowance for Sales Discounts, $0; and Accounts Receivable, $5,000. Of the $5,000 of receivables, $1,000 are within a 2% discount period, meaning that it expects buyers to take $20 in future-period discounts arising from this period's sales.

a. Prepare the December 31 year-end adjusting journal entry for future sales discounts.

b. Assume the same facts above *and* that there is a $5 year-end unadjusted credit balance in Allowance for Sales Discounts. Prepare the December 31 year-end adjusting journal entry for future sales discounts.

c. Is Allowance for Sales Discounts a contra asset or a contra liability account?

Exercise 4-20ᴮ
Recording estimates of future discounts
P6

Chico Company allows its customers to return merchandise within 30 days of purchase.

- At December 31, the end of its first year of operations, Chico estimates future-period merchandise returns of $60,000 (cost of $22,500) related to its current-year sales.
- A few days later, on January 3, a customer returns merchandise with a selling price of $2,000 for a cash refund; the returned merchandise cost $750 and is returned to inventory as it is not defective.

a. Prepare the December 31 year-end adjusting journal entry for estimated future sales returns and allowances (revenue side).

b. Prepare the December 31 year-end adjusting journal entry for estimated future inventory returns and allowances (cost side).

c. Prepare the January 3 journal entries to record the merchandise returned.

Exercise 4-21ᴮ
Recording estimates of future returns
P6

Lopez Company reports unadjusted first-year merchandise sales of $100,000 and cost of merchandise sales of $30,000.

a. Compute gross profit (using the unadjusted numbers above).

b. The company expects future returns and allowances equal to 5% of sales and 5% of cost of sales.

   1. Prepare the year-end adjusting entry to record the sales expected to be refunded.

   2. Prepare the year-end adjusting entry to record the cost side of sales returns and allowances.

   3. Recompute gross profit using the adjusted numbers from parts 1 and 2.

c. Is Sales Refund Payable an asset, liability, or equity account?

d. Is Inventory Returns Estimated an asset, liability, or equity account?

Exercise 4-22ᴮ
Recording estimates of future returns
P6

Refer to Exercise 4-7 and prepare journal entries to record each of the merchandising transactions assuming that the *perpetual inventory system* and the *net method* are used by both the buyer and the seller.

Exercise 4-23ᶜ
Recording sales, purchases, shipping, and returns: buyer and seller—perpetual and net method **P7**

Piere Imports uses the perpetual system in accounting for merchandise inventory and had the following transactions during the month of October. Prepare entries to record these transactions assuming that Piere Imports records invoices (*a*) at gross amounts and (*b*) at net amounts.

Oct. 2   Purchased merchandise at a $3,000 price ($2,940 net), invoice dated October 2, terms 2/10, n/30.
     10   Returned $500 ($490 net) of merchandise purchased on October 2 and debited its account payable for that amount.
     17   Purchased merchandise at a $5,400 price ($5,292 net), invoice dated October 17, terms 2/10, n/30.
     27   Paid for the merchandise purchased on October 17, less the discount.
     31   Paid for the merchandise purchased on October 2.

Exercise 4-24ᶜ
Recording purchases, sales, returns, and discounts: buyer and seller—perpetual and both net & gross methods
P7

Exercise 4-25
Purchasing transactions

P1

Prepare journal entries to record the following transactions of Recycled Fashion retail store. Recycled Fashion uses a perpetual inventory system and the gross method.

Mar. 3 Purchased $1,150 of merchandise made from recycled material from GreenWorld Company with credit terms of 2/15, n/60, invoice dated March 3, and FOB shipping point.
4 Paid $75 cash for shipping charges on the March 3 purchase.
5 Returned to GreenWorld unacceptable merchandise that had an invoice price of $150.
18 Paid GreenWorld for the March 3 purchase, net of the discount and the returned merchandise.
19 Purchased $425 of fair trade merchandise from PeopleFirst Corp. with credit terms of 1/10, n/30, invoice dated March 19, and FOB destination.
21 After negotiations, received from PeopleFirst a $25 allowance (for scuffed merchandise) toward the $425 owed on the March 19 purchase.
29 Sent check to PeopleFirst paying for the March 19 purchase, net of the allowance and the discount.

PROBLEM SET A

Problem 4-1A
Preparing journal entries for merchandising activities—perpetual system

P1   P2

Check July 12, Dr. Cash, $882
July 16, Cr. Cash, $5,940

July 24, Cr. Cash, $1,960
July 30, Dr. Cash, $1,078

Prepare journal entries to record the following merchandising transactions of Cabela's, which uses the perpetual inventory system and the gross method. *Hint:* It will help to identify each receivable and payable; for example, record the purchase on July 1 in Accounts Payable—Boden.

July 1 Purchased merchandise from Boden Company for $6,000 under credit terms of 1/15, n/30, FOB shipping point, invoice dated July 1.
2 Sold merchandise to Creek Co. for $900 under credit terms of 2/10, n/60, FOB shipping point, invoice dated July 2. The merchandise had cost $500.
3 Paid $125 cash for freight charges on the purchase of July 1.
8 Sold merchandise that had cost $1,300 for $1,700 cash.
9 Purchased merchandise from Leight Co. for $2,200 under credit terms of 2/15, n/60, FOB destination, invoice dated July 9.
11 Returned $200 of merchandise purchased on July 9 from Leight Co. and debited its account payable for that amount.
12 Received the balance due from Creek Co. for the invoice dated July 2, net of the discount.
16 Paid the balance due to Boden Company within the discount period.
19 Sold merchandise that cost $800 to Art Co. for $1,200 under credit terms of 2/15, n/60, FOB shipping point, invoice dated July 19.
21 Gave a price reduction (allowance) of $100 to Art Co. for merchandise sold on July 19 and credited Art's accounts receivable for that amount.
24 Paid Leight Co. the balance due, net of discount.
30 Received the balance due from Art Co. for the invoice dated July 19, net of discount.
31 Sold merchandise that cost $4,800 to Creek Co. for $7,000 under credit terms of 2/10, n/60, FOB shipping point, invoice dated July 31.

Problem 4-2A
Preparing journal entries for merchandising activities—perpetual system

P1   P2

Check Aug. 9, Dr. Delivery Expense, $125

Aug. 18, Cr. Cash, $4,950

Prepare journal entries to record the following merchandising transactions of Lowe's, which uses the perpetual inventory system and the gross method. *Hint:* It will help to identify each receivable and payable; for example, record the purchase on August 1 in Accounts Payable—Aron.

Aug. 1 Purchased merchandise from Aron Company for $7,500 under credit terms of 1/10, n/30, FOB destination, invoice dated August 1.
5 Sold merchandise to Baird Corp. for $5,200 under credit terms of 2/10, n/60, FOB destination, invoice dated August 5. The merchandise had cost $4,000.
8 Purchased merchandise from Waters Corporation for $5,400 under credit terms of 1/10, n/45, FOB shipping point, invoice dated August 8.
9 Paid $125 cash for shipping charges related to the August 5 sale to Baird Corp.
10 Baird returned merchandise from the August 5 sale that had cost Lowe's $400 and was sold for $600. The merchandise was restored to inventory.
12 After negotiations with Waters Corporation concerning problems with the purchases on August 8, Lowe's received a price reduction from Waters of $400 off the $5,400 of goods purchased. Lowe's debited accounts payable for $400.
14 At Aron's request, Lowe's paid $200 cash for freight charges on the August 1 purchase, reducing the amount owed (accounts payable) to Aron.
15 Received balance due from Baird Corp. for the August 5 sale less the return on August 10.
18 Paid the amount due Waters Corporation for the August 8 purchase less the price allowance from August 12.

[continued on next page]

19 Sold merchandise to Tux Co. for $4,800 under credit terms of n/10, FOB shipping point, invoice dated August 19. The merchandise had cost $2,400.

22 Tux requested a price reduction on the August 19 sale because the merchandise did not meet specifications. Lowe's gave a price reduction (allowance) of $500 to Tux and credited Tux's accounts receivable for that amount.

29 Received Tux's cash payment for the amount due from the August 19 sale less the price allowance from August 22.

Aug. 29, Dr. Cash, $4,300

30 Paid Aron Company the amount due from the August 1 purchase.

Valley Company's adjusted trial balance on August 31, its fiscal year-end, follows. It categorizes the following accounts as selling expenses: Sales Salaries Expense, Rent Expense—Selling Space, Store Supplies Expense, and Advertising Expense. It categorizes the remaining expenses as general and administrative.

Problem 4-3A
Computing merchandising amounts and formatting income statements

C2   P4

	Debit	Credit
Merchandise inventory (ending)	$ 41,000	
Other (noninventory) assets	130,100	
Total liabilities........................		$ 25,000
Common stock		10,000
Retained earnings.....................		94,550
Dividends	8,000	
Sales		225,600
Sales discounts.......................	2,250	
Sales returns and allowances	12,000	
Cost of goods sold	74,500	
Sales salaries expense..................	32,000	
Rent expense—Selling space.............	8,000	
Store supplies expense	1,500	
Advertising expense....................	13,000	
Office salaries expense	28,500	
Rent expense—Office space	3,600	
Office supplies expense.... ...	400	
Totals..............................	$355,150	$355,150

Beginning merchandise inventory was $25,400. Supplementary records of merchandising activities for the year ended August 31 reveal the following itemized costs.

Invoice cost of merchandise purchases	$92,000	Purchases returns and allowances..........	$ 4,500
Purchases discounts received	2,000	Costs of transportation-in	4,600

Required

1. Compute the company's net sales for the year.
2. Compute the company's total cost of merchandise purchased for the year.
3. Prepare a multiple-step income statement that includes separate categories for net sales, cost of goods sold, selling expenses, and general and administrative expenses.
4. Prepare a single-step income statement that includes these expense categories: cost of goods sold, selling expenses, and general and administrative expenses.

Check   (2) $90,100

(3) Gross profit, $136,850;
Net income, $49,850

(4) Total expenses, $161,500

Use the data for Valley Company in Problem 4-3A to complete the following requirement.

Required

Prepare closing entries as of August 31 (the perpetual inventory system is used).

Problem 4-4A
Preparing closing entries and interpreting information about discounts and returns   C2   P3

The following unadjusted trial balance is prepared at fiscal year-end for Nelson Company. Nelson Company uses a perpetual inventory system. It categorizes the following accounts as selling expenses: Depreciation Expense—Store Equipment, Sales Salaries Expense, Rent Expense—Selling Space, Store Supplies Expense, and Advertising Expense. It categorizes the remaining expenses as general and administrative.

Problem 4-5A
Preparing adjusting entries and income statements; computing gross margin, acid-test, and current ratios

A1   A2   P3   P4

NELSON COMPANY Unadjusted Trial Balance January 31		
	Debit	Credit
Cash	$ 1,000	
Merchandise inventory	12,500	
Store supplies	5,800	
Prepaid insurance	2,400	
Store equipment	42,900	
Accumulated depreciation—Store equipment		$ 15,250
Accounts payable		10,000
Common stock		5,000
Retained earnings		27,000
Dividends	2,200	
Sales		111,950
Sales discounts	2,000	
Sales returns and allowances	2,200	
Cost of goods sold	38,400	
Depreciation expense—Store equipment	0	
Sales salaries expense	17,500	
Office salaries expense	17,500	
Insurance expense	0	
Rent expense—Selling space	7,500	
Rent expense—Office space	7,500	
Store supplies expense	0	
Advertising expense	9,800	
Totals	$169,200	$169,200

Required

1. Prepare adjusting journal entries to reflect each of the following:
   a. Store supplies still available at fiscal year-end amount to $1,750.
   b. Expired insurance, an administrative expense, is $1,400 for the fiscal year.
   c. Depreciation expense on store equipment, a selling expense, is $1,525 for the fiscal year.
   d. To estimate shrinkage, a physical count of ending merchandise inventory is taken. It shows $10,900 of inventory is still available at fiscal year-end.

Check (2) Gross profit, $67,750

2. Prepare a multiple-step income statement for the year ended January 31 that begins with gross sales and includes separate categories for net sales, cost of goods sold, selling expenses, and general and administrative expenses.

(3) Total expenses, $106,775; Net income, $975

3. Prepare a single-step income statement for the year ended January 31.

4. Compute the current ratio, acid-test ratio, and gross margin ratio as of January 31. (Round ratios to two decimals.)

PROBLEM SET B

Problem 4-1B

Preparing journal entries for merchandising activities—perpetual system

P1   P2

Prepare journal entries to record the following merchandising transactions of IKEA, which uses the perpetual inventory system and gross method. *Hint:* It will help to identify each receivable and payable; for example, record the purchase on May 2 in Accounts Payable—Havel.

May 2   Purchased merchandise from Havel Co. for $10,000 under credit terms of 1/15, n/30, FOB shipping point, invoice dated May 2.
    4   Sold merchandise to Rath Co. for $11,000 under credit terms of 2/10, n/60, FOB shipping point, invoice dated May 4. The merchandise had cost $5,600.
    5   Paid $250 cash for freight charges on the purchase of May 2.
    9   Sold merchandise that had cost $2,000 for $2,500 cash.
    10   Purchased merchandise from Duke Co. for $3,650 under credit terms of 2/15, n/60, FOB destination, invoice dated May 10.
    12   Returned $650 of merchandise purchased on May 10 from Duke Co. and debited its account payable for that amount.

Check May 14, Dr. Cash, $10,780
May 17, Cr. Cash, $9,900

    14   Received the balance due from Rath Co. for the invoice dated May 4, net of the discount.
    17   Paid the balance due to Havel Co. within the discount period.

[continued on next page]

20   Sold merchandise that cost $1,450 to Tamer Co. for $2,800 under credit terms of 2/15, n/60, FOB shipping point, invoice dated May 20.

22   Gave a price reduction (allowance) of $300 to Tamer Co. for merchandise sold on May 20 and credited Tamer's accounts receivable for that amount.

25   Paid Duke Co. the balance due, net of the discount.

30   Received the balance due from Tamer Co. for the invoice dated May 20, net of discount and allowance.   May 30, Dr. Cash, $2,450

31   Sold merchandise that cost $3,600 to Rath Co. for $7,200 under credit terms of 2/10, n/60, FOB shipping point, invoice dated May 31.

Prepare journal entries to record the following merchandising transactions of Menards, which applies the perpetual inventory system and gross method. *Hint:* It will help to identify each receivable and payable; for example, record the purchase on July 3 in Accounts Payable—OLB.

July 3   Purchased merchandise from OLB Corp. for $15,000 under credit terms of 1/10, n/30, FOB destination, invoice dated July 3.

7   Sold merchandise to Brill Co. for $11,500 under credit terms of 2/10, n/60, FOB destination, invoice dated July 7. The merchandise had cost $7,750.

10   Purchased merchandise from Rupert Co. for $14,200 under credit terms of 1/10, n/45, FOB shipping point, invoice dated July 10.

11   Paid $300 cash for shipping charges related to the July 7 sale to Brill Co.

12   Brill returned merchandise from the July 7 sale that had cost Menards $1,450 and been sold for $2,000. The merchandise was restored to inventory.

14   After negotiations with Rupert Co. concerning problems with the merchandise purchased on July 10, Menards received a price reduction from Rupert of $1,200. Menards debited accounts payable for $1,200.

15   At OLB's request, Menards paid $200 cash for freight charges on the July 3 purchase, reducing the amount owed (accounts payable) to OLB.

17   Received balance due from Brill Co. for the July 7 sale less the return on July 12.

20   Paid the amount due Rupert Co. for the July 10 purchase less the price reduction granted on July 14.

21   Sold merchandise to Brown for $11,000 under credit terms of 1/10, n/30, FOB shipping point, invoice dated July 21. The merchandise had cost $7,000.

24   Brown requested a price reduction on the July 21 sale because the merchandise did not meet specifications. Menards gave a price reduction (allowance) of $1,000 to Brown and credited Brown's accounts receivable for that amount.

30   Received Brown's cash payment for the amount due from the July 21 sale less the price allowance from July 24.

31   Paid OLB Corp. the amount due from the July 3 purchase.

Problem 4-2B
Preparing journal entries for merchandising activities—perpetual system

P1   P2

Check   July 17, Dr. Cash, $9,310

July 30, Dr. Cash, $9,900

July 31, Cr. Cash, $14,800

Barkley Company's adjusted trial balance on March 31, its fiscal year-end, follows. It categorizes the following accounts as selling expenses: Sales Salaries Expense, Rent Expense—Selling Space, Store Supplies Expense, and Advertising Expense. It categorizes the remaining expenses as general and administrative.

Problem 4-3B
Computing merchandising amounts and formatting income statements

C1   C2   P4

	Debit	Credit
Merchandise inventory (ending)	$ 56,500	
Other (noninventory) assets..............	202,600	
Total liabilities.........................		$ 42,500
Common stock		10,000
Retained earnings......................		154,425
Dividends	3,000	
Sales		332,650
Sales discounts........................	5,875	
Sales returns and allowances	20,000	
Cost of goods sold	115,600	
Sales salaries expense...................	44,500	
Rent expense—Selling space.............	16,000	
Store supplies expense	3,850	
Advertising expense....................	26,000	
Office salaries expense	40,750	
Rent expense—Office space	3,800	
Office supplies expense.................	1,100	
Totals..............................	$539,575	$539,575

Beginning merchandise inventory was $37,500. Supplementary records of merchandising activities for the year ended March 31 reveal the following itemized costs.

Invoice cost of merchandise purchases	$138,500	Purchases returns and allowances............	$6,700
Purchases discounts received	2,950	Costs of transportation-in	5,750

Required

1. Compute the company's net sales for the year.

Check (2) $134,600

(3) Gross profit, $191,175; Net income, $55,175

(4) Total expenses, $251,600

2. Compute the company's total cost of merchandise purchased for the year.

3. Prepare a multiple-step income statement that includes separate categories for net sales, cost of goods sold, selling expenses, and general and administrative expenses.

4. Prepare a single-step income statement that includes these expense categories: cost of goods sold, selling expenses, and general and administrative expenses.

Problem 4-4B

Preparing closing entries and interpreting information about discounts and returns C2 P3

Use the data for Barkley Company in Problem 4-3B to complete the following requirement.

Required

Prepare closing entries as of March 31 (the perpetual inventory system is used).

Problem 4-5B

Preparing adjusting entries and income statements; computing gross margin, acid-test, and current ratios

P3 P4 A1 A2

The following unadjusted trial balance is prepared at fiscal year-end for Foster Products Company. Foster Products Company uses a perpetual inventory system. It categorizes the following accounts as selling expenses: Depreciation Expense—Store Equipment, Sales Salaries Expense, Rent Expense—Selling Space, Store Supplies Expense, and Advertising Expense. It categorizes the remaining expenses as general and administrative.

FOSTER PRODUCTS COMPANY Unadjusted Trial Balance October 31	Debit	Credit
Cash	$ 7,400	
Merchandise inventory	24,000	
Store supplies	9,700	
Prepaid insurance	6,600	
Store equipment	81,800	
Accumulated depreciation—Store equipment		$ 32,000
Accounts payable		18,000
Common stock		3,000
Retained earnings		40,000
Dividends	2,000	
Sales		227,100
Sales discounts	1,000	
Sales returns and allowances	5,000	
Cost of goods sold	75,800	
Depreciation expense—Store equipment	0	
Sales salaries expense	31,500	
Office salaries expense	31,500	
Insurance expense	0	
Rent expense—Selling space	13,000	
Rent expense—Office space	13,000	
Store supplies expense	0	
Advertising expense	17,800	
Totals	$320,100	$320,100

Required

1. Prepare adjusting journal entries to reflect each of the following:

   a. Store supplies still available at fiscal year-end amount to $3,700.

   b. Expired insurance, an administrative expense, is $2,800 for the fiscal year.

[continued on next page]

c. Depreciation expense on store equipment, a selling expense, is $3,000 for the fiscal year.

d. To estimate shrinkage, a physical count of ending merchandise inventory is taken. It shows $21,300 of inventory is still available at fiscal year-end.

2. Prepare a multiple-step income statement for the year ended October 31 that begins with gross sales and includes separate categories for net sales, cost of goods sold, selling expenses, and general and administrative expenses.

3. Prepare a single-step income statement for the year ended October 31.

4. Compute the current ratio, acid-test ratio, and gross margin ratio as of October 31. (Round ratios to two decimals.)

Check   (2) Gross profit, $142,600

(3) Total expenses, $197,100; Net income, $24,000

This serial problem began in Chapter 1 and continues through most of the book. If previous chapter segments were not completed, the serial problem can begin at this point.

SERIAL PROBLEM
Business Solutions

P1   P2   P3   P4

SP 4   Santana Rey created **Business Solutions** on October 1, 2019. The company has been successful, and its list of customers has grown. To accommodate the growth, the accounting system is modified to set up separate accounts for each customer. The following chart of accounts includes the account number used for each account and any balance as of December 31, 2019. Santana Rey decided to add a fourth digit with a decimal point to the 106 account number that had been used for the single Accounts Receivable account. This change allows the company to continue using the existing chart of accounts.

No.	Account Title	Dr.	Cr.
101	Cash	$48,372	
106.1	Alex's Engineering Co.	0	
106.2	Wildcat Services	0	
106.3	Easy Leasing	0	
106.4	IFM Co.	3,000	
106.5	Liu Corp.	0	
106.6	Gomez Co.	2,668	
106.7	Delta Co.	0	
106.8	KC, Inc.	0	
106.9	Dream, Inc.	0	
119	Merchandise inventory	0	
126	Computer supplies	580	
128	Prepaid insurance	1,665	
131	Prepaid rent	825	
163	Office equipment	8,000	
164	Accumulated depreciation—Office equipment		$ 400
167	Computer equipment	20,000	
168	Accumulated depreciation—Computer equipment		1,250
201	Accounts payable		1,100

No.	Account Title	Dr.	Cr.
210	Wages payable		$ 500
236	Unearned computer services revenue		1,500
307	Common stock		73,000
318	Retained earnings		7,360
319	Dividends	$0	
403	Computer services revenue		0
413	Sales		0
414	Sales returns and allowances	0	
415	Sales discounts	0	
502	Cost of goods sold	0	
612	Depreciation expense—Office equipment	0	
613	Depreciation expense—Computer equipment	0	
623	Wages expense	0	
637	Insurance expense	0	
640	Rent expense	0	
652	Computer supplies expense	0	
655	Advertising expense	0	
676	Mileage expense	0	
677	Miscellaneous expenses	0	
684	Repairs expense—Computer	0	

In response to requests from customers, S. Rey will begin selling computer software. The company will extend credit terms of 1/10, n/30, FOB shipping point, to all customers who purchase this merchandise. However, no cash discount is available on consulting fees. Additional accounts (Nos. 119, 413, 414, 415, and 502) are added to its general ledger to accommodate the company's new merchandising activities. Its transactions for January through March follow.

©Alexander Image/Shutterstock

Jan.   4   The company paid cash to Lyn Addie for five days' work at the rate of $125 per day. Four of the five days relate to wages payable that were accrued in the prior year.

5   Santana Rey invested an additional $25,000 cash in the company in exchange for more common stock.

7   The company purchased $5,800 of merchandise from Kansas Corp. with terms of 1/10, n/30, FOB shipping point, invoice dated January 7.

9   The company received $2,668 cash from Gomez Co. as full payment on its account.

11   The company completed a five-day project for Alex's Engineering Co. and billed it $5,500, which is the total price of $7,000 less the advance payment of $1,500. The company debited Unearned Computer Services Revenue for $1,500.

13   The company sold merchandise with a retail value of $5,200 and a cost of $3,560 to Liu Corp., invoice dated January 13.

15   The company paid $600 cash for freight charges on the merchandise purchased on January 7.

16   The company received $4,000 cash from Delta Co. for computer services provided.

17   The company paid Kansas Corp. for the invoice dated January 7, net of the discount.

20   The company gave a price reduction (allowance) of $500 to Liu Corp. and credited Liu's accounts receivable for that amount.

22   The company received the balance due from Liu Corp., net of the discount and the allowance.

24   The company returned defective merchandise to Kansas Corp. and accepted a credit against future purchases (debited accounts payable). The defective merchandise invoice cost, net of the discount, was $496.

26   The company purchased $9,000 of merchandise from Kansas Corp. with terms of 1/10, n/30, FOB destination, invoice dated January 26.

26   The company sold merchandise with a $4,640 cost for $5,800 on credit to KC, Inc., invoice dated January 26.

31   The company paid cash to Lyn Addie for 10 days' work at $125 per day.

Feb. 1   The company paid $2,475 cash to Hillside Mall for another three months' rent in advance.

3   The company paid Kansas Corp. for the balance due, net of the cash discount, less the $496 credit from merchandise returned on January 24.

5   The company paid $600 cash to Facebook for an advertisement to appear on February 5 only.

11   The company received the balance due from Alex's Engineering Co. for fees billed on January 11.

15   The company paid a $4,800 cash dividend.

23   The company sold merchandise with a $2,660 cost for $3,220 on credit to Delta Co., invoice dated February 23.

26   The company paid cash to Lyn Addie for eight days' work at $125 per day.

27   The company reimbursed Santana Rey $192 cash for business automobile mileage. The company recorded the reimbursement as "Mileage Expense."

Mar. 8   The company purchased $2,730 of computer supplies from Harris Office Products on credit with terms of n/30, FOB destination, invoice dated March 8.

9   The company received the balance due from Delta Co. for merchandise sold on February 23.

11   The company paid $960 cash for minor repairs to the company's computer.

16   The company received $5,260 cash from Dream, Inc., for computing services provided.

19   The company paid the full amount due of $3,830 to Harris Office Products, consisting of amounts created on December 15 (of $1,100) and March 8.

24   The company billed Easy Leasing for $9,047 of computing services provided.

25   The company sold merchandise with a $2,002 cost for $2,800 on credit to Wildcat Services, invoice dated March 25.

30   The company sold merchandise with a $1,048 cost for $2,220 on credit to IFM Company, invoice dated March 30.

31   The company reimbursed Santana Rey $128 cash for business automobile mileage. The company recorded the reimbursement as "Mileage Expense."

The following additional facts are available for preparing adjustments on March 31 prior to financial statement preparation.

a. The March 31 amount of computer supplies still available totals $2,005.

b. Prepaid insurance coverage of $555 expired during this three-month period.

c. Lyn Addie has not been paid for seven days of work at the rate of $125 per day.

d. Prepaid rent of $2,475 expired during this three-month period.

e. Depreciation on the computer equipment for January 1 through March 31 is $1,250.

f. Depreciation on the office equipment for January 1 through March 31 is $400.

g. The March 31 amount of merchandise inventory still available totals $704.

Required

Check   (2) Ending balances at March 31: Cash, $68,057; Sales, $19,240

(3) Unadj. TB totals, $151,557; Adj. TB totals, $154,082

1. Prepare journal entries to record each of the January through March transactions.

2. Post the journal entries in part 1 to the accounts in the company's general ledger. *Note:* Begin with the ledger's post-closing adjusted balances as of December 31, 2019.

3. Prepare a 6-column work sheet (similar to the one shown in Exhibit 3.13) that includes the unadjusted trial balance, the March 31 adjustments (*a*) through (*g*), and the adjusted trial balance. Do not prepare closing entries and do not journalize the adjustments or post them to the ledger.

[continued on next page]

4. Prepare an income statement (from the adjusted trial balance in part 3) for the three months ended March 31, 2020. (*a*) Use a single-step format. List all expenses without differentiating between selling expenses and general and administrative expenses. (*b*) Use a multiple-step format that begins with gross sales (service revenues plus gross product sales) and includes separate categories for net sales, cost of goods sold, selling expenses, and general and administrative expenses. Categorize the following accounts as selling expenses: Wages Expense, Mileage Expense, and Advertising Expense. Categorize the remaining expenses as general and administrative.

(4) Net income, $18,833

5. Prepare a statement of retained earnings (from the adjusted trial balance in part 3) for the three months ended March 31, 2020.

6. Prepare a classified balance sheet (from the adjusted trial balance) as of March 31, 2020.

(6) Total assets, $120,268

The **General Ledger** tool in *Connect* automates several of the procedural steps in the accounting cycle so that the accounting professional can focus on the impacts of each transaction on the various financial reports. The following General Ledger questions highlight the operating cycle of a merchandising company. In each case, the trial balance is automatically updated from the journal entries recorded.

GENERAL LEDGER PROBLEM

GL 4-1 Based on Problem 4-1A

GL 4-3 Based on Problem 4-5A

GL 4-2 Based on Problem 4-2A

Accounting Analysis

AA 4-1 Refer to **Apple**'s financial statements in Appendix A to answer the following.

Required

1. Assume that the amounts reported for inventories and cost of sales reflect items purchased in a form ready for resale. Compute the net cost of goods purchased for the year ended September 30, 2017.

2. Compute the current ratio and acid-test ratio as of September 30, 2017, and September 24, 2016.

3. Does Apple's 2017 current ratio outperform or underperform the (assumed) industry average of 1.5?

4. Does Apple's 2017 acid-test ratio outperform or underperform the (assumed) industry average of 1.0?

COMPANY ANALYSIS

A1

APPLE

AA 4-2 Key comparative figures for **Apple** and **Google** follow.

COMPARATIVE ANALYSIS

A2

APPLE
GOOGLE

$ millions	Apple		Google	
	Current Year	Prior Year	Current Year	Prior Year
Net sales	$229,234	$215,639	$110,855	$90,272
Cost of sales	141,048	131,376	45,583	35,138

Required

1. Compute the amount of gross margin and the gross margin ratio for the two years shown for each of these companies.

2. Which company earns more in gross margin for each dollar of net sales for the current year?

3. Do (*a*) Apple's and (*b*) Google's current-year gross margins underperform or outperform the industry (assumed) average of 35.0%?

4. Are (*a*) Apple's and (*b*) Google's current-year gross margins on a favorable or unfavorable trend?

AA 4-3 Key comparative figures for **Samsung**, **Apple**, and **Google** follow.

GLOBAL ANALYSIS

A2 P4

APPLE
GOOGLE
Samsung

In millions	Net Sales	Cost of Sales
Samsung	₩239,575,376	₩129,290,661
Apple	$ 229,234	$ 141,048
Google	$ 110,855	$ 45,583

Required

1. Compute the gross margin ratio for each of the three companies.
2. Is Samsung's gross margin ratio better or worse than (*a*) Apple's ratio? (*b*) Google's?
3. Do (*a*) Apple, (*b*) Google, and (*c*) Samsung use single-step or multiple-step income statements?

Beyond the Numbers

ETHICS CHALLENGE

C1   P2

BTN 4-1   Amy Martin is a student who plans to attend approximately four professional events a year at her college. Each event necessitates a financial outlay of $100 to $200 for a new suit and accessories. After incurring a major hit to her savings for the first event, Amy developed a different approach. She buys the suit on credit the week before the event, wears it to the event, and returns it the next week to the store for a full refund on her charge card.

Required

1. Comment on the ethics exhibited by Amy and possible consequences of her actions.
2. How does the merchandising company account for the suits that Amy returns?

COMMUNICATING IN PRACTICE

C2   P3   P5

BTN 4-2   You are the financial officer for Music Plus, a retailer that sells goods for home entertainment needs. The business owner, Vic Velakturi, recently reviewed the annual financial statements you prepared and sent you an e-mail stating that he thinks you overstated net income. He explains that although he has invested a great deal in security, he is sure shoplifting and other forms of inventory shrinkage have occurred, but he does not see any deduction for shrinkage on the income statement. The store uses a perpetual inventory system.

Required

Prepare a brief memorandum that responds to the owner's concerns.

TAKING IT TO THE NET

C1   A2

BTN 4-3   Access the SEC's EDGAR database (**SEC.gov**) and obtain the March 21, 2017, filing of its fiscal 2017 10-K report (for year ended January 28, 2017) for **J. Crew Group, Inc.** (ticker: JCG).

Required

Prepare a table that reports the gross margin ratios for J. Crew using the revenues and cost of goods sold data from J. Crew's income statement for each of its most recent three years. Analyze and comment on the trend in its gross margin ratio.

TEAMWORK IN ACTION

C1   C2

BTN 4-4   Official Brands's general ledger and supplementary records at the end of its current period reveal the following.

Sales, gross	$600,000	Merchandise inventory (beginning of period)	$ 98,000
Sales returns & allowances	20,000	Invoice cost of merchandise purchases	360,000
Sales discounts	13,000	Purchases discounts received	9,000
Cost of transportation-in	22,000	Purchases returns and allowances	11,000
Operating expenses	50,000	Merchandise inventory (end of period)	84,000

Required

1. *Each* member of the team is to assume responsibility for computing *one* of the following items. You are not to duplicate your teammates' work. Get any necessary amounts to compute your item from the appropriate teammate. Each member is to explain his or her computation to the team in preparation for reporting to the class.

   a. Net sales

   b. Total cost of merchandise purchases

   c. Cost of goods sold

   d. Gross profit

   e. Net income

2. Check your net income with the instructor. If correct, proceed to step 3.
3. Assume that a physical inventory count finds that actual ending inventory is $76,000. Discuss how this affects previously computed amounts in step 1.

Point: In teams of four, assign the same student *a* and *e*. Rotate teams for reporting on a different computation and the analysis in step 3.

ENTREPRENEURIAL DECISION

C1   C2   P1

BTN 4-5   Refer to the opening feature about **Build-A-Bear Workshop** and its founder Maxine Clark. Assume the business reports current annual sales at approximately $1 million and prepares the following income statement.

BUILD-A-BEAR WORKSHOP Income Statement For Year Ended January 31, 2018	
Net sales	$1,000,000
Cost of sales	610,000
Expenses (other than cost of sales)	200,000
Net income	$ 190,000

Assume the business sells to individuals and retailers, ranging from small shops to large chains. Assume that they currently offer credit terms of 1/15, n/60, and ship FOB destination. To improve their cash flow, they are considering changing credit terms to 3/10, n/30. In addition, they propose to change shipping terms to FOB shipping point. They expect that the increase in discount rate will increase net sales by 9%, but the gross margin ratio (and ratio of cost of sales divided by net sales) is expected to remain unchanged. They also expect that delivery expenses will be zero under this proposal; thus, expenses other than cost of sales are expected to increase only 6%.

Required

1. Prepare a forecasted income statement for the year ended January 31, 2019, based on the proposal.

2. Based on the forecasted income statement alone (from your part 1 solution), do you recommend that the business implement the new sales policies? Explain.

3. What else should the business consider before deciding whether to implement the new policies? Explain.

HITTING THE ROAD

C1   P2

Point: This activity complements the Ethics Challenge assignment.

BTN 4-6   Arrange an interview (in person or by phone) with the manager of a retail shop in a mall or in the downtown area of your community. Explain to the manager that you are a student studying merchandising activities and the accounting for sales returns and sales allowances. Ask the manager what the store policy is regarding returns. Also find out if sales allowances are ever negotiated with customers. Inquire whether management perceives that customers are abusing return policies and what actions management takes to counter potential abuses. Be prepared to discuss your findings in class.

5 Inventories and Cost of Sales

Learning Objectives

CONCEPTUAL

C1 Identify the items making up merchandise inventory.

C2 Identify the costs of merchandise inventory.

ANALYTICAL

A1 Analyze the effects of inventory methods for both financial and tax reporting.

A2 Analyze the effects of inventory errors on current and future financial statements.

A3 Assess inventory management using both inventory turnover and days' sales in inventory.

PROCEDURAL

P1 Compute inventory in a perpetual system using the methods of specific identification, FIFO, LIFO, and weighted average.

P2 Compute the lower of cost or market amount of inventory.

P3 *Appendix 5A*—Compute inventory in a periodic system using the methods of specific identification, FIFO, LIFO, and weighted average.

P4 *Appendix 5B*—Apply both the retail inventory and gross profit methods to estimate inventory.

Shake It Up

"Show guests you care"—**DANNY MEYER**

NEW YORK—Danny Meyer opened his first **Shake Shack** (**ShakeShack.com**) restaurant in Madison Square Park. The first Shake Shack was a hot dog stand! While much has changed since the first Shack, Danny's commitment to high-quality ingredients has not.

"We call it fine-casual," explains Danny. "Shake Shack . . . is proving that people don't want to go backwards in terms of how their food was sourced, how it was cooked."

Managing this "modern-day roadside burger stand" was not easy. Danny's Shack grew from "$5,000 worth of hamburgers" to "$30,000-plus" of hamburgers per day. Danny needed an accounting system to track everything.

"The thinking back then was, to have a successful restaurant, the owner had to be there 24/7," says Danny. To expand Shake Shack, that had to change. Danny put in an inventory system for each of his Shacks. "Great companies," insists Danny, "figured [inventory] out."

To ensure fresh sourced ingredients were available at the Shacks, Danny set up an inventory tracking system. He prepared and read inventory reports and applied inventory management tools. His inventory system tracks all transactions, and he regularly reviews accounting data in making key decisions.

"You need to get your ducks in a line," asserts Danny. This means that Shake Shack must successfully manage its inventory, even as growth continues.

©Monica Schipper/NYCWFF/Getty Images

To be successful, Danny insists that "the numbers add up." Once your financial house is in order, explains Danny, "you need to take more risk." He adds, "The best start-ups are businesses that find a unique way to solve problems for people—sometimes problems that people didn't even know they had."

Sources: *Shake Shack website,* January 2019; *Fool.com,* December 2016; *Eater.com,* September 2016; *Inc.com,* May 2015

INVENTORY BASICS

Determining Inventory Items

Merchandise inventory includes all goods that a company owns and holds for sale. This is true regardless of where the goods are located when inventory is counted. Special attention is directed at goods in transit, goods on consignment, and goods that are damaged or obsolete.

C1

Identify the items making up merchandise inventory.

Goods in Transit   Does a buyer's inventory include goods in transit from a supplier? If ownership has passed to the buyer, the goods are included in the buyer's inventory. We determine this by reviewing shipping terms.

- FOB shipping point—goods are included in buyer's inventory once they are shipped.
- FOB destination—goods are included in buyer's inventory after arrival at their destination.

Goods on Consignment   Goods on consignment are goods shipped by the owner, called the **consignor,** to another party, the **consignee.** A consignee sells goods for the owner. The consignor owns the consigned goods and reports them in its inventory. For example, **Upper Deck** pays sports celebrities such as Russell Wilson of the Seattle Seahawks to sign memorabilia, which are offered to card shops on consignment. Upper Deck, the consignor, reports these items in its inventory until sold. The consignee *never* reports consigned goods in inventory.

Goods Damaged or Obsolete   Damaged, obsolete (out-of-date), and deteriorated goods are not reported in inventory if they cannot be sold. If these goods can be sold at a lower price, they are included in inventory at **net realizable value.** Net realizable value is sales price minus the cost of making the sale. A loss is recorded when the damage or obsolescence occurs.

©Aleksandar Georgiev/Getty Images

Ethical Risk

Eyes in the Sky   One of the largest builders, **Homex**, was accused of faking the construction and sale of 100,000 homes. How were they caught? When the SEC used satellite imagery to confirm the existence of homes, they found nothing but bare soil. SEC 2017-60 ■

Determining Inventory Costs

C2

Identify the costs of merchandise inventory.

Merchandise inventory includes costs to bring an item to a salable condition and location. Inventory costs include invoice cost minus any discount, plus any other costs. Other costs include shipping, storage, import duties, and insurance. The *expense recognition principle* says that inventory costs are expensed as cost of goods sold when inventory is sold.

Internal Controls and Taking a Physical Count

Fraud: Auditors observe employees as they count inventory. Auditors also take their own count to ensure accuracy.

Events can cause the Inventory account balance to be different than the actual inventory available. Such events include theft, loss, damage, and errors. Thus, nearly all companies take a *physical count of inventory* at least once each year. This physical count is used to adjust the Inventory account balance to the actual inventory available.

■ **Decision Insight**

In Control   A company applies internal controls when taking a physical count of inventory that usually include the following to minimize fraud and to increase reliability.

Point: The Inventory account has *subsidiary ledgers* that contain a separate record (units and costs) for each separate product.

- *Prenumbered inventory tickets* are distributed to *counters*—each ticket must be accounted for.
- Counters of inventory are assigned and do not include those responsible for inventory.
- Counters confirm the existence, amount, and condition of inventory.
- A second count is taken by a different counter.
- A manager confirms all inventories are ticketed once, and only once. ■

NEED-TO-KNOW 5-1

Inventory Items and Costs

C1 C2

Do More: QS 5-1, QS 5-2, QS 5-23, E 5-1, E 5-2

1. A master carver of wooden birds operates her business out of a garage. At the end of the current period, the carver has 17 units (carvings) in her garage, 3 of which were damaged by water and cannot be sold. She also has another 5 units in her truck, ready to deliver per a customer order, terms FOB destination, and another 11 units out on consignment at retail stores. How many units does she include in the business's period-end inventory?

2. A distributor of artistic iron-based fixtures acquires a piece for $1,000, terms FOB shipping point. Additional costs in obtaining it and offering it for sale include $150 for transportation-in, $300 for import duties, $100 for insurance during shipment, $200 for advertising, a $50 voluntary gratuity to the delivery person, $75 for enhanced store lighting, and $250 for sales staff salaries. For computing inventory, what cost is assigned to this artistic piece?

Solutions

1.

Units in ending inventory	
Units in storage.	17 units
Less damaged (unsalable) units.	(3)
Plus units in transit	5
Plus units on consignment.	11
Total units in ending inventory.	30 units

2.

Merchandise cost	$1,000
Plus:	
Transportation-in	150
Import duties	300
Insurance	100
Total inventory cost.	$1,550

INVENTORY COSTING UNDER A PERPETUAL SYSTEM

When identical items are purchased at different costs, we must decide which amounts to record in cost of goods sold and which amounts remain in inventory. Four methods are used to assign costs to inventory and to cost of goods sold: (1) specific identification; (2) first-in, first-out (FIFO); (3) last-in, first-out (LIFO); and (4) weighted average. Exhibit 5.1 shows the frequency in use of these methods.

Each method has a pattern for how costs flow through inventory. The cost flow assumption does not have to match the actual physical flow of goods. For example, **Kroger**'s grocery chain sells food first-in, first-out, meaning they sell the oldest food in inventory first. However, Kroger can use last-in, first-out to assign costs to food sold. With the exception of specific identification, the **physical flow and cost flow do not have to be the same**.

EXHIBIT 5.1

Frequency in Use of Inventory Methods

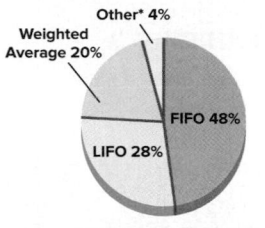

*Includes specific identification.

Inventory Cost Flow Assumptions

To show inventory cost flow assumptions, assume that three identical units are purchased separately at the following three dates and costs: May 1 at $45, May 3 at $65, and May 6 at $70. One unit is then sold on May 7 for $100. Exhibit 5.2 shows the flow of costs to either cost of goods sold on the income statement or inventory reported on the balance sheet for FIFO, LIFO, and weighted average.

Point: Cost of goods sold is abbreviated COGS.

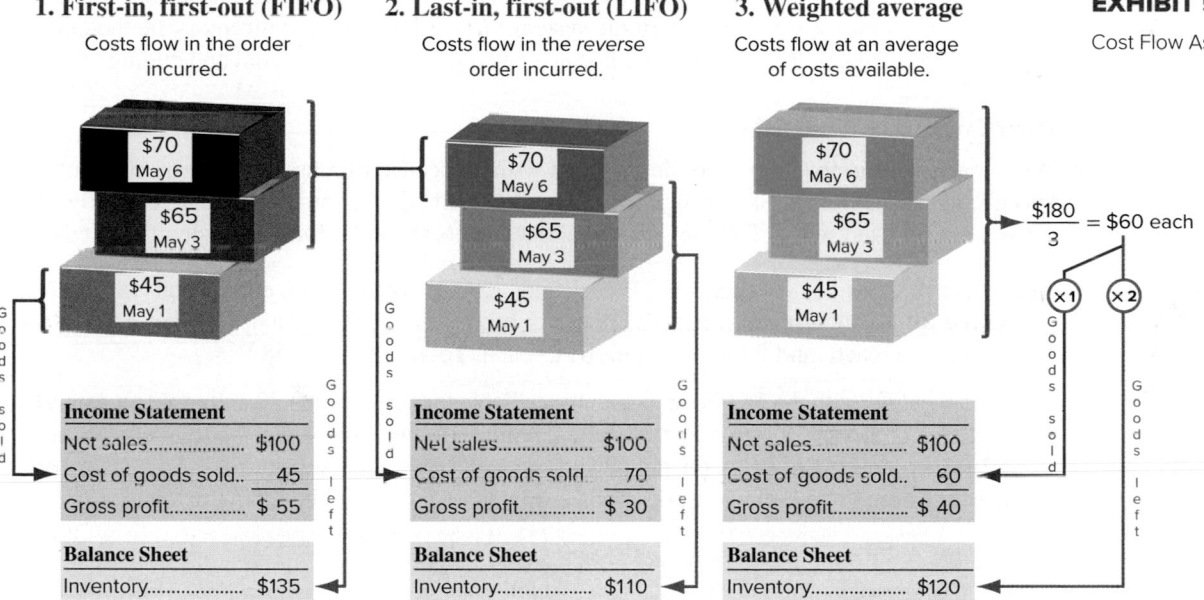

EXHIBIT 5.2

Cost Flow Assumptions

(1) *FIFO assumes costs flow in the order incurred.* The unit purchased on May 1 for $45 is the earliest cost incurred—it is sent to cost of goods sold on the income statement first. The remaining two units ($65 and $70) are reported in inventory on the balance sheet.

(2) *LIFO assumes costs flow in the reverse order incurred.* The unit purchased on May 6 for $70 is the most recent cost incurred—it is sent to cost of goods sold on the income statement. The remaining two units ($45 and $65) are reported in inventory on the balance sheet.

(3) *Weighted average assumes costs flow at an average of the costs available.* The units available at the May 7 sale average $60 in cost, computed as ($45 + $65 + $70)/3. One unit's $60 average cost is sent to cost of goods sold on the income statement. The remaining two units' average costs are reported in inventory at $120 on the balance sheet.

Cost flow assumptions impact gross profit and inventory numbers. Exhibit 5.2 shows that gross profit ranges from $30 to $55 due to the cost flow assumption.

Point: Recall inventory cost flow.

Beginning inventory **+** Net purchases

= Merchandise available for sale

Ending inventory **+** Cost of goods sold

The following sections on inventory costing use the *perpetual system*. Appendix 5A uses the periodic system. An instructor can choose to cover either one or both systems. If the perpetual system is skipped, then read Appendix 5A and return to the "Valuing Inventory at LCM and the Effects of Inventory Errors" section.

Inventory Costing Illustration

This section demonstrates inventory costing methods. We use information from Trekking, a sporting goods store. Among its products, Trekking sells one type of mountain bike whose sales are directed at resorts that provide inexpensive bikes for guest use. We use Trekking's data from August. Its mountain bike (unit) inventory at the beginning of August and its purchases and sales during August are in Exhibit 5.3. It ends August with 12 bikes in inventory.

EXHIBIT 5.3

Purchases and Sales
of Goods

©Michael DeYoung/Blend Images

Date	Activity	Units Acquired at Cost	Units Sold at Retail	Unit Inventory
Aug. 1	Beginning inventory.......	10 units @ $ 91 = $ 910		10 units
Aug. 3	Purchases..............	15 units @ $106 = $ 1,590		25 units
Aug. 14	Sales..................		20 units @ $130	5 units
Aug. 17	Purchases..............	20 units @ $115 = $ 2,300		25 units
Aug. 28	Purchases..............	10 units @ $119 = $ 1,190		35 units
Aug. 30	Sales..................		23 units @ $150	**12 units**
	Totals	**55 units** → $5,990	**43 units** ←	
		Units available for sale / Goods available for sale	Units sold	Units left

Trekking uses the **perpetual inventory system**, which means that its Merchandise Inventory account is updated for each purchase and sale of inventory. (Appendix 5A describes the assignment of costs to inventory using a periodic system.) Regardless of what inventory method is used, cost of goods available for sale must be allocated between cost of goods sold and ending inventory.

Specific Identification

When each item in inventory can be matched with a specific purchase and invoice, we can use **specific identification** or **SI** to assign costs. We also need sales records that identify exactly which items were sold and when. Trekking's internal documents show the following specific unit sales.

August 14   Sold 8 bikes costing $91 each and 12 bikes costing $106 each. Total cost = $2,000.
August 30   Sold 2 bikes costing $91 each, 3 bikes costing $106 each, 15 bikes costing $115 each, and 3 bikes costing $119 each. Total cost = $2,582.

Exhibit 5.4 begins with the $5,990 in total units available for sale. For the 20 units sold on August 14, the total cost of sales is $2,000. Next, for the 23 units sold on August 30, the total cost of sales is $2,582. The total cost of sales for the period is $4,582. We then subtract this $4,582 in cost of goods sold from the $5,990 in cost of goods available to get $1,408 in ending inventory.

EXHIBIT 5.4

Specific Identification
Computations

Total cost of 55 units available for sale (from Exhibit 5.3)		$ 5,990
Cost of goods sold		
Aug. 14 (8 @ $91) + (12 @ $106)..	$2,000	
Aug. 30 (2 @ $91) + (3 @ $106) + (15 @ $115) + (3 @ $119).................	2,582	**4,582**
Ending inventory		**$1,408**

Merchandise Inventory (SI)			
Aug. 1	910		
Aug. 3	1,590		
		Aug. 14	2,000
Aug. 17	2,300		
Aug. 28	1,190		
		Aug. 30	2,582
Aug. 31	1,408		

Trekking's cost of goods sold reported on the income statement is **$4,582**, and ending inventory reported on the balance sheet is **$1,408**. The following graphic shows this flow of costs.

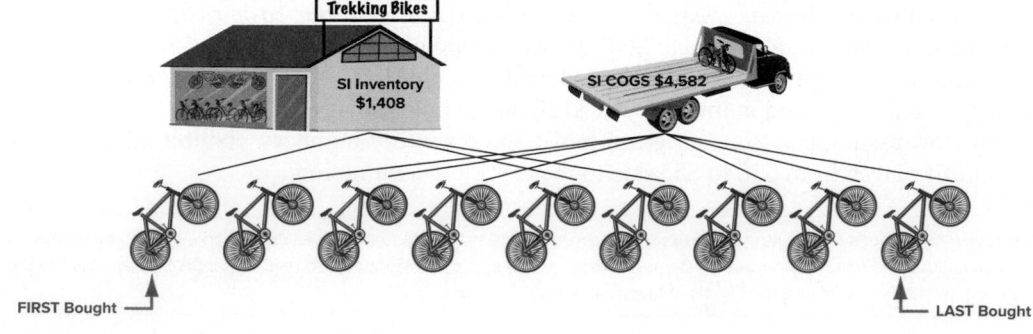

FIRST Bought   LAST Bought

First-In, First-Out

First-in, first-out (FIFO) assumes that inventory items are sold in the order acquired. When sales occur, the costs of the earliest units acquired are charged to cost of goods sold. This leaves the costs from the most recent purchases in ending inventory.

Exhibit 5.5 starts with beginning inventory of 10 bikes at $91 each.

August 3	Purchased 15 bikes costing $106 each for $1,590. Inventory now consists of 10 bikes at $91 each and 15 bikes at $106 each, for a total of $2,500.
August 14	Sold 20 bikes—applying FIFO, the first 10 sold cost $91 each and the next 10 sold cost $106 each, for a total cost of $1,970. This leaves 5 bikes costing $106 each, or $530, in inventory.
August 17	Purchased 20 bikes costing $115 each, and on August 28, purchased another 10 bikes costing $119 each, for a total of 35 bikes costing $4,020 in inventory.
August 30	Sold 23 bikes—applying FIFO, the first 5 bikes sold cost $106 each and the next 18 sold cost $115 each, for a total of $2,600. This leaves 12 bikes costing $1,420 in ending inventory.

Point: "Goods Purchased" column is identical for all methods.

EXHIBIT 5.5

FIFO Computations— Perpetual System

Date	Goods Purchased	Cost of Goods Sold	Inventory Balance
Aug. 1	Beginning balance		10 @ $ 91 = $ 910
Aug. 3	15 @ $106 = $1,590		10 @ $ 91 15 @ $106 } = $ 2,500
Aug. 14		10 @ $ 91 = $ 910 10 @ $106 = $1,060 } = $1,970	5 @ $106 = $ 530
Aug. 17	20 @ $115 = $2,300		5 @ $106 20 @ $115 } = $ 2,830
Aug. 28	10 @ $119 = $1,190		5 @ $106 20 @ $115 10 @ $119 } = $ 4,020
Aug. 30		5 @ $106 = $ 530 18 @ $115 = $2,070 } = $2,600	2 @ $115 10 @ $119 } = $1,420
		$4,570	

Merchandise Inventory (FIFO)

Aug. 1	910			
Aug. 3	1,590		Aug. 14	1,970
Aug. 17	2,300			
Aug. 28	1,190			
			Aug. 30	2,600
Aug. 31	1,420			

Trekking's cost of goods sold reported on its income statement is **$4,570** ($1,970 + $2,600), and its ending inventory reported on the balance sheet is **$1,420**.

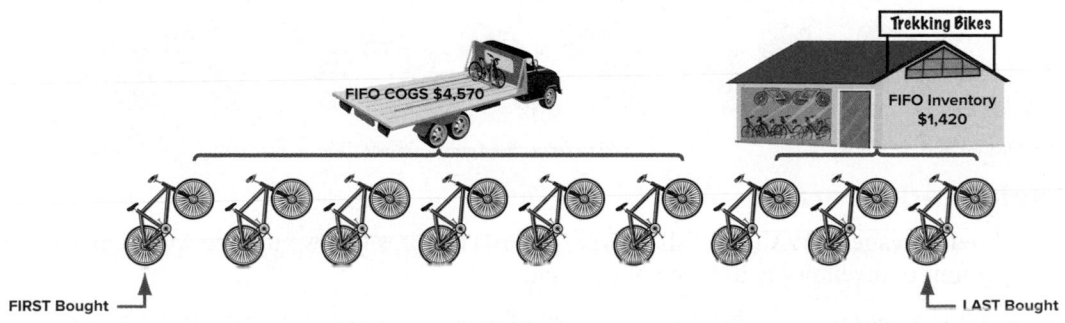

Last-In, First-Out

Last-in, first-out (LIFO) assumes that the most recent purchases are sold first. These more recent costs are charged to the goods sold, and the costs of the earliest purchases are assigned to inventory.

Point: By assigning costs from the most recent purchases to cost of goods sold, LIFO comes closest to matching current costs of goods sold with revenues.

Exhibit 5.6 starts with beginning inventory of 10 bikes at $91 each.

August 3   Purchased 15 bikes costing $106 each for $1,590. Inventory now consists of 10 bikes at $91 each and 15 bikes at $106 each, for a total of $2,500.

August 14   Sold 20 bikes—applying LIFO, the first 15 sold are from the most recent purchase costing $106 each, and the next 5 sold are from the next most recent purchase costing $91 each, for a total of $2,045. This leaves 5 bikes costing $91 each, or $455, in inventory.

August 17   Purchased 20 bikes costing $115 each, and on August 28, purchased another 10 bikes costing $119 each, for a total of 35 bikes costing $3,945 in inventory.

August 30   Sold 23 bikes—applying LIFO, the first 10 bikes sold are from the most recent purchase costing $119 each, and the next 13 sold are from the next most recent purchase costing $115 each, for a total of $2,685. This leaves 12 bikes costing $1,260 in ending inventory.

EXHIBIT 5.6

LIFO Computations—
Perpetual System

Date	Goods Purchased	Cost of Goods Sold	Inventory Balance
Aug. 1	Beginning balance		10 @ $ 91 = $ 910
Aug. 3	15 @ $106 = $1,590		10 @ $ 91 / 15 @ $106 } = $ 2,500
Aug. 14		15 @ $106 = $1,590 / 5 @ $ 91 = $ 455 } = $2,045	5 @ $ 91 = $ 455
Aug. 17	20 @ $115 = $2,300		5 @ $ 91 / 20 @ $115 } = $2,755
Aug. 28	10 @ $119 = $1,190		5 @ $ 91 / 20 @ $115 / 10 @ $119 } = $3,945
Aug. 30		10 @ $119 = $1,190 / 13 @ $115 = $1,495 } = $2,685 — $4,730	5 @ $ 91 / 7 @ $115 } = $1,260

Merchandise Inventory (LIFO)

Aug. 1	910		
Aug. 3	1,590		
		Aug. 14	2,045
Aug. 17	2,300		
Aug. 28	1,190		
		Aug. 30	2,685
Aug. 31	1,260		

Trekking's cost of goods sold reported on the income statement is **$4,730** ($2,045 + $2,685), and its ending inventory reported on the balance sheet is **$1,260**.

FIRST Bought   *LIFO perpetual applied at each sale date.   LAST Bought

Weighted Average

Weighted average or **WA** (also called **average cost**) requires that we use the weighted average cost per unit of inventory at the time of each sale.

$$\frac{\text{Weighted average cost per unit}}{\text{at time of each sale}} = \frac{\text{Cost of goods available for sale (at each sale)}}{\text{Number of units available for sale (at each sale)}}$$

Exhibit 5.7 starts with beginning inventory of 10 bikes at $91 each.

August 3   Purchased 15 bikes costing $106 each for $1,590. Inventory now consists of 10 bikes at $91 each and 15 bikes at $106 each, for a total of $2,500. The average cost per bike for that inventory is $100, computed as $2,500/(10 bikes + 15 bikes).

August 14 Sold 20 bikes—applying WA, the 20 sold are assigned the $100 average cost, for a total of $2,000. This leaves 5 bikes with an average cost of $100 each, or $500, in inventory.

August 17 Purchased 20 bikes costing $2,300, and on August 28, purchased another 10 bikes costing $1,190, for a total of 35 bikes costing $3,990 in inventory at August 28. The average cost per bike for the August 28 inventory is $114, computed as $3,990/35 bikes.

August 30 Sold 23 bikes—applying WA, the 23 sold are assigned the $114 average cost, for a total of $2,622. This leaves 12 bikes costing $1,368 in ending inventory.

Date	Goods Purchased	Cost of Goods Sold	Inventory Balance
Aug. 1	Beginning balance		10 @ $ 91 = $ 910 (10 @ $ 91 per unit)
Aug. 3	15 @ $106 = $1,590		10 @ $ 91 15 @ $106 } = $2,500 (25 @ $100 per unit)[a]
Aug. 14		20 @ $100 = **$2,000**	5 @ $100 = $ 500 (5 @ $100 per unit)[b]
Aug. 17	20 @ $115 = $2,300		5 @ $100 20 @ $115 } = $2,800 (25 @ $112 per unit)[c]
Aug. 28	10 @ $119 = $1,190		25 @ $112 10 @ $119 } = $3,990 (35 @ $114 per unit)[d]
Aug. 30		23 @ $114 = **$2,622**	12 @ $114 = **$1,368** (12 @ $114 per unit)[e]
		$4,622	

[a]$100 per unit = ($2,500 inventory balance ÷ 25 units in inventory).
[b]$100 per unit = ($500 inventory balance ÷ 5 units in inventory).
[c]$112 per unit = ($2,800 inventory balance ÷ 25 units in inventory).
[d]$114 per unit = ($3,990 inventory balance ÷ 35 units in inventory).
[e]$114 per unit = ($1,368 inventory balance ÷ 12 units in inventory).

EXHIBIT 5.7

Weighted Average Computations—Perpetual System

Merchandise Inventory (WA)			
Aug. 1	910		
Aug. 3	1,590		
		Aug. 14	2,000
Aug. 17	2,300		
Aug. 28	1,190		
		Aug. 30	2,622
Aug. 31	1,368		

Trekking's cost of goods sold reported on the income statement is **$4,622** ($2,000 + $2,622), and its ending inventory reported on the balance sheet is **$1,368**.

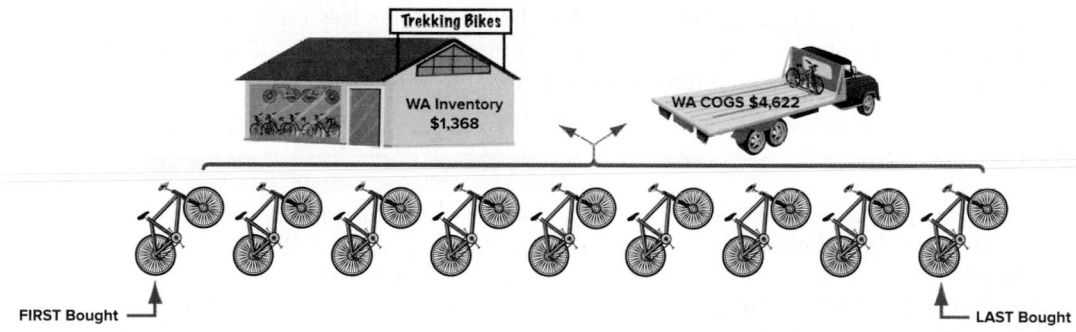

Point: WA perpetual applied at each sale date.

Ethical Risk

Kickbacks and Invoice Fraud Inventory safeguards include restricted access, use of authorized requisitions, and security measures. Proper accounting includes matching inventory received with purchase order terms and quality requirements, preventing misstatements, and controlling access to records. A study reports that 35% of employees in purchasing and procurement observed improper kickbacks or gifts from suppliers. ■

Financial Statement Effects of Costing Methods

When purchase prices do not change, each inventory costing method assigns the same cost amounts to inventory and to cost of goods sold. When purchase prices are different, the methods assign different cost amounts. We show these differences in Exhibit 5.8 using Trekking's data.

A1

Analyze the effects of inventory methods for both financial and tax reporting.

Rising Costs When purchase costs *regularly rise,* as in Trekking's case, the following occurs.

- FIFO reports the lowest cost of goods sold—yielding the highest gross profit and net income.
- LIFO reports the highest cost of goods sold—yielding the lowest gross profit and net income.
- Weighted average yields results between FIFO and LIFO.

EXHIBIT 5.8

Financial Statement
Effects of Inventory
Costing Methods

Trekking Company For Month Ended August 31	Specific Identification	FIFO	LIFO	Weighted Average
Income Statement				
Sales...............................	$ 6,050	$ 6,050	$ 6,050	$ 6,050
Cost of goods sold.................	4,582	4,570	4,730	4,622
Gross profit	1,468	1,480	1,320	1,428
Expenses	450	450	450	450
Income before taxes	1,018	1,030	870	978
Income tax expense (30%)	305	309	261	293
Net income	$ 713	$ 721	$ 609	$ 685
Balance Sheet				
Inventory...........................	$1,408	$1,420	$1,260	$1,368

Falling Costs   When costs *regularly decline,* the reverse occurs for FIFO and LIFO.

- FIFO gives the highest cost of goods sold—yielding the lowest gross profit and income.
- LIFO gives the lowest cost of goods sold—yielding the highest gross profit and income.

Method Advantages   Each method offers advantages.

- FIFO—inventory on the balance sheet approximates its current cost; it also follows the actual flow of goods for most businesses.

Point: LIFO inventory is often less than the inventory's replacement cost because LIFO inventory is valued using the oldest inventory purchase costs.

- LIFO—cost of goods sold on the income statement approximates its current cost; it also better matches current costs with revenues.
- Weighted average—smooths out erratic changes in costs.
- Specific identification—matches the costs of items with the revenues they generate.

Tax Effects of Costing Methods

Inventory costs affect net income and have potential tax effects. Exhibit 5.8 shows that Trekking gains a temporary tax advantage by using LIFO because it has less income to be taxed. Many companies use LIFO for this reason. The IRS requires that when LIFO is used for tax reporting, it also must be used for financial reporting—called *LIFO conformity rule.*

■ **Decision Ethics**

Inventory Manager   Your compensation as inventory manager includes a bonus plan based on gross profit. Your superior asks your opinion on changing the inventory costing method from FIFO to LIFO. As costs are expected to continue to rise, your superior predicts that LIFO would match higher current costs against sales, thereby lowering taxable income (and gross profit). What do you recommend? ■   *Answer:* It seems your company can save (or at least postpone) taxes by switching to LIFO, but the switch is likely to reduce bonus money that you believe you have earned and deserve. Your best decision is to tell your superior about the tax savings with LIFO. You should discuss your bonus plan and how this is likely to hurt you unfairly.

 **5-2**

Perpetual SI, FIFO, LIFO, and WA

P1

A company reported the following December purchase and sales data for its only product.

Date	Activities	Units Acquired at Cost	Units Sold at Retail
Dec. 1	Beginning inventory	5 units @ $3.00 = $ 15.00	
Dec. 8	Purchase	10 units @ $4.50 = 45.00	
Dec. 9	Sales...........................		8 units @ $7.00
Dec. 19	Purchase	13 units @ $5.00 = 65.00	
Dec. 24	Sales...........................		18 units @ $8.00
Dec. 30	Purchase	8 units @ $5.30 = 42.40	
Totals	....	36 units $167.40	26 units

The company uses a *perpetual inventory system.* Determine the cost assigned to ending inventory and to cost of goods sold using (a) specific identification, (b) FIFO, (c) LIFO, and (d) weighted average. (Round per unit costs and inventory amounts to cents.)

For specific identification, ending inventory consists of 10 units, where 8 are from the December 30 purchase and 2 are from the December 8 purchase. Specific unit sales follow.

Dec. 9 Sold 2 units costing $3.00 each and 6 units costing $4.50 each. Total cost = $33.00.

Dec. 24 Sold 3 units costing $3.00 each, 2 units costing $4.50 each, and 13 units costing $5.00 each. Total cost = $83.00.

Solutions

a. Specific identification: Ending inventory—eight units from December 30 purchase and two units from December 8 purchase.

Specific Identification	Ending Inventory	Cost of Goods Sold
(8 × $5.30) + (2 × $4.50)	$51.40	
(5 × $3.00) + (8 × $4.50) + (13 × $5.00) + (0 × $5.30)		
or $167.40 [Total Goods Available] − $51.40 [Ending Inventory].		$116.00

Merchandise Inventory (SI)

Beg. inventory	15.00		
Dec. 8	45.00		
		Dec. 9	33.00
Dec. 19	65.00		
		Dec. 24	83.00
Dec. 30	42.40		
End. inventory	51.40		

b. FIFO—Perpetual.

Date	Goods Purchased	Cost of Goods Sold	Inventory Balance
12/1			5 @ $3.00 = $15.00
12/8	10 @ $4.50		5 @ $3.00 ⎱ = $60.00 10 @ $4.50 ⎰
12/9		5 @ $3.00 ⎱ = $ 28.50 3 @ $4.50 ⎰	7 @ $4.50 = $31.50
12/19	13 @ $5.00		7 @ $4.50 ⎱ = $96.50 13 @ $5.00 ⎰
12/24		7 @ $4.50 ⎱ = $ 86.50 11 @ $5.00 ⎰	2 @ $5.00 = $10.00
12/30	8 @ $5.30		2 @ $5.00 ⎱ = $52.40 8 @ $5.30 ⎰
		$115.00	

Merchandise Inventory (FIFO)

Beg. inventory	15.00		
Dec. 8	45.00		
		Dec. 9	28.50
Dec. 19	65.00		
		Dec. 24	86.50
Dec. 30	42.40		
End. inventory	52.40		

OR "short-cut" FIFO—Perpetual.

FIFO	Ending Inventory	Cost of Goods Sold
(8 × $5.30) + (2 × $5.00)	$52.40	
(5 × $3.00) + (10 × $4.50) + (11 × $5.00)		
or $167.40 [Total Goods Available] − $52.40 [Ending Inventory].		$115.00

c. LIFO—Perpetual.

Date	Goods Purchased	Cost of Goods Sold	Inventory Balance
12/1			5 @ $3.00 = $15.00
12/8	10 @ $4.50		5 @ $3.00 ⎱ = $60.00 10 @ $4.50 ⎰
12/9		8 @ $4.50 = $ 36.00	5 @ $3.00 ⎱ = $24.00 2 @ $4.50 ⎰
12/19	13 @ $5.00		5 @ $3.00 2 @ $4.50 ⎬ = $89.00 13 @ $5.00
12/24		13 @ $5.00 2 @ $4.50 ⎬ = $ 83.00 3 @ $3.00	2 @ $3.00 = $ 6.00
12/30	8 @ $5.30		2 @ $3.00 ⎱ = $48.40 8 @ $5.30 ⎰
		$119.00	

Merchandise Inventory (LIFO)

Beg. inventory	15.00		
Dec. 8	45.00		
		Dec. 9	36.00
Dec. 19	65.00		
		Dec. 24	83.00
Dec. 30	42.40		
End. inventory	48.40		

d. Weighted Average—Perpetual.

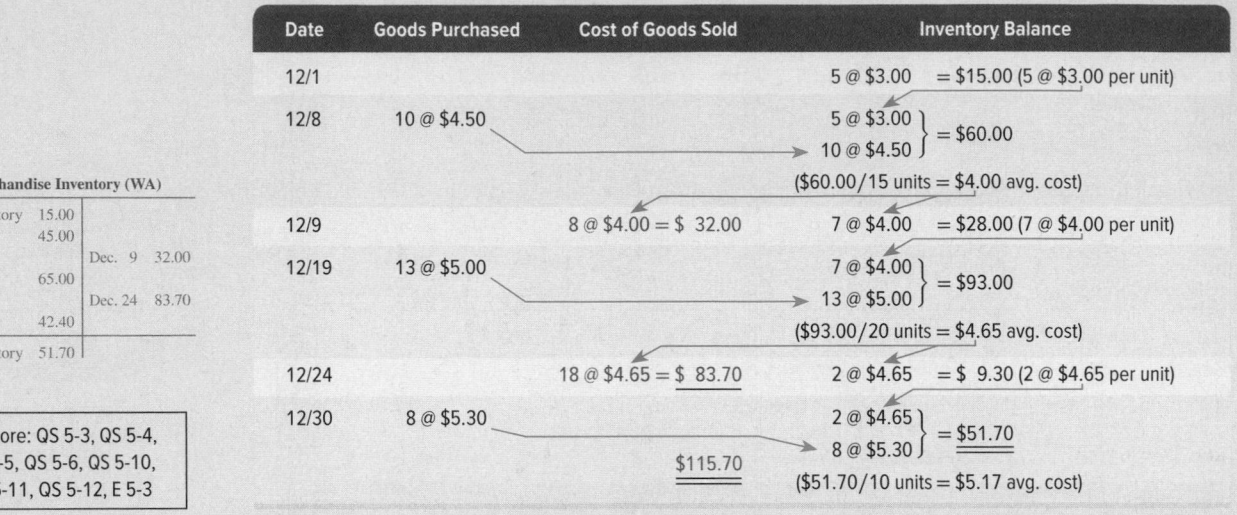

Date	Goods Purchased	Cost of Goods Sold	Inventory Balance
12/1			5 @ $3.00 = $15.00 (5 @ $3.00 per unit)
12/8	10 @ $4.50		5 @ $3.00 10 @ $4.50 } = $60.00 ($60.00/15 units = $4.00 avg. cost)
12/9		8 @ $4.00 = $ 32.00	7 @ $4.00 = $28.00 (7 @ $4.00 per unit)
12/19	13 @ $5.00		7 @ $4.00 13 @ $5.00 } = $93.00 ($93.00/20 units = $4.65 avg. cost)
12/24		18 @ $4.65 = $ 83.70	2 @ $4.65 = $ 9.30 (2 @ $4.65 per unit)
12/30	8 @ $5.30		2 @ $4.65 8 @ $5.30 } = $51.70
		$115.70	($51.70/10 units = $5.17 avg. cost)

Merchandise Inventory (WA)

Beg. inventory	15.00		
Dec. 8	45.00		
		Dec. 9	32.00
Dec. 19	65.00		
		Dec. 24	83.70
Dec. 30	42.40		
End. inventory	51.70		

> Do More: QS 5-3, QS 5-4, QS 5-5, QS 5-6, QS 5-10, QS 5-11, QS 5-12, E 5-3

VALUING INVENTORY AT LCM AND THE EFFECTS OF INVENTORY ERRORS

This section covers how market value and inventory errors impact financial statements.

Lower of Cost or Market

P2

Compute the lower of cost or market amount of inventory.

After companies apply one of four costing methods (FIFO, LIFO, weighted average, or specific identification), inventory is reviewed to ensure it is reported at the **lower of cost or market (LCM).**

Computing the Lower of Cost or Market   *Market* in the term *LCM* is *replacement cost* for LIFO, but *net realizable value* for the other three methods—advanced courses cover specifics. A decline in market value means a loss of value in inventory. When market value is lower than cost of inventory, a loss is recorded. When market value is higher than cost of inventory, no adjustment is made.

Point: LCM applied to each individual item always yields the lowest inventory.

    LCM is applied in one of three ways: (1) to each individual item separately, (2) to major categories of items, or (3) to the whole of inventory. With the increasing use of technology and inventory tracking, companies increasingly apply LCM to each individual item separately. Accordingly, we show that method only; advanced courses cover other methods. To demonstrate LCM, we apply it to the ending inventory of a motorsports retailer in Exhibit 5.9.

EXHIBIT 5.9

Lower of Cost or Market Computations

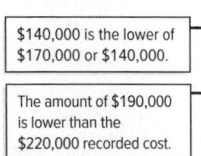

$140,000 is the lower of $170,000 or $140,000.

The amount of $190,000 is lower than the $220,000 recorded cost.

Inventory Items	Units	Per Unit Cost	Per Unit Market	Total Cost	Total Market	LCM Applied to Items
Roadster............	20	$8,500	$7,000	$170,000	$140,000	$ 140,000
Sprint	10	5,000	6,000	50,000	60,000	50,000
Totals				$220,000		**$190,000**

For Roadster, $140,000 is the lower of the $170,000 cost and the $140,000 market. For Sprint, $50,000 is the lower of the $50,000 cost and the $60,000 market. This yields a $190,000 reported inventory, computed from $140,000 for Roadster plus $50,000 for Sprint.

Recording the Lower of Cost or Market   Inventory is adjusted downward when total "LCM applied to items" is less than total cost of inventory. To demonstrate, if LCM is applied in Exhibit 5.9, the Merchandise Inventory account must be adjusted from the $220,000 recorded cost down to the $190,000 LCM amount as follows.

Cost of Goods Sold...............................	30,000	
Merchandise Inventory		30,000
Adjust inventory cost to market.		

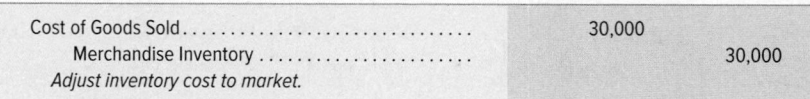

A company has the following products in its ending inventory, along with cost and market values. (a) Compute the lower of cost or market for its inventory when applied *separately to each product*. (b) If the market amount is less than the recorded cost of the inventory, then record the December 31 LCM adjustment to the Merchandise Inventory account.

NEED-TO-KNOW 5-3

LCM Method

P2

	Units	Cost per Unit	Market per Unit
Road bikes	5	$1,000	$800
Mountain bikes...........	4	500	600
Town bikes	10	400	450

Solution

a.

Inventory Items	Units	Cost per Unit	Market per Unit	Total Cost	Total Market	LCM Items
Road bikes	5	$1,000	$800	$ 5,000	$4,000	$ 4,000
Mountain bikes..............	4	500	600	2,000	2,400	2,000
Town bikes	10	400	450	4,000	4,500	4,000
Totals......................				$11,000		$ 10,000
LCM applied to each product....						$10,000

b.

Dec. 31	Cost of Goods Sold	1,000	
	Merchandise Inventory.......................................		1,000
	Adjust inventory cost to market ($11,000 − $10,000).		

Do More: QS 5-19, E 5-10

Financial Statement Effects of Inventory Errors

An inventory error causes misstatements in cost of goods sold, gross profit, net income, current assets, and equity. It also causes misstatements in the next period's statements because ending inventory of one period is the beginning inventory of the next. As we consider financial statement effects, we recall the following *inventory relation*.

A2

Analyze the effects of inventory errors on current and future financial statements.

Beginning inventory	**+**	Net purchases	**−**	Ending inventory	**=**	Cost of goods sold

Income Statement Effects Exhibit 5.10 shows the effects of inventory errors in the current and next period's income statements.

- **Row 1, Year 1.** Understating ending inventory overstates cost of goods sold. This is because we subtract a smaller ending inventory in computing cost of goods sold. A higher cost of goods sold yields a lower income.
- **Row 1, Year 2.** Understated ending inventory for Year 1 becomes an understated beginning inventory for Year 2. If beginning inventory is understated, cost of goods sold is understated (because we are starting with a smaller amount). A lower cost of goods sold yields a higher income.
- **Row 2, Year 1.** Overstating ending inventory understates cost of goods sold. A lower cost of goods sold yields a higher income.
- **Row 2, Year 2.** Overstated ending inventory for Year 1 becomes an overstated beginning inventory for Year 2. If beginning inventory is overstated, cost of goods sold is overstated. A higher cost of goods sold yields a lower income.

EXHIBIT 5.10

Effects of Inventory Errors
on the Income Statement

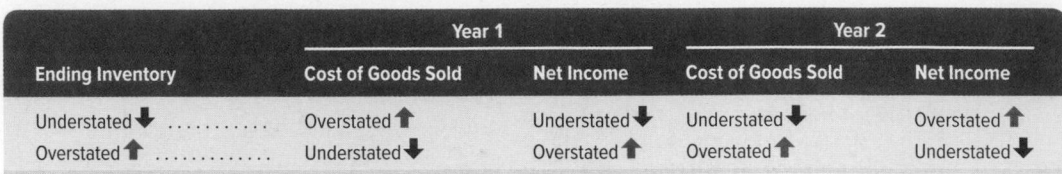

	Year 1			Year 2	
Ending Inventory	Cost of Goods Sold	Net Income		Cost of Goods Sold	Net Income
Understated ⬇	Overstated ⬆	Understated ⬇		Understated ⬇	Overstated ⬆
Overstated ⬆	Understated ⬇	Overstated ⬆		Overstated ⬆	Understated ⬇

Inventory Error Example
Consider an inventory error for a company with $100,000 in sales for each of Year 1, Year 2, and Year 3. If this company has a steady $20,000 inventory level and makes $60,000 in purchases in each year, its cost of goods sold is $60,000 and its gross profit is $40,000.

Year 1 Understated Inventory: Year 1 Impact   Assume the company makes an error in computing its Year 1 ending inventory and reports $16,000 instead of the correct amount of $20,000. The effects of this error are in Exhibit 5.11. The $4,000 understatement of Year 1 ending inventory causes a $4,000 overstatement in Year 1 cost of goods sold and a $4,000 understatement in both gross profit and net income for Year 1.

EXHIBIT 5.11

Effects of Inventory Errors
on Three Periods' Income
Statements

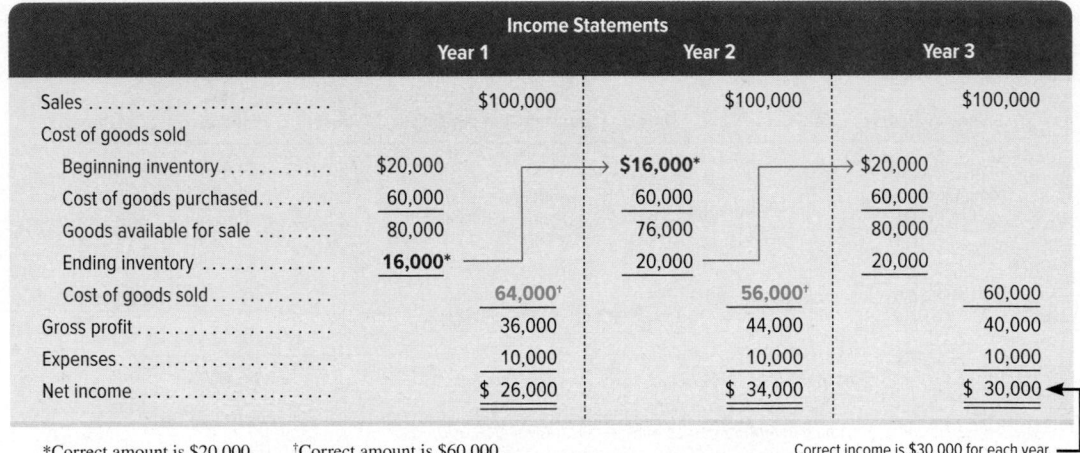

	Income Statements		
	Year 1	Year 2	Year 3
Sales	$100,000	$100,000	$100,000
Cost of goods sold			
Beginning inventory............	$20,000	**$16,000***	$20,000
Cost of goods purchased........	60,000	60,000	60,000
Goods available for sale	80,000	76,000	80,000
Ending inventory	**16,000***	20,000	20,000
Cost of goods sold	64,000†	56,000†	60,000
Gross profit	36,000	44,000	40,000
Expenses......................	10,000	10,000	10,000
Net income	$ 26,000	$ 34,000	$ 30,000

*Correct amount is $20,000.   †Correct amount is $60,000.   Correct income is $30,000 for each year.

Example: If Year 1 ending inventory in Exhibit 5.11 is overstated by $3,000, cost of goods sold is understated by $3,000 in Year 1 and overstated by $3,000 in Year 2. Net income is overstated in Year 1 and understated in Year 2. Assets and equity are overstated in Year 1.

Year 1 Understated Inventory: Year 2 Impact   The Year 1 understated ending inventory becomes the Year 2 understated beginning inventory. This error causes an understatement in Year 2 cost of goods sold and a $4,000 overstatement in both gross profit and net income for Year 2.

Year 1 Understated Inventory: Year 3 Impact   The Year 1 ending inventory error affects only that period and the next. It does not affect Year 3 results or any period thereafter.

Balance Sheet Effects
Understating ending inventory understates both current and total assets. An understatement in ending inventory also yields an understatement in equity because of the understatement in net income. Exhibit 5.12 shows the effects of inventory errors on the current period's balance sheet amounts.

EXHIBIT 5.12

Effects of Inventory
Errors on Current Period's
Balance Sheet

Ending Inventory	Assets	Equity
Understated ⬇	Understated ⬇	Understated ⬇
Overstated ⬆	Overstated ⬆	Overstated ⬆

 **5-4**

Effects of Inventory
Errors

A2

A company had $10,000 of sales, and it purchased merchandise costing $7,000 in each of Year 1, Year 2, and Year 3. It also maintained a $2,000 physical inventory from the beginning to the end of that three-year period. In accounting for inventory, it made an error at the end of Year 1 that caused its Year 1 ending inventory to appear on its statements as $1,600 rather than the correct $2,000. (a) Determine the correct amount of the company's gross profit in each of Year 1, Year 2, and Year 3. (b) Prepare comparative income statements as in Exhibit 5.11 to show the effect of this error on the company's cost of goods sold and gross profit for each of Year 1, Year 2, and Year 3.

Solution

a. Correct gross profit = $10,000 − $7,000 = $3,000 (for each year).

b. Cost of goods sold and gross profit figures follow.

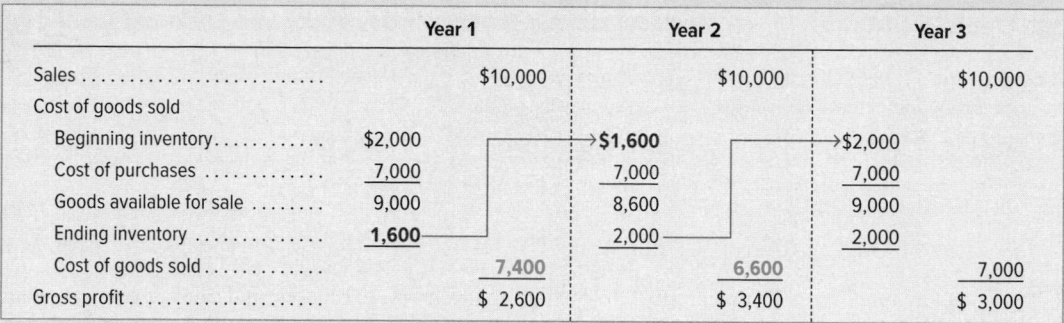

	Year 1		Year 2		Year 3
Sales		$10,000		$10,000		$10,000
Cost of goods sold						
Beginning inventory.	$2,000		→$1,600		→$2,000	
Cost of purchases	7,000		7,000		7,000	
Goods available for sale	9,000		8,600		9,000	
Ending inventory	1,600		2,000		2,000	
Cost of goods sold		7,400		6,600		7,000
Gross profit		$ 2,600		$ 3,400		$ 3,000

Combined income for the 3 years is $9,000 ($2,600 + $3,400 + $3,000), which is correct, meaning the inventory error is "self-correcting" (even though individual years' inventory amounts are in error).

Do More: QS 5-20, E 5-12

 **Inventory Turnover and Days' Sales in Inventory** ☐☐☐ **Decision Analysis**

Inventory Turnover

Inventory turnover, also called *merchandise inventory turnover,* is defined in Exhibit 5.13. Inventory turnover tells how many *times* a company turns over (sells) its inventory in a period. It is used to assess whether management is doing a good job controlling the amount of inventory. A low ratio means the company may have more inventory than it needs. A very high ratio means inventory might be too low. This can cause lost sales if customers must back-order merchandise. Inventory turnover has no simple rule except to say *a high ratio is preferable if inventory is adequate to meet demand.*

$$\text{Inventory turnover} = \frac{\text{Cost of goods sold}}{\text{Average inventory}}$$

Days' Sales in Inventory

Days' sales in inventory is a ratio that shows how much inventory is available in terms of the number of days' sales. It can be interpreted as the number of days one can sell from existing inventory if no new items are purchased. This ratio reveals the buffer against out-of-stock inventory and is useful in evaluating how quickly inventory is being sold. It is defined in Exhibit 5.14. Days' sales in inventory uses *ending* inventory, whereas inventory turnover uses *average* inventory.

$$\text{Days' sales in inventory} = \frac{\text{Ending inventory}}{\text{Cost of goods sold}} \times 365$$

Analysis of Inventory Management

Merchandisers must plan and control inventory purchases and sales. **Costco**'s inventory at the end of the current year was $9,834 million. This inventory was 57% of its current assets and 27% of its total assets. We apply the analysis tools in this section to Costco and **Walmart**, as shown in Exhibit 5.15.

Company	Figure ($ millions)	Current Year	1 Year Ago	2 Years Ago
Costco	Cost of goods sold	$111,882	$102,901	$101,065
	Ending inventory.	$ 9,834	$ 8,969	$ 8,908
	Inventory turnover	**11.9** times	**11.5** times	**11.6** times
	Days' sales in inventory	**32.1** days	**31.8** days	**32.2** days
Walmart	Inventory turnover	8.3 times	8.1 times	8.1 times
	Days' sales in inventory	43.5 days	45.0 days	45.1 days

Costco's current year inventory turnover of 11.9 times means that it turns over its inventory 11.9 times per year. Costco's inventory turnover exceeded Walmart's turnover in each of the last three years. This is a positive for Costco, as we prefer inventory turnover to be high provided inventory is not out of stock and the company is not losing customers. Days' sales in inventory of 32.1 days means that Costco is carrying 32.1 days of sales in inventory. This inventory buffer seems sufficient. As long as Costco is not at risk of running out of stock, it prefers its assets not be tied up in inventory.

A3
Assess inventory management using both inventory turnover and days' sales in inventory.

EXHIBIT 5.13
Inventory Turnover

Point: Low inventory turnover can reveal obsolescence.

Point: Inventory turnover is higher and days' sales in inventory is lower for industries such as foods.

EXHIBIT 5.14
Days' Sales in Inventory

EXHIBIT 5.15
Inventory Turnover and Days' Sales in Inventory for Costco and Walmart

Point: Take care when comparing turnover ratios across companies that use different costing methods (such as FIFO and LIFO).

■ Decision Maker

Entrepreneur   Your retail store has an inventory turnover of 5.0 and a days' sales in inventory of 73 days. The industry norm for inventory turnover is 4.4 and for days' sales in inventory is 74 days. What is your assessment of inventory management? ■   *Answer:* Your inventory turnover is higher than the norm, whereas days' sales in inventory approximates the norm. Because your turnover is already 14% better than average, you should probably direct attention to days' sales in inventory. You should see if you can reduce the level of inventory while maintaining service to customers. Given your higher turnover, you should be able to hold less inventory.

NEED-TO-KNOW 5-5

COMPREHENSIVE 1

Perpetual Method:
Computing Inventory
Using LIFO, FIFO, WA,
and SI; Financial
Statement Impacts; and
Inventory Errors

Craig Company buys and sells one product. Its beginning inventory, purchases, and sales during calendar-year 2019 follow.

Date	Activity	Units Acquired at Cost	Units Sold at Retail	Unit Inventory
Jan. 1	Beg. inventory...........	400 units @ $14 = $ 5,600		400 units
Jan. 15	Sale..................		200 units @ $30	200 units
Mar. 10	Purchase..............	200 units @ $15 = $ 3,000		400 units
Apr. 1	Sale..................		200 units @ $30	200 units
May 9	Purchase..............	300 units @ $16 = $ 4,800		500 units
Sep. 22	Purchase..............	250 units @ $20 = $ 5,000		750 units
Nov. 1	Sale..................		300 units @ $35	450 units
Nov. 28	Purchase..............	100 units @ $21 = $ 2,100		550 units
	Totals.................	1,250 units $20,500	700 units	

Additional tracking data for specific identification: (1) January 15 sale—200 units @ $14, **(2)** April 1 sale—200 units @ $15, and **(3)** November 1 sale—200 units @ $14 and 100 units @ $20.

Required

1. Compute the cost of goods available for sale.
2. Apply the four methods of inventory costing (FIFO, LIFO, weighted average, and specific identification) to compute ending inventory and cost of goods sold under each method using the *perpetual system*.
3. Compute gross profit earned by the company for each of the four costing methods in part 2. Also, report the inventory amount reported on the balance sheet for each of the four methods.
4. In preparing financial statements for year 2019, the financial officer was instructed to use FIFO but failed to do so and instead computed cost of goods sold according to LIFO, which led to a $1,400 overstatement in cost of goods sold from using LIFO. Determine the impact on year 2019's income from the error. Also determine the effect of this error on year 2020's income. Assume no income taxes.
5. Management wants a report that shows how changing from FIFO to another method would change net income. Prepare a table showing (1) the cost of goods sold amount under each of the four methods, (2) the amount by which each cost of goods sold total is different from the FIFO cost of goods sold, and (3) the effect on net income if another method is used instead of FIFO.

PLANNING THE SOLUTION

● Compute cost of goods available for sale by multiplying the units of beginning inventory and each purchase by their unit costs to determine the total cost of goods available for sale.
● Prepare a perpetual FIFO table starting with beginning inventory and showing how inventory changes after each purchase and after each sale (see Exhibit 5.5).
● Prepare a perpetual LIFO table starting with beginning inventory and showing how inventory changes after each purchase and after each sale (see Exhibit 5.6).
● Make a table of purchases and sales recalculating the average cost of inventory prior to each sale to arrive at the weighted average cost of ending inventory. Total the average costs associated with each sale to determine cost of goods sold (see Exhibit 5.7).
● Prepare a table showing the computation of cost of goods sold and ending inventory using the specific identification method (see Exhibit 5.4).
● Compare the year-end 2019 inventory amounts under FIFO and LIFO to determine the misstatement of year 2019 income that results from using LIFO. The errors for years 2019 and 2020 are equal in amount but opposite in effect.
● Create a table showing cost of goods sold under each method and how net income would differ from FIFO net income if an alternate method were adopted.

SOLUTION

1. Cost of goods available for sale (this amount is the same for all methods).

Date		Units	Unit Cost	Cost
Jan. 1	Beg. inventory..............	400	$14	$ 5,600
Mar. 10	Purchase..................	200	15	3,000
May 9	Purchase..................	300	16	4,800
Sep. 22	Purchase..................	250	20	5,000
Nov. 28	Purchase..................	100	21	2,100
	Total goods available for sale	1,250		$20,500

2a. FIFO **perpetual** method.

Date	Goods Purchased	Cost of Goods Sold	Inventory Balance	
Jan. 1	Beginning balance		400 @ $14	= $ 5,600
Jan. 15		200 @ $14 = $2,800	200 @ $14	= $ 2,800
Mar. 10	200 @ $15 = $3,000		200 @ $14 200 @ $15	= $ 5,800
Apr. 1		200 @ $14 = $2,800	200 @ $15	= $ 3,000
May 9	300 @ $16 = $4,800		200 @ $15 300 @ $16	= $ 7,800
Sep. 22	250 @ $20 = $5,000		200 @ $15 300 @ $16 250 @ $20	= $ 12,800
Nov. 1		200 @ $15 = $3,000 100 @ $16 = $1,600	200 @ $16 250 @ $20	= $ 8,200
Nov. 28	100 @ $21 = $2,100		200 @ $16 250 @ $20 100 @ $21	= **$10,300**
Total cost of goods sold		**$10,200**		

Note: **In a classroom situation,** once we compute cost of goods available for sale, we can compute the amount for either cost of goods sold or ending inventory—it is a matter of preference. **In practice,** the costs of items sold are identified as sales are made and immediately transferred from the Inventory account to the Cost of Goods Sold account. The previous solution showing the line-by-line approach illustrates actual application in practice. The following alternate solutions illustrate that, once the concepts are understood, other solution approaches are available. Although this is only shown for FIFO, it could be shown for all methods.

Alternate Methods to Compute FIFO Perpetual Numbers

[FIFO Alternate No. 1: Computing ending inventory first]

Cost of goods available for sale (from part 1).....			$ 20,500
Ending inventory*			
Nov. 28	Purchase (100 @ $21)...........	$2,100	
Sep. 22	Purchase (250 @ $20)..........	5,000	
May 9	Purchase (200 @ $16)..........	3,200	
Ending inventory...........................			10,300
Cost of goods sold			**$10,200**

[FIFO Alternate No. 2: Computing cost of goods sold first]

Cost of goods available for sale (from part 1).......			$ 20,500
Cost of goods sold			
Jan. 15	Sold (200 @ $14)	$2,800	
Apr. 1	Sold (200 @ $14)	2,800	
Nov. 1	Sold (200 @ $15 and 100 @ $16)	4,600	10,200
Ending inventory.............................			**$10,300**

*FIFO assumes that the earlier costs are the first to flow out; thus, we determine
ending inventory by assigning the most recent costs to the remaining items.

2b. LIFO **perpetual** method.

Date	Goods Purchased	Cost of Goods Sold	Inventory Balance	
Jan. 1	Beginning balance		400 @ $14	= $ 5,600
Jan. 15		200 @ $14 = $2,800	200 @ $14	= $ 2,800
Mar. 10	200 @ $15 = $3,000		200 @ $14 200 @ $15	= $ 5,800
Apr. 1		200 @ $15 = $3,000	200 @ $14	= $ 2,800
May 9	300 @ $16 = $4,800		200 @ $14 300 @ $16	= $ 7,600
Sep. 22	250 @ $20 = $5,000		200 @ $14 300 @ $16 250 @ $20	= $12,600
Nov. 1		250 @ $20 = $5,000 50 @ $16 = $ 800	200 @ $14 250 @ $16	= $ 6,800
Nov. 28	100 @ $21 = $2,100		200 @ $14 250 @ $16 100 @ $21	= **$ 8,900**
Total cost of goods sold		**$11,600**		

2c. Weighted average **perpetual** method.

Date	Goods Purchased	Cost of Goods Sold	Inventory Balance	
Jan. 1	Beginning balance		400 @ $14.00 ($5,600/400 units	= $ 5,600 = $14.00 avg. cost)
Jan. 15		200 @ $14.00 = $ 2,800	200 @ $14.00	= $ 2,800
Mar. 10	200 @ $15.00 = $3,000		200 @ $14.00 200 @ $15.00 ($5,800/400 units	= $ 5,800 = $14.50 avg. cost)
Apr. 1		200 @ $14.50 = $ 2,900	200 @ $14.50	= $ 2,900
May 9	300 @ $16.00 = $4,800		200 @ $14.50 300 @ $16.00 ($7,700/500 units	= $ 7,700 = $15.40 avg. cost)
Sep. 22	250 @ $20.00 = $5,000		500 @ $15.40 250 @ $20.00 ($12,700/750 units	= $ 12,700 = $16.93[†] avg. cost)
Nov. 1		300 @ $16.93 = $ 5,079	450 @ $16.93	= $ 7,618.50
Nov. 28	100 @ $21.00 = $2,100		450 @ $16.93 100 @ $21.00 ($9,718.50/550 units	= **$9,718.50** = $17.67 avg. cost)
Total cost of goods sold*		**$10,779**		

*Cost of goods sold ($10,779) plus ending inventory ($9,718.50) is $2.50 less than the cost of goods available for sale ($20,500) due to rounding.

[†]Rounded to 2 decimal places.

2d. Specific identification method.

Cost of goods available for sale (from part 1)...............			$ 20,500
Ending inventory*			
May 9 Purchase (300 @ $16)......................		$4,800	
Sep. 22 Purchase (150 @ $20).....................		3,000	
Nov. 28 Purchase (100 @ $21).....................		2,100	
Ending inventory.......................................			9,900
Cost of goods sold			$10,600

*The additional tracking data provided are used to identify the items in ending inventory.

3.

	FIFO	LIFO	Weighted Average	Specific Identification
Income Statement				
Sales*	$ 22,500	$22,500	$ 22,500	$22,500
Cost of goods sold	10,200	11,600	10,779	10,600
Gross profit.....................	$ 12,300	$10,900	$ 11,721	$11,900
Balance Sheet				
Inventory	$10,300	$ 8,900	$9,718.50	$ 9,900

*Sales = (200 units × $30) + (200 units × $30) + (300 units × $35) = $22,500

4. Mistakenly using LIFO when FIFO should have been used overstates cost of goods sold in year 2019 by $1,400, which is the difference between the FIFO and LIFO amounts of ending inventory. It understates income in 2019 by $1,400. In year 2020, income is overstated by $1,400 because of the understatement in beginning inventory.

5. Analysis of the effects of alternative inventory methods.

	Cost of Goods Sold	Difference from FIFO Cost of Goods Sold	Effect on Net Income If Adopted Instead of FIFO
FIFO.........................	$10,200	—	—
LIFO.........................	11,600	+$1,400	$1,400 lower
Weighted average	10,779	+ 579	579 lower
Specific identification..........	10,600	+ 400	400 lower

Craig Company buys and sells one product. Its beginning inventory, purchases, and sales during calendar-year 2019 follow.

NEED-TO-KNOW 5-6

COMPREHENSIVE 2

Periodic Method: Computing Inventory Using LIFO, FIFO, WA, and SI; Financial Statement Impacts; and Inventory Errors

Date	Activity	Units Acquired at Cost	Units Sold at Retail	Unit Inventory
Jan. 1	Beg. inventory...........	400 units @ $14 = $ 5,600		400 units
Jan. 15	Sale		200 units @ $30	200 units
Mar. 10	Purchase...............	200 units @ $15 = $ 3,000		400 units
Apr. 1	Sale		200 units @ $30	200 units
May 9	Purchase...............	300 units @ $16 = $ 4,800		500 units
Sep. 22	Purchase...............	250 units @ $20 = $ 5,000		750 units
Nov. 1	Sale		300 units @ $35	450 units
Nov. 28	Purchase...............	100 units @ $21 = $ 2,100		550 units
	Totals..................	1,250 units $20,500	700 units	

Additional tracking data for specific identification: (**1**) January 15 sale—200 units @ $14, (**2**) April 1 sale—200 units @ $15, and (**3**) November 1 sale—200 units @ $14 and 100 units @ $20.

208   Chapter 5   Inventories and Cost of Sales

Required

1. Compute the cost of goods available for sale.
2. Apply the four methods of inventory costing (FIFO, LIFO, weighted average, and specific identification) to compute ending inventory and cost of goods sold under each method using the *periodic system*.
3. Compute gross profit earned by the company for each of the four costing methods in part 2. Also, report the inventory amount reported on the balance sheet for each of the four methods.
4. In preparing financial statements for year 2019, the financial officer was instructed to use FIFO but failed to do so and instead computed cost of goods sold according to LIFO. Determine the impact of the error on year 2019's income. Also determine the effect of this error on year 2020's income. Assume no income taxes.

PLANNING THE SOLUTION

- Compute cost of goods available for sale by multiplying the units of beginning inventory and each purchase by their unit costs to determine the total cost of goods available for sale.
- Prepare a periodic FIFO computation starting with cost of units available and subtracting FIFO ending inventory amounts to obtain FIFO cost of goods sold (see Exhibit 5A.3).
- Prepare a periodic LIFO computation starting with cost of units available and subtracting LIFO ending inventory amounts to obtain LIFO cost of goods sold (see Exhibit 5A.4).
- Compute weighted average ending inventory and cost of goods sold using the three-step process illustrated in Exhibits 5A.5a and 5A.5b.
- Prepare a table showing the computation of cost of goods sold and ending inventory using the specific identification method (see Exhibit 5A.2).
- Compare the year-end 2019 inventory amounts under FIFO and LIFO to determine the misstatement of year 2019 income that results from using LIFO. The errors for years 2019 and 2020 are equal in amount but opposite in effect.

SOLUTION

1. Cost of goods available for sale (this amount is the same for all methods).

Date		Units	Unit Cost	Cost
Jan. 1	Beg. inventory............	400	$14	$ 5,600
Mar. 10	Purchase................	200	15	3,000
May 9	Purchase................	300	16	4,800
Sep. 22	Purchase................	250	20	5,000
Nov. 28	Purchase................	100	21	2,100
	Total goods available for sale	1,250		$20,500

2a. FIFO **periodic** method.

Cost of goods available for sale (from part 1)....		$ 20,500
Ending inventory*		
Nov. 28	Purchase (100 @ $21).......... $2,100	
Sep. 22	Purchase (250 @ $20)......... 5,000	
May 9	Purchase (200 @ $16)......... 3,200	
Ending inventory.........................		10,300
Cost of goods sold		$10,200

*FIFO assumes that the earlier costs are the first to flow out; thus, we determine ending inventory by assigning the most recent costs to the remaining items.

2b. LIFO **periodic** method.

Cost of goods available for sale (from part 1)....		$ 20,500
Ending inventory†		
Jan. 1	Beg. inventory (400 @ $14) ... $5,600	
Mar. 10	Purchase (150 @ $15)........ 2,250	
Ending inventory.........................		7,850
Cost of goods sold		$12,650

†LIFO assumes that the most recent (newest) costs are the first to flow out; thus, we determine ending inventory by assigning the earliest (oldest) costs to the remaining items.

2c. Weighted average **periodic** method.

Step 1:	400 units @ $14 = $ 5,600
	200 units @ $15 = 3,000
	300 units @ $16 = 4,800
	250 units @ $20 = 5,000
	100 units @ $21 = 2,100
	1,250 units **$20,500**

Step 2: $20,500/1,250 units = **$16.40** weighted average cost per unit

Step 3: Total cost of 1,250 units available for sale . . . . $ 20,500
Less **ending inventory** priced on a weighted average
cost basis: 550 units at $16.40 each   9,020
Cost of goods sold (700 units at $16.40 each) **$11,480**

2d. Specific identification method.

Cost of goods available for sale (from part 1). . .	$ 20,500
Ending inventory*	
May 9 Purchase (300 @ $16). $4,800	
Sep. 22 Purchase (150 @ $20). 3,000	
Nov. 28 Purchase (100 @ $21). 2,100	
Ending inventory.	**9,900**
Cost of goods sold	**$10,600**

*The additional tracking data provided are used to identify the items in ending inventory.

3.

	FIFO	LIFO	Weighted Average	Specific Identification
Income Statement				
Sales*	$ 22,500	$22,500	$ 22,500	$22,500
Cost of goods sold	10,200	12,650	11,480	10,600
Gross profit.	$ 12,300	$ 9,850	$ 11,020	$11,900
Balance Sheet				
Inventory	$10,300	$ 7,850	$ 9,020	$ 9,900

*Sales = (200 units × $30) + (200 units × $30) + (300 units × $35) = $22,500

4. Mistakenly using LIFO, when FIFO should have been used, overstates cost of goods sold in year 2019 by $2,450, which is the difference between the FIFO and LIFO amounts of ending inventory. It understates income in 2019 by $2,450. In year 2020, income is overstated by $2,450 because of the understatement in beginning inventory.

Inventory Costing under a Periodic System   5A

This section demonstrates inventory costing methods. We use information from Trekking, a sporting goods store. Among its many products, Trekking sells one type of mountain bike whose sales are directed at resorts that provide inexpensive bikes for guest use. We use Trekking's data from August. Its mountain bike (unit) inventory at the beginning of August and its purchases and sales during August are shown in Exhibit 5A.1. It ends August with 12 bikes remaining in inventory.

P3

Compute inventory in a periodic system using the methods of specific identification, FIFO, LIFO, and weighted average.

EXHIBIT 5A.1

Purchases and Sales of Goods

Date	Activity	Units Acquired at Cost	Units Sold at Retail	Unit Inventory
Aug. 1	Beginning inventory.	10 units @ $ 91 = $ 910		10 units
Aug. 3	Purchases.	15 units @ $106 = $ 1,590		25 units
Aug. 14	Sales.		20 units @ $130	5 units
Aug. 17	Purchases.	20 units @ $115 = $ 2,300		25 units
Aug. 28	Purchases.	10 units @ $119 = $ 1,190		35 units
Aug. 30	Sales.		23 units @ $150	**12 units**
	Totals	**55 units** **$5,990**	**43 units**	

Units available for sale | Goods available for sale | Units sold | Units left

Trekking uses the **periodic inventory system**, which means that its Merchandise Inventory account is updated at the end of each period (monthly for Trekking) to reflect purchases and sales. Regardless of what inventory method is used, cost of goods available for sale must be allocated between cost of goods sold and ending inventory. (Many companies use the periodic system for tracking costs [not so much for sales]. Reasons include the use of standard costs by some companies and dollar-value LIFO by others. Also, the methods of specific identification and FIFO, used by a majority of companies, give the same result under the periodic and the perpetual systems.)

Specific Identification

When each item in inventory can be matched with a specific purchase and invoice, we can use **specific identification** or **SI** to assign costs. We also need sales records that identify exactly which items were sold and when. Trekking's internal documents show the following specific unit sales.

August 14   Sold 8 bikes costing $91 each and 12 bikes costing $106 each. Total cost = $2,000.
August 30   Sold 2 bikes costing $91 each, 3 bikes costing $106 each, 15 bikes costing $115 each, and 3 bikes costing $119 each. Total cost = $2,582.

Exhibit 5A.2 begins with the $5,990 in total units available for sale. For the 20 units sold on August 14, the total cost of sales is $2,000. Next, for the 23 units sold on August 30, the total cost of sales is $2,582. The total cost of sales for the period is $4,582. We then subtract this $4,582 in cost of goods sold from the $5,990 in cost of goods available to get $1,408 in ending inventory.

EXHIBIT 5A.2

Specific Identification Computations

Total cost of 55 units available for sale (from Exhibit 5A.1).		$ 5,990
Cost of goods sold		
Aug. 14 (8 @ $91) + (12 @ $106).	$2,000	
Aug. 30 (2 @ $91) + (3 @ $106) + (15 @ $115) + (3 @ $119).	2,582	**4,582**
Ending inventory		**$1,408**

Trekking's cost of goods sold reported on the income statement is **$4,582**, and ending inventory reported on the balance sheet is **$1,408**. The following graphic shows these cost flows.

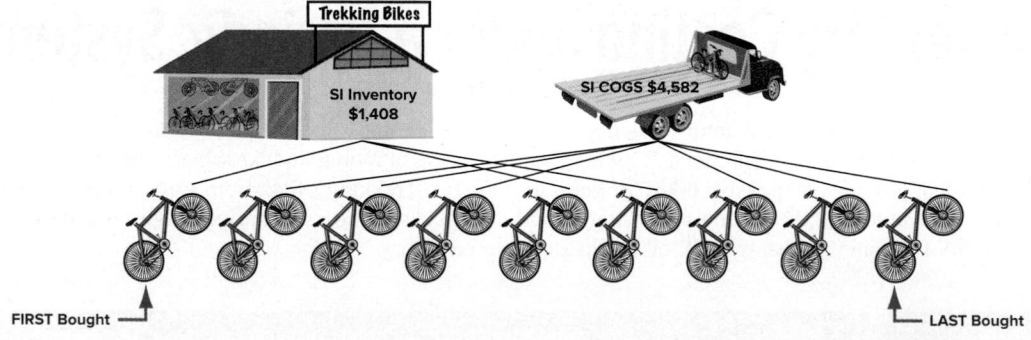

First-In, First-Out

First-in, first-out (FIFO) assumes that inventory items are sold in the order acquired. When sales occur, the costs of the earliest units acquired are charged to cost of goods sold. This leaves the costs from the most recent purchases in ending inventory.

Exhibit 5A.3 starts with $5,990 in total units available for sale. Applying FIFO, the 12 units in ending inventory are reported at the cost of the most recent 12 purchases. Reviewing purchases in reverse order, we assign costs to the 12 bikes in ending inventory as follows: $119 cost to 10 bikes and $115 cost to 2 bikes. This yields $1,420 in ending inventory. We subtract this $1,420 in ending inventory from $5,990 in cost of goods available to get $4,570 in cost of goods sold.

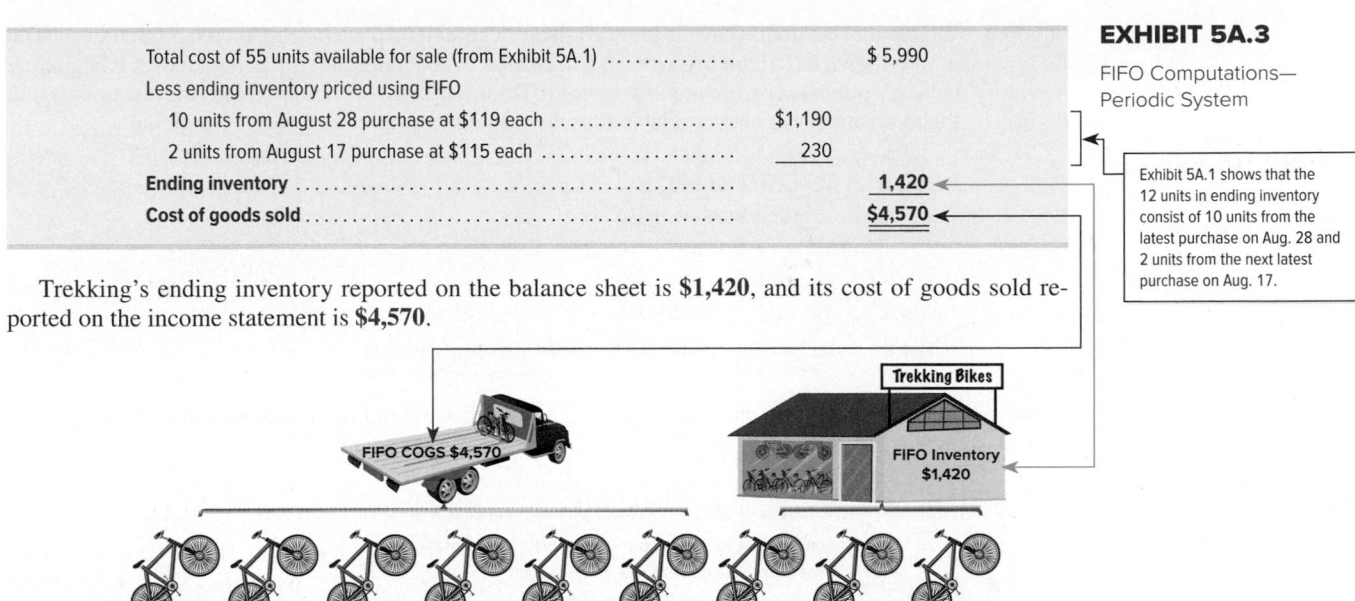

Total cost of 55 units available for sale (from Exhibit 5A.1)		$ 5,990
Less ending inventory priced using FIFO		
10 units from August 28 purchase at $119 each	$1,190	
2 units from August 17 purchase at $115 each	230	
Ending inventory		1,420
Cost of goods sold		$4,570

Exhibit 5A.1 shows that the 12 units in ending inventory consist of 10 units from the latest purchase on Aug. 28 and 2 units from the next latest purchase on Aug. 17.

Trekking's ending inventory reported on the balance sheet is **$1,420**, and its cost of goods sold reported on the income statement is **$4,570**.

Last-In, First-Out

Last-in, first-out (LIFO) assumes that the most recent purchases are sold first. These more recent costs are charged to goods sold, and the costs of the earliest purchases are assigned to inventory.

Point: By assigning costs from the most recent purchases to cost of goods sold, LIFO comes closest to matching current costs of goods sold with revenues.

Exhibit 5A.4 starts with $5,990 in total units available for sale. Applying LIFO, the 12 units in ending inventory are reported at the cost of the earliest 12 purchases. Reviewing the earliest purchases in order, we assign costs to the 12 bikes in ending inventory as follows: $91 cost to 10 bikes and $106 cost to 2 bikes. This yields $1,122 in ending inventory. We subtract this $1,122 in ending inventory from $5,990 in cost of goods available to get $4,868 in cost of goods sold.

Total cost of 55 units available for sale (from Exhibit 5A.1).		$ 5,990
Less ending inventory priced using LIFO		
10 units in beginning inventory at $91 each	$910	
2 units from August 3 purchase at $106 each.	212	
Ending inventory.		1,122
Cost of goods sold		$4,868

Exhibit 5A.1 shows that the 12 units in ending inventory consist of 10 units from the earliest purchase (beg. inv.) and 2 units from the next earliest purchase on Aug. 3.

Trekking's ending inventory reported on the balance sheet is **$1,122**, and its cost of goods sold reported on the income statement is **$4,868**.

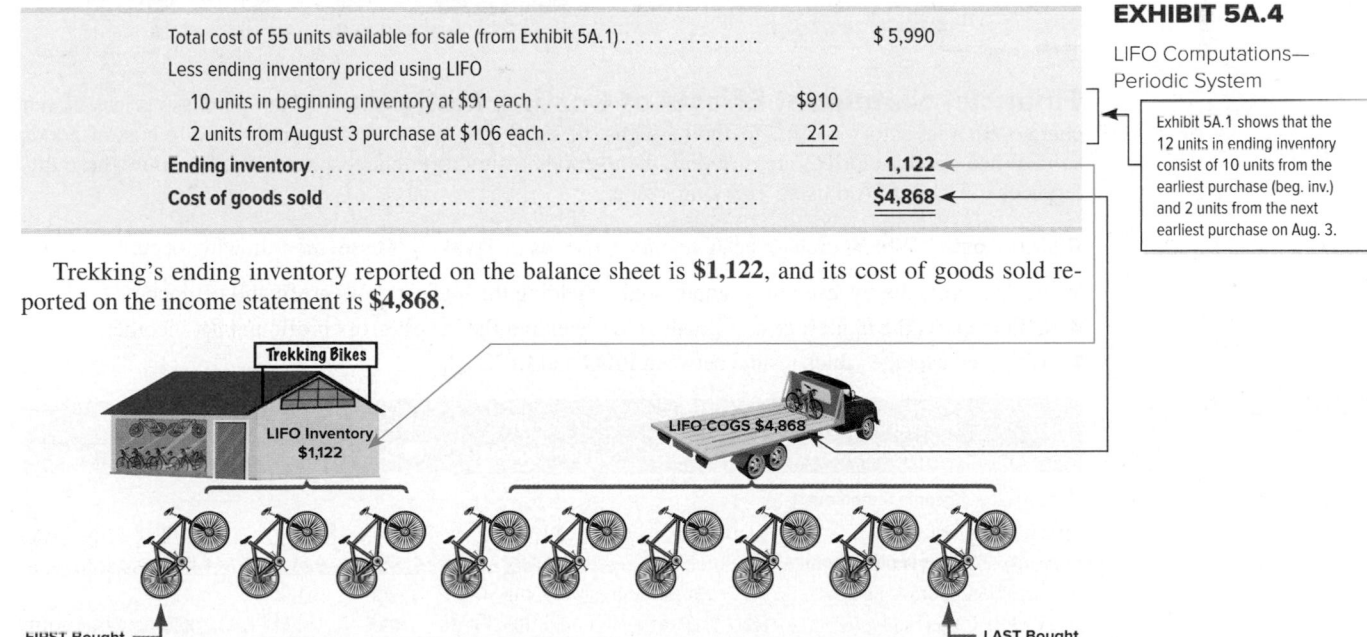

Weighted Average

Weighted average or **WA** (also called **average cost**) requires that we use the average cost per unit of inventory at the end of the period. Weighted average cost per unit equals the cost of goods available for sale divided by the units available. The weighted average method has three steps. The first two steps are shown in Exhibit 5A.5a. Step 1 in Exhibit 5A.5a multiplies the per unit cost for beginning inventory and each purchase by the number of units (from Exhibit 5A.1). Step 2 adds these amounts and divides by the total number of units available for sale to find the weighted average cost per unit.

EXHIBIT 5A.5a

Weighted Average Cost per Unit

Step 1:	10 units @ $ 91 =	$ 910	
	15 units @ $106 =	1,590	
	20 units @ $115 =	2,300	
	10 units @ $119 =	1,190	
	55	**$5,990**	
Step 2:	$5,990/55 units = **$108.91** weighted average cost per unit		

Step 3 uses the weighted average cost per unit to assign costs to ending inventory and to cost of goods sold, as shown in Exhibit 5A.5b.

EXHIBIT 5A.5b

Weighted Average Computations—Periodic

Step 3:	Total cost of 55 units available for sale (from Exhibit 5A.1)	$ 5,990
	Less **ending inventory** priced on a weighted average cost basis: 12 units at $108.91 each (from Exhibit 5A.5a)	**1,307**
	Cost of goods sold (43 units at $108.91 each)	**$4,683**

Trekking's ending inventory reported on the balance sheet is **$1,307**, and its cost of goods sold reported on the income statement is **$4,683**.

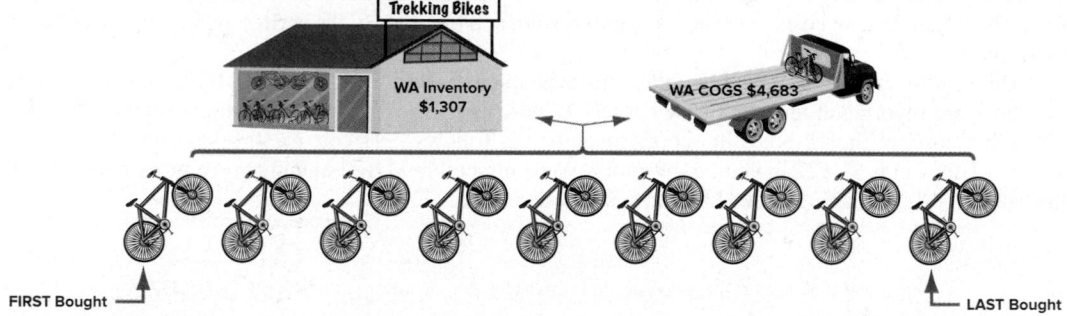

Financial Statement Effects of Costing Methods

When purchase prices do not change, each inventory costing method assigns the same cost amounts to inventory and to cost of goods sold. When purchase prices are different, the methods assign different cost amounts. We show these differences in Exhibit 5A.6 using Trekking's data.

Rising Costs   When purchase costs *regularly rise,* as in Trekking's case, the following occurs.

● FIFO reports the lowest cost of goods sold—yielding the highest gross profit and net income.
● LIFO reports the highest cost of goods sold—yielding the lowest gross profit and net income.
● Weighted average yields results between FIFO and LIFO.

EXHIBIT 5A.6

Financial Statement Effects of Inventory Costing Methods

Trekking Company For Month Ended August 31	Specific Identification	FIFO	LIFO	Weighted Average
Income Statement				
Sales.	$ 6,050	$ 6,050	$ 6,050	$ 6,050
Cost of goods sold.	**4,582**	**4,570**	**4,868**	**4,683**
Gross profit	1,468	1,480	1,182	1,367
Expenses	450	450	450	450
Income before taxes	1,018	1,030	732	917
Income tax expense (30%)	305	309	220	275
Net income	**$ 713**	**$ 721**	**$ 512**	**$ 642**
Balance Sheet				
Inventory.	**$1,408**	**$1,420**	**$1,122**	**$1,307**

Falling Costs   When costs *regularly decline,* the reverse occurs for FIFO and LIFO. FIFO gives the highest cost of goods sold—yielding the lowest gross profit and income. LIFO gives the lowest cost of goods sold—yielding the highest gross profit and income.

Method Advantages   Each method offers advantages.

- FIFO—inventory on the balance sheet approximates its current cost; it also follows the actual flow of goods for most businesses.
- LIFO—cost of goods sold on the income statement approximates its current cost; it also better matches current costs with revenues.
- Weighted average—smooths out erratic changes in costs.
- Specific identification—matches the costs of items with the revenues they generate.

Point: LIFO inventory is often less than the inventory's replacement cost because LIFO inventory is valued using the oldest inventory purchase costs.

A company reported the following December purchases and sales data for its only product.

NEED-TO-KNOW **5-7**

Periodic SI, FIFO, LIFO, and WA

P3

Date	Activities	Units Acquired at Cost	Units Sold at Retail
Dec. 1	Beginning inventory	5 units @ $3.00 = $ 15.00	
Dec. 8	Purchase	10 units @ $4.50 = 45.00	
Dec. 9	Sales.		8 units @ $7.00
Dec. 19	Purchase	13 units @ $5.00 = 65.00	
Dec. 24	Sales.		18 units @ $8.00
Dec. 30	Purchase	8 units @ $5.30 = 42.40	
Totals	. . . .	36 units $167.40	26 units

The company uses a *periodic inventory system.* Determine the cost assigned to ending inventory and to cost of goods sold using (a) specific identification, (b) FIFO, (c) LIFO, and (d) weighted average. (Round per unit costs and inventory amounts to cents.) For specific identification, ending inventory consists of 10 units, where 8 are from the December 30 purchase and 2 are from the December 8 purchase.

Solutions

a. Specific identification: Ending inventory—eight units from December 30 purchase and two units from December 8 purchase.

Specific Identification	Ending Inventory	Cost of Goods Sold
(8 × $5.30) + (2 × $4.50)	$51.40	
(5 × $3.00) + (8 × $4.50) + (13 × $5.00) + (0 × $5.30)		
or $167.40 [Total Goods Available] − $51.40 [Ending Inventory].		$116.00

b. FIFO—Periodic.

FIFO	Ending Inventory	Cost of Goods Sold
(8 × $5.30) + (2 × $5.00)	$52.40	
(5 × $3.00) + (10 × $4.50) + (11 × $5.00)		
or $167.40 [Total Goods Available] − $52.40 [Ending Inventory].		$115.00

c. LIFO—Periodic.

LIFO	Ending Inventory	Cost of Goods Sold
(5 × $3.00) + (5 × $4.50)	$37.50	
(8 × $5.30) + (13 × $5.00) + (5 × $4.50)		
or $167.40 [Total Goods Available] − $37.50 [Ending Inventory].		$129.90

d. WA—Periodic.

Do More: QS 5-7, QS 5-8, QS 5-9, QS 5-14, QS 5-15, QS 5-16, QS 5-17, E 5-5

WA	Ending Inventory	Cost of Goods Sold
10 × $4.65 (computed from $167.40/36)	$46.50	
26 × $4.65 (computed from $167.40/36)		
or $167.40 [Total Goods Available] − $46.50 [Ending Inventory].		$120.90

APPENDIX

5B Inventory Estimation Methods

P4 Apply both the retail inventory and gross profit methods to estimate inventory.

Inventory sometimes is estimated for two reasons. First, companies often report **interim financial statements** (financial statements prepared for periods of less than one year), but they only annually take a physical count of inventory. Second, companies may require an inventory estimate if some casualty such as fire or flood makes taking a physical count impossible. Estimates are usually only required for companies that use the periodic system. Companies using a perpetual system would presumably have updated inventory data.

This appendix describes two methods to estimate inventory.

Retail Inventory Method To avoid the time-consuming process of taking a physical inventory, some companies use the **retail inventory method** to estimate cost of goods sold and ending inventory.

The retail inventory method uses a three-step process to estimate ending inventory. We need to know the amount of inventory a company had at the beginning of the period in both *cost* and *retail* amounts. We already explained how to compute the cost of inventory. The *retail amount of inventory* is measured using selling prices of inventory items. We also need to know the net amount of goods purchased (minus returns, allowances, and discounts) in the period, both at cost and at retail. The amount of net sales at retail also is needed. The process is shown in Exhibit 5B.1.

EXHIBIT 5B.1

Retail Inventory Method of Inventory Estimation

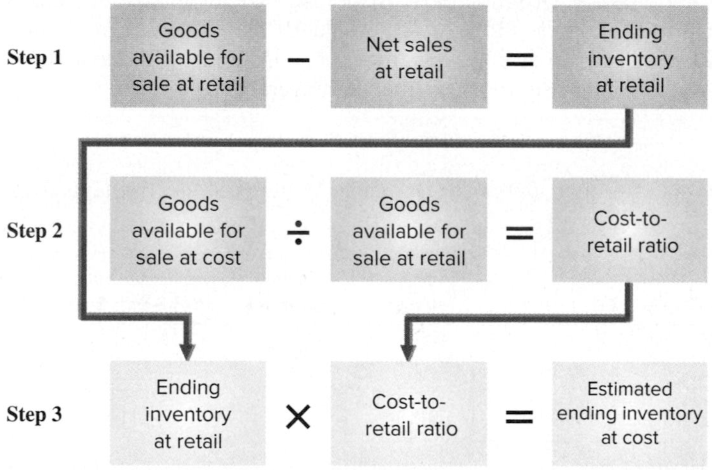

The reasoning behind the retail inventory method is that if we can get a good estimate of the cost-to-retail ratio, we can multiply ending inventory at retail by this ratio to estimate ending inventory at cost. Exhibit 5B.2 shows how these steps are applied to estimate ending inventory. First, we find that $100,000 of goods (at retail selling prices) were available for sale. A total of $70,000 of these

EXHIBIT 5B.2

Estimated Inventory Using the Retail Inventory Method

		At Cost	At Retail
	Goods available for sale		
	Beginning inventory	$ 20,500	$ 34,500
	Cost of goods purchased	39,500	65,500
Step 1:	Goods available for sale	60,000	100,000
	Deduct net sales at retail		**70,000**
	Ending inventory at retail		**$ 30,000**
Step 2:	**Cost-to-retail ratio: ($60,000 ÷ $100,000) = 60%**		
Step 3:	**Estimated ending inventory at cost ($30,000 × 60%)**	**$18,000**	

goods were sold, leaving $30,000 (retail value) of merchandise in ending inventory. Second, the cost of these goods is 60% of the $100,000 retail value. Third, because cost for these goods is 60% of retail, the estimated cost of ending inventory is $18,000.

Gross Profit Method The **gross profit method** estimates the cost of ending inventory by applying the gross profit ratio to net sales (at retail). This type of estimate often is used when inventory is destroyed, lost, or stolen. This method uses the historical relation between cost of goods sold and net sales to estimate the proportion of cost of goods sold making up current sales. This cost of goods sold estimate is then subtracted from cost of goods available for sale to estimate the ending inventory at cost. These two steps are shown in Exhibit 5B.3.

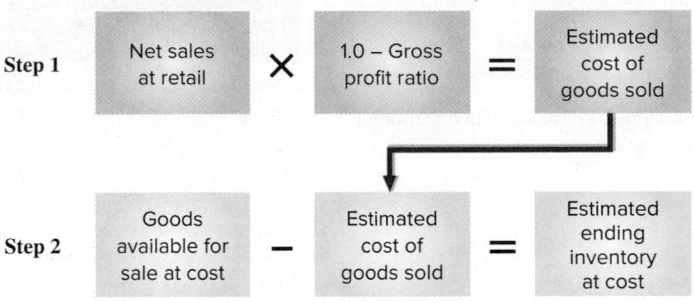

EXHIBIT 5B.3

Gross Profit Method of Inventory Estimation

To demonstrate, assume that a company's inventory is destroyed by fire in March. When the fire occurs, the company's accounts show the following balances for January through March: Net Sales, $30,000; Beginning Inventory, $12,000 (at January 1); and Cost of Goods Purchased, $20,500. If this company's gross profit ratio is 30%, then 30% of each net sales dollar is gross profit and 70% is cost of goods sold. We show in Exhibit 5B.4 how this 70% is used to estimate lost inventory of $11,500.

EXHIBIT 5B.4

Estimated Inventory Using the Gross Profit Method

Goods available for sale		
Beginning inventory, January 1	$12,000	
Cost of goods purchased	20,500	
Goods available for sale (at cost)	32,500	
Net sales at retail		$30,000
Step 1: Estimated cost of goods sold ($30,000 × 70%)	(21,000)	× 0.70
Step 2: Estimated March inventory at cost	$11,500	

Using the retail method and the following data, estimate the cost of ending inventory.

	Cost	Retail
Beginning inventory	$324,000	$530,000
Cost of goods purchased	195,000	335,000
Net sales		320,000

NEED-TO-KNOW 5-8

Retail Inventory Estimation

P4

Solution

Estimated ending inventory (at cost) is $327,000. It is computed as follows.

Step 1: ($530,000 + $335,000) − $320,000 = $545,000

Step 2: $\frac{\$324,000 + \$195,000}{\$530,000 + \$335,000} = 60\%$

Step 3: $545,000 × 60% = \underline{\$327,000}$

Do More: QS 5-22, E 5-16, E 5-17, P 5-9

Summary: Cheat Sheet

INVENTORY BASICS

FOB shipping point: Goods are included in buyer's inventory once they are shipped.
FOB destination: Goods are included in buyer's inventory after arrival at their destination.

Consignee: Never reports consigned goods in inventory; stays in consignor's inventory until sold.
Merchandise inventory: Includes any *necessary* costs to make an item ready for sale. Examples—shipping, storage, import fees, and insurance.

INVENTORY COSTING

FIFO: Earliest units purchased are the first to be reported as cost of goods sold.

LIFO: Latest units purchased are the first to be reported as cost of goods sold.

Weighted average: The weighted average cost per unit (formula below) of inventory at the time of each sale is reported as cost of goods sold.

$$\frac{\text{Cost of goods available for sale (at each sale)}}{\text{Number of units available for sale (at each sale)}}$$

Specific identification: Each unit is assigned a cost, and when that unit is sold, its cost is reported as cost of goods sold.

Cost Flow Assumptions Example

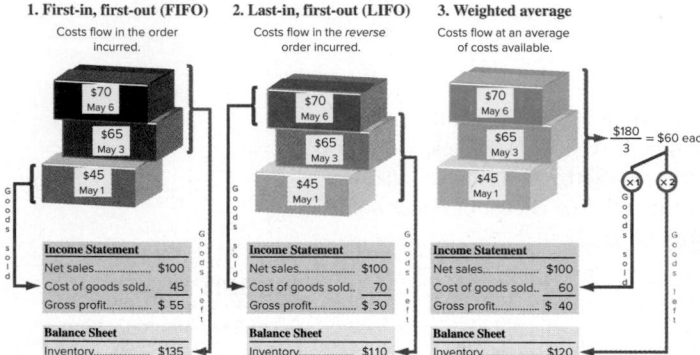

1. First-in, first-out (FIFO)
Costs flow in the order incurred.

2. Last-in, first-out (LIFO)
Costs flow in the *reverse* order incurred.

3. Weighted average
Costs flow at an average of costs available.

Income Statement	
Net sales	$100
Cost of goods sold	45
Gross profit	$ 55

Balance Sheet	
Inventory	$135

Income Statement	
Net sales	$100
Cost of goods sold	70
Gross profit	$ 30

Balance Sheet	
Inventory	$110

Income Statement	
Net sales	$100
Cost of goods sold	60
Gross profit	$ 40

Balance Sheet	
Inventory	$120

$\frac{\$180}{3} = \$60$ each

Financial Statement Effects

Rising Costs—FIFO reports lowest cost of goods sold and highest net income. LIFO reports highest cost of goods sold and lowest income. Weighted average reports results in between LIFO and FIFO.

Falling Costs—FIFO reports highest cost of goods sold and lowest net income. LIFO reports lowest cost of goods sold and highest income.

INVENTORY VALUATION, ERRORS, & ANALYSIS

Lower of cost or market (LCM): When market value of inventory is lower than its cost, a loss is recorded. When market value is higher than cost of inventory, no adjustment is made.

LCM Example (applied to individual items separately)

Inventory Items	Units	Per Unit Cost	Per Unit Market	Total Cost	Total Market	LCM Applied to Items
Roadster	20	$8,500	$7,000	$170,000	$140,000	$ 140,000
Sprint	10	5,000	6,000	50,000	60,000	50,000
Totals				$220,000		$190,000

Roadster: $140,000 is the lower of the $170,000 cost and $140,000 market.
Sprint: $50,000 is the lower of the $50,000 cost and $60,000 market.
LCM: Results in a $190,000 reported inventory.

LCM Journal Entry: To get from $220,000 reported inventory to the $190,000 LCM inventory, make the following entry.

Cost of Goods Sold	30,000	
Merchandise Inventory		30,000

Effects of Overstated or Understated Inventory for Income Statement

	Year 1			Year 2	
Ending Inventory	Cost of Goods Sold	Net Income		Cost of Goods Sold	Net Income
Understated ↓	Overstated ↑	Understated ↓		Understated ↓	Overstated ↑
Overstated ↑	Understated ↓	Overstated ↑		Overstated ↑	Understated ↓

Effects of Overstated or Understated Inventory for Balance Sheet

Ending Inventory	Assets	Equity
Understated ↓	Understated ↓	Understated ↓
Overstated ↑	Overstated ↑	Overstated ↑

Multiple Choice Quiz

Use the following information from Marvel Company for the month of July to answer questions 1 through 4.

July 1	Beginning inventory	75 units @ $25 each
July 3	Purchase	348 units @ $27 each
July 8	Sale	300 units
July 15	Purchase	257 units @ $28 each
July 23	Sale	275 units

1. **Perpetual:** Assume that Marvel uses a *perpetual* FIFO inventory system. What is the dollar value of its ending inventory?
   a. $2,940
   b. $2,685
   c. $2,625
   d. $2,852
   e. $2,705

2. **Perpetual:** Assume that Marvel uses a *perpetual* LIFO inventory system. What is the dollar value of its ending inventory?
   a. $2,940
   b. $2,685
   c. $2,625
   d. $2,852
   e. $2,705

3. **Perpetual and Periodic:** Assume that Marvel uses a specific identification inventory system. Its ending inventory consists of 20 units from beginning inventory, 40 units from the July 3 purchase, and 45 units from the July 15 purchase. What is the dollar value of its ending inventory?

   a. $2,940   **c.** $2,625   **e.** $2,840

   b. $2,685   **d.** $2,852

4.ᴬ **Periodic:** Assume that Marvel uses a *periodic* FIFO inventory system. What is the dollar value of its ending inventory?

   a. $2,940   **c.** $2,625   **e.** $2,705

   b. $2,685   **d.** $2,852

5.ᴬ **Periodic:** A company reports the following beginning inventory and purchases, and it ends the period with 30 units in inventory.

Beginning inventory.........	100 units at $10 cost per unit
Purchase 1	40 units at $12 cost per unit
Purchase 2	20 units at $14 cost per unit

   i) Compute ending inventory using the FIFO *periodic* system.

   a. $400   **b.** $1,460   **c.** $1,360   **d.** $300

   ii) Compute cost of goods sold using the LIFO *periodic* system.

   a. $400   **b.** $1,460   **c.** $1,360   **d.** $300

6. A company has cost of goods sold of $85,000 and ending inventory of $18,000. Its days' sales in inventory equals

   a. 49.32 days.   **c.** 4.72 days.   **e.** 1,723.61 days.

   b. 0.21 day.   **d.** 77.29 days.

ANSWERS TO MULTIPLE CHOICE QUIZ

1. a; FIFO perpetual

Date	Goods Purchased	Cost of Goods Sold	Inventory Balance
July 1			75 units @ $25 = $ 1,875
July 3	348 units @ $27 = $9,396		75 units @ $25 348 units @ $27 } = $11,271
July 8		75 units @ $25 225 units @ $27 } = $ 7,950	123 units @ $27 = $ 3,321
July 15	257 units @ $28 = $7,196		123 units @ $27 257 units @ $28 } = $10,517
July 23		123 units @ $27 152 units @ $28 } = $ 7,577 $15,527	105 units @ $28 = **$2,940**

2. b; LIFO perpetual

Date	Goods Purchased	Cost of Goods Sold	Inventory Balance
July 1			75 units @ $25 = $ 1,875
July 3	348 units @ $27 = $9,396		75 units @ $25 348 units @ $27 } = $11,271
July 8		300 units @ $27 = $ 8,100	75 units @ $25 48 units @ $27 } = $ 3,171
July 15	257 units @ $28 = $7,196		75 units @ $25 48 units @ $27 257 units @ $28 } = $10,367
July 23		257 units @ $28 18 units @ $27 } = $ 7,682 $15,782	75 units @ $25 30 units @ $27 } = **$ 2,685**

3. e; Specific identification (perpetual and periodic are identical for specific identification)—Ending inventory computation follows.

20 units @ $25	$ 500
40 units @ $27	1,080
45 units @ $28	1,260
105 units	$2,840

4. a; FIFO periodic. Ending inventory computation: 105 units @ $28 each = $2,940. (*Hint:* FIFO periodic inventory computation is identical to the FIFO perpetual inventory computation.)

5. **i)** a; FIFO periodic inventory = $(20 \times \$14) + (10 \times \$12)$
   $$= \$400$$

   ii) b; LIFO periodic cost of goods sold = $(20 \times \$14) + (40 \times \$12) + (70 \times \$10) = \$1,460$

6. d; Days' sales in inventory = (Ending inventory/Cost of goods sold) $\times 365 = (\$18,000/\$85,000) \times 365$
   $$= \underline{77.29 \text{ days}}$$

A(B) *Superscript letter A or B denotes assignments based on Appendix 5A or 5B.*

[i] Icon denotes assignments that involve decision making.

Discussion Questions

1. Describe how costs flow from inventory to cost of goods sold for the following methods: (*a*) FIFO and (*b*) LIFO.

2. Where is the amount of merchandise inventory disclosed in the financial statements?

3. [i] If costs are declining, will the LIFO or FIFO method of inventory valuation yield the lower cost of goods sold? Why?

4. [i] If inventory errors are said to correct themselves, why are accounting users concerned when such errors are made?

5. Explain the following statement: "Inventory errors correct themselves."

6. What is the meaning of *market* as it is used in determining the lower of cost or market for inventory?

7. What factors contribute to (or cause) inventory shrinkage?

8.B When preparing interim financial statements, what two methods can companies utilize to estimate cost of goods sold and ending inventory?

9. Refer to **Apple**'s financial statements in Appendix A. On September 30, 2017, what **APPLE** percent of current assets is represented by inventory?

10. Refer to **Apple**'s financial statements in Appendix A and compute its cost of goods **APPLE** available for sale for the year ended September 30, 2017.

11. Refer to **Samsung**'s financial statements in Appendix A. Compute its cost of goods **Samsung** available for sale for the year ended December 31, 2017.

12. Refer to **Samsung**'s financial statements in Appendix A. What percent of its cur- **Samsung** rent assets is inventory as of December 31, 2017 and 2016?

McGraw Hill connect

QUICK STUDY

QS 5-1
Inventory ownership
C1

Homestead Crafts, a distributor of handmade gifts, operates out of owner Emma Finn's house. At the end of the current period, Emma looks over her inventory and finds that she has

- 1,300 units (products) in her basement, 20 of which were damaged by water and cannot be sold.
- 350 units in her van, ready to deliver per a customer order, terms FOB destination.
- 80 units out on consignment to a friend who owns a retail store.

How many units should Emma include in her company's period-end inventory?

QS 5-2
Inventory costs
C2

A car dealer acquires a used car for $14,000, with terms FOB shipping point. Compute total inventory costs assigned to the used car if additional costs include

- $250 for transportation-in.
- $300 for shipping insurance.
- $900 for car import duties.
- $150 for advertising.
- $1,250 for sales staff salaries.
- $180 for trimming shrubs.

QS 5-3
Computing goods available for sale   **P1**

Wattan Company reports beginning inventory of 10 units at $60 each. Every week for four weeks it purchases an additional 10 units at respective costs of $61, $62, $65, and $70 per unit for weeks 1 through 4. Compute the cost of goods available for sale and the units available for sale for this four-week period. Assume that no sales occur during those four weeks.

QS 5-4
Perpetual: Inventory costing with FIFO

P1

A company reports the following beginning inventory and two purchases for the month of January. On January 26, the company sells 350 units. Ending inventory at January 31 totals 150 units.

	Units	Unit Cost
Beginning inventory on January 1.............	320	$3.00
Purchase on January 9......................	80	3.20
Purchase on January 25....................	100	3.34

Required

Assume the perpetual inventory system is used. Determine the costs assigned to ending inventory when costs are assigned based on the FIFO method. (Round per unit costs and inventory amounts to cents.)

Refer to the information in QS 5-4 and assume the perpetual inventory system is used. Determine the costs assigned to ending inventory when costs are assigned based on LIFO. (Round per unit costs and inventory amounts to cents.)

QS 5-5
Perpetual: Inventory costing with LIFO **P1**

Refer to the information in QS 5-4 and assume the perpetual inventory system is used. Determine the costs assigned to ending inventory when costs are assigned based on the weighted average method. (Round per unit costs and inventory amounts to cents.)

QS 5-6
Perpetual: Inventory costing with weighted average **P1**

Refer to the information in QS 5-4 and assume the periodic inventory system is used. Determine the costs assigned to ending inventory when costs are assigned based on the FIFO method. (Round per unit costs and inventory amounts to cents.)

QS 5-7^A
Periodic: Inventory costing with FIFO **P3**

Refer to the information in QS 5-4 and assume the periodic inventory system is used. Determine the costs assigned to ending inventory when costs are assigned based on the LIFO method. (Round per unit costs and inventory amounts to cents.)

QS 5-8^A
Periodic: Inventory costing with LIFO **P3**

Refer to the information in QS 5-4 and assume the periodic inventory system is used. Determine the costs assigned to ending inventory when costs are assigned based on the weighted average method. (Round per unit costs and inventory amounts to cents.)

QS 5-9^A
Periodic: Inventory costing with weighted average **P3**

Trey Monson starts a merchandising business on December 1 and enters into the following three inventory purchases. Also, on December 15, Monson sells 15 units for $20 each.

QS 5-10
Perpetual: Assigning costs with FIFO

P1

Purchases on December 7......	10 units @ $ 6.00 cost
Purchases on December 14.....	20 units @ $12.00 cost
Purchases on December 21.....	15 units @ $14.00 cost

Required

Monson uses a perpetual inventory system. Determine the costs assigned to the December 31 ending inventory based on the FIFO method. (Round per unit costs and inventory amounts to cents.)

Refer to the information in QS 5-10 and assume the perpetual inventory system is used. Determine the costs assigned to ending inventory when costs are assigned based on the LIFO method. (Round per unit costs and inventory amounts to cents.)

QS 5-11
Perpetual: Inventory costing with LIFO **P1**

Refer to the information in QS 5-10 and assume the perpetual inventory system is used. Determine the costs assigned to ending inventory when costs are assigned based on the weighted average method. (Round per unit costs and inventory amounts to cents.)

QS 5-12
Perpetual: Inventory costing with weighted average **P1**

Refer to the information in QS 5-10 and assume the perpetual inventory system is used. Determine the costs assigned to ending inventory when costs are assigned based on specific identification. Of the units sold, eight are from the December 7 purchase and seven are from the December 14 purchase. (Round per unit costs and inventory amounts to cents.)

QS 5-13
Perpetual: Inventory costing with specific identification **P1**

Refer to the information in QS 5-10 and assume the periodic inventory system is used. Determine the costs assigned to ending inventory when costs are assigned based on the FIFO method. (Round per unit costs and inventory amounts to cents.)

QS 5-14^A
Periodic: Inventory costing with FIFO **P3**

Refer to the information in QS 5-10 and assume the periodic inventory system is used. Determine the costs assigned to ending inventory when costs are assigned based on the LIFO method. (Round per unit costs and inventory amounts to cents.)

QS 5-15^A
Periodic: Inventory costing with LIFO **P3**

QS 5-16ᴬ
Periodic: Inventory costing with weighted average   **P3**

Refer to the information in QS 5-10 and assume the periodic inventory system is used. Determine the costs assigned to ending inventory when costs are assigned based on the weighted average method. (Round per unit costs and inventory amounts to cents.)

QS 5-17ᴬ
Periodic: Inventory costing with specific identification   **P3**

Refer to the information in QS 5-10 and assume the periodic inventory system is used. Determine the costs assigned to ending inventory when costs are assigned based on specific identification. Of the units sold, eight are from the December 7 purchase and seven are from the December 14 purchase. (Round per unit costs and inventory amounts to cents.)

QS 5-18
Contrasting inventory costing methods

A1

Identify the inventory costing method (SI, FIFO, LIFO, or WA) best described by each of the following separate statements. Assume a period of increasing costs.

_____ **1.** Results in the highest cost of goods sold.

_____ **2.** Yields the highest net income.

_____ **3.** Has the lowest tax expense because of reporting the lowest net income.

_____ **4.** Better matches current costs with revenues.

_____ **5.** Precisely matches the costs of items with the revenues they generate.

QS 5-19
Applying LCM to inventories

P2

Ames Trading Co. has the following products in its ending inventory. Compute lower of cost or market for inventory applied separately to each product.

Product	Quantity	Cost per Unit	Market per Unit
Mountain bikes...........	11	$600	$550
Skateboards	13	350	425
Gliders..................	26	800	700

QS 5-20
Inventory errors

A2

In taking a physical inventory at the end of Year 1, Grant Company forgot to count certain units and understated ending inventory by $10,000. Determine how this error affects each of the following.

a. Year 1 cost of goods sold   **c.** Year 2 cost of goods sold

b. Year 1 net income   **d.** Year 2 net income

QS 5-21
Analyzing inventory   **A3**

Endor Company begins the year with $140,000 of goods in inventory. At year-end, the amount in inventory has increased to $180,000. Cost of goods sold for the year is $1,200,000. Compute Endor's inventory turnover and days' sales in inventory. Assume there are 365 days in the year.

QS 5-22ᴮ
Estimating inventories—gross profit method

P4

Confucius Bookstore's inventory is destroyed by a fire on September 5. The following data for the current year are available from the accounting records. Estimate the cost of the inventory destroyed.

Beginning inventory, Jan. 1	$190,000
Jan. 1 through Sept. 5 purchases (net).............	$352,000
Jan. 1 through Sept. 5 sales (net)	$685,000
Current year's estimated gross profit rate	44%

QS 5-23
Inventory costs

C2

A solar panel dealer acquires a used panel for $9,000, with terms FOB shipping point. Compute total inventory costs assigned to the used panel if additional costs include

- $1,500 for sales staff salaries.   • $135 for shipping insurance.
- $280 for transportation-in by train.   • $550 for used panel restoration.
- $110 for online advertising.   • $300 for lawn care.

 connect®

EXERCISES

Exercise 5-1
Inventory ownership   **C1**

1. At year-end, Barr Co. had shipped $12,500 of merchandise FOB destination to Lee Co. Which company should include the $12,500 of merchandise in transit as part of its year-end inventory?

2. Parris Company has shipped $20,000 of goods to Harlow Co., and Harlow Co. has arranged to sell the goods for Parris. Identify the consignor and the consignee. Which company should include any unsold goods as part of its inventory?

Walberg Associates, antique dealers, purchased goods for $75,000. Terms of the purchase were FOB shipping point, and the cost of transporting the goods to Walberg Associates's warehouse was $2,400. Walberg Associates insured the shipment at a cost of $300. Prior to putting the goods up for sale, they cleaned and refurbished them at a cost of $980. Determine the cost of inventory.

Exercise 5-2
Inventory costs
C2

Laker Company reported the following January purchases and sales data for its only product.

Date	Activities	Units Acquired at Cost	Units Sold at Retail
Jan. 1	Beginning inventory	140 units @ $6.00 = $ 840	
Jan. 10	Sales........................		100 units @ $15
Jan. 20	Purchase	60 units @ $5.00 = 300	
Jan. 25	Sales........................		80 units @ $15
Jan. 30	Purchase	180 units @ $4.50 = 810	
	Totals	380 units $1,950	180 units

Exercise 5-3
Perpetual: Inventory costing methods
P1

Required

The company uses a perpetual inventory system. Determine the cost assigned to ending inventory and to cost of goods sold using (*a*) specific identification, (*b*) weighted average, (*c*) FIFO, and (*d*) LIFO. (Round per unit costs and inventory amounts to cents.) For specific identification, ending inventory consists of 200 units, where 180 are from the January 30 purchase, 5 are from the January 20 purchase, and 15 are from beginning inventory.

Check   Ending inventory: LIFO, $930; WA, $918

Use the data in Exercise 5-3 to prepare comparative income statements for the month of January for Laker Company similar to those shown in Exhibit 5.8 for the four inventory methods. Assume expenses are $1,250 and the applicable income tax rate is 40%. (Round amounts to cents.)

1. Which method yields the highest net income?
2. Does net income using weighted average fall above, between, or below that using FIFO and LIFO?
3. If costs were rising instead of falling, which method would yield the highest net income?

Exercise 5-4
Perpetual: Income effects of inventory methods

A1

Refer to the information in Exercise 5-3 and assume the periodic inventory system is used. Determine the costs assigned to ending inventory and to cost of goods sold using (*a*) specific identification, (*b*) weighted average, (*c*) FIFO, and (*d*) LIFO. (Round per unit costs and inventory amounts to cents.) For specific identification, ending inventory consists of 200 units, where 180 are from the January 30 purchase, 5 are from the January 20 purchase, and 15 are from beginning inventory.

Exercise 5-5ᴬ
Periodic: Inventory costing
P3

Use the data and results from Exercise 5-5 to prepare comparative income statements for the month of January for the company similar to those shown in Exhibit 5.8 for the four inventory methods. Assume expenses are $1,250 and the applicable income tax rate is 40%. (Round amounts to cents.)

Exercise 5-6ᴬ
Periodic: Income effects of inventory methods

P3   A1

Required

1. Which method yields the highest net income?
2. Does net income using weighted average fall above, between, or below that using FIFO and LIFO?
3. If costs were rising instead of falling, which method would yield the highest net income?

Hemming Co. reported the following current-year purchases and sales for its only product.

Date	Activities	Units Acquired at Cost	Units Sold at Retail
Jan. 1	Beginning inventory.............	200 units @ $10 = $ 2,000	
Jan. 10	Sales........................		150 units @ $40
Mar. 14	Purchase	350 units @ $15 = 5,250	
Mar. 15	Sales........................		300 units @ $40
July 30	Purchase	450 units @ $20 = 9,000	
Oct. 5	Sales........................		430 units @ $40
Oct. 26	Purchase	100 units @ $25 = 2,500	
	Totals	1,100 units $18,750	880 units

Exercise 5-7
Perpetual: Inventory costing methods—FIFO and LIFO
P1

Required

Hemming uses a perpetual inventory system. Determine the costs assigned to ending inventory and to cost of goods sold using (*a*) FIFO and (*b*) LIFO. (*c*) Compute the gross margin for each method. (Round amounts to cents.)

Exercise 5-8

Specific identification   **P1**

Refer to the information in Exercise 5-7. Ending inventory consists of 45 units from the March 14 purchase, 75 units from the July 30 purchase, and all 100 units from the October 26 purchase. Using the specific iden- tification method, compute (*a*) the cost of goods sold and (*b*) the gross profit. (Round amounts to cents.)

Exercise 5-9[A]

Periodic: Inventory costing   **P3**

Refer to the information in Exercise 5-7 and assume the periodic inventory system is used. Determine the costs assigned to ending inventory and to cost of goods sold using (*a*) FIFO and (*b*) LIFO. (*c*) Compute the gross margin for each method.

Exercise 5-10

Lower of cost or market

P2

Martinez Company's ending inventory includes the following items. Compute the lower of cost or market for ending inventory applied separately to each product.

Product	Units	Cost per Unit	Market per Unit
Helmets..........	24	$50	$54
Bats............	17	78	72
Shoes...........	38	95	91
Uniforms........	42	36	36

Exercise 5-11

Comparing LIFO numbers to FIFO numbers; ratio analysis

A1   **A3**

Cruz Company uses LIFO for inventory costing and reports the following financial data. It also recom- puted inventory and cost of goods sold using FIFO for comparison purposes.

	Year 2	Year 1
LIFO inventory........................	$160	$110
LIFO cost of goods sold	740	680
FIFO inventory........................	240	110
FIFO cost of goods sold	660	645
Current assets (using LIFO)	220	180
Current assets (using FIFO).............	300	180
Current liabilities......................	200	170

1. Compute its current ratio, inventory turnover, and days' sales in inventory for Year 2 using (*a*) LIFO numbers and (*b*) FIFO numbers. (Round answers to one decimal.)
2. Comment on and interpret the results of part 1.

Exercise 5-12

Analyzing inventory errors

A2

Vibrant Company had $850,000 of sales in each of Year 1, Year 2, and Year 3, and it purchased merchan- dise costing $500,000 in each of those years. It also maintained a $250,000 physical inventory from the beginning to the end of that three-year period. In accounting for inventory, it made an error at the end of Year 1 that caused its Year 1 ending inventory to appear on its statements as $230,000 rather than the correct $250,000.

1. Determine the correct amount of the company's gross profit in each of Year 1, Year 2, and Year 3.
2. Prepare comparative income statements as in Exhibit 5.11 to show the effect of this error on the com- pany's cost of goods sold and gross profit for each of Year 1, Year 2, and Year 3.

Exercise 5-13

Inventory turnover and days' sales in inventory

A3

Use the following information for Palmer Co. to compute inventory turnover for Year 3 and Year 2, and its days' sales in inventory at December 31, Year 3 and Year 2. (Round answers to one decimal.) Comment on Palmer's efficiency in using its assets to increase sales from Year 2 to Year 3.

	Year 3	Year 2	Year 1
Cost of goods sold	$643,825	$426,650	$391,300
Ending inventory.............	97,400	87,750	92,500

Lopez Company reported the following current-year data for its only product. The company uses a periodic inventory system, and its ending inventory consists of 150 units—50 from each of the last three purchases. Determine the cost assigned to ending inventory and to cost of goods sold using (*a*) specific identification, (*b*) weighted average, (*c*) FIFO, and (*d*) LIFO. (Round per unit costs and inventory amounts to cents.) (*e*) Which method yields the highest net income?

Exercise 5-14ᴬ
Periodic: Cost flow assumptions
P3

Jan.	1	Beginning inventory	96 units @ $2.00 = $	192
Mar.	7	Purchase	220 units @ $2.25 =	495
July	28	Purchase	544 units @ $2.50 =	1,360
Oct.	3	Purchase	480 units @ $2.80 =	1,344
Dec.	19	Purchase	160 units @ $2.90 =	464
		Totals	1,500 units	$3,855

Check   Inventory; LIFO, $313.50; FIFO, $435.00

Flora's Gifts reported the following current-month data for its only product. The company uses a periodic inventory system, and its ending inventory consists of 60 units—50 units from the January 6 purchase and 10 units from the January 25 purchase. Determine the cost assigned to ending inventory and to cost of goods sold using (*a*) specific identification, (*b*) weighted average, (*c*) FIFO, and (*d*) LIFO. (Round per unit costs and inventory amounts to cents.) (*e*) Which method yields the lowest net income?

Exercise 5-15ᴬ
Periodic: Cost flow assumptions
P3

Jan.	1	Beginning inventory	138 units @ $3.00 = $	414
Jan.	6	Purchase	300 units @ $2.80 =	840
Jan.	17	Purchase	540 units @ $2.30 =	1,242
Jan.	25	Purchase	22 units @ $2.00 =	44
		Totals	1,000 units	$2,540

Check   Inventory: LIFO, $180.00; FIFO, $131.40

Dakota Company had net sales (at retail) of $260,000. The following additional information is available from its records. Use the retail inventory method to estimate Dakota's year-end inventory at cost

Exercise 5-16ᴮ
Estimating ending inventory—retail method
P4

	At Cost	At Retail
Beginning inventory	$ 63,800	$128,400
Cost of goods purchased	115,060	196,800

Check   End. inventory at cost, $35,860

On January 1, JKR Shop had $225,000 of beginning inventory at cost. In the first quarter of the year, it purchased $795,000 of merchandise, returned $11,550, and paid freight charges of $18,800 on purchased merchandise, terms FOB shipping point. The company's gross profit averages 30%, and the store had $1,000,000 of net sales (at retail) in the first quarter of the year.
   Use the gross profit method to estimate its cost of inventory at the end of the first quarter.

Exercise 5-17ᴮ
Estimating ending inventory—gross profit method   **P4**

Tree Seedlings has the following current-year purchases and sales for its only product.

Exercise 5-18
Perpetual inventory costing
P1

Date	Activities	Units Acquired at Cost	Units Sold at Retail
Jan.	1	Beginning inventory...........	40 units @ $2 = $ 80	
Jan.	3	Sales.......................		30 units @ $8
Feb.	14	Purchase....................	70 units @ $3 = $210	
Feb.	15	Sales.......................		60 units @ $8
June	30	Purchase....................	90 units @ $4 = $360	
Nov.	6	Sales.......................		86 units @ $8
Nov.	19	Purchase....................	20 units @ $5 = $100	
		Totals	220 units $750	176 units

Required

The company uses a perpetual inventory system. Determine the costs assigned to ending inventory and to cost of goods sold using (*a*) FIFO and (*b*) LIFO. (*c*) Compute the gross margin for each method.

Exercise 5-19[A]
Periodic inventory costing

P3

Refer to the information in Exercise 5-18 and assume the periodic inventory system is used. Determine the costs assigned to ending inventory and to cost of goods sold using (*a*) FIFO and (*b*) LIFO. (*c*) Compute the gross margin for each method.

 connect

PROBLEM SET A

Problem 5-1A
Perpetual: Alternative cost flows

P1

Warnerwoods Company uses a perpetual inventory system. It entered into the following purchases and sales transactions for March. (For specific identification, the March 9 sale consisted of 80 units from beginning inventory and 340 units from the March 5 purchase; the March 29 sale consisted of 40 units from the March 18 purchase and 120 units from the March 25 purchase.)

Date	Activities	Units Acquired at Cost	Units Sold at Retail
Mar. 1	Beginning inventory............	100 units @ $50.00 per unit	
Mar. 5	Purchase.....................	400 units @ $55.00 per unit	
Mar. 9	Sales		420 units @ $85.00 per unit
Mar. 18	Purchase.....................	120 units @ $60.00 per unit	
Mar. 25	Purchase.....................	200 units @ $62.00 per unit	
Mar. 29	Sales		160 units @ $95.00 per unit
	Totals.......................	820 units	580 units

Required

Check   (3) Ending inventory: FIFO, $14,800; LIFO, $13,680; WA, $14,352
(4) LIFO gross profit, $17,980

1. Compute cost of goods available for sale and the number of units available for sale.
2. Compute the number of units in ending inventory.
3. Compute the cost assigned to ending inventory using (*a*) FIFO, (*b*) LIFO, (*c*) weighted average, and (*d*) specific identification. (Round all amounts to cents.)
4. Compute gross profit earned by the company for each of the four costing methods in part 3.

Problem 5-2A[A]
Periodic: Alternative cost flows

P3

Refer to the information in Problem 5-1A and assume the periodic inventory system is used.

Required

1. Compute cost of goods available for sale and the number of units available for sale.
2. Compute the number of units in ending inventory.
3. Compute the cost assigned to ending inventory using (*a*) FIFO, (*b*) LIFO, (*c*) weighted average, and (*d*) specific identification. (Round all amounts to cents.)
4. Compute gross profit earned by the company for each of the four costing methods in part 3.

Problem 5-3A
Perpetual: Alternative cost flows

P1

Montoure Company uses a perpetual inventory system. It entered into the following calendar-year purchases and sales transactions. (For specific identification, units sold consist of 600 units from beginning inventory, 300 from the February 10 purchase, 200 from the March 13 purchase, 50 from the August 21 purchase, and 250 from the September 5 purchase.)

Date	Activities	Units Acquired at Cost	Units Sold at Retail
Jan. 1	Beginning inventory............	600 units @ $45.00 per unit	
Feb. 10	Purchase.....................	400 units @ $42.00 per unit	
Mar. 13	Purchase.....................	200 units @ $27.00 per unit	
Mar. 15	Sales		800 units @ $75.00 per unit
Aug. 21	Purchase.....................	100 units @ $50.00 per unit	
Sep. 5	Purchase.....................	500 units @ $46.00 per unit	
Sep. 10	Sales		600 units @ $75.00 per unit
	Totals.......................	1,800 units	1,400 units

Required

1. Compute cost of goods available for sale and the number of units available for sale.
2. Compute the number of units in ending inventory.
3. Compute the cost assigned to ending inventory using (*a*) FIFO, (*b*) LIFO, (*c*) weighted average, and (*d*) specific identification. (Round all amounts to cents.)
4. Compute gross profit earned by the company for each of the four costing methods in part 3.

Check   (3) Ending inventory: FIFO, $18,400; LIFO, $18,000; WA, $17,760 (4) LIFO gross profit, $45,800

Analysis Component

5. The company's manager earns a bonus based on a percent of gross profit. Which method of inventory costing produces the highest bonus for the manager?

Refer to the information in Problem 5-3A and assume the periodic inventory system is used.

Problem 5-4A[A]
Periodic: Alternative cost flows

P3

Required

1. Compute cost of goods available for sale and the number of units available for sale.
2. Compute the number of units in ending inventory.
3. Compute the cost assigned to ending inventory using (*a*) FIFO, (*b*) LIFO, (*c*) weighted average, and (*d*) specific identification. (Round all amounts to cents.)
4. Compute gross profit earned by the company for each of the four costing methods in part 3.

Analysis Component

5. The company's manager earns a bonus based on a percentage of gross profit. Which method of inventory costing produces the highest bonus for the manager?

A physical inventory of Liverpool Company taken at December 31 reveals the following.

Problem 5-5A
Lower of cost or market

P2

Item	Units	Cost per Unit	Market per Unit
Car audio equipment			
Speakers	345	$ 90	$ 98
Stereos	260	111	100
Amplifiers	326	86	95
Subwoofers	204	52	41
Security equipment			
Alarms	480	150	125
Locks	291	93	84
Cameras	212	310	322
Binocular equipment			
Tripods	185	70	84
Stabilizers	170	97	105

Required

1. Compute the lower of cost or market for the inventory applied separately to each item.
2. If the market amount is less than the recorded cost of the inventory, then record the LCM adjustment to the Merchandise Inventory account.

Check   (1) $273,054

Navajo Company's financial statements show the following. The company recently discovered that in making physical counts of inventory, it had made the following errors: Year 1 ending inventory is understated by $56,000 and Year 2 ending inventory is overstated by $20,000.

Problem 5-6A
Analysis of inventory errors

A2

For Year Ended December 31		Year 1	Year 2	Year 3
(a)	Cost of goods sold	$ 615,000	$ 957,000	$ 780,000
(b)	Net income	230,000	285,000	241,000
(c)	Total current assets	1,255,000	1,365,000	1,200,000
(d)	Total equity	1,387,000	1,530,000	1,242,000

Required

1. For each key financial statement figure—(a), (b), (c), and (d) above—prepare a table similar to the following to show the adjustments necessary to correct the reported amounts.

Figure: _____	Year 1	Year 2	Year 3
Reported amount	_____	_____	_____
Adjustments for: Year 1 error..................	_____	_____	_____
Year 2 error..................	_____	_____	_____
Corrected amount	_____	_____	_____

Check (1) Corrected net income: Year 1, $286,000; Year 2, $209,000; Year 3, $261,000

2. What is the total error in combined net income for the three-year period resulting from the inventory errors? Explain.

Problem 5-7A^A

Periodic: Alternative cost flows   **P3**

Seminole Co. began the year with 23,000 units of product in its January 1 inventory costing $15 each. It made four purchases of its product during the year as follows. The company uses a periodic inventory system. On December 31, a physical count reveals that 40,000 units of its product remain in inventory.

Mar. 7	30,000 units @ $18.00 each	Aug. 1	23,000 units @ $25.00 each
May 25	39,000 units @ $20.00 each	Nov. 10	35,000 units @ $26.00 each

Required

Check (2) Cost of goods sold: FIFO, $2,115,000; LIFO, $2,499,000; WA, $2,310,000

1. Compute the number and total cost of the units available for sale during the year.

2. Compute the amounts assigned to ending inventory and the cost of goods sold using (a) FIFO, (b) LIFO, and (c) weighted average. (Round all amounts to cents.)

Problem 5-8A^A

Periodic: Income comparisons and cost flows

A1   P3

QP Corp. sold 4,000 units of its product at $50 per unit during the year and incurred operating expenses of $5 per unit in selling the units. It began the year with 700 units in inventory and made successive purchases of its product as follows.

Jan. 1	Beginning inventory............	700 units @ $18.00 per unit
Feb. 20	Purchase	1,700 units @ $19.00 per unit
May 16	Purchase	800 units @ $20.00 per unit
Oct. 3	Purchase	500 units @ $21.00 per unit
Dec. 11	Purchase	2,300 units @ $22.00 per unit
	Total	6,000 units

Required

Check (1) Net income: FIFO, $61,200; LIFO, $57,180; WA, $59,196

1. Prepare comparative income statements similar to Exhibit 5.8 for the three inventory costing methods of FIFO, LIFO, and weighted average. (Round all amounts to cents.) Include a detailed cost of goods sold section as part of each statement. The company uses a periodic inventory system, and its income tax rate is 40%.

2. How would the financial results from using the three alternative inventory costing methods change if the company had been experiencing *declining* costs in its purchases of inventory?

3. What advantages and disadvantages are offered by using (a) LIFO and (b) FIFO? Assume the continuing trend of *increasing* costs.

Problem 5-9A^B

Retail inventory method

P4

The records of Alaska Company provide the following information for the year ended December 31.

	At Cost	At Retail
Beginning inventory, January 1	$ 469,010	$ 928,950
Cost of goods purchased	3,376,050	6,381,050
Sales		5,595,800
Sales returns...........................		42,800

Required

Check (1) Inventory, $924,182 cost

(2) Inventory shortage at cost, $36,873

1. Use the retail inventory method to estimate the company's year-end inventory at cost.

2. A year-end physical inventory at retail prices yields a total inventory of $1,686,900. Prepare a calculation showing the company's loss from shrinkage at cost and at retail.

Wayward Company wants to prepare interim financial statements for the first quarter. The company wishes to avoid making a physical count of inventory. Wayward's gross profit rate averages 34%. The following information for the first quarter is available from its records.

Problem 5-10Aᴮ
Gross profit method **P4**

Beginning inventory, January 1	$ 302,580
Cost of goods purchased	941,040
Sales	1,211,160
Sales returns	8,410

Required

Use the gross profit method to estimate the company's first-quarter ending inventory.

Check Estimated ending inventory, $449,805

Ming Company uses a perpetual inventory system. It entered into the following purchases and sales transactions for April. (For specific identification, the April 9 sale consisted of 8 units from beginning inventory and 27 units from the April 6 purchase; the April 30 sale consisted of 12 units from beginning inventory, 3 units from the April 6 purchase, and 10 units from the April 25 purchase.)

PROBLEM SET B

Problem 5-1B
Perpetual: Alternative cost flows

P1

Date	Activities	Units Acquired at Cost	Units Sold at Retail
Apr. 1	Beginning inventory	20 units @ $3,000.00 per unit	
Apr. 6	Purchase	30 units @ $3,500.00 per unit	
Apr. 9	Sales		35 units @ $12,000.00 per unit
Apr. 17	Purchase	5 units @ $4,500.00 per unit	
Apr. 25	Purchase	10 units @ $4,800.00 per unit	
Apr. 30	Sales		25 units @ $14,000.00 per unit
	Total	65 units	60 units

Required

1. Compute cost of goods available for sale and the number of units available for sale.

2. Compute the number of units in ending inventory.

3. Compute the cost assigned to ending inventory using (*a*) FIFO, (*b*) LIFO, (*c*) weighted average, and (*d*) specific identification. (Round all amounts to cents.)

4. Compute gross profit earned by the company for each of the four costing methods in part 3.

Check (3) Ending inventory: FIFO, $24,000; LIFO, $15,000; WA, $20,000
(4) LIFO gross profit, $549,500

Refer to the information in Problem 5-1B and assume the periodic inventory system is used.

Problem 5-2Bᴬ
Periodic: Alternative cost flows

P3

Required

1. Compute cost of goods available for sale and the number of units available for sale.

2. Compute the number of units in ending inventory.

3. Compute the cost assigned to ending inventory using (*a*) FIFO, (*b*) LIFO, (*c*) weighted average, and (*d*) specific identification. (Round all amounts to cents.)

4. Compute gross profit earned by the company for each of the four costing methods in part 3.

Aloha Company uses a perpetual inventory system. It entered into the following calendar-year purchases and sales transactions. (For specific identification, the May 9 sale consisted of 80 units from beginning inventory and 100 units from the May 6 purchase; the May 30 sale consisted of 200 units from the May 6 purchase and 100 units from the May 25 purchase.)

Problem 5-3B
Perpetual: Alternative cost flows

P1

Date	Activities	Units Acquired at Cost	Units Sold at Retail
May 1	Beginning inventory	150 units @ $300.00 per unit	
May 6	Purchase	350 units @ $350.00 per unit	
May 9	Sales		180 units @ $1,200.00 per unit
May 17	Purchase	80 units @ $450.00 per unit	
May 25	Purchase	100 units @ $458.00 per unit	
May 30	Sales		300 units @ $1,400.00 per unit
	Total	680 units	480 units

Required

1. Compute cost of goods available for sale and the number of units available for sale.

2. Compute the number of units in ending inventory.

3. Compute the cost assigned to ending inventory using (*a*) FIFO, (*b*) LIFO, (*c*) weighted average, and (*d*) specific identification. (Round all amounts to cents.)

4. Compute gross profit earned by the company for each of the four costing methods in part 3.

Analysis Component

5. If the company's manager earns a bonus based on a percent of gross profit, which method of inventory costing will the manager likely prefer?

Problem 5-4B^A

Periodic: Alternative
cost flows

P3

Refer to the information in Problem 5-3B and assume the periodic inventory system is used.

Required

1. Compute cost of goods available for sale and the number of units available for sale.

2. Compute the number of units in ending inventory.

3. Compute the cost assigned to ending inventory using (*a*) FIFO, (*b*) LIFO, (*c*) weighted average, and (*d*) specific identification. (Round all amounts to cents.)

4. Compute gross profit earned by the company for each of the four costing methods in part 3.

Analysis Component

5. If the company's manager earns a bonus based on a percentage of gross profit, which method of inventory costing will the manager likely prefer?

Problem 5-5B

Lower of cost or market

P2

A physical inventory of Office Necessities Company taken at December 31 reveals the following.

Item	Units	Cost per Unit	Market per Unit
Office furniture			
Desks	536	$261	$305
Chairs	395	227	256
Mats	687	49	43
Bookshelves	421	93	82
Filing cabinets			
Two-drawer	114	81	70
Four-drawer	298	135	122
Lateral	75	104	118
Office equipment			
Projectors	370	168	200
Copiers	475	317	288
Phones	302	125	117

Required

1. Compute the lower of cost or market for the inventory applied separately to each item.

2. If the market amount is less than the recorded cost of the inventory, then record the LCM adjustment to the Merchandise Inventory account.

Problem 5-6B

Analysis of inventory errors

A2

Hallam Company's financial statements show the following. The company recently discovered that in making physical counts of inventory, it had made the following errors: Year 1 ending inventory is overstated by $18,000 and Year 2 ending inventory is understated by $26,000.

For Year Ended December 31	Year 1	Year 2	Year 3
(*a*) Cost of goods sold	$207,200	$213,800	$197,030
(*b*) Net income	175,800	212,270	184,910
(*c*) Total current assets.	276,000	277,500	272,950
(*d*) Total equity	314,000	315,000	346,000

Required

1. For each key financial statement figure—(a), (b), (c), and (d) above—prepare a table similar to the following to show the adjustments necessary to correct the reported amounts.

Figure: _____	Year 1	Year 2	Year 3
Reported amount			
Adjustments for: Year 1 error..................			
Year 2 error..................			
Corrected amount			

Check   (1) Corrected net income: Year 1, $157,800; Year 2, $256,270; Year 3, $158,910

2. What is the total error in combined net income for the three-year period resulting from the inventory errors? Explain.

Seneca Co. began the year with 6,500 units of product in its January 1 inventory costing $35 each. It made four purchases of its product during the year as follows. The company uses a periodic inventory system. On December 31, a physical count reveals that 8,500 units of its product remain in inventory.

Problem 5-7B[A]

Periodic: Alternative cost flows

P3

Jan. 4	11,500 units @ $33 each	July 9	11,000 units @ $29 each
May 18	13,400 units @ $32 each	Nov. 21	7,600 units @ $27 each

Required

1. Compute the number and total cost of the units available for sale during the year.
2. Compute the amounts assigned to ending inventory and the cost of goods sold using (a) FIFO, (b) LIFO, and (c) weighted average. (Round all amounts to cents.)

Check   (2) Cost of goods sold: FIFO, $1,328,700; LIFO, $1,266,500; WA, $1,294,800

Shepard Company sold 4,000 units of its product at $100 per unit during the year and incurred operating expenses of $15 per unit in selling the units. It began the year with 840 units in inventory and made successive purchases of its product as follows.

Problem 5-8B[A]

Periodic: Income comparisons and cost flows

A1   P3

Jan.	1	Beginning inventory	840 units @ $58 per unit
Apr.	2	Purchase	600 units @ $59 per unit
June	14	Purchase	1,205 units @ $61 per unit
Aug.	29	Purchase	700 units @ $64 per unit
Nov.	18	Purchase	1,655 units @ $65 per unit
		Total	5,000 units

Required

1. Prepare comparative income statements similar to Exhibit 5.8 for the three inventory costing methods of FIFO, LIFO, and weighted average. (Round all amounts to cents.) Include a detailed cost of goods sold section as part of each statement. The company uses a periodic inventory system, and its income tax rate is 40%.
2. How would the financial results from using the three alternative inventory costing methods change if the company had been experiencing decreasing prices in its purchases of inventory?
3. What advantages and disadvantages are offered by using (a) LIFO and (b) FIFO? Assume the continuing trend of increasing costs.

Check   (1) Net income: LIFO, $52,896; FIFO, $57,000; WA, $55,200

The records of Macklin Co. provide the following information for the year ended December 31.

Problem 5-9B[B]

Retail inventory method

P4

	At Cost	At Retail
Beginning inventory, January 1	$ 90,022	$115,610
Cost of goods purchased	502,250	761,830
Sales		782,300
Sales returns		3,460

Required

1. Use the retail inventory method to estimate the company's year-end inventory.
2. A year-end physical inventory at retail prices yields a total inventory of $80,450. Prepare a calculation showing the company's loss from shrinkage at cost and at retail.

Check   (1) Inventory, $66,555 cost

(2) Inventory shortage at cost, $12,251.25

Problem 5-10B[B]
Gross profit method
P4

Otingo Equipment Co. wants to prepare interim financial statements for the first quarter. The company wishes to avoid making a physical count of inventory. Otingo's gross profit rate averages 35%. The following information for the first quarter is available from its records.

Beginning inventory, January 1	$ 802,880
Cost of goods purchased	2,209,636
Sales	3,760,260
Sales returns	79,300

Check Est. ending inventory, $619,892

Required

Use the gross profit method to estimate the company's first-quarter ending inventory.

SERIAL PROBLEM
Business Solutions

A3 P2

©Alexander Image/Shutterstock

This serial problem began in Chapter 1 and continues through most of the book. If previous chapter segments were not completed, the serial problem can begin at this point.

SP 5
Part A

Santana Rey of **Business Solutions** is evaluating her inventory to determine whether it must be adjusted based on lower of cost or market rules. Business Solutions has three different types of software in its inventory, and the following information is available for each.

Inventory Items	Units	Cost per Unit	Market per Unit
Office productivity	3	$ 76	$ 74
Desktop publishing.	2	103	100
Accounting	3	90	96

Required

Compute the lower of cost or market for ending inventory assuming Rey applies the lower of cost or market rule to each product in inventory. Must Rey adjust the reported inventory value? Explain.

Part B

Selected accounts and balances for the three months ended March 31, 2020, for Business Solutions follow.

Beginning inventory, January 1	$ 0
Cost of goods sold	14,052
Ending inventory, March 31	704

Required

1. Compute inventory turnover and days' sales in inventory for the three months ended March 31, 2020.
2. Assess the company's performance if competitors average 15 times for inventory turnover and 25 days for days' sales in inventory.

Accounting Analysis

COMPANY ANALYSIS

C2 A3

APPLE

AA 5-1 Use **Apple**'s financial statements in Appendix A to answer the following.

Required

1. What amount of inventories did Apple report as a current asset (*a*) on September 30, 2017? (*b*) On September 24, 2016?
2. Inventories make up what percent of total assets (*a*) on September 30, 2017? (*b*) On September 24, 2016?
3. Assuming Apple has enough inventory to meet demand, does Apple prefer inventory to be a lower or higher percentage of total assets?
4. Compute (*a*) inventory turnover for fiscal year ended September 30, 2017, and (*b*) days' sales in inventory as of September 30, 2017.

AA 5-2   Comparative figures for **Apple** and **Google** follow.

	Apple			Google		
$ millions	Current Year	One Year Prior	Two Years Prior	Current Year	One Year Prior	Two Years Prior
Inventory.............	$ 4,855	$ 2,132	$ 2,349	$ 749	$ 268	$ 491
Cost of sales..........	141,048	131,376	140,089	45,583	35,138	28,164

Required

1. Compute inventory turnover for each company for the most recent two years shown.
2. Compute days' sales in inventory for each company for the three years shown.
3. In the current year, does (*a*) Apple's and (*b*) Google's inventory turnover underperform or outperform the industry (assumed) average of 15?

AA 5-3   Key figures for **Samsung** follow.

₩ millions	Current Year	One Year Prior	Two Years Prior
Inventory.............	₩ 24,983,355	₩ 18,353,503	₩ 18,811,794
Cost of sales..........	129,290,661	120,277,715	123,482,118

Required

1. Compute Samsung's (*a*) inventory turnover and (*b*) days' sales in inventory for the most recent two years.
2. Is Samsung's inventory turnover on a favorable or unfavorable trend?
3. In the current year, does Samsung's inventory turnover underperform or outperform the industry (assumed) average of 15?

Beyond the Numbers

BTN 5-1   Golf Challenge Corp. is a retail sports store carrying golf apparel and equipment. The store is at the end of its second year of operation and is struggling. A major problem is that its cost of inventory has continually increased in the past two years. In the first year of operations, the store assigned inventory costs using LIFO. A loan agreement the store has with its bank, its prime source of financing, requires the store to maintain a certain profit margin and current ratio. The store's owner is currently looking over Golf Challenge's preliminary financial statements for its second year. The numbers are not favorable. The only way the store can meet the financial ratios agreed on with the bank is to change from LIFO to FIFO. The store originally decided on LIFO because of its tax advantages. The owner recalculates ending inventory using FIFO and submits those numbers and statements to the loan officer for the required bank review. The owner thankfully reflects on the available latitude in choosing the inventory costing method.

Required

1. How does Golf Challenge's use of FIFO improve its net profit margin and current ratio?
2. Is the action by Golf Challenge's owner ethical? Explain.

BTN 5-2   You are a financial adviser with a client in the wholesale produce business that just completed its first year of operations. Due to weather conditions, the cost of acquiring produce to resell has escalated during the latter part of this period. Your client, Javonte Gish, mentions that because her business sells perishable goods, she has striven to maintain a FIFO flow of goods. Although sales are good, the increasing cost of inventory has put the business in a tight cash position. Gish has expressed concern regarding the ability of the business to meet income tax obligations.

Required

Prepare a memorandum that identifies, explains, and justifies the inventory method you recommend that Ms. Gish adopt.

BTN 5-3   Access the September 30, 2017, 10-K report for **Apple, Inc.** (ticker: AAPL), filed on November 3, 2017, from the EDGAR filings at **SEC.gov**.

Required

1. What products are manufactured by Apple?

2. What inventory method does Apple use? *Hint:* See Note 1 to its financial statements.

3. Compute its gross margin and gross margin ratio for the 2017 fiscal year. Comment on your computations—assume an industry average of 40% for the gross margin ratio.

4. Compute its inventory turnover and days' sales in inventory for the year ended September 30, 2017. Comment on your computations—assume an industry average of 15 for inventory turnover and 9 for days' sales in inventory.

BTN 5-4   Each team member has the responsibility to become an expert on an inventory method. This expertise will be used to facilitate teammates' understanding of the concepts relevant to that method.

1. Each learning team member should select an area for expertise by choosing one of the following inventory methods: specific identification, LIFO, FIFO, or weighted average.

Point: Step 1 allows four choices or areas for expertise. Larger teams will have some duplication of choice, but the specific identification method should not be duplicated.

2. Form expert teams made up of students who have selected the same area of expertise. The instructor will identify where each expert team will meet.

3. Using the following data, each expert team must collaborate to develop a presentation that illustrates the relevant concepts and procedures for its inventory method. Each team member must write the presentation in a format that can be shown to the learning team.

Data

The company uses a *perpetual* inventory system. It had the following beginning inventory and current-year purchases of its product.

Jan. 1	Beginning inventory	50 units @ $100 = $ 5,000
Jan. 14	Purchase	150 units @ $120 = 18,000
Apr. 30	Purchase	200 units @ $150 = 30,000
Sep. 26	Purchase	300 units @ $200 = 60,000

The company transacted sales on the following dates at a $350 per unit sales price.

Jan. 10	30 units..........	specific cost: 30 @ $100
Feb. 15	100 units..........	specific cost: 100 @ $120
Oct. 5	350 units..........	specific cost: 100 @ $150 and 250 @ $200

Concepts and Procedures to Illustrate in Expert Presentation

a. Identify and compute the costs to assign to the units sold. (Round per unit costs to three decimals.)

b. Identify and compute the costs to assign to the units in ending inventory. (Round inventory balances to the dollar.)

c. How likely is it that this inventory costing method will reflect the actual physical flow of goods? How relevant is that factor in determining whether this is an acceptable method to use?

d. What is the impact of this method versus others in determining net income and income taxes?

e. How closely does the ending inventory amount reflect replacement cost?

4. Re-form learning teams. In rotation, each expert is to present to the team the presentation developed in part 3. Experts are to encourage and respond to questions.

BTN 5-5   Review the chapter's opening feature highlighting Danny Meyer and **Shake Shack**. Assume that the business consistently maintains an inventory level of $30,000, meaning that its average and ending inventory levels are the same. Also assume its annual cost of sales is $120,000. To cut costs, the business proposes to slash inventory to a constant level of $15,000 with no impact on cost of sales. The business plans to work with suppliers to get quicker deliveries and to order smaller quantities more often.

Required

1. Compute the company's inventory turnover and its days' sales in inventory under (*a*) current conditions and (*b*) proposed conditions.

2. Evaluate and comment on the merits of the proposal given your analysis for part 1. Identify any concerns you might have about the proposal.

BTN 5-6 Visit four retail stores with another classmate. In each store, identify whether the store uses a bar coding system to help manage its inventory. Try to find at least one store that does not use bar coding. If a store does not use bar coding, ask the store's manager or clerk whether he or she knows which type of inventory method the store employs. Create a table that shows columns for the name of store visited, type of merchandise sold, use or nonuse of bar coding, and the inventory method used if bar coding is not employed. You also might inquire as to what the store's inventory turnover is and how often physical inventory is taken.

HITTING THE ROAD

C1   C2

6 Cash, Fraud, and Internal Control

Chapter Preview

FRAUD AND INTERNAL CONTROL

C1 Purpose and principles of controls

Technology and controls

Limitations of controls

NTK 6-1

CONTROL OF CASH

C2 Definition and reporting of cash

P1 Control of cash receipts and cash payments

NTK 6-2

TOOLS OF CONTROL AND ANALYSIS

P2 Control of petty cash

P3 Bank reconciliation as a control tool

A1 Assessing liquidity

NTK 6-3, 6-4

Learning Objectives

CONCEPTUAL

C1 Define internal control and identify its purpose and principles.

C2 Define cash and cash equivalents and explain how to report them.

ANALYTICAL

A1 Compute the days' sales uncollected ratio and use it to assess liquidity.

PROCEDURAL

P1 Apply internal control to cash receipts and payments.

P2 Explain and record petty cash fund transactions.

P3 Prepare a bank reconciliation.

P4 *Appendix 6A*—Describe use of documentation and verification to control cash payments.

Taking Care of Business

©Jin Lee/Bloomberg/Getty Images

"Take the risks"—**SHEILA MARCELO**

WALTHAM, MA—Sheila Marcelo was in college when her first child was born. "We had to scramble for child care throughout our college years," recalls Sheila. "It was harder than it should have been."

The struggle to find child care led Sheila to start **Care.com** (**Care.com**). Care.com matches caregivers with families online.

A key part of Care.com's business is its internal control systems. Sheila explains that controls are important to Care.com's future, to the integrity of its systems, and to the trust of its members. Her controls extend to monitoring transactions and safeguarding its assets and members.

Sheila insists that controls raise productivity, cut expenses, reduce fraud, and enhance the member experience. "People fear finance [and accounting] courses," admits Sheila. "[But] if you want to be an entrepreneur," declares Sheila, "don't underestimate the value of skills learned in those classes."

Sheila offers two suggestions for pursuing a business. First, "don't worry about how you're being perceived . . . about fitting into the mold." Second, "to grow in leadership, you have to be a narcissist." Adds Sheila, "Focus on yourself, understand yourself, take time for yourself. It will make you a better leader."

Sources: *Care.com website,* January 2019; *EAK,* October 2016; *Business Insider,* March 2014; *Boston Globe,* August 2014; *Bloomberg,* September 2012

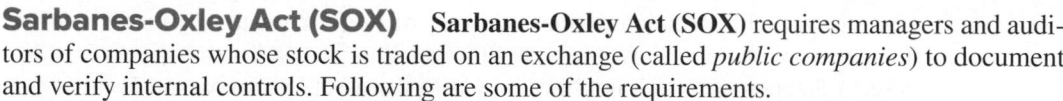

FRAUD AND INTERNAL CONTROL

Purpose of Internal Control

Managers or owners of small businesses often control the entire operation. They know if the business is actually receiving the assets and services it paid for. Most companies, however, cannot maintain personal supervision and must rely on internal controls.

C1
Define internal control and identify its purpose and principles.

Internal Control System   Managers use an internal control system to monitor and control business activities. An **internal control system** is policies and procedures used to

- Protect assets.
- Ensure reliable accounting.
- Promote efficient operations.
- Uphold company policies.

Managers use internal control systems to prevent avoidable losses, plan operations, and monitor company and employee performance. For example, internal controls for **UnitedHealth Group** protect patient records and privacy.

©Wright Studio/Shutterstock

Sarbanes-Oxley Act (SOX)   Sarbanes-Oxley Act (SOX) requires managers and auditors of companies whose stock is traded on an exchange (called *public companies*) to document and verify internal controls. Following are some of the requirements.

- The company must have effective internal controls.
- Auditors must evaluate internal controls.
- Violators receive harsh penalties—up to 25 years in prison with fines.
- Auditors' work is overseen by the *Public Company Accounting Oversight Board* (PCAOB).

Committee of Sponsoring Organizations (COSO)   Committee of Sponsoring Organizations (COSO) lists five ingredients of internal control that add to the quality of accounting information.

- **Control environment**—company structure, ethics, and integrity for internal control.
- **Risk assessment**—identify, analyze, and manage risk factors.
- **Control activities**—policies and procedures to reduce risk of loss.
- **Information & communication**—reports to internal and external parties.
- **Monitoring**—regular review of internal control effectiveness.

Principles of Internal Control

Internal control varies from company to company, but internal control principles apply to all companies. The **principles of internal control** are to

1. Establish responsibilities.
2. Maintain adequate records.
3. Insure assets and bond key employees.
4. Separate recordkeeping from custody of assets.
5. Divide responsibility for related transactions.
6. Apply technological controls.
7. Perform regular and independent reviews.

A control system is only as strong as its weakest link

Point: Many companies have a mandatory vacation policy for employees who handle cash. When another employee must cover for the one on vacation, it is more difficult to hide cash frauds.

Establish Responsibilities   Responsibility for a task should be clearly established and assigned to one person. When a problem occurs in a company where responsibility is not established, determining who is at fault is difficult. For example, if two salesclerks share the same cash register and cash is missing, neither clerk can be held accountable. To prevent this problem, a company can use separate cash drawers for each clerk.

Maintain Adequate Records   Good recordkeeping helps protect assets and helps managers monitor company activities. When there are detailed records of equipment, for example, items are unlikely to be lost or stolen without detection. Similarly, transactions are less likely to be entered in wrong accounts if a chart of accounts is used. Preprinted forms are also part of good internal control. When sales slips are properly designed, employees can record information efficiently with fewer errors. When sales slips are prenumbered, each slip is the responsibility of one salesperson, preventing the salesperson from stealing cash by making a sale and destroying the sales slip. Computerized point-of-sale systems achieve the same control results.

Courtesy of Commercial Collection Agency Association of the Commercial Law League of America

Point: ACFE estimates that employee fraud costs more than $150,000 per incident.

Insure Assets and Bond Key Employees   Assets should be insured against losses, and employees handling lots of cash and easily transferable assets should be bonded. An employee is *bonded* when a company purchases an insurance policy, or a bond, against theft by that employee. Bonding discourages theft because bonded employees know the bonding company will pursue reported theft.

Separate Recordkeeping from Custody of Assets   A person who controls or has access to an asset must not have access to that asset's accounting records. This principle reduces the risk of theft or waste of an asset because the person with control over it knows that another person keeps its records. Also, a recordkeeper who does not have access to the asset has no reason to falsify records. This means that to steal an asset and hide the theft from the records, two or more people must *collude*—or agree in secret to commit the fraud.

Divide Responsibility for Related Transactions   Responsibility for a transaction should be divided between two or more individuals or departments. This ensures the work of one person acts as a check on the other to prevent fraud and errors. This principle, called *separation of duties,* does not mean duplication of work. For example, when a company orders inventory, the task should be split among several employees. One employee submits a request to purchase inventory, a second employee approves the request, a third employee makes the payment, and a fourth employee records the transaction.

Apply Technological Controls   Cash registers, time clocks, and ID scanners are examples of devices that can improve internal control. A cash register with a locked-in tape or electronic file makes a record of each cash sale. A time clock records the exact hours worked by an employee. ID scanners limit access to authorized individuals.

Perform Regular and Independent Reviews   Regular reviews of internal controls help ensure that procedures are followed. These reviews are preferably done by auditors not directly involved in the activities. Auditors evaluate the efficiency and effectiveness of internal controls. Many companies pay for audits by independent auditors. These auditors test the company's financial records and evaluate the effectiveness of internal controls.

 Decision Maker

Entrepreneur   As owner of a start-up surfboard company, you hire a systems analyst. The analyst sees that your company employs only two workers. She says that as owner you must serve as a compensating control. What does the analyst mean? ■   *Answer:* Transaction authorization, recording, and asset custody are ideally handled by three employees. Many small businesses do not employ three workers. In such cases, an owner must make sure that the lack of separation of duties does not result in fraud.

©EpicStockMedia/iStockphoto/ Getty Images

Technology, Fraud, and Internal Control

Principles of internal control are relevant no matter what the technological state of the accounting system, from manual to fully automated. Technology allows us quicker access to information and improves managers' abilities to monitor and control business activities. This section describes technological impacts we must be alert to.

Reduced Processing Errors   Technology reduces, but does not eliminate, errors in processing information. Less human involvement can cause data entry errors to go undiscovered. Also, errors in software can produce consistent but inaccurate processing of transactions.

Point: Internal control failure reduces confidence in financial statements.

More Extensive Testing of Records   When accounting records are kept manually, only small samples of data are usually checked for accuracy. When data are accessible using technology, large samples or even the entire database can be tested quickly.

New Evidence of Processing   Technology makes it possible to record additional transaction details not possible with manual systems. For example, a system can record who made the entry, the date and time, the source of the entry, and so on. This means that internal control depends more on the design and operation of the information system and less on the analysis of its resulting documents.

Point: To assess a company's internal controls, review the auditor's report, management report on controls (if available), management discussion and analysis, and financial press.

Separation of Duties   A company with few employees risks losing separation of duties. For example, the person who designs the information system should not operate it. The company also must separate control over programs and files from the activities related to cash receipts and payments. For example, a computer operator should not control check-writing activities.

Increased E-Commerce   **Amazon** and **eBay** are examples of successful e-commerce companies. All e-commerce transactions involve at least three risks: (1) credit card number theft, (2) computer viruses, and (3) impersonation or identity theft. Companies use technological internal controls to combat these risks.

 Decision Insight

Butterfingers   Internal control failures can cost a company and its customers millions. Amazon learned the hard way when its web services failed. This failure led hundreds of websites to slow down. Reports say this failure cost companies in the S&P 500 index $150 million. The culprit? A typo in Amazon's code. ■

Limitations of Internal Control

Internal controls have limitations from (1) human error or fraud and (2) the cost-benefit principle.

   Human error occurs from carelessness, misjudgment, or confusion. *Human fraud* is intentionally defeating internal controls, such as management override, for personal gain. Human fraud is driven by the *triple threat* of fraud.

- **Opportunity**—internal control weaknesses in a business.
- **Pressure**—financial, family, and societal stresses to succeed.
- **Rationalization**—employees justifying fraudulent behavior.

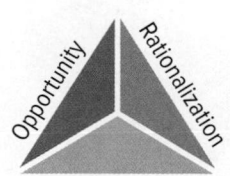

Financial Pressure

The *cost-benefit principle* says that the costs of internal controls must not exceed their benefits. Analysis of costs and benefits considers all factors, including morale. For example, most companies have a legal right to read employees' e-mails but rarely do unless there is evidence of potential harm.

Hacker's Guide to Cyberspace

Pharming Viruses attached to e-mails and websites monitor keystrokes; when you sign on to financial websites, it steals your passwords.

Phishing Hackers send e-mails to you posing as banks; you are asked for information using fake websites where they steal your passwords and personal data.

Wi-Phishing Cybercrooks set up wireless networks hoping you will use them to connect to the web; passwords and data are stolen when you connect.

Bot-Networking Hackers send out spam and viruses from your PC.

Typo-Squatting Hackers set up websites with addresses similar to legit businesses; when you make a typo and hit their sites, they infect your PC.

NEED-TO-KNOW 6-1

Internal Controls

C1

Identify each of the following as a (a) purpose of an internal control system, (b) principle of internal control, or (c) limitation of internal control.

____ **1.** Protect assets
____ **2.** Establish responsibilities
____ **3.** Human error
____ **4.** Maintain adequate records
____ **5.** Apply technological controls
____ **6.** Ensure reliable accounting
____ **7.** Insure assets and bond key employees
____ **8.** Human fraud
____ **9.** Separate recordkeeping from custody of assets
____ **10.** Divide responsibility for related transactions
____ **11.** Cost-benefit principle
____ **12.** Promote efficient operations
____ **13.** Perform regular and independent reviews
____ **14.** Uphold company policies

Solution

1. a **2.** b **3.** c **4.** b **5.** b **6.** a **7.** b **8.** c **9.** b **10.** b **11.** c **12.** a **13.** b **14.** a

Do More: QS 6-1, E 6-1, E 6-2, E 6-3, P 6-1

CONTROL OF CASH

C2 _____

Define cash and cash equivalents and explain how to report them.

Cash is easily hidden and moved. Internal controls protect cash and meet three guidelines.

1. Handling cash is separate from recordkeeping of cash.
2. Cash receipts are promptly deposited in a bank.
3. Cash payments are made by check or electronic funds transfer (EFT).

The first guideline applies separation of duties to minimize errors and fraud. When duties are separated, two or more people must collude to steal cash and hide this action. The second guideline uses immediate deposits of all cash receipts to produce an independent record of the cash received. It also reduces the chance of cash theft (or loss). The third guideline uses payments by check to develop an independent record of cash payments. It also reduces the risk of cash theft (or loss).

Cash, Cash Equivalents, and Liquidity

Liquidity refers to a company's ability to pay for its current liabilities. Cash and similar assets are called **liquid assets** because they can be readily used to pay for liabilities.

Cash includes currency, coins, and deposits in bank accounts. Cash also includes items that can be deposited in these accounts such as customer checks, cashier's checks, certified checks, and money orders. **Cash equivalents** are short-term, highly liquid investment assets meeting two criteria: (1) readily convertible to a known cash amount and (2) close enough to their due date so that their market value will not greatly change. Only investments within three months of their due date usually meet these criteria. Cash equivalents are short-term investments such as U.S. Treasury bills. Most companies combine cash equivalents with cash on the balance sheet.

Point: The most liquid assets are usually reported first on a balance sheet; the least liquid assets are reported last.

Point: Companies invest idle cash in cash equivalents to increase income.

Cash Management

A common reason companies fail is inability to manage cash. Companies must plan both cash receipts and cash payments. Goals of cash management are to

1. Plan cash receipts to meet cash payments when due.
2. Keep a minimum level of cash necessary to operate.

The *treasurer* is responsible for cash management. Effective cash management involves applying the following cash management strategies.

- **Encourage collection of receivables.** The quicker customers and others pay the company, the quicker it can use the money. Some companies offer discounts for quicker payments.
- **Delay payment of liabilities.** The more delayed a company is in paying others, the more time it has to use the money. Companies regularly wait to pay bills until the last day allowed.
- **Keep only necessary assets.** Acquiring expensive and rarely used assets can cause cash shortages. Some companies lease warehouses or rent equipment to avoid large up-front payments.
- **Plan expenditures.** Companies must look at seasonal and business cycles to plan expenditures when money is available.
- **Invest excess cash.** Excess cash earns no return and should be invested in productive assets like factories. Excess cash from seasonal cycles can be placed in a short-term investment for interest.

Control of Cash Receipts

Internal control of cash receipts ensures that cash received is properly recorded and deposited. Cash receipts arise from transactions such as cash sales, collections of customer accounts, receipts of interest, bank loans, sales of assets, and owner investments. This section explains internal control over two types of cash receipts: over-the-counter and by mail.

P1

Apply internal control to cash receipts and payments.

Over-the-Counter Cash Receipts

Over-the-counter cash sales should be recorded on a cash register after each sale, and customers should get a receipt. Cash registers should hold a permanent, locked-in record of each transaction. The register is often linked with the accounting system. Less advanced registers record each transaction on a paper tape or electronic file locked inside the register.

Custody over cash should be separate from recordkeeping. The clerk who has access to cash in the register should not have access to its record. At the end of the clerk's work period, the clerk should count the cash in the register, record the amount, and turn over the cash and record to the company cashier. The cashier, like the clerk, has access to the cash but should not have access to accounting records (or the register tape or file). A third employee, often a supervisor, compares the record of total register transactions with the cash receipts reported by the cashier. This record is used for a journal entry recording over-the-counter cash receipts. The third employee has access to the records for cash but not to the actual cash. The clerk and the cashier have access to cash but not to the accounting

Point: Many businesses have signs that read: If you receive no receipt, your purchase is free! This helps ensure that clerks ring up all transactions on registers.

records. None of them can make a mistake or steal cash without the difference being noticed (see the following diagram).

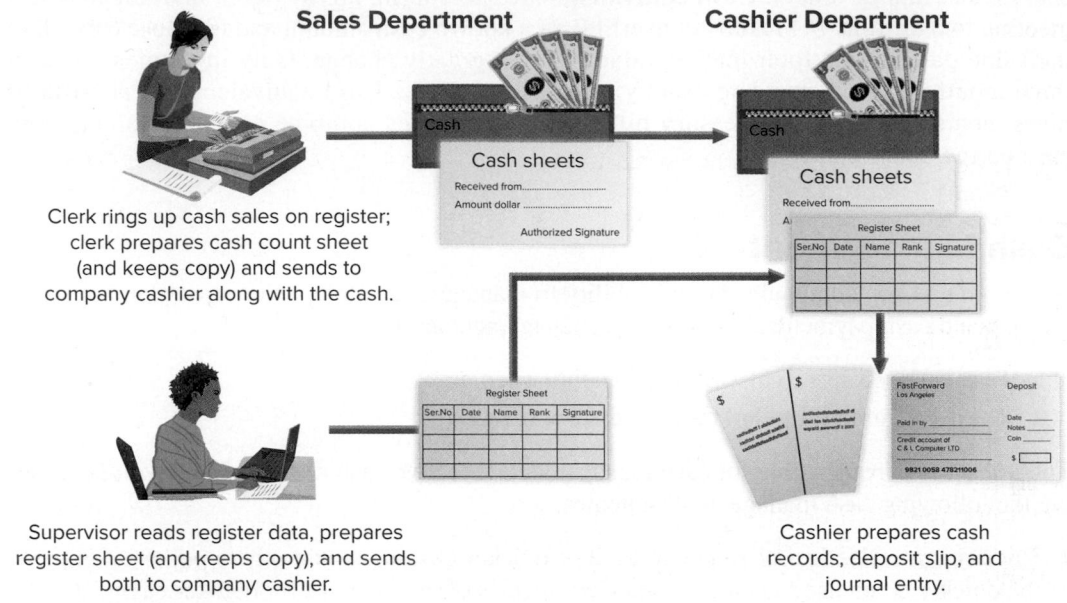

Sales Department

Clerk rings up cash sales on register; clerk prepares cash count sheet (and keeps copy) and sends to company cashier along with the cash.

Supervisor reads register data, prepares register sheet (and keeps copy), and sends both to company cashier.

Cashier Department

Cashier prepares cash records, deposit slip, and journal entry.

Cash Over and Short

One or more customers can be given too much or too little change. This means that at the end of a work period, the cash in a cash register might not equal the record of cash receipts. This difference is reported in the **Cash Over and Short** account, also called *Cash Short and Over,* which is an income statement account recording the income effects of cash overages and cash shortages. If a cash register's record shows $550 but the count of cash in the register is $555, the entry to record cash sales and its overage is

Assets = Liabilities + Equity
+555   +   5
                   +550

Cash..	555	
Cash Over and Short		**5**
Sales...		550
Record cash sales and a cash overage.		

Alternatively, if a cash register's record shows $625 but the count of cash in the register is $621, the entry to record cash sales and its shortage is

Assets = Liabilities + Equity
+621   –   4
                   +625

Cash..	621	
Cash Over and Short.................................	**4**	
Sales...		625
Record cash sales and a cash shortage.		

Because customers are more likely to dispute being shortchanged than being given too much change, the Cash Over and Short account usually has a debit balance. A debit balance reflects an expense. It is reported on the income statement as part of selling, general, and administrative expenses. (Because the amount is usually small, it is often reported as part of *miscellaneous expenses*—or as part of *miscellaneous revenues* if it has a credit balance.)

Cash Receipts by Mail

Two people are assigned the task of opening the mail. In this case, theft of cash receipts by mail requires collusion between these two employees. The person(s) opening the mail enters a list (in triplicate) of money received. This list has each sender's name, the amount, and an explanation of why the money was sent. The first copy is sent with the money to the cashier. A second copy is sent to the recordkeeper. A third copy is kept by the person(s) who opened the mail. The cashier deposits the money in a bank, and the recordkeeper records the amounts received.

This process is good internal control because the bank's record of cash deposited must agree with the records from each of the three. If the mail person(s) does not report all receipts correctly, customers will question their account balances. If the cashier does not deposit all the cash, the bank balance does not agree with the recordkeeper's cash balance. The recordkeeper does not have access to cash and has no opportunity to steal cash. This system makes errors and fraud highly unlikely. The exception is employee collusion.

Decision Insight

Cash Register Insight   Walmart uses a network of information links with its point-of-sale cash registers to coordinate sales, purchases, and distribution. Its stores ring up tens of thousands of separate sales on heavy days. By using cash register information, the company can fix pricing mistakes quickly and capitalize on sales trends. ■

©Amble Design/Shutterstock

Control of Cash Payments

Control of cash payments is important as most large thefts occur from payment of fictitious invoices. One key to controlling cash payments is to require all payments to be made by check. The only exception is small payments made from petty cash. Another key is to deny access to accounting records to anyone other than the owner who has the authority to sign checks. A small-business owner often signs checks and knows that the items being paid for are actually received. Large businesses cannot maintain personal supervision and must rely on internal controls described here, including the voucher system and petty cash system.

Cash Budget   Projected cash receipts and cash payments are summarized in a *cash budget*. If there is enough cash for operations, companies wish to minimize the cash they hold because of its risk of theft and its low return versus other assets.

Voucher System of Control   A **voucher system** is a set of procedures and approvals designed to control cash payments and the acceptance of liabilities that consist of

- Verifying, approving, and recording liabilities for cash payment.
- Issuing checks for payment of verified, approved, and recorded liabilities.

A voucher system's control over cash payments begins when a company incurs a liability that will result in cash payment. The system only allows authorized departments and individuals to incur liabilities and limits the type of liabilities. In a large retail store, for example, only a purchasing department is authorized to incur liabilities for inventory. Purchasing, receiving, and paying for merchandise are divided among several departments (or individuals). These departments include the one requesting the purchase, the purchasing department, the receiving department, and the accounting department.

To coordinate and control responsibilities of these departments, a company uses several different business documents. Exhibit 6.1 shows how documents are accumulated in a **voucher,** which is an internal document (or file) used to collect information to control cash payments and to ensure that a transaction is properly recorded. This specific example begins with a *purchase requisition* and ends with issuing a *check*.

Point: A purchase requisition is a request to purchase merchandise.

A voucher system should be applied to all payments (except those using petty cash). When a company receives a monthly telephone bill, it should review the charges, prepare a voucher (file), and insert the bill. This transaction is then recorded. If the amount is due, a check is issued. If not, the voucher is filed for payment on its due date. Without records, an employee could collude with a supplier to get more than one payment, payment for excessive amounts, or payment for goods and services not received. A voucher system helps prevent such frauds.

Ethical Risk

Cash Fraud   The Association of Certified Fraud Examiners (ACFE) reports that 87% of fraud is from asset theft. Of those asset thefts, a few stand out—in both frequency and median loss. Namely, cash is most frequently stolen through billing (22%) and theft (20%), followed by expense reimbursements (14%), skimming (12%), check tampering (11%), and payroll (9%). Interestingly, the average loss per incident is greatest for check tampering ($158,000) and billing ($100,000). *Source:* "Report to the Nations," ACFE. ■

EXHIBIT 6.1

Document Flow in
a Voucher System

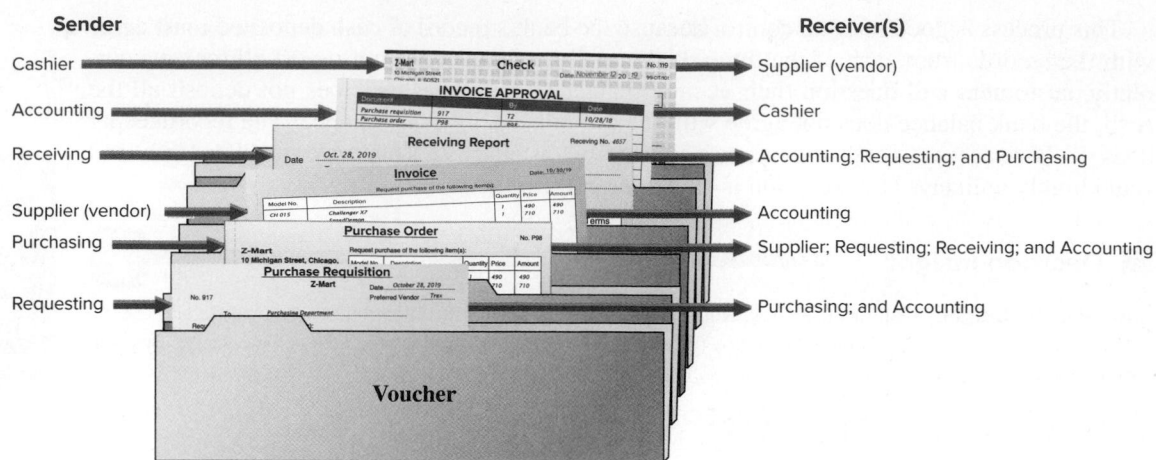

NEED-TO-KNOW 6-2

Control of Cash Receipts
and Payments

P1 C2

Do More: QS 6-2, QS 6-4,
QS 6-5, E 6-4, E 6-5, E 6-6,
E 6-7

Which of the following statements are true regarding the control of cash receipts and cash payments?

_____ **1.** Over-the-counter cash sales should be recorded on a cash register after each sale.

_____ **2.** Custody over cash should be separate from the recordkeeping of cash.

_____ **3.** For control of cash receipts that arrive through the mail, two people should be present for opening that mail.

_____ **4.** One key to controlling cash payments is to require that no expenditures be made by check; instead, all expenditures should be made from petty cash.

_____ **5.** A voucher system of control should be applied only to purchases of inventory and never to other expenditures.

Solution

1. True   **2.** True   **3.** True   **4.** False   **5.** False

---

P2 _____

Explain and record petty
cash fund transactions.

Petty Cash System of Control   To avoid writing checks for small amounts, a company sets up a **petty cash** system. *Petty cash payments* are small payments for items such as shipping fees, minor repairs, and low-cost supplies.

Operating a Petty Cash Fund   A petty cash fund requires estimating the amount of small payments to be made during a short period such as a week or month. A check is then drawn by the company cashier for an amount slightly in excess of this estimate. The check is cashed and given to an employee called the *petty cashier* or *petty cash custodian*. The petty cashier keeps this cash safe, makes payments from the fund, and keeps records of it in a secure *petty cashbox*.

EXHIBIT 6.2

Petty Cash Receipt

Z-Mart   No. 9
PETTY CASH RECEIPT

For *Office supplies used*
Date *November 15, 2019*
Charge to *Office Supplies Exp.*
Amount *$4.75*
Approved by *JL Gale*

Received by *DL Fall*

Point: Companies use surprise
petty cash counts for verification.

When a cash payment is made, the person receiving payment signs a prenumbered *petty cash receipt,* also called *petty cash ticket*—see Exhibit 6.2. The petty cash receipt is then placed in the petty cashbox with the remaining money. Under this system, the total of all receipts plus the remaining cash equals the total fund amount. A $100 petty cash fund, for example, contains any combination of cash and petty cash receipts that totals $100 (examples are $80 cash plus $20 in receipts, or $10 cash plus $90 in receipts).

The petty cash fund is reimbursed when it is nearing zero and at the end of an accounting period. The petty cashier sorts the paid receipts by the type of expense or account and then totals the receipts. The petty cashier gives all paid receipts to the company cashier, who stamps all receipts *paid* so they cannot be reused, files them for recordkeeping, and gives the petty cashier a check. When this check is cashed and the money placed in the cashbox, the total money in the cashbox is restored to its original amount. The fund is now ready for a new cycle of petty cash payments.

Illustrating a Petty Cash Fund Assume Z-Mart sets up a petty cash fund on November 1. A $75 check is drawn, cashed, and the proceeds given to the petty cashier. The entry to record the setup of this petty cash fund is

Nov. 1	Petty Cash	75	
	Cash		75
	Establish a petty cash fund.		

Assets = Liabilities + Equity
+75
−75

After the petty cash fund is established, the Petty Cash account is not debited or credited again unless the amount of the fund is changed.

Next, assume that Z-Mart's petty cashier makes several November payments from petty cash. On November 27, after making a $46.50 cash payment for tile cleaning, only $3.70 cash remains in the fund. The petty cashier then summarizes and totals the petty cash receipts as shown in Exhibit 6.3.

Petty Cash Payments Report	
Miscellaneous Expense	
Nov. 27 Tile cleaning	$ 46.50
Merchandise Inventory (transportation-in)	
Nov. 5 Transport of merchandise purchased	15.05
Delivery Expense	
Nov. 18 Customer's package delivered	5.00
Office Supplies Expense	
Nov. 15 Purchase of office supplies immediately used	4.75
Total	**$71.30**

EXHIBIT 6.3

Petty Cash Payments Report

Point: This report also can include receipt number and names of those who approved and received cash payment (see **Need-to-Know 6-3**).

The petty cash payments report and all receipts are given to the company cashier in exchange for a $71.30 check to reimburse the fund. The petty cashier cashes the check and puts the $71.30 cash in the petty cashbox. The company records this reimbursement as follows. A petty cash fund is usually reimbursed at the end of an accounting period so that expenses are recorded in the proper period, even if the fund is not low on money.

Nov. 27	Miscellaneous Expenses..................................	46.50	
	Merchandise Inventory	15.05	
	Delivery Expense..	5.00	
	Office Supplies Expense	4.75	
	Cash*..		71.30
	*Reimburse petty cash. *$75 fund bal. − $3.70 cash remaining.*		

Assets = Liabilities + Equity
−71.30   −46.50
+15.05   − 5.00
               − 4.75

Increasing or Decreasing a Petty Cash Fund A decision to increase or decrease a petty cash fund is often made when reimbursing it. Assume Z-Mart decides to *increase* its petty cash fund from $75 to $100 on November 27 when it reimburses the fund. The entries required are to (1) reimburse the fund as usual (see the preceding November 27 entry) and (2) increase the fund amount as follows.

Nov. 27	Petty Cash	25	
	Cash		25
	Increase petty cash fund from $75 to $100.		

Instead, if it *decreases* the petty cash fund from $75 to $55 on November 27, the entry is

Nov. 27	Cash..	20	
	Petty Cash...		20
	Decrease petty cash fund from $75 to $55.		

Summary of Petty Cash Accounting			
Event	Petty Cash	Cash	Expenses
Set up fund	Dr.	Cr.	—
Reimburse fund.	—	Cr.	Dr.
Increase fund	Dr.	Cr.	—
Decrease fund.	Cr.	Dr.	—

$200 Petty Cash Fund

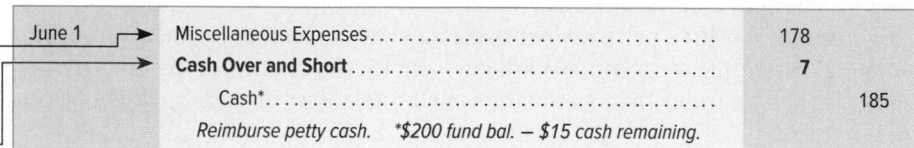

$15 Cash $7 Short $178 Receipts

Cash Over and Short   Sometimes a petty cashier fails to get a receipt for payment or overpays for the amount due. When this occurs and the fund is later reimbursed, the petty cash payments report plus the cash remaining will not equal the fund balance. This mistake causes the fund to be *short*. This shortage is recorded as an expense in the reimbursing entry with a debit to the Cash Over and Short account. (An *overage* in the petty cash fund is recorded with a credit to Cash Over and Short in the reimbursing entry.)

Following is the June 1 entry to reimburse a $200 petty cash fund when its payments report shows $178 in miscellaneous expenses and only $15 cash remains.

June 1	Miscellaneous Expenses.	178	
	Cash Over and Short.	7	
	Cash*.		185
	*Reimburse petty cash. *$200 fund bal. − $15 cash remaining.*		

Ethical Risk

Get Clued In   There are clues to fraudulent activities. Clues from accounting include (1) an increase in customer refunds—could be fake, (2) missing documents—could be used for fraud, (3) differences between bank deposits and cash receipts—could be cash embezzled, and (4) delayed recording—could reflect fraudulent records. Clues from employees include (1) lifestyle change—could be embezzlement, (2) too close with suppliers—could signal fraudulent transactions, and (3) refusal to leave job, even for vacations—could conceal fraudulent activities. ■

NEED-TO-KNOW 6-3

Petty Cash System

P2

Bacardi Company established a $150 petty cash fund with Eminem as the petty cashier. When the fund balance reached $19 cash, Eminem prepared a petty cash payments report, which follows.

Petty Cash Payments Report				
Receipt No.	Account Charged		Approved by	Received by
12	Delivery Expense	$ 29	Eminem	A. Smirnoff
13	Merchandise Inventory	18	Eminem	J. Daniels
15	(Omitted).	32	Eminem	C. Carlsberg
16	Miscellaneous Expense	41	(Omitted)	J. Walker
	Total	$120		

Required

1. Identify four internal control weaknesses from the petty cash payments report.

2. Prepare general journal entries to record
   a. Establishment of the petty cash fund.
   b. Reimbursement of the fund. (Assume for this part only that petty cash Receipt No. 15 was issued for miscellaneous expenses.)

3. What is the Petty Cash account balance immediately before reimbursement? After reimbursement?

Solution

1. Four internal control weaknesses that are apparent from the payments report include
   a. Petty cash Receipt No. 14 is missing. This raises questions about the petty cashier's management of the fund.
   b. The $19 cash balance means that $131 has been withdrawn ($150 − $19 = $131). However, the total amount of the petty cash receipts is only $120 ($29 + $18 + $32 + $41). The fund is $11 short of cash ($131 − $120 = $11). Management should investigate.
   c. The petty cashier (Eminem) did not sign petty cash Receipt No. 16. This could have been a mistake on his part or he might not have authorized the payment.
   d. Petty cash Receipt No. 15 does not say which account to charge. Management should check with C. Carlsberg and the petty cashier (Eminem) about the transaction. Without further information, debit Miscellaneous Expense.

2. Petty cash general journal entries.

    a. Entry to establish the petty cash fund.
    b. Entry to reimburse the fund.

Petty Cash..........................	150
Cash..........................	150

Delivery Expense	29	
Merchandise Inventory	18	
Miscellaneous Expense ($41 + $32)	73	
Cash Over and Short	11	
Cash ($150 fund bal. − $19 cash rem.).....		131

3. The Petty Cash account balance *always* equals its fund balance, in this case $150. This account balance does not change unless the fund is increased or decreased.

> Do More: QS 6-6, E 6-8, E 6-9, E 6-10, P 6-2, P 6-3

BANKING ACTIVITIES AS CONTROLS

Basic Bank Services

Banks safeguard cash and provide detailed records of cash transactions. They provide services and documents that help control cash, which is the focus of this section.

Bank Account, Deposit, and Check   A *bank account* is used to deposit money for safekeeping and helps control withdrawals. Persons authorized to write checks on the account must sign a **signature card,** which the bank uses to verify signatures.

    Each bank deposit has a **deposit ticket,** which lists items such as currency, coins, and checks deposited along with amounts. The bank gives the customer a receipt as proof of the deposit. Exhibit 6.4 shows a deposit ticket.

Point: Firms often have multiple bank accounts for different needs and for specific transactions such as payroll.

EXHIBIT 6.4

Deposit Ticket

To withdraw money, the depositor can use a **check,** which is a document telling the bank to pay a specified amount to a designated recipient. A check involves three parties: a *maker* who signs the check, a *payee* who is the recipient, and a *bank* (or *payer*) on which the check is drawn. The bank provides the depositor the checks. Exhibit 6.5 shows one type of check. It has an optional *remittance advice* explaining the payment. The *memo* line is used for an explanation.

Electronic Funds Transfer   **Electronic funds transfer (EFT)** is the electronic transfer of cash from one party to another. Companies are increasingly using EFT because of its convenience and low cost. Payroll, rent, utilities, insurance, and interest payments are usually done by EFT. The bank statement lists cash withdrawals by EFT with the checks and other deductions. Cash receipts by EFT are listed with deposits and other additions.

EXHIBIT 6.5

Check with Remittance
Advice

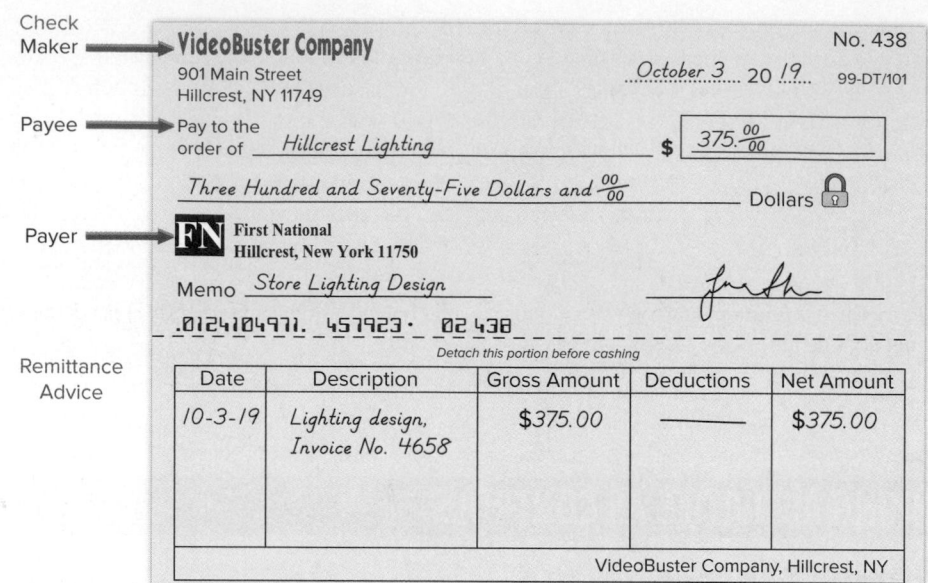

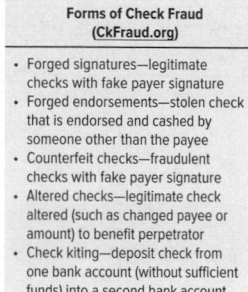

Forms of Check Fraud
(CkFraud.org)

- Forged signatures—legitimate checks with fake payer signature
- Forged endorsements—stolen check that is endorsed and cashed by someone other than the payee
- Counterfeit checks—fraudulent checks with fake payer signature
- Altered checks—legitimate check altered (such as changed payee or amount) to benefit perpetrator
- Check kiting—deposit check from one bank account (without sufficient funds) into a second bank account

Bank Statement

Point: Good control is to send a copy of the bank statement directly to a party without access to cash or recordkeeping.

Usually once a month, the bank sends a **bank statement** showing the account activity. Different banks use different formats for their bank statements, but all of them include the following.

1. Beginning-of-period account balance.
2. Checks and other debits decreasing the account during the period.
3. Deposits and other credits increasing the account during the period.
4. End-of-period account balance.

Exhibit 6.6 shows one type of bank statement. Part Ⓐ of Exhibit 6.6 summarizes changes in the account. Ⓑ lists paid checks along with other debits. Ⓒ lists deposits and credits to the account.

Canceled checks are checks the bank has paid and deducted from the customer's account. We say such checks *cleared the bank*. Other usual deductions on a bank statement include (1) bank

EXHIBIT 6.6

Bank Statement

Bank's Liability to VideoBuster

	Sep. 30 bal.	1,610
	CRs	1,163
DRs 723		
	Oct. 31 bal.	2,050

Point: Debit memos (DM) from the bank produce credits on the depositor's books. Credit memos (CM) from the bank produce debits on the depositor's books.

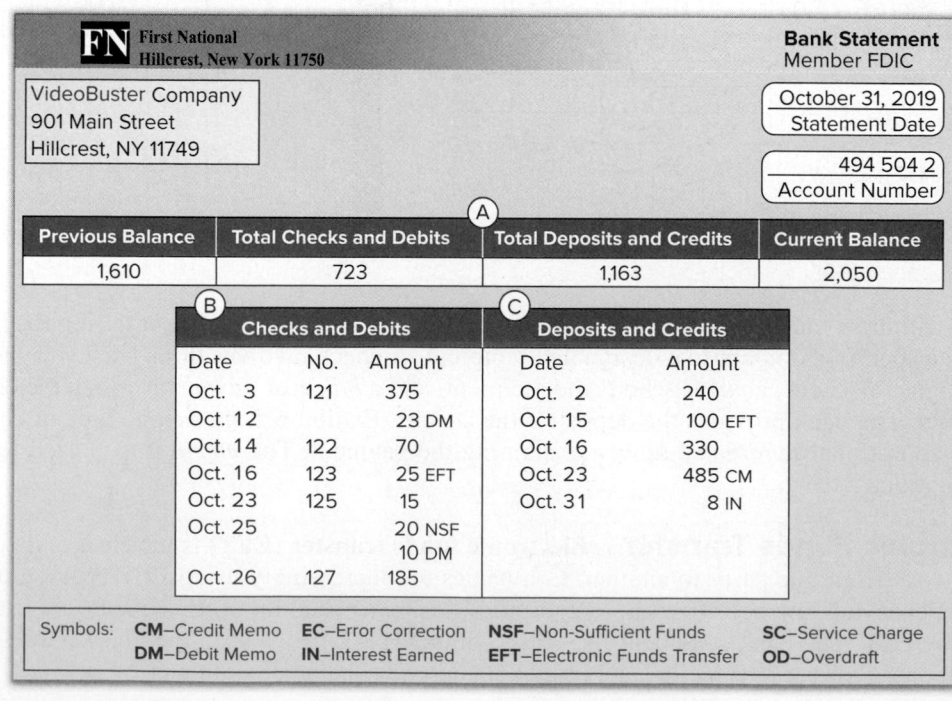

service fees, (2) checks deposited that are uncollectible, (3) corrections of previous errors, (4) withdrawals through automated teller machines (ATMs), and (5) payments arranged in advance by a depositor. A **debit memorandum** notifies a depositor of a deduction.

Increases to the depositor's account include amounts the bank collects on behalf of the depositor and the corrections of previous errors. A **credit memorandum** notifies the depositor of all increases. Banks that pay interest on checking accounts credit interest earned to the depositor's account each period. In Exhibit 6.6, the bank credits $8 of interest to the account.

Bank Reconciliation

The balance of a checking account on the bank statement rarely equals the depositor's book balance (from its records). This is due to information that one party has that the other does not. We must therefore verify the accuracy of both the depositor's records and the bank's records. To do this, we prepare a **bank reconciliation** to explain differences between the checking account balance in the depositor's records and the balance on the bank statement. The following explains bank and book adjustments.

Bank Balance Adjustments

+ **Deposits in transit** (or **outstanding deposits**). **Deposits in transit** are deposits made and recorded in the depositor's books but not yet listed on the bank statement. For example, companies can make deposits (in the night depository) after the bank is closed. If such a deposit occurred on a bank statement date, it would not appear on this period's statement. The bank would record such a deposit on the next business day, and it would appear on the next period's bank statement. Deposits mailed to the bank near the end of a period also can be in transit and not listed on the bank statement.

− **Outstanding checks. Outstanding checks** are checks written by the depositor, subtracted on the depositor's books, and sent to the payees but not yet turned in for payment at the bank statement date.

± **Bank errors.** Any errors made by the bank are accounted for in the reconciliation. To find errors, we (a) compare deposits on the bank statement with deposits in the accounting records and (b) compare canceled checks on the bank statement with checks recorded in the accounting records.

Book Balance Adjustments

+ **Interest earned and unrecorded cash receipts.** Banks sometimes collect notes for depositors. Banks also receive electronic funds transfers to the depositor's account. When a bank collects an item, it is added to the depositor's account, less any service fee. The bank statement also includes any interest earned.

− **Bank fees and NSF checks.** A company sometimes deposits another party's check that is uncollectible. This check is called a *nonsufficient funds (NSF)* check. The bank initially credits (increases) the depositor's account for the check. When the check is uncollectible, the bank debits (reduces) the depositor's account for that check. The bank may charge the depositor a fee for processing an uncollectible check. Other bank charges include printing new checks and service fees.

± **Book errors.** Any errors made by the depositor in the company books are accounted for in the reconciliation. To find errors, we use the same procedures described in the "Bank errors" section above.

Adjustments Summary   Following is a summary of bank and book adjustments. Each of these items has already been recorded by either the bank or the company, but not both.

Bank Balance Adjustments	Book Balance Adjustments
Add deposits in transit.	Add interest earned and unrecorded cash receipts.
Subtract outstanding checks.	Subtract bank fees and NSF checks.
Add or subtract corrections of bank errors.	Add or subtract corrections of book errors.

Point: Your checking account is a liability from the bank's perspective (but an asset from yours). When you make a deposit, they "credit your account." Credits increase the bank's liability to you. When you write a check or use your debit card, the bank decreases its liability to you; they "debit your account." Debits decrease the bank's liability to you.

P3 _____
Prepare a bank reconciliation.

Point: *Books* refer to accounting records.

Point: The person preparing the bank reconciliation should not be responsible for processing cash receipts, managing checks, or maintaining cash records.

Point: Businesses with few employees often allow record-keepers to both write checks and keep the general ledger. If this is done, the owner must do the bank reconciliation.

Bank Reconciliation Demonstration
In preparing the bank reconciliation, refer to Exhibit 6.7 and steps ❶ through ❽.

❶ Enter VideoBuster's bank balance of $2,050 taken from the bank statement.

❷ Add any unrecorded deposits and bank errors that understate the bank balance to the bank balance. VideoBuster's $145 deposit in the bank's night depository on October 31 is not listed on its bank statement.

Point: Outstanding checks are identified by comparing canceled checks on the bank statement with checks recorded. This includes identifying any outstanding checks listed on the *previous* period's bank reconciliation that are not included in the canceled checks on this period's bank statement.

❸ Subtract any outstanding checks and bank errors that overstate the bank balance from the bank balance. VideoBuster's comparison of canceled checks with its books shows two checks outstanding: No. 124 for $150 and No. 126 for $200.

❹ Compute the *adjusted bank balance.*

❺ Enter VideoBuster's cash account book balance of $1,405 taken from its accounting records.

❻ Add any unrecorded cash receipts, interest earned, and errors understating the book balance to the book balance. VideoBuster's bank statement shows the bank collected a note receivable and increased VideoBuster's account for $485. The bank statement also shows $8 for interest earned that was not yet recorded on the books.

❼ Subtract any unrecorded bank fees, NSF checks, and errors overstating the book balance from the book balance. Deductions on VideoBuster's bank statement that are not yet recorded include (a) a $23 charge for check printing and (b) an NSF check for $30. (The NSF check is dated October 16 and was in the book balance.)

❽ Compute the *adjusted book balance.*

Verify that the two adjusted balances from steps 4 and 8 are equal (reconciled).

EXHIBIT 6.7

Bank Reconciliation

	VIDEOBUSTER Bank Reconciliation October 31, 2019						
①	Bank statement balance...........		$ 2,050	⑤	Book balance......................		$ 1,405
②	Add			⑥	Add		
	Deposit of Oct. 31 in transit......		145		Collected note	$485	
			2,195		Interest earned.................	8	493
③	Deduct						1,898
	Outstanding checks			⑦	Deduct		
	No. 124....................	$150			Check printing charge	23	
	No. 126....................	200	350		NSF check.....................	30	53
④	**Adjusted bank balance...........**		**$1,845**	⑧	**Adjusted book balance............**		**$1,845**

Balances are equal (reconciled)

Adjusting Entries from a Bank Reconciliation
A bank reconciliation often finds unrecorded items that need recording by the company. In VideoBuster's reconciliation, the adjusted balance of $1,845 is the correct balance as of October 31. But the company's accounting records show a $1,405 balance. We make adjusting entries so that the book balance equals the adjusted balance. **Only items impacting the *book balance* need entries.** Exhibit 6.7 shows that four entries are required.

Collection of Note The first entry is to record collection of a note receivable by the bank.

Assets = Liabilities + Equity
+485
−485

Oct. 31	Cash	485	
	Notes Receivable		485
	Record note collected by bank.		

Interest Earned The second entry records interest earned.

Assets = Liabilities + Equity
+8   +8

Oct. 31	Cash	8	
	Interest Revenue...............................		8
	Record interest earned in checking account.		

Check Printing   The third entry records expenses for the check printing charge.

Oct. 31	Miscellaneous Expenses................................	23	
	Cash..		23
	Check printing charge.		

Assets = Liabilities + Equity
−23   −23

NSF Check   The fourth entry records the NSF check that is returned as uncollectible. The check was from T. Woods in payment of his account. The bank deducted $30 total from VideoBuster's account. This means the entry must reverse the effects of the original entry when the check was received.

Point: The company will try to collect the $30 from the customer.

Oct. 31	Accounts Receivable—T. Woods........................	30	
	Cash..		30
	Charge Woods's account for $30 NSF check.		

Assets = Liabilities + Equity
+30
−30

After these four entries are recorded, the book balance of cash is adjusted to the correct amount of $1,845 (the adjusted book balance). The Cash T-account to the side shows the computation, where entries match the steps in Exhibit 6.7.

Point: Need-to-Know 6-4 shows an adjusting entry for an error correction.

Cash			
Unadj. bal.	1,405		
⑥	485	⑦	23
⑥	8	⑦	30
Adj. bal.	1,845		

Ethical Risk

Cause for Alarm   The Association of Certified Fraud Examiners (ACFE) reports that the primary factor contributing to fraud is the lack of internal controls (30%), followed by the override of existing controls (19%), lack of management review (18%), poor tone at the top (10%), and lack of competent oversight (8%). These findings highlight the importance of internal controls over cash. *Source: "Report to the Nations," ACFE.* ∎

©Redpixel.pl/Shutterstock

The following information is available to reconcile Gucci's book balance of cash with its bank statement cash balance as of December 31.

a. The December 31 cash balance according to the accounting records is $1,610, and the bank statement cash balance for that date is $1,900.

b. Gucci's December 31 daily cash receipts of $800 were placed in the bank's night depository on December 31 but do not appear on the December 31 bank statement.

c. Gucci's comparison of canceled checks with its books shows three checks outstanding: No. 6242 for $200, No. 6273 for $400, and No. 6282 for $100.

d. When the December checks are compared with entries in the accounting records, it is found that Check No. 6267 had been correctly drawn (taken from the bank) for $340 to pay for office supplies but was erroneously entered in the accounting records as $430.

e. The bank statement shows the bank collected a note receivable and increased Gucci's account for $470. Gucci had not recorded this transaction before receiving the statement.

f. The bank statement included an NSF check for $150 received from Prada Inc. in payment of its account. It also included a $20 charge for check printing. Gucci had not recorded these transactions before receiving the statement.

NEED-TO-KNOW 6-4

Bank Reconciliation

P3

Required

1. Prepare the bank reconciliation for this company as of December 31.

2. Prepare the journal entries to make Gucci's book balance of cash equal to the reconciled cash balance as of December 31.

Solutions

Part 1

		GUCCI		
		Bank Reconciliation		
		December 31		

Bank statement balance............		$1,900	Book balance		$1,610
Add			Add		
Deposit of Dec. 31..............		800	Error (Ck. 6267)	$ 90	
		2,700	Collected note	470	560
					2,170
Deduct			Deduct		
Outstanding Checks No. 6242	$200		NSF check	150	
6273	400		Printing fee.............	20	
6282	100	700			170
Adjusted bank balance............		$2,000	Adjusted book balance		$2,000

> Do More: QS 6-7, QS 6-8, QS 6-9, E 6-11, E 6-12, E 6-13, E 6-14, P 6-4, P 6-5

Part 2

Dec. 31	Cash	90	
	Office Supplies		90
	Correct an entry error.		
Dec. 31	Cash	470	
	Notes Receivable		470
	Record note collection.		

Dec. 31	Accounts Receivable—Prada Inc.......	150	
	Cash.........................		150
	Charge account for NSF check.		
Dec. 31	Miscellaneous Expenses.............	20	
	Cash.........................		20
	Record check printing charge.		

 Decision Analysis  **Days' Sales Uncollected**

A1

Compute the days' sales uncollected ratio and use it to assess liquidity.

One measure of how quickly a company can convert its accounts receivable into cash is the **days' sales uncollected,** also called *days' sales in receivables*, which is defined in Exhibit 6.8.

EXHIBIT 6.8

Days' Sales Uncollected

$$\text{Days' sales uncollected} = \frac{\text{Accounts receivable}}{\text{Net sales}} \times 365$$

We use days' sales uncollected to estimate how much time is likely to pass before the current amount of accounts receivable is received in cash. It is used to determine if cash is being collected quickly enough to pay upcoming obligations.

Days' sales uncollected are shown for **Starbucks** and **Jack in the Box** in Exhibit 6.9.

EXHIBIT 6.9

Analysis Using Days' Sales Uncollected

Company	Figure ($ millions)	Current Year	1 Year Ago	2 Years Ago
Starbucks	Accounts receivable....................	$ 870	$ 769	$ 719
	Net sales............................	$22,387	$21,316	$19,163
	Days' sales uncollected	**14.2 days**	**13.2 days**	**13.7 days**
Jack in the Box	Accounts receivable....................	$ 69	$ 73	$ 48
	Net sales............................	$ 1,554	$ 1,599	$ 1,540
	Days' sales uncollected	**16.2 days**	**16.7 days**	**11.4 days**

Days' sales uncollected for Starbucks is 14.2 days for the current year, computed as ($870/$22,387) × 365 days. This means it takes 14.2 days to collect cash from ending accounts receivable. This number reflects one or more of the following factors: a company's ability to collect receivables, customer financial health, customer payment strategies, and discount terms. To further assess Starbucks, we compare it to Jack in the Box. We see that Starbucks's 14.2 days' sales uncollected is better than Jack in the Box's 16.2 days' sales uncollected for the current year. Starbucks took less time to collect its receivables. The less time money is tied up in receivables, the better.

■ Decision Maker

Sales Representative   The sales staff are told to help reduce days' sales uncollected for cash management purposes. What can you, a salesperson, do to reduce days' sales uncollected? ■   *Answer:* A salesperson can (1) push cash sales over credit, (2) identify customers most delayed in their payments and require earlier payments or cash sales, and (3) eliminate credit sales to customers that never pay.

Prepare a bank reconciliation for Jamboree Enterprises for the month ended November 30. The following information is available as of November 30.

a. On November 30, the company's book balance of cash is $16,380, but its bank statement shows a $38,520 balance.

b. Checks No. 2024 for $4,810 and No. 2026 for $5,000 are outstanding.

c. In comparing the canceled checks on the bank statement with the entries in the accounting records, it is found that Check No. 2025 in payment of rent is correctly drawn (taken from the bank) for $1,000 but is erroneously entered in the accounting records as $880.

d. The November 30 deposit of $17,150 was placed in the night depository after banking hours on that date, and this amount does not appear on the bank statement.

e. In reviewing the bank statement, a check written by Jumbo Enterprises in the amount of $160 was erroneously drawn against Jamboree's account.

f. The bank statement says that the bank collected a $30,000 note and $900 of interest was earned. These transactions were not recorded by Jamboree prior to receiving the statement.

g. The bank statement lists a $1,100 NSF check received from a customer, Marilyn Welch. Jamboree had not recorded the return of this check before receiving the statement.

h. Bank service charges for November total $40. These charges were not recorded by Jamboree before receiving the statement.

> **NEED-TO-KNOW** 6-5
>
> **COMPREHENSIVE**
>
> Preparing Bank Reconciliation and Adjusting Entries

PLANNING THE SOLUTION

● Set up a bank reconciliation (as in Exhibit 6.7).

● Examine each item *a* through *h* to determine whether it affects the book or the bank balance and whether it should be added or subtracted.

● After all items are analyzed, complete the reconciliation and arrive at a reconciled balance between the bank side and the book side.

● For each reconciling item on the book side, prepare an adjusting entry. Additions to the book side require an adjusting entry that debits Cash. Deductions on the book side require an adjusting entry that credits Cash.

SOLUTION

JAMBOREE ENTERPRISES Bank Reconciliation November 30					
Bank statement balance.......		$ 38,520	Book balance		$ 16,380
Add			Add		
Deposit of Nov. 30	$17,150		Collection of note	$30,000	
Bank error (Jumbo)	160	17,310	Interest earned.............	900	30,900
		55,830			47,280
Deduct			Deduct		
Outstanding checks			NSF check (M. Welch)........	1,100	
No. 2024...............	4,810		Recording error (No. 2025) ...	120	
No. 2026...............	5,000	9,810	Service charge	40	1,260
Adjusted bank balance		**$46,020**	**Adjusted book balance**.......		**$46,020**

Required Adjusting Entries for Jamboree

Nov. 30	Cash	30,000	
	Notes Receivable		30,000
	Record collection of note.		
Nov. 30	Cash	900	
	Interest Revenue.................		900
	Record collection of revenue.		
Nov. 30	Accounts Receivable—M. Welch	1,100	
	Cash............................		1,100
	Reinstate account due from an NSF check.		

Nov. 30	Rent Expense	120	
	Cash............................		120
	Correct recording error on Check No. 2025.		
Nov. 30	Miscellaneous Expenses	40	
	Cash............................		40
	Record bank service charges.		

APPENDIX

6A   Documentation and Verification

P4

Describe use of documentation and verification to control cash payments.

This appendix covers the documents of a voucher system of control.

Purchase Requisition   Department managers are usually not allowed to place orders directly with suppliers for control purposes. Instead, a department manager must inform the purchasing department of its needs by preparing and signing a **purchase requisition,** which lists the merchandise requested to be purchased—see Exhibit 6A.1. Two copies of the purchase requisition are sent to the purchasing department, which then sends one copy to the accounting department. When the accounting department receives a purchase requisition, it creates and maintains a voucher for this transaction. The requesting department keeps a third copy.

EXHIBIT 6A.1

Purchase Requisition

Z-Mart

PURCHASE REQUISITION   No. 917

| From | Sporting Goods Department | Date | October 28, 2019 |
| To | Purchasing Department | Preferred Vendor | Trex |

Request purchase of the following item(s):

MODEL NO.	DESCRIPTION	QUANTITY
CH 015	Toddler—Challenger X7	1
SD 099	Boys/Girls—Speed Demon	1

Reason for Request   Replenish inventory
Approval for Request   T.Z.

For Purchasing Department use only: Order Date _10-30-19_   P.O. No. _P98_

Purchase Order   A **purchase order** is a document the purchasing department uses to place an order with a **vendor** (seller or supplier). A purchase order authorizes a vendor to ship merchandise at the stated price and terms—see Exhibit 6A.2. When the purchasing department receives a purchase requisition, it prepares at least five copies of a purchase order. The copies are distributed as follows: *copy 1* to the vendor as a purchase request to ship merchandise; *copy 2,* along with a copy of the purchase requisition, to the accounting department, where it is entered in the voucher and used in approving payment of the invoice; *copy 3* to the requesting department to inform its manager of the purchase; *copy 4* to the receiving department without order quantity so it can compare with goods received and provide an independent count of goods received; and *copy 5* kept on file by the purchasing department.

Point: This appendix shows one example of a common voucher system design, but *not* the only design.

Invoice   An **invoice** is an itemized statement of goods prepared by the vendor listing the customer's name, items sold, sales prices, and terms of sale. An invoice is also a bill sent to the buyer from the supplier. From the vendor's point of view, it is a *sales invoice.* The buyer, or **vendee,** treats it as a *purchase*

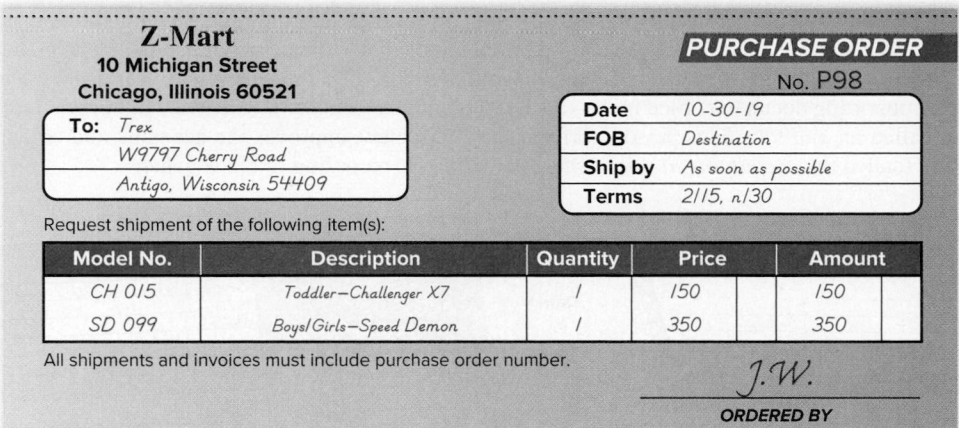

EXHIBIT 6A.2

Purchase Order

Point: Shipping terms and credit terms are shown on the purchase order.

invoice. The invoice is sent to the buyer's accounting department, where it is placed in the voucher (Refer back to Exhibit 4.6, which shows Z-Mart's purchase invoice.)

Receiving Report

Many companies have a receiving department to receive all merchandise and purchased assets. When each shipment arrives, this receiving department counts the goods and checks them for damage and agreement with the purchase order. It then prepares four or more copies of a **receiving report,** which is used within the company to notify that ordered goods have been received and to describe the quantities and condition of the goods. One copy is sent to accounting and placed in the voucher. Copies also are sent to the requesting department and the purchasing department to notify them that the goods have arrived. The receiving department keeps a copy in its files.

Invoice Approval

When a receiving report arrives, the accounting department should have copies of the following documents in the voucher: purchase requisition, purchase order, and invoice. With the information in these documents, the accounting department can record the purchase and approve its payment. In approving an invoice for payment, it checks and compares information across all documents. To verify this information and to ensure that no step is missing, it often uses an **invoice approval,** also called *check authorization*—see Exhibit 6A.3. An invoice approval is a checklist of steps necessary for approving an invoice for recording and payment. It is a separate document either filed in the voucher or preprinted (or stamped) on the voucher.

INVOICE APPROVAL			BY	DATE
DOCUMENT				
Purchase requisition		917	TZ	10-28-19
Purchase order		P98	JW	10-30-19
Receiving report		R85	SK	11-03-19
Invoice:		4657		11-12-19
Price			JK	11-12-19
Calculations			JK	11-12-19
Terms			JK	11-12-19
Approved for payment			BC	

EXHIBIT 6A.3

Invoice Approval

As each step in the checklist is approved, the person initials the invoice approval and records the current date. Final approval means the following steps have occurred.

1. **Requisition check:** Items on invoice are requested per purchase requisition.
2. **Purchase order check:** Items on invoice are ordered per purchase order.
3. **Receiving report check:** Items on invoice are received per receiving report.
4. **Invoice check: Price:** Invoice prices are as agreed with the vendor.
   Calculations: Invoice has no mathematical errors.
   Terms: Terms are as agreed with the vendor.

Point: Recording a purchase is initiated by an invoice approval, not an invoice. An invoice approval verifies that the amount is consistent with that requested, ordered, and received. This controls and verifies purchases and related liabilities.

Point: Auditors, when auditing inventory, check a sampling of purchases by reviewing the purchase order, receiving report, and invoice.

Voucher

Once an invoice has been checked and approved, the voucher is complete. A complete voucher is a record summarizing a transaction. Once the voucher certifies a transaction, it authorizes recording an obligation. A voucher also contains approval for paying the obligation on an appropriate date.

Completion of a voucher usually requires a person to enter certain information on both the inside and outside of the voucher. Typical information required on the inside of a voucher is on the left-hand side of Exhibit 6A.4, and that for the outside is on the right-hand side. This information is taken from the invoice and the supporting documents filed in the voucher. A complete voucher is sent to an authorized individual (often called an *auditor*). This person performs a final review, approves the accounts and amounts for debiting (called the *accounting distribution*), and authorizes recording of the voucher.

EXHIBIT 6A.4

A Voucher

After a voucher is approved and recorded (in a journal called a **voucher register**), it is filed by its due date. A check is then sent on the payment date from the cashier, the voucher is marked "paid," and the voucher is sent to the accounting department and recorded (in a journal called the **check register**). The person issuing checks relies on the approved voucher and its signed supporting documents as proof that an obligation has been incurred and must be paid. The purchase requisition and purchase order confirm the purchase was authorized. The receiving report shows that items have been received, and the invoice approval form verifies that the invoice has been checked for errors. There is little chance for error and even less chance for fraud without collusion unless all the documents and signatures are forged.

Summary: Cheat Sheet

FRAUD AND INTERNAL CONTROL

Principles of Internal Control

Establish responsibilities: Responsibility for a task should be assigned to one person. If responsibility is not established, determining who is at fault is difficult.

Maintain adequate records: Good recordkeeping helps protect assets and helps managers monitor company activities.

Insure assets and bond key employees: Assets should be insured, and employees handling cash and easily transferable assets should be bonded.

Separate recordkeeping from custody of assets: An employee who has access to an asset must not have access to that asset's accounting records.

Divide responsibility for related transactions: Responsibility for a transaction should be divided between two or more individuals or departments. One person's work is a check on the others to prevent errors. This is *not* duplication of work.

Apply technological controls: Use technology such as ID scanners to protect assets and improve control.

Perform regular and independent reviews: Regular reviews of internal controls should be performed by outside reviewers, preferably auditors.

CONTROL OF CASH

Cash account: Includes currency, coins, checks, and deposits in bank accounts.

Cash equivalents: Short-term, liquid investment assets meeting two criteria: (1) convertible to a known cash amount and (2) close to their due date, usually within 3 months. An example is a U.S. Treasury bill.

Cash management strategies: (a) Encourage early collection of receivables, (b) delay payment of liabilities, (c) keep only necessary assets, (d) plan expenditures, and (e) invest excess cash.

Over-the-Counter Cash Receipt Control Procedures

- Sales are recorded on a cash register after each sale, and customers are given a receipt.
- Cash registers hold a locked-in record of each transaction and often are linked with the accounting system.
- Custody over cash is separate from recordkeeping. The clerk who has access to cash in the register cannot access accounting records. The recordkeeper cannot access the cash.

Cash Over and Short Journal Entries

If cash received is *more* than recorded cash sales:

Cash	555	
Cash Over and Short		5
Sales.		550

If cash received is *less* than recorded cash sales:

Cash	621	
Cash Over and Short	4	
Sales.		625

Cash Receipts by Mail Control Procedures

- Two people are tasked with opening mail. Theft of cash would require collusion between these two employees.
- A list (in triplicate) is kept of each sender's name, the amount, and an explanation of why money was sent. The first copy is sent with the money to the cashier. A second copy is sent to the recordkeeper. The employees who opened the mail keep the third copy. The cashier deposits the money in a bank, and the recordkeeper records amounts received.
- No employee has access to both accounting records and cash.

Cash Payment Control Procedures
- Require all payments to be made by check or EFT. The only exception is small payments made from petty cash.
- Deny access to records to employees who can sign checks (other than the owner).

Voucher system: Set of procedures to control cash payments. Applied to all payments.

TOOLS OF CONTROL AND ANALYSIS

Petty cash: System of control used for small payments.

Entry to set up a petty cash fund:

Petty Cash	75	
Cash		75

Reimburse and record expenses for petty cash:

Miscellaneous Expenses	46.50	
Merchandise Inventory	15.05	
Delivery Expense	5.00	
Office Supplies Expense	4.75	
Cash		71.30

Increasing a petty cash fund (after reimbursement):

Petty Cash	25	
Cash		25

Decreasing a petty cash fund (after reimbursement):

Cash	20	
Petty Cash		20

Petty cash fund has unexplained shortage:

Miscellaneous Expenses	178	
Cash Over and Short	7	
Cash		185

Canceled checks: Checks the bank has paid and deducted from the customer's account.

Bank reconciliation adjustments:

Bank Balance Adjustments	Book Balance Adjustments
Add deposits in transit.	Add interest earned and unrecorded cash receipts.
Subtract outstanding checks.	Subtract bank fees and NSF checks.
Add or subtract corrections of bank errors.	Add or subtract corrections of book errors.

Adjusting Entries from Bank Reconciliation—Examples

Collection of note:

Cash	485	
Notes Receivable		485

Interest earned:

Cash	8	
Interest Revenue		8

Bank fees:

Miscellaneous Expenses	23	
Cash		23

NSF checks:

Accounts receivable–Name	30	
Cash		30

Key Terms

Bank reconciliation (247)
Bank statement (246)
Canceled checks (246)
Cash (239)
Cash equivalents (239)
Cash Over and Short (240)
Check (245)
Check register (254)
Committee of Sponsoring Organizations (COSO) (235)
Credit memorandum (247)
Days' sales uncollected (250)
Debit memorandum (247)
Deposit ticket (245)
Deposits in transit (247)
Electronic funds transfer (EFT) (245)
Internal control system (235)
Invoice (252)
Invoice approval (253)
Liquid assets (238)
Liquidity (238)
Outstanding checks (247)
Petty cash (242)
Principles of internal control (236)
Purchase order (252)
Purchase requisition (252)
Receiving report (253)
Sarbanes-Oxley Act (SOX) (235)
Signature card (245)
Vendee (252)
Vendor (252)
Voucher (241)
Voucher register (254)
Voucher system (241)

Multiple Choice Quiz

1. The following information is available for Hapley Co.
- November 30 bank statement shows a $1,895 balance.
- The general ledger shows a $1,742 balance at November 30.
- A $795 deposit placed in the bank's night depository on November 30 does not appear on the November 30 bank statement.
- Outstanding checks amount to $638 at November 30.
- A customer's $320 note was collected by the bank and deposited in Hapley's account in November.

- A bank service charge of $10 is deducted by the bank and appears on the November 30 bank statement.

How will the customer's note appear on Hapley's November 30 bank reconciliation?
- **a.** $320 appears as an addition to the book balance of cash.
- **b.** $320 appears as a deduction from the book balance of cash.
- **c.** $320 appears as an addition to the bank balance of cash.
- **d.** $320 appears as a deduction from the bank balance of cash.
- **e.** $335 appears as an addition to the bank balance of cash.

2. Using the information from question 1, what is the reconciled balance on Hapley's November 30 bank reconciliation?

   a. $2,052   **c.** $1,742   **e.** $1,184

   b. $1,895   **d.** $2,201

3. A company needs to replenish its $500 petty cash fund. Its petty cashbox has $75 cash and petty cash receipts of $420. The journal entry to replenish the fund includes

   a. A debit to Cash for $75.

   b. A credit to Cash for $75.

   c. A credit to Petty Cash for $420.

   d. A credit to Cash Over and Short for $5.

   e. A debit to Cash Over and Short for $5.

4. A company had net sales of $84,000 and accounts receivable of $6,720. Its days' sales uncollected is

   a. 3.2 days.   **c.** 230.0 days.   **e.** 12.5 days.

   b. 18.4 days.   **d.** 29.2 days.

ANSWERS TO MULTIPLE CHOICE QUIZ

1. a; recognizes cash collection of note by bank.

2. a; the bank reconciliation follows.

Bank Reconciliation November 30			
Balance per bank statement....	$1,895	Balance per books........	$1,742
Add: Deposit in transit.........	795	Add: Note collected.......	320
Deduct: Outstanding checks....	(638)	Deduct: Service charge....	(10)
Reconciled balance...........	$2,052	Reconciled balance.......	$2,052

3. e; The entry follows.

Debits to expenses (or assets)..........	420
Cash Over and Short..................	5
Cash	425

4. d; ($6,720/$84,000) × 365 = <u>29.2 days</u>

---

^A *Superscript letter A denotes assignments based on Appendix 6A.*

  Icon denotes assignments that involve decision making.

Discussion Questions

1. List the seven broad principles of internal control.

2. Internal control procedures are important in every business, but at what stage in the development of a business do they become especially critical?

3. Why should responsibility for related transactions be divided among different departments or individuals?

4. Why should the person who keeps the records of an asset not be the person responsible for its custody?

5. When a store purchases merchandise, why are individual departments not allowed to directly deal with suppliers?

6. What are the limitations of internal controls?

7. Which of the following assets—inventory, building, accounts receivable, or cash—is most liquid? Which is least liquid?

8. What is a petty cash receipt? Who should sign it?

9. Why should cash receipts be deposited on the day of receipt?

10. **Apple**'s statement of cash flows in Appendix A **APPLE** describes changes in cash and cash equivalents for the year ended September 30, 2017. What total amount is provided (used) by investing activities? What amount is provided (used) by financing activities?

11. Refer to **Google**'s financial statements in Appendix A. Identify Google's net earnings (income) for the year ended December 31, 2017. Is its net earnings equal to the change in cash and cash equivalents for the year? Explain the difference between net earnings and the change in cash and cash equivalents. **GOOGLE**

12. Refer to **Samsung**'s balance sheet in Appendix A. How does its cash (titled "Cash and cash equivalents") compare with its other current assets (in both amount and percent) as of December 31, 2017? Compare and assess its cash at December 31, 2017, with its cash at December 31, 2016. **Samsung**

13. **Samsung**'s statement of cash flows in Appendix A reports the change in cash and equivalents for the year ended December 31, 2017. Identify the cash generated (or used) by operating activities, by investing activities, and by financing activities. **Samsung**

connect

QUICK STUDY

QS 6-1

Internal control objectives

C1

Indicate which statements are true and which are false.

_____ **1.** Separation of recordkeeping for assets from the custody over assets helps reduce fraud.

_____ **2.** The primary objective of internal control procedures is to safeguard the business against theft from government agencies.

_____ **3.** Internal control procedures should be designed to protect assets from waste and theft.

_____ **4.** Separating the responsibility for a transaction between two or more individuals or departments will not help prevent someone from creating a fictitious invoice and paying the money to himself.

COSO lists five components of internal control: control environment, risk assessment, control activities, information and communication, and monitoring. Indicate the COSO component that matches with each of the following internal control activities.

QS 6-2
COSO internal control components
C1

___ **a.** Independent review of controls
___ **b.** Executives' strong ethics
___ **c.** Reporting of control effectiveness
___ **d.** Analyses of fraud risk factors

Choose from the following list of terms and phrases to best complete the following statements.

QS 6-3
Cash and equivalents
C2

a. Cash
b. Cash equivalents
c. Outstanding check
d. Liquidity
e. Cash over and short
f. Voucher system

___ **1.** The _____ category includes currency, coins, and deposits in bank accounts.
___ **2.** The term _____ refers to a company's ability to pay for its current liabilities.
___ **3.** The _____ category includes short-term, highly liquid investment assets that are readily convertible to a known cash amount and sufficiently close to their due dates so that their market value will not greatly change.

Identify each of the following statements as either true or false.

QS 6-4
Internal control for cash
P1

___ **a.** A guideline for safeguarding cash is that all cash receipts be deposited monthly or yearly.
___ **b.** A voucher system of control is a control system exclusively for cash receipts.
___ **c.** A guideline for safeguarding cash is to separate the duties of those who have custody of cash from those who keep cash records.
___ **d.** Separation of duties eliminates the possibility of collusion to steal an asset and hide the theft from the records.

Record the journal entry for Sales and for Cash Over and Short for each of the following separate situations.

QS 6-5
Cash Over and Short
P1

a. The cash register's record shows $420 of cash sales, but the count of cash in the register is $430.
b. The cash register's record shows $980 of cash sales, but the count of cash in the register is $972.

---

1. Brooks Agency set up a petty cash fund for $150. At the end of the current period, the fund contained $28 and had the following receipts: entertainment, $70; postage, $30; and printing, $22. Prepare journal entries to record (a) establishment of the fund and (b) reimbursement of the fund at the end of the current period.

QS 6-6
Petty cash accounting
P2

2. Identify the two events from the following that cause a Petty Cash account to be credited in a journal entry.

___ **a.** Fund amount is being reduced.
___ **b.** Fund amount is being increased.
___ **c.** Fund is being eliminated.
___ **d.** Fund is being established.

For *a* through *g*, indicate whether its amount (1) affects the bank or book side of a bank reconciliation, (2) is an addition or a subtraction in a bank reconciliation, and (3) requires an adjusting journal entry.

QS 6-7
Bank reconciliation
P3

	Bank or Book Side	Add or Subtract	Adj. Entry or Not
a. Interest on cash balance.			
b. Bank service charges			
c. Minimum balance bank fee			
d. Outstanding checks			
e. Collection of note by bank			
f. NSF checks			
g. Outstanding deposits			

Nolan Company's Cash account shows a $22,352 debit balance and its bank statement shows $21,332 on deposit at the close of business on June 30. Prepare a bank reconciliation using the following information.

QS 6-8
Bank reconciliation
P3

a. Outstanding checks as of June 30 total $3,713.
b. The June 30 bank statement lists $41 in bank service charges; the company has not yet recorded the cost of these services.

[continued on next page]

c. In reviewing the bank statement, a $90 check written by the company was mistakenly recorded in the company's books as $99.

d. June 30 cash receipts of $4,724 were placed in the bank's night depository after banking hours and were not recorded on the June 30 bank statement.

e. The bank statement included a $23 credit for interest earned on the company's cash in the bank. The company has not yet recorded interest earned.

QS 6-9

Bank reconciliation

P3

Organic Food Co.'s Cash account shows a $5,500 debit balance and its bank statement shows $5,160 on deposit at the close of business on August 31. Prepare a bank reconciliation using the following information.

a. August 31 cash receipts of $1,240 were placed in the bank's night depository after banking hours and were not recorded on the August 31 bank statement.

b. The bank statement shows a $120 NSF check from a customer; the company has not yet recorded this NSF check.

c. Outstanding checks as of August 31 total $1,120.

d. In reviewing the bank statement, an $80 check written by Organic Fruits was mistakenly drawn against Organic Food's account.

e. The August 31 bank statement lists $20 in bank service charges; the company has not yet recorded the cost of these services.

QS 6-10

Days' sales uncollected

A1

The following annual account balances are from Armour Sports at December 31.

	Year 2	Year 1
Accounts receivable	$ 100,000	$ 85,000
Net sales	2,500,000	2,000,000

a. What is the change in the number of days' sales uncollected between Year 1 and Year 2? (Round the number of days to one decimal.)

b. From the analysis in part *a*, is the company's collection of receivables improving?

QS 6-11ᴬ

Documents in a voucher system **P4**

Management uses a voucher system to help control and monitor cash payments. Which one or more of the four documents listed below are prepared as part of a voucher system of control?

_____ **a.** Purchase order   _____ **b.** Outstanding check   _____ **c.** Invoice   _____ **d.** Voucher

---

connect

EXERCISES

Exercise 6-1

Analyzing internal control

C1

Identify the internal control principle that was violated in each of the following separate situations.

a. The recordkeeper left town after the owner discovered a large sum of money had disappeared. An audit found that the recordkeeper had written and signed several checks made payable to his fiancée and recorded the checks as salaries expense.

b. An employee was put in charge of handling cash. That employee later stole cash from the business. The company incurred an *uninsured* loss of $184,000.

c. There is $500 in cash missing from a cash register drawer. Three salesclerks shared the cash register drawer, so the owner cannot determine who is at fault.

Exercise 6-2

Applying internal control principles

C1

Whole Fruits Market took the following actions to improve internal controls. For each of the following actions, identify the internal control principle the company followed.

a. Prohibit the recordkeeper from having control over cash.

b. Purchased an insurance (bonding) policy against losses from theft by a cashier.

c. Each cashier is designated a specific cash drawer and is solely responsible for cash in that drawer.

d. Detailed records of inventory are kept to ensure items lost or stolen do not go unnoticed.

e. Digital time clocks are used to register which employees are at work at what times.

f. External auditors are regularly hired to evaluate internal controls.

Determine whether each procedure described below is an internal control strength or weakness; then identify the internal control principle violated or followed for each procedure.

1. The same employee requests, records, and makes payment for purchases of inventory.
2. The company saves money by having employees involved in operations perform the only review of internal controls.
3. Time is saved by not updating records for use of supplies.
4. The recordkeeper is not allowed to write checks or initiate EFTs.
5. Each salesclerk is in charge of her own cash drawer.

Exercise 6-3
Internal control strengths and weaknesses
C1

Determine whether each policy below is good or bad cash management; then identify the cash management strategy violated or followed for each policy.

1. Bills are paid as soon as they are received.
2. Cash receipts and cash payments are regularly planned and reviewed.
3. Excess cash is put in checking accounts, earning no interest income.
4. Customers are regularly allowed to pay after due dates without concern.
5. Rarely used equipment is rented rather than purchased.

Exercise 6-4
Cash management strategies
C2

Specter Co. combines cash and cash equivalents on the balance sheet. Using the following information, determine the amount reported on the year-end balance sheet for cash and cash equivalents.
- $3,000 cash deposit in checking account.
- $20,000 bond investment due in 20 years.
- $5,000 U.S. Treasury bill due in 1 month.
- $200, 3-year loan to an employee.
- $1,000 of currency and coins.
- $500 of accounts receivable.

Exercise 6-5
Cash and cash equivalents
C2

Determine whether each cash receipts procedure is an internal control strength or weakness.

1. If a salesclerk makes an error in recording a cash sale, she can access the register's electronic record to correct the transaction
2. All sales transactions, even those for less than $1, are recorded on a cash register.
3. Two employees are tasked with opening mail that contains cash receipts.
4. One of the two employees tasked with opening mail is also the recordkeeper for the business.
5. The supervisor has access to both cash and the accounting records.
6. Receipts are given to customers only for sales that are above $20.

Exercise 6-6
Control of cash receipts
P1

Determine whether each cash payment procedure is an internal control strength or weakness.

1. A voucher system is used for all payments of liabilities.
2. The owner of a small business has authority to write and sign checks.
3. When the owner is out of town, the recordkeeper is in charge of signing checks.
4. To save time, all departments are allowed to incur liabilities.
5. Payments over $100 are made by check.
6. Requesting and receiving merchandise are handled by the same department.

Exercise 6-7
Voucher system and control of cash payments
P1

Waupaca Company establishes a $350 petty cash fund on September 9. On September 30, the fund shows $104 in cash along with receipts for the following expenditures: transportation-in, $40; postage expenses, $123; and miscellaneous expenses, $80. The petty cashier could not account for a $3 shortage in the fund.
The company uses the perpetual system in accounting for merchandise inventory. Prepare (1) the September 9 entry to establish the fund, (2) the September 30 entry to reimburse the fund, and (3) an October 1 entry to increase the fund to $400.

Exercise 6-8
Petty cash fund with a shortage P2

Check (2) Cr. Cash, $246 and (3) Cr. Cash, $50

EcoMart establishes a $1,050 petty cash fund on May 2. On May 30, the fund shows $326 in cash along with receipts for the following expenditures: transportation-in, $120; postage expenses, $369; and miscellaneous expenses, $240. The petty cashier could not account for a $5 overage in the fund. The company uses the perpetual system in accounting for merchandise inventory.
Prepare the (1) May 2 entry to establish the fund, (2) May 30 entry to reimburse the fund [*Hint:* Credit Cash Over and Short for $5 and credit Cash for $724], and (3) June 1 entry to increase the fund to $1,200.

Exercise 6-9
Petty cash fund with an overage
P2

Exercise 6-10

Petty cash fund accounting

P2

Check (3) Cr. Cash, $162 & $250

Palmona Co. establishes a $200 petty cash fund on January 1. On January 8, the fund shows $38 in cash along with receipts for the following expenditures: postage, $74; transportation-in, $29; delivery expenses, $16; and miscellaneous expenses, $43.

Palmona uses the perpetual system in accounting for merchandise inventory. Prepare journal entries to (1) establish the fund on January 1, (2) reimburse it on January 8, and (3) both reimburse the fund and increase it to $450 on January 8, assuming no entry in part 2. *Hint:* Make two separate entries for part 3.

Exercise 6-11

Bank reconciliation and adjusting entries

P3

Prepare a table with the following headings for a monthly bank reconciliation dated September 30.

Item	Bank Balance	Book Balance		Shown or Not Shown on Reconciliation
	Add or Subtract	Add or Subtract	Dr. or Cr.	Shown or Not Shown

Indicate whether each item should be added to or deducted from the book or bank balance and whether it should or should not appear on the September 30 reconciliation. For items that add or deduct from the book balance column, place a *Dr.* or *Cr.* after the "Add" or "Deduct" to show the accounting impact on Cash.

1. NSF check from a customer is shown on the bank statement but not yet recorded by the company.
2. Interest earned on the September cash balance in the bank is not yet recorded by the company.
3. Deposit made on September 5 and processed by the bank on September 6.
4. Checks written by another depositor but mistakenly charged against this company's account.
5. Bank service charge for September is not yet recorded by the company.
6. Checks outstanding on August 31 that cleared the bank in September.
7. Check written against the company's account and cleared by the bank; erroneously not recorded by the company's recordkeeper.
8. A note receivable is collected by the bank for the company, but it is not yet recorded by the company.
9. Checks written and mailed to payees on October 2.
10. Checks written by the company and mailed to payees on September 30.
11. Night deposit made on September 30 after the bank closed.
12. Bank fees for check printing are not yet recorded by the company.

Exercise 6-12

Bank reconciliation

P3

Del Gato Clinic's Cash account shows an $11,589 debit balance and its bank statement shows $10,555 on deposit at the close of business on June 30. Prepare its bank reconciliation using the following information.

a. Outstanding checks as of June 30 total $1,829.

b. The June 30 bank statement lists a $16 bank service charge.

c. Check No. 919, listed with the canceled checks, was correctly drawn for $467 in payment of a utility bill on June 15. Del Gato Clinic mistakenly recorded it with a debit to Utilities Expense and a credit to Cash in the amount of $476.

Check Reconciled bal., $11,582

d. The June 30 cash receipts of $2,856 were placed in the bank's night depository after banking hours and were not recorded on the June 30 bank statement.

Exercise 6-13

Adjusting entries from bank reconciliation   **P3**

Prepare the adjusting journal entries that Del Gato Clinic must record as a result of preparing the bank reconciliation in Exercise 6-12.

Exercise 6-14

Bank reconciliation

P3

Wright Company's Cash account shows a $27,500 debit balance and its bank statement shows $25,800 on deposit at the close of business on May 31. Prepare its bank reconciliation using the following information.

a. The May 31 bank statement lists $100 in bank service charges; the company has not yet recorded the cost of these services.

b. Outstanding checks as of May 31 total $5,600.

c. May 31 cash receipts of $6,200 were placed in the bank's night depository after banking hours and were not recorded on the May 31 bank statement.

d. In reviewing the bank statement, a $400 check written by Smith Company was mistakenly drawn against Wright's account.

Check Reconciled bal., $26,800

e. The bank statement shows a $600 NSF check from a customer; the company has not yet recorded this NSF check.

Barga Co.'s net sales for Year 1 and Year 2 are $730,000 and $1,095,000, respectively. Its year-end balances of accounts receivable follow: Year 1, $65,000; and Year 2, $123,000.

a. Compute its days' sales uncollected at the end of each year. Round the number of days to one decimal.

b. Did days' sales uncollected improve or worsen in Year 2 versus Year 1?

Exercise 6-15
Liquid assets and accounts receivable   A1

Match each document in a voucher system with its description.

Document	Description
1. Purchase requisition	____ **A.** An itemized statement of goods prepared by the vendor listing the customer's name, items sold, sales prices, and terms of sale.
2. Purchase order	
3. Invoice	____ **B.** An internal file used to store documents and information to control cash payments and to ensure that a transaction is properly authorized and recorded.
4. Receiving report	
5. Invoice approval	____ **C.** A document used to place an order with a vendor that authorizes the vendor to ship ordered merchandise at the stated price and terms.
6. Voucher	
	____ **D.** A checklist of steps necessary for the approval of an invoice for recording and payment; also known as a check authorization.
	____ **E.** A document used by department managers to inform the purchasing department to place an order with a vendor.
	____ **F.** A document used to notify the appropriate persons that ordered goods have arrived, including a description of the quantities and condition of goods.

Exercise 6-16ᴬ
Documents in a voucher system
P4

---

connect

Following are five separate cases involving internal control issues.

a. Chi Han receives all incoming customer cash receipts for her employer and posts the customer payments to their respective accounts.

b. At Tico Company, Julia and Trevor alternate lunch hours. Julia is the petty cash custodian, but if someone needs petty cash when she is at lunch, Trevor fills in as custodian.

c. Nori Nozumi posts all patient charges and payments at the Hopeville Medical Clinic. Each night Nori backs up the computerized accounting system but does not password lock her computer.

d. Ben Shales prides himself on hiring quality workers who require little supervision. As office manager, Ben gives his employees full discretion over their tasks and for years has seen no reason to perform independent reviews of their work.

e. Carla Farah's manager has told her to reduce costs. Carla decides to raise the deductible on the plant's property insurance from $5,000 to $10,000. This cuts the property insurance premium in half. In a related move, she decides that bonding the plant's employees is a waste of money because the company has not experienced any losses due to employee theft. Carla saves the entire amount of the bonding insurance premium by dropping the bonding insurance.

PROBLEM SET A

Problem 6-1A
Analyzing internal control

C1

Required

1. For each case, identify the principle(s) of internal control that is violated.

2. Recommend what should be done to adhere to principles of internal control in each case.

Kiona Co. set up a petty cash fund for payments of small amounts. The following transactions involving the petty cash fund occurred in May (the last month of the company's fiscal year).

May 1   Prepared a company check for $300 to establish the petty cash fund.

    15   Prepared a company check to replenish the fund for the following expenditures made since May 1.
        a.   Paid $88 for janitorial expenses.
        b.   Paid $53.68 for miscellaneous expenses.
        c.   Paid postage expenses of $53.50.
        d.   Paid $47.15 to Facebook for advertising expense.
        e.   Counted $62.15 remaining in the petty cashbox.

    16   Prepared a company check for $200 to increase the fund to $500.

Problem 6-2A
Establishing, reimbursing, and adjusting petty cash
P2

[continued on next page]

31　The petty cashier reports that $288.20 cash remains in the fund. A company check is drawn to replenish the fund for the following expenditures made since May 15.
　　f.　Paid postage expenses of $147.36.
　　g.　Reimbursed the office manager for mileage expense, $23.50.
　　h.　Paid $34.75 in delivery expense for products to a customer, terms FOB destination.

31　The company decides that the May 16 increase in the fund was too large. It reduces the fund by $100, leaving a total of $400.

Required

Prepare journal entries to establish the fund on May 1, to replenish it on May 15 and on May 31, and to reflect any increase or decrease in the fund balance on May 16 and May 31.

Problem 6-3A
Establishing, reimbursing, and increasing petty cash
P2

Nakashima Gallery had the following petty cash transactions in February of the current year. Nakashima uses the perpetual system to account for merchandise inventory.

Feb.　2　Wrote a $400 check to establish a petty cash fund.
　　　　5　Purchased paper for the copier for $14.15 that is immediately used.
　　　　9　Paid $32.50 shipping charges (transportation-in) on merchandise purchased for resale, terms FOB shipping point. These costs are added to merchandise inventory.
　　　12　Paid $7.95 postage to deliver a contract to a client.
　　　14　Reimbursed Adina Sharon, the manager, $68 for mileage on her car.
　　　20　Purchased office paper for $67.77 that is immediately used.
　　　23　Paid a courier $20 to deliver merchandise sold to a customer, terms FOB destination.
　　　25　Paid $13.10 shipping charges (transportation-in) on merchandise purchased for resale, terms FOB shipping point. These costs are added to merchandise inventory.
　　　27　Paid $54 for postage expenses.
　　　28　The fund had $120.42 remaining in the petty cashbox. Sorted the petty cash receipts by accounts affected and exchanged them for a check to reimburse the fund for expenditures.
　　　28　The petty cash fund amount is increased by $100 to a total of $500.

Required

1. Prepare the journal entry to establish the petty cash fund.

2. Prepare a petty cash payments report for February with these categories: delivery expense, mileage expense, postage expense, merchandise inventory (for transportation-in), and office supplies expense.

3. Prepare the journal entries for part 2 to both (*a*) reimburse and (*b*) increase the fund amount.

Problem 6-4A
Preparing a bank reconciliation and recording adjustments
P3

The following information is available to reconcile Branch Company's book balance of cash with its bank statement cash balance as of July 31.

a. On July 31, the company's Cash account has a $27,497 debit balance, but its July bank statement shows a $27,233 cash balance.

b. Check No. 3031 for $1,482, Check No. 3065 for $382, and Check No. 3069 for $2,281 are outstanding checks as of July 31.

c. Check No. 3056 for July rent expense was correctly written and drawn for $1,270 but was erroneously entered in the accounting records as $1,250.

d. The July bank statement shows the bank collected $7,955 cash on a note for Branch. Branch had not recorded this event before receiving the statement.

e. The bank statement shows an $805 NSF check. The check had been received from a customer, Evan Shaw. Branch has not yet recorded this check as NSF.

f. The July statement shows a $25 bank service charge. It has not yet been recorded in miscellaneous expenses because no previous notification had been received.

g. Branch's July 31 daily cash receipts of $11,514 were placed in the bank's night depository on that date but do not appear on the July 31 bank statement.

Required

1. Prepare the bank reconciliation for this company as of July 31.

2. Prepare the journal entries necessary to make the company's book balance of cash equal to the reconciled cash balance as of July 31.

Chavez Company most recently reconciled its bank statement and book balances of cash on August 31 and it reported two checks outstanding, No. 5888 for $1,028 and No. 5893 for $494. Check No. 5893 was still outstanding as of September 30. The following information is available for its September 30 reconciliation.

Problem 6-5A
Preparing a bank reconciliation and recording adjustments

P3

From the September 30 Bank Statement

PREVIOUS BALANCE	TOTAL CHECKS AND DEBITS	TOTAL DEPOSITS AND CREDITS	CURRENT BALANCE
16,800	9,617	11,270	18,453

CHECKS AND DEBITS			DEPOSITS AND CREDITS	
Date	No.	Amount	Date	Amount
Sep. 3	5888	1,028	Sep. 5	1,103
Sep. 4	5902	719	Sep. 12	2,226
Sep. 7	5901	1,824	Sep. 21	4,093
Sep. 17		600 NSF	Sep. 25	2,351
Sep. 20	5905	937	Sep. 30	12 IN
Sep. 22	5903	399	Sep. 30	1,485 CM
Sep. 22	5904	2,090		
Sep. 28	5907	213		
Sep. 29	5909	1,807		

From Chavez Company's Accounting Records

Cash Receipts Deposited		
Date		Cash Debit
Sep.	5	1,103
	12	2,226
	21	4,093
	25	2,351
	30	1,682
		11,455

Cash Payments	
Check No.	Cash Credit
5901	1,824
5902	719
5903	399
5904	2,060
5905	937
5906	982
5907	213
5908	388
5909	1,807
	9,329

Cash						Acct. No. 101
Date		Explanation	PR	Debit	Credit	Balance
Aug.	31	Balance				15,278
Sep.	30	Total receipts	R12	11,455		26,733
	30	Total payments	D23		9,329	17,404

Additional Information (*a*) Check No. 5904 is correctly drawn for $2,090 to pay for computer equipment; however, the recordkeeper misread the amount and entered it in the accounting records with a debit to Computer Equipment and a credit to Cash of $2,060. (*b*) The NSF check shown in the statement was originally received from a customer, S. Nilson, in payment of her account. Its return has not yet been recorded by the company. (*c*) The credit memorandum (CM) is from the collection of a $1,485 note for Chavez Company by the bank. The collection is not yet recorded.

Required

1. Prepare the September 30 bank reconciliation for this company.
2. Prepare journal entries to adjust the book balance of cash to the reconciled balance.

Check (1) Reconciled balance, $18,271; (2) Cr. Notes Receivable, $1,485

Following are five separate cases involving internal control issues.

a. Tywin Company keeps very poor records of its equipment. Instead, the company asserts its employees are honest and would never steal from the company.

b. Marker Theater has a computerized order-taking system for its tickets. The system is backed up once a year.

c. Sutton Company has two employees handling acquisitions of inventory. One employee places purchase orders and pays vendors. The second employee receives the merchandise.

PROBLEM SET B

Problem 6-1B
Analyzing internal control

C1

d. The owner of Super Pharmacy uses a check software/printer to prepare checks, making it difficult for anyone to alter the amount of a check. The check software/printer, which is not password protected, is on the owner's desk in an office that contains company checks and is normally unlocked.

e. To ensure the company retreat would not be cut, the manager of Lavina Company decided to save money by canceling the external audit of internal controls.

Required

1. For each case, identify the principle(s) of internal control that is violated.

2. Recommend what should be done to adhere to principles of internal control in each case.

Problem 6-2B

Establishing, reimbursing, and adjusting petty cash

P2

Moya Co. establishes a petty cash fund for payments of small amounts. The following transactions involving the petty cash fund occurred in January (the last month of the company's fiscal year).

Jan. 3   A company check for $150 is written and made payable to the petty cashier to establish the petty cash fund.

14   A company check is written to replenish the fund for the following expenditures made since January 3.

    a.   Purchased office supplies for $14.29 that are immediately used.

    b.   Paid $19.60 COD shipping charges on merchandise purchased for resale, terms FOB shipping point. Moya uses the perpetual system to account for inventory.

    c.   Paid $38.57 to All-Tech for repairs expense to a computer.

    d.   Paid $12.82 for items classified as miscellaneous expenses.

    e.   Counted $62.28 remaining in the petty cashbox.

15   Prepared a company check for $50 to increase the fund to $200.

31   The petty cashier reports that $17.35 remains in the fund. A company check is written to replenish the fund for the following expenditures made since January 14.

    f.   Paid $50 to *The Smart Shopper* in advertising expense for January's newsletter.

    g.   Paid $48.19 for postage expenses.

    h.   Paid $78 to Smooth Delivery for delivery expense of merchandise, terms FOB destination.

31   The company decides that the January 15 increase in the fund was too little. It increases the fund by another $50.

Required

Check   Cr. to Cash:
Jan. 14, $87.72;
Jan. 31 (total), $232.65

Prepare journal entries (in dollars and cents) to establish the fund on January 3, to replenish it on January 14 and January 31, and to reflect any increase or decrease in the fund balance on January 15 and 31.

Problem 6-3B

Establishing, reimbursing, and increasing petty cash

P2

Blues Music Center had the following petty cash transactions in March of the current year. Blues uses the perpetual system to account for merchandise inventory.

Mar. 5   Wrote a $250 check to establish a petty cash fund.

6   Paid $12.50 shipping charges (transportation-in) on merchandise purchased for resale, terms FOB shipping point. These costs are added to merchandise inventory.

11   Paid $10.75 in delivery expense on merchandise sold to a customer, terms FOB destination.

12   Purchased office file folders for $14.13 that are immediately used.

14   Reimbursed Bob Geldof, the manager, $11.65 for office supplies purchased and used.

18   Purchased office printer paper for $20.54 that is immediately used.

27   Paid $45.10 shipping charges (transportation-in) on merchandise purchased for resale, terms FOB shipping point. These costs are added to merchandise inventory.

28   Paid postage expense of $18.

30   Reimbursed Geldof $56.80 for mileage expense.

31   Cash of $61.53 remained in the fund. Sorted the petty cash receipts by accounts affected and exchanged them for a check to reimburse the fund for expenditures.

31   The petty cash fund amount is increased by $50 to a total of $300.

Required

1. Prepare the journal entry to establish the petty cash fund.

Check   (2) Total expenses, $189.47
(3*a* & 3*b*) Total Cr. to Cash, $238.47

2. Prepare a petty cash payments report for March with these categories: delivery expense, mileage expense, postage expense, merchandise inventory (for transportation-in), and office supplies expense.

3. Prepare the journal entries for part 2 to both (*a*) reimburse and (*b*) increase the fund amount.

The following information is available to reconcile Severino Co.'s book balance of cash with its bank statement cash balance as of December 31.

a. The December 31 cash balance according to the accounting records is $32,878.30, and the bank statement cash balance for that date is $46,822.40.

b. Check No. 1242 for $410.40, Check No. 1273 for $4,589.30, and Check No. 1282 for $400 are outstanding checks as of December 31.

c. Check No. 1267 had been correctly drawn for $3,456 to pay for office supplies but was erroneously entered in the accounting records as $3,465.

d. The bank statement shows a $762.50 NSF check received from a customer, Titus Industries, in payment of its account. The statement also shows a $99 bank fee in miscellaneous expenses for check printing. Severino had not yet recorded these transactions.

e. The bank statement shows that the bank collected $18,980 cash on a note receivable for the company. Severino did not record this transaction before receiving the statement.

f. Severino's December 31 daily cash receipts of $9,583.10 were placed in the bank's night depository on that date but do not appear on the December 31 bank statement.

Required

1. Prepare the bank reconciliation for this company as of December 31.

2. Prepare the journal entries necessary to make the company's book balance of cash equal to the reconciled cash balance as of December 31.

Problem 6-4B
Preparing a bank reconciliation and recording adjustments
P3

Check (1) Reconciled balance, $51,005.80; (2) Cr. Notes Receivable, $18,980.00

Shamara Systems most recently reconciled its bank balance on April 30 and reported two checks outstanding at that time, No. 1771 for $781 and No. 1780 for $1,425.90. Check No. 1780 was still outstanding as of May 31. The following information is available for its May 31 reconciliation.

Problem 6-5B
Preparing a bank reconciliation and recording adjustments
P3

From the May 31 Bank Statement

PREVIOUS BALANCE	TOTAL CHECKS AND DEBITS	TOTAL DEPOSITS AND CREDITS	CURRENT BALANCE
18,290.70	13,094.80	16,566.80	21,762.70

CHECKS AND DEBITS			DEPOSITS AND CREDITS	
Date	No.	Amount	Date	Amount
May 1	1771	781.00	May 4	2,438.00
May 2	1783	382.50	May 14	2,898.00
May 4	1782	1,285.50	May 22	1,801.80
May 11	1784	1,449.60	May 25	7,350.00 CM
May 18		431.80 NSF	May 26	2,079.00
May 25	1787	8,032.50		
May 26	1785	63.90		
May 29	1788	654.00		
May 31		14.00 SC		

From Shamara Systems's Accounting Records

Cash Receipts Deposited		Cash Payments	
Date	Cash Debit	Check No.	Cash Credit
May 4	2,438.00	1782	1,285.50
14	2,898.00	1783	382.50
22	1,801.80	1784	1,449.60
26	2,079.00	1785	63.90
31	2,727.30	1786	353.10
	11,944.10	1787	8,032.50
		1788	644.00
		1789	639.50
			12,850.60

Cash						Acct. No. 101
Date		Explanation	PR	Debit	Credit	Balance
Apr.	30	Balance				16,083.80
May	31	Total receipts	R7	11,944.10		28,027.90
	31	Total payments	D8		12,850.60	15,177.30

[continued on next page]

Additional Information (*a*) Check No. 1788 is correctly drawn for $654 to pay for May utilities; however, the recordkeeper misread the amount and entered it in the accounting records with a debit to Utilities Expense and a credit to Cash for $644. The bank paid and deducted the correct amount. (*b*) The NSF check shown in the statement was originally received from a customer, W. Sox, in payment of her account. The company has not yet recorded its return. (*c*) The credit memorandum (CM) is from a $7,350 note that the bank collected for the company. The collection has not yet been recorded.

Required

Check   (1) Reconciled balance, $22,071.50; (2) Cr. Notes Receivable, $7,350.00

1. Prepare the May 31 bank reconciliation for Shamara Systems.

2. Prepare journal entries to adjust the book balance of cash to the reconciled balance.

SERIAL PROBLEM
Business Solutions

P3

©Alexander Image/Shutterstock

This serial problem began in Chapter 1 and continues through most of the book. If previous chapter segments were not completed, the serial problem can begin at this point.

SP 6   Santana Rey receives the March bank statement for **Business Solutions** on April 11, 2020. The March 31 bank statement shows an ending cash balance of $67,566. The general ledger Cash account, No. 101, shows an ending cash balance per books of $68,057 as of March 31 (prior to any reconciliation). A comparison of the bank statement with the general ledger Cash account, No. 101, reveals the following.

a. The bank erroneously cleared a $500 check against the company account in March that S. Rey did not issue. The check was actually issued by Business Systems.

b. On March 25, the bank statement lists a $50 charge for a safety deposit box. Santana has not yet recorded this expense.

c. On March 26, the bank statement lists a $102 charge for printed checks that Business Solutions ordered from the bank. Santana has not yet recorded this expense.

d. On March 31, the bank statement lists $33 interest earned on Business Solutions's checking account for the month of March. Santana has not yet recorded this revenue.

e. S. Rey notices that the check she issued for $128 on March 31, 2020, has not yet cleared the bank.

f. S. Rey verifies that all deposits made in March do appear on the March bank statement.

Required

Check   (1) Adj. bank bal., $67,938

1. Prepare a bank reconciliation for Business Solutions for the month ended March 31, 2020.

2. Prepare any necessary adjusting entries. Use Miscellaneous Expenses, No. 677, for any bank charges. Use Interest Revenue, No. 404, for any interest earned on the checking account for March.

GENERAL LEDGER PROBLEM

The **General Ledger** tool in Connect automates several of the procedural steps in the accounting cycle so that the financial professional can focus on the impacts of each transaction on the various financial reports.

GL 6-1   General Ledger assignment GL 6-1, based on Problem 6-2A, focuses on transactions related to the petty cash fund and highlights the impact each transaction has on net income, if any. Prepare the journal entries related to the petty cash fund and assess the impact of each transaction on the company's net income, if any.

Accounting Analysis

COMPANY ANALYSIS

C2 A1

APPLE

AA 6-1   Use **Apple**'s financial statements in Appendix A to answer the following.

1. Identify the total amount of cash and cash equivalents for fiscal years ended (*a*) September 30, 2017, and (*b*) September 24, 2016.

2. Compute cash and cash equivalents as a percent (rounded to one decimal) of total current assets, total current liabilities, total shareholders' equity, and total assets at fiscal year-end for both 2017 and 2016.

3. Compute the percent change (rounded to one decimal) between the beginning and ending year amounts of cash and cash equivalents for fiscal years ended (*a*) September 30, 2017, and (*b*) September 24, 2016.

4. Compute the days' sales uncollected (rounded to one decimal) as of (*a*) September 30, 2017, and (*b*) September 24, 2016.

5. Does Apple's collection of receivables show a favorable or unfavorable change?

AA 6-2   Key comparative figures for **Apple** and **Google** follow.

$ millions	Apple		Google	
	Current Year	Prior Year	Current Year	Prior Year
Accounts receivable	$ 17,874	$ 15,754	$ 18,336	$14,137
Net sales	229,234	215,639	110,855	90.272

COMPARATIVE ANALYSIS

A1

APPLE

GOOGLE

Required

1. Compute days' sales uncollected (rounded to one decimal) for (*a*) Apple and (*b*) Google for the current and prior years.

2. Which company had more success collecting receivables?

AA 6-3   Key figures for **Samsung** follow.

₩ millions	Current Year	Prior Year
Cash.........................	₩ 30,545,130	₩ 32,111,442
Accounts receivable	31,804,956	27,800,408
Current assets.................	146,982,464	141,429,704
Total assets	301,752,090	262,174,324
Current liabilities...............	67,175,114	54,704,095
Shareholders' equity	214,491,428	192,963,033
Net sales.....................	239,575,376	201,866,745

GLOBAL ANALYSIS

C2   A1

Samsung

Required

1. Compute cash and cash equivalents as a percent (rounded to one decimal) of total current assets, total assets, total current liabilities, and total shareholders' equity for both years.

2. Compute the percentage change (rounded to one decimal) between the current year and prior year cash balances.

3. Compute the days' sales uncollected (rounded to one decimal) at the end of both the (*a*) current year and (*b*) prior year.

4. Does Samsung's collection of receivables show a favorable or unfavorable change?

Beyond the Numbers

BTN 6-1   Harriet Knox, Ralph Patton, and Marcia Diamond work for a family physician, Dr. Gwen Conrad, who is in private practice. Dr. Conrad is knowledgeable about office management practices and has segregated the cash receipt duties as follows. Knox opens the mail and prepares a triplicate list of money received. She sends one copy of the list to Patton, the cashier, who deposits the receipts daily in the bank. Diamond, the recordkeeper, receives a copy of the list and posts payments to patients' accounts. About once a month the office clerks have an expensive lunch they pay for as follows. First, Patton

ETHICS CHALLENGE

C1

endorses a patient's check in Dr. Conrad's name and cashes it at the bank. Knox then destroys the remittance advice accompanying the check. Finally, Diamond posts payment to the customer's account as a miscellaneous credit. The three justify their actions by their relatively low pay and knowledge that Dr. Conrad will likely never miss the money.

Required

1. Who is the best person in Dr. Conrad's office to reconcile the bank statement?
2. Would a bank reconciliation uncover this office fraud?
3. What are some procedures to detect this type of fraud?
4. Suggest additional internal controls that Dr. Conrad could implement.

COMMUNICATING IN PRACTICE

P4

BTN 6-2   Assume you are a business consultant. The owner of a company sends you an e-mail expressing concern that the company is not taking advantage of its discounts offered by vendors. The company currently uses the gross method of recording purchases. The owner is considering a review of all invoices and payments from the previous period. Due to the volume of purchases, however, the owner recognizes that this is time-consuming and costly. The owner *seeks your advice about monitoring purchase discounts* in the future. Provide a response in memorandum form. *Hint:* It will help to review the recording of purchase discounts in Appendix 4C.

TAKING IT TO THE NET

C1   P1

BTN 6-3   Visit the Association of Certified Fraud Examiners website and open the "2016 Report to the Nations" (**s3-us-west-2.amazonaws.com/acfepublic/2016-report-to-the-nations.pdf**). Read the two-page Executive Summary and fill in the following blanks.

1. The median loss for all cases in our study was _____, with _____ of cases causing losses of $1 million or more.
2. The typical organization loses _____ of revenues in a given year as a result of fraud.
3. The median duration—the amount of time from when the fraud commenced until it was detected—for the fraud cases reported to us was _____.
4. Asset misappropriation was by far the most common form of occupational fraud, occurring in more than _____ of cases, but causing the smallest median loss of _____.
5. Financial statement fraud was on the other end of the spectrum, occurring in less than 10% of cases but causing a median loss of _____. Corruption cases fell in the middle, with _____ of cases and a median loss of _____.
6. The most common detection method in our study was _____ (39.1% of cases).
7. Approximately _____ of the cases reported to us targeted privately held or publicly owned companies. These for-profit organizations suffered the largest median losses among the types of organizations analyzed, at _____ and _____, respectively.

TEAMWORK IN ACTION

C1

BTN 6-4   Organize the class into teams. Each team must prepare a list of 10 internal controls a consumer could observe in a typical retail department store. When called upon, the team's spokesperson must be prepared to share controls identified by the team that have not been shared by another team's spokesperson.

BTN 6-5   Review the opening feature of this chapter that highlights Sheila Marcelo and her company **Care.com**. Her company plans to open a kiosk in the Ferry Building in San Francisco to sell Care.com shirts, hats, and other merchandise. Other retail outlets and expansion plans may be in the works.

Required

1. List the seven principles of internal control and explain how a retail outlet might implement each of the principles in its store.
2. Do you believe that a retail outlet will need to add controls to the business as it expands? Explain.

BTN 6-6   Visit an area of your college that serves the student community with either products or services. Some examples are food services, libraries, and bookstores. Identify and describe between four and eight internal controls being implemented.

7 Accounting for Receivables

Chapter Preview

VALUING RECEIVABLES	DIRECT WRITE-OFF METHOD	ALLOWANCE METHOD	ESTIMATING BAD DEBTS	NOTES RECEIVABLE
C1 Sales on credit	**P1** Recording bad debts	**P2** Recording bad debts	**P3** Percent of sales	**C2** Maturity and interest
Sales on store card	Recovery of bad debts	Writing off bad debts	Percent of receivables	**P4** Accounting for notes
Sales on bank card	When to use direct write-off	Recovery of bad debts	Aging of receivables	**C3** Selling and pledging
Sales on installment				**A1** Receivable turnover
NTK 7-1	**NTK 7-2**	**NTK 7-3**	**NTK 7-4**	**NTK 7-5**

Learning Objectives

CONCEPTUAL

C1 Describe accounts receivable and how they occur and are recorded.

C2 Describe a note receivable, the computation of its maturity date, and the recording of its existence.

C3 Explain how receivables can be converted to cash before maturity.

ANALYTICAL

A1 Compute accounts receivable turnover and use it to help assess financial condition.

PROCEDURAL

P1 Apply the direct write-off method to accounts receivable.

P2 Apply the allowance method to accounts receivable.

P3 Estimate uncollectibles based on sales and accounts receivable.

P4 Record the honoring and dishonoring of a note and adjustments for interest.

At Face Value

"Taking initiative pays off"—**SHERYL SANDBERG**

MENLO PARK, CA—Many know the story of how Mark Zuckerberg started **Facebook** (**Facebook.com**) in his college dorm room. How Facebook went from a "cool website" to a profitable company is less well known.

It began at a Christmas party when Sheryl Sandberg met Mark. "We talked for probably an hour by the door," recalls Mark. After much convincing, Sheryl joined Facebook as its chief operating officer.

Sheryl began by reviewing Facebook's financial statements and was alarmed by the lack of revenue and receivables. "There was this open question," explains Sheryl. "Could we make money . . . ever?" She organized a meeting where ideas such as charging a subscription fee and inserting ads were proposed.

As we now know, Facebook committed to an ad-focused model. The strategy was a huge success, and revenues and receivables soared. Sheryl then moved to her next challenge: managing accounts receivable.

Sheryl and Mark saw that decisions on credit sales and extending credit were impacting income. To combat risk of loss, credit is extended to customers who make timely payments.

©Kim White/Bloomberg/Getty Images

Sheryl and Mark also look at cash inflow patterns to estimate uncollectibles and minimize bad debts.

Sheryl enjoys Facebook's success, but her passion is "mission-based." She explains: "I believe strongly in what Facebook's doing. That's why I get up and go to work every day."

Sources: *Facebook website,* January 2019; *BSR.org,* April 2016; *McKinsey,* April 2013; *New Yorker,* July 2011

VALUING ACCOUNTS RECEIVABLE

A *receivable* is an amount due from another party. The two most common receivables are accounts receivable and notes receivable. Other receivables include interest receivable, rent receivable, tax refund receivable, and receivables from employees.

Accounts receivable are amounts due from customers for credit sales. Exhibit 7.1 shows amounts of receivables and their percent of total assets for some well-known companies.

C1
Describe accounts receivable and how they occur and are recorded.

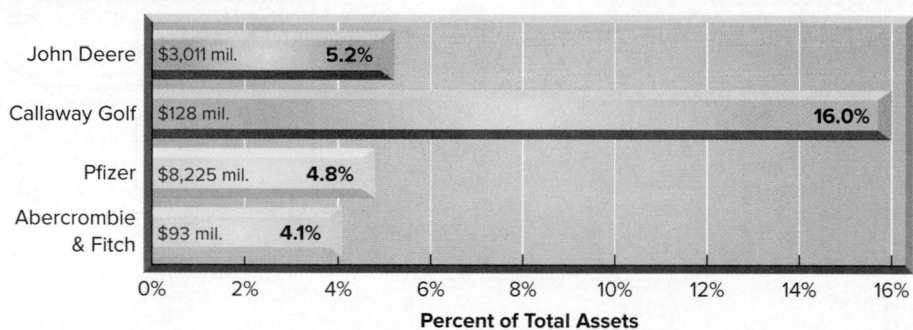

EXHIBIT 7.1

Accounts Receivable for Selected Companies

Sales on Credit Credit sales are recorded by increasing (debiting) Accounts Receivable. The general ledger has a single Accounts Receivable account (called a *control* account). A company uses a separate account for each customer to track how much that customer purchases, has already paid, and still owes. A supplementary record has a separate account for each customer and is called the *accounts receivable ledger* (or *accounts receivable subsidiary ledger*).

Exhibit 7.2 shows the relation between the Accounts Receivable account in the general ledger and its customer accounts in the accounts receivable ledger for TechCom, a small wholesaler. TechCom's accounts receivable reports a $3,000 ending balance for June 30. TechCom has two credit customers: CompStore and RDA Electronics. Its *schedule of accounts receivable* shows that the $3,000 balance of the Accounts Receivable account in the general ledger equals the total of its two customers' balances in the accounts receivable ledger.

EXHIBIT 7.2

General Ledger and the Accounts Receivable Ledger (before July 1 transactions)

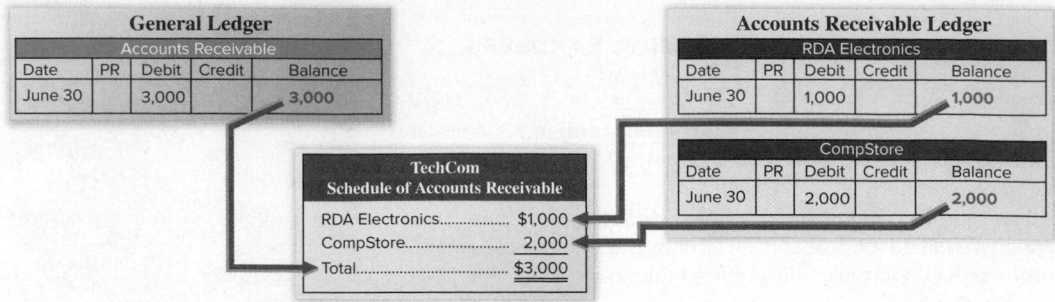

General Ledger				
Accounts Receivable				
Date	PR	Debit	Credit	Balance
June 30		3,000		3,000

TechCom
Schedule of Accounts Receivable
RDA Electronics................. $1,000
CompStore......................... 2,000
Total.................................... $3,000

Accounts Receivable Ledger				
RDA Electronics				
Date	PR	Debit	Credit	Balance
June 30		1,000		1,000

CompStore				
Date	PR	Debit	Credit	Balance
June 30		2,000		2,000

EXHIBIT 7.3

Accounts Receivable Transactions

Assets = Liabilities + Equity
+950   +950

Assets = Liabilities + Equity
+720
−720

To see how to record accounts receivable from credit sales, we look at two transactions between TechCom and its credit customers—see Exhibit 7.3. The first is a credit sale of $950 to CompStore. The second is a collection of $720 from RDA Electronics from a prior credit sale.

July 1	Accounts Receivable—CompStore	950	
	Sales		950
	*Record credit sales.**		
July 1	Cash	720	
	Accounts Receivable—RDA Electronics..............		720
	Record collection of credit sales.		

*We omit the entry to Dr. Cost of Sales and Cr. Inventory to focus on sales and receivables; no sales returns and allowances are expected.

Exhibit 7.4 shows the general ledger and the accounts receivable ledger after recording the two July 1 transactions. The general ledger shows the effects of the sale, the collection, and the resulting balance of $3,230. These transactions are also shown in the individual customer accounts: RDA Electronics's ending balance is $280 and CompStore's ending balance is $2,950. The $3,230 total of customer accounts equals the balance of the Accounts Receivable account in the general ledger.

EXHIBIT 7.4

General Ledger and the Accounts Receivable Ledger (after July 1 transactions)

General Ledger				
Accounts Receivable				
Date	PR	Debit	Credit	Balance
June 30		3,000		3,000
July 1		950		3,950
July 1			720	**3,230**

TechCom
Schedule of Accounts Receivable
RDA Electronics................. $ 280
CompStore......................... 2,950
Total.................................... $3,230

Accounts Receivable Ledger				
RDA Electronics				
Date	PR	Debit	Credit	Balance
June 30		1,000		1,000
July 1			720	**280**

CompStore				
Date	PR	Debit	Credit	Balance
June 30		2,000		2,000
July 1		950		**2,950**

Sales on Store Credit Cards   Like TechCom, many large retailers such as **Home Depot** sell on credit. Many also have their own credit cards to grant credit to approved customers and to earn interest on any balance past due. The entries in this case are the same as those for TechCom except for added interest revenue as follows.

Assets = Liabilities + Equity
+1,000   +1,000

Assets = Liabilities + Equity
+15   +15

Nov. 1	Accounts Receivable	1,000	
	Sales		1,000
	Record sales on store credit card.		
Dec. 31	Accounts Receivable	15	
	Interest Revenue......................................		15
	Interest of $15 earned on store card sales past due.		

Sales on Bank Credit Cards

Most companies allow customers to pay using bank (or third-party) credit cards, such as **Visa**, **Mastercard**, or **American Express**, and debit cards. Sellers allow customers to use credit cards and debit cards for several reasons. First, the seller does not have to decide who gets credit and how much. Second, the seller avoids the risk of customers not paying (this risk is transferred to the card company). Third, the seller typically receives cash from the card company sooner than had it granted credit directly to customers. Fourth, more credit options for customers can lead to more sales.

©Science Photo Library/Image Source

The seller pays a fee when a card is used by the customer, often ranging from 1% to 5% of card sales. This fee reduces the cash received by the seller. If TechCom has $100 of credit card sales with a 4% fee, the entry follows. Some sellers report Credit Card Expense in the income statement as a discount subtracted from sales to get net sales. Other sellers report it as a selling expense or an administrative expense. In this text, we report credit card expense as a selling expense.

Point: JCPenney reported third-party credit card costs exceeding $10 million.

July 15	Cash...	96	
	Credit Card Expense...	4	
	Sales..		100
	*Record credit card sales less a 4% credit card expense.**		

Assets = Liabilities + Equity
+96   +100
                                  −4

*We omit the entry to Dr. Cost of Sales and Cr. Inventory to focus on credit card expense.

◼ Decision Insight

Credit or Debit? A credit card is authorization by the card company of a line of credit for the buyer—hence, the term *credit card*. A buyer's debit card purchase reduces the buyer's Cash account balance at the card company, which is often a bank. Because the buyer's Cash account balance is a liability (with a credit balance) for the card company to the buyer, the card company would debit that account for a buyer's purchase—hence, the term *debit card*. ◼

Sales on Installment

Many companies allow their credit customers to make periodic payments over several months. For example, **Harley-Davidson** reports more than $2 billion in installment receivables. The seller reports such assets as *installment accounts* (or *finance*) *receivable,* which are amounts owed by customers from credit sales for which payment is required in periodic amounts. Most installment receivables require interest payments, and they can be either current or noncurrent assets depending on the time of repayment.

©PhotoAlto

◼ Decision Maker

Entrepreneur As a small retailer, you are considering allowing customers to use credit cards. Until now, your store accepted only cash. What analysis do you use to decide? ◼ *Answer:* This analysis must weigh benefits versus costs. The main benefit is the potential to increase sales by attracting customers who prefer credit cards. The main cost is the fee charged by the credit card company. We must estimate the expected increase in sales from allowing credit cards and then subtract (1) normal costs and expenses and (2) card fees from the expected sales increase. If analysis shows an increase in profit, the store should probably accept credit cards.

A small retailer accepts credit cards and has its own store credit card. Prepare journal entries to record the following transactions for the retailer. (The retailer uses the perpetual inventory system.)

Jan. 2 Sold merchandise for $1,000 (that had cost $600) and accepted the customer's AA Bank Card. AA charges a 5% fee.

6 Sold merchandise for $400 (that had cost $300) and accepted the customer's VIZA Card. VIZA charges a 3% fee.

31 Recognized the $75 interest revenue earned on its store credit card for January.

 **NEED-TO-KNOW** 7-1

Credit Card Sales

C1

Solution

Jan. 2	Cash	950	
	Credit Card Expense*	50	
	Sales		1,000
	*Record credit card sales less 5% fee. *($1,000 × 0.05)*		
Jan. 2	Cost of Goods Sold	600	
	Merchandise Inventory		600
	Record cost of sales.		
Jan. 6	Cash	388	
	Credit Card Expense†	12	
	Sales		400
	Record credit card sales less 3% fee. †($400 × 0.03)		
Jan. 6	Cost of Goods Sold	300	
	Merchandise Inventory		300
	Record cost of sales.		
Jan. 31	Accounts Receivable	75	
	Interest Revenue		75
	Record interest earned from store credit card.		

Do More: QS 7-1, E 7-2, E 7-3

DIRECT WRITE-OFF METHOD

P1

Apply the direct write-off method to accounts receivable.

When a company directly grants credit to customers, it expects some customers will not pay what they promised. The accounts of these customers are *uncollectible accounts,* or **bad debts.** Uncollectible accounts are an expense of selling on credit. Why do companies sell on credit if they expect uncollectible accounts? The answer is that companies believe that granting credit will increase total sales enough to offset bad debts. Companies use two methods for uncollectible accounts: (1) direct write-off method and (2) allowance method.

Recording and Writing Off Bad Debts   The **direct write-off method** records the loss from an uncollectible account receivable when it is determined to be uncollectible. No attempt is made to predict bad debts expense. If TechCom determines on January 23 that it cannot collect $520 owed by its customer J. Kent, it records the loss as follows. The debit in this entry charges the uncollectible amount directly to the current period's Bad Debts Expense account. The credit removes its balance from the Accounts Receivable account.

Point: Managers realize that some credit sales will be uncollectible, but which credit sales is unknown.

Assets = Liabilities + Equity
−520   −520

Jan. 23	Bad Debts Expense	520	
	Accounts Receivable—J. Kent		520
	Write off an uncollectible account.		

Recovering a Bad Debt   Sometimes an account written off is later collected. If the account of J. Kent that was written off directly to Bad Debts Expense is later collected in full, then we record two entries.

Point: Recovery of a bad debt always requires two journal entries.

Assets = Liabilities + Equity
+520   +520

Assets = Liabilities + Equity
+520
−520

Mar. 11	Accounts Receivable—J. Kent	520	
	Bad Debts Expense		520
	Reinstate account previously written off.		
Mar. 11	Cash	520	
	Accounts Receivable—J. Kent		520
	Record full payment of account.		

Assessing the Direct Write-Off Method   Many publicly traded companies and thousands of privately held companies use the direct write-off method; they include

Rand Medical Billing, Gateway Distributors, First Industrial Realty, New Frontier Energy, Globalink, Solar3D, and **Sub Surface Waste Management**. The following disclosure by **Pharma-Bio Serv** is the usual justification: Bad debts are mainly accounted for using the direct write-off method . . . this method approximates that of the allowance method.

Companies weigh at least two concepts when considering use of the direct write-off method. (1) Expense recognition requires expenses be reported in the same period as the sales they helped produce. The direct write-off method usually does *not* best match sales and expenses because bad debts expense is not recorded until an account becomes uncollectible, which often occurs in a period after the credit sale. (2) The materiality constraint permits use of the direct write-off method when its results are similar to using the allowance method. Otherwise, companies must use the allowance method.

Direct write-off method

Advantages:
- Simple
- No estimates needed

Disadvantages:
- Receivables and income temporarily overstated
- Bad debts expense often not matched with sales

A retailer uses the direct write-off method. Record the following transactions.

Feb. 14   The retailer determines that it cannot collect $400 of its accounts receivable from a customer named ZZZ Company.

Apr. 1   ZZZ Company unexpectedly pays its account in full to the retailer, which then records its recovery of this bad debt.

NEED-TO-KNOW 7-2

Entries under Direct Write-Off Method

P1

Solution

Feb. 14	Bad Debts Expense	400	
	Accounts Receivable—ZZZ Co.		400
	Write off an account.		
Apr. 1	Accounts Receivable—ZZZ Co.	400	
	Bad Debts Expense...............................		400
	Reinstate an account previously written off.		
Apr. 1	Cash	400	
	Accounts Receivable—ZZZ Co.		400
	Record cash received on account.		

Do More: QS 7-2, QS 7-3, E 7-4

ALLOWANCE METHOD

The **allowance method** for bad debts matches the *estimated* loss from uncollectible accounts receivable against the sales they helped produce. We use estimated losses because when sales occur, sellers do not know which customers will not pay. This means that at the end of each period, the allowance method requires an estimate of the total bad debts expected from that period's sales. This method has two advantages over the direct write-off method: (1) It records estimated bad debts expense in the period when the related sales are recorded and (2) it reports accounts receivable on the balance sheet at the estimated amount to be collected.

P2

Apply the allowance method to accounts receivable.

Recording Bad Debts Expense   The allowance method estimates bad debts expense at the end of each accounting period and records it with an adjusting entry. TechCom had credit sales of $300,000 in its first year of operations. At the end of the first year, $20,000 of credit sales were uncollected. Based on the experience of similar businesses, TechCom estimates that $1,500 of its accounts receivable is uncollectible and makes the following adjusting entry.

Method	Bad Debts Expense Recorded . . .
Direct write-off. . .	*In future,* when accounts are uncollectible.
Allowance.	*Currently,* using estimated uncollectibles.

Dec. 31	Bad Debts Expense	1,500	
	Allowance for Doubtful Accounts..................		1,500
	Record estimated bad debts.		

Assets = Liabilities + Equity
−1,500   −1,500

The estimated Bad Debts Expense of $1,500 is reported on the income statement (as either a selling expense or an administrative expense). The **Allowance for Doubtful Accounts** is a contra asset account. TechCom's account balances for Accounts Receivable and the Allowance for Doubtful Accounts follow.

Accounts Receivable			
Dec. 31	20,000		

Allowance for Doubtful Accounts			
		Dec. 31	1,500

The Allowance for Doubtful Accounts credit balance of $1,500 reduces accounts receivable to its **realizable value,** which is the amount expected to be received. Although credit customers owe $20,000 to TechCom, only $18,500 is expected from customers. (TechCom still bills its customers for $20,000.) In the balance sheet, the Allowance for Doubtful Accounts is subtracted from Accounts Receivable and is often reported as follows.

Current assets
Accounts receivable...................................... $20,000
Less allowance for doubtful accounts...................... 1,500 $18,500

Sometimes the Allowance for Doubtful Accounts is not reported separately as follows.

Current assets
Accounts receivable (net of $1,500 doubtful accounts).......... $18,500

Writing Off a Bad Debt   When specific accounts become uncollectible, they are written off against the Allowance for Doubtful Accounts. TechCom decides that J. Kent's $520 account is uncollectible and makes the following entry to write it off.

Assets = Liabilities + Equity
+520
−520

Jan. 23	Allowance for Doubtful Accounts	520	
	Accounts Receivable—J. Kent		520
	Write off an uncollectible account.		

Point: Bad Debts Expense is not debited in the write-off because it was recorded in the period when sales occurred.

This entry removes $520 from the Accounts Receivable account (and the subsidiary ledger). The general ledger accounts appear as follows.

Accounts Receivable			
Dec. 31	20,000	Jan. 23	**520**

Allowance for Doubtful Accounts			
Jan. 23	**520**	Dec. 31	1,500

Point: In posting a write-off, the Explanation column shows the reason for this credit so it is not misinterpreted as payment in full.

The write-off does *not* affect the realizable value of accounts receivable; see Exhibit 7.5. Neither total assets nor net income is affected by the write-off of a specific account. Instead, both assets and net income are affected in the period when bad debts expense is predicted and recorded with an adjusting entry.

EXHIBIT 7.5

Realizable Value before and after Write-Off of a Bad Debt

	Before Write-Off	After Write-Off
Accounts receivable	$ 20,000	$ 19,480
Less allowance for doubtful accounts	1,500	980
Realizable value of accounts receivable	$18,500	$18,500

Exhibit 7.6 portrays the allowance method. It shows the creation of the allowance for future write-offs—adding to a cookie jar. It also shows the decrease of the allowance through write-offs—taking cookies from the jar.

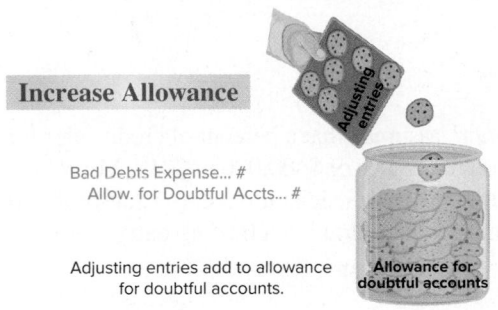

EXHIBIT 7.6

Increases and Decreases to the Allowance for Doubtful Accounts

Increase Allowance

Bad Debts Expense... #
Allow. for Doubtful Accts... #

Adjusting entries add to allowance for doubtful accounts.

Decrease Allowance

Write-offs

Allow. for Doubtful Accts... #
Accts Receivable—J.Kent... #

Bad debt write-offs subtract from allowance for doubtful accounts.

Recovering a Bad Debt

If an account that was written off is later collected, two entries are made. The first is to reverse the write-off and reinstate the customer's account. The second is to record the collection of the reinstated account. If on March 11 Kent pays in full his account previously written off, the entries are

Mar. 11	Accounts Receivable—J. Kent............................	520	
	Allowance for Doubtful Accounts...................		520
	Reinstate account previously written off.		
Mar. 11	Cash...	520	
	Accounts Receivable—J. Kent		520
	Record full payment of account.		

Assets = Liabilities + Equity
+520
−520

Assets = Liabilities + Equity
+520
−520

Kent paid the entire amount previously written off, but sometimes a customer pays only a portion. If we believe this customer will later pay in full, we return the entire amount owed to accounts receivable (in the first entry only). If we expect no further collection, we return only the amount paid.

A retailer uses the allowance method. Record the following transactions.

Dec. 31   The retailer estimates $3,000 of its accounts receivable are uncollectible at its year-end.
Feb. 14   The retailer determines that it cannot collect $400 of its accounts receivable from a customer named ZZZ Company.
Apr. 1   ZZZ Company unexpectedly pays its account in full to the retailer, which then records its recovery of this bad debt.

NEED-TO-KNOW 7-3

Entries under Allowance Method

P2

Solution

Dec. 31	Bad Debts Expense	3,000	
	Allowance for Doubtful Accounts...................		3,000
	Record estimated bad debts.		
Feb. 14	Allowance for Doubtful Accounts	400	
	Accounts Receivable—ZZZ Co.		400
	Write off an account.		
Apr. 1	Accounts Receivable—ZZZ Co.........................	400	
	Allowance for Doubtful Accounts...................		400
	Reinstate an account previously written off.		
Apr. 1	Cash...	400	
	Accounts Receivable—ZZZ Co.		400
	Record cash received on account.		

Do More: QS 7-4, QS 7-5, E 7-5

ESTIMATING BAD DEBTS

P3 _____

Estimate uncollectibles based on sales and accounts receivable.

Point: Focus on *credit* sales because cash sales do not produce bad debts.

Assets = Liabilities + Equity
−2,400   −2,400

Bad Debts Expense	
Unadj. bal.	0
Adj. (% sales)	**2,400**
Est. bal.	2,400

Point: When using the *percent of sales method* for estimating uncollectibles, and because the "Unadj. bal." in Bad Debts Expense is always $0, the adjusting entry amount always equals the % of sales.

Bad debts expense is estimated under the allowance method. This section covers methods for estimating bad debts expense.

Percent of Sales Method

The *percent of sales method,* or *income statement method,* assumes that a percent of credit sales for the period is uncollectible. For example, Musicland has credit sales of $400,000 in 2019. Musicland estimates 0.6% of credit sales to be uncollectible. This means Musicland expects $2,400 of bad debts expense from its sales ($400,000 × 0.006) and makes the following adjusting entry.

Dec. 31*	Bad Debts Expense	2,400	
	Allowance for Doubtful Accounts.		2,400
	Record estimated bad debts.		

*The adjusting entry applies our three-step adjusting entry process:
Step 1: Current balance for Bad Debts Expense is $0 debit (as the expense account was closed in prior period).
Step 2: Current balance for Bad Debts Expense should be $2,400 debit.
Step 3: Record entry to get from step 1 to step 2.

Allowance for Doubtful Accounts, a balance sheet account, is not closed at period end. Unless a company is in its first period of operations, its Allowance for Doubtful Accounts balance rarely equals the Bad Debts Expense balance. (When computing bad debts expense as a percent of sales, managers monitor and adjust the percent so it is not too high or too low.)

Percent of Receivables Method

The *percent of accounts receivable method,* also called a *balance sheet method,* assumes that a percent of a company's receivables is uncollectible. This percent is based on experience and economic trends. Total receivables is multiplied by this percent to get the estimated uncollectible amount as reported in the balance sheet as Allowance for Doubtful Accounts.

Assume Musicland has $50,000 of accounts receivable on December 31, 2019. It estimates 5% of its receivables is uncollectible. This means that *after* the adjusting entry is posted, we want the Allowance for Doubtful Accounts to show a $2,500 credit balance (5% of $50,000). Musicland's beginning balance is $2,200 on December 31, 2018—see Exhibit 7.7.

EXHIBIT 7.7

Allowance for Doubtful Accounts after Bad Debts Adjusting Entry

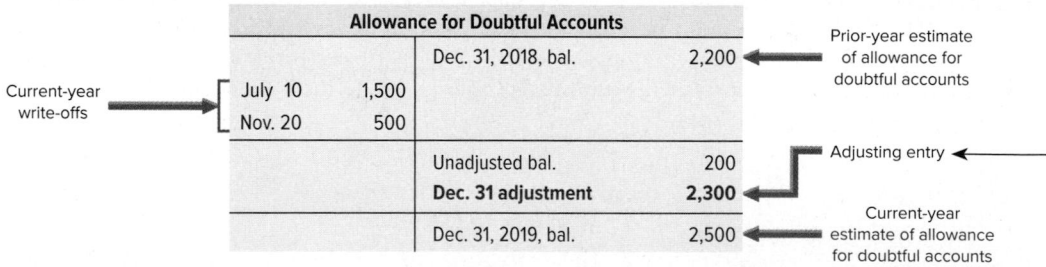

During 2019, accounts of customers are written off on July 10 and November 20. The account has a $200 credit balance *before* the December 31, 2019, adjustment. The adjusting entry to give the allowance account the estimated $2,500 balance is

Assets = Liabilities + Equity
−2,300   −2,300

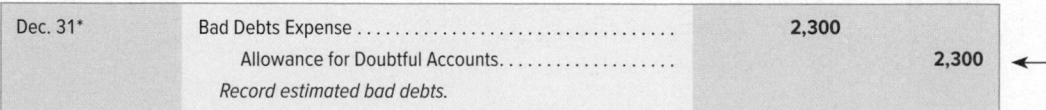

Dec. 31*	Bad Debts Expense	2,300	
	Allowance for Doubtful Accounts.		2,300
	Record estimated bad debts.		

*The adjusting entry applies our three-step adjusting entry process:
Step 1: Current balance for Allowance account is $200 credit.
Step 2: Current balance for Allowance account should be $2,500 credit.
Step 3: Record entry to get from step 1 to step 2.

■ **Decision Insight**

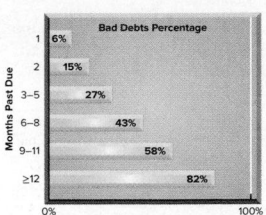

For the Ages Unlike wine, accounts receivable do not improve with age. The longer a receivable is past due, the less likely it is to be collected. An *aging schedule* uses this knowledge to estimate bad debts. The chart here is from a survey that reported estimates of bad debts for receivables grouped by how long they were past their due dates. Each company sets its own estimates based on its customers and its customers' payment patterns. ■

Aging of Receivables Method

The **aging of accounts receivable** method, also called a *balance sheet method,* is applied like the percent of receivables method except that several percentages are used (versus one) to estimate the allowance. Each receivable is classified by how long it is past its due date. Then estimates of uncollectible amounts are made assuming that the longer an amount is past due, the more likely it is uncollectible. After the amounts are classified (or aged), experience is used to estimate the percent of each uncollectible class. These percents are multiplied by the amounts in each class to get the estimated balance of the Allowance for Doubtful Accounts. An example schedule is shown in Exhibit 7.8.

Exhibit 7.8 lists each customer's balance assigned to one of five classes based on its days past due. The amounts in each class are totaled and multiplied by the estimated percent of uncollectible accounts for each class.

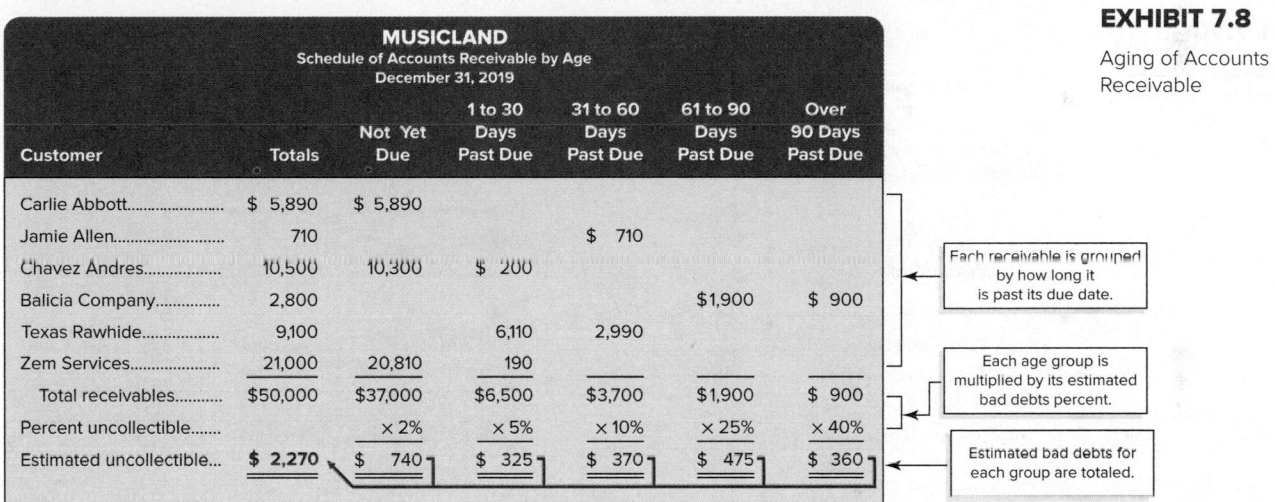

EXHIBIT 7.8

Aging of Accounts Receivable

To explain, Musicland has $3,700 in accounts receivable that are 31 to 60 days past due. Management estimates 10% of the amounts in this class are uncollectible, or a total of $370 ($3,700 × 10%). Similar analysis is done for each class. The final total of $2,270 ($740 + $325 + $370 + $475 + $360) shown in the first column is the estimated balance for the Allowance for Doubtful Accounts. Exhibit 7.9 shows that because the allowance account has an unadjusted

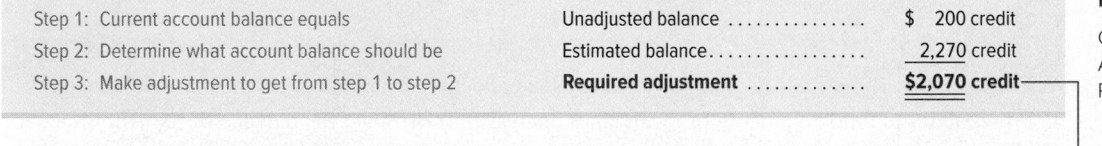

EXHIBIT 7.9

Computation of the Required Adjustment for the Accounts Receivable Method

credit balance of $200, the required adjustment to the Allowance for Doubtful Accounts is $2,070. (We can use a T-account for this analysis as shown to the side.) This analysis yields the following end-of-period adjusting entry.

Allowance for Doubtful Accounts		
	Unadj. bal.	200
	Req. adj.	**2,070**
	Est. bal.	2,270

Dec. 31	Bad Debts Expense	2,070	
	Allowance for Doubtful Accounts.		2,070
	Record estimated bad debts.		

Assets = Liabilities + Equity
−2,070   −2,070

Point: A debit balance implies that write-offs for that period exceed the total allowance.

Allowance for Doubtful Accounts

Unadj. bal. 500	
	Req. adj. 2,770
	Est. bal. 2,270

Unadjusted Debit Balance in the Allowance Account   If the allowance account had an unadjusted *debit* balance of $500 (instead of the $200 credit balance), its required adjustment is computed as follows. (A T-account can be used for this analysis as shown to the side.)

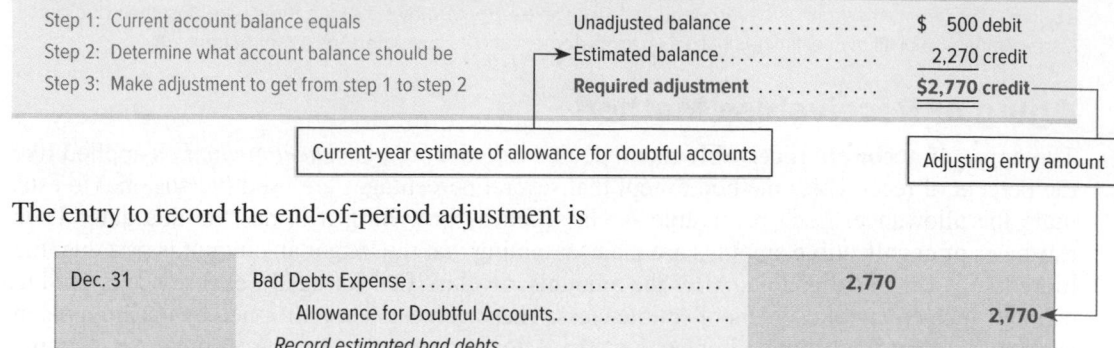

Step 1: Current account balance equals   Unadjusted balance .... $ 500 debit
Step 2: Determine what account balance should be   Estimated balance................   2,270 credit
Step 3: Make adjustment to get from step 1 to step 2   Required adjustment .... $2,770 credit

Current-year estimate of allowance for doubtful accounts

Adjusting entry amount

The entry to record the end-of-period adjustment is

Assets = Liabilities + Equity
−2,770   −2,770

Dec. 31	Bad Debts Expense	2,770	
	Allowance for Doubtful Accounts..................		2,770
	Record estimated bad debts.		

Point: Credit approval is usually not assigned to the selling dept. because its goal is to increase sales, and it may approve customers at the cost of increased bad debts.

EXHIBIT 7.10

Methods to Estimate Bad Debts under the Allowance Method

Estimating Bad Debts—Summary of Methods   Exhibit 7.10 summarizes the three estimation methods. The aging of accounts receivable method focuses on specific accounts and is usually the most reliable of the estimation methods.

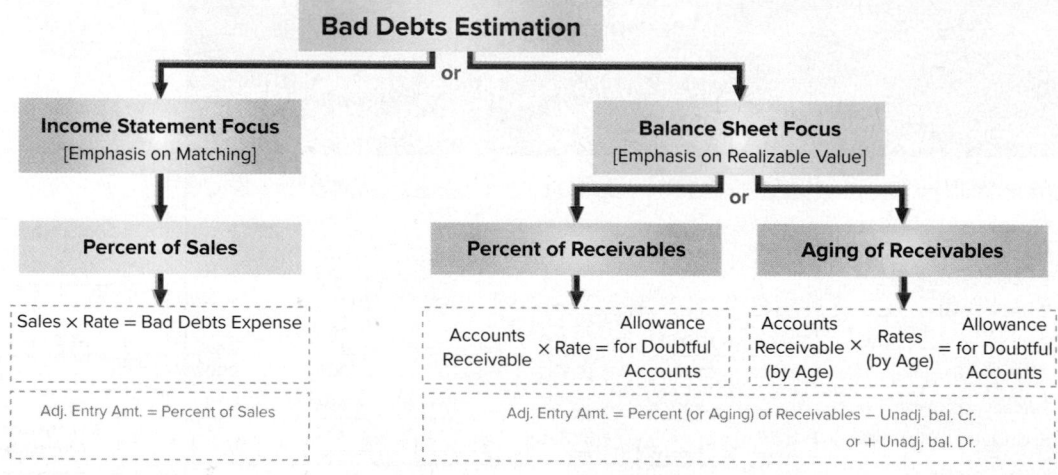

Bad Debts Estimation
or

Income Statement Focus
[Emphasis on Matching]

Balance Sheet Focus
[Emphasis on Realizable Value]
or

Percent of Sales

Percent of Receivables

Aging of Receivables

Sales × Rate = Bad Debts Expense

$$\text{Accounts Receivable} \times \text{Rate} = \text{Allowance for Doubtful Accounts}$$

$$\text{Accounts Receivable (by Age)} \times \text{Rates (by Age)} = \text{Allowance for Doubtful Accounts}$$

Adj. Entry Amt. = Percent of Sales

Adj. Entry Amt. = Percent (or Aging) of Receivables − Unadj. bal. Cr.
or + Unadj. bal. Dr.

©kali9/Getty Images

■ **Decision Maker**

Labor Union   One week prior to labor contract negotiations, financial statements are released showing no income growth. A 10% growth was predicted. Your analysis finds that the company increased its allowance for uncollectibles from 1.5% to 4.5% of receivables. Without this change, income would show a 9% growth. Does this analysis impact negotiations? ■   *Answer:* Yes, this information is likely to impact negotiations. The obvious question is why the company greatly increased this allowance. The large increase means a substantial increase in bad debts expense and a decrease in earnings. This change (coming prior to labor negotiations) also raises concerns because it reduces labor's bargaining power. We want to ask management for documentation justifying this increase.

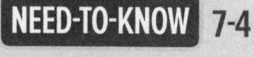 **NEED-TO-KNOW** 7-4

Estimating Bad Debts

P3

At its December 31 year-end, a company estimates uncollectible accounts using the allowance method.

1. It prepared the following aging of receivables analysis. (a) Estimate the balance of the Allowance for Doubtful Accounts using the aging of accounts receivable method. (b) Prepare the adjusting entry to record bad debts expense using the estimate from part *a*. Assume the unadjusted balance in the Allowance for Doubtful Accounts is a $10 debit.

			Days Past Due			
	Total	0	1 to 30	31 to 60	61 to 90	Over 90
Accounts receivable............	$2,600	$2,000	$300	$80	$100	$120
Percent uncollectible		1%	2%	5%	7%	10%

2. Refer to the data in part 1. (a) Estimate the balance of the Allowance for Doubtful Accounts assuming the company uses 2% of total accounts receivable to estimate uncollectibles instead of the aging of receivables method in part 1. (b) Prepare the adjusting entry to record bad debts expense using the estimate from part 2*a*. Assume the unadjusted balance in the Allowance for Doubtful Accounts is a $4 credit.

3. Refer to the data in part 1. (a) Estimate the balance of the uncollectibles assuming the company uses 0.5% of annual credit sales (annual credit sales were $10,000). (b) Prepare the adjusting entry to record bad debts expense using the estimate from part 3*a*. Assume the unadjusted balance in the Allowance for Doubtful Accounts is a $4 credit.

Solutions

1a. Computation of the estimated balance of the allowance for uncollectibles.

Not due	$2,000 × 0.01 =	$20
1 to 30	300 × 0.02 =	6
31 to 60	80 × 0.05 =	4
61 to 90	100 × 0.07 =	7
Over 90	120 × 0.10 =	12
		$49 credit

Do More: QS 7-7, QS 7-8, QS 7-9, E 7-6, E 7-7, E 7-8, E 7-9, E 7-10, E 7-11

1b.

Dec. 31	Bad Debts Expense	59	
	Allowance for Doubtful Accounts		59
	*Record estimated bad debts.**		

Allowance for Doubtful Accounts

Unadj. Dec. 31	10		
		Adj. Dec. 31	59
		Est. bal. Dec. 31	49

Step 1:	Current account balance equals	*Unadjusted balance	$10 debit
Step 2:	Determine what account balance should be	Estimated balance	49 credit
Step 3:	Make adjustment to get from step 1 to step 2	Required adjustment	$59 credit

2a. Computation of the estimated balance of the allowance for uncollectibles.

$2,600 × 0.02 = $52 credit

2b.

Dec. 31	Bad Debts Expense	48	
	Allowance for Doubtful Accounts		48
	*Record estimated bad debts.**		

Allowance for Doubtful Accounts

		Unadj. Dec. 31	4
		Adj. Dec. 31	48
		Est. bal. Dec. 31	52

Step 1:	Current account balance equals	*Unadjusted balance	$ 4 credit
Step 2:	Determine what account balance should be	Estimated balance	52 credit
Step 3:	Make adjustment to get from step 1 to step 2	Required adjustment	$48 credit

3a. Computation of the estimated balance of the bad debts expense.

$10,000 × 0.005 = $50 credit

3b.

Dec. 31	Bad Debts Expense	50	
	Allowance for Doubtful Accounts		50
	Record estimated bad debts.		

Bad Debts Expense

Unadj. Dec. 31	0	
Adj. Dec. 31	50	
Est. bal. Dec. 31	50	

NOTES RECEIVABLE

A **promissory note** is a written promise to pay a specified amount, usually with interest, either on demand or at a stated future date. Promissory notes are used in many transactions, including paying for products and services and lending and borrowing money. Sellers sometimes ask for a note to replace an account receivable when a customer requests more time to pay a past-due account. Sellers prefer notes when the credit period is long and when the receivable is for a large amount. If a lawsuit is needed to collect from a customer, a note is the customer's written promise to pay the debt, its amount, and its terms.

C2

Describe a note receivable, the computation of its maturity date, and the recording of its existence.

Exhibit 7.11 shows a promissory note dated July 10, 2019. For this note, Julia Browne promises to pay TechCom or to its order a specified amount ($1,000), called the **principal of a note,** at a stated future date (October 8, 2019). As the one who signed the note and promised to pay it, Browne is the **maker of the note.** As the person to whom the note is payable, TechCom is the **payee of the note.** To Browne, the note is a liability called a *note payable*. To TechCom, the same note is an asset called a *note receivable*. This note's interest rate is 12%, as written on the note. **Interest** is the charge for using the money until its due date. To a borrower, interest is an expense. To a lender, it is revenue.

EXHIBIT 7.11

Promissory Note

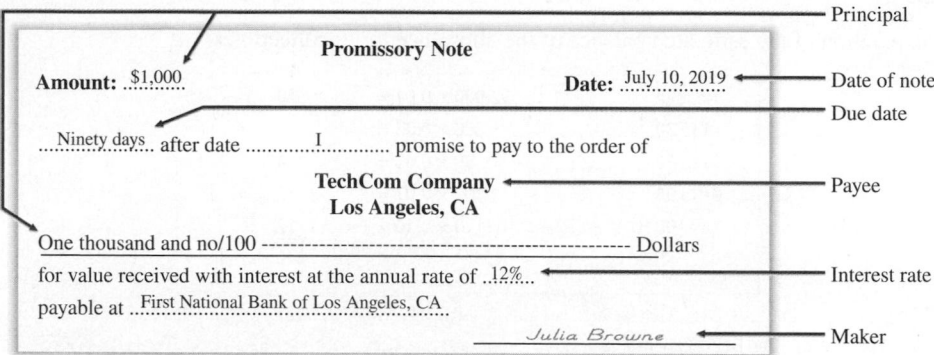

Computing Maturity and Interest

This section covers a note's maturity date, period covered, and interest computation.

Maturity Date and Period   The **maturity date of a note** is the day the note (principal and interest) must be repaid. The *period* of a note is the time from the note's (contract) date to its maturity date. Many notes mature in less than a full year, and the period they cover is often expressed in days. As an example, a five-day note dated June 15 matures and is due on June 20. A 90-day note dated July 10 matures on October 8. This count is shown in Exhibit 7.12. The period of a note is sometimes expressed in months or years. When months are used, the note is payable in the month of its maturity on the *same day of the month* as its original date. A nine-month note dated July 10, for example, is payable on April 10. The same rule applies when years are used.

Point: When counting days, omit the day a note is issued, but count the due date.

EXHIBIT 7.12

Maturity Date Computation

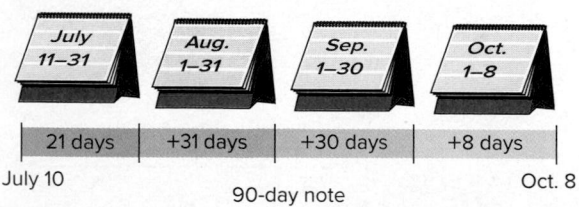

Days in July.	31
Minus the date of the note.	10
Days remaining in July.	21 ← July 11–31
Add days in August.	31 ← Aug. 1–31
Add days in September	30 ← Sep. 1–30
Days to equal 90 days, or **maturity date of October 8**.	8 ← Oct. 1–8
Period of the note in days	90

Point: Excel for maturity date.

	A	B
1	Note date	10-Jul
2	# of days	90
3	Maturity	

=B1+B2 = 8-Oct

EXHIBIT 7.13

Computation of Interest Formula

Interest Computation   *Interest* is the cost of borrowing money for the borrower and the profit from lending money for the lender. Unless otherwise stated, the rate of interest on a note is the rate charged for the use of principal for one year (*annual rate*). The formula for computing interest on a note is in Exhibit 7.13.

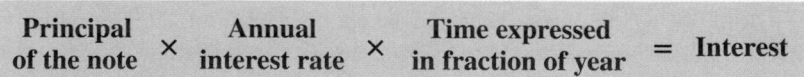

| Principal of the note | × | Annual interest rate | × | Time expressed in fraction of year | = | Interest |

To simplify interest computations, a year is commonly treated as having 360 days (called the *banker's rule* and widely used in business transactions). **We treat a year as having 360 days**

for interest computations in examples and assignments. Using the promissory note in Exhibit 7.11, where we have a 90-day, 12%, $1,000 note, the total interest follows.

$$\$1,000 \times 12\% \times \frac{90}{360} = \$1,000 \times 0.12 \times 0.25 = \$30$$

Point: If the *banker's rule* is <u>not</u> used, interest is **$29.589041**. The *banker's rule* yields $30, which is easier to account for than $29.589041.

Point: *Maturity value* of a note equals principal plus interest earned.

Recording Notes Receivable

Notes receivable are usually recorded in a single Notes Receivable account to simplify record-keeping. To show how we record receipt of a note, we use the $1,000, 90-day, 12% promissory note in Exhibit 7.11. TechCom received this note at the time of a product sale to Julia Browne. This is recorded as

July 10*	Notes Receivable.....................................	1,000	
	Sales		1,000
	Sold goods in exchange for a 90-day, 12% note.		

Assets = Liabilities + Equity
+1,000   +1,000

*We omit the entry to Dr. Cost of Sales and Cr. Inventory to focus on sales and receivables.

When a seller accepts a note from an overdue customer to grant a time extension on a past-due account receivable, it often will collect part of the past-due balance in cash. Assume that Tech-Com agreed to accept $232 in cash along with a $600, 60-day, 15% note from Jo Cook to settle her $832 past-due account. TechCom makes the following entry.

Oct. 5	Cash	232	
	Notes Receivable.....................................	600	
	Accounts Receivable—J. Cook.....................		832
	Received cash and note to settle account.		

Assets = Liabilities + Equity
+232
+600
−832

Valuing and Settling Notes

Recording an Honored Note
The principal and interest of a note are due on its maturity date. The maker of the note usually *honors* the note and pays it in full. When J. Cook pays the note above on its due date, TechCom records it as follows. Interest revenue, or *interest earned*, is reported on the income statement.

P4

Record the honoring and dishonoring of a note and adjustments for interest.

Dec. 4	Cash	615	
	Notes Receivable		600
	Interest Revenue...............................		15
	Collect note with interest of $600 × 15% × 60/360.		

Assets = Liabilities + Equity
+615   +15
−600

Recording a Dishonored Note
When a note's maker does not pay at maturity, the note is *dishonored*. Dishonoring a note does not mean the maker no longer has to pay. The payee still tries to collect. How do companies report this? The balance of the Notes Receivable account should only include notes that have not matured. When a note is dishonored, we remove the amount of this note from Notes Receivable and charge it back to an account receivable from its maker. Assume that J. Cook dishonors the note at maturity. The following records the dishonoring of the note.

Dec. 4	Accounts Receivable—J. Cook	615	
	Interest Revenue...............................		15
	Notes Receivable		600
	Charge account of J. Cook for a dishonored note and interest of $600 × 15% × 60/360.		

Assets = Liabilities + Equity
+615   +15
−600

Charging a dishonored note to accounts receivable does two things. First, it removes the note from the Notes Receivable account and records the dishonored note in the maker's account. Second, if the maker of the dishonored note asks for credit in the future, his or her account will show the dishonored note.

Recording End-of-Period Interest Adjustment   When notes receivable are outstanding at period-end, any accrued interest is recorded. Assume on December 16 TechCom accepts a $3,000, 60-day, 12% note from a customer. When TechCom's accounting period ends on December 31, $15 of interest has accrued on this note ($3,000 × 12% × 15/360). The following adjusting entry records this revenue.

Assets = Liabilities + Equity
+15   +15

Dec. 31	Interest Receivable	15	
	Interest Revenue................................		15
	Record accrued interest earned.		

Interest revenue is on the income statement, and interest receivable is on the balance sheet as a current asset. When the December 16 note is collected on February 14, TechCom's entry to record the cash receipt is

Assets = Liabilities + Equity
+3,060   +45
−15
−3,000

Feb. 14	Cash	3,060	
	Interest Revenue................................		45
	Interest Receivable..............................		15
	Notes Receivable		3,000
	Received payment of note and its interest.		

Total interest on the 60-day note is $60 ($3,000 × 12% × 60/360). The $15 credit to Interest Receivable is the collection of interest accrued from the December 31 entry. The $45 interest revenue is from holding the note from January 1 to February 14.

NEED-TO-KNOW 7-5

Honoring and
Dishonoring Notes

C2   P4

Ace Company purchases $1,400 of merchandise from Zitco on December 16. Zitco accepts Ace's $1,400, 90-day, 12% note as payment. Zitco's accounting period ends on December 31.

a. Prepare entries for Zitco on December 16 and December 31.
b. Prepare Zitco's March 16 entry if Ace dishonors the note.
c. Instead of the facts in part *b*, prepare Zitco's March 16 entry if Ace honors the note.
d. Assume the facts in part *b* (Ace dishonors the note). Then, on March 31, Zitco writes off the receivable from Ace Company. Prepare that write-off entry assuming that Zitco uses the allowance method.

Solution

a.

Dec. 16	Note Receivable—Ace..............................	1,400	
	Sales		1,400
Dec. 31	Interest Receivable	7	
	Interest Revenue *($1,400 × 12% × 15/360)*......		7

b.

Mar. 16	Accounts Receivable—Ace	1,442	
	Interest Revenue *($1,400 × 12% × 75/360)*......		35
	Interest Receivable..............................		7
	Notes Receivable—Ace		1,400

c.

Mar. 16	Cash	1,442	
	Interest Revenue................................		35
	Interest Receivable..............................		7
	Notes Receivable—Ace		1,400

d.

Mar. 31	Allowance for Doubtful Accounts	1,442	
	Accounts Receivable—Ace.....................		1,442

Do More: QS 7-10, QS 7-11,
QS 7-12, QS 7-13, E 7-12,
E 7-13, E 7-14, E 7-15

Disposal of Receivables

Companies convert receivables to cash before they are due if they need cash or do not want to deal with collecting receivables. This is usually done by (1) selling them or (2) using them as security for a loan.

Selling Receivables   A company can sell its receivables to a finance company or bank. The buyer, called a *factor,* acquires ownership of the receivables and receives cash when they come due. The seller is charged a *factoring fee.* By incurring a factoring fee, the seller gets cash earlier and can pass the risk of bad debts to the factor. The seller also avoids costs of billing and accounting for receivables. If TechCom sells $20,000 of its accounts receivable and is charged a 4% factoring fee, it records this sale as follows.

Aug. 15	Cash...	19,200	
	Factoring Fee Expense.............................	800	
	Accounts Receivable...............................		20,000
	Sold accounts receivable for cash less 4% fee.		

Pledging Receivables   A company can borrow money by *pledging* its receivables as security for the loan. If the borrower defaults on (does not pay) the loan, the lender is paid from the cash receipts of the receivables. The borrower discloses pledging receivables in financial statement footnotes. If TechCom borrows $35,000 and pledges its receivables as security, it records

Aug. 20	Cash...	35,000	
	Notes Payable.....................................		35,000
	Borrow with a note secured by pledging receivables.		

■ **Decision Maker**

Analyst/Auditor   You are reviewing accounts receivable. Over the past five years, the allowance account as a percentage of gross accounts receivable shows a steady downward trend. What does this finding suggest? ■ *Answer:* The downward trend means the company is reducing the relative amount charged to bad debts expense each year. This could be to increase net income. Alternatively, collections may have improved and fewer bad debts are justified.

©Rawpixel.com/Shutterstock

Accounts Receivable Turnover  **Decision Analysis**

Accounts receivable turnover helps assess the quality and liquidity of receivables. *Quality* of receivables is the likelihood of collection without loss. *Liquidity* of receivables is the speed of collection. **Accounts receivable turnover** measures how often, on average, receivables are collected during the period and is defined in Exhibit 7.14.

$$\text{Accounts receivable turnover} = \frac{\text{Net sales}}{\text{Average accounts receivable, net}}$$

EXHIBIT 7.14

Accounts Receivable Turnover

The denominator is the *average* accounts receivable, net balance, computed as (Beginning balance + Ending balance) ÷ 2. TechCom has an accounts receivable turnover of 5.1. This means its average accounts receivable balance is converted into cash 5.1 times during the period, which is pictured here.

A1

Compute accounts receivable turnover and use it to help assess financial condition.

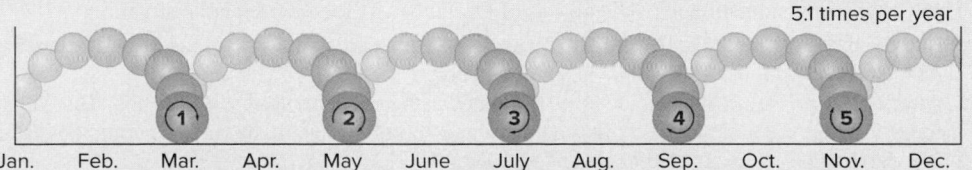

Accounts receivable turnover shows how well management is doing in granting credit to customers. A high turnover suggests that management should consider using less strict credit terms to increase sales. A low turnover suggests management should consider more strict credit terms and more aggressive collection efforts to avoid having assets tied up in accounts receivable.

Exhibit 7.15 shows accounts receivable turnover for **Visa** and **Mastercard**.

EXHIBIT 7.15

Analysis Using Accounts
Receivable Turnover

Company	Figure ($ millions)	Current Year	1 Year Ago	2 Years Ago
Visa	Net sales...............................	$18,358	$15,082	$13,880
	Average accounts receivable, net...........	$ 1,087	$ 944	$ 835
	Accounts receivable turnover.............	**16.9**	**16.0**	**16.6**
Mastercard	Net sales...............................	$12,497	$10,776	$ 9,667
	Average accounts receivable, net...........	$ 1,693	$ 1,248	$ 1,094
	Accounts receivable turnover.............	**7.4**	**8.6**	**8.8**

Visa's current year turnover is 16.9, computed as $18,358/$1,087 ($ millions). This means that Visa's average accounts receivable balance was converted into cash 16.9 times in the current year. Its turnover slightly increased in the current year (16.9) compared with one year ago (16.0). Visa's turnover also exceeds that for Mastercard in each of these three years. Both Visa and Mastercard seem to be doing an adequate job of managing receivables.

■ **Decision Maker**

Family Physician   Your medical practice is barely profitable, so you hire an analyst. The analyst says, *"Accounts receivable turnover is too low. Tighter credit policies are recommended along with discontinuing service to those most delayed in payments."* What actions do you take? ■   *Answer:* Both suggestions are probably financially wise recommendations, but we may be troubled by eliminating services to those less able to pay. One alternative is to follow the recommendations but start a care program directed at patients less able to pay for services. This allows you to continue services to patients less able to pay and to discontinue services to patients able but unwilling to pay.

NEED-TO-KNOW 7-6

COMPREHENSIVE

Recording Accounts
and Notes Receivable
Transactions; Estimating
Bad Debts

Clayco Company completes the following transactions during the year.

July 14   Writes off a $750 account receivable arising from a sale to Briggs Company that dates to 10 months ago. (Clayco Company uses the allowance method.)

    30   Clayco Company receives a $1,000, 90-day, 10% note in exchange for merchandise sold to Sumrell Company (the merchandise cost $600).

Aug. 15   Receives $2,000 cash plus a $10,000 note from JT Co. in exchange for merchandise that sells for $12,000 (its cost is $8,000). The note is dated August 15, bears 12% interest, and matures in 120 days.

Nov. 1   Completes a $200 credit card sale with a 4% fee (the cost of sales is $150). The cash is transferred immediately from the credit card company.

     3   Sumrell Company refuses to pay the note that was due to Clayco Company on October 28. Prepare the journal entry to charge the dishonored note plus accrued interest to Sumrell Company's accounts receivable.

     5   Completes a $500 credit card sale with a 5% fee (the cost of sales is $300). The cash is transferred immediately from the credit card company.

    15   Receives the full amount of $750 from Briggs Company that was previously written off on July 14. Record the bad debts recovery.

Dec. 13   Receives payment of principal plus interest from JT for the August 15 note.

Required

1. Prepare Clayco Company's journal entries to record these transactions.

2. Prepare a year-end adjusting journal entry as of December 31 for each separate situation.

    a. Bad debts are estimated to be $20,400 by aging accounts receivable. The unadjusted balance of the Allowance for Doubtful Accounts is a $1,000 debit.

    b. Alternatively, assume that bad debts are estimated using the percent of sales method. The Allowance for Doubtful Accounts had a $1,000 debit balance before adjustment, and the company estimates bad debts to be 1% of its credit sales of $2,000,000.

PLANNING THE SOLUTION

● Examine each transaction to determine the accounts affected, and then record the entries.

● For the year-end adjustment, record the bad debts expense for the two approaches.

SOLUTION

1.

July 14	Allowance for Doubtful Accounts	750	
	Accounts Receivable—Briggs Co.		750
	Wrote off an uncollectible account.		
July 30	Notes Receivable—Sumrell Co.	1,000	
	Sales		1,000
	Sold merchandise for a 90-day,		
	10% note.		
July 30	Cost of Goods Sold	600	
	Merchandise Inventory.		600
	Record the cost of July 30 sale.		
Aug. 15	Cash	2,000	
	Notes Receivable—JT Co.	10,000	
	Sales		12,000
	Sold merchandise for $2,000 cash		
	and $10,000 note.		
Aug. 15	Cost of Goods Sold	8,000	
	Merchandise Inventory.		8,000
	Record the cost of Aug. 15 sale.		
Nov. 1	Cash	192	
	Credit Card Expense	8	
	Sales		200
	Record credit card sale less a 4%		
	credit card expense.		
Nov. 1	Cost of Goods Sold	150	
	Merchandise Inventory.		150
	Record the cost of Nov. 1 sale.		

Nov. 3	Accounts Receivable—Sumrell Co.	1,025	
	Interest Revenue.		25
	Notes Receivable—Sumrell Co.		1,000
	Charge account of Sumrell Co.		
	for a $1,000 dishonored note and		
	interest of $1,000 × 10% × 90/360.		
Nov. 5	Cash	475	
	Credit Card Expense	25	
	Sales		500
	Record credit card sale less a		
	5% credit card expense.		
Nov. 5	Cost of Goods Sold	300	
	Merchandise Inventory.		300
	Record the cost of Nov. 5 sale.		
Nov. 15	Accounts Receivable—Briggs Co.	750	
	Allowance for Doubtful Accounts. . . .		750
	Reinstate account of Briggs Co.		
	previously written off.		
Nov. 15	Cash	750	
	Accounts Receivable—Briggs Co.		750
	Cash received in full payment of account.		
Dec. 13	Cash	10,400	
	Interest Revenue.		400
	Note Receivable—JT Co.		10,000
	Collect note with interest of		
	$10,000 × 12% × 120/360.		

2a. Aging of accounts receivable method.

Dec. 31	Bad Debts Expense	21,400	
	Allowance for Doubtful Accounts.		21,400
	Adjust allowance account from a $1,000 debit		
	balance to a $20,400 credit balance.		

2b. Percent of sales method. (For the income statement approach, which requires estimating bad debts as a percent of sales or credit sales, the Allowance for Doubtful Accounts balance is *not* considered when making the adjusting entry.)

Dec. 31	Bad Debts Expense	20,000	
	Allowance for Doubtful Accounts.		20,000
	Record bad debts expense as 1% × $2,000,000		
	of credit sales.		

Summary: Cheat Sheet

VALUING RECEIVABLES

Accounts Receivable: Amounts due from customers for credit sales.

Credit sales and later collection:

Accounts Receivable—CompStore	950	
Sales.		950
Cash	720	
Accounts Receivable—RDA Electronics		720

Store credit card interest revenue:

Accounts Receivable	15	
Interest Revenue		15

Sales using bank credit card:

Cash	96	
Credit Card Expense.	4	
Sales.		100

DIRECT WRITE-OFF METHOD

Direct write-off method: Record bad debt expense when an account is determined to be uncollectible.

Writing off a bad debt under *direct method*:

Bad Debts Expense	520	
Accounts Receivable—J. Kent...............		520

Bad debt later recovered under *direct method*:

Accounts Receivable—J. Kent	520	
Bad Debts Expense.........................		520
Cash	520	
Accounts Receivable—J. Kent................		520

ALLOWANCE METHOD

Allowance method: Matches estimated loss from uncollectible accounts receivable against the sales they helped produce.

Estimating bad debts:

Bad Debts Expense	1,500	
Allowance for Doubtful Accounts..............		1,500

Allowance for Doubtful Accounts: A contra asset account that reduces accounts receivable.

Writing off a bad debt under *allowance method*:

Allowance for Doubtful Accounts	520	
Accounts Receivable—J. Kent................		520

Bad debt is later recovered under *allowance method*:

Accounts Receivable—J. Kent	520	
Allowance for Doubtful Accounts..............		520
Cash	520	
Accounts Receivable—J. Kent................		520

ESTIMATING BAD DEBTS

When using the allowance method, we often use one of the following methods to estimate bad debts.
- **Percent of sales:** Uses a percent of credit sales for the period to estimate bad debts.
- **Percent of accounts receivable:** Uses a percent of accounts receivable to estimate bad debts.
- **Aging of accounts receivable:** Applies several percentages to accounts receivable to estimate bad debts.

NOTES RECEIVABLE

Note receivable: A promise to pay a specified amount of money at a future date.
Principal of a note: Amount promised to be repaid.
Maturity date: Day the note must be repaid.

Interest formula (year assumed to have 360 days):

Principal of the note	×	Annual interest rate	×	Time expressed in fraction of year	=	Interest

Note receivable from sales:

Notes Receivable	1,000	
Sales......................................		1,000

Note receivable and cash in exchange for accounts receivable:

Cash	232	
Notes Receivable	600	
Accounts Receivable—J. Cook		832

Note is *honored*; cash received in full (with interest):

Cash	615	
Notes Receivable..........................		600
Interest Revenue		15

Note is *dishonored*; receivable and interest recorded:

Accounts Receivable—J. Cook....................	615	
Interest Revenue		15
Notes Receivable..........................		600

Accrue interest on note receivable:

Interest Receivable............................	15	
Interest Revenue		15

Note is *honored*; when note term runs over two periods:

Cash	3,060	
Interest Revenue		45
Interest Receivable		15
Notes Receivable..........................		3,000

Factoring (selling) receivables: Accounts receivable are sold to a bank and the seller is charged a *factoring fee*.

Sale of receivables for cash with a charged factor fee:

Cash	19,200	
Factoring Fee Expense..........................	800	
Accounts Receivable.......................		20,000

Pledging of receivables: Borrowing money by *pledging* receivables as security for a loan. Borrower discloses pledging in notes to financial statement.

Key Terms

Accounts receivable (271)	Bad debts (274)	Payee of the note (282)
Accounts receivable turnover (285)	Direct write-off method (274)	Principal of a note (282)
Aging of accounts receivable (279)	Interest (282)	Promissory note (or note) (281)
Allowance for Doubtful Accounts (276)	Maker of the note (282)	Realizable value (276)
Allowance method (275)	Maturity date of a note (282)	

Multiple Choice Quiz

1. A company's Accounts Receivable balance at its December 31 year-end is $125,650, and its Allowance for Doubtful Accounts has a credit balance of $328 before year-end adjustment. Its net sales are $572,300. It estimates that 4% of outstanding accounts receivable are uncollectible. What amount of bad debts expense is recorded at December 31?
   - **a.** $5,354
   - **b.** $328
   - **c.** $5,026
   - **d.** $4,698
   - **e.** $34,338

2. A company's Accounts Receivable balance at its December 31 year-end is $489,300, and its Allowance for Doubtful Accounts has a debit balance of $554 before year-end adjustment. Its net sales are $1,300,000. It estimates that 6% of outstanding accounts receivable are uncollectible. What amount of bad debts expense is recorded at December 31?
   - **a.** $29,912
   - **b.** $28,804
   - **c.** $78,000
   - **d.** $29,358
   - **e.** $554

3. Total interest to be earned on a $7,500, 5%, 90-day note is
   - **a.** $93.75.
   - **b.** $375.00.
   - **c.** $1,125.00.
   - **d.** $31.25.
   - **e.** $125.00.

4. A company receives a $9,000, 8%, 60-day note. The maturity value of the note is
   - **a.** $120.
   - **b.** $9,000.
   - **c.** $9,120.
   - **d.** $720.
   - **e.** $9,720.

5. A company has net sales of $489,600 and average accounts receivable of $40,800. What is its accounts receivable turnover?
   - **a.** 0.08
   - **b.** 30.41
   - **c.** 1,341.00
   - **d.** 12.00
   - **e.** 111.78

ANSWERS TO MULTIPLE CHOICE QUIZ

1. d; Desired balance in Allowance for Doubtful Accounts = $ 5,026 cr.
   ($125,650 × 0.04)
   Current balance in Allowance for Doubtful Accounts = (328) cr.
   Bad debts expense to be recorded = $ 4,698

2. a; Desired balance in Allowance for Doubtful Accounts = $ 29,358 cr.
   ($489,300 × 0.06)
   Current balance in Allowance for Doubtful Accounts = 554 dr.
   Bad debts expense to be recorded = $29,912

3. a; $7,500 × 0.05 × 90/360 = $93.75

4. c; Principal amount $9,000
   Interest accrued . . . . 120 ($9,000 × 0.08 × 60/360)
   Maturity value $9,120

5. d; $489,600/$40,800 = 12

Ⓘ Icon denotes assignments that involve decision making.

Discussion Questions

1. Ⓘ How do sellers benefit from allowing their customers to use credit cards?
2. Ⓘ Why does the direct write-off method of accounting for bad debts usually fail to match revenues and expenses?
3. Explain the accounting constraint of materiality.
4. Why might a business prefer a note receivable to an account receivable?
5. Explain why writing off a bad debt against the Allowance for Doubtful Accounts does not reduce the estimated realizable value of a company's accounts receivable.

6. Ⓘ Why does the Bad Debts Expense account usually not have the same adjusted balance as the Allowance for Doubtful Accounts?
7. Ⓘ Refer to the financial statements and notes **APPLE** of **Apple** in Appendix A. In its presentation of accounts receivable on the balance sheet, how does it title accounts receivable? What does it report for its allowance as of September 30, 2017?
8. Ⓘ Refer to the balance sheet of **Google** in **GOOGLE** Appendix A. Does it use the direct write-off

method or allowance method in accounting for its accounts receivable? What is the realizable value of its receivables balance as of December 31, 2017?

"Trade receivables," on its December 31, 2017, balance sheet?

9. Refer to the financial statements of **Samsung** in Appendix A. What is the **Samsung** amount of Samsung's accounts receivable, titled as

10. Refer to the December 31, 2017, financial statements of **Samsung** in Appendix A. **Samsung** Does Samsung report its accounts receivable, titled as "Trade receivables," as a current or noncurrent asset?

---

connect

QUICK STUDY

QS 7-1
Credit card sales
C1

Prepare journal entries for the following credit card sales transactions (the company uses the perpetual inventory system).

1. Sold $20,000 of merchandise, which cost $15,000, on Mastercard credit cards. Mastercard charges a 5% fee.

2. Sold $5,000 of merchandise, which cost $3,000, on an assortment of bank credit cards. These cards charge a 4% fee.

QS 7-2
Direct write-off method
P1

Solstice Company determines on October 1 that it cannot collect $50,000 of its accounts receivable from its customer, P. Moore. Apply the direct write-off method to record this loss as of October 1.

QS 7-3
Recovering a bad debt
P1

Solstice Company determines on October 1 that it cannot collect $50,000 of its accounts receivable from its customer, P. Moore. It uses the direct write-off method to record this loss as of October 1. On October 30, P. Moore unexpectedly pays his account in full to Solstice Company. Record Solstice's entries for recovery of this bad debt.

QS 7-4
Distinguishing between allowance method and direct write-off method
P1   P2

Indicate whether each statement best describes the allowance (A) method or the direct write-off (DW) method.

_____ **1.** Does not predict bad debts expense.

_____ **2.** Accounts receivable on the balance sheet is reported at net realizable value.

_____ **3.** The write-off of a specific account does not affect net income.

_____ **4.** When an account is written off, the debit is to Bad Debts Expense.

_____ **5.** Usually does *not* best match sales and expenses because bad debts expense is not recorded until an account becomes uncollectible, which usually occurs in a period after the credit sale.

_____ **6.** Estimates bad debts expense related to the sales recorded in that period.

QS 7-5
Allowance method for bad debts
P2

Gomez Corp. uses the allowance method to account for uncollectibles. On January 31, it wrote off an $800 account of a customer, C. Green. On March 9, it receives a $300 payment from Green.

1. Prepare the journal entry for January 31.

2. Prepare the journal entries for March 9; assume no additional money is expected from Green.

QS 7-6
Reporting allowance for doubtful accounts
P2

On December 31 of Swift Co.'s first year, $50,000 of accounts receivable is not yet collected. Swift estimates that $2,000 of its accounts receivable is uncollectible and recorded the year-end adjusting entry.

1. Compute the realizable value of accounts receivable reported on Swift's year-end balance sheet.

2. On January 1 of Swift's second year, it writes off a customer's account for $300. Compute the realizable value of accounts receivable on January 1 after the write-off.

QS 7-7
Percent of accounts receivable method
P3

Warner Company's year-end unadjusted trial balance shows accounts receivable of $99,000, allowance for doubtful accounts of $600 (credit), and sales of $280,000. Uncollectibles are estimated to be 1.5% of accounts receivable.

1. Prepare the December 31 year-end adjusting entry for uncollectibles.

2. What amount would have been used in the year-end adjusting entry if the allowance account had a year-end unadjusted debit balance of $300?

Warner Company's year-end unadjusted trial balance shows accounts receivable of $99,000, allowance for doubtful accounts of $600 (credit), and sales of $140,000. Uncollectibles are estimated to be 1% of sales. Prepare the December 31 year-end adjusting entry for uncollectibles.

QS 7-8
Percent of sales method
P3

Net Zero Products, a wholesaler of sustainable raw materials, prepares the following aging of receivables analysis. (1) Estimate the balance of the Allowance for Doubtful Accounts using the aging of accounts receivable method. (2) Prepare the adjusting entry to record bad debts expense assuming the unadjusted balance in the Allowance for Doubtful Accounts is a $1,000 credit.

QS 7-9
Aging of receivables method
P3

		Days Past Due				
	Total	0	1 to 30	31 to 60	61 to 90	Over 90
Accounts receivable............	$115,200	$80,000	$18,000	$7,200	$4,000	$6,000
Percent uncollectible		1%	3%	5%	8%	11%

Determine the maturity date and compute interest for each note.

QS 7-10
Computing note interest and maturity date
C2

Note	Contract Date	Principal	Interest Rate	Period of Note (Term)
1.............	March 1	$10,000	6%	60 days
2.............	May 15	15,000	8	90 days
3.............	October 20	8,000	4	45 days

On August 2, Jun Co. receives a $6,000, 90-day, 12% note from customer Ryan Albany as payment on his $6,000 account receivable. (1) Compute the maturity date for this note. (2) Prepare Jun's journal entry for August 2.

QS 7-11
Note receivable
C2

On August 2, Jun Co. receives a $6,000, 90-day, 12% note from customer Ryan Albany as payment on his $6,000 account receivable. Prepare Jun's journal entry assuming the note is honored by the customer on October 31 of that same year.

QS 7-12
Note receivable honored
P4

On December 1, Daw Co. accepts a $10,000, 45-day, 6% note from a customer. (1) Prepare the year-end adjusting entry to record accrued interest revenue on December 31. (2) Prepare the entry required on the note's maturity date assuming it is honored.

QS 7-13
Note receivable interest and maturity **P4**

Record the sale by Balus Company of $125,000 in accounts receivable on May 1. Balus is charged a 2.5% factoring fee.

QS 7-14
Factoring receivables **C3**

Selected accounts from Fair Trader Co.'s adjusted trial balance for the year ended December 31 follow. Prepare its income statement.

QS 7-15
Preparing an income statement
P2 P4 C3

Factoring fees	$ 300	Interest revenue........................	$ 3,000
Insurance expense......................	4,000	Salaries expense	22,000
Sales......................................	50,000	Supplies expense......................	200
Rent expense	15,000	Bad debt expense	1,000

Selected accounts from Bennett Co.'s adjusted trial balance for the year ended December 31 follow. Prepare a classified balance sheet. *Note:* Allowance for doubtful accounts is subtracted from accounts receivable on the company's balance sheet.

QS 7-16
Preparing a balance sheet
P2 P4 C3

Prepaid rent	$ 1,000	Accounts payable......................	$2,500
Accounts receivable....................	10,000	Allowance for doubtful accounts..........	500
Cash	12,000	Notes payable (due in 10 years)	6,000
Total equity..............................	18,000	Notes receivable (due in 4 years)	4,000

QS 7-17

Accounts receivable turnover

A1

The following data are for Ruggers Company. Compute and interpret its accounts receivable turnover for the current year (competitors average a turnover of 7.5).

	Current Year	1 Year Ago
Accounts receivable, net	$153,400	$138,500
Net sales	861,105	910,600

![connect]

EXERCISES

Vail Company recorded the following transactions during November.

Exercise 7-1

Accounts receivable subsidiary ledger; schedule of accounts receivable

C1

Nov. 5	Accounts Receivable—Ski Shop	4,615	
	Sales		4,615
10	Accounts Receivable—Welcome Enterprises	1,350	
	Sales		1,350
13	Accounts Receivable—Zia Natara.....................	832	
	Sales		832
21	Sales Returns and Allowances	209	
	Accounts Receivable—Zia Natara		209
30	Accounts Receivable—Ski Shop	2,713	
	Sales		2,713

1. Open a general ledger having T-accounts for Accounts Receivable, Sales, and Sales Returns and Allowances. Also open an accounts receivable subsidiary ledger having a T-account for each of its three customers. Post these entries to both the general ledger and the accounts receivable ledger.

Check Accounts Receivable ending balance, $9,301

2. Prepare a schedule of accounts receivable (see Exhibit 7.4) and compare its total with the balance of the Accounts Receivable controlling account as of November 30.

Exercise 7-2

Accounting for credit card sales

C1

Levine Company uses the perpetual inventory system. Prepare journal entries to record the following credit card transactions of Levine Company.

Apr. 8 Sold merchandise for $8,400 (that had cost $6,000) and accepted the customer's Suntrust Bank Card. Suntrust charges a 4% fee.

12 Sold merchandise for $5,600 (that had cost $3,500) and accepted the customer's Continental Card. Continental charges a 2.5% fee.

Exercise 7-3

Sales on store credit card

C1

Z-Mart uses the perpetual inventory system and has its own credit card. Z-Mart charges a per-month interest fee for any unpaid balance on its store credit card at each month-end.

Apr. 30 Z-Mart sold merchandise for $1,000 (that had cost $650) and accepted the customer's Z-Mart store credit card.

May 31 Z-Mart recorded $4 of interest earned from its store credit card as of this month-end.

Exercise 7-4

Direct write-off method

P1

Dexter Company uses the direct write-off method. Prepare journal entries to record the following transactions.

Mar. 11 Dexter determines that it cannot collect $45,000 of its accounts receivable from Leer Co.

29 Leer Co. unexpectedly pays its account in full to Dexter Company. Dexter records its recovery of this bad debt.

Exercise 7-5

Writing off receivables

P2

On January 1, Wei Company begins the accounting period with a $30,000 credit balance in Allowance for Doubtful Accounts.

a. On February 1, the company determined that $6,800 in customer accounts was uncollectible; specifically, $900 for Oakley Co. and $5,900 for Brookes Co. Prepare the journal entry to write off those two accounts.

b. On June 5, the company unexpectedly received a $900 payment on a customer account, Oakley Company, that had previously been written off in part a. Prepare the entries to reinstate the account and record the cash received.

At year-end (December 31), Chan Company estimates its bad debts as 1% of its annual credit sales of $487,500. Chan records its bad debts expense for that estimate. On the following February 1, Chan decides that the $580 account of P. Park is uncollectible and writes it off as a bad debt. On June 5, Park unexpectedly pays the amount previously written off.

Prepare Chan's journal entries to record the transactions of December 31, February 1, and June 5.

Exercise 7-6
Percent of sales method; write-off

P3

Mazie Supply Co. uses the percent of accounts receivable method. On December 31, it has outstanding accounts receivable of $55,000, and it estimates that 2% will be uncollectible.

Prepare the year-end adjusting entry to record bad debts expense under the assumption that the Allowance for Doubtful Accounts has (a) a $415 credit balance before the adjustment and (b) a $291 debit balance before the adjustment.

Exercise 7-7
Percent of accounts receivable method

P3

Daley Company prepared the following aging of receivables analysis at December 31.

Exercise 7-8
Aging of receivables method

P3

			Days Past Due			
	Total	0	1 to 30	31 to 60	61 to 90	Over 90
Accounts receivable.............	$570,000	$396,000	$90,000	$36,000	$18,000	$30,000
Percent uncollectible		1%	2%	5%	7%	10%

a. Estimate the balance of the Allowance for Doubtful Accounts using aging of accounts receivable.

b. Prepare the adjusting entry to record bad debts expense using the estimate from part *a*. Assume the unadjusted balance in the Allowance for Doubtful Accounts is a $3,600 credit.

c. Prepare the adjusting entry to record bad debts expense using the estimate from part *a*. Assume the unadjusted balance in the Allowance for Doubtful Accounts is a $100 debit.

Refer to the information in Exercise 7-8 to complete the following requirements.

a. Estimate the balance of the Allowance for Doubtful Accounts assuming the company uses 4.5% of total accounts receivable to estimate uncollectibles, instead of the aging of receivables method.

b. Prepare the adjusting entry to record bad debts expense using the estimate from part *a*. Assume the unadjusted balance in the Allowance for Doubtful Accounts is a $12,000 credit.

c. Prepare the adjusting entry to record bad debts expense using the estimate from part *a*. Assume the unadjusted balance in the Allowance for Doubtful Accounts is a $1,000 debit.

Exercise 7-9
Percent of receivables method

P3

Following is a list of credit customers along with their amounts owed and the days past due at December 31. Following that list are five classifications of accounts receivable and estimated bad debts percent for each class.

1. Create an aging of accounts receivable schedule similar to Exhibit 7.8 and calculate the estimated balance for the Allowance for Doubtful Accounts.

2. Assuming an unadjusted credit balance of $100, record the required adjustment to the Allowance for Doubtful Accounts.

Exercise 7-10
Aging of receivables schedule

P3

Customer	Accounts Receivable	Days Past Due
BCC Company	$4,000	12
Lannister Co.	1,000	0
Mike Properties	5,000	107
Ted Reeves	500	72
Jen Steffens	2,000	35

Days Past Due	0	1 to 30	31 to 60	61 to 90	Over 90
Percent uncollectible	1%	3%	5%	8%	12%

At December 31, Folgeys Coffee Company reports the following results for its calendar year.

Exercise 7-11
Estimating bad debts

P3

Cash sales..........................	$900,000	Credit sales	$300,000

Its year-end unadjusted trial balance includes the following items.

Accounts receivable............	$125,000 debit	Allowance for doubtful accounts.....	$5,000 debit

Check Dr. Bad Debts
Expense: (1) $9,000

1. Prepare the adjusting entry to record bad debts expense assuming uncollectibles are estimated to be 3% of credit sales.

2. Prepare the adjusting entry to record bad debts expense assuming uncollectibles are estimated to be 1% of total sales.

(3) $12,500

3. Prepare the adjusting entry to record bad debts expense assuming uncollectibles are estimated to be 6% of year-end accounts receivable.

Exercise 7-12

Notes receivable transactions **C2**

Check Dec. 31, Cr. Interest Revenue, $38

Prepare journal entries for the following transactions of Danica Company.

Dec. 13   Accepted a $9,500, 45-day, 8% note in granting Miranda Lee a time extension on her past-due account receivable.

31   Prepared an adjusting entry to record the accrued interest on the Lee note.

Exercise 7-13

Notes receivable transactions **P4**

Check Jan. 27, Dr. Cash, $9,595

June 1, Dr. Cash, $5,125

Refer to the information in Exercise 7-12 and prepare the journal entries for the *following year* for Danica Company.

Jan. 27   Received Lee's payment for principal and interest on the note dated December 13.

Mar. 3   Accepted a $5,000, 10%, 90-day note in granting a time extension on the past-due account receivable of Tomas Company.

17   Accepted a $2,000, 30-day, 9% note in granting H. Cheng a time extension on his past-due account receivable.

Apr. 16   Cheng dishonored his note.

May 1   Wrote off the Cheng account against the Allowance for Doubtful Accounts.

June 1   Received the Tomas payment for principal and interest on the note dated March 3.

Exercise 7-14

Honoring a note

P4

Prepare journal entries to record transactions for Vitalo Company.

Nov. 1   Accepted a $6,000, 180-day, 8% note from Kelly White in granting a time extension on her past-due account receivable.

Dec. 31   Adjusted the year-end accounts for the accrued interest earned on the White note.

Apr. 30   White honored her note when presented for payment.

Exercise 7-15

Dishonoring a note

P4

Prepare journal entries to record the following transactions of Ridge Company.

Mar. 21   Accepted a $9,500, 180-day, 8% note from Tamara Jackson in granting a time extension on her past-due account receivable.

Sep. 17   Jackson dishonored her note.

Dec. 31   After trying several times to collect, Ridge Company wrote off Jackson's account against the Allowance for Doubtful Accounts.

Exercise 7-16

Selling and pledging accounts receivable

C3

On November 30, Petrov Co. has $128,700 of accounts receivable and uses the perpetual inventory system. (1) Prepare journal entries to record the following transactions. (2) Which transaction would most likely require a note to the financial statements?

Dec. 4   Sold $7,245 of merchandise (that had cost $5,000) to customers on credit, terms n/30.

9   Sold $20,000 of accounts receivable to Main Bank. Main charges a 4% factoring fee.

17   Received $5,859 cash from customers in payment on their accounts.

27   Borrowed $10,000 cash from Main Bank, pledging $12,500 of accounts receivable as security for the loan.

Exercise 7-17

Accounts receivable turnover

A1

The following information is from the annual financial statements of Raheem Company. (1) Compute its accounts receivable turnover for Year 2 and Year 3. (2) Assuming its competitor has a turnover of 11, is Raheem performing better or worse at collecting receivables than its competitor?

	Year 3	Year 2	Year 1
Net sales.....................................	$405,140	$335,280	$388,000
Accounts receivable, net (year-end)	44,800	41,400	34,800

≋ connect

Mayfair Co. completed the following transactions and uses a perpetual inventory system.

June 4   Sold $650 of merchandise on credit (that had cost $400) to Natara Morris, terms n/15.

     5   Sold $6,900 of merchandise (that had cost $4,200) to customers who used their Zisa cards. Zisa charges a 3% fee.

     6   Sold $5,850 of merchandise (that had cost $3,800) to customers who used their Access cards. Access charges a 2% fee.

     8   Sold $4,350 of merchandise (that had cost $2,900) to customers who used their Access cards. Access charges a 2% fee.

   13   Wrote off the account of Abigail McKee against the Allowance for Doubtful Accounts. The $429 balance in McKee's account was from a credit sale last year.

   18   Received Morris's check in full payment for the June 4 purchase.

Required

Prepare journal entries to record the preceding transactions and events.

PROBLEM SET A

Problem 7-1A
Sales on account and credit card sales

C1

Check   June 18, Dr. Cash, $650

At December 31, Hawke Company reports the following results for its calendar year.

| Cash sales............... | $1,905,000 | Credit sales.................... | $5,682,000 |

In addition, its unadjusted trial balance includes the following items.

| Accounts receivable........... | $1,270,100 debit | Allowance for doubtful accounts..... | $16,580 debit |

Required

1. Prepare the adjusting entry to record bad debts under each separate assumption.
   a. Bad debts are estimated to be 1.5% of credit sales.
   b. Bad debts are estimated to be 1% of total sales.
   c. An aging analysis estimates that 5% of year-end accounts receivable are uncollectible.

2. Show how Accounts Receivable and the Allowance for Doubtful Accounts appear on its December 31 balance sheet given the facts in part 1a.

3. Show how Accounts Receivable and the Allowance for Doubtful Accounts appear on its December 31 balance sheet given the facts in part 1c.

Problem 7-2A
Estimating and reporting bad debts

P2   P3

Check   Bad Debts Expense:
(1a) $85,230, (1c) $80,085

On December 31, Jarden Co.'s Allowance for Doubtful Accounts has an unadjusted credit balance of $14,500. Jarden prepares a schedule of its December 31 accounts receivable by age.

Problem 7-3A
Aging accounts receivable and accounting for bad debts

P2   P3

	A	B	C
1	**Accounts**	**Age of**	**Expected Percent**
2	**Receivable**	**Accounts Receivable**	**Uncollectible**
3	$830,000	Not yet due	1.25%
4	254,000	1 to 30 days past due	2.00
5	86,000	31 to 60 days past due	6.50
6	38,000	61 to 90 days past due	32.75
7	12,000	Over 90 days past due	68.00

Required

1. Compute the required balance of the Allowance for Doubtful Accounts at December 31 using an aging of accounts receivable.

2. Prepare the adjusting entry to record bad debts expense at December 31.

Analysis Component

3. On June 30 of the next year, Jarden concludes that a customer's $4,750 receivable is uncollectible and the account is written off. Does this write-off directly affect Jarden's net income?

Check   (2) Dr. Bad Debts Expense, $27,150

Problem 7-4A
Accounts receivable
transactions and bad debts
adjustments

C1   P2   P3

Check   (*d*) Dr. Bad Debts
Expense, $28,169

(*h*) Dr. Bad Debts Expense,
$32,199

Liang Company began operations in Year 1. During its first two years, the company completed a number of transactions involving sales on credit, accounts receivable collections, and bad debts. These transactions are summarized as follows.

Year 1

a. Sold $1,345,434 of merchandise (that had cost $975,000) on credit, terms n/30.

b. Wrote off $18,300 of uncollectible accounts receivable.

c. Received $669,200 cash in payment of accounts receivable.

d. In adjusting the accounts on December 31, the company estimated that 1.5% of accounts receivable would be uncollectible.

Year 2

e. Sold $1,525,634 of merchandise on credit (that had cost $1,250,000), terms n/30.

f. Wrote off $27,800 of uncollectible accounts receivable.

g. Received $1,204,600 cash in payment of accounts receivable.

h. In adjusting the accounts on December 31, the company estimated that 1.5% of accounts receivable would be uncollectible.

Required

Prepare journal entries to record Liang's summarized transactions and its year-end adjustments to record bad debts expense. (The company uses the perpetual inventory system, and it applies the allowance method for its accounts receivable. Round to the nearest dollar.)

Problem 7-5A
Analyzing and journalizing
notes receivable
transactions

C2   C3   P4

Check   Feb. 14, Cr. Interest
Revenue, $108

May 31, Cr. Interest Revenue,
$122

Nov. 2, Cr. Interest Revenue,
$35

The following transactions are from Ohlm Company.

Year 1

Dec. 16   Accepted a $10,800, 60-day, 8% note in granting Danny Todd a time extension on his past-due account receivable.

      31   Made an adjusting entry to record the accrued interest on the Todd note.

Year 2

Feb. 14   Received Todd's payment of principal and interest on the note dated December 16.

Mar. 2   Accepted a $6,100, 8%, 90-day note in granting a time extension on the past-due account receivable from Midnight Co.

      17   Accepted a $2,400, 30-day, 7% note in granting Ava Privet a time extension on her past-due account receivable.

Apr. 16   Privet dishonored her note.

May 31   Midnight Co. dishonored its note.

Aug. 7   Accepted a $7,440, 90-day, 10% note in granting a time extension on the past-due account receivable of Mulan Co.

Sep. 3   Accepted a $2,100, 60-day, 10% note in granting Noah Carson a time extension on his past-due account receivable.

Nov. 2   Received payment of principal plus interest from Carson for the September 3 note.

Nov. 5   Received payment of principal plus interest from Mulan for the August 7 note.

Dec. 1   Wrote off the Privet account against the Allowance for Doubtful Accounts.

Required

1. Prepare journal entries to record these transactions and events.

Analysis Component

2. If Ohlm pledged its receivables as security for a loan from the bank, where on the financial statements does it disclose this pledge of receivables?

Archer Co. completed the following transactions and uses a perpetual inventory system.

Aug. 4   Sold $3,700 of merchandise on credit (that had cost $2,000) to McKenzie Carpenter, terms n/10.
    10   Sold $5,200 of merchandise (that had cost $2,800) to customers who used their Commerce Bank credit cards. Commerce charges a 3% fee.
    11   Sold $1,250 of merchandise (that had cost $900) to customers who used their Goldman cards. Goldman charges a 2% fee.
    14   Received Carpenter's check in full payment for the August 4 purchase.
    15   Sold $3,250 of merchandise (that had cost $1,758) to customers who used their Goldman cards. Goldman charges a 2% fee.
    22   Wrote off the account of Craw Co. against the Allowance for Doubtful Accounts. The $498 balance in Craw Co.'s account was from a credit sale last year.

PROBLEM SET B

Problem 7-1B
Sales on account and credit card sales **C1**

Check Aug. 14, Dr. Cash, $3,700

Required

Prepare journal entries to record the preceding transactions and events.

At December 31, Ingleton Company reports the following results for the year.

Cash sales.................	$1,025,000	Credit sales	$1,342,000

In addition, its unadjusted trial balance includes the following items.

Accounts receivable...........	$575,000 debit	Allowance for doubtful accounts	$7,500 credit

Problem 7-2B
Estimating and reporting bad debts

P2 **P3**

Required

1. Prepare the adjusting entry to record bad debts under each separate assumption.
    a. Bad debts are estimated to be 2.5% of credit sales.
    b. Bad debts are estimated to be 1.5% of total sales.
    c. An aging analysis estimates that 6% of year-end accounts receivable are uncollectible.
2. Show how Accounts Receivable and the Allowance for Doubtful Accounts appear on its December 31 balance sheet given the facts in part 1a.
3. Show how Accounts Receivable and the Allowance for Doubtful Accounts appear on its December 31 balance sheet given the facts in part 1c.

Check Dr. Bad Debts Expense: (1b) $35,505, (1c) $27,000

At December 31, Hovak Co.'s Allowance for Doubtful Accounts has an unadjusted debit balance of $3,400. Hovak prepares a schedule of its December 31 accounts receivable by age.

Problem 7-3B
Aging accounts receivable and accounting for bad debts

P2 **P3**

	A	B	C
1	**Accounts**	**Age of**	**Expected Percent**
2	**Receivable**	**Accounts Receivable**	**Uncollectible**
3	$396,400	Not yet due	2.0%
4	277,800	1 to 30 days past due	4.0
5	48,000	31 to 60 days past due	8.5
6	6,600	61 to 90 days past due	39.0
7	2,800	Over 90 days past due	82.0

Required

1. Compute the required balance of the Allowance for Doubtful Accounts at December 31 using an aging of accounts receivable.
2. Prepare the adjusting entry to record bad debts expense at December 31.

Check (2) Dr. Bad Debts Expense, $31,390

Analysis Component

3. On July 31 of the following year, Hovak concludes that a customer's $3,455 receivable is uncollectible and the account is written off. Does this write-off directly affect Hovak's net income?

Problem 7-4B

Accounts receivable
transactions and bad debts
adjustments

C1 P2 P3

Check (*d*) Dr. Bad Debts
Expense, $11,287

(*h*) Dr. Bad Debts Expense,
$9,773

Sherman Co. began operations in Year 1. During its first two years, the company completed several transactions involving sales on credit, accounts receivable collections, and bad debts. These transactions are summarized as follows.

Year 1

a. Sold $685,350 of merchandise on credit (that had cost $500,000), terms n/30.

b. Received $482,300 cash in payment of accounts receivable.

c. Wrote off $9,350 of uncollectible accounts receivable.

d. In adjusting the accounts on December 31, the company estimated that 1% of accounts receivable would be uncollectible.

Year 2

e. Sold $870,220 of merchandise on credit (that had cost $650,000), terms n/30.

f. Received $990,800 cash in payment of accounts receivable.

g. Wrote off $11,090 of uncollectible accounts receivable.

h. In adjusting the accounts on December 31, the company estimated that 1% of accounts receivable would be uncollectible.

Required

Prepare journal entries to record Sherman's summarized transactions and its year-end adjusting entries to record bad debts expense. (The company uses the perpetual inventory system, and it applies the allowance method for its accounts receivable.)

Problem 7-5B

Analyzing and journalizing
notes receivable
transactions

C2 C3 P4

Check Jan. 30, Cr. Interest
Revenue, $32

Apr. 30, Cr. Interest Revenue,
$124

Sep. 19, Cr. Interest Revenue,
$190

The following transactions are from Springer Company.

Year 1

Nov. 1   Accepted a $4,800, 90-day, 8% note in granting Steve Julian a time extension on his past-due account receivable.

Dec. 31   Made an adjusting entry to record the accrued interest on the Julian note.

Year 2

Jan. 30   Received Julian's payment for principal and interest on the note dated November 1.

Feb. 28   Accepted a $12,600, 30-day, 8% note in granting a time extension on the past-due account receivable from King Co.

Mar. 1   Accepted a $6,200, 60-day, 12% note in granting Myron Shelley a time extension on his past-due account receivable.

     30   The King Co. dishonored its note.

Apr. 30   Received payment of principal plus interest from M. Shelley for the March 1 note.

June 15   Accepted a $2,000, 72-day, 8% note in granting a time extension on the past-due account receivable of Ryder Solon.

     21   Accepted a $9,500, 90-day, 8% note in granting J. Felton a time extension on his past-due account receivable.

Aug. 26   Received payment of principal plus interest from R. Solon for the June 15 note.

Sep. 19   Received payment of principal plus interest from J. Felton for the June 21 note.

Nov. 30   Wrote off King's account against the Allowance for Doubtful Accounts.

Required

1. Prepare journal entries to record these transactions and events.

Analysis Component

2. If Springer pledged its receivables as security for a loan from the bank, where on the financial statements does it disclose this pledge of receivables?

SERIAL PROBLEM

Business Solutions

P1 P2

This serial problem began in Chapter 1 and continues through most of the book. If previous chapter segments were not completed, the serial problem can begin at this point.

SP 7   Santana Rey, owner of **Business Solutions**, realizes that she needs to begin accounting for bad debts expense. Assume that Business Solutions has total revenues of $44,000 during the first three months of 2020 and that the Accounts Receivable balance on March 31, 2020, is $22,867.

Required

1. Prepare the adjusting entry to record bad debts expense on March 31, 2020, under each separate assumption. There is a zero unadjusted balance in the Allowance for Doubtful Accounts at March 31.

   a. Bad debts are estimated to be 1% of total revenues.

   b. Bad debts are estimated to be 2% of accounts receivable. (Round to the dollar.)

2. Assume that Business Solutions's Accounts Receivable balance at June 30, 2020, is $20,250 and that one account of $100 has been written off against the Allowance for Doubtful Accounts since March 31, 2020. If Rey uses the method in part 1b, what adjusting journal entry is made to recognize bad debts expense on June 30, 2020?

3. Should Rey consider adopting the direct write-off method of accounting for bad debts expense rather than one of the allowance methods considered in part 1? Explain.

©Alexander Image/Shutterstock
Check (2) Dr. Bad Debts Expense, $48

The **General Ledger** tool in Connect automates several of the procedural steps in accounting so that the financial professional can focus on the impacts of each transaction on various financial reports and performance measures.

GL 7-1 General Ledger assignment GL 7-1, based on Problem 7-5A, focuses on transactions related to accounts and notes receivable and highlights the impact each transaction has on interest revenue.

GENERAL LEDGER PROBLEM

Accounting Analysis

AA 7-1 Use **Apple**'s financial statements in Appendix A to answer the following.

1. What is the amount of Apple's accounts receivable as of September 30, 2017?
2. Compute Apple's accounts receivable turnover as of September 30, 2017.
3. How long does it take, *on average,* for the company to collect receivables for the fiscal year ended September 30, 2017?
4. Apple's most liquid assets include (*a*) cash and cash equivalents, (*b*) short-term marketable securities, (*c*) accounts receivable, and (*d*) inventory. Compute the percentage that these liquid assets (in total) make up of current liabilities as of September 30, 2017, and as of September 24, 2016.
5. Did Apple's liquid assets as a percentage of current liabilities improve or worsen as of its fiscal 2017 year-end compared to its fiscal 2016 year-end?

COMPANY ANALYSIS

A1

APPLE

AA 7-2 Comparative figures for **Apple** and **Google** follow.

$ millions	Apple			Google		
	Current Year	One Year Prior	Two Years Prior	Current Year	One Year Prior	Two Years Prior
Accounts receivable, net ..	$ 17,874	$ 15,754	$ 16,849	$ 18,336	$14,137	$11,556
Net sales	229,234	215,639	233,715	110,855	90,272	74,909

COMPARATIVE ANALYSIS

A1 P2

APPLE
GOOGLE

Required

1. Compute the accounts receivable turnover for (*a*) Apple and (*b*) Google for each of the two most recent years using the data shown.
2. Compute how many days, *on average,* it takes to collect receivables for the two most recent years for (*a*) Apple and (*b*) Google.
3. Which company more quickly collects its accounts receivable in the current year?

Hint: Average collection period equals 365 divided by the accounts receivable turnover.

GLOBAL ANALYSIS

C1   A1

Samsung

AA 7-3   Key figures for **Samsung** follow.

₩ millions	Current Year	One Year Prior	Two Years Prior
Accounts receivable, net	₩ 27,695,995	₩ 24,279,211	₩ 25,168,026
Sales	239,575,376	201,866,745	200,653,482

1. Compute its accounts receivable turnover for the current year.

2. How long does it take on average for Samsung to collect receivables in the current year?

3. In the current year, does Samsung's accounts receivable turnover underperform or outperform the industry (assumed) average of 7?

Beyond the Numbers

ETHICS CHALLENGE

P2   P3

BTN 7-1   Anton Blair is the manager of a medium-size company. A few years ago, Blair persuaded the owner to base a part of his compensation on the net income the company earns each year. Each December he estimates year-end financial figures in anticipation of the bonus he will receive. If the bonus is not as high as he would like, he offers several recommendations to the accountant for year-end adjustments. One of his favorite recommendations is for the controller to reduce the estimate of doubtful accounts.

Required

1. What effect does lowering the estimate for doubtful accounts have on the income statement and balance sheet?

2. Do you believe Blair's recommendation to adjust the allowance for doubtful accounts is within his rights as manager, or do you believe this action is an ethics violation? Justify your response.

3. What type of internal control(s) might be useful for this company in overseeing the manager's recommendations for accounting changes?

COMMUNICATING IN PRACTICE

P2   P3

BTN 7-2   As the accountant for Pure-Air Distributing, you attend a sales managers' meeting devoted to a discussion of credit policies. At the meeting, you report that bad debts expense is estimated to be $59,000 and accounts receivable at year-end amount to $1,750,000 less a $43,000 allowance for doubtful accounts. Sid Omar, a sales manager, expresses confusion over why bad debts expense and the allowance for doubtful accounts are different amounts. Write a one-page memorandum to him explaining why a difference in bad debts expense and the allowance for doubtful accounts is not unusual. The company estimates bad debts expense as 2% of sales.

TAKING IT TO THE NET

C1   P3

BTN 7-3   Access **eBay**'s February 6, 2017, filing of its 10-K report for the year ended December 31, 2016, at **SEC.gov**.

Required

1. What is the amount of eBay's net accounts receivable at December 31, 2016, and at December 31, 2015?

2. "Financial Statement Schedule II" of its 10-K report lists eBay's allowance for doubtful accounts (including authorized credits). For the two years ended December 31, 2016 and 2015, identify its allowance for doubtful accounts (including authorized credits), and then compute it as a percent of gross accounts receivable.

3. Do you believe that these percentages are reasonable based on what you know about eBay? Explain.

TEAMWORK IN ACTION

P2   P3

BTN 7-4   Each member of a team is to participate in estimating uncollectibles using the aging schedule and percents shown in Problem 7-3A. The division of labor is up to the team. Your goal is to accurately complete this task as soon as possible. After estimating uncollectibles, check your estimate with the instructor. If the estimate is correct, the team then should prepare the adjusting entry and the presentation of accounts receivable (net) for the December 31 year-end balance sheet.

BTN 7-5 Sheryl Sandberg and Mark Zuckerberg of **Facebook** are introduced in the chapter's opening feature. Assume that they are considering two options.

Plan A. Facebook would begin selling access to a premium version of its website. The new online customers would use their credit cards. The company has the capability of selling the premium service with no additional investment in hardware or software. Annual credit sales are expected to increase by $250,000.

Costs associated with Plan A: Additional wages related to these new sales are $135,500; credit card fees will be 4.75% of sales; and additional recordkeeping costs will be 6% of sales. Premium service sales will reduce advertising revenues for Facebook by $8,750 annually because some customers will now only use the premium service.

Plan B. The company would begin selling Facebook merchandise. It would make additional annual credit sales of $500,000.

Costs associated with Plan B: Cost of these new sales is $375,000; additional recordkeeping and shipping costs will be 4% of sales; and uncollectible accounts will be 6.2% of sales.

Required

1. Compute the additional annual net income or loss expected under (*a*) Plan A and (*b*) Plan B.
2. Should the company pursue either plan? Discuss both the financial and nonfinancial factors relevant to this decision.

BTN 7-6 Many commercials include comments similar to the following: "We accept **VISA**" or "We do not accept **American Express**." Conduct your own research by contacting at least five companies via interviews, phone calls, or the Internet to determine the reason(s) companies discriminate in their use of credit cards. Collect information on the fees charged by the different cards for the companies contacted. (The instructor can assign this as a team activity.)

ENTREPRENEURIAL DECISION

C1

Check (1*b*) Additional net income, $74,000

HITTING THE ROAD

C1

8 Accounting for Long-Term Assets

Chapter Preview

PLANT ASSETS

C1 Cost determination

P1 Depreciation

C2 Partial years and changes in estimates

C3 Additional expenditures

P2 Disposal

NTK 8-1, 8-2, 8-3

NATURAL RESOURCES

P3 Cost determination

Depletion

Presentation

Plant assets tied into extracting resources

NTK 8-4

INTANGIBLE ASSETS

P4 Cost determination

Amortization

Types of intangibles

A1 Analyze asset usage

NTK 8-5

Learning Objectives

CONCEPTUAL

C1 Compute the cost of plant assets.

C2 Explain depreciation for partial years and changes in estimates.

C3 Distinguish between revenue and capital expenditures, and account for them.

ANALYTICAL

A1 Compute total asset turnover and apply it to analyze a company's use of assets.

PROCEDURAL

P1 Compute and record depreciation using the straight-line, units-of-production, and declining-balance methods.

P2 Account for asset disposal through discarding or selling an asset.

P3 Account for natural resource assets and their depletion.

P4 Account for intangible assets.

P5 *Appendix 8A—Account for asset exchanges.*

Crafting the Dream

"Strive to surpass yourself"—**DEB CAREY**

NEW GLARUS, WI—Deb Carey told her husband Dan, "I could start a brewery and you could work for me." A few days later, she recalls, "We were bidding on equipment from a brew pub." Dan reminded her, "But we don't have any money." Deb declared, "I'm going to sell the house!" Soon, she says, **New Glarus Brewing** (**NewGlarusBrewing.com**) was up and running.

"In that first year," explains Deb, "we had no money, and we were working from 5 a.m. to midnight." Deb focused on the business. She stresses that long-term assets in the brewery such as brew houses, packaging lines, and fermentation cellars are expensive but key to success. Financing that equipment, buildings, and other assets, she says, is not easy.

A constant challenge for Deb and Dan is maintaining the right kind and amount of assets to meet business demands and be profitable. "Machinery cannot be divorced from the process," insists Dan. "You have to work with the strengths and weaknesses of your machinery."

Deb explains that success depends on monitoring and controlling the types and costs of long-term assets. Each of her tangible and intangible assets commands Deb's attention. She accounts for, manages, and focuses on recovering all costs of those acquisitions.

©Cooper Hedberg/Bloomberg/Getty Images

Their company is on a roll—employing nearly 150 workers, offering unique products such as Spotted Cow, and generating over 250,000 barrels. Adds Deb, running a company "is like having a big family."

Sources: *New Glarus Brewing website*, January 2019; *Wisconsin State Journal*, July 2011; *NBC 26 Green Bay*, February 2018; *Daily Dose*, October 2017

Section 1—Plant Assets

Plant assets are tangible assets used in a company's operations that have a useful life of more than one accounting period. Plant assets are also called *plant and equipment; property, plant and equipment (PP&E);* or *fixed assets.* Exhibit 8.1 shows plant assets as a percentage of total assets for several companies.

Plant assets are set apart from other assets by two important features. First, *plant assets are used in operations.* A computer purchased to resell is reported on the balance sheet as inventory. If the same computer is used in operations, it is a plant asset. Another example is land held for expansion, which is reported as a long-term investment. Instead, if this land holds a factory used in operations, the land is a plant asset.

The second important feature is that *plant assets have useful lives extending over more than one accounting period.* This makes plant assets different from current assets such as supplies that are normally used up within one period.

Exhibit 8.2 shows four issues in accounting for plant assets: (1) computing the costs of plant assets, (2) allocating the costs of plant assets, (3) accounting for subsequent expenditures to plant assets, and (4) recording the disposal of plant assets. The following sections discuss these issues.

EXHIBIT 8.1

Plant Assets of Selected Companies

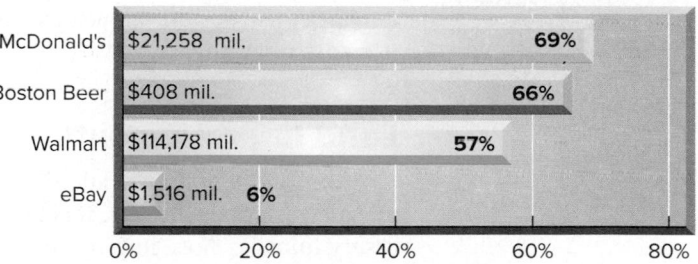

McDonald's	$21,258 mil.	69%
Boston Beer	$408 mil.	66%
Walmart	$114,178 mil.	57%
eBay	$1,516 mil.	6%

As a Percentage of Total Assets

Point: *Capital-intensive* refers to companies with large amounts of plant assets.

EXHIBIT 8.2

Issues in Accounting for Plant Assets

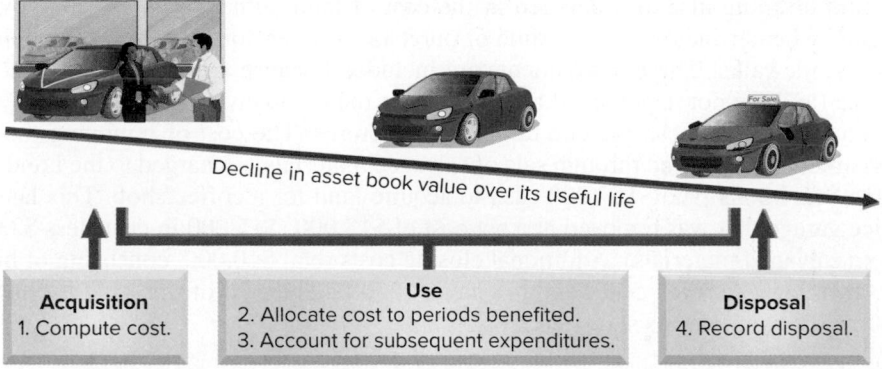

Decline in asset book value over its useful life

Acquisition	**Use**	**Disposal**
1. Compute cost.	2. Allocate cost to periods benefited. 3. Account for subsequent expenditures.	4. Record disposal.

COST DETERMINATION

C1 ─────────
Compute the cost of plant assets.

Plant assets are recorded at cost when acquired. **Cost** includes all expenditures necessary to get an asset in place and ready for use. The cost of a machine, for example, includes its invoice cost minus any discount, plus necessary shipping, assembling, installing, and testing costs. Examples are the costs of building a base for a machine, installing electrical hookups, and testing the asset before using it in operations.

To be recorded as part of the cost of a plant asset, an expenditure must be normal, reasonable, and necessary in preparing it for its intended use. If an asset is damaged during unpacking, the repairs are not added to its cost. Instead, they are charged to an expense account. Costs to modify or customize a new plant asset are added to the asset's cost. This section explains how to determine the cost of plant assets for its four major classes.

Machinery and Equipment

The costs of machinery and equipment consist of all costs normal and necessary to purchase them and prepare them for their intended use. These include the purchase price, taxes, transportation charges, insurance while in transit, and the installing, assembling, and testing of the machinery and equipment.

Buildings

©Syda Productions/Shutterstock

A Building account consists of the costs of purchasing or constructing a building that is used in operations. A purchased building's costs include its purchase price, taxes, title fees, and lawyer fees. Its costs also include all expenditures to ready it for its intended use, including necessary repairs or renovations. When a company constructs a building or any plant asset for its own use, its costs include materials and labor plus indirect overhead cost. Overhead includes heat, lighting, power, and depreciation on machinery used to construct the asset. Costs of construction also include design fees, building permits, and insurance during construction. However, costs such as insurance to cover the asset *after* it is being used are operating expenses.

Land Improvements

Point: Entry for cash purchase of land improvements:
Land Improvements. . . . .   #
    Cash. . . . .   #

Land improvements are additions to land and have limited useful lives. Examples are parking lots, driveways, walkways, fences, and lighting systems. Land improvements include costs necessary to make those improvements ready for their intended use.

Land

Land is the earth's surface and has an indefinite (unlimited) life. Land includes costs necessary to make it ready for its intended use. When land is purchased for a building site, its cost includes the total amount paid for the land, including real estate commissions, title insurance fees, legal fees, and any accrued property taxes paid by the purchaser. Payments for surveying, clearing, grading, and draining also are included in the cost of land. Other costs include government assessments, whether incurred at the time of purchase or later, for items such as public roads, sewers, and sidewalks. These assessments are included because they permanently add to the land's value (and are not depreciated as they are not the company's responsibility). Land purchased as a building site can include unwanted structures. The cost of removing those structures, less amounts recovered through sale of salvaged materials, is charged to the Land account.

Assume **Starbucks** paid $167,000 cash to acquire land for a coffee shop. This land had an old service garage that was removed at a net cost of $13,000 ($15,000 in costs less $2,000 proceeds from salvaged materials). Additional closing costs total $10,000, consisting of brokerage fees ($8,000), legal fees ($1,500), and title costs ($500). The cost of this land to Starbucks is $190,000 and is computed as shown in Exhibit 8.3.

Cash price of land.	$ 167,000
Net cost of garage removal	13,000
Closing costs.	10,000
Cost of land	**$190,000**

Entry for cash purchase of land:

Land.	190,000	
Cash		190,000
Record purchase of land.		

EXHIBIT 8.3

Computing and Recording
Cost of Land

Lump-Sum Purchase

Plant assets sometimes are purchased as a group in a single transaction for a lump-sum price. This transaction is called a *lump-sum purchase,* or *group, bulk,* or *basket purchase.* When this occurs, we allocate the cost to the assets acquired based on their *relative market* (or *appraised) values.* Assume **CarMax** paid $90,000 cash to acquire a group of items consisting of a building appraised at $60,000 and land appraised at $40,000. The $90,000 cost is allocated based on appraised values as shown in Exhibit 8.4. The entry to record the lump-sum purchase also is shown in Exhibit 8.4.

	Appraised Value	Percent of Total	Apportioned Cost
Building...	$ 60,000	60% ($60,000/$100,000)	**$54,000** ($90,000 × 60%)
Land	40,000	40 ($40,000/$100,000)	**36,000** ($90,000 × 40%)
Totals	$100,000	100%	$ 90,000

Entry for lump-sum cash purchase:

Building.	54,000	
Land	36,000	
Cash.		90,000
Record costs of plant assets.		

EXHIBIT 8.4

Computing and
Recording Costs
in a Lump-Sum
Purchase

Compute the recorded cost of a new machine given the following payments related to its purchase: gross purchase price, $700,000; sales tax, $49,000; purchase discount taken, $21,000; freight cost—terms FOB shipping point, $3,500; normal assembly costs, $3,000; cost of necessary machine platform, $2,500; and cost of parts used in maintaining machine, $4,200.

Solution

$737,000 = $700,000 + $49,000 − $21,000 + $3,500 + $3,000 + $2,500

NEED-TO-KNOW 8-1

Cost Determination

C1

Do More: QS 8-1, QS 8-2,
E 8-1, E 8-2, E 8-3

DEPRECIATION

Depreciation is the process of allocating the cost of a plant asset to expense while it is in use. Depreciation does not measure the decline in the asset's market value or its physical deterioration. This section covers computing depreciation.

Factors in Computing Depreciation

Factors that determine depreciation are (1) cost, (2) salvage value, and (3) useful life.

Cost   The cost of a plant asset consists of all necessary and reasonable expenditures to acquire it and to prepare it for its intended use.

Salvage Value   The **salvage value,** also called *residual value* or *scrap value,* is an estimate of the asset's value at the end of its useful life. This is the amount the owner expects to receive from disposing of the asset at the end of its useful life. If the asset is expected to be traded in on a new asset, its salvage value is the expected trade-in value.

Useful Life   The **useful life** of a plant asset is the length of time it is used in a company's operations. Useful life, or *service life,* might not be as long as the asset's total productive life. For example, the productive life of a computer can be eight years or more. Some companies, however, trade in old computers for new ones every two years. In this case, these computers

P1_____

Compute and record depreciation using the straight-line, units-of-production, and declining-balance methods.

Point: If we expect disposal costs, the salvage value equals the expected amount from disposal less any disposal costs.

Point: Useful life and salvage value are estimates.

have a two-year useful life. The useful life of a plant asset is impacted by inadequacy and obso-lescence. **Inadequacy** is the inability of a plant asset to meet its demands. **Obsolescence** is the process of becoming outdated and no longer used.

©Fuse/Getty Images

■ **Decision Insight**

Sweet Life   The useful life of plant assets is different for each company. **Hershey Foods** and **Tootsie Roll** are competitors and apply similar manufacturing processes, but their equipment's life expectancies are different. Hershey depreciates equipment over 3 to 15 years, but Tootsie Roll depreciates them over 5 to 20 years. Such differences impact financial statements. ■

Depreciation Methods

Depreciation methods are used to allocate a plant asset's cost over its useful life. The most frequently used method is the straight-line method. The units-of-production and double-declining methods are also commonly used. We explain all three methods. Computations in this section use information about a machine used by **Reebok** and **Adidas** to inspect athletic shoes before packaging. Data for this machine are in Exhibit 8.5.

EXHIBIT 8.5

Data for Inspection Machine

Cost.................	$10,000	Useful life:	
Salvage value..........	1,000	Accounting periods........	5 years
Depreciable cost.......	$ 9,000	Units inspected...........	36,000 shoes

Straight-Line Method   **Straight-line depreciation** charges the same amount to each period of the asset's useful life. A two-step process is used. We first compute the *depreciable cost* of the asset, also called *cost to be depreciated*. It is computed as asset total cost minus salvage value. Second, depreciable cost is divided by the number of accounting periods in the asset's useful life. The computation for the inspection machine is in Exhibit 8.6.

EXHIBIT 8.6

Straight-Line Depreciation
Formula and Example

Point: Excel for SLN.

	A	B
1	Cost	$10,000
2	Salvage	$1,000
3	Life	5
4	SLN depr.	

=SLN(B1,B2,B3) = $1,800

Assets = Liabilities + Equity
−1,800   −1,800

$$\frac{\text{Cost} - \text{Salvage value}}{\text{Useful life in periods}} = \frac{\$10,000 - \$1,000}{5 \text{ years}} = \$1,800 \text{ per year}$$

If this machine is purchased on December 31, 2018, and used during its predicted useful life of five years, the straight-line method allocates equal depreciation to each of the years 2019 through 2023. We make the following adjusting entry at the end of each of the five years to record straight-line depreciation.

Dec. 31	Depreciation Expense	1,800	
	Accumulated Depreciation—Machinery		1,800
	Record annual depreciation.		

The $1,800 Depreciation Expense is reported on the income statement. The $1,800 **Accumulated Depreciation is a contra asset account to the Machinery account on the balance sheet.** The left graph in Exhibit 8.7 shows the $1,800 per year expense reported in each of the five years. The right graph shows the Machinery account balance (net) on each of the six December 31 balance sheets.

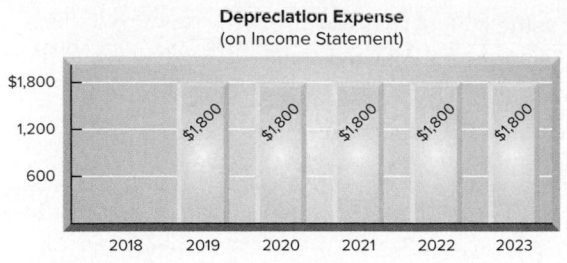

Depreciation Expense
(on Income Statement)

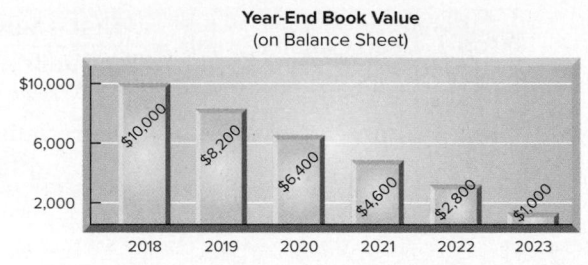

Year-End Book Value
(on Balance Sheet)

EXHIBIT 8.7

Financial
Statement Effects
of Straight-Line
Depreciation

The net balance sheet amount is the **asset book value,** or *book value,* and is computed as the asset's total cost minus accumulated depreciation. For example, at the end of Year 2 (December 31, 2020), its book value is $6,400, which is $10,000 minus $3,600 (2 years × $1,800), and is reported in the balance sheet as follows.

Book value = Cost − Accumulated depreciation

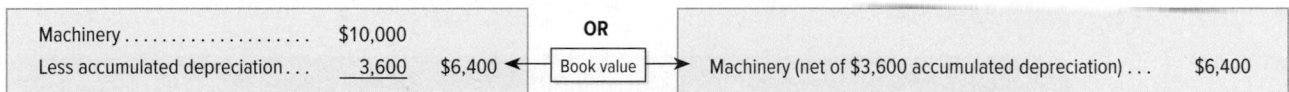

We also can compute the *straight-line depreciation rate,* which is 100% divided by the number of periods in the asset's useful life. For the inspection machine, this rate is 20% (100% ÷ 5 years, or 20% per period). We use this rate, along with other information, to compute the machine's *straight-line depreciation schedule* shown in Exhibit 8.8. This exhibit shows (1) straight-line depreciation is the same each period, (2) accumulated depreciation is the total of current and prior periods' depreciation expense, and (3) book value declines each period until it equals salvage value.

Point: Once an asset's book value equals its salvage value, depreciation stops.

Example: If salvage value of the machine is $2,500, what is the annual depreciation? *Answer:* ($10,000 − $2,500)/ 5 years = $1,500 per year

EXHIBIT 8.8

Straight-Line Depreciation Schedule

| Annual Period | Depreciation for the Period | | | End of Period | |
	Depreciable Cost*	Depreciation Rate	Depreciation Expense	Accumulated Depreciation	Book Value†
2018	—	—	—	—	$10,000
2019	$9,000	20%	**$1,800**	$1,800	8,200
2020	9,000	20	**1,800**	3,600	6,400
2021	9,000	20	**1,800**	5,400	4,600
2022	9,000	20	**1,800**	7,200	2,800
2023	9,000	20	**1,800**	9,000	**1,000** ◀
			$9,000 ◀		

Salvage value is not depreciated.

$10,000 cost − $1,000 salvage

*$10,000 − $1,000.   †Book value is total cost minus accumulated depreciation.

Units-of-Production Method

The use of some plant assets varies greatly from one period to the next. For example, a builder might use a piece of equipment for a month and then not use it again for several months. When equipment use varies from period to period, the units-of-production depreciation method can better match expenses with revenues. **Units-of-production depreciation** charges a varying amount for each period depending on an asset's *usage.*

A two-step process is used. We first compute *depreciation per unit* as the asset's total cost minus salvage value and then divide by the total units expected to be produced during its useful life. Units of production can be expressed in product or other units such as hours used or miles driven. The second step is to compute depreciation for the period by multiplying the units produced in the period by the depreciation per unit. The computation for the machine described in Exhibit 8.5 is in Exhibit 8.9. *Note:* 7,000 shoes are inspected and sold in its first year.

EXHIBIT 8.9

Units-of-Production
Depreciation Formula
and Example

$$\text{Step 1 Depreciation per unit} = \frac{\text{Cost} - \text{Salvage value}}{\text{Total units of production}} = \frac{\$10,000 - \$1,000}{36,000 \text{ shoes}} = \$0.25 \text{ per shoe}$$

$$\text{Step 2 Depreciation expense} = \text{Depreciation per unit} \times \text{Units produced in period}$$
$$\$0.25 \text{ per shoe} \times 7,000 \text{ shoes} = \$1,750$$

Example: Refer to Exhibit 8.10. If the number of shoes inspected in 2023 is 5,500, what is depreciation for 2023? *Answer:* $1,250 (never depreciate below salvage value)

Using data on the number of units inspected (shoes produced) by the machine, we compute the *units-of-production depreciation schedule* in Exhibit 8.10. For example, depreciation for the first year is $1,750 (7,000 shoes at $0.25 per shoe). Depreciation for the second year is $2,000 (8,000 shoes at $0.25 per shoe). Exhibit 8.10 shows (1) depreciation expense depends on unit output, (2) accumulated depreciation is the total of current and prior periods' depreciation expense, and (3) book value declines each period until it equals salvage value.

EXHIBIT 8.10

Units-of-Production
Depreciation Schedule

	Depreciation for the Period			End of Period	
Annual Period	Number of Units	Depreciation per Unit	Depreciation Expense	Accumulated Depreciation	Book Value
2018	—	—	—	—	$10,000
2019	7,000	$0.25	**$1,750**	$1,750	8,250
2020	8,000	0.25	**2,000**	3,750	6,250
2021	9,000	0.25	**2,250**	6,000	4,000
2022	7,000	0.25	**1,750**	7,750	2,250
2023	5,000	0.25	**1,250**	9,000	**1,000**
	36,000 units	$10,000 cost − $1,000 salvage	**$9,000**	Salvage value is not depreciated.	

$$\text{SL rate} = \frac{100\%}{\text{Useful life}}$$

$$\text{DDB rate} = \frac{200\%}{\text{Useful life}}$$

Point: Excel for DDB.

	A	B
1	Cost	$10,000
2	Salvage	$1,000
3	Life	5
4	DDB depr.	
5	1	
6	2	
7	etc.	

=DDB(B1,B2,B3,A5) = $4,000
=DDB(B1,B2,B3,A6) = $2,400

Declining-Balance Method

An **accelerated depreciation method** has more depreciation in the early years and less depreciation in later years. The most common accelerated method is the **declining-balance method,** which uses a depreciation rate that is a multiple of the straight-line rate. A common depreciation rate is double the straight-line rate. This is called *double-declining-balance (DDB)*. This is done in three steps.

1. Compute the asset's straight-line depreciation rate.
2. Double the straight-line rate.
3. Compute depreciation by multiplying this rate by the asset's beginning-period book value.

Let's return to the machine in Exhibit 8.5 and use double-declining-balance to compute depreciation. Exhibit 8.11 shows the first-year depreciation computation. The three steps are (1) divide 100% by five years to get the straight-line rate of 20%, or 1/5, per year; (2) double this 20% rate to get the declining-balance rate of 40%, or 2/5, per year; and (3) compute depreciation as 40%, or 2/5, multiplied by the beginning-period book value.

EXHIBIT 8.11

Double-Declining-Balance
Depreciation Formula*

Step 1 Straight-line rate = 100% ÷ Useful life = 100% ÷ 5 years = 20%

Step 2 Double-declining-balance rate = 2 × Straight-line rate = 2 × 20% = 40%

Step 3 Depreciation expense = Double-declining-balance rate × Beginning-period book value
40% × $10,000 = $4,000 (for 2019)

*In simple form: DDB depreciation = (2 × Beginning-period book value)/Useful life.

The *double-declining-balance depreciation schedule* is in Exhibit 8.12. The schedule follows the formula except for year 2023, when depreciation is $296. This $296 is not equal to 40% × $1,296, or $518.40. If we had used the $518.40 for depreciation in 2023, the ending book value would equal $777.60, which is less than the $1,000 salvage value. Instead, the $296 is computed as $1,296 book value minus $1,000 salvage value (for the year when DDB depreciation cuts into salvage value).

Example: What is the DDB depreciation in year 2022 if salvage value is $2,000? *Answer:* $2,160 − $2,000 = $160

EXHIBIT 8.12

Double-Declining-Balance Depreciation Schedule

	Depreciation for the Period			End of Period	
Annual Period	Beginning-of-Period Book Value	Depreciation Rate	Depreciation Expense	Accumulated Depreciation	Book Value
2018	—	—	—	—	$10,000
2019	$10,000	40%	**$4,000**	$4,000	6,000
2020	6,000	40	**2,400**	6,400	3,600
2021	3,600	40	**1,440**	7,840	2,160
2022	2,160	40	**864**	8,704	1,296
2023	1,296	40	**296***	9,000	**1,000**
			$9,000		

Salvage value is not depreciated.

$10,000 cost − $1,000 salvage

*Year 2023 depreciation is $1,296 − $1,000 = $296 (never depreciate book value below salvage value).

Comparing Depreciation Methods

Exhibit 8.13 shows depreciation for each year under the three methods. While depreciation per period differs, total depreciation of $9,000 is the same over the useful life.

EXHIBIT 8.13

Depreciation Expense for the Different Methods

Period	Straight-Line	Units-of-Production	Double-Declining-Balance
2019	$1,800	$1,750	$4,000
2020	1,800	2,000	2,400
2021	1,800	2,250	1,440
2022	1,800	1,750	864
2023	1,800	1,250	296
Totals	$9,000	$9,000	$9,000

Most Popular Methods

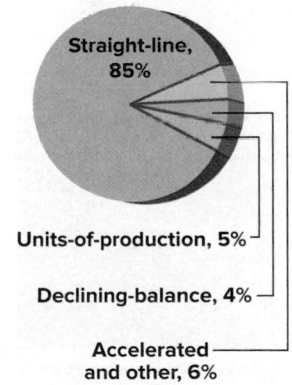

Straight-line, 85%

Units-of-production, 5%

Declining-balance, 4%

Accelerated and other, 6%

Depreciation for Tax Reporting

Many companies use accelerated depreciation in computing taxable income. Reporting higher depreciation expense in the early years of an asset's life reduces the company's taxable income in those years and increases it in later years. The goal is to *postpone* its tax payments. The U.S. tax law has rules for depreciating assets. These rules include the **Modified Accelerated Cost Recovery System (MACRS),** which allows straight-line depreciation for some assets but requires accelerated depreciation for most kinds of assets. MACRS is *not* acceptable for financial reporting because it does not consider an asset's useful life or salvage value.

Partial-Year Depreciation

When an asset is purchased or sold at a time other than the beginning or end of an accounting period, depreciation is recorded for part of that period.

C2

Explain depreciation for partial years and changes in estimates.

Mid-Period Asset Purchase Assume that the machine in Exhibit 8.5 is purchased and placed in service on October 1, 2018, and the annual accounting period ends on December 31. Because this machine is used for three months in 2018, the calendar-year income statement reports depreciation for those three months. Using straight-line depreciation, we compute three months' depreciation of $450 as follows.

$$\frac{\$10,000 - \$1,000}{5 \text{ years}} \times \frac{3}{12} = \$450$$

Mid-Period Asset Sale   Assume that the machine above is sold on June 1, 2023. Depreciation is recorded in 2023 for the period January 1 through June 1 as follows.

$$\frac{\$10,000 - \$1,000}{5 \text{ years}} \times \frac{5}{12} = \$750$$

Change in Estimates

Depreciation is based on estimates of salvage value and useful life. If our estimate of an asset's useful life and/or salvage value changes, what should we do? The answer is to use the new estimate to compute depreciation for current and future periods. Revising an estimate of the useful life or salvage value of a plant asset is called a **change in an accounting estimate** and only affects current and future financial statements. We do not go back and restate (change) prior years' statements. This applies to all depreciation methods.

Let's return to the machine in Exhibit 8.8 using straight-line depreciation. At the beginning of this asset's third year, its book value is $6,400. Assume that at the beginning of its third year, the estimated number of years remaining in its useful life changes from three to four years *and* its estimate of salvage value changes from $1,000 to $400. Depreciation for each of the four remaining years is computed as in Exhibit 8.14.

Annual Period	Original Depreciation	Revised Depreciation
2018	—	—
2019	$1,800	$1,800
2020	1,800	1,800
2021	1,800	1,500
2022	1,800	1,500
2023	1,800	1,500
2024	—	1,500
	$9,000	$9,600

EXHIBIT 8.14

Computing Revised Straight-Line Depreciation

$$\frac{\text{Book value} - \text{Revised salvage value}}{\text{Revised remaining useful life}} = \frac{\$6,400 - \$400}{4 \text{ years}} = \$1,500 \text{ per year}$$

Reporting Depreciation

Some companies, such as **O'Reilly Auto**, report both the cost and accumulated depreciation of plant assets on the balance sheet. **Apple** and many other companies show plant assets on one line with the net amount of cost minus accumulated depreciation. When this is done, accumulated depreciation is disclosed in a note—see Appendix A for Apple.

Impairment   When there is a *permanent decline* in the fair value of an asset relative to its book value, the company writes down the asset to this fair value. This is called an asset **impairment.** Assume equipment has a book value of $800 and a fair (market) value of $750, *and* this $50 decline in value meets the impairment test (details are in advanced courses). The impairment entry is

Impairment Loss...	50	
Accumulated Depreciation—Equipment		50
Record impairment of equipment.		

■ **Decision Ethics**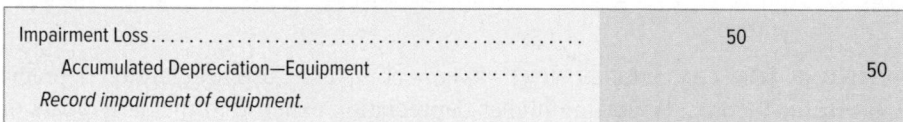

Controller   You are the controller for a struggling wingsuit company. Depreciation is its largest expense. Competitors depreciate equipment over three years. The company president tells you to revise useful lives of equipment from three to six years. What should you do? ■   *Answer:* The president's instructions may be an honest and reasonable prediction of the future. However, you might confront the president if you believe the aim is only to increase income.

©Cultura Creative/Alamy Stock Photo

NEED-TO-KNOW **8-2**

Depreciation Computations

C2   P1

Part 1. A machine costing $22,000 with a five-year life and an estimated $2,000 salvage value is installed on January 1. The manager estimates the machine will produce 1,000 units of product during its life. It actually produces the following units: 200 in Year 1, 400 in Year 2, 300 in Year 3, 80 in Year 4, and 30 in Year 5. The total units produced by the end of Year 5 exceed the original estimate—this difference was not predicted. (The machine must not be depreciated below its estimated salvage value.) Compute depreciation expense for each year and total depreciation for all years combined under straight-line, units-of-production, and double-declining-balance.

Part 2. In early January, a company acquires equipment for $3,800. The company estimates this equipment has a useful life of three years and a salvage value of $200. On January 1 of the third year, the company changes its estimates to a total four-year useful life and zero salvage value. Using the straight-line method, what is depreciation expense for the third year?

Solution—Part 1

Year	Straight-Line[a]	Units-of-Production[b]	Double-Declining-Balance[c]
1.	$ 4,000	$ 4,000	$ 8,800
2.	4,000	8,000	5,280
3.	4,000	6,000	3,168
4.	4,000	1,600	1,901
5.	4,000	400	851
Totals.	$20,000	$20,000	$20,000

[a]Straight-line: Cost per year = ($22,000 − $2,000)/5 years = $4,000 per year

[b]Units-of-production: Cost per unit = ($22,000 − $2,000)/1,000 units = $20 per unit

Year	Units	Depreciation per Unit	Depreciation	Accum. Deprec.	Book Value
1.	200	$20	$ 4,000	$ 4,000	$18,000
2.	400	20	8,000	12,000	10,000
3.	300	20	6,000	18,000	4,000
4.	80	20	1,600	19,600	2,400
5.	30	20	400*	20,000*	2,000
Total			$20,000		

*30 × $20 = $600; however, $600 would make accumulated depreciation exceed the $20,000 total
depreciable cost. This means we take only enough depreciation in Year 5, or $400, to decrease book value
to the asset's $2,000 salvage value (never lower).

[c]Double-declining-balance: (100%/5) × 2 = 40% depreciation rate

Year	Beginning Book Value	Annual Depreciation (40% of book value)	Accumulated Depreciation at Year-End	Ending Book Value ($22,000 cost less accumulated depreciation)
1.	$22,000	$ 8,800	$ 8,800	$13,200
2.	13,200	5,280	14,080	7,920
3.	7,920	3,168	17,248	4,752
4.	4,752	1,901*	19,149	2,851
5.	2,851	851†	20,000	2,000
Total		$20,000		

*Rounded to the nearest dollar.
†Set depreciation in Year 5 to reduce book value to the $2,000 salvage value; namely, instead of $1,140
  ($2,851 × 40%), we use the maximum of $851 ($2,851 − $2,000).

Solution—Part 2

($3,800 − $200)/3 years = $1,200 (original depreciation per year)

$1,200 × 2 years = $2,400 (accumulated depreciation at date of change in estimate)

($3,800 − $2,400)/2 years = **$700** (revised depreciation)

Do More: QS 8-3
through QS 8-8, E 8-4
through E 8-13

ADDITIONAL EXPENDITURES

Plant assets require maintenance, repairs, and improvements. We must decide whether to
expense or capitalize these expenditures (to capitalize is to increase the asset account).

Revenue expenditures, also called *income statement expenditures,* are costs that do not
materially increase the plant asset's life or capabilities. They are recorded as expenses on the
current-period income statement.

Capital expenditures, also called *balance sheet expenditures,* are costs of plant assets that
provide benefits for longer than the current period. They increase the asset on the balance sheet.

C3

Distinguish between
revenue and capital
expenditures, and
account for them.

Ordinary Repairs

Ordinary repairs are expenditures to keep an asset in good operating condition. Ordinary repairs do not extend an asset's useful life or increase its productivity beyond original expectations. Examples are normal costs of cleaning, lubricating, changing oil, and replacing small parts of a machine. Ordinary repairs are *revenue expenditures.* This means their costs are reported as expenses on the current-period income statement. Following this rule, **Brunswick** reports that "maintenance and repair costs are expensed as incurred." If Brunswick's current-year repair costs are $9,500, it makes the following entry.

Assets = Liabilities + Equity
−9,500   −9,500

Dec. 31	Repairs Expense	9,500	
	Cash		9,500
	Record ordinary repairs of equipment.		

Betterments and Extraordinary Repairs

Betterments and extraordinary repairs are *capital expenditures.*

Additional Expenditures	Examples	Expense Timing	Entry	
Ordinary repairs	• Cleaning • Lubricating • Adjusting • Repainting	Expensed currently	Repairs Expense. . . . . Cash	# #
Betterments and extraordinary repairs	• Replacing main parts • Major asset expansions	Expensed in future	Asset (such as Equip.) Cash	# #

Example: Assume a firm owns a web server. Identify each cost as a revenue or capital expenditure: (1) purchase price, (2) necessary wiring, (3) platform for operation, (4) circuits to increase capacity, (5) monthly cleaning, (6) repair of a faulty switch, and (7) replacement of a worn fan. *Answer:* Capital expenditures: 1, 2, 3, 4; Revenue expenditures: 5, 6, 7.

Betterments (Improvements)

Betterments, or *improvements,* are expenditures that make a plant asset more efficient or productive. A betterment often involves adding a component to an asset or replacing an old component with a better one and does not always increase useful life. An example is replacing manual controls on a machine with automatic controls. One special type of betterment is an *addition,* such as adding a new dock to a warehouse. Because a betterment benefits future periods, it is debited to the asset account as a capital expenditure. The new book value (less salvage value) is then depreciated over the asset's remaining useful life. Assume a company pays $8,000 for a machine with an eight-year useful life and no salvage value. After three years and $3,000 of depreciation, it adds an automated control system to the machine at a cost of $1,800. The cost of the betterment is added to the Machinery account with the following entry.

Assets = Liabilities + Equity
+1,800
−1,800

Jan. 2	Machinery	1,800	
	Cash		1,800
	Record installation of automated system.		

Point: Both extraordinary repairs and betterments require revising future depreciation.

After this entry, the remaining cost to be depreciated is $6,800, computed as $8,000 − $3,000 + $1,800. Depreciation for the remaining five years is $1,360 per year, computed as $6,800/5 years.

Extraordinary Repairs (Replacements)

Extraordinary repairs are expenditures that extend the asset's useful life beyond its original estimate. Their costs are debited to the asset account.

Source: NASA/Tony Gray and Kevin O'Connell

■ Decision Insight

To the Moon and Back   SpaceX made history when it relaunched a used Falcon 9 rocket. This was the first time an orbital rocket was launched into space a second time. SpaceX made extraordinary repairs to the rocket to make this relaunch possible. However, these repairs were considerably less costly than building a new rocket for tens of millions of dollars. ■

DISPOSALS OF PLANT ASSETS

Disposal of plant assets occurs in one of three ways: discarding, sale, or exchange. Discarding and selling are covered here; Appendix 8A covers exchanges. The steps for disposing plant assets are in Exhibit 8.15.

1. Record depreciation up to the date of disposal—this also updates Accumulated Depreciation.
2. Record the removal of the disposed asset's account balances—including its accumulated depreciation.
3. Record any cash (and/or other assets) received or paid in the disposal.
4. Record any gain or loss—equal to the value of any assets received minus the disposed asset's book value.

EXHIBIT 8.15

Accounting for Disposals of Plant Assets

Discarding Plant Assets

A plant asset is *discarded* when it is no longer useful to the company and it has no market value. Assume that a machine costing $9,000 with accumulated depreciation of $9,000 is discarded. When accumulated depreciation equals the asset's cost, it is said to be *fully depreciated* (zero book value). The entry to record the discarding of this asset is

P2

Account for asset disposal through discarding or selling an asset.

June 5	Accumulated Depreciation—Machinery	9,000	
	Machinery......................................		9,000
	Discarding of fully depreciated machinery.		

Assets = Liabilities + Equity
+9,000
−9,000

This entry reflects all four steps of Exhibit 8.15. Step 1 is unnecessary because the machine is fully depreciated. Step 2 is reflected in the debit to Accumulated Depreciation and credit to Machinery. Because no other asset is involved, step 3 is irrelevant. Finally, because book value is zero and no other asset is involved, no gain or loss is recorded in step 4.

How do we account for discarding an asset that is not fully depreciated or one whose depreciation is not up-to-date? To answer this, consider equipment costing $8,000 with accumulated depreciation of $6,000 on December 31 of the prior fiscal year-end. This equipment is being depreciated by $1,000 per year using the straight-line method over eight years with zero salvage. On July 1 of the current year it is discarded. Step 1 is to bring depreciation up-to-date.

Point: Recording depreciation expense up-to-date gives an up-to-date book value for determining gain or loss.

July 1	Depreciation Expense	500	
	Accumulated Depreciation—Equipment............		500
	Record 6 months' depreciation ($1,000 × 6/12).		

Assets = Liabilities + Equity
−500   −500

Steps 2 through 4 of Exhibit 8.15 are reflected in the second (and final) entry.

July 1	Accumulated Depreciation—Equipment..................	6,500	
	Loss on Disposal of Equipment........................	1,500	
	Equipment.....................................		8,000
	Discard equipment with a $1,500 book value.		

Assets = Liabilities + Equity
+6,500   −1,500
−8,000

This loss is computed by comparing the equipment's $1,500 book value ($8,000 − $6,000 − $500) with the zero net cash proceeds. The loss is reported in the Other Expenses and Losses section of the income statement. Discarding an asset can sometimes require a cash payment that would increase the loss.

Selling Plant Assets

To demonstrate selling plant assets, consider BTO's March 31 sale of equipment that cost $16,000 and has accumulated depreciation of $12,000 at December 31 of the prior year-end. Annual depreciation on this equipment is $4,000 using straight-line. Step 1 of this sale is to record depreciation expense and update accumulated depreciation to March 31 of the current year.

Mar. 31	Depreciation Expense	1,000	
	Accumulated Depreciation—Equipment............		1,000
	Record 3 months' depreciation ($4,000 × 3/12).		

Assets = Liabilities + Equity
−1,000   −1,000

Steps 2 through 4 need one final entry that depends on the amount received from the sale. We cover three different possibilities.

Sale at Book Value   If BTO receives $3,000 cash, an amount equal to the equipment's book value as of March 31 (book value = $16,000 − $12,000 − $1,000), no gain or loss is recorded. The entry is

Sale price = Book value → No gain or loss

Assets = Liabilities + Equity
+3,000
+13,000
−16,000

Mar. 31	Cash.	3,000	
	Accumulated Depreciation—Equipment	13,000	
	Equipment		16,000
	Record sale of equipment for no gain or loss.		

Sale above Book Value   If BTO receives $7,000, an amount that is $4,000 above the equipment's $3,000 book value as of March 31, a gain is recorded. The entry is

Sale price > Book value → Gain

Assets = Liabilities + Equity
+7,000   +4,000
+13,000
−16,000

Mar. 31	Cash.	7,000	
	Accumulated Depreciation—Equipment	13,000	
	Gain on Disposal of Equipment.		4,000
	Equipment		16,000
	Record sale of equipment for a $4,000 gain.		

Sale below Book Value   If BTO receives $2,500, an amount that is $500 below the equipment's $3,000 book value as of March 31, a loss is recorded. The entry is

Sale price < Book value → Loss

Assets = Liabilities + Equity
+2,500   −500
+13,000
−16,000

Mar. 31	Cash.	2,500	
	Loss on Disposal of Equipment	500	
	Accumulated Depreciation—Equipment	13,000	
	Equipment		16,000
	Record sale of equipment for a $500 loss.		

NEED-TO-KNOW 8-3

Additional Expenditures and Asset Disposals

C3 P2

Part 1. A company pays $1,000 for equipment expected to last four years and have a $200 salvage value. Prepare journal entries to record the following costs related to the equipment.

a. During the second year of the equipment's life, $400 cash is paid for a new component expected to materially increase the equipment's productivity.

b. During the third year, $250 cash is paid for normal repairs necessary to keep the equipment in good working order.

c. During the fourth year, $500 is paid for repairs expected to increase the useful life of the equipment from four to five years.

Part 2. A company owns a machine that cost $500 and has accumulated depreciation of $400. Prepare the entry to record the disposal of the machine on January 2 in each separate situation.

a. The company disposed of the machine, receiving nothing in return.

b. The company sold the machine for $80 cash.

c. The company sold the machine for $100 cash.

d. The company sold the machine for $110 cash.

Solution—Part 1

a.

Year 2	Equipment	400	
	Cash.		400
	Record betterment.		

b.

Year 3	Repairs Expense	250	
	Cash.		250
	Record ordinary repairs.		

c.

Year 4	Equipment	500	
	Cash......................................		500
	Record extraordinary repairs.		

Do More: QS 8-9, QS 8-10, E 8-14, E 8-15, E 8-16, E 8-17

Solution—Part 2   (*Note:* Book value of machine = $500 − $400 = $100)

a. Disposed of at no value.

Jan. 2	Loss on Disposal of Machine............	100	
	Accumulated Depreciation—Machine.....	400	
	Machine.......................		500
	Record disposal of machine.		

c. Sold for $100 cash.

Jan. 2	Cash	100	
	Accumulated Depreciation—Machine.....	400	
	Machine.......................		500
	Record sale of machine at book value.		

b. Sold for $80 cash.

Jan. 2	Cash	80	
	Loss on Sale of Machine	20	
	Accumulated Depreciation—Machine.....	400	
	Machine.......................		500
	Record sale of machine below book value.		

d. Sold for $110 cash.

Jan. 2	Cash	110	
	Accumulated Depreciation—Machine.....	400	
	Gain on Sale of Machine...........		10
	Machine.......................		500
	Record sale of machine above book value.		

Section 2—Natural Resources

Natural resources are assets that are physically consumed when used. Examples are standing timber, mineral deposits, and oil and gas fields. These assets are soon-to-be inventories of raw materials after cutting, mining, or pumping. Until that conversion happens, they are reported as noncurrent assets under either plant assets or their own category using titles such as *Timber-lands, Mineral deposits,* or *Oil reserves.*

P3

Account for natural resource assets and their depletion.

Cost Determination and Depletion

Natural resources are recorded at cost, which includes all expenditures necessary to acquire the resource and prepare it for use. **Depletion** is the process of allocating the cost of a natural resource to the period when it is consumed. Natural resources are reported on the balance sheet at cost minus *accumulated depletion.* The depletion expense per period is usually based on units extracted from cutting, mining, or pumping. This is similar to units-of-production depreciation.

To demonstrate, consider a mineral deposit with an estimated 250,000 tons of available ore. It is purchased for $500,000, and we expect zero salvage value. The depletion charge per ton of ore mined is $2, computed as $500,000 ÷ 250,000 tons. If 85,000 tons are mined and sold in the first year, the depletion charge for that year is $170,000. These computations are in Exhibit 8.16.

Step 1   Depletion per unit $= \dfrac{\text{Cost} - \text{Salvage value}}{\text{Total units of capacity}} = \dfrac{\$500{,}000 - \$0}{250{,}000 \text{ tons}} = \$2 \text{ per ton}$

Step 2 Depletion expense = Depletion per unit × Units extracted and sold in period
$= \$2 \times 85{,}000 = \$170{,}000$

EXHIBIT 8.16

Depletion Formula and Example

Depletion expense for the first year is recorded as follows.

Dec. 31	Depletion Expense—Mineral Deposit....................	170,000	
	Accumulated Depletion—Mineral Deposit...........		170,000
	Record depletion of the mineral deposit.		

Assets = Liabilities + Equity
−170,000   −170,000

The period-end balance sheet reports the mineral deposit as shown in Exhibit 8.17.

EXHIBIT 8.17

Balance Sheet Presentation
of Natural Resources

Mineral deposit	$500,000	
Less accumulated depletion	**170,000**	$330,000

Because all 85,000 tons of the mined ore are sold during the year, the entire $170,000 of depletion is reported on the income statement. If some of the ore remains unsold at year-end, the depletion related to the unsold ore is carried forward on the balance sheet and reported as Ore Inventory, a current asset. Altering our example, assume that of the 85,000 tons mined the first year, only 70,000 tons are sold. We record depletion of $140,000 (70,000 tons × $2 depletion per unit) and the remaining ore inventory of $30,000 (15,000 tons × $2 depletion per unit) as follows.

Assets = Liabilities + Equity
−170,000   −140,000
+30,000

Dec. 31	Depletion Expense—Mineral Deposit	140,000	
	Ore Inventory	30,000	
	Accumulated Depletion—Mineral Deposit		170,000
	Record depletion and inventory of mineral deposit.		

Plant Assets Tied into Extracting

Mining, cutting, or pumping natural resources requires machinery, equipment, and buildings. When the usefulness of these plant assets is directly related to the depletion of a natural resource, their costs are depreciated using the units-of-production method in proportion to the depletion of the natural resource. For example, if a machine is permanently installed in a mine and 10% of the ore is mined and sold in the period, then 10% of the machine's cost (minus any salvage value) is depreciated. The same procedure is used when a machine is abandoned once resources are extracted. If the machine will be used at another site when extraction is complete, it is depreciated over its own useful life.

©GIRODJL/Shutterstock

Ethical Risk

Lost Cause   Long-term assets must be safeguarded against theft, misuse, and damage. Controls include use of security tags, monitoring of rights infringements, and approvals of asset disposals. A study reports that 43% of employees in operations and services witnessed the wasting, mismanaging, or abusing of assets in the past year (KPMG). ∎

NEED-TO-KNOW 8-4

Depletion Accounting

P3

A company acquires a zinc mine at a cost of $750,000 on January 1. At that same time, it incurs additional costs of $100,000 to access the mine, which is estimated to hold 200,000 tons of zinc. The estimated value of the land after the zinc is removed is $50,000.

1. Prepare the January 1 entry(ies) to record the cost of the zinc mine.

2. Prepare the December 31 year-end adjusting entry if 50,000 tons of zinc are mined, but only 40,000 tons are sold the first year.

Solution

1.

Jan. 1	Zinc Mine	850,000	
	Cash.		850,000
	Record cost of zinc mine.		

2. Depletion per unit = ($750,000 + $100,000 − $50,000)/200,000 tons = $4.00 per ton

Dec. 31	Depletion Expense—Zinc Mine.	160,000	
	Zinc Inventory	40,000	
	Accumulated Depletion—Zinc Mine.		200,000
	Record depletion of zinc mine (50,000 × $4.00).		

Do More: QS 8-11, E 8-18,
P 8-7

Section 3—Intangible Assets

Intangible assets are nonphysical assets used in operations that give companies long-term rights or competitive advantages. Examples are patents, copyrights, licenses, leaseholds, franchises, and trademarks. Lack of physical substance does not always mean an intangible asset. For example, notes and accounts receivable lack physical substance but are not intangibles. This section covers common types of intangible assets.

P4

Account for intangible assets.

Cost Determination and Amortization

An intangible asset is recorded at cost when purchased. Intangibles can have limited lives or indefinite lives. If an intangible has a **limited life,** its cost is expensed over its estimated useful life using **amortization.** If an intangible asset has an **indefinite life**—meaning that no legal, competitive, economic, or other factors limit its useful life—it is not amortized. (If an intangible with an indefinite life is later judged to have a limited life, it is amortized over that limited life.)

Amortization of intangible assets is similar to depreciation. However, only the straight-line method is used for amortizing intangibles *unless* the company can show that another method is preferred. Amortization is recorded in a contra account, Accumulated Amortization. The acquisition cost of intangible assets is disclosed along with the accumulated amortization. The disposal of an intangible asset involves removing its book value, recording any other asset(s) received or given up, and recognizing any gain or loss for the difference.

Many intangibles have limited lives due to laws, contracts, or other reasons. Examples are patents, copyrights, and leaseholds. The cost of intangible assets is amortized over the periods expected to benefit from their use, but this period cannot be longer than the assets' legal existence. Other intangibles such as trademarks and trade names have indefinite lives and are not amortized. An intangible asset that is not amortized is tested annually for **impairment**—if necessary, an impairment loss is recorded. (Details are in advanced courses.)

Intangible assets are often in a separate section of the balance sheet immediately after plant assets. For example, **Nike** follows this approach in reporting nearly $300 million of intangible assets in its balance sheet, plus $140 million in goodwill. Companies usually disclose their amortization periods for intangibles. The remainder of our discussion focuses on accounting for specific types of intangible assets.

©Michael DeYoung/Blend Images

Types of Intangibles

Patents   The federal government grants patents to encourage the invention of new technology and processes. A **patent** is an exclusive right granted to its owner to manufacture and sell a patented item or to use a process for 20 years. When patent rights are purchased, the cost to acquire the rights is debited to an account called Patents. If the owner engages in lawsuits to successfully defend a patent, the cost of lawsuits is debited to the Patents account; if the defense is unsuccessful, the book value of the patent is expensed. However, the costs of research and development leading to a new patent are expensed when incurred.

A patent's cost is amortized over its estimated useful life (not to exceed 20 years). If we purchase a patent costing $25,000 with a useful life of 10 years, we make the following adjusting entry at the end of each of the 10 years to amortize one-tenth of its cost. The $2,500 debit to Amortization Expense is on the income statement as a cost of the patented product or service. The Accumulated Amortization—Patents account is a contra asset account to Patents.

Dec. 31	Amortization Expense—Patents	2,500	
	Accumulated Amortization—Patents		2,500
	Amortize patent costs over its useful life.		

Assets = Liabilities + Equity
−2,500   −2,500

Copyrights   A **copyright** gives its owner the exclusive right to publish and sell a musical, literary, or artistic work during the life of the creator plus 70 years, although the useful life of most copyrights is much shorter. The costs of a copyright are amortized over its useful life. The only identifiable cost of many copyrights is the fee paid to the Copyright Office. Identifiable costs of a copyright are capitalized (recorded in an asset account) and amortized by debiting an account called Amortization Expense—Copyrights.

Franchises and Licenses   **Franchises** and **licenses** are rights that a company or government grants an entity to sell a product or service under specified conditions. Many organizations grant franchise and license rights—**Anytime Fitness**, **Firehouse Subs**, and **Major League Baseball** are just a few examples. The costs of franchises and licenses are debited to a Franchises and Licenses asset account and are amortized over the life of the agreement. If an agreement is for an indefinite time, those costs are not amortized.

Trademarks and Trade Names   A **trademark** or **trade (brand) name** is a symbol, name, phrase, or jingle identified with a company, product, or service. Examples are Nike Swoosh, Big Mac, Coca-Cola, and Corvette. Ownership and exclusive right to use a trademark or trade name often are granted to the company that used it first. Ownership is best established by registering a trademark or trade name with the government's Patent Office. The cost of developing, maintaining, or enhancing the value of a trademark or trade name (such as advertising) is charged to expense when incurred. If a trademark or trade name is purchased, however, its cost is debited to an asset account and then amortized over its expected life. If the company plans to renew indefinitely its right to the trademark or trade name, the cost is not amortized.

Goodwill   **Goodwill** is the amount by which a company's value exceeds the value of its individual assets and liabilities. This implies that the company as a whole has certain valuable attributes not measured in assets and liabilities. These can include superior management, skilled workforce, good supplier or customer relations, quality products or services, good location, or other competitive advantages.

　　Goodwill is only recorded when an entire company or business segment is purchased. Purchased goodwill is computed as purchase price of the company minus the market value of net assets (excluding goodwill). **Google** paid $1.19 billion to acquire **YouTube**; about $1.13 of the $1.19 billion was for goodwill. Goodwill is recorded as an asset, and it is *not* amortized. Instead, goodwill is annually tested for impairment. (Details are in advanced courses.)

Right-of-Use Asset (Lease)   Property is rented under a contract called a **lease.** The property's owner, called the **lessor,** grants the lease. The one who secures the right to possess and use the property is called the **lessee.** A **leasehold** is the rights the lessor grants to the lessee under the terms of the lease.

Lease or Buy   Some advantages of leasing an asset versus buying it are that

- Little or no up-front payment is normally required (making it more affordable).
- Lease terms often allow exchanges to trade up on leased assets (reducing obsolescence).

Lease Accounting   For noncurrent leases, the lessee records a "Right-of-Use Asset" and "Lease Liability" equal to the value of lease payments. At each period-end, the lessee records amortization with a debit to Amortization Expense and a credit to Accumulated Amortization—Right-of-Use Asset.

Leasehold Improvements   A lessee sometimes pays for improvements to the leased property such as partitions, painting, and storefronts. These improvements are called **leasehold improvements,** and the lessee debits these costs to a Leasehold Improvements account. The lessee amortizes these costs over the life of the lease or the life of the improvements, whichever

---

Point: McDonald's "golden arches" are one of the world's most valuable trademarks, yet this asset is not on McDonald's balance sheet.

Point: Amortization of goodwill is different for financial accounting and tax accounting. The IRS requires the amortization of goodwill over 15 years.

Example: Assume goodwill has a book value of $500, an implied fair value of $475, *and* this $25 decline in value meets the impairment test. The impairment entry is

Impairment Loss   25
　　Goodwill   25

Point: At lease start:
Right-of-Use Asset . . . .   #
　　Lease Liability . . . .   #
　　　At each period-end:
Amortization Expense . . . .   #
　　Acc Amor—RoU Asset . . .   #

Point: A Leasehold account implies existence of future benefits that the lessee controls because of a prepayment. It also meets the definition of an asset.

is shorter. The amortization entry *debits* Amortization Expense—Leasehold Improvements and *credits* Accumulated Amortization—Leasehold Improvements.

Other Intangibles

There are other types of intangible assets such as software, non-compete covenants, customer lists, and so forth. Accounting for them is the same as for other intangibles.

Research and Development

Research and development costs are expenditures to discover new products, new processes, or knowledge. Creating patents, copyrights, and innovative products and services requires research and development costs. **The costs of research and development are expensed when incurred** because it is difficult to predict the future benefits from research and development. GAAP does **not** include them as intangible assets.

■ **Decision Insight**

Free Mickey The Walt Disney Company successfully lobbied Congress to extend copyright protection from the life of the creator plus 50 years to the life of the creator plus 70 years. This extension allows the company to protect its characters for 20 additional years before the right to use them enters the public domain. Mickey Mouse is now protected by copyright law until 2023. The law is officially termed the Copyright Term Extension Act (CTEA), but it is also known as the Mickey Mouse Protection Act. ■

©Yoshikazu Tsuno/AFP/Getty Images

Part 1. A publisher purchases the copyright on a book for $1,000 on January 1 of this year. The copyright lasts five more years. The company plans to sell prints for seven years. Prepare entries to record the purchase of the copyright on January 1 and its annual amortization on December 31.

Part 2. On January 3 of this year, a retailer pays $9,000 to modernize its store. Improvements include lighting, partitions, and a sound system. These improvements are estimated to yield benefits for five years. The retailer leases its store and has three years remaining on its lease. Prepare the entry to record (a) the cost of modernization and (b) amortization at the end of this year.

Part 3. On January 6 of this year, a company pays $6,000 for a patent with a remaining 12-year legal life to produce a supplement expected to be marketable for 3 years. Prepare entries to record its acquisition and the December 31 amortization entry.

NEED-TO-KNOW **8-5**

Accounting for Intangibles

P4 ▶

Solution—Part 1

Jan. 1	Copyright...	1,000	
	Cash		1,000
	Record purchase of copyright.		
Dec. 31	Amortization Expense—Copyright	200	
	Accumulated Amortization—Copyright....................		200
	Record amortization of copyright ($1,000/5 years).		

Solution—Part 2

a.

Jan. 3	Leasehold Improvements....................................	9,000	
	Cash		9,000
	Record leasehold improvements.		

b.

Dec. 31	Amortization Expense—Leasehold Improvements	3,000	
	Accumulated Amortization—Leasehold Improvements........		3,000
	*Record amortization of leasehold over remaining lease life.**		

*Amortization = $9,000/3-year lease term = $3,000 per year.

Solution—Part 3

Jan. 6	Patents..	6,000	
	Cash		6,000
	Record purchase of patent.		
Dec. 31	Amortization Expense*	2,000	
	Accumulated Amortization—Patents.....................		2,000
	*Record amortization of patent. *$6,000/3 years = $2,000*		

Do More: QS 8-12, QS 8-13, E 8-19, E 8-20

Decision Analysis ▢▢▢   **Total Asset Turnover**

One important measure of a company's ability to use its assets efficiently and effectively is **total asset turnover,** defined in Exhibit 8.18.

EXHIBIT 8.18

Total Asset Turnover

$$\text{Total asset turnover} = \frac{\text{Net sales}}{\text{Average total assets}}$$

A1

Compute total asset turnover and apply it to analyze a company's use of assets.

Net sales is net amounts earned from the sale of products and services. Average total assets is (Current period-end total assets + Prior period-end total assets)/2. A higher total asset turnover means a company is generating more net sales for each dollar of assets. Management is evaluated on efficient and effective use of total assets by looking at total asset turnover.

Let's look at total asset turnover in Exhibit 8.19 for two competing companies: **Starbucks** and **Jack in the Box**.

EXHIBIT 8.19

Analysis Using Total Asset Turnover

Company	Figure ($ millions)	Current Year	1 Year Ago	2 Years Ago
Starbucks	Net sales.............................	$22,387	$21,316	$19,163
	Average total assets....................	$14,339	$13,364	$11,585
	Total asset turnover	**1.56**	**1.60**	**1.65**
Jack in the Box	Net sales.............................	$1,554	$1,599	$1,540
	Average total assets....................	$1,289	$1,326	$1,287
	Total asset turnover	**1.21**	**1.21**	**1.20**

To show how we use total asset turnover, let's look at Starbucks. We express Starbucks's use of assets in generating net sales by saying "it turned its assets over 1.56 times during the current year." This means that each $1.00 of assets produced $1.56 of net sales.

Is a total asset turnover of 1.56 good or bad? All companies want a high total asset turnover. Interpreting the total asset turnover requires an understanding of company operations. Some operations are capital-intensive, meaning that a relatively large amount is invested in plant assets to generate sales. This results in a lower total asset turnover. Other companies' operations are labor-intensive, meaning that they generate sales using people instead of assets. In that case, we expect a higher total asset turnover.

Starbucks's turnover is higher than that for Jack in the Box. However, Starbucks's total asset turnover decreased over the last three years. To maintain a strong total asset turnover, Starbucks must grow sales at a rate equal to, or higher than, its total asset growth.

■ **Decision Maker** ━━━━━━━━━━━━━━━━━━━━

Environmentalist A paper manufacturer claims it cannot afford more environmental controls. It points to its low total asset turnover of 1.9 and argues that it cannot compete with companies whose total asset turnover is much higher. Examples cited are food stores (5.5) and auto dealers (3.8). How do you respond? ■ *Answer:* The paper manufacturer's comparison of its total asset turnover with food stores and auto dealers is misdirected. You need to collect data from competitors in the paper industry to show that a 1.9 total asset turnover is about the norm for this industry.

On July 1, 2018, Tulsa Company pays $600,000 to acquire a fully equipped factory. The purchase includes the following assets and information.

COMPREHENSIVE

Acquisition, Cost Allocation, and Disposal of Tangible and Intangible Assets

Asset	Appraised Value	Salvage Value	Useful Life	Depreciation Method
Land...........................	$160,000			Not depreciated
Land improvements	80,000	$ 0	10 years	Straight-line
Building........................	320,000	100,000	10 years	Double-declining-balance
Machinery......................	240,000	20,000	10,000 units	Units-of-production
Total...........................	$800,000			

Required

1. Allocate the total $600,000 purchase cost among the separate assets.

2. Compute the 2018 (six months) and 2019 depreciation expense for each asset, and compute the company's total depreciation expense for both years. The machinery produced 700 units in 2018 and 1,800 units in 2019.

3. On the last day of calendar-year 2020, Tulsa discarded equipment that had been on its books for five years. The equipment's original cost was $12,000 (estimated life of five years) and its salvage value was $2,000. No depreciation had been recorded for the fifth year when the disposal occurred. Journalize the fifth year of depreciation (straight-line method) and the asset's disposal.

4. At the beginning of year 2020, Tulsa purchased a patent for $100,000 cash. The company estimated the patent's useful life to be 10 years. Journalize the patent acquisition and its amortization for the year 2020.

5. Late in the year 2020, Tulsa acquired an ore deposit for $600,000 cash. It added roads and built mine shafts for an additional cost of $80,000. Salvage value of the mine is estimated to be $20,000. The company estimated 330,000 tons of available ore. In year 2020, Tulsa mined and sold 10,000 tons of ore. Journalize the mine's acquisition and its first year's depletion.

6.ᴬ (This question applies to this chapter's Appendix coverage.) On the first day of 2020, Tulsa exchanged the machinery that was acquired on July 1, 2018, along with $5,000 cash for machinery with a $210,000 market value. Journalize the exchange of these assets assuming the exchange has commercial substance. (Refer to background information in parts 1 and 2.)

PLANNING THE SOLUTION

● Complete a three-column table showing the following amounts for each asset: appraised value, percent of total value, and apportioned cost.

● Using allocated costs, compute depreciation for 2018 (only one-half year) and 2019 (full year) for each asset. Summarize those computations in a table showing total depreciation for each year.

● Depreciation must be recorded up-to-date before discarding an asset. Calculate and record depreciation expense for the fifth year using the straight-line method. Record the loss on the disposal as well as the removal of the discarded asset and its accumulated depreciation.

● Record the patent (an intangible asset) at its purchase price. Use straight-line amortization over its useful life to calculate amortization expense.

● Record the ore deposit (a natural resource asset) at its cost, including any added costs to ready the mine for use. Calculate depletion per ton using the depletion formula. Multiply the depletion per ton by the amount of tons mined and sold to calculate depletion expense for the year.

● Gains and losses on asset exchanges that have commercial substance are recognized. Make a journal entry to add the acquired machinery and remove the old machinery, along with its accumulated depreciation, and to record the cash given in the exchange.

SOLUTION

1. Allocation of the total cost of $600,000 among the separate assets.

Asset	Appraised Value	Percent of Total Value	Apportioned Cost
Land........................	$160,000	20%	$120,000 ($600,000 × 20%)
Land improvements	80,000	10	60,000 ($600,000 × 10%)
Building.....................	320,000	40	240,000 ($600,000 × 40%)
Machinery...................	240,000	30	180,000 ($600,000 × 30%)
Total........................	$800,000	100%	$ 600,000

2. Depreciation for each asset. (Land is not depreciated.)

Land Improvements

Cost..	$ 60,000
Salvage value...	0
Depreciable cost	$ 60,000
Useful life	10 years
Annual depreciation expense ($60,000/10 years)	$ 6,000
2018 depreciation ($6,000 × 6/12)..........................	**$ 3,000**
2019 depreciation	**$ 6,000**

Building

Straight-line rate = 100%/10 years = 10%
Double-declining-balance rate = 10% × 2 = 20%

2018 depreciation ($240,000 × 20% × 6/12)	**$ 24,000**
2019 depreciation [($240,000 − $24,000) × 20%]..............	**$ 43,200**

Machinery

Cost..	$180,000
Salvage value...	20,000
Depreciable cost	$160,000
Total expected units of production	10,000 units
Depreciation per unit ($160,000/10,000 units)	$ 16
2018 depreciation ($16 × 700 units)........................	**$ 11,200**
2019 depreciation ($16 × 1,800 units)	**$ 28,800**

Total depreciation expense for each year.

	2018	2019
Land improvements	$ 3,000	$ 6,000
Building.....................	24,000	43,200
Machinery...................	11,200	28,800
Total.......................	$38,200	$78,000

3. Record the depreciation up-to-date on the discarded asset.

Depreciation Expense—Equipment	2,000	
Accumulated Depreciation—Equipment................................		2,000
Record depreciation on date of disposal: ($12,000 − $2,000)/5.		

Record the removal of the discarded asset and its loss on disposal.

Accumulated Depreciation—Equipment	10,000	
Loss on Disposal of Equipment...	2,000	
Equipment...		12,000
Record the discarding of equipment with a $2,000 book value.		

4.

Patent..	100,000	
Cash		100,000
Record patent acquisition.		

Amortization Expense—Patent..	10,000	
Accumulated Amortization—Patent....................................		10,000
Record amortization expense: $100,000/10 years = $10,000.		

5.

Ore Deposit	680,000	
Cash		680,000
Record ore deposit acquisition and its related costs.		

Depletion Expense—Ore Deposit...	20,000	
Accumulated Depletion—Ore Deposit................................		20,000
Record depletion expense: ($680,000 − $20,000)/330,000 tons = $2 per ton.		
10,000 tons mined and sold × $2 = $20,000 depletion.		

6.ᴬ Record the asset exchange: The book value on the exchange date is $180,000 (cost) − $40,000 (accumulated depreciation). The book value of the machinery given up in the exchange ($140,000) plus the $5,000 cash paid is less than the $210,000 value of the machine acquired. The entry to record this exchange of assets that has commercial substance and recognizes the $65,000 gain ($210,000 − $140,000 − $5,000) is

Machinery (new)	210,000	
Accumulated Depreciation—Machinery (old)	40,000	
Machinery (old)...		180,000
Cash		5,000
Gain on Exchange of Assets...		65,000
Record exchange with commercial substance of old equipment		
plus cash for new equipment.		

Exchanging Plant Assets

8A

Many plant assets such as machinery, automobiles, and equipment are exchanged for newer assets. In a typical exchange of plant assets, a *trade-in allowance* is received on the old asset and the balance is paid in cash. Accounting for the exchange of assets depends on whether the transaction has *commercial substance*. An exchange has commercial substance if the company's future cash flows change as a result of the exchange of one asset for another asset. If an asset exchange has commercial substance, a gain or loss is recorded based on the difference between the book value of the asset(s) given up and the market value of the asset(s) received. Because most exchanges have commercial substance, we cover gains and losses for only that situation. Advanced courses cover exchanges without commercial substance.

Exchange with Commercial Substance: A Loss   A company acquires $42,000 in new equipment. In exchange, the company pays $33,000 cash and trades in old equipment. The old equipment originally cost $36,000 and has accumulated depreciation of $20,000, which implies a $16,000 book value at the time of exchange. This exchange has commercial substance and the old equipment has a trade-in allowance of $9,000. This exchange yields a loss as computed in the middle (Loss) columns of Exhibit 8A.1; the loss is computed as Asset received − Assets given = $42,000 − $49,000 = $(7,000). We also can compute the loss as Trade-in allowance − Book value of assets given = $9,000 − $16,000 = $(7,000).

EXHIBIT 8A.1

Computing Gain or Loss on Asset Exchange with Commercial Substance

Asset Exchange Has Commercial Substance	Loss		Gain	
Market value of asset received		$42,000		$42,000
Book value of assets given:				
Equipment ($36,000 − $20,000)	$16,000		$16,000	
Cash	33,000	49,000	23,000	39,000
Gain (loss) on exchange		**$(7,000)**		**$ 3,000**

The entry to record this asset exchange and the loss follows.

Assets = Liabilities + Equity
+42,000   −7,000
+20,000
−36,000
−33,000

Jan. 3	Equipment (new)	42,000	
	Loss on Exchange of Assets	7,000	
	Accumulated Depreciation—Equipment (old)	20,000	
	Equipment (old)		36,000
	Cash.......................................		33,000
	Record exchange (with commercial substance) of old equipment and cash for new equipment.		

Point: "New" and "old" equipment are for illustration only. Both the debit and credit are to the same Equipment account.

Exchange with Commercial Substance: A Gain   Let's assume the same facts as in the preceding asset exchange *except that the company pays $23,000 cash, not $33,000, with the trade-in.* This exchange has commercial substance and the old equipment has a trade-in allowance of $19,000. This exchange yields a gain as computed in the right-most (Gain) columns of Exhibit 8A.1; the gain is computed as Asset received − Assets given = $42,000 − $39,000 = $3,000. We also can compute the gain as Trade-in allowance − Book value of assets given = $19,000 − $16,000 = $3,000. The entry to record this asset exchange and the gain follows.

Assets = Liabilities + Equity
+42,000   +3,000
+20,000
−36,000
−23,000

Jan. 3	Equipment (new)	42,000	
	Accumulated Depreciation—Equipment (old)	20,000	
	Equipment (old)		36,000
	Cash.......................................		23,000
	Gain on Exchange of Assets......................		3,000
	Record exchange (with commercial substance) of old equipment and cash for new equipment.		

NEED-TO-KNOW 8-7

Asset Exchange

P5

A company acquires $45,000 in new web servers. In exchange, the company trades in old web servers along with a cash payment. The old servers originally cost $30,000 and had accumulated depreciation of $23,400 at the time of the trade. Prepare entries to record the trade under two different assumptions where (a) the exchange has commercial substance and the old servers have a trade-in allowance of $3,000 and (b) the exchange has commercial substance and the old servers have a trade-in allowance of $7,000.

Solution

a.

Equipment (new)	45,000	
Loss on Exchange of Assets	3,600	
Accumulated Depreciation—Equipment (old)	23,400	
Equipment (old)		30,000
Cash ($45,000 − $3,000)		42,000

b.

Equipment (new)	45,000	
Accumulated Depreciation—Equipment (old)	23,400	
Equipment (old)		30,000
Cash ($45,000 − $7,000)		38,000
Gain on Exchange of Assets........................		400

Do More: QS 8-16, E 8-23, E 8-24

Summary: Cheat Sheet

PLANT ASSETS

Cost of plant assets: Normal, reasonable, and necessary costs in preparing an asset for its intended use. If an asset is damaged during unpacking, the repairs are not added to its cost. Instead, they are charged to an expense account.

Machinery and equipment: Cost includes purchase price, taxes, transportation, insurance while in transit, installation, assembly, and testing.
Building: A purchased building's costs include its purchase price, real estate fees, taxes, title fees, and attorney fees. A constructed building's costs include construction costs and insurance during construction, but not insurance after it is completed.

Land improvements: Additions to land that have limited useful lives. Examples are parking lots, driveways, and lights.

Land: Has an indefinite (unlimited) life and costs include real estate commissions, clearing, grading, and draining.

Lump-sum purchase: Plant assets purchased as a group for a single lump-sum price. We allocate the cost to the assets acquired based on their relative market (or appraised) values.

	Appraised Value	Percent of Total	Apportioned Cost		Entry for lump-sum cash purchase:		
Building...	$ 60,000	60% ($60,000/$100,000)	**$54,000** ($90,000 × 60%)		Building...............	54,000	
Land	40,000	40 ($40,000/$100,000)	**36,000** ($90,000 × 40%)		Land	36,000	
Totals.....	$100,000	100%	$ 90,000		Cash............		90,000
					Record costs of plant assets.		

Depreciation: Process of allocating the cost of a plant asset to expense while it is in use.

Salvage value: Estimate of the asset's value at the end of its useful life.

Useful life: Length of time a plant asset is to be used in operations.

Record depreciation expense:

Depreciation Expense	1,800	
Accumulated Depreciation—"Asset Type".......		1,800

Straight-line depreciation: Charges the same amount of depreciation expense in each period of the asset's useful life.

Straight-line depreciation formula:

$$\text{Depreciation expense} = \frac{\text{Cost} - \text{Salvage value}}{\text{Useful life in periods}}$$

Asset book value (or book value): Computed as the asset's total cost minus accumulated depreciation.

Units-of-production depreciation: Charges a varying amount for each period depending on an asset's usage.

Units-of-production formula:

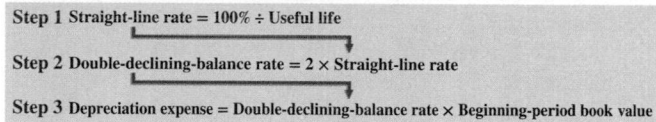

Step 1 Depreciation per unit = $\dfrac{\text{Cost} - \text{Salvage value}}{\text{Total units of production}}$

Step 2 Depreciation expense = Depreciation per unit × Units produced in period

Double-declining-balance depreciation: Charges more depreciation in early years and less depreciation in later years.

Double-declining-balance formula:

Step 1 Straight-line rate = 100% ÷ Useful life

Step 2 Double-declining-balance rate = 2 × Straight-line rate

Step 3 Depreciation expense = Double-declining-balance rate × Beginning-period book value

Change in an accounting estimate: For plant assets, it is changing the estimate of useful life or salvage value. It only affects current and future depreciation expense. Do not go back and change prior years' depreciation.

Straight-line depreciation after change in accounting estimate:

$$\frac{\text{Book value} - \text{Revised salvage value}}{\text{Revised remaining useful life}}$$

Impairment: Permanent decline in the fair value of an asset relative to its book value.

Impairment Loss.................................	50	
Accumulated Depreciation—Equipment		50

Ordinary repairs (revenue expenditure): Expenditures to keep an asset in good operating condition. They do not increase useful life or productivity. Include cleaning, changing oil, and minor repairs.

Repairs Expense...............................	9,500	
Cash.......................................		9,500

Betterments (capital expenditure): Expenditures to make a plant asset more efficient or productive. Include upgrading components and adding additions onto plant assets.

Extraordinary repairs (capital expenditure): Expenditures that extend the asset's useful life beyond its original estimate.

Betterments and extraordinary repairs: These expenditures are "capitalized" by adding their costs to the plant asset.

"Plant Asset"....................................	1,800	
Cash.......................................		1,800

Before discarding, selling, or exchanging a plant asset: Must record depreciation up to that date.

Depreciation Expense	500	
Accumulated Depreciation—Equipment		500

Discarding *fully* depreciated asset:

Accumulated Depreciation—Machinery	9,000	
Machinery		9,000

Discarding *partially* depreciated asset: Loss is the book value (Cost − Accumulated depreciation) of the asset when discarded.

Accumulated Depreciation—Equipment.............	6,500	
Loss on Disposal of Equipment	1,500	
Equipment		8,000

Sale of asset at book value: If sale price = book value, no gain or loss.

Cash	3,000	
Accumulated Depreciation—Equipment.............	13,000	
Equipment		16,000

Sale of asset *above* book value: If sale price > book value → gain.

Cash	7,000	
Accumulated Depreciation—Equipment.............	13,000	
Gain on Disposal of Equipment...............		4,000
Equipment		16,000

Sale of asset *below* book value: If sale price < book value → loss.

Cash	2,500	
Loss on Disposal of Equipment	500	
Accumulated Depreciation—Equipment.............	13,000	
Equipment		16,000

NATURAL RESOURCES

Natural resources: Assets that are physically consumed when used. Examples are standing timber, mineral deposits, and oil and gas fields.

Depletion: Process of allocating the cost of a natural resource.

Depletion formula:

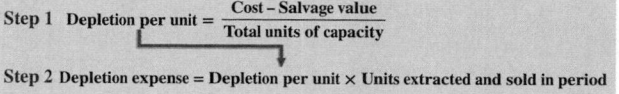

Step 1 Depletion per unit = $\dfrac{\text{Cost} - \text{Salvage value}}{\text{Total units of capacity}}$

Step 2 Depletion expense = Depletion per unit × Units extracted and sold in period

Depletion expense (when *all* units extracted are sold):

Depletion Expense—Mineral Deposit	170,000	
Accumulated Depletion—Mineral Deposit		170,000

Depletion expense (when *not all* units extracted are sold):

Depletion Expense—Mineral Deposit	140,000	
Ore Inventory	30,000	
Accumulated Depletion—Mineral Deposit		170,000

INTANGIBLE ASSETS

Intangible assets: Nonphysical assets (used in operations) that give companies long-term rights, privileges, or competitive advantages.

Amortization: Intangible assets with limited useful lives require amortization. It is similar to depreciation and uses the shorter of the legal life or useful life of the intangible for straight-line amortization.

Amortization Expense—Patents..................	2,500	
Accumulated Amortization—Patents		2,500

Patent: Exclusive right to manufacture and sell a patented item or to use a process for 20 years.

Copyright: Exclusive right to publish and sell a musical, literary, or artistic work during the life of the creator plus 70 years.

Franchises or licenses: Rights to sell a product or service under specified conditions.

Trademark or trade (brand) name: A symbol, name, phrase, or jingle identified with a company, product, or service.

Goodwill: Amount by which a company's value exceeds the value of its individual assets and liabilities (net assets). Goodwill is only recorded when an entire company or business segment is purchased. Not amortized, but tested for impairment.

Right-of-use asset (lease): Rights the lessor grants to the lessee under terms of the lease.

Leasehold improvements: Improvements to a leased (rented) property such as partitions, painting, and storefronts. The lessee amortizes these costs over the life of the lease or the life of the improvements, whichever is shorter.

Key Terms

Accelerated depreciation method (308)
Amortization (317)
Asset book value (307)
Betterments (312)
Capital expenditures (311)
Change in an accounting estimate (310)
Copyright (318)
Cost (304)
Declining-balance method (308)
Depletion (315)
Depreciation (305)
Extraordinary repairs (312)
Franchises (318)
Goodwill (318)

Impairment (310, 317)
Inadequacy (306)
Indefinite life (317)
Intangible assets (317)
Land improvements (304)
Lease (318)
Leasehold (318)
Leasehold improvements (318)
Lessee (318)
Lessor (318)
Licenses (318)
Limited life (317)
Modified Accelerated Cost Recovery System (MACRS) (309)

Natural resources (315)
Obsolescence (306)
Ordinary repairs (312)
Patent (317)
Plant assets (303)
Research and development costs (319)
Revenue expenditures (311)
Salvage value (305)
Straight-line depreciation (306)
Total asset turnover (320)
Trademark or trade (brand) name (318)
Units-of-production depreciation (307)
Useful life (305)

Multiple Choice Quiz

1. A company paid $326,000 for property that included land, land improvements, and a building. The land was appraised at $175,000, the land improvements were appraised at $70,000, and the building was appraised at $105,000. What is the allocation of costs to the three assets?
   a. Land, $150,000; Land Improvements, $60,000; Building, $90,000
   b. Land, $163,000; Land Improvements, $65,200; Building, $97,800
   c. Land, $150,000; Land Improvements, $61,600; Building, $92,400
   d. Land, $159,000; Land Improvements, $65,200; Building, $95,400
   e. Land, $175,000; Land Improvements, $70,000; Building, $105,000

2. A company purchased a truck for $35,000 on January 1, 2019. The truck is estimated to have a useful life of four years and a salvage value of $1,000. Assuming that the company uses straight-line depreciation, what is depreciation expense for the year ended December 31, 2020?
   a. $8,750   c. $8,500   e. $25,500
   b. $17,500   d. $17,000

3. A company purchased machinery for $10,800,000 on January 1, 2019. The machinery has a useful life of 10 years and an estimated salvage value of $800,000. What is depreciation expense for the year ended December 31, 2020, assuming that the double-declining-balance method is used?
   a. $2,160,000   c. $1,728,000   e. $1,600,000
   b. $3,888,000   d. $2,000,000

4. A company sold a machine that originally cost $250,000 for $120,000 when accumulated depreciation on the machine was $100,000. The gain or loss recorded on the sale of this machine is
   a. $0 gain or loss.   d. $30,000 gain.
   b. $120,000 gain.   e. $150,000 loss.
   c. $30,000 loss.

5. A company had average total assets of $500,000, gross sales of $575,000, and net sales of $550,000. The company's total asset turnover is
   a. 1.15.   d. 0.87.
   b. 1.10.   e. 1.05.
   c. 0.91.

ANSWERS TO MULTIPLE CHOICE QUIZ

1. b;

	Appraisal Value	%	Total Cost	Allocated
Land..............	$175,000	50%	$326,000	$163,000
Land improvements ..	70,000	20	326,000	65,200
Building............	105,000	30	326,000	97,800
Totals.............	$350,000			$326,000

2. c; ($35,000 − $1,000)/4 years = $8,500 per year

3. c; 2019: $10,800,000 × (2 × 10%) = $2,160,000
    2020: ($10,800,000 − $2,160,000) × (2 × 10%) = $1,728,000

4. c;

Cost of machine	$250,000
Accumulated depreciation	100,000
Book value	150,000
Cash received.....................	120,000
Loss on sale	$ 30,000

5. b; $550,000/$500,000 = 1.10

---

^{A} *Superscript letter A denotes assignments based on Appendix 8A.*

 Icon denotes assignments that involve decision making.

Discussion Questions

1. What characteristics of a plant asset make it different from other assets?

2. What is the general rule for cost inclusion for plant assets?

3. What is different between land and land improvements?

4. Why is the cost of a lump-sum purchase allocated to the individual assets acquired?

5. Does the balance in the Accumulated Depreciation—Machinery account represent funds to replace the machinery when it wears out? If not, what does it represent?

6. Why is the Modified Accelerated Cost Recovery System not generally accepted for financial accounting purposes?

7. What is the difference between ordinary repairs and extraordinary repairs? How should each be recorded?

8. Identify events that might lead to disposal of a plant asset.

9. What is the process of allocating the cost of natural resources to expense as they are used?

10. Is the declining-balance method an acceptable way to compute depletion of natural resources? Explain.

11. What are the characteristics of an intangible asset?

12. What general procedures are applied in accounting for the acquisition and potential cost allocation of intangible assets?

13. When do we know that a company has goodwill? When can goodwill appear in a company's balance sheet?

14. Assume that a company buys another business and pays for its goodwill. If the company plans to incur costs each year to maintain the value of the goodwill, must it also amortize this goodwill?

15. How is total asset turnover computed? Why would a financial statement user be interested in total asset turnover?

16. On its recent balance sheet in Appendix A, **APPLE** Apple lists its plant assets as "Property, plant and equipment, net." What does "net" mean in this title?

17. Refer to **Google**'s recent balance sheet in **GOOGLE** Appendix A. What is the book value of its total net property, plant, and equipment assets at December 31, 2017?

18. Refer to **Samsung**'s balance sheet in **Samsung** Appendix A. What does it title its plant assets? What is the book value of its plant assets at December 31, 2017?

19. Refer to **Samsung**'s December 31, 2017, **Samsung** balance sheet in Appendix A. What long-term assets discussed in this chapter are reported by the company?

20. Identify the main difference between (*a*) plant assets and current assets, (*b*) plant assets and inventory, and (*c*) plant assets and long-term investments.

---

connect

Kegler Bowling buys scorekeeping equipment with an invoice cost of $190,000. The electrical work required for the installation costs $20,000. Additional costs are $4,000 for delivery and $13,700 for sales tax. During the installation, the equipment was damaged and the cost of repair was $1,850.

  What is the total recorded cost of the scorekeeping equipment?

QUICK STUDY

QS 8-1
Cost of plant assets

C1

QS 8-2

Assigning costs to plant assets

C1

Listed below are costs (or discounts) to purchase or construct new plant assets. (1) Indicate whether the costs should be *expensed* or *capitalized* (meaning they are included in the cost of the plant assets on the balance sheet). (2) For costs that should be capitalized, indicate in which category of plant assets (Equipment, Building, or Land) the related costs should be recorded on the balance sheet.

Expensed or Capitalized	Asset Category	
_____	_____	**1.** Wages paid to train employees to use new equipment.
_____	_____	**2.** Invoice cost paid for new equipment.
_____	_____	**3.** Early payment discount taken on the purchase of new equipment.
_____	_____	**4.** Realtor commissions incurred on land purchased.
_____	_____	**5.** Property taxes on land incurred after it was purchased.
_____	_____	**6.** Costs of oil for the truck used to deliver new equipment.
_____	_____	**7.** Costs to lay foundation for a new building.
_____	_____	**8.** Insurance on a new building during its construction.

QS 8-3

Straight-line depreciation

P1

On January 1, the Matthews Band pays $65,800 for sound equipment. The band estimates it will use this equipment for four years and perform 200 concerts. It estimates that after four years it can sell the equipment for $2,000. During the first year, the band performs 45 concerts.

Compute the first-year depreciation using the straight-line method.

QS 8-4

Units-of-production depreciation   P1

On January 1, the Matthews Band pays $65,800 for sound equipment. The band estimates it will use this equipment for four years and perform 200 concerts. It estimates that after four years it can sell the equipment for $2,000. During the first year, the band performs 45 concerts.

Compute the first-year depreciation using the units-of-production method.

QS 8-5

Double-declining-balance method   P1

A building is acquired on January 1 at a cost of $830,000 with an estimated useful life of eight years and salvage value of $75,000. Compute depreciation expense for the first three years using the double-declining-balance method.

QS 8-6

Straight-line, partial-year depreciation   C2

On October 1, Organic Farming purchases wind turbines for $140,000. The wind turbines are expected to last six years, have a salvage value of $20,000, and be depreciated using the straight-line method.

1. Compute depreciation expense for the last three months of the first year.

2. Compute depreciation expense for the second year.

QS 8-7

Computing revised depreciation

C2

On January 1, the Matthews Band pays $65,800 for sound equipment. The band estimates it will use this equipment for four years and after four years it can sell the equipment for $2,000. Matthews Band uses straight-line depreciation but realizes at the start of the second year that this equipment will last only a total of three years. The salvage value is not changed.

Compute the revised depreciation for both the second and third years.

QS 8-8

Recording plant asset impairment   C2

Equipment has a book value of $16,000 and a fair value of $14,750. The decline in value meets the impairment test. Prepare the entry to record this $1,250 impairment.

QS 8-9

Revenue and capital expenditures

C3

1. Classify the following as either a revenue expenditure (RE) or a capital expenditure (CE).

    ____ **a.** Paid $40,000 cash to replace a motor on equipment that extends its useful life by four years.

    ____ **b.** Paid $200 cash per truck for the cost of their annual tune-ups.

    ____ **c.** Paid $175 for the monthly cost of replacement filters on an air-conditioning system.

    ____ **d.** Completed an addition to a building for $225,000 cash.

2. Prepare the journal entries to record the four transactions from part 1.

QS 8-10

Disposal of assets   P2

Garcia Co. owns equipment that cost $76,800, with accumulated depreciation of $40,800. Record the sale of the equipment under the following three separate cases assuming Garcia sells the equipment for (1) $47,000 cash, (2) $36,000 cash, and (3) $31,000 cash.

Perez Company acquires an ore mine at a cost of $1,400,000. It incurs additional costs of $400,000 to access the mine, which is estimated to hold 1,000,000 tons of ore. The estimated value of the land after the ore is removed is $200,000.

1. Prepare the entry(ies) to record the cost of the ore mine.

2. Prepare the year-end adjusting entry if 180,000 tons of ore are mined and sold the first year.

QS 8-11
Natural resources and depletion
P3

Identify the following as intangible assets (IA), natural resources (NR), or some other asset (O).

_____ **a.** Oil well   _____ **d.** Gold mine   _____ **g.** Franchise

_____ **b.** Trademark   _____ **e.** Building   _____ **h.** Coal mine

_____ **c.** Leasehold   _____ **f.** Copyright   _____ **i.** Salt mine

QS 8-12
Classifying assets
P3   P4

On January 1 of this year, Diaz Boutique pays $105,000 to modernize its store. Improvements include new floors, ceilings, wiring, and wall coverings. These improvements are estimated to yield benefits for 10 years. Diaz leases (does not own) its store and has eight years remaining on the lease. Prepare the entry to record (1) the cost of modernization and (2) amortization at the end of this current year.

QS 8-13
Intangible assets and amortization   **P4**

Selected accounts from Westeros Co.'s adjusted trial balance for the year ended December 31 follow. Prepare its income statement.

Sales	$30,000	Depreciation expense	$ 5,000
Repairs expense	500	Salaries expense	10,000
Depletion expense	4,000	Amortization expense	2,000

QS 8-14
Preparing an income statement
P1   P3   P4

Aneko Company reports the following: net sales of $14,800 for Year 2 and $13,990 for Year 1; end-of-year total assets of $19,100 for Year 2 and $17,900 for Year 1. (1) Compute total asset turnover for Year 2. (2) Aneko's competitor has a turnover of 2.0. Is Aneko performing better or worse than its competitor based on total asset turnover?

QS 8-15
Computing total asset turnover   **A1**

Caleb Co. owns a machine that had cost $42,400 with accumulated depreciation of $18,400. Caleb exchanges the machine for a newer model that has a market value of $52,000.

1. Record the exchange assuming Caleb paid $30,000 cash and the exchange has commercial substance.

2. Record the exchange assuming Caleb paid $22,000 cash and the exchange has commercial substance.

QS 8-16^A
Asset exchange
P5

---

connect

Rizio Co. purchases a machine for $12,500, terms 2/10, n/60, FOB shipping point. Rizio paid within the discount period and took the $250 discount. Transportation costs of $360 were paid by Rizio. The machine required mounting and power connections costing $895. Another $475 is paid to assemble the machine, and $40 of materials are used to get it into operation. During installation, the machine was damaged and $180 worth of repairs were made. Compute the cost recorded for this machine.

EXERCISES

Exercise 8-1
Cost of plant assets
C1

Cala Manufacturing purchases land for $390,000 as part of its plans to build a new plant. The company pays $33,500 to tear down an old building on the lot and $47,000 to fill and level the lot. It also pays construction costs of $1,452,200 for the new building and $87,800 for lighting and paving a parking area. Prepare a single journal entry to record these costs incurred by Cala, all of which are paid in cash.

Exercise 8-2
Recording costs of assets
C1

Rodriguez Company pays $395,380 for real estate with land, land improvements, and a building. Land is appraised at $157,040; land improvements are appraised at $58,890; and the building is appraised at $176,670. Allocate the total cost among the three assets and prepare the journal entry to record the purchase.

Exercise 8-3
Lump-sum purchase of plant assets   **C1**

Ramirez Company installs a computerized manufacturing machine in its factory at the beginning of the year at a cost of $43,500. The machine's useful life is estimated at 10 years, or 385,000 units of product, with a $5,000 salvage value. During its second year, the machine produces 32,500 units of product. Determine the machine's second-year depreciation under the straight-line method.

Exercise 8-4
Straight-line depreciation
P1

Exercise 8-5
Units-of-production
depreciation   **P1**

Ramirez Company installs a computerized manufacturing machine in its factory at the beginning of the year at a cost of $43,500. The machine's useful life is estimated at 10 years, or 385,000 units of product, with a $5,000 salvage value. During its second year, the machine produces 32,500 units of product. Determine the machine's second-year depreciation using the units-of-production method.

Exercise 8-6
Double-declining-balance
depreciation   **P1**

Ramirez Company installs a computerized manufacturing machine in its factory at the beginning of the year at a cost of $43,500. The machine's useful life is estimated at 10 years, or 385,000 units of product, with a $5,000 salvage value. During its second year, the machine produces 32,500 units of product. Determine the machine's second-year depreciation using the double-declining-balance method.

Exercise 8-7
Straight-line depreciation
P1

NewTech purchases computer equipment for $154,000 to use in operating activities for the next four years. It estimates the equipment's salvage value at $25,000. Prepare a table showing depreciation and book value for each of the four years assuming straight-line depreciation.

Exercise 8-8
Double-declining-balance
depreciation   **P1**

NewTech purchases computer equipment for $154,000 to use in operating activities for the next four years. It estimates the equipment's salvage value at $25,000. Prepare a table showing depreciation and book value for each of the four years assuming double-declining-balance depreciation.

Exercise 8-9
Straight-line depreciation
and income effects

P1

Tory Enterprises pays $238,400 for equipment that will last five years and have a $43,600 salvage value. By using the equipment in its operations for five years, the company expects to earn $88,500 annually, after deducting all expenses except depreciation. Prepare a table showing income before depreciation, depreciation expense, and net (pretax) income for each year and for the total five-year period, assuming straight-line depreciation is used.

Exercise 8-10
Double-declining-balance
depreciation   **P1**

Check   Year 3 NI, $54,170

Tory Enterprises pays $238,400 for equipment that will last five years and have a $43,600 salvage value. By using the equipment in its operations for five years, the company expects to earn $88,500 annually, after deducting all expenses except depreciation. Prepare a table showing income before depreciation, depreciation expense, and net (pretax) income for each year and for the total five-year period, assuming double-declining-balance depreciation is used.

Exercise 8-11
Straight-line, partial-year
depreciation   **C2**

On April 1, Cyclone Co. purchases a trencher for $280,000. The machine is expected to last five years and have a salvage value of $40,000. Compute depreciation expense at December 31 for both the first year and second year assuming the company uses the straight-line method.

Exercise 8-12
Double-declining-
balance, partial-year
depreciation   **C2**

On April 1, Cyclone Co. purchases a trencher for $280,000. The machine is expected to last five years and have a salvage value of $40,000. Compute depreciation expense at December 31 for both the first year and second year assuming the company uses the double-declining-balance method.

Exercise 8-13
Revising depreciation
C2

Check   (2) $3,710

Apex Fitness Club uses straight-line depreciation for a machine costing $23,860, with an estimated four-year life and a $2,400 salvage value. At the beginning of the third year, Apex determines that the machine has three more years of remaining useful life, after which it will have an estimated $2,000 salvage value. Compute (1) the machine's book value at the end of its second year and (2) the amount of depreciation for each of the final three years given the revised estimates.

Exercise 8-14
Ordinary repairs,
extraordinary repairs,
and betterments

C3

Oki Company pays $264,000 for equipment expected to last four years and have a $29,000 salvage value. Prepare journal entries to record the following costs related to the equipment.

1. Paid $22,000 cash for a new component that increased the equipment's productivity.
2. Paid $6,250 cash for minor repairs necessary to keep the equipment working well.
3. Paid $14,870 cash for significant repairs to increase the useful life of the equipment from four to seven years.

Martinez Company owns a building that appears on its prior year-end balance sheet at its original $572,000 cost less $429,000 accumulated depreciation. The building is depreciated on a straight-line basis assuming a 20-year life and no salvage value. During the first week in January of the current calendar year, major structural repairs are completed on the building at a $68,350 cost. The repairs extend its useful life for 5 years beyond the 20 years originally estimated.

1. Determine the building's age (plant asset age) as of the prior year-end balance sheet date.
2. Prepare the entry to record the cost of the structural repairs that are paid in cash.
3. Determine the book value of the building immediately after the repairs are recorded.
4. Prepare the entry to record the current calendar year's depreciation.

Exercise 8-15
Extraordinary repairs; plant asset age

C3

Check (3) $211,350

Diaz Company owns a machine that cost $250,000 and has accumulated depreciation of $182,000. Prepare the entry to record the disposal of the machine on January 1 in each separate situation.

1. The machine needed extensive repairs and was not worth repairing. Diaz disposed of the machine, receiving nothing in return.
2. Diaz sold the machine for $35,000 cash.
3. Diaz sold the machine for $68,000 cash.
4. Diaz sold the machine for $80,000 cash.

Exercise 8-16
Disposal of assets

P2

Rayya Co. purchases a machine for $105,000 on January 1, 2019. Straight-line depreciation is taken each year for four years assuming a seven-year life and no salvage value. The machine is sold on July 1, 2023, during its fifth year of service. Prepare entries to record the partial year's depreciation on July 1, 2023, and to record the sale under each separate situation.

1. The machine is sold for $45,500 cash.   2. The machine is sold for $25,000 cash.

Exercise 8-17
Partial-year depreciation; disposal of plant asset

P2

Montana Mining Co. pays $3,721,000 for an ore deposit containing 1,525,000 tons. The company installs machinery in the mine costing $213,500. Both the ore and machinery will have no salvage value after the ore is completely mined. Montana mines and sells 166,200 tons of ore during the year. Prepare the year-end entries to record both the ore deposit depletion and the mining machinery depreciation. Mining machinery depreciation should be in proportion to the mine's depletion.

Exercise 8-18
Depletion of natural resources

P3

Milano Gallery purchases the copyright on a painting for $418,000 on January 1. The copyright is good for 10 more years, after which the copyright will expire and anyone can make prints. The company plans to sell prints for 11 years. Prepare entries to record the purchase of the copyright on January 1 and its annual amortization on December 31.

Exercise 8-19
Amortization of intangible assets P4

Robinson Company purchased Franklin Company at a price of $2,500,000. The fair market value of the net assets purchased equals $1,800,000.

1. What is the amount of goodwill that Robinson records at the purchase date?
2. Does Robinson amortize goodwill at year-end for financial reporting purposes? If so, over how many years is it amortized?
3. Robinson believes that its employees provide superior customer service, and through their efforts, Robinson believes it has created $900,000 of goodwill. Should Robinson Company record this goodwill?

Exercise 8-20
Goodwill

P4

Selected accounts from Gregor Co.'s adjusted trial balance for the year ended December 31 follow. Prepare a classified balance sheet.

Exercise 8-21
Preparing a balance sheet

P1   P3   P4

Total equity	$50,000	Accounts payable...	$ 2,000
Patents	4,000	Accumulated depreciation—Equipment	13,000
Cash	6,000	Notes payable (due in 9 years)	11,000
Land	30,000	Goodwill	5,000
Equipment	20,000	Accumulated depletion—Silver mine	3,000
Silver mine	15,000	Accumulated amortization—Patents	1,000

Lok Co. reports net sales of $5,856,480 for Year 2 and $8,679,690 for Year 3. End-of-year balances for total assets are Year 1, $1,686,000; Year 2, $1,800,000; and Year 3, $1,982,000. (a) Compute Lok's total asset turnover for Year 2 and Year 3. (b) Lok's competitor has a turnover of 3.0. Is Lok performing better or worse than its competitor on the basis of total asset turnover?

Exercise 8-22
Evaluating efficient use of assets A1

Exercise 8-23ᴬ

Exchanging assets

P5

Check (2) $14,500

Gilly Construction trades in an old tractor for a new tractor, receiving a $29,000 trade-in allowance and paying the remaining $83,000 in cash. The old tractor had cost $96,000 and had accumulated depreciation of $52,500. Answer the following questions assuming the exchange has commercial substance.

1. What is the book value of the old tractor at the time of exchange?
2. What is the loss on this asset exchange?
3. What amount should be recorded (debited) in the asset account for the new tractor?

Exercise 8-24ᴬ

Recording plant asset disposals

P5

Check (3) Dr. Loss on Exchange, $4,375

On January 2, Bering Co. disposes of a machine costing $44,000 with accumulated depreciation of $24,625. Prepare the entries to record the disposal under each separate situation.

1. The machine is sold for $18,250 cash.
2. The machine is traded in for a new machine having a $60,200 cash price. A $25,000 trade-in allowance is received, and the balance is paid in cash. Assume the asset exchange has commercial substance.
3. The machine is traded in for a new machine having a $60,200 cash price. A $15,000 trade-in allowance is received, and the balance is paid in cash. Assume the asset exchange has commercial substance.

⊪ connect

PROBLEM SET A

Problem 8-1A

Plant asset costs; depreciation methods

C1   P1

Check (2) $30,000

(3) $10,800

Timberly Construction makes a lump-sum purchase of several assets on January 1 at a total cash price of $900,000. The estimated market values of the purchased assets are building, $508,800; land, $297,600; land improvements, $28,800; and four vehicles, $124,800.

Required

1. Allocate the lump-sum purchase price to the separate assets purchased. Prepare the journal entry to record the purchase.
2. Compute the first-year depreciation expense on the building using the straight-line method, assuming a 15-year life and a $27,000 salvage value.
3. Compute the first-year depreciation expense on the land improvements assuming a five-year life and double-declining-balance depreciation.

Analysis Component

4. Compared to straight-line depreciation, does accelerated depreciation result in payment of less total taxes over the asset's life?

Problem 8-2A

Depreciation methods

P1

A machine costing $257,500 with a four-year life and an estimated $20,000 salvage value is installed in Luther Company's factory on January 1. The factory manager estimates the machine will produce 475,000 units of product during its life. It actually produces the following units: 220,000 in Year 1, 124,600 in Year 2, 121,800 in Year 3, and 15,200 in Year 4. The total number of units produced by the end of Year 4 exceeds the original estimate—this difference was not predicted. *Note:* The machine cannot be depreciated below its estimated salvage value.

Required

Prepare a table with the following column headings and compute depreciation for each year (and total depreciation of all years combined) for the machine under each depreciation method.

Check Year 4: units-of-production depreciation, $4,300; DDB depreciation, $12,187

Year	Straight-Line	Units-of-Production	Double-Declining-Balance

---

Problem 8-3A

Asset cost allocation; straight-line depreciation

C1   P1

On January 1, Mitzu Co. pays a lump-sum amount of $2,600,000 for land, Building 1, Building 2, and Land Improvements 1. Building 1 has no value and will be demolished. Building 2 will be an office and is appraised at $644,000, with a useful life of 20 years and a $60,000 salvage value. Land Improvements 1 is valued at $420,000 and is expected to last another 12 years with no salvage value. The land is valued at $1,736,000. The company also incurs the following additional costs.

Cost to demolish Building 1	$ 328,400	Cost of additional land grading	$175,400
Cost to construct Building 3, having a useful life of 25 years and a $392,000 salvage value. . . .	2,202,000	Cost of new Land Improvements 2, having a 20-year useful life and no salvage value	164,000

Required

1. Prepare a table with the following column headings: Land, Building 2, Building 3, Land Improvements 1, and Land Improvements 2. Allocate the costs incurred by Mitzu to the appropriate columns and total each column.

2. Prepare a single journal entry to record all the incurred costs assuming they are paid in cash on January 1.

3. Using the straight-line method, prepare the December 31 adjusting entries to record depreciation for the first year these assets were in use.

Check (1) Land costs, $2,115,800; Building 2 costs, $598,000

(3) Depr.—Land Improv. 1 and 2, $32,500 and $8,200

Champion Contractors completed the following transactions involving equipment.

Year 1

Jan. 1 Paid $287,600 cash plus $11,500 in sales tax and $1,500 in transportation (FOB shipping point) for a new loader. The loader is estimated to have a four-year life and a $20,600 salvage value. Loader costs are recorded in the Equipment account.

    3 Paid $4,800 to install air-conditioning in the loader to enable operations under harsher conditions. This increased the estimated salvage value of the loader by another $1,400.

Dec. 31 Recorded annual straight-line depreciation on the loader.

Year 2

Jan. 1 Paid $5,400 to overhaul the loader's engine, which increased the loader's estimated useful life by two years.

Feb. 17 Paid $820 for minor repairs to the loader after the operator backed it into a tree.

Dec. 31 Recorded annual straight-line depreciation on the loader.

Required

Prepare journal entries to record these transactions and events.

Problem 8-4A
Computing and revising depreciation; revenue and capital expenditures

C1 C2 C3

Check Dec. 31, Year 1: Dr. Depr. Expense—Equip., $70,850

Dec. 31, Year 2: Dr. Depr. Expense—Equip., $43,590

Yoshi Company completed the following transactions and events involving its delivery trucks.

Year 1

Jan. 1 Paid $20,515 cash plus $1,485 in sales tax for a new delivery truck estimated to have a five-year life and a $2,000 salvage value. Delivery truck costs are recorded in the Trucks account.

Dec. 31 Recorded annual straight-line depreciation on the truck.

Year 2

Dec. 31 The truck's estimated useful life was changed from five to four years, and the estimated salvage value was increased to $2,400. Recorded annual straight-line depreciation on the truck.

Year 3

Dec. 31 Recorded annual straight-line depreciation on the truck.

    31 Sold the truck for $5,300 cash.

Required

Prepare journal entries to record these transactions and events.

Problem 8-5A
Computing and revising depreciation; selling plant assets

C2 P1 P2

Check Dec. 31, Year 2: Dr. Depr. Expense—Trucks, $5,200

Dec. 31, Year 3: Dr. Loss on Disposal of Trucks, $2,300

Onslow Co. purchased a used machine for $178,000 cash on January 2. On January 3, Onslow paid $2,840 to wire electricity to the machine and an additional $1,160 to secure it in place. The machine will be used for six years and have a $14,000 salvage value. Straight-line depreciation is used. On December 31, at the end of its fifth year in operations, it is disposed of.

Required

1. Prepare journal entries to record the machine's purchase and the costs to ready it for use. Cash is paid for all costs incurred.

2. Prepare journal entries to record depreciation of the machine at December 31 of (a) its first year of operations and (b) the year of its disposal.

3. Prepare journal entries to record the machine's disposal under each separate situation: (a) it is sold for $15,000 cash; (b) it is sold for $50,000 cash; and (c) it is destroyed in a fire and the insurance company pays $30,000 cash to settle the loss claim.

Problem 8-6A
Disposal of plant assets

C1 P1 P2

Check (2b) Depr. Exp., $28,000

(3c) Dr. Loss from Fire, $12,000

Problem 8-7A

Natural resources

P3

On July 23 of the current year, Dakota Mining Co. pays $4,715,000 for land estimated to contain 5,125,000 tons of recoverable ore. It installs and pays for machinery costing $410,000 on July 25. The company removes and sells 480,000 tons of ore during its first five months of operations ending on December 31. Depreciation of the machinery is in proportion to the mine's depletion as the machinery will be abandoned after the ore is mined.

Required

Check   (c) Depletion, $441,600

(d) Depreciation, $38,400

Prepare entries to record (a) the purchase of the land, (b) the cost and installation of machinery, (c) the first five months' depletion assuming the land has a net salvage value of zero after the ore is mined, and (d) the first five months' depreciation on the machinery.

Analysis Component

(e) If the machine will be used at another site when extraction is complete, how would we depreciate this machine?

Problem 8-8A

Right-of-use lease asset

P4

On January 1, Falk Company signed a contract to lease space in a building for three years. The current value of the three lease payments is $270,000.

Required

Prepare entries for Falk to record (a) the lease asset and obligation at January 1 and (b) the $90,000 straight-line amortization at December 31 of the first year.

PROBLEM SET B

Problem 8-1B

Plant asset costs; depreciation methods

C1   P1

Check   (2) $65,000

(3) $50,400

Nagy Company makes a lump-sum purchase of several assets on January 1 at a total cash price of $1,800,000. The estimated market values of the purchased assets are building, $890,000; land, $427,200; land improvements, $249,200; and five trucks, $213,600.

Required

1. Allocate the lump-sum purchase price to the separate assets purchased. Prepare the journal entry to record the purchase.

2. Compute the first-year depreciation expense on the building using the straight-line method, assuming a 12-year life and a $120,000 salvage value.

3. Compute the first-year depreciation expense on the land improvements assuming a 10-year life and double-declining-balance depreciation.

Analysis Component

4. Compared to straight-line depreciation, does accelerated depreciation result in payment of less total taxes over the asset's life?

Problem 8-2B

Depreciation methods

P1

On January 1, Manning Co. purchases and installs a new machine costing $324,000 with a five-year life and an estimated $30,000 salvage value. Management estimates the machine will produce 1,470,000 units of product during its life. Actual production of units is as follows: 355,600 in Year 1, 320,400 in Year 2, 317,000 in Year 3, 343,600 in Year 4, and 138,500 in Year 5. The total number of units produced by the end of Year 5 exceeds the original estimate—this difference was not predicted. *Note:* The machine cannot be depreciated below its estimated salvage value.

Required

Prepare a table with the following column headings and compute depreciation for each year (and total depreciation of all years combined) for the machine under each depreciation method.

Check   DDB Depreciation, Year 3, $46,656; U-of-P Depreciation, Year 4, $68,720

Year	Straight-Line	Units-of-Production	Double-Declining-Balance

Problem 8-3B

Asset cost allocation; straight-line depreciation

C1   P1

On January 1, ProTech Co. pays a lump-sum amount of $1,550,000 for land, Building A, Building B, and Land Improvements B. Building A has no value and will be demolished. Building B will be an office and is appraised at $482,800, with a useful life of 15 years and a $99,500 salvage value. Land Improvements B is valued at $142,000 and is expected to last another five years with no salvage value. The land is valued at $795,200. The company also incurs the following additional costs.

Cost to demolish Building A	$ 122,000	Cost of additional land grading	$174,500
Cost to construct Building C, having a useful life . . of 20 years and a $258,000 salvage value.	1,458,000	Cost of new Land Improvements C, having a 10-year useful life and no salvage value	103,500

Required

1. Prepare a table with the following column headings: Land, Building B, Building C, Land Improvements B, and Land Improvements C. Allocate the costs incurred by ProTech to the appropriate columns and total each column.

2. Prepare a single journal entry to record all incurred costs assuming they are paid in cash on January 1.

3. Using the straight-line method, prepare the December 31 adjusting entries to record depreciation for the first year these assets were in use.

Check (1) Land costs, $1,164,500; Building B costs, $527,000

(3) Depr.—Land Improv. B and C, $31,000 and $10,350

Mercury Delivery Service completed the following transactions involving equipment.

Year 1

Jan. 1 Paid $25,860 cash plus $1,810 in sales tax for a new delivery van that was estimated to have a five-year life and a $3,670 salvage value. Van costs are recorded in the Equipment account.
      3 Paid $1,850 to install sorting racks in the van for more accurate and quicker delivery of packages. This increases the estimated salvage value of the van by another $230.
Dec. 31 Recorded annual straight-line depreciation on the van.

Year 2

Jan. 1 Paid $2,064 to overhaul the van's engine, which increased the van's useful life by two years.
May 10 Paid $800 for minor repairs to the van after the driver backed it into a loading dock.
Dec. 31 Recorded annual straight-line depreciation on the van.

Required

Prepare journal entries to record these transactions and events.

Problem 8-4B
Computing and revising depreciation; revenue and capital expenditures
C1 C2 C3

Check Dec. 31, Year 1: Dr. Depr. Expense—Equip., $5,124

Dec. 31, Year 2: Dr. Depr. Expense—Equip., $3,760

York Instruments completed the following transactions and events involving its machinery.

Year 1

Jan. 1 Paid $107,800 cash plus $6,470 in sales tax for a new machine. The machine is estimated to have a six-year life and a $9,720 salvage value.
Dec. 31 Recorded annual straight-line depreciation on the machinery.

Year 2

Dec. 31 The machine's estimated useful life was changed from six to four years, and the estimated salvage value was increased to $14,345. Recorded annual straight-line depreciation on the machinery.

Year 3

Dec. 31 Recorded annual straight-line depreciation on the machinery.
      31 Sold the machine for $25,240 cash.

Required

Prepare journal entries to record these transactions and events.

Problem 8-5B
Computing and revising depreciation; selling plant assets
C2 P1 P2

Check Dec. 31, Year 2: Dr. Depr. Expense— Machinery, $27,500

Dec. 31, Year 3: Dr. Loss on Disposal of Machinery, $16,605

On January 1, Walker purchased a used machine for $150,000. On January 4, Walker paid $3,510 to wire electricity to the machine and an additional $4,600 to secure it in place. The machine will be used for seven years and have an $18,110 salvage value. Straight-line depreciation is used. On December 31, at the end of its sixth year of use, the machine is disposed of.

Required

1. Prepare journal entries to record the machine's purchase and the costs to ready it for use. Cash is paid for all costs incurred.

2. Prepare journal entries to record depreciation of the machine at December 31 of (a) its first year of operations and (b) the year of its disposal.

3. Prepare journal entries to record the machine's disposal under each separate situation: (a) it is sold for $28,000 cash; (b) it is sold for $52,000 cash; and (c) it is destroyed in a fire and the insurance company pays $25,000 cash to settle the loss claim.

Problem 8-6B
Disposal of plant assets
C1 P1 P2

Check (2b) Depr. Exp., $20,000

(3c) Dr. Loss from Fire, $13,110

Problem 8-7B

Natural resources

P3

On February 19 of the current year, Quartzite Co. pays $5,400,000 for land estimated to contain 4 million tons of recoverable ore. It installs and pays for machinery costing $400,000 on March 21. The company removes and sells 254,000 tons of ore during its first nine months of operations ending on December 31. Depreciation of the machinery is in proportion to the mine's depletion as the machinery will be abandoned after the ore is mined.

Required

Check (c) Depletion, $342,900
(d) Depreciation, $25,400

Prepare entries to record (*a*) the purchase of the land, (*b*) the cost and installation of the machinery, (*c*) the first nine months' depletion assuming the land has a net salvage value of zero after the ore is mined, and (*d*) the first nine months' depreciation on the machinery.

Analysis Component

(*e*) If the machine will be used at another site when extraction is complete, how would we depreciate this machine?

Problem 8-8B

Right-of-use lease asset

P4

On January 1, Mason Co. entered into a three-year lease on a building. The current value of the three lease payments is $60,000.

Required

Prepare entries for Mason to record (*a*) the lease asset and obligation at January 1 and (*b*) the $20,000 straight-line amortization at December 31 of the first year.

SERIAL PROBLEM

Business Solutions

A1   P1

©Alexander Image/Shutterstock

This serial problem began in Chapter 1 and continues through most of the book. If previous chapter segments were not completed, the serial problem can begin at this point.

SP 8   Selected ledger account balances for **Business Solutions** follow.

	For Three Months Ended December 31, 2019	For Three Months Ended March 31, 2020
Office equipment	$ 8,000	$ 8,000
Accumulated depreciation—Office equipment	400	800
Computer equipment	20,000	20,000
Accumulated depreciation—Computer equipment.	1,250	2,500
Total revenue	31,284	44,000
Total assets	83,460	120,268

Required

1. Assume that Business Solutions does not acquire additional office equipment or computer equipment in 2020. Compute amounts for *the year ended* December 31, 2020, for Depreciation Expense—Office Equipment and for Depreciation Expense—Computer Equipment (assume use of the straight-line method).

2. Given the assumptions in part 1, what is the book value of both the office equipment and the computer equipment as of December 31, 2020?

Check (3) Three-month (annual) turnover = 0.43 (1.73 annual)

3. Compute the three-month total asset turnover for Business Solutions as of March 31, 2020. Use total revenue for the numerator and average the December 31, 2019, total assets and the March 31, 2020, total assets for the denominator. Interpret its total asset turnover if competitors average 2.5 for annual periods. (Round turnover to two decimals.)

Accounting Analysis

COMPANY ANALYSIS

A1

APPLE

AA 8-1   Refer to **Apple**'s financial statements in Appendix A to answer the following.

1. What percent of the original cost of Apple's Property, Plant and Equipment account remains to be depreciated as of (*a*) September 30, 2017, and (*b*) September 24, 2016? Assume these assets have no salvage value and the entire account is depreciable. *Hint:* Accumulated Depreciation is listed under "Property, Plant and Equipment" in the notes to Apple's financial statements in Appendix A.

2. Much research and development is needed to create the next iPhone. Does Apple capitalize and amortize research and development costs over the life of the product, or are research and development costs expensed as incurred?

3. Compute Apple's total asset turnover for the year ended (*a*) September 30, 2017, and (*b*) September 24, 2016. Assume total assets at September 26, 2015, are $290,345 ($ millions).

4. Using the results in part 3, is the change in Apple's asset turnover favorable or unfavorable?

AA 8-2   Comparative figures for **Apple** and **Google** follow.

	Apple			Google		
$ millions	Current Year	One Year Prior	Two Years Prior	Current Year	One Year Prior	Two Years Prior
Total assets	$375,319	$321,686	$290,345	$197,295	$167,497	$147,461
Net sales	229,234	215,639	233,715	110,855	90,272	74,989

Required

1. Compute total asset turnover for the most recent two years for Apple and Google using the data shown.

2. In the current year, which company is more efficient in generating net sales given total assets?

3. Does each company's asset turnover underperform or outperform the industry (assumed) asset turnover of 0.5 for (*a*) Apple and (*b*) Google?

AA 8-3   Comparative figures for **Samsung**, **Apple**, and **Google** follow.

	Samsung			Apple		Google	
In millions	Current Year	Prior Year	Two Years Prior	Current Year	Prior Year	Current Year	Prior Year
Total assets . . .	₩301,752,090	₩262,174,324	₩242,179,521	$375,319	$321,686	$197,295	$167,497
Net sales	239,575,376	201,866,745	200,653,482	229,234	215,639	110,855	90,272

Required

1. Compute total asset turnover for the most recent two years for Samsung using the data shown.

2. Is the change in Samsung's asset turnover favorable or unfavorable?

3. For the current year, is Samsung's asset turnover better or worse than the asset turnover for (*a*) Apple and (*b*) Google?

Beyond the Numbers

BTN 8-1   Flo Choi owns a small business and manages its accounting. Her company just finished a year in which a large amount of borrowed funds was invested in a new building addition as well as in equipment and fixture additions. Choi's banker requires her to submit semiannual financial statements so he can monitor the financial health of her business. He has warned her that if profit margins erode, he might raise the interest rate on the borrowed funds to reflect the increased loan risk from the bank's point of view. Choi knows profit margin is likely to decline this year. As she prepares year-end adjusting entries, she decides to apply the following depreciation rule: All asset additions are considered to be in use on the first day of the following month. (The previous rule assumed assets are in use on the first day of the month nearest to the purchase date.)

Required

1. Identify decisions that managers like Choi must make in applying depreciation methods.
2. Is Choi's rule an ethical violation, or is it a legitimate decision in computing depreciation?
3. How will Choi's new depreciation rule affect the profit margin of her business?

COMMUNICATING IN PRACTICE

A1

BTN 8-2   Teams are to select an industry, and each team member is to select a different company in that industry. Each team member is to acquire the financial statements (Form 10-K) of the company selected—see the company's website or the SEC's EDGAR database (**SEC.gov**). Use the financial statements to compute total asset turnover. Communicate with teammates via a meeting, e-mail, or telephone to discuss the meaning of this ratio, how different companies compare to each other, and the industry norm. The team must prepare a one-page report that describes the ratios for each company and identifies the conclusions reached during the team's discussion.

TAKING IT TO THE NET

P4

BTN 8-3   Access the **Yahoo!** (renamed as Altaba, ticker: AABA) 10-K report for the year ended December 31, 2016, filed on March 1, 2017, at **SEC.gov**.

Required

1. What amount of goodwill is reported on Yahoo!'s balance sheet? What percentage of total assets does its goodwill represent? Is goodwill a major asset for Yahoo!? Explain.
2. Compute the change in goodwill from December 31, 2015, to December 31, 2016. Comment on the change in goodwill over this period.
3. Locate Note 6 to its financial statements. What are the three categories of intangible assets that Yahoo! reports at December 31, 2016? What proportion of total assets do the intangibles represent?
4. What does Yahoo! indicate is the life of "Tradenames, trademarks, and domain names" according to its Note 6?

TEAMWORK IN ACTION

P1

Point: This activity can follow an overview of each method. Step 1 allows for three areas of expertise. Larger teams will have some duplication of areas, but the straight-line choice should not be duplicated. Expert teams can use the book and consult with the instructor.

BTN 8-4   Each team member is to become an expert on one depreciation method to facilitate teammates' understanding of that method. Follow these procedures:

a. Each team member is to select an area of expertise from one of the following depreciation methods: straight-line, units-of-production, or double-declining-balance.

b. Expert teams are to be formed from those who have selected the same area of expertise. The instructor will identify the location where each expert team meets.

c. Using the following data, expert teams are to collaborate and develop a presentation answering the requirements. Expert team members must write the presentation in a format they can show to their learning teams.

Data and Requirements On January 8, 2017, Whitewater Riders purchases a van to transport rafters back to the point of departure at the conclusion of the rafting adventures they operate. The cost of the van is $44,000. It has an estimated salvage value of $2,000 and is expected to be used for four years and driven 60,000 miles. The van is driven 12,000 miles in 2017; 18,000 miles in 2018; 21,000 in 2019; and 10,000 in 2020.

1. Compute the annual depreciation expense for each year of the van's estimated useful life.
2. Explain when and how annual depreciation is recorded.
3. Explain the impact on income of this depreciation method versus others over the van's life.
4. Identify the van's book value for each year of its life and illustrate the reporting of this amount for any one year.

d. Re-form original learning teams. In rotation, experts are to present to their teams the results from part *c*. Experts are to encourage and respond to questions.

BTN 8-5 Review the chapter's opening feature involving Deb and Dan Carey and their company, **New Glarus Brewing Company**. Assume that the company currently has net sales of $8,000,000 and that it is planning an expansion that will increase net sales by $4,000,000. To accomplish this expansion, the company must increase its average total assets from $2,500,000 to $3,000,000.

ENTREPRENEURIAL DECISION

A1

Required

1. Compute the company's total asset turnover under (*a*) current conditions and (*b*) proposed conditions.
2. Evaluate and comment on the merits of the proposal given the analysis in part 1. Identify any concerns we would express about the proposal.

BTN 8-6 Team up with one or more classmates for this activity. Identify companies in your community or area that must account for at least one of the following assets: natural resource, patent, lease, leasehold improvement, copyright, trademark, or goodwill. You might find a company that has more than one type of asset. Once you identify a company with a specific asset, describe the accounting this company uses to allocate the cost of that asset to the periods that benefit from its use.

HITTING THE ROAD

P3   P4

9 Accounting for Current Liabilities

Chapter Preview

KNOWN LIABILITIES

C1 Reporting liabilities

C2 Sales taxes payable

Unearned revenues

P1 Short-term notes

NTK 9-1

PAYROLL LIABILITIES

P2 Employee payroll and deductions

P3 Employer payroll taxes

Multi-period liabilities

NTK 9-2

ESTIMATED LIABILITIES

P4 Reporting for:

Health and pension

Vacation benefits

Bonus plans

Warranty liabilities

NTK 9-3

CONTINGENCIES AND ANALYSIS

C3 Accounting for contingencies:

Probable

Possible

Remote

A1 Times interest earned

NTK 9-4

Learning Objectives

CONCEPTUAL

C1 Describe current and long-term liabilities and their characteristics.

C2 Identify and describe known current liabilities.

C3 Explain how to account for contingent liabilities.

ANALYTICAL

A1 Compute the times interest earned ratio and use it to analyze liabilities.

PROCEDURAL

P1 Prepare entries to account for short-term notes payable.

P2 Compute and record *employee* payroll deductions and liabilities.

P3 Compute and record *employer* payroll expenses and liabilities.

P4 Account for estimated liabilities, including warranties and bonuses.

P5 *Appendix 9A*—Identify and describe the details of payroll reports, records, and procedures.

Sounds Like a Winner!

"Good stuff doesn't come easy"—**TIM WESTERGREN**

OAKLAND, CA—"I was a senior in college," recalls Tim Westergren, "when unbeknownst to me, I decided to become an entrepreneur." Tim was playing in a band and considering ways to discover new music.

"I shared the idea with a former college classmate, Jon Kraft . . . and in a matter of weeks it went from 'we have an idea' to 'we have a business plan and we're pitching it.'" The business Tim and Jon built is now known as **Pandora Media** (**Pandora.com**), an Internet radio that plays music based on the listener's preferences.

Tim and Jon started Pandora with financing help. However, within a year of starting the business, Tim and Jon ran out of money.

"We weren't paying our employees," admits Tim. "About 50 or 55 people worked without getting paid for over two years during that time." To keep the business afloat, Tim and Jon learned about managing current liabilities for payroll, supplies, employee benefits, vacations, training, and taxes.

Tim and Jon insist that effective management of liabilities, especially payroll and employee benefits, is crucial for new businesses. Tim and Jon's ability to juggle their current liabilities enabled them to "hang on" for those crucial first two years.

"Business is an execution game," insists Tim, "not an invention game."

©Jason Davis/Pandora Media/Getty Images

Tim encourages people to start a business doing something they love. "If you're doing it because you love it and because it has meaning for you," proclaims Tim, "then you can't really fail."

Sources: *Pandora website,* January 2019; *Billboard.com,* March 2016; *Fortune,* June 2015; *Washington Post,* February 2015; *GreenBiz,* November 2012

KNOWN LIABILITIES

Characteristics of Liabilities

This section discusses characteristics of liabilities and how liabilities are classified.

Defining Liabilities   A *liability* is a probable future payment of assets or services that a company is presently obligated to make as a result of past transactions or events. This definition includes three elements that are shown in Exhibit 9.1. No liability is reported when one or more of those elements are missing. For example, companies expect to pay wages in future years, but these future payments are *not* liabilities because no past event such as employee work resulted in a present obligation. Instead, liabilities are recorded when employees perform work and earn wages.

C1 _____
Describe current and long-term liabilities and their characteristics.

Due to a past transaction or event . . .

company has a present obligation

. . . for future payment of assets or services.

Past   Present   Future

EXHIBIT 9.1

Characteristics of a Liability

Point: Most liability accounts use *payable* or *unearned* in their titles.

Classifying Liabilities   Liabilities are classified as either current or long term.

Current Liabilities   **Current liabilities,** or *short-term liabilities,* **are liabilities due *within one year*** (or the company's operating cycle if longer). Most are paid using current assets or by creating other current liabilities. Common examples are accounts payable, short-term notes

Point: For simplicity we assume an operating cycle of one year.

341

payable, wages payable, warranty liabilities, and taxes payable. Some liabilities do not have a fixed due date but instead are payable on the creditor's demand. These are reported as current liabilities because of the possibility of payment in the near term.

Current liabilities differ across companies because they depend on the type of company operations. For example, **MGM Resorts** reports casino outstanding chip liability. **Harley-Davidson** reports different current liabilities such as warranty, recall, and dealer incentive liabilities. Exhibit 9.2 shows current liabilities as a percentage of total liabilities for selected companies.

EXHIBIT 9.2

Current Liabilities as a Percentage of Total Liabilities

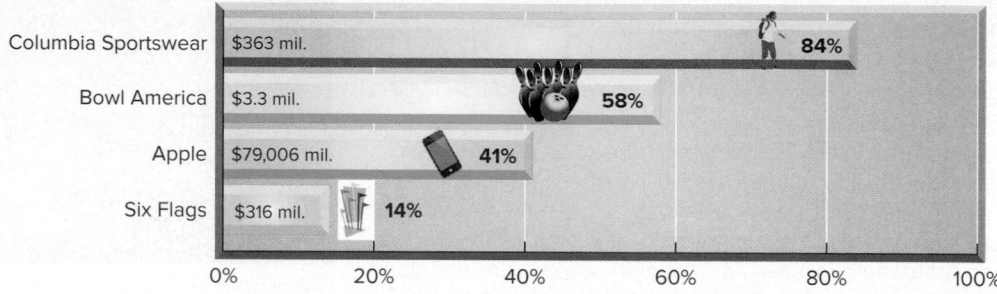

Long-Term Liabilities   **Long-term liabilities** are obligations due *after* one year (or the company's operating cycle if longer). They include long-term notes payable, warranty liabilities, lease liabilities, and bonds payable. For example, **Domino's Pizza** reports long-term liabilities of $2,196 million. A single liability can be divided between the current and noncurrent sections if a company expects to make payments toward it in both the short and long term. Domino's reports long-term debt of $2,149 million and current portion of long-term debt of $39 million. The current portion is reported in current liabilities.

Uncertainty in Liabilities   Accounting for liabilities involves answering three important questions: Whom to pay? When to pay? How much to pay? Answers are usually decided when a liability is incurred. For example, if a company has a $100 account payable to a firm, payable on March 15, the answers are clear. However, answers to one or more of these three questions are uncertain for some liabilities.

Uncertainty in Whom to Pay   Liabilities can involve uncertainty in whom to pay. For example, a company can create a liability with a known amount when issuing a note that is payable to its holder. In this case, a specific amount is payable to the note's holder at a specified date, but the company does not know who the holder is until that date. Despite this uncertainty, the company reports this liability on its balance sheet.

Uncertainty in When to Pay   A company can have an obligation of a specific amount to a known creditor but not know when it must be paid. For example, a law firm can accept fees in advance from a client who plans to use the firm's services in the future. This means that the firm has a liability that it settles by providing services at an unknown future date. Although this uncertainty exists, the law firm's balance sheet must report this liability. These types of obligations are reported as current liabilities because they are likely to be settled in the short term.

Uncertainty in How Much to Pay   A company can be aware of an obligation but not know how much it will be required to pay. For example, a company using electrical power is billed only after the meter has been read. This cost is incurred and the liability created before a bill is received. A liability to the power company is reported as an estimated amount if the balance sheet is prepared before a bill arrives.

Examples of Known Liabilities

C2

Identify and describe known current liabilities.

Known liabilities are measurable obligations arising from agreements, contracts, or laws. Known liabilities include accounts payable, notes payable, payroll obligations, sales taxes, and unearned revenues.

Accounts Payable

Accounts payable, or trade accounts payable, are amounts owed to suppliers for products or services purchased on credit. Accounts payable are a focus of the merchandising chapter.

Sales Taxes Payable

Nearly all states and many cities levy taxes on retail sales. Sales taxes are shown as a percent of selling prices. The seller collects sales taxes from customers when sales occur and sends these collections to the government. Because sellers currently owe these collections to the government, this amount is a current liability. If **Home Depot** sells materials on August 31 for $6,000 cash that are subject to a 5% sales tax, the revenue portion of this transaction is recorded as follows. Later, when Home Depot sends the $300 collected to the government, it debits Sales Taxes Payable and credits Cash.

Aug. 31	Cash..	6,300	
	Sales...		6,000
	Sales Taxes Payable ($6,000 × 0.05)		300
	*Record cash sales and 5% sales tax.**		
	*We also Dr. Cost of Sales and Cr. Inventory for cost of sales.		

Assets = Liabilities + Equity
+6,300   +300   +6,000

Unearned Revenues

Unearned revenues, or *deferred revenues,* are amounts received in advance from customers for future products or services. Unearned revenues arise with airline ticket sales, magazine subscriptions, construction projects, hotel reservations, gift card sales, and custom orders. Advance ticket sales for sporting events or concerts are other examples. If **Selena Gomez** sells $5 million in tickets for eight concerts, the entry is

©Dwphotos/Shutterstock

June 30	Cash...	5,000,000	
	Unearned Ticket Revenue............................		5,000,000
	Record sale of tickets for eight concerts.		

Assets = Liabilities + Equity
+5,000,000   +5,000,000

Unearned Ticket Revenue is reported as a current liability. As each concert is played, 1/8 of the liability is satisfied and 1/8 of the revenue is earned—this entry follows.

Point: To *defer* a revenue means to postpone recording a revenue collected in advance.

Oct. 31	Unearned Ticket Revenue	625,000	
	Ticket Revenue		625,000
	Record concert revenues earned ($5,000,000 × 1/8).		

Assets = Liabilities + Equity
           −625,000   +625,000

Short-Term Notes Payable

A **short-term note payable** is a written promise to pay a specified amount on a stated future date within one year. Notes can be sold or transferred. Most notes payable bear interest. The written documentation with notes is helpful in resolving legal disputes. We describe two transactions that create notes payable.

P1_____

Prepare entries to account for short-term notes payable.

Note Given to Extend Credit Period   A company can replace an account payable with a note payable. A common example is a creditor that requires an interest-bearing note for an overdue account payable. Assume that on August 23, Brady asks to extend its past-due $600 account payable to McGraw. After negotiations, McGraw agrees to accept $100 cash and a 60-day, 12%, $500 note payable to replace the account payable. Brady records the following.

Point: Note requirements: (1) unconditional promise, (2) in writing, (3) specific amount, and (4) stated due date.

Aug. 23	Accounts Payable—McGraw...............................	600	
	Cash		100
	Notes Payable—McGraw...............................		500
	Sent cash and a note for payment on account.		

Assets = Liabilities + Equity
−100   −600
            +500

	A	B
1	Principal	$500
2	Rate	12%
3	Issue date	8/23
4	Days	60
5	Accrued interest	←

=ACCRINTM(B3,B3+B4,B2,B1,2)=$10

Assets = Liabilities + Equity
−510   −500   −10

Point: Firms commonly compute interest using a 360-day year, called the *banker's rule*.

Point: A loan is reported as an asset (receivable) on a bank's balance sheet.

Assets = Liabilities + Equity
+2,000   +2,000

Point: Excel for accrued interest.

	A	B
1	Principal	$2,000
2	Rate	12%
3	Issue date	9/30
4	Days	60
5	Accrued interest	←

=ACCRINTM(B3,B3+B4,B2,B1,2)=$40

Assets = Liabilities + Equity
−2,040   −2,000   −40

Signing the note changes Brady's debt from an account payable to a note payable. McGraw prefers the note payable over the account payable because it earns interest and it is written documentation of the debt's existence, term, and amount. When the note comes due, Brady pays the note and interest to McGraw and records this entry.

Oct. 22	Notes Payable—McGraw	500	
	Interest Expense	10	
	Cash..		510
	Paid note with interest ($500 × 12% × 60/360).		

Interest expense is computed by multiplying the principal of the note ($500) by the annual interest rate (12%) for the fraction of the year the note is outstanding (60 days/360 days).

Note Given to Borrow from Bank

A bank requires a borrower to sign a note when making a loan. When the note comes due, the borrower repays the note with an amount larger than the amount borrowed. The difference between the amount borrowed and the amount repaid is *interest*. The amount borrowed is called *principal* or *face value* of the note. Assume that a company borrows $2,000 from a bank at 12% annual interest. The loan is made on September 30, 2019, and is due in 60 days. The note says: *"I promise to pay $2,000 plus interest at 12% within 60 days after September 30."* The borrower records its receipt of cash and the new liability with this entry.

Sep. 30	Cash	2,000	
	Notes Payable		2,000
	Borrowed $2,000 cash with a 60-day, 12%, $2,000 note.		

When principal and interest are paid, the borrower records payment with this entry.

Nov. 29	Notes Payable	2,000	
	Interest Expense	40	
	Cash..		2,040
	Paid note with interest ($2,000 × 12% × 60/360).		

When Note Extends over Two Periods

When a note is issued in one period but paid in the next, interest expense is recorded in each period based on the number of days the note extends over each period. Assume a company borrows $2,000 cash on December 16, 2019, at 12% annual interest. This 60-day note matures on February 14, 2020, and the company's fiscal year ends on December 31. This means 15 of the 60 days are in 2019 and 45 of the 60 days are in 2020. Interest for these two periods is:

- 12/16/2019 to 12/31/2019 = 15 days. Interest expense = $2,000 × 12% × 15/360 = $10.
- 01/01/2020 to 02/14/2020 = 45 days. Interest expense = $2,000 × 12% × 45/360 = $30.

The borrower records the 2019 expense with the following adjusting entry.

Assets = Liabilities + Equity
           +10   −10

Dec. 31, 2019	Interest Expense	10	
	Interest Payable		10
	Record accrued interest ($2,000 × 12% × 15/360).		

When this note is paid on February 14, the borrower records 45 days of interest expense in 2020 and removes the balances of the two liability accounts.

Assets = Liabilities + Equity
−2,040   −10   −30
               −2,000

Feb. 14, 2020	Interest Expense*	30	
	Interest Payable.....................................	10	
	Notes Payable	2,000	
	Cash..		2,040
	Paid note with interest. *$2,000 × 12% × 45/360*		

■ **Decision Insight**

Debt to Pay   Franchisors such as **Pizza Hut** and **Papa John's** use notes to help entrepreneurs acquire their own franchises, including notes to pay for the franchise fee and equipment. Payments on these notes are usually collected monthly and often are secured by the franchisees' assets. For example, a **McDonald's** franchise can cost from under $200,000 to over $2 million, depending on the type selected. ■

Part 1. A retailer sells merchandise for $500 cash on June 30 (cost of merchandise is $300). The retailer collects 7% sales tax. Record the entry for the $500 sale and its applicable sales tax. Also record the entry that shows the taxes collected being sent to the government on July 15.

Part 2. A ticket agency receives $40,000 cash in advance ticket sales for Haim's upcoming four-date tour. Record the advance ticket sales on April 30. Record the revenue earned for the first concert date of May 15, assuming it represents one-fourth of the advance ticket sales.

Part 3. On November 25 of the current year, a company borrows $8,000 cash by signing a 90-day, 5% note payable with a face value of $8,000. (a) Compute the accrued interest payable on December 31 of the current year, (b) prepare the journal entry to record the accrued interest expense at December 31 of the current year, and (c) prepare the journal entry to record payment of the note at maturity.

NEED-TO-KNOW 9-1

Accounting for Known Liabilities

C2   P1

Point: *Maturity date* is the day a note's principal and interest are due. *Maturity value* is a note's principal plus interest owed on its maturity date.

Solution—Part 1

June 30	Cash	535	
	Sales		500
	Sales Taxes Payable		35
	Record cash sales and 7% sales tax.		
June 30	Cost of Goods Sold	300	
	Merchandise Inventory...........................		300
	Record cost of June 30 sales.		
July 15	Sales Taxes Payable................................	35	
	Cash..		35
	Record sales taxes sent to govt.		

Solution—Part 2

Apr. 30	Cash	40,000	
	Unearned Ticket Revenue		40,000
	Record sales in advance of concerts.		
May 15	Unearned Ticket Revenue............................	10,000	
	Earned Ticket Revenue		10,000
	Record concert revenues earned ($40,000 × 1/4).		

Point: Accrued interest, 11/25–12/31.

	A	B
1	Principal	$8,000
2	Rate	5%
3	Issue date	11/25
4	Days	36
5	Accrued interest	◄—

=ACCRINTM(B3,B3+B4,B2,B1,2)=$40—

Solution—Part 3

a.

Computation of interest payable at December 31:	
Days from November 25 to December 31	36 days
Accrued interest (5% × $8,000 × 36/360).....................	<u>$40</u>

Point: Accrued interest, 1/1–2/23.

	A	B
1	Principal	$8,000
2	Rate	5%
3	Issue date	11/25
4	Days	54
5	Accrued interest	◄—

=ACCRINTM(B3,B3+B4,B2,B1,2)=$60—

b.

Dec. 31	Interest Expense	40	
	Interest Payable		40
	Record accrued interest (5% × $8,000 × 36/360).		

Point: Feb. 23 entry assumes no reversing entry was made.

c.

Feb. 23	Interest Expense	60	
	Interest Payable....................................	40	
	Notes Payable	8,000	
	Cash..		8,100
	Record payment of note plus interest		
	(5% × $8,000 × 90/360 = $100 total interest)		
	(5% × $8,000 × 54/360 = $60 interest expense).		

Do More: QS 9-2, QS 9-3, QS 9-4, E 9-2, E 9-3, E 9-4

PAYROLL LIABILITIES

Payroll liabilities are from salaries and wages, employee benefits, and payroll taxes levied on the employer. For example, **Boston Beer** reports current payroll liabilities of more than $14 million from accrued "employee wages, benefits and reimbursements."

P2

Compute and record *employee* payroll deductions and liabilities.

EMPLOYEE Payroll and Deductions

Gross pay is the total compensation an employee earns including wages, salaries, commissions, bonuses, and any compensation earned before deductions such as taxes. (*Wages* usually refer to payments to employees at an hourly rate. *Salaries* usually refer to payments to employees at a monthly or yearly rate.) **Net pay,** or *take-home pay,* is gross pay minus all deductions. **Payroll deductions,** or *withholdings,* are amounts withheld from an employee's gross pay, either required or voluntary. Required deductions result from laws and include income taxes and Social Security taxes. Voluntary deductions, at an employee's option, include pension and health contributions, health and life insurance premiums, union dues, and donations.

Point: Deductions at some companies, such as those for insurance coverage, are "required" under labor contracts.

Exhibit 9.3 shows typical employee payroll deductions. The employer withholds payroll deductions from employees' pay and sends this money to the designated group or government. The employer records payroll deductions as current liabilities until these amounts are sent. This section covers major payroll deductions.

EXHIBIT 9.3

Payroll Deductions

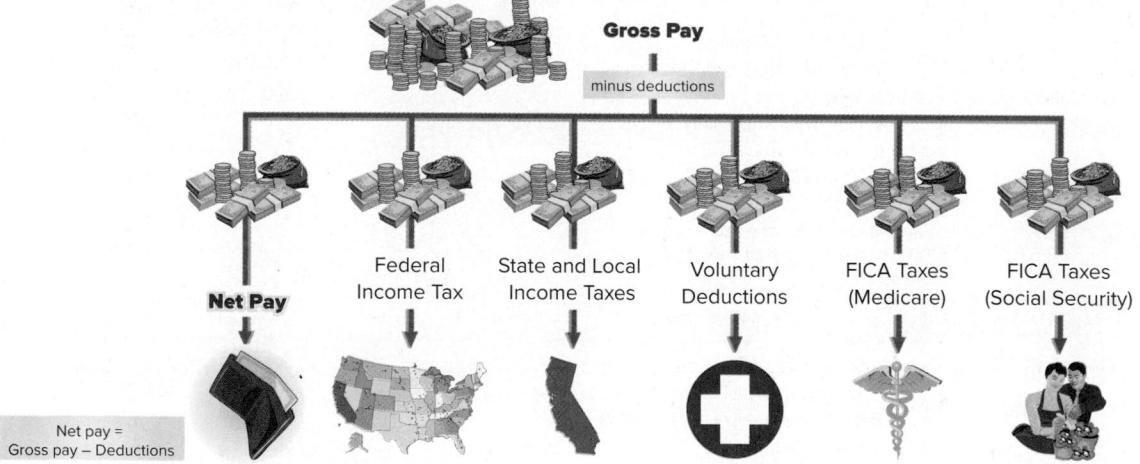

Employee FICA Taxes   Employers withhold **Federal Insurance Contributions Act (FICA) taxes** from employees' pay. Employers separate FICA taxes into two groups.

1. **Social Security taxes**—withholdings to cover retirement, disability, and survivorship.
2. **Medicare taxes**—withholdings to cover medical benefits.

Taxes for Social Security and Medicare are computed separately. For 2018, the amount withheld from each employee's pay for Social Security tax is 6.2% of the first $128,400 the employee earns in the calendar year. The Medicare tax is 1.45% of *all* amounts the employee earns; there is no maximum limit to Medicare tax. A 0.9% *Additional Medicare Tax* is imposed on the high-income employee for pay usually in excess of $200,000 (this additional tax is *not* imposed on the employer, whereas the others are). Until the taxes are sent to the Internal Revenue Service (IRS), they are included in employers' current liabilities. For any changes in rates or earnings levels, check **IRS.gov** or **SSA.gov**.

Point: Sources of U.S. tax receipts:
50%   Personal income tax
35%   FICA and FUTA taxes
10%   Corporate income tax
  5%   Other taxes

Employee Income Tax   Most employers withhold federal income tax from each employee's paycheck. The amount withheld is computed using IRS tables. The amount depends on the employee's income and the number of *withholding allowances* the employee claims. Allowances reduce taxes owed to the government. Employees can claim allowances for themselves and their dependents. Until the government is paid, withholdings are reported as a current liability on the employer's balance sheet.

Employee Voluntary Deductions

Voluntary deduction withholdings come from employee requests, contracts, unions, or other agreements. They include charitable giving, medical and life insurance premiums, pension contributions, and union dues. Until they are paid, voluntary withholdings are reported as part of employers' current liabilities.

Employee Payroll Recording

Employers accrue payroll expenses and liabilities at the end of each pay period. Assume that an employee earns a salary of $2,000 per month. At the end of January, the employer's entry to accrue payroll expenses and liabilities for this employee is

Jan. 31	Salaries Expense	2,000	
	FICA—Social Security Taxes Payable (6.2%)		124
	FICA—Medicare Taxes Payable (1.45%)		29
	Employee Federal Income Taxes Payable*		213
	Employee Medical Insurance Payable*		85
	Employee Union Dues Payable*		25
	Salaries Payable		1,524
	Record accrued payroll for January.		
	*Amounts taken from employer's accounting records.		

Assets = Liabilities + Equity
+124   −2,000
+29
+213
+85
+25
+1,524

Salaries Expense (debit) shows that the employee earns a gross salary of $2,000. The first five payables (credits) show the liabilities the employer owes on behalf of this employee to cover FICA taxes, income taxes, medical insurance, and union dues. The Salaries Payable account (credit) records the $1,524 net pay the employee receives from the $2,000 gross pay earned. The February 1 entry to record cash payment to this employee is

Feb. 1	Salaries Payable.....................................	1,524	
	Cash		1,524
	Record payment of payroll.		

EMPLOYER Payroll Taxes

Employers must pay payroll taxes in addition to those required of employees. Employer taxes include FICA and unemployment taxes.

Employer FICA Tax

Employers must pay FICA taxes on their payroll. For 2018, the employer must pay Social Security tax of 6.2% on the first $128,400 earned by each employee and 1.45% Medicare tax on all earnings of each employee. An employer's tax is credited to the same FICA Taxes Payable accounts used to record the Social Security and Medicare taxes withheld from employees.

Employer Unemployment Taxes

The federal government works with states in a joint federal and state unemployment insurance program. Each state has its own program. These programs provide unemployment benefits to qualified workers.

Federal Unemployment Tax Act (FUTA) Employers must pay a federal unemployment tax on wages and salaries earned by their employees. For the recent year, employers were required to pay FUTA taxes of as much as 6.0% of the first $7,000 earned by each employee. This federal tax can be reduced by a credit of up to 5.4% for taxes paid to a state program. As a result, the net federal unemployment tax is often 0.6%.

State Unemployment Tax Act (SUTA) All states fund their unemployment insurance programs by placing a payroll tax on employers. (A few states require employees to make a contribution. In the book's assignments, we assume this tax is only levied on the employer.) In most states, the base rate for SUTA taxes is 5.4% of the first $7,000 earned by each employee (the dollar level varies by state). This base rate is adjusted according to an employer's merit rating.

P3

Compute and record *employer* payroll expenses and liabilities.

Point: A self-employed person must pay both the employee and employer FICA taxes.

The state assigns a **merit rating** based on a company's stability in employing workers. A good rating reflects stability in employment and means an employer can pay less than the 5.4% base rate. A low rating means high turnover or seasonal hirings and layoffs.

Recording Employer Payroll Taxes   Employer payroll taxes are an added expense beyond the wages and salaries earned by employees. These taxes are often recorded in an entry separate from the one recording payroll expenses and deductions. Assume that the $2,000 recorded salaries expense from the previous example is earned by an employee whose earnings have not yet reached $5,000 for the year. This means the entire salaries expense for this period is subject to tax because year-to-date pay is under $7,000. Consequently, the FICA portion of the employer's tax is $153, computed by multiplying both the 6.2% and 1.45% by the $2,000 gross pay. Assume that the federal unemployment tax rate is 0.6% and the state unemployment tax rate is 5.4%. This means state unemployment (SUTA) taxes are $108 (5.4% of the $2,000 gross pay) and federal unemployment (FUTA) taxes are $12 (0.6% of $2,000). The entry to record the employer's payroll tax expense and related liabilities is

Assets = Liabilities + Equity
+124   −273
+29
+108
+12

Jan. 31	Payroll Taxes Expense	273	
	FICA—Social Security Taxes Payable (6.2%)		124
	FICA—Medicare Taxes Payable (1.45%)		29
	State Unemployment Taxes Payable		108
	Federal Unemployment Taxes Payable		12
	Record employer payroll taxes.		

Internal Control of Payroll

Internal controls are crucial for payroll because of a high risk of fraud and error. Exhibit 9.4 identifies and explains four key areas of payroll activities that we aim to *separate and monitor*.

EXHIBIT 9.4

Internal Controls in Four Key Areas of Payroll

Employee Hiring	**Payroll Preparation**	**Timekeeping**	**Payroll Payment**

Duty: Authorize, hire, and fire.
Aim: Keep fake workers off payroll.

Duty: Verify tax rates and payroll amounts.
Aim: Rates updated and amounts accurate.

Duty: Track and verify time worked.
Aim: Paid for time worked only.

Duty: Sign and issue prenumbered checks.
Aim: Checks valid, secured, and correct.

Ethical Risk

Ceridian Connection reports: 8.5% of fraud is tied to payroll; $72,000 is the median loss per payroll fraud; and 24 months is the median time to uncover payroll fraud.

Payroll Fraud   Probably the greatest number of frauds involve payroll. Controls include proper approvals and processes for employee additions, deletions, and pay rate changes. A common fraud is a manager adding a fictitious employee to the payroll and then cashing the fictitious employee's check. A study reports that 42% of employees in operations and service areas witnessed violations of employee wage, overtime, or benefit rules in the past year. Another 33% observed falsifying of time and expense reports (KPMG). ■

Multi-Period Known Liabilities

Many known liabilities extend over multiple periods. These often include unearned revenues and notes payable. For example, if **Sports Illustrated** sells a three-year digital magazine subscription, it records amounts received for this subscription in an Unearned Subscription Revenues account. Amounts in this account are liabilities, but are they current or long term? They are *both*. The portion of the Unearned Subscription Revenues account that will be fulfilled in the next year is reported as a current liability. The remaining portion is reported as a long-term liability.

The same analysis applies to notes payable. For example, a borrower reports a three-year note payable as a long-term liability in the first two years it is outstanding. In the third year, the borrower reclassifies this note as a current liability because it is due within one year. The **current portion of long-term debt** is that part of long-term debt due within one year. Long-term debt is reported under long-term liabilities, but the *current portion due* is reported under current liabilities. Assume that a $7,500 debt is paid in installments of $1,500 per year for five years. The $1,500 due within the year is reported as a current liability. No journal entry is necessary for this reclassification. Instead, we simply classify the amounts for debt as either current or long term when the balance sheet is prepared.

Point: Some accounting systems make an entry to transfer the current amount due out of Long-Term Debt and into the Current Portion of Long-Term Debt as follows:

Long-Term Debt 1,500
   Current Portion
      of L-T Debt   1,500

■ Decision Ethics

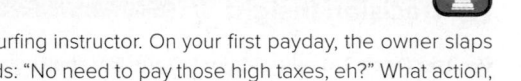

Summer Intern   You take a summer job working as a windsurfing instructor. On your first payday, the owner slaps you on the back, gives you full payment in cash, winks, and adds: "No need to pay those high taxes, eh?" What action, if any, do you take? ■   *Answer:* You do not want to be an accomplice to unlawful payroll activities. Not paying federal and state taxes on wages is illegal and unethical. One action is to request payment by check. If this fails, you must consider quitting.

A company's first weekly pay period of the year ends on January 8. Sales employees earned $30,000 and office employees earned $20,000 in salaries. The employees are to have withheld from their salaries FICA Social Security taxes at the rate of 6.2%, FICA Medicare taxes at the rate of 1.45%, $9,000 of federal income taxes, $2,000 of medical insurance deductions, and $1,000 of pension contributions. No employee earned more than $7,000 in the first pay period.

NEED-TO-KNOW 9-2

Payroll Liabilities

P2   P3

Part 1. Compute FICA Social Security taxes payable and FICA Medicare taxes payable. Prepare the journal entry to record the company's January 8 (employee) payroll expenses and liabilities.

Part 2. Prepare the journal entry to record the company's (employer) payroll taxes resulting from the January 8 payroll. Its state unemployment tax rate is 5.4% on the first $7,000 paid to each employee. The federal unemployment tax rate is 0.6%.

Solution—Part 1

Jan. 8	Sales Salaries Expense	30,000	
	Office Salaries Expense	20,000	
	FICA—Social Security Taxes Payable*		3,100
	FICA—Medicare Taxes Payable†		725
	Employee Fed. Income Taxes Payable		9,000
	Employee Med. Insurance Payable . .		2,000
	Employee Pensions Payable		1,000
	Salaries Payable		34,175
	Record payroll for period.		
	*$50,000 × 6.2% = $3,100		
	†$50,000 × 1.45% = $725		

Solution—Part 2

Jan. 8	Payroll Taxes Expense	6,825	
	FICA—Social Security Taxes Payable .		3,100
	FICA—Medicare Taxes Payable		725
	State Unemployment Taxes Payable*		2,700
	Federal Unemployment Taxes Payable†		300
	Record employer payroll taxes.		
	*$50,000 × 5.4% = $2,700		
	†$50,000 × 0.6% = $300		

Do More: QS 9-5, QS 9-6, E 9-5,
E 9-6, E 9-7, E 9-8, E 9-9

ESTIMATED LIABILITIES

An **estimated liability** is a known obligation of an uncertain amount that can be reasonably estimated. Common examples are employee benefits such as pensions, health care, and vacation pay, and warranties offered by a seller.

P4

Account for estimated liabilities, including warranties and bonuses.

Health and Pension Benefits

Many companies provide **employee benefits.** An employer often pays all or part of medical, dental, life, and disability insurance. Many employers also contribute to *pension plans,* which are agreements by employers to provide benefits (payments) to employees after retirement. Many companies also provide medical care and insurance benefits to their retirees. Assume an employer agrees to (1) pay $8,000 for medical insurance and (2) contribute an additional 10% of the employees' $120,000 gross salaries to a retirement program. The entry to record these accrued benefits is

Assets = Liabilities + Equity
+8,000   −20,000
+12,000

Dec. 31	Employee Benefits Expense	20,000	
	Employee Medical Insurance Payable		8,000
	Employee Retirement Program Payable		12,000
	Record costs of employee benefits.		

■ Decision Insight

Rest on One's Laurels   **Major League Baseball** was the first pro sport to set up a pension, originally up to $100 per month depending on years played. Many former players now take home six-figure pensions. Cal Ripken Jr.'s pension at age 62 is estimated at $180,000 per year (he played 21 seasons). The same applies to Ichiro Suzuki, who has played 17 seasons—see photo. The requirement is 43 games for a full pension and just one game for full medical benefits for life. ■

©Imac/Alamy Stock Photo

Point: An *accrued expense* is an unpaid expense and is also called an *accrued liability.*

Vacation Benefits

Many employers offer paid vacation benefits, or *paid absences.* Vacation benefits are estimated and expensed in the period when employees earn them. Assume that salaried employees earn 2 weeks' paid vacation per year. The year-end adjusting entry to record $3,200 of accrued vacation benefits follows.

Assets = Liabilities + Equity
+3,200   −3,200

Dec. 31	Vacation Benefits Expense	3,200	
	Vacation Benefits Payable		3,200
	Record vacation benefits accrued.		

Vacation Benefits Expense is an operating expense, and Vacation Benefits Payable is a current liability. When an employee takes a one-week vacation, the employer reduces (debits) Vacation Benefits Payable and credits Cash.

Assets = Liabilities + Equity
−400   −400

Jan. 20	Vacation Benefits Payable.	400	
	Cash.		400
	Record vacation benefits taken.		

Bonus Plans

Many companies offer bonuses to employees, and many of the bonuses depend on net income. Assume that an employer gives a bonus to its employees based on the company's annual net income (to be equally shared by all). The year-end adjusting entry to record a $10,000 bonus is

Assets = Liabilities + Equity
+10,000   −10,000

Dec. 31	Employee Bonus Expense.	10,000	
	Bonus Payable		10,000
	Record expected bonus costs.		

Warranty Liabilities

A **warranty** is a seller's obligation to replace or fix a product (or service) that fails to perform as expected within a specified period. For example, new **Ford** cars are sold with a warranty covering parts for a specified period of time. The seller reports the expected warranty expense in the period

when revenue from the sale of the product or service is reported. The seller reports this warranty liability, even though the existence, amount, payee, and date of future payments are uncertain. This is because warranty costs are probable and the amount can be estimated using past experience.

Assume a dealer sells a car for $16,000 on December 1, 2019, with a one-year or 12,000-mile warranty covering parts. Experience shows that warranty expense is 4% of a car's selling price, or $640 in this case ($16,000 × 4%). The dealer records the estimated expense and liability related to this sale with this entry.

Dec. 1	Warranty Expense	640	
	Estimated Warranty Liability		640
	Record estimated warranty expense.		

Assets = Liabilities + Equity
    +640   −640

This entry alternatively could be made as part of end-of-period adjustments. Either way, the estimated warranty expense is reported on the 2019 income statement and the warranty liability on the 2019 balance sheet. Continuing this example, assume the customer brings the car in for warranty repairs on January 9, 2020. The dealer fixes the car by replacing parts costing $200. The entry to record the repair is

Jan. 9	Estimated Warranty Liability	200	
	Auto Parts Inventory		200
	Record costs of warranty repairs.		

Assets = Liabilities + Equity
 −200   −200

This entry reduces the balance of the Estimated Warranty Liability account, but no expense is recorded in 2020 for the repair. Warranty expense was previously recorded in 2019, the year the car was sold with the warranty. Finally, what happens if total warranty expenses are more or less than the estimated 4%, or $640? The answer is that management should monitor actual warranty expenses to see if a 4% rate is accurate. If not, the rate is changed for future periods.

Multi-Period Estimated Liabilities

Estimated liabilities can be both current and long term. For example, pension liabilities to employees are long term to workers who will not retire within the next year. For employees who are retired or will retire within the next year, a portion of pension liabilities is current. Other examples include employee health benefits and warranties.

■ **Decision Insight**

Promises, Promises   When we purchase a new laptop at **Best Buy**, a sales clerk commonly asks: *"Do you want the Geek Squad Protection Plan?"* Best Buy earns about a 60% profit margin on such warranty contracts, and those contracts are a large part of its profit—see table (*BusinessWeek*). ■

Warranties as a percent of sales	4%
Warranties as a percent of operating profit....	45%

Part 1. A company's salaried employees earn two weeks' vacation per year. The company estimated and must expense $9,000 of accrued vacation benefits for the year. (a) Prepare the year-end adjusting entry to record accrued vacation benefits. (b) Prepare the entry on May 1 of the next year when an employee takes a one-week vacation and is paid $450 cash for that week.

Part 2. For the current year ended December 31, a company has implemented an employee bonus program based on its net income, which employees share equally. Its bonus expense is $40,000. (a) Prepare the journal entry at December 31 of the current year to record the bonus due. (b) Prepare the journal entry at January 20 of the following year to record payment of that bonus to employees.

Part 3. On June 11 of the current year, a retailer sells a trimmer for $400 with a one-year warranty that covers parts. Warranty expense is estimated at 5% of sales. On March 24 of the next year, the trimmer is brought in for repairs covered under the warranty requiring $15 in materials taken from the Repair Parts Inventory. Prepare the (a) June 11 entry to record the trimmer sale—ignore the cost of sales part of this sales entry—and (b) March 24 entry to record warranty repairs.

 **NEED-TO-KNOW** 9-3

Estimated Liabilities

P4

Solution—Part 1

a.

Dec. 31	Vacation Benefits Expense	9,000	
	Vacation Benefits Payable		9,000
	Record vacation benefits accrued.		

b.

May 1	Vacation Benefits Payable	450	
	Cash....................		450
	Record vacation benefits taken.		

Solution—Part 2

a.

Dec. 31	Employee Bonus Expense	40,000	
	Bonus Payable		40,000
	Record expected bonus costs.		

b.

Jan. 20	Bonus Payable	40,000	
	Cash....................		40,000
	Record payment of bonus.		

Solution—Part 3

June 11	Cash	400	
	Sales		400
	Record trimmer sales.		
June 11	Warranty Expense	20	
	Estimated Warranty Liability		20
	Record estimated warranty expense ($400 × 5%).		
Mar. 24	Estimated Warranty Liability	15	
	Repair Parts Inventory		15
	Record cost of warranty repairs.		

Do More: QS 9-7, QS 9-8, QS 9-9, QS 9-10, E 9-10, E 9-11, E 9-12, E 9-13

CONTINGENT LIABILITIES

C3

Explain how to account for contingent liabilities.

A **contingent liability** is a potential obligation that depends on a future event arising from a past transaction or event. An example is a pending lawsuit. Here, a past transaction or event leads to a lawsuit whose financial outcome depends on the result of the suit.

Accounting for Contingent Liabilities

Accounting for contingent liabilities depends on the likelihood that a future event will occur and the ability to estimate the future amount owed if this event occurs. Three different possibilities are shown in Exhibit 9.5: record liability with a journal entry, disclose in notes to financial statements, or no disclosure.

EXHIBIT 9.5

Accounting for Contingent Liabilities

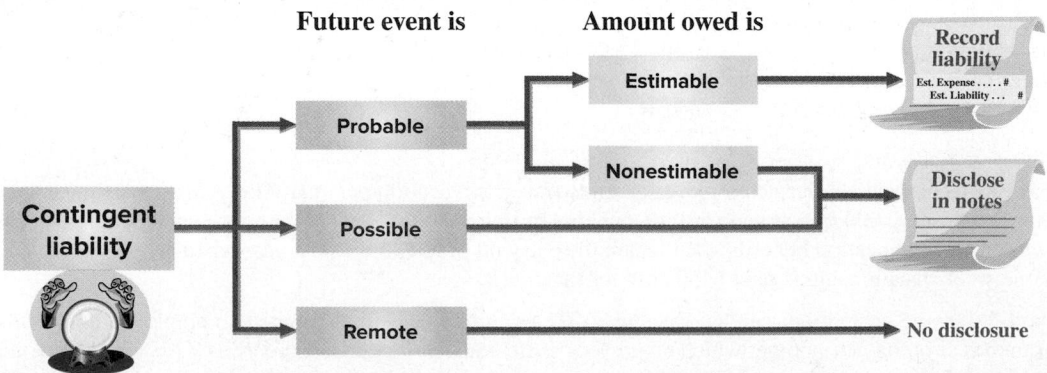

The conditions that determine each of these three possibilities follow.

Point: A contingency is an *if.* Namely, *if* a future event occurs, then financial consequences are likely for the entity.

1. **Record liability.** The future event is *probable* (likely) and the amount owed can be *reasonably estimated.* Examples are warranties, vacation pay, and income taxes.
2. **Disclose in notes.** The future event is *reasonably possible* (could occur).
3. **No disclosure.** The future event is *remote* (unlikely).

Applying Rules of Contingent Liabilities

This section covers common contingent liabilities.

Potential Legal Claims   Many companies are sued or at risk of being sued. The accounting issue is whether the defendant records a liability or discloses a contingent liability in its notes while a lawsuit is outstanding and not yet settled. The answer is that a potential claim is recorded *only* if payment for damages is probable and the amount can be reasonably estimated. If the potential claim cannot be reasonably estimated but is reasonably possible, it is disclosed. For example, **Ford** includes the following note in its annual report: "Various legal actions, proceedings, and claims are pending . . . arising out of alleged defects in our products."

Debt Guarantees   Sometimes a company guarantees the payment of debt owed by a supplier, customer, or another company. The guarantor usually discloses the guarantee in its financial statement notes as a contingent liability. If it is probable that the debtor will default, the guarantor reports the guarantee as a liability. The **Boston Celtics** report a unique guarantee: "Contracts provide for guaranteed payments which must be paid even if the employee [player] is injured or terminated."

Other Contingencies   Other examples of contingencies include environmental damages, possible tax assessments, insurance losses, and government investigations. **Chevron**, for example, reports that it "is subject to loss contingencies . . . related to environmental matters. . . . The amount of additional future costs are not fully determinable." Many of Chevron's contingencies are revealed only in notes.

Uncertainties That Are Not Contingencies

All organizations face uncertainties from future events such as natural disasters and new technologies. These uncertainties are not contingent liabilities because they are future events *not* arising from past transactions. Accordingly, they are not disclosed.

The following legal claims exist for a company. Identify the accounting treatment for each claim as either (a) a liability that is recorded or (b) an item described in notes to its financial statements.

1. The company (defendant) estimates that a pending lawsuit could result in damages of $500,000; it is reasonably possible that the plaintiff will win the case.

2. The company faces a probable loss on a pending lawsuit; the amount is not reasonably estimable.

3. The company estimates environmental damages in a pending case at $900,000 with a high probability of losing the case.

NEED-TO-KNOW 9-4

Contingent Liabilities

C3

Solution

1. (b); reason—is reasonably estimated but not a probable loss.

2. (b); reason—probable loss but cannot be reasonably estimated.

3. (a); reason—can be reasonably estimated and loss is probable.

Do More: QS 9-11, E 9-14

Times Interest Earned Ratio **Decision Analysis**

Interest expense is often called a *fixed expense* because it usually does not vary due to short-term changes in sales or other operating activities. While fixed expenses can be good when a company is growing, they create risk. The risk is that a company might be unable to pay fixed expenses if sales decline. Consider Diego Co.'s results for 2019 and two possible outcomes for year 2020 in Exhibit 9.6. Expenses excluding interest are expected to remain at 75% of sales. Expenses that change with sales volume are *variable expenses*. Interest expense is fixed at $60 per year.

A1

Compute the times interest earned ratio and use it to analyze liabilities.

EXHIBIT 9.6

Actual and Projected
Results

$ millions	2019	2020 Projections	
		Sales Increase	Sales Decrease
Sales	$600	$900	$300
Expenses (75% of sales)	450	675	225
Income before interest	150	225	75
Interest expense (fixed)	60	60	60
Net income.....................	$ 90	$165	$ 15

The Sales Increase column of Exhibit 9.6 shows that Diego's net income increases by 83% to $165 if sales increase by 50% to $900. The Sales Decrease column shows that net income decreases by 83% if sales decline by 50%. These results show that the amount of fixed interest expense affects a company's risk of its ability to pay interest. One measure of "ability to pay" is the **times interest earned** ratio in Exhibit 9.7.

EXHIBIT 9.7

Times Interest Earned

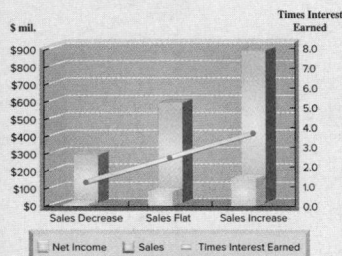

$$\text{Times interest earned} = \frac{\text{Income before interest expense and income taxes}}{\text{Interest expense}}$$

For 2019, Diego's times interest earned is computed as $150/$60, or 2.5 times. This ratio means that Diego has low to moderate risk because its sales must decline sharply before it is unable to pay its interest expenses. If times interest earned falls below around 1.5, a company will likely be at risk of not being able to pay its liabilities.

■ **Decision Maker**

Entrepreneur You wish to invest in a franchise for either one of two national chains. Each franchise has an expected annual net income *after* interest and taxes of $100,000. Net income for the first franchise includes a regular fixed interest charge of $200,000. The fixed interest charge for the second franchise is $40,000. Which franchise is riskier to you if sales forecasts are not met? ■ *Answer:* Times interest earned for the first franchise is 1.5 [($100,000 + $200,000)/$200,000], whereas it is 3.5 for the second [($100,000 + $40,000)/$40,000]. This shows the first franchise is more at risk of incurring a loss if its sales decline.

NEED-TO-KNOW 9-5

COMPREHENSIVE

Accounting for Current
Liabilities Including
Warranties, Notes,
Contingencies, Payroll,
and Income Taxes

The following transactions took place at Kern Co. during its recent calendar-year reporting period.

a. In September, Kern sold $140,000 of merchandise covered by a 180-day warranty. Prior experience shows that costs of the warranty equal 5% of sales. Compute September's warranty expense and prepare the adjusting journal entry for the warranty liability as recorded at September 30. Also prepare the journal entry on October 8 to record a $300 cash payment to provide warranty service on an item sold in September.

b. On October 12, Kern replaced an overdue $10,000 account payable by paying $2,500 cash and signing a note for $7,500. The note matures in 90 days and has a 12% interest rate. Prepare the entries recorded on October 12, December 31, and January 10.

c. In late December, Kern is facing a product liability suit filed by an unhappy customer. Kern's lawyer says it will probably suffer a loss from the lawsuit, but the amount is impossible to estimate.

d. Sally Bline works for Kern. For the pay period ended November 30, her gross earnings are $3,000. Bline has $800 deducted for federal income taxes and $200 for state income taxes from each paycheck. Additionally, a $35 premium for health insurance and a $10 donation to United Way are deducted. Bline pays FICA Social Security taxes at a rate of 6.2% and FICA Medicare taxes at a rate of 1.45%. She has not earned enough this year to be exempt from any FICA taxes. Journalize the accrual of salaries expense for Bline by Kern.

e. On November 1, Kern borrows $5,000 cash from a bank in return for a 60-day, 12%, $5,000 note. Record the note's issuance on November 1 and its repayment with interest on December 31.

f.ᴮ *(Part f covers Appendix 9B.)* Kern has estimated and recorded its quarterly income tax payments. In reviewing its year-end tax adjustments, it identifies an additional $5,000 of income taxes expense that should be recorded. A portion of this additional expense, $1,000, is deferred to future years. Record this year-end income taxes expense adjusting entry.

g. For this calendar year, Kern's net income is $1,000,000, its interest expense is $275,000, and its income taxes expense is $225,000. Compute Kern's times interest earned ratio.

PLANNING THE SOLUTION

- For *a*, compute the warranty expense for September and record it with an estimated liability. Record the October payment as a decrease in the liability.
- For *b*, eliminate the liability for the account payable and create the liability for the note payable. Compute interest expense for the 80 days that the note is outstanding in the current year and record it as a liability. Record the payment of the note, being sure to include the interest for the 10 days in January.
- For *c*, decide whether the company's contingent liability needs to be disclosed or accrued (recorded) according to the two necessary criteria: probable loss and reasonably estimable.
- For *d*, set up payable accounts for all items in Bline's paycheck that require deductions. After all deductions, credit the remaining amount to Salaries Payable.
- For *e*, record the issuance of the note. Compute 60 days' interest due.
- For *f*, determine how much of the income taxes expense is payable in the current year and how much needs to be deferred (see Appendix 9B).
- For *g*, apply and compute times interest earned.

SOLUTION

a. Warranty expense = 5% × $140,000 = $7,000

Sep. 30	Warranty Expense	7,000	
	Estimated Warranty Liability		7,000
	Record warranty expense for month.		
Oct. 8	Estimated Warranty Liability	300	
	Cash		300
	Record cost of warranty service.		

b. Interest expense for current year = 12% × $7,500 × 80/360 = $200
Interest expense for following year = 12% × $7,500 × 10/360 = $25

Oct. 12	Accounts Payable	10,000	
	Notes Payable		7,500
	Cash		2,500
	Paid $2,500 cash and gave a 90-day, 12% note to extend due date on the account.		
Dec. 31	Interest Expense	200	
	Interest Payable		200
	Accrue interest on note payable.		
Jan. 10	Interest Expense	25	
	Interest Payable	200	
	Notes Payable	7,500	
	Cash		7,725
	Paid note with interest, including accrued interest payable.		

c. Disclose the pending lawsuit in the financial statement notes. Although the loss is probable, no liability is accrued because the loss cannot be reasonably estimated.

d.

Nov. 30	Salaries Expense	3,000.00	
	FICA—Social Security Taxes Payable (6.2%)		186.00
	FICA—Medicare Taxes Payable (1.45%)		43.50
	Employee Federal Income Taxes Payable		800.00
	Employee State Income Taxes Payable		200.00
	Employee Medical Insurance Payable		35.00
	Employee United Way Payable		10.00
	Salaries Payable		1,725.50
	Record Bline's accrued payroll.		

e.

Nov. 1	Cash	5,000	
	Notes Payable		5,000
	Borrowed cash with a 60-day, 12% note.		

When the note and interest are paid 60 days later, Kern Co. records this entry.

Dec. 31	Notes Payable	5,000	
	Interest Expense	100	
	Cash		5,100
	Paid note with interest ($5,000 × 12% × 60/360).		

f.[B]

Dec. 31	Income Taxes Expense	5,000	
	Income Taxes Payable		4,000
	Deferred Income Tax Liability		1,000
	Record added income taxes expense and the deferred tax liability.		

g. Times interest earned $= \dfrac{\$1,000,000 + \$275,000 + \$225,000}{\$275,000} = \underline{\underline{5.45 \text{ times}}}$

9A

Payroll Reports, Records, and Procedures

P5

Identify and describe the details of payroll reports, records, and procedures.

This appendix focuses on payroll accounting reports, records, and procedures.

Payroll Reports Most employees and employers are required to pay local, state, and federal payroll taxes. Payroll expenses are liabilities to individual employees, to federal and state governments, and to other organizations such as insurance companies. Employers are required to prepare and submit reports explaining how they computed these payments.

Reporting FICA Taxes and Income Taxes The Federal Insurance Contributions Act (FICA) requires each employer to file an Internal Revenue Service (IRS) **Form 941,** the *Employer's Quarterly Federal Tax Return,* within one month after the end of each calendar quarter. A sample Form 941 is shown in Exhibit 9A.1 for Phoenix Sales & Service, a landscape design company. Accounting information and software are helpful in tracking payroll transactions and reporting the accumulated information on Form 941. Specifically, the employer reports total wages subject to income tax withholding on line 2 of Form 941. (For simplicity, this appendix uses *wages* to refer to both wages and salaries.) The income tax withheld is reported on line 3. The combined amount of employee and employer FICA (Social Security) taxes for Phoenix Sales & Service is reported on line 5a (taxable Social Security wages, $36,599 × 12.4% = $4,538.28). The 12.4% is the sum of the Social Security tax withheld, computed as 6.2% tax withheld from the employee wages for the quarter, plus the 6.2% tax levied on the employer. The combined amount of employee Medicare wages is reported on line 5c. The 2.9% is the sum of 1.45% withheld from employee wages for the quarter plus 1.45% tax levied on the employer. Total FICA taxes are reported on line 5e and are added to the total income taxes withheld of $3,056.47 to yield a total of $8,656.12. For this year, assume that income up to $128,400 is subject to Social Security tax. There is no income limit on amounts subject to Medicare tax. Congress sets rates owed for Social Security tax (and it typically changes each year).

Point: Deposits for federal payroll taxes must be made by electronic funds transfer (EFT).

Federal depository banks are authorized to accept deposits of amounts payable to the federal government. Deposit requirements depend on the amount of tax owed. For example, when the sum of FICA taxes plus the employee income taxes is less than $2,500 for a quarter, the taxes can be paid when Form 941 is filed.

Reporting FUTA Taxes and SUTA Taxes An employer's federal unemployment taxes (FUTA) are reported on an annual basis by filing an *Annual Federal Unemployment Tax Return,* IRS **Form 940.** It must be mailed on or before January 31 following the end of each tax year. Ten more days are allowed if all required tax deposits are filed on a timely basis and the full amount of tax is paid on or before January 31. FUTA payments are made quarterly to a federal depository bank if the total amount due exceeds $500. If $500 or less

Form 941 Employer's QUARTERLY Federal Tax Return
Department of the Treasury — Internal Revenue Service

(EIN) Employer identification number 8 6 – 3 2 1 4 5 8 7

Name (not your trade name) Phoenix Sales & Service

Trade name (if any)

Address 1214 Mill Road
Number Street

Phoenix AZ 85621
City State ZIP code

Report for this Quarter ...
(Check one.)
☐ 1: January, February, March
☐ 2: April, May, June
☐ 3: July, August, September
☒ 4: October, November, December

Part 1: Answer these questions for this quarter.

1 Number of employees who received wages, tips, or other compensation for the pay period including: Mar. 12 (Quarter 1), June 12 (Quarter 2), Sept. 12 (Quarter 3), Dec. 12 (Quarter 4) — 1 — 2

2 Wages, tips, and other compensation — 2 — 36,599.00

3 Total income tax withheld from wages, tips, and other compensation — 3 — 3,056.47

4 If no wages, tips, and other compensation are subject to social security or Medicare tax ☐ Check and go to line 6.

5 Taxable social security and Medicare wages and tips:

	Column 1		Column 2
5a Taxable social security wages	36,599.00	× .124 =	4,538.28
5b Taxable social security tips		× .124 =	
5c Taxable Medicare wages & tips	36,599.00	× .029 =	1,061.37
5d Taxable wages & tips subject to Additional Medicare Tax withholding		× 0.009 =	
5e Add Column 2 from lines 5a, 5b, 5c, and 5d		5e	5,599.65

5f Section 3121(q) Notice and Demand–Tax due to unreported tips (see instructions) — 5f

6 Total taxes before adjustments. Add lines 3, 5e, and 5f — 6 — 8,656.12

7 Current quarter's adjustment for fractions of cents — 7

8 Current quarter's adjustment for sick pay — 8

9 Current quarter's adjustments for tips and group-term life insurance — 9

10 Total taxes after adjustments. Combine lines 6 through 9 — 10 — 8,656.12

11 Qualified small business payroll tax credit for increasing research activities. Attach Form 8974 — 11

12 Total taxes after adjustments and credits. Subtract line 11 from line 10 — 12 — 8,656.12

13 Total deposits for this quarter, including overpayment applied from a prior quarter and overpayments applied from Form 941-X, 941-X (PR), 944-X, or 944-X (SP) filed in the current quarter — 13 — 8,656.12

14 Balance due. If line 12 is more than line 13, enter the difference and see instructions — 14 — 0.00

15 Overpayment. If line 13 is more than line 12, enter the difference — Check one: ☐ Apply to next return. ☐ Send a refund.

Part 2: Tell us about your deposit schedule and tax liability for this quarter.

If you are unsure about whether you are a monthly schedule depositor or a semiweekly schedule depositor, see section 11 of Pub. 15.

16 Check one: ☐ Line 12 on this return is less than $2,500 or line 12 (line 10 if the prior quarter was the fourth quarter of last year) on the return for the prior quarter was less than $2,500, and you didn't incur a $100,000 next-day deposit obligation during the current quarter. If line 12 (line 10 if the prior quarter was the fourth quarter of last year) for the prior quarter was less than $2,500 but line 12 on this return is $100,000 or more, you must provide a record of your federal tax liability. If you are a monthly schedule depositor, complete the deposit schedule below; if you are a semiweekly schedule depositor, attach Schedule B (Form 941). Go to Part 3.

☒ You were a monthly schedule depositor for the entire quarter. Enter your tax liability for each month and total liability for the quarter, then go to Part 3.

Tax liability: Month 1 3,079.11
Month 2 2,049.77
Month 3 3,527.24
Total liability for quarter 8,656.12 Total must equal line 12.

☐ You were a semiweekly schedule depositor for any part of this quarter. Fill out Schedule B (Form 941): Report of Tax Liability for Semiweekly Schedule Depositors, and attach it to Form 941.

Part 3: Tell us about your business. If a question does NOT apply to your business, leave it blank.

17 If your business has closed or you stopped paying wages ☐ Check here, and enter the final date you paid wages ___/___/___

18 If you are a seasonal employer and you do not have to file a return for every quarter of the year ☐ Check here.

Part 4: May we speak with your third-party designee?

Do you want to allow an employee, a paid tax preparer, or another person to discuss this return with the IRS? See the instructions for details.
☐ Yes. Designee's name and phone number
Select a 5-digit Personal Identification Number (PIN) to use when talking to the IRS.
☒ No.

Part 5: Sign here. You MUST complete both pages of Form 941 and SIGN it.

Under penalties of perjury, I declare that I have examined this return, including accompanying schedules and statements, and to the best of my knowledge and belief, it is true, correct, and complete. Declaration of preparer (other than taxpayer) is based on all information of which preparer has any knowledge.

✗ Sign your name here
Print your name here
Print your title here
Date ___/___/___
Best daytime phone

EXHIBIT 9A.1

Form 941

Point: Line 5a shows the matching nature of FICA tax as 6.2% × 2, or 12.4%, which is shown as 0.124.

Point: Auditors rely on the four 941 Forms filed during a year when auditing a company's annual wages and salaries expense account.

is due, the taxes are remitted annually. Requirements for paying and reporting state unemployment taxes (SUTA) vary depending on the laws of each state. Most states require quarterly payments and reports.

Reporting Wages and Salaries Employers are required to give each employee an annual report of his or her wages subject to FICA and federal income taxes along with the amounts of these taxes withheld. This report is called a *Wage and Tax Statement,* or **Form W-2.** It must be given to employees before January 31 following the year covered by the report. Exhibit 9A.2 shows Form W-2 for one of the

Form W-2 Wage and Tax Statement
Copy 1–For State, City, or Local Tax Department
Department of Treasury—Internal Revenue Service

a Control number AR101 22222 OMB No. 1545-0006

b Employer identification number (EIN) 86-3214587

c Employer's name, address and ZIP code
Phoenix Sales & Service
1214 Mill Road
Phoenix, AZ 85621

d Employee's social security number 333-22-9999

e Employee's first name and initial Robert J. Last name Austin

f Employee's address and ZIP code
18 Roosevelt Blvd., Apt. C
Tempe, AZ 86322

1 Wages, tips, other compensation 4,910.00
2 Federal income tax withheld 333.37
3 Social security wages 4,910.00
4 Social security tax withheld 304.42
5 Medicare wages and tips 4,910.00
6 Medicare tax withheld 71.20
7 Social security tips
8 Allocated tips
9 Advance EIC payment
10 Dependent care benefits
11 Nonqualified plans
12a Code
13 Statutory employee / Retirement plan / Third-party sick pay
12b Code
14 Other
12c Code

15 State Employer's state ID number AZ 13-902319
16 State wages, tips, etc. 4,910.00
17 State income tax 26.68
18 Local wages, tips, etc.
19 Local income tax
20 Locality name

EXHIBIT 9A.2

Form W-2

employees at Phoenix Sales & Service. Copies of Form W-2 must be sent to the Social Security Administration, where the amount of the employee's wages subject to FICA taxes and FICA taxes withheld are posted to each employee's Social Security account. These posted amounts become the basis for determining an employee's retirement and survivors' benefits. The Social Security Administration also transmits to the IRS the amount of each employee's wages subject to federal income taxes and the amount of taxes withheld.

Payroll Records   Employers must keep payroll records in addition to reporting and paying taxes. These records usually include a payroll register and an individual earnings report for each employee.

Payroll Register   A **payroll register** usually shows the pay period dates, hours worked, gross pay, deductions, and net pay of each employee for each pay period. Exhibit 9A.3 shows a payroll register for Phoenix Sales & Service. It is organized into nine columns:

Col. A   Employee Identification (ID); Employee name; Social Security number (SS No.); Reference (check number); and Date (date check issued)
Col. B   Pay Type (regular and overtime)
Col. C   Pay Hours (number of hours worked as regular and overtime)
Col. D   Gross Pay (amount of gross pay)
Col. E   FIT (federal income taxes withheld); FUTA (federal unemployment taxes)
Col. F   SIT (state income taxes withheld); SUTA (state unemployment taxes)
Col. G   FICA-SS_EE (Social Security taxes withheld, employee); FICA-SS_ER (Social Security taxes, employer)
Col. H   FICA-Med_EE (Medicare tax withheld, employee); FICA-Med_ER (Medicare tax, employer)
Col. I   Net Pay (gross pay less amounts withheld from employees)

Net pay for each employee is computed as gross pay minus the items on the first line of columns E through H. The employer's payroll tax for each employee is computed as the sum of items on the third line of columns E through H. A payroll register includes all data necessary to record payroll. In some software programs, the entries to record payroll are made in a special *payroll journal*.

EXHIBIT 9A.3

Payroll Register

A	B	C	D	E	F	G	H	I
			Phoenix Sales & Service Payroll Register For Week Ended Jan. 8, 2019					
Employee ID Employee SS No. Refer., Date	**Gross Pay**			**FIT** [blank] **FUTA**	**SIT** [blank] **SUTA**	**FICA-SS_EE** [blank] **FICA-SS_ER**	**FICA-Med_EE** [blank] **FICA-Med_ER**	**Net Pay**
	Pay Type	**Pay Hours**	**Gross Pay**					
AR101 Robert Austin 333-22-9999 9001, 1/8/19	Regular Overtime	40.00 0.00	400.00 0.00 400.00	−28.99 −2.40	−2.32 −10.80	−24.80 −24.80	−5.80 −5.80	338.09
CJ102 Judy Cross 299-11-9201 9002, 1/8/19	Regular Overtime	40.00 1.00	560.00 21.00 581.00	−52.97 −3.49	−4.24 −15.69	−36.02 −36.02	−8.42 −8.42	479.35
DJ103 John Diaz 444-11-9090 9003, 1/8/19	Regular Overtime	40.00 2.00	560.00 42.00 602.00	−48.33 −3.61	−3.87 −16.25	−37.32 −37.32	−8.73 −8.73	503.75
KK104 Kay Keife 909-11-3344 9004, 1/8/19	Regular Overtime	40.00 0.00	560.00 0.00 560.00	−68.57 −3.36	−5.49 −15.12	−34.72 −34.72	−8.12 −8.12	443.10
ML105 Lee Miller 444-56-3211 9005, 1/8/19	Regular Overtime	40.00 0.00	560.00 0.00 560.00	−34.24 −3.36	−2.74 −15.12	−34.72 −34.72	−8.12 −8.12	480.18
SD106 Dale Sears 909-33-1234 9006, 1/8/19	Regular Overtime	40.00 0.00	560.00 0.00 560.00	−68.57 −3.36	−5.49 −15.12	−34.72 −34.72	−8.12 −8.12	443.10
Totals	Regular Overtime	240.00 3.00	3,200.00 63.00 3,263.00	−301.67 −19.58	−24.15 −88.10	−202.30 −202.30	−47.31 −47.31	2,687.57

Point: Gross Pay column shows regular hours worked on the first line multiplied by regular pay rate. Overtime hours multiplied by the overtime premium rate equals overtime pay on the second line. For this company, workers earn 150% of their regular rate for hours in excess of 40 per week.

Payroll Check Payment of payroll is usually done by check or electronic funds transfer. Exhibit 9A.4 shows a *payroll check* for a Phoenix employee. This check includes a detachable *statement of earnings* (at top) showing gross pay, deductions, and net pay.

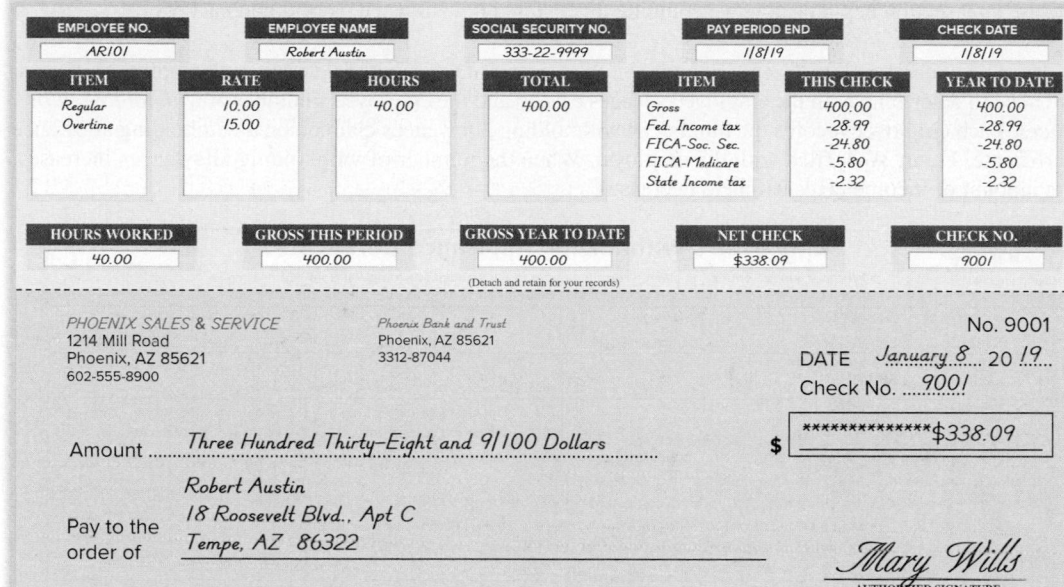

EXHIBIT 9A.4

Check and Statement of Earnings

Employee Earnings Report An **employee earnings report** is a cumulative record of an employee's hours worked, gross earnings, deductions, and net pay. Payroll information on this report is taken from the payroll register. The employee earnings report for R. Austin at Phoenix Sales & Service is shown in Exhibit 9A.5. An employee earnings report accumulates information that can show when an employee's

EXHIBIT 9A.5

Employee Earnings Report

Phoenix Sales & Service Employee Earnings Report For Month Ended Dec. 31, 2019								
Employee ID Employee SS No.	Date Reference	Gross Pay	FIT [blank] FUTA	SIT [blank] SUTA	FICA-SS_EE [blank] FICA-SS_ER	FICA-Med_EE [blank] FICA-Med_ER	Net Pay	
Beginning balance for Robert Austin	11/26/19 (balance)	2,910.00	−188.42	−15.08	−180.42	−42.20	2,483.88	
			−17.46	−78.57	−180.42	−42.20		
AR101 Robert Austin 333-22-9999	12/03/19 9049	400.00	−28.99	−2.32	−24.80	−5.80	338.09	
			−2.40	−10.80	−24.80	−5.80		
AR101 Robert Austin 333-22-9999	12/10/19 9055	400.00	−28.99	−2.32	−24.80	−5.80	338.09	
			−2.40	−10.80	−24.80	−5.80		
AR101 Robert Austin 333-22-9999	12/17/19 9061	400.00	−28.99	−2.32	−24.80	−5.80	338.09	
			−2.40	−10.80	−24.80	−5.80		
AR101 Robert Austin 333-22-9999	12/24/19 9067	400.00	−28.99	−2.32	−24.80	−5.80	338.09	
			−2.40	−10.80	−24.80	−5.80		
AR101 Robert Austin 333-22-9999	12/31/19 9073	400.00	−28.99	−2.32	−24.80	−5.80	338.09	
			−2.40	−10.80	−24.80	−5.80		
Total 5-wk month thru 12/31/19		2,000.00	−144.95	−11.60	−124.00	−29.00	1,690.45	
			−12.00	−54.00	−124.00	−29.00		
Year-to-date total for Robert Austin	12/31/19 (balance)	4,910.00	−333.37	−26.68	−304.42	−71.20	4,174.33	
			−29.46	−132.57	−304.42	−71.20		

Point: Year-end balances agree with W-2.

earnings reach the tax-exempt points for FICA, FUTA, and SUTA taxes. It also gives data an employer needs to prepare Form W-2.

Payroll Procedures

Employers must be able to compute federal income tax for payroll purposes. This section explains how we compute this tax and how to use a payroll bank account.

Computing Federal Income Taxes   To compute the amount of taxes withheld from each employee's wages, we need to determine both the employee's wages earned and the employee's number of *withholding allowances*. Each employee records the number of withholding allowances claimed on a withholding allowance certificate, **Form W-4,** filed with the employer. When the number of withholding allowances increases, the amount of income taxes withheld decreases.

Employers often use a **wage bracket withholding table** similar to the one shown in Exhibit 9A.6 to compute the **federal income taxes withheld** from each employee's gross pay. The table in Exhibit 9A.6 is for a single employee paid weekly. Tables also are provided for married employees and for biweekly, semimonthly, and monthly pay periods (most payroll software includes these tables). When using a wage bracket withholding table to compute federal income tax withheld from an employee's gross wages, we need to locate an employee's wage bracket within the first two columns. We then find the amount withheld by looking in the withholding allowance column for that employee.

EXHIBIT 9A.6

Wage Bracket
Withholding Table

If the wages are—		And the number of withholding allowances claimed is—										
At least	But less than	0	1	2	3	4	5	6	7	8	9	10
		The amount of income tax to be withheld is—										
$600	$610	$76	$67	$58	$49	$39	$30	$21	$12	$6	$0	$0
610	620	79	69	59	50	41	32	22	13	7	1	0
620	630	81	70	61	52	42	33	24	15	8	2	0
630	640	84	72	62	53	44	35	25	16	9	3	0
640	650	86	73	64	55	45	36	27	18	10	4	0
650	660	89	75	65	56	47	38	28	19	11	5	0
660	670	91	76	67	58	48	39	30	21	12	6	0
670	680	94	78	68	59	50	41	31	22	13	7	1
680	690	96	81	70	61	51	42	33	24	14	8	2
690	700	99	83	71	62	53	44	34	25	16	9	3
700	710	101	86	73	64	54	45	35	27	17	10	4
710	720	104	88	74	65	56	47	37	28	19	11	5
720	730	106	91	76	67	57	48	39	30	20	12	6
730	740	109	93	78	68	59	50	40	31	22	13	7
740	750	111	96	80	70	60	51	42	33	23	14	8

Payroll Bank Account   Companies with few employees often pay them with checks drawn on the company's regular bank account. Companies with many employees often use a special **payroll bank account** to pay employees. When this account is used, a company either (1) draws one check for total payroll on the regular bank account and deposits it in the payroll bank account or (2) executes an *electronic funds transfer* to the payroll bank account. Individual payroll checks are then drawn on this payroll bank account. Because only one check for the total payroll is drawn on the regular bank account each payday, use of a special payroll bank account helps with internal control. It also helps in reconciling the regular bank account. When companies use a payroll bank account, they usually include check numbers in the payroll register. The payroll register in Exhibit 9A.3 shows check numbers in column A. For instance, Check No.

9001 is issued to Robert Austin. With this information, the payroll register serves as a supplementary record of wages earned by and paid to employees.

Who Pays What Payroll Taxes and Benefits
We conclude this appendix with the following table identifying who pays which payroll taxes and which common employee benefits such as medical, disability, pension, charitable, and union costs. Who pays which employee benefits, and what portion, is subject to agreements between companies and their workers. Also, self-employed workers must pay both the employer and employee FICA taxes for Social Security and Medicare.

Year-To-Date Pay	Employer Taxes	Employee Taxes
$0 to $7,000	FICA—Medicare FICA—Social Security FUTA SUTA	FICA—Medicare FICA—Social Security State & Federal Income Tax
$7,000 to $128,400	FICA—Medicare FICA—Social Security	FICA—Medicare FICA—Social Security State & Federal Income Tax
Above $128,400	FICA—Medicare	FICA—Medicare State & Federal Income Tax

Employer Payroll Taxes and Costs	Employee Payroll Deductions
• FICA—Social Security taxes	• FICA—Social Security taxes
• FICA—Medicare taxes	• FICA—Medicare taxes
• FUTA (federal unemployment taxes)	• Federal income taxes
• SUTA (state unemployment taxes)	• State and local income taxes
• Share of medical coverage, if any	• Share of medical coverage, if any
• Share of pension coverage, if any	• Share of pension coverage, if any
• Share of other benefits, if any	• Share of other benefits, if any

Point: IRS reports average (effective) income tax rates for categories of income earners:

Top 1%. 24%
Top 5%. 20%
Top 10% 18%
Lower 50% . . . . <2%

APPENDIX

Corporate Income Taxes
9B

This appendix covers current liabilities for income taxes of C corporations. Income tax on sole proprietorships, partnerships, S corporations, and LLCs is computed on their owner's tax filings and is not covered here.

Income Tax Liabilities   Corporations are subject to income taxes and must estimate their income tax liability when preparing financial statements. Because income tax expense is created by earning income, a liability is incurred when income is earned. This tax must be paid quarterly. Consider a corporation that prepares monthly financial statements. Based on its income in January, this corporation estimates that it owes income taxes of $12,100. The following adjusting entry records this estimate.

Jan. 31	Income Taxes Expense	12,100	
	Income Taxes Payable		12,100
	Accrue January income taxes.		

Assets = Liabilities + Equity
+12,100   −12,100

The tax liability is recorded each month until the first quarterly payment is made. If the company's estimated taxes for this first quarter total $30,000, the entry to record its payment is

Apr. 10	Income Taxes Payable	30,000	
	Cash.		30,000
	Paid estimated first-quarter income taxes.		

Assets = Liabilities + Equity
−30,000   −30,000

This process of accruing and then paying estimated income taxes continues through the year. When annual financial statements are prepared at year-end, the corporation knows its actual total income and the actual amount of income taxes it must pay. This information allows it to accurately record income taxes expense for the fourth quarter so that the total of the four quarters' expense amounts equals the actual taxes paid to the government.

Deferred Income Tax Liabilities   An income tax liability for corporations can arise when the amount of income before taxes that the corporation reports on its income statement is not the same as the amount of income reported on its income tax return. This difference occurs because income tax laws and GAAP measure income differently. Differences between tax laws and GAAP arise because Congress uses tax laws to generate receipts, stimulate the economy, and influence behavior, whereas GAAP is intended to provide financial information useful for business decisions. Also, tax accounting often follows the cash basis, whereas GAAP follows the accrual basis.

Some differences between tax laws and GAAP are temporary. *Temporary differences* arise when the tax return and the income statement report a revenue or expense in different years. As an example, companies are often able to deduct higher amounts of depreciation in the early years of an asset's life and smaller amounts in later years for tax reporting in comparison to GAAP. This means that in the early years, depreciation for tax reporting is often more than depreciation on the income statement. In later years, depreciation for tax reporting is often less than depreciation on the income statement. When temporary differences exist between taxable income on the tax return and the income before taxes on the income statement, corporations compute income taxes expense based on the income reported on the income statement. The result is that income taxes expense reported in the income statement is often different from the amount of income taxes payable to the government. This difference is the **deferred income tax liability.**

Assume that in recording its usual quarterly income tax payments, a corporation computes $25,000 of income taxes expense. It also determines that only $21,000 is currently due and $4,000 is deferred to future years (a timing difference). The entry to record this end-of-period adjustment is

Point: For a temporary difference, if GAAP income exceeds taxable income, a deferred tax liability is created. If GAAP income is initially less than taxable income, a deferred tax asset is created.

Assets = Liabilities + Equity
+21,000   −25,000
+4,000

Dec. 31	Income Taxes Expense	25,000	
	Income Taxes Payable		21,000
	Deferred Income Tax Liability		4,000
	Record tax expense and deferred tax liability.		

The credit to Income Taxes Payable is the amount currently due to be paid. The credit to Deferred Income Tax Liability is tax payments deferred until future years when the temporary difference reverses.

Deferred Income Tax Assets   Temporary differences also can cause a company to pay income taxes *before* they are reported on the income statement. If so, the company reports a *Deferred Income Tax Asset* on its balance sheet.

Summary: Cheat Sheet

KNOWN LIABILITIES

Current liabilities (or short-term liabilities): Liabilities due *within* one year.
Long-term liabilities: Liabilities due *after* one year.

Sales tax collection:

Cash	6,300	
Sales..................................		6,000
Sales Taxes Payable		300

Unearned revenues (or deferred revenues): Amount received in advance from customers for future products or services; to record cash received in advance.

Cash	5,000,000	
Unearned Revenue		5,000,000

Unearned revenue is earned: To record service or product delivered.

Unearned Revenue..........................	625,000	
Revenue............................		625,000

Short-term note payable: A written promise to pay a specified amount on a stated future date within one year.

Note given to replace accounts payable (partial cash paid):

Accounts Payable...........................	600	
Cash................................		100
Notes Payable		500

Note given to borrow cash:

Cash	2,000	
Notes Payable		2,000

Note and interest paid:

Notes Payable.....................................	500	
Interest Expense	10	
Cash.......................................		510

Interest expense incurred but not yet paid:

Interest Expense	10	
Interest Payable		10

Interest formula (year assumed to have 360 days):

$$\text{Principal of the note} \times \text{Annual interest rate} \times \text{Time expressed in fraction of year} = \text{Interest}$$

PAYROLL LIABILITIES

Gross pay: Total compensation an employee earns before deductions such as taxes.

Payroll deductions (or withholdings): Amounts withheld from an employee's gross pay, either required or voluntary.

FICA—Social Security taxes payable: Withholdings to cover retirement, disability, and survivorship. Social Security tax is 6.2% of the first $128,400 the employee earns for the year.

FICA—Medicare taxes payable: Withholdings to cover medical benefits. The Medicare tax is 1.45% of all amounts the employee earns; there is no maximum limit to Medicare tax.

Employee federal income taxes payable: Federal income tax withheld from each employee's paycheck.

Employee voluntary deductions: Voluntary withholdings for things such as union dues, charitable giving, and health insurance.

Employee payroll taxes:

Salaries Expense	2,000	
FICA—Social Security Taxes Payable (6.2%)		124
FICA—Medicare Taxes Payable (1.45%)		29
Employee Federal Income Taxes Payable		213
Employee Medical Insurance Payable		85
Employee Union Dues Payable		25
Salaries Payable		1,524

Payment of salary to employees:

Salaries Payable..............................	1,524	
Cash		1,524

Federal Unemployment Tax Act (FUTA): Employers pay a federal unemployment tax on wages and salaries earned by their employees. FUTA taxes are between 0.6% and 6.0% of the first $7,000 earned by each employee.

State Unemployment Tax Act (SUTA): Employers pay a state unemployment tax on wages and salaries earned by their employees. SUTA taxes are up to 5.4% of the first $7,000 earned by each employee.

Employer payroll taxes expense:

Payroll Taxes Expense	273	
FICA—Social Security Taxes Payable (6.2%)		124
FICA—Medicare Taxes Payable (1.45%)		29
State Unemployment Taxes Payable		108
Federal Unemployment Taxes Payable		12

ESTIMATED LIABILITIES

Health and pension benefits:

Employee Benefits Expense......................	20,000	
Employee Medical Insurance Payable		8,000
Employee Retirement Program Payable		12,000

Accrual of vacation benefits (also called *paid absences*):

Vacation Benefits Expense	3,200	
Vacation Benefits Payable		3,200

Vacation benefits are used:

Vacation Benefits Payable	400	
Cash		400

Bonus plan accrued:

Employee Bonus Expense	10,000	
Bonus Payable		10,000

Warranty: A seller's obligation to replace or fix a product (or service) that fails to perform as expected within a specified period. Warranty expense is recorded in the period when revenue from the sale of the product or service is reported.

Warranty expense accrued:

Warranty Expense	640	
Estimated Warranty Liability		640

Warranty repairs and replacements:

Estimated Warranty Liability	200	
Auto Parts Inventory		200

CONTINGENCIES AND ANALYSIS

Contingent liability: A potential liability that depends on a future event arising from a past transaction or event. An example is a pending lawsuit.

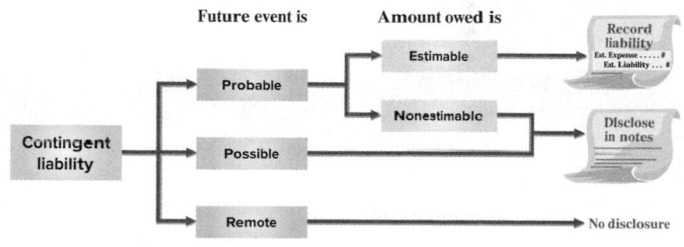

Key Terms

Multiple Choice Quiz

1. On December 1, a company signed a $6,000, 90-day, 5% note payable, with principal plus interest due on March 1 of the following year. What amount of interest expense should be accrued at December 31 on the note?

   a. $300   **c.** $100   **e.** $0

   b. $25   **d.** $75

2. An employee earned $50,000 during the year. FICA tax for Social Security is 6.2% and FICA tax for Medicare is 1.45%. The employer's share of FICA taxes is

   a. $0; employee's pay exceeds FICA limit.

   b. $0; FICA is not an employer tax.

   c. $3,100.

   d. $725.

   e. $3,825.

3. Assume the FUTA tax rate is 0.6% and the SUTA tax rate is 5.4%. Both taxes are applied to the first $7,000 of an employee's pay. What is the total unemployment tax an employer must pay on an employee's annual wages of $40,000?

   a. $2,400

   b. $420

   c. $42

   d. $378

   e. $0; employee's wages exceed the $7,000 maximum.

4. A company sold 10,000 TVs in July and estimates warranty expense for these TVs to be $25,000. During July, 80 TVs were serviced under warranty at a cost of $18,000. The credit balance in the Estimated Warranty Liability account at July 1 was $26,000. What is the company's warranty expense for the month of July?

   a. $51,000   **c.** $25,000   **e.** $18,000

   b. $1,000   **d.** $33,000

5. AXE Co. is the defendant in a lawsuit. AXE reasonably estimates that this pending lawsuit will result in damages of $99,000. It is probable that AXE will lose the case. What should AXE do?

   a. Record a liability   **c.** Have no disclosure

   b. Disclose in notes

ANSWERS TO MULTIPLE CHOICE QUIZ

1. b; $6,000 × 0.05 × 30/360 = $25
2. e; $50,000 × (0.062 + 0.0145) = $3,825
3. b; $7,000 × (0.006 + 0.054) = $420

4. c; $25,000
5. a; Reason—it is reasonably estimated and is a probable loss. AXE would record an estimated legal expense and liability.

$^{A(B)}$ Superscript letter A or B denotes assignments based on Appendix 9A or 9B.

Icon denotes assignments that involve decision making.

Discussion Questions

1. What is the difference between a current and a long-term liability?

2. What is an estimated liability?

3. What are the three important questions concerning the uncertainty of liabilities?

4. What is the combined amount (in percent) of the employee and employer Social Security tax rate? (Assume wages do not exceed $128,400 per year.)

5. What is the current Medicare tax rate? This rate is applied to what maximum level of salary and wages?

6. Which payroll taxes are the employee's responsibility and which are the employer's responsibility?

7. What determines the amount deducted from an employee's wages for federal income taxes?

8. What is an employer's unemployment merit rating? How are these ratings assigned to employers?

9. Why are warranty liabilities usually recognized on the balance sheet as liabilities even when they are uncertain?

10. Suppose a company has a facility located where disastrous weather conditions often occur. Should it report a probable loss from a future disaster as a liability on its balance sheet? Explain.

11.^{A} What is a wage bracket withholding table?

12.^{A} What amount of income tax is withheld from the salary of an employee who is single with two withholding allowances and earns $725 per week? What if the employee earns $625 and has no withholding allowances? (Use Exhibit 9A.6.)

13. Refer to **Apple**'s balance sheet in Appendix A. What is the amount of Apple's accounts payable as of September 30, 2017?   **APPLE**

14. Refer to **Google**'s balance sheet in Appendix A. What "accrued" expenses (liabilities) does Google report at December 31, 2017?   **GOOGLE**

15. Refer to **Samsung**'s balance sheet in Appendix A. List Samsung's current liabilities as of December 31, 2017.   **Samsung**

16. Refer to **Samsung**'s recent balance sheet in Appendix A. What current liabilities related to income taxes are on its balance sheet? Explain the meaning of each income tax account identified.   **Samsung**

connect

Which of the following items are normally classified as current liabilities for a company that has a one-year operating cycle?

_____ **1.** Portion of long-term note due in 10 months.

_____ **2.** Note payable maturing in 2 years.

_____ **3.** Note payable due in 18 months.

_____ **4.** Accounts payable due in 11 months.

_____ **5.** FICA taxes payable.

_____ **6.** Salaries payable.

QUICK STUDY

QS 9-1
Classifying liabilities
C1

Dextra Computing sells merchandise for $6,000 cash on September 30 (cost of merchandise is $3,900). Dextra collects 5% sales tax. (1) Record the entry for the $6,000 sale and its sales tax. (2) Record the entry that shows Dextra sending the sales tax on this sale to the government on October 15.

QS 9-2
Accounting for sales taxes
C2

Ticketsales, Inc., receives $5,000,000 cash in advance ticket sales for a four-date tour of Bon Jovi. Record the advance ticket sales on October 31. Record the revenue earned for the first concert date of November 5, assuming it represents one-fourth of the advance ticket sales.

QS 9-3
Unearned revenue   **C2**

On November 7, Mura Company borrows $160,000 cash by signing a 90-day, 8%, $160,000 note payable. (1) Compute the accrued interest payable on December 31; (2) prepare the journal entry to record the accrued interest expense at December 31; and (3) prepare the journal entry to record payment of the note at maturity on February 5.

QS 9-4
Interest-bearing note
transactions   **P1**

On January 15, the end of the first pay period of the year, North Company's employees earned $35,000 of sales salaries. Withholdings from the employees' salaries include FICA Social Security taxes at the rate of 6.2%, FICA Medicare taxes at the rate of 1.45%, $6,500 of federal income taxes, $772.50 of medical insurance deductions, and $120 of union dues. No employee earned more than $7,000 in this first period. Prepare the journal entry to record North Company's January 15 salaries expense and related liabilities. (Round amounts to cents.)

QS 9-5
Recording employee
payroll taxes
P2

Merger Co. has 10 employees, each of whom earns $2,000 per month and has been employed since January 1. FICA Social Security taxes are 6.2% of the first $128,400 paid to each employee, and FICA Medicare taxes are 1.45% of gross pay. FUTA taxes are 0.6% and SUTA taxes are 5.4% of the first $7,000 paid to each employee. Prepare the March 31 journal entry to record the March payroll taxes expense.

QS 9-6
Recording employer
payroll taxes   **P3**

Noura Company offers an annual bonus to employees (to be shared equally) if the company meets certain net income goals. Prepare the journal entry to record a $15,000 bonus owed (but not yet paid) to its workers at calendar year-end.

QS 9-7
Accounting for bonuses
P4

Chavez Co.'s salaried employees earn four weeks' vacation per year. Chavez estimated and must expense $8,000 of accrued vacation benefits for the year. (*a*) Prepare the December 31 year-end adjusting entry for accrued vacation benefits. (*b*) Prepare the entry on April 1 of the next year when an employee takes a one-week vacation and is paid $500 cash for that week.

QS 9-8
Accounting for vacations
P4

On September 1, Home Store sells a mower (that costs $200) for $500 cash with a one-year warranty that covers parts. Warranty expense is estimated at 8% of sales. On January 24 of the following year, the mower is brought in for repairs covered under the warranty requiring $35 in materials taken from the Repair Parts Inventory. Prepare the September 1 entry to record the mower sale (and cost of sale) and the January 24 entry to record the warranty repairs.

QS 9-9
Recording warranty repairs
P4

Riverrun Co. provides medical care and insurance benefits to its retirees. In the current year, Riverrun agrees to pay $5,500 for medical insurance and contribute an additional $9,000 to a retirement program. Record the entry for these accrued (but unpaid) benefits on December 31.

QS 9-10
Accounting for health and
pension benefits   **P4**

Huprey Co. is the defendant in the following legal claims. For each of the following claims, indicate whether Huprey should (*a*) record a liability, (*b*) disclose in notes, or (*c*) have no disclosure.

_____ **1.** Huprey can reasonably estimate that a pending lawsuit will result in damages of $1,250,000. It is probable that Huprey will lose the case.

_____ **2.** It is reasonably possible that Huprey will lose a pending lawsuit. The loss cannot be estimated.

_____ **3.** Huprey is being sued for damages of $2,000,000. It is very unlikely (remote) that Huprey will lose the case.

QS 9-11
Accounting for
contingent liabilities
C3

QS 9-12
Times interest earned
A1

Park Company reports interest expense of $145,000 and income before interest expense and income taxes of $1,885,000. (1) Compute its times interest earned. (2) Park's competitor's times interest earned is 4.0. Is Park in a better or worse position than its competitor to make interest payments if the economy turns bad?

QS 9-13ᴬ
Federal income tax withholdings
P5

Organic Farmers Co-Op has three employees and pays them weekly. Using the withholding bracket table in Exhibit 9A.6, determine each employee's federal income tax withholding.

1. Maria earns $735 per week and claims three withholding allowances.
2. Jeff earns $607 per week and claims five withholding allowances.
3. Alicia earns $704 per week and does not claim any withholding allowances.

QS 9-14ᴬ
Net pay and tax computations
P5

The payroll records of Speedy Software show the following information about Marsha Gottschalk, an employee, for the weekly pay period ending September 30. Gottschalk is single and claims one allowance. Compute her Social Security tax (6.2%), Medicare tax (1.45%), federal income tax withholding (use the withholding table in Exhibit 9A.6), state income tax (1.0%), and net pay for the current pay period. Round tax amounts to the nearest cent.

Total (gross) earnings for current pay period	$ 740
Cumulative earnings of previous pay periods	$9,700

Check   Net pay, $579.99

QS 9-15ᴮ
Recording deferred income tax liability   **P4**

Sera Corporation has made and recorded its quarterly income tax payments. After a final review of taxes for the year, the company identifies an additional $40,000 of income tax expense that should be recorded. A portion of this additional expense, $6,000, is deferred for payment in future years. Record Sera's year-end adjusting entry for income tax expense.

📶 connect

EXERCISES

Exercise 9-1
Classifying liabilities
C1

The following items appear on the balance sheet of a company with a one-year operating cycle. Identify the proper classification of each item as follows: *C* if it is a current liability, *L* if it is a long-term liability, or *N* if it is not a liability.

_____ **1.** Notes payable (due in 13 to 24 months).   _____ **6.** FUTA taxes payable.
_____ **2.** Notes payable (due in 6 to 11 months).   _____ **7.** Accounts receivable.
_____ **3.** Notes payable (mature in five years).   _____ **8.** Sales taxes payable.
_____ **4.** Current portion of long-term debt.   _____ **9.** Salaries payable.
_____ **5.** Notes payable (due in 120 days).   _____ **10.** Wages payable.

Exercise 9-2
Recording known current liabilities
C2

1. On July 15, Piper Co. sold $10,000 of merchandise (costing $5,000) for cash. The sales tax rate is 4%. On August 1, Piper sent the sales tax collected from the sale to the government. Record entries for the July 15 and August 1 transactions.

2. On November 3, the **Milwaukee Bucks** sold a six-game pack of advance tickets for $300 cash. On November 20, the Bucks played the first game of the six-game pack (this represented one-sixth of the advance ticket sales). Record the entries for the November 3 and November 20 transactions.

Exercise 9-3
Accounting for note payable   **P1**

Check   (2b) Interest expense, $2,200

Sylvestor Systems borrows $110,000 cash on May 15 by signing a 60-day, 12%, $110,000 note.

1. On what date does this note mature?
2. Prepare the entries to record (*a*) issuance of the note and (*b*) payment of the note at maturity.

Exercise 9-4
Interest-bearing notes payable with year-end adjustments   **P1**

Check   (2) $3,000
(3) $1,500

Keesha Co. borrows $200,000 cash on November 1 of the current year by signing a 90-day, 9%, $200,000 note.

1. On what date does this note mature?
2. How much interest expense is recorded in the current year? (Assume a 360-day year.)
3. How much interest expense is recorded in the following year? (Assume a 360-day year.)
4. Prepare journal entries to record (*a*) issuance of the note, (*b*) accrual of interest on December 31, and (*c*) payment of the note at maturity.

BMX Company has one employee. FICA Social Security taxes are 6.2% of the first $128,400 paid to its employee, and FICA Medicare taxes are 1.45% of gross pay. For BMX, its FUTA taxes are 0.6% and SUTA taxes are 5.4% of the first $7,000 paid to its employee. Compute BMX's amounts for each of these four taxes as applied to the employee's gross earnings for September under each of three separate situations (a), (b), and (c). Round amounts to cents.

Exercise 9-5
Computing payroll taxes
P2   P3

	Gross Pay through August 31	Gross Pay for September
a.	$ 6,400	$ 800
b.	2,000	2,100
c.	122,100	8,000

Check (a) FUTA, $3.60; SUTA, $32.40

Using the data in *situation (a)* of Exercise 9-5, prepare the employer's September 30 journal entries to record salary expense and its related payroll liabilities for this employee. The employee's federal income taxes withheld by the employer are $80 for this pay period. Round amounts to cents.

Exercise 9-6
Payroll-related journal entries **P2**

Using the data in *situation (a)* of Exercise 9-5, prepare the employer's September 30 journal entries to record the *employer's* payroll taxes expense and its related liabilities. Round amounts to cents.

Exercise 9-7
Payroll-related journal entries **P3**

The following monthly data are taken from Ramirez Company at July 31: sales salaries, $200,000; office salaries, $160,000; federal income taxes withheld, $90,000; state income taxes withheld, $20,000; Social Security taxes withheld, $22,320; Medicare taxes withheld, $5,220; medical insurance premiums, $7,000; life insurance premiums, $4,000; union dues deducted, $1,000; and salaries subject to unemployment taxes, $50,000. The employee pays 40% of medical and life insurance premiums.

Prepare journal entries to record (1) accrued payroll, including employee deductions, for July; (2) cash payment of the net payroll (salaries payable) for July; (3) accrued employer payroll taxes, and other related employment expenses, for July—assume that FICA taxes are identical to those on employees and that SUTA taxes are 5.4% and FUTA taxes are 0.6%; and (4) cash payment of all liabilities related to the July payroll.

Exercise 9-8
Recording payroll
P2   P3

Mest Company has nine employees. FICA Social Security taxes are 6.2% of the first $128,400 paid to each employee, and FICA Medicare taxes are 1.45% of gross pay. FUTA taxes are 0.6% and SUTA taxes are 5.4% of the first $7,000 paid to each employee. Cumulative pay for the current year for each of its employees follows.

Exercise 9-9
Computing payroll taxes
P2   P3

Employee	Cumulative Pay	Employee	Cumulative Pay	Employee	Cumulative Pay
Ken S.	$ 6,000	Michelle W.	$143,500	Lori K.	$130,900
Tim V.	40,400	Michael M.	106,900	Kitty O.	36,900
Steve S.	87,000	Zach R.	128,400	John W.	4,000

a. Prepare a table with the following six column headings. Compute the amounts in this table for each employee and then total the numerical columns.

Employee	Cumulative Pay	Pay Subject to FICA Social Security	Pay Subject to FICA Medicare	Pay Subject to FUTA Taxes	Pay Subject to SUTA Taxes

b. For the company, compute each total for FICA Social Security taxes, FICA Medicare taxes, FUTA taxes, and SUTA taxes. *Hint:* Remember to include in those totals any employee share of taxes that the company must collect. Round amounts to cents.

Hitzu Co. sold a copier (that costs $4,800) for $6,000 cash with a two-year parts warranty to a customer on August 16 of Year 1. Hitzu expects warranty costs to be 4% of dollar sales. It records warranty expense with an adjusting entry on December 31. On January 5 of Year 2, the copier requires on-site repairs that are completed the same day. The repairs cost $209 for materials taken from the repair parts inventory. These are the only repairs required in Year 2 for this copier.

1. How much warranty expense does the company report for this copier in Year 1?
2. How much is the estimated warranty liability for this copier as of December 31 of Year 1?
3. How much is the estimated warranty liability for this copier as of December 31 of Year 2?
4. Prepare journal entries to record (a) the copier's sale; (b) the adjustment to recognize the warranty expense on December 31 of Year 1; and (c) the repairs that occur on January 5 of Year 2.

Exercise 9-10
Warranty expense and liability computations and entries
P4
Check (1) $240

(3) $31

Exercise 9-11
Recording bonuses
P4

For the year ended December 31, Lopez Company implements an employee bonus program based on company net income, which the employees share equally. Lopez's bonus expense is computed as $14,563.
1. Prepare the journal entry at December 31 to record the bonus due the employees.
2. Prepare the later journal entry at January 19 to record payment of the bonus to employees.

Exercise 9-12
Accounting for estimated liabilities
P4

Prepare adjusting entries at December 31 for Maxum Company's year-end financial statements for each of the following separate transactions.
1. Employees earn vacation pay at a rate of one day per month. Maxum estimated and must expense $13,000 of accrued vacation benefits for the year.
2. During December, Maxum Company sold 12,000 units of a product that carries a 60-day warranty. December sales for this product total $460,000. The company expects 10% of the units to need warranty repairs, and it estimates the average repair cost per unit will be $15.

Exercise 9-13
Accounting for health and pension benefits
P4

Vander Co. provides medical care and insurance benefits to its retirees. In the current year, Vander agrees to pay $9,500 for medical insurance and contribute an additional 5% of the employees' $200,000 gross salaries to a retirement program. (1) Record the entry for these accrued (but unpaid) benefits on December 31. (2) Assuming $5,000 of the retirement benefits are not to be paid for five years, how should this amount be reported on the current balance sheet?

Exercise 9-14
Accounting for contingent liabilities
C3

For each separate situation, indicate whether Cruz Company should (a) record a liability, (b) disclose in notes, or (c) have no disclosure.
1. Cruz Company guarantees the $100,000 debt of a supplier. It is not probable that the supplier will default on the debt.
2. A disgruntled employee is suing Cruz Company. Legal advisers believe that the company will likely need to pay damages, but the amount cannot be reasonably estimated.

Exercise 9-15
Preparing a balance sheet
C1 P2 P3

Selected accounts from Lue Co.'s adjusted trial balance for the year ended December 31 follow. Prepare a classified balance sheet.

Total equity	$30,000	Employee federal income taxes payable	$9,000
Equipment	40,000	Federal unemployment taxes payable	200
Salaries payable	34,000	FICA—Medicare taxes payable	725
Accounts receivable	5,100	FICA—Social Security taxes payable	3,100
Cash	50,000	Employee medical insurance payable	2,000
Current portion of long-term debt	4,000	State unemployment taxes payable	1,800
Notes payable (due in 6 years)	10,000	Sales tax payable (due in 2 weeks)	275

Exercise 9-16
Computing and interpreting times interest earned
A1

Use the following information from separate companies a through d to compute times interest earned. Which company indicates the strongest ability to pay interest expense as it comes due?

	Net Income (Loss)	Interest Expense	Income Taxes
a.	$119,000	$44,000	$35,000
b.	135,000	16,000	25,000
c.	138,000	12,000	30,000
d.	314,000	14,000	50,000

Check (b) 11.0

Exercise 9-17ᴮ
Accounting for income taxes P4

Nishi Corporation prepares financial statements for each month-end. As part of its accounting process, estimated income taxes are accrued each month for 30% of the current month's net income. The income taxes are paid in the first month of each quarter for the amount accrued for the prior quarter. The following information is available for the fourth quarter of the year just ended. When tax computations are completed on January 20 of the following year, Nishi determines that the quarter's Income Taxes Payable account balance should be $28,300 on December 31 of the year just ended (its unadjusted balance is $24,690).

| October net income ...... $28,600 | November net income..... $19,100 | December net income ..... $34,600 |

1. Determine the amount of the accounting adjustment (dated as of December 31) to get the correct ending balance in the Income Taxes Payable account.

2. Prepare journal entries to record (*a*) the December 31 adjustment to the Income Taxes Payable account and (*b*) the later January 20 payment of the fourth-quarter taxes.

Check   (1) $3,610

Lenny Florita, an unmarried employee, works 48 hours in the week ended January 12. His pay rate is $14 per hour, and his wages have deductions for FICA Social Security, FICA Medicare, and federal income taxes. He claims two withholding allowances.

Compute his regular pay, overtime pay (Lenny earns $21 per hour for each hour over 40 per week), and gross pay. Then compute his FICA tax deduction (6.2% for the Social Security portion and 1.45% for the Medicare portion), income tax deduction (use the wage bracket withholding table from Exhibit 9A.6), total deductions, and net pay. Round tax amounts to the nearest cent.

Exercise 9-18ᴬ
Computing gross and net pay
P5

Check   Net pay, $596.30

Stark Company has five employees. Employees paid by the hour earn $10 per hour for the regular 40-hour workweek and $15 per hour beyond the 40 hours per week. Hourly employees are paid every two weeks, but salaried employees are paid monthly on the last biweekly payday of each month. FICA Social Security taxes are 6.2% of the first $128,400 paid to each employee, and FICA Medicare taxes are 1.45% of gross pay. FUTA taxes are 0.6% and SUTA taxes are 5.4% of the first $7,000 paid to each employee. The company has a benefits plan that includes medical insurance, life insurance, and retirement funding for employees. Under this plan, employees must contribute 5% of their gross income as a payroll withholding, which the company matches with *double* the amount. Following is the partially completed payroll register for the biweekly period ending August 31, which is the last payday of August.

Exercise 9-19ᴬ
Preparing payroll register and related entries
P5

Employee	Cumulative Pay (Excludes Current Period)	Pay Type	Pay Hours	Gross Pay	FIT / SIT	FUTA / SUTA	FICA-SS_EE / FICA-SS_ER	FICA-Med_EE / FICA-Med_ER	EE-Ben_Plan Withholding / ER-Ben_Plan Expense	Employee Net Pay (Current Period)
Kathleen	$126,600.00	Salary	—	$7,000.00	$2,000.00 / 300.00					
Anthony	6,800.00	Salary	—	500.00	80.00 / 20.00				25.00 / 50.00	
Nichole	15,100.00	Regular / Overtime	80 / 8		110.00 / 25.00					
Zoey	6,500.00	Regular / Overtime	80 / 4		100.00 / 22.00					
Gracie	5,000.00	Regular / Overtime	74 / 0	740.00 / 0.00	90.00 / 21.00					
Totals	$160,000.00				2,380.00 / 388.00					

Note: Table abbreviations follow those in Exhibit 9A.3; "Ben_Plan" refers to employee (EE) withholding or the employer (ER) expense for the benefits plan.

a. Complete this payroll register by filling in all cells for the pay period ended August 31. *Hint:* See Exhibit 9A.5 for guidance. Round amounts to cents.

b. Prepare the August 31 journal entry to record the accrued biweekly payroll and related liabilities for deductions.

c. Prepare the August 31 journal entry to record the employer's cash payment of the net payroll of part *b*.

d. Prepare the August 31 journal entry to record the employer's payroll taxes including the contribution to the benefits plan.

e. Prepare the August 31 journal entry to pay all liabilities (except for the net payroll in part *c*) for this biweekly period.

PROBLEM SET A

Problem 9-1A
Short-term notes payable transactions and entries

P1

Tyrell Co. entered into the following transactions involving short-term liabilities.

Year 1

Apr. 20	Purchased $40,250 of merchandise on credit from Locust, terms n/30.
May 19	Replaced the April 20 account payable to Locust with a 90-day, 10%, $35,000 note payable along with paying $5,250 in cash.
July 8	Borrowed $80,000 cash from NBR Bank by signing a 120-day, 9%, $80,000 note payable.
?	Paid the amount due on the note to Locust at the maturity date.
?	Paid the amount due on the note to NBR Bank at the maturity date.
Nov. 28	Borrowed $42,000 cash from Fargo Bank by signing a 60-day, 8%, $42,000 note payable.
Dec. 31	Recorded an adjusting entry for accrued interest on the note to Fargo Bank.

Year 2

?	Paid the amount due on the note to Fargo Bank at the maturity date.

Required

Check (2) Locust, $875

(3) $308

(4) $252

1. Determine the maturity date for each of the three notes described.
2. Determine the interest due at maturity for each of the three notes. Assume a 360-day year.
3. Determine the interest expense recorded in the adjusting entry at the end of Year 1.
4. Determine the interest expense recorded in Year 2.
5. Prepare journal entries for all the preceding transactions and events.

Problem 9-2A
Entries for payroll transactions

P2 P3

On January 8, the end of the first weekly pay period of the year, Regis Company's employees earned $22,760 of office salaries and $65,840 of sales salaries. Withholdings from the employees' salaries include FICA Social Security taxes at the rate of 6.2%, FICA Medicare taxes at the rate of 1.45%, $12,860 of federal income taxes, $1,340 of medical insurance deductions, and $840 of union dues. No employee earned more than $7,000 in this first period.

Required

Check (1) Cr. Salaries Payable, $66,782.10

(2) Dr. Payroll Taxes Expense, $12,093.90

1. Calculate FICA Social Security taxes payable and FICA Medicare taxes payable. Prepare the journal entry to record Regis Company's January 8 *employee* payroll expenses and liabilities. Round amounts to cents.

2. Prepare the journal entry to record Regis's *employer* payroll taxes resulting from the January 8 payroll. Regis's state unemployment tax rate is 5.4% of the first $7,000 paid to each employee. The federal unemployment tax rate is 0.6%. Round amounts to cents.

Problem 9-3A
Payroll expenses, withholdings, and taxes

P2 P3

Paloma Co. has four employees. FICA Social Security taxes are 6.2% of the first $128,400 paid to each employee, and FICA Medicare taxes are 1.45% of gross pay. Also, for the first $7,000 paid to each employee, the company's FUTA taxes are 0.6% and SUTA taxes are 5.4%. The company is preparing its payroll calculations for the week ended August 25. Payroll records show the following information for the company's four employees.

	A	B	C	D
1		**Gross Pay**	**Current Week**	
2	**Name**	**through Aug. 18**	**Gross Pay**	**Income Tax Withholding**
3	Dali	$127,300	$2,000	$284
4	Trey	127,500	900	145
5	Kiesha	6,900	450	39
6	Chee	1,250	400	30

In addition to gross pay, the company must pay two-thirds of the $60 per employee weekly health insurance; each employee pays the remaining one-third. The company also contributes an extra 8% of each employee's gross pay (at no cost to employees) to a pension fund.

Required

Compute the following for the week ended August 25 (round amounts to the nearest cent):

1. Each employee's FICA withholdings for Social Security.
2. Each employee's FICA withholdings for Medicare.

Check (3) $176.70

3. Employer's FICA taxes for Social Security.

4. Employer's FICA taxes for Medicare.

5. Employer's FUTA taxes.

6. Employer's SUTA taxes.

7. Each employee's net (take-home) pay.

8. Employer's total payroll-related expense for each employee.

(4) $54.38

(5) $3.00

(7) Total net pay, $2,940.92

On October 29, Lobo Co. began operations by purchasing razors for resale. The razors have a 90-day warranty. When a razor is returned, the company discards it and mails a new one from merchandise inventory to the customer. The company's cost per new razor is $20 and its retail selling price is $75. The company expects warranty costs to equal 8% of dollar sales. The following transactions occurred.

Problem 9-4A
Estimating warranty
expense and liability
P4

Nov. 11   Sold 105 razors for $7,875 cash.

   30   Recognized warranty expense related to November sales with an adjusting entry.

Dec. 9   Replaced 15 razors that were returned under the warranty.

   16   Sold 220 razors for $16,500 cash.

   29   Replaced 30 razors that were returned under the warranty.

   31   Recognized warranty expense related to December sales with an adjusting entry.

Jan. 5   Sold 150 razors for $11,250 cash.

   17   Replaced 50 razors that were returned under the warranty.

   31   Recognized warranty expense related to January sales with an adjusting entry.

Required

1. Prepare journal entries to record these transactions and adjustments.

2. How much warranty expense is reported for November and for December?

3. How much warranty expense is reported for January?

4. What is the balance of the Estimated Warranty Liability account as of December 31?

5. What is the balance of the Estimated Warranty Liability account as of January 31?

Check   (3) $900

(4) $1,050 Cr.

(5) $950 Cr.

Shown here are condensed income statements for two different companies (assume no income taxes).

Problem 9-5A
Computing and analyzing
times interest earned

A1

Miller Company	
Sales	$1,000,000
Variable expenses (80%)	800,000
Income before interest.............	200,000
Interest expense (fixed)	60,000
Net income	$ 140,000

Weaver Company	
Sales	$1,000,000
Variable expenses (60%)	600,000
Income before interest.............	400,000
Interest expense (fixed)	260,000
Net income	$ 140,000

Required

1. Compute times interest earned for Miller Company and for Weaver Company.

2. What happens to each company's net income if sales increase by 30%?

3. What happens to each company's net income if sales increase by 50%?

4. What happens to each company's net income if sales decrease by 10%?

5. What happens to each company's net income if sales decrease by 40%?

Check   (2) Miller net income,
$200,000 (43% increase)

(4) Weaver net income,
$100,000 (29% decrease)

Analysis Component

6. Which company would have a greater ability to pay interest expense if sales were to decrease?

Francisco Company has 10 employees, each of whom earns $2,800 per month and is paid on the last day of each month. All 10 have been employed continuously at this amount since January 1. On March 1, the following accounts and balances exist in its general ledger.

Problem 9-6A[A]
Entries for payroll
transactions
P5

a. FICA—Social Security Taxes Payable, $3,472; FICA—Medicare Taxes Payable, $812. (The balances of these accounts represent total liabilities for *both* the employer's and employees' FICA taxes for the February payroll only.)

b. Employees' Federal Income Taxes Payable, $4,000 (liability for February only).

c. Federal Unemployment Taxes Payable, $336 (liability for January and February together).

d. State Unemployment Taxes Payable, $3,024 (liability for January and February together).

[continued on next page]

The company had the following payroll transactions.

Mar. 15   Issued check payable to Swift Bank, a federal depository bank authorized to accept employers' payments of FICA taxes and employee income tax withholdings. The $8,284 check is in payment of the February FICA and employee income taxes.

Check March 31: Salaries
Payable, $21,858

Mar. 31   Recorded the journal entry for the March salaries payable. Then recorded the cash payment of the March payroll (the company issued checks payable to each employee in payment of the March payroll). The payroll register shows the following summary totals for the March pay period.

	Salaries				Federal	
Office Salaries	Shop Salaries	Gross Pay	FICA Taxes*	Income Taxes	Net Pay
$11,200	$16,800	$28,000	$1,736	$4,000	$21,858
			$ 406		

*FICA taxes are Social Security and Medicare, respectively.

March 31: Dr. Payroll Taxes
Expense, $2,982

Mar. 31   Recorded the employer's payroll taxes resulting from the March payroll. The company has a state unemployment tax rate of 5.4% on the first $7,000 paid to each employee. The federal rate is 0.6%.

April 15: Cr. Cash, $8,284
(Swift Bank)

Apr. 15   Issued check to Swift Bank in payment of the March FICA and employee income taxes.

Apr. 15   Issued check to the State Tax Commission for the January, February, and March state unemployment taxes. Filed the check and the first-quarter tax return with the Commission.

Apr. 30   Issued check payable to Swift Bank in payment of the employer's FUTA taxes for the first quarter of the year.

Apr. 30   Filed Form 941 with the IRS, reporting the FICA taxes and the employees' federal income tax withholdings for the first quarter.

Required

Prepare journal entries to record these transactions and events.

PROBLEM SET B

Warner Co. entered into the following transactions involving short-term liabilities.

Problem 9-1B

Short-term notes payable transactions and entries

P1

Year 1

Apr. 22   Purchased $5,000 of merchandise on credit from Fox-Pro, terms n/30.

May 23   Replaced the April 22 account payable to Fox-Pro with a 60-day, 15% $4,600 note payable along with paying $400 in cash.

July 15   Borrowed $12,000 cash from Spring Bank by signing a 120-day, 10%, $12,000 note payable.

___?___   Paid the amount due on the note to Fox-Pro at maturity.

___?___   Paid the amount due on the note to Spring Bank at maturity.

Dec. 6   Borrowed $8,000 cash from City Bank by signing a 45-day, 9%, $8,000 note payable.

Dec. 31   Recorded an adjusting entry for accrued interest on the note to City Bank.

Year 2

___?___   Paid the amount due on the note to City Bank at maturity.

Required

Check (2) Fox-Pro, $115
(3) $50
(4) $40

1. Determine the maturity date for each of the three notes described.
2. Determine the interest due at maturity for each of the three notes. Assume a 360-day year.
3. Determine the interest expense recorded in the adjusting entry at the end of Year 1.
4. Determine the interest expense recorded in Year 2.
5. Prepare journal entries for all the preceding transactions and events.

Problem 9-2B

Entries for payroll transactions

P2   P3

Tavella Company's first weekly pay period of the year ends on January 8. On that date, Tavella's sales employees earned $34,745, office employees earned $21,225, and delivery employees earned $1,030 in salaries. The employees are to have withheld from their salaries FICA Social Security taxes at the rate of 6.2%, FICA Medicare taxes at the rate of 1.45%, $8,625 of federal income taxes, $1,160 of medical insurance deductions, and $138 of union dues. No employee earned more than $7,000 in the first pay period.

Required

1. Calculate FICA Social Security taxes payable and FICA Medicare taxes payable. Prepare the journal entry to record Tavella Company's January 8 *employee* payroll expenses and liabilities. Round amounts to cents.

2. Prepare the journal entry to record Tavella's *employer* payroll taxes resulting from the January 8 payroll. Tavella's state unemployment tax rate is 5.4% of the first $7,000 paid to each employee. The federal unemployment tax rate is 0.6%. Round amounts to cents.

Check (1) Cr. Salaries Payable, $42,716.50

(2) Dr. Payroll Taxes Expense, $7,780.50

Fishing Guides Co. has four employees. FICA Social Security taxes are 6.2% of the first $128,400 paid to each employee, and FICA Medicare taxes are 1.45% of gross pay. Also, for the first $7,000 paid to each employee, the company's FUTA taxes are 0.6% and SUTA taxes are 5.4%. The company is preparing its payroll calculations for the week ended September 30. Payroll records show the following information for the company's four employees.

Problem 9-3B
Payroll expenses, withholdings, and taxes
P2   P3

	A	B	C	D
1		Gross Pay	Current Week	
2	Name	through Sep. 23	Gross Pay	Income Tax Withholding
3	Ahmed	$126,800	$2,500	$198
4	Carlos	126,885	1,515	182
5	Jun	6,650	475	32
6	Marie	23,700	1,000	68

In addition to gross pay, the company must pay 60% of the $50 per employee weekly health insurance; each employee pays the remaining 40%. The company also contributes an extra 5% of each employee's gross pay (at no cost to employees) to a pension fund.

Required

Compute the following for the week ended September 30 (round amounts to the nearest cent):

1. Each employee's FICA withholdings for Social Security.
2. Each employee's FICA withholdings for Medicare.
3. Employer's FICA taxes for Social Security.
4. Employer's FICA taxes for Medicare.
5. Employer's FUTA taxes.
6. Employer's SUTA taxes.
7. Each employee's net (take-home) pay.
8. Employer's total payroll-related expense for each employee.

Check (3) $284.58

(4) $79.61

(5) $2.10

(7) Total net pay, $4,565.81

On November 10, Lee Co. began operations by purchasing coffee grinders for resale. The grinders have a 60-day warranty. When a grinder is returned, the company discards it and mails a new one from merchandise inventory to the customer. The company's cost per new grinder is $24 and its retail selling price is $50. The company expects warranty costs to equal 10% of dollar sales. The following transactions occurred.

Problem 9-4B
Estimating warranty expense and liability
P4

Nov. 16 Sold 50 grinders for $2,500 cash.
    30 Recognized warranty expense related to November sales with an adjusting entry.
Dec. 12 Replaced six grinders that were returned under the warranty.
    18 Sold 200 grinders for $10,000 cash.
    28 Replaced 17 grinders that were returned under the warranty.
    31 Recognized warranty expense related to December sales with an adjusting entry.

Jan. 7 Sold 40 grinders for $2,000 cash.
    21 Replaced 36 grinders that were returned under the warranty.
    31 Recognized warranty expense related to January sales with an adjusting entry.

Required

1. Prepare journal entries to record these transactions and adjustments.
2. How much warranty expense is reported for November and for December?
3. How much warranty expense is reported for January?
4. What is the balance of the Estimated Warranty Liability account as of December 31?
5. What is the balance of the Estimated Warranty Liability account as of January 31?

Check (3) $200

(4) $698 Cr.

(5) $34 Cr.

Problem 9-5B
Computing and analyzing
times interest earned

A1

Shown here are condensed income statements for two different companies (assume no income taxes).

Ellis Company	
Sales	$240,000
Variable expenses (50%)	120,000
Income before interest.............	120,000
Interest expense (fixed)	90,000
Net income	$ 30,000

Seidel Company	
Sales	$240,000
Variable expenses (75%)	180,000
Income before interest.............	60,000
Interest expense (fixed)	30,000
Net income	$ 30,000

Required

1. Compute times interest earned for Ellis Company and for Seidel Company.

2. What happens to each company's net income if sales increase by 10%?

Check (3) Ellis net income,
$78,000 (160% increase)
(4) Seidel net income,
$18,000 (40% decrease)

3. What happens to each company's net income if sales increase by 40%?

4. What happens to each company's net income if sales decrease by 20%?

5. What happens to each company's net income if sales decrease by 50%?

Analysis Component

6. Which company would have a greater ability to pay interest expense if sales were to decrease?

Problem 9-6B^A
Entries for payroll
transactions

P5

MLS Company has five employees, each of whom earns $1,600 per month and is paid on the last day of each month. All five have been employed continuously at this amount since January 1. On June 1, the following accounts and balances exist in its general ledger.

a. FICA—Social Security Taxes Payable, $992; FICA—Medicare Taxes Payable, $232. (The balances of these accounts represent total liabilities for *both* the employer's and employees' FICA taxes for the May payroll only.)

b. Employees' Federal Income Taxes Payable, $1,050 (liability for May only).

c. Federal Unemployment Taxes Payable, $66 (liability for April and May together).

d. State Unemployment Taxes Payable, $594 (liability for April and May together).

The company had the following payroll transactions.

June 15   Issued check payable to Security Bank, a federal depository bank authorized to accept employers' payments of FICA taxes and employee income tax withholdings. The $2,274 check is in payment of the May FICA and employee income taxes.

Check June 30: Cr. Salaries
Payable, $6,338

30   Recorded the journal entry for the June salaries payable. Then recorded the cash payment of the June payroll (the company issued checks payable to each employee in payment of the June payroll). The payroll register shows the following summary totals for the June pay period.

Salaries				Federal	
Office Salaries	Shop Salaries	Gross Pay	FICA Taxes*	Income Taxes	Net Pay
$3,800	$4,200	$8,000	$496	$1,050	$6,338
			$116		

*FICA taxes are Social Security and Medicare, respectively.

Check June 30: Dr. Payroll
Taxes Expense, $612
July 15: Cr. Cash, $2,274
(Security Bank)

30   Recorded the employer's payroll taxes resulting from the June payroll. The company has a state unemployment tax rate of 5.4% on the first $7,000 paid to each employee. The federal rate is 0.6%.

July 15   Issued check payable to Security Bank in payment of the June FICA and employee income taxes.

15   Issued check to the State Tax Commission for the April, May, and June state unemployment taxes. Filed the check and the second-quarter tax return with the State Tax Commission.

31   Issued check payable to Security Bank in payment of the employer's FUTA taxes for the first quarter of the year.

31   Filed Form 941 with the IRS, reporting the FICA taxes and the employees' federal income tax withholdings for the second quarter.

Required

Prepare journal entries to record the transactions and events.

This serial problem began in Chapter 1 and continues through most of the book. If previous chapter segments were not completed, the serial problem can begin at this point.

SP 9 Review the February 26 and March 25 transactions for **Business Solutions** (SP 4) from Chapter 4.

Feb. 26 The company paid cash to Lyn Addie for eight days' work at $125 per day.
Mar. 25 The company sold merchandise with a $2,002 cost for $2,800 on credit to Wildcat Services, invoice dated March 25.

Required

1. Assume that Lyn Addie is an unmarried employee. Her $1,000 of wages have deductions for FICA Social Security taxes, FICA Medicare taxes, and federal income taxes. Her federal income taxes for this pay period total $159. Compute her net pay for the eight days' work paid on February 26. Round amounts to the nearest cent.

2. Record the journal entry to reflect the payroll payment to Lyn Addie as computed in part 1.

3. Record the journal entry to reflect the (employer) payroll tax expenses for the February 26 payroll payment. Assume Lyn Addie has not met earnings limits for FUTA and SUTA (the FUTA rate is 0.6% and the SUTA rate is 5.4% for the company). Round amounts to the nearest cent.

4. Record the entry(ies) for the merchandise sold on March 25 if a 4% sales tax rate applies.

©Alexander Image/Shutterstock

CP 9 Bug-Off Exterminators provides pest control services and sells extermination products manufactured by other companies. The following six-column table contains the company's unadjusted trial balance as of December 31, 2019.

December 31, 2019	Unadjusted Trial Balance		Adjustments		Adjusted Trial Balance	
Cash	$ 17,000					
Accounts receivable	4,000					
Allowance for doubtful accounts		$ 828				
Merchandise inventory	11,700					
Trucks	32,000					
Accum. depreciation—Trucks		0				
Equipment	45,000					
Accum. depreciation—Equipment		12,200				
Accounts payable		5,000				
Estimated warranty liability		1,400				
Unearned services revenue		0				
Interest payable		0				
Long-term notes payable		15,000				
Common stock		10,000				
Retained earnings		49,700				
Dividends	10,000					
Extermination services revenue		60,000				
Interest revenue		872				
Sales (of merchandise)		71,026				
Cost of goods sold	46,300					
Depreciation expense—Trucks	0					
Depreciation expense—Equipment	0					
Wages expense	35,000					
Interest expense	0					
Rent expense	9,000					
Bad debts expense	0					
Miscellaneous expense	1,226					
Repairs expense	8,000					
Utilities expense	6,800					
Warranty expense	0					
Totals	$226,026	$226,026				

The following information in *a* through *h* applies to the company at the end of the current year.

a. The bank reconciliation as of December 31, 2019, includes the following facts.

Cash balance per bank	$15,100	Deposit in transit................................	$2,450
Cash balance per books..............	17,000	Interest earned (on bank account).................	52
Outstanding checks	1,800	Bank service charges (miscellaneous expense)	15

Reported on the bank statement is a canceled check that the company failed to record. (Information from the bank reconciliation allows you to determine the amount of this check, which is a payment on an account payable.)

b. An examination of customers' accounts shows that accounts totaling $679 should be written off as uncollectible. Using an aging of receivables, the company determines that the ending balance of the Allowance for Doubtful Accounts should be $700.

c. A truck is purchased and placed in service on January 1, 2019. Its cost is being depreciated with the straight-line method using the following facts and estimates.

Original cost........	$32,000	Expected salvage value	$8,000	Useful life (years)	4

d. Two items of equipment (a sprayer and an injector) were purchased and put into service in early January 2017. They are being depreciated with the straight-line method using these facts and estimates.

	Sprayer	Injector
Original cost	$27,000	$18,000
Expected salvage value	$ 3,000	$ 2,500
Useful life (years)	8	5

e. On August 1, 2019, the company is paid $3,840 cash in advance to provide monthly service for an apartment complex for one year. The company began providing the services in August. When the cash was received, the full amount was credited to the Extermination Services Revenue account.

f. The company offers a warranty for the services it sells. The expected cost of providing warranty service is 2.5% of the extermination services revenue of $57,760 for 2019. No warranty expense has been recorded for 2019. All costs of servicing warranties in 2019 were properly debited to the Estimated Warranty Liability account.

g. The $15,000 long-term note is an 8%, five-year, interest-bearing note with interest payable annually on December 31. The note was signed with First National Bank on December 31, 2019.

h. The ending inventory of merchandise is counted and determined to have a cost of $11,700. Bug-Off uses a perpetual inventory system.

Required

1. Use the preceding information to determine amounts for the following items.

Check (1*a*) Reconciled cash bal. $15,750
(1*b*) $551 credit

   a. Correct (reconciled) ending balance of Cash; and the amount of the omitted check.

   b. Adjustment needed to obtain the correct ending balance of the Allowance for Doubtful Accounts.

   c. Depreciation expense for the truck used during year 2019.

   d. Depreciation expense for the two items of equipment used during year 2019.

   e. The adjusted 2019 ending balances of the Extermination Services Revenue and Unearned Services Revenue accounts.

(1*f*) Estimated Warranty Liability, $2,844 Cr.

   f. The adjusted 2019 ending balances of the Warranty Expense and the Estimated Warranty Liability accounts.

   g. The adjusted 2019 ending balances of the Interest Expense and the Interest Payable accounts. (Round amounts to nearest whole dollar.)

(2) Adjusted trial balance totals, $238,207

2. Use the results of part 1 to complete the six-column table by first entering the appropriate adjustments for items *a* through *g* and then completing the Adjusted Trial Balance columns. *Hint:* Item *b* requires two adjustments.

3. Prepare journal entries to record the adjustments entered on the six-column table. Assume Bug-Off's adjusted balance for Merchandise Inventory matches the year-end physical count.

(4) Net income, $9,274; Total assets, $82,771

4. Prepare a single-step income statement, a statement of retained earnings (cash dividends during 2019 were $10,000), and a classified balance sheet.

GL 9-1 General Ledger assignment GL 9-1, based on Problem 9-1A, focuses on transactions related to accounts and notes payable and highlights the impact each transaction has on interest expense, if any. Prepare the journal entries related to accounts and notes payable; the schedules for accounts payable and notes payable are automatically completed using the **General Ledger** tool. Compute both the amount and timing of interest expense for each note. Prepare the subsequent-period journal entries related to accrued interest.

GENERAL LEDGER PROBLEM

Accounting Analysis

AA 9-1 Use the table below and **Apple**'s financial statements in Appendix A to answer the following.

COMPANY ANALYSIS

A1 P4

APPLE

$ millions	2017	2016	2015
Interest expense..........	$2,323	$1,456	$733

1. Compute times interest earned for each of the three years shown.
2. Is Apple in a good or bad position to pay interest obligations? Assume an industry average of 10.
3. Identify Apple's total accrued expenses in 2017.

AA 9-2 Key figures for **Apple** and **Google** follow.

COMPARATIVE ANALYSIS

A1

APPLE
GOOGLE

	Apple			Google		
$ millions	Current Year	One Year Prior	Two Years Prior	Current Year	One Year Prior	Two Years Prior
Net income	$48,351	$45,687	$53,394	$12,662	$19,478	$16,348
Income taxes............	15,738	15,685	19,121	14,531	4,672	3,303
Interest expense.........	2,323	1,456	733	109	124	104

Required

1. Compute times interest earned for the three years' data shown for each company.
2. In the current year, and using times interest earned, which company appears better able to pay interest obligations?
3. In the current year, and using times interest earned, is the company in a good or bad position to pay interest obligations for (*a*) Apple and (*b*) Google? Assume an industry average of 10.

AA 9-3 Comparative figures for **Samsung**, **Apple**, and **Google** follow.

GLOBAL ANALYSIS

A1

Samsung
APPLE
GOOGLE

	Samsung		Apple		Google	
In millions	Current Year	Prior Year	Current Year	Prior Year	Current Year	Prior Year
Net income......................	₩42,186,747	₩22,726,092	$48,351	$45,687	$12,662	$19,478
Income taxes....................	14,009,220	7,987,560	15,738	15,685	14,531	4,672
Interest expense................	655,402	587,831	2,323	1,456	109	124

Required

1. Compute the times interest earned ratio for the most recent two years for Samsung using the data shown.
2. Is the change in Samsung's times interest earned ratio favorable or unfavorable?
3. In the current year, is Samsung's times interest earned ratio better or worse than the same ratio for (*a*) Apple and (*b*) Google?

Beyond the Numbers

ETHICS CHALLENGE

P4

BTN 9-1 Cameron Bly is a sales manager for an automobile dealership. He earns a bonus each year based on revenue from the number of autos sold in the year less related warranty expenses. Actual warranty expenses have varied over the prior 10 years from a low of 3% of an automobile's selling price to a high of 10%. In the past, Bly has tended to estimate warranty expenses on the high end to be conservative. He must work with the dealership's accountant at year-end to arrive at the warranty expense accrual for cars sold each year.

1. Does the warranty accrual decision create any ethical dilemma for Bly?

2. Because warranty expenses vary, what percent do you think Bly should choose for the current year? Justify your response.

COMMUNICATING IN PRACTICE

C3

BTN 9-2 Dusty Johnson is the accounting and finance manager for a manufacturer. At year-end, he must determine how to account for the company's contingencies. His manager, Tom Pretti, objects to Johnson's proposal to recognize an expense and a liability for warranty service on units of a new product introduced in the fourth quarter. Pretti comments, "There's no way we can estimate this warranty cost. We don't owe anyone anything until a product fails and it is returned. Let's report an expense if and when we do any warranty work."

Required

Prepare a one-page memorandum for Johnson to send to Pretti defending his proposal.

TAKING IT TO THE NET

C1   A1

BTN 9-3 Access the March 1, 2017, filing of the December 31, 2016, annual 10-K report of **McDonald's Corporation** (ticker: MCD), which is available from **SEC.gov**.

Required

1. Identify the current liabilities on McDonald's balance sheet as of December 31, 2016.

2. Use the consolidated statement of income for the year ended December 31, 2016, to compute McDonald's times interest earned ratio. Comment on the result. Assume an industry average of 5.0.

TEAMWORK IN ACTION

C2   P1

BTN 9-4 Assume that your team is in business and you must borrow $6,000 cash for short-term needs. You have been shopping banks for a loan, and you have the following two options.

A. Sign a $6,000, 90-day, 10% interest-bearing note dated June 1.

B. Sign a $6,000, 120-day, 8% interest-bearing note dated June 1.

Required

1. Discuss these two options and determine the better choice. Ensure that all teammates concur with the decision and understand the rationale.

2. Each member of the team is to prepare *one* of the following journal entries.

    a. Option A—at date of issuance.

    b. Option B—at date of issuance.

    c. Option A—at maturity date.

    d. Option B—at maturity date.

3. In rotation, each member is to explain to the team the entry he or she prepared in part 2. Ensure that all team members concur with and understand the entries.

4. Assume that the funds are borrowed on December 1 (instead of June 1) and your business operates on a calendar-year reporting period. Each member of the team is to prepare *one* of the following entries.

    a. Option A—the year-end adjustment.

    b. Option B—the year-end adjustment.

    c. Option A—at maturity date.

    d. Option B—at maturity date.

5. In rotation, each member is to explain to the team the entry he or she prepared in part 4. Ensure that all team members concur with and understand the entries.

BTN 9-5 Review the chapter's opening feature about Tim Westergren and the business he founded, **Pandora**. Assume that he is considering expanding the business to Europe and that the current abbreviated income statement appears as follows.

PANDORA Income Statement For Year Ended December 31	
Sales	$1,000,000
Operating expenses (55%)	550,000
Net income	$ 450,000

Assume also that the company currently has no interest-bearing debt. If it expands to Europe, it will require a $300,000 loan. The company has found a bank that will loan it the money on a 7% note payable. The company believes that, at least for the first few years, sales in Europe will equal $250,000 and that all expenses at both locations will continue to equal 55% of sales.

Required

1. Prepare an income statement (showing three separate columns for current operations, European, and total) for the company assuming that it borrows the funds and expands to Europe. Annual revenues for current operations are expected to remain at $1,000,000.
2. Compute the company's times interest earned under the expansion assumptions in part 1.
3. Assume sales in Europe are $400,000. Prepare an income statement (with columns for current operations, European, and total) for the company and compute times interest earned.
4. Assume sales in Europe are $100,000. Prepare an income statement (with columns for current operations, European, and total) for the company and compute times interest earned.
5. Comment on your results from parts 1 through 4.

BTN 9-6 Check the Social Security Administration website (SSA.gov) to locate the Social Security office near you. Visit the office to request a personal earnings and estimate form. Fill out the form and mail according to the instructions. You will receive a statement from the Social Security Administration regarding your earnings history and future Social Security benefits you can receive. (Formerly the request could be made online. The online service has been discontinued and is now under review by the Social Security Administration due to security concerns; however, it might once again be available online.) It is good to request an earnings and benefit statement every 5 to 10 years to make sure you have received credit for all wages earned and for which you and your employer have paid taxes into the system.

HITTING THE ROAD

P2

10 Accounting for Long-Term Liabilities

Chapter Preview

BOND BASICS

A1 Bond financing

Bond trading

P1 Par bonds

NTK 10-1

DISCOUNT BONDS

Discount or premium

P2 Bond payments

Amortize discount

Straight-line

NTK 10-2

PREMIUM BONDS

P3 Bond payments

Amortize premium

Straight-line

P4 Bond retirement

NTK 10-3

LONG-TERM NOTES

C1 Recording notes

DEBT ANALYSIS

A2 Debt features

A3 Debt-to-equity

NTK 10-4

Learning Objectives

CONCEPTUAL

C1 Explain the types of notes and prepare entries to account for notes.

C2 *Appendix 10A*—Explain and compute bond pricing.

C3 *Appendix 10C*—Describe accounting for leases and pensions.

ANALYTICAL

A1 Compare bond financing with stock financing.

A2 Assess debt features and their implications.

A3 Compute the debt-to-equity ratio and explain its use.

PROCEDURAL

P1 Record issuance and interest expense for par bonds.

P2 Record issuance and amortization of discount bonds using the straight-line method.

P3 Record issuance and amortization of premium bonds using the straight-line method.

P4 Record the retirement of bonds.

P5 *Appendix 10B*—Compute and record amortization of a bond discount using the effective interest method.

P6 *Appendix 10B*—Compute and record amortization of a bond premium using the effective interest method.

At Face Value

"Believe in your product"—**SCOTT BORBA**

OAKLAND, CA—Joey Shamah, a college student, met Scott Borba at a party. The two men talked at length, but it was not your typical "party" talk. Instead, they discussed the women's cosmetics market!

Scott explains that he saw "all these women with Louis Vuitton purses . . . buying truckloads of lip balms and nail polishes" from 99 cent stores. "There's a major market here," insists Scott.

Joey and Scott agreed to work together to fill this market void by forming **e.l.f. Cosmetics** (**elfCosmetics.com**). "We felt women shouldn't have to skip lunch or not go out for dinner or have other cutbacks to afford makeup," recalls Joey.

As e.l.f. grows, Joey and Scott make decisions on how to finance that growth. Up to now, they have used a mix of long-term debt and equity.

Financing a large part of their business with long-term debt requires that Joey and Scott carefully manage liabilities. This is especially true with long-term financing from sources such as notes and bonds. They also know that retaining more equity in the business helped them personally when e.l.f. issued stock.

©Clemens Bilan/Douglas/Getty Images

Joey and Scott welcome the financial rewards, yet they insist e.l.f. is about making the consumer feel more confident. "The consumer feels better inside" from using e.l.f. products, claims Scott. "There's more of a glimmer."

Sources: *e.l.f. Cosmetics website*, January 2019; *CNN*, January 2006

BASICS OF BONDS

This section explains bonds and reasons for issuing them. Both for-profit and nonprofit companies, as well as governmental units, such as nations, states, cities, and schools, issue bonds.

Bond Financing

Projects that need a lot of money often are financed with bonds. A **bond** is its issuer's written promise to pay the par value of the bond with interest. The **par value of a bond,** or *face value,* is paid at a stated future date called the *maturity date.* Most bonds require the issuer to make semiannual (twice a year) interest payments. Interest is computed by multiplying the par value by the bond's contract rate.

A1

Compare bond financing with stock financing.

Advantages of Bonds   There are three main advantages of bond financing.

1. *Bonds do not affect owner control.* Equity affects ownership in a company, but bonds do not. A person who contributes $1,000 of a company's $10,000 equity financing typically controls one-tenth of the company. A person who owns a $1,000, 11%, 20-year bond has no ownership.

2. *Interest on bonds is tax deductible.* Bond interest payments are tax deductible, but distributions to owners are not. A corporation with no bond financing, $15,000 in pretax income, and a 40% tax rate pays $6,000 ($15,000 × 40%) in taxes. Instead, if it issues bonds and pays $10,000 in bond interest expense, then taxes paid are only $2,000 ([$15,000 − $10,000] × 40%).

3. *Bonds can increase return on equity.* A company that earns a higher return with borrowed funds than it pays in interest on those funds increases its return on equity. This process is called *financial leverage,* or *trading on the equity.*

To demonstrate the third point, consider Magnum Co., which has $1,000 in equity and is planning a $500 expansion ($ millions). Magnum predicts the expansion will increase income by $125 before paying interest. It currently earns $100 per year and has no interest expense. Magnum is considering three plans. Plan A is to not expand. Plan B is to expand and raise $500 from equity financing. Plan C is to expand and issue $500 of bonds that pay 10% annual interest ($50). Exhibit 10.1 shows how these plans affect net income, equity, and return on equity (Net

EXHIBIT 10.1

Financing with Bonds versus Equity

$ millions	Plan A: Do Not Expand	Plan B: Equity Financing	Plan C: Bond Financing
Income before interest expense	$ 100	$ 225	$ 225
Interest expense	—	—	(50)
Net income	**$ 100**	**$ 225**	**$ 175**
Equity	$1,000	$1,500	$1,000
Return on equity	**10.0%**	**15.0%**	**17.5%**

Example: Compute return on equity for all three plans if Magnum is subject to a 40% income tax. *Answer* ($ mil.):

A = 6.0% ($100[1 − 0.4]/$1,000)

B = 9.0% ($225[1 − 0.4]/$1,500)

C = 10.5% ($175[1 − 0.4]/$1,000)

income/Equity). Magnum earns a higher return on equity under Plan C to issue bonds. Income under Plan C ($175) is smaller than under Plan B ($225), but the return on equity is larger because of less equity investment.

Disadvantages of Bonds

There are two main disadvantages of bond financing.

1. *Bonds can decrease return on equity.* When a company earns a lower return with the borrowed funds than it pays in interest, it decreases return on equity. This is more likely when a company has low income or losses.

Point: There are nearly 5 million individual U.S. bond issues, compared to about 12,000 individual U.S. stocks.

2. *Bonds require payment of both periodic interest and the par value at maturity.* Bond payments are a burden when income and cash flow are low. Equity does not require payments because withdrawals (dividends) are optional.

EXHIBIT 10.2

Bond Certificate

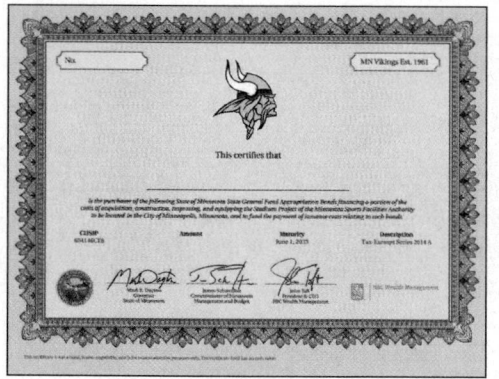

Courtesy of RBC Wealth Management

Bond Issuing

Bond issuances state the number of bonds authorized, their par value, and the contract interest rate. The legal contract between the issuer and the bondholders is called the **bond indenture.** A bondholder may receive a **bond certificate,** which is evidence of the company's debt—see Exhibit 10.2.

Bond Trading

A bond *issue* is the sale of bonds, usually in denominations of $1,000 or $5,000. After bonds are issued, they often are bought and sold among investors, meaning that a bond probably has had many owners before it matures. When bonds are bought and sold, they have a market value (price). Bond market values are shown as a percent of par (face) value. For example, a bond trading at 103½ is bought or sold for 103.5% of par value. A bond trading at 95 is bought or sold at 95% of par value.

Point: A bond with a par value of $1,000 trading at 103½ sells for $1,035 ($1,000 × 1.035).

■ Decision Insight

Quotes The **IBM** bond quote here is interpreted (left to right) as **Bonds,** issuer name; **Rate,** contract interest rate (4%); **Mat,** matures in year 2042 when principal is paid; **Yld,** yield rate (3.81%) of bond at current price; **Vol,** dollar worth ($110,000) of trades (in 1,000s); **Close,** closing price (103.08) for the day as percentage of par value; **Chg,** change (+0.73%) in closing price from prior day's close. ■

Bonds	Rate	Mat	Yld	Vol	Close	Chg
IBM	4	42	3.81	110	103.08	+0.73%

PAR BONDS

P1

Record issuance and interest expense for par bonds.

Bonds issued at par value are called **par bonds.** Assume **Nike** issues $100,000 of 8%, two-year bonds dated December 31, 2019, that mature on December 31, 2021, and pay interest semiannually each June 30 and December 31. If all bonds are sold at par value, Nike records the sale as follows.

Assets = Liabilities + Equity
+100,000   +100,000

Dec. 31, 2019	Cash	100,000	
	Bonds Payable		100,000
	Sold bonds at par.		

Nike records the first semiannual interest payment as follows. The same entry is made *every* six months, including at the maturity date.

June 30, 2020	Bond Interest Expense.............................	4,000	
	Cash..		4,000
	Paid semiannual interest (8% × $100,000 × 1/2 year).		

Assets = Liabilities + Equity
−4,000   −4,000

When the bonds mature, Nike records its payment of principal as follows.

Dec. 31, 2021	Bonds Payable	100,000	
	Cash..		100,000
	Paid bond principal at maturity.		

Assets = Liabilities + Equity
−100,000   −100,000

A company issues 8%, two-year bonds on December 31, 2019, with a par value of $7,000 and semiannual interest payments. On the issue date, the annual market rate for these bonds is 8%, which implies a selling price of $7,000. Prepare journal entries to record (a) the issuance of bonds on December 31, 2019; (b) the first through fourth interest payments on each June 30 and December 31; and (c) the maturity of the bonds on December 31, 2021.

NEED-TO-KNOW 10-1

Recording Par Value Bonds

P1

Solution

a.

Dec. 31, 2019	Cash	7,000	
	Bonds Payable.................................		7,000
	Sold bonds at par.		

b. The following entry is made for each of the four interest payments of June 30 and December 31 for both 2020 and 2021.

2020–2021	Bond Interest Expense.............................	280	
June 30 and	Cash..		280
Dec. 31	*Pay semiannual interest ($7,000 × 8% × 1/2).*		

c.

Dec. 31, 2021	Bonds Payable	7,000	
	Cash..		7,000
	Record maturity and payment of bonds.		

Do More: QS 10-2, QS 10-3, E 10-2, E 10-3

DISCOUNT BONDS

This section covers bond issuances *below par,* called **discount bonds**.

Bond Discount or Premium

The bond issuer pays the bond interest rate, called the **contract rate** (also called *coupon rate, stated rate,* or *nominal rate*). The annual interest paid is computed by multiplying the bond par value by the contract rate. The contract rate is usually stated on an annual basis, even if interest is paid semiannually. For example, a $1,000, 8% bond paying interest semiannually pays annual interest of $80 (8% × $1,000) in two semiannual payments of $40 each.

The contract rate sets the interest paid in *cash,* which is not necessarily the *bond interest expense* for the issuer. Bond interest expense depends on the bond's market value at issuance. The bond's **market rate** of interest is the rate that borrowers are willing to pay and lenders are willing to accept for a bond and its risk level. As bond risk increases, the market rate increases to compensate bond purchasers.

EXHIBIT 10.3

Relation between Bond Issue Price, Contract Rate, and Market Rate

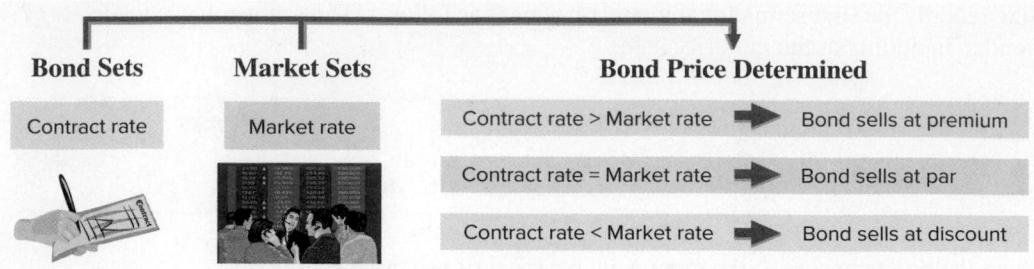

Bond Sets	Market Sets	Bond Price Determined	
Contract rate	Market rate	Contract rate > Market rate ➡	Bond sells at premium
		Contract rate = Market rate ➡	Bond sells at par
		Contract rate < Market rate ➡	Bond sells at discount

When the contract rate and market rate are equal, a bond sells at par value. If they are not equal, it is sold at a *premium* above par value or at a *discount* below par value. Exhibit 10.3 shows the relation between the contract rate, the market rate, and a bond's issue price.

Issuing Bonds at a Discount

P2

Record issuance and amortization of discount bonds using the straight-line method.

A **discount on bonds payable** occurs when a company issues bonds with a contract rate less than the market rate. This means the issue price is less than par value—the issuer gets less money at issuance than what the issuer must pay back at maturity. Assume **Fila** issues bonds with a $100,000 par value, an 8% annual contract rate (paid semiannually), and a two-year life. These bonds sell at a discount price of 96.400 (meaning 96.400% of par value, or $96,400); we show how to compute bond prices in Appendix 10A.

Cash Payments with Discount Bonds   These bonds require Fila to pay

1. Par value of $100,000 cash at the end of the bonds' two-year life.
2. Semiannual cash interest payments of $4,000 ($100,000 × 8% × 1/2 year).

The pattern of cash receipts and payments for Fila bonds is shown in Exhibit 10.4.

EXHIBIT 10.4

Discount Bond Cash Receipts and Payments

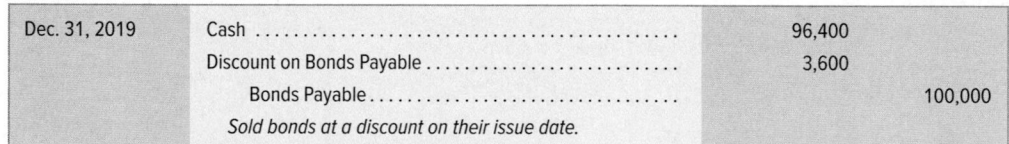

Recording Issuance of Discount Bonds   When Fila accepts $96,400 cash for its bonds on the issue date of December 31, 2019, it records the sale as follows.

Assets = Liabilities + Equity
+96,400   +100,000
          −3,600

Dec. 31, 2019	Cash	96,400	
	Discount on Bonds Payable	3,600	
	Bonds Payable...............................		100,000
	Sold bonds at a discount on their issue date.		

Point: Book value at issuance always equals the issuer's cash borrowed.

Bonds payable are reported as a long-term liability on Fila's December 31, 2019, balance sheet as in Exhibit 10.5. A discount is subtracted from par value to get the **carrying (book) value of bonds.** Discount on Bonds Payable is a contra liability account.

EXHIBIT 10.5

Balance Sheet Presentation of Bond Discount

Long-term liabilities
Bonds payable, 8%, due December 31, 2021 .... $100,000
Less discount on bonds payable......................   3,600 $96,400 ◀ [Carrying (book) value]

Amortizing Discount Bonds   Fila receives $96,400 for its bonds; in return it must pay bondholders $100,000 when the bonds mature in two years (plus four interest payments). Panel A in Exhibit 10.6 shows that the four $4,000 interest payments plus the $3,600 bond discount equals total bond interest expense of $19,600.

The total $19,600 bond interest expense is allocated over the four semiannual periods in the bonds' life, and the bonds' carrying value is updated at each balance sheet date. This is done using

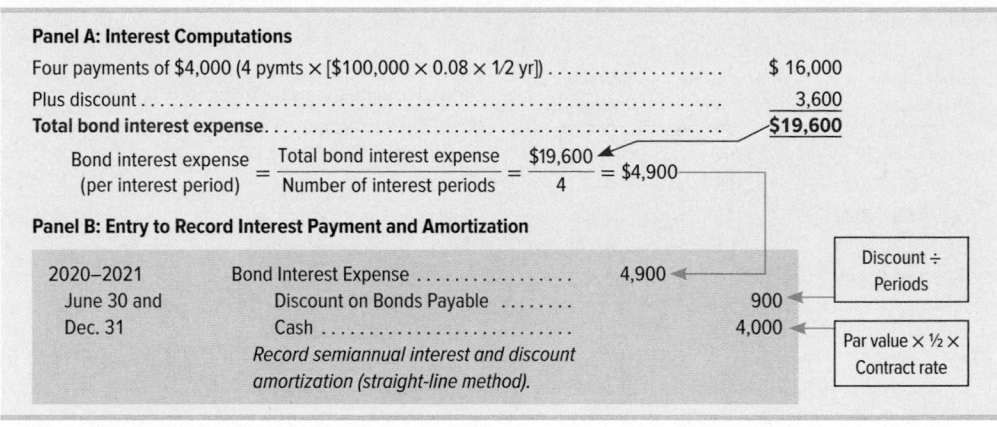

Panel A: Interest Computations

Four payments of $4,000 (4 pymts × [$100,000 × 0.08 × 1⁄2 yr]) . . . . $ 16,000

Plus discount   3,600

Total bond interest expense $19,600

$$\text{Bond interest expense (per interest period)} = \frac{\text{Total bond interest expense}}{\text{Number of interest periods}} = \frac{\$19,600}{4} = \$4,900$$

Panel B: Entry to Record Interest Payment and Amortization

2020–2021	Bond Interest Expense	4,900	
June 30 and	Discount on Bonds Payable		900
Dec. 31	Cash		4,000
	Record semiannual interest and discount amortization (straight-line method).		

Discount ÷ Periods

Par value × ½ × Contract rate

EXHIBIT 10.6

Interest Computation and Entry for Discount Bonds

Bonds Payable

	12/31/2019	100,000
	6/30/2020	—
	12/31/2020	—
	6/30/2021	—
12/31/2021 100,000		
	12/31/2021	0

Discount on Bonds Payable

12/31/2019 3,600		
	6/30/2020	900
	12/31/2020	900
	6/30/2021	900
	12/31/2021	900
	12/31/2021	0

the straight-line method (or the effective interest method in Appendix 10B). Both methods reduce the bond discount to zero over the bond life. This process is called *amortizing a bond discount*.

Straight-Line Method   **Straight-line bond amortization** allocates equal bond interest expense to each interest period. We divide the total bond interest expense of $19,600 by 4 (number of semiannual periods in bonds' life). This gives a bond interest expense of $4,900 per period. Panel B of Exhibit 10.6 shows how the issuer records bond interest expense and updates the bond liability account at the end of *each* of the four semiannual interest periods (June 30, 2020, through December 31, 2021).

Exhibit 10.7 shows the pattern of decreases in the Discount on Bonds Payable account and the pattern of increases in the bonds' carrying value. Three points summarize the discount bonds' straight-line amortization.

Point: Another way to compute bond interest expense: (1) Divide the $3,600 discount by 4 periods to get $900 amortized each period. (2) Add $900 to the $4,000 cash payment to get bond interest expense of $4,900 per period.

EXHIBIT 10.7

Straight-Line Amortization of Bond Discount

Semiannual Period-End	Unamortized Discount*	Carrying Value†
(0) 12/31/2019	$3,600	$ 96,400
(1) 6/30/2020	2,700	97,300
(2) 12/31/2020	1,800	98,200
(3) 6/30/2021	900	99,100
(4) **12/31/2021**	**0**	**100,000**

The columns always sum to par value for discount bonds.

*Total bond discount of $3,600 less accumulated periodic amortization of $900 per semiannual interest period.

†Bond par value of $100,000 less unamortized discount.

1. At issuance, the $96,400 carrying value equals the $100,000 par value minus the $3,600 unamortized discount.

2. During the bonds' life, the (unamortized) discount decreases each period by the $900 amortization ($3,600/4), and carrying value (par value less unamortized discount) increases each period by $900.

3. At maturity, unamortized discount equals zero, and carrying value equals the $100,000 par value that the issuer pays the holder.

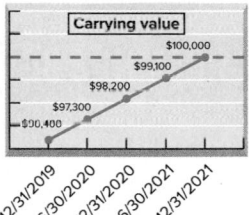

Point: Amortization always gets the carrying value of a bond closer to its par value.

■ **Decision Insight** ━━━━━━━━━━━━━━━━━━━

Ratings Game   Many bond buyers rely on rating services such as **Standard & Poor's**, **Moody's**, and **Fitch** to assess bond risk. These services analyze financial statements and other factors in setting ratings. Standard & Poor's ratings, from best quality to default, are AAA, AA, A, BBB, BB, B, CCC, CC, C, and D. Bonds rated in the A and B range are referred to as *investment grade;* lower-rated bonds are considered riskier. ■

A company issues 8%, two-year bonds on December 31, 2019, with a par value of $7,000 and semiannual interest payments. On the issue date, the annual market rate for these bonds is 10%, which implies a selling price of 96.46 or $6,752. (a) Prepare an amortization table like Exhibit 10.7 for these bonds; use the straight-line method to amortize the discount. Then prepare journal entries to record (b) the issuance of bonds on December 31, 2019; (c) the first through fourth interest payments on each June 30 and December 31; and (d) the maturity of the bonds on December 31, 2021.

NEED-TO-KNOW 10-2

Recording Discount Bonds

P2

Solution

a.

Semiannual Period-End		Unamortized Discount	Carrying Value
(0)	12/31/2019....	$248	$6,752
(1)	6/30/2020....	186	6,814
(2)	12/31/2020....	124	6,876
(3)	6/30/2021....	62	6,938
(4)	12/31/2021 ...	0	7,000

Interest computations for solutions a, b, and c

Four interest payments of $280	
(4 pymts × [$7,000 × 0.08 × 1/2 yr])	$1,120
Plus discount	248
Total bond interest expense................	$1,368
Divided by number of periods	÷ 4
Bond interest expense per period...........	$ 342

Point: Straight-line amortization is GAAP when the effect of using it approximates effective interest amortization.

Bonds Payable

	12/31/2019	7,000	
	6/30/2020	—	
	12/31/2020	—	
	6/30/2021	—	
12/31/2021 7,000			
	12/31/2021	0	

Discount on Bonds Payable

12/31/2019 248			
	6/30/2020	62	
	12/31/2020	62	
	6/30/2021	62	
	12/31/2021	62	
	12/31/2021	0	

Do More: QS 10-5, QS 10-7, QS 10-8, E 10-4, E 10-5, E 10-6, P 10-1

b.

Dec. 31, 2019	Cash	6,752	
	Discount on Bonds Payable............................	248	
	Bonds Payable		7,000
	Sold bonds at discount.		

c. The following entry is made for each of the four interest payments on June 30 and December 31 for both 2020 and 2021.

2020–2021	Bond Interest Expense	342	
June 30 and	Discount on Bonds Payable*		62
Dec. 31	Cash†		280
	Pay semiannual interest and record amortization.		

*$248/4   †$7,000 × 8% × 1/2

d.

Dec. 31, 2021	Bonds Payable	7,000	
	Cash		7,000
	Record maturity and payment of bonds.		

PREMIUM BONDS

This section covers bond issuances *above par,* called **premium bonds.**

Issuing Bonds at a Premium

P3

Record issuance and amortization of premium bonds using the straight-line method.

When the contract rate is higher than the market rate, the bonds sell at a price higher than par value—the issuer gets more money at issuance than what the issuer must pay back at maturity. The amount by which the bond price exceeds par value is the **premium on bonds.** Assume **Adidas** issues bonds with a $100,000 par value, a 12% annual contract rate, semiannual interest payments, and a two-year life. The Adidas bonds sell at a premium price of 103.600 (meaning 103.600% of par value, or $103,600); we show how to compute bond prices in Appendix 10A.

Cash Payments with Premium Bonds   These bonds require Adidas to pay

Point: Contract rate *yields* cash interest payment. **Market** rate *yields* interest expense.

1. Par value of $100,000 cash at the end of the bonds' two-year life.
2. Semiannual cash interest payments of $6,000 ($100,000 × 12% × 1/2 year).

The pattern of cash receipts and payments for Adidas bonds is shown in Exhibit 10.8.

EXHIBIT 10.8

Premium Bond Cash Receipts and Payments

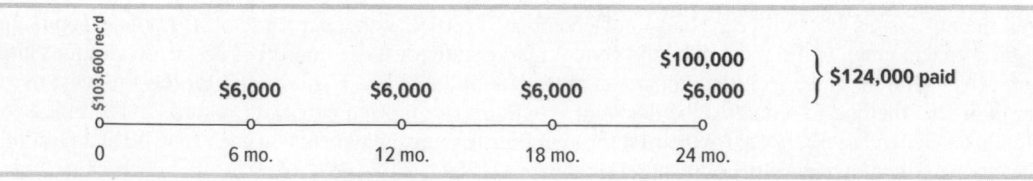

Recording Issuance of Premium Bonds

When Adidas receives $103,600 cash for its bonds on the issue date of December 31, 2019, it records this as follows.

Dec. 31, 2019	Cash	103,600	
	Premium on Bonds Payable		3,600
	Bonds Payable................................		100,000
	Sold bonds at a premium on their issue date.		

Assets = Liabilities + Equity
+103,600   +100,000
                +3,600

Bonds payable are reported as a long-term liability on Adidas's December 31, 2019, balance sheet as in Exhibit 10.9. A premium is added to par value to get the carrying (book) value of bonds. Premium on Bonds Payable is an adjunct ("add-on") liability account.

Long-term liabilities		
Bonds payable, 12%, due December 31, 2021.............	$100,000	
Plus premium on bonds payable.......................	**3,600**	$103,600

EXHIBIT 10.9

Balance Sheet Presentation of Bond Premium

Amortizing Premium Bonds

Adidas receives $103,600 for its bonds. In return, it pays bondholders $100,000 after two years (plus four interest payments). Panel A of Exhibit 10.10 shows that the four $6,000 interest payments minus the $3,600 bond premium equals total bond interest expense of $20,400. The premium is subtracted because it reduces the issuer's cost. Total bond interest expense is allocated over the four semiannual periods using the straight-line method (or the effective interest method in Appendix 10B).

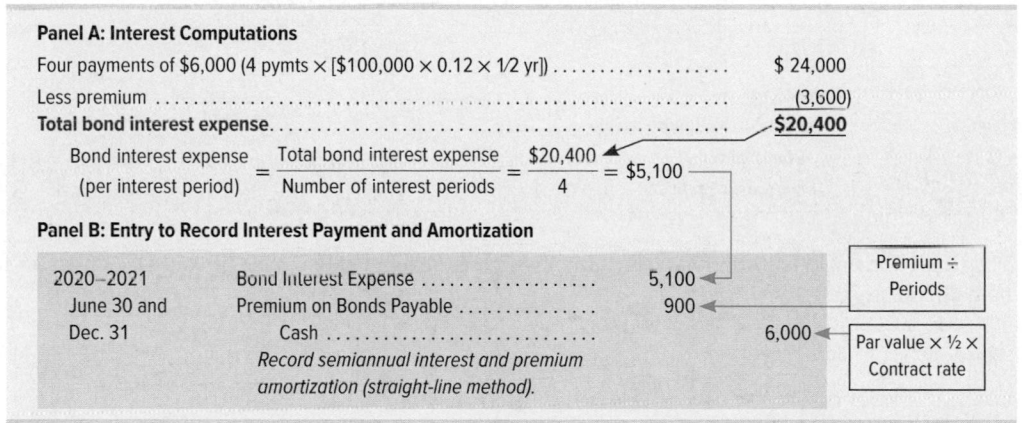

Panel A: Interest Computations

Four payments of $6,000 (4 pymts × [$100,000 × 0.12 × 1/2 yr])	$ 24,000
Less premium	(3,600)
Total bond interest expense..	**$20,400**

$$\frac{\text{Bond interest expense}}{\text{(per interest period)}} = \frac{\text{Total bond interest expense}}{\text{Number of interest periods}} = \frac{\$20,400}{4} = \$5,100$$

Panel B: Entry to Record Interest Payment and Amortization

2020–2021	Bond Interest Expense	5,100	
June 30 and	Premium on Bonds Payable	900	
Dec. 31	Cash		6,000
	Record semiannual interest and premium		
	amortization (straight-line method).		

Premium ÷ Periods

Par value × 1/2 × Contract rate

EXHIBIT 10.10

Interest Computation and Entry for Premium Bonds

Bonds Payable

		12/31/2019	100,000
		6/30/2020	—
		12/31/2020	—
		6/30/2021	—
12/31/2021	100,000		
		12/31/2021	0

Premium on Bonds Payable

		12/31/2019	3,600
6/30/2020	900		
12/31/2020	900		
6/30/2021	900		
12/31/2021	900		
		12/31/2021	0

Straight-Line Method

The straight-line method allocates equal bond interest expense to each semiannual interest period. We divide the total bond interest expense of $20,400 by 4 (number of semiannual periods in bonds' life). This gives bond interest expense of $5,100 per period. Panel B of Exhibit 10.10 shows how Adidas records bond interest expense and updates the balance of the bond liability account for *each* semiannual period (June 30, 2020, through December 31, 2021).

Exhibit 10.11 shows the pattern of decreases in the unamortized Premium on Bonds Payable account and

Point: A premium decreases Bond Interest Expense; a discount increases it.

EXHIBIT 10.11

Straight-Line Amortization of Bond Premium

Semiannual Period-End	Unamortized Premium*	Carrying Value†
(0) 12/31/2019	$3,600	$103,600
(1) 6/30/2020	2,700	102,700
(2) 12/31/2020	1,800	101,800
(3) 6/30/2021	900	100,900
(4) 12/31/2021	0	100,000

During the bond life, carrying value is adjusted to par and the amortized premium to zero.

*Total bond premium of $3,600 less accumulated periodic amortization of $900 per semiannual interest period.

†Bond par value of $100,000 plus unamortized premium.

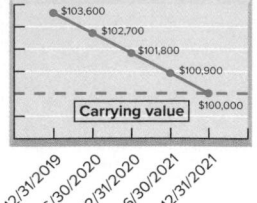

in the bonds' carrying value. Three points summarize straight-line amortization of premium bonds.

1. At issuance, the $103,600 carrying value equals the $100,000 par value plus the $3,600 unamortized premium.
2. During the bonds' life, the (unamortized) premium decreases each period by the $900 amortization ($3,600/4), and carrying value decreases each period by the same $900.
3. At maturity, unamortized premium equals zero, and carrying value equals the $100,000 par value that the issuer pays the holder.

NEED-TO-KNOW 10-3

Recording Premium Bonds

P3

A company issues 8%, two-year bonds on December 31, 2019, with a par value of $7,000 and semiannual interest payments. On the issue date, the annual market rate for these bonds is 6%, which implies a selling price of 103.71 or $7,260. (a) Prepare an amortization table like Exhibit 10.11 for these bonds; use the straight-line method to amortize the premium. Then prepare journal entries to record (b) the issuance of bonds on December 31, 2019; (c) the first through fourth interest payments on each June 30 and December 31; and (d) the maturity of the bonds on December 31, 2021.

Solution

a.

Semiannual Period-End	Unamortized Premium	Carrying Value
(0) 12/31/2019....	$260	$7,260
(1) 6/30/2020....	195	7,195
(2) 12/31/2020....	130	7,130
(3) 6/30/2021....	65	7,065
(4) 12/31/2021....	0	7,000

Interest computations for solutions *a, b,* and *c*	
Four interest payments of $280	
(4 pymts × [$7,000 × 0.08 × 1/2 yr])	$1,120
Less premium	260
Total bond interest expense..............	$ 860
Divided by number of periods	÷ 4
Bond interest expense per period.........	$ 215

Bonds Payable

	12/31/2019	7,000
	6/30/2020	—
	12/31/2020	—
	6/30/2021	—
12/31/2021 7,000		
	12/31/2021	0

b.

Dec. 31, 2019	Cash..	7,260	
	Premium on Bonds Payable		260
	Bonds Payable		7,000
	Sold bonds at premium.		

Premium on Bonds Payable

	12/31/2019	260
6/30/2020 65		
12/31/2020 65		
6/30/2021 65		
12/31/2021 65		
	12/31/2021	0

c. The following entry is made for each of the four interest payments on June 30 and December 31 for both 2020 and 2021.

2020–2021	Bond Interest Expense	215	
June 30 and	Premium on Bonds Payable*	65	
Dec. 31	Cash†		280
	Pay semiannual interest and record amortization.		

*$260/4   †$7,000 × 8% × 1/2

d.

Dec. 31, 2021	Bonds Payable	7,000	
	Cash		7,000
	Record maturity and payment of bonds.		

Do More: QS 10-9, E 10-8, E 10-9, P 10-2, P 10-3

Bond Retirement

P4 _____

Record the retirement of bonds.

This section covers the retirement of bonds.

Bond Retirement at Maturity   The carrying value of bonds at maturity always equals par value. For example, both Exhibits 10.7 (a discount) and 10.11 (a premium) show that the carrying value of bonds at maturity equals par value ($100,000). Retirement of these bonds at maturity, assuming interest is already paid and recorded, is as follows.

Dec. 31, 2021	Bonds Payable.....................................	100,000	
	Cash...		100,000
	Record retirement of bonds at maturity.		

Assets = Liabilities + Equity
−100,000 −100,000

Bond Retirement before Maturity

Issuers sometimes retire some or all of their bonds before maturity. If interest rates decline, an issuer may want to replace high-interest-paying bonds with new low-interest bonds. There are two common ways to retire bonds before maturity.

Point: Bond retirement is also called *bond redemption.*

- **Exercise a call option.** An issuer can reserve the right to retire bonds early by issuing *callable bonds.* This gives the issuer an option to *call* the bonds before they mature by paying the par value plus a *call premium.*
- **Open market purchase.** The issuer can repurchase them from bondholders at current market price.

Whether bonds are called or purchased, the issuer is likely to pay a price different from their carrying value. The issuer records a difference between the bonds' carrying value and the amount paid as a gain or loss. Assume that **Puma** issued callable bonds with a par value of $100,000. The call option requires Puma to pay a call premium of $3,000 to bondholders plus the par value. Next, assume that after the June 30 interest payment, the bonds have a carrying value of $104,500. Then on July 1, Puma calls these bonds and pays $103,000 to bondholders. Puma records a $1,500 gain from the difference between the bonds' carrying value of $104,500 and the retirement price of $103,000 as follows.

July 1	Bonds Payable.....................................	100,000	
	Premium on Bonds Payable	4,500	
	Gain on Bond Retirement.........................		1,500
	Cash..		103,000
	Record retirement of bonds before maturity.		

Assets = Liabilities + Equity
−103,000 −100,000 +1,500
              −4,500

Convertible Bond

Bond Retirement by Conversion

Holders of *convertible bonds* have the right to convert their bonds to stock. When conversion occurs, the bonds' carrying value is transferred to equity accounts and no gain or loss is recorded. (Convertible bonds are described further in the Decision Analysis section of this chapter.) Assume that on January 1 the $100,000 par value bonds of **Converse**, with a carrying value of $100,000, are converted to 15,000 shares of $2 par value common stock. The entry to record this conversion follows (market prices of the bonds and stock are *not* relevant to this entry).

Jan. 1	Bonds Payable.....................................	100,000	
	Common Stock		30,000
	Paid-In Capital in Excess of Par Value		70,000
	Record retirement of bonds by conversion.		

Assets = Liabilities + Equity
−100,000 +30,000
              +70,000

■ **Decision Insight** ━━━━━━━━━━━━━━━━━━━━━━━━━━━━

Junk Bonds Junk bonds are company bonds with low credit ratings due to a higher likelihood of nonpayment. On the upside, the high risk of junk bonds can yield high returns if the issuer repays its debt. Investors in junk bonds identify and buy bonds with low credit ratings when they believe those bonds will survive and pay their debts. Financial statements are used to identify junk bonds that are better than what their ratings would suggest. ■

LONG-TERM NOTES PAYABLE

C1
Explain the types of notes and prepare entries to account for notes.

Like bonds, notes are issued in exchange for assets such as cash. Unlike bonds, notes are usually issued to a *single* lender such as a bank. An issuer initially records a note at its selling price—the note's face value minus any discount or plus any premium. Over the note's life, the amount of interest expense allocated to each period is computed by multiplying the market rate (at issuance of the note) by the beginning-of-period note balance. The note's carrying (book) value at any time equals its face value minus any unamortized discount or plus any unamortized premium.

Installment Notes

An **installment note** is a liability requiring a series of payments to the lender. Installment notes are common for franchises and other businesses when lenders and borrowers agree to spread payments over time.

Issuance of Notes   Assume Foghog borrows $60,000 from a bank to purchase equipment. It signs an 8% installment note requiring three annual payments of principal plus interest. Foghog records the note's issuance at January 1, 2019, as follows.

Assets = Liabilities + Equity
+60,000   +60,000

Jan. 1	Cash	60,000	
	Notes Payable..................................		60,000
	Borrowed $60,000 by signing 8%, three-year note.		

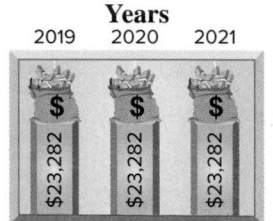
Years
2019   2020   2021
$23,282 $23,282 $23,282

Payments of Principal and Interest   Payments on an installment note include accrued interest expense plus part of the amount borrowed (the *principal*). For this section, let's consider an installment note with equal payments. The equal total payments pattern has changing amounts of both interest and principal. Foghog borrows $60,000 by signing a $60,000 note that requires three *equal payments* of $23,282 at each year-end. Exhibit 10.12 shows the pattern of equal total payments and its two parts, interest and principal. Column A shows the note's beginning balance. Column B shows accrued interest at 8% of the beginning note balance. Column C shows the portion that reduces the principal owed, which equals total payment in column D minus interest expense in column B. Column E shows the note's year-end balance.

EXHIBIT 10.12

Installment Note:
Equal Total Payments
Amortization Schedule

Point: Installment note payments.

	A	B
1	Rate per period	8%
2	Number of periods	3
3	Loan amount	$60,000
4	Loan payments	←

=−PMT(B1,B2,B3)=$23,282

Point: Principal portion of note payments.

	A	B
1	Rate per period	8%
2	Number of periods	3
3	Loan amount	$60,000
4	Period	Principal
5	1	←
6	2	←
7	3	←

=−PPMT(B1,A5,B2,B3)=$18,482
=−PPMT(B1,A6,B2,B3)=$19,961
=−PPMT(B1,A7,B2,B3)=$21,557

			Payments		
	(A)	**(B)** Debit Interest Expense	+	**(C)** Debit Notes Payable	=	**(D)** Credit Cash	**(E)** Ending Balance
Period Ending Date	**Beginning Balance**	**8% × (A)**		**(D) − (B)**		**(computed)**	**(A) − (C)**
(1) **12/31/2019**	**$60,000**	**$4,800**		**$ 18,482**		**$23,282**	**$41,518**
(2) 12/31/2020	41,518	3,321		19,961		23,282	21,557
(3) 12/31/2021	21,557	1,725		21,557		23,282	0
		$9,846		**$60,000**		**$69,846**	

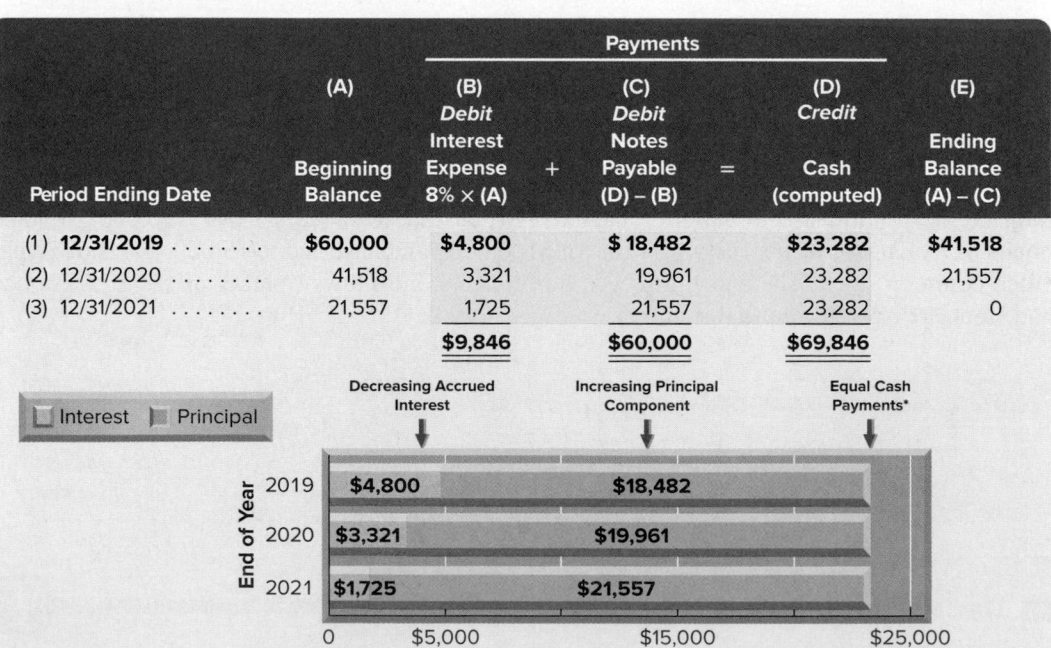

☐ Interest ■ Principal

Decreasing Accrued Interest   Increasing Principal Component   Equal Cash Payments*

End of Year
2019 $4,800 | $18,482
2020 $3,321 | $19,961
2021 $1,725 | $21,557

0   $5,000 $15,000 $25,000

*Table B.3 in Appendix B is used to compute the dollar amount of three payments that equal the initial note balance of $60,000 at 8% interest. We go to Table B.3, row 3, and across to the 8% column, where the present value factor is 2.5771. The dollar amount is then computed by solving the following equation. The amount is computed by dividing $60,000 by 2.5771, yielding $23,282.

Table	Present Value Factor		Dollar Amount		Present Value
B.3	2.5771	×	?	=	$60,000

The three $23,282 cash payments are equal, but accrued interest decreases each year because the principal balance of the note decreases. As the amount of interest decreases each year, the portion of each payment applied to principal increases. This pattern is shown in the lower part of Exhibit 10.12. Foghog uses the amounts in Exhibit 10.12 to record its first two payments (for years 2019 and 2020) as follows. Foghog records a similar entry but with different amounts for the last payment. After three years, the Notes Payable account balance is zero.

Dec. 31, 2019	Interest Expense.....................................	4,800	
	Notes Payable.......................................	18,482	
	Cash		23,282
	Record first installment payment.		

Assets = Liabilities + Equity
−23,282   −18,482   −4,800

Dec. 31, 2020	Interest Expense.....................................	3,321	
	Notes Payable.......................................	19,961	
	Cash		23,282
	Record second installment payment.		

Assets = Liabilities + Equity
−23,282   −19,961   −3,321

Mortgage Notes and Bonds

A **mortgage** is a legal agreement that helps protect a lender if a borrower does not make required payments on notes or bonds. A mortgage gives the lender a right to be paid from the cash proceeds of the sale of a borrower's assets identified in the mortgage. A *mortgage contract* describes the mortgage terms. *Mortgage notes* pledge title to specific assets as security for the note. Mortgage notes are popular in the purchase of homes and plant assets. *Mortgage bonds* are backed by the issuer's assets. Accounting for mortgage notes and bonds is similar to that for unsecured notes and bonds, except that the mortgage agreement must be disclosed. For example, **TIBCO Software** reports that its "mortgage note payable . . . is collateralized by the commercial real property acquired."

Ethical Risk

Lurking Debt   A study reports that 29% of employees in finance and accounting witnessed the falsifying or manipulating of accounting information in the past year. This includes nondisclosure of some long-term liabilities. Another study reports that most people committing fraud (36%) work in the finance function of their firm (KPMG). ■

On January 1, 2019, a company borrows $1,000 cash by signing a four-year, 5% installment note. The note requires four equal payments of $282, consisting of accrued interest and principal on December 31 of each year from 2019 through 2022.

1. Prepare an amortization table for this installment note like the one in Exhibit 10.12.
2. Prepare journal entries to record the loan on January 1, 2019, and the four payments from December 31, 2019, through December 31, 2022.

NEED-TO-KNOW 10-4

Recording Installment Note

C1

Solution

1. Amortization table for loan.

	(A)	(B)		(C)		(D)	(E)
		Payments					
		Debit		*Debit*		*Credit*	
	Beginning Balance	**Interest Expense**		**Notes Payable**		**Cash**	**Ending Balance**
Period Ending Date	**[Prior (E)]**	**[5% × (A)]**	**+**	**[(D) − (B)]**	**=**	**[computed]**	**[(A) − (C)]**
2019.................	$1,000	$ 50		$ 232		$ 282†	$768
2020.................	768	38		244		282	524
2021.................	524	26		256		282	268
2022.................	268	14*		268		282	0
		$128		$1,000		$1,128	

*Adjusted for rounding.   †Amount of each payment = Initial note balance/PV of annuity for 4 periods at 5% (from Table B.3)
= $1,000/3.5460 = $282 (rounded)

Point: An *annuity* is a series of equal payments occurring at equal time intervals.

2.

Jan. 1, 2019	Cash	1,000	
	Notes Payable		1,000
	Borrowed $1,000 by giving a note.		
Dec. 31, 2019	Interest Expense	50	
	Notes Payable	232	
	Cash.........................		282
	Record first installment payment.		
Dec. 31, 2020	Interest Expense	38	
	Notes Payable	244	
	Cash.........................		282
	Record second installment payment.		

Dec. 31, 2021	Interest Expense	26	
	Notes Payable	256	
	Cash.........................		282
	Record third installment payment.		
Dec. 31, 2022	Interest Expense	14	
	Notes Payable	268	
	Cash.........................		282
	Record fourth installment payment.		

> Do More: QS 10-12, E 10-12, E 10-13, P 10-5

Decision Analysis ⬛⬛⬛   Debt Features and the Debt-to-Equity Ratio

A2

Assess debt features and their implications.

Secured Debt

Unsecured Debt

Features of Bonds and Notes

This section covers features of debt securities.

Secured or Unsecured   **Secured bonds** (and notes) have specific assets of the issuer pledged (or *mortgaged*) as collateral. If the issuer does not pay its debt, the secured holders can demand that the collateral be sold and the proceeds used to pay the obligation. **Unsecured bonds** (and notes), also called *debentures,* are backed by the issuer's general credit standing and are riskier than secured debt.

Term or Serial   **Term bonds** (and notes) mature on one specified date. **Serial bonds** (and notes) mature at more than one date (often in series) and thus are usually repaid over a number of periods. For instance, $100,000 of serial bonds might mature at the rate of $10,000 each year from 6 to 15 years after they are issued. **Sinking fund bonds** reduce the holder's risk by requiring the issuer to set aside assets to pay debt in a *sinking fund.*

Registered or Bearer   Bonds issued in the names and addresses of their holders are **registered bonds.** The issuer makes bond payments by sending checks (or cash transfers) to registered holders. Bonds payable to whoever holds them (the *bearer*) are called **bearer bonds** or *unregistered bonds*. The holder of a bearer bond is presumed to be its rightful owner. Many bearer bonds are also **coupon bonds.** This term reflects interest coupons that are attached to the bonds. When each coupon matures, the holder presents it to a bank or broker for collection.

Convertible Debt

Callable Debt

Convertible and/or Callable   **Convertible bonds** (and notes) can be exchanged for a fixed number of shares of the issuing corporation's stock. Convertible debt offers holders the potential to profit from increases in stock price. Holders still receive interest while the debt is held and the par value if they hold the debt to maturity. In most cases, the holders decide whether and when to convert debt to stock. **Callable bonds** (and notes) give the issuer the option to retire them at a stated dollar amount before maturity.

A3

Compute the debt-to-equity ratio and explain its use.

Debt-to-Equity Ratio

A company financed mainly with debt is more risky because liabilities must be repaid with interest, whereas equity financing does not. A measure to assess the risk of a company's financing structure is the **debt-to-equity ratio** (see Exhibit 10.13).

EXHIBIT 10.13

Debt-to-Equity Ratio

$$\text{Debt-to-equity} = \frac{\text{Total liabilities}}{\text{Total equity}}$$

The debt-to-equity ratios for **Nike** and **Under Armour** are in Exhibit 10.14. Nike's current-year debt-to-equity ratio is 0.87, meaning that debtholders contributed $0.87 for each $1 contributed by equity holders. This implies a low-risk financing structure for Nike and is similar to its competitors. In comparison, Under Armour's current-year ratio is 0.98. Analysis across the years shows that Nike's debt-to-equity ratio has risen to a riskier level in recent years. In the case of Nike, the increase in debt-to-equity ratio is less concerning as it has historically earned higher returns with this financing than the interest rate it pays. Still, investors and debtholders will continue to monitor Nike's debt-to-equity ratio to be sure it does not reach risky levels.

Company	$ millions	Current Year	1 Year Ago	2 Years Ago
Nike	Total liabilities........................	$10,852	$ 9,138	$ 8,890
	Total equity	$12,407	$12,258	$12,707
	Debt-to-equity......................	**0.87**	**0.75**	**0.70**
Under Armour	Total liabilities........................	$ 1,988	$ 1,613	$ 1,198
	Total equity	$ 2,019	$ 2,031	$ 1,668
	Debt-to-equity......................	**0.98**	**0.79**	**0.72**

EXHIBIT 10.14

Analysis using
Debt-to-Equity Ratio

■ Decision Maker

Bond Investor   You plan to purchase bonds from one of two companies in the same industry that are similar in size and performance. The first company has $350,000 in total liabilities and $1,750,000 in equity. The second company has $1,200,000 in total liabilities and $1,000,000 in equity. Which company's bonds are less risky based on the debt-to-equity ratio? ■   *Answer:* The debt-to-equity ratio for the first company is 0.2 ($350,000/$1,750,000) and for the second is 1.2 ($1,200,000/$1,000,000), suggesting that financing for the second company is riskier than for the first.

Water Sports Company (WSC) patented and successfully test-marketed a new product. To produce and market the new product, WSC needs to raise $800,000 of financing. On January 1, 2019, the company obtained the money in two ways.

NEED-TO-KNOW 10-5

COMPREHENSIVE

Accounting for
Bonds and Notes—
Amortization, Journal
Entries, and Disposal

a. WSC signed a $400,000, 10% installment note to be repaid with five equal annual installments of $105,519 to be made on December 31 of 2019 through 2023.

b. WSC issued five-year bonds with a par value of $400,000 for $430,881 cash on January 1, 2019. The bonds have a 12% annual contract rate and pay interest on June 30 and December 31. The bonds' annual market rate is 10%.

Required

1. For the installment note, (a) prepare an amortization table similar to Exhibit 10.12 and (b) prepare the journal entry for the first payment.

2. For the bonds, (a) prepare the January 1, 2019, journal entry to record their issuance; (b) prepare an amortization table using the straight-line method; (c) prepare the June 30, 2019, journal entry to record the first interest payment; and (d) prepare a journal entry to record retiring the bonds at a $416,000 call price on January 1, 2021.

3.ᴮ Using Appendix 10B, redo parts 2(b), 2(c), and 2(d) assuming the bonds are amortized using the effective interest method.

PLANNING THE SOLUTION

● For the installment note, prepare a table similar to Exhibit 10.12 and use the numbers in the table's first line for the journal entry.

● Record the bonds' issuance. Next, prepare an amortization table like Exhibit 10.11 (and Exhibit 10B.2) and use it to get the numbers for the journal entry. Also use the table to find the carrying value as of the date of the bonds' retirement needed for the journal entry.

SOLUTION

Part 1: Installment Note

a. An amortization table for the long-term note payable follows.

	(a)	Payments			(e)
		(b) Debit Interest Expense	(c) Debit Notes Payable	(d) Credit Cash	
Annual Period Ending	Beginning Balance	10% × (a)	+ (d) − (b) =	Cash (computed)	Ending Balance (a) − (c)
(1) 12/31/2019	$400,000	$ 40,000	$ 65,519	$105,519*	$334,481
(2) 12/31/2020	334,481	33,448	72,071	105,519	262,410
(3) 12/31/2021	262,410	26,241	79,278	105,519	183,132
(4) 12/31/2022	183,132	18,313	87,206	105,519	95,926
(5) 12/31/2023	95,926	9,593	95,926	105,519	0
		$127,595	$400,000	$527,595	

*Annual payment = Note balance / PV annuity factor = $400,000/3.7908 = $105,519
(The present value annuity factor is for five payments at a rate of 10%.)

b. Journal entry for December 31, 2019, payment.

Dec. 31	Interest Expense	40,000	
	Notes Payable	65,519	
	Cash...		105,519
	Record first installment payment.		

Part 2: Bonds (Straight-Line Amortization)

a. Journal entry for January 1, 2019, issuance.

Jan. 1	Cash	430,881	
	Premium on Bonds Payable.......................		30,881
	Bonds Payable		400,000
	Sold bonds at a premium.		

Point: Bond issue price equals present value of its future cash payments discounted at bond's market rate.

Cash Flow	Table	Present Value Factor*	Amount	Present Value
Par (maturity) value	B.1 in App. B (PV of 1)	0.6139	× $400,000 =	$245,560
Interest payments	B.3 in App. B (PV of annuity)	7.7217	× 24,000 =	185,321
Price of bond				$430,881

*Present value factors are for 10 payments using a semiannual market rate of 5%.

b. The straight-line amortization table for premium bonds follows. The semiannual discount amortization is $3,088, computed as $30,881/10 periods.

Semiannual Period-End	Unamortized Discount	Carrying Value
(0) 1/1/2019	$ 30,881	$ 430,881
(1) 6/30/2019	27,793	427,793
(2) 12/31/2019	24,705	424,705
(3) 6/30/2020	21,617	421,617
(4) 12/31/2020	18,529	418,529
(5) 6/30/2021	15,441	415,441
(6) 12/31/2021	12,353	412,353
(7) 6/30/2022	9,265	409,265
(8) 12/31/2022	6,177	406,177
(9) 6/30/2023	3,089	403,089
(10) 12/31/2023	0*	400,000

*Adjusted for rounding.

c. Journal entry for June 30, 2019, bond payment.

June 30	Bond Interest Expense	20,912	
	Premium on Bonds Payable	3,088	
	Cash.......................................		24,000
	Paid semiannual interest on bonds.		

d. Journal entry for January 1, 2021, bond retirement (use carrying value as of 12/31/2020).

Jan. 1	Bonds Payable......................................	400,000	
	Premium on Bonds Payable	18,529	
	Cash.......................................		416,000
	Gain on Retirement of Bonds......................		2,529
	Record bond retirement for cash.		

Part 3: Bonds (Effective Interest Amortization)—Using Appendix 10B

b. The effective interest amortization table for premium bonds.

Semiannual Interest Period	(A) Cash Interest Paid 6% × $400,000	(B) Interest Expense 5% × Prior (E)	(C) Premium Amortization (A) – (B)	(D) Unamortized Premium Prior (D) – (C)	(E) Carrying Value $400,000 + (D)
(0) 1/1/2019				$30,881	$430,881
(1) 6/30/2019	$ 24,000	$ 21,544	$ 2,456	28,425	428,425
(2) 12/31/2019	24,000	21,421	2,579	25,846	425,846
(3) 6/30/2020	24,000	21,292	2,708	23,138	423,138
(4) 12/31/2020	24,000	21,157	2,843	20,295	420,295
(5) 6/30/2021	24,000	21,015	2,985	17,310	417,310
(6) 12/31/2021	24,000	20,866	3,134	14,176	414,176
(7) 6/30/2022	24,000	20,709	3,291	10,885	410,885
(8) 12/31/2022	24,000	20,544	3,456	7,429	407,429
(9) 6/30/2023	24,000	20,371	3,629	3,800	403,800
(10) 12/31/2023	24,000	20,200*	3,800	0	400,000
	$240,000	$209,119	$30,881		

*Adjusted for rounding.

Point: Using effective interest, carrying value is also computed as the present value of all remaining payments, discounted using the market rate at issuance.

c. Journal entry for June 30, 2019, bond payment.

June 30	Bond Interest Expense	21,544	
	Premium on Bonds Payable	2,456	
	Cash.......................................		24,000
	Paid semiannual interest on bonds.		

d. Journal entry for January 1, 2021, bond retirement (use carrying value as of 12/31/2020).

Jan. 1	Bonds Payable......................................	400,000	
	Premium on Bonds Payable	20,295	
	Cash.......................................		416,000
	Gain on Retirement of Bonds......................		4,295
	Record bond retirement for cash.		

Bond Pricing

This section shows how to price the **Fila** discount bond and the **Adidas** premium bond described earlier.

C2

Explain and compute bond pricing.

Present Value of Discount Bonds   The issue price of bonds is the present value of the bonds' cash payments, discounted at the bonds' market rate. The annual market rate is 10.031% for the Fila bonds. However, for simplicity, we **assume a 10% annual rate** in this appendix. When computing the present value of the Fila bonds, we use *semiannual* compounding periods because this is the time between interest payments; the annual market rate of 10% is considered a semiannual rate of 5%. Also, the two-year bond life is viewed as four semiannual periods. The price computation has two parts.

1 Find the present value of the $100,000 par value paid at maturity.

2 Find the present value of the four semiannual payments of $4,000 each; see Exhibit 10.4.

The present values are found using Excel or a calculator (see directions to the side). We also can find present values if the market rate is in *present value tables*. Appendix B at the end of this book shows present value tables and describes their use. Table B.1 in Appendix B is used for the single $100,000 maturity payment, and Table B.3 in Appendix B is used for the $4,000 series of interest payments. The annual market rate is 10%, or 5% semiannually. In this case, we go to Table B.1, row 4, and across to the 5% column to identify the present value factor of 0.8227 for the maturity payment. Next, we go to Table B.3, row 4, and across to the 5% column, where the present value factor is 3.5460 for the interest payments. We compute bond price by multiplying the cash flow payments by their present value factors and adding them—see Exhibit 10A.1.

Point: Excel for bond pricing.

	A	B
1	Annual contract rate	8%
2	Annual market rate	10%
3	Payments within yr	2
4	Years to maturity	2
5	Par (face) value	$100,000
6	Issue price	

=−PV(B2/B3,B3*B4,B5*B1/B3,B5)
=$96,454

EXHIBIT 10A.1

Computing Issue Price for Fila Discount Bonds

Calculator
N = 4   PMT = 4,000
I/Yr = 5   FV = 100,000

PV = **96,454**

Cash Flow	Table	Present Value Factor		Amount		Present Value
$100,000 par (maturity) value............	B.1 (PV of 1)	0.8227	×	$100,000	=	$ 82,270
$4,000 interest payments	B.3 (PV of ann.)	3.5460	×	4,000	=	14,184
Price of bond........................		(using a 5% semiannual market rate)				**$96,454**

Present Value of Premium Bonds

We compute the issue price of the Adidas bonds by using the market rate to compute the present value of the bonds' future cash flows. The annual market rate is 9.97% for the Adidas bonds. However, for simplicity, we **assume a 10% annual rate** in this appendix. When computing the present value of these bonds, we again use *semiannual* compounding periods because this is the time between interest payments. The annual 10% market rate is applied as a semiannual rate of 5%, and the two-year bond life is viewed as four semiannual periods. The computation has two parts.

1 Find the present value of the $100,000 par value paid at maturity.

2 Find the present value of the four payments of $6,000 each; see Exhibit 10.8.

These present values are found using Excel or a calculator (see directions to the side). We also can find present value if the market rate is in present value tables. The annual market rate is 10%, or 5% semiannually. In this case, go to Table B.1, row 4, and across to the 5% column, where the present value factor is 0.8227 for the maturity payment. Second, go to Table B.3, row 4, and across to the 5% column, where the present value factor is 3.5460 for the series of interest payments. The bonds' price is computed by multiplying the cash flow payments by their present value factors and adding them—see Exhibit 10A.2.

Point: Excel for bond pricing.

	A	B
1	Annual contract rate	12%
2	Annual market rate	10%
3	Payments within yr	2
4	Years to maturity	2
5	Par (face) value	$100,000
6	Issue price	

=−PV(B2/B3,B3*B4,B5*B1/B3,B5)
=$103,546

EXHIBIT 10A.2

Computing Issue Price for Adidas Premium Bonds

Calculator
N = 4   PMT = 6,000
I/Yr = 5   FV = 100,000

PV = **103,546**

Cash Flow	Table	Present Value Factor		Amount		Present Value
$100,000 par (maturity) value............	B.1 (PV of 1)	0.8227	×	$100,000	=	$ 82,270
$6,000 interest payments	B.3 (PV of ann.)	3.5460	×	6,000	=	21,276
Price of bond........................		(using a 5% semiannual market rate)				**$103,546**

Point: Calculator inputs defined:
N   Number of semiannual periods
I/Yr Market rate per semiannual period
FV   Future (maturity) value
PMT Payment (interest) per semiannual period
PV   Price (present value)

■ Decision Insight

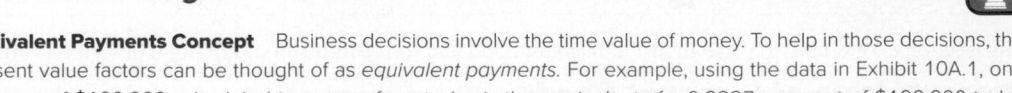

Equivalent Payments Concept   Business decisions involve the time value of money. To help in those decisions, the present value factors can be thought of as *equivalent payments*. For example, using the data in Exhibit 10A.1, one payment of $100,000 scheduled two years from today is the *equivalent* of a 0.8227 payment of $100,000 today (assuming a market with 10% return). Similarly, four semiannual payments of $4,000 over the next two years are the equivalent of 3.5460 payments of $4,000 today (again, assuming a 10% return). ■

Effective Interest Amortization

10B

Effective Interest Amortization of Discount Bonds The **effective interest method** allocates total bond interest expense over the bonds' life in a way that yields a constant rate of interest. This constant rate of interest is the market rate at the issue date. This means bond interest expense for a period equals the carrying value of the bond at the beginning of that period multiplied by the market rate when issued.

Exhibit 10B.1 shows an effective interest amortization table for **Fila** bonds (as described in Exhibit 10.4). The key difference between the effective interest and straight-line methods is computing bond interest expense. Instead of assigning an equal amount of bond interest expense to each period, the effective interest method assigns a bond interest expense amount that increases over the life of a discount bond. **Both methods allocate the same $19,600 of total bond interest expense over the bonds' life, but in different patterns.** Specifically, the amortization table in Exhibit 10B.1 shows that the balance of the discount (column D) is amortized until it reaches zero. Also, the bonds' carrying value (column E) changes each period until it equals par value at maturity. Compare columns D and E to the columns in Exhibit 10.7 to see the amortization patterns. Total bond interest expense is $19,600, consisting of $16,000 of semiannual cash payments and $3,600 of the original bond discount, the same for both methods.

P5

Compute and record amortization of a bond discount using the effective interest method.

Point: Contract rate determines cash interest paid, but market rate determines the actual interest expense.

	Bonds: $100,000 Par Value, Semiannual Interest Payments, Two-Year Life, 4% Semiannual Contract Rate, 5.0155% Semiannual Market Rate				
Semiannual Interest Period-End	(A) Cash Interest Paid 4% × $100,000	(B) Bond Interest Expense 5.0155% × Prior (E)	(C) Discount Amortization (B) − (A)	(D) Unamortized Discount Prior (D) − (C)	(E) Carrying Value $100,000 − (D)
(0) 12/31/2019				$3,600	$ 96,400
(1) 6/30/2020	$4,000	$ 4,835	$ 835	2,765	97,235
(2) 12/31/2020	4,000	4,877	877	1,888	98,112
(3) 6/30/2021	4,000	4,921	921	967	99,033
(4) 12/31/2021	4,000	4,967	967	0	100,000
	$16,000	$19,600	$3,600		

Column (**A**) is the par value ($100,000) multiplied by the semiannual contract rate (4%).
Column (**B**) is the prior period's carrying value multiplied by the semiannual market rate (5.0155%).
Column (**C**) is the difference between interest paid and bond interest expense, or [(B) − (A)].
Column (**D**) is the prior period's unamortized discount less the current period's discount amortization.
Column (**E**) is the par value less unamortized discount, or [$100,000 − (D)].

EXHIBIT 10B.1

Effective Interest Amortization of Bond Discount

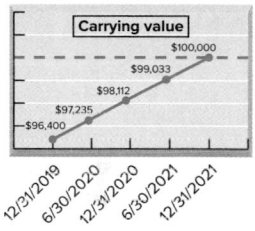

Except for differences in amounts, journal entries recording the expense and updating the liability balance are the same under the effective interest method and the straight-line method. We use the numbers in Exhibit 10B.1 to record each semiannual entry during the bonds' two-year life (June 30, 2020, through December 31, 2021). The interest payment entry at the end of the first semiannual period is

June 30, 2020	Bond Interest Expense	4,835	
	Discount on Bonds Payable		835
	Cash		4,000
	Record semiannual interest and discount amortization (effective interest method).		

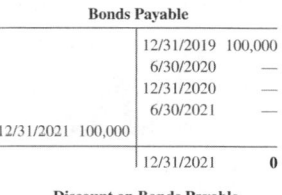

Bonds Payable

	12/31/2019	100,000
	6/30/2020	—
	12/31/2020	—
	6/30/2021	—
12/31/2021 100,000		
	12/31/2021	0

Discount on Bonds Payable

12/31/2019	3,600		
		6/30/2020	835
		12/31/2020	877
		6/30/2021	921
		12/31/2021	967
12/31/2021	0		

Effective Interest Amortization of Premium Bonds Exhibit 10B.2 shows the amortization table using the effective interest method for **Adidas** bonds (as described in Exhibit 10.8). Column A lists the semiannual cash payments. Column B shows the amount of bond interest expense, computed as the 4.9851% semiannual market rate at issuance multiplied by the beginning-of-period carrying value. The amount of cash paid in column A is larger than the bond interest expense because the

P6

Compute and record amortization of a bond premium using the effective interest method.

cash payment is based on the higher 6% semiannual contract rate. The excess cash payment over the interest expense reduces the principal. These amounts are shown in column C. Column E shows the carrying value after deducting the amortized premium in column C from the prior period's carrying value. Column D shows the premium's reduction by periodic amortization.

EXHIBIT 10B.2

Effective Interest
Amortization of Bond
Premium

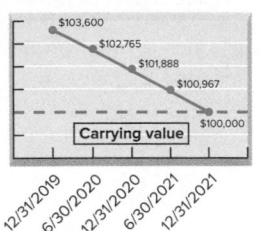

Bonds Payable

	12/31/2019	100,000
	6/30/2020	—
	12/31/2020	—
	6/30/2021	—
12/31/2021 100,000		
	12/31/2021	0

Premium on Bonds Payable

	12/31/2019	3,600
6/30/2020 835		
12/31/2020 877		
6/30/2021 921		
12/31/2021 967		
	12/31/2021	0

		Bonds: $100,000 Par Value, Semiannual Interest Payments, Two-Year Life, 6% Semiannual Contract Rate, 4.9851% Semiannual Market Rate				
	Semiannual Interest Period-End	(A) Cash Interest Paid 6% × $100,000	(B) Bond Interest Expense 4.9851% × Prior (E)	(C) Premium Amortization (A) – (B)	(D) Unamortized Premium Prior (D) – (C)	(E) Carrying Value $100,000 + (D)
(0)	12/31/2019				$3,600	$103,600
(1)	6/30/2020	$ 6,000	$ 5,165	$ 835	2,765	102,765
(2)	12/31/2020	6,000	5,123	877	1,888	101,888
(3)	6/30/2021	6,000	5,079	921	967	100,967
(4)	12/31/2021	6,000	5,033	967	0	100,000
		$24,000	$20,400	$3,600		

Column (**A**) is the par value ($100,000) multiplied by the semiannual contract rate (6%).
Column (**B**) is the prior period's carrying value multiplied by the semiannual market rate (4.9851%).
Column (**C**) is the difference between interest paid and bond interest expense, or [(A) – (B)].
Column (**D**) is the prior period's unamortized premium less the current period's premium amortization.
Column (**E**) is the par value plus unamortized premium, or [$100,000 + (D)].

When the issuer makes the first semiannual interest payment, it records the following. Similar entries with different amounts are recorded at each payment date until the bond matures at the end of 2021. The effective interest method yields decreasing amounts of bond interest expense and increasing amounts of premium amortization over the bonds' life.

June 30, 2020	Bond Interest Expense	5,165	
	Premium on Bonds Payable	835	
	Cash		6,000
	Record semiannual interest and premium amortization (effective interest method).		

APPENDIX

10C

Leases and Pensions

C3

Describe accounting for leases and pensions.

Lease Liabilities   A **lease** is an agreement between a *lessor* (owner) and a *lessee* (renter or tenant) that gives the lessee the right to use the asset for a period of time in return for cash (rent) payments. The financing of leases is a $1 trillion industry. The advantages of lease financing include no up-front, full cash payment and the potential to deduct rental payments from taxable income.

Leases are classified as either finance leases or operating leases. In either case, for noncurrent leases the lessee records a "Right-of-Use Asset" and "Lease Liability" equal to the present value of lease payments. At each period-end, the lessee records financing expense differently depending on whether it's a finance lease or operating lease.

Finance Leases   **Finance leases** are long-term leases where the lessee receives substantially all remaining benefits of the asset. A *finance lease* meets one or more of five criteria: (1) transfers ownership of lease asset to lessee, (2) has a purchase option that lessee is reasonably certain to exercise, (3) lease term is for major part of the lease asset's remaining economic life, (4) present value of lease payments equals or exceeds substantially all of the lease asset's fair value, or (5) the lease asset is specialized and expected to have no alternative use to lessor at lease-end.

A finance lease is similar to the financing of an asset purchase. Examples include most leases of airplanes, delivery trucks, medical equipment, railcars, and department store buildings. The lessee records the leased item as its own asset along with a lease liability at the start of the lease term; the amount recorded equals the present value of all lease payments.

Lease Start and First Payment Assume KDI Co. enters into a three-year lease of a building in which it sells sporting equipment. The lease is accounted for as a finance lease, it requires three $21,000 payments (the first at the *beginning* of the lease and the others at December 31 of 2019 and 2020), and the present value of its annual lease payments is $60,000 (implying a 5.086% discount rate). KDI records the asset and liability along with the first-period lease payment as follows. KDI reports the right-of-use lease asset as a long-term asset and the lease liability as a long-term liability. The portion of the lease liability expected to be paid in the next year is reported as a current liability.

Jan. 1, 2019	Right-of-Use Asset.	60,000	
	Lease Liability		60,000
	Record right-of-use asset and lease liability.		
Jan. 1, 2019	Lease Liability	21,000	
	Cash.		21,000
	Record beginning-year cash lease payment.		

Lease Asset Amortization At each year-end, KDI records amortization on the right-of-use asset (assume straight-line amortization, three-year lease term, and no salvage value) as follows.

Dec. 31, 2019	Amortization Expense	20,000	
	Accumulated Amortization—Right-of-Use Asset.		20,000
	Record amortization on right-of-use asset. ($60,000—$0)/3 yrs		

Lease Payment for Liability and Interest KDI accrues interest expense on the lease liability at each year-end. Interest expense is computed by multiplying the lease liability by the interest rate on the lease. It records interest expense as part of its $21,000 annual lease payment as follows (for its first year).

Dec. 31, 2019	Interest Expense	1,984	
	Lease Liability	19,016	
	Cash.		21,000
	*Record lease payment for interest and lease liability.**		

*Numbers are from a *lease payment schedule* as follows.

	(A)	(B)		(C)	(D)	(E)
		Debit		*Debit*	*Credit*	
		Interest on	+			=	Ending Balance
	Beginning Balance	Lease Liability		Lease Liability	Cash Lease	of Lease Liability
Date	of Lease Liability	5.086% × (A)		(D) – (B)	Payment	(A) – (C)
Jan. 1, 2019	**$60,000**	▮▮▮▮▮		**$21,000**	**$21,000**	**$39,000**
Dec 31, 2019	39,000	$1,984		19,016	21,000	19,984
Dec 31, 2020	19,984	1,016		19,984	21,000	0
		$3,000		**$60,000**	**$63,000**	

KDI's entries for the final two years of this lease follow.

Dec. 31, 2020	Amortization Expense.	20,000	
	Accumulated Amortization—Right-of-Use Asset		20,000
	Record amortization on right-of-use asset.		
Dec. 31, 2020	Interest Expense	1,016	
	Lease Liability	19,984	
	Cash		21,000
	Record lease payment for interest and lease liability.		
Dec. 31, 2021	Amortization Expense.	20,000	
	Accumulated Amortization—Right-of-Use Asset		20,000
	Record amortization on right-of-use asset.		

Operating Leases

Operating leases are long-term leases that do not meet any of the five criteria for finance leases.

Lease Start and Payments We prepare journal entries using the same *lease payment schedule* shown for the finance lease above. Recall this is a three-year lease that requires three $21,000 payments (the first at the *beginning* of the lease and the others at December 31 of 2019 and 2020), with a present value of its annual lease payments of $60,000 (implying a 5.086% discount rate). All entries under the finance lease apply here, but amounts for amortization entries differ.

Lease Amortization   Total amortization for the lease life is the same for finance and operating leases. The difference is the yearly asset amortization. Those entries follow using the amortization calculated below.

		2019	2020	2021
Dec. 31	Amortization Expense............................	19,016	19,984	21,000
	Accumulated Amortization—Right-of-Use Asset....	19,016	19,984	21,000
	Record amortization on right-of-use asset. *			

	Amortization*	=	Lease Payment	−	Interest on Lease Liability
For 2019 ...	**$19,016**	=	$21,000	−	$1,984
For 2020 ...	**$19,984**	=	$21,000	−	$1,016
For 2021 ...	**$21,000**	=	$21,000	−	$ 0

Point: In the income statement for an operating lease, Amortization Exp. and Interest Exp. are combined as one line item, "Lease Expense." The balance sheet and ledger keep them separate.

Short-Term Leases   **Short-term leases** have lease terms of 12 months or less and do not have long-term purchase options. Examples include most car and apartment rental agreements. The lessee records such lease payments as expenses. The lessee does not report the leased item as an asset or a liability (it is the lessor's asset). If **Verizon** leases a kiosk from the mall for $300 per month, its entry follows.

July 4	Rental Expense	300	
	Cash...		300
	Record short-term lease rental payment.		

Pension Liabilities

A **pension plan** is an agreement for the employer to provide benefits (payments) to employees after they retire. Some employers pay the full cost of the pension, and some pay part of the cost. An employer records its payment into a pension plan with a debit to Pension Expense and a credit to Cash. A *plan administrator* invests the payments in pension assets and makes benefit payments to *pension recipients* (retired employees).

Point: Fringe benefits are often 40% or more of salaries and wages, and pension benefits make up nearly 15% of fringe benefits.

Defined Benefit Plan   *Defined benefit plans* give workers defined future benefits; the employer's contributions vary, depending on assumptions about future pension assets and liabilities. A pension liability is reported when the accumulated benefit obligation is *more than* the plan assets, called an *underfunded plan.* The accumulated benefit obligation is the present value of promised future pension payments to retirees. *Plan assets* refer to the market value of pension assets. A pension asset is reported when the accumulated benefit obligation is *less than* the plan assets, called an *overfunded plan.* An employer reports pension expense when employees earn wages, which is sometimes decades before it pays pension benefits to employees.

Point: Two types of pension plans are (1) *defined benefit plan*—the retirement benefit is defined and the employer estimates the contribution necessary to pay these benefits—and (2) *defined contribution plan*—the pension contribution is defined and the employer and/or employee contribute amounts specified in the pension agreement.

Other Postretirement Benefits   *Other postretirement benefits* refer to nonpension benefits such as health care and life insurance benefits. Costs of these benefits are estimated and liabilities accrued when the employees earn them. Many of these benefits are not funded.

Summary: Cheat Sheet

BOND BASICS AND PAR BONDS

Bond advantages: Bonds do not affect owner control, interest on bonds is tax deductible, and bonds can potentially increase return on equity.
Bond disadvantages: Bonds can potentially decrease return on equity and require payments of both periodic interest and the par value at maturity.

Bonds issued at *par value* (called *par bonds*):

Cash	100,000	
Bonds Payable...........................		100,000

Par bonds semiannual interest payment:

Bond Interest Expense.........................	4,000	
Cash...................................		4,000

Maturity of bonds (payment of par): When the bond issuer pays the par value back to the bondholder.

Bonds Payable	100,000	
Cash....................................		100,000

DISCOUNT BONDS

Contract rate: The interest the bond issuer pays in cash.
Market rate: The interest rate that borrowers are willing to pay and lenders are willing to accept.

Contract rate > Market rate ➡	Bond sells at premium
Contract rate = Market rate ➡	Bond sells at par
Contract rate < Market rate ➡	Bond sells at discount

Bond prices: A $1,000 bond with a price of 96.400 is sold for $964. A $1,000 bond with a price of 103½ is sold for $1,035.
Carrying (book) value of a bond: Equals bond par value plus any premium or minus any discount.
Discount bonds: Bonds issued with a contract rate that is *less* than the market rate.

Issuance of discount bonds:

Cash	96,400	
Discount on Bonds Payable	3,600	
Bonds Payable		100,000

Reporting of discount bonds:

Long-term liabilities		
Bonds payable, 8%, due December 31, 2021	$100,000	
Less discount on bonds payable	3,600	$96,400

Amortizing discount bonds (straight-line method):

Panel A: Interest Computations

Four payments of $4,000 (4 pymts × [$100,000 × 0.08 × 1/2 yr])	$ 16,000
Plus discount	3,600
Total bond interest expense	**$19,600**

$$\text{Bond interest expense (per interest period)} = \frac{\text{Total bond interest expense}}{\text{Number of interest periods}} = \frac{\$19,600}{4} = \$4,900$$

Panel B: Entry to Record Interest Payment and Amortization

2020–2021	Bond Interest Expense	4,900	Discount ÷ Periods
June 30 and	Discount on Bonds Payable	900	
Dec. 31	Cash	4,000	Par value × ½ × Contract rate

Straight-line discount bond amortization table:

Semiannual Period-End	Unamortized Discount	Carrying Value
(0) 12/31/2019	$3,600	$ 96,400
(1) 6/30/2020	2,700	97,300
(2) 12/31/2020	1,800	98,200
(3) 6/30/2021	900	99,100
(4) **12/31/2021**	0	100,000

PREMIUM BONDS

Premium bonds: Bonds issued with a contract rate *higher* than the market rate.

Issuance of premium bonds:

Cash	103,600	
Premium on Bonds Payable		3,600
Bonds Payable		100,000

Reporting of premium bonds:

Long-term liabilities		
Bonds payable, 12%, due December 31, 2021	$100,000	
Plus premium on bonds payable	3,600	$103,600

Amortizing premium bonds (straight-line method):

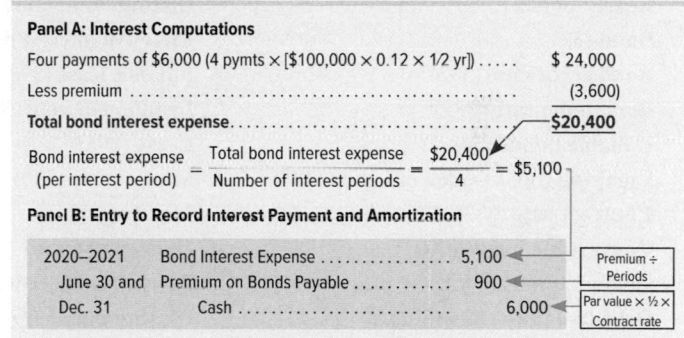

Panel A: Interest Computations

Four payments of $6,000 (4 pymts × [$100,000 × 0.12 × 1/2 yr])	$ 24,000
Less premium	(3,600)
Total bond interest expense	**$20,400**

$$\text{Bond interest expense (per interest period)} = \frac{\text{Total bond interest expense}}{\text{Number of interest periods}} = \frac{\$20,400}{4} = \$5,100$$

Panel B: Entry to Record Interest Payment and Amortization

2020–2021	Bond Interest Expense	5,100	Premium ÷ Periods
June 30 and	Premium on Bonds Payable	900	
Dec. 31	Cash	6,000	Par value × ½ × Contract rate

Straight-line premium bond amortization table:

Semiannual Period-End	Unamortized Premium	Carrying Value
(0) 12/31/2019	$3,600	$103,600
(1) 6/30/2020	2,700	102,700
(2) 12/31/2020	1,800	101,800
(3) 6/30/2021	900	100,900
(4) 12/31/2021	0	100,000

BOND RETIREMENT

Bond retirement by call option: Some bonds give issuers an option to call the bonds before they mature by paying par value plus a call premium. Record a gain if carrying value is *greater* than retirement price (shown here). Record a loss if carrying value is *less* than retirement price.

Bonds Payable	100,000	
Premium on Bonds Payable	4,500	
Gain on Bond Retirement		1,500
Cash		103,000

Bond retirement by conversion: Holders of convertible bonds can convert their bonds to stock. No gain or loss is recorded. Bonds are converted to stock at the bonds' carrying value.

Bonds Payable	100,000	
Common Stock		30,000
Paid-In Capital in Excess of Par Value		70,000

LONG-TERM NOTES

Installment note: A liability requiring a series of payments to the lender. Usually issued to a single lender, such as a bank.

Payments of principal and interest payments for note: Payments on an installment note include accrued interest expense plus part of the amount borrowed (the principal).

| | (A) | Payments | | | (E) |
| | | (B)
Debit
Interest
Expense
8% × (A) | (C)
Debit
Notes
Payable
(D) – (B) | (D)
Credit
Cash
(computed) | |
Period Ending Date	Beginning Balance	+	=		Ending Balance (A) – (C)
(1) 12/31/2019	$60,000	$4,800	$ 18,482	$23,282	$41,518
(2) 12/31/2020.	41,518	3,321	19,961	23,282	21,557
(3) 12/31/2021	21,557	1,725	21,557	23,282	0
		$9,846	$60,000	$69,846	

Issuance of notes:

Cash........................	60,000	
Notes Payable.............		60,000

Note installment payments:

Dec. 31, 2019	Interest Expense	4,800	
	Notes Payable	18,482	
	Cash		23,282

Dec. 31, 2020	Interest Expense	3,321	
	Notes Payable	19,961	
	Cash		23,282

Key Terms

Bearer bonds (392)	Discount on bonds payable (384)	Premium on bonds (386)
Bond (381)	Effective interest method (397)	Registered bonds (392)
Bond certificate (382)	Finance lease (398)	Secured bonds (392)
Bond indenture (382)	Installment note (390)	Serial bonds (392)
Callable bonds (392)	Lease (398)	Short-term lease (400)
Carrying (book) value of bonds (384)	Market rate (383)	Sinking fund bonds (392)
Contract rate (383)	Mortgage (391)	Straight-line bond amortization (385)
Convertible bonds (392)	Operating lease (399)	Term bonds (392)
Coupon bonds (392)	Par value of a bond (381)	Unsecured bonds (392)
Debt-to-equity ratio (392)	Pension plan (400)	

Multiple Choice Quiz

1. A bond traded at 97½ means that
  a. The bond pays 97½% interest.
  b. The bond trades at $975 per $1,000 bond.
  c. The market rate of interest is below the contract rate of interest for the bond.
  d. The bonds can be retired at $975 each.
  e. The bond's interest rate is 2½%.

2. A bondholder that owns a $1,000, 6%, 15-year (term) bond has
  a. The right to receive $1,000 at maturity.
  b. Ownership rights in the bond-issuing entity.
  c. The right to receive $60 per month until maturity.
  d. The right to receive $1,900 at maturity.
  e. The right to receive $600 per year until maturity.

3. A company issues 8%, 20-year bonds with a par value of $500,000. The current market rate for the bonds is 8%. The amount of interest owed to the bondholders for each semi-annual interest payment is
  a. $40,000.   **c.** $20,000.   **e.** $400,000.
  b. $0.   **d.** $800,000.

4. A company issued five-year, 5% bonds with a par value of $100,000. The company received $95,735 for the bonds. Using the straight-line method, the company's interest expense for the first semiannual interest period is
  a. $2,926.50.   **c.** $2,500.00.   **e.** $9,573.50.
  b. $5,853.00.   **d.** $5,000.00.

5. A company issued eight-year, 5% bonds with a par value of $350,000. The company received proceeds of $373,745. Interest is payable semiannually. The amount of premium amortized for the first semiannual interest period, assuming straight-line bond amortization, is
  a. $2,698.   **c.** $8,750.   **e.** $1,484.
  b. $23,745.   **d.** $9,344.

ANSWERS TO MULTIPLE CHOICE QUIZ

1. b
2. a
3. c; $500,000 × 0.08 × ½ year = $20,000

4. a; Cash interest paid = $100,000 × 5% × ½ year = $2,500
    Discount amortization = ($100,000 − $95,735)/10 periods = $426.50
    Interest expense = $2,500.00 + $426.50 = $2,926.50
5. e; ($373,745 − $350,000)/16 periods = $1,484

A(B,C) *Superscript letter A, B, or C denotes assignments based on Appendix 10A, 10B, or 10C.*

🔲 Icon denotes assignments that involve decision making.

Discussion Questions

1. What is the main difference between notes payable and bonds payable?

2. What is the main difference between a bond and a share of stock?

3. 🔲 What is the advantage of issuing bonds instead of obtaining financing from the company's owners?

4. What is a bond indenture? What provisions are usually included in it?

5. What are the *contract* rate and the *market* rate for bonds?

6. 🔲 What factors affect the market rates for bonds?

7.B 🔲 Does the straight-line or effective interest method produce an interest expense allocation that yields a constant rate of interest over a bond's life? Explain.

8. Explain the concept of accrued interest on bonds at the end of an accounting period.

9. 🔲 If you know the par value of bonds, the contract rate, and the market rate, how do you compute the bonds' price?

10. What is the issue price of a $2,000 bond sold at 98¼? What is the issue price of a $6,000 bond sold at 101½?

11. Describe the debt-to-equity ratio and explain how creditors and owners use this ratio to evaluate a company's risk.

12. 🔲 What obligation does an entrepreneur (owner) have to investors that purchase bonds to finance the business?

13. Refer to **Apple**'s annual report in Appendix A. Is there any indication that Apple has issued long-term debt? **APPLE**

14. Refer to the statements for **Samsung** in Appendix A. By what amount did **Samsung** Samsung's long-term borrowings increase or decrease in 2017?

15. Refer to the statement of cash flows for **Samsung** in Appendix A. For the year **Samsung** ended December 31, 2017, what was the amount for repayment of long-term borrowings and debentures?

16. Refer to the statements for **Google** in **GOOGLE** Appendix A. For the year ended December 31, 2017, what was its debt-to-equity ratio? What does this ratio tell us?

17.C When can a lease create both an asset and a liability for the lessee?

18.C Compare and contrast a finance lease with an operating lease.

19.C Describe the two basic types of pension plans.

🔲 connect

> *Round dollar amounts to the nearest whole dollar for all assignments in this chapter.*

Identify the following as either an advantage (A) or a disadvantage (D) of bond financing for a company.

_____ **a.** Bonds do not affect owner control.

_____ **b.** A company earns a lower return with borrowed funds than it pays in interest.

_____ **c.** A company earns a higher return with borrowed funds than it pays in interest.

_____ **d.** Bonds require payment of periodic interest.

_____ **e.** Interest on bonds is tax deductible.

_____ **f.** Bonds require payment of par value at maturity.

QUICK STUDY

QS 10-1
Advantages of bond financing
A1

Dunphy Company issued $10,000 of 6%, 10-year bonds at par value on January 1. Interest is paid semiannually each June 30 and December 31. Prepare the entries for (*a*) the issuance of the bonds and (*b*) the first interest payment on June 30.

QS 10-2
Issuing bonds at par   **P1**

Madrid Company plans to issue 8% bonds with a par value of $4,000,000. The company sells $3,600,000 of the bonds at par on January 1. The remaining $400,000 sells at par on July 1. The bonds pay interest semiannually on June 30 and December 31.

1. Record the entry for the first interest payment on June 30.

2. Record the entry for the July 1 cash sale of bonds.

QS 10-3
Issuing bonds at par
P1

On January 1, Renewable Energy issues bonds that have a $20,000 par value, mature in eight years, and pay 12% interest semiannually on June 30 and December 31.

1. Prepare the journal entry for issuance assuming the bonds are issued at (*a*) 99 and (*b*) 103½.

2. How much interest does the company pay (in cash) to its bondholders every six months if the bonds are sold at par?

QS 10-4
Recording bond issuance and interest

P1   P2   P3 🔲

Enviro Company issues 8%, 10-year bonds with a par value of $250,000 and semiannual interest payments. On the issue date, the annual market rate for these bonds is 10%, which implies a selling price of 87½. Prepare the journal entry for the issuance of the bonds for cash on January 1.

QS 10-5
Journalizing discount bond issuance   **P2**

QS 10-6
Journalizing premium bond issuance **P3**

Garcia Company issues 10%, 15-year bonds with a par value of $240,000 and semiannual interest payments. On the issue date, the annual market rate for these bonds is 8%, which implies a selling price of 117¼. Prepare the journal entry for the issuance of these bonds for cash on January 1.

QS 10-7
Straight-Line:
Discount bond computations
P2

Enviro Company issues 8%, 10-year bonds with a par value of $250,000 and semiannual interest payments. On the issue date, the annual market rate for these bonds is 10%, which implies a selling price of 87½. The straight-line method is used to allocate interest expense.

1. What are the issuer's cash proceeds from issuance of these bonds?
2. What total amount of bond interest expense will be recognized over the life of these bonds?
3. What is the amount of bond interest expense recorded on the first interest payment date?

QS 10-8
Recording bond issuance and discount amortization
P2

Snap Company issues 10%, five-year bonds, on January 1 of this year, with a par value of $100,000 and semiannual interest payments. Use the following bond amortization table and prepare journal entries to record (a) the issuance of bonds on January 1, (b) the first interest payment on June 30, and (c) the second interest payment on December 31.

Semiannual Period-End	Unamortized Discount	Carrying Value
(0) January 1, issuance	$7,360	$92,640
(1) June 30, first payment	6,624	93,376
(2) December 31, second payment.	5,888	94,112

QS 10-9
Straight-Line: Premium bond computations
P3

Enviro Company issues 8%, 10-year bonds with a par value of $250,000 and semiannual interest payments. On the issue date, the annual market rate for these bonds is 5%, which implies a selling price of 123.375. The straight-line method is used to allocate interest expense.

1. What are the issuer's cash proceeds from issuance of these bonds?
2. What total amount of bond interest expense will be recognized over the life of these bonds?
3. What is the amount of bond interest expense recorded on the first interest payment date?

QS 10-10
Bond retirement by call option **P4**

On July 1, Aloha Co. exercises a call option that requires Aloha to pay $408,000 for its outstanding bonds that have a carrying value of $416,000 and a par value of $400,000. The company exercises the call option after the semiannual interest is paid the day before on June 30. Record the entry to retire the bonds.

QS 10-11
Bond retirement by stock conversion **P4**

On January 1, the $3,000,000 par value bonds of Spitz Company with a carrying value of $3,000,000 are converted to 1,000,000 shares of $1 par value common stock. Record the entry for the conversion of the bonds.

QS 10-12
Issuance and interest for installment note
C1

On January 1, MM Co. borrows $340,000 cash from a bank and in return signs an 8% installment note for five annual payments of $85,155 each.

1. Prepare the journal entry to record issuance of the note.
2. For the first $85,155 annual payment at December 31, what amount goes toward interest expense? What amount goes toward principal reduction of the note?

QS 10-13
Bond features and terminology
A2

Select the description that best fits each term or phrase.

A. Records and tracks the bondholders' names.
B. Is unsecured; backed only by the issuer's credit standing.
C. Has varying maturity dates for amounts owed.
D. The legal contract between the issuer and the bondholders.
E. Can be exchanged for shares of the issuer's stock.
F. Is unregistered; interest is paid to whoever possesses them.
G. Maintains a separate asset account from which bondholders are paid at maturity.
H. Pledges specific assets of the issuer as collateral.

_____ **1.** Registered bond   _____ **5.** Convertible bond
_____ **2.** Serial bond   _____ **6.** Bond indenture
_____ **3.** Secured bond   _____ **7.** Sinking fund bond
_____ **4.** Bearer bond   _____ **8.** Debenture

Compute the debt-to-equity ratio for each of the following companies. Which company appears to have a riskier financing structure?

	Atlanta Company	Spokane Company
Total liabilities	$429,000	$ 549,000
Total equity	572,000	1,830,000

QS 10-14
Debt-to-equity ratio
A3

Compute the selling price of 8%, 10-year bonds with a par value of $250,000 and semiannual interest payments. The annual market rate for these bonds is 10%. Use present value tables B.1 and B.3 in Appendix B.

QS 10-15ᴬ
Computing bond price C2

Compute the selling price of 10%, 15-year bonds with a par value of $240,000 and semiannual interest payments. The annual market rate for these bonds is 8%. Use present value tables B.1 and B.3 in Appendix B.

QS 10-16ᴬ
Computing bond price C2

Garcia Company issues 10%, 15-year bonds with a par value of $240,000 and semiannual interest payments. On the issue date, the annual market rate for these bonds is 14%, which implies a selling price of 75¼. The effective interest method is used to allocate interest expense.
1. What are the issuer's cash proceeds from issuance of these bonds?
2. What total amount of bond interest expense will be recognized over the life of these bonds?
3. What amount of bond interest expense is recorded on the first interest payment date?

QS 10-17ᴮ
Effective Interest: Bond discount computations
P5

Garcia Company issues 10%, 15-year bonds with a par value of $240,000 and semiannual interest payments. On the issue date, the annual market rate for these bonds is 8%, which implies a selling price of 117¼. The effective interest method is used to allocate interest expense.
1. What are the issuer's cash proceeds from issuance of these bonds?
2. What total amount of bond interest expense will be recognized over the life of these bonds?
3. What amount of bond interest expense is recorded on the first interest payment date?

QS 10-18ᴮ
Effective Interest: Bond premium computations
P6

Jin Li, an employee of ETrain.com, leases a car at O'Hare Airport for a three-day business trip. The rental cost is $250. Prepare the entry by ETrain.com to record Jin Li's short-term car lease cost.

QS 10-19ᶜ
Recording short-term leases C3

Algoma, Inc., signs a five-year lease for office equipment with Office Solutions. The present value of the lease payments is $15,499. Prepare the journal entry that Algoma records at the inception of this finance lease.

QS 10-20ᶜ
Recording leases C3

connect

No-Toxic-Toys currently has $200,000 of equity and is planning an $80,000 expansion to meet increasing demand for its product. The company currently earns $50,000 in net income, and the expansion will yield $25,000 in additional income before any interest expense.
  The company has three options: (1) do not expand, (2) expand and issue $80,000 in debt that requires payments of 8% annual interest, or (3) expand and raise $80,000 from equity financing. For each option, compute (a) net income and (b) return on equity (Net income ÷ Equity). Ignore any income tax effects.

EXERCISES
Exercise 10-1
Debt versus equity financing
A1

Brussels Enterprises issues bonds at par dated January 1, 2019, that have a $3,400,000 par value, mature in four years, and pay 9% interest semiannually on June 30 and December 31.
1. Record the entry for the issuance of bonds for cash on January 1.
2. Record the entry for the first semiannual interest payment and the second semiannual interest payment.
3. Record the entry for the maturity of the bonds on December 31, 2022 (assume semiannual interest is already recorded).

Exercise 10-2
Recording bond issuance at par, interest payments, and bond maturity
P1

Exercise 10-3
Recording bond issuance and interest
P1

On January 1, Boston Enterprises issues bonds that have a $3,400,000 par value, mature in 20 years, and pay 9% interest semiannually on June 30 and December 31. The bonds are sold at par.

1. How much interest will Boston pay (in cash) to the bondholders every six months?

2. Prepare journal entries to record (*a*) the issuance of bonds on January 1, (*b*) the first interest payment on June 30, and (*c*) the second interest payment on December 31.

3. Prepare the journal entry for issuance assuming the bonds are issued at (*a*) 98 and (*b*) 102.

Exercise 10-4
Straight-Line: Amortization of bond discount
P2

Tano Company issues bonds with a par value of $180,000 on January 1, 2019. The bonds' annual contract rate is 8%, and interest is paid semiannually on June 30 and December 31. The bonds mature in three years. The annual market rate at the date of issuance is 10%, and the bonds are sold for $170,862.

1. What is the amount of the discount on these bonds at issuance?

2. How much total bond interest expense will be recognized over the life of these bonds?

3. Prepare a straight-line amortization table like Exhibit 10.7 for these bonds.

Exercise 10-5
Straight-Line:
Recording bond issuance and discount amortization
P2

Paulson Company issues 6%, four-year bonds, on January 1 of this year, with a par value of $200,000 and semiannual interest payments. Use the following bond amortization table and prepare journal entries to record (*a*) the issuance of bonds on January 1, (*b*) the first interest payment on June 30, and (*c*) the second interest payment on December 31.

Semiannual Period-End	Unamortized Discount	Carrying Value
(0)　January 1, issuance	$13,466	$186,534
(1)　June 30, first payment	11,782	188,218
(2)　December 31, second payment　. . .	10,098	189,902

Exercise 10-6
Straight-Line:
Recording bond issuance and discount amortization
P2

Dobbs Company issues 5%, two-year bonds, on December 31, 2019, with a par value of $200,000 and semiannual interest payments. Use the following bond amortization table and prepare journal entries to record (*a*) the issuance of bonds on December 31, 2019; (*b*) the first through fourth interest payments on each June 30 and December 31; and (*c*) the maturity of the bonds on December 31, 2021.

Semiannual Period-End	Unamortized Discount	Carrying Value
(0)　12/31/2019　.	$12,000	$188,000
(1)　　6/30/2020　.	9,000	191,000
(2)　12/31/2020　.	6,000	194,000
(3)　　6/30/2021　.	3,000	197,000
(4)　12/31/2021　.	0	200,000

Exercise 10-7
Straight-Line:
Amortization table and bond interest expense
P2

Duval Co. issues four-year bonds with a $100,000 par value on January 1, 2019, at a price of $95,952. The annual contract rate is 7%, and interest is paid semiannually on June 30 and December 31.

1. Prepare a straight-line amortization table like Exhibit 10.7 for these bonds.

2. Prepare journal entries to record the first two interest payments.

3. Prepare the journal entry for maturity of the bonds on December 31, 2022 (assume semiannual interest is already recorded).

Exercise 10-8
Straight-Line:
Recording bond issuance and premium amortization
P3

Wookie Company issues 10%, five-year bonds, on January 1 of this year, with a par value of $200,000 and semiannual interest payments. Use the following bond amortization table and prepare journal entries to record (*a*) the issuance of bonds on January 1, (*b*) the first interest payment on June 30, and (*c*) the second interest payment on December 31.

Semiannual Period-End	Unamortized Premium	Carrying Value
(0)　January 1, issuance	$16,222	$216,222
(1)　June 30, first payment	14,600	214,600
(2)　December 31, second payment　. . .	12,978	212,978

Quatro Co. issues bonds dated January 1, 2019, with a par value of $400,000. The bonds' annual contract rate is 13%, and interest is paid semiannually on June 30 and December 31. The bonds mature in three years. The annual market rate at the date of issuance is 12%, and the bonds are sold for $409,850.

1. What is the amount of the premium on these bonds at issuance?

2. How much total bond interest expense will be recognized over the life of these bonds?

3. Prepare a straight-line amortization table like Exhibit 10.11 for these bonds.

Exercise 10-9
Straight-Line:
Amortization of bond premium
P3

Tyrell Company issued callable bonds with a par value of $10,000. The call option requires Tyrell to pay a call premium of $500 plus par (or a total of $10,500) to bondholders to retire the bonds. On July 1, Tyrell exercises the call option. The call option is exercised after the semiannual interest is paid the day before on June 30. Record the entry to retire the bonds under each separate situation.

1. The bonds have a carrying value of $9,000.

2. The bonds have a carrying value of $11,000.

Exercise 10-10
Bond retirement by call option
P4

On January 1, 2019, Shay Company issues $700,000 of 10%, 15-year bonds. The bonds sell for $684,250. Six years later, on January 1, 2025, Shay retires these bonds by buying them on the open market for $731,500. All interest is accounted for and paid through December 31, 2024, the day before the purchase. The straight-line method is used to amortize any bond discount.

1. What is the amount of the discount on the bonds at issuance?

2. How much amortization of the discount is recorded on the bonds for the entire period from January 1, 2019, through December 31, 2024?

3. What is the carrying (book) value of the bonds as of the close of business on December 31, 2024?

4. Prepare the journal entry to record the bond retirement.

Exercise 10-11
Straight-Line: Bond computations, amortization, and bond retirement
P2 **P4**

On January 1, 2019, Eagle Company borrows $100,000 cash by signing a four-year, 7% installment note. The note requires four equal payments of $29,523, consisting of accrued interest and principal on December 31 of each year from 2019 through 2022. Prepare an amortization table for this installment note like the one in Exhibit 10.12.

Exercise 10-12
Installment note amortization table **C1**

Use the information in Exercise 10-12 to prepare the journal entries for Eagle to record the note's issuance and each of the four payments.

Exercise 10-13
Installment note entries
C1

Selected accounts from WooHoo Co.'s adjusted trial balance for the year ended December 31 follow. Prepare the liabilities section of its classified balance sheet.

Exercise 10-14
Reporting liabilities section of balance sheet
C1 **P2**

Notes payable (due in 5 years)	$ 3,000	Discount on bonds payable.	$400
Accounts payable.	500	Wages payable.	200
Bonds payable (due in 10 years).	10,000	Interest payable (due in 2 weeks).	100
Machinery.	4,500	Sales tax payable.	50

Montclair Company is considering a project that will require a $500,000 loan. It presently has total liabilities of $220,000 and total assets of $620,000.

1. Compute Montclair's (a) current debt-to-equity ratio and (b) the debt-to-equity ratio assuming it borrows $500,000 to fund the project.

2. If Montclair borrows the funds, does its financing structure become more or less risky?

Exercise 10-15
Applying debt-to-equity ratio
A3

Bringham Company issues bonds with a par value of $800,000. The bonds mature in 10 years and pay 6% annual interest in semiannual payments. The annual market rate for the bonds is 8%.

1. Compute the price of the bonds as of their issue date.

2. Prepare the journal entry to record the bonds' issuance.

Exercise 10-16[A]
Computing bond interest and price; recording bond issuance **C2**

Exercise 10-17^A Computing bond interest and price; recording bond issuance **C2**	Citywide Company issues bonds with a par value of $150,000. The bonds mature in five years and pay 10% annual interest in semiannual payments. The annual market rate for the bonds is 8%. **1.** Compute the price of the bonds as of their issue date. **2.** Prepare the journal entry to record the bonds' issuance.
Exercise 10-18^B **Effective Interest:** Amortization of bond discount **P5**	Stanford issues bonds dated January 1, 2019, with a par value of $500,000. The bonds' annual contract rate is 9%, and interest is paid semiannually on June 30 and December 31. The bonds mature in three years. The annual market rate at the date of issuance is 12%, and the bonds are sold for $463,140. **1.** What is the amount of the discount on these bonds at issuance? **2.** How much total bond interest expense will be recognized over the life of these bonds? **3.** Prepare an effective interest amortization table like Exhibit 10B.1 for these bonds.
Exercise 10-19^B **Effective Interest:** Amortization of bond premium **P6**	Quatro Co. issues bonds dated January 1, 2019, with a par value of $400,000. The bonds' annual contract rate is 13%, and interest is paid semiannually on June 30 and December 31. The bonds mature in three years. The annual market rate at the date of issuance is 12%, and the bonds are sold for $409,850. **1.** What is the amount of the premium on these bonds at issuance? **2.** How much total bond interest expense will be recognized over the life of these bonds? **3.** Prepare an effective interest amortization table like Exhibit 10B.2 for these bonds.
Exercise 10-20^C Identifying finance and operating leases **C3**	In each of the following separate cases, indicate whether the company has entered into a finance lease or an operating lease. _____ **1.** The lessor retains title to the asset, and the lease term is 3 years on an asset that has a 10-year useful life. _____ **2.** The title is transferred to the lessee. The lessee can purchase the asset for $1 at the end of the lease, and the lease term is five years. The leased asset has an expected useful life of six years. _____ **3.** The present value of the lease payments is 95% of the leased asset's market value, and the lease term is 90% of the leased asset's useful life.
Exercise 10-21^C Accounting for finance lease **C3**	On January 1, Harbor (lessee) signs a five-year lease for equipment that is accounted for as a finance lease. The lease requires five $10,000 lease payments (the first at the beginning of the lease and the remaining four at December 31 of years 1, 2, 3, and 4), and the present value of the five annual lease payments is $41,000, based on an 11% interest rate. **1.** Prepare the January 1 journal entry Harbor records at inception of the lease for any asset or liability. **2.** Prepare the January 1 entry Harbor records for the first $10,000 cash lease payment. **3.** If the leased asset has a five-year useful life with no salvage value, prepare the December 31 journal entry Harbor records each year for amortization of the leased asset.
Exercise 10-22^C Analyzing lease purchase options **C3**	**General Motors** advertised three alternatives for a 25-month lease on a new Tahoe: (1) zero dollars down and a lease payment of $1,750 per month for 25 months, (2) $5,000 down and $1,500 per month for 25 months, or (3) $38,500 down and no payments for 25 months. Use the present value Table B.3 in Appendix B to determine which is the best alternative for the customer (assume you have enough cash to accept any alternative and the annual interest rate is 12% compounded monthly).

connect

PROBLEM SET A	Hillside issues $4,000,000 of 6%, 15-year bonds dated January 1, 2019, that pay interest semiannually on June 30 and December 31. The bonds are issued at a price of $3,456,448.
Problem 10-1A **Straight-Line:** Amortization of bond discount **P2** **Check** (3) $4,143,552 (4) 12/31/2020 carrying value, $3,528,920	**Required** **1.** Prepare the January 1 journal entry to record the bonds' issuance. **2.** For each semiannual period, compute (*a*) the cash payment, (*b*) the straight-line discount amortization, and (*c*) the bond interest expense. **3.** Determine the total bond interest expense to be recognized over the bonds' life. **4.** Prepare the first two years of a straight-line amortization table like Exhibit 10.7. **5.** Prepare the journal entries to record the first two interest payments.

Refer to the bond details in Problem 10-1A, *except* assume that the bonds are issued at a price of $4,895,980.

Required

1. Prepare the January 1 journal entry to record the bonds' issuance.
2. For each semiannual period, compute (*a*) the cash payment, (*b*) the straight-line premium amortization, and (*c*) the bond interest expense.
3. Determine the total bond interest expense to be recognized over the bonds' life.
4. Prepare the first two years of a straight-line amortization table like Exhibit 10.11.
5. Prepare the journal entries to record the first two interest payments.

Problem 10-2A
Straight Line:
Amortization of bond premium

P3

Check (3) $2,704,020
(4) 12/31/2020 carrying value, $4,776,516

Ellis Company issues 6.5%, five-year bonds dated January 1, 2019, with a $250,000 par value. The bonds pay interest on June 30 and December 31 and are issued at a price of $255,333. The annual market rate is 6% on the issue date.

Required

1. Calculate the total bond interest expense over the bonds' life.
2. Prepare a straight-line amortization table like Exhibit 10.11 for the bonds' life.
3. Prepare the journal entries to record the first two interest payments.

Problem 10-3A
Straight-Line:
Amortization of bond premium

P3

Check (2) 6/30/2021 carrying value, $252,668

Legacy issues $325,000 of 5%, four-year bonds dated January 1, 2019, that pay interest semiannually on June 30 and December 31. They are issued at $292,181 when the market rate is 8%.

Required

1. Prepare the January 1 journal entry to record the bonds' issuance.
2. Determine the total bond interest expense to be recognized over the bonds' life.
3. Prepare a straight-line amortization table like the one in Exhibit 10.7 for the bonds' first two years.
4. Prepare the journal entries to record the first two interest payments.

Problem 10-4A
Straight-Line:
Amortization of bond discount **P2**

Check (2) $97,819
(3) 12/31/2020 carrying value, $308,589

On November 1, 2019, Norwood borrows $200,000 cash from a bank by signing a five-year installment note bearing 8% interest. The note requires equal payments of $50,091 each year on October 31.

Required

1. Complete an amortization table for this installment note similar to the one in Exhibit 10.12.
2. Prepare the journal entries in which Norwood records (*a*) accrued interest as of December 31, 2019 (the end of its annual reporting period), and (*b*) the first annual payment on the note.

Problem 10-5A
Installment notes

C1

Check (1) 10/31/2023 ending balance, $46,382

At the end of the current year, the following information is available for both Pulaski Company and Scott Company.

Problem 10-6A
Applying the debt-to-equity ratio

A3

	Pulaski Company	Scott Company
Total assets	$860,000	$440,000
Total liabilities	360,000	240,000
Total equity	500,000	200,000

Required

1. Compute the debt-to-equity ratios for both companies.
2. Which company has the riskier financing structure?

Hartford Research issues bonds dated January 1 that pay interest semiannually on June 30 and December 31. The bonds have a $40,000 par value and an annual contract rate of 10%, and they mature in 10 years.

Required

For each separate situation, (*a*) determine the bonds' issue price on January 1 and (*b*) prepare the journal entry to record their issuance.

1. The market rate at the date of issuance is 8%.
2. The market rate at the date of issuance is 10%.
3. The market rate at the date of issuance is 12%.

Problem 10-7A^A
Computing bond price and recording issuance

C2

Check (1) Premium, $5,437

(3) Discount, $4,588

Problem 10-8A[B]

Effective Interest:

Amortization of bond

discount   **P5**

Check (2) $97,819

(3) 12/31/2020 carrying value, $307,308

Refer to the bond details in Problem 10-4A.

Required

1. Prepare the January 1 journal entry to record the bonds' issuance.
2. Determine the total bond interest expense to be recognized over the bonds' life.
3. Prepare an effective interest amortization table like the one in Exhibit 10B.1 for the bonds' first two years.
4. Prepare the journal entries to record the first two interest payments.

Problem 10-9A[B]

Effective Interest:

Amortization of bond

premium   **P6**

Check (2) 6/30/2021 carrying value, $252,865

Refer to the bond details in Problem 10-3A.

Required

1. Compute the total bond interest expense over the bonds' life.
2. Prepare an effective interest amortization table like the one in Exhibit 10B.2 for the bonds' life.
3. Prepare the journal entries to record the first two interest payments.

Problem 10-10A[B]

Effective Interest:

Amortization of bond

P6

Check (3) 6/30/2020 carrying value, $182,448

Ike issues $180,000 of 11%, three-year bonds dated January 1, 2019, that pay interest semiannually on June 30 and December 31. They are issued at $184,566 when the market rate is 10%.

Required

1. Prepare the January 1 journal entry to record the bonds' issuance.
2. Determine the total bond interest expense to be recognized over the bonds' life.
3. Prepare an effective interest amortization table like Exhibit 10B.2 for the bonds' first two years.
4. Prepare the journal entries to record the first two interest payments.

Problem 10-11A[C]

Accounting for finance lease

C3

On January 1, Rogers (lessee) signs a three-year lease for machinery that is accounted for as a finance lease. The lease requires three $18,000 lease payments (the first at the beginning of the lease and the remaining two at December 31 of Year 1 and Year 2). The present value of the three annual lease payments is $51,000, using a 6.003% interest rate. The lease payment schedule follows.

	(A)	(B) Debit Interest on Lease Liability 6.003% × (A)	+	(C) Debit Lease Liability (D) − (B)	=	(D) Credit Cash Lease Payment	(E) Ending Balance of Lease Liability (A) − (C)
Date	Beginning Balance of Lease Liability						
Jan. 1, Year 1	$51,000			$18,000		$18,000	$33,000
Dec. 31, Year 1....	33,000	$1,981		16,019		18,000	16,981
Dec. 31, Year 2 ...	16,981	1,019		16,981		18,000	0
		$3,000		$51,000		$54,000	

Required

1. Prepare the January 1 journal entry at the start of the lease to record any asset or liability.
2. Prepare the January 1 journal entry to record the first $18,000 cash lease payment.
3. Prepare the December 31 journal entry to record straight-line amortization with zero salvage value at the end of (a) Year 1, (b) Year 2, and (c) Year 3.
4. Prepare the December 31 journal entry to record the $18,000 cash lease payment at the end of (a) Year 1 and (b) Year 2.

Problem 10-12A[C]

Accounting for operating lease

C3

Refer to the lease details in Problem 10-11A. Assume that this lease is classified as an operating lease instead of a finance lease.

Required

1. Prepare the January 1 journal entry at the start of the lease to record any asset or liability.
2. Prepare the January 1 journal entry to record the first $18,000 cash lease payment.
3. Prepare the December 31 journal entry to record amortization at the end of (a) Year 1, (b) Year 2, and (c) Year 3.
4. Prepare the December 31 journal entry to record the $18,000 cash lease payment at the end of (a) Year 1 and (b) Year 2.

Romero issues $3,400,000 of 10%, 10-year bonds dated January 1, 2019, that pay interest semiannually on June 30 and December 31. The bonds are issued at a price of $3,010,000.

Required

1. Prepare the January 1 journal entry to record the bonds' issuance.
2. For each semiannual period, compute (*a*) the cash payment, (*b*) the straight-line discount amortization, and (*c*) the bond interest expense.
3. Determine the total bond interest expense to be recognized over the bonds' life.
4. Prepare the first two years of a straight-line amortization table like Exhibit 10.7.
5. Prepare the journal entries to record the first two interest payments.

PROBLEM SET B

Problem 10-1B
Straight-Line: Amortization of bond discount

P2

Check (3) $3,790,000
(4) 6/30/2020 carrying value, $3,068,500

Refer to the bond details in Problem 10-1B, *except* assume that the bonds are issued at a price of $4,192,932.

Required

1. Prepare the January 1 journal entry to record the bonds' issuance.
2. For each semiannual period, compute (*a*) the cash payment, (*b*) the straight-line premium amortization, and (*c*) the bond interest expense.
3. Determine the total bond interest expense to be recognized over the bonds' life.
4. Prepare the first two years of a straight-line amortization table like Exhibit 10.11.
5. Prepare the journal entries to record the first two interest payments.

Problem 10-2B
Straight-Line: Amortization of bond premium

P3

Check (3) $2,607,068
(4) 6/30/2020 carrying value, $4,073,991

Ripkin Company issues 9%, five-year bonds dated January 1, 2019, with a $320,000 par value. The bonds pay interest on June 30 and December 31 and are issued at a price of $332,988. Their annual market rate is 8% on the issue date.

Required

1. Calculate the total bond interest expense over the bonds' life.
2. Prepare a straight-line amortization table like Exhibit 10.11 for the bonds' life.
3. Prepare the journal entries to record the first two interest payments.

Problem 10-3B
Straight-Line: Amortization of bond premium

P3

Check (2) 6/30/2021 carrying value, $326,493

Gomez issues $240,000 of 6%, 15-year bonds dated January 1, 2019, that pay interest semiannually on June 30 and December 31. They are issued at $198,494 when the market rate is 8%.

Required

1. Prepare the January 1 journal entry to record the bonds' issuance.
2. Determine the total bond interest expense to be recognized over the life of the bonds.
3. Prepare a straight-line amortization table like the one in Exhibit 10.7 for the bonds' first two years.
4. Prepare the journal entries to record the first two interest payments.

Analysis Component

5. Assume the market rate at issuance is 4% instead of 8%. Without providing numbers, describe how this change affects the amounts reported on Gomez's financial statements.

Problem 10-4B
Straight-Line: Amortization of bond discount

P2

Check (2) $257,506
(3) 6/30/2020 carrying value, $202,646

On October 1, 2019, Gordon borrows $150,000 cash from a bank by signing a three-year installment note bearing 10% interest. The note requires equal payments of $60,316 each year on September 30.

Required

1. Complete an amortization table for this installment note similar to the one in Exhibit 10.12.
2. Prepare the journal entries to record (*a*) accrued interest as of December 31, 2019 (the end of its annual reporting period), and (*b*) the first annual payment on the note.

Problem 10-5B
Installment notes

C1

Check (1) 9/30/2021 ending balance, $54,836

Problem 10-6B

Applying the debt-to-equity ratio

A3

At the end of the current year, the following information is available for both Atlas Company and Bryan Company.

	Atlas Company	Bryan Company
Total assets	$180,000	$750,000
Total liabilities	80,000	562,500
Total equity	100,000	187,500

Required

1. Compute the debt-to-equity ratios for both companies.
2. Which company has the riskier financing structure?

Problem 10-7B[A]

Computing bond price and recording issuance

C2

Check (1) Premium, $6,948

(3) Discount, $6,326

Flagstaff Systems issues bonds dated January 1 that pay interest semiannually on June 30 and December 31. The bonds have a $90,000 par value and an annual contract rate of 12%, and they mature in five years.

Required

For each separate situation, (a) determine the bonds' issue price on January 1 and (b) prepare the journal entry to record their issuance.

1. The market rate at the date of issuance is 10%.
2. The market rate at the date of issuance is 12%.
3. The market rate at the date of issuance is 14%.

Problem 10-8B[B]

Effective Interest:

Amortization of bond discount P5

Check (2) $257,506

(3) 6/30/2020 carrying value, $200,803

Refer to the bond details in Problem 10-4B.

Required

1. Prepare the January 1 journal entry to record the bonds' issuance.
2. Determine the total bond interest expense to be recognized over the bonds' life.
3. Prepare an effective interest amortization table like the one in Exhibit 10B.1 for the bonds' first two years.
4. Prepare the journal entries to record the first two interest payments.

Problem 10-9B[B]

Effective Interest:

Amortization of bond premium P6

Check (2) 6/30/2021 carrying value, $327,136

Refer to the bond details in Problem 10-3B.

Required

1. Compute the total bond interest expense over the bonds' life.
2. Prepare an effective interest amortization table like the one in Exhibit 10B.2 for the bonds' life.
3. Prepare the journal entries to record the first two interest payments.

Problem 10-10B[B]

Effective Interest:

Amortization of bond

P6

Check (3) 6/30/2020 carrying value, $479,202

Valdez issues $450,000 of 13%, four-year bonds dated January 1, 2019, that pay interest semiannually on June 30 and December 31. They are issued at $493,608 when the market rate is 10%.

Required

1. Prepare the January 1 journal entry to record the bonds' issuance.
2. Determine the total bond interest expense to be recognized over the bonds' life.
3. Prepare an effective interest amortization table like the one in Exhibit 10B.2 for the bonds' first two years.
4. Prepare the journal entries to record the first two interest payments.

Analysis Component

5. Assume that the market rate at issuance is 14% instead of 10%. Without presenting numbers, describe how this change affects the amounts reported on Valdez's financial statements.

On January 1, Kwak (lessee) signs a three-year lease for equipment that is accounted for as a finance lease. The lease requires three $14,000 lease payments (the first at the beginning of the lease and the remaining two at December 31 of Year 1 and Year 2). The present value of the three annual lease payments is $39,000, using a 7.9% interest rate. The lease payment schedule follows.

Problem 10-11B[C]

Accounting for finance lease

C3

	(A)	Payments			(E)
		(B)	(C)	(D)	
		Debit	*Debit*	*Credit*	
		Interest on			Ending Balance
	Beginning Balance	Lease Liability +	Lease Liability =	Cash Lease	of Lease Liability
Date	of Lease Liability	7.9% × (A)	(D) − (B)	Payment	(A) − (C)
Jan. 1, Year 1	$39,000		$14,000	$14,000	$25,000
Dec. 31, Year 1 ...	25,000	$1,975	12,025	14,000	12,975
Dec. 31, Year 2 ...	12,975	1,025	12,975	14,000	0
		$3,000	$39,000	$42,000	

Required

1. Prepare the January 1 journal entry at the start of the lease to record any asset or liability.
2. Prepare the January 1 journal entry to record the first $14,000 cash lease payment.
3. Prepare the December 31 journal entry to record straight-line amortization with zero salvage value at the end of (*a*) Year 1, (*b*) Year 2, and (*c*) Year 3.
4. Prepare the December 31 journal entry to record the $14,000 cash lease payment at the end of (*a*) Year 1 and (*b*) Year 2.

Refer to the lease details in Problem 10-11B. Assume that this lease is classified as an operating lease instead of a finance lease.

Problem 10-12B[C]

Accounting for operating lease

C3

Required

1. Prepare the January 1 journal entry at the start of the lease to record any asset or liability.
2. Prepare the January 1 journal entry to record the first $14,000 cash lease payment.
3. Prepare the December 31 journal entry to record amortization at the end of (*a*) Year 1, (*b*) Year 2, and (*c*) Year 3.
4. Prepare the December 31 journal entry to record the $14,000 cash lease payment at the end of (*a*) Year 1 and (*b*) Year 2.

This serial problem began in Chapter 1 and continues through most of the book. If previous chapter segments were not completed, the serial problem can begin at this point.

SERIAL PROBLEM
Business Solutions

A1   A3

SP 10   Santana Rey has consulted with her local banker and is considering financing an expansion of her business by obtaining a long-term bank loan. Selected account balances at March 31, 2020, for **Business Solutions** follow.

| Total assets .... | $120,268 | Total liabilities .... | $875 | Total equity .... | $119,393 |

Required

1. The bank has offered a long-term secured note to Business Solutions. The bank's loan procedures require that a client's debt-to-equity ratio not exceed 0.8. As of March 31, 2020, what is the maximum amount that Business Solutions could borrow from this bank?
2. If Business Solutions borrows the maximum amount allowed from the bank, what percentage of assets would be financed (*a*) by debt and (*b*) by equity?
3. What are some factors Santana Rey should consider before borrowing the funds?

©Alexander Image/Shutterstock

Check   (1) $94,639

Accounting Analysis

**COMPANY
ANALYSIS**

A1   A2

APPLE

AA 10-1   Use **Apple**'s financial statements in Appendix A to answer the following.

1. Identify Apple's long-term debt as reported on its balance sheet at (*a*) September 30, 2017, and (*b*) September 24, 2016.
2. Calculate the percentage change in long-term debt from September 24, 2016, to September 30, 2017.
3. If Apple's reported long-term debt continues on the current trend, do we expect total interest expense to increase or decrease?

**COMPARATIVE
ANALYSIS**

A3

**APPLE
GOOGLE**

AA 10-2   Key figures for **Apple** and **Google** follow.

$ millions	Apple		Google	
	Current Year	Prior Year	Current Year	Prior Year
Total assets	$375,319	$321,686	$197,295	$167,497
Total liabilities	241,272	193,437	44,793	28,461
Total equity	134,047	128,249	152,502	139,036

Required

1. Compute the debt-to-equity ratios for Apple and Google for both the current year and the prior year.
2. Use the ratios from part 1 to determine which company's financing structure is least risky.
3. Is its debt-to-equity ratio more risky or less risky compared to the industry (assumed) average of 0.5 for (*a*) Apple and (*b*) Google?

GLOBAL ANALYSIS

A3

**Samsung
APPLE
GOOGLE**

AA 10-3   Selected results from **Samsung**, **Apple**, and **Google** follow.

In millions	Samsung		Apple	Google
	Current Year	Prior Year	Current Year	Current Year
Total assets............	₩301,752,090	₩262,174,324	$375,319	$197,295
Total liabilities	87,260,662	69,211,291	241,272	44,793
Total equity............	214,491,428	192,963,033	134,047	152,502

Required

1. Compute Samsung's debt-to-equity ratio for the current year and the prior year.
2. Is Samsung's financing structure more risky or less risky in the current year versus the prior year?
3. In the current year, is Samsung's financing structure more risky or less risky than (*a*) Apple's and (*b*) Google's?

Beyond the Numbers

**ETHICS
CHALLENGE**

C3   A1

BTN 10-1   Traverse County needs a new county government building that would cost $10 million. The politicians feel that voters will not approve a municipal bond issue to fund the building because it would increase taxes. They opt to have a state bank issue $10 million of tax-exempt securities to pay for the building construction. The county then will make yearly lease payments (of principal and interest) to repay the obligation. Unlike conventional municipal bonds, the lease payments are not binding obligations on the county and, therefore, require no voter approval.

Required

1. Do you think the actions of the politicians and the bankers in this situation are ethical?
2. In terms of risk, how do the tax-exempt securities used to pay for the building compare to a conventional municipal bond issued by Traverse County?

**COMMUNICATING
IN PRACTICE**

P3

BTN 10-2   Your business associate mentions that she is considering investing in corporate bonds currently selling at a premium. She says that because the bonds are selling at a premium, they are highly valued and her investment will yield more than the going rate of return for the risk involved. Reply with a memorandum to confirm or correct your associate's interpretation of premium bonds.

BTN 10-3 Access the March 23, 2017, filing of the 10-K report of **Home Depot** for the year ended January 29, 2017, from **SEC.gov** (ticker: HD). Refer to Home Depot's balance sheet, including its note 4 (on debt).

TAKING IT TO THE NET

A2

Required

1. Identify Home Depot's long-term liabilities and the amounts for those liabilities from Home Depot's balance sheet at January 29, 2017.

2. Review Home Depot's note 4. The note reports that as of January 29, 2017, it had $2.947 billion of "5.875% Senior Notes; due December 16, 2036; interest payable semiannually on June 16 and December 16." These notes have a face value of $3.0 billion and were originally issued at $2.958 billion.

   a. Why would Home Depot issue $3.0 billion of its notes for only $2.958 billion?

   b. How much cash interest must Home Depot pay each June 16 and December 16 on these notes?

BTN 10-4ᴮ Break into teams and complete the following requirements related to *effective interest* amortization for a premium bond.

TEAMWORK IN ACTION

P5 P6

1. Each team member is to independently prepare a blank table with proper headings for amortization of a bond premium. When all have finished, compare tables and ensure that all are in agreement.

Parts 2 and 3 require use of these facts: On January 1, 2019, McElroy issues $100,000, 9%, five-year bonds at 104.1. The market rate at issuance is 8%. McElroy pays interest semiannually on June 30 and December 31.

2. In rotation, *each* team member must explain how to complete *one* line of the bond amortization table, including all computations for his or her line. All members are to fill in their tables during this process. You need not finish the table; stop after all members have explained a line.

3. In rotation, *each* team member is to identify a separate column of the table and indicate what the final number in that column will be and explain the reasoning.

4. Reach a team consensus as to what the total bond interest expense on this bond issue will be if the bond is not retired before maturity.

Hint: Rotate teams to report on parts 4 and 5. Consider requiring entries for issuance and interest payments.

5. As a team, prepare a list of similarities and differences between the amortization table just prepared and the amortization table if the bond had been issued at a discount.

BTN 10-5 Joey Shamah and Scott Borba are the founders of **e.l.f. Cosmetics**. Assume that the company currently has $250,000 in equity and is considering a $100,000 expansion to meet increased demand. The $100,000 expansion would yield $16,000 in additional annual income before interest expense. Assume that the business currently earns $40,000 annual income before interest expense of $10,000, yielding a return on equity of 12% ($30,000/$250,000). To fund the expansion, the company is considering the issuance of a 10-year, $100,000 note with annual interest payments (the principal due at the end of 10 years).

ENTREPRENEURIAL DECISION

A1

Required

1. Using return on equity as the decision criterion, show computations to support or reject the expansion if interest on the $100,000 note is (*a*) 10%, (*b*) 15%, (*c*) 16%, (*d*) 17%, and (*e*) 20%.

2. What general rule do the results in part 1 illustrate?

BTN 10-6 Visit your city or county library. Ask the librarian to help you locate the most recent financial records of your city or county government. Examine those records.

HITTING THE ROAD

A1

Required

1. Determine the amount of long-term bonds and notes currently outstanding.

2. Read the supporting information to your municipality's financial statements and record

   a. The market interest rate(s) when the bonds and/or notes were issued.

   b. The date(s) when the bonds and/or notes will mature.

   c. Any rating(s) on the bonds and/or notes received from **Moody's Investors Service, Standard & Poor's Ratings Services, Fitch Ratings**, or another rating agency.

---

11 Corporate Reporting and Analysis

Chapter Preview

COMMON STOCK

C1 Stock basics

P1 Stock issuance:

Par value

No-par value

Stated value

Noncash assets

NTK 11-1

DIVIDENDS

P2 Cash dividends

Stock dividends

Stock splits

NTK 11-2

PREFERRED STOCK

C2 Issuance

Dividend preferences

Rationale

NTK 11-3

TREASURY STOCK

P3 Purchasing treasury stock

Reissuing treasury stock

NTK 11-4

REPORTING AND ANALYSIS

C3 Retained earnings and equity

A1 EPS

A2 PE ratio

A3 Dividend yield

A4 Book value

NTK 11-5

Learning Objectives

CONCEPTUAL

C1 Identify characteristics of corporations and their organization.

C2 Explain characteristics of, and distribute dividends between, common and preferred stock.

C3 Explain the items reported in retained earnings.

ANALYTICAL

A1 Compute earnings per share and describe its use.

A2 Compute price-earnings ratio and describe its use in analysis.

A3 Compute dividend yield and explain its use in analysis.

A4 Compute book value and explain its use in analysis.

PROCEDURAL

P1 Record the issuance of corporate stock.

P2 Record transactions involving cash dividends, stock dividends, and stock splits.

P3 Record purchases and sales of treasury stock.

Point of View

SAN FRANCISCO—"When I was in business school, I was thinking about doing something entrepreneurial," recalls Jeremy Stoppelman. "I'd always read the little vignettes about how someone started a small business."

"Word of mouth was the best way to find local businesses," explains Jeremy. "If we could find a way to capture that and bring it online, that would be powerful." To turn his idea into a business, Jeremy and his co-founders built **Yelp** (**Yelp.com**). Yelp publishes crowdsourced reviews about local businesses.

In the first few years of business, Jeremy had to make crucial decisions regarding creditor versus equity financing. When **Google** offered to purchase his business, Jeremy had to learn about stock types and ways to finance Yelp.

"I felt like we built this company," recalls Jeremy, "there's no fundamental reason for us to sell." Instead of selling to Google, and armed with knowledge of equity financing, Jeremy raised money from individual investors. Also, instead of paying dividends, he reinvested Yelp income into the company.

©Maria J. Avila/MCT/Newscom

Jeremy has some advice: "Building a great company takes time. If it's not something you're passionate about . . . you're not going to make it."

Sources: *Yelp website*, January 2019; *Yelp Foundation*, January 2018; *Time*, December 2014

CORPORATE FORM OF ORGANIZATION

A **corporation** is an entity that is separate from its owners and has many of the same rights as a person. Owners of corporations are called *stockholders* or *shareholders*. Corporations are separated into two types. A *privately held* (or *closely held*) corporation does not offer its stock for public sale and usually has few stockholders. A *publicly held* corporation offers its stock for public sale and can have thousands of stockholders. *Public sale* means selling and trading stock on an organized stock market.

C1

Identify characteristics of corporations and their organization.

Corporate Advantages

- **Separate legal entity:** A corporation has many of the same rights, duties, and responsibilities as a person. It takes actions through its agents, who are its officers and managers.
- **Limited liability:** Stockholders are not liable for corporate actions or debt.
- **Transferable ownership rights:** Transfer of shares from one stockholder to another has no direct effect on operations except when it causes a change in directors who oversee the corporation.
- **Continuous life:** A corporation's life is indefinite because it is not tied to the physical lives of its owners.
- **No mutual agency for stockholders:** Stockholders, who are not officers and managers, cannot bind the corporation to contracts—called *lack of mutual agency*.
- **Easier capital accumulation:** Buying stock is attractive to investors because of the advantages above, which helps corporations collect large sums of money.

Corporate Disadvantages

- **Government regulation:** A corporation must follow a state's incorporation laws. Proprietorships and partnerships avoid many of these.
- **Corporate taxation:** Corporations pay many of the same taxes as proprietorships and partnerships plus *additional* taxes. The most burdensome are federal and state corporate income taxes that together can take 21% or more of pretax income. Also, corporate income is usually taxed a second time as part of stockholders' personal income when they receive cash dividends. This is called *double taxation*.

■ **Decision Insight**

Artificial Unintelligence **Dow Jones** newswire mistakenly published a bogus news story about **Google** acquiring **Apple** for $9 billion. Informed investors were not fooled, as Apple's market value was over $700 billion. However, bots designed to purchase stock of any company rumored of being acquired instantaneously purchased millions of shares of Apple. This event revealed how bots are increasingly impacting our financial markets. ■

Corporate Organization and Management

Incorporation   A corporation is created by getting a charter from a state government. A charter application is signed by the prospective stockholders called *incorporators* or *promoters* and then filed with the state. When the application process is complete and fees paid, the charter is issued and the corporation is formed. Investors then purchase the corporation's stock, meet as stockholders, and elect a board of directors.

Organization Expenses   **Organization expenses** (or *organization costs*) are the costs to start a corporation; they include legal fees, promoters' fees, and payments for a charter. The corporation records (debits) these costs to *Organization Expenses*. Organization costs are expensed as incurred.

EXHIBIT 11.1

Corporate Structure

> *Corporate governance* is the system by which companies are directed and controlled.

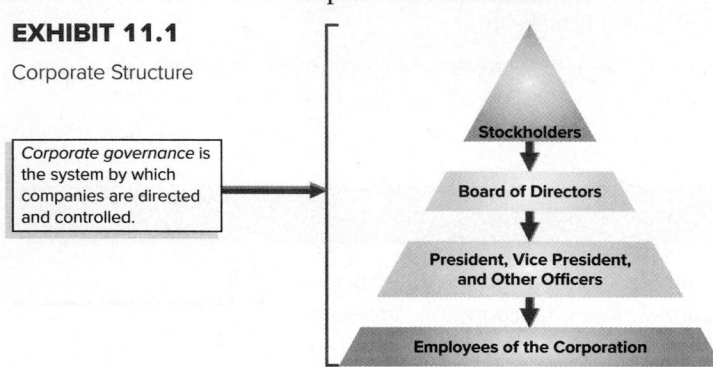

Management   Stockholders control a corporation by electing a *board of directors,* or *directors*. A stockholder usually has one vote for each share of stock owned. This control relation is shown in Exhibit 11.1. Directors are responsible for overseeing corporate activities. A board is in charge of hiring and firing key executives who manage day-to-day operations. A corporation's chief executive officer (CEO) is often its president. Several vice presidents are commonly assigned to specific areas such as finance, production, and marketing.

Point: *Bylaws* are guidelines that govern the corporation.

A corporation usually holds a stockholder meeting at least once a year to elect directors. Stockholders who do not attend stockholders' meetings can give their voting rights to an agent by signing a **proxy,** a document that gives a designated agent the right to vote the stock.

■ **Decision Insight**

Keep the Faith   Sources for start-up money include (1) "angel" investors such as family, friends, or anyone who believes in a company; (2) employees, investors, and even suppliers; and (3) venture capitalists (investors) who have a record of entrepreneurial success. ■

Corporate Stockholders

Rights of Stockholders   Stockholders have *specific* rights under the corporation's charter and *general* rights under state law. Stockholders also have the right to receive timely financial reports. When a corporation has only one class of stock, it is called **common stock.** State laws vary, but common stockholders usually have the right to

Point: While rare, not all common stock has voting rights; **Google's** C Class shares are nonvoting.

Point: Green Bay Packers are the only nonprofit, community-owned major professional team.

- Vote at stockholders' meetings (or register proxy votes).
- Sell or dispose of their stock.
- Purchase their proportional share of any common stock later issued. This **preemptive right** protects stockholders' proportionate interest. For example, a stockholder who owns 25% of a corporation's stock has the first opportunity to buy 25% of any new stock issued.
- Receive the same dividend, if any, on each common share.
- Share in any assets remaining after creditors and preferred stockholders are paid if the corporation is liquidated. Each common share receives the same amount.

Stock Certificates and Transfer A corporation sometimes gives a *stock certificate* as proof of share ownership. Exhibit 11.2 shows a stock certificate issued by the **Green Bay Packers**. A certificate shows the company name, stockholder name, number of shares, and other information. Issuance of paper certificates is becoming less common.

Registrar and Transfer Agents If a corporation's stock is traded on a stock exchange, the corporation has a registrar and a transfer agent. A *registrar* keeps a list of stockholders for stockholder meetings and dividend payments. A *transfer agent* assists with purchases and sales of shares. Registrars and transfer agents are usually large banks or trust companies.

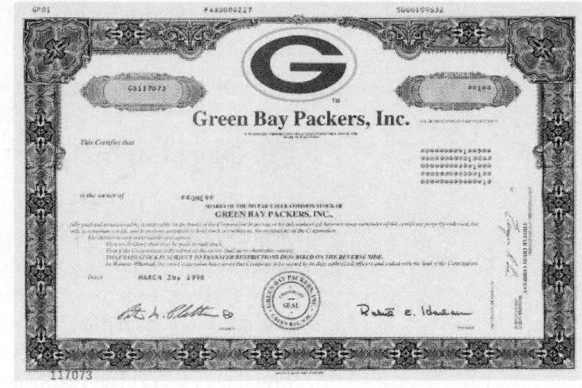
Courtesy of JJW Images

EXHIBIT 11.2

Stock Certificate

Corporate Stock

Capital stock is shares issued to obtain capital (owner financing).

Authorized Stock **Authorized stock** is the number of shares that a corporation's charter allows it to sell. The number of authorized shares usually exceeds the number of shares issued (and outstanding) by a large amount. *Outstanding stock* is stock held by stockholders. No journal entry is required for stock authorization. A corporation discloses the number of shares authorized in the equity section of its balance sheet or notes. **Apple**'s balance sheet reports 12.6 billion common shares authorized.

Selling (Issuing) Stock A corporation can sell stock directly or indirectly. To *sell directly,* it offers its stock to buyers. This type of sale is common with privately held corporations. To *sell indirectly,* a corporation pays a brokerage house (investment banker) to sell its stock. Some brokerage houses *underwrite* stock, meaning they buy the stock from the corporation and resell it to investors.

Market Value of Stock **Market value per share** is the price at which a stock is bought and sold. Expected future income, dividends, growth, and economic factors influence market value. The current market value of previously issued shares does not impact the issuing corporation's stockholders' equity.

Classes of Stock When all authorized shares have the same rights and characteristics, the stock is called *common stock*. A corporation sometimes issues more than one class of stock, including preferred stock and different classes of common stock. **American Greetings** has two types of common stock: Class A stock has 1 vote per share and Class B stock has 10 votes per share.

Par Value Stock **Par value stock** is stock that has a **par value,** which is an amount assigned per share by the corporation in its charter. **Monster Worldwide**'s common stock has a par value of $0.001. Other commonly assigned par values are $5, $1 and $0.01. There is no restriction on assigned par value. In many states, the par value of a stock establishes **minimum legal capital,** which is the least amount that the buyers of stock must contribute to the corporation or be at risk to pay creditors at a future date.

No-Par Value Stock **No-par value stock,** or *no-par stock,* is stock *not* assigned an amount per share by the corporate charter. There is no minimum legal capital with no-par stock.

Stated Value Stock **Stated value stock** is no-par stock that has an assigned "stated" value per share. Stated value per share is the minimum legal capital per share in this case.

Stockholders' Equity A corporation's equity is called **stockholders' equity,** or *shareholders' equity*. Exhibit 11.3 shows stockholders' equity consists of (1) paid-in (or contributed) capital and (2) retained

Subcategories of Authorized Stock

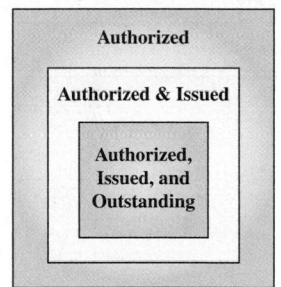

Innermost box would show a decline in shares issued if a company buys back its issued stock.

Point: Managers set a low par value when minimum legal capital or state issuance taxes are based on par.

Point: Par, no-par, and stated value do *not* affect the stock's market value.

EXHIBIT 11.3

Equity Composition

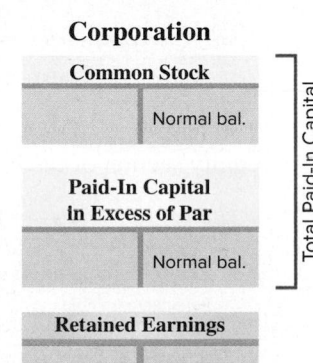

earnings. **Paid-in capital** is the total amount of cash and other assets the corporation receives from its stockholders in exchange for its stock. **Retained earnings** is the cumulative net income (and loss) not distributed as dividends to its stockholders.

■ Decision Insight

Stock Quote   The **AT&T** stock quote is interpreted as (left to right): **Hi,** highest price in past 52 weeks; **Lo,** lowest price in past 52 weeks; **Sym,** company exchange symbol;

52 Weeks									
Hi	Lo	Sym	Div	Yld %	PE	Hi	Lo	Close	Net Chg
42.70	32.55	T	2.00	5.24	7.95	38.31	37.77	37.81	+0.53

Div, dividends paid per share in past year; **Yld %,** dividend divided by closing price; **PE,** stock price per share divided by earnings per share; **Hi,** highest price for the day; **Lo,** lowest price for the day; **Close,** closing price for the day; **Net Chg,** change in closing price from prior day. ■

COMMON STOCK

P1 _____

Record the issuance of corporate stock.

Issuance of stock affects paid-in (contributed) capital accounts; retained earnings is unaffected.

Issuing Par Value Stock

Par value stock can be issued at par, at a premium (above par), or at a discount (below par). Cash or other assets are received in exchange for stock.

Issuing Par Value Stock at Par   When common stock is issued at par value, we record both the asset(s) received and the par value stock issued. The entry to record Dillon's issuance of 30,000 shares of $10 par value stock for $300,000 cash on June 5 follows.

Assets = Liabilities + Equity
+300,000   +300,000

June 5	Cash	300,000	
	Common Stock, $10 Par Value*		300,000
	Issued 30,000 shares of $10 par value stock at par.		

*$10 par value × 30,000 shares

Issuing Par Value Stock at a Premium   A **premium on stock** occurs when a corporation sells its stock for more than par (or stated) value. If Dillon issues its $10 par value common stock at $12 per share, its stock is sold at a $2 per share premium. The premium, called **paid-in capital in excess of par value,** is reported as part of equity; it is not revenue and is not listed on the income statement. The entry to issue 30,000 shares of $10 par value stock for $12 per share follows.

Point: Paid-In Capital in Excess of Par Value is also called *Additional Paid-In Capital.*

Assets = Liabilities + Equity
+360,000   +300,000
                  +60,000

June 5	Cash	360,000	
	Common Stock, $10 Par Value*		300,000
	Paid-In Capital in Excess of Par Value, Common Stock†		**60,000**
	Sold and issued 30,000 shares of $10 par value common stock at $12 per share.		

*$10 par value × 30,000 shares   †[$12 issue price − $10 par value] × 30,000 shares

Point: The phrase *paid-in capital* is interchangeable with *contributed capital.*

The Paid-In Capital in Excess of Par Value account is added to the par value of the stock in the equity section of the balance sheet, as shown in Exhibit 11.4.

EXHIBIT 11.4

Stockholders' Equity for Stock Issued at a Premium

Common stock—$10 par value; 50,000 shares authorized; 30,000 shares issued and outstanding	$300,000
Paid-in capital in excess of par value, common stock	**60,000**
Retained earnings*	65,000
Total stockholders' equity..	$425,000

*This is the company's first year of operations, with income of $65,000 and no dividends.

Issuing Par Value Stock at a Discount A **discount on stock** occurs when it is sold for less than par value. Most states prohibit this. If stock is issued at a discount, the amount by which issue price is less than par is debited to a *Discount on Common Stock* account, a contra to the Common Stock account, and its balance is subtracted from the par value of stock.

Issuing No-Par Value Stock

When no-par stock is issued, the amount the corporation receives is credited to a no-par stock account. The entry to issue 1,000 shares of no-par common stock for $40 cash per share follows.

Oct. 20	Cash	40,000	
	Common Stock, No-Par Value*		40,000
	Issued 1,000 shares of no-par stock at $40 per share.		

Assets = Liabilities + Equity
+40,000   +40,000

*$40 issue price × 1,000 no-par shares

Issuing Stated Value Stock

When stated value stock is issued, the stated value is credited to the stock account. Any amount above the stated value is credited to Paid-In Capital in Excess of Stated Value, which is reported in stockholders' equity. The entry to issue 1,000 shares of no-par common stock having a stated value of $40 per share in return for $50 cash per share follows.

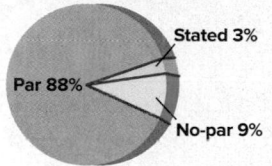
Frequency of Stock Types
Stated 3%
Par 88%
No-par 9%

Oct. 20	Cash	50,000	
	Common Stock, $40 Stated Value*		40,000
	Paid-In Capital in Excess of Stated Value, Common Stock† ...		10,000
	Issued 1,000 shares of $40 per share stated value stock at $50 per share.		

Assets = Liabilities + Equity
+50,000   +40,000
                    +10,000

*$40 stated value × 1,000 shares   †[$50 issue price − $40 stated value] × 1,000 shares

Issuing Stock for Noncash Assets

A corporation can receive assets other than cash in exchange for its stock. (It also can take liabilities such as a mortgage on property received.) The corporation records the assets received at their market values as of the transaction date. The stock given in exchange is recorded at its par (or stated) value with any excess recorded in the Paid-In Capital in Excess of Par (or Stated) Value account. (If no-par stock is issued, the stock is recorded at the assets' market value.) The entry to record receipt of land valued at $105,000 in return for 4,000 shares of $20 par value common stock is

Point: Stock issued for noncash assets is recorded at the market value of either the stock or the noncash assets, whichever is more determinable.

June 10	Land	105,000	
	Common Stock, $20 Par Value*		80,000
	Paid-In Capital in Excess of Par Value, Common Stock†		25,000
	Exchanged 4,000 shares of $20 par value stock for land.		

Assets = Liabilities + Equity
+105,000   +80,000
                    +25,000

*$20 par value × 4,000 shares   †$105,000 asset value − $80,000 par value

A corporation sometimes gives shares of its stock to promoters in exchange for their work in organizing the corporation, which it records as organization expenses. The entry to issue 600 shares of $15 par value common stock for $12,000 of organizing work is

June 5	Organization Expenses...............................	12,000	
	Common Stock, $15 Par Value*		9,000
	Paid-In Capital in Excess of Par Value, Common Stock†		3,000
	Gave promoters 600 shares of $15 par value common stock in exchange for their services.		

Assets = Liabilities + Equity
                    −12,000
                    +9,000
                    +3,000

*$15 par value × 600 shares   †$12,000 services value − $9,000 par value

 **11-1**

Recording Stock
Issuance

P1

Prepare journal entries to record the following four separate issuances of stock.

1. Issued 80 shares of $5 par value common stock for $700 cash.
2. Issued 40 shares of no-par common stock to promoters in exchange for their efforts, estimated to be worth $800. The stock has a $1 per share stated value.
3. Issued 40 shares of no-par common stock in exchange for land estimated to be worth $800. The stock has no stated value.
4. Issued 20 shares of no-par common stock with a stated value of $30 per share for $900 cash.

Solution

1.

Cash	700	
Common Stock, $5 Par Value*		400
Paid-In Capital in Excess of Par Value, Common Stock† ..		300
Issued common stock for cash.		

*80 shares × $5 per share = $400   †$700 − $400 = $300

2.

Organization Expenses	800	
Common Stock, $1 Stated Value		40
Paid-In Capital in Excess of Stated Value, Common Stock...		760
Issued stock to promoters.		

3.

Land	800	
Common Stock, No-Par Value......................		800
Issued stock in exchange for land.		

Do More: QS 11-2, QS 11-3, QS 11-4, QS 11-5, E 11-3, E 11-4, E 11-5

4.

Cash	900	
Common Stock, $30 Stated Value*..................		600
Paid-In Capital in Excess of Stated Value, Common Stock† ..		300
Issued stated value stock for cash.		

*20 shares × $30 stated value = $600   †$900 − $600 = $300

DIVIDENDS

P2 _____

Record transactions involving cash dividends, stock dividends, and stock splits.

Point: Amazon has never declared a cash dividend.

Percent of Corporations Paying Dividends

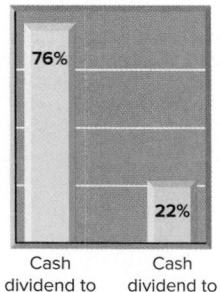

Cash dividend to common   Cash dividend to preferred

Assets = Liabilities + Equity
         +5,000   −5,000

Cash Dividends

The board of directors decides whether to pay cash dividends. The directors may decide to keep the cash to invest in the corporation's growth, to meet emergencies, or to pay off debt. Alternatively, many corporations pay cash dividends to their stockholders at regular dates.

Accounting for Cash Dividends

Dividend payment has three important dates: declaration, record, and payment. **Date of declaration** is the date the directors vote to declare and pay a dividend. This creates a legal liability of the corporation to its stockholders. **Date of record** is the date for identifying those stockholders to receive dividends. Persons who own stock on the date of record receive dividends. **Date of payment** is the date when the corporation makes payment.

Cash Dividend Dates

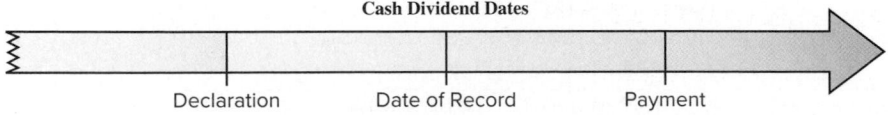

Declaration   Date of Record   Payment

The entry for a January 9 *declaration* of a $1 per share cash dividend by Z-Tech with 5,000 outstanding shares follows. Common Dividend Payable is a current liability.

Date of Declaration—Cash Dividend

Jan. 9	Retained Earnings....................................	5,000	
	Common Dividend Payable*		5,000
	Declared $1 per common share cash dividend.†		

*$1 per share declared dividend × 5,000 outstanding shares
†To aid learning and show how dividends impact retained earnings, we **debit** (reduce) **Retained Earnings** on the date of declaration in this chapter and all assignments. We normally debit Dividends; then, at period-end, Dividends is closed to Retained Earnings. The effect is the same: Retained earnings is decreased from dividends.

The *date of record* for this dividend is January 22. **No journal entry is made on the date of record.**

The February 1 *date of payment* entry removes the liability and reduces cash.

Date of Payment—Cash Dividend

Feb. 1	Common Dividend Payable	5,000	
	Cash		5,000
	Paid $1 per common share cash dividend.		

Assets = Liabilities + Equity
−5,000   −5,000

Deficits and Cash Dividends   A corporation with a debit (abnormal) balance for Retained Earnings has a **retained earnings deficit,** which occurs when a company has cumulative losses and/or pays more dividends than total earnings from current and prior years. A deficit reduces equity, as shown in Exhibit 11.5. Most states prohibit a corporation with a deficit from paying a cash dividend to protect creditors. Another type of dividend is a **liquidating cash dividend,** or *liquidating dividend,* where a corporation returns a portion of the capital contributed back to stockholders.

Point: The Retained Earnings Deficit account is also called *Accumulated Deficit.*

Common stock—$10 par value, 5,000 shares authorized, issued, and outstanding	$50,000
Retained earnings deficit	(6,000)
Total stockholders' equity..	$44,000

EXHIBIT 11.5

Stockholders' Equity with a Deficit

Stock Dividends

A **stock dividend,** declared by a corporation's directors, is a distribution of additional shares of its own stock to its stockholders without any payment in return. Stock dividends and cash dividends are different. A stock dividend does not reduce assets and equity but instead transfers a portion of equity from retained earnings to contributed capital.

Reasons for Stock Dividends   Stock dividends are given for at least two reasons. First, stock dividends keep the market price of the stock affordable. When a corporation has a stock dividend, it increases the number of outstanding shares, which lowers the per share stock price. Second, a stock dividend shows management's confidence that the company is doing well and will continue to do well.

Accounting for Stock Dividends   A stock dividend transfers part of retained earnings to contributed capital accounts, called *capitalizing* retained earnings. Accounting for a stock dividend depends on whether it is a small or large stock dividend.

- A **small stock dividend** is a distribution of 25% or less of previously outstanding shares. It is recorded by capitalizing retained earnings for an amount equal to the *market value* of the shares to be distributed.
- A **large stock dividend** is a distribution of more than 25% of previously outstanding shares. It is recorded by capitalizing retained earnings for the *par or stated value* of the stock.

Hint: Five Steps to Record Stock Dividends

Step 1: Identify number of shares outstanding.
Step 2: Identify the stock dividend percentage.
Step 3: Compute number of new shares (step 1 × step 2).
Step 4: Value new shares at market (small stock dividend) *or* par (large stock dividend).
Step 5: Determine debit (reduction) to Retained Earnings (step 3 × step 4).

The equity section of Quest's balance sheet just *before* its declaration of a stock dividend on December 31 follows.

Stockholders' Equity	Before Dividend
Common stock—$10 par value, 15,000 shares authorized, 10,000 shares issued and outstanding......	$100,000
Paid-in capital in excess of par value, common stock	8,000
Retained earnings..	35,000
Total stockholders' equity	$143,000

Small Stock Dividend   Assume that Quest declares a 10% stock dividend on December 31. This stock dividend of 1,000 shares, computed as 10% of its 10,000 outstanding shares, is to be distributed on January 20 to the stockholders of record on January 15. Because the market price of Quest's stock on December 31 is $15 per share, this small stock dividend declaration is recorded as follows.

Date of Declaration—Small Stock Dividend

Assets = Liabilities + Equity
−15,000
+10,000
+ 5,000

Dec. 31	Retained Earnings......................................	15,000	
	Common Stock Dividend Distributable*.............		10,000
	Paid-In Capital in Excess of Par Value, Common Stock†		5,000
	Declared a 10% stock dividend of 1,000 shares.		

*10% dividend × 10,000 outstanding shares × $10 par value
†10% dividend × 10,000 outstanding shares × [$15 market price − $10 par value]

The balance sheet changes in three ways when a small stock dividend is declared.

Point: The term *distributable* (not *payable*) is used for stock dividends. A stock dividend is never a liability because it never reduces assets.

Point: The credit to Paid-In Capital in Excess of Par Value is recorded when the stock dividend is declared. This account is not affected when stock is later distributed.

- Common Stock Dividend Distributable, an equity account that exists only until the shares are distributed, increases by $10,000.
- Paid-in capital in excess of par increases by $5,000, which is the amount in excess of par (or stated) value.
- Retained earnings decreases by $15,000, reflecting the increase in both common stock and paid-in capital in excess of par.

The impacts on stockholders' equity from the 10% stock dividend are in Exhibit 11.6.

EXHIBIT 11.6

Stockholders' Equity before, during, and after a Stock Dividend

Stockholders' Equity	Before Dividend	Date of Declaration	Date of Payment	After Dividend
Common stock—$10 par value, 15,000 shares authorized, 10,000 shares issued and outstanding...........	$100,000	$	$+10,000	$110,000
Common stock dividend distributable—1,000 shares...........	0	+10,000	−10,000	0
Paid-in capital in excess of par value, common stock	8,000	+ 5,000		13,000
Retained earnings..	35,000	−15,000		20,000
Total stockholders' equity	$143,000	$ 0	$ 0	$143,000

No entry is made on the date of record for a stock dividend. However, on January 20, the date of payment, Quest distributes the new shares and records the entry below (numbers from the "Payment" column of Exhibit 11.6). The combined effect of these entries is to transfer (or capitalize) $15,000 of retained earnings to paid-in capital accounts (see far right column of Exhibit 11.6). A stock dividend has no effect on the ownership percentage of stockholders.

Point: A stock dividend does not affect total assets or total equity.

Date of Payment—Small Stock Dividend

Assets = Liabilities + Equity
−10,000
+10,000

Jan. 20	Common Stock Dividend Distributable	10,000	
	Common Stock, $10 Par Value		10,000
	Record issuance of common stock dividend.		

Large Stock Dividend   A corporation capitalizes retained earnings equal to the par or stated value of the newly issued shares for a large stock dividend. Suppose Quest declares a stock dividend of 30% instead of 10% on December 31. Because this dividend is more than 25%, it is a large stock dividend. This means the par value of the 3,000 (10,000 outstanding shares × 30%) dividend shares is capitalized at the date of declaration with the entry below. This transaction decreases retained earnings and increases contributed capital by $30,000.

Date of Declaration—Large Stock Dividend

Assets = Liabilities + Equity
−30,000
+30,000

Dec. 31	Retained Earnings......................................	30,000	
	Common Stock Dividend Distributable*.............		30,000
	Declared a 30% stock dividend of 3,000 shares.		

*30% dividend × 10,000 outstanding shares × $10 par value

On the date of payment, the company makes the following entry.

Jan. 15	Common Stock Dividend Distributable	30,000	
	Common Stock, $10 Par Value		30,000

Stock Splits

A **stock split** is the distribution of additional shares to stockholders according to their percent ownership. When a stock split occurs, the corporation "calls in" its outstanding shares and issues more than one new share in exchange for each old share. Splits can be done in any ratio. **Apple** did a 7-for-1 stock split. Stock splits reduce the par or stated value per share. The reasons for stock splits are similar to those for stock dividends, including affordability and management confidence.

Assume CTI has 100,000 outstanding shares of $20 par value common stock with a current market value of $88 per share. A 2-for-1 stock split cuts par value in half as it replaces 100,000 shares of $20 par value stock with 200,000 shares of $10 par value stock. The split does not affect any equity amounts reported on the balance sheet or any individual stockholder's percent ownership. *No journal entry is made*. The only effect on the accounts is a change in the stock account description. After the split, CTI changes its stock account title to *Common Stock, $10 Par Value*. The stock's description on the balance sheet also changes to reflect the additional issued and outstanding shares and the new par value.

Before 5 : 1 Split: 1 share, $50 par

After 5 : 1 Split: 5 shares, $10 par

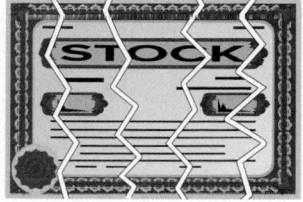

Financial Statement Effects of Dividends and Splits

	Cash Dividend	Small Stock Dividend	Large Stock Dividend	Stock Split
Total assets	**Decrease**	No change	No change	No change
Total liabilities	No change	No change	No change	No change
Total stockholders' equity	**Decrease**	No change	No change	No change
Common stock	No change	Increase	Increase	No change
Paid-in capital in excess of par	No change	Increase	No change	No change
Retained earnings	**Decrease**	**Decrease**	**Decrease**	No change

 ■ **Decision Maker**

Entrepreneur   A company you co-founded and own stock in announces a 50% stock dividend. Has the value of your stock investment increased, decreased, or remained the same? Would it make a difference if it was a 3-for-2 stock split executed in the form of a dividend? ■   *Answer:* The stock dividend does not affect the value of your investment or give you income. However, a stock dividend can reveal positive expectations and also improve a stock's marketability by making it more affordable. The same answer applies to the 3-for-2 stock split.

Point: A reverse stock split is the opposite of a stock split and results in fewer shares. It increases the par or stated value per share.

A company began the current year with the following balances in its stockholders' equity accounts.

Common stock—$10 par, 500 shares authorized, 200 shares issued and outstanding	$2,000
Paid-in capital in excess of par, common stock	1,000
Retained earnings.	5,000
Total.	$8,000

NEED-TO-KNOW 11-2

Recording Dividends

P2

All outstanding common stock was issued for $15 per share when the company was created. Prepare journal entries to account for the following transactions during the current year.

Jan. 10   The board declared a $0.10 cash dividend per share to shareholders of record on January 28.
Feb. 15   Paid the cash dividend declared on January 10.
Mar. 31   Declared a 20% stock dividend when the market value of the stock was $18 per share.
May   1   Distributed the stock dividend declared on March 31.
Dec.   1   Declared a 40% stock dividend when the market value of the stock was $25 per share.
Dec. 31   Distributed the stock dividend declared on December 1.

Solution

Jan. 10	Retained Earnings[a]	20	
	Common Dividend Payable		20
	Declared a $0.10 per share cash dividend.		
	[a]200 outstanding shares × $0.10		
Feb. 15	Common Dividend Payable...................................	20	
	Cash..		20
	Paid $0.10 per share cash dividend.		
Mar. 31	Retained Earnings[b]	720	
	Common Stock Dividend Distributable[c]...................		400
	Paid-In Capital in Excess of Par Value, Common Stock		320
	Declared a small stock dividend of 20%, or		
	40 shares; market value is $18 per share.		
	[b]200 outstanding shares × 20% × $18 market		
	[c]40 new shares × $10 par		
May 1	Common Stock Dividend Distributable.........................	400	
	Common Stock		400
	Distributed 40 shares of common stock.		
Dec. 1	Retained Earnings[d]	960	
	Common Stock Dividend Distributable		960
	Declared a large stock dividend of 40%, or 96 shares		
	(40% × [200 + 40]); par value is $10 per share.		
	[d]240 outstanding shares × 40% × $10 par		
Dec. 31	Common Stock Dividend Distributable.........................	960	
	Common Stock		960
	Distributed 96 shares of common stock.		

Do More: QS 11-6, QS 11-7, QS 11-8, QS 11-9, QS 11-10, E 11-6, E 11-7, E 11-8

PREFERRED STOCK

C2

Explain characteristics of, and distribute dividends between, common and preferred stock.

Preferred stock has special rights that give it priority (or senior status) over common stock in one or more areas. Special rights usually include a preference for receiving dividends and assets in liquidation. Preferred stock has the rights of common stock unless the corporate charter excludes them. A common exclusion is the right to vote.

Issuance of Preferred Stock

Preferred stock is recorded in its own separate capital accounts. If Dillon issues 50 shares of $100 par value preferred stock for $6,000 cash, the entry is

Assets = Liabilities + Equity
+6,000   +5,000
                               +1,000

July 1	Cash...	6,000	
	Preferred Stock, $100 Par Value*..................		5,000
	Paid-In Capital in Excess of Par Value, Preferred Stock[†] ..		1,000
	Issued preferred stock for cash.		

*$100 par value × 50 shares   [†]$6,000 cash − [$100 par value × 50 shares]

The equity section of the year-end balance sheet for Dillon, including preferred stock, is in Exhibit 11.7. (The entry for issuing no-par preferred stock is similar to issuing no-par common stock. Also, the entry for issuing preferred stock for noncash assets is similar to that for common stock.)

EXHIBIT 11.7

Stockholders' Equity with Common and Preferred Stock

Stockholders' Equity	
Preferred stock—$100 par value; 1,000 shares authorized; 50 shares issued and outstanding............	$ 5,000
Paid-in capital in excess of par value, preferred stock	1,000
Common stock—$10 par value; 50,000 shares authorized; 30,000 shares issued and outstanding............	300,000
Retained earnings..	65,000
Total stockholders' equity	$371,000

Dividend Preference of Preferred Stock

Preferred stock has preference for dividends, meaning that preferred stockholders are paid their dividends before any dividends are paid to common stockholders. A preference for dividends does *not* guarantee dividends. If the directors do not declare a dividend, neither the preferred nor the common stockholders get dividends.

Cumulative or Noncumulative   Most preferred stock has a cumulative dividend right.

- **Cumulative preferred stock** gives its owners a right to be paid both the current and all prior periods' unpaid dividends before any dividend is paid to common stockholders. When preferred stock is cumulative and the directors either do not declare a dividend to preferred stockholders or declare one that does not cover the total amount of cumulative dividend, the unpaid dividend amount is called **dividend in arrears.** Accumulation of dividends in arrears on cumulative preferred stock does not guarantee they will be paid. Dividend in arrears is not a liability and is usually reported in notes to financial statements.

Point: Dividend preference does not mean that preferred stockholders get more dividends than common stockholders.

- **Noncumulative preferred stock** does not have rights to prior periods' unpaid dividends if they were not declared in those prior periods. It does have rights to current-period dividends.

To show the difference between cumulative and noncumulative preferred stock, assume that a corporation's outstanding stock includes

- 1,000 shares of $100 par, 9% preferred stock—with *potential* dividends of $9,000 per year (1,000 shares × $100 par × 9%).
- 4,000 shares of $50 par value common stock.

During 2018, the first year of operations, the directors declare cash dividends of $5,000. In 2019, they declare cash dividends of $42,000. Exhibit 11.8 shows the allocation of dividends. If the preferred stock is cumulative, the $4,000 in arrears is paid in 2019 before any other dividends are paid—shown in green below. With noncumulative preferred, the preferred stockholders never receive the $4,000 skipped in 2018.

EXHIBIT 11.8

Allocation of Dividends: Cumulative vs. Noncumulative

Preferred Stock Is Cumulative	Preferred	Common
Year 2018	$ 5,000	$ 0
Year 2019		
Step 1: Dividend in arrears	$ 4,000	
Step 2: Current year's preferred dividend	9,000	
Step 3: Remainder to common		$29,000
Totals for year 2019	$13,000	$29,000
Totals for 2018–2019	$18,000	$29,000

Preferred Stock Is Noncumulative	Preferred	Common
Year 2018	$ 5,000	$ 0
Year 2019		
Step 1: Current year's preferred dividend	$ 9,000	
Step 2: Remainder to common		$33,000
Totals for 2018–2019	$14,000	$33,000

Participating or Nonparticipating   Most preferred stock is nonparticipating.

- **Nonparticipating preferred stock** limits dividends each year. Once preferred stockholders receive a stated amount, the common stockholders get any and all additional dividends.
- **Participating preferred stock** allows preferred stockholders to share with common stockholders any dividends paid in excess of the amount stated on the preferred stock. This participation feature applies after common stockholders get dividends equal to the preferred stock's dividend percent.

Reasons for Issuing Preferred Stock

Preferred stock is issued for several reasons. One reason is to raise money without giving up control. We can, for example, raise money by issuing preferred stock with no voting rights.

A second reason is to boost the return earned by common stockholders. Suppose a corporation's organizers expect to earn an annual after-tax income of $22,000 on an investment of $200,000. If they sell $200,000 worth of common stock, the $22,000 income produces an 11%

Frequency of Preferred Stock

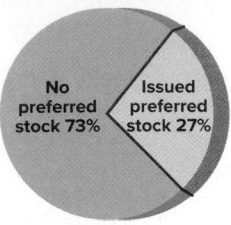

No preferred stock 73%   Issued preferred stock 27%

return ($22,000/$200,000). If they issue $150,000 of 8% preferred stock to outsiders and $50,000 of common stock to themselves, their own return increases to 20% ([$22,000 − $12,000]/$50,000).

Use of preferred stock to increase return to common stockholders is an example of **financial leverage.** As a general rule, when the dividend rate on preferred stock is less than the rate the corporation earns on its assets, issuing preferred stock increases the rate earned by common stockholders.

Other reasons for issuing preferred stock include its appeal to some investors who believe that the corporation's common stock is too risky or that the expected return on common stock is too low.

■ Decision Maker

Concert Organizer Assume that you alter your business strategy from organizing concerts targeted at under 1,000 people to those targeted at between 5,000 and 20,000 people. You also incorporate because of an increased risk of lawsuits and a desire to issue stock for financing. It is important that you control the company for decisions on whom to schedule. What types of stock do you offer? ■ *Answer:* You have two options: (1) different classes of common stock or (2) common and preferred stock. You want to own stock that has all or a majority of voting power. The other class of stock, whether common or preferred, would have limited or no voting rights. In this way, you keep control and are able to raise money.

NEED-TO-KNOW 11-3

Allocating Cash Dividends

C2

A company's outstanding stock consists of 80 shares of *noncumulative* 5% preferred stock with a $5 par value and also 200 shares of common stock with a $1 par value. During its first three years of operation, the corporation declared and paid the following total cash dividends.

2018 total cash dividends $15	2019 total cash dividends. . . . $5	2020 total cash dividends. $200

Part 1. Determine the amount of dividends paid each year to each of the two classes of stockholders: preferred and common. Also compute the total dividends paid to each class for the three years combined.

Part 2. Determine the amount of dividends paid each year to each of the two classes of stockholders assuming that the preferred stock is *cumulative.* Also determine the total dividends paid to each class for the three years combined.

Solution—Part 1

	Noncumulative Preferred	Common
2018 ($15 paid)		
Preferred*.	$15	
Common—remainder.		$ 0
Total for the year	$15	$ 0
2019 ($5 paid)		
Preferred*.	$ 5	
Common—remainder.		$ 0
Total for the year	$ 5	$ 0
2020 ($200 paid)		
Preferred*.	$20	
Common—remainder.		$180
Total for the year	$20	$180
2018–2020 (combined $220 paid)		
Total for three years.	$40	$180

*Holders of noncumulative preferred stock are entitled to no more than $20 of dividends in any one year (5% × $5 × 80 shares).

Do More: QS 11-11, QS 11-12, QS 11-13, QS 11-14, E 11-9, E 11-10, E 11-11

Solution—Part 2

	Cumulative Preferred	Common
2018 ($15 paid)		
Preferred*.	$15	
Common—remainder.		$ 0
Total for the year	$15	$ 0
(Note: $5 in preferred dividends in arrears; [$20 × 1 yr] − $15 paid.)		
2019 ($5 paid)		
Preferred—arrears from 2018.	$ 5	
Preferred*.	0	
Common—remainder.		$ 0
Total for the year	$ 5	$ 0
(Note: $20 in preferred dividends in arrears; [$20 × 2 yrs] − $15 paid − $5 paid.)		
2020 ($200 paid)		
Preferred—arrears from 2019.	$20	
Preferred*.	20	
Common—remainder.		$160
Total for the year	$40	$160
(Note: $0 in preferred dividends in arrears; [$20 × 3 yrs] − $15 paid − $5 paid − $40 paid.)		
2018–2020 (combined $220 paid)		
Total for three years.	$60	$160

*Holders of cumulative preferred stock are entitled to $20 of dividends declared in any year (5% × $5 × 80 shares) plus any dividends in arrears.

TREASURY STOCK

Corporations buy back their own stock for several reasons: (1) to use their shares to acquire another corporation, (2) to avoid a takeover of the company, (3) to give them to employees as compensation, and (4) to maintain a strong market for their stock or to show confidence in the current price.

A corporation's reacquired shares are called **treasury stock,** which is similar to unissued stock in several ways: (1) neither treasury stock nor unissued stock is an asset, (2) neither receives cash dividends or stock dividends, and (3) neither has voting rights.

P3

Record purchases and sales of treasury stock.

Corporations and Treasury Stock

With treasury stock 62%   No treasury stock 38%

Purchasing Treasury Stock

Purchasing treasury stock reduces the corporation's assets and equity by equal amounts. We describe the *cost method* of accounting for treasury stock, which is the most popular method. (The *par value* method is explained in advanced courses.) The simple balance sheet below shows Cyber Inc.'s account balances *before* any treasury stock purchase (Cyber has no liabilities).

Assets		Stockholders' Equity	
Cash.................	$ 30,000	Common stock—$10 par; 10,000 shares authorized, issued, and outstanding...............	$100,000
Other assets...........	95,000	Retained earnings.................................	25,000
Total assets...........	$125,000	Total stockholders' equity..........................	$125,000

Cyber then purchases 1,000 of its own shares for $11,500. The entry below reduces equity with a debit to the **Treasury Stock account, which is a contra equity account.**

May 1	Treasury Stock, Common*	11,500	
	Cash...		11,500
	Purchased 1,000 treasury shares at $11.50 per share.		

*$11.50 cost per share × 1,000 shares

Assets = Liabilities + Equity
−11,500   −11,500

The balance sheet below shows account balances *after* this transaction. The treasury stock purchase reduces Cyber's cash, total assets, and total equity by $11,500 but does not reduce Common Stock or Retained Earnings. The stock description says that 1,000 issued shares are in treasury, leaving only 9,000 shares still outstanding. The description for retained earnings says that it is partly restricted.

Point: A treasury stock purchase is also called a *stock buyback*.

Assets		Stockholders' Equity	
Cash.................	$ 18,500	Common stock—$10 par; 10,000 shares authorized and issued; 1,000 shares in treasury	$100,000
Other assets...........	95,000	Retained earnings, $11,500 restricted by treasury stock purchase...	25,000
		Less cost of treasury stock.................................	**(11,500)**
Total assets...........	$113,500	Total stockholders' equity....................................	$113,500

Reissuing Treasury Stock

Treasury stock can be reissued by selling it at cost, above cost, or below cost.

Selling Treasury Stock at Cost If treasury stock is reissued at cost, the entry is the reverse of the one made to record the purchase. If on May 21 Cyber reissues 100 of the treasury shares purchased on May 1 at the same $11.50 per share cost, the entry is

Assets = Liabilities + Equity
+1,150   +1,150

May 21	Cash..	1,150	
	Treasury Stock, Common*.......................		1,150
	Received $11.50 per share for 100 treasury		
	shares costing $11.50 per share.		

*$11.50 cost per share × 100 shares

Selling Treasury Stock *above* Cost

If treasury stock is sold for more than cost, the amount received in excess of cost is credited to the Paid-In Capital, Treasury Stock account. This account is reported as a separate item in the stockholders' equity section. No "gain" is ever reported from the sale of treasury stock. If Cyber receives $12 cash per share on June 3 for 400 treasury shares costing $11.50 per share, the entry is

Assets = Liabilities + Equity
+4,800   +4,600
                +200

June 3	Cash..	4,800	
	Treasury Stock, Common*.......................		4,600
	Paid-In Capital, Treasury Stock†.................		**200**
	Received $12 per share for 400 treasury		
	shares costing $11.50 per share.		

*$11.50 cost per share × 400 shares   †[$12 issue price − $11.50 cost per share] × 400 shares

Selling Treasury Stock *below* Cost

When treasury stock is sold below cost, the entry depends on whether the Paid-In Capital, Treasury Stock account has a credit balance. If it has a zero balance, the excess of cost over the sales price is debited to Retained Earnings. If the Paid-In Capital, Treasury Stock account has a credit balance, it is debited for the excess of the cost over the selling price but not to exceed the credit balance. When the credit balance is eliminated, any remaining difference between the cost and selling price is debited to Retained Earnings. If Cyber sells its remaining 500 shares of treasury stock at $10 per share on July 10, equity is reduced by $750 (500 shares × $1.50 per share excess of cost over selling price), as shown below. This entry eliminates the $200 credit balance in the Paid-In Capital account created on June 3 and then reduces the Retained Earnings balance by the remaining $550. A company never reports a "loss" from the sale of treasury stock.

Point: Paid-In Capital, Treasury Stock account can have a zero or credit balance but never a debit balance.

Assets = Liabilities + Equity
+5,000   −200
                −550
                +5,750

July 10	Cash..	5,000	
	Paid-In Capital, Treasury Stock*	**200**	
	Retained Earnings†.................................	**550**	
	Treasury Stock, Common‡.......................		5,750
	Received $10 per share for 500 treasury shares		
	costing $11.50 per share.		

*[$10 issue price − $11.50 cost per share] × 500 shares; not to exceed $200
†For any amount exceeding $200 in Paid-In Capital, Treasury Stock   ‡$11.50 cost per share × 500 shares

---

NEED-TO-KNOW 11-4

Recording Treasury Stock

P3

A company began the current year with the following balances in its stockholders' equity accounts.

Common stock—$10 par, 500 shares authorized, 200 shares issued and outstanding	$2,000
Paid-in capital in excess of par, common stock	1,000
Retained earnings...	5,000
Total...	$8,000

All outstanding common stock was issued for $15 per share when the company was created. Prepare journal entries to account for the following transactions during the current year.

July 1   Purchased 30 shares of treasury stock at $20 per share.
Sep. 1   Sold 20 treasury shares at $26 cash per share.
Dec. 1   Sold the remaining 10 shares of treasury stock at $7 cash per share.

Solution

July 1	Treasury Stock, Common[a]	600	
	Cash		600
	Purchased 30 common shares at $20 per share.		
	[a]30 shares × $20 cost		
Sep. 1	Cash[b]	520	
	Treasury Stock, Common[c]		400
	Paid-In Capital, Treasury Stock		120
	Sold 20 treasury shares at $26 per share.		
	[b]20 shares × $26 reissue price [c]20 shares × $20 cost		
Dec. 1	Cash[d]	70	
	Paid-In Capital, Treasury Stock[e]	120	
	Retained Earnings	10	
	Treasury Stock, Common[f]		200
	Sold 10 treasury shares at $7 per share.		
	[d]10 shares × $7 reissue price		
	[e]Not to exceed existing balance [f]10 shares × $20 cost		

Treasury Stock, Common

July 1	600	Sep. 1	400
		Dec. 1	200
End. bal.	0		

Do More: QS 11-15, E 11-12

REPORTING OF EQUITY

Statement of Retained Earnings

C3

Explain the items reported in retained earnings.

Retained earnings generally consists of cumulative net income minus any net losses and dividends declared. Retained earnings does *not* mean that a certain amount of cash or other assets is available to pay stockholders. For example, **Abercrombie & Fitch** has $2,474,703 thousand in retained earnings, but only $547,189 thousand in cash.

Restrictions and Appropriations   **Restricted retained earnings** are statutory and contractual restrictions. A common *statutory* (or *legal*) *restriction* is to limit treasury stock purchases to the amount of retained earnings. A common *contractual restriction* is a loan agreement that restricts paying dividends beyond a specified amount of retained earnings. Restrictions are usually described in the notes. **Appropriated retained earnings** is a voluntary transfer of amounts from the Retained Earnings account to the Appropriated Retained Earnings account to inform users of special activities that require funds.

Prior Period Adjustments   **Prior period adjustments** are corrections of material errors in past financial statements. These errors include math errors, improper accounting, and missed facts. Prior period adjustments are reported in the *statement of retained earnings,* net of any income tax effects. Prior period adjustments result in changing the beginning balance of retained earnings for *events occurring prior to the earliest period reported in the current set of financial statements.* Assume that ComUS made an error two years ago in a journal entry for the purchase of land by incorrectly debiting an expense account. When this is discovered in the current year, the statement of retained earnings includes a prior period adjustment, as shown in Exhibit 11.9.

Statement of Retained Earnings	
Retained earnings, Dec. 31, 2018, as previously reported	$4,700
Prior period adjustment	
Cost of land incorrectly expensed (net of $60 of income tax benefit) ...	200
Retained earnings, Dec. 31, 2018, as adjusted	4,900
Plus net income	800
Less cash dividends declared	(300)
Retained earnings, Dec. 31, 2019....................................	$5,400

EXHIBIT 11.9

Statement of Retained Earnings with a Prior Period Adjustment

Many items reported in financial statements are based on estimates. Future events reveal that some estimates were inaccurate even when based on the best data available at the time. These inaccuracies are *not* considered errors and are *not* reported as prior period adjustments. Instead, they are **changes in accounting estimates** and are accounted for in current and future periods.

Statement of Stockholders' Equity

A **statement of stockholders' equity** lists the beginning and ending balances of key equity accounts and describes the changes that occur during the period. Exhibit 11.10 shows a condensed statement for **Apple.**

EXHIBIT 11.10

Statement of Stockholders' Equity

APPLE

Statement of Stockholders' Equity $ millions, shares in thousands	Common Stock Shares	Common Stock Amount	Retained Earnings	Other	Total Equity
Beginning balance	5,336,166	$31,251	$96,364	$ 634	$128,249
Net income	—	—	48,351	—	48,351
Issuance of common stock.	36,531	(913)	(581)	—	(1,494)
Repurchase of common stock & other.	(246,496)	5,529	(33,001)	(784)	(28,256)
Cash dividends	—	—	(12,803)	—	(12,803)
Ending balance	5,126,201	$35,867	$98,330	$(150)	$134,047

Ethical Risk

Fake News   Fake information can be used to pump up stock price and cause uninformed investors to buy the stock and drive up its price. After that, those who released fake information dump the stock at an inflated price. When later information reveals that the stock is overvalued, its price declines and investors still holding the stock lose value. This scheme is called *pump 'n dump*. A 15-year-old allegedly made about $1 million in one of the most infamous cases of pump 'n dump. (SEC Release No. 7891) ■

 **Decision Analysis** ▢▢▢ **Earnings per Share, Price-Earnings Ratio, Dividend Yield, and Book Value per Share**

A1

Compute earnings per share and describe its use.

Earnings per Share

Earnings per share, also called *EPS* or *net income per share,* is the income earned per share of outstanding common stock. The **basic earnings per share** formula is in Exhibit 11.11. When a company has no preferred stock, then preferred dividends are zero. The weighted-average common shares outstanding is measured over the income reporting period; its computation is explained in advanced courses.

EXHIBIT 11.11

Basic Earnings per Share

$$\text{Basic earnings per share} = \frac{\text{Net income} - \text{Preferred dividends}}{\text{Weighted-average common shares outstanding}}$$

Point: Diluted EPS is another EPS measure covered in advanced courses.

Assume Quantum Co. earns $40,000 net income in 2019 and declares dividends of $7,500 on its noncumulative preferred stock. (If preferred stock is *non*cumulative, preferred dividends are only subtracted if dividends are *declared* in that same period. If preferred stock is cumulative, preferred dividends are subtracted whether declared or not.) Quantum has 5,000 weighted-average common shares outstanding during 2019. Its basic EPS is $6.50, computed as ($40,000 − $7,500) / 5,000 shares.

A2

Compute price-earnings ratio and describe its use in analysis.

Price-Earnings Ratio

A comparison of a company's EPS and its market value per share reveals market expectations. This comparison is made using a **price-earnings (or PE) ratio,** also called *price earnings* or *price to earnings*. Some analysts interpret this ratio as what price the market is willing to pay for a company's current earnings stream. Price-earnings ratios differ across companies that have similar earnings because of either higher or lower expectations of future earnings. The price-earnings ratio is in Exhibit 11.12.

EXHIBIT 11.12

Price-Earnings Ratio

$$\text{Price-earnings ratio} = \frac{\text{Market value (price) per share}}{\text{Earnings per share}}$$

Point: The average PE ratio of stocks in the 1950–2019 period is about 14.

Price-earnings ratios for **Visa** and **Mastercard** follow. Both companies have relatively high PE ratios, showing that investors have high expectations of future earnings for both. Based on Mastercard's higher PE versus Visa, one interpretation is the market is willing to pay more for Mastercard's current earnings stream.

Company	Market Value per Share	Earnings per Share	P/E Ratio
Visa.............	$105.24	$2.80	37.6
Mastercard........	$151.36	$3.67	41.2

■ Decision Maker

Money Manager   You plan to invest in one of two companies identified as having identical future prospects. One has a PE of 19 and the other a PE of 25. Which do you invest in? ■   *Answer:* Because one company requires a payment of $19 for each $1 of earnings and the other requires $25, you prefer the stock with a PE of 19; it is a better deal given identical prospects.

Dividend Yield

Investors buy company stock to get a return from either or both cash dividends and stock price increases. Stocks that pay large dividends on a regular basis, called *income stocks,* are attractive to investors who want recurring cash flows from their investments. In contrast, *growth stocks* pay little or no cash dividends but are attractive to investors because of expected stock price increases. One way to help identify whether a stock is an income stock or a growth stock is to analyze its dividend yield. **Dividend yield** is defined in Exhibit 11.13.

$$\text{Dividend yield} = \frac{\text{Annual cash dividends per share}}{\text{Market value per share}}$$

The table below shows recent dividend and stock price data for **Amazon** and **Altria Group** to compute dividend yield. Dividend yield is zero for Amazon, implying it is a growth stock. An investor in Amazon expects increases in stock prices (and eventual cash from the sale of stock). Altria has a dividend yield of 5.0%, implying it is an income stock for which dividends are important in assessing its value.

Company	Cash Dividends per Share	Market Value per Share	Dividend Yield
Amazon	$0.00	$1,603	0.0%
Altria Group	$2.80	$ 56	5.0%

A3

Compute dividend yield and explain its use in analysis.

EXHIBIT 11.13

Dividend Yield

Point: The *payout ratio* equals cash dividends declared on common stock divided by net income. A low payout ratio suggests that it is retaining earnings for growth.

Book Value per Share

Book value per common share, defined in Exhibit 11.14, is the amount of equity applicable to *common* shares on a per share basis. Book value per share is the value per share if a company is liquidated at balance sheet amounts. Book value is also the starting point in many stock valuation models, merger negotiations, price setting for public utilities, and loan contracts. The main limitation in using book value is that the difference between market value and recorded value of assets and liabilities can be large.

$$\text{Book value per common share} = \frac{\text{Stockholders' equity applicable to common shares}}{\text{Number of common shares outstanding}}$$

Consider LTD's equity in the table below. At the current date there are two years of preferred dividends in arrears.

A4

Compute book value and explain its use in analysis.

EXHIBIT 11.14

Book Value per Common Share

Preferred stock—$100 par value, 7% cumulative, 2,000 shares authorized, 1,000 shares issued and outstanding.....	$100,000
Common stock—$25 par value, 12,000 shares authorized, 10,000 shares issued and outstanding..............	250,000
Paid-in capital in excess of par value, common stock	15,000
Retained earnings...	82,000
Total stockholders' equity	$447,000

LTD's book value computations follow. Equity allocated to any preferred shares is removed before the book value of common shares is computed.

Total stockholders' equity		$447,000
Less equity applicable to preferred shares: Par value (1,000 shares × $100)	$100,000	
Dividends in arrears ($100,000 × 7% × 2 years) ...	14,000	(114,000)
Equity applicable to common shares..........................		$333,000
Book value per common share ($333,000/10,000 shares)		$ 33.30

 **11-5**

COMPREHENSIVE

Issuance of, and
Dividends to, Common
and Preferred Stock;
Reporting of
Stockholders' Equity

Barton Corporation began operations on January 1, 2018. The following transactions relating to stock-holders' equity occurred in the first two years of the company's operations.

2018

Jan. 1 Authorized the issuance of 2 million shares of $5 par value common stock and 100,000 shares of $100 par value, 10% cumulative preferred stock.

   2 Issued 200,000 shares of common stock for $12 cash per share.

   3 Issued 100,000 shares of common stock in exchange for a building valued at $820,000 and merchandise inventory valued at $380,000.

   4 Paid $10,000 cash to the company's founders for organization activities.

   5 Issued 12,000 shares of preferred stock for $110 cash per share.

2019

June 4 Issued 100,000 shares of common stock for $15 cash per share.

Required

1. Prepare journal entries to record these transactions.

2. Prepare the stockholders' equity section of the balance sheet as of December 31, 2018 and 2019.

3. Prepare a table showing dividend allocations for 2018 and 2019 assuming Barton declares the follow-ing cash dividends: 2018, $50,000, and 2019, $300,000.

4. Prepare the January 2, 2018, entry for issuance of 200,000 shares of common stock for $12 cash per share if

   a. Common stock is no-par stock without a stated value.

   b. Common stock is no-par stock with a stated value of $10 per share.

PLANNING THE SOLUTION

- Record journal entries for the transactions for 2018 and 2019.
- Determine the balances for the 2018 and 2019 equity accounts for the balance sheet.
- Prepare the contributed capital portion of the 2018 and 2019 balance sheets.
- Prepare a table similar to Exhibit 11.8 showing dividend allocations for 2018 and 2019.
- Record the issuance of common stock under both specifications of no-par stock.

SOLUTION

1. Journal entries.

Jan. 2, 2018	Cash...	2,400,000	
	Common Stock, $5 Par Value.....................		1,000,000
	Paid-In Capital in Excess of Par Value, Common Stock..		1,400,000
	Issued 200,000 shares of common stock.		
Jan. 3, 2018	Building	820,000	
	Merchandise Inventory	380,000	
	Common Stock, $5 Par Value.....................		500,000
	Paid-In Capital in Excess of Par Value, Common Stock....		700,000
	Issued 100,000 shares of common stock.		
Jan. 4, 2018	Organization Expenses	10,000	
	Cash.......................................		10,000
	Paid founders for organization costs.		
Jan. 5, 2018	Cash	1,320,000	
	Preferred Stock, $100 Par Value		1,200,000
	Paid-In Capital in Excess of Par Value, Preferred Stock....		120,000
	Issued 12,000 shares of preferred stock.		
June 4, 2019	Cash	1,500,000	
	Common Stock, $5 Par Value.....................		500,000
	Paid-In Capital in Excess of Par Value, Common Stock....		1,000,000
	Issued 100,000 shares of common stock.		

2. Balance sheet presentations (at December 31 year-end).

Stockholders' Equity	2019	2018
Preferred stock—$100 par value, 10% cumulative, 100,000 shares authorized, 12,000 shares issued and outstanding.....................	$1,200,000	$1,200,000
Paid-in capital in excess of par value, preferred stock...........................	120,000	120,000
Total paid-in capital by preferred stockholders.................................	1,320,000	1,320,000
Common stock—$5 par value, 2,000,000 shares authorized, 300,000 shares issued and outstanding in 2018, and 400,000 shares issued and outstanding in 2019............................	2,000,000	1,500,000
Paid-in capital in excess of par value, common stock..........................	3,100,000	2,100,000
Total paid-in capital by common stockholders	5,100,000	3,600,000
Total paid-in capital..	$6,420,000	$4,920,000

3. Dividend allocation table.

	Common	Preferred
2018 ($50,000)		
Preferred—current year (12,000 shares × $10 = $120,000)	$ 0	$ 50,000
Common—remainder (300,000 shares outstanding)	0	0
Total for the year...	$ 0	$ 50,000
2019 ($300,000)		
Preferred—dividend in arrears from 2018 ($120,000 − $50,000)	$ 0	$ 70,000
Preferred—current year	0	120,000
Common—remainder (400,000 shares outstanding)	110,000	0
Total for the year...	$110,000	$190,000

4. Journal entries.

a. For 2018 (no-par stock without a stated value).

Jan. 2	Cash..	2,400,000	
	Common Stock, No-Par Value....................		2,400,000
	Issued 200,000 shares of no-par stock at $12 per share.		

b. For 2018 (no-par stock with a stated value).

Jan. 2	Cash..	2,400,000	
	Common Stock, $10 Stated Value		2,000,000
	Paid-In Capital in Excess of Stated Value, Common Stock .		400,000
	Issued 200,000 shares of $10 stated value common stock at $12 per share.		

Summary: Cheat Sheet

COMMON STOCK

Corporate advantages: Separate legal entity, limited liability, transferable ownership, continuous life, no mutual agency for shareholders, and easier capital accumulation.

Corporate disadvantages: More government regulation and corporate income taxes (double taxation).

Issuing common stock at par value:

Cash	300,000	
Common Stock, $10 Par Value		300,000

Issuing common stock above par: When market value > par value.

Cash	360,000	
Common Stock, $10 Par Value		300,000
Paid-In Capital in Excess of Par Value, Common Stock .		60,000

Issuing no-par common stock:

Cash	40,000	
Common Stock, No-Par Value		40,000

Issuing stated value common stock: When market value > stated value.

Cash	50,000
Common Stock, $40 Stated Value	40,000
Paid-in Capital in Excess of Stated Value, Common Stock	10,000

Issuing common stock for noncash assets:

Land	105,000
Common Stock, $20 Par Value	80,000
Paid-In Capital in Excess of Par Value, Common Stock	25,000

Issuing common stock in exchange for services:

Organization Expenses	12,000
Common Stock, $15 Par Value	9,000
Paid-In Capital in Excess of Par Value, Common Stock	3,000

DIVIDENDS

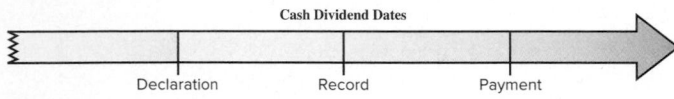

Cash Dividend Dates

Declaration   Record   Payment

Cash dividend—Date of declaration:

Retained Earnings	5,000
Common Dividend Payable......................	5,000

Cash dividend—Date of record: No entry is made.

Cash dividend—Date of payment:

Common Dividend Payable	5,000
Cash	5,000

Small stock dividend: Distribution of 25% or less of previously outstanding shares. Retained earnings is capitalized for an amount equal to *market value* of shares.

Small stock dividend—Date of declaration:

Retained Earnings	15,000
Common Stock Dividend Distributable............	10,000
Paid-In Capital in Excess of Par Value, Common Stock	5,000

Small stock dividend—Date of payment:

Common Stock Dividend Distributable	10,000
Common Stock, $10 Par Value	10,000

Large stock dividend: Distribution of more than 25% of previously outstanding shares. Retained earnings is capitalized for an amount equal to *par* or *stated value* of shares.

Large stock dividend—Date of declaration:

Retained Earnings	30,000
Common Stock Dividend Distributable............	30,000

Large stock dividend—Date of payment:

Common Stock Dividend Distributable	30,000
Common Stock, $10 Par Value	30,000

Stock split: Distribution of additional shares to stockholders according to percent ownership. It does not affect any equity balances. No journal entry is made. Only effect is a change in stock account description.

PREFERRED STOCK

Issuing preferred stock: When market value > par value.

Cash	6,000
Preferred Stock, $100 Par Value................	5,000
Paid-In Capital in Excess of Par Value, Preferred Stock	1,000

Cumulative preferred stock: Preferred stockholders are paid both current and all prior periods' unpaid dividends before any dividend is paid to common stockholders.

Dividend in arrears: Unpaid dividends due to cumulative preferred stock.

Noncumulative preferred stock: Does not have rights to prior periods' unpaid dividends, only current-period dividends.

TREASURY STOCK

Treasury stock: Shares reacquired by the company. It reduces equity and does not receive dividends.

Treasury Stock, Common........................	11,500
Cash	11,500

Treasury stock in stockholders' equity:

Stockholders' Equity	
Common stock—$10 par; 10,000 shares authorized and issued; 1,000 shares in treasury	$100,000
Retained earnings, $11,500 restricted by treasury stock purchase	25,000
Less cost of treasury stock	**(11,500)**
Total stockholders' equity	$113,500

Selling treasury stock at cost:

Cash	1,150
Treasury Stock, Common......................	1,150

Selling treasury stock above cost: When sale price > reacquisition price.

Cash	4,800
Treasury Stock, Common......................	4,600
Paid-In Capital, Treasury Stock	200

Selling treasury stock below cost: When sale price < reacquisition price.

Cash	5,000
Paid-In Capital, Treasury Stock	200
Retained Earnings	550
Treasury Stock, Common......................	5,750

REPORTING AND ANALYSIS

Prior period adjustments: Corrections of material errors in past financial statements. Errors include math errors, improper accounting, and missed facts. Prior period adjustments are reported in statement of retained earnings, net of any income tax effects.

Changes in accounting estimates: Revised estimates that were inaccurate even when based on the best data available at the time. These are not errors and are *not* reported as prior period adjustments. Instead, they are accounted for in current and future periods.

Statement of Retained Earnings	
Retained earnings, Dec. 31, 2018, as previously reported	$4,700
Prior period adjustment	
Cost of land incorrectly expensed (net of $60 of income tax benefit) ...	**200**
Retained earnings, Dec. 31, 2018, as adjusted	4,900
Plus net income.......................................	800
Less cash dividends declared	(300)
Retained earnings, Dec. 31, 2019..............................	$5,400

Key Terms

Appropriated retained earnings (431)	Earnings per share (EPS) (432)	Preferred stock (426)
Authorized stock (419)	Financial leverage (428)	Premium on stock (420)
Basic earnings per share (432)	Large stock dividend (423)	Price-earnings (PE) ratio (432)
Book value per common share (433)	Liquidating cash dividend (423)	Prior period adjustment (431)
Capital stock (419)	Market value per share (419)	Proxy (418)
Change in an accounting estimate (432)	Minimum legal capital (419)	Restricted retained earnings (431)
Common stock (418)	Noncumulative preferred stock (427)	Retained earnings (420)
Corporation (417)	Nonparticipating preferred stock (427)	Retained earnings deficit (423)
Cumulative preferred stock (427)	No-par value stock (419)	Reverse stock split (425)
Date of declaration (422)	Organization expenses (costs) (418)	Small stock dividend (423)
Date of payment (422)	Paid-in capital (420)	Stated value stock (419)
Date of record (422)	Paid-in capital in excess of par value (420)	Statement of stockholders' equity (432)
Diluted earnings per share (432)	Par value (419)	Stock dividend (423)
Discount on stock (421)	Par value stock (419)	Stock split (425)
Dividend in arrears (427)	Participating preferred stock (427)	Stockholders' equity (419)
Dividend yield (433)	Preemptive right (418)	Treasury stock (429)

Multiple Choice Quiz

1. A corporation issues 6,000 shares of $5 par value common stock for $8 cash per share. The entry to record this transaction includes

  a. A debit to Paid-In Capital in Excess of Par Value for $18,000.

  b. A credit to Common Stock for $48,000.

  c. A credit to Paid-In Capital in Excess of Par Value for $30,000.

  d. A credit to Cash for $48,000.

  e. A credit to Common Stock for $30,000.

2. A company reports net income of $75,000. Its weighted-average common shares outstanding is 19,000. It has no other stock outstanding. Its earnings per share is

  a. $4.69.   **c.** $3.75.   **e.** $4.41.

  b. $3.95.   **d.** $2.08.

3. A company has 5,000 shares of $100 par preferred stock and 50,000 shares of $10 par common stock outstanding. Its total stockholders' equity is $2,000,000. Its book value per common share is

  a. $100.00.   **c.** $40.00.   **e.** $36.36.

  b. $10.00.   **d.** $30.00.

4. A company paid cash dividends of $0.81 per share. Its earnings per share is $6.95 and its market price per share is $45.00. Its dividend yield is

  a. 1.8%.   **c.** 15.4%.   **e.** 8.6%.

  b. 11.7%.   **d.** 55.6%.

5. A company's shares have a market value of $85 per share. Its net income is $3,500,000, and its weighted-average common shares outstanding is 700,000. Its price-earnings ratio is

  a. 5.9.   **c.** 17.0.   **e.** 41.2.

  b. 425.0.   **d.** 10.4.

ANSWERS TO MULTIPLE CHOICE QUIZ

1. e; Entry to record this stock issuance follows.

Cash (6,000 × $8)	48,000	
Common Stock (6,000 × $5)		30,000
Paid-In Capital in Excess of Par Value, Common Stock		18,000

2. b; $75,000/19,000 shares = $3.95 per share

3. d; Preferred stock = 5,000 × $100 = $500,000; Book value per share = ($2,000,000 − $500,000)/50,000 shares = $30 per common share

4. a; $0.81/$45.00 = 1.8%

5. c; Earnings per share = $3,500,000/700,000 shares = $5 per share; PE ratio = $85/$5 = 17.0

🛈 Icon denotes assignments that involve decision making.

Discussion Questions

1. What are organization expenses? Provide examples.

2. How are organization expenses reported?

3. 🛈 Who is responsible for overseeing corporate activities?

4. What is the difference between authorized shares and outstanding shares?

5. What is the preemptive right of common stockholders?

6. List the general rights of common stockholders.

7. What is the difference between the market value per share and the par value per share?

8. Identify and explain the importance of the three dates relevant to corporate dividends.

9. Why is the term *liquidating dividend* used to describe cash dividends debited against paid-in capital accounts?

10. 🔲 How does declaring a stock dividend affect the corporation's assets, liabilities, and total equity? What are the effects of the eventual distribution of that stock?

11. 🔲 What is the difference between a stock dividend and a stock split?

12. How does the purchase of treasury stock affect the purchaser's assets and total equity?

13. How are EPS results computed for a corporation with a simple capital structure?

14. How is book value per share computed for a corporation with no preferred stock? What is the main limitation of using book value per share to value a corporation?

15. Refer to **Apple**'s fiscal 2017 balance sheet in Appendix A. How many shares of common **APPLE** stock are authorized? How many shares of common stock are issued and outstanding?

16. 🔲 Refer to the 2017 balance sheet for **GOOGLE** Google in Appendix A. What is the par value per share of its preferred stock? Suggest a rationale for the amount of par value it assigned.

17. 🔲 Refer to the financial statements for **Samsung** Samsung in Appendix A. How much were its cash payments for treasury stock acquisitions for the year ended December 31, 2017?

QUICK STUDY

QS 11-1

Characteristics of corporations

C1

Identify which of the following statements are true for the corporate form of organization.

_____ **1.** Ownership rights cannot be easily transferred.

_____ **2.** Owners have unlimited liability for corporate debts.

_____ **3.** Capital is more easily accumulated than with most other forms of organization.

_____ **4.** Corporate income that is distributed to shareholders is usually taxed twice.

_____ **5.** It is a separate legal entity.

_____ **6.** It has a limited life.

_____ **7.** Owners are not agents of the corporation.

QS 11-2

Issuance of common stock

P1

Prepare the journal entry to record Zende Company's issuance of 75,000 shares of $5 par value common stock assuming the shares sell for

a. $5 cash per share.   **b.** $6 cash per share.

QS 11-3

Issuance of par and stated value common stock   P1

Prepare the journal entry to record Jevonte Company's issuance of 36,000 shares of its common stock assuming the shares have a

a. $2 par value and sell for $18 cash per share.   **b.** $2 stated value and sell for $18 cash per share.

QS 11-4

Issuance of no-par common stock   P1

Prepare the journal entry to record Autumn Company's issuance of 63,000 shares of no-par value common stock assuming the shares

a. Sell for $29 cash per share.   **b.** Are exchanged for land valued at $1,827,000.

QS 11-5

Issuance of common stock

P1

Prepare the issuer's journal entry for each of the following separate transactions.

a. On March 1, Atlantic Co. issues 42,500 shares of $4 par value common stock for $297,500 cash.

b. On April 1, OP Co. issues no-par value common stock for $70,000 cash.

c. On April 6, MPG issues 2,000 shares of $25 par value common stock for $45,000 of inventory, $145,000 of machinery, and acceptance of a $94,000 note payable.

QS 11-6

Accounting for cash dividends

P2

Prepare journal entries to record the following transactions for Emerson Corporation.

July 15   Declared a cash dividend payable to common stockholders of $165,000.
Aug. 15   Date of record is August 15 for the cash dividend declared on July 15.
Aug. 31   Paid the dividend declared on July 15.

QS 11-7

Accounting for small stock dividends   P2

Epic Inc. has 10,000 shares of $2 par value common stock outstanding. Epic declares a 5% stock dividend on July 1 when the stock's market value is $8 per share. The stock dividend is distributed on July 20. Prepare journal entries for (a) declaration and (b) distribution of the stock dividend.

The stockholders' equity section of Jun Co.'s balance sheet as of April 1 follows. On April 2, Jun declares and distributes a 10% stock dividend. The stock's per share market value on April 2 is $20 (prior to the dividend). Prepare the stockholders' equity section immediately after the stock dividend is distributed.

QS 11-8
Accounting for small stock dividend
P2

Common stock—$5 par value, 375,000 shares authorized, 200,000 shares issued and outstanding.........	$1,000,000
Paid-in capital in excess of par value, common stock	600,000
Retained earnings...	833,000
Total stockholders' equity	$2,433,000

Belkin Inc. has 100,000 shares of $3 par value common stock outstanding. Belkin declares a 40% stock dividend on March 2 when the stock's market value is $72 per share. Prepare the journal entry for declaration of the stock dividend.

QS 11-9
Accounting for large stock dividends **P2**

Indicate whether each of the following statements regarding dividends is true or false.

_____ **1.** Cash and stock dividends reduce retained earnings.

_____ **2.** Dividends payable is recorded at the time a cash dividend is declared.

_____ **3.** The date of record is the date a cash dividend is paid to stockholders.

_____ **4.** Stock dividends help keep the market price of stock affordable.

QS 11-10
Accounting for dividends
P2

1. Prepare the journal entry to record Tamas Company's issuance of 5,000 shares of $100 par value, 7% cumulative preferred stock for $102 cash per share.

2. Assuming the facts in part 1, if Tamas declares a year-end cash dividend, what is the amount of dividend paid to preferred shareholders? (Assume no dividends in arrears.)

QS 11-11
Preferred stock issuance and dividends **C2**

Stockholders' equity of Ernst Company consists of 80,000 shares of $5 par value, 8% cumulative preferred stock and 250,000 shares of $1 par value common stock. Both classes of stock have been outstanding since the company's inception. Ernst did not declare any dividends in the prior year, but it now declares and pays a $110,000 cash dividend at the current year-end. Determine the amount distributed to each class of stockholders for this two-year-old company.

QS 11-12
Dividend allocation between classes of shareholders **C2**

Green Planet Corp. has 5,000 shares of noncumulative 10% preferred stock with a $2 par value and 17,000 shares of common stock with a $0.01 par value. During its first two years of operation, Green Planet declared and paid the following total cash dividends. Compute the dividends paid *each year* to each of the two classes of stockholders: preferred and common.

QS 11-13
Dividends on noncumulative preferred stock
C2

Year 1 total cash dividends	$800	Year 2 total cash dividends	$1,700

Use the information in QS 11-13 to compute the dividends paid *each year* to each of the two classes of stockholders assuming that the preferred stock is *cumulative*.

QS 11-14
Dividends on cumulative preferred stock **C2**

On May 3, Zirbal Corporation purchased 4,000 shares of its own stock for $36,000 cash. On November 4, Zirbal reissued 850 shares of this treasury stock for $8,500. Prepare the May 3 and November 4 journal entries to record Zirbal's purchase and reissuance of treasury stock.

QS 11-15
Purchase and sale of treasury stock **P3**

Identify whether stockholders' equity would increase (I), decrease (D), or have no effect (NE) as a result of each separate transaction listed below.

_____ **1.** A stock dividend equal to 30% of the previously outstanding shares is declared.

_____ **2.** New shares of common stock are issued for cash.

_____ **3.** Treasury shares of common stock are purchased.

_____ **4.** Cash dividends are paid to shareholders.

QS 11-16
Impacts of stock issuances, dividends, splits, and treasury transactions
P2 P3

On December 31, Westworld Inc. has the following equity accounts and balances: Retained Earnings, $45,000; Common Stock, $1,000; Treasury Stock, $2,000; Paid-In Capital in Excess of Par Value, Common Stock, $39,000; Preferred Stock, $7,000; and Paid-In Capital in Excess of Par Value, Preferred Stock, $3,000. Prepare the stockholders' equity section of Westworld's balance sheet.

QS 11-17
Preparing stockholders' equity section
C2 P1 P3

QS 11-18
Accounting for changes in estimates; error adjustments

C3

For each situation, identify whether it is treated as a prior period adjustment or change in accounting estimate.

1. A review of notes payable discovers that three years ago the company reported the entire amount of a payment (principal and interest) on an installment note payable as interest expense. This mistake had a material effect on net income in that year.

2. After using an expected useful life of seven years and no salvage value to depreciate its office equipment over the preceding three years, the company decided early this year that the equipment will last only two more years.

3. Upon reviewing customer contracts, the company realizes it mistakenly reported $150,000 in revenue instead of the actual amount earned of $15,000. This mistake occurred two years ago and had a material effect on financial statements.

QS 11-19
Determining retained earnings balance   C3

On January 1, Payson Inc. had a retained earnings balance of $20,000. During the year, Payson reported net income of $30,000 and paid cash dividends of $17,000. Calculate the retained earnings balance at its December 31 year-end.

QS 11-20
Basic earnings per share   A1

Murray Company reports net income of $770,000 for the year. It has no preferred stock, and its weighted-average common shares outstanding is 280,000 shares. Compute its basic earnings per share.

QS 11-21
Basic earnings per share   A1

Epic Company earned net income of $900,000 this year. There were 400,000 weighted-average common shares outstanding, and preferred shareholders received a $20,000 cash dividend. Compute Epic Company's basic earnings per share.

QS 11-22
Price-earnings ratio

A2

Compute Topp Company's price-earnings ratio if its common stock has a market value of $20.54 per share and its EPS is $3.95. Its key competitor, Lower Deck, has a PE ratio of 9.5. For which company does the market have higher expectations of future performance?

QS 11-23
Dividend yield   A3

Foxburo Company expects to pay a $2.34 per share cash dividend this year on its common stock. The current market value of Foxburo stock is $32.50 per share. Compute the expected dividend yield. If a competitor with a dividend yield of 3% is considered an income stock, would we classify Foxburo as a growth or an income stock?

QS 11-24
Book value per common share

A4

The stockholders' equity section of Montel Company's balance sheet follows. No preferred dividends are in arrears at the current date. Determine the book value per share of the common stock.

Preferred stock—5% cumulative, $10 par value, 20,000 shares authorized, issued, and outstanding	$ 200,000
Common stock—$5 par value, 200,000 shares authorized, 150,000 shares issued and outstanding.	750,000
Retained earnings.	900,000
Total stockholders' equity	$1,850,000

■ connect·

EXERCISES

Exercise 11-1
Characteristics of corporations

C1

Next to each corporate characteristic 1 through 8, enter the letter of the description that best relates to it.

_____ **1.** Owner authority and control

_____ **2.** Ease of formation

_____ **3.** Transferability of ownership

_____ **4.** Ability to raise large capital amounts

_____ **5.** Duration of life

_____ **6.** Owner liability

_____ **7.** Legal status

_____ **8.** Tax status of income

a. Requires government approval

b. Corporate income is taxed

c. Separate legal entity

d. Readily transferred

e. One vote per share

f. High ability

g. Unlimited

h. Limited

Exercise 11-2
Rights of stockholders

C1

Indicate which activities of Stockton Corporation violated the rights of a stockholder who owned one share of common stock.

1. Did not allow the stockholder to sell the stock to her brother.

2. Rejected the stockholder's request to be put in charge of its retail store.

3. Paid the stockholder a smaller dividend per share than another common stockholder.

4. Rejected the stockholder's request to vote via proxy because she was home sick.

5. In liquidation, paid the common shareholder after all creditors were already paid.

Rodriguez Corporation issues 19,000 shares of its common stock for $152,000 cash on February 20. Prepare journal entries to record this event under each of the following separate situations.

1. The stock has a $2 par value.   **3.** The stock has a $5 stated value.

2. The stock has neither par nor stated value.

Exercise 11-3
Accounting for par, stated, and no-par stock issuances
P1

Prepare journal entries to record each of the following four separate issuances of stock.

1. A corporation issued 4,000 shares of $5 par value common stock for $35,000 cash.

2. A corporation issued 2,000 shares of no-par common stock to its promoters in exchange for their efforts, estimated to be worth $40,000. The stock has a $1 per share stated value.

3. A corporation issued 2,000 shares of no-par common stock to its promoters in exchange for their efforts, estimated to be worth $40,000. The stock has no stated value.

4. A corporation issued 1,000 shares of $50 par value preferred stock for $60,000 cash.

Exercise 11-4
Recording stock issuances
P1

Sudoku Company issues 7,000 shares of $7 par value common stock in exchange for land and a building. The land is valued at $45,000 and the building at $85,000. Prepare the journal entry to record issuance of the stock in exchange for the land and building.

Exercise 11-5
Stock issuance for noncash assets   P1

On June 30, Sharper Corporation's stockholders' equity section of its balance sheet appears as follows before any stock dividend or split. Sharper declares and immediately distributes a 50% stock dividend. After the distribution is made, (1) prepare the updated stockholders' equity section and (2) compute the number of shares outstanding.

Exercise 11-6
Large stock dividend
P2

Common stock—$10 par value, 50,000 shares issued and outstanding	$ 500,000
Paid-in capital in excess of par value, common stock	200,000
Retained earnings	660,000
Total stockholders' equity	$1,360,000

Refer to the information in Exercise 11-6. Assume that instead of distributing a stock dividend, Sharper did a 3-for-1 stock split. After the split, (1) prepare the updated stockholders' equity section and (2) compute the number of shares outstanding. *Hint:* A 3-for-1 split means that each *old* share is replaced with 3 *new* shares.

Exercise 11-7
Stock split   P2

The stockholders' equity section of TVX Company on February 4 follows.

Exercise 11-8
Small stock dividend
P2

Common stock—$10 par value, 150,000 shares authorized, 60,000 shares issued and outstanding	$ 600,000
Paid-in capital in excess of par value, common stock	425,000
Retained earnings	550,000
Total stockholders' equity	$1,575,000

On February 5, the directors declare a 20% stock dividend distributable on February 28 to the February 15 stockholders of record. The stock's market value is $40 per share on February 5 before the stock dividend.

1. Prepare entries to record both the dividend declaration and its distribution.

2. Prepare the stockholders' equity section after the stock dividend is distributed. (Assume no other changes to equity.)

Match each description with the characteristic of preferred stock that it best describes.

A. Cumulative   **B.** Noncumulative   **C.** Nonparticipating   **D.** Participating

____ **1.** Receives current and all past dividends before common stockholders receive any dividends.

____ **2.** Receives dividends exceeding the stated rate under certain conditions.

____ **3.** Not entitled to receive dividends in excess of the stated rate.

____ **4.** Loses any dividends that are not declared in the current year.

Exercise 11-9
Identifying characteristics of preferred stock
C2

York's outstanding stock consists of 80,000 shares of *noncumulative* 7.5% preferred stock with a $5 par value and also 200,000 shares of common stock with a $1 par value. During its first four years of operation, the corporation declared and paid the following total cash dividends. Determine the amount of dividends paid each year to each of the two classes of stockholders: preferred and common. Also compute the total dividends paid to each class for the four years combined.

Exercise 11-10
Dividends on common and noncumulative preferred stock
C2

Year 1 total cash dividends	$20,000	Year 3 total cash dividends	$200,000
Year 2 total cash dividends	28,000	Year 4 total cash dividends	350,000

Check   4-year total paid to preferred, $108,000

Exercise 11-11

Dividends on common and cumulative preferred stock

C2

Use the data in Exercise 11-10 to determine the amount of dividends paid each year to each of the two classes of stockholders assuming that the preferred stock is *cumulative*. Also determine the total dividends paid to each class for the four years combined.

Exercise 11-12

Recording and reporting treasury stock transactions

P3

On October 10, the stockholders' equity section of Sherman Systems appears as follows.

Common stock—$10 par value, 72,000 shares authorized, issued, and outstanding......	$ 720,000
Paid-in capital in excess of par value, common stock	216,000
Retained earnings.	864,000
Total stockholders' equity	$1,800,000

1. Prepare journal entries to record the following transactions for Sherman Systems.

    a. Purchased 5,000 shares of its own common stock at $25 per share on October 11.

    b. Sold 1,000 treasury shares on November 1 for $31 cash per share.

Check (1c) Dr. Retained Earnings, $14,000

    c. Sold all remaining treasury shares on November 25 for $20 cash per share.

2. Prepare the stockholders' equity section after the October 11 treasury stock purchase.

Exercise 11-13

Preparing stockholders' equity section

C2   C3   P1   P3

In Draco Corporation's first year of business, the following transactions affected its equity accounts. Prepare the stockholders' equity section of Draco's balance sheet as of December 31.

- Issued 4,000 shares of $2 par value common stock for $18. It authorized 20,000 shares.
- Issued 1,000 shares of 12%, $10 par value preferred stock for $23. It authorized 3,000 shares.
- Reacquired 200 shares of common stock for $30 each.
- Retained earnings is impacted by reported net income of $50,000 and cash dividends of $15,000.

Exercise 11-14

Determining retained earnings balance

C3

Tuscan Inc. had a retained earnings balance of $60,000 at December 31, 2018. During the year, Tuscan had the following selected transactions. Calculate the retained earnings balance at December 31, 2019.

- Reported net income of $100,000.
- Revised an estimate of a machine's salvage value. Depreciation increased by $1,000 per year.
- An error was discovered. Three years ago, a purchase of a building was incorrectly expensed. The effect is understated retained earnings of $12,000 (net of tax benefit).
- Paid cash dividends of $33,000.

Exercise 11-15

Preparing a statement of retained earnings

C3

The following information is from Amos Company for the year ended December 31, 2019. Prepare a statement of retained earnings for Amos Company.

- Retained earnings at December 31, 2018 (before discovery of error), $1,375,000.
- Cash dividends declared and paid during the year, $43,000.
- Two years ago, it forgot to record depreciation expense of $55,500 (net of tax benefit).
- The company earned $126,000 in net income this year.

Exercise 11-16

Earnings per share

A1

Ecker Company reports $2,700,000 of net income and declares $388,020 of cash dividends on its preferred stock for the year. At year-end, the company had 678,000 weighted-average shares of common stock.

1. What amount of net income is available to common stockholders?

Check (2) $3.41

2. What is the company's basic EPS?

Exercise 11-17

Earnings per share

A1

Kelley Company reports $960,000 of net income and declares $120,000 of cash dividends on its preferred stock for the year. At year-end, the company had 400,000 weighted-average shares of common stock.

1. What amount of net income is available to common stockholders?

Check (2) $2.10

2. What is the company's basic EPS? Round your answer to the nearest whole cent.

Compute the price-earnings ratio for each of these four separate companies. For which of these four companies does the market have the lowest expectation of future performance?

Exercise 11-18
Price-earnings ratio
computation and
interpretation

A2

	A	B	C
1	**Company**	**Earnings per Share**	**Market Value per Share**
2	Hilton	$12.00	$176.40
3	SPG	10.00	96.00
4	Hyatt	7.50	93.75
5	Accor	50.00	250.00

Compute the dividend yield for each of these four separate companies. Which company's stock would probably *not* be classified as an income stock?

Exercise 11-19
Dividend yield computation
and interpretation

A3

	A	B	C
1	**Company**	**Annual Cash Dividend per Share**	**Market Value per Share**
2	Etihad	$16.06	$220.00
3	United	13.86	132.00
4	Lingus	3.96	72.00
5	Allied	0.48	80.00

The equity section of Cyril Corporation's balance sheet shows the following.

Exercise 11-20
Book value per share

A4

Preferred stock—6% cumulative, $25 par value, 10,000 shares issued and outstanding....................	$ 250,000
Common stock $8 par value, 100,000 shares issued and outstanding	800,000
Retained earnings...	535,000
Total stockholders' equity	$1,585,000

Determine the book value per share of common stock under two separate situations.

1. No preferred dividends are in arrears at the current date.

2. Three years of preferred dividends are in arrears at the current date.

Check (1) Book value of
common, $13.35 per share

Alexander Corporation reports the following components of stockholders' equity at December 31, 2018.

Exercise 11-21
Cash dividends, treasury
stock, and statement of
retained earnings

C3   P2   P3

Common stock—$25 par value, 50,000 shares authorized, 30,000 shares issued and outstanding...........	$ 750,000
Paid-in capital in excess of par value, common stock	50,000
Retained earnings...	340,000
Total stockholders' equity	$1,140,000

During 2019, the following transactions affected its stockholders' equity accounts.

Jan. 2	Purchased 3,000 shares of its own stock at $25 cash per share.
Jan. 7	Directors declared a $1.50 per share cash dividend payable on February 28 to the February 9 stockholders of record.
Feb. 28	Paid the dividend declared on January 7.
July 9	Sold 1,200 of its treasury shares at $30 cash per share.
Aug. 27	Sold 1,500 of its treasury shares at $20 cash per share.
Sep. 9	Directors declared a $2 per share cash dividend payable on October 22 to the September 23 stockholders of record.
Oct. 22	Paid the dividend declared on September 9.
Dec. 31	Closed the $52,000 credit balance (from net income) in the Income Summary account to Retained Earnings.

Required

1. Prepare journal entries to record each of these transactions.

2. Prepare a statement of retained earnings for the year ended December 31, 2019.

3. Prepare the stockholders' equity section of the company's balance sheet as of December 31, 2019.

PROBLEM SET A

Problem 11-1A
Stockholders' equity
transactions and analysis

P1   A4

Kinkaid Co. was incorporated at the beginning of this year and had a number of transactions. The following journal entries impacted its stockholders' equity during its first year of operations.

a.	Cash	300,000	
	Common Stock, $25 Par Value		250,000
	Paid-In Capital in Excess of Par Value, Common Stock		50,000
b.	Organization Expenses	150,000	
	Common Stock, $25 Par Value		125,000
	Paid-In Capital in Excess of Par Value, Common Stock		25,000
c.	Cash	43,000	
	Accounts Receivable	15,000	
	Building..	81,500	
	Notes Payable		59,500
	Common Stock, $25 Par Value...........................		50,000
	Paid-In Capital in Excess of Par Value, Common Stock		30,000
d.	Cash	120,000	
	Common Stock, $25 Par Value		75,000
	Paid-In Capital in Excess of Par Value, Common Stock		45,000

Required

1. Explain the transaction(s) underlying each journal entry (*a*) through (*d*).

Check (2) 20,000 shares

(3) $650,000

2. How many shares of common stock are outstanding at year-end?

3. What is the total paid-in capital at year-end?

4. What is the book value per share of the common stock at year-end if total paid-in capital plus retained earnings equals $695,000?

Problem 11-2A
Cash dividends, treasury
stock, and statement of
retained earnings

C3   P2   P3

Kohler Corporation reports the following components of stockholders' equity at December 31, 2018.

Common stock—$10 par value, 100,000 shares authorized, 40,000 shares issued and outstanding..........	$400,000
Paid-in capital in excess of par value, common stock	60,000
Retained earnings...	270,000
Total stockholders' equity	$730,000

During 2019, the following transactions affected its stockholders' equity accounts.

Jan. 2   Purchased 4,000 shares of its own stock at $20 cash per share.
Jan. 5   Directors declared a $2 per share cash dividend payable on February 28 to the February 5 stockholders of record.
Feb. 28   Paid the dividend declared on January 5.
July 6   Sold 1,500 of its treasury shares at $24 cash per share.
Aug. 22   Sold 2,500 of its treasury shares at $17 cash per share.
Sep. 5   Directors declared a $2 per share cash dividend payable on October 28 to the September 25 stockholders of record.
Oct. 28   Paid the dividend declared on September 5.
Dec. 31   Closed the $388,000 credit balance (from net income) in the Income Summary account to Retained Earnings.

Required

1. Prepare journal entries to record each of these transactions.

Check (2) Ending retained
earnings, $504,500

2. Prepare a statement of retained earnings for the year ended December 31, 2019.

3. Prepare the stockholders' equity section of the company's balance sheet as of December 31, 2019.

At September 30, the end of Beijing Company's third quarter, the following stockholders' equity accounts are reported.

Common stock, $12 par value.	$360,000
Paid-in capital in excess of par value, common stock	90,000
Retained earnings.	320,000

Problem 11-3A
Equity analysis—journal entries and account balances

P2

In the fourth quarter, the following entries related to its equity are recorded.

Oct. 2	Retained Earnings.	60,000	
	Common Dividend Payable.		60,000
Oct. 25	Common Dividend Payable	60,000	
	Cash		60,000
Oct. 31	Retained Earnings.	75,000	
	Common Stock Dividend Distributable.		36,000
	Paid-In Capital in Excess of Par Value, Common Stock		39,000
Nov. 5	Common Stock Dividend Distributable	36,000	
	Common Stock, $12 Par Value		36,000
Dec. 1	Memo—Change the title of the Common Stock account to reflect the new par value of $4.		
Dec. 31	Income Summary	210,000	
	Retained Earnings		210,000

Required

1. Explain the transaction(s) underlying each journal entry.
2. Complete the following table showing the equity account balances at each indicated date (take into account the beginning balances from September 30).

	Sep. 30	Oct. 2	Oct. 25	Oct. 31	Nov. 5	Dec. 1	Dec. 31
Common stock	$ 360,000	$ ____	$ ____	$ ____	$ ____	$ ____	$ ____
Common stock dividend distributable	0	____	____	____	____	____	____
Paid-in capital in excess of par, common stock	90,000	____	____	____	____	____	____
Retained earnings	320,000	____	____	____	____	____	____
Total equity	$ 770,000	$ ____	$ ____	$ ____	$ ____	$ ____	$ ____

Check   Total equity: Oct. 2, $710,000; Dec. 31, $920,000

The equity sections for Atticus Group at the beginning of the year (January 1) and end of the year (December 31) follow.

Problem 11-4A
Analyzing changes in stockholders' equity accounts

C3   P2   P3

Stockholders' Equity (January 1)

Common stock—$4 par value, 100,000 shares authorized, 40,000 shares issued and outstanding.	$160,000
Paid-in capital in excess of par value, common stock	120,000
Retained earnings.	320,000
Total stockholders' equity	$600,000

Stockholders' Equity (December 31)

Common stock—$4 par value, 100,000 shares authorized, 47,400 shares issued, 3,000 shares in treasury.	$189,600
Paid-in capital in excess of par value, common stock	179,200
Retained earnings ($30,000 restricted by treasury stock).	400,000
	768,800
Less cost of treasury stock.	(30,000)
Total stockholders' equity	$738,800

The following transactions and events affected its equity during the year.

Jan.   5   Declared a $0.50 per share cash dividend, date of record January 10.
Mar. 20   Purchased treasury stock for cash.
Apr.   5   Declared a $0.50 per share cash dividend, date of record April 10.
July   5   Declared a $0.50 per share cash dividend, date of record July 10.
July 31   Declared a 20% stock dividend when the stock's market value was $12 per share.
Aug. 14   Issued the stock dividend that was declared on July 31.
Oct.   5   Declared a $0.50 per share cash dividend, date of record October 10.

Required

1. How many common shares are outstanding on each cash dividend date?
2. What is the total dollar amount for each of the four cash dividends?

Check   (3) $88,800

3. What is the amount of retained earnings transferred to paid-in capital accounts (capitalized) for the stock dividend?

(4) $10

4. What is the per share cost of the treasury stock purchased?

(5) $248,000

5. How much net income did the company earn this year?

Problem 11-5A
Computing book values
and dividend allocations

C2   A4

Raphael Corporation's balance sheet shows the following stockholders' equity section.

Preferred stock—5% cumulative, $___ par value, 1,000 shares authorized, issued, and outstanding............	$ 50,000
Common stock—$___ par value, 4,000 shares authorized, issued, and outstanding	80,000
Retained earnings..	150,000
Total stockholders' equity	$280,000

Required

1. What are the par values of the corporation's preferred stock and its common stock?
2. If no dividends are in arrears at the current date, what is the book value per share of common stock? Round per share value to the nearest cent.

Check   (3) Book value of
common, $56.25

3. If two years' preferred dividends are in arrears at the current date, what is the book value per share of common stock? Round per share value to the nearest cent.
4. If two years' preferred dividends are in arrears at the current date and the board of directors declares cash dividends of $11,500, what total amount will be paid to the preferred and to the common shareholders?

PROBLEM SET B

Weiss Company was incorporated at the beginning of this year and had a number of transactions. The following journal entries impacted its stockholders' equity during its first year of operations.

Problem 11-1B
Stockholders' equity
transactions and analysis

P1   A4

a.	Cash	120,000	
	Common Stock, $1 Par Value..............................		3,000
	Paid-In Capital in Excess of Par Value, Common Stock..........		117,000
b.	Organization Expenses	40,000	
	Common Stock, $1 Par Value..............................		1,000
	Paid-In Capital in Excess of Par Value, Common Stock..........		39,000
c.	Cash	13,300	
	Accounts Receivable	8,000	
	Building..	37,000	
	Notes Payable..		18,300
	Common Stock, $1 Par Value..............................		800
	Paid-In Capital in Excess of Par Value, Common Stock..........		39,200
d.	Cash	60,000	
	Common Stock, $1 Par Value..............................		1,200
	Paid-In Capital in Excess of Par Value, Common Stock..........		58,800

Required

1. Explain the transaction(s) underlying each journal entry (a) through (d).

Check   (2) 6,000 shares

2. How many shares of common stock are outstanding at year-end?

3. What is the total paid-in capital at year-end?   (3) $260,000

4. What is the book value per share of the common stock at year-end if total paid-in capital plus retained earnings equals $283,200?

Balthus Corp. reports the following components of stockholders' equity at December 31, 2018.

Common stock—$1 par value, 320,000 shares authorized, 200,000 shares issued and outstanding............	$ 200,000
Paid-in capital in excess of par value, common stock	1,400,000
Retained earnings...	2,160,000
Total stockholders' equity	$3,760,000

Problem 11-2B
Cash dividends, treasury stock, and statement of retained earnings

C3   P2   P3

It completed the following transactions related to stockholders' equity during 2019.

Jan. 10   Purchased 40,000 shares of its own stock at $12 cash per share.
Mar.   2   Directors declared a $1.50 per share cash dividend payable on March 31 to the March 15 stockholders of record.
Mar. 31   Paid the dividend declared on March 2.
Nov. 11   Sold 24,000 of its treasury shares at $13 cash per share.
Nov. 25   Sold 16,000 of its treasury shares at $9.50 cash per share.
Dec.   1   Directors declared a $2.50 per share cash dividend payable on January 2 to the December 10 stockholders of record.
Dec. 31   Closed the $1,072,000 credit balance (from net income) in the Income Summary account to Retained Earnings.

Required

1. Prepare journal entries to record each of these transactions.

2. Prepare a statement of retained earnings for the year ended December 31, 2019.   **Check**   (2) Ending retained earnings, $2,476,000

3. Prepare the stockholders' equity section of the company's balance sheet as of December 31, 2019.

At December 31, the end of Chilton Communication's third quarter, the following stockholders' equity accounts are reported.

Common stock, $10 par value..................................	$ 960,000
Paid-in capital in excess of par value, common stock	384,000
Retained earnings...	1,600,000

Problem 11-3B
Equity analysis—journal entries and account balances

P2

In the fourth quarter, the following entries related to its equity are recorded.

Jan. 17	Retained Earnings...	96,000	
	Common Dividend Payable...............................		96,000
Feb. 5	Common Dividend Payable	96,000	
	Cash..		96,000
Feb. 28	Retained Earnings...	252,000	
	Common Stock Dividend Distributable......................		120,000
	Paid-In Capital in Excess of Par Value, Common Stock		132,000
Mar. 14	Common Stock Dividend Distributable	120,000	
	Common Stock, $10 Par Value		120,000
Mar. 25	Memo—Change the title of the Common Stock account to reflect the new par value of $5.		
Mar. 31	Income Summary	720,000	
	Retained Earnings		720,000

Required

1. Explain the transaction(s) underlying each journal entry.

2. Complete the following table showing the equity account balances at each indicated date (take into account the beginning balances from December 31).

	Dec. 31	Jan. 17	Feb. 5	Feb. 28	Mar. 14	Mar. 25	Mar. 31
Common stock	$ 960,000	$____	$____	$____	$____	$____	$____
Common stock dividend distributable	0	____	____	____	____	____	____
Paid-in capital in excess of par, common stock	384,000	____	____	____	____	____	____
Retained earnings	1,600,000	____	____	____	____	____	____
Total equity	$ 2,944,000	$____	$____	$____	$____	$____	$____

Check Total equity: Jan. 17, $2,848,000; Mar. 31, $3,568,000

Problem 11-4B

Analyzing changes in stockholders' equity accounts

C3 P2 P3

The equity sections for Hovo Corp. at the beginning of the year (January 1) and end of the year (December 31) follow.

Stockholders' Equity (January 1)

Common stock—$20 par value, 30,000 shares authorized, 17,000 shares issued and outstanding.............	$340,000
Paid-in capital in excess of par value, common stock	60,000
Retained earnings...	270,000
Total stockholders' equity	$670,000

Stockholders' Equity (December 31)

Common stock—$20 par value, 30,000 shares authorized, 19,000 shares issued, 1,000 shares in treasury......	$380,000
Paid-in capital in excess of par value, common stock	104,000
Retained earnings ($40,000 restricted by treasury stock)..	295,200
	779,200
Less cost of treasury stock...	(40,000)
Total stockholders' equity	$739,200

The following transactions and events affected its equity during the year.

Feb. 15 Declared a $0.40 per share cash dividend, date of record five days later.
Mar. 2 Purchased treasury stock for cash.
May 15 Declared a $0.40 per share cash dividend, date of record five days later.
Aug. 15 Declared a $0.40 per share cash dividend, date of record five days later.
Oct. 4 Declared a 12.5% stock dividend when the stock's market value is $42 per share.
Oct. 20 Issued the stock dividend that was declared on October 4.
Nov. 15 Declared a $0.40 per share cash dividend, date of record five days later.

Required

1. How many common shares are outstanding on each cash dividend date?
2. What is the total dollar amount for each of the four cash dividends?
3. What is the amount of retained earnings transferred to paid-in capital accounts (capitalized) for the stock dividend?
4. What is the per share cost of the treasury stock purchased?
5. How much net income did the company earn this year?

Check (3) $84,000

(4) $40

(5) $136,000

Problem 11-5B

Computing book values and dividend allocations

C2 A4

Soltech Company's balance sheet shows the following stockholders' equity section.

Preferred stock—8% cumulative, $___ par value, 1,500 shares authorized, issued, and outstanding...........	$ 375,000
Common stock—$___ par value, 18,000 shares authorized, issued, and outstanding	900,000
Retained earnings...	1,125,000
Total stockholders' equity	$2,400,000

Required

1. What are the par values of the corporation's preferred stock and its common stock?

2. If no dividends are in arrears at the current date, what is the book value per share of common stock? Round per share value to the nearest cent.

3. If two years' preferred dividends are in arrears at the current date, what is the book value per share of common stock? Round per share value to the nearest cent.

4. If two years' preferred dividends are in arrears at the current date and the board of directors declares cash dividends of $100,000, what total amount will be paid to the preferred and to the common shareholders?

Check   (3) Book value of common, $109.17

This serial problem began in Chapter 1 and continues through most of the book. If previous chapter segments were not completed, the serial problem can begin at this point.

SP 11   Santana Rey created **Business Solutions** on October 1, 2019. The company has been successful, and Santana plans to expand her business. She believes that an additional $86,000 is needed and is investigating three funding sources.

a. Santana's sister Cicely is willing to invest $86,000 in the business as a common shareholder. Because Santana currently has about $129,000 invested in the business, Cicely's investment will mean that Santana will maintain about 60% ownership and Cicely will have 40% ownership of Business Solutions.

b. Santana's uncle Marcello is willing to invest $86,000 in the business as a preferred shareholder. Marcello would purchase 860 shares of $100 par value, 7% preferred stock.

c. Santana's banker is willing to lend her $86,000 on a 7%, 10-year note payable. She would make monthly payments of $1,000 per month for 10 years.

SERIAL PROBLEM
Business Solutions

P1   C1   C2

©Alexander Image/Shutterstock

Required

1. Prepare the journal entry to reflect the initial $86,000 investment under each of the options (*a*), (*b*), and (*c*).

2. Evaluate the three proposals for expansion, providing the pros and cons of each option.

3. Which option do you recommend Santana adopt? Explain.

The following **General Ledger** assignments highlight the impact, or lack thereof, on financial statements from equity-based transactions.

GL 11-1   General Ledger assignment 11-1 is adapted from Problem 11-2A, including beginning equity balances. Prepare journal entries related to treasury stock, cash dividends, and net income. Then prepare the statement of retained earnings and the stockholders' equity section of the balance sheet.

GL 11-2   General Ledger assignment 11-2 is adapted from Problem 11-4A, including beginning and ending equity balances. Prepare journal entries related to cash dividends and stock dividends. Calculate the number of shares outstanding, the amount of net income, and the amount of retained earnings to be capitalized as a result of the stock dividend, if any.

**GENERAL
LEDGER
PROBLEM**

Accounting Analysis

AA 11-1   Use **Apple**'s financial statements in Appendix A to answer the following.

1. How many shares of Apple common stock are issued and outstanding at (*a*) September 30, 2017, and (*b*) September 24, 2016?

2. What is the total amount of cash dividends paid to common stockholders for the years ended (*a*) September 30, 2017, and (*b*) September 24, 2016?

3. Identify basic EPS amounts for fiscal years (*a*) 2017 and (*b*) 2016.

4. Is the change in Apple's EPS from 2016 to 2017 favorable or unfavorable?

5. If Apple buys back outstanding shares from investors, would you expect EPS to increase or decrease from the buyback?

**COMPANY
ANALYSIS**

C2   A1   A4

APPLE

**COMPARATIVE
ANALYSIS**

A1 A2 A3 A4

**APPLE
GOOGLE**

AA 11-2 Use the following comparative figures for **Apple** and **Google**.

Key Figures	Apple	Google
Net income (in millions)	$ 48,351	$ 12,662
Cash dividends declared per common share	$ 2.40	$ 0.00
Common shares outstanding (in millions)	5,126.201	694.783
Weighted-average common shares outstanding (in millions)	5,217.242	693.049
Market value (price) per share	$ 154.12	$1,046.40
Equity applicable to common shares (in millions)	$ 134,047	$ 152,502

Required

1. Compute the book value per common share for each company using these data.
2. Compute the basic EPS for each company using these data.
3. Compute the dividend yield for each company using these data.
4. Compute the price-earnings ratio for each company using these data.
5. Based on the PE ratio, for which company do investors have greater expectations about future performance?

GLOBAL ANALYSIS

C3   A1

Samsung

AA 11-3 Use the following financial information for **Samsung**.

Net income less dividends available to preferred shares (in millions)	₩ 36,323,611
Number of common shares outstanding (in millions)	119.688
Weighted-average common shares outstanding (in millions)	121.132
Equity applicable to common shares (in millions)	₩214,371,961

Required

1. Compute book value per share for Samsung.
2. Compute earnings per share (EPS) for Samsung.
3. If Samsung buys back outstanding shares from investors, would we expect EPS to increase or decrease from the buyback?

Beyond the Numbers

**ETHICS
CHALLENGE**

C3

BTN 11-1 Harriet Moore is an accountant for New World Pharmaceuticals. Her duties include tracking research and development spending in the new product development division. Over the course of the past six months, Harriet has noticed that a great deal of funds have been spent on a particular project for a new drug. She hears "through the grapevine" that the company is about to patent the drug and expects it to be a major advance in antibiotics. Harriet believes that this new drug will greatly improve company perfor-mance and will cause the company's stock to increase in value. Harriet decides to purchase shares of New World in order to benefit from this expected increase.

Required

What are Harriet's ethical responsibilities, if any, with respect to the information she has learned through her duties as an accountant for New World Pharmaceuticals? What are the implications of her planned purchase of New World shares?

**COMMUNICATING
IN PRACTICE**

A1   A2

Hint: Make a slide of each team's memo for a class discussion.

BTN 11-2 Teams are to select an industry, and each team member is to select a different company in that industry. Each team member then is to acquire the selected company's financial statements (or Form 10-K) from the SEC site (**SEC.gov**). Use these data to identify basic EPS. Use the financial press (or **finance.yahoo.com**) to determine the market price of this stock, and then compute the price-earnings ratio. Communicate with teammates via a meeting, e-mail, or telephone to discuss the meaning of this ratio, how companies compare, and the industry norm. The team must prepare a single memorandum reporting the ratio for each company and identifying the team conclusions or consensus of opinion. The memorandum is to be duplicated and distributed to the instructor and teammates.

BTN 11-3 Access the March 1, 2017, filing of the 2016 calendar-year 10-K report of **McDonald's** (ticker: MCD) from **SEC.gov**.

TAKING IT TO THE NET

C1 C3

Required

1. Review McDonald's balance sheet and identify how many classes of stock it has issued.

2. What are the par values, number of authorized shares, and number of issued shares of the classes of stock you identified in part 1?

3. Review its statement of cash flows and identify what total amount of cash it paid in 2016 to purchase treasury stock.

4. What amount did McDonald's pay out in common stock cash dividends for 2016?

BTN 11-4 This activity requires teamwork to reinforce understanding of accounting for treasury stock.

1. Write a brief team statement (*a*) generalizing what happens to a corporation's financial position when it engages in a stock buyback and (*b*) identifying reasons why a corporation would engage in this activity.

2. Assume that an entity acquires 100 shares of its $100 par value common stock at a cost of $134 cash per share. Discuss the entry to record this acquisition. Next, assign *each* team member to prepare *one* of the following entries (assume each entry applies to all shares).

   a. Reissue treasury shares at cost.

   b. Reissue treasury shares at $150 per share.

   c. Reissue treasury shares at $120 per share; assume the paid-in capital account from treasury shares has a $1,500 balance.

   d. Reissue treasury shares at $120 per share; assume the paid-in capital account from treasury shares has a $1,000 balance.

   e. Reissue treasury shares at $120 per share; assume the paid-in capital account from treasury shares has a zero balance.

3. In sequence, each member is to present his/her entry to the team and explain the *similarities* and *differences* between that entry and the previous entry.

TEAMWORK IN ACTION

P3

Hint: Instructor must be sure each team accurately completes part 1 before proceeding.

BTN 11-5 Assume that **Yelp** decides to launch a new website to market discount bookkeeping services to consumers. This chain, named Aladin, requires $500,000 of start-up capital. The founder contributes $375,000 of personal assets in return for 15,000 shares of common stock, but he must raise another $125,000 in cash. There are two alternative plans for raising the additional cash.

ENTREPRENEURIAL DECISION

C2 P2

- *Plan A* is to sell 3,750 shares of common stock to one or more investors for $125,000 cash.

- *Plan B* is to sell 1,250 shares of cumulative preferred stock to one or more investors for $125,000 cash (this preferred stock would have a $100 par value, have an annual 8% dividend rate, and be issued at par).

1. If the new business is expected to earn $72,000 of after-tax net income in the first year, what rate of return on beginning equity will the founder earn under each alternative plan? Which plan will provide the higher expected return?

2. If the new business is expected to earn $16,800 of after-tax net income in the first year, what rate of return on beginning equity will the founder earn under each alternative plan? Which plan will provide the higher expected return?

3. Analyze and interpret the differences between the results for parts 1 and 2.

BTN 11-6 Review 30 to 60 minutes of financial news programming on television. Take notes on companies that are catching analysts' attention. You might hear reference to over- and undervaluation of firms and to reports about PE ratios, dividend yields, and earnings per share. Be prepared to give a brief description to the class of your observations.

HITTING THE ROAD

A1 A2 A3

---

12 Reporting Cash Flows

Chapter Preview

BASICS OF CASH FLOW REPORTING

C1 Purpose, measurement, and classification

Noncash activities

P1 Format and preparation

NTK 12-1

CASH FLOWS FROM OPERATING

P2 Indirect method

Illustration of indirect method

Summary of indirect method adjustments

NTK 12-2

CASH FLOWS FROM INVESTING

P3 Three-step process of analysis

Analyzing noncurrent assets

Analyzing other assets

NTK 12-3

CASH FLOWS FROM FINANCING

P3 Three-step process of analysis

Analyzing noncurrent liabilities

Analyzing equity

Summary using T-accounts

A1 Analyzing cash

NTK 12-4

Learning Objectives

CONCEPTUAL

C1 Distinguish between operating, investing, and financing activities, and describe how noncash investing and financing activities are disclosed.

ANALYTICAL

A1 Analyze the statement of cash flows and apply the cash flow on total assets ratio.

PROCEDURAL

P1 Prepare a statement of cash flows.

P2 Compute cash flows from operating activities using the indirect method.

P3 Determine cash flows from both investing and financing activities.

P4 *Appendix 12A*—Illustrate use of a spreadsheet to prepare a statement of cash flows.

P5 *Appendix 12B*—Compute cash flows from operating activities using the direct method.

True Colors

"Work with people who have faith in you"
—BARBARA BRADLEY

FORT WAYNE, IN—"I never saw myself going into business," recalls Barbara Bradley. Until one day, "we were at the airport when we noticed no one was carrying anything colorful or fun. So we decided to start a company to make handbags and luggage for women," exclaims Barbara.

Barbara and her co-founder had no cash, so they borrowed $250 and started "cutting fabric out on a Ping-Pong table," explains Barbara. "We decided to name the company **Vera Bradley (VeraBradley.com)** after [my mother]."

As the business grew, Barbara had to manage cash flows. "The first year, we did $10,000 in sales," proclaims Barbara. "Then things got chaotic." While cash flows from operations were good, the business had to expand to meet demand.

"We went to a bank, seeking a $5,000 loan," says Barbara. The loan was a welcome cash inflow that allowed the company to "build its own building!"

Barbara admits that she's "not a great finance [and accounting] person," but she insists that accounting and attention to cash flows are key to running a successful business.

©Robin Marchant/Vera Bradley/Getty Images

Although cash may be king, Barbara insists that "business is all about forming relationships. My father always said, 'In business, you sell yourself first, your company second, and the product third,' and he was right."

Sources: *Vera Bradley website,* January 2019; *Vera Bradley Foundation,* January 2019; *Fortune,* October 2015

BASICS OF CASH FLOW REPORTING

Purpose of the Statement of Cash Flows

The **statement of cash flows** reports cash receipts (inflows) and cash payments (outflows) for a period. Cash flows are separated into operating, investing, and financing activities. The details of sources and uses of cash make this statement useful. The statement of cash flows helps answer

- What explains the change in the cash balance?
- Where does a company spend its cash?
- How does a company receive its cash?
- Why do income and cash flows differ?

Importance of Cash Flows

Information about cash flows influences decisions. Cash flows help users decide whether a company has enough cash to pay its debts. They also help evaluate a company's ability to pursue opportunities. Managers use cash flow information to plan day-to-day operations and make long-term investment decisions.

W. T. Grant Co. is a classic example of the importance of cash flows. Grant reported net income of more than $40 million per year for three consecutive years. At that same time, cash outflow was more than $90 million by the end of that three-year period. Grant soon went bankrupt. Users who relied only on Grant's income numbers were caught off guard.

Measurement of Cash Flows

Cash flows include both *cash* and *cash equivalents*. The statement of cash flows explains the difference between the beginning and ending balances of cash and cash equivalents. We continue to use the phrases *cash flows* and the *statement of cash flows,* but remember that both phrases refer to cash *and* cash equivalents. Because cash and cash equivalents are combined, the statement of cash flows does not report transactions *between* cash and cash equivalents, such as cash paid to purchase cash equivalents and cash received from selling cash equivalents.

A cash equivalent has two criteria: (1) be readily convertible to a known amount of cash and (2) be sufficiently close to its maturity so its market value is unaffected by interest rate changes. **American Express** defines its cash equivalents as including "highly liquid investments with original maturities of 90 days or less."

Cash Equivalents

Classification of Cash Flows

Cash receipts and cash payments are classified in one of three categories: operating, investing, or financing activities. A net cash inflow (source) occurs when the receipts in a category exceed the payments. A net cash outflow (use) occurs when the payments in a category exceed the receipts.

Operating Activities

Operating activities include transactions and events that affect net income. Examples are the production and purchase of inventory, the sale of goods and services to customers, and the expenditures to operate the business. Not all items in income, such as unusual gains and losses, are operating activities (we discuss these exceptions later). Exhibit 12.1 lists common cash inflows and outflows from operating activities.

EXHIBIT 12.1

Cash Flows from Operating Activities

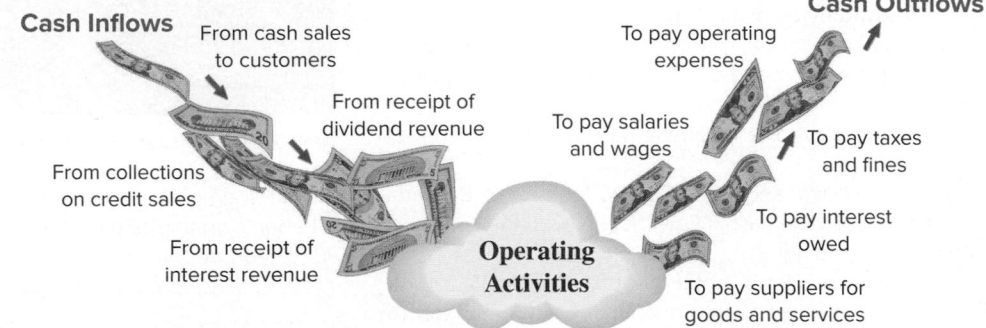

Investing Activities

Investing activities include transactions and events that come from the purchase and sale of long-term assets. They also include (1) the purchase and sale of short-term investments and (2) lending and collecting money for notes receivable. Exhibit 12.2 lists examples of cash flows from investing activities. Cash from collecting the principal on notes is an investing activity. However, collecting interest on notes is an operating activity; also, if a note results from sales to customers, it is an operating activity.

Point: For simplicity, we assume purchases and sales of equity and debt securities are investing activities.

EXHIBIT 12.2

Cash Flows from Investing Activities

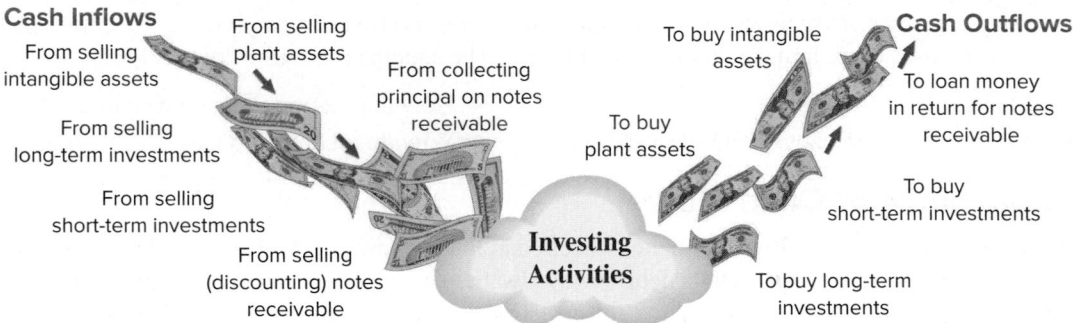

Financing Activities

Financing activities include transactions and events that affect long-term liabilities and equity. Examples are (1) getting cash from issuing debt and repaying debt and (2) receiving cash from or distributing cash to owners. Borrowing and repaying principal on both short- and long-term debt are financing activities. However, payments of interest are operating activities. Exhibit 12.3 lists examples of cash flows from financing activities.

EXHIBIT 12.3

Cash Flows from Financing Activities

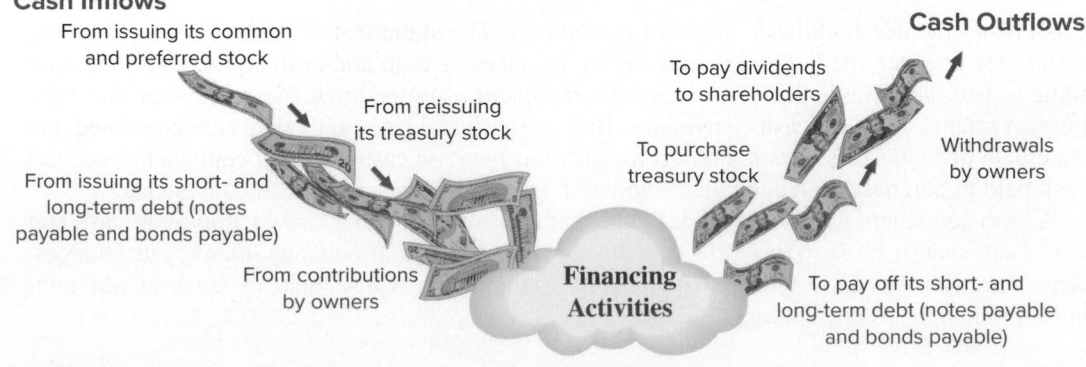

Link between Classification of Cash Flows and the Balance Sheet   Operating, investing, and financing activities are loosely linked to different parts of the balance sheet. Operating activities are affected by changes in current assets and current liabilities (and the income statement). Investing activities are affected by changes in long-term assets. Financing activities are affected by changes in long-term liabilities and equity. These links are shown in Exhibit 12.4. Exceptions to these links include (1) current assets *unrelated* to operations—such as short-term notes receivable from noncustomers and from investment securities, which are investing activities, and (2) current liabilities *unrelated* to operations—such as short-term notes payable and dividends payable, which are financing activities.

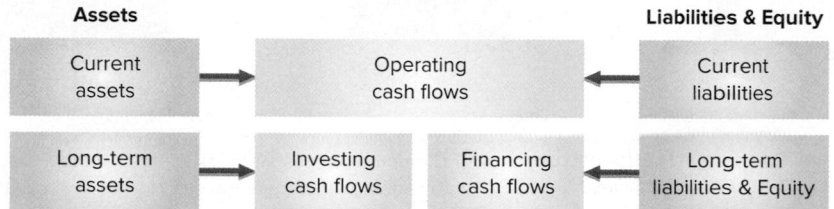

EXHIBIT 12.4

Linkage of Cash Flow Classifications to the Balance Sheet

Noncash Investing and Financing

Some investing and financing activities do not affect cash flows. One example is the purchase of long-term assets using a long-term note payable (loan). This transaction impacts both investing and financing activities but does not impact current-period cash. Such transactions are reported at the bottom of the statement of cash flows or in a note to the statement—Exhibit 12.5 has examples.

● Retirement of debt by issuing equity stock.

● Conversion of preferred stock to common stock.

● Lease of assets in a long-term lease transaction.

● Purchase of long-term assets by issuing a note or bond.

● Exchange of noncash assets for other noncash assets.

● Purchase of noncash assets by issuing equity or debt.

EXHIBIT 12.5

Examples of Noncash Investing and Financing Activities

Format of the Statement of Cash Flows

A statement of cash flows reports cash flows from three activities: operating, investing, and financing. Exhibit 12.6 shows the usual format. The statement shows the net increase or decrease from those activities and ties it into the cash balance. Any noncash investing and financing transactions are disclosed in a note or separate schedule.

P1_____

Prepare a statement of cash flows.

EXHIBIT 12.6

Format of the Statement of Cash Flows

COMPANY NAME		
Statement of Cash Flows		
For *period* Ended *date*		
Cash flows from operating activities		
[Compute operating cash flows using indirect or direct method]		
Net cash provided (used) by operating activities	$ #	
Cash flows from investing activities		
[List of individual inflows and outflows]		
Net cash provided (used) by investing activities	#	
Cash flows from financing activities		
[List of individual inflows and outflows]		
Net cash provided (used) by financing activities	#	
Net increase (decrease) in cash.	$ #	
Cash (and equivalents) balance at prior period-end.	#	
Cash (and equivalents) balance at current period-end	$ #	

Separate schedule or note disclosure of any noncash investing and financing transactions is required.

Preparing the Statement of Cash Flows

Preparing a statement of cash flows has five steps, shown in Exhibit 12.7. Computing the net increase or net decrease in cash is a simple but crucial computation. It equals the current period's cash balance minus the prior period's cash balance. This is the *bottom-line* figure for the statement of cash flows and is a check on accuracy.

EXHIBIT 12.7

Five Steps in Preparing the Statement of Cash Flows

1 Compute net increase or decrease in cash.

2 Compute net cash from or for operating activities.

3 Compute net cash from or for investing activities.

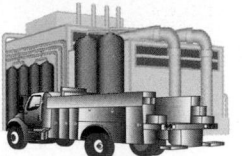

4 Compute net cash from or for financing activities.

5 Compute net cash from all sources; then *prove* it by adding it to beginning cash to get ending cash.

Analyzing the Cash Account   A company's cash receipts and cash payments are recorded in its Cash account. The Cash account is one place to look for information about cash flows. The summarized Cash T-account of Genesis, Inc., is in Exhibit 12.8. Preparing a statement of cash flows requires classifying each cash inflow or outflow as an operating, investing, or financing activity.

EXHIBIT 12.8

Summarized Cash Account

Cash			
Balance, Dec. 31, 2018	12,000		
Receipts from customers	570,000	Payments for inventory	319,000
Receipts from asset sales	2,000	Payments for operating exp.	218,000
Receipts from stock issuance ..	15,000	Payments for interest	8,000
		Payments for taxes	5,000
		Payments for notes retirement ...	18,000
		Payments for dividends	14,000
Balance, Dec. 31, 2019	17,000		

Analyzing Noncash Accounts   A second approach to preparing the statement of cash flows analyzes noncash accounts and uses double-entry accounting. Exhibit 12.9 uses the accounting equation to show the relation between the Cash account and the noncash balance sheet accounts. We can explain changes in cash and prepare a statement of cash flows by analyzing changes in liability accounts, equity accounts, and noncash asset accounts (along with income statement accounts).

EXHIBIT 12.9

Relation between Cash and Noncash Accounts

$$\textbf{Cash} = \textbf{Liabilities} + \textbf{Equity} - \textbf{Noncash assets}$$

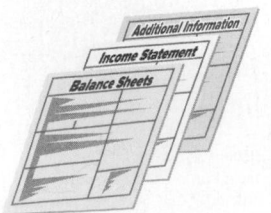

Information to Prepare the Statement   Information to prepare the statement of cash flows comes from three sources: (1) comparative balance sheets, (2) the current income statement, and (3) additional information. Comparative balance sheets are used to compute changes in noncash accounts from the beginning to the end of the period. The current income statement is used to help compute cash flows from operating activities. Additional information includes details that help explain cash flows and noncash activities.

■ **Decision Maker**

Entrepreneur   You are considering purchasing a start-up business that recently reported a $110,000 annual net loss and a $225,000 annual net cash inflow. How are these results possible? ■ *Answer:* Several factors can explain an increase in net cash flows when a net loss is reported, including (1) early recognition of expenses relative to revenues generated (such as research and development), (2) cash advances on long-term sales contracts not yet recognized in income, (3) issuances of debt or equity for cash to finance expansion, (4) cash sale of assets, (5) delay of cash payments, and (6) cash prepayment on sales.

Classify each of the following cash flows as operating, investing, or financing activities.

___ **a.** Purchase equipment for cash		___ **g.** Cash paid for utilities	
___ **b.** Cash payment of wages		___ **h.** Cash paid to acquire investments	
___ **c.** Issuance of stock for cash		___ **i.** Cash paid to retire debt	
___ **d.** Receipt of cash dividends from investments		___ **j.** Cash received as interest on Investments	
___ **e.** Cash collections from customers		___ **k.** Cash received from selling investments	
___ **f.** Note payable issued for cash		___ **l.** Cash received from a bank loan	

NEED-TO-KNOW 12-1

Classifying Cash Flows

C1   P1 ▶

Solution

a. Investing	**c.** Financing	**e.** Operating	**g.** Operating	**i.** Financing	**k.** Investing
b. Operating	**d.** Operating	**f.** Financing	**h.** Investing	**j.** Operating	**l.** Financing

Do More: QS 12-1, QS 12-2, E 12-1

CASH FLOWS FROM OPERATING

Indirect and Direct Methods of Reporting

Cash flows provided (used) by operating activities are reported using the *direct method* or the *indirect method.* **These two different methods apply only to the operating activities section.**

- The **direct method** separately lists operating cash receipts (such as cash received from customers) and operating cash payments (such as cash paid for inventory). The cash payments are then subtracted from cash receipts.

- The **indirect method** reports net income and then adjusts it for items that do not affect cash. It does *not* report individual items of cash inflows and cash outflows from operating activities.

The net cash amount provided by operating activities is *identical* under both the direct and indirect methods. The difference is with the computation and presentation. The indirect method is arguably easier. Nearly all companies report operating cash flows using the indirect method, including **Apple**, **Google**, and **Samsung** in Appendix A.

Operating

Demonstration Data   Exhibit 12.10 shows Genesis's income statement and balance sheets. We use this information to prepare a statement of cash flows that explains the $5,000 increase in cash.

Applying the Indirect Method

Net income is computed using accrual accounting. Revenues and expenses rarely match the receipt and payment of cash. The indirect method adjusts net income to get the net cash provided or used by operating activities. We begin with Genesis's income of $38,000 and adjust it

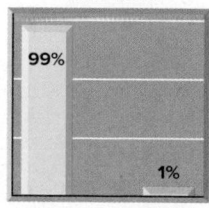

Firms Using Indirect vs. Direct

99%

1%

Indirect   Direct

GENESIS
Income Statement
For Year Ended December 31, 2019

Sales		$590,000
Cost of goods sold	$300,000	
Wages and other operating expenses.	216,000	
Interest expense.	7,000	
Depreciation expense	24,000	(547,000)
		43,000
Other gains (losses)		
Loss on sale of plant assets	(6,000)	
Gain on retirement of notes	16,000	10,000
Income before taxes.		53,000
Income taxes expense		(15,000)
Net income		$ 38,000

Additional information for 2019

a. The accounts payable balances result from inventory purchases.

b. Purchased $60,000 in plant assets by issuing $60,000 of notes payable.

c. Sold plant assets with a book value of $8,000 (original cost of $20,000 and accumulated depreciation of $12,000) for $2,000 cash, yielding a $6,000 loss.

d. Received $15,000 cash from issuing 3,000 shares of common stock.

e. Paid $18,000 cash to retire notes with a $34,000 book value, yielding a $16,000 gain.

f. Declared and paid cash dividends of $14,000.

GENESIS
Balance Sheets
December 31, 2019 and 2018

	2019	2018	Change
Assets			
Current assets			
Cash	$ 17,000	$ 12,000	$ 5,000 Increase
Accounts receivable	60,000	40,000	20,000 Increase
Inventory	84,000	70,000	14,000 Increase
Prepaid expenses	6,000	4,000	2,000 Increase
Total current assets	167,000	126,000	
Long-term assets			
Plant assets	250,000	210,000	40,000 Increase
Accumulated depreciation	(60,000)	(48,000)	12,000 Increase
Total assets.	$357,000	$288,000	
Liabilities			
Current liabilities			
Accounts payable.	$ 35,000	$ 40,000	$ 5,000 Decrease
Interest payable.	3,000	4,000	1,000 Decrease
Income taxes payable	22,000	12,000	10,000 Increase
Total current liabilities	60,000	56,000	
Long-term notes payable.	90,000	64,000	26,000 Increase
Total liabilities.	150,000	120,000	
Equity			
Common stock, $5 par.	95,000	80,000	15,000 Increase
Retained earnings	112,000	88,000	24,000 Increase
Total equity	207,000	168,000	
Total liabilities and equity	$357,000	$288,000	

EXHIBIT 12.10

Financial Statements

to get cash provided by operating activities of $20,000—see Exhibit 12.11. There are two types of adjustments: ① Adjustments to income statement items that do not impact cash and ② Adjustments for changes in current assets and current liabilities (linked to operating activities). Nearly all companies group adjustments into these two types, including Apple, Google, and Samsung in Appendix A.

EXHIBIT 12.11

Operating Activities Section—Indirect Method

GENESIS
Statement of Cash Flows—Operating Section under Indirect Method
For Year Ended December 31, 2019

Cash flows from operating activities	
Net income	$ 38,000
Adjustments to reconcile net income to net cash provided by operating activities	
Income statement items not affecting cash	
① Depreciation expense.	24,000
Loss on sale of plant assets	6,000
Gain on retirement of notes	(16,000)
Changes in current assets and liabilities	
Increase in accounts receivable.	(20,000)
Increase in inventory.	(14,000)
② Increase in prepaid expenses	(2,000)
Decrease in accounts payable	(5,000)
Decrease in interest payable	(1,000)
Increase in income taxes payable	10,000
Net cash provided by operating activities	**$20,000**

① **Adjustments for Income Statement Items Not Affecting Cash** Some

expenses and losses subtracted from net income were not cash outflows. Examples are depreciation, amortization, depletion, bad debts expense, loss from an asset sale, and loss from retirement of notes payable. The indirect method requires that

> **Expenses and losses with no cash outflows are added back to net income.**

These expenses and losses did *not* reduce cash, and adding them back cancels their deductions from net income. Any cash received or paid from a transaction that yields a loss, such as from an asset sale or payoff of a note, is reported under investing or financing activities.

When net income has revenues and gains that are not cash inflows, the indirect method requires that

> **Revenues and gains with no cash inflows are subtracted from net income.**

Section ① of Exhibit 12.11 shows three adjustments for items that did not impact cash for Genesis.

Depreciation Depreciation expense is Genesis's only operating item in net income that had no effect on cash flows. We add back the $24,000 depreciation expense to net income because depreciation did not reduce cash.

Loss on Sale of Plant Assets Genesis reported a $6,000 loss on sale of plant assets that reduced net income but did not affect cash flows. This $6,000 loss is added back to net income because it is not a cash outflow.

Gain on Retirement of Debt A $16,000 gain on retirement of debt increased net income but did not affect cash flows. This $16,000 gain is subtracted from net income because it was not a cash inflow.

② **Adjustments for Changes in Current Assets and Current Liabilities** This

section covers adjustments for changes in current assets and current liabilities.

Adjustments for Changes in Current Assets

> **Decreases in current assets are added to net income.**

> **Increases in current assets are subtracted from net income.**

Adjustments for Changes in Current Liabilities

> **Increases in current liabilities are added to net income.**

> **Decreases in current liabilities are subtracted from net income.**

The lower section of Exhibit 12.11 shows adjustments to the three noncash current assets and three current liabilities for Genesis. We explain each adjustment next.

Accounts Receivable The $20,000 increase in the current asset of accounts receivable is subtracted from income (showing less cash available). This increase means Genesis collects less cash than is reported in sales. To help see this, we use *account analysis.* This involves setting up a T-account, entering **in black** the balances and entries we know, and computing **in red** the cash receipts or payments. We see cash receipts are $20,000 less than sales, which is why we subtract $20,000 from income in computing the cash flow.

P2
Compute cash flows from operating activities using the indirect method.

Point: An income statement reports revenues, gains, expenses, and losses on an accrual basis. The statement of cash flows reports cash received and cash paid for operating, financing, and investing activities.

Point: Section ② adjustments.

	Account Increases	Account Decreases
Current assets	Subtract from net income	Add to net income
Current liabilities . . .	Add to net income	Subtract from net income

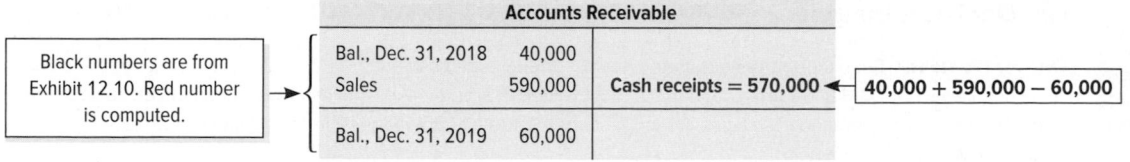

Accounts Receivable				
Bal., Dec. 31, 2018	40,000			
Sales	590,000	Cash receipts = 570,000 ◄	40,000 + 590,000 − 60,000	
Bal., Dec. 31, 2019	60,000			

Black numbers are from Exhibit 12.10. Red number is computed.

Inventory			
Bal., Dec. 31, 2018	70,000		
Purchases =	**314,000**	Cost of goods sold	300,000
Bal., Dec. 31, 2019	84,000		

Inventory   The $14,000 increase in inventory is subtracted from income. The T-account shows that purchases are $14,000 more than cost of goods sold. This means that cost of goods sold excludes $14,000 of inventory purchased this year, which is why we subtract $14,000 from income in computing cash flow.

Prepaid Expenses			
Bal., Dec. 31, 2018	4,000		
Cash payments =	**218,000**	Wages and other operating exp.	216,000
Bal., Dec. 31, 2019	6,000		

Prepaid Expenses   The $2,000 increase in prepaid expenses is subtracted from income. The T-account shows that cash paid is $2,000 more than expenses recorded, which is why we subtract $2,000 from income in computing cash flow.

Accounts Payable			
		Bal., Dec. 31, 2018	40,000
Cash payments =	**319,000**	Purchases	314,000
		Bal., Dec. 31, 2019	35,000

Accounts Payable   The $5,000 decrease in accounts payable is subtracted from income. The T-account shows that cash paid is $5,000 more than purchases recorded, which is why we subtract $5,000 from income in computing cash flow.

Interest Payable			
		Bal., Dec. 31, 2018	4,000
Cash paid for interest =	8,000	Interest expense	7,000
		Bal., Dec. 31, 2019	3,000

Interest Payable   The $1,000 decrease in interest payable is subtracted from income. The T-account shows that cash paid is $1,000 more than interest expense recorded, which is why we subtract $1,000 from income in computing cash flow.

Income Taxes Payable			
		Bal., Dec. 31, 2018	12,000
Cash paid for taxes =	5,000	Income taxes expense	15,000
		Bal., Dec. 31, 2019	22,000

Income Taxes Payable   The $10,000 increase in income taxes payable is added to income. The T-account shows that cash paid is $10,000 less than tax expense recorded, which is why we add $10,000 to income in computing cash flow.

Summary of Adjustments for Indirect Method

Exhibit 12.12 summarizes the adjustments to net income under the indirect method.

EXHIBIT 12.12

Summary of Adjustments for Operating Activities—Indirect Method

---

Net Income (or Loss)

① Adjustments for operating items not providing or using cash

  + Noncash expenses and losses

    Examples: Expenses for depreciation, depletion, and amortization; losses from disposal of long-term assets and from retirement of debt

  − Noncash revenues and gains

    Examples: Gains from disposal of long-term assets and from retirement of debt

② Adjustments for changes in current assets and current liabilities

  + Decrease in noncash current operating asset

  − Increase in noncash current operating asset

  + Increase in current operating liability

  − Decrease in current operating liability

Net cash provided (used) by operating activities

©Mark Lennihan/AP Images

▪ Decision Insight ━━━━━━━━━━━━━━━━━━━━

One for the Road   Even though **Tesla** reported net losses and large cash outflows, its market value tripled in five years. Tesla now rivals both **GM** and **Ford** as one of the most valued U.S. automakers. Investors are counting on Tesla's Model 3 to create positive operating cash flows. So far, Tesla has funded its operations with cash inflows from stock and debt issuances. ▪

A company's current-year income statement and selected balance sheet data at December 31 of the current and prior years follow. Prepare the operating activities section of the statement of cash flows using the indirect method for the current year.

Income Statement For Current Year Ended December 31	
Sales revenue	$120
Expenses: Cost of goods sold.	50
Depreciation expense.	30
Salaries expense.	17
Interest expense	3
Net income.	$ 20

Selected Balance Sheet Accounts		
At December 31	Current Yr	Prior Yr
Accounts receivable	$12	$10
Inventory	6	9
Accounts payable	7	11
Salaries payable	8	3
Interest payable.	1	0

Solution

Cash Flows from Operating Activities—Indirect Method For Current Year Ended December 31		
Cash flows from operating activities		
Net income.		$20
Adjustments to reconcile net income to net cash provided by operating activities		
Income statement items not affecting cash		
Depreciation expense	$30	
Changes in current assets and current liabilities		
Increase in accounts receivable	(2)	
Decrease in inventory	3	
Decrease in accounts payable.	(4)	
Increase in salaries payable	5	
Increase in interest payable.	1	33
Net cash provided by operating activities		$53

Do More: QS 12-3, QS 12-4, QS 12-5, QS 12-6, QS 12-7, E 12-2, E 12-3, E 12-4, E 12-5, E 12-6, E 12-7

CASH FLOWS FROM INVESTING

To compute cash flows from investing activities, we analyze changes in (1) all long-term asset accounts and (2) any current accounts for notes receivable and investments in securities. **Reporting of investing activities is identical under the direct method and indirect method.**

Three-Step Analysis

To determine cash provided or used by investing activities: (1) identify changes in investing-related accounts, (2) explain these changes using T-accounts and reconstructed entries, and (3) report the cash flow effects.

P3

Determine cash flows from both investing and financing activities.

Analyzing Noncurrent Assets

Genesis both purchased and sold long-term assets during the period. These transactions are investing activities and are analyzed in this section.

Plant Asset Transactions

First Step   Analyze Genesis's Plant Assets account and its Accumulated Depreciation account to identify changes in those accounts. Comparative balance sheets in Exhibit 12.10 show a $40,000 increase in plant assets from $210,000 to $250,000 and a $12,000 increase in accumulated depreciation from $48,000 to $60,000.

Point: Investing activities include (1) purchasing and selling long-term assets, (2) lending and collecting on notes receivable, and (3) purchasing and selling short-term investments other than cash equivalents and trading securities.

Second Step   Items *b* and *c* of the additional information in Exhibit 12.10 relate to plant assets. Recall that the Plant Assets account is impacted by both asset purchases and sales; its Accumulated Depreciation account is increased by depreciation and decreased by the removal of accumulated depreciation in asset sales. To explain changes in these accounts and to identify their cash flow effects, we prepare *reconstructed entries, which is our attempt to re-create actual entries made by the preparer.* Item *b* says Genesis purchased plant assets of $60,000 by issuing $60,000 in notes payable. The reconstructed entry is

| Reconstruction | Plant Assets .... | 60,000 | |
| | Notes Payable... | | 60,000 |

Item *c* says Genesis sold plant assets costing $20,000 (with $12,000 of accumulated depreciation) for $2,000 cash, resulting in a $6,000 loss. The reconstructed entry is

Reconstruction	**Cash**..	**2,000**	
	Accumulated Depreciation	12,000	
	Loss on Sale of Plant Assets	6,000	
	Plant Assets...		20,000

We also reconstruct the entry for depreciation from the income statement, which does not impact cash.

| Reconstruction | Depreciation Expense .... | 24,000 | |
| | Accumulated Depreciation................................ | | 24,000 |

The three reconstructed entries are shown in the following T-accounts. This reconstruction analysis is complete in that changes in the long-term asset accounts are entirely explained.

Plant Assets			
Bal., Dec. 31, 2018	210,000		
Purchase	**60,000**	**Sale**	**20,000**
Bal., Dec. 31, 2019	250,000		

Accumulated Depreciation—Plant Assets			
		Bal., Dec. 31, 2018	48,000
Sale	**12,000**	**Depr. expense**	**24,000**
		Bal., Dec. 31, 2019	60,000

Third Step   Look at the reconstructed entries to identify cash flows. The identified cash flows are reported in the investing section of the statement.

Cash flows from investing activities	
Cash received from sale of plant assets	$2,000

Example: If a plant asset costing $40,000 with $37,000 of accumulated depreciation is sold at a $3,000 gain, what is the cash flow? *Answer:* +$6,000

The $60,000 purchase in item *b,* paid for by issuing notes, is a noncash investing and financing activity. It is reported in a note or in a separate schedule to the statement.

Noncash investing and financing activity	
Purchased plant assets with issuance of notes	$60,000

Additional Long-Term Assets   Genesis did not have any additional noncurrent assets (or nonoperating current assets). If such assets do exist, we analyze and report investing cash flows using the same three-step process.

Ethical Risk

Location, Location, Location   Cash flows can be delayed or accelerated at period-end to improve or reduce current-period cash flows. Cash flows also can be misclassified. We know cash outflows under operating activities are viewed as expense payments. However, cash outflows under investing activities are viewed as a sign of growth potential. This requires investors to review where cash flows are reported. ■

Use the following information to determine this company's cash flows from investing activities.

a. A factory with a book value of $100 and an original cost of $800 was sold at a loss of $10.

b. Paid $70 cash for new equipment.

c. Long-term stock investments were sold for $20 cash, yielding a loss of $4.

d. Sold land costing $175 for $160 cash, yielding a loss of $15.

Solution

Cash flows from investing activities	
Cash received from sale of factory (from *a**—also see margin entry)	$ 90
Cash paid for new equipment (from *b*)	(70)
Cash received from sale of long-term investments (from *c*).	20
Cash received from sale of land (from *d*)	160
Net cash provided by investing activities	$200

**Cash received from sale of factory = Book value − Loss = $100 − $10 = $90.

NEED-TO-KNOW 12-3

Reporting Investing
Cash Flows

P3

Reconstruction for part *a*.
Cash.............. **90**
Loss on asset sale.... 10
    Factory (BV) 100

Do More: QS 12-8, QS 12-9,
QS 12-10, QS 12-11, QS 12-12,
QS 12-13, E 12-8

CASH FLOWS FROM FINANCING

To compute cash flows from financing activities, we analyze changes in all noncurrent liability accounts (including the current portion of any notes and bonds) and equity accounts. These accounts include long-term debt, notes payable, bonds payable, common stock, and retained earnings. **Reporting of financing activities is identical under the direct method and indirect method.**

Three-Step Analysis

To determine cash provided or used by financing activities: (1) identify changes in financing-related accounts, (2) explain these changes using T-accounts and reconstructed entries, and (3) report the cash flow effects.

Analyzing Noncurrent Liabilities

Genesis retired notes payable by paying cash. This is a change in noncurrent liabilities.

Point: Examples of financing activities are (1) receiving cash from issuing debt or repaying amounts borrowed and (2) receiving cash from or distributing cash to owners.

Notes Payable Transactions

First Step   Review comparative balance sheets in Exhibit 12.10, which shows an increase in notes payable from $64,000 to $90,000.

Second Step   Item *e* of the additional information in Exhibit 12.10 reports that notes with a carrying value of $34,000 are retired for $18,000 cash, resulting in a $16,000 gain. The reconstructed entry is

Reconstruction	Notes Payable	34,000	
	Gain on retirement of debt......................		16,000
	Cash		**18,000**

Item *b* of the additional information reports that Genesis purchased plant assets costing $60,000 by issuing $60,000 in notes payable. This $60,000 increase to notes payable is reported as a noncash investing and financing transaction. The Notes Payable account is explained by these reconstructed entries.

		Notes Payable	
		Bal., Dec. 31, 2018	64,000
Retired notes	**34,000**	**Issued notes**	**60,000**
		Bal., Dec. 31, 2019	90,000

Third Step   Report cash paid for the notes retirement in the financing activities section.

Cash flows from financing activities	
Cash paid to retire notes	$(18,000)

Analyzing Equity

Genesis had two equity transactions. The first is the issuance of common stock for cash. The second is the declaration and payment of cash dividends.

Common Stock Transactions

First Step   Review the comparative balance sheets in Exhibit 12.10, which show an increase in common stock from $80,000 to $95,000.

Second Step   Item *d* of the additional information in Exhibit 12.10 reports that 3,000 shares of common stock are issued at par for $5 per share. The reconstructed entry and the complete Common Stock T-account follow.

Reconstruction	Cash.	15,000	
	Common Stock		15,000

Common Stock		
	Bal., Dec. 31, 2018	80,000
	Issued stock	**15,000**
	Bal., Dec. 31, 2019	95,000

Third Step   Report cash received from stock issuance in the financing activities section.

Cash flows from financing activities	
Cash received from issuing stock	$15,000

Retained Earnings Transactions

First Step   Review the comparative balance sheets in Exhibit 12.10, which show an increase in retained earnings from $88,000 to $112,000.

Second Step   Item *f* of the additional information in Exhibit 12.10 reports that cash dividends of $14,000 are paid. The reconstructed entry follows.

Reconstruction	Retained Earnings	14,000	
	Cash		**14,000**

Retained Earnings also is impacted by net income of $38,000. (Net income is covered in operating activities.) The reconstructed Retained Earnings account follows.

Retained Earnings			
		Bal., Dec. 31, 2018	88,000
Cash dividend	**14,000**	**Net income**	**38,000**
		Bal., Dec. 31, 2019	112,000

Point: Stock dividends and splits do not impact cash.

Third Step   Report cash paid for dividends in the financing activities section.

Cash flows from financing activities	
Cash paid for dividends.	$(14,000)

Proving Cash Balances

The final stage in preparing the statement is to report the beginning and ending cash balances and prove that the *net change in cash* is explained by operating, investing, and financing cash flows. The last three rows of Exhibit 12.13 show that the $5,000 net increase in cash, from $12,000 at the beginning of the period to $17,000 at the end, is reconciled by net cash flows from operating ($20,000 inflow), investing ($2,000 inflow), and financing ($17,000 outflow) activities.

GENESIS Statement of Cash Flows (Indirect Method) For Year Ended December 31, 2019		
Cash flows from operating activities		
Net income		$ 38,000
Adjustments to reconcile net income to net cash provided by operating activities		
Income statement items not affecting cash		
Depreciation expense	24,000	
Loss on sale of plant assets..................................	6,000	
Gain on retirement of notes	(16,000)	
Changes in current assets and liabilities		
Increase in accounts receivable	(20,000)	
Increase in inventory.......................................	(14,000)	
Increase in prepaid expenses...............................	(2,000)	
Decrease in accounts payable	(5,000)	
Decrease in interest payable................................	(1,000)	
Increase in income taxes payable...........................	10,000	
Net cash provided by operating activities.....................		$ 20,000
Cash flows from investing activities		
Cash received from sale of plant assets	2,000	
Net cash provided by investing activities		2,000
Cash flows from financing activities		
Cash received from issuing stock	15,000	
Cash paid to retire notes	(18,000)	
Cash paid for dividends	(14,000)	
Net cash used in financing activities		(17,000)
Net increase in cash		$ 5,000
Cash balance at prior year-end		12,000
Cash balance at current year-end		$ 17,000

EXHIBIT 12.13

Complete Statement of Cash Flows—Indirect Method

 Decision Maker

Reporter   Management is in labor contract negotiations and grants you an interview. It highlights a total net cash outflow of $550,000 (which includes net cash outflows of $850,000 for investing activities and $350,000 for financing activities). What is your assessment of this company? ■   *Answer:* An initial reaction from the $550,000 decrease in net cash is not positive. However, closer scrutiny shows a more positive picture. Cash flow from operations is $650,000, computed as [?] – $850,000 – $350,000 = $(550,000).

Use the following information to determine cash flows from financing activities.

a. Issued common stock for $40 cash.

b. Paid $70 cash to retire a note payable at its $70 maturity value.

c. Paid cash dividend of $15.

d. Paid $5 cash to acquire its treasury stock.

Solution

Cash flows from financing activities	
Cash received from issuance of common stock (from *a*)	$ 40
Cash paid to settle note payable (from *b*).....................	(70)
Cash paid for dividend (from *c*)	(15)
Cash paid to acquire treasury stock (from *d*)	(5)
Net cash used by financing activities	$(50)

 12-4

Reporting Financing Cash Flows

P3

Do More: QS 12-14, QS 12-15, QS 12-16, QS 12-17, E 12-9

SUMMARY USING T-ACCOUNTS

Exhibit 12.14 uses T-accounts to summarize how changes in Genesis's noncash balance sheet accounts affect its cash inflows and outflows (dollar amounts in thousands). The top of the exhibit shows Genesis's Cash T-account, and the lower part shows T-accounts for its remaining balance sheet accounts. We see that the $20,000 net cash provided by operating activities and the $5,000 net increase in cash shown in the Cash T-account agree with the same figures in the statement of cash flows in Exhibit 12.13. We explain Exhibit 12.14 in five parts.

a. Entry (1) records $38 net income on the credit side of the Retained Earnings account and the debit side of the Cash account. This $38 net income in the Cash T-account is adjusted until it reflects the $5 net increase in cash.

b. Entries (2) through (4) add the $24 depreciation and $6 loss on asset sale to net income and subtract the $16 gain on retirement of notes.

c. Entries (5) through (10) adjust net income for changes in current asset and current liability accounts.

EXHIBIT 12.14

Balance Sheet T-Accounts to Explain the Change in Cash ($ thousands)

d. Entry (11) records the noncash investing and financing transaction involving a $60 purchase of assets by issuing $60 of notes.

e. Entries (12) and (13) record the $15 stock issuance and the $14 dividend.

Cash			
(1) Net income	38		
(2) Depreciation	24	(4) Gain on retirement of notes	16
(3) Loss on sale of plant assets	6		
(10) Increase in income taxes payable	10	(5) Increase in accounts receivable	20
		(6) Increase in inventory	14
		(7) Increase in prepaid expense	2
		(8) Decrease in accounts payable	5
		(9) Decrease in interest payable	1
Net cash provided by operating activities [O]	20		
(3) Cash received from sale of plant assets [I]	2	(4) Cash paid to retire notes [F]	18
(12) Cash received from issuing stock [F]	15	(13) Cash paid for dividends [F]	14
Net increase in cash	5		

Info to prepare statement of cash flows

Accounts Receivable			
Beg.	40		
(5)	20		
End.	60		

Inventory			
Beg.	70		
(6)	14		
End.	84		

Prepaid Expenses			
Beg.	4		
(7)	2		
End.	6		

Plant Assets			
Beg.	210		
		(3)	20
(11)	60		
End.	250		

Accumulated Depreciation			
		Beg.	48
(3)	12	(2)	24
		End.	60

Accounts Payable			
		Beg.	40
(8)	5		
		End.	35

Interest Payable			
		Beg.	4
(9)	1		
		End.	3

Income Taxes Payable			
		Beg.	12
		(10)	10
		End.	22

Long-Term Notes Payable			
		Beg.	64
(4)	34		
		(11)	60
		End.	90

Common Stock			
		Beg.	80
		(12)	15
		End.	95

Retained Earnings			
		Beg.	88
		(1)	38
(13)	14		
		End.	112

Cash Flow Analysis □□□ **Decision Analysis**

Analyzing Cash Sources and Uses

A1

Analyze the statement of cash flows and apply the cash flow on total assets ratio.

Managers review cash flows for business decisions. Creditors evaluate a company's ability to generate enough cash to pay debt. Investors assess cash flows before buying and selling stock.

To effectively evaluate cash flows, we separately analyze investing, financing, and operating activities. Consider data from three different companies in Exhibit 12.15 that operate in the same industry and have been in business for several years. Each company has the same $15,000 net increase in cash, but its sources and uses of cash flows are different. BMX's operating activities provide net cash flows of $90,000, allowing it to purchase plant assets of $48,000 and repay $27,000 of its debt. ATV's operating activities provide $40,000 of cash flows, limiting its purchase of plant assets to $25,000. Trex's $15,000

EXHIBIT 12.15

Cash Flows of Competing Companies

$ thousands	BMX	ATV	Trex
Cash provided (used) by operating activities . . .	$90,000	$40,000	$(24,000)
Cash provided (used) by investing activities			
Proceeds from sale of plant assets.			26,000
Purchase of plant assets	(48,000)	(25,000)	
Cash provided (used) by financing activities			
Proceeds from issuance of debt			13,000
Repayment of debt	(27,000)		
Net increase (decrease) in cash	$15,000	$15,000	$ 15,000

net cash increase is due to selling plant assets and incurring additional debt. Its operating activities yield a cash outflow of $24,000. Overall, analysis of cash flows reveals that BMX is more capable of generating future cash flows than is ATV or Trex.

■ Decision Insight

Free Cash Flows Many investors use cash flows to value company stock. However, cash-based valuation models often yield different stock values due to differences in measurement of cash flows. Most models require cash flows that are "free" for distribution to shareholders. These *free cash flows* are defined as cash flows available to shareholders after operating asset reinvestments and debt payments. A company's growth and financial flexibility depend on adequate free cash flows. ■

Point: Cash flow from operations
  – Capital expenditures
  – Debt repayments
  = Free cash flows

Cash Flow on Total Assets

Cash flow information can help measure a company's ability to meet its obligations, pay dividends, expand operations, and obtain financing. The **cash flow on total assets** ratio is in Exhibit 12.16.

EXHIBIT 12.16

Cash Flow on Total Assets

$$\text{Cash flow on total assets} = \frac{\text{Cash flow from operations}}{\text{Average total assets}}$$

This ratio measures actual cash flows and is not affected by accounting recognition and measurement. It can help estimate the amount and timing of cash flows from operating activities.

The cash flow on total assets for competitors **Nike** and **Under Armour** are in Exhibit 12.17. In all years, Nike's cash flow on total assets ratio exceeded Under Armour's ratio. This means that Nike did a better job of generating operating cash flows given its assets. However, Nike's cash flow on total assets declined from two years ago, which is not a positive result. At the same time, Under Armour's lower and uneven cash flow on total assets make it difficult to predict the amount and timing of its cash flows.

EXHIBIT 12.17

Cash Flow on Total Assets for Two Competitors

Company	Figure ($ millions)	Current Year	1 Year Ago	2 Years Ago
Nike	Operating cash flows	$ 3,640	$ 3,096	$ 4,680
	Average total assets.	$22,328	$21,497	$20,096
	Cash flow on total assets.	**16.3%**	**14.4%**	**23.3%**
Under Armour	Operating cash flows	$ 234	$ 364	$ 15
	Average total assets.	$ 3,825	$ 3,255	$ 2,479
	Cash flow on total assets.	**6.1%**	**11.2%**	**0.6%**

NEED-TO-KNOW 12-5

COMPREHENSIVE

Preparing Statement of
Cash Flows—Indirect
and Direct Methods

Comparative balance sheets, an income statement, and additional information follow.

UMA COMPANY Balance Sheets December 31, 2019 and 2018		
	2019	**2018**
Assets		
Cash	$ 43,050	$ 23,925
Accounts receivable	34,125	39,825
Inventory	156,000	146,475
Prepaid expenses	3,600	1,650
Total current assets	236,775	211,875
Equipment	135,825	146,700
Accum. depreciation—Equipment	(61,950)	(47,550)
Total assets	$310,650	$311,025
Liabilities		
Accounts payable	$ 28,800	$ 33,750
Income taxes payable	5,100	4,425
Dividends payable	0	4,500
Total current liabilities	33,900	42,675
Bonds payable	0	37,500
Total liabilities	33,900	80,175
Equity		
Common stock, $10 par	168,750	168,750
Retained earnings	108,000	62,100
Total liabilities and equity	$310,650	$311,025

UMA COMPANY Income Statement For Year Ended December 31, 2019		
Sales		$446,100
Cost of goods sold	$222,300	
Other operating expenses	120,300	
Depreciation expense	25,500	(368,100)
		78,000
Other gains (losses)		
Loss on sale of equipment	3,300	
Loss on retirement of bonds	825	(4,125)
Income before taxes		73,875
Income tax expense		(13,725)
Net income		$ 60,150

Additional Information

a. Equipment costing $21,375 with accumulated depreciation of $11,100 is sold for cash.

b. Equipment purchases are for cash.

c. Accumulated Depreciation is affected by depreciation expense and the sale of equipment.

d. The balance of Retained Earnings is affected by dividend declarations and net income.

e. All sales are made on credit.

f. All inventory purchases are on credit.

g. Accounts Payable balances result from inventory purchases.

h. Prepaid expenses relate to "other operating expenses."

Required

1. Prepare a statement of cash flows using the indirect method for year 2019.

2.B Prepare a statement of cash flows using the direct method for year 2019.

PLANNING THE SOLUTION

- Prepare two blank statements of cash flows with sections for operating, investing, and financing activities using the (1) indirect method format and (2) direct method format.
- Compute the cash paid for equipment and the cash received from the sale of equipment using the additional information provided along with the amount for depreciation expense and the change in the balances of Equipment and Accumulated Depreciation. Use T-accounts to help chart the effects of the sale and purchase of equipment on the balances of the Equipment account and the Accumulated Depreciation account.
- Compute the effect of net income on the change in the Retained Earnings account balance. Assign the difference between the change in retained earnings and the amount of net income to dividends declared. Adjust the dividends declared amount for the change in the Dividends Payable balance.
- Compute cash received from customers, cash paid for inventory, cash paid for other operating expenses, and cash paid for taxes.
- Enter the cash effects of reconstruction entries to the appropriate section(s) of the statement.
- Total each section of the statement, determine the total net change in cash, and add it to the beginning balance to get the ending balance of cash.

SOLUTION

Supporting computations for cash receipts and cash payments.

(1) Cost of equipment sold*	$ 21,375
Accumulated depreciation of equipment sold	(11,100)
Book value of equipment sold	10,275
Loss on sale of equipment	(3,300)
Cash received from sale of equipment	**$ 6,975**
Cost of equipment sold	$ 21,375
Less decrease in the Equipment account balance	(10,875)
Cash paid for new equipment	**$10,500**
(2) Loss on retirement of bonds	$ 825
Carrying value of bonds retired	37,500
Cash paid to retire bonds	**$38,325**

(3) Net income	$ 60,150
Less increase in retained earnings	45,900
Dividends declared	14,250
Plus decrease in dividends payable	4,500
Cash paid for dividends	**$ 18,750**
(4)ᴮ Sales	$ 446,100
Add decrease in accounts receivable	5,700
Cash received from customers	**$451,800**
(5)ᴮ Cost of goods sold	$ 222,300
Plus increase in inventory	9,525
Purchases	231,825
Plus decrease in accounts payable	4,950
Cash paid for inventory	**$236,775**
(6)ᴮ Other operating expenses	$ 120,300
Plus increase in prepaid expenses	1,950
Cash paid for other operating expenses	**$122,250**
(7)ᴮ Income tax expense	$ 13,725
Less increase in income taxes payable	(675)
Cash paid for income taxes	**$ 13,050**

*Supporting T-account analysis for part 1 follows.

Equipment				Accumulated Depreciation—Equipment		
Bal., Dec. 31, 2018	146,700				Bal., Dec. 31, 2018	47,550
Cash purchase	10,500	Sale 21,375	Sale 11,100		Depr. expense	25,500
Bal., Dec. 31, 2019	135,825				Bal., Dec. 31, 2019	61,950

1. Indirect method.

UMA COMPANY
Statement of Cash Flows (Indirect Method)
For Year Ended December 31, 2019

Cash flows from operating activities		
Net income	$ 60,150	
Adjustments to reconcile net income to net cash provided by operating activities		
Income statement items not affecting cash		
Depreciation expense	25,500	
Loss on sale of plant assets	3,300	
Loss on retirement of bonds	825	
Changes in current assets and current liabilities		
Decrease in accounts receivable	5,700	
Increase in inventory	(9,525)	
Increase in prepaid expenses	(1,950)	
Decrease in accounts payable	(4,950)	
Increase in income taxes payable	675	
Net cash provided by operating activities		$ 79,725
Cash flows from investing activities		
Cash received from sale of equipment	6,975	
Cash paid for equipment	(10,500)	
Net cash used in investing activities		(3,525)
Cash flows from financing activities		
Cash paid to retire bonds payable	(38,325)	
Cash paid for dividends	(18,750)	
Net cash used in financing activities		(57,075)
Net increase in cash		$ 19,125
Cash balance at prior year-end		23,925
Cash balance at current year-end		$ 43,050

2ᴮ Direct method (Appendix 12B).

UMA COMPANY
Statement of Cash Flows (Direct Method)
For Year Ended December 31, 2019

Cash flows from operating activities		
Cash received from customers	$ 451,800	
Cash paid for inventory	(236,775)	
Cash paid for other operating expenses	(122,250)	
Cash paid for income taxes	(13,050)	
Net cash provided by operating activities		$ 79,725
Cash flows from investing activities		
Cash received from sale of equipment	6,975	
Cash paid for equipment	(10,500)	
Net cash used in investing activities		(3,525)
Cash flows from financing activities		
Cash paid to retire bonds payable	(38,325)	
Cash paid for dividends	(18,750)	
Net cash used in financing activities		(57,075)
Net increase in cash		$ 19,125
Cash balance at prior year-end		23,925
Cash balance at current year-end		$ 43,050

12A

Spreadsheet Preparation of the Statement of Cash Flows

P4

Illustrate use of a spread-sheet to prepare a statement of cash flows.

This appendix explains how to use a spreadsheet (work sheet) to prepare the statement of cash flows under the indirect method.

Preparing the Indirect Method Spreadsheet

A *spreadsheet*, also called *work sheet*, can help us prepare a statement of cash flows. To demonstrate, we return to the comparative balance sheets and income statement shown in Exhibit 12.10. We use letters *a* through *g* to code changes in accounts, and letters *h* through *m* for additional information, to prepare the statement of cash flows.

a. Net income is $38,000.

b. Accounts receivable increase by $20,000.

c. Inventory increases by $14,000.

d. Prepaid expenses increase by $2,000.

e. Accounts payable decrease by $5,000.

f. Interest payable decreases by $1,000.

g. Income taxes payable increase by $10,000.

h. Depreciation expense is $24,000.

i. Plant assets costing $20,000 with accumulated depreciation of $12,000 are sold for $2,000 cash. This yields a loss on sale of assets of $6,000.

j. Notes with a book value of $34,000 are retired with a cash payment of $18,000, yielding a $16,000 gain on retirement.

k. Plant assets costing $60,000 are purchased with an issuance of notes payable for $60,000.

l. Issued 3,000 shares of common stock for $15,000 cash.

m. Paid cash dividends of $14,000.

Exhibit 12A.1 shows the indirect method spreadsheet for Genesis. We enter both beginning and ending balance sheet amounts on the spreadsheet. We also enter information in the Analysis of Changes columns (keyed to the additional information items *a* through *m*) to explain changes in the accounts and determine the cash flows for operating, investing, and financing activities. Information about noncash investing and financing activities is reported near the bottom.

Entering the Analysis of Changes on the Spreadsheet

The following steps are used to complete the spreadsheet after the beginning and ending balances of the balance sheet accounts are entered.

① Enter net income as the first item in the statement of cash flows section for computing operating cash inflow (debit) and as a credit to Retained Earnings. **(Entry *a*)**

② In the statement of cash flows section, adjustments to net income are entered as debits if they increase cash flows and as credits if they decrease cash flows. Applying this rule, adjust net income for the change in each noncash current asset and current liability account related to operating activities. For each adjustment to net income, the offsetting debit or credit must help reconcile the beginning and ending balances of a current asset or current liability account. **(Entries *b* through *g*)**

③ Enter adjustments to net income for income statement items not providing or using cash in the period. For each adjustment, the offsetting debit or credit must help reconcile a noncash balance sheet account. **(Entry *h*)**

④ Adjust net income to eliminate any gains or losses from investing and financing activities. Because the cash from a gain must be excluded from operating activities, the gain is entered as a credit in the operating activities section. Losses are entered as debits. For each adjustment, the related debit and/or credit must help reconcile balance sheet accounts and involve reconstructed entries to show the cash flow from investing or financing activities. **(Entries *i* and *j*)**

⑤ After reviewing any unreconciled balance sheet accounts and related information, enter the remaining reconciling entries for investing and financing activities. Examples are purchases of plant assets,

EXHIBIT 12A.1

Spreadsheet for Preparing Statement of Cash Flows—Indirect Method

GENESIS
Spreadsheet for Statement of Cash Flows—Indirect Method
For Year Ended December 31, 2019

	Dec. 31, 2018		Analysis of Changes Debit		Analysis of Changes Credit	Dec. 31, 2019
Balance Sheet—Debit Bal. Accounts						
Cash	$ 12,000					$ 17,000
Accounts receivable	40,000	(b)	$ 20,000			60,000
Inventory	70,000	(c)	14,000			84,000
Prepaid expenses	4,000	(d)	2,000			6,000
Plant assets	210,000	(k1)	60,000	(i)	$ 20,000	250,000
	$336,000					$417,000
Balance Sheet—Credit Bal. Accounts						
Accumulated depreciation	$ 48,000	(i)	12,000	(h)	24,000	$ 60,000
Accounts payable	40,000	(e)	5,000			35,000
Interest payable	4,000	(f)	1,000			3,000
Income taxes payable	12,000			(g)	10,000	22,000
Notes payable	64,000	(j)	34,000	(k2)	60,000	90,000
Common stock, $5 par value	80,000			(l)	15,000	95,000
Retained earnings	88,000	(m)	14,000	(a)	38,000	112,000
	$336,000					$417,000
Statement of Cash Flows						
Operating activities						
Net income		(a)	38,000			
Increase in accounts receivable				(b)	20,000	
Increase in inventory				(c)	14,000	
Increase in prepaid expenses				(d)	2,000	
Decrease in accounts payable				(e)	5,000	
Decrease in interest payable				(f)	1,000	
Increase in income taxes payable		(g)	10,000			
Depreciation expense		(h)	24,000			
Loss on sale of plant assets		(i)	6,000			
Gain on retirement of notes				(j)	16,000	
Investing activities						
Receipts from sale of plant assets		(i)	2,000			
Financing activities						
Payment to retire notes				(j)	18,000	
Receipts from issuing stock		(l)	15,000			
Payment of cash dividends				(m)	14,000	
Noncash Investing and Financing Activities						
Purchase of plant assets with notes		(k2)	60,000	(k1)	60,000	
			$317,000		$317,000	

issuances of long-term debt, stock issuances, and dividend payments. Some of these may require entries in the noncash investing and financing section of the spreadsheet. (**Entries k through m**)

⑥ Check accuracy by totaling the Analysis of Changes columns and by determining that the change in each balance sheet account has been explained (reconciled).

Because adjustments i, j, and k are more challenging, we show them in the following debit and credit format. These entries are for purposes of our understanding; they are *not* the entries actually made in the journals. Changes in the Cash account are identified as sources or uses of cash.

i.	Cash—Receipt from sale of plant assets **(source of cash)**	2,000	
	Loss from sale of plant assets	6,000	
	Accumulated depreciation	12,000	
	Plant assets		20,000
	Describe sale of plant assets.		
j.	Notes payable	34,000	
	Cash—Payments to retire notes **(use of cash)**		**18,000**
	Gain on retirement of notes		16,000
	Describe retirement of notes.		
k1.	Plant assets	60,000	
	Cash—Purchase of plant assets financed by notes		**60,000**
	Describe purchase of plant assets.		
k2.	Cash—Purchase of plant assets financed by notes	**60,000**	
	Notes payable		60,000
	Issue notes for purchase of assets.		

12B

Direct Method of Reporting Operating Cash Flows

P5

Compute cash flows from operating activities using the direct method.

We compute operating cash flows under the direct method by adjusting accrual-based income statement items to the cash basis as follows.

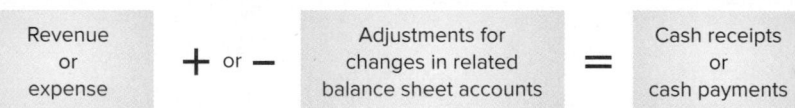

The framework for reporting cash receipts and cash payments for the operating section under the direct method is shown in Exhibit 12B.1.

EXHIBIT 12B.1

Major Classes of Operating Cash Flows

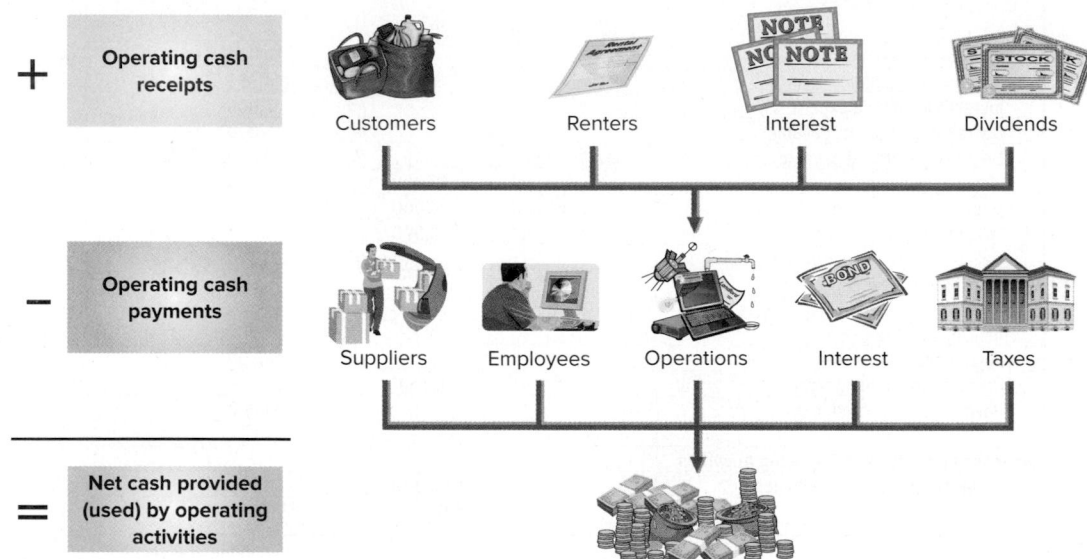

Operating Cash Receipts

The financial statements and additional information reported by Genesis in Exhibit 12.10 show one cash receipt: sales to customers. We start with sales to customers as reported on the income statement and then adjust it to get cash received from customers.

Cash Received from Customers   If all sales are for cash, cash received from customers equals the sales reported on the income statement. When some or all sales are on credit, we must adjust the amount of sales for the change in Accounts Receivable. To help us compute cash receipts, we use a T-account that includes accounts receivable balances for Genesis on December 31, 2018 and 2019. The beginning balance is $40,000 and the ending balance is $60,000. Next, the income statement shows sales of $590,000, which is put on the debit side. We now reconstruct the account to determine the cash receipts from customers are $570,000, computed as $40,000 + $590,000 − [?] = $60,000.

Point: An accounts receivable increase implies that cash received from customers is less than sales (the converse is also true).

Reconstructed Entry
Cash..........	570,000	
Accts Recble....	20,000	
Sales		590,000

Accounts Receivable			
Bal., Dec. 31, 2018	40,000		
Sales	590,000	Cash receipts =	570,000
Bal., Dec. 31, 2019	60,000		

Example: If the ending balance of Accounts Receivable is $20,000 (instead of $60,000), what is cash received from customers?
Answer: $610,000

Cash receipts also can be computed as sales of $590,000 minus a $20,000 increase in accounts receivable. This computation is in Exhibit 12B.2. Genesis reports the $570,000 cash received from customers as a cash inflow from operating activities.

$$\text{Cash received from customers} = \text{Sales} \quad \begin{array}{l} \text{+ \textbf{Decrease} in accounts receivable} \\ \text{or} \\ \text{− \textbf{Increase} in accounts receivable} \end{array}$$

EXHIBIT 12B.2

Formula to Compute Cash Received from Customers— Direct Method

Other Cash Receipts   Other common cash receipts involve rent, interest, and dividends. We compute cash received from these items by subtracting an increase in their receivable or adding a decrease. For example, if rent receivable increases in the period, cash received from renters is less than rent revenue reported on the income statement. If rent receivable decreases, cash received is more than reported rent revenue. The same applies to interest and dividends.

Operating Cash Payments
The financial statements and additional information for Genesis in Exhibit 12.10 show four operating expenses: cost of goods sold; wages and other operating expenses; interest expense; and taxes expense. We analyze each expense to compute its cash impact.

Cash Paid for Inventory   We compute cash paid for inventory by analyzing both cost of goods sold and inventory. If all inventory purchases are for cash and the balance of Inventory is unchanged, the amount of cash paid for inventory equals cost of goods sold—an uncommon situation. Instead, there normally is some change in the Inventory balance. Also, some or all purchases are often made on credit, which changes the Accounts Payable balance. When the balances of both Inventory and Accounts Payable change, we must adjust the cost of goods sold for changes in both accounts to compute cash paid for inventory. This is a two-step adjustment.

First, we use the change in the account balance of Inventory, along with the cost of goods sold amount, to compute cost of purchases for the period. An increase in inventory means that we bought more than we sold, and we add this inventory increase to cost of goods sold to compute cost of purchases. A decrease in inventory means that we bought less than we sold, and we subtract the inventory decrease from cost of goods sold to compute purchases. We show the *first step* by reconstructing the Inventory account. We determine purchases to be $314,000, computed as cost of goods sold of $300,000 plus the $14,000 increase in inventory.

Inventory			
Bal., Dec. 31, 2018	70,000		
Purchases =	314,000	Cost of goods sold	300,000
Bal., Dec. 31, 2019	84,000		

The second step uses the change in the balance of Accounts Payable, and the cost of purchases, to compute cash paid for inventory. A decrease in accounts payable means that we paid for more goods than we acquired this period, and we would add the accounts payable decrease to cost of purchases to compute cash paid for inventory. An increase in accounts payable means that we paid for less than the amount of goods acquired, and we would subtract the accounts payable increase from purchases to compute cash paid for inventory. The *second step* is applied to Genesis by reconstructing its Accounts Payable account to get cash paid of $319,000 (or $40,000 + $314,000 − [?] = $35,000).

Accounts Payable			
		Bal., Dec. 31, 2018	40,000
Cash payments =	319,000	Purchases	314,000
		Bal., Dec. 31, 2019	35,000

Reconstructed Entry

COGS	300,000	
Inventory	14,000	
Accounts Payable . .	5,000	
Cash.		319,000

Alternatively, cash paid for inventory is equal to purchases of $314,000 plus the $5,000 decrease in accounts payable. The $319,000 cash paid for inventory is reported as a cash outflow under operating activities. This two-step adjustment to cost of goods sold to compute cash paid for inventory is in Exhibit 12B.3.

Example: If the ending balances of Inventory and Accounts Payable are $60,000 and $50,000, respectively (instead of $84,000 and $35,000), what is cash paid for inventory? *Answer:* $280,000

EXHIBIT 12B.3

Two Steps to Compute Cash Paid for Inventory— Direct Method

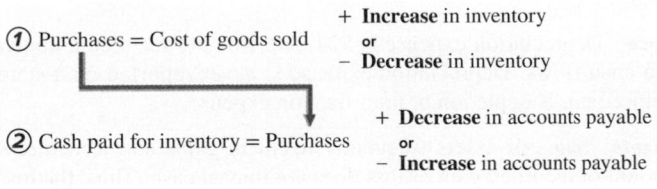

$$\text{\textcircled{1} Purchases} = \text{Cost of goods sold} \quad \begin{array}{l} \text{+ \textbf{Increase} in inventory} \\ \text{or} \\ \text{− \textbf{Decrease} in inventory} \end{array}$$

$$\text{\textcircled{2} Cash paid for inventory} = \text{Purchases} \quad \begin{array}{l} \text{+ \textbf{Decrease} in accounts payable} \\ \text{or} \\ \text{− \textbf{Increase} in accounts payable} \end{array}$$

Cash Paid for Wages and Operating Expenses (Excluding Depreciation) The Genesis income statement shows wages and other operating expenses of $216,000 (see Exhibit 12.10). To compute cash paid for wages and other operating expenses, we adjust for any changes in related balance sheet accounts. We begin by looking for any prepaid expenses and accrued liabilities related to wages and other operating expenses in the balance sheets in Exhibit 12.10. The balance sheets show prepaid expenses but no accrued liabilities. Thus, the adjustment is only for the change in prepaid expenses. The adjustment is computed by assuming that all cash paid for wages and other operating expenses is initially debited to Prepaid Expenses. This assumption allows us to reconstruct the Prepaid Expenses account to get cash paid of $218,000.

Point: A decrease in prepaid expenses implies that reported expenses include an amount(s) that did not require a cash outflow in the period.

Reconstructed Entry

Wages & Other Exp. .	216,000	
Prepaid Expenses . .	2,000	
Cash.		218,000

Prepaid Expenses			
Bal., Dec. 31, 2018	4,000		
Cash payments =	**218,000**	Wages and other operating exp.	216,000
Bal., Dec. 31, 2019	6,000		

Cash paid also can be calculated as reported expenses of $216,000 plus the $2,000 increase in prepaid expenses. Exhibit 12B.4 summarizes the adjustments to wages (including salaries) and other operating expenses.

EXHIBIT 12B.4

Formula to Compute Cash Paid for Wages and Operating Expenses—Direct Method

$$\begin{matrix} \text{Cash paid for} \\ \text{wages and other} \\ \text{operating expenses} \end{matrix} = \begin{matrix} \text{Wages and} \\ \text{other} \\ \text{operating} \\ \text{expenses} \end{matrix} \quad \begin{matrix} \text{+ \textbf{Increase} in prepaid} \\ \text{expenses} \\ or \\ \text{- \textbf{Decrease} in prepaid} \\ \text{expenses} \end{matrix} \quad \begin{matrix} \text{+ \textbf{Decrease} in accrued} \\ \text{liabilities} \\ or \\ \text{- \textbf{Increase} in accrued} \\ \text{liabilities} \end{matrix}$$

Cash Paid for Accrued Liabilities The Genesis balance sheet did not report accrued liabilities, but we include them in the formula to explain the adjustment to cash when they do exist. A decrease in accrued liabilities means that we paid cash for more goods or services than received this period, so cash paid is higher than the recorded expense. Alternatively, an increase in accrued liabilities implies that we paid less cash than what was received, so cash paid is less than the recorded expense.

Cash Paid for Interest and Income Taxes Computing operating cash flows for interest and taxes requires adjustments for amounts reported on the income statement for changes in related balance sheet accounts. The Genesis income statement shows interest expense of $7,000 and income taxes expense of $15,000. To compute the cash paid, we adjust interest expense for the change in interest payable and adjust income taxes expense for the change in income taxes payable. These computations involve reconstructing both liability accounts and show cash paid for interest of $8,000 and cash paid for income taxes of $5,000.

Reconstructed Entry

Interest Expense	7,000	
Interest Payable.	1,000	
Cash.		8,000

Reconstructed Entry

Income Tax Exp.	15,000	
Income Tax Pay. . . .	10,000	
Cash.		5,000

Interest Payable			
		Bal., Dec. 31, 2018	4,000
Cash paid for interest = 8,000		Interest expense	7,000
		Bal., Dec. 31, 2019	3,000

Income Taxes Payable			
		Bal., Dec. 31, 2018	12,000
Cash paid for taxes = 5,000		Income taxes expense	15,000
		Bal., Dec. 31, 2019	22,000

The formulas to compute these amounts are in Exhibit 12B.5. Both of these cash payments are reported as operating cash outflows.

EXHIBIT 12B.5

Formulas to Compute Cash Paid for Both Interest and Taxes—Direct Method

$$\begin{matrix} \text{Cash paid} \\ \text{for interest} \end{matrix} = \text{Interest expense} \quad \begin{matrix} \text{+ \textbf{Decrease} in interest payable} \\ or \\ \text{- \textbf{Increase} in interest payable} \end{matrix}$$

$$\begin{matrix} \text{Cash paid} \\ \text{for taxes} \end{matrix} = \text{Income taxes expense} \quad \begin{matrix} \text{+ \textbf{Decrease} in income taxes payable} \\ or \\ \text{- \textbf{Increase} in income taxes payable} \end{matrix}$$

Analyzing Additional Expenses, Gains, and Losses Genesis has three more items reported on its income statement: depreciation, loss on sale of assets, and gain on retirement of debt. We consider each for its potential cash effects.

Depreciation Expense Depreciation expense is $24,000. It is often called a *noncash expense* because depreciation has no cash flows. Depreciation expense is *never* reported on a statement of cash flows using the direct method; nor is depletion or amortization expense.

Loss on Sale of Assets Sales of assets frequently result in gains and losses reported as part of net income, but the amount of recorded gain or loss does *not* impact cash. Thus, the loss or gain on a sale of assets is *never* reported on a statement of cash flows using the direct method.

Gain on Retirement of Debt Retirement of debt usually yields a gain or loss reported as part of net income, but that gain or loss does *not* impact cash. Thus, the loss or gain from retirement of debt is *never* reported on a statement of cash flows using the direct method.

Summary of Adjustments for Direct Method Exhibit 12B.6 summarizes common adjustments for net income to yield net cash provided (used) by operating activities under the direct method.

EXHIBIT 12B.6

Summary of Selected Adjustments for Direct Method

Item	From Income Statement	Adjustments to Obtain Cash Flow Numbers	
Receipts			
From sales	Sales Revenue	+ Decrease in Accounts Receivable – Increase in Accounts Receivable	
From rent	Rent Revenue	+ Decrease in Rent Receivable – Increase in Rent Receivable	
From interest	Interest Revenue	+ Decrease in Interest Receivable – Increase in Interest Receivable	
From dividends	Dividend Revenue	+ Decrease in Dividends Receivable – Increase in Dividends Receivable	
Payments			
To suppliers	Cost of Goods Sold	+ Increase in Inventory – Decrease in Inventory	+ Decrease in Accounts Payable – Increase in Accounts Payable
For operations	Operating Expense	+ Increase in Prepaids – Decrease in Prepaids	+ Decrease in Accrued Liabilities – Increase in Accrued Liabilities
To employees	Wages (Salaries) Expense	+ Decrease in Wages (Salaries) Payable – Increase in Wages (Salaries) Payable	
For interest	Interest Expense	+ Decrease in Interest Payable – Increase in Interest Payable	
For taxes	Income Tax Expense	+ Decrease in Income Tax Payable – Increase in Income Tax Payable	

Point: The FASB requires a reconciliation of net income to net cash provided (used) by operating activities when the direct method is used. This reconciliation follows the operating activities section using the indirect method.

Direct Method Format of Operating Activities Section Exhibit 12B.7 shows the Genesis statement of cash flows using the direct method. Operating cash outflows are subtracted from operating cash inflows to get net cash provided (used) by operating activities.

EXHIBIT 12B.7

Statement of Cash Flows— Direct Method

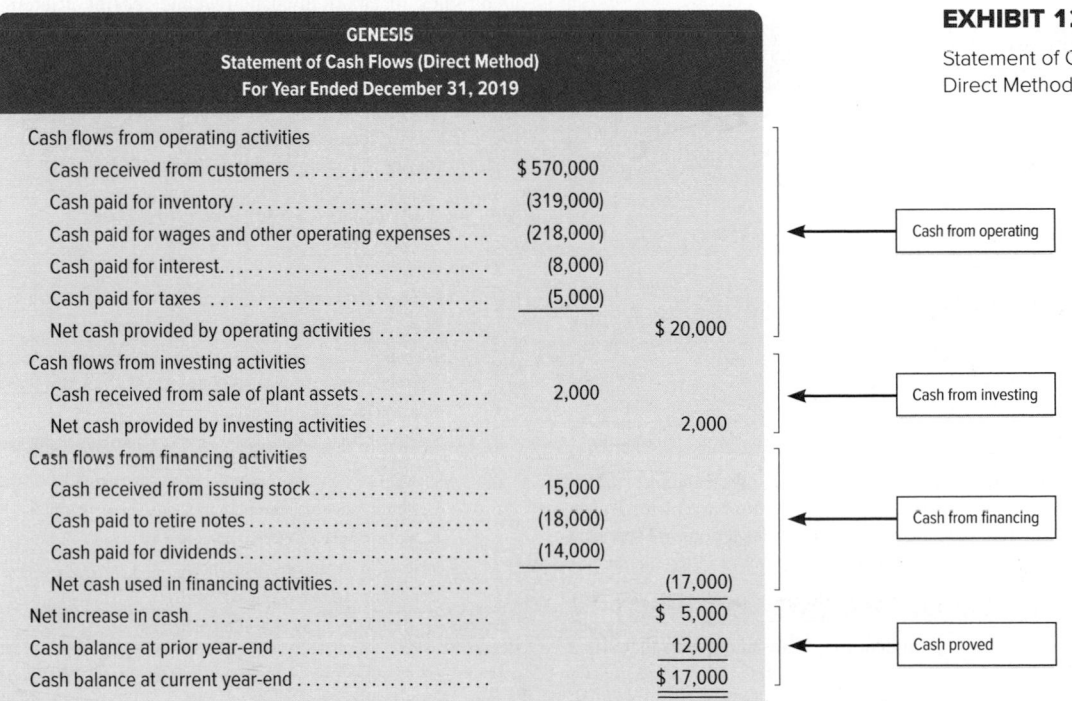

GENESIS Statement of Cash Flows (Direct Method) For Year Ended December 31, 2019		
Cash flows from operating activities		
Cash received from customers	$ 570,000	
Cash paid for inventory	(319,000)	
Cash paid for wages and other operating expenses	(218,000)	
Cash paid for interest.	(8,000)	
Cash paid for taxes	(5,000)	
Net cash provided by operating activities		$ 20,000
Cash flows from investing activities		
Cash received from sale of plant assets	2,000	
Net cash provided by investing activities		2,000
Cash flows from financing activities		
Cash received from issuing stock	15,000	
Cash paid to retire notes	(18,000)	
Cash paid for dividends.	(14,000)	
Net cash used in financing activities.		(17,000)
Net increase in cash		$ 5,000
Cash balance at prior year-end		12,000
Cash balance at current year-end		$ 17,000

Cash from operating

Cash from investing

Cash from financing

Cash proved

NEED-TO-KNOW 12-6

Reporting Operating
Cash Flows (Direct)

P5

A company's current-year income statement and selected balance sheet data at December 31 of the current and prior years follow. Prepare the operating activities section of the statement of cash flows using the direct method for the current year.

Income Statement For Current Year Ended December 31	
Sales revenue	$120
Expenses: Cost of goods sold.............	50
Depreciation expense..........	30
Salaries expense..............	17
Interest expense	3
Net income..........................	$ 20

Selected Balance Sheet Accounts		
At December 31	**Current Yr**	**Prior Yr**
Accounts receivable	$12	$10
Inventory	6	9
Accounts payable	7	11
Salaries payable	8	3
Interest payable........	1	0

Solution

Cash Flows from Operating Activities—Direct Method For Current Year Ended December 31	
Cash flows from operating activities*	
Cash received from customers	$118
Cash paid for inventory	(51)
Cash paid for salaries	(12)
Cash paid for interest............................	(2)
Net cash provided by operating activities...............	$53

Do More: QS 12-21, QS 12-22, QS 12-23, QS 12-24, QS 12-25, QS 12-26, QS 12-27, E 12-15, E 12-16, E 12-17, E 12-18, E 12-19

*Supporting computations:
Cash received from customers = Sales of $120 − Accounts Receivable increase of $2.
Cash paid for inventory = COGS of $50 − Inventory decrease of $3 + Accounts Payable decrease of $4.
Cash paid for salaries = Salaries Expense of $17 − Salaries Payable increase of $5.
Cash paid for interest = Interest Expense of $3 − Interest Payable increase of $1.

Summary: Cheat Sheet

BASICS OF CASH FLOW REPORTING

Format for statement of cash flows:

COMPANY NAME Statement of Cash Flows For *period* Ended *date*	
Cash flows from operating activities	
[Compute operating cash flows using indirect or direct method]	
Net cash provided (used) by operating activities..	$ #
Cash flows from investing activities	
[List of individual inflows and outflows]	
Net cash provided (used) by investing activities..	#
Cash flows from financing activities	
[List of individual inflows and outflows]	
Net cash provided (used) by financing activities	#
Net increase (decrease) in cash	$ #
Cash (and equivalents) balance at prior period-end	#
Cash (and equivalents) balance at current period-end	$ #

Separate schedule or note disclosure of any noncash investing and financing transactions is required.

Noncash investing and financing activities: Some investing and financing activities do not affect cash flows, such as the purchase of long-term assets using a long-term note payable (loan). Such transactions are reported at the bottom of the statement of cash flows or in a note to the statement.

CASH FLOWS FROM OPERATING—INDIRECT

Operating activities: Generally include transactions and events that affect net income.

Operating cash inflow examples: Cash sales to customers, collections on credit sales, receipt of dividend revenue, receipt of interest revenue.

Operating cash outflow examples: Cash to pay salaries and wages, pay operating expenses, pay suppliers for goods and services, pay interest owed, pay taxes and fines.

Indirect method: Reports net income and then adjusts it for items that do not affect cash. Indirect method only affects the presentation of operating cash flows, not investing or financing sections.

Summary of adjustments for *indirect* method:

Net Income (or Loss)

(1) Adjustments for operating items not providing or using cash

   + Noncash expenses and losses

   Examples: Expenses for depreciation, depletion, and amortization; losses from disposal of long-term assets and from retirement of debt

   − Noncash revenues and gains

   Examples: Gains from disposal of long-term assets and from retirement of debt

(2) Adjustments for changes in current assets and current liabilities

   + Decrease in noncash current operating asset

   − Increase in noncash current operating asset

   + Increase in current operating liability

   − Decrease in current operating liability

Net cash provided (used) by operating activities

CASH FLOWS FROM INVESTING

Investing activities: Generally include transactions and events that come from the purchase and sale of long-term assets.

Investing cash inflow examples: Cash from selling plant assets, selling intangible assets, selling short-term and long-term investments, selling notes receivable, collecting principal (but *not* interest) on notes receivable.

Investing cash outflow examples: Cash to buy plant assets, buy intangible assets, buy short-term and long-term investments, loan money in return for notes receivable.

Example of investing section format:

Cash flows from investing activities		
Cash received from sale of plant assets.............	$2,000	
Net cash provided by investing activities............		$2,000

CASH FLOWS FROM FINANCING

Financing activities: Generally include transactions and events that affect long-term liabilities and equity.

Financing cash inflow examples: Cash from issuing common and preferred stock, issuing short- and long-term debt (notes payable and bonds payable), reissuing treasury stock.

Financing cash outflow examples: Cash to pay dividends to shareholders, pay off short- and long-term debt (notes payable and bonds payable), purchase treasury stock.

Example of financing section format:

Cash flows from financing activities	
Cash received from issuing stock..............	$ 15,000
Cash paid to retire notes....................	(18,000)
Cash paid for dividends.....................	(14,000)
Net cash used in financing activities...........	$(17,000)

CASH FLOWS FROM OPERATING—DIRECT

Direct method: Separately lists operating cash receipts and operating cash payments. Cash payments are subtracted from cash receipts. Unlike the indirect method, it does not start with net income. This only affects the operating section of the statement of cash flows.

Summary of adjustments for *direct* method:

Item	From Income Statement	Adjustments to Obtain Cash Flow Numbers
Receipts		
From sales	Sales Revenue	+ Decrease in Accounts Receivable / − Increase in Accounts Receivable
From rent	Rent Revenue	+ Decrease in Rent Receivable / − Increase in Rent Receivable
From interest	Interest Revenue	+ Decrease in Interest Receivable / − Increase in Interest Receivable
From dividends	Dividend Revenue	+ Decrease in Dividends Receivable / − Increase in Dividends Receivable
Payments		
To suppliers	Cost of Goods Sold	+ Increase in Inventory / − Decrease in Inventory + Decrease in Accounts Payable / − Increase in Accounts Payable
For operations	Operating Expense	+ Increase in Prepaids / − Decrease in Prepaids + Decrease in Accrued Liabilities / − Increase in Accrued Liabilities
To employees	Wages (Salaries) Expense	+ Decrease in Wages (Salaries) Payable / − Increase in Wages (Salaries) Payable
For interest	Interest Expense	+ Decrease in Interest Payable / − Increase in Interest Payable
For taxes	Income Tax Expense	+ Decrease in Income Tax Payable / − Increase in Income Tax Payable

Key Terms

Cash flow on total assets (467)

Direct method (457)

Financing activities (457)

Indirect method (457)

Investing activities (454)

Operating activities (454)

Statement of cash flows (453)

Multiple Choice Quiz

1. A company uses the indirect method to determine its cash flows from operating activities. Use the following information to determine its net cash provided or used by operating activities.

Net income	$15,200
Depreciation expense	10,000
Cash payment on note payable............	8,000
Gain on sale of land	3,000
Increase in inventory	1,500
Increase in accounts payable..............	2,850

   a. $23,550 used by operating activities
   b. $23,550 provided by operating activities
   c. $15,550 provided by operating activities
   d. $42,400 provided by operating activities
   e. $20,850 provided by operating activities

2. A machine with a cost of $175,000 and accumulated depreciation of $94,000 is sold for $87,000 cash. The amount reported as a source of cash under cash flows from investing activities is
   a. $81,000.
   b. $6,000.
   c. $87,000.
   d. $0; this is a financing activity.
   e. $0; this is an operating activity.

3. A company settles a long-term note payable plus interest by paying $68,000 cash toward the principal amount and $5,440 cash for interest. The amount reported as a use of cash under cash flows from financing activities is
   a. $0; this is an investing activity.
   b. $0; this is an operating activity.
   c. $73,440.
   d. $68,000.
   e. $5,440.

4. The following information is available regarding a company's annual salaries and wages. What amount of cash is paid for salaries and wages?

Salaries and wages expense	$255,000
Salaries and wages payable, prior year-end.	8,200
Salaries and wages payable, current year-end.	10,900

   a. $252,300   **c.** $255,000   **e.** $235,900
   b. $257,700   **d.** $274,100

5. The following information is available for a company. What amount of cash is paid for inventory for the current year?

Cost of goods sold	$545,000
Inventory, prior year-end	105,000
Inventory, current year-end	112,000
Accounts payable, prior year-end	98,500
Accounts payable, current year-end	101,300

   a. $545,000   **c.** $540,800   **e.** $549,200
   b. $554,800   **d.** $535,200

ANSWERS TO MULTIPLE CHOICE QUIZ

1. b;

Net income	$15,200
Depreciation expense	10,000
Gain on sale of land	(3,000)
Increase in inventory	(1,500)
Increase in accounts payable.	2,850
Net cash provided by operations.	$23,550

2. c; Cash received from sale of machine is reported as an investing activity.

3. d; FASB requires cash interest paid to be reported under operating.

4. a; Cash paid for salaries and wages = $255,000 + $8,200 − $10,900 = $252,300

5. e; Increase in inventory = $112,000 − $105,000 = $7,000
Increase in accounts payable = $101,300 − $98,500 = $2,800
Cash paid for inventory = $545,000 + $7,000 − $2,800 = $549,200

[A(B)] *Superscript letter A or B denotes assignments based on Appendix 12A or 12B.*

[I] Icon denotes assignments that involve decision making.

Discussion Questions

1. What is the reporting purpose of the statement of cash flows? Identify at least two questions that this statement can answer.

2. What are some investing activities reported on the statement of cash flows?

3. What are some financing activities reported on the statement of cash flows?

4.[B] Describe the direct method of reporting cash flows from operating activities.

5.[B] When a statement of cash flows is prepared using the direct method, what are some of the operating cash flows?

6. Describe the indirect method of reporting cash flows from operating activities.

7. Where on the statement of cash flows is the payment of cash dividends reported?

8. [I] Assume that a company purchases land for $1,000,000, paying $400,000 cash and borrowing the remainder with a long-term note payable. How should this transaction be reported on a statement of cash flows?

9. [I] On June 3, a company borrows $200,000 cash by giving its bank a 90-day, interest-bearing note. On the statement of cash flows, where should this be reported?

10. [I] If a company reports positive net income for the year, can it also show a net cash outflow from operating activities? Explain.

11. [I] Is depreciation a source of cash flow?

12. [I] Refer to **Apple**'s statement of cash flows in Appendix A. (*a*) Which method is used to compute its net cash provided by operating activities? (*b*) Its balance sheet shows an increase in accounts receivable from September 24, 2016, to September 30, 2017; why is this increase in accounts receivable subtracted when computing net cash provided by operating activities for the fiscal year ended September 30, 2017?   **APPLE**

13. [I] Refer to **Google**'s statement of cash flows in Appendix A. What are its cash flows from financing activities for the year ended December 31, 2017? List the items and amounts.   **GOOGLE**

14. [I] Refer to **Samsung**'s 2017 statement of cash flows in Appendix A. List its cash flows from operating activities, investing activities, and financing activities.   **Samsung**

15. [I] Refer to **Samsung**'s statement of cash flows in Appendix A. What investing activities result in cash outflows for the year ended December 31, 2017? List items and amounts.   **Samsung**

[Mc Graw Hill] **connect**

QUICK STUDY

QS 12-1

Classifying transactions by activity

C1 [I]

Classify the following cash flows as either operating (O), investing (I), or financing (F) activities.

  ____ **1.** Sold stock investments for cash.
  ____ **2.** Received cash payments from customers.
  ____ **3.** Paid cash for wages and salaries.
  ____ **4.** Purchased inventories with cash.
  ____ **5.** Paid cash dividends.

  ____ **6.** Issued common stock for cash.
  ____ **7.** Received cash interest on a note.
  ____ **8.** Paid cash interest on outstanding notes.
  ____ **9.** Received cash from sale of land.
  ____ **10.** Paid cash for property taxes on building.

Label the following headings, line items, and notes with the numbers *1* through *13* according to their sequential order (from top to bottom) for presentation on the statement of cash flows.

____ **a.** "Cash flows from investing activities" title

____ **b.** "For *period* Ended *date*" heading

____ **c.** "Cash flows from operating activities" title

____ **d.** Company name

____ **e.** Schedule or note disclosure of noncash investing and financing transactions

____ **f.** "Statement of Cash Flows" heading

____ **g.** Net increase (decrease) in cash. . . . . $

____ **h.** Net cash provided (used) by operating activities . . . . $

____ **i.** Cash (and equivalents) balance at prior period-end . . . . $

____ **j.** Net cash provided (used) by financing activities . . . . $

____ **k.** "Cash flows from financing activities" title

____ **l.** Net cash provided (used) by investing activities. . . . . $

____ **m.** Cash (and equivalents) balance at current period-end . . . . $

QS 12-2
Statement of cash flows

P1

Bryant Co. reports net income of $20,000. For the year, depreciation expense is $7,000 and the company reports a gain of $3,000 from sale of machinery. It also had a $2,000 loss from retirement of notes. Compute cash flows from operations using the *indirect* method.

QS 12-3
Indirect: Computing cash flows from operations   **P2**

Cain Inc. reports net income of $15,000. Its comparative balance sheet shows the following changes: accounts receivable increased $6,000; inventory decreased $8,000; prepaid insurance decreased $1,000; accounts payable increased $3,000; and taxes payable decreased $2,000. Compute cash flows from operations using the *indirect* method.

QS 12-4
Indirect: Computing cash flows from operations   **P2**

For each separate company, compute cash flows from operations using the *indirect method.*

QS 12-5
Indirect: Computing cash flows from operations

P2

	Twix	Dots	Skor
Net income	$ 4,000	$100,000	$72,000
Depreciation expense	30,000	8,000	24,000
Accounts receivable increase (decrease)	40,000	20,000	(4,000)
Inventory increase (decrease)	(20,000)	(10,000)	10,000
Accounts payable increase (decrease)	24,000	(22,000)	14,000
Accrued liabilities increase (decrease)	(44,000)	12,000	(8,000)

Use the following information to determine cash flows from operating activities using the *indirect method.*

QS 12-6
Indirect: Computing cash from operations   **P2**

MOSS COMPANY
Income Statement
For Year Ended December 31, 2019

Sales		$515,000
Cost of goods sold		331,600
Gross profit		183,400
Operating expenses		
Depreciation expense . . .	$ 36,000	
Other expenses	121,500	157,500
Income before taxes.		25,900
Income taxes expense		7,700
Net income		$ 18,200

MOSS COMPANY
Selected Balance Sheet Information
December 31, 2019 and 2018

	2019	2018
Current assets		
Cash	$84,650	$26,800
Accounts receivable.	25,000	32,000
Inventory.	60,000	54,100
Current liabilities		
Accounts payable.	30,400	25,700
Income taxes payable . . .	2,050	2,200

QS 12-7

Indirect: Computing cash from operations   P2

CRUZ, INC.
Comparative Balance Sheets

At December 31	2019	2018
Assets		
Cash.	$ 94,800	$ 24,000
Accounts receivable, net	41,000	51,000
Inventory	85,800	95,800
Prepaid expenses	5,400	4,200
Total current assets	227,000	175,000
Furniture	109,000	119,000
Accum. depreciation—Furniture	(17,000)	(9,000)
Total assets	$319,000	$285,000
Liabilities and Equity		
Accounts payable	$ 15,000	$ 21,000
Wages payable	9,000	5,000
Income taxes payable	1,400	2,600
Total current liabilities	25,400	28,600
Notes payable (long-term)	29,000	69,000
Total liabilities	54,400	97,600
Equity		
Common stock, $5 par value	229,000	179,000
Retained earnings	35,600	8,400
Total liabilities and equity	$319,000	$285,000

CRUZ, INC.
Income Statement
For Year Ended December 31, 2019

Sales		$488,000
Cost of goods sold		314,000
Gross profit		174,000
Operating expenses		
Depreciation expense	$37,600	
Other expenses	89,100	126,700
Income before taxes		47,300
Income taxes expense		17,300
Net income		$ 30,000

Required

Use the *indirect method* to prepare the operating activities section of Cruz's statement of cash flows.

QS 12-8

Computing cash from asset sales

P3

The following information is from Ellerby Company's comparative balance sheets. The current-year income statement reports depreciation expense on furniture of $18,000. During the year, furniture costing $52,500 was sold for its book value. Compute cash received from the sale of furniture.

At December 31	Current Year	Prior Year
Furniture	$132,000	$ 184,500
Accumulated depreciation—Furniture	(88,700)	(110,700)

QS 12-9

Computing investing cash flows

P3

Indicate the effect each separate transaction has on *investing* cash flows.

a. Sold a truck costing $40,000, with $22,000 of accumulated depreciation, for $8,000 cash. The sale results in a $10,000 loss.

b. Sold a machine costing $10,000, with $8,000 of accumulated depreciation, for $5,000 cash. The sale results in a $3,000 gain.

c. Purchased stock investments for $16,000 cash. The purchaser believes the stock is worth at least $30,000.

QS 12-10

Computing investing cash flows

P3

The plant assets section of the comparative balance sheets of Anders Company is reported below.

ANDERS COMPANY
Comparative Year-End Balance Sheets

Plant assets	2019	2018
Equipment	$ 180,000	$ 270,000
Accumulated depreciation—Equipment	(100,000)	(210,000)
Equipment, net	$ 80,000	$ 60,000
Buildings	$ 380,000	$ 400,000
Accumulated depreciation—Buildings	(100,000)	(285,000)
Buildings, net	$ 280,000	$ 115,000

Refer to the balance sheet data above from Anders Company. During 2019, equipment with a book value of $40,000 and an original cost of $210,000 was sold at a loss of $3,000.
1. How much cash did Anders receive from the sale of equipment?
2. How much depreciation expense was recorded on equipment during 2019?
3. What was the cost of new equipment purchased by Anders during 2019?

Refer to the balance sheet data in QS 12-10 from Anders Company. During 2019, a building with a book value of $70,000 and an original cost of $300,000 was sold at a gain of $60,000.
1. How much cash did Anders receive from the sale of the building?
2. How much depreciation expense was recorded on buildings during 2019?
3. What was the cost of buildings purchased by Anders during 2019?

QS 12-11
Computing investing cash flows
P3

Compute cash flows from investing activities using the following company information.

Sale of short-term stock investments	$ 6,000	Cash purchase of used equipment	$5,000
Cash collections from customers.	16,000	Depreciation expense	2,000

QS 12-12
Computing cash flows from investing
P3

Refer to the data in QS 12-7.

Furniture costing $55,000 is sold at its book value in 2019. Acquisitions of furniture total $45,000 cash, on which no depreciation is necessary because it is acquired at year-end. What is the cash inflow from the sale of furniture?

QS 12-13
Computing cash from asset sales   P3

Indicate the effect, if any, that each separate transaction has on *financing* cash flows.
a. Notes payable with a carrying value of $15,000 are retired for $16,000 cash, resulting in a $1,000 gain.
b. Paid cash dividends of $11,000 to common stockholders.
c. Acquired $20,000 worth of machinery in exchange for common stock.

QS 12-14
Computing financing cash flows
P3

The following information is from Princeton Company's comparative balance sheets.

At December 31	Current Year	Prior Year
Common stock, $10 par value.	$105,000	$100,000
Paid-in capital in excess of par	567,000	342,000
Retained earnings.	313,500	287,500

The company's net income for the current year ended December 31 was $48,000.
1. Compute the cash received from the sale of its common stock during the current year.
2. Compute the cash paid for dividends during the current year.

QS 12-15
Computing financing cash flows
P3

Compute cash flows from financing activities using the following company information.

Cash received from short-term note payable	$20,000	Cash dividends paid	$16,000
Purchase of short-term stock investments	5,000	Interest paid	8,000

QS 12-16
Computing cash flows from financing
P3

Refer to the data in QS 12-7.
1. Assume that all common stock is issued for cash. What amount of cash dividends is paid during 2019?
2. Assume that no additional notes payable are issued in 2019. What cash amount is paid to reduce the notes payable balance in 2019?

QS 12-17
Computing financing cash outflows   P3

Use the following information for VPI Co. to prepare a statement of cash flows for the year ended December 31 using the *indirect* method.

Cash balance at prior year-end	$40,000	Gain on sale of machinery.	$ 2,000
Increase in inventory	5,000	Cash received from sale of machinery	9,500
Depreciation expense	4,000	Increase in accounts payable	1,500
Cash received from issuing stock	8,000	Net income.	23,000
Cash paid for dividends	1,000	Decrease in accounts receivable	3,000

QS 12-18
Indirect: Preparing statement of cash flows
P2   P3

QS 12-19

Interpreting disclosures on sources and uses of cash

A1

Financial data from three competitors in the same industry follow.

1. Rank the three companies from high to low on cash from operating activities.
2. Which company has the largest cash outflow for investing activities?
3. Which company has the largest cash inflow from financing activities?
4. Which company has the highest cash flow on total assets ratio?

	Mancala	Yahtzee	Cluedo
Cash provided (used) by operating activities	$ 70,000	$ 60,000	$ (24,000)
Cash provided (used) by investing activities	(28,000)	(34,000)	26,000
Cash provided (used) by financing activities	(6,000)	0	23,000
Net increase (decrease) in cash	$ 36,000	$ 26,000	$ 25,000
Average total assets	$790,000	$625,000	$300,000

QS 12-20ᴬ

Recording entries in a spreadsheet

P4

A company uses a spreadsheet to prepare its statement of cash flows. Indicate whether each of the following items would be recorded in the Debit column or Credit column of the spreadsheet's *statement of cash flows section*.

a. Decrease in accounts payable
b. Payment of cash dividends
c. Increase in accounts receivable
d. Loss on sale of machinery
e. Net income
f. Increase in interest payable

QS 12-21ᴮ

Direct: Computing cash receipts from operations

P5

Russell Co. reports sales revenue of $30,000 and interest revenue of $5,000. Its comparative balance sheet shows that accounts receivable decreased $4,000 and interest receivable increased $1,000. Compute cash provided by operating activities using the *direct* method.

QS 12-22ᴮ

Direct: Computing cash payments to suppliers **P5**

Bioware Co. reports cost of goods sold of $42,000. Its comparative balance sheet shows that inventory decreased $7,000 and accounts payable increased $5,000. Compute cash payments to suppliers using the *direct* method.

QS 12-23ᴮ

Direct: Computing cash paid for operations **P5**

BTN Inc. reports operating expenses of $27,000. Its comparative balance sheet shows that accrued liabilities decreased $6,000 and prepaid expenses increased $2,000. Compute cash used in operating activities using the *direct* method.

QS 12-24ᴮ

Direct: Computing cash flows

P5

For each separate case, compute the required cash flow information for BioClean.

Case A: Compute cash interest received		**Case B:** Compute cash paid for wages	
Interest revenue	$5,000	Wages expense	$9,000
Interest receivable, beginning of year.	600	Wages payable, beginning of year	2,200
Interest receivable, end of year	1,700	Wages payable, end of year	1,000

QS 12-25ᴮ

Direct: Computing cash received from customers

P5

Refer to the data in QS 12-7.

1. How much cash is received from sales to customers for year 2019?
2. What is the net increase or decrease in the Cash account for year 2019?

QS 12-26ᴮ

Direct: Computing operating cash outflows

P5

Refer to the data in QS 12-7.

1. How much cash is paid to acquire inventory during year 2019?
2. How much cash is paid for "other expenses" during year 2019? *Hint:* Examine prepaid expenses and wages payable.

QS 12-27ᴮ

Direct: Computing cash from operations **P5**

Refer to the data in QS 12-7.

Use the *direct method* to prepare the operating activities section of Cruz's statement of cash flows.

connect

Indicate where each item would appear on a statement of cash flows using the *indirect method* by placing an *x* in the appropriate column.

	Statement of Cash Flows			Noncash Investing and Financing Activities	Not Reported on Statement or in Notes
	Operating Activities	Investing Activities	Financing Activities		
a. Declared and paid a cash dividend	——	——	——	——	——
b. Recorded depreciation expense	——	——	——	——	——
c. Paid cash to settle long-term note payable . . .	——	——	——	——	——
d. Prepaid expenses increased in the year	——	——	——	——	——
e. Accounts receivable decreased in the year . . .	——	——	——	——	——
f. Purchased land by issuing common stock	——	——	——	——	——
g. Inventory increased in the year	——	——	——	——	——
h. Sold equipment for cash, yielding a loss	——	——	——	——	——
i. Accounts payable decreased in the year	——	——	——	——	——
j. Income taxes payable increased in the year . . .	——	——	——	——	——

EXERCISES

Exercise 12-1
Indirect:
Classifying cash flows

C1

Hampton Company reports the following information for its recent calendar year. Prepare the operating activities section of the statement of cash flows using the *indirect method*.

Income Statement Data	
Sales.	$160,000
Expenses: Cost of goods sold.	100,000
Salaries expense	24,000
Depreciation expense	12,000
Net income.	$ 24,000

Selected Year-End Balance Sheet Data	
Accounts receivable increase	$10,000
Inventory decrease	16,000
Salaries payable increase	1,000

Exercise 12-2
Indirect: Reporting cash flows from operations

P2

Arundel Company disclosed the following information for its recent calendar year. Prepare the operating activities section of the statement of cash flows using the *indirect method*.

Income Statement Data	
Revenues.	$100,000
Expenses: Salaries expense	84,000
Utilities expense	14,000
Depreciation expense	14,600
Other expenses	3,400
Net loss	$ (16,000)

Selected Year-End Balance Sheet Data	
Accounts receivable decrease	$24,000
Purchased a machine for cash	10,000
Salaries payable increase	18,000
Other accrued liabilities decrease	8,000

Exercise 12-3
Indirect: Reporting cash flows from operations

P2

Using the following income statement and additional year-end information, prepare the operating activities section of the statement of cash flows using the *indirect method*.

SONAD COMPANY Income Statement For Year Ended December 31		
Sales		$1,828,000
Cost of goods sold		991,000
Gross profit		837,000
Operating expenses		
Salaries expense	$245,535	
Depreciation expense	44,200	
Rent expense	49,600	
Amortization expense—Patents	4,200	
Utilities expense.	18,125	361,660
		475,340
Gain on sale of equipment		6,200
Net income		$ 481,540

Selected Year-End Balance Sheet Data	
Accounts receivable . .	$30,500 increase
Inventory	25,000 increase
Accounts payable	12,500 decrease
Salaries payable	3,500 decrease

Exercise 12-4
Indirect: Cash flows from operating activities

P2

Exercise 12-5

Indirect: Cash flows from operating activities

P2

Fitz Company reports the following information. Use the *indirect method* to prepare the operating activities section of its statement of cash flows for the year ended December 31.

Selected Annual Income Statement Data		Selected Year-End Balance Sheet Data	
Net income	$374,000	Accounts receivable decrease	$17,100
Depreciation expense	44,000	Inventory decrease	42,000
Amortization expense.	7,200	Prepaid expenses increase.	4,700
Gain on sale of plant assets.	6,000	Accounts payable decrease	8,200
		Salaries payable increase.	1,200

Exercise 12-6

Indirect: Cash flows from operating activities

P2

Salud Company reports the following information. Use the *indirect method* to prepare the operating activities section of its statement of cash flows for the year ended December 31.

Selected Annual Income Statement Data		Selected Year-End Balance Sheet Data	
Net income	$400,000	Accounts receivable increase.	$40,000
Depreciation expense	80,000	Prepaid expenses decrease.	12,000
Gain on sale of machinery	20,000	Accounts payable increase.	6,000
		Wages payable decrease	2,000

Exercise 12-7

Indirect: Reporting cash flows from operations

P2

Prepare the operating activities section of the statement of cash flows for GreenGarden using the *indirect method*.

Annual Income Statement Data		Selected Year-End Balance Sheet Data	
Sales.	$50,000	Prepaid expenses increase.	$3,000
Expenses: Cost of goods sold.	30,000	Inventory increase	500
Wages expense	10,000	Accounts payable decrease	1,000
Amortization expense	1,500		
Net income.	$ 8,500		

Exercise 12-8

Cash flows from investing activities

P3

Use the following information to determine cash flows from investing activities.

a. Equipment with a book value of $65,300 and an original cost of $133,000 was sold at a loss of $14,000.

b. Paid $89,000 cash for a new truck.

c. Sold land costing $154,000 for $198,000 cash, yielding a gain of $44,000.

d. Stock investments were sold for $60,800 cash, yielding a gain of $4,150.

Exercise 12-9

Cash flows from financing activities

P3

Use the following information to determine cash flows from financing activities.

a. Net income was $35,000.

b. Issued common stock for $64,000 cash.

c. Paid cash dividend of $14,600.

d. Paid $50,000 cash to settle a note payable at its $50,000 maturity value.

e. Paid $12,000 cash to acquire its treasury stock.

f. Purchased equipment for $39,000 cash.

Exercise 12-10

Reconstructed entries

P3

For each of the following separate transactions, (*a*) prepare the reconstructed journal entry and (*b*) identify the effect it has, if any, on the *investing section* or *financing section* of the statement of cash flows.

1. Sold a building costing $30,000, with $20,000 of accumulated depreciation, for $8,000 cash, resulting in a $2,000 loss.

2. Acquired machinery worth $10,000 by issuing $10,000 in notes payable.

3. Issued 1,000 shares of common stock at par for $2 per share.

4. Notes payable with a carrying value of $40,000 were retired for $47,000 cash, resulting in a $7,000 loss.

The following financial statements and additional information are reported. (1) Prepare a statement of cash flows using the *indirect method* for the year ended June 30, 2019. (2) Compute the company's cash flow on total assets ratio for fiscal year 2019.

Exercise 12-11
Indirect: Preparing statement of cash flows
A1 P2 P3

IKIBAN INC.
Income Statement
For Year Ended June 30, 2019

Sales		$678,000
Cost of goods sold		411,000
Gross profit		267,000
Operating expenses		
Depreciation expense	$58,600	
Other expenses	67,000	
Total operating expenses		125,600
		141,400
Other gains (losses)		
Gain on sale of equipment		2,000
Income before taxes		143,400
Income taxes expense		43,890
Net income		$ 99,510

Additional Information

a. A $30,000 note payable is retired at its $30,000 carrying (book) value in exchange for cash.
b. The only changes affecting retained earnings are net income and cash dividends paid.
c. New equipment is acquired for $57,600 cash.
d. Received cash for the sale of equipment that had cost $40,000, yielding a $2,000 gain.
e. Prepaid Expenses and Wages Payable relate to Other Expenses on the income statement.
f. All purchases and sales of inventory are on credit.

IKIBAN INC.
Comparative Balance Sheets

At June 30	2019	2018
Assets		
Cash	$ 87,500	$ 44,000
Accounts receivable, net	65,000	51,000
Inventory	63,800	86,500
Prepaid expenses	4,400	5,400
Total current assets	220,700	186,900
Equipment	124,000	115,000
Accum. depreciation—Equipment	(27,000)	(9,000)
Total assets	$317,700	$292,900
Liabilities and Equity		
Accounts payable	$ 25,000	$ 30,000
Wages payable	6,000	15,000
Income taxes payable	3,400	3,800
Total current liabilities	34,400	48,800
Notes payable (long term)	30,000	60,000
Total liabilities	64,400	108,800
Equity		
Common stock, $5 par value	220,000	160,000
Retained earnings	33,300	24,100
Total liabilities and equity	$317,700	$292,900

Check (1b) Cash paid for dividends, $90,310
(1d) Cash received from equip. sale, $10,000

Use the following information to prepare a statement of cash flows for the current year using the *indirect method*.

Exercise 12-12
Indirect: Preparing statement of cash flows
P2 P3

MONTGOMERY INC.
Comparative Balance Sheets

At December 31	Current Year	Prior Year
Assets		
Cash	$ 30,400	$ 30,550
Accounts receivable, net	10,050	12,150
Inventory	90,100	70,150
Total current assets	130,550	112,850
Equipment	49,900	41,500
Accum. depreciation—Equipment	(22,500)	(15,300)
Total assets	$157,950	$139,050
Liabilities and Equity		
Accounts payable	$ 23,900	$ 25,400
Salaries payable	500	600
Total current liabilities	24,400	26,000
Equity		
Common stock, no par value	110,000	100,000
Retained earnings	23,550	13,050
Total liabilities and equity	$157,950	$139,050

MONTGOMERY INC.
Income Statement
For Current Year Ended December 31

Sales		$45,575
Cost of goods sold		(18,950)
Gross profit		26,625
Operating expenses		
Depreciation expense	$7,200	
Other expenses	5,550	
Total operating expenses		12,750
Income before taxes		13,875
Income tax expense		3,375
Net income		$10,500

Additional Information on Current-Year Transactions

a. No dividends are declared or paid.
b. Issued additional stock for $10,000 cash.
c. Purchased equipment for cash; no equipment was sold.

Exercise 12-13

Analyzing cash flow on
total assets   A1

A company reported average total assets of $1,240,000 in Year 1 and $1,510,000 in Year 2. Its net operating cash flow was $102,920 in Year 1 and $138,920 in Year 2. (1) Calculate its cash flow on total assets ratio for both years. (2) Did its cash flow on total assets improve in Year 2 versus Year 1?

Exercise 12-14^A

Indirect: Cash flows
spreadsheet

P4

Complete the following spreadsheet in preparation of the statement of cash flows. (The statement of cash flows is not required.) Prepare the spreadsheet as in Exhibit 12A.1 under the *indirect method*. Identify the debits and credits in the Analysis of Changes columns with letters that correspond to the following transactions and events *a* through *h*.

a. Net income for the year was $100,000.

b. Dividends of $80,000 cash were declared and paid.

c. The only noncash expense was $70,000 of depreciation.

d. Purchased plant assets for $70,000 cash.

e. Notes payable of $20,000 were issued for $20,000 cash.

f. $70,000 increase in accounts receivable.

g. $20,000 decrease in inventory.

h. $10,000 decrease in accounts payable.

SCORETECK CORPORATION					
Spreadsheet for Statement of Cash Flows—Indirect Method					
For Year Ended December 31, 2019					
			Analysis of Changes		
	Dec. 31, 2018		Debit	Credit	Dec. 31, 2019
Balance Sheet—Debit Bal. Accounts					
Cash	$ 80,000				$ 60,000
Accounts receivable	120,000				190,000
Inventory	250,000				230,000
Plant assets	600,000				670,000
	$1,050,000				$1,150,000
Balance Sheet—Credit Bal. Accounts					
Accumulated depreciation	$ 100,000				$ 170,000
Accounts payable	150,000				140,000
Notes payable	370,000				390,000
Common stock	200,000				200,000
Retained earnings	230,000				250,000
	$1,050,000				$1,150,000
Statement of Cash Flows					
Operating activities					
Net income					
Increase in accounts receivable					
Decrease in inventory					
Decrease in accounts payable					
Depreciation expense					
Investing activities					
Cash paid to purchase plant assets					
Financing activities					
Cash paid for dividends					
Cash from issuance of notes					

Exercise 12-15^B

Direct: Classifying cash
flows

C1   P5

Indicate where each item would appear on a statement of cash flows using the *direct method* by placing an *x* in the appropriate column.

	Statement of Cash Flows			Noncash Investing and Financing Activities	Not Reported on Statement or in Notes
	Operating Activities	Investing Activities	Financing Activities		
a. Retired long-term notes payable by issuing common stock	____	____	____	____	____
b. Paid cash toward accounts payable . . .	____	____	____	____	____
c. Sold inventory for cash	____	____	____	____	____
d. Paid cash dividends	____	____	____	____	____
e. Accepted note receivable in exchange for plant assets	____	____	____	____	____
f. Recorded depreciation expense	____	____	____	____	____
g. Paid cash to acquire treasury stock . . .	____	____	____	____	____
h. Collected cash from sales	____	____	____	____	____
i. Borrowed cash from bank by signing a nine-month note payable	____	____	____	____	____
j. Paid cash to purchase a patent	____	____	____	____	____

For each of the following separate cases, compute the required cash flow information.

| | **Exercise 12-16^B** |

Exercise 12-16^B
Direct: Computing
cash flows
P5

Case X: Compute cash received from customers		**Case Z:** Compute cash paid for inventory	
Sales......................................	$515,000	Cost of goods sold	$525,000
Accounts receivable, Beginning balance....	27,200	Inventory, Beginning balance	158,600
Accounts receivable, Ending balance	33,600	Accounts payable, Beginning balance ...	66,700
Case Y: Compute cash paid for rent		Inventory, Ending balance	130,400
Rent expense.........................	$139,800	Accounts payable, Ending balance	82,000
Rent payable, Beginning balance.........	7,800		
Rent payable, Ending balance	6,200		

Refer to the information in Exercise 12-11. Using the *direct method,* prepare the statement of cash flows for the year ended June 30, 2019.

Exercise 12-17^B
Direct: Preparing statement
of cash flows   **P5**

Refer to information in Exercise 12-4. Use the *direct method* to prepare the operating activities section of Sonad's statement of cash flows.

Exercise 12-18^B
Direct: Cash flows from
operating activities   **P5**

Use the following information about Ferron Company to prepare a complete statement of cash flows (*direct method*) for the current year ended December 31. Use a note disclosure for any noncash investing and financing activities.

Exercise 12-19^B
Direct: Preparing
statement of cash flows
and supporting note

P5

Cash and cash equivalents,		Cash received in exchange for six-month	
Dec. 31 prior year end....................	$ 10,000	note payable...........................	$ 35,000
Cash and cash equivalents,		Land purchased by issuing long-term	
Dec. 31 current year-end.................	148,000	note payable..........................	105,250
Cash received as interest...................	3,500	Cash paid for store equipment..............	24,750
Cash paid for salaries.....................	76,500	Cash dividends paid	10,000
Bonds payable retired by issuing common		Cash paid for other expenses...............	20,000
stock (no gain or loss on retirement)	185,500	Cash received from customers..............	495,000
Cash paid to retire long-term notes payable ...	100,000	Cash paid for inventory....................	254,500
Cash received from sale of equipment	60,250		

The following Cash T-account shows the total debits and total credits to the Cash account of Thomas Corporation for the current year.

1. Prepare a complete statement of cash flows for the current year using the *direct method.*
2. Refer to the statement of cash flows prepared for part 1 to answer the following questions. (*a*) Which section—operating, investing, or financing—shows the largest cash (i) inflow and (ii) outflow? (*b*) What is the largest individual item among the investing cash outflows? (*c*) Are the cash proceeds larger from issuing notes or issuing stock? (*d*) Does the company have a net cash inflow or outflow from borrowing activities?

Exercise 12-20^B
Direct: Preparing
statement of cash flows
from Cash T-account

P1   P3   P5

Cash			
Balance, Dec. 31, prior year	333,000		
Receipts from customers	5,000,000	Payments for inventory	2,590,000
Receipts from dividends	208,400	Payments for wages	550,000
Receipts from land sale	220,000	Payments for rent	320,000
Receipts from machinery sale	710,000	Payments for interest	218,000
Receipts from issuing stock	1,540,000	Payments for taxes	450,000
Receipts from borrowing	3,600,000	Payments for machinery	2,236,000
		Payments for stock investments	1,260,000
		Payments for note payable	386,000
		Payments for dividends	500,000
		Payments for treasury stock	218,000
Balance, Dec. 31, current year	?		

PROBLEM SET A

Problem 12-1A

Indirect: Computing cash flows from operations

P2

Lansing Company's current-year income statement and selected balance sheet data at December 31 of the current and prior years follow.

LANSING COMPANY Selected Balance Sheet Accounts		
At December 31	**Current Year**	**Prior Year**
Accounts receivable........	$5,600	$5,800
Inventory................	1,980	1,540
Accounts payable.........	4,400	4,600
Salaries payable...........	880	700
Utilities payable...........	220	160
Prepaid insurance.........	260	280
Prepaid rent	220	180

LANSING COMPANY Income Statement For Current Year Ended December 31	
Sales revenue	$97,200
Expenses	
Cost of goods sold	42,000
Depreciation expense............	12,000
Salaries expense................	18,000
Rent expense	9,000
Insurance expense	3,800
Interest expense................	3,600
Utilities expense	2,800
Net income......................	$ 6,000

Required

Check   Cash from operating activities, $17,780

Prepare the operating activities section of the statement of cash flows using the *indirect method* for the current year.

Problem 12-2A[B]

Direct: Computing cash flows from operations

P5

Refer to the information in Problem 12-1A.

Required

Prepare the operating activities section of the statement of cash flows using the *direct method* for the current year.

Problem 12-3A

Indirect: Statement of cash flows

A1   P2   P3

Forten Company's current-year income statement, comparative balance sheets, and additional information follow. For the year, (1) all sales are credit sales, (2) all credits to Accounts Receivable reflect cash receipts from customers, (3) all purchases of inventory are on credit, (4) all debits to Accounts Payable reflect cash payments for inventory, and (5) Other Expenses are paid in advance and are initially debited to Prepaid Expenses.

FORTEN COMPANY Income Statement For Current Year Ended December 31		
Sales		$582,500
Cost of goods sold		285,000
Gross profit............................		297,500
Operating expenses		
Depreciation expense	$ 20,750	
Other expenses	132,400	153,150
Other gains (losses)		
Loss on sale of equipment............		(5,125)
Income before taxes....................		139,225
Income taxes expense		24,250
Net income		$114,975

FORTEN COMPANY Comparative Balance Sheets December 31		
	Current Year	**Prior Year**
Assets		
Cash......................................	$ 49,800	$ 73,500
Accounts receivable	65,810	50,625
Inventory	275,656	251,800
Prepaid expenses	1,250	1,875
Total current assets.......................	392,516	377,800
Equipment	157,500	108,000
Accum. depreciation—Equipment	(36,625)	(46,000)
Total assets	$513,391	$439,800
Liabilities and Equity		
Accounts payable	$ 53,141	$114,675
Short-term notes payable	10,000	6,000
Total current liabilities.....................	63,141	120,675
Long-term notes payable	65,000	48,750
Total liabilities	128,141	169,425
Equity		
Common stock, $5 par value	162,750	150,250
Paid-in capital in excess of par, common stock ...	37,500	0
Retained earnings	185,000	120,125
Total liabilities and equity	$513,391	$439,800

Additional Information on Current-Year Transactions

a. The loss on the cash sale of equipment was $5,125 (details in b).

b. Sold equipment costing $46,875, with accumulated depreciation of $30,125, for $11,625 cash.

c. Purchased equipment costing $96,375 by paying $30,000 cash and signing a long-term note payable for the balance.

d. Borrowed $4,000 cash by signing a short-term note payable.

e. Paid $50,125 cash to reduce the long-term notes payable.

f. Issued 2,500 shares of common stock for $20 cash per share.

g. Declared and paid cash dividends of $50,100.

Required

1. Prepare a complete statement of cash flows using the *indirect method* for the current year. Disclose any noncash investing and financing activities in a note.

Check   Cash from operating activities, $40,900

Analysis Component

2. Analyze and discuss the statement of cash flows prepared in part 1, giving special attention to the wisdom of the cash dividend payment.

Refer to the information reported about Forten Company in Problem 12-3A.

Problem 12-4A^A
Indirect: Cash flows spreadsheet
P4

Required

Prepare a complete statement of cash flows using a spreadsheet as in Exhibit 12A.1 using the *indirect method*. Identify the debits and credits in the Analysis of Changes columns with letters that correspond to the following list of transactions and events.

a. Net income was $114,975.
b. Accounts receivable increased.
c. Inventory increased.
d. Prepaid expenses decreased.
e. Accounts payable decreased.
f. Depreciation expense was $20,750.

g. Sold equipment costing $46,875, with accumulated depreciation of $30,125, for $11,625 cash. This yielded a loss of $5,125.
h. Purchased equipment costing $96,375 by paying $30,000 cash and
(i.) by signing a long-term note payable for the balance.
j. Borrowed $4,000 cash by signing a short-term note payable.
k. Paid $50,125 cash to reduce the long-term notes payable.
l. Issued 2,500 shares of common stock for $20 cash per share.
m. Declared and paid cash dividends of $50,100.

Check   Analysis of Changes column totals, $600,775

Refer to Forten Company's financial statements and related information in Problem 12-3A.

Problem 12-5A^B
Direct: Statement of cash flows **P5**

Required

Prepare a complete statement of cash flows using the *direct method*. Disclose any noncash investing and financing activities in a note.

Check   Cash used in financing activities, $(46,225)

Golden Corp.'s current-year income statement, comparative balance sheets, and additional information follow. For the year, (1) all sales are credit sales, (2) all credits to Accounts Receivable reflect cash receipts from customers, (3) all purchases of inventory are on credit, (4) all debits to Accounts Payable reflect cash payments for inventory, (5) Other Expenses are all cash expenses, and (6) any change in Income Taxes Payable reflects the accrual and cash payment of taxes.

Problem 12-6A
Indirect: Statement of cash flows
P2   P3

GOLDEN CORPORATION Comparative Balance Sheets		
At December 31	**Current Year**	**Prior Year**
Assets		
Cash	$ 164,000	$107,000
Accounts receivable	83,000	71,000
Inventory	601,000	526,000
Total current assets	848,000	704,000
Equipment	335,000	299,000
Accum. depreciation—Equipment	(158,000)	(104,000)
Total assets	$1,025,000	$899,000
Liabilities and Equity		
Accounts payable	$ 87,000	$ 71,000
Income taxes payable	28,000	25,000
Total current liabilities	115,000	96,000
Equity		
Common stock, $2 par value	592,000	568,000
Paid-in capital in excess of par value, common stock	196,000	160,000
Retained earnings	122,000	75,000
Total liabilities and equity	$1,025,000	$899,000

GOLDEN CORPORATION Income Statement For Current Year Ended December 31		
Sales		$1,792,000
Cost of goods sold		1,086,000
Gross profit		706,000
Operating expenses		
Depreciation expense	$ 54,000	
Other expenses	494,000	548,000
Income before taxes		158,000
Income taxes expense		22,000
Net income		$ 136,000

Additional Information on Current-Year Transactions
a. Purchased equipment for $36,000 cash.
b. Issued 12,000 shares of common stock for $5 cash per share.
c. Declared and paid $89,000 in cash dividends.

Required

Prepare a complete statement of cash flows using the *indirect method* for the current year.

Problem 12-7A^A
Indirect: Cash flows
spreadsheet

P4

Refer to the information reported about Golden Corporation in Problem 12-6A.

Required

Prepare a complete statement of cash flows using a spreadsheet as in Exhibit 12A.1 under the *indirect method*. Identify the debits and credits in the Analysis of Changes columns with letters that correspond to the following list of transactions and events.

a. Net income was $136,000.
b. Accounts receivable increased.
c. Inventory increased.
d. Accounts payable increased.
e. Income taxes payable increased.

f. Depreciation expense was $54,000.
g. Purchased equipment for $36,000 cash.
h. Issued 12,000 shares at $5 cash per share.
i. Declared and paid $89,000 of cash dividends.

Problem 12-8A^B
Direct: Statement of
cash flows **P5**

Refer to Golden Corporation's financial statements and related information in Problem 12-6A.

Required

Prepare a complete statement of cash flows using the *direct method* for the current year.

PROBLEM SET B

Problem 12-1B
Indirect: Computing cash
flows from operations

P2

Salt Lake Company's current-year income statement and selected balance sheet data at December 31 of the current and prior years follow.

SALT LAKE COMPANY
Income Statement
For Current Year Ended December 31

Sales revenue	$156,000
Expenses	
Cost of goods sold	72,000
Depreciation expense...........	32,000
Salaries expense................	20,000
Rent expense	5,000
Insurance expense	2,600
Interest expense................	2,400
Utilities expense	2,000
Net income......................	$ 20,000

SALT LAKE COMPANY
Selected Balance Sheet Accounts

At December 31	Current Year	Prior Year
Accounts receivable........	$3,600	$3,000
Inventory.................	860	980
Accounts payable..........	2,400	2,600
Salaries payable...........	900	600
Utilities payable	200	0
Prepaid insurance..........	140	180
Prepaid rent	100	200

Required

Prepare the operating activities section of the statement of cash flows using the *indirect method* for the current year.

Problem 12-2B^B
Direct: Computing cash
flows from operations

P5

Refer to the information in Problem 12-1B.

Required

Prepare the operating activities section of the statement of cash flows using the *direct method* for the current year.

Problem 12-3B
Indirect: Statement of
cash flows

A1 P2 P3

Gazelle Corporation's current-year income statement, comparative balance sheets, and additional information follow. For the year, (1) all sales are credit sales, (2) all credits to Accounts Receivable reflect cash receipts from customers, (3) all purchases of inventory are on credit, (4) all debits to Accounts Payable reflect cash payments for inventory, and (5) Other Expenses are paid in advance and are initially debited to Prepaid Expenses.

GAZELLE CORPORATION Comparative Balance Sheets December 31		
	Current Year	**Prior Year**
Assets		
Cash..............................	$123,450	$ 61,550
Accounts receivable	77,100	80,750
Inventory	240,600	250,700
Prepaid expenses	15,100	17,000
Total current assets.................	456,250	410,000
Equipment	262,250	200,000
Accum. depreciation—Equipment	(110,750)	(95,000)
Total assets	$607,750	$515,000
Liabilities and Equity		
Accounts payable	$ 17,750	$102,000
Short-term notes payable	15,000	10,000
Total current liabilities...............	32,750	112,000
Long-term notes payable	100,000	77,500
Total liabilities	132,750	189,500
Equity		
Common stock, $5 par	215,000	200,000
Paid-in capital in excess		
of par, common stock.............	30,000	0
Retained earnings..................	230,000	125,500
Total liabilities and equity	$607,750	$515,000

GAZELLE CORPORATION Income Statement For Current Year Ended December 31		
Sales		$1,185,000
Cost of goods sold		595,000
Gross profit		590,000
Operating expenses		
Depreciation expense	$ 38,600	
Other expenses	362,850	
Total operating expenses.........		401,450
		188,550
Other gains (losses)		
Loss on sale of equipment.......		(2,100)
Income before taxes.............		186,450
Income taxes expense		28,350
Net income		$ 158,100

Additional Information on Current-Year Transactions

a. The loss on the cash sale of equipment was $2,100 (details in *b*).

b. Sold equipment costing $51,000, with accumulated depreciation of $22,850, for $26,050 cash.

c. Purchased equipment costing $113,250 by paying $43,250 cash and signing a long-term note payable for the balance.

d. Borrowed $5,000 cash by signing a short-term note payable.

e. Paid $47,500 cash to reduce the long-term notes payable.

f. Issued 3,000 shares of common stock for $15 cash per share.

g. Declared and paid cash dividends of $53,600.

Required

1. Prepare a complete statement of cash flows using the *indirect method* for the current year. Disclose any noncash investing and financing activities in a note.

Check   Cash from operating activities, $130,200

Analysis Component

2. Analyze and discuss the statement of cash flows prepared in part 1, giving special attention to the wisdom of the cash dividend payment.

Refer to the information reported about Gazelle Corporation in Problem 12-3B.

Problem 12-4B[A]
Indirect: Cash flows spreadsheet

P4

Required

Prepare a complete statement of cash flows using a spreadsheet as in Exhibit 12A.1 using the *indirect method*. Identify the debits and credits in the Analysis of Changes columns with letters that correspond to the following list of transactions and events.

a. Net income was $158,100.

b. Accounts receivable decreased.

c. Inventory decreased.

d. Prepaid expenses decreased.

e. Accounts payable decreased.

f. Depreciation expense was $38,600.

g. Sold equipment costing $51,000, with accumulated depreciation of $22,850, for $26,050 cash. This yielded a loss of $2,100.

h. Purchased equipment costing $113,250 by paying $43,250 cash and **(i.)** by signing a long-term note payable for the balance.

j. Borrowed $5,000 cash by signing a short-term note payable.

k. Paid $47,500 cash to reduce the long-term notes payable.

l. Issued 3,000 shares of common stock for $15 cash per share.

m. Declared and paid cash dividends of $53,600.

Check   Analysis of Changes column totals, $681,950

Problem 12-5B[B]
Direct: Statement of
cash flows   **P5**

Check   Cash used in
financing activities, $(51,100)

Refer to Gazelle Corporation's financial statements and related information in Problem 12-3B.

Required

Prepare a complete statement of cash flows using the *direct method*. Disclose any noncash investing and financing activities in a note.

Problem 12-6B
Indirect: Statement of
cash flows

P2   P3

Satu Company's current-year income statement, comparative balance sheets, and additional information follow. For the year, (1) all sales are credit sales, (2) all credits to Accounts Receivable reflect cash receipts from customers, (3) all purchases of inventory are on credit, (4) all debits to Accounts Payable reflect cash payments for inventory, (5) Other Expenses are cash expenses, and (6) any change in Income Taxes Payable reflects the accrual and cash payment of taxes.

SATU COMPANY Comparative Balance Sheets		
At December 31	**Current Year**	**Prior Year**
Assets		
Cash............................	$ 58,750	$ 28,400
Accounts receivable	20,222	25,860
Total current assets................	78,972	54,260
Inventory	165,667	140,320
Equipment	107,750	77,500
Accum. depreciation—Equipment	(46,700)	(31,000)
Total assets	$305,689	$241,080
Liabilities and Equity		
Accounts payable	$ 20,372	$157,530
Income taxes payable	2,100	6,100
Total current liabilities..............	22,472	163,630
Equity		
Common stock, $5 par value	40,000	25,000
Paid-in capital in excess		
of par, common stock.............	68,000	20,000
Retained earnings..................	175,217	32,450
Total liabilities and equity...........	$305,689	$241,080

SATU COMPANY Income Statement For Current Year Ended December 31		
Sales		$750,800
Cost of goods sold		269,200
Gross profit		481,600
Operating expenses		
Depreciation expense	$ 15,700	
Other expenses	173,933	189,633
Income before taxes.........		291,967
Income taxes expense		89,200
Net income		$202,767

Additional Information on Current-Year Transactions
  a. Purchased equipment for $30,250 cash.
  b. Issued 3,000 shares of common stock for $21 cash per share.
  c. Declared and paid $60,000 of cash dividends.

Check   Cash from operating
activities, $57,600

Required

Prepare a complete statement of cash flows using the *indirect method* for the current year.

Problem 12-7B[A]
Indirect: Cash flows
spreadsheet

P4

Refer to the information reported about Satu Company in Problem 12-6B.

Required

Prepare a complete statement of cash flows using a spreadsheet as in Exhibit 12A.1 under the *indirect method*. Identify the debits and credits in the Analysis of Changes columns with letters that correspond to the following list of transactions and events.

  a. Net income was $202,767.
  b. Accounts receivable decreased.
  c. Inventory increased.
  d. Accounts payable decreased.
  e. Income taxes payable decreased.

  f. Depreciation expense was $15,700.
  g. Purchased equipment for $30,250 cash.
  h. Issued 3,000 shares at $21 cash per share.
  i. Declared and paid $60,000 of cash dividends.

Check   Analysis of Changes
column totals, $543,860

Problem 12-8B[B]
Direct: Statement of
cash flows   **P5**

Check   Cash provided by
financing activities, $3,000

Refer to Satu Company's financial statements and related information in Problem 12-6B.

Required

Prepare a complete statement of cash flows using the *direct method* for the current year.

This serial problem began in Chapter 1 and continues through most of the book. If previous chapter segments were not completed, the serial problem can begin at this point.

SERIAL PROBLEM
Business Solutions **(Indirect)**

P2   P3

©Alexander Image/Shutterstock

SP 12   Santana Rey, owner of **Business Solutions**, decides to prepare a statement of cash flows for her business. (Although the serial problem allowed for various ownership changes in earlier chapters, we will prepare the statement of cash flows using the following financial data.)

BUSINESS SOLUTIONS Comparative Balance Sheets December 31, 2019, and March 31, 2020		
	Mar. 31, 2020	**Dec. 31, 2019**
Assets		
Cash	$ 68,057	$48,372
Accounts receivable....................	22,867	5,668
Inventory..............................	704	0
Computer supplies	2,005	580
Prepaid insurance......................	1,110	1,665
Prepaid rent	825	825
Total current assets	95,568	57,110
Office equipment	8,000	8,000
Accumulated depreciation—Office equipment	(800)	(400)
Computer equipment....................	20,000	20,000
Accumulated depreciation— Computer equipment...................	(2,500)	(1,250)
Total assets............................	$120,268	$83,460
Liabilities and Equity		
Accounts payable.......................	$ 0	$ 1,100
Wages payable.........................	875	500
Unearned computer service revenue	0	1,500
Total current liabilities	875	3,100
Equity		
Common stock	98,000	73,000
Retained earnings.......................	21,393	7,360
Total liabilities and equity..................	$120,268	$83,460

BUSINESS SOLUTIONS Income Statement For Three Months Ended March 31, 2020		
Computer services revenue..............		$25,307
Net sales		18,693
Total revenue		44,000
Cost of goods sold	$14,052	
Depreciation expense—Office equipment ...	400	
Depreciation expense— Computer equipment.................	1,250	
Wages expense........................	3,250	
Insurance expense.....................	555	
Rent expense	2,475	
Computer supplies expense	1,305	
Advertising expense....................	600	
Mileage expense	320	
Repairs expense—Computer.............	960	
Total expenses		25,167
Net income		$18,833

Required

Prepare a statement of cash flows for Business Solutions using the *indirect method* for the three months ended March 31, 2020. Recall that owner Santana Rey contributed $25,000 to the business in exchange for additional stock in the first quarter of 2020 and has received $4,800 in cash dividends.

Check   Cash flows used by operations: $(515)

The following **General Ledger** assignments highlight the impact, or lack thereof, on the statement of cash flows from summary journal entries derived from consecutive trial balances. Prepare summary journal entries reflecting changes in consecutive trial balances. Then prepare the statement of cash flows (direct method) from those entries. Finally, prepare the reconciliation to the indirect method for net cash provided (used) by operating activities.

GL 12-1   General Ledger assignment based on Exercise 12-11

GL 12-2   General Ledger assignment based on Problem 12-1

GL 12-3   General Ledger assignment based on Problem 12-6

GENERAL LEDGER PROBLEM

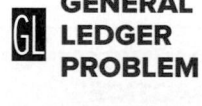

Accounting Analysis

AA 12-1   Use **Apple**'s financial statements in Appendix A to answer the following.

1. Is Apple's statement of cash flows prepared under the direct method or the indirect method?
2. For each fiscal year 2017, 2016, and 2015, identify the amount of cash provided by operating activities and cash paid for dividends.
3. In 2017, did Apple have sufficient cash flows from operations to pay dividends?
4. Did Apple spend more or less cash to repurchase common stock in 2017 versus 2016?

COMPANY ANALYSIS

A1    **APPLE**

COMPARATIVE ANALYSIS

A1

APPLE

GOOGLE

AA 12-2 Key figures for **Apple** and **Google** follow.

$ millions	Apple			Google		
	Current Year	1 Year Prior	2 Years Prior	Current Year	1 Year Prior	2 Years Prior
Operating cash flows	$ 63,598	$ 65,824	$ 81,266	$ 37,091	$ 36,036	$ 26,572
Total assets	375,319	321,686	290,345	197,295	167,497	147,461

Required

1. Compute the recent two years' cash flow on total assets ratios for Apple and Google.
2. For the current year, which company has the better cash flow on total assets ratio?
3. For the current year, does cash flow on total assets outperform or underperform the industry (assumed) average of 15% for (*a*) Apple and (*b*) Google?

GLOBAL ANALYSIS

C1

Samsung

APPLE

GOOGLE

AA 12-3 Key comparative information for **Samsung**, **Apple**, and **Google** follows.

In millions	Samsung			Apple		Google	
	Current Year	1 Year Prior	2 Years Prior	Current Year	1 Year Prior	Current Year	1 Year Prior
Operating cash flows	₩ 62,162,041	₩ 47,385,644	₩ 40,061,761	$ 63,598	$ 65,824	$ 37,091	$ 36,036
Total assets	301,752,090	262,174,324	242,179,521	375,319	321,686	197,295	167,497

Required

1. Compute the recent two years' cash flow on total assets ratio for Samsung.
2. Is the change in Samsung's cash flow on total assets ratio favorable or unfavorable?
3. For the current year, is Samsung's cash flow on total assets ratio better or worse than (*a*) Apple's and (*b*) Google's?

Beyond the Numbers

ETHICS CHALLENGE

C1   A1

BTN 12-1 Katie Murphy is preparing for a meeting with her banker. Her business is finishing its fourth year of operations. In the first year, it had negative cash flows from operations. In the second and third years, cash flows from operations were positive. However, inventory costs rose significantly in Year 4, and cash flows from operations will probably be down 25%. Murphy wants to secure a line of credit from her banker as a financing buffer. From experience, she knows the banker will scrutinize operating cash flows for Years 1 through 4 and will want a projected number for Year 5. Murphy knows that a steady progression upward in operating cash flows for Years 1 through 4 will help her case. She decides to use her discretion as owner and considers several business actions that will turn her operating cash flow in Year 4 from a decrease to an increase.

Required

1. Identify two business actions Murphy might take to improve cash flows from operations.
2. Comment on the ethics and possible consequences of Murphy's decision to pursue these actions.

COMMUNICATING IN PRACTICE

C1

BTN 12-2 Your friend, Diana Wood, recently completed the second year of her business and just received annual financial statements from her accountant. Wood finds the income statement and balance sheet informative but does not understand the statement of cash flows. She says the first section is especially confusing because it contains a lot of additions and subtractions that do not make sense to her. Wood adds, "The income statement tells me the business is more profitable than last year and that's most important. If I want to know how cash changes, I can look at comparative balance sheets."

Required

Write a half-page memorandum to your friend explaining the purpose of the statement of cash flows. Speculate as to why the first section is so confusing and how it might be rectified.

TAKING IT TO THE NET

A1

BTN 12-3 Access the April 14, 2016, filing of the 10-K report (for year ending December 31, 2015) of **Mendocino Brewing Company, Inc.** (ticker: MENB) at **SEC.gov**.

Required

1. Does Mendocino Brewing use the direct or indirect method to construct its consolidated statement of cash flows?

2. For the year ended December 31, 2015, what is the largest item in reconciling the net income (or loss) to net cash provided by operating activities?

3. In the recent two years, has the company been more successful in generating operating cash flows or in generating net income? Identify the figures to support the answer.

4. In the year ended December 31, 2015, what was the largest cash outflow for investing activities *and* for financing activities?

5. What item(s) does the company report as supplemental cash flow information?

6. Does the company report any noncash financing activities for 2015? Identify them, if any.

BTN 12-4 Team members are to coordinate and independently answer one question within each of the following three sections. Team members should then report to the team and confirm or correct teammates' answers.

1. Answer *one* of the following questions about the statement of cash flows: (*a*) What are this statement's reporting objectives? (*b*) What two methods are used to prepare it? Identify similarities and differences between them. (*c*) What steps are followed to prepare the statement? (*d*) What types of analyses are often made from this statement's information?

2. Identify and explain the adjustment from net income to obtain cash flows from operating activities using the indirect method for *one* of the following items: (*a*) Noncash operating revenues and expenses. (*b*) Nonoperating gains and losses. (*c*) Increases and decreases in noncash current assets. (*d*) Increases and decreases in current liabilities.

3.[B] Identify and explain the formula for computing cash flows from operating activities using the direct method for *one* of the following items: (*a*) Cash receipts from sales to customers. (*b*) Cash paid for inventory. (*c*) Cash paid for wages and operating expenses. (*d*) Cash paid for interest and taxes.

BTN 12-5 Review the chapter's opener involving **Vera Bradley** and its founder, Barbara Bradley.

Required

1. In a business such as Vera Bradley, monitoring cash flow is always a priority. Explain how cash flow can lag behind net income.

2. What are potential sources of financing for Vera Bradley's future expansion?

ENTREPRENEURIAL DECISION

C1 A1

BTN 12-6 Jenna and Matt Wilder are completing their second year operating Mountain High, a downhill ski area and resort. Mountain High reports a net loss of $(10,000) for its second year, which includes an $85,000 unusual loss from fire. This past year also involved major purchases of plant assets for renovation and expansion, yielding a year-end total asset amount of $800,000. Mountain High's net cash outflow for its second year is $(5,000); a summarized version of its statement of cash flows follows.

ENTREPRENEURIAL DECISION

C1 A1

Net cash flow provided by operating activities	$ 295,000
Net cash flow used by investing activities	(310,000)
Net cash flow provided by financing activities	10,000

Required

Write a one-page memorandum to the Wilders evaluating Mountain High's current performance and assessing its future. Give special emphasis to cash flow data and their interpretation.

BTN 12-7 Visit **The Motley Fool**'s web page on cash flow based valuation (**Fool.com/how-to-invest/how-to-value-stocks-cash-flow-based-valuations.aspx**).

Required

1. How does the Motley Fool define cash flow? What is the reasoning for this definition?

2. Per the Fool's instruction, why do analysts focus on earnings before interest and taxes (EBIT)?

3. Visit other links at this website that interest you such as "How to Read a Balance Sheet," or find out what the "Fool's Ratio" is. Write a half-page report on what you find.

HITTING THE ROAD

C1

13 Analysis of Financial Statements

Chapter Preview

BASICS OF ANALYSIS	HORIZONTAL ANALYSIS	VERTICAL ANALYSIS	RATIO ANALYSIS AND REPORTING
C1 Analysis purpose	**P1** Application of:	**P2** Application of:	**P3** Liquidity and efficiency
Building blocks	Comparative balance sheets	Common-size balance sheet	Solvency
C2 Standards for comparisons	Comparative income statements	Common-size income statement	Profitability
Analysis tools	Trend analysis	Common-size graphics	Market prospects
			A1 Analysis reports
	NTK 13-1	**NTK 13-2**	**NTK 13-3**

Learning Objectives

CONCEPTUAL

C1 Explain the purpose and identify the building blocks of analysis.

C2 Describe standards for comparisons in analysis.

ANALYTICAL

A1 Summarize and report results of analysis.

A2 *Appendix 13A*—Explain the form and assess the content of a complete income statement.

PROCEDURAL

P1 Explain and apply methods of horizontal analysis.

P2 Describe and apply methods of vertical analysis.

P3 Define and apply ratio analysis.

Numbers Rule

"Expect to win!"—**CARLA HARRIS**

NEW YORK—"I grew up as an only child in a no-nonsense, no-excuses household," recalls Carla Harris. "My parents gave me the sense that I was supposed to do well." Fast-forward and Carla is now vice chair of **Morgan Stanley**'s (**MorganStanley.com**) prized Global Wealth Management division and past-chair of the Morgan Stanley Foundation.

Carla Harris and her colleagues at Morgan Stanley analyze financial statements for profit. One of Morgan Stanley's key tools for analysis is *ModelWare*. ModelWare is a framework to analyze the nuts and bolts of companies' financial statements and then to compare those companies head-to-head. One of its key aims is to provide comparable information that focuses on sustainable performance.

Morgan Stanley uses the accounting numbers in financial statements to produce comparable metrics using techniques such as horizontal and vertical analysis. It also computes financial ratios for analysis and interpretation. Those ratios include return on equity, return on assets, asset turnover, profit margin, price-to-earnings, and many other accounting measures. The focus is to uncover the drivers of profitability and to predict future levels of those drivers.

Carla has experienced much success through analyzing financial statements. As Carla likes to say, "I'm tough and

©Jonathan Leibson/AOL/Getty Images

analytical!" She says that people do not take full advantage of information available in financial statements.

Carla plays by the rules and asserts that those with accounting know-how continue to earn profits from financial statement analysis and interpretation. Carla is proud of her success and adds: "Always start from a place of doing the right thing."

Sources: *Morgan Stanley website*, January 2019; *MorganStanleyIQ*, November 2007; *Alumni.HBS.edu/Stories*, September 2006; *Fortune*, August 2013 and March 2016

BASICS OF ANALYSIS

Financial statement analysis applies analytical tools to financial statements and related data for making business decisions.

C1_____

Explain the purpose and identify the building blocks of analysis.

Purpose of Analysis

Internal users of accounting information manage and operate the company. They include managers, officers, and internal auditors. The purpose of financial statement analysis for internal users is to provide information to improve efficiency and effectiveness.

External users of accounting information are *not* directly involved in running the company. External users use financial statement analysis to pursue their own goals. Shareholders and creditors assess company performance to make investing and lending decisions. A board of directors analyzes financial statements to monitor management's performance. External auditors use financial statements to assess "fair presentation" of financial results.

Point: Financial statement analysis is a topic on the CPA, CMA, CIA, and CFA exams.

The common goal of these users is to evaluate company performance and financial condition. This includes evaluating past and current performance, current financial position, and future performance and risk.

Building Blocks of Analysis

Financial statement analysis focuses on one or more of the four *building blocks* of financial statement analysis. The four building blocks cover different, but interrelated, aspects of financial condition or performance.

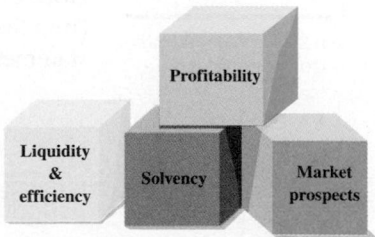

- **Liquidity** and **efficiency**—ability to meet short-term obligations and to efficiently generate revenues.
- **Solvency**—ability to meet long-term obligations and generate future revenues.
- **Profitability**—ability to provide financial rewards to attract and retain financing.
- **Market prospects**—ability to generate positive market expectations.

Information for Analysis

Financial analysis uses **general-purpose financial statements** that include the (1) income statement, (2) balance sheet, (3) statement of stockholders' equity (or statement of retained earnings), (4) statement of cash flows, and (5) notes to these statements.

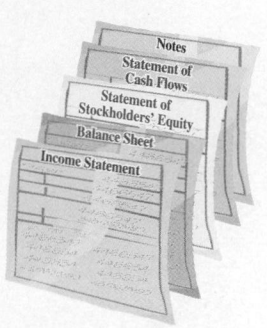

Financial reporting is the communication of financial information useful for making investment, credit, and other business decisions. Financial reporting includes general-purpose financial statements, information from SEC 10-K and other filings, press releases, shareholders' meetings, forecasts, management letters, and auditors' reports.

Management's Discussion and Analysis (MD&A) is one example of useful information outside usual financial statements. **Apple**'s MD&A (available at **Investor.Apple.com** and "Item 7" in the annual report) begins with an overview, followed by critical accounting policies and estimates. It then discusses operating results followed by financial condition (liquidity, capital resources, and cash flows). The final few parts discuss risks. The MD&A is an excellent starting point in understanding a company's business.

Standards for Comparisons

C2

Describe standards for comparisons in analysis.

When analyzing financial statements, we use the following standards (benchmarks) for comparisons. Benchmarks from a competitor or group of competitors are often best. Intracompany and industry measures are also good. Guidelines can be applied, but only if they seem reasonable given recent experience.

Point: Each chapter's Accounting Analysis problems cover *intra-company* analysis. *Comparative Analysis* problems cover competitor analysis (**Apple** vs. **Google** vs. **Samsung**).

- *Intracompany*—The company's current performance is compared to its prior performance and its relations between financial items. Apple's current net income, for example, can be compared with its prior years' net income and in relation to its revenues or total assets.
- *Competitor*—Competitors provide standards for comparisons. **Coca-Cola**'s profit margin can be compared with **PepsiCo**'s profit margin.
- *Industry*—Industry statistics provide standards of comparisons. **Intel**'s profit margin can be compared with the industry's profit margin.
- *Guidelines (rules of thumb)*—Standards of comparison can develop from experience. Examples are the 2:1 level for the current ratio or 1:1 level for the acid-test ratio.

Tools of Analysis

There are three common tools of financial statement analysis. This chapter describes these analysis tools and how to apply them.

1. **Horizontal analysis**—comparison of financial condition and performance across time.
2. **Vertical analysis**—comparison of financial condition and performance to a base amount.
3. **Ratio analysis**—measurement of key relations between financial statement items.

■ **Decision Insight**

Stock in Trade   *Blue chips* are stocks of big, established companies. The phrase comes from poker, where the most valuable chips are blue. *Brokers* execute orders to buy or sell stock. The term comes from wine retailers—individuals who broach (break) wine casks. ■

HORIZONTAL ANALYSIS

P1

Explain and apply methods of horizontal analysis.

Horizontal analysis is the review of financial statement data *across time*. *Horizontal* comes from the left-to-right (or right-to-left) movement of our eyes as we review comparative financial statements across time.

Comparative Statements

Comparative financial statements show financial amounts in side-by-side columns on a single statement, called a *comparative format*. Using **Apple**'s financial statements, this section explains how to compute dollar changes and percent changes for comparative statements.

Dollar Changes and Percent Changes

Dollar Changes and Percent Changes   Comparing financial statements is often done by analyzing dollar amount changes and percent changes in line items. Both analyses are relevant because small dollar changes can yield large percent changes inconsistent with their importance. A 50% change from a base figure of $100 is less important than a 50% change from a base amount of $100,000. We compute the *dollar change* for a financial statement item as follows.

$$\text{Dollar change} = \text{Analysis period amount} - \text{Base period amount}$$

Analysis period refers to the financial statements under analysis, and *base period* refers to the financial statements used for comparison. The prior year is commonly used as a base period. We compute the *percent change* as follows.

$$\text{Percent change (\%)} = \frac{\text{Analysis period amount} - \text{Base period amount}}{\text{Base period amount}} \times 100$$

We must know a few rules in working with percent changes. Let's look at four separate cases.

- **Cases A and B:** When a negative amount is in one period and a positive amount is in the other, we cannot compute a meaningful percent change.
- **Case C:** When no amount is in the base period, no percent change is computable.
- **Case D:** When a positive amount is in the base period and zero is in the analysis period, the decrease is 100%.

Example: When there is a value in the base period and zero in the analysis period, the decrease is 100%. Why isn't the reverse situation an increase of 100%? *Answer:* A 100% increase of zero is still zero.

Case	Analysis Period	Base Period	Change Analysis Dollar	Change Analysis Percent
A	$ 1,500	$(4,500)	$ 6,000	—
B	(1,000)	2,000	(3,000)	—
C	8,000	—	8,000	—
D	0	10,000	(10,000)	(100%)

Comparative Balance Sheets

Comparative Balance Sheets   Analysis of comparative financial statements begins by focusing on large dollar and percent changes. We then identify the reasons and implications for these changes. We also review small changes when we expected large changes.

Exhibit 13.1 shows comparative balance sheets for **Apple Inc.** (ticker: AAPL). A few items stand out on the asset side. Apple's short-term marketable securities increased by 15.5%, and its long-term marketable securities increased by 14.2%. This combined for a large $31,505 million increase in securities. In response, Apple raised its dividend and announced plans to spend at least $210 billion buying back stock by the end of the next year. Dividends and share repurchase plans are likely to slow Apple's growth of short-term securities. Other notable increases occur with (1) property, plant and equipment, partially related to its new headquarters, and (2) inventories, which had a high percentage increase but relatively small dollar increase.

On Apple's financing side, we see its overall 16.7% increase is driven by a 24.7% increase in liabilities; equity increased only 4.5%. The largest increase is from long-term debt, which increased by $21,780 million, or 28.9%. Much of this increase results from bond offerings by Apple to take advantage of low interest rates. We also see a modest increase of 2.0% ($1,966 million) in retained earnings, which was increased by a strong income of $48,351 million and reduced by cash dividends and stock repurchases.

Comparative Income Statements

Comparative Income Statements   Exhibit 13.2 shows Apple's comparative income statements. Apple reports an increase in sales of 6.3%. Cost of sales increased to a greater extent than sales (7.4%), which is not a positive sign. The 10.7% increase in operating expenses is primarily driven by the 15.3% increase in research and development costs, from which management and investors hope to reap future income. While Apple's net income increased just 5.8%, its basic earnings per share increased 11.0%. This is largely due to Apple's share buyback program.

EXHIBIT 13.1

Comparative Balance Sheets

APPLE

APPLE INC. Comparative Year-End Balance Sheets				
$ millions	Current Yr	Prior Yr	Dollar Change	Percent Change
Assets				
Cash and cash equivalents	$ 20,289	$ 20,484	$ (195)	(1.0)%
Short-term marketable securities	53,892	46,671	7,221	15.5
Accounts receivable, net	17,874	15,754	2,120	13.5
Inventories	4,855	2,132	2,723	127.7
Vendor non-trade receivables	17,799	13,545	4,254	31.4
Other current assets	13,936	8,283	5,653	68.2
Total current assets	128,645	106,869	21,776	20.4
Long-term marketable securities	194,714	170,430	24,284	14.2
Property, plant and equipment, net	33,783	27,010	6,773	25.1
Goodwill	5,717	5,414	303	5.6
Acquired intangible assets, net	2,298	3,206	(908)	(28.3)
Other non-current assets	10,162	8,757	1,405	16.0
Total assets	$375,319	$321,686	$53,633	16.7
Liabilities				
Accounts payable	$ 49,049	$ 37,294	$11,755	31.5%
Accrued expenses	25,744	22,027	3,717	16.9
Deferred revenue	7,548	8,080	(532)	(6.6)
Commercial paper	11,977	8,105	3,872	47.8
Current portion of long-term debt	6,496	3,500	2,996	85.6
Total current liabilities	100,814	79,006	21,808	27.6
Deferred revenue—non-current	2,836	2,930	(94)	(3.2)
Long-term debt	97,207	75,427	21,780	28.9
Other non-current liabilities	40,415	36,074	4,341	12.0
Total liabilities	241,272	193,437	47,835	24.7
Stockholders' Equity				
Common stock	35,867	31,251	4,616	14.8
Retained earnings	98,330	96,364	1,966	2.0
Accumulated other comprehensive income	(150)	634	(784)	—
Total stockholders' equity	134,047	128,249	5,798	4.5
Total liabilities and stockholders' equity	$375,319	$321,686	$53,633	16.7

EXHIBIT 13.2

Comparative Income Statements

APPLE

APPLE INC. Comparative Income Statements				
$ millions, except per share	Current Yr	Prior Yr	Dollar Change	Percent Change
Net sales	$229,234	$215,639	$13,595	6.3%
Cost of sales	141,048	131,376	9,672	7.4
Gross margin	88,186	84,263	3,923	4.7
Research and development	11,581	10,045	1,536	15.3
Selling, general and administrative	15,261	14,194	1,067	7.5
Total operating expenses	26,842	24,239	2,603	10.7
Operating income	61,344	60,024	1,320	2.2
Other income, net	2,745	1,348	1,397	103.6
Income before provision for income taxes	64,089	61,372	2,717	4.4
Provision for income taxes	15,738	15,685	53	0.3
Net income	$ 48,351	$ 45,687	2,664	5.8
Basic earnings per share	$ 9.27	$ 8.35	$ 0.92	11.0
Diluted earnings per share	$ 9.21	$ 8.31	$ 0.90	10.8

Point: Percent change is also computed by dividing the current period by the prior period and then subtracting 1.0.

Trend Analysis

Trend analysis is computing trend percents that show patterns in data across periods. Trend percent is computed as follows.

$$\text{Trend percent (\%)} = \frac{\text{Analysis period amount}}{\text{Base period amount}} \times 100$$

Financial Results

Point: *Index* refers to the comparison of the analysis period to the base period. Percents determined for each period are called *index numbers.*

Trend analysis is shown in Exhibit 13.3 using data from Apple's current and prior financial statements.

$ millions	Current Yr	1 Yr Ago	2 Yrs Ago	3 Yrs Ago	4 Yrs Ago
Net sales....................	$229,234	$215,639	$233,715	$182,795	$170,910
Cost of sales.................	141,048	131,376	140,089	112,258	106,606
Operating expenses...........	26,842	24,239	22,396	18,034	15,305

EXHIBIT 13.3

Sales and Expenses

The trend percents—using data from Exhibit 13.3—are shown in Exhibit 13.4. The base period is the number reported four years ago, and the trend percent is computed for each year by dividing that year's amount by the base period amount. For example, the net sales trend percent for the current year is 134.1%, computed as $229,234/$170,910.

Point: Trend analysis expresses a percent of base, not a percent of change.

In trend percent	Current Yr	1 Yr Ago	2 Yrs Ago	3 Yrs Ago	4 Yrs Ago
Net sales....................	134.1%	126.2%	136.7%	107.0%	100.0%
Cost of sales.................	132.3	123.2	131.4	105.3	100.0
Operating expenses...........	175.4	158.4	146.3	117.8	100.0

EXHIBIT 13.4

Trend Percents for Sales and Expenses

Exhibit 13.5 shows the trend percents from Exhibit 13.4 in a *line graph,* which helps us see trends and detect changes in direction or magnitude. It shows that the trend line for operating expenses exceeds net sales in each of the years shown. This is not positive for Apple. Apple's net income will suffer if expenses rise faster than sales.

Exhibit 13.6 compares Apple's revenue trend line to those of **Google** and **Samsung**. Google was able to grow revenue in each year relative to the base year. Apple was able to grow revenue overall in the last five years, but at a slower pace than Google. Samsung's revenue was mainly flat.

Trend analysis can show relations between items on different

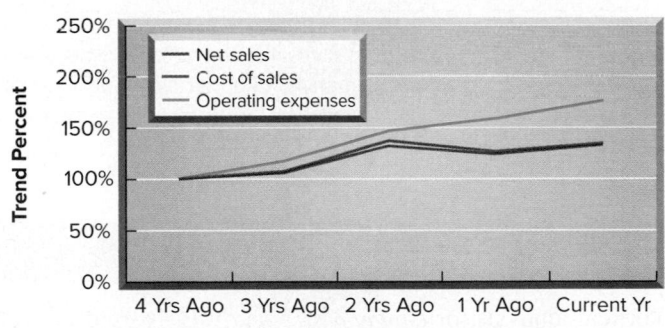

EXHIBIT 13.5

Trend Percent Lines for Apple's Sales and Expenses

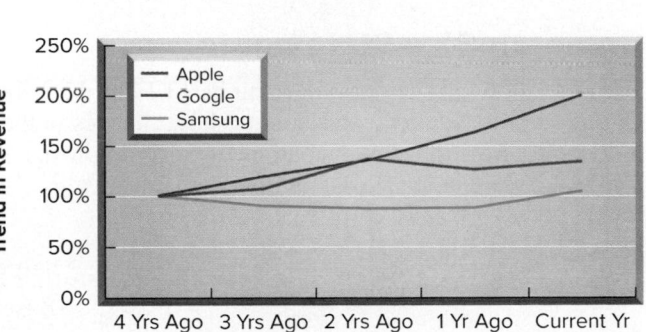

EXHIBIT 13.6

Revenue Trend Percent Lines—Apple, Google, and Samsung

APPLE

GOOGLE

Samsung

EXHIBIT 13.7

Sales and Asset Data for Apple

$ millions	Current Yr	4 Yrs Ago	Change
Net sales..............	$229,234	$170,910	34.1%
Total assets............	375,319	207,000	81.3

financial statements. Exhibit 13.7 compares Apple's net sales and total assets. The increase in total assets (81.3%) has exceeded the increase in net sales (34.1%). Is this result favorable or not? One interpretation is that Apple was *less* efficient in using its assets in the current year versus four years ago.

■ **Decision Maker**

Auditor Your tests reveal a 3% increase in sales from $200,000 to $206,000 and a 4% decrease in expenses from $190,000 to $182,400. Both changes are within your "reasonableness" criterion of ±5%, and thus you don't pursue additional tests. The audit partner in charge questions your lack of follow-up and mentions the *joint relation* between sales and expenses. What is the partner referring to? ■ *Answer:* Both *individual* accounts (sales and expenses) yield percent changes within the ±5% acceptable range. However, a *joint analysis* shows an increase in sales and a decrease in expenses producing a more than 5% increase in income. This client's profit margin is 11.46% (($206,000 − $182,400)/$206,000) for the current year compared with 5.0% (($200,000 − $190,000)/$200,000) for the prior year—a 129% increase!

NEED-TO-KNOW 13-1

Horizontal Analysis

P1

Compute trend percents for the following accounts using 3 Years Ago as the base year. Indicate whether the trend appears to be favorable or unfavorable for each account.

$ millions	Current Yr	1 Yr Ago	2 Yrs Ago	3 Yrs Ago
Sales	$500	$350	$250	$200
Cost of goods sold	400	175	100	50

Solution

$ millions	Current Yr	1 Yr Ago	2 Yrs Ago	3 Yrs Ago
Sales	250%	175%	125%	100%
	($500/$200)	($350/$200)	($250/$200)	($200/$200)
Cost of goods sold	800%	350%	200%	100%
	($400/$50)	($175/$50)	($100/$50)	($50/$50)

Analysis: The trend in sales is favorable; however, we need more information about economic conditions and competitors' performances to better assess it. Cost of goods sold also is rising (as expected with increasing sales). However, cost of goods sold is rising faster than the increase in sales, which is bad news.

Do More: QS 13-3, QS 13-4, E 13-3

VERTICAL ANALYSIS

P2_____

Describe and apply methods of vertical analysis.

Vertical analysis, or *common-size analysis,* is used to evaluate individual financial statement items or a group of items. *Vertical* comes from the up-down [or down-up] movement of our eyes as we review common-size financial statements.

Common-Size Statements

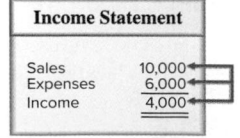

Income Statement	
Sales	10,000
Expenses	6,000
Income	4,000

Point: Numerator and denominator in common-size percent are taken from the same financial statement and from the same period.

The comparative statements in Exhibits 13.1 and 13.2 show the change in each item over time. **Common-size financial statements** show changes in the relative importance of each financial statement item. All individual amounts in common-size statements are shown in common-size percents. A *common-size percent* is calculated as

$$\text{Common-size percent (\%)} = \frac{\text{Analysis amount}}{\text{Base amount}} \times 100$$

Common-Size Balance Sheets

Common-size statements show each item as a percent of a *base amount,* which for a common-size balance sheet is total assets. The base amount is assigned a value of 100%. (Total liabilities plus equity also equals 100% because this amount equals total assets.) We then compute a common-size percent for each asset, liability, and equity item using total assets as the base amount.

Exhibit 13.8 shows common-size comparative balance sheets for **Apple**. Two results that stand out on both a magnitude and percentage basis include (1) issuance of long-term debt—a 2.5% increase from 23.4% to 25.9%, the largest of any liability, and (2) a 3.8% decrease in retained earnings and 1% decrease in cash and cash equivalents, largely the result of cash dividends and stock buybacks. The absence of other substantial changes in Apple's balance sheet suggests a mature company, but with some lack of focus as evidenced by the large amounts for securities. This buildup in securities is a concern as the return on securities is historically smaller than the return on operating assets.

Point: Common-size statements often are used to compare companies in the same industry.

Common-Size Income Statements

Analysis also involves the use of a common-size income statement. Revenue is the base amount, which is assigned a value of 100%. Each income statement item is shown as a percent of revenue. If we think of the 100% revenue amount

EXHIBIT 13.8

Common-Size Comparative Balance Sheets

APPLE

APPLE INC. Common-Size Comparative Year-End Balance Sheets			Common-Size Percents*	
$ millions	Current Yr	Prior Yr	Current Yr	Prior Yr
Assets				
Cash and cash equivalents	$ 20,289	$ 20,484	5.4%	6.4%
Short-term marketable securities	53,892	46,671	14.4	14.5
Accounts receivable, net	17,874	15,754	4.8	4.9
Inventories	4,855	2,132	1.3	0.7
Vendor non-trade receivables.	17,799	13,545	4.7	4.2
Other current assets.	13,936	8,283	3.7	2.6
Total current assets	128,645	106,869	34.3	33.2
Long-term marketable securities	194,714	170,430	51.9	53.0
Property, plant and equipment, net	33,783	27,010	9.0	8.4
Goodwill	5,717	5,414	1.5	1.7
Acquired intangible assets, net.	2,298	3,206	0.6	1.0
Other non-current assets.	10,162	8,757	2.7	2.7
Total assets.	$375,319	$321,686	100.0%	100.0%
Liabilities				
Accounts payable.	$ 49,049	$ 37,294	13.1%	11.6%
Accrued expenses	25,744	22,027	6.9	6.8
Deferred revenue.	7,548	8,080	2.0	2.5
Commercial paper	11,977	8,105	3.2	2.5
Current portion of long-term debt.	6,496	3,500	1.7	1.1
Total current liabilities	100,814	79,006	26.9	24.6
Deferred revenue—noncurrent.	2,836	2,930	0.8	0.9
Long-term debt.	97,207	75,427	25.9	23.4
Other non-current liabilties	40,415	36,074	10.8	11.2
Total liabilities.	241,272	193,437	64.3	60.1
Stockholders' Equity				
Common stock	35,867	31,251	9.6	9.7
Retained earnings	98,330	96,364	26.2	30.0
Accumulated other comprehensive income	(150)	634	0.0	0.2
Total stockholders' equity	134,047	128,249	35.7	39.9
Total liabilities and stockholders' equity.	$375,319	$321,686	100.0%	100.0%

*Percents are rounded to tenths and thus may not exactly sum to totals and subtotals.

EXHIBIT 13.9

Common-Size Comparative
Income Statements

APPLE

APPLE INC. Common-Size Comparative Income Statements				
			Common-Size Percents*	
$ millions	Current Yr	Prior Yr	Current Yr	Prior Yr
Net sales	$229,234	$215,639	100.0%	100.0%
Cost of sales	141,048	131,376	61.5	60.9
Gross margin.	88,186	84,263	38.5	39.1
Research and development	11,581	10,045	5.1	4.7
Selling, general and administrative	15,261	14,194	6.7	6.6
Total operating expenses	26,842	24,239	11.7	11.2
Operating income	61,344	60,024	26.8	27.8
Other income, net	2,745	1,348	1.2	0.6
Income before provision for income taxes	64,089	61,372	28.0	28.5
Provision for income taxes	15,738	15,685	6.9	7.3
Net income	$ 48,351	$ 45,687	21.1%	21.2%

*Percents are rounded to tenths and thus may not exactly sum to totals and subtotals.

as representing one sales dollar, the remaining items show how each revenue dollar is distributed among costs, expenses, and income.

Exhibit 13.9 shows common-size comparative income statements for each dollar of Apple's net sales. The past two years' common-size numbers are similar with two exceptions. One is the increase of 0.4 cents in research and development costs, which can be a positive development if these costs lead to future revenues. Another is the increase in cost of sales of 0.6 cent and increase in selling, general and administrative costs of 0.1 cent. We must monitor the growth in these expenses.

EXHIBIT 13.10

Common-Size Graphic of
Income Statement

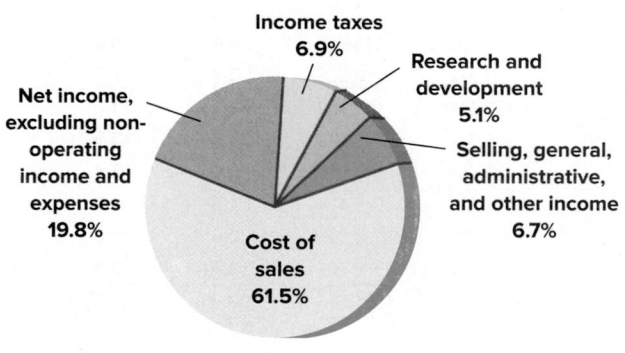

Common-Size Graphics

Exhibit 13.10 is a graphic of Apple's current-year common-size income statement. This pie chart shows the contribution of each cost component of net sales for net income.

Exhibit 13.11 takes data from Apple's *Segments* footnote. The exhibit shows the level of net sales for each of Apple's five operating segments. Its Americas segment generates $96.6 billion net sales, which is roughly 42% of its total sales. Within each bar is that segment's operating income margin (Operating income/Segment net sales). The Americas segment has a 32% operating income margin. This type of graphic can raise questions about the profitability of each segment and lead to discussion of further expansions into more profitable segments. For example, the Japan segment has an operating margin of 46%. A natural question for management is what potential is there to expand sales into the Japan segment and maintain

EXHIBIT 13.11

Sales and Operating
Income Margin Breakdown
by Segment

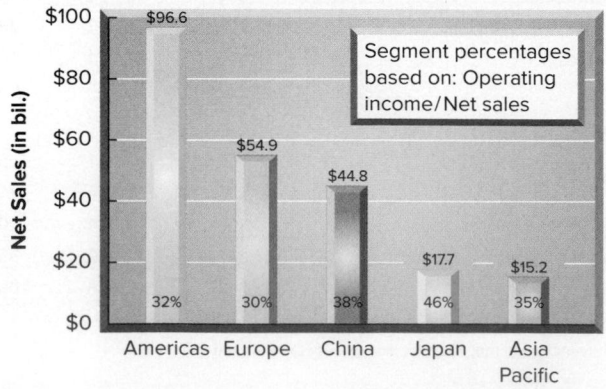

this operating margin? This type of analysis can help determine strategic plans.

Graphics also are used to identify (1) sources of financing, including the distribution among current liabilities, noncurrent liabilities, and equity capital, and (2) focuses of investing activities, including the distribution among current and noncurrent assets. Exhibit 13.12 shows a common-size graphic of Apple's assets, a high percentage of which are in securities, followed by property, plant and equipment.

Common-size financial statements are useful in comparing companies. Exhibit 13.13 shows common-size graphics of Apple, **Google**, and **Samsung** on financing sources. This graphic shows the larger percent of equity financing for Google versus Apple and Samsung. It also shows the larger noncurrent debt financing of Apple versus Google and Samsung. Comparison of a company's common-size statements with competitors' or industry common-size statistics alerts us to differences in the structure of its financial statements.

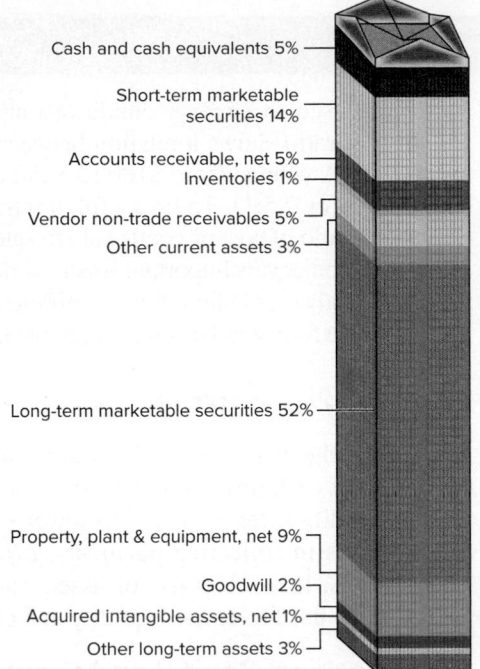

EXHIBIT 13.12

Common-Size Graphic of Asset Components

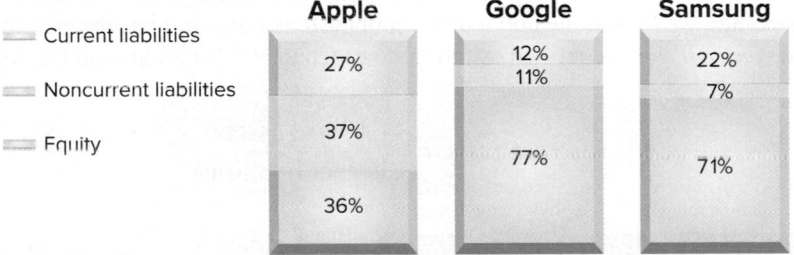

EXHIBIT 13.13

Common-Size Graphic of Financing Sources— Competitor Analysis

APPLE

GOOGLE

Samsung

Ethical Risk

Truth Be Told   In a survey of nearly 200 CFOs of large companies, roughly 20% say that firms use accounting tools to report earnings that do not fully reflect the firms' underlying operations. One goal of financial analysis is to see through such ploys. The top reasons CFOs gave for this were to impact stock price, hit an earnings target, and influence executive pay (*The Wall Street Journal*). ∎

Express the following comparative income statements in common-size percents and assess whether this company's situation has improved in the current year.

Comparative Income Statements		
For Years Ended December 31	Current Yr	Prior Yr
Sales	$800	$500
Total expenses	560	400
Net income	$240	$100

Solution

	Current Yr	Prior Yr
Sales	100% ($800/$800)	100% ($500/$500)
Total expenses	70% ($560/$800)	80% ($400/$500)
Net income	30%	20%

Analysis: This company's situation has improved. This is evident from its substantial increase in net income as a percent of sales for the current year (30%) relative to the prior year (20%). Further, the company's sales increased from $500 to $800 (while expenses declined as a percent of sales from 80% to 70%).

NEED-TO-KNOW 13-2

Vertical Analysis

P2

Do More: QS 13-5, E 13-4, E 13-5, E 13-6

RATIO ANALYSIS

P3
Define and apply ratio analysis.

Ratios are used to uncover conditions and trends difficult to detect by looking at individual amounts. A ratio shows a relation between two amounts. It can be shown as a percent, rate, or proportion. A change from $100 to $250 can be shown as (1) 150% increase, (2) 2.5 times, or (3) 2.5 to 1 (or 2.5:1). To be useful, a ratio must show an economically important relation. For example, a ratio of cost of goods sold to sales is useful, but a ratio of freight costs to patents is not.

This section covers important financial ratios organized into the four building blocks of financial statement analysis: (1) liquidity and efficiency, (2) solvency, (3) profitability, and (4) market prospects. We use four standards for comparison: intracompany, competitor, industry, and guidelines.

Liquidity and Efficiency

Liquidity is the availability of resources to pay short-term cash requirements. It is affected by the timing of cash inflows and outflows along with prospects for future performance. A lack of liquidity often is linked to lower profitability. To creditors, lack of liquidity can cause delays in collecting payments. *Efficiency* is how productive a company is in using its assets. Inefficient use of assets can cause liquidity problems. This section covers key ratios used to assess liquidity and efficiency.

Working Capital and Current Ratio   The amount of current assets minus current liabilities is called **working capital,** or *net working capital.* A company that runs low on working capital is less likely to pay debts or to continue operating. When evaluating a company's working capital, we look at the dollar amount of current assets minus current liabilities *and* at their ratio. The *current ratio* is defined as follows (see Chapter 3 for additional explanation).

$$\text{Current ratio} = \frac{\text{Current assets}}{\text{Current liabilities}}$$

EXHIBIT 13.14

Apple's Working Capital and Current Ratio

Current ratio
Google = 5.14
Samsung = 2.19
Industry = 2.5

$ millions	Current Yr	Prior Yr
Current assets.............	$128,645	$106,869
Current liabilities...........	100,814	79,006
Working capital...........	$ 27,831	$ 27,863
Current ratio		
$128,645/$100,814 =	1.28 to 1	
$106,869/$79,006 =		1.35 to 1

Apple's working capital and current ratio are shown in Exhibit 13.14. Also, **Google**'s (5.14), **Samsung**'s (2.19), and the industry's (2.5) current ratios are shown in the margin. Although its ratio (1.28) is lower than competitors' ratios, Apple is not in danger of defaulting on loan payments. A high current ratio suggests a strong ability to meet current obligations. An excessively high current ratio means that the company has invested too much in current assets compared to current obligations. An excessive investment in current assets is not an efficient use of funds because current assets normally earn a low return on investment (compared with long-term assets).

Many analysts use a guideline of 2:1 (or 1.5:1) for the current ratio. A 2:1 or higher ratio is considered low risk in the short run. Analysis of the current ratio, and many other ratios, must consider type of business, composition of current assets, and turnover rate of current asset components.

- **Business Type**   A service company that grants little or no credit and carries few inventories can probably operate on a current ratio of less than 1:1 if its revenues generate enough cash to pay its current liabilities. On the other hand, a company selling high-priced clothing or furniture requires a higher ratio because of difficulties in judging customer demand and cash receipts.

- **Asset Composition**   The composition of assets is important to assess short-term liquidity. For instance, cash, cash equivalents, and short-term investments are more liquid than accounts and notes receivable. An excessive amount of receivables and inventory weakens a company's ability to pay current liabilities.

- **Turnover Rate**   Asset turnover measures efficiency in using assets. A measure of asset efficiency is revenue generated.

Decision Maker

Banker   A company requests a one-year, $200,000 loan for expansion. This company's current ratio is 4:1, with current assets of $160,000. Key competitors have a current ratio of 1.9:1. Using this information, do you approve the loan? ■   *Answer:* The loan application is likely approved for at least two reasons. First, the current ratio suggests an ability to meet short-term obligations. Second, current assets of $160,000 and a current ratio of 4:1 imply current liabilities of $40,000 (one-fourth of current assets) and a working capital excess of $120,000. The working capital is 60% of the loan.

Acid-Test Ratio
Quick assets are cash, short-term investments, and current receivables. These are the most liquid types of current assets. The *acid-test ratio,* also called *quick ratio* and introduced in Chapter 4, evaluates a company's short-term liquidity.

$$\text{Acid-test ratio} = \frac{\text{Cash} + \text{Short-term investments} + \text{Current receivables}}{\text{Current liabilities}}$$

Apple's acid-test ratio is computed in Exhibit 13.15. Apple's acid-test ratio (0.91) is lower than those for Google (4.97), Samsung (1.71), and the 1:1 common guideline for an acceptable acid-test ratio. As with analysis of the current ratio, we must consider other factors. How frequently a company converts its current assets into cash also affects its ability to pay current obligations. This means analysis of short-term liquidity should consider receivables and inventories, which we cover next.

$ millions	Current Yr	Prior Yr
Cash and equivalents............	$ 20,289	$20,484
Short-term securities	53,892	46,671
Current receivables	17,874	15,754
Total quick assets..............	$ 92,055	$82,909
Current liabilities...............	$100,814	$79,006
Acid-test ratio		
$92,055/$100,814 =	0.91 to 1	
$82,909/$79,006 =		1.05 to 1

EXHIBIT 13.15
Acid-Test Ratio

Acid-test ratio
Google = 4.97
Samsung = 1.71
Industry = 0.9

Accounts Receivable Turnover
Accounts receivable turnover measures how frequently a company converts its receivables into cash. This ratio is defined as follows (see Chapter 7 for additional explanation). Apple's accounts receivable turnover is computed next to the formula ($ millions). Apple's turnover of 13.6 exceeds Google's 6.8 and Samsung's 9.2 turnover. Accounts receivable turnover is high when accounts receivable are quickly collected. A high turnover is favorable because it means the company does not tie up assets in accounts receivable. However, accounts receivable turnover can be too high; this can occur when credit terms are so restrictive that they decrease sales.

Accounts receivable turnover
Google = 6.8
Samsung = 9.2
Industry = 5.0

$$\frac{\text{Accounts receivable}}{\text{turnover}} = \frac{\text{Net sales}}{\text{Average accounts receivable, net}} = \frac{\$229,234}{(\$15,754 + \$17,874)/2} = 13.6 \text{ times}$$

Inventory Turnover
Inventory turnover measures how long a company holds inventory before selling it. It is defined as follows (see Chapter 5 for additional explanation). Next to the formula we compute Apple's inventory turnover at 40.4. Apple's inventory turnover is higher than Samsung's 6.0 but lower than Google's 89.6. A company with a high turnover requires a smaller investment in inventory than one producing the same sales with a lower turnover. However, high inventory turnover can be bad if inventory is so low that stock-outs occur.

$$\text{Inventory turnover} = \frac{\text{Cost of goods sold}}{\text{Average inventory}} = \frac{\$141,048}{(\$2,132 + \$4,855)/2} = 40.4 \text{ times}$$

Inventory turnover
Google = 89.6
Samsung = 6.0
Industry = 7.0

©VCG/Getty Images

Days' Sales Uncollected
Days' sales uncollected measures how frequently a company collects accounts receivable and is defined as follows (Chapter 6 provides additional explanation). Apple's days' sales uncollected of 28.5 days is shown next to the formula. Both Google's days' sales uncollected of 60.4 days and Samsung's 48.5 days are more than the 28.5 days for Apple. Days' sales uncollected is more meaningful if we know company credit terms. A rough

guideline states that days' sales uncollected should not exceed $1\frac{1}{3}$ times the days in its (1) credit period, *if* discounts are not offered, or (2) discount period, *if* favorable discounts are offered.

Days' sales uncollected
Google = 60.4
Samsung = 48.5

$$\text{Days' sales uncollected} = \frac{\text{Accounts receivable, net}}{\text{Net sales}} \times 365 = \frac{\$17,874}{\$229,234} \times 365 = 28.5 \text{ days}$$

Days' Sales in Inventory

Point: *Average collection period* is estimated by dividing 365 by the accounts receivable turnover ratio. For example, 365 divided by an accounts receivable turnover of 12.6 indicates a 29-day average collection period.

Days' sales in inventory is used to evaluate inventory liquidity. We compute days' sales in inventory as follows (Chapter 5 provides additional explanation). Apple's days' sales in inventory of 12.6 days is shown next to the formula. If the products in Apple's inventory are in demand by customers, this formula estimates that its inventory will be converted into receivables (or cash) in 12.6 days. If all of Apple's sales were credit sales, the conversion of inventory to receivables in 12.6 days *plus* the conversion of receivables to cash in 28.5 days implies that inventory will be converted to cash in about 41.1 days (12.6 + 28.5).

Days' sales in inventory
Google = 6.0
Samsung = 70.5
Industry = 35

$$\text{Days' sales in inventory} = \frac{\text{Ending inventory}}{\text{Cost of goods sold}} \times 365 = \frac{\$4,855}{\$141,048} \times 365 = 12.6 \text{ days}$$

Total Asset Turnover

Total asset turnover measures a company's ability to use its assets to generate sales and reflects on operating efficiency. The definition of this ratio follows (Chapter 8 offers additional explanation). Apple's total asset turnover of 0.66 is shown next to the formula. Apple's turnover is greater than that for Google (0.61), but not Samsung (0.85).

Total asset turnover
Google = 0.61
Samsung = 0.85
Industry = 1.1

$$\text{Total asset turnover} = \frac{\text{Net sales}}{\text{Average total assets}} = \frac{\$229,234}{(\$375,319 + \$321,686)/2} = 0.66 \text{ times}$$

Solvency

Solvency is a company's ability to meet long-term obligations and generate future revenues. Analysis of solvency is long term and uses broader measures than liquidity. An important part of solvency analysis is a company's capital structure. *Capital structure* is a company's makeup of equity and debt financing. Our analysis here focuses on a company's ability to both meet its obligations and provide security to its creditors *over the long run.*

Debt Ratio and Equity Ratio

Point: For analysis purposes, noncontrolling interest is usually included in equity.

One part of solvency analysis is to assess a company's mix of debt and equity financing. The *debt ratio* (described in Chapter 2) shows total liabilities as a percent of total assets. The **equity ratio** shows total equity as a percent of total assets. Apple's debt and equity ratios follow. Apple's ratios reveal more debt than equity. A company is considered less risky if its capital structure (equity plus debt) has more equity. Debt is considered more risky because of its required payments for interest and principal. Stockholders cannot require payment from the company. However, debt can increase income for stockholders if the company earns a higher return than interest paid on the debt.

Point: Total of debt and equity ratios always equals 100%.

Debt ratio :: Equity ratio
Google = 22.7% :: 77.3%
Samsung = 28.9% :: 71.1%
Industry = 35% :: 65%

$ millions	Current Yr	Ratios	
Total liabilities.....................	$241,272	64.3%	[Debt ratio]
Total equity	134,047	35.7%	[Equity ratio]
Total liabilities and equity............	$375,319	100.0%	

Debt-to-Equity Ratio

The *debt-to-equity* ratio is another measure of solvency. We compute the ratio as follows (Chapter 10 offers additional explanation). Apple's debt-to-equity ratio of 1.80 is shown next to the formula. Apple's ratio is higher than those of Google (0.29) and Samsung (0.41), and greater than the industry ratio of 0.6. Apple's capital structure has more debt than equity. Debt must be repaid with interest, while equity does not. Debt payments can be burdensome when the industry and/or the economy experience a downturn.

$$\text{Debt-to-equity ratio} = \frac{\text{Total liabilities}}{\text{Total equity}} = \frac{\$241,272}{\$134,047} = 1.80$$

Debt-to-equity
Google = 0.29
Samsung = 0.41
Industry = 0.6

Times Interest Earned The amount of income before subtracting interest expense and income tax expense is the amount available to pay interest expense. The following *times interest earned* ratio measures a company's ability to pay interest (see Chapter 9 for additional explanation).

$$\text{Times interest earned} = \frac{\text{Income before interest expense and income tax expense}}{\text{Interest expense}}$$

The larger this ratio is, the less risky the company is for creditors. One guideline says that creditors are reasonably safe if the company has a ratio of two or more. Apple's times interest earned ratio of 28.6 follows. It suggests that creditors have little risk of nonrepayment.

$$\frac{\$48,351 + \$2,323 + \$15,738}{\$2,323} = 28.6 \text{ times}$$

Times interest earned
Google = 250.5
Samsung = 86.7

Profitability

Profitability is a company's ability to earn an adequate return. This section covers key profitability measures.

Profit Margin *Profit margin* measures a company's ability to earn net income from sales (Chapter 3 offers additional explanation). Apple's profit margin of 21.1% is shown next to the formula. To evaluate profit margin, we must consider the industry. For instance, an appliance company might require a profit margin of 15%, whereas a retail supermarket might require a profit margin of 2%. Apple's 21.1% profit margin is better than Google's 11.4%, Samsung's 17.6%, and the industry's 11% margin.

$$\text{Profit margin} = \frac{\text{Net income}}{\text{Net sales}} = \frac{\$48,351}{\$229,234} = 21.1\%$$

Profit margin
Google = 11.4%
Samsung = 17.6%
Industry = 11%

Return on Total Assets *Return on total assets* is defined as follows. Apple's return on total assets of 13.9% is shown next to the formula. Apple's 13.9% return on total assets is higher than Google's 6.9% and the industry's 8%, but lower than Samsung's 15.0%. We also should evaluate any trend in the return.

$$\text{Return on total assets} = \frac{\text{Net income}}{\text{Average total assets}} = \frac{\$48,351}{(\$375,319 + \$321,686)/2} = 13.9\%$$

Return on total assets
Google = 6.9%
Samsung = 15.0%
Industry = 8%

The relation between profit margin, total asset turnover, and return on total assets follows.

$$\text{Profit margin} \times \text{Total asset turnover} = \text{Return on total assets}$$
$$\frac{\text{Net income}}{\text{Net sales}} \times \frac{\text{Net sales}}{\text{Average total assets}} = \frac{\text{Net income}}{\text{Average total assets}}$$

Both profit margin and total asset turnover affect operating efficiency, as measured by return on total assets. This formula is applied to Apple as follows. This analysis shows that Apple's superior return on assets versus that of Google is driven by its high profit margin and good asset turnover.

$$21.1\% \times 0.66 = 13.9\% \text{ (with rounding)}$$

Google = 11.4% × 0.61 ≈ 6.9%
Samsung = 17.6% × 0.85 ≈ 15.0%
(with rounding)

Return on Common Stockholders' Equity   The most important goal in operating a company is to earn income for its owner(s). *Return on common stockholders' equity* measures a company's ability to earn income for common stockholders and is defined as follows.

$$\text{Return on common stockholders' equity} = \frac{\text{Net income} - \text{Preferred dividends}}{\text{Average common stockholders' equity}}$$

Apple's return on common stockholders' equity is computed as follows. The denominator in this computation is the book value of common equity. Dividends on cumulative preferred stock are subtracted from income whether they are declared or are in arrears. If preferred stock is non-cumulative, its dividends are subtracted only if declared. Apple's 36.9% return on common stockholders' equity is superior to Google's 8.7% and Samsung's 20.5%.

Return on common equity
Google = 8.7%
Samsung = 20.5%
Industry = 15%

$$\frac{\$48,351 - \$0}{(\$128,249 + \$134,047)/2} = 36.9\%$$

■ **Decision Insight**

Take It to the Street   *Wall Street* is synonymous with financial markets, but its name comes from the street location of the original New York Stock Exchange. The street's name comes from stockades built by early settlers to protect New York from pirate attacks. ■

Market Prospects

Market measures are useful for analyzing corporations with publicly traded stock. These market measures use stock price, which reflects the market's (public's) expectations for the company. This includes market expectations of both company return and risk.

Price-Earnings Ratio   Computation of the *price-earnings ratio* follows (Chapter 11 provides additional explanation). This ratio is used to measure market expectations for future growth. The market price of Apple's common stock at the start of the current fiscal year was $154.12. Using Apple's $9.27 basic earnings per share, we compute its price-earnings ratio as follows. Apple's price-earnings ratio is less than that for Samsung and Google, but it is higher than the industry norm for this period.

Point: Low expectations = low PE.
High expectations = high PE.

$$\text{Price-earnings ratio} = \frac{\text{Market price per common share}}{\text{Earnings per share}} = \frac{\$154.12}{\$9.27} = 16.6$$

PE (year-end)
Google = 57.3
Samsung = 22.9
Industry = 11

Dividend Yield   *Dividend yield* is used to compare the dividend-paying performance of different companies. We compute dividend yield as follows (Chapter 11 offers additional explanation). Apple's dividend yield of 1.6%, based on its fiscal year-end market price per share of $154.12 and its $2.40 cash dividends per share, is shown next to the formula. Some companies, such as Google, do not pay dividends because they reinvest the cash to grow their businesses in the hope of generating greater future earnings and dividends.

Dividend yield
Google = 0.0%
Samsung = 1.6%

$$\text{Dividend yield} = \frac{\text{Annual cash dividends per share}}{\text{Market price per share}} = \frac{\$2.40}{\$154.12} = 1.6\%$$

©Partner Media GmbH/Alamy Stock Photo

■ **Decision Insight**

Bull Session   A *bear market* is a declining market. The phrase comes from bear-skin hunters who sold the skins before the bears were caught. The term *bear* was then used to describe investors who sold shares they did not own in anticipation of a price decline. A *bull market* is a rising market. This phrase comes from the once-popular sport of bear and bull baiting. The term *bull* means the opposite of *bear*. ■

Summary of Ratios

Exhibit 13.16 summarizes the ratios illustrated in this chapter and throughout the book.

EXHIBIT 13.16

Financial Statement Analysis Ratios

Ratio	Formula	Measure of
Liquidity and Efficiency		
Current ratio	$= \dfrac{\text{Current assets}}{\text{Current liabilities}}$	Short-term debt-paying ability
Acid-test ratio	$= \dfrac{\text{Cash + Short-term investments + Current receivables}}{\text{Current liabilities}}$	Immediate short-term debt-paying ability
Accounts receivable turnover	$= \dfrac{\text{Net sales}}{\text{Average accounts receivable, net}}$	Efficiency of collection
Inventory turnover	$= \dfrac{\text{Cost of goods sold}}{\text{Average inventory}}$	Efficiency of inventory management
Days' sales uncollected	$= \dfrac{\text{Accounts receivable, net}}{\text{Net sales}} \times 365$	Liquidity of receivables
Days' sales in inventory	$= \dfrac{\text{Ending inventory}}{\text{Cost of goods sold}} \times 365$	Liquidity of inventory
Total asset turnover	$= \dfrac{\text{Net sales}}{\text{Average total assets}}$	Efficiency of assets in producing sales
Solvency		
Debt ratio	$= \dfrac{\text{Total liabilities}}{\text{Total assets}}$	Creditor financing and leverage
Equity ratio	$= \dfrac{\text{Total equity}}{\text{Total assets}}$	Owner financing
Debt-to-equity ratio	$= \dfrac{\text{Total liabilities}}{\text{Total equity}}$	Debt versus equity financing
Times interest earned	$= \dfrac{\text{Income before interest expense and income tax expense}}{\text{Interest expense}}$	Protection in meeting interest payments
Profitability		
Profit margin ratio	$= \dfrac{\text{Net income}}{\text{Net sales}}$	Net income in each sales dollar
Gross margin ratio	$= \dfrac{\text{Net sales - Cost of goods sold}}{\text{Net sales}}$	Gross margin in each sales dollar
Return on total assets	$= \dfrac{\text{Net income}}{\text{Average total assets}}$	Overall profitability of assets
Return on common stockholders' equity	$= \dfrac{\text{Net income - Preferred dividends}}{\text{Average common stockholders' equity}}$	Profitability of owner investment
Book value per common share	$= \dfrac{\text{Shareholders' equity applicable to common shares}}{\text{Number of common shares outstanding}}$	Liquidation at reported amounts
Basic earnings per share	$= \dfrac{\text{Net income - Preferred dividends}}{\text{Weighted-average common shares outstanding}}$	Net income per common share
Market Prospects		
Price-earnings ratio	$= \dfrac{\text{Market price per common share}}{\text{Earnings per share}}$	Market value relative to earnings
Dividend yield	$= \dfrac{\text{Annual cash dividends per share}}{\text{Market price per share}}$	Cash return per common share

NEED-TO-KNOW 13-3

Ratio Analysis

P3

For each ratio listed, identify whether the change in ratio value from the prior year to the current year is favorable or unfavorable.

Ratio	Current Yr	Prior Yr	Ratio	Current Yr	Prior Yr
1. Profit margin	6%	8%	4. Accounts receivable turnover	8.8	9.4
2. Debt ratio.	50%	70%	5. Basic earnings per share	$2.10	$2.00
3. Gross margin	40%	36%	6. Inventory turnover.	3.6	4.0

Solution

Ratio	Current Yr	Prior Yr	Change
1. Profit margin ratio	6%	8%	Unfavorable
2. Debt ratio.	50%	70%	Favorable
3. Gross margin ratio.	40%	36%	Favorable
4. Accounts receivable turnover.	8.8	9.4	Unfavorable
5. Basic earnings per share	$2.10	$2.00	Favorable
6. Inventory turnover.	3.6	4.0	Unfavorable

Do More: QS 13-6 through
QS 13-13, E 13-7, E 13-8,
E 13-9, E 13-10, E 13-11,
P 13-4

 **Decision Analysis** **Analysis Reporting**

A1

Summarize and report
results of analysis.

A *financial statement analysis report* usually consists of six sections.

1. **Executive summary**—brief analysis of results and conclusions.
2. **Analysis overview**—background on the company, its industry, and the economy.
3. **Evidential matter**—financial statements and information used in the analysis, including ratios, trends, comparisons, and all analytical measures used.
4. **Assumptions**—list of assumptions about a company's industry and economic environment, and other assumptions underlying estimates.
5. **Key factors**—list of favorable and unfavorable factors, both quantitative and qualitative, for company performance; usually organized by areas of analysis.
6. **Inferences**—forecasts, estimates, interpretations, and conclusions of the analysis report.

We must remember that the user dictates relevance, meaning that the analysis report should include a brief table of contents to help readers focus on those areas most relevant to their decisions. Finally, writing is important. Mistakes in grammar and errors of fact compromise the report's credibility.

 Decision Insight

Short and Sweet *Short selling* refers to selling stock before you buy it. Here's an example: You borrow 100 shares of **Nike** stock, sell them at $55 each, and receive money from their sale. You then wait. You hope that Nike's stock price falls to, say, $50 each and you can replace the borrowed stock for less than you sold it, reaping a profit of $5 each less any transaction costs. ■

NEED-TO-KNOW 13-4

COMPREHENSIVE

Applying Horizontal,
Vertical, and Ratio
Analyses

Use the following financial statements of Precision Co. to complete these requirements.

1. Prepare comparative income statements showing the percent increase or decrease for the current year in comparison to the prior year.
2. Prepare common-size comparative balance sheets for both years.
3. Compute the following ratios for the current year and identify each one's building block category for financial statement analysis.

a. Current ratio
b. Acid-test ratio
c. Accounts receivable turnover
d. Days' sales uncollected
e. Inventory turnover
f. Debt ratio

g. Debt-to-equity ratio
h. Times interest earned
i. Profit margin ratio
j. Total asset turnover
k. Return on total assets
l. Return on common stockholders' equity

PRECISION COMPANY Comparative Income Statements		
For Years Ended December 31	**Current Yr**	**Prior Yr**
Sales	$2,486,000	$2,075,000
Cost of goods sold	1,523,000	1,222,000
Gross profit	963,000	853,000
Operating expenses		
Advertising expense.	145,000	100,000
Sales salaries expense.	240,000	280,000
Office salaries expense	165,000	200,000
Insurance expense.	100,000	45,000
Supplies expense.	26,000	35,000
Depreciation expense	85,000	75,000
Miscellaneous expenses	17,000	15,000
Total operating expenses	778,000	750,000
Operating income.	185,000	103,000
Interest expense.	44,000	46,000
Income before taxes.	141,000	57,000
Income tax expense	47,000	19,000
Net income	$ 94,000	$ 38,000
Earnings per share	$ 0.99	$ 0.40

PRECISION COMPANY Comparative Year-End Balance Sheets		
At December 31	**Current Yr**	**Prior Yr**
Assets		
Current assets		
Cash	$ 79,000	$ 42,000
Short-term investments	65,000	96,000
Accounts receivable, net	120,000	100,000
Merchandise inventory	250,000	265,000
Total current assets	514,000	503,000
Plant assets		
Store equipment, net.	400,000	350,000
Office equipment, net	45,000	50,000
Buildings, net	625,000	675,000
Land	100,000	100,000
Total plant assets	1,170,000	1,175,000
Total assets	$1,684,000	$1,678,000
Liabilities		
Current liabilities		
Accounts payable.	$ 164,000	$ 190,000
Short-term notes payable	75,000	90,000
Taxes payable.	26,000	12,000
Total current liabilities	265,000	292,000
Long-term liabilities		
Notes payable (secured by mortgage on buildings)	400,000	420,000
Total liabilities.	665,000	712,000
Stockholders' Equity		
Common stock, $5 par value	475,000	475,000
Retained earnings.	544,000	491,000
Total stockholders' equity	1,019,000	966,000
Total liabilities and equity.	$1,684,000	$1,678,000

PLANNING THE SOLUTION

- Set up a four-column income statement; enter the current-year and prior-year amounts in the first two columns and then enter the dollar change in the third column and the percent change from the prior year in the fourth column.

- Set up a four-column balance sheet; enter the current-year and prior-year year end amounts in the first two columns and then compute and enter the amount of each item as a percent of total assets.

- Compute the required ratios using the data provided. Use the average of beginning and ending amounts when appropriate (see Exhibit 13.16 for definitions).

SOLUTION

1.

PRECISION COMPANY Comparative Income Statements				
For Years Ended December 31	**Current Yr**	**Prior Yr**	**Dollar Change**	**Percent Change**
Sales	$2,486,000	$2,075,000	$411,000	19.8%
Cost of goods sold	1,523,000	1,222,000	301,000	24.6
Gross profit	963,000	853,000	110,000	12.9
Operating expenses				
Advertising expense.	145,000	100,000	45,000	45.0
Sales salaries expense.	240,000	280,000	(40,000)	(14.3)
Office salaries expense	165,000	200,000	(35,000)	(17.5)
Insurance expense.	100,000	45,000	55,000	122.2
Supplies expense.	26,000	35,000	(9,000)	(25.7)
Depreciation expense	85,000	75,000	10,000	13.3
Miscellaneous expenses	17,000	15,000	2,000	13.3
Total operating expenses	778,000	750,000	28,000	3.7
Operating income.	185,000	103,000	82,000	79.6
Interest expense.	44,000	46,000	(2,000)	(4.3)
Income before taxes.	141,000	57,000	84,000	147.4
Income tax expense	47,000	19,000	28,000	147.4
Net income	$ 94,000	$ 38,000	$ 56,000	147.4
Earnings per share	$ 0.99	$ 0.40	$ 0.59	147.5

2.

	PRECISION COMPANY			
	Common-Size Comparative Year-End Balance Sheets			
			Common-Size Percents	
At December 31	Current Yr	Prior Yr	Current Yr*	Prior Yr*
Assets				
Current assets				
Cash	$ 79,000	$ 42,000	4.7%	2.5%
Short-term investments	65,000	96,000	3.9	5.7
Accounts receivable, net	120,000	100,000	7.1	6.0
Merchandise inventory...............	250,000	265,000	14.8	15.8
Total current assets	514,000	503,000	30.5	30.0
Plant assets				
Store equipment, net	400,000	350,000	23.8	20.9
Office equipment, net................	45,000	50,000	2.7	3.0
Buildings, net	625,000	675,000	37.1	40.2
Land.............................	100,000	100,000	5.9	6.0
Total plant assets	1,170,000	1,175,000	69.5	70.0
Total assets	$1,684,000	$1,678,000	100.0%	100.0%
Liabilities				
Current liabilities				
Accounts payable...................	$ 164,000	$ 190,000	9.7%	11.3%
Short-term notes payable	75,000	90,000	4.5	5.4
Taxes payable......................	26,000	12,000	1.5	0.7
Total current liabilities	265,000	292,000	15.7	17.4
Long-term liabilities				
Notes payable (secured by				
mortgage on buildings)	400,000	420,000	23.8	25.0
Total liabilities	665,000	712,000	39.5	42.4
Stockholders' Equity				
Common stock, $5 par value	475,000	475,000	28.2	28.3
Retained earnings....................	544,000	491,000	32.3	29.3
Total stockholders' equity..............	1,019,000	966,000	60.5	57.6
Total liabilities and equity..............	$1,684,000	$1,678,000	100.0%	100.0%

*Columns do not always exactly add to 100 due to rounding.

3. Ratios:

a. Current ratio: $514,000/$265,000 = 1.9:1 (liquidity and efficiency)

b. Acid-test ratio: ($79,000 + $65,000 + $120,000)/$265,000 = 1.0:1 (liquidity and efficiency)

c. Average receivables: ($120,000 + $100,000)/2 = $110,000
Accounts receivable turnover: $2,486,000/$110,000 = 22.6 times (liquidity and efficiency)

d. Days' sales uncollected: ($120,000/$2,486,000) × 365 = 17.6 days (liquidity and efficiency)

e. Average inventory: ($250,000 + $265,000)/2 = $257,500
Inventory turnover: $1,523,000/$257,500 = 5.9 times (liquidity and efficiency)

f. Debt ratio: $665,000/$1,684,000 = 39.5% (solvency)

g. Debt-to-equity ratio: $665,000/$1,019,000 = 0.65 (solvency)

h. Times interest earned: $185,000/$44,000 = 4.2 times (solvency)

i. Profit margin ratio: $94,000/$2,486,000 = 3.8% (profitability)

j. Average total assets: ($1,684,000 + $1,678,000)/2 = $1,681,000
Total asset turnover: $2,486,000/$1,681,000 = 1.48 times (liquidity and efficiency)

k. Return on total assets: $94,000/$1,681,000 = 5.6% or 3.8% × 1.48 = 5.6% (profitability)

l. Average total common equity: ($1,019,000 + $966,000)/2 = $992,500
Return on common stockholders' equity: $94,000/$992,500 = 9.5% (profitability)

Sustainable Income

13A

A2

Explain the form and assess the content of a complete income statement.

When a company's activities include income-related events not part of its normal, continuing operations, it must disclose these events. To alert users to these activities, companies separate the income statement into continuing operations, discontinued segments, comprehensive income, and earnings per share. Exhibit 13A.1 shows such an income statement for ComUS. These separations help us measure *sustainable income,* which is the income level most likely to continue into the future. Sustainable income is commonly used in performance measures.

EXHIBIT 13A.1

Income Statement (all-inclusive) for a Corporation

ComUS		
Income Statement		
For Year Ended December 31		
Net sales		$8,478,000
Operating expenses		
Cost of goods sold	$5,950,000	
Depreciation expense	35,000	
Other selling, general, and administrative expenses	515,000	
Interest expense	20,000	
① Total operating expenses		(6,520,000)
Other unusual and/or infrequent gains (losses)		
Loss on plant relocation		(45,000)
Gain on sale of surplus land		72,000
Income from continuing operations before taxes		1,985,000
Income tax expense		(595,500)
Income from continuing operations		1,389,500
Discontinued segment		
② Income from operating Division A (net of $180,000 taxes)	420,000	
Loss on disposal of Division A (net of $66,000 tax benefit)	(154,000)	266,000
Net income		$ 1,655,500
Earnings per common share (200,000 outstanding shares)		
③ Income from continuing operations		$ 6.95
Discontinued operations		1.33
Net income (basic earnings per share)		$ 8.28

① **Continuing Operations** Section ① shows revenues, expenses, and income from continuing operations. This information is used to predict future operations, and most view this section as the most important.

Gains and losses that are normal and frequent are reported as part of continuing operations. Gains and losses that are either unusual and/or infrequent are reported as part of continuing operations *but after* the normal revenues and expenses. Items considered unusual and/or infrequent include (1) property taken away by a foreign government, (2) condemning of property, (3) prohibiting use of an asset from a new law, (4) losses and gains from an unusual and infrequent calamity ("act of God"), and (5) financial effects of labor strikes.

Point: FASB no longer allows *extraordinary items.*

② **Discontinued Segments** A **business segment** is a part of a company that is separated by its products/services or by geographic location. A segment has assets, liabilities, and financial results of operations that can be separated from those of other parts of the company. A gain or loss from selling or closing down a segment is separately reported. Section ② of Exhibit 13A.1 reports both (a) income from operating the discontinued segment before its disposal and (b) the loss from disposing of the segment's net assets. The income tax effects of each are reported separately from the income tax expense in section ①.

③ **Earnings per Share** Section ③ of Exhibit 13A.1 reports earnings per share for both continuing operations and discontinued segments (when they both exist). Earnings per share is covered in Chapter 11.

Changes in Accounting Principles Changes in accounting principles require retrospective application to prior periods' financial statements. *Retrospective application* means applying a different accounting principle to prior periods as if that principle had always been used. Retrospective application enhances the consistency of financial information between periods, which improves the usefulness of information, especially with comparative analyses.

 Decision Maker

Small Business Owner   You own an orange grove near Jacksonville, Florida. A bad frost destroys about one-half of your oranges. You are currently preparing an income statement for a bank loan. Where on the income statement do you report the loss of oranges? ■   *Answer:* The frost loss is likely unusual, meaning it is reported in the nonrecurring section of continuing operations. Managers would highlight this loss apart from ongoing, normal results so that the bank views it separately from normal operations.

Summary: Cheat Sheet

BASICS OF ANALYSIS

Liquidity and efficiency: Ability to meet short-term obligations and efficiently generate revenues.

Solvency: Ability to meet long-term obligations and generate future revenues.

Profitability: Ability to provide financial rewards to attract and retain financing.

Market prospects: Ability to generate positive market expectations.

General-purpose financial statements: Include the (1) income statement, (2) balance sheet, (3) statement of stockholders' equity (or statement of retained earnings), (4) statement of cash flows, and (5) notes to these statements.

HORIZONTAL ANALYSIS

Comparative financial statements: Show financial amounts in side-by-side columns on a single statement.

Analysis period: The financial statements under analysis.

Base period: The financial statements used for comparison. The prior year is commonly used as a base period.

Dollar change formula:

> **Dollar change = Analysis period amount − Base period amount**

Percent change formula:

$$\text{Percent change (\%)} = \frac{\text{Analysis period amount} - \text{Base period amount}}{\text{Base period amount}} \times 100$$

Apple comparative balance sheet: The prior year is the base period and current year is the analysis period.

$ millions	Current Yr	Prior Yr	Dollar Change	Percent Change
Assets				
Cash and cash equivalents............	$20,289	$20,484	$ (195)	(1.0)%
Short-term marketable securities.......	53,892	46,671	7,221	15.5
Accounts receivable, net..............	17,874	15,754	2,120	13.5

Trend analysis: Computing trend percents that show patterns in data across periods.

$$\text{Trend percent (\%)} = \frac{\text{Analysis period amount}}{\text{Base period amount}} \times 100$$

Apple trend analysis: 4 years ago is the base period, and each subsequent year is the analysis period.

In trend percent	Current Yr	1 Yr Ago	2 Yrs Ago	3 Yrs Ago	4 Yrs Ago
Net sales................	134.1%	126.2%	136.7%	107.0%	100.0%
Cost of sales.............	132.3	123.2	131.4	105.3	100.0
Operating expenses........	175.4	158.4	146.3	117.8	100.0

VERTICAL ANALYSIS

Common-size financial statements: Show changes in the relative importance of each financial statement item. All individual amounts in common-size statements are shown in common-size percents.

Common-size percent formula:

$$\text{Common-size percent (\%)} = \frac{\text{Analysis amount}}{\text{Base amount}} \times 100$$

Base amount: Comparative balance sheets use total assets, and comparative income statements use net sales.

Apple common-size balance sheet:

$ millions			Common-Size Percents	
$ millions	Current Yr	Prior Yr	Current Yr	Prior Yr
Goodwill	5,717	5,414	1.5%	1.7%
Acquired intangible assets, net	2,298	3,206	0.6	1.0
Other assets	10,162	8,757	2.7	2.7
Total assets	$375,319	$321,686	100.0	100.0

Apple common-size income statement:

$ millions			Common-Size Percents	
$ millions	Current Yr	Prior Yr	Current Yr	Prior Yr
Net sales	$229,234	$215,639	100.0%	100.0%
Cost of sales	141,048	131,376	61.5	60.9
Gross margin	88,186	84,263	38.5	39.1

RATIO ANALYSIS AND REPORTING

Ratio	Formula
Liquidity and Efficiency	
Current ratio	$= \dfrac{\text{Current assets}}{\text{Current liabilities}}$
Acid-test ratio	$= \dfrac{\text{Cash + Short-term investments + Current receivables}}{\text{Current liabilities}}$
Accounts receivable turnover	$= \dfrac{\text{Net sales}}{\text{Average accounts receivable, net}}$
Inventory turnover	$= \dfrac{\text{Cost of goods sold}}{\text{Average inventory}}$
Days' sales uncollected	$= \dfrac{\text{Accounts receivable, net}}{\text{Net sales}} \times 365$
Days' sales in inventory	$= \dfrac{\text{Ending inventory}}{\text{Cost of goods sold}} \times 365$
Total asset turnover	$= \dfrac{\text{Net sales}}{\text{Average total assets}}$
Solvency	
Debt ratio	$= \dfrac{\text{Total liabilities}}{\text{Total assets}}$
Equity ratio	$= \dfrac{\text{Total equity}}{\text{Total assets}}$
Debt-to-equity ratio	$= \dfrac{\text{Total liabilities}}{\text{Total equity}}$
Times interest earned	$= \dfrac{\text{Income before interest expense and income tax expense}}{\text{Interest expense}}$
Profitability	
Profit margin ratio	$= \dfrac{\text{Net income}}{\text{Net sales}}$
Gross margin ratio	$= \dfrac{\text{Net sales} - \text{Cost of goods sold}}{\text{Net sales}}$
Return on total assets	$= \dfrac{\text{Net income}}{\text{Average total assets}}$
Return on common stockholders' equity	$= \dfrac{\text{Net income} - \text{Preferred dividends}}{\text{Average common stockholders' equity}}$
Basic earnings per share	$= \dfrac{\text{Net income} - \text{Preferred dividends}}{\text{Weighted-average common shares outstanding}}$
Market Prospects	
Price-earnings ratio	$= \dfrac{\text{Market price per common share}}{\text{Earnings per share}}$
Dividend yield	$= \dfrac{\text{Annual cash dividends per share}}{\text{Market price per share}}$

Key Terms

Business segment (515)
Common-size financial statement (502)
Comparative financial statement (498)
Efficiency (497)
Equity ratio (508)
Financial reporting (498)

Financial statement analysis (497)
General-purpose financial
statements (498)
Horizontal analysis (498)
Liquidity (497)
Market prospects (497)

Profitability (497)
Ratio analysis (498)
Solvency (497)
Vertical analysis (498)
Working capital (506)

Multiple Choice Quiz

1. A company's sales in the prior year were $300,000 and in the current year were $351,000. Using the prior year as the base year, the sales trend percent for the current year is
   a. 17%.
   b. 85%.
   c. 100%.
   d. 117%.
   e. 48%.

Use the following information for questions 2 through 5.

ELLA COMPANY Balance Sheet December 31			
Assets		**Liabilities**	
Cash	$ 86,000	Current liabilities	$124,000
Accounts receivable	76,000	Long-term liabilities	90,000
Merchandise inventory	122,000	**Equity**	
Prepaid insurance	12,000	Common stock	300,000
Long-term investments	98,000	Retained earnings	316,000
Plant assets, net	436,000		
Total assets	$830,000	Total liabilities and equity	$830,000

2. What is Ella Company's current ratio?
   a. 0.69
   b. 1.31
   c. 3.88
   d. 6.69
   e. 2.39

3. What is Ella Company's acid-test ratio?
   a. 2.39
   b. 0.69
   c. 1.31
   d. 6.69
   e. 3.88

4. What is Ella Company's debt ratio?
   a. 25.78%
   b. 100.00%
   c. 74.22%
   d. 137.78%
   e. 34.74%

5. What is Ella Company's equity ratio?
   a. 25.78%
   b. 100.00%
   c. 34.74%
   d. 74.22%
   e. 137.78%

ANSWERS TO MULTIPLE CHOICE QUIZ

1. d; ($351,000/$300,000) × 100 = 117%
2. e; ($86,000 + $76,000 + $122,000 + $12,000)/$124,000 = 2.39
3. c; ($86,000 + $76,000)/$124,000 = 1.31
4. a; ($124,000 + $90,000)/$830,000 = 25.78%
5. d; ($300,000 + $316,000)/$830,000 = 74.22%

[A] *Superscript letter A denotes assignments based on Appendix 13A.*

Icon denotes assignments that involve decision making.

Discussion Questions

1. Explain the difference between financial reporting and financial statements.
2. What is the difference between comparative financial statements and common-size comparative statements?
3. Which items are usually assigned a 100% value on (a) a common-size balance sheet and (b) a common-size income statement?
4. What three factors would influence your evaluation as to whether a company's current ratio is good or bad?
5. Suggest several reasons why a 2:1 current ratio might not be adequate for a particular company.
6. Why is working capital given special attention in the process of analyzing balance sheets?
7. What does the number of days' sales uncollected indicate?
8. What does a relatively high accounts receivable turnover indicate about a company's short-term liquidity?
9. Why is a company's capital structure, as measured by debt and equity ratios, important to financial statement analysts?
10. How does inventory turnover provide information about a company's short-term liquidity?

11. 🛈 What ratios would you compute to evaluate management performance?

12. 🛈 Why would a company's return on total assets be different from its return on common stockholders' equity?

13. Where on the income statement does a company report an unusual gain not expected to occur more often than once every two years or so?

14. Refer to **Apple**'s financial statements in Appendix A. Compute its profit margin for the years ended September 30, 2017, and September 24, 2016.   **APPLE**

15. Refer to **Google**'s financial statements in Appendix A to compute its equity ratio as of December 31, 2017, and December 31, 2016.   **GOOGLE**

16. Refer to **Samsung**'s financial statements in Appendix A. Compute its debt ratio as of December 31, 2017, and December 31, 2016.   **Samsung**

17. Use **Samsung**'s financial statements in Appendix A to compute its return on total assets for fiscal year ended December 31, 2017.   **Samsung**

Mc Graw Hill Education ■ **connect**

QUICK STUDY

QS 13-1
Financial reporting
C1

Identify which of the following items are *not* included as part of general-purpose financial statements but are part of financial reporting.

____ **a.** Income statement
____ **b.** Balance sheet
____ **c.** Shareholders' meetings
____ **d.** Financial statement notes
____ **e.** Company news releases

____ **f.** Statement of cash flows
____ **g.** Stock price information and analysis
____ **h.** Statement of shareholders' equity
____ **i.** Management discussion and analysis of financial performance

---

QS 13-2
Standard of comparison
C2

Identify which standard of comparison, (*a*) intracompany, (*b*) competitor, (*c*) industry, or (*d*) guidelines, best describes each of the following examples.

____ **1.** Compare **Ford**'s return on assets to **GM**'s return on assets.
____ **2.** Compare a company's acid-test ratio to the 1:1 rule of thumb.
____ **3.** Compare **Netflix**'s current-year sales to its prior-year sales.
____ **4.** Compare **McDonald**'s profit margin to the fast-food industry profit margin.

QS 13-3
Horizontal analysis
P1

Compute the annual dollar changes and percent changes for each of the following accounts.

	Current Yr	Prior Yr
Short-term investments	$374,634	$234,000
Accounts receivable	97,364	101,000
Notes payable....................	0	88,000

QS 13-4
Trend percents
P1

Use the following information to determine the prior-year and current-year trend percents for net sales using the prior year as the base year.

$ thousands	Current Yr	Prior Yr
Net sales........................	$801,810	$453,000
Cost of goods sold	392,887	134,088

QS 13-5
Common-size analysis   **P2**

Refer to the information in QS 13-4. Determine the prior-year and current-year common-size percents for cost of goods sold using net sales as the base.

QS 13-6
Computing current ratio
and acid-test ratio   **P3**

Pritchett Co. reported the following year-end data: cash of $15,000; short-term investments of $5,000; accounts receivable (current) of $8,000; inventory of $20,000; prepaid (current) assets of $6,000; and total current liabilities of $20,000. Compute the (*a*) current ratio and (*b*) acid-test ratio. Round to one decimal.

QS 13-7
Computing accounts
receivable turnover and
days' sales uncollected   **P3**

Mifflin Co. reported the following for the current year: net sales of $60,000; cost of goods sold of $38,000; beginning balance in accounts receivable of $14,000; and ending balance in accounts receivable of $6,000. Compute (*a*) accounts receivable turnover and (*b*) days' sales uncollected. Round to one decimal. *Hint:* Recall that accounts receivable turnover uses average accounts receivable and days' sales uncollected uses the ending balance in accounts receivable.

SCC Co. reported the following for the current year: net sales of $48,000; cost of goods sold of $40,000; beginning balance in inventory of $2,000; and ending balance in inventory of $8,000. Compute (a) inventory turnover and (b) days' sales in inventory. *Hint:* Recall that inventory turnover uses average inventory and days' sales in inventory uses the ending balance in inventory.

QS 13-8
Computing inventory turnover and days' sales in inventory **P3**

Dundee Co. reported the following for the current year: net sales of $80,000; cost of goods sold of $60,000; beginning balance of total assets of $115,000; and ending balance of total assets of $85,000. Compute total asset turnover. Round to one decimal.

QS 13-9
Computing total asset turnover **P3**

Paddy's Pub reported the following year-end data: income before interest expense and income tax expense of $30,000; cost of goods sold of $17,000; interest expense of $1,500; total assets of $70,000; total liabilities of $20,000; and total equity of $50,000. Compute the (a) debt-to-equity ratio and (b) times interest earned. Round to one decimal.

QS 13-10
Computing debt-to-equity ratio and times interest earned **P3**

Edison Co. reported the following for the current year: net sales of $80,000; cost of goods sold of $56,000; net income of $16,000; beginning balance of total assets of $60,000; and ending balance of total assets of $68,000. Compute (a) profit margin and (b) return on total assets.

QS 13-11
Computing profit margin and return on total assets **P3**

Franklin Co. reported the following year-end data: net income of $220,000; annual cash dividends per share of $3; market price per (common) share of $150; and earnings per share of $10. Compute the (a) price-earnings ratio and (b) dividend yield.

QS 13-12
Computing price-earnings ratio and dividend yield **P3**

For each ratio listed, identify whether the change in ratio value from the prior year to the current year is usually regarded as favorable or unfavorable.

QS 13-13
Ratio interpretation

P3

Ratio	Current Yr	Prior Yr	Ratio	Current Yr	Prior Yr
___ 1. Profit margin......	9%	8%	___ 5. Accounts receivable turnover.....	5.5	6.7
___ 2. Debt ratio........	47%	42%	___ 6. Basic earnings per share........	$1.25	$1.10
___ 3. Gross margin	34%	46%	___ 7. Inventory turnover.............	3.6	3.4
___ 4. Acid-test ratio.....	1.00	1.15	___ 8. Dividend yield	2.0%	1.2%

Morgan Company and Parker Company are similar firms operating in the same industry. Write a half-page report comparing Morgan and Parker using the available information. Your discussion should include their ability to meet current obligations and to use current assets efficiently.

QS 13-14
Analyzing short-term financial condition

A1

	Morgan			Parker		
	Current Yr	1 Yr Ago	2 Yrs Ago	Current Yr	1 Yr Ago	2 Yrs Ago
Current ratio	1.7	1.6	2.1	3.2	2.7	1.9
Acid-test ratio	1.0	1.1	1.2	2.8	2.5	1.6
Accounts receivable turnover	30.5	25.2	29.2	16.4	15.2	16.0
Merchandise inventory turnover	24.2	21.9	17.1	14.5	13.0	12.6
Working capital	$70,000	$58,000	$52,000	$131,000	$103,000	$78,000

Team Project: Assume that the two companies apply for a one-year loan from the team. Identify additional information the companies must provide before the team can make a loan decision.

Which of the following gains or losses would Organic Foods account for as unusual and/or infrequent?

a. A hurricane destroys rainwater tanks that result in a loss for Organic Foods.

b. The used vehicle market is weak and Organic Foods is forced to sell its used delivery truck at a loss.

c. Organic Foods owns an organic farm in Venezuela that is seized by the government. The company records a loss.

QS 13-15^A
Identifying unusual and/or infrequent gains or losses

A2

■ connect

EXERCISES

Match the ratio to the building block of financial statement analysis to which it best relates.

A. Liquidity and efficiency   **B.** Solvency   **C.** Profitability   **D.** Market prospects

Exercise 13-1

Building blocks of analysis

C1

_____ **1.** Equity ratio

_____ **2.** Return on total assets

_____ **3.** Dividend yield

_____ **4.** Book value per common share

_____ **5.** Days' sales in inventory

_____ **6.** Accounts receivable turnover

_____ **7.** Debt-to-equity ratio

_____ **8.** Times interest earned

_____ **9.** Gross margin ratio

_____ **10.** Acid-test ratio

Exercise 13-2

Identifying financial ratios

C2

Identify which of the following six metrics *a* through *f* best completes questions 1 through 3 below.

a. Days' sales uncollected

b. Accounts receivable turnover

c. Working capital

d. Return on total assets

e. Total asset turnover

f. Profit margin

1. Which two ratios are key components in measuring a company's operating efficiency? _____ _____
Which ratio summarizes these two components? _____

2. What measure reflects the difference between current assets and current liabilities? _____

3. Which two short-term liquidity ratios measure how frequently a company collects its accounts?
_____ _____

Exercise 13-3

Computing and analyzing trend percents

P1

Compute trend percents for the following accounts using 2015 as the base year. For each of the three accounts, state whether the situation as revealed by the trend percents appears to be favorable or unfavorable.

	2019	2018	2017	2016	2015
Sales	$282,880	$270,800	$252,600	$234,560	$150,000
Cost of goods sold	128,200	122,080	115,280	106,440	67,000
Accounts receivable	18,100	17,300	16,400	15,200	9,000

Exercise 13-4

Computing and interpreting common-size percents

P2

Compute common-size percents for the following comparative income statements (round percents to one decimal). Using the common-size percents, which item is most responsible for the decline in net income?

GOMEZ CORPORATION		
Comparative Income Statements		
For Years Ended December 31	Current Yr	Prior Yr
Sales	$740,000	$625,000
Cost of goods sold	560,300	290,800
Gross profit	179,700	334,200
Operating expenses	128,200	218,500
Net income	$ 51,500	$115,700

Exercise 13-5

Determining income effects from common-size and trend percents

P1   P2

Common-size and trend percents for Roxi Company's sales, cost of goods sold, and expenses follow. Determine whether net income increased, decreased, or remained unchanged in this three-year period.

	Common-Size Percents			Trend Percents		
	Current Yr	1 Yr Ago	2 Yrs Ago	Current Yr	1 Yr Ago	2 Yrs Ago
Sales...................	100.0%	100.0%	100.0%	105.4%	104.2%	100.0%
Cost of goods sold........	63.4	61.9	59.1	113.1	109.1	100.0
Total expenses...........	15.3	14.8	15.1	106.8	102.1	100.0

Exercise 13-6

Common-size percents

P2

Simon Company's year-end balance sheets follow. (1) Express the balance sheets in common-size percents. Round percents to one decimal. (2) Assuming annual sales have not changed in the last three years, is the change in accounts receivable as a percentage of total assets favorable or unfavorable? (3) Is the change in merchandise inventory as a percentage of total assets favorable or unfavorable?

At December 31	Current Yr	1 Yr Ago	2 Yrs Ago
Assets			
Cash.	$ 31,800	$ 35,625	$ 37,800
Accounts receivable, net	89,500	62,500	50,200
Merchandise inventory.	112,500	82,500	54,000
Prepaid expenses.	10,700	9,375	5,000
Plant assets, net	278,500	255,000	230,500
Total assets	$523,000	$445,000	$377,500
Liabilities and Equity			
Accounts payable	$129,900	$ 75,250	$ 51,250
Long-term notes payable secured by mortgages on plant assets	98,500	101,500	83,500
Common stock, $10 par value.	163,500	163,500	163,500
Retained earnings.	131,100	104,750	79,250
Total liabilities and equity.	$523,000	$445,000	$377,500

Refer to Simon Company's balance sheets in Exercise 13-6. (1) Compute the current ratio for each of the three years. Did the current ratio improve or worsen over the three-year period? (2) Compute the acid-test ratio for each of the three years. Did the acid-test ratio improve or worsen over the three-year period? Round ratios to two decimals.

Exercise 13-7
Analyzing liquidity
P3

Refer to the Simon Company information in Exercise 13-6. The company's income statements for the current year and one year ago follow. Assume that all sales are on credit and then compute (1) days' sales uncollected, (2) accounts receivable turnover, (3) inventory turnover, and (4) days' sales in inventory. For each ratio, determine if it improved or worsened in the current year. Round to one decimal.

Exercise 13-8
Analyzing and interpreting liquidity
P3

For Year Ended December 31	Current Yr		1 Yr Ago	
Sales		$673,500		$532,000
Cost of goods sold	$411,225		$345,500	
Other operating expenses	209,550		134,980	
Interest expense.	12,100		13,300	
Income tax expense	9,525		8,845	
Total costs and expenses.		642,400		502,625
Net income		$ 31,100		$ 29,375
Earnings per share		$ 1.90		$ 1.80

Refer to the Simon Company information in Exercises 13-6 and 13-8. For both the current year and one year ago, compute the following ratios: (1) debt ratio and equity ratio—percent rounded to one decimal, (2) debt-to-equity ratio—rounded to two decimals; based on debt-to-equity ratio, does the company have more or less debt in the current year versus one year ago? and (3) times interest earned—rounded to one decimal. Based on times interest earned, is the company more or less risky for creditors in the current year versus one year ago?

Exercise 13-9
Analyzing risk and capital structure
P3

Refer to Simon Company's financial information in Exercises 13-6 and 13-8. For both the current year and one year ago, compute the following ratios: (1) profit margin ratio—percent rounded to one decimal; did profit margin improve or worsen in the current year versus one year ago? (2) total asset turnover—rounded to one decimal, and (3) return on total assets—percent rounded to one decimal. Based on return on total assets, did Simon's operating efficiency improve or worsen in the current year versus one year ago?

Exercise 13-10
Analyzing efficiency and profitability
P3

Refer to Simon Company's financial information in Exercises 13-6 and 13-8. Additional information about the company follows. For both the current year and one year ago, compute the following ratios: (1) return on common stockholders' equity—percent rounded to one decimal, (2) dividend yield—percent rounded to one decimal, and (3) price-earnings ratio on December 31—rounded to one decimal. Assuming Simon's competitor has a price-earnings ratio of 10, which company has higher market expectations for future growth?

Exercise 13-11
Analyzing profitability
P3

Common stock market price, December 31, current year.	$30.00	Annual cash dividends per share in current year	$0.29
Common stock market price, December 31, 1 year ago	28.00	Annual cash dividends per share 1 year ago.	0.24

Exercise 13-12

Computing current ratio
and profit margin

P3

Nintendo Company, Ltd., recently reported the following financial information (amounts in millions). Compute Nintendo's current ratio and profit margin. Round to two decimals.

Current assets..........................	$ 9,036	Net sales................................	$4,464
Total assets..............................	11,477	Net income.............................	146
Current liabilities	871		

Exercise 13-13

Analyzing efficiency and
profitability

P3

Following are data for BioBeans and GreenKale, which sell organic produce and are of similar size.

1. Compute the profit margin and the return on total assets for both companies.
2. Based on analysis of these two measures, which company is the preferred investment?

	BioBeans	GreenKale
Average total assets...........	$187,500	$150,000
Net sales....................	75,000	60,000
Net income	15,000	9,000

Exercise 13-14

Reconstructing an income
statement with ratios

P3

Following is an incomplete current-year income statement.

Income Statement	
Net sales...	$ (a)
Cost of goods sold	(b)
Selling, general, and administrative expenses..........	7,000
Income tax expense...............................	2,000
Net income	(c)

Determine amounts *a, b,* and *c.* Additional information follows:

- Return on total assets is 16% (average total assets is $68,750).
- Inventory turnover is 5 (average inventory is $6,000).
- Accounts receivable turnover is 8 (average accounts receivable is $6,250).

Exercise 13-15

Analyzing efficiency and
financial leverage

A1

Roak Company and Clay Company are similar firms that operate in the same industry. Clay began operations two years ago and Roak started five years ago. In the current year, both companies pay 6% interest on their debt to creditors. The following additional information is available.

	Roak Company			Clay Company		
	Current Yr	1 Yr Ago	2 Yrs Ago	Current Yr	1 Yr Ago	2 Yrs Ago
Total asset turnover	3.1	2.8	3.0	1.7	1.5	1.1
Return on total assets	7.4%	7.0%	6.9%	4.8%	4.5%	3.2%
Profit margin ratio	2.4%	2.5%	2.3%	2.8%	3.0%	2.9%
Sales..................	$410,000	$380,000	$396,000	$210,000	$170,000	$110,000

Write a half-page report comparing Roak and Clay using the available information. Your analysis should include their ability to use assets efficiently to produce profits. Comment on their success in employing financial leverage in the current year.

Exercise 13-16

Interpreting financial ratios

A1   **P3**

Refer to the information in Exercise 13-15.

1. Which company has the better (*a*) profit margin, (*b*) asset turnover, and (*c*) return on assets?
2. Which company has the better rate of growth in sales?
3. Did Roak successfully use financial leverage in the current year? Did Clay?

Exercise 13-17ᴬ

Income statement
categories

A2

In the current year, Randa Merchandising, Inc., sold its interest in a chain of wholesale outlets, taking the company completely out of the wholesaling business. The company still operates its retail outlets. A listing of the major sections of an income statement follows.

A. Net sales less operating expense section

B. Other unusual and/or infrequent gains (losses)

C. Taxes reported on income (loss) from continuing operations

D. Income (loss) from operating a discontinued segment, or gain (loss) from its disposal

Indicate where each of the following income-related items for this company appears on its current-year income statement by writing the letter of the appropriate section in the blank beside each item.

Section	Item	Debit	Credit
_____	1. Net sales		$2,900,000
_____	2. Gain on state's condemnation of company property		230,000
_____	3. Cost of goods sold	$1,480,000	
_____	4. Income tax expense	217,000	
_____	5. Depreciation expense	232,000	
_____	6. Gain on sale of wholesale business segment, net of tax		775,000
_____	7. Loss from operating wholesale business segment, net of tax . . .	444,000	
_____	8. Loss of assets from meteor strike	640,000	

Use the financial data for Randa Merchandising, Inc., in Exercise 13-17ᴬ to prepare its December 31 year-end income statement. Ignore the earnings per share section.

Exercise 13-18ᴬ
Income statement presentation   **A2**

connect

Selected comparative financial statements of Haroun Company follow.

PROBLEM SET A

Problem 13-1A
Calculating and analyzing trend percents

P1

HAROUN COMPANY
Comparative Income Statements
For Years Ended December 31

$ thousands	2019	2018	2017	2016	2015	2014	2013
Sales	$1,694	$1,496	$1,370	$1,264	$1,186	$1,110	$928
Cost of goods sold	1,246	1,032	902	802	752	710	586
Gross profit	448	464	468	462	434	400	342
Operating expenses . . .	330	256	234	170	146	144	118
Net income	$ 118	$ 208	$ 234	$ 292	$ 288	$ 256	$224

HAROUN COMPANY
Comparative Year-End Balance Sheets

At December 31, $ thousands	2019	2018	2017	2016	2015	2014	2013
Assets							
Cash.	$ 58	$ 78	$ 82	$ 84	$ 88	$ 86	$ 89
Accounts receivable, net . . .	490	514	466	360	318	302	216
Merchandise inventory.	1,838	1,364	1,204	1,032	936	810	615
Other current assets.	36	32	14	34	28	28	9
Long-term investments.	0	0	0	146	146	146	146
Plant assets, net	2,020	2,014	1,752	944	978	860	725
Total assets	$4,442	$4,002	$3,518	$2,600	$2,494	$2,232	$1,800
Liabilities and Equity							
Current liabilities.	$1,220	$1,042	$ 718	$ 614	$ 546	$ 522	$ 282
Long-term liabilities	1,294	1,140	1,112	570	580	620	400
Common stock	1,000	1,000	1,000	850	850	650	650
Other paid-in capital.	250	250	250	170	170	150	150
Retained earnings.	678	570	438	396	348	290	318
Total liabilities and equity. . .	$4,442	$4,002	$3,518	$2,600	$2,494	$2,232	$1,800

Required

1. Compute trend percents for all components of both statements using 2013 as the base year. Round percents to one decimal.

Analysis Component

2. Refer to the results from part 1. (*a*) Did sales grow steadily over this period? (*b*) Did net income as a percent of sales grow over the past four years? (*c*) Did inventory increase over this period?

Problem 13-2A
Ratios, common-size
statements, and trend
percents

P1   P2   P3

Selected comparative financial statements of Korbin Company follow.

KORBIN COMPANY			
Comparative Income Statements			
For Years Ended December 31	2019	2018	2017
Sales	$555,000	$340,000	$278,000
Cost of goods sold	283,500	212,500	153,900
Gross profit	271,500	127,500	124,100
Selling expenses.	102,900	46,920	50,800
Administrative expenses	50,668	29,920	22,800
Total expenses	153,568	76,840	73,600
Income before taxes.	117,932	50,660	50,500
Income tax expense	40,800	10,370	15,670
Net income	$ 77,132	$ 40,290	$ 34,830

KORBIN COMPANY			
Comparative Balance Sheets			
At December 31	2019	2018	2017
Assets			
Current assets.	$ 52,390	$ 37,924	$ 51,748
Long-term investments.	0	500	3,950
Plant assets, net	100,000	96,000	60,000
Total assets	$152,390	$134,424	$115,698
Liabilities and Equity			
Current liabilities.	$ 22,800	$ 19,960	$ 20,300
Common stock	72,000	72,000	60,000
Other paid-in capital.	9,000	9,000	6,000
Retained earnings.	48,590	33,464	29,398
Total liabilities and equity. . . .	$152,390	$134,424	$115,698

Required

1. Compute each year's current ratio. Round ratios to one decimal.
2. Express the income statement data in common-size percents. Round percents to two decimals.

3. Express the balance sheet data in trend percents with 2017 as base year. Round percents to two decimals.

Analysis Component

4. Refer to the results from parts 1, 2, and 3. (*a*) Did cost of goods sold make up a greater portion of sales for the most recent year? (*b*) Did income as a percent of sales improve in the most recent year? (*c*) Did plant assets grow over this period?

Problem 13-3A
Transactions, working
capital, and liquidity ratios

P3

Plum Corporation began the month of May with $700,000 of current assets, a current ratio of 2.50:1, and an acid-test ratio of 1.10:1. During the month, it completed the following transactions (the company uses a perpetual inventory system).

May	2	Purchased $50,000 of merchandise inventory on credit.
	8	Sold merchandise inventory that cost $55,000 for $110,000 cash.
	10	Collected $20,000 cash on an account receivable.
	15	Paid $22,000 cash to settle an account payable.
	17	Wrote off a $5,000 bad debt against the Allowance for Doubtful Accounts account.

	22	Declared a $1 per share cash dividend on its 50,000 shares of outstanding common stock.
	26	Paid the dividend declared on May 22.
	27	Borrowed $100,000 cash by giving the bank a 30-day, 10% note.

	28	Borrowed $80,000 cash by signing a long-term secured note.
	29	Used the $180,000 cash proceeds from the notes to buy new machinery.

Required

Prepare a table, similar to the following, showing Plum's (1) current ratio, (2) acid-test ratio, and (3) working capital after each transaction. Round ratios to two decimals.

	A	B	C	D	E	F	G
1		Current	Quick	Current	Current	Acid-Test	Working
2	Transaction	Assets	Assets	Liabilities	Ratio	Ratio	Capital
3	Beginning	$700,000	—	—	2.50	1.10	—

Selected current year-end financial statements of Cabot Corporation follow. All sales were on credit; selected balance sheet amounts at December 31 of the *prior year* were inventory, $48,900; total assets, $189,400; common stock, $90,000; and retained earnings, $33,748.

Problem 13-4A
Calculating financial statement ratios

P3

CABOT CORPORATION Balance Sheet December 31 of Current Year			
Assets		**Liabilities and Equity**	
Cash.	$ 10,000	Accounts payable.	$ 17,500
Short-term investments . .	8,400	Accrued wages payable.	3,200
Accounts receivable, net .	33,700	Income taxes payable	3,300
Merchandise inventory. . .	32,150	Long-term note payable, secured	
Prepaid expenses.	2,650	by mortgage on plant assets.	63,400
Plant assets, net	153,300	Common stock	90,000
		Retained earnings	62,800
Total assets.	$240,200	Total liabilities and equity	$240,200

CABOT CORPORATION Income Statement For Current Year Ended December 31	
Sales	$448,600
Cost of goods sold	297,250
Gross profit	151,350
Operating expenses	98,600
Interest expense.	4,100
Income before taxes.	48,650
Income tax expense	19,598
Net income	$ 29,052

Required

Compute the following: (1) current ratio, (2) acid-test ratio, (3) days' sales uncollected, (4) inventory turnover, (5) days' sales in inventory, (6) debt-to-equity ratio, (7) times interest earned, (8) profit margin ratio, (9) total asset turnover, (10) return on total assets, and (11) return on common stockholders' equity. Round to one decimal place; for part 6, round to two decimals.

Check Acid-test ratio, 2.2 to 1; Inventory turnover, 7.3

Summary information from the financial statements of two companies competing in the same industry follows.

Problem 13-5A
Comparative ratio analysis

P3

	Barco Company	Kyan Company		Barco Company	Kyan Company
Data from the current year-end balance sheets			**Data from the current year's income statement**		
Assets			Sales.	$770,000	$880,200
Cash.	$ 19,500	$ 34,000	Cost of goods sold.	585,100	632,500
Accounts receivable, net	46,500	64,600	Interest expense	7,900	13,000
Merchandise inventory.	84,440	132,500	Income tax expense	14,800	24,300
Prepaid expenses.	5,000	6,950	Net income	162,200	210,400
Plant assets, net	290,000	304,400	Basic earnings per share.	4.51	5.11
Total assets.	$445,440	$542,450	Cash dividends per share	3.81	3.93
Liabilities and Equity			**Beginning-of-year balance sheet data**		
Current liabilities.	$ 61,340	$ 93,300	Accounts receivable, net.	$ 29,800	$ 54,200
Long-term notes payable	80,800	101,000	Merchandise inventory	55,600	107,400
Common stock, $5 par value	180,000	206,000	Total assets	398,000	382,500
Retained earnings.	123,300	142,150	Common stock, $5 par value	180,000	206,000
Total liabilities and equity.	$445,440	$542,450	Retained earnings	98,300	93,600

Required

1. For both companies compute the (*a*) current ratio, (*b*) acid-test ratio, (*c*) accounts receivable turnover, (*d*) inventory turnover, (*e*) days' sales in inventory, and (*f*) days' sales uncollected. Round to one decimal place. Identify the company you consider to be the better short-term credit risk and explain why.

2. For both companies compute the (*a*) profit margin ratio, (*b*) total asset turnover, (*c*) return on total assets, and (*d*) return on common stockholders' equity. Assuming that each company's stock can be purchased at $75 per share, compute their (*e*) price-earnings ratios and (*f*) dividend yields. Round to one decimal place. Identify which company's stock you would recommend as the better investment and explain why.

Problem 13-6A^A
Income statement computations and format

A2

Selected account balances from the adjusted trial balance for Olinda Corporation as of its calendar year-end December 31 follow.

	Debit	Credit
a. Interest revenue		$ 14,000
b. Depreciation expense—Equipment	$ 34,000	
c. Loss on sale of equipment	25,850	
d. Accounts payable		44,000
e. Other operating expenses	106,400	
f. Accumulated depreciation—Equipment		71,600
g. Gain from settlement of lawsuit		44,000
h. Accumulated depreciation—Buildings		174,500
i. Loss from operating a discontinued segment (pretax)	18,250	
j. Gain on insurance recovery of tornado damage		20,000
k. Net sales		998,000
l. Depreciation expense—Buildings	52,000	
m. Correction of overstatement of prior year's sales (pretax)	16,000	
n. Gain on sale of discontinued segment's assets (pretax)		34,000
o. Loss from settlement of lawsuit	23,250	
p. Income tax expense	?	
q. Cost of goods sold	482,500	

Required

Answer each of the following questions by providing supporting computations.

1. Assume that the company's income tax rate is 30% for all items. Identify the tax effects and after-tax amounts of the three items labeled pretax.

2. Compute the amount of income from continuing operations before income taxes. What is the amount of the income tax expense? What is the amount of income from continuing operations?

3. What is the total amount of after-tax income (loss) associated with the discontinued segment?

4. What is the amount of net income for the year?

PROBLEM SET B

Selected comparative financial statements of Tripoly Company follow.

Problem 13-1B
Calculating and analyzing trend percents

P1

TRIPOLY COMPANY Comparative Income Statements For Years Ended December 31							
$ thousands	2019	2018	2017	2016	2015	2014	2013
Sales	$560	$610	$630	$680	$740	$770	$860
Cost of goods sold	276	290	294	314	340	350	380
Gross profit	284	320	336	366	400	420	480
Operating expenses	84	104	112	126	140	144	150
Net income	$200	$216	$224	$240	$260	$276	$330

TRIPOLY COMPANY Comparative Year-End Balance Sheets							
At December 31, $ thousands	2019	2018	2017	2016	2015	2014	2013
Assets							
Cash.......................	$ 44	$ 46	$ 52	$ 54	$ 60	$ 62	$ 68
Accounts receivable, net	130	136	140	144	150	154	160
Merchandise inventory........	166	172	178	180	186	190	208
Other current assets..........	34	34	36	38	38	40	40
Long-term investments........	36	30	26	110	110	110	110
Plant assets, net	510	514	520	412	420	428	454
Total assets	$920	$932	$952	$938	$964	$984	$1,040
Liabilities and Equity							
Current liabilities.............	$148	$156	$186	$190	$210	$260	$ 280
Long-term liabilities	92	120	142	148	194	214	260
Common stock	160	160	160	160	160	160	160
Other paid-in capital..........	70	70	70	70	70	70	70
Retained earnings............	450	426	394	370	330	280	270
Total liabilities and equity......	$920	$932	$952	$938	$964	$984	$1,040

Required

1. Compute trend percents for all components of both statements using 2013 as the base year. Round percents to one decimal.

Check (1) 2019, Total assets trend, 88.5%

Analysis Component

2. Analyze and comment on the financial statements and trend percents from part 1.

Selected comparative financial statement information of Bluegrass Corporation follows.

Problem 13-2B
Ratios, common-size statements, and trend percents

P1 P2 P3

BLUEGRASS CORPORATION Comparative Year-End Balance Sheets			
At December 31	2019	2018	2017
Assets			
Current assets................	$ 54,860	$ 32,660	$ 36,300
Long-term investments.........	0	1,700	10,600
Plant assets, net	112,810	113,660	79,000
Total assets	$167,670	$148,020	$125,900
Liabilities and Equity			
Current liabilities..............	$ 22,370	$ 19,180	$ 16,500
Common stock	46,500	46,500	37,000
Other paid-in capital..........	13,850	13,850	11,300
Retained earnings.............	84,950	68,490	61,100
Total liabilities and equity........	$167,670	$148,020	$125,900

BLUEGRASS CORPORATION Comparative Income Statements			
For Years Ended December 31	2019	2018	2017
Sales	$198,800	$166,000	$143,800
Cost of goods sold	108,890	86,175	66,200
Gross profit..................	89,910	79,825	77,600
Selling expenses.............	22,680	19,790	18,000
Administrative expenses	16,760	14,610	15,700
Total expenses	39,440	34,400	33,700
Income before taxes..........	50,470	45,425	43,900
Income tax expense	6,050	5,910	5,300
Net income	$ 44,420	$ 39,515	$ 38,600

Required

1. Compute each year's current ratio. Round ratios to one decimal.

2. Express the income statement data in common-size percents. Round percents to two decimals.

3. Express the balance sheet data in trend percents with 2017 as the base year. Round percents to two decimals.

Check (3) 2019, Total assets trend, 133.18%

Analysis Component

4. Comment on any significant relations revealed by the ratios and percents computed.

Problem 13-3B

Transactions, working capital, and liquidity ratios   P3

Check   June 3: Current ratio, 2.88; Acid-test ratio, 2.40

June 30: Working capital, $(10,000); Current ratio, 0.97

Koto Corporation began the month of June with $300,000 of current assets, a current ratio of 2.5:1, and an acid-test ratio of 1.4:1. During the month, it completed the following transactions (the company uses a perpetual inventory system).

June 1   Sold merchandise inventory that cost $75,000 for $120,000 cash.
       3   Collected $88,000 cash on an account receivable.
       5   Purchased $150,000 of merchandise inventory on credit.
       7   Borrowed $100,000 cash by giving the bank a 60-day, 10% note.
      10   Borrowed $120,000 cash by signing a long-term secured note.
      12   Purchased machinery for $275,000 cash.
      15   Declared a $1 per share cash dividend on its 80,000 shares of outstanding common stock.
      19   Wrote off a $5,000 bad debt against the Allowance for Doubtful Accounts account.
      22   Paid $12,000 cash to settle an account payable.
      30   Paid the dividend declared on June 15.

Required

Prepare a table, similar to the following, showing the company's (1) current ratio, (2) acid-test ratio, and (3) working capital after each transaction. Round ratios to two decimals.

	A	B	C	D	E	F	G
1		**Current Assets**	**Quick Assets**	**Current Liabilities**	**Current Ratio**	**Acid-Test Ratio**	**Working Capital**
2	**Transaction**						
3	Beginning	$300,000	—	—	2.50	1.40	—

Problem 13-4B

Calculating financial statement ratios

P3

Selected current year-end financial statements of Overton Corporation follow. (All sales were on credit; selected balance sheet amounts at December 31 of the *prior year* were inventory, $17,400; total assets, $94,900; common stock, $35,500; and retained earnings, $18,800.)

OVERTON CORPORATION
Income Statement
For Current Year Ended December 31

Sales	$315,500
Cost of goods sold	236,100
Gross profit	79,400
Operating expenses	49,200
Interest expense	2,200
Income before taxes	28,000
Income tax expense	4,200
Net income	$ 23,800

OVERTON CORPORATION
Balance Sheet
December 31 of Current Year

Assets		Liabilities and Equity	
Cash.	$ 6,100	Accounts payable.	$ 11,500
Short-term investments	6,900	Accrued wages payable.	3,300
Accounts receivable, net . . .	15,100	Income taxes payable	2,600
Merchandise inventory.	13,500	Long-term note payable, secured	
Prepaid expenses.	2,000	by mortgage on plant assets. . . .	30,000
Plant assets, net	73,900	Common stock, $5 par value.	35,000
		Retained earnings	35,100
Total assets.	$117,500	Total liabilities and equity	$117,500

Required

Check   Acid-test ratio, 1.6 to 1; Inventory turnover, 15.3

Compute the following: (1) current ratio, (2) acid-test ratio, (3) days' sales uncollected, (4) inventory turnover, (5) days' sales in inventory, (6) debt-to-equity ratio, (7) times interest earned, (8) profit margin ratio, (9) total asset turnover, (10) return on total assets, and (11) return on common stockholders' equity. Round to one decimal place; for part 6, round to two decimals.

Problem 13-5B

Comparative ratio analysis   P3

Summary information from the financial statements of two companies competing in the same industry follows.

	Fargo Company	Ball Company		Fargo Company	Ball Company
Data from the current year-end balance sheets			**Data from the current year's income statement**		
Assets			Sales..........................	$393,600	$667,500
Cash.................................	$ 20,000	$ 36,500	Cost of goods sold..................	290,600	480,000
Accounts receivable, net	88,700	79,500	Interest expense	5,900	12,300
Merchandise inventory................	86,800	82,000	Income tax expense	5,700	12,300
Prepaid expenses....................	9,700	10,100	Net income	33,850	61,700
Plant assets, net	176,900	252,300	Basic earnings per share.............	1.27	2.19
Total assets........................	$382,100	$460,400			
Liabilities and Equity			**Beginning-of-year balance sheet data**		
Current liabilities.....................	$ 90,500	$ 97,000	Accounts receivable, net..............	$ 72,200	$ 73,300
Long-term notes payable..............	93,000	93,300	Merchandise inventory	105,100	80,500
Common stock, $5 par value...........	133,000	141,000	Total assets	383,400	443,000
Retained earnings....................	65,600	129,100	Common stock, $5 par value	133,000	141,000
Total liabilities and equity.............	$382,100	$460,400	Retained earnings..................	49,100	109,700

Required

1. For both companies compute the (*a*) current ratio, (*b*) acid-test ratio, (*c*) accounts receivable turnover, (*d*) inventory turnover, (*e*) days' sales in inventory, and (*f*) days' sales uncollected. Round to one decimal place. Identify the company you consider to be the better short-term credit risk and explain why.

Check (1) Fargo: Accounts receivable turnover, 4.9; Inventory turnover, 3.0

2. For both companies compute the (*a*) profit margin ratio, (*b*) total asset turnover, (*c*) return on total assets, and (*d*) return on common stockholders' equity. Assuming that each company paid cash dividends of $1.50 per share and each company's stock can be purchased at $25 per share, compute their (*e*) price-earnings ratios and (*f*) dividend yields. Round to one decimal place; for part *b*, round to two decimals. Identify which company's stock you would recommend as the better investment and explain why.

(2) Ball: Profit margin, 9.2%; PE, 11.4

Selected account balances from the adjusted trial balance for Harbor Corp. as of its calendar year-end December 31 follow.

Problem 13-6B[A]
Income statement computations and format

A2

	Debit	Credit
a. Accumulated depreciation—Buildings		$ 400,000
b. Interest revenue...		20,000
c. Net sales...		2,640,000
d. Income tax expense..	$?	
e. Loss on hurricane damage	48,000	
f. Accumulated depreciation—Equipment.......................		220,000
g. Other operating expenses...................................	328,000	
h. Depreciation expense—Equipment...........................	100,000	
i. Loss from settlement of lawsuit	36,000	
j. Gain from settlement of lawsuit		68,000
k. Loss on sale of equipment...................................	24,000	
l. Loss from operating a discontinued segment (pretax).............	120,000	
m. Depreciation expense—Buildings.............................	156,000	
n. Correction of overstatement of prior year's expense (pretax).......		48,000
o. Cost of goods sold...	1,040,000	
p. Loss on sale of discontinued segment's assets (pretax)	180,000	
q. Accounts payable..		132,000

Required

Answer each of the following questions by providing supporting computations.

1. Assume that the company's income tax rate is 25% for all items. Identify the tax effects and after-tax amounts of the three items labeled pretax.

2. What is the amount of income from continuing operations before income taxes? What is the amount of income tax expense? What is the amount of income from continuing operations?

Check   (3) $(225,000)
(4) $522,000

3. What is the total amount of after-tax income (loss) associated with the discontinued segment?

4. What is the amount of net income for the year?

SERIAL PROBLEM
Business Solutions

P3

©Alexander Image/Shutterstock

This serial problem began in Chapter 1 and continues through most of the book. If previous chapter segments were not completed, the serial problem can begin at this point.

SP 13 Use the following selected data from **Business Solutions**'s income statement for the three months ended March 31, 2020, and from its March 31, 2020, balance sheet to complete the requirements.

Computer services revenue.......	$25,307	Net income.........	$ 18,833	Current liabilities	$ 875
Net sales (of goods)	18,693	Quick assets........	90,924	Total liabilities	875
Total sales and revenue	44,000	Current assets	95,568	Total equity.........	119,393
Cost of goods sold	14,052	Total assets	120,268		

Required

1. Compute the gross margin ratio (both with and without services revenue) and net profit margin ratio (round the percent to one decimal).

2. Compute the current ratio and acid-test ratio (round to one decimal).

3. Compute the debt ratio and equity ratio (round the percent to one decimal).

4. What percent of its assets are current? What percent are long term? Round percents to one decimal.

Accounting Analysis

COMPANY ANALYSIS

A1 P1 P2

APPLE

AA 13-1 Use **Apple**'s financial statements in Appendix A to answer the following.

1. Using fiscal 2015 as the base year, compute trend percents for fiscal years 2015, 2016, and 2017 for net sales, cost of sales, operating income, other income (expense) net, provision for income taxes, and net income. Round percents to one decimal.

2. Compute common-size percents for fiscal years 2016 and 2017 for the following categories of assets: (*a*) total current assets; (*b*) property, plant and equipment, net; and (*c*) goodwill plus acquired intangible assets, net. Round percents to one decimal.

3. Using current assets as a percent of total assets to measure liquidity, did Apple's asset makeup become more liquid or less liquid in 2017?

COMPARATIVE ANALYSIS

C2 P2

APPLE
GOOGLE

AA 13-2 Key figures for **Apple** and **Google** follow.

$ millions	Apple	Google	$ millions	Apple	Google
Cash and equivalents.............	$20,289	$ 10,715	Cost of sales	$141,048	$ 45,583
Accounts receivable, net	17,874	18,336	Revenues.............	229,234	110,855
Inventories	4,855	749	Total assets	375,319	197,295
Retained earnings...............	98,330	113,247			

Required

1. Compute common-size percents for each of the companies using the data provided. Round percents to one decimal.

2. If Google decided to pay a dividend, would retained earnings as a percent of total assets increase or decrease?

3. Which company has a higher gross margin ratio on sales?

AA 13-3   Key figures for **Samsung** follow (in ₩ millions).

Cash and equivalents...............	₩ 30,545,130	Cost of sales......................	₩129,290,661
Accounts receivable, net............	27,695,995	Revenues........................	239,575,376
Inventories.......................	24,983,355	Total assets.......................	301,752,090
Retained earnings.................	215,811,200		

Required

1. Compute common-size percents for Samsung using the data provided. Round percents to one decimal.
2. What is Samsung's gross margin ratio on sales?
3. Does Samsung's gross margin ratio outperform or underperform the industry (assumed) average of 25%?

Beyond the Numbers

BTN 13-1   As Beacon Company controller, you are responsible for informing the board of directors about its financial activities. At the board meeting, you present the following information.

	2019	2018	2017
Sales trend percent......................	147.0%	135.0%	100.0%
Selling expenses to sales..................	10.1%	14.0%	15.6%
Sales to plant assets ratio	3.8 to 1	3.6 to 1	3.3 to 1
Current ratio...........................	2.9 to 1	2.7 to 1	2.4 to 1
Acid-test ratio	1.1 to 1	1.4 to 1	1.5 to 1
Inventory turnover	7.8 times	9.0 times	10.2 times
Accounts receivable turnover	7.0 times	7.7 times	8.5 times
Total asset turnover	2.9 times	2.9 times	3.3 times
Return on total assets....................	10.4%	11.0%	13.2%
Return on stockholders' equity	10.7%	11.5%	14.1%
Profit margin ratio.......................	3.6%	3.8%	4.0%

After the meeting, the company's CEO holds a press conference with analysts in which she mentions the following ratios.

	2019	2018	2017
Sales trend percent......................	147.0%	135.0%	100.0%
Selling expenses to sales..................	10.1%	14.0%	15.6%
Sales to plant assets ratio	3.8 to 1	3.6 to 1	3.3 to 1
Current ratio...........................	2.9 to 1	2.7 to 1	2.4 to 1

Required

1. Why do you think the CEO decided to report 4 ratios instead of the 11 prepared?
2. Comment on the possible consequences of the CEO's reporting of the ratios selected.

BTN 13-2   Each team is to select a different industry, and each team member is to select a different company in that industry and acquire its financial statements. Use those statements to analyze the company, including at least one ratio from each of the four building blocks of analysis. When necessary, use the financial press to determine the market price of its stock. Communicate with teammates via a meeting, e-mail, or telephone to discuss how different companies compare to each other and to industry norms. The team is to prepare a single one-page memorandum reporting on its analysis and the conclusions reached.

TAKING IT TO THE NET

P3

BTN 13-3   Access the February 21, 2017, filing of the December 31, 2016, 10-K report of **The Hershey Company** (ticker: HSY) at **SEC.gov** and complete the following requirements.

Required

Compute or identify the following profitability ratios of Hershey for its years ending December 31, 2016, *and* December 31, 2015. Interpret its profitability using the results obtained for these two years.

1. Profit margin ratio (round the percent to one decimal).
2. Gross profit ratio (round the percent to one decimal).
3. Return on total assets (round the percent to one decimal). (Total assets at year-end 2014 were $5,622,870 in thousands.)
4. Return on common stockholders' equity (round the percent to one decimal). (Total shareholders' equity at year-end 2014 was $1,519,530 in thousands.)
5. Basic net income per common share (round to the nearest cent).

TEAMWORK IN ACTION

P1   P2   P3

Hint: Pairing within teams may be necessary for part 2. Use as an in-class activity or as an assignment. Consider presentations to the entire class using team rotation with slides.

BTN 13-4   A team approach to learning financial statement analysis is often useful.

Required

1. Each team should write a description of horizontal and vertical analysis that all team members agree with and understand. Illustrate each description with an example.
2. *Each* member of the team is to select *one* of the following categories of ratio analysis. Explain what the ratios in that category measure. Choose one ratio from the category selected, present its formula, and explain what it measures.

   a. Liquidity and efficiency   **c.** Profitability
   b. Solvency   **d.** Market prospects

3. Each team member is to present his or her notes from part 2 to teammates. Team members are to confirm or correct other teammates' presentations.

ENTREPRENEURIAL DECISION

A1   P1   P2   P3

BTN 13-5   Assume that Carla Harris of **Morgan Stanley** (**MorganStanley.com**) has impressed you with the company's success and its commitment to ethical behavior. You learn of a staff opening at Morgan Stanley and decide to apply for it. Your resume is successfully screened from those received and you advance to the interview process. You learn that the interview consists of analyzing the following financial facts and answering analysis questions below. (The data are taken from a small merchandiser in outdoor recreational equipment.)

	2019	2018	2017
Sales trend percents......................	137.0%	125.0%	100.0%
Selling expenses to sales...................	9.8%	13.7%	15.3%
Sales to plant assets ratio	3.5 to 1	3.3 to 1	3.0 to 1
Current ratio	2.6 to 1	2.4 to 1	2.1 to 1
Acid-test ratio	0.8 to 1	1.1 to 1	1.2 to 1
Merchandise inventory turnover	7.5 times	8.7 times	9.9 times
Accounts receivable turnover	6.7 times	7.4 times	8.2 times
Total asset turnover	2.6 times	2.6 times	3.0 times
Return on total assets.....................	8.8%	9.4%	11.1%
Return on equity.........................	9.75%	11.50%	12.25%
Profit margin ratio........................	3.3%	3.5%	3.7%

Required

Use these data to answer each of the following questions with explanations.

1. Is it becoming easier for the company to meet its current liabilities on time and to take advantage of any available cash discounts? Explain.
2. Is the company collecting its accounts receivable more rapidly? Explain.

3. Is the company's investment in accounts receivable decreasing? Explain.

4. Is the company's investment in plant assets increasing? Explain.

5. Is the owner's investment becoming more profitable? Explain.

6. Did the dollar amount of selling expenses decrease during the three-year period? Explain.

BTN 13-6   You are to devise an investment strategy to enable you to accumulate $1,000,000 by age 65. Start by making some assumptions about your salary. Next, compute the percent of your salary that you will be able to save each year. If you will receive any lump-sum monies, include those amounts in your calculations. Historically, stocks have delivered average annual returns of around 10%. Given this history, you probably should not assume that you will earn above 10% on the money you invest. It is not necessary to specify exactly what types of assets you will buy for your investments; just assume a rate you expect to earn. Use the future value tables in Appendix B to calculate how your savings will grow. Experiment a bit with your figures to see how much less you have to save if you start at, for example, age 25 versus age 35 or 40. (For this assignment, do not include inflation in your calculations.)

HITTING THE ROAD

C1   P3

Financial Statement Information

This appendix includes financial information for (1) **Apple**, (2) **Google**, and (3) **Samsung**. Apple states that it designs, manufactures, and markets mobile communication and media devices, personal computers, and portable digital music players, and sells a variety of related software, services, peripherals, networking solutions, and third-party digital content and applications; it competes with both Google and Samsung in the United States and globally. The information in this appendix is taken from annual 10-K reports (or annual report for Samsung) filed with the SEC or other regulatory agency. An **annual report** is a summary of a company's financial results for the year along with its current financial condition and future plans. This report is directed to external users of financial information, but it also affects the actions and decisions of internal users.

A company often uses an annual report to showcase itself and its products. Many annual reports include photos, diagrams, and illustrations related to the company. The primary objective of annual reports, however, is the financial section, which communicates much information about a company, with most data drawn from the accounting information system. The content of a typical annual report's financial section follows.

- Letter to Shareholders
- Financial History and Highlights
- Quantitative and Qualitative Disclosures about Risk Factors
- Management Discussion and Analysis
- Management's Report on Financial Statements and on Internal Controls
- Report of Independent Accountants (Auditor's Report) and on Internal Controls
- Financial Statements
- Notes to Financial Statements
- Directors, Officers, and Corporate Governance
- Executive Compensation
- Accounting Fees and Services

This appendix provides the financial statements for Apple (plus selected notes), Google, and Samsung. The appendix is organized as follows:

- **Apple A-2** through **A-9**
- **Google A-10** through **A-13**
- **Samsung A-14** through **A-17**

APPLE
GOOGLE
Samsung

Many assignments at the end of each chapter refer to information in this appendix. We encourage readers to spend time with these assignments; they are especially useful in showing the relevance and diversity of accounting and reporting.

Special note: The SEC maintains the EDGAR (**E**lectronic **D**ata **G**athering, **A**nalysis, and **R**etrieval) database at **SEC.gov** for U.S. filers. The **Form 10-K** is the annual report form for most companies. It provides electronically accessible information. The **Form 10-KSB** is the annual report form filed by small businesses. It requires slightly less information than the Form 10-K. One of these forms must be filed within 90 days after the company's fiscal year-end. (Forms 10-K405, 10-KT, 10-KT405, and 10-KSB405 are slight variations of the usual form due to certain regulations or rules.)

APPLE

Apple Inc.
CONSOLIDATED BALANCE SHEETS
(In millions, except number of shares which are reflected in thousands and par value)

	September 30, 2017	September 24, 2016
ASSETS		
Current assets		
Cash and cash equivalents	$ 20,289	$ 20,484
Short-term marketable securities	53,892	46,671
Accounts receivable, less allowances of $58 and $53, respectively	17,874	15,754
Inventories	4,855	2,132
Vendor non-trade receivables	17,799	13,545
Other current assets	13,936	8,283
Total current assets	128,645	106,869
Long-term marketable securities	194,714	170,430
Property, plant and equipment, net	33,783	27,010
Goodwill	5,717	5,414
Acquired intangible assets, net	2,298	3,206
Other non-current assets	10,162	8,757
Total assets	$ 375,319	$ 321,686
LIABILITIES AND SHAREHOLDERS' EQUITY		
Current liabilities		
Accounts payable	$ 49,049	$ 37,294
Accrued expenses	25,744	22,027
Deferred revenue	7,548	8,080
Commercial paper	11,977	8,105
Current portion of long-term debt	6,496	3,500
Total current liabilities	100,814	79,006
Deferred revenue, non-current	2,836	2,930
Long-term debt	97,207	75,427
Other non-current liabilities	40,415	36,074
Total liabilities	241,272	193,437
Commitments and contingencies		
Shareholders' equity		
Common stock and additional paid-in capital, $0.00001 par value: 12,600,000 shares authorized; 5,126,201 and 5,336,166 shares issued and outstanding, respectively	35,867	31,251
Retained earnings	98,330	96,364
Accumulated other comprehensive income (loss)	(150)	634
Total shareholders' equity	134,047	128,249
Total liabilities and shareholders' equity	$ 375,319	$ 321,686

See accompanying Notes to Consolidated Financial Statements.

Apple Inc.
CONSOLIDATED STATEMENTS OF OPERATIONS
(In millions, except number of shares which are reflected in thousands and per share amounts)

Years ended	September 30, 2017	September 24, 2016	September 26, 2015
Net sales	$ 229,234	$ 215,639	$ 233,715
Cost of sales	141,048	131,376	140,089
Gross margin	88,186	84,263	93,626
Operating expenses			
Research and development	11,581	10,045	8,067
Selling, general and administrative	15,261	14,194	14,329
Total operating expenses	26,842	24,239	22,396
Operating income	61,344	60,024	71,230
Other income (expense), net	2,745	1,348	1,285
Income before provision for income taxes	64,089	61,372	72,515
Provision for income taxes	15,738	15,685	19,121
Net income	$ 48,351	$ 45,687	$ 53,394
Earnings per share:			
Basic	$ 9.27	$ 8.35	$ 9.28
Diluted	$ 9.21	$ 8.31	$ 9.22
Shares used in computing earnings per share:			
Basic	5,217,242	5,470,820	5,753,421
Diluted	5,251,692	5,500,281	5,793,069
Cash dividends declared per share	$ 2.40	$ 2.18	$ 1.98

See accompanying Notes to Consolidated Financial Statements.

Apple Inc.
CONSOLIDATED STATEMENTS OF COMPREHENSIVE INCOME
(In millions)

Years ended	September 30, 2017	September 24, 2016	September 26, 2015
Net income	$ 48,351	$ 45,687	$ 53,394
Other comprehensive income (loss):			
Change in foreign currency translation, net of tax effects of $(77), $8 and $201, respectively	224	75	(411)
Change in unrealized gains/losses on derivative instruments:			
Change in fair value of derivatives, net of tax benefit (expense) of $(478), $(7) and $(441), respectively	1,315	7	2,905
Adjustment for net (gains) losses realized and included in net income, net of tax expense (benefit) of $475, $131 and $630, respectively	(1,477)	(741)	(3,497)
Total change in unrealized gains/losses on derivative instruments, net of tax	(162)	(734)	(592)
Change in unrealized gains/losses on marketable securities:			
Change in fair value of marketable securities, net of tax benefit (expense) of $425, $(863) and $264, respectively	(782)	1,582	(483)
Adjustment for net (gains) losses realized and included in net income, net of tax expense (benefit) of $35, $(31), and $(32), respectively	(64)	56	59
Total change in unrealized gains/losses on marketable securities, net of tax	(846)	1,638	(424)
Total other comprehensive income (loss)	(784)	979	(1,427)
Total comprehensive income	$ 47,567	$ 46,666	$ 51,967

See accompanying Notes to Consolidated Financial Statements.

APPLE

Apple Inc.
CONSOLIDATED STATEMENTS OF SHAREHOLDERS' EQUITY
(In millions, except number of shares which are reflected in thousands)

	Common Stock and Additional Paid-In Capital		Retained Earnings	Accumulated Other Comprehensive Income (Loss)	Total Shareholders' Equity
	Shares	Amount			
Balances as of September 27, 2014	5,866,161	$ 23,313	$ 87,152	$ 1,082	$ 111,547
Net income	—	—	53,394	—	53,394
Other comprehensive income (loss)	—	—	—	(1,427)	(1,427)
Dividends and dividend equivalents declared	—	—	(11,627)	—	(11,627)
Repurchase of common stock	(325,032)	—	(36,026)	—	(36,026)
Share-based compensation	—	3,586	—	—	3,586
Common stock issued, net of shares withheld for employee taxes	37,624	(231)	(609)	—	(840)
Tax benefit from equity awards, including transfer pricing adjustments	—	748	—	—	748
Balances as of September 26, 2015	5,578,753	$ 27,416	$ 92,284	$ (345)	$ 119,355
Net income	—	—	45,687	—	45,687
Other comprehensive income (loss)	—	—	—	979	979
Dividends and dividend equivalents declared	—	—	(12,188)	—	(12,188)
Repurchase of common stock	(279,609)	—	(29,000)	—	(29,000)
Share-based compensation	—	4,262	—	—	4,262
Common stock issued, net of shares withheld for employee taxes	37,022	(806)	(419)	—	(1,225)
Tax benefit from equity awards, including transfer pricing adjustments	—	379	—	—	379
Balances as of September 24, 2016	5,336,166	$ 31,251	$ 96,364	$ 634	$ 128,249
Net income	—	—	48,351	—	48,351
Other comprehensive income (loss)	—	—	—	(784)	(784)
Dividends and dividend equivalents declared	—	—	(12,803)	—	(12,803)
Repurchase of common stock	(246,496)	—	(33,001)	—	(33,001)
Share-based compensation	—	4,909	—	—	4,909
Common stock issued, net of shares withheld for employee taxes	36,531	(913)	(581)	—	(1,494)
Tax benefit from equity awards, including transfer pricing adjustments	—	620	—	—	620
Balances as of September 30, 2017	5,126,201	$ 35,867	$ 98,330	$ (150)	$ 134,047

See accompanying Notes to Consolidated Financial Statements.

APPLE

Apple Inc.
CONSOLIDATED STATEMENTS OF CASH FLOWS
(In millions)

Years ended	September 30, 2017	September 24, 2016	September 26, 2015
Cash and cash equivalents, beginning of the year	$ 20,484	$ 21,120	$ 13,844
Operating activities:			
Net income	48,351	45,687	53,394
Adjustments to reconcile net income to cash generated by operating activities:			
Depreciation and amortization	10,157	10,505	11,257
Share-based compensation expense	4,840	4,210	3,586
Deferred income tax expense	5,966	4,938	1,382
Other	(166)	486	385
Changes in operating assets and liabilities:			
Accounts receivable, net	(2,093)	527	417
Inventories	(2,723)	217	(238)
Vendor non-trade receivables	(4,254)	(51)	(3,735)
Other current and non-current assets	(5,318)	1,055	(283)
Accounts payable	9,618	1,837	5,001
Deferred revenue	(626)	(1,554)	1,042
Other current and non-current liabilities	(154)	(2,033)	9,058
Cash generated by operating activities	63,598	65,824	81,266
Investing activities:			
Purchases of marketable securities	(159,486)	(142,428)	(166,402)
Proceeds from maturities of marketable securities	31,775	21,258	14,538
Proceeds from sales of marketable securities	94,564	90,536	107,447
Payments made in connection with business acquisitions, net	(329)	(297)	(343)
Payments for acquisition of property, plant and equipment	(12,451)	(12,734)	(11,247)
Payments for acquisition of intangible assets	(344)	(814)	(241)
Payments for strategic investments, net	(395)	(1,388)	—
Other	220	(110)	(26)
Cash used in investing activities	(46,446)	(45,977)	(56,274)
Financing activities:			
Proceeds from issuance of common stock	555	495	543
Excess tax benefits from equity awards	627	407	749
Payments for taxes related to net share settlement of equity awards	(1,874)	(1,570)	(1,499)
Payments for dividends and dividend equivalents	(12,769)	(12,150)	(11,561)
Repurchases of common stock	(32,900)	(29,722)	(35,253)
Proceeds from issuance of term debt, net	28,662	24,954	27,114
Repayments of term debt	(3,500)	(2,500)	—
Change in commercial paper, net	3,852	(397)	2,191
Cash used in financing activities	(17,347)	(20,483)	(17,716)
Increase (decrease) in cash and cash equivalents	(195)	(636)	7,276
Cash and cash equivalents, end of the year	$ 20,289	$ 20,484	$ 21,120
Supplemental cash flow disclosure:			
Cash paid for income taxes, net	$ 11,591	$ 10,444	$ 13,252
Cash paid for interest	$ 2,092	$ 1,316	$ 514

See accompanying Notes to Consolidated Financial Statements.

APPLE INC.
SELECTED NOTES TO CONSOLIDATED FINANCIAL STATEMENTS

Basis of Presentation and Preparation

In the opinion of the Company's management, the consolidated financial statements reflect all adjustments, which are normal and recurring in nature, necessary for fair financial statement presentation.

The Company's fiscal year is the 52 or 53-week period that ends on the last Saturday of September. The Company's fiscal year 2017 included 53 weeks and ended on September 30, 2017. A 14th week was included in the first fiscal quarter of 2017, as is done every five or six years, to realign the Company's fiscal quarters with calendar quarters. The Company's fiscal years 2016 and 2015 ended on September 24, 2016 and September 26, 2015, respectively, and spanned 52 weeks each. Unless otherwise stated, references to particular years, quarters, months and periods refer to the Company's fiscal years ended in September and the associated quarters, months and periods of those fiscal years.

Revenue Recognition

Net sales consist primarily of revenue from the sale of hardware, software, digital content and applications, accessories, and service and support contracts. The Company recognizes revenue when persuasive evidence of an arrangement exists, delivery has occurred, the sales price is fixed or determinable and collection is probable. Product is considered delivered to the customer once it has been shipped and title, risk of loss and rewards of ownership have been transferred. For most of the Company's product sales, these criteria are met at the time the product is shipped. For online sales to individuals, for some sales to education customers in the U.S., and for certain other sales, the Company defers revenue until the customer receives the product because the Company retains a portion of the risk of loss on these sales during transit. For payment terms in excess of the Company's standard payment terms, revenue is recognized as payments become due unless the Company has positive evidence that the sales price is fixed or determinable, such as a successful history of collection, without concession, on comparable arrangements. The Company recognizes revenue from the sale of hardware products, software bundled with hardware that is essential to the functionality of the hardware and third-party digital content sold on the iTunes Store in accordance with general revenue recognition accounting guidance. The Company recognizes revenue in accordance with industry-specific software accounting guidance for the following types of sales transactions: (i) standalone sales of software products, (ii) sales of software upgrades and (iii) sales of software bundled with hardware not essential to the functionality of the hardware.

For the sale of most third-party products, the Company recognizes revenue based on the gross amount billed to customers because the Company establishes its own pricing for such products, retains related inventory risk for physical products, is the primary obligor to the customer and assumes the credit risk for amounts billed to its customers. For third-party applications sold through the App Store and Mac App Store and certain digital content sold through the iTunes Store, the Company does not determine the selling price of the products and is not the primary obligor to the customer. Therefore, the Company accounts for such sales on a net basis by recognizing in net sales only the commission it retains from each sale. The portion of the gross amount billed to customers that is remitted by the Company to third-party app developers and certain digital content owners is not reflected in the Company's Consolidated Statements of Operations.

The Company records deferred revenue when it receives payments in advance of the delivery of products or the performance of services. This includes amounts that have been deferred for unspecified and specified software upgrade rights and non-software services that are attached to hardware and software products. The Company sells gift cards redeemable at its retail and online stores, and also sells gift cards redeemable on iTunes Store, App Store, Mac App Store, TV App Store and iBooks Store for the purchase of digital content and software. The Company records deferred revenue upon the sale of the card, which is relieved upon redemption of the card by the customer. Revenue from AppleCare service and support contracts is deferred and recognized over the service coverage periods. AppleCare service and support contracts typically include extended phone support, repair services, web-based support resources and diagnostic tools offered under the Company's standard limited warranty.

The Company records reductions to revenue for estimated commitments related to price protection and other customer incentive programs. For transactions involving price protection, the Company recognizes revenue net of the estimated amount to be refunded. For the Company's other customer incentive programs, the estimated cost of these programs is recognized at the later of the date at which the Company has sold the product or the date at which the program is offered. The Company also records reductions to revenue for expected future product returns based on the Company's historical experience. Revenue is recorded net of taxes collected from customers that are remitted to governmental authorities, with the collected taxes recorded as current liabilities until remitted to the relevant government authority.

For multi-element arrangements that include hardware products containing software essential to the hardware product's functionality, undelivered software elements that relate to the hardware product's essential software, and undelivered non-software services, the Company allocates revenue to all deliverables based on their relative selling prices.

For sales of qualifying versions of iPhone, iPad, iPod touch, Mac, Apple Watch and Apple TV, the Company has

Apple Inc. Notes—continued

indicated it may from time to time provide future unspecified software upgrades to the device's essential software and/or non-software services free of charge. The Company has identified up to three deliverables regularly included in arrangements involving the sale of these devices. The Company allocates revenue between these deliverables using the relative selling price method. Revenue allocated to the delivered hardware and the related essential software is recognized at the time of sale, provided the other conditions for revenue recognition have been met. Revenue allocated to the embedded unspecified software upgrade rights and the non-software services is deferred and recognized on a straight-line basis over the estimated period the software upgrades and non-software services are expected to be provided. Cost of sales related to delivered hardware and related essential software, including estimated warranty costs, are recognized at the time of sale. Costs incurred to provide non-software services are recognized as cost of sales as incurred, and engineering and sales and marketing costs are recognized as operating expenses as incurred.

Shipping Costs

Amounts billed to customers related to shipping and handling are classified as revenue, and the Company's shipping and handling costs are classified as cost of sales.

Warranty Costs

The Company generally provides for the estimated cost of hardware and software warranties in the period the related revenue is recognized. The Company assesses the adequacy of its accrued warranty liabilities and adjusts the amounts as necessary based on actual experience and changes in future estimates.

Software Development Costs

Research and development ("R&D") costs are expensed as incurred. Development costs of computer software to be sold, leased, or otherwise marketed are subject to capitalization beginning when a product's technological feasibility has been established and ending when a product is available for general release to customers. In most instances, the Company's products are released soon after technological feasibility has been established and as a result software development costs were expensed as incurred.

Advertising Costs

Advertising costs are expensed as incurred and included in selling, general and administrative expenses.

Other Income and Expense

$ millions	2017	2016	2015
Interest and dividend income	$ 5,201	$ 3,999	$2,921
Interest expense	(2,323)	(1,456)	(733)
Other expense, net	(133)	(1,195)	(903)
Total other income (expense), net	$ 2,745	$ 1,348	$1,285

Earnings Per Share

Basic earnings per share is computed by dividing income available to common shareholders by the weighted-average number of shares of common stock outstanding during the period. Diluted earnings per share is computed by dividing income available to common shareholders by the weighted-average number of shares of common stock outstanding during the period increased to include the number of additional shares of common stock that would have been outstanding if the potentially dilutive securities had been issued.

Cash Equivalents and Marketable Securities

All highly liquid investments with maturities of three months or less at the date of purchase are classified as cash equivalents. The Company's marketable debt and equity securities have been classified and accounted for as available-for-sale. Management determines the appropriate classification of its investments at the time of purchase and reevaluates the classifications at each balance sheet date. The Company classifies its marketable debt securities as either short-term or long-term based on each instrument's underlying contractual maturity date. Marketable debt securities with maturities of 12 months or less are classified as short-term and marketable debt securities with maturities greater than 12 months are classified as long-term. Marketable equity securities, including mutual funds, are classified as either short-term or long-term based on the nature of each security and its availability for use in current operations. The Company's marketable debt and equity securities are carried at fair value, with unrealized gains and losses, net of taxes, reported as a component of accumulated other comprehensive income/(loss) ("AOCI") in shareholders' equity, with the exception of unrealized losses believed to be other-than-temporary which are reported in earnings in the current period. The cost of securities sold is based upon the specific identification method.

Accounts Receivable (Trade Receivables)

The Company has considerable trade receivables outstanding with its third-party cellular network carriers, wholesalers, retailers, value-added resellers, small and mid-sized businesses and education, enterprise and government customers.

As of September 30, 2017, the Company had two customers that individually represented 10% or more of total trade receivables, each of which accounted for 10%. As of September 24, 2016, the Company had one customer that represented 10% or more of total trade receivables, which accounted for 10%. The Company's cellular network carriers accounted for 59% and 63% of trade receivables as of September 30, 2017 and September 24, 2016, respectively.

Allowance for Doubtful Accounts

The Company records its allowance for doubtful accounts based upon its assessment of various factors, including

Apple Inc. Notes—continued

historical experience, age of the accounts receivable balances, credit quality of the Company's customers, current economic conditions and other factors that may affect the customers' abilities to pay.

Inventories

Inventories are stated at the lower of cost, computed using the first-in, first-out method, and net realizable value. Any adjustments to reduce the cost of inventories to their net realizable value are recognized in earnings in the current period.

Property, Plant and Equipment

Property, plant and equipment are stated at cost. Depreciation is computed by use of the straight-line method over the estimated useful lives of the assets, which for buildings is the lesser of 30 years or the remaining life of the underlying building; between one and five years for machinery and equipment, including product tooling and manufacturing process equipment; and the shorter of lease term or useful life for leasehold improvements. The Company capitalizes eligible costs to acquire or develop internal-use software that are incurred subsequent to the preliminary project stage. Capitalized costs related to internal-use software are amortized using the straight-line method over the estimated useful lives of the assets, which range from three to five years. Depreciation and amortization expense on property and equipment was $8.2 billion, $8.3 billion and $9.2 billion during 2017, 2016 and 2015, respectively.

Property, Plant and Equipment, Net

($ millions)	2017	2016
Land and buildings	$ 13,587	$ 10,185
Machinery, equipment and internal-use software	54,210	44,543
Leasehold improvements	7,279	6,517
Gross property, plant and equipment	75,076	61,245
Accumulated depreciation and amortization	(41,293)	(34,235)
Total property, plant and equipment, net	$ 33,783	$ 27,010

Long-Lived Assets Including Goodwill and Other Acquired Intangible Assets

The Company reviews property, plant and equipment, inventory component prepayments and identifiable intangibles, excluding goodwill and intangible assets with indefinite useful lives, for impairment. Long-lived assets are reviewed for impairment whenever events or changes in circumstances indicate the carrying amount of an asset may not be recoverable. Recoverability of these assets is measured by comparison of their carrying amounts to future undiscounted cash flows the assets are expected to generate. If property, plant and equipment, inventory component prepayments and certain identifiable intangibles are considered to be impaired, the impairment to be recognized equals the amount by which the carrying value of the asset exceeds its fair value.

The Company does not amortize goodwill and intangible assets with indefinite useful lives; rather, such assets are required to be tested for impairment at least annually or sooner if events or changes in circumstances indicate that the assets may be impaired. The Company performs its goodwill and intangible asset impairment tests in the fourth quarter of each year. The Company did not recognize any impairment charges related to goodwill or indefinite lived intangible assets during 2017, 2016 and 2015. For purposes of testing goodwill for impairment, the Company established reporting units based on its current reporting structure. Goodwill has been allocated to these reporting units to the extent it relates to each reporting unit. In 2017 and 2016, the Company's goodwill was primarily allocated to the Americas and Europe reporting units.

The Company amortizes its intangible assets with definite useful lives over their estimated useful lives and reviews these assets for impairment. The Company typically amortizes its acquired intangible assets with definite useful lives over periods from three to seven years.

Acquired Intangible Assets

The Company's acquired intangible assets with definite useful lives primarily consist of patents and licenses. The following table summarizes the components of acquired intangible asset balances as of September 30, 2017. Amortization expense related to acquired intangible assets was $1.2 billion in 2017.

$ millions	Gross Carrying Amount	Accumulated Amortization	Net Carrying Amount
Definite-lived and amortizable acquired intangible assets	$ 7,507	$ (5,309)	$ 2,198
Indefinite-lived and non-amortizable acquired intangible assets	100	—	100
Total acquired intangible assets	$ 7,607	$ (5,309)	$ 2,298

Fair Value Measurements

The Company applies fair value accounting for all financial assets and liabilities and non-financial assets and liabilities that are recognized or disclosed at fair value in the financial statements on a recurring basis. The Company defines fair value as the price that would be received from selling an asset or paid to transfer a liability in an orderly transaction between market participants at the measurement date. When determining the fair value measurements for assets and liabilities that are required to be recorded at fair value, the Company considers the principal or most advantageous market in which the Company would transact and the market-based risk measurements or assumptions that market participants would use to price the asset or liability, such as risks inherent in valuation techniques, transfer restrictions and credit risk. Fair value is estimated by applying the following hierarchy,

Apple Inc. Notes—continued

which prioritizes the inputs used to measure fair value into three levels and bases the categorization within the hierarchy upon the lowest level of input that is available and significant to the fair value measurement:

Level 1—Quoted prices in active markets for identical assets or liabilities.
Level 2—Observable inputs other than quoted prices in active markets for identical assets and liabilities, quoted prices for identical or similar assets or liabilities in inactive markets, or other inputs that are observable or can be corroborated by observable market data for substantially the full term of the assets or liabilities.
Level 3—Inputs that are generally unobservable and typically reflect management's estimate of assumptions that market participants would use in pricing the asset or liability.

The Company's valuation techniques used to measure the fair value of money market funds and certain marketable equity securities were derived from quoted prices in active markets for identical assets or liabilities. The valuation techniques used to measure the fair value of the Company's debt instruments and all other financial instruments, all of which have counterparties with high credit ratings, were valued based on quoted market prices or model-driven valuations using significant inputs derived from or corroborated by observable market data.

In accordance with the fair value accounting requirements, companies may choose to measure eligible financial instruments and certain other items at fair value. The Company has not elected the fair value option for any eligible financial instruments.

Accrued Warranty and Indemnification

The following table shows changes in the Company's accrued warranties and related costs for 2017 and 2016:

$ millions	2017	2016
Beginning accrued warranty and related costs	$ 3,702	$ 4,780
Cost of warranty claims	(4,322)	(4,663)
Accruals for product warranty	4,454	3,585
Ending accrued warranty and related costs	$ 3,834	$ 3,702

Term Debt

As of September 30, 2017, the Company had outstanding floating- and fixed-rate notes with varying maturities for an aggregate principal amount of $104.0 billion (collectively the "Notes"). The Notes are senior unsecured obligations, and interest is payable in arrears.

The Company recognized $2.2 billion, $1.4 billion and $722 million of interest expense on its term debt for 2017, 2016 and 2015, respectively.

As of September 30, 2017 and September 24, 2016, the fair value of the Company's Notes, based on Level 2 inputs, was $106.1 billion and $81.7 billion, respectively.

Dividends

The Company declared and paid cash dividends per share during the periods presented as follows:

	2017		2016	
	Dividends Per Share	Amount (in millions)	Dividends Per Share	Amount (in millions)
Fourth quarter	$ 0.63	$ 3,252	$ 0.57	$ 3,071
Third quarter	0.63	3,281	0.57	3,117
Second quarter	0.57	2,988	0.52	2,879
First quarter	0.57	3,042	0.52	2,898
Total cash dividends declared and paid	$ 2.40	$ 12,563	$ 2.18	$ 11,965

Segment Information and Geographic Data

Net sales by product (mil.)	2017	2016	2015
iPhone	$141,319	$136,700	$155,041
iPad	19,222	20,628	23,227
Mac	25,850	22,831	25,471
Services	29,980	24,348	19,909
Other Products	12,863	11,132	10,067
Total net sales	$229,234	$215,639	$233,715

Reportable segment (mil.)	2017	2016	2015
Americas:			
Net sales	$96,600	$ 86,613	$ 93,864
Operating income	$30,684	$ 28,172	$ 31,186
Europe:			
Net sales	$54,938	$ 49,952	$ 50,337
Operating income	$16,514	$ 15,348	$ 16,527
Greater China:			
Net sales	$44,764	$ 48,492	$ 58,715
Operating income	$17,032	$ 18,835	$ 23,002
Japan:			
Net sales	$17,733	$ 16,928	$ 15,706
Operating income	$ 8,097	$ 7,165	$ 7,617
Rest of Asia Pacific:			
Net sales	$15,199	$ 13,654	$ 15,093
Operating income	$ 5,304	$ 4,781	$ 5,518

A reconciliation of the Company's segment operating income to the Consolidated Statements of Operations for 2017, 2016 and 2015 is as follows:

$ millions	2017	2016	2015
Segment operating income	$ 77,631	$ 74,301	$83,850
Research and development expense	(11,581)	(10,045)	(8,067)
Other corporate expenses, net	(4,706)	(4,232)	(4,553)
Total operating income	$ 61,344	$ 60,024	$71,230

APPLE

Google Inc. (Alphabet Inc.)[a]
CONSOLIDATED BALANCE SHEETS
**(In millions, except share and par value amounts which are reflected in thousands,
and par value per share amounts)**

	As of December 31, 2016	As of December 31, 2017
Assets		
Current assets		
Cash and cash equivalents	$ 12,918	$ 10,715
Marketable securities	73,415	91,156
Total cash, cash equivalents, and marketable securities	86,333	101,871
Accounts receivable, net of allowance of $467 and $674	14,137	18,336
Income taxes receivable, net	95	369
Inventory	268	749
Other current assets	4,575	2,983
Total current assets	105,408	124,308
Non-marketable investments	5,878	7,813
Deferred income taxes	383	680
Property and equipment, net	34,234	42,383
Intangible assets, net	3,307	2,692
Goodwill	16,468	16,747
Other non-current assets	1,819	2,672
Total assets	$ 167,497	$ 197,295
Liabilities and Stockholders' Equity		
Current liabilities		
Accounts payable	$ 2,041	$ 3,137
Accrued compensation and benefits	3,976	4,581
Accrued expenses and other current liabilities	6,144	10,177
Accrued revenue share	2,942	3,975
Deferred revenue	1,099	1,432
Income taxes payable, net	554	881
Total current liabilities	16,756	24,183
Long-term debt	3,935	3,969
Deferred revenue, non-current	202	340
Income taxes payable, non-current	4,677	12,812
Deferred income taxes	226	430
Other long-term liabilities	2,665	3,059
Total liabilities	28,461	44,793
Commitments and contingencies		
Stockholders' equity:		
Convertible preferred stock, $0.001 par value per share, 100,000 shares authorized; no shares issued and outstanding	0	0
Class A and Class B common stock, and Class C capital stock and additional paid-in capital, $0.001 par value per share: 15,000,000 shares authorized (Class A 9,000,000, Class B 3,000,000, Class C 3,000,000); 691,293 (Class A 296,992, Class B 47,437, Class C 346,864) and 694,783 (Class A 298,470, Class B 46,972, Class C 349,341) shares issued and outstanding	36,307	40,247
Accumulated other comprehensive loss	(2,402)	(992)
Retained earnings	105,131	113,247
Total stockholders' equity	139,036	152,502
Total liabilities and stockholders' equity	$ 167,497	$ 197,295

[a]Google is part of Alphabet, but we loosely refer to Alphabet as "Google" because of its global familiarity and that Google provides 99% of Alphabet's $110,855 billion in revenues.

See accompanying notes.

Google Inc. (Alphabet Inc.)[a]
CONSOLIDATED STATEMENTS OF INCOME
(In millions)

Year Ended December 31	2015	2016	2017
Revenues	$ 74,989	$ 90,272	$ 110,855
Costs and expenses			
Cost of revenues	28,164	35,138	45,583
Research and development	12,282	13,948	16,625
Sales and marketing	9,047	10,485	12,893
General and administrative	6,136	6,985	6,872
European Commission fine	0	0	2,736
Total costs and expenses	55,629	66,556	84,709
Income from operations	19,360	23,716	26,146
Other income (expense), net	291	434	1,047
Income before income taxes	19,651	24,150	27,193
Provision for income taxes	3,303	4,672	14,531
Net income	$ 16,348	$ 19,478	$ 12,662
Less: Adjustment Payment to Class C capital stockholders	522	0	0
Net income available to all stockholders	$ 15,826	$ 19,478	$ 12,662

[a]Google is part of Alphabet, but we loosely refer to Alphabet as "Google" because of its global familiarity and that Google provides 99% of Alphabet's $110,855 billion in revenues.

See accompanying notes.

Google Inc. (Alphabet Inc.)[a]
CONSOLIDATED STATEMENTS OF COMPREHENSIVE INCOME
(In millions)

Year Ended December 31	2015	2016	2017
Net income	$ 16,348	$ 19,478	$ 12,662
Other comprehensive income (loss):			
Change in foreign currency translation adjustment	(1,067)	(599)	1,543
Available-for-sale investments:			
Change in net unrealized gains (losses)	(715)	(314)	307
Less: reclassification adjustment for net (gains) losses included in net income	208	221	105
Net change (net of tax effect of $29, $0, and $0)	(507)	(93)	412
Cash flow hedges:			
Change in net unrealized gains (losses)	676	515	(638)
Less: reclassification adjustment for net (gains) losses included in net income	(1,003)	(351)	93
Net change (net of tax effect of $115, $64, and $247)	(327)	164	(545)
Other comprehensive income (loss)	(1,901)	(528)	1,410
Comprehensive income	$ 14,447	$ 18,950	$ 14,072

[a]Google is part of Alphabet, but we loosely refer to Alphabet as "Google" because of its global familiarity and that Google provides 99% of Alphabet's $110,855 billion in revenues.

See accompanying notes.

Google Inc. (Alphabet Inc.)[a]
CONSOLIDATED STATEMENTS OF STOCKHOLDERS' EQUITY
(In millions, except share amounts which are reflected in thousands)

	Class A and Class B Common Stock, Class C Capital Stock and Additional Paid-In Capital		Accumulated Other Comprehensive Income (Loss)	Retained Earnings	Total Stockholders' Equity
	Shares	Amount			
Balance as of December 31, 2014	680,172 $	28,767 $	27 $	75,066 $	103,860
Common and capital stock issued	8,714	664	0	0	664
Stock-based compensation expense	0	5,151	0	0	5,151
Stock-based compensation tax benefits	0	815	0	0	815
Tax withholding related to vesting of restricted stock units	0	(2,779)	0	0	(2,779)
Repurchases of capital stock	(2,391)	(111)	0	(1,669)	(1,780)
Adjustment Payment to Class C capital stockholders	853	475	0	(522)	(47)
Net income	0	0	0	16,348	16,348
Other comprehensive loss	0	0	(1,901)	0	(1,901)
Balance as of December 31, 2015	687,348	32,982	(1,874)	89,223	120,331
Cumulative effect of accounting change	0	180	0	(133)	47
Common and capital stock issued	9,106	298	0	0	298
Stock-based compensation expense	0	6,700	0	0	6,700
Tax withholding related to vesting of restricted stock units	0	(3,597)	0	0	(3,597)
Repurchases of capital stock	(5,161)	(256)	0	(3,437)	(3,693)
Net income	0	0	0	19,478	19,478
Other comprehensive loss	0	0	(528)	0	(528)
Balance as of December 31, 2016	691,293	36,307	(2,402)	105,131	139,036
Cumulative effect of accounting change	0	0	0	(15)	(15)
Common and capital stock issued	8,652	212	0	0	212
Stock-based compensation expense	0	7,694	0	0	7,694
Tax withholding related to vesting of restricted stock units	0	(4,373)	0	0	(4,373)
Repurchases of capital stock	(5,162)	(315)	0	(4,531)	(4,846)
Sale of subsidiary shares	0	722	0	0	722
Net income	0	0	0	12,662	12,662
Other comprehensive loss	0	0	1,410	0	1,410
Balance as of December 31, 2017	694,783 $	40,247 $	(992) $	113,247 $	152,502

[a]Google is part of Alphabet, but we loosely refer to Alphabet as "Google" because of its global familiarity and that Google provides 99% of Alphabet's $110,855 billion in revenues.

See accompanying notes.

Google Inc. (Alphabet Inc.)[a]
CONSOLIDATED STATEMENTS OF CASH FLOWS
(In millions)

Year Ended December 31	2015	2016	2017
Operating activities			
Net income	$ 16,348	$ 19,478	$ 12,662
Adjustments:			
Depreciation and impairment of property and equipment	4,132	5,267	6,103
Amortization and impairment of intangible assets	931	877	812
Stock-based compensation expense	5,203	6,703	7,679
Deferred income taxes	(179)	(38)	258
Loss on marketable and non-marketable investments, net	334	275	194
Other	212	174	137
Changes in assets and liabilities, net of effects of acquisitions:			
Accounts receivable	(2,094)	(2,578)	(3,768)
Income taxes, net	(179)	3,125	8,211
Other assets	(318)	312	(2,164)
Accounts payable	203	110	731
Accrued expenses and other liabilities	1,597	1,515	4,891
Accrued revenue share	339	593	955
Deferred revenue	43	223	390
Net cash provided by operating activities	26,572	36,036	37,091
Investing activities			
Purchases of property and equipment	(9,950)	(10,212)	(13,184)
Proceeds from disposals of property and equipment	35	240	99
Purchases of marketable securities	(74,368)	(84,509)	(92,195)
Maturities and sales of marketable securities	62,905	66,895	73,959
Purchases of non-marketable investments	(2,326)	(1,109)	(1,745)
Maturities and sales of non-marketable investments	154	494	533
Cash collateral related to securities lending	(350)	(2,428)	0
Investments in reverse repurchase agreements	425	450	0
Acquisitions, net of cash acquired, and purchases of intangible assets	(236)	(986)	(287)
Proceeds from collection of notes receivable	0	0	1,419
Net cash used in investing activities	(23,711)	(31,165)	(31,401)
Financing activities			
Net payments related to stock-based award activities	(2,375)	(3,304)	(4,166)
Adjustment Payment to Class C capital stockholders	(47)	0	0
Repurchases of capital stock	(1,780)	(3,693)	(4,846)
Proceeds from issuance of debt, net of costs	13,705	8,729	4,291
Repayments of debt	(13,728)	(10,064)	(4,377)
Proceeds from sale of subsidiary shares	0	0	800
Net cash used in financing activities	(4,225)	(8,332)	(8,298)
Effect of exchange rate changes on cash and cash equivalents	(434)	(170)	405
Net decrease in cash and cash equivalents	(1,798)	(3,631)	(2,203)
Cash and cash equivalents at beginning of period	18,347	16,549	12,918
Cash and cash equivalents at end of period	$ 16,549	$ 12,918	$ 10,715
Supplemental disclosures of cash flow information			
Cash paid for taxes, net of refunds	$ 3,651	$ 1,643	$ 6,191
Cash paid for interest, net of amounts capitalized	$ 96	$ 84	$ 84

[a]Google is part of Alphabet, but we loosely refer to Alphabet as "Google" because of its global familiarity and that Google provides 99% of Alphabet's $110,855 billion in revenues.

See accompanying notes.

Samsung Electronics Co., Ltd. and Subsidiaries
CONSOLIDATED STATEMENTS OF FINANCIAL POSITION

(In millions of Korean won)	December 31, 2017	December 31, 2016
Assets	KRW	KRW
Current assets		
Cash and cash equivalents	30,545,130	32,111,442
Short-term financial instruments	49,447,696	52,432,411
Short-term available-for-sale financial assets	3,191,375	3,638,460
Trade receivables	27,695,995	24,279,211
Non-trade receivables	4,108,961	3,521,197
Advance payments	1,753,673	1,439,938
Prepaid expenses	3,835,219	3,502,083
Inventories	24,983,355	18,353,503
Other current assets	1,421,060	1,315,653
Assets held-for-sale	—	835,806
Total current assets	**146,982,464**	**141,429,704**
Non-current assets		
Long-term available-for-sale financial assets	7,752,180	6,804,276
Held-to-maturity financial assets	106,751	—
Investment in associates and joint ventures	6,802,351	5,837,884
Property, plant and equipment	111,665,648	91,473,041
Intangible assets	14,760,483	5,344,020
Long-term prepaid expenses	3,434,375	3,834,831
Net defined benefit assets	825,892	557,091
Deferred income tax assets	5,061,687	5,321,450
Other non-current assets	4,360,259	1,572,027
Total assets	**301,752,090**	**262,174,324**
Liabilities and Equity		
Current liabilities		
Trade payables	9,083,907	6,485,039
Short-term borrowings	15,767,619	12,746,789
Other payables	13,899,633	11,525,910
Advances received	1,249,174	1,358,878
Withholdings	793,582	685,028
Accrued expenses	13,996,273	12,527,300
Income tax payable	7,408,348	2,837,353
Current portion of long-term liabilities	278,619	1,232,817
Provisions	4,294,820	4,597,417
Other current liabilities	403,139	351,176
Liabilities held-for-sale	—	356,388
Total current liabilities	**67,175,114**	**54,704,095**
Non-current liabilities		
Debentures	953,361	58,542
Long-term borrowings	1,814,446	1,244,238
Long-term other payables	2,043,729	3,317,054
Net defined benefit liabilities	389,922	173,656
Deferred income tax liabilities	11,710,781	7,293,514
Provisions	464,324	358,126
Other non-current liabilities	2,708,985	2,062,066
Total liabilities	**87,260,662**	**69,211,291**
Equity attributable to owners of the parent		
Preference shares	119,467	119,467
Ordinary shares	778,047	778,047
Share premium	4,403,893	4,403,893
Retained earnings	215,811,200	193,086,317
Other components of equity	(13,899,191)	(11,934,586)
Accumulated other comprehensive income attributable to assets held for-sale	—	(28,810)
	207,213,416	**186,424,328**
Non-controlling interests	7,278,012	6,538,705
Total equity	**214,491,428**	**192,963,033**
Total liabilities and equity	**301,752,090**	**262,174,324**

The above consolidated statement of financial position should be read in conjunction with the accompanying notes.

Samsung Electronics Co., Ltd. and Subsidiaries
CONSOLIDATED STATEMENTS OF PROFIT OR LOSS

For the year ended December 31	2017	2016
(In millions of Korean won)	KRW	KRW
Revenue	239,575,376	201,866,745
Cost of sales	129,290,661	120,277,715
Gross profit	**110,284,715**	**81,589,030**
Selling and administrative expenses	56,639,677	52,348,358
Operating profit	**53,645,038**	**29,240,672**
Other non-operating income	3,010,657	3,238,261
Other non-operating expense	1,419,648	2,463,814
Share of profit of associates and joint ventures	201,442	19,501
Financial income	9,737,391	11,385,645
Financial expense	8,978,913	10,706,613
Profit before income tax	**56,195,967**	**30,713,652**
Income tax expense	14,009,220	7,987,560
Profit for the period	**42,186,747**	**22,726,092**
Profit attributable to owners of the parent	41,344,569	22,415,655
Profit attributable to non-controlling interests	842,178	310,437
Earnings per share		
—Basic	299,868	157,967
—Diluted	299,868	157,967

The above consolidated statement of financial position should be read in conjunction with the accompanying notes.

Samsung Electronics Co., Ltd. and Subsidiaries
CONSOLIDATED STATEMENTS OF COMPREHENSIVE INCOME

For the year ended December 31	2017	2016
(In millions of Korean won)	KRW	KRW
Profit for the period	42,186,747	22,726,092
Other comprehensive income (loss)		
Items not to be reclassified to profit or loss subsequently:		
Remeasurement of net defined benefit liabilities, net of tax	414,247	963,602
Shares of other comprehensive income (loss) of associates and joint ventures, net of tax	(6,347)	50,438
Items to be reclassified to profit or loss subsequently:		
Changes in value of available-for-sale financial assets, net of tax	511,207	(23,839)
Share of other comprehensive income (loss) of associates and joint ventures, net of tax	(49,256)	(130,337)
Foreign currency translation, net of tax	(6,334,987)	1,131,536
Gain (loss) on valuation of derivatives	(37,121)	—
Other comprehensive income (loss) for the period, net of tax	**(5,502,257)**	**1,991,400**
Total comprehensive income for the period	**36,684,490**	**24,717,492**
Comprehensive income attributable to:		
Owners of the parent	35,887,505	24,310,814
Non-controlling interests	796,985	406,678

The above consolidated statement of financial position should be read in conjunction with the accompanying notes.

SAMSUNG

Samsung Electronics Co., Ltd. and Subsidiaries
CONSOLIDATED STATEMENTS OF CHANGES IN EQUITY

In millions of Korean won	Preference shares	Ordinary shares	Share premium	Retained earnings	Other Components of equity	Accumulated other comprehensive income attributable to assets held-for-sale	Equity attributable to owners of the parent	Non controlling interests	Total
Balance as at January 1, 2016	119,467	778,047	4,403,893	185,132,014	(17,580,451)	23,797	172,876,767	6,183,038	179,059,805
Profit for the period	—	—	—	22,415,655	—	—	22,415,655	310,437	22,726,092
Changes in value of available-for-sale financial assets, net of tax	—	—	—	—	(87,706)	(23,797)	(111,503)	87,664	(23,839)
Share of other comprehensive income (loss) of associates and joint ventures, net of tax	—	—	—	—	(80,146)	212	(79,934)	35	(79,899)
Foreign currency translation, net of tax	—	—	—	—	1,160,316	—	1,160,316	(28,780)	1,131,536
Remeasurement of net defined benefit liabilities, net of tax	—	—	—	—	926,280	—	926,280	37,322	963,602
Classified as held-for-sale	—	—	—	—	29,022	(29,022)	—	—	—
Total comprehensive income (loss)	—	—	—	22,415,655	1,947,766	(52,607)	24,310,814	406,678	24,717,492
Dividends	—	—	—	(3,061,361)	—	—	(3,061,361)	(65,161)	(3,126,522)
Capital transaction under common control	—	—	—	—	(37)	—	(37)	12,272	12,235
Changes in consolidated entities	—	—	—	—	—	—	—	1,790	1,790
Acquisition of treasury stock	—	—	—	—	(7,707,938)	—	(7,707,938)	—	(7,707,938)
Retirement of treasury stock	—	—	—	(11,399,991)	11,399,991	—	—	—	—
Others	—	—	—	—	6,083	—	6,083	88	6,171
Total transactions with owners	—	—	—	(14,461,352)	3,698,099	—	(10,763,253)	(51,011)	(10,814,264)
Balance as at December 31, 2016	119,467	778,047	4,403,893	193,086,317	(11,934,586)	(28,810)	186,424,328	6,538,705	192,963,033
Profit for the period	—	—	—	41,344,569	—	—	41,344,569	842,178	42,186,747
Changes in value of available-for-sale financial assets, net of tax	—	—	—	—	489,150	—	489,150	22,057	511,207
Share of other comprehensive income (loss) of associates and joint ventures, net of tax	—	—	—	—	(54,300)	—	(54,300)	(1,303)	(55,603)
Foreign currency translation, net of tax	—	—	—	—	(6,289,926)	28,810	(6,261,116)	(73,871)	(6,334,987)
Remeasurement of net defined benefit liabilities, net of tax	—	—	—	—	406,323	—	406,323	7,924	414,247
Gain (loss) on valuation of derivatives	—	—	—	—	(37,121)	—	(37,121)	—	(37,121)
Total comprehensive income (loss)	—	—	—	41,344,569	(5,485,874)	28,810	35,887,505	796,985	36,684,490
Dividends	—	—	—	(6,747,123)	—	—	(6,747,123)	(64,277)	(6,811,400)
Capital transaction under common control	—	—	—	—	(2,992)	—	(2,992)	15,114	12,122
Changes in consolidated entities	—	—	—	—	(2,699)	—	(2,699)	(9,352)	(12,051)
Acquisition of treasury stock	—	—	—	—	(8,350,424)	—	(8,350,424)	—	(8,350,424)
Retirement of treasury stock	—	—	—	(11,872,563)	11,872,563	—	—	—	—
Others	—	—	—	—	4,821	—	4,821	837	5,658
Total transactions with owners	—	—	—	(18,619,686)	3,521,269	—	(15,098,417)	(57,678)	(15,156,095)
Balance as at December 31, 2017	119,467	778,047	4,403,893	215,811,200	(13,899,191)	—	207,213,416	7,278,012	214,491,428

The above consolidated statement of financial position should be read in conjunction with the accompanying notes.

SAMSUNG

Samsung Electronics Co., Ltd. and Subsidiaries
CONSOLIDATED STATEMENTS OF CASH FLOWS

For the year ended December 31	2017	2016
(In millions of Korean won)	KRW	KRW
Cash flows from operating activities		
Profit for the period	42,186,747	22,726,092
Adjustments	36,211,232	30,754,471
Changes in assets and liabilities arising from operating activities	(10,620,547)	(1,180,953)
Cash generated from operations	67,777,432	52,299,610
Interest received	1,581,117	1,405,085
Interest paid	(542,715)	(443,838)
Dividends received	173,305	256,851
Income tax paid	(6,827,098)	(6,132,064)
Net cash inflow from operating activities	**62,162,041**	**47,385,644**
Cash flows from investing activities		
Net decrease (increase) in short-term financial instruments	387,627	(6,780,610)
Disposal of short-term available-for-sale financial assets	499,856	3,010,003
Acquisition of short-term available-for-sale financial assets	—	(2,129,551)
Disposal of long-term financial instruments	1,750,221	789,862
Acquisition of long-term financial instruments	(1,079,355)	(1,741,547)
Disposal of long-term available-for-sale financial assets	191,826	2,010,356
Acquisition of long-term available-for-sale financial assets	(358,497)	(1,498,148)
Acquisition of held-to-maturity financial assets	(106,751)	—
Disposal of investment in associates and joint ventures	355,926	2,280,203
Acquisition of investment in associates and joint ventures	(25,293)	(84,306)
Disposal of property, plant and equipment	308,354	270,874
Acquisition of property, plant and equipment	(42,792,234)	(24,142,973)
Disposal of intangible assets	733	6,944
Acquisition of intangible assets	(983,740)	(1,047,668)
Cash outflow from business combinations	(8,754,268)	(622,050)
Cash inflow from business transfers	1,248,834	—
Others	(28,455)	19,936
Net cash outflow from investing activities	**(49,385,216)**	**(29,658,675)**
Cash flows from financing activities		
Net increase in short-term borrowings	2,730,676	1,351,037
Acquisition of treasury stock	(8,350,424)	(7,707,938)
Proceeds from long-term borrowings and debentures	998,311	1,041,743
Repayment of long-term borrowings and debentures	(1,140,803)	(252,846)
Dividends paid	(6,804,297)	(3,114,742)
Net increase in non-controlling interests	5,670	13,232
Net cash outflow from financing activities	**(12,560,867)**	**(8,669,514)**
Effect of exchange rate changes on cash and cash equivalents	(1,782,270)	417,243
Net (decrease) increase in cash and cash equivalents	**(1,566,312)**	**9,474,698**
Cash and cash equivalents		
Beginning of the period	32,111,442	22,636,744
End of the period	30,545,130	32,111,442

The above consolidated statements of cash flows should be read in conjunction with the accompanying notes.

SAMSUNG

B Time Value of Money

Learning Objectives

CONCEPTUAL

C1 Describe the earning of interest and the concepts of present and future values.

PROCEDURAL

P1 Apply present value concepts to a single amount by using interest tables.

P2 Apply future value concepts to a single amount by using interest tables.

P3 Apply present value concepts to an annuity by using interest tables.

P4 Apply future value concepts to an annuity by using interest tables.

PRESENT AND FUTURE VALUE CONCEPTS

The old saying "Time is money" means that as time passes, the values of assets and liabilities change. This change is due to *interest,* which is a borrower's payment to the owner of an asset for its use. The most common example of interest is a savings account. Cash in the account earns interest paid by the financial institution. An example of a liability is a car loan. As we carry the balance of the loan, we accumulate interest costs on it. We must ultimately repay this loan with interest.

Present and future value computations enable us to measure or estimate the interest component of holding assets or liabilities over time. The present value computation is used to compute the value of future-day assets *today.* The future value computation is used to compute the value of present-day assets *at a future date.* The first section focuses on the present value of a single amount. The second section focuses on the future value of a single amount. Then both the present and future values of a series of amounts (called an *annuity*) are defined and explained.

C1

Describe the earning of interest and the concepts of present and future values.

■ Decision Insight

What's Five Million Worth?   Robert Miles, a maintenance worker, purchased a scratch-off ticket that won him a $5 million jackpot. The $5 million payout was offered to Miles as a $250,000 annuity for 20 years **or** as a lump-sum payment of $3,210,000, which is about $2,124,378 after taxes. ■

PRESENT VALUE OF A SINGLE AMOUNT

Graph of PV of a Single Amount   We graphically express the present value, called *p*, of a single future amount, called *f*, that is received or paid at a future date in Exhibit B.1.

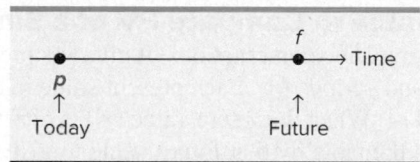

EXHIBIT B.1

Present Value of a Single Amount Diagram

Formula of PV of a Single Amount   The formula to compute the present value of a single amount is shown in Exhibit B.2, where *p* = present value (PV); *f* = future value (FV); *i* = rate of interest per period; and *n* = number of periods. (Interest is also called the *discount,* and interest rate is also called the *discount rate.*)

$$p = \frac{f}{(1+i)^n}$$

P1

Apply present value concepts to a single amount by using interest tables.

EXHIBIT B.2

Present Value of a Single Amount Formula

Illustration of PV of a Single Amount for One Period   To illustrate present value concepts, assume that we need $220 one period from today. We want to know how much we must invest now, for one period, at an interest rate of 10% to provide for this $220. For this illustration, the *p*, or present value, is the unknown amount—the specifics are shown graphically as follows.

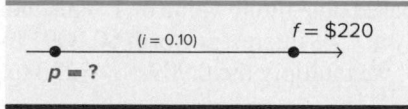

Conceptually, we know *p* must be less than $220. This is clear from the answer to: Would we rather have $220 today or $220 at some future date? If we had $220 today, we could invest it and see it grow to something more than $220 in the future. Therefore, we would prefer the $220 today. This means that if we were promised $220 in the future, we would take less than $220 today. But how much less? To answer that question, we compute an estimate of the present value of the $220 to be received one period from now using the formula in Exhibit B.2 as follows.

$$p = \frac{f}{(1 + i)^n} = \frac{\$220}{(1 + 0.10)^1} = \$200$$

We interpret this result to say that given an interest rate of 10%, we are indifferent between $200 today or $220 at the end of one period.

Point: Excel for PV.

	A	B
1	Future value	$242
2	Periods	2
3	Period int. rate	10%
4	Present value	

=−PV(B3,B2,0,B1) = $200

Illustration of PV of a Single Amount for Multiple Periods   We can use this formula to compute the present value for *any number of periods*. To illustrate, consider a payment of $242 at the end of two periods at 10% interest. The present value of this $242 to be received two periods from now is computed as follows.

$$p = \frac{f}{(1 + i)^n} = \frac{\$242}{(1 + 0.10)^2} = \$200$$

I will pay your allowance at the end of the month. Do you want to wait or receive its present value today?

Together, these results tell us we are indifferent between $200 today, or $220 one period from today, or $242 two periods from today given a 10% interest rate per period.

The number of periods (n) in the present value formula does not have to be expressed in years. Any period of time such as a day, a month, a quarter, or a year can be used. Whatever period is used, the interest rate (i) must be compounded for the same period. This means that if a situation expresses n in months and i equals 12% per year, then i is transformed into interest earned per month (or 1%). In this case, interest is said to be *compounded monthly*. For example, the present value of $1 when n is 12 months and i is 12% compounded monthly follows.

$$p = \frac{1}{(1 + 0.01)^{12}} = \$0.8874$$

Using Present Value Table to Compute PV of a Single Amount   A present value table helps us with present value computations. It gives us present values (factors) for a variety of both interest rates (i) and periods (n). Each present value in a present value table assumes that the future value (f) equals 1. When the future value (f) is different from 1, we simply multiply the present value (p) from the table by that future value to give us the estimate. The formula used to construct a table of present values for a single future amount of 1 is shown in Exhibit B.3.

EXHIBIT B.3

Present Value of 1 Formula

$$p = \frac{1}{(1 + i)^n}$$

This formula is identical to that in Exhibit B.2 except that f equals 1. Table B.1 at the end of this appendix is such a present value table. It is often called a **present value of 1 table**. A present value table has three factors: p, i, and n. Knowing two of these three factors allows us to compute the third. (A fourth is f, but, as already explained, we need only multiply the 1 used in the formula by f.) To illustrate the use of a present value table, consider three cases.

Case 1   Solve for p when knowing i and n. To show how we use a present value table, let's look again at how we estimate the present value of $220 (the f value) at the end of one period ($n = 1$) where the interest rate (i) is 10%. To solve this case, we go to the present value table (Table B.1) and look in the row for one period and in the column for 10% interest. Here we find a present value (p) of 0.9091 based on a future value of 1. This means, for instance, that $1 to be received one period from today at 10% interest is worth $0.9091 today. Because the future value in this case is not $1 but $220, we multiply the 0.9091 by $220 to get an answer of $200.

Case 2   Solve for n when knowing p and i. To illustrate, assume a $100,000 future value ($f$) that is worth $13,000 today ($p$) using an interest rate of 12% (i) but where n is unknown. In particular, we want to know how many periods (n) there are between the present value and the future value. To put this in context, it would fit a situation in which we want to retire with $100,000 but currently have only $13,000 that is earning a 12% return and we are unable to save additional money. How long will it be before we can retire? To answer this, we go to Table B.1 and look in the 12% interest column. Here we find a column of present values (p) based on a future value of 1. To use the present value table for this solution, we must divide $13,000 ($p$) by $100,000 ($f$), which equals 0.1300. This is necessary because *a present value table defines* f *equal to 1, and* p *as a fraction of 1.* We look for a value nearest to 0.1300 (p), which we find in the row for 18 periods (n). This means that the present value of $100,000 at the end of 18 periods at 12% interest is $13,000; alternatively stated, we must work 18 more years.

Case 3   Solve for *i* when knowing *p* and *n*. In this case, we have, say, a $120,000 future value ($f$) worth $60,000 today ($p$) when there are nine periods (n) between the present and future values, but the interest rate is unknown. As an example, suppose we want to retire with $120,000 in nine years, but we have only $60,000 and we are unable to save additional money. What interest rate must we earn to retire with $120,000 in nine years? To answer this, we go to the present value table (Table B.1) and look in the row for nine periods. To use the present value table, we must divide $60,000 ($p$) by $120,000 ($f$), which equals 0.5000. Recall that this step is necessary because a present value table defines f equal to 1 and p as a fraction of 1. We look for a value in the row for nine periods that is nearest to 0.5000 (p), which we find in the column for 8% interest (i). This means that the present value of $120,000 at the end of nine periods at 8% interest is $60,000 or, in our example, we must earn 8% annual interest to retire in nine years.

A company is considering an investment expected to yield $70,000 after six years. If this company demands an 8% return, how much is it willing to pay for this investment today?

NEED-TO-KNOW B-1

Present Value of a Single Amount

Solution

Today's value = $70,000 × 0.6302 = $44,114 (using PV factor from Table B.1, $i = 8\%$, $n = 6$)

P1

FUTURE VALUE OF A SINGLE AMOUNT

Formula of FV of a Single Amount   We must modify the formula for the present value of a single amount to obtain the formula for the future value of a single amount. In particular, we multiply both sides of the equation in Exhibit B.2 by $(1 + i)^n$ to get the result shown in Exhibit B.4.

$$f = p \times (1 + i)^n$$

Illustration of FV of a Single Amount for One Period   The future value (f) is defined in terms of p, i, and n. We can use this formula to determine that $200 ($p$) invested for one period (n) at an interest rate of 10% (i) yields a future value of $220 as follows.

$$
\begin{aligned}
f &= p \times (1 + i)^n \\
&= \$200 \times (1 + 0.10)^1 \\
&= \$220
\end{aligned}
$$

Illustration of FV of a Single Amount for Multiple Periods   This formula can be used to compute the future value of an amount for *any number of periods* into the future. To illustrate, assume that $200 is invested for three periods at 10%. The future value of this $200 is $266.20, computed as follows.

$$
\begin{aligned}
f &= p \times (1 + i)^n \\
&= \$200 \times (1 + 0.10)^3 \\
&= \$200 \times 1.3310 \\
&= \$266.20
\end{aligned}
$$

Using Future Value Table to Compute FV of a Single Amount   A future value table makes it easier for us to compute future values (f) for many different combinations of interest rates (i) and time periods (n). Each future value in a future value table assumes the present value (p)

P2

Apply future value concepts to a single amount by using interest tables.

EXHIBIT B.4

Future Value of a Single Amount Formula

Point: The FV factor in Table B.2 when $n = 3$ and $i = 10\%$ is 1.3310.

Point: Excel for FV.

	A	B
1	Present value	$200
2	Periods	3
3	Period int. rate	10%
4	Future value	

=−FV(B3,B2,0,B1) = $266.20

is 1. If the future amount is something other than 1, we multiply our answer by that amount. The formula used to construct a table of future values (factors) for a single amount of 1 is in Exhibit B.5.

EXHIBIT B.5

Future Value of 1 Formula

$$f = (1 + i)^n$$

Table B.2 at the end of this appendix shows a table of future values for a current amount of 1. This type of table is called a **future value of 1 table**.

Point:
1/PV factor = FV factor.
1/FV factor = PV factor.

There are some important relations between Tables B.1 and B.2. In Table B.2, for the row where $n = 0$, the future value is 1 for each interest rate. This is because no interest is earned when time does not pass. We also see that Tables B.1 and B.2 report the same information but in a different manner. In particular, one table is simply the *reciprocal* of the other. To illustrate this inverse relation, let's say we invest $100 for a period of five years at 12% per year. How much do we expect to have after five years? We can answer this question using Table B.2 by finding the future value (f) of 1, for five periods from now, compounded at 12%. From that table we find $f = 1.7623$. If we start with $100, the amount it accumulates to after five years is $176.23 ($100 × 1.7623). We can alternatively use Table B.1. Here we find that the present value (p) of 1, discounted five periods at 12%, is 0.5674. Recall the inverse relation between present value and future value. This means that $p = 1/f$ (or equivalently, $f = 1/p$). We can compute the future value of $100 invested for five periods at 12% as follows: $f = $100 × (1/0.5674) = $176.24 (which equals the $176.23 just computed, except for a 1 cent rounding difference).

Point: The FV factor when $n = 2$ and $i = 10\%$, is 1.2100. Its reciprocal, 0.8264, is the PV factor when $n = 2$ and $i = 10\%$.

A future value table has three factors: f, i, and n. Knowing two of these three factors allows us to compute the third. To illustrate, consider three possible cases.

Case 1   Solve for f when knowing i and n. Our preceding example fits this case. We found that $100 invested for five periods at 12% interest accumulates to $176.24.

Case 2   Solve for n when knowing f and i. In this case, we have, say, $2,000 ($p$) and we want to know how many periods (n) it will take to accumulate to $3,000 ($f$) at 7% interest ($i$). To answer this, we go to the future value table (Table B.2) and look in the 7% interest column. Here we find a column of future values (f) based on a present value of 1. To use a future value table, we must divide $3,000 ($f$) by $2,000 ($p$), which equals 1.500. This is necessary because *a future value table defines* p *equal to 1, and* f *as a multiple of 1*. We look for a value nearest to 1.50 (f), which we find in the row for six periods (n). This means that $2,000 invested for six periods at 7% interest accumulates to $3,000.

Case 3   Solve for i when knowing f and n. In this case, we have, say, $2,001 ($p$), and in nine years ($n$) we want to have $4,000 ($f$). What rate of interest must we earn to accomplish this? To answer that, we go to Table B.2 and search in the row for nine periods. To use a future value table, we must divide $4,000 ($f$) by $2,001 ($p$), which equals 1.9990. Recall that this is necessary because a future value table defines p equal to 1 and f as a multiple of 1. We look for a value nearest to 1.9990 (f), which we find in the column for 8% interest (i). This means that $2,001 invested for nine periods at 8% interest accumulates to $4,000.

■ Decision Maker ──────────────────────────

Entrepreneur   You are a retailer planning a sale on a security system that requires no payments for two years. At the end of two years, buyers must pay the full amount. The system's suggested retail price is $4,100, but you are willing to sell it today for $3,000 cash. What is your sale price if payment will not occur for two years and the market interest rate is 10%? ■   *Answer:* This is a present value question. The interest rate (10%) and present value ($3,000) are known, but the payment required two years later is unknown. The two-year-later price of $3,630 is computed as $3,000 × 1.10 × 1.10. The $3,630 two years from today is equivalent to $3,000 today.

NEED-TO-KNOW B-2

Future Value of a Single Amount

P2

Assume that you win a $150,000 cash sweepstakes today. You decide to deposit this cash in an account earning 8% annual interest, and you plan to quit your job when the account equals $555,000. How many years will it be before you can quit working?

Solution

Future value factor = $555,000/$150,000 = 3.7000

Searching for 3.7 in the 8% column of Table B.2 shows you cannot quit working for <u>17 years</u> if your deposit earns 8% interest.

PRESENT VALUE OF AN ANNUITY

Graph of PV of an Annuity   An *annuity* is a series of equal payments occurring at equal intervals. One example is a series of three annual payments of $100 each. An *ordinary annuity* is defined as equal end-of-period payments at equal intervals. An ordinary annuity of $100 for three periods and its present value (p) are illustrated in Exhibit B.6.

P3
Apply present value concepts to an annuity by using interest tables.

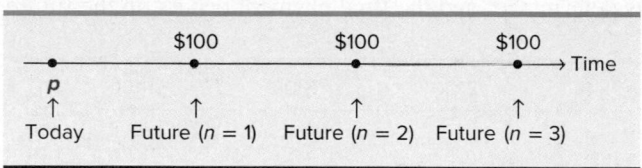

EXHIBIT B.6
Present Value of an Ordinary Annuity Diagram

Formula and Illustration of PV of an Annuity   One way to compute the present value of an ordinary annuity is to find the present value of each payment using our present value formula from Exhibit B.3. We then add each of the three present values. To illustrate, let's look at three $100 payments at the end of each of the next three periods with an interest rate of 15%. Our present value computations are

$$p = \frac{\$100}{(1+0.15)^1} + \frac{\$100}{(1+0.15)^2} + \frac{\$100}{(1+0.15)^3} = \$228.32$$

Using Present Value Table to Compute PV of an Annuity   This computation is identical to computing the present value of each payment (from Table B.1) and taking their sum or, alternatively, adding the values from Table B.1 for each of the three payments and multiplying their sum by the $100 annuity payment.

A more direct way is to use a present value of annuity table. Table B.3 at the end of this appendix is one such table. This table is called a **present value of an annuity of 1 table**. If we look at Table B.3 where $n = 3$ and $i = 15\%$, we see the present value is 2.2832. This means that the present value of an annuity of 1 for three periods, with a 15% interest rate, equals 2.2832.

A present value of an annuity formula is used to construct Table B.3. It also can be constructed by adding the amounts in a present value of 1 table. To illustrate, we use Tables B.1 and B.3 to confirm this relation for the prior example.

From Table B.1		From Table B.3	
$i = 15\%, n = 1$	0.8696		
$i = 15\%, n = 2$	0.7561		
$i = 15\%, n = 3$	0.6575		
Total..................	2.2832	$i = 15\%, n = 3$	2.2832

Point: Excel for PV annuity.

	A	B
1	Payment	$100
2	Periods	3
3	Period int. rate	15%
4	Present value	

=−PV(B3,B2,B1) = $228.32

We also can use business calculators or spreadsheet programs to find the present value of an annuity.

■ Decision Insight

Count Your Blessings   "I don't have good luck—I'm blessed," proclaimed Andrew "Jack" Whittaker, a sewage treatment contractor, after winning the largest ever undivided jackpot in a U.S. lottery. Whittaker had to choose between $315 million in 30 annual installments or $170 million in one lump sum ($112 million after-tax). ■

A company is considering an investment that would produce payments of $10,000 every six months for three years. The first payment would be received in six months. If this company requires an 8% annual return, what is the maximum amount it is willing to pay for this investment today?

NEED-TO-KNOW B-3

Present Value of an Annuity

P3

Solution

Maximum paid = $10,000 × 5.2421 = $52,421 (using PV of annuity factor from Table B.3, $i = 4\%$, $n = 6$)

FUTURE VALUE OF AN ANNUITY

P4
—————
Apply future value concepts to an annuity by using interest tables.

Graph of FV of an Annuity
The future value of an *ordinary annuity* is the accumulated value of each annuity payment with interest as of the date of the final payment. To illustrate, let's consider the earlier annuity of three annual payments of $100. Exhibit B.7 shows the point in time for the future value (f). The first payment is made two periods prior to the point when future value is determined, and the final payment occurs on the future value date.

EXHIBIT B.7

Future Value of an Ordinary Annuity Diagram

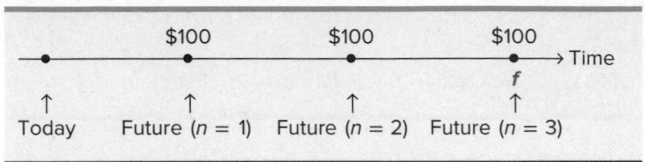

Point: An ordinary annuity is a series of equal cash flows, with the payment at the *end* of each period.

Formula and Illustration of FV of an Annuity
One way to compute the future value of an annuity is to use the formula to find the future value of *each* payment and add them. If we assume an interest rate of 15%, our calculation is

$$f = \$100 \times (1 + 0.15)^2 + \$100 \times (1 + 0.15)^1 + \$100 \times (1 + 0.15)^0 = \$347.25$$

This is identical to using Table B.2 and summing the future values of each payment, or adding the future values of the three payments of 1 and multiplying the sum by $100.

Using Future Value Table to Compute FV of an Annuity
A more direct way is to use a table showing future values of annuities. Such a table is called a **future value of an annuity of 1 table**. Table B.4 at the end of this appendix is one such table. Note that in Table B.4 when $n = 1$, the future values equal 1 ($f = 1$) for all rates of interest. This is because such an annuity consists of only one payment, and the future value is determined on the date of that payment—no time passes between the payment and its future value. The future value of an annuity formula is used to construct Table B.4. We also can construct it by adding the amounts from a future value of 1 table. To illustrate, we use Tables B.2 and B.4 to confirm this relation for the prior example.

Point: Excel for FV annuity.

	A	B
1	Payment	$100
2	Periods	3
3	Period int. rate	15%
4	Future value	

=−FV(B3,B2,B1) = $347.25

From Table B.2		From Table B.4	
$i = 15\%, n = 0$	1.0000		
$i = 15\%, n = 1$	1.1500		
$i = 15\%, n = 2$	1.3225		
Total	3.4725	$i = 15\%, n = 3$	3.4725

Note that the future value in Table B.2 is 1.0000 when $n = 0$, but the future value in Table B.4 is 1.0000 when $n = 1$. Is this a contradiction? No. When $n = 0$ in Table B.2, the future value is determined on the date when a single payment occurs. This means that no interest is earned because no time has passed, and the future value equals the payment. Table B.4 describes annuities with equal payments occurring at the end of each period. When $n = 1$, the annuity has one payment, and its future value equals 1 on the date of its final and only payment. Again, no time passes between the payment and its future value date.

NEED-TO-KNOW B-4

Future Value of an Annuity

P4

A company invests $45,000 per year for five years at 12% annual interest. Compute the value of this annuity investment at the end of five years.

Solution

Future value = $45,000 × 6.3528 = $285,876 (using FV of annuity factor from Table B.4, $i = 12\%, n = 5$)

Summary: Cheat Sheet

PV OF A SINGLE AMOUNT

$$p = \frac{f}{(1+i)^n}$$

where p = present value (PV); f = future value (FV); i = rate of interest per period; and n = number of periods. Excel follows:

Point: Excel for PV.

	A	B
1	Future value	$242
2	Periods	2
3	Period int. rate	10%
4	Present value	

=−PV(B3,B2,0,B1) = $200

PV OF AN ANNUITY

$$p = f \times \left[1 - \frac{1}{(1+i)^n}\right]/i$$

where p = present value (PV); f = future value (FV); i = rate of interest per period; and n = number of periods. Excel follows:

Point: Excel for PV annuity.

	A	B
1	Payment	$100
2	Periods	3
3	Period int. rate	15%
4	Present value	

=−PV(B3,B2,B1) = $228.32

FV OF A SINGLE AMOUNT

$$f = p \times (1+i)^n$$

where p = present value (PV); f = future value (FV); i = rate of interest per period; and n = number of periods. Excel follows:

Point: Excel for FV.

	A	B
1	Present value	$200
2	Periods	3
3	Period int. rate	10%
4	Future value	

=−FV(B3,B2,0,B1) = $266.20

FV OF AN ANNUITY

$$f = p \times [(1+i)^n - 1]/i$$

where p = present value (PV); f = future value (FV); i = rate of interest per period; and n = number of periods. Excel follows:

Point: Excel for FV annuity.

	A	B
1	Payment	$100
2	Periods	3
3	Period int. rate	15%
4	Future value	

=−FV(B3,B2,B1) = $347.25

connect

Assume that you must estimate what the future value will be two years from today using the *future value of 1 table* (Table B.2). Which interest rate column *and* number-of-periods row do you use when working with the following rates?

1. 12% annual rate, compounded annually
2. 6% annual rate, compounded semiannually
3. 8% annual rate, compounded quarterly
4. 12% annual rate, compounded monthly (the answer for number-of-periods in part 4 is not shown in Table B.2)

QUICK STUDY

QS B-1
Identifying interest rates in tables
C1

Ken Francis is offered the possibility of investing $2,745 today; in return, he would receive $10,000 after 15 years. What is the annual rate of interest for this investment? (Use Table B.1.)

QS B-2
Interest rate on an investment P1

Megan Brink is offered the possibility of investing $6,651 today at 6% interest per year in a desire to accumulate $10,000. How many years must Brink wait to accumulate $10,000? (Use Table B.1.)

QS B-3
Number of periods of an investment P1

Flaherty is considering an investment that, if paid for immediately, is expected to return $140,000 five years from now. If Flaherty demands a 9% return, how much is she willing to pay for this investment?

QS B-4
Present value of an amount P1

CII, Inc., invests $630,000 in a project expected to earn a 12% annual rate of return. The earnings will be reinvested in the project each year until the entire investment is liquidated 10 years later. What will the cash proceeds be when the project is liquidated?

QS B-5
Future value of an amount P2

Beene Distributing is considering a project that will return $150,000 annually at the end of each year for the next six years. If Beene demands an annual return of 7% and pays for the project immediately, how much is it willing to pay for the project?

QS B-6
Present value of an annuity P3

Claire Fitch is planning to begin an individual retirement program in which she will invest $1,500 at the end of each year. Fitch plans to retire after making 30 annual investments in the program earning a return of 10%. What is the value of the program on the date of the last payment (30 years from the present)?

QS B-7
Future value of an annuity P4

EXERCISES

Exercise B-1
Present value of an
amount P1

Mike Derr Company expects to earn 10% per year on an investment that will pay $606,773 six years from now. Use Table B.1 to compute the present value of this investment. (Round the amount to the nearest dollar.)

Exercise B-2
Present value of an
amount P1

On January 1, a company agrees to pay $20,000 in three years. If the annual interest rate is 10%, determine how much cash the company can borrow with this agreement.

Exercise B-3
Number of periods of an
investment P2

Tom Thompson expects to invest $10,000 at 12% and, at the end of a certain period, receive $96,463. How many years will it be before Thompson receives the payment? (Use Table B.2.)

Exercise B-4
Interest rate on an
investment P2

Bill Padley expects to invest $10,000 for 25 years, after which he wants to receive $108,347. What rate of interest must Padley earn? (Use Table B.2.)

Exercise B-5
Future value of an
amount P2

Mark Welsch deposits $7,200 in an account that earns interest at an annual rate of 8%, compounded quarterly. The $7,200 plus earned interest must remain in the account 10 years before it can be withdrawn. How much money will be in the account at the end of 10 years?

Exercise B-6
Future value of an
amount P2

Catten, Inc., invests $163,170 today earning 7% per year for nine years. Use Table B.2 to compute the future value of the investment nine years from now. (Round the amount to the nearest dollar.)

Exercise B-7
Interest rate on an
investment P3

Jones expects an immediate investment of $57,466 to return $10,000 annually for eight years, with the first payment to be received one year from now. What rate of interest must Jones earn? (Use Table B.3.)

Exercise B-8
Number of periods of an
investment P3

Keith Riggins expects an investment of $82,014 to return $10,000 annually for several years. If Riggins earns a return of 10%, how many annual payments will he receive? (Use Table B.3.)

Exercise B-9
Present value of an
annuity P3

Dave Krug finances a new automobile by paying $6,500 cash and agreeing to make 40 monthly payments of $500 each, the first payment to be made one month after the purchase. The loan bears interest at an annual rate of 12%. What is the cost of the automobile?

Exercise B-10
Present values of annuities
P3

C&H Ski Club recently borrowed money and agreed to pay it back with a series of six annual payments of $5,000 each. C&H subsequently borrows more money and agrees to pay it back with a series of four annual payments of $7,500 each. The annual interest rate for both loans is 6%.

1. Use Table B.1 to find the present value of these two separate annuities. (Round amounts to the nearest dollar.)
2. Use Table B.3 to find the present value of these two separate annuities. (Round amounts to the nearest dollar.)

Exercise B-11
Present value with
semiannual compounding
C1 P3

Otto Co. borrows money on April 30, 2019, by promising to make four payments of $13,000 each on November 1, 2019; May 1, 2020; November 1, 2020; and May 1, 2021.

1. How much money is Otto able to borrow if the interest rate is 8%, compounded semiannually?
2. How much money is Otto able to borrow if the interest rate is 12%, compounded semiannually?
3. How much money is Otto able to borrow if the interest rate is 16%, compounded semiannually?

Exercise B-12
Present value of bonds
P1 P3

Spiller Corp. plans to issue 10%, 15-year, $500,000 par value bonds payable that pay interest semiannually on June 30 and December 31. The bonds are dated December 31, 2019, and are issued on that date. If the market rate of interest for the bonds is 8% on the date of issue, what will be the total cash proceeds from the bond issue?

Compute the amount that can be borrowed under each of the following circumstances:

1. A promise to repay $90,000 seven years from now at an interest rate of 6%.

2. An agreement made on February 1, 2019, to make three separate payments of $20,000 on February 1 of 2020, 2021, and 2022. The annual interest rate is 10%.

Exercise B-13
Present value of an amount and of an annuity
P1   P3

Algoe expects to invest $1,000 annually for 40 years to yield an accumulated value of $154,762 on the date of the last investment. For this to occur, what rate of interest must Algoe earn? (Use Table B.4.)

Exercise B-14
Interest rate on an investment   **P4**

Steffi Derr expects to invest $10,000 annually that will earn 8%. How many annual investments must Derr make to accumulate $303,243 on the date of the last investment? (Use Table B.4.)

Exercise B-15
Number of periods of an investment   **P4**

Kelly Malone plans to have $50 withheld from her monthly paycheck and deposited in a savings account that earns 12% annually, compounded monthly. If Malone continues with her plan for two and one-half years, how much will be accumulated in the account on the date of the last deposit?

Exercise B-16
Future value of an annuity   **P4**

Starr Company decides to establish a fund that it will use 10 years from now to replace an aging production facility. The company will make a $100,000 initial contribution to the fund and plans to make quarterly contributions of $50,000 beginning in three months. The fund earns 12%, compounded quarterly. What will be the value of the fund 10 years from now?

Exercise B-17
Future value of an amount plus an annuity
P2   P4

---

a. How much would you have to deposit today if you wanted to have $60,000 in four years? Annual interest rate is 9%.

b. Assume that you are saving up for a trip around the world when you graduate in two years. If you can earn 8% on your investments, how much would you have to deposit today to have $15,000 when you graduate?

c. Would you rather have $463 now or $1,000 ten years from now? Assume that you can earn 9% on your investments.

d. Assume that a college parking sticker today costs $90. If the cost of parking is increasing at the rate of 5% per year, how much will the college parking sticker cost in eight years?

e. Assume that the average price of a new home is $158,500. If the cost of a new home is increasing at a rate of 10% per year, how much will a new home cost in eight years?

f. An investment will pay you $10,000 in 10 years *and* it also will pay you $400 at the end of *each* of the next 10 years (Years 1 through 10). If the annual interest rate is 6%, how much would you be willing to pay today for this type of investment?

g. A college student is reported in the newspaper as having won $10,000,000 in the Kansas State Lottery. However, as is often the custom with lotteries, she does *not* actually receive the entire $10 million now. Instead she will receive $500,000 at the end of the year for *each* of the next 20 years. If the annual interest rate is 6%, what is the present value (today's amount) that she won? (Ignore taxes.)

Exercise B-18
Practical applications of the time value of money
P1   P2   P3   P4

For each of the following situations, identify (1) the case as either (*a*) a present or a future value and (*b*) a single amount or an annuity, (2) the table you would use in your computations (but do not solve the problem), and (3) the interest rate and time periods you would use.

a. You need to accumulate $10,000 for a trip you wish to take in four years. You are able to earn 8% compounded semiannually on your savings. You plan to make only one deposit and let the money accumulate for four years. How would you determine the amount of the one-time deposit?

b. Assume the same facts as in part (*a*) except that you will make semiannual deposits to your savings account.

c. You want to retire after working 40 years with savings in excess of $1,000,000. You expect to save $4,000 a year for 40 years and earn an annual rate of interest of 8%. Will you be able to retire with more than $1,000,000 in 40 years? Explain.

d. A sweepstakes agency names you a grand prize winner. You can take $225,000 immediately or elect to receive annual installments of $30,000 for 20 years. You can earn 10% annually on any investments you make. Which prize do you choose to receive?

Exercise B-19
Using present and future value tables
C1   P1   P2   P3   P4

TABLE B.1*

Present Value of 1

$$p = 1/(1 + i)^n$$

Periods	1%	2%	3%	4%	5%	6%	7%	8%	9%	10%	12%	15%	Periods
						Rate							
1	0.9901	0.9804	0.9709	0.9615	0.9524	0.9434	0.9346	0.9259	0.9174	0.9091	0.8929	0.8696	1
2	0.9803	0.9612	0.9426	0.9246	0.9070	0.8900	0.8734	0.8573	0.8417	0.8264	0.7972	0.7561	2
3	0.9706	0.9423	0.9151	0.8890	0.8638	0.8396	0.8163	0.7938	0.7722	0.7513	0.7118	0.6575	3
4	0.9610	0.9238	0.8885	0.8548	0.8227	0.7921	0.7629	0.7350	0.7084	0.6830	0.6355	0.5718	4
5	0.9515	0.9057	0.8626	0.8219	0.7835	0.7473	0.7130	0.6806	0.6499	0.6209	0.5674	0.4972	5
6	0.9420	0.8880	0.8375	0.7903	0.7462	0.7050	0.6663	0.6302	0.5963	0.5645	0.5066	0.4323	6
7	0.9327	0.8706	0.8131	0.7599	0.7107	0.6651	0.6227	0.5835	0.5470	0.5132	0.4523	0.3759	7
8	0.9235	0.8535	0.7894	0.7307	0.6768	0.6274	0.5820	0.5403	0.5019	0.4665	0.4039	0.3269	8
9	0.9143	0.8368	0.7664	0.7026	0.6446	0.5919	0.5439	0.5002	0.4604	0.4241	0.3606	0.2843	9
10	0.9053	0.8203	0.7441	0.6756	0.6139	0.5584	0.5083	0.4632	0.4224	0.3855	0.3220	0.2472	10
11	0.8963	0.8043	0.7224	0.6496	0.5847	0.5268	0.4751	0.4289	0.3875	0.3505	0.2875	0.2149	11
12	0.8874	0.7885	0.7014	0.6246	0.5568	0.4970	0.4440	0.3971	0.3555	0.3186	0.2567	0.1869	12
13	0.8787	0.7730	0.6810	0.6006	0.5303	0.4688	0.4150	0.3677	0.3262	0.2897	0.2292	0.1625	13
14	0.8700	0.7579	0.6611	0.5775	0.5051	0.4423	0.3878	0.3405	0.2992	0.2633	0.2046	0.1413	14
15	0.8613	0.7430	0.6419	0.5553	0.4810	0.4173	0.3624	0.3152	0.2745	0.2394	0.1827	0.1229	15
16	0.8528	0.7284	0.6232	0.5339	0.4581	0.3936	0.3387	0.2919	0.2519	0.2176	0.1631	0.1069	16
17	0.8444	0.7142	0.6050	0.5134	0.4363	0.3714	0.3166	0.2703	0.2311	0.1978	0.1456	0.0929	17
18	0.8360	0.7002	0.5874	0.4936	0.4155	0.3503	0.2959	0.2502	0.2120	0.1799	0.1300	0.0808	18
19	0.8277	0.6864	0.5703	0.4746	0.3957	0.3305	0.2765	0.2317	0.1945	0.1635	0.1161	0.0703	19
20	0.8195	0.6730	0.5537	0.4564	0.3769	0.3118	0.2584	0.2145	0.1784	0.1486	0.1037	0.0611	20
25	0.7798	0.6095	0.4776	0.3751	0.2953	0.2330	0.1842	0.1460	0.1160	0.0923	0.0588	0.0304	25
30	0.7419	0.5521	0.4120	0.3083	0.2314	0.1741	0.1314	0.0994	0.0754	0.0573	0.0334	0.0151	30
35	0.7059	0.5000	0.3554	0.2534	0.1813	0.1301	0.0937	0.0676	0.0490	0.0356	0.0189	0.0075	35
40	0.6717	0.4529	0.3066	0.2083	0.1420	0.0972	0.0668	0.0460	0.0318	0.0221	0.0107	0.0037	40

*Used to compute the present value of a known future amount. For example: How much would you need to invest today at 10% compounded semiannually to accumulate $5,000 in 6 years from today? Using the factors of $n = 12$ and $i = 5\%$ (12 semiannual periods and a semiannual rate of 5%), the factor is 0.5568. You would need to invest $2,784 today ($5,000 × 0.5568).

TABLE B.2†

Future Value of 1

$$f = (1 + i)^n$$

Periods	1%	2%	3%	4%	5%	6%	7%	8%	9%	10%	12%	15%	Periods
						Rate							
0	1.0000	1.0000	1.0000	1.0000	1.0000	1.0000	1.0000	1.0000	1.0000	1.0000	1.0000	1.0000	0
1	1.0100	1.0200	1.0300	1.0400	1.0500	1.0600	1.0700	1.0800	1.0900	1.1000	1.1200	1.1500	1
2	1.0201	1.0404	1.0609	1.0816	1.1025	1.1236	1.1449	1.1664	1.1881	1.2100	1.2544	1.3225	2
3	1.0303	1.0612	1.0927	1.1249	1.1576	1.1910	1.2250	1.2597	1.2950	1.3310	1.4049	1.5209	3
4	1.0406	1.0824	1.1255	1.1699	1.2155	1.2625	1.3108	1.3605	1.4116	1.4641	1.5735	1.7490	4
5	1.0510	1.1041	1.1593	1.2167	1.2763	1.3382	1.4026	1.4693	1.5386	1.6105	1.7623	2.0114	5
6	1.0615	1.1262	1.1941	1.2653	1.3401	1.4185	1.5007	1.5869	1.6771	1.7716	1.9738	2.3131	6
7	1.0721	1.1487	1.2299	1.3159	1.4071	1.5036	1.6058	1.7138	1.8280	1.9487	2.2107	2.6600	7
8	1.0829	1.1717	1.2668	1.3686	1.4775	1.5938	1.7182	1.8509	1.9926	2.1436	2.4760	3.0590	8
9	1.0937	1.1951	1.3048	1.4233	1.5513	1.6895	1.8385	1.9990	2.1719	2.3579	2.7731	3.5179	9
10	1.1046	1.2190	1.3439	1.4802	1.6289	1.7908	1.9672	2.1589	2.3674	2.5937	3.1058	4.0456	10
11	1.1157	1.2434	1.3842	1.5395	1.7103	1.8983	2.1049	2.3316	2.5804	2.8531	3.4785	4.6524	11
12	1.1268	1.2682	1.4258	1.6010	1.7959	2.0122	2.2522	2.5182	2.8127	3.1384	3.8960	5.3503	12
13	1.1381	1.2936	1.4685	1.6651	1.8856	2.1329	2.4098	2.7196	3.0658	3.4523	4.3635	6.1528	13
14	1.1495	1.3195	1.5126	1.7317	1.9799	2.2609	2.5785	2.9372	3.3417	3.7975	4.8871	7.0757	14
15	1.1610	1.3459	1.5580	1.8009	2.0789	2.3966	2.7590	3.1722	3.6425	4.1772	5.4736	8.1371	15
16	1.1726	1.3728	1.6047	1.8730	2.1829	2.5404	2.9522	3.4259	3.9703	4.5950	6.1304	9.3576	16
17	1.1843	1.4002	1.6528	1.9479	2.2920	2.6928	3.1588	3.7000	4.3276	5.0545	6.8660	10.7613	17
18	1.1961	1.4282	1.7024	2.0258	2.4066	2.8543	3.3799	3.9960	4.7171	5.5599	7.6900	12.3755	18
19	1.2081	1.4568	1.7535	2.1068	2.5270	3.0256	3.6165	4.3157	5.1417	6.1159	8.6128	14.2318	19
20	1.2202	1.4859	1.8061	2.1911	2.6533	3.2071	3.8697	4.6610	5.6044	6.7275	9.6463	16.3665	20
25	1.2824	1.6406	2.0938	2.6658	3.3864	4.2919	5.4274	6.8485	8.6231	10.8347	17.0001	32.9190	25
30	1.3478	1.8114	2.4273	3.2434	4.3219	5.7435	7.6123	10.0627	13.2677	17.4494	29.9599	66.2118	30
35	1.4166	1.9999	2.8139	3.9461	5.5160	7.6861	10.6766	14.7853	20.4140	28.1024	52.7996	133.1755	35
40	1.4889	2.2080	3.2620	4.8010	7.0400	10.2857	14.9745	21.7245	31.4094	45.2593	93.0510	267.8635	40

†Used to compute the future value of a known present amount. For example: What is the accumulated value of $3,000 invested today at 8% compounded quarterly for 5 years? Using the factors of $n = 20$ and $i = 2\%$ (20 quarterly periods and a quarterly interest rate of 2%), the factor is 1.4859. The accumulated value is $4,457.70 ($3,000 × 1.4859).

$$p = \left[1 - \frac{1}{(1+i)^n}\right]/i$$

TABLE B.3‡

Present Value of an Annuity of 1

Periods	Rate												Periods
	1%	2%	3%	4%	5%	6%	7%	8%	9%	10%	12%	15%	
1	0.9901	0.9804	0.9709	0.9615	0.9524	0.9434	0.9346	0.9259	0.9174	0.9091	0.8929	0.8696	1
2	1.9704	1.9416	1.9135	1.8861	1.8594	1.8334	1.8080	1.7833	1.7591	1.7355	1.6901	1.6257	2
3	2.9410	2.8839	2.8286	2.7751	2.7232	2.6730	2.6243	2.5771	2.5313	2.4869	2.4018	2.2832	3
4	3.9020	3.8077	3.7171	3.6299	3.5460	3.4651	3.3872	3.3121	3.2397	3.1699	3.0373	2.8550	4
5	4.8534	4.7135	4.5797	4.4518	4.3295	4.2124	4.1002	3.9927	3.8897	3.7908	3.6048	3.3522	5
6	5.7955	5.6014	5.4172	5.2421	5.0757	4.9173	4.7665	4.6229	4.4859	4.3553	4.1114	3.7845	6
7	6.7282	6.4720	6.2303	6.0021	5.7864	5.5824	5.3893	5.2064	5.0330	4.8684	4.5638	4.1604	7
8	7.6517	7.3255	7.0197	6.7327	6.4632	6.2098	5.9713	5.7466	5.5348	5.3349	4.9676	4.4873	8
9	8.5660	8.1622	7.7861	7.4353	7.1078	6.8017	6.5152	6.2469	5.9952	5.7590	5.3282	4.7716	9
10	9.4713	8.9826	8.5302	8.1109	7.7217	7.3601	7.0236	6.7101	6.4177	6.1446	5.6502	5.0188	10
11	10.3676	9.7868	9.2526	8.7605	8.3064	7.8869	7.4987	7.1390	6.8052	6.4951	5.9377	5.2337	11
12	11.2551	10.5753	9.9540	9.3851	8.8633	8.3838	7.9427	7.5361	7.1607	6.8137	6.1944	5.4206	12
13	12.1337	11.3484	10.6350	9.9856	9.3936	8.8527	8.3577	7.9038	7.4869	7.1034	6.4235	5.5831	13
14	13.0037	12.1062	11.2961	10.5631	9.8986	9.2950	8.7455	8.2442	7.7862	7.3667	6.6282	5.7245	14
15	13.8651	12.8493	11.9379	11.1184	10.3797	9.7122	9.1079	8.5595	8.0607	7.6061	6.8109	5.8474	15
16	14.7179	13.5777	12.5611	11.6523	10.8378	10.1059	9.4466	8.8514	8.3126	7.8237	6.9740	5.9542	16
17	15.5623	14.2919	13.1661	12.1657	11.2741	10.4773	9.7632	9.1216	8.5436	8.0216	7.1196	6.0472	17
18	16.3983	14.9920	13.7535	12.6593	11.6896	10.8276	10.0591	9.3719	8.7556	8.2014	7.2497	6.1280	18
19	17.2260	15.6785	14.3238	13.1339	12.0853	11.1581	10.3356	9.6036	8.9501	8.3649	7.3658	6.1982	19
20	18.0456	16.3514	14.8775	13.5903	12.4622	11.4699	10.5940	9.8181	9.1285	8.5136	7.4694	6.2593	20
25	22.0232	19.5235	17.4131	15.6221	14.0939	12.7834	11.6536	10.6748	9.8226	9.0770	7.8431	6.4641	25
30	25.8077	22.3965	19.6004	17.2920	15.3725	13.7648	12.4090	11.2578	10.2737	9.4269	8.0552	6.5660	30
35	29.4086	24.9986	21.4872	18.6646	16.3742	14.4982	12.9477	11.6546	10.5668	9.6442	8.1755	6.6166	35
40	32.8347	27.3555	23.1148	19.7928	17.1591	15.0463	13.3317	11.9246	10.7574	9.7791	8.2438	6.6418	40

†Used to calculate the present value of a series of equal payments made at the end of each period. For example: What is the present value of $2,000 per year for 10 years assuming an annual interest rate of 9%? For ($n = 10$, $i = 9\%$), the PV factor is 6.4177. $2,000 per year for 10 years is the equivalent of $12,835 today ($2,000 × 6.4177).

TABLE B.4§

Future Value of an Annuity of 1

$$f = [(1+i)^n - 1]/i$$

Periods	Rate												Periods
	1%	2%	3%	4%	5%	6%	7%	8%	9%	10%	12%	15%	
1	1.0000	1.0000	1.0000	1.0000	1.0000	1.0000	1.0000	1.0000	1.0000	1.0000	1.0000	1.0000	1
2	2.0100	2.0200	2.0300	2.0400	2.0500	2.0600	2.0700	2.0800	2.0900	2.1000	2.1200	2.1500	2
3	3.0301	3.0604	3.0909	3.1216	3.1525	3.1836	3.2149	3.2464	3.2781	3.3100	3.3744	3.4725	3
4	4.0604	4.1216	4.1836	4.2465	4.3101	4.3746	4.4399	4.5061	4.5731	4.6410	4.7793	4.9934	4
5	5.1010	5.2040	5.3091	5.4163	5.5256	5.6371	5.7507	5.8666	5.9847	6.1051	6.3528	6.7424	5
6	6.1520	6.3081	6.4684	6.6330	6.8019	6.9753	7.1533	7.3359	7.5233	7.7156	8.1152	8.7537	6
7	7.2135	7.4343	7.6625	7.8983	8.1420	8.3938	8.6540	8.9228	9.2004	9.4872	10.0890	11.0668	7
8	8.2857	8.5830	8.8923	9.2142	9.5491	9.8975	10.2598	10.6366	11.0285	11.4359	12.2997	13.7268	8
9	9.3685	9.7546	10.1591	10.5828	11.0266	11.4913	11.9780	12.4876	13.0210	13.5795	14.7757	16.7858	9
10	10.4622	10.9497	11.4639	12.0061	12.5779	13.1808	13.8164	14.4866	15.1929	15.9374	17.5487	20.3037	10
11	11.5668	12.1687	12.8078	13.4864	14.2068	14.9716	15.7836	16.6455	17.5603	18.5312	20.6546	24.3493	11
12	12.6825	13.4121	14.1920	15.0258	15.9171	16.8699	17.8885	18.9771	20.1407	21.3843	24.1331	29.0017	12
13	13.8093	14.6803	15.6178	16.6268	17.7130	18.8821	20.1406	21.4953	22.9534	24.5227	28.0291	34.3519	13
14	14.9474	15.9739	17.0863	18.2919	19.5986	21.0151	22.5505	24.2149	26.0192	27.9750	32.3926	40.5047	14
15	16.0969	17.2934	18.5989	20.0236	21.5786	23.2760	25.1290	27.1521	29.3609	31.7725	37.2797	47.5804	15
16	17.2579	18.6393	20.1569	21.8245	23.6575	25.6725	27.8881	30.3243	33.0034	35.9497	42.7533	55.7175	16
17	18.4304	20.0121	21.7616	23.6975	25.8404	28.2129	30.8402	33.7502	36.9737	40.5447	48.8837	65.0751	17
18	19.6147	21.4123	23.4144	25.6454	28.1324	30.9057	33.9990	37.4502	41.3013	45.5992	55.7497	75.8364	18
19	20.8109	22.8406	25.1169	27.6712	30.5390	33.7600	37.3790	41.4463	46.0185	51.1591	63.4397	88.2118	19
20	22.0190	24.2974	26.8704	29.7781	33.0660	36.7856	40.9955	45.7620	51.1601	57.2750	72.0524	102.4436	20
25	28.2432	32.0303	36.4593	41.6459	47.7271	54.8645	63.2490	73.1059	84.7009	98.3471	133.3339	212.7930	25
30	34.7849	40.5681	47.5754	56.0849	66.4388	79.0582	94.4608	113.2832	136.3075	164.4940	241.3327	434.7451	30
35	41.6603	49.9945	60.4621	73.6522	90.3203	111.4348	138.2369	172.3168	215.7108	271.0244	431.6635	881.1702	35
40	48.8864	60.4020	75.4013	95.0255	120.7998	154.7620	199.6351	259.0565	337.8824	442.5926	767.0914	1,779.0903	40

§Used to calculate the future value of a series of equal payments made at the end of each period. For example: What is the future value of $4,000 per year for 6 years assuming an annual interest rate of 8%? For ($n = 6$, $i = 8\%$), the FV factor is 7.3359. $4,000 per year for 6 years accumulates to $29,343.60 ($4,000 × 7.3359).

C Investments

Appendix Preview

BASICS OF INVESTMENTS

C1 Short- vs. long-term

Debt vs. equity

Classification and reporting summary

DEBT INVESTMENTS

Recording debt investments

P1 Trading securities

P2 Held-to-maturity securities

P3 Available-for-sale securities

NTK C-1, C-2, C-3

EQUITY INVESTMENTS

Recording equity investments

P4 Insignificant influence

P5 Significant influence

C2 Controlling influence

NTK C-4, C-5

REPORTING AND ANALYSIS

Summary of debt and equity investments

Comprehensive income

A1 Return on assets components

NTK C-6

Learning Objectives

CONCEPTUAL

C1 Distinguish between debt and equity securities and between short-term and long-term investments.

C2 Describe how to report equity securities with controlling influence.

ANALYTICAL

A1 Compute and analyze the components of return on total assets.

PROCEDURAL

P1 Account for debt securities as trading.

P2 Account for debt securities as held-to-maturity.

P3 Account for debt securities as available-for-sale.

P4 Account for equity securities with insignificant influence.

P5 Account for equity securities with significant influence.

BASICS OF INVESTMENTS

In prior chapters we covered the reporting of both equity (common and preferred stock) and debt (bonds and notes) from the seller's (also called *issuer* or *investee*) standpoint. **This appendix covers the reporting of both equity and debt from the buyer's (or *investor*) standpoint.**

Purposes and Types of Investments

Companies make investments for at least three reasons. (1) Companies invest their *extra cash* to earn more income. (2) Some entities, such as mutual funds and pension funds, are set up to earn income from investments. (3) Companies make investments for strategic reasons such as investments in competitors, suppliers, and customers. Exhibit C.1 shows short-term (ST) and long-term (LT) investments as a percent of total assets for several companies.

Short-Term Investments **Short-term investments,** or *marketable securities,* are investments that (1) management intends to convert to cash within one year or the operating cycle, whichever is longer, and (2) are readily convertible to cash. These investments usually mature between 3 and 12 months. Cash equivalents are not short-term investments because they usually mature within 3 months. Short-term investments are current assets.

Long-Term Investments **Long-term investments** are investments that are not readily convertible to cash or are not intended to be converted into cash in the short term. Long-term investments also include funds designated for a special purpose, such as investments in land or other assets not used in operations. Long-term investments are noncurrent assets.

Debt Securities versus Equity Securities Investments in securities include both debt and equity securities. *Debt securities* reflect a creditor relation such as investments in notes, bonds, and certificates of deposit; they are issued by governments, companies, and individuals. *Equity securities* reflect an owner relation such as investments in shares of stock issued by companies.

Classification and Reporting

Accounting for investments in securities depends on three factors: (1) security type, either debt or equity; (2) the company's intent to hold the security either short term or long term; and (3) the investor's percentage of ownership in the other company's (investee's) equity securities. Exhibit C.2 identifies six classes of securities using these three factors.

C1_____

Distinguish between debt and equity securities and between short-term and long-term investments.

EXHIBIT C.1

Investments of Selected Companies

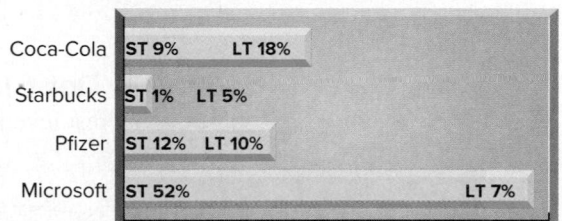

Percent of total assets

Investee's Balance Sheet — Investor's Balance Sheet

Liabilities — Assets
Notes Payable ←→ Debt Investments
Bonds Payable
Equity
Common Stock ←→ Equity Investments
Preferred Stock

EXHIBIT C.2

Investments in Securities

Debt Investments			Equity Investments		
Held-to-Maturity	**Trading**	**Available-for-Sale**	**Insignificant Influence**	**Significant Influence**	**Controlling Influence**
Debt securities intended to be held until maturity	Debt securities that are actively traded	Debt securities that are not HTM or Trading	Equity securities with insignificant influence	Equity securities with significant influence	Equity securities with controlling influence

Debt Investments

Debt Investments—Basics

This section covers the purchase, sale, and any interest received for **debt investments** (also called *debt securities*).

Recording Acquisition Debt investments are recorded at cost when purchased. Assume that Ling Co. paid $30,000 on July 1, 2019, to buy Dell's 7%, two-year bonds payable with a $30,000 par value. The bonds pay interest semiannually on December 31 and June 30. The entry to record this purchase follows.

©Scott Olson/Getty Images

<table>
<tr><td>Assets = Liabilities + Equity
+30,000
−30,000</td><td>July 1, 2019</td><td>Debt Investments . . . .
    Cash . . . .
Purchased bonds as debt investments.</td><td>30,000

    30,000</td></tr>
</table>

Recording Interest Interest revenue for debt investments is recorded when earned. On December 31, 2019, Ling records cash receipt of interest as follows. The $1,050 interest earned from July 1 to December 31 is computed as Principal × Annual rate × Fraction of year.

<table>
<tr><td>Assets = Liabilities + Equity
+1,050   +1,050</td><td>Dec. 31, 2019</td><td>Cash . . . .
    Interest Revenue . . . .
Record interest earned ($30,000 × 7% × 6/12).</td><td>1,050

    1,050</td></tr>
</table>

Reporting Debt Investments Ling's financial statements at December 31, 2019, report the interest revenue and the investment as shown in Exhibit C.3.

EXHIBIT C.3

Financial Statement Presentation of Debt Investments

On the income statement for year 2019:		On the December 31, 2019, balance sheet:	
Interest revenue	**$ 1,050**	**Debt investments**	**$30,000**

Maturity When bonds mature, we record the proceeds (assuming interest was already recorded).

<table>
<tr><td>Assets = Liabilities + Equity
+30,000
−30,000</td><td>July 1, 2021</td><td>Cash . . . .
    Debt Investments . . . .
Received cash from matured bonds.</td><td>30,000

    30,000</td></tr>
</table>

Point: It is common to add the security name to the account title to track as a subsidiary ledger. For example, the Debt Investments account can be titled Debt Investments (Dell).

The cost of a debt security can be either higher or lower than its maturity value. When the investment is long term, the difference between cost and maturity value is amortized as an adjustment to interest revenue over the remaining life of the security. We assume for simplicity that the cost of a long-term debt security equals its maturity value for all assignments.

DEBT INVESTMENTS—TRADING

P1

Account for debt securities as trading.

Trading securities are *debt* investments that the company actively buys and sells for profit. **Trading securities are *always* current assets.**

The portfolio of trading securities is reported at fair value; this requires a "fair value adjustment" from the cost of the portfolio. A *portfolio* is a group of securities. **Any unrealized gain (or loss) from a change in the fair value of the portfolio of trading securities is reported on the income statement.**

Recording Fair Value TechCom's portfolio of trading securities had a total cost of $11,500 and a fair value of $13,000 on December 31, 2019, the first year it held trading securities. The difference between the $11,500 cost and the $13,000 fair value is a $1,500 gain. It is an **unrealized gain** because it is not yet confirmed by actual sales of securities. The fair value adjustment for trading securities is recorded with an adjusting entry at the end of each period to equal the difference between the portfolio's cost and its fair value. TechCom records this gain as follows.

Point: Fair Value Adj. is a balance sheet account with either a debit balance (Fair value > Cost) or credit balance (Fair value < Cost).

<table>
<tr><td>Assets = Liabilities + Equity
+1,500   +1,500</td><td>Dec. 31, 2019</td><td>Fair Value Adjustment—Trading. . . . .
    Unrealized Gain—Income . . . .
Record unrealized gain in trading securities.</td><td>1,500

    1,500</td></tr>
</table>

This adjustment is computed using our three-step adjusting process.

Step 1:	Determine what unadjusted balance equals: Fair Value Adj.–Trading = $0.	
Step 2:	Determine what adjusted balance should equal: Fair Value Adj.–Trading = $1,500 Dr.	
	Explanation: $13,000 fair value > $11,500 cost; thus Fair Value Adj.–Trading requires a $1,500 debit to be at fair value.	
Step 3:	Record the $1,500 adjusting entry to get from step 1 to step 2.	
	Explanation: This means a $1,500 debit to Fair Value Adj.–Trading and a $1,500 credit to Unrealized Gain–Income.	

Unadj. bal. is rarely $0; it is $0 here because it's the first year.

Example: If TechCom's trading securities have a cost of $14,800 and a fair value of $16,100 at Dec. 31, 2020, its adjusting entry is

Unreal. Loss—Income...   200
  Fair Value Adj.—Trading   200

This is computed as:

$1,500 Beg. Dr. bal. + $200 Cr. = $1,300 End. Dr. bal.

Reporting Fair Value   The **unrealized gain (or loss)** is reported in the Other Revenues and Gains (or Expenses and Losses) section on the income statement. Unrealized Gain—Income (or Unrealized Loss—Income) is a *temporary* account that is closed to Income Summary at the end of each period. Fair Value Adjustment—Trading is a *permanent* asset account that adjusts the reported value of the trading securities portfolio from its prior-period fair value to the current period fair value. The total cost of the trading securities portfolio is maintained in one account, and the fair value adjustment is recorded in a separate account. For example, TechCom's investment in trading securities is reported in current assets as follows.

Current Assets		
Debt investments—Trading (at cost)	$11,500	
Fair value adjustment—Trading.	1,500	
Debt investments—Trading (at fair value).		$13,000
or simply		
Debt investments—Trading (at fair value; cost is $11,500)		$13,000

Debt Investments–Trading

1/1/2019	0	
Purch.	11,500	
12/31/2019	11,500	

Fair Value Adj.–Trading

1/1/2019	0	
Adj.	**1,500**	
12/31/2019	1,500	

Selling Trading Securities   When individual trading securities are sold, the difference between the net proceeds (sale price minus fees) and the cost of the individual trading securities sold is recorded as a gain or a loss. **Any prior-period fair value adjustment to the portfolio is *not* used to compute the gain or loss from the sale of individual trading securities.** This is because the balance in the Fair Value Adjustment account is for the entire portfolio, not individual securities. If TechCom sold some of its trading securities that had cost $100 for $120 cash on January 9, 2020, it records the following.

Jan. 9, 2020	Cash	120	
	Debt Investments—Trading.		100
	Gain on Sale of Debt Investments.		20
	Sold trading securities costing $100 for $120 cash.		

Assets = Liabilities + Equity
+120   +20
−100

A gain is reported in the Other Revenues and Gains section on the income statement, and a loss is reported in Other Expenses and Losses. When the period-end fair value adjustment for the portfolio of trading securities is computed, it excludes the cost and fair value of any securities sold.

Point: This is a *realized* $20 gain—realized by actual sale.

Berkshire Co. purchases debt investments in trading securities at a cost of $130 on July 1. (This is its first and only purchase of trading securities.) On December 30, Berkshire received $1 of interest from its trading securities. At year-end December 31, the trading securities had a fair value of $140.

a. Prepare the July 1 purchase entry of trading securities.

b. Prepare the December 30 entry for receipt of cash interest.

c. Prepare the December 31 year-end adjusting entry for the trading securities' portfolio.

NEED-TO-KNOW C-1

Trading Securities

P1

d. Explain how each account in entry *c* is reported in financial statements.

e. Prepare the January 3 entry when a portion of its trading securities (that had cost $33) is sold for $36.

Solution

a.

July 1	Debt Investments—Trading............................	130	
	Cash..		130
	Record purchase of trading securities.		

b.

Dec. 30	Cash	1	
	Interest Revenue.............................		1
	Record interest received on trading securities.		

Fair Value Adj.–Trading

Unadj. bal.	0	
Adj.	10	
Dec. 31	10	

c.

Dec. 31	Fair Value Adjustment—Trading	10	
	Unrealized Gain—Income......................		10
	Record unrealized gain in fair value of trading securities.		

d. (i) The $10 debit in the Fair Value Adjustment—Trading account is an adjunct asset account in the balance sheet. It increases the $130 balance of the Debt Investments—Trading account to its $140 fair value.

(ii) The $10 credit for Unrealized Gain is reported in the Other Revenues and Gains section of the income statement.

e.

Jan. 3	Cash	36	
	Gain on Sale of Debt Investments		3
	Debt Investments—Trading		33
	Record sale of trading securities.		

Do More: QS C-3, QS C-4, QS C-5, E C-2, P C-1

DEBT INVESTMENTS—HELD-TO-MATURITY

P2

Account for debt securities as held-to-maturity.

Held-to-maturity (HTM) securities are *debt* securities a company intends and is able to hold until maturity. They are reported in current assets if their maturity dates are within one year or the operating cycle, whichever is longer. Otherwise, they are classified as long-term investments.

The cost of a debt security can be either higher or lower than its maturity value. When the investment is long term, the difference between cost and maturity value is amortized over the remaining life of the security. We assume for simplicity that the cost of a long-term HTM debt security equals its maturity value for all assignments.

Recording Acquisition and Interest   All HTM securities are recorded at cost when purchased, and interest revenue is recorded when earned—see earlier "basic" entries.

Reporting HTM Securities at Cost   The portfolio of HTM securities is usually reported at (amortized) cost, which is explained in advanced courses. **There is *no* fair value adjustment to the portfolio of HTM securities—neither to short-term nor long-term portfolios.**

Prepare journal entries to record the following transactions involving short-term debt investments.

a. On May 15, paid $100 cash to purchase Muni's 120-day short-term debt securities ($100 principal), dated May 15, that pay 6% interest (categorized as held-to-maturity securities).

b. On September 13, received a check from Muni in payment of the principal and 120 days' interest on the debt securities purchased in transaction *a*.

NEED-TO-KNOW C-2

Held-to-Maturity
Securities

P2

Solution

a.

May 15	Debt Investments—HTM	100	
	Cash...		100
	Purchased 120-day, 6% debt securities.		

b.

Sep. 13	Cash..	102	
	Debt Investments—HTM		100
	Interest Revenue................................		2
	Collect $100 principal plus interest of $100 × 6% × 120/360.		

Do More: QS C-6, E C-3

DEBT INVESTMENTS—AVAILABLE-FOR-SALE

Available-for-sale (AFS) securities are *debt* investments not classified as trading or held-to-maturity securities. If the intent is to sell AFS securities within the longer of one year or the operating cycle, they are classified as short-term investments. Otherwise, they are classified as long-term investments.

Companies adjust the cost of the portfolio of AFS securities for changes in fair value. This is done with a fair value adjustment to its portfolio cost. **Any unrealized gain or loss for the portfolio of AFS securities is *not* reported on the income statement. It is reported in the equity section of the balance sheet** (as part of *comprehensive income,* covered later).

P3

Account for debt securities as available-for-sale.

Recording Fair Value Assume that Mitsu Co. had no prior investments in available-for-sale securities other than those purchased in the current period. Exhibit C.4 shows the cost and fair value of the portfolio of investments on December 31, 2019, the end of its reporting period.

	Cost	Fair Value	Unrealized Gain (Loss)
Apple bonds	$30,000	$29,050	$ (950)
Intex notes	43,000	45,500	2,500
Total...............	$73,000	$74,550	$1,550

EXHIBIT C.4

Cost and Fair Value of Available-for-Sale Securities

Example: If fair value in Exhibit C.4 is $70,000 (instead of $74,550), what entry is made? *Answer:*
Unreal. Loss—Equity . . . 3,000
    Fair Value Adj.—AFS . .   3,000

The year-end adjusting entry to record the fair value of the portfolio of investments follows.

Dec. 31, 2019	Fair Value Adjustment—Available-for-Sale	1,550	
	Unrealized Gain—Equity		1,550
	Record adjustment to fair value of AFS securities.		

Assets = Liabilities + Equity
+1,550   +1,550

Reporting Fair Value

Exhibit C.5 shows the December 31, 2019, balance sheet—it assumes these investments are long term, but they also can be short term. It is also common to combine the cost of investments with the balance in the Fair Value Adjustment account and report the net as a single amount.

EXHIBIT C.5

Balance Sheet Presentation of Available-for-Sale Securities

Debt Investments–AFS	
1/1/2019	0
Purch.	73,000
12/31/2019	73,000

Fair Value Adj.–AFS	
1/1/2019	0
Adj.	**1,550**
12/31/2019	1,550

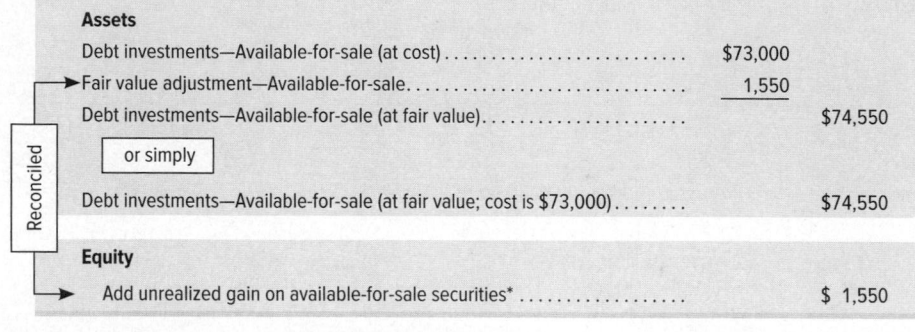

Assets	
Debt investments—Available-for-sale (at cost)	$73,000
Fair value adjustment—Available-for-sale.	1,550
Debt investments—Available-for-sale (at fair value).	$74,550
or simply	
Debt investments—Available-for-sale (at fair value; cost is $73,000).	$74,550
Equity	
Add unrealized gain on available-for-sale securities*	$ 1,550

Reconciled

*Included under Accumulated Other Comprehensive Income.

Reporting for Next Year

Let's extend this example and assume that at the end of its next year, December 31, 2020, Mitsu's portfolio of long-term AFS securities has an $81,000 cost and an $82,000 fair value. The year-end adjustment is computed using our three-step adjusting process.

Step 1:	Determine what unadjusted balance equals: Fair Value Adj.–AFS = $1,550 Dr. (from Exhibit C.5).
Step 2:	Determine what adjusted balance should equal: Fair Value Adj.–AFS = $1,000 Dr.
	Explanation: $82,000 fair value > $81,000 cost; thus Fair Value Adj.–AFS must have a $1,000 Dr. bal. so securities are at fair value.
Step 3:	Record the $550 adjusting entry to get from step 1 to step 2.
	Explanation: This implies a $550 credit to Fair Value Adj.–AFS (and a $550 debit to Unrealized Gain).

It records the year-end adjustment to fair value as follows.

Dec. 31, 2020	Unrealized Gain—Equity.	**550**	
	Fair Value Adjustment—Available-for-Sale		**550**
	Record adjustment to fair value of AFS securities.		

The effects of the 2019 and 2020 securities transactions are shown in the following T-accounts.

Unrealized Gain—Equity			
		Bal. 12/31/19	1,550
Adj. 12/31/20	**550**		
		Bal. 12/31/20	**1,000**

Fair Value Adjustment—Available-for-Sale			
Bal. 12/31/19	1,550		
		Adj. 12/31/20	**550**
Bal. 12/31/20	**1,000**		

Selling AFS Securities

Accounting for the sale of individual AFS securities is identical to accounting for the sale of trading securities. When individual AFS securities are sold, the difference between the cost of the individual securities sold and the net proceeds (sale price less fees) is recorded as a gain or loss on sale of debt investments.

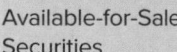

NEED-TO-KNOW C-3

Available-for-Sale Securities

P3

Gard Company completes the following transactions related to its short-term debt investments.

May 8	Purchased FedEx notes as a short-term investment in available-for-sale securities for $12,975.
Sep. 2	Sold part of its investment in FedEx notes for $4,475, which had cost $4,325.
Oct. 2	Purchased Ajay bonds for $25,600 as a short-term investment in available-for-sale securities.

Required

1. Prepare journal entries for the transactions.
2. Prepare a year-end adjusting journal entry as of December 31 if the fair values of the debt securities held by Gard are $9,600 for FedEx and $22,000 for Ajay. (This year is the first year Gard Company acquired short-term debt investments.)

Solution

1.

May 8	Debt Investments—AFS	12,975	
	Cash.		12,975
	Purchased FedEx notes.		
Sep. 2	Cash	4,475	
	Gain on Sale of Debt Investment		150
	Debt Investments—AFS		4,325
	Sold a portion of its FedEx notes		
Oct. 2	Debt Investments—AFS	25,600	
	Cash.		25,600
	Purchased Ajay bonds.		

2. Computation of unrealized gain or loss, along with the adjusting entry, follows.

Debt Investments in Available-for-Sale Securities	Total Cost	Total Fair Value	Unrealized Gain (Loss)
FedEx.	$ 8,650*	$ 9,600	
Ajay	25,600	22,000	
Totals.	$34,250	$31,600	$(2,650)

*$12,975 − $4,325

Debt Investments–AFS

Jan. 1	0		
May 8	12,975		
		Sep. 2	4,325
Oct. 2	25,600		
Dec. 31 bal.	34,250		

Fair Value Adj.–AFS

Jan. 1	0		
		Dec. 31 adj.	2,650
		Dec. 31 bal.	2,650

Dec. 31	Unrealized Loss—Equity	2,650	
	Fair Value Adjustment—Available-for-Sale		2,650
	Record unrealized loss in fair value of ST AFS portfolio.		

Do More: QS C-7, QS C-8, QS C-9, QS C-10, E C-4, E C-5, E C-6

Equity Investments

This section covers **equity investments** (also called *equity securities*). Exhibit C.6 summarizes the accounting for equity investments based on an investor's ownership in the stock. We cover each of these three cases.

Insignificant Influence	Significant Influence	Controlling
Fair value method (under 20%)	**Equity method** (20% to 50%)	**Consolidation method** (more than 50%)

0%   20%   50%   100%
Investor's percent ownership of a company's stock

EXHIBIT C.6

Accounting for Equity Investments by Percent of Ownership

EQUITY INVESTMENTS—INSIGNIFICANT INFLUENCE, UNDER 20%

When an investor has insignificant influence over another company, presumably when it owns less than 20% of voting stock, the stock investment is reported at fair value. Stock investments are classified as short or long term based on managers' intent and the stock's marketability. Any cash dividends are recorded as dividend revenue.

P4

Account for equity securities with insignificant influence.

Recording Acquisition

Equity investments are recorded at cost when acquired, including any commissions and brokerage fees paid. Assume ITI purchases 100 shares of Lynx common stock for $7,000 on October 10, 2019. After the purchase, ITI has insignificant influence over Lynx. It records this purchase as follows.

Assets = Liabilities + Equity
+7,000
−7,000

Oct. 10	Stock Investments	7,000	
	Cash		7,000
	Purchased 100 shares of Lynx.		

Recording Dividends

If ITI receives $10 in dividends on November 1 from its stock investment, it records the following.

Assets = Liabilities + Equity
+10   +10

Nov. 1	Cash	10	
	Dividend Revenue		10
	Record dividend received on stock investments.		

Recording Fair Value

The stock investments portfolio is reported at fair value; this requires a "fair value adjustment" from cost of the portfolio. **Any unrealized gain (or loss) from a change in the fair value of this portfolio of stock investments is reported on the income statement.**

Assume ITI's portfolio of stock investments with insignificant influence has a total cost of $7,000 and a fair value of $9,000 on December 31, 2019, the first year it held these securities. The difference between the $7,000 cost and the $9,000 fair value is a $2,000 **unrealized gain.** The fair value adjustment is recorded at the end of each period to equal the difference between the portfolio's cost and its fair value. ITI records this gain as follows.

Assets = Liabilities + Equity
+2,000   +2,000

Dec. 31	Fair Value Adjustment—Stock	2,000	
	Unrealized Gain—Income		2,000
	Record unrealized gain in stock investments.		

This adjustment is computed using our three-step adjusting process.

> Unadj. bal. is rarely $0; it is $0 here because it's the first year.

Step 1:	Determine what unadjusted balance equals: Fair Value Adj.–Stock = $0.
Step 2:	Determine what adjusted balance should equal: Fair Value Adj.–Stock = $2,000 Dr.
	Explanation: $9,000 fair value > $7,000 cost; thus Fair Value Adj.–Stock requires a $2,000 debit to be at fair value.
Step 3:	Record the $2,000 adjusting entry to get from step 1 to step 2.
	Explanation: This means a $2,000 debit to Fair Value Adj.–Stock and a $2,000 credit to Unrealized Gain–Income.

Example: If cost is $10,000 and fair value is $8,500 at Dec. 31, 2020, it records the following adjustment:
Unreal. Loss—Income 3,500
   Fair Value Adj.—Stock   3,500

The FVA—Stock Cr. is computed as: $2,000 Beg. Dr. bal. + **$3,500 Cr.** = $1,500 End. Cr. bal.

Reporting Fair Value

The **unrealized gain (or loss)** is reported in the Other Revenues and Gains (or Expenses and Losses) section on the income statement. Unrealized Gain (or Loss)—Income is a *temporary* account that is closed to Income Summary at the end of each period. Fair Value Adjustment—Stock is a *permanent* asset account that adjusts the reported value of the stock investments portfolio from its prior-period fair value to the current-period fair value. The total cost of the portfolio is kept in one account, and the fair value adjustment is kept in a separate account. ITI's stock investment is reported in its assets.

Stock Investments

1/1/2019	0	
Purch.	7,000	
12/31/2019	7,000	

Fair Value Adj.–Stock

1/1/2019	0	
Adj.	**2,000**	
12/31/2019	2,000	

Assets

Stock investments (at cost)	$7,000	
Fair value adjustment—Stock	2,000	
Stock investments (at fair value)		$9,000

or simply

Stock investments (at fair value; cost is $7,000)		$9,000

Selling Stock Investments   When individual stock investments are sold, the difference between the net proceeds (sale price minus fees) and the cost of the individual stocks that are sold is recorded as a gain or a loss. **Any prior-period fair value adjustment to the portfolio is *not* used to compute the gain or loss from the sale of individual stocks.** This is because the balance in the Fair Value Adjustment account is for the entire portfolio, not individual stocks. If ITI sold some of its stock investments that had cost $500 for $800 cash on March 9, 2020, it records the following. A gain is reported in the Other Revenues and Gains section on the income statement and a loss is reported in Other Expenses and Losses.

Mar. 9	Cash	800	
	Stock Investments		500
	Gain on Sale of Stock Investments		300
	Sold stock investments costing $500 for $800 cash.		

Assets = Liabilities + Equity
+800 +300
−500

Derr Co. purchases stock investments (with insignificant influence) at a cost of $250 on December 15. This is its first and only purchase of such securities. On December 28, Derr received a $15 cash dividend from the stock investments. At year-end December 31, the stock investments had a fair value of $200.

a. Prepare the December 15 purchase entry for stock investments.
b. Prepare the December 28 receipt of cash dividends entry.
c. Prepare the December 31 year-end adjusting entry for the stock investments' portfolio.
d. Explain how each account in entry *c* is reported in financial statements.
e. Prepare the January 3 entry when a portion of its stock investments (that had cost $37) is sold for $40.

NEED-TO-KNOW C-4

Stock Investments with Insignificant Influence (<20%)

P4

Solution

a.
Dec. 15	Stock Investments	250	
	Cash......................................		250
	Record purchase of stock investments.		

b.
Dec. 28	Cash	15	
	Dividend Revenue............................		15
	Record dividend received on stock investments.		

c.
Dec. 31	Unrealized Loss—Income	50	
	Fair Value Adjustment—Stock		50
	Record unrealized loss in stock investments.		

Fair Value Adj.–Stock
Unadj. bal. 0
Adj. 50
Dec. 31 50

d. (i) The $50 credit in the Fair Value Adjustment—Stock account is a contra asset account in the balance sheet. It decreases the $250 balance of the Stock Investments account to its $200 fair value.
   (ii) The $50 debit for Unrealized Loss is reported in the Other Expenses and Losses section of the income statement.

e.
Jan. 3	Cash	40	
	Gain on Sale of Stock Investments		3
	Stock Investments............................		37
	Record sale of stock investments.		

Do More: QS C-11, QS C-12, QS C-13, E C-7, E C-8, E C-9, E C-10

EQUITY INVESTMENTS—SIGNIFICANT INFLUENCE, 20% TO 50%

A long-term investment classified as **equity securities with significant influence** means that the investor has significant influence over the investee. An investor that owns between 20% and 50% of a company's voting stock usually has significant influence. The **equity method** is used for long-term investments in equity securities with significant influence, which is explained in this section.

P5

Account for equity securities with significant influence.

Recording Acquisition

Long-term investments in equity securities with significant influence are recorded at cost when acquired. Micron Co. records the purchase of 3,000 shares (30%) of Star Co. common stock at a total cost of $70,000 on January 1, 2019, as follows.

Assets = Liabilities + Equity
+70,000
−70,000

Jan. 1	Equity Method Investments	70,000	
	Cash		70,000
	Record purchase of 3,000 Star shares.		

Recording Share of Earnings

When the investee reports its earnings, the investor records its share of those earnings in its investment account. Assume that Star reports net income of $20,000 for 2019. Micron records its 30% share of those earnings—see entry below. The debit increases Micron's equity in Star. The credit is 30% of Star's net income. Earnings from Equity Method Investments is a *temporary* account (closed to Income Summary at each period-end) and is reported on the investor's (Micron's) income statement. If the investee incurs a net loss instead of net income, the investor records its share of the loss and reduces (credits) its investments account.

Assets = Liabilities + Equity
+6,000   +6,000

Dec. 31	Equity Method Investments	6,000	
	Earnings from Equity Method Investments...........		6,000
	Record 30% equity in investee's $20,000 earnings.		

Recording Share of Dividends

Cash dividends received by an investor from an investee under the equity method are accounted for as a conversion of one asset to another. Dividends reduce the Equity Method Investments account. Assume Star pays a total of $10,000 in cash dividends on its common stock. Micron records its 30% share of these dividends received on January 9, 2020, as follows.

Assets = Liabilities + Equity
+3,000
−3,000

Jan. 9	Cash	3,000	
	Equity Method Investments		3,000
	Record 30% share of $10,000 dividend paid by Star.		

Reporting Investments with Significant Influence

The book value of investments under the equity method equals the cost of investments *plus* the investor's share of net income or loss and *minus* its share of dividends. **The Equity Method Investments account is not adjusted to fair value.** After Micron records these transactions, its Equity Method Investments account appears as in Exhibit C.7. Micron's account balance on January 9, 2020, for its investment in Star is $73,000. This is the investment's cost *plus* Micron's share of Star's earnings *minus* Micron's share of Star's cash dividends.

EXHIBIT C.7

Investment in Star Common Stock (ledger T-account)

Equity Method Investments			
1/1/2019 Investment acquisition	70,000		
12/31/2019 Share of earnings	6,000		
12/31/2019 Balance	76,000		
		1/9/2020 Share of dividend	3,000
1/9/2020 Balance	73,000		

Selling Investments with Significant Influence

When equity method investments are sold, the gain or loss is computed by comparing proceeds from the sale with the book value of the investments on the sale date. If Micron sells all of its Star stock for $80,000 on January 10, 2020, it records the sale as follows.

Assets = Liabilities + Equity
+80,000   +7,000
−73,000

Jan. 10	Cash	80,000	
	Equity Method Investments		73,000
	Gain on Sale of Stock Investments................		7,000
	Sold 3,000 shares of stock for $80,000.		

Prepare entries to record the following transactions of Garcia Company.

NEED-TO-KNOW **C-5**

Equity Method
Investments

P5 ▶

2019

Jan. 1   Purchased 400 shares of Lopez Co. common stock for $3,000 cash. Lopez has 1,000 shares of common stock outstanding, and its policies will be significantly influenced by Garcia.

Aug. 1   Lopez declared and paid a cash dividend of $2 per share.

Dec. 31 Lopez reported net income for the year of $2,500.

2020

Aug. 1   Lopez declared and paid a cash dividend of $2.25 per share.

Dec. 31 Lopez reported net income for the year of $2,750.

2021

Jan. 1   Garcia sold 100 shares of Lopez for $1,300 cash.

Solution

Jan. 1, 2019	Equity Method Investments	3,000	
	Cash.....................................		3,000
	*Record purchase of investment.**		

*Garcia's investment is 40% of Lopez's stock (400/1,000). Garcia uses the equity method.

Aug. 1, 2019	Cash	800	
	Equity Method Investments		800
	Record receipt of cash dividend (400 × $2).		
Dec. 31, 2019	Equity Method Investments	1,000	
	Earnings from Equity Method Investments		1,000
	Record equity in investee earnings ($2,500 × 40%).		

Aug. 1, 2020	Cash	900	
	Equity Method Investments		900
	Record receipt of cash dividend (400 × $2.25).		
Dec. 31, 2020	Equity Method Investments	1,100	
	Earnings from Equity Method Investments		1,100
	Record equity in investee earnings ($2,750 × 40%).		

Jan. 1, 2021	Cash	1,300	
	Gain on Sale of Stock Investments		450
	Equity Method Investments*		850
	Record sale of investment.		

*Book value (Lopez stock) at 1/1/2021.

Original cost...	$3,000
Less 2019 dividends.................................	(800)
Plus share of 2019 earnings	1,000
Less 2020 dividends.................................	(900)
Plus share of 2020 earnings	1,100
Book value at date of sale............................	$3,400
Book value of shares sold ($3,400 × [100/400])	$ 850

Do More: QS C-15, E C-12,
E C-13, E C-14

EQUITY INVESTMENTS—CONTROLLING INFLUENCE, MORE THAN 50%

A long-term investment classified as **equity securities with controlling influence** means that the investor has a controlling influence over the investee. An investor who owns more than 50% of a company's voting stock has control over the investee. This investor can dominate all other shareholders in electing the corporation's board of directors and has control over the investee's management.

C2

Describe how to report equity securities with controlling influence.

©Tim Greenway/Portland Press
Herald/Getty Images

The *consolidation method* is used for long-term investments in equity securities with controlling influence. The investor reports *consolidated financial statements* when owning such securities. The controlling investor is called the **parent** and the investee is called the **subsidiary.** Many companies are parents with subsidiaries. **Amazon** is the parent of Whole Foods Market, Zappos, and other subsidiaries. When a company operates as a parent with subsidiaries, each entity maintains separate accounting records.

Consolidated financial statements show the financial statements of all entities under the parent's control, including all subsidiaries. These statements are prepared as if the business were organized as one entity. The individual assets and liabilities of the parent and its subsidiaries are combined on one balance sheet. Their revenues and expenses also are combined on one income statement, and their cash flows are combined on one statement of cash flows. Preparing consolidated financial statements is covered in advanced courses.

Accounting Summary for Debt and Equity Investments

Exhibit C.8 summarizes accounting for debt and equity investments.

EXHIBIT C.8

Accounting for Investments in Securities

Classification	Investments Account Reported at
Short-Term Investment in Securities	
Debt Investments—Held-to-Maturity...................	Cost (without any discount or premium amortization)
Debt Investments—Trading...........................	Fair value (with fair value adjustment to income)
Debt Investments—Available-for-Sale.................	Fair value (with fair value adjustment to equity)
Stock Investments—insignificant influence..............	Fair value (with fair value adjustment to income)
Long-Term Investment in Securities	
Debt Investments—Held-to-Maturity	Cost (with any discount or premium amortized)
Debt Investments—Available-for-Sale	Fair value (with fair value adjustment to equity)
Stock Investments—insignificant influence..............	Fair value (with fair value adjustment to income)
Equity Method Investments—significant influence	Equity method (no fair value adjustment)
Consolidated Investments—controlling influence	Consolidation method (no fair value adjustment)

Computing and Reporting Comprehensive Income   **Comprehensive income** is all changes in equity during a period except those from owners' investments and dividends. Specifically, comprehensive income is computed by adding *other comprehensive income* to or subtracting it from net income.

Statement of Comprehensive Income	
Net income..	$ #
Other comprehensive income.........................	#
Comprehensive income..............................	$ #

Frequently consists of:
Change in value of available-for-sale investment, net of tax
Change in foreign currency translation adjustment
Change in cash flow hedges, net of tax

Other comprehensive income includes **unrealized** gains and losses on available-for-sale securities, foreign currency translation adjustments, and other adjustments. (*Accumulated other comprehensive income* is the cumulative impact for all periods of *other comprehensive income*.) Comprehensive income is reported in financial statements in one of two ways.

1. On a separate *statement of comprehensive income* that follows the income statement.
2. On the lower section of the income statement (as a single continuous *statement of income and comprehensive income*).

Option 1 is most common. **Google**, for example, reports a statement of comprehensive income following its income statement (see Appendix A).

GOOGLE

A company's **return on total assets** (or *return on assets*) is used to assess financial performance. The return on total assets can be separated into two components, profit margin and total asset turnover, for additional analyses. Exhibit C.9 shows how these two components determine return on total assets.

A1

Compute and analyze the components of return on total assets.

$$\frac{\text{Net income}}{\text{Average total assets}} = \frac{\text{Net income}}{\text{Net sales}} \times \frac{\text{Net sales}}{\text{Average total assets}}$$

Return on total assets = Profit margin × Total asset turnover

EXHIBIT C.9

Components of Return on Total Assets

Profit margin reflects the percent of net income in each dollar of net sales. Total asset turnover reflects a company's ability to produce net sales from total assets. All companies want a high return on total assets. By considering these two components, we can often discover strengths and weaknesses not revealed by return on total assets alone. This improves our ability to assess future performance and company strategy.

Costco's return on total assets and its components are in Exhibit C.10.

EXHIBIT C.10

Components of Return on Total Assets for Two Competitors

| | Costco | | | | | Walmart |
Year	Return on Total Assets	=	Profit Margin	×	Total Asset Turnover	Return on Total Assets
Current Year	7.8%	=	2.1%	×	3.7	7.2%
1 Year Ago	7.2%	=	2.0%	×	3.6	7.5%
2 Years Ago	7.0%	=	2.0%	×	3.5	8.4%

Costco's return on total assets improved over the three-year period. This increase is driven by both an increase in profit margin and in total asset turnover. Costco increased its return on total assets during a time when other retailers like **Walmart** have struggled. To continue this trend, Costco's management must increase net income while keeping total asset turnover steady or at least at a level where it does not decrease return on total assets.

■ **Decision Maker**

Retailer   You are an owner of a retail store. The store's recent annual performance reveals (industry norms in parentheses) return on total assets = 11% (11.2%); profit margin = 4.4% (3.5%); and total asset turnover = 2.5 (3.2). What does your analysis reveal? ■   *Answer:* The store's 11% return on assets is similar to the 11.2% industry norm. However, the store's 4.4% profit margin is much higher than the 3.5% norm, but the 2.5 asset turnover is much lower than the 3.2 norm. The poor turnover suggests that this store is less efficient in using assets. It must focus on increasing sales or reducing assets.

The following transactions relate to Brown Company's long-term investments. Brown did not own any long-term investments prior to these transactions. Show (1) the necessary journal entries and (2) the relevant portions of each year's balance sheet and income statement that reflect these transactions for both years.

 **NEED-TO-KNOW** C-6

COMPREHENSIVE

Accounting for Equity Securities with Insignificant Influence and for Equity Securities with Significant Influence

2019

Sep. 9   Purchased 1,000 shares of Packard common stock for $80,000 cash. These shares represent 30% of Packard's outstanding shares.

Oct. 2   Purchased 2,000 shares of AT&T common stock for $60,000 cash as a long-term investment. These shares represent less than a 1% ownership in AT&T.

      17   Purchased as a long-term investment 1,000 shares of Apple common stock for $40,000 cash. These shares are less than 1% of Apple's outstanding shares.

Nov. 1   Received $5,000 cash dividend from Packard.

      30   Received $3,000 cash dividend from AT&T.

Dec. 15   Received $1,400 cash dividend from Apple.

      31   Packard's net income for this year is $70,000.

[continued on next page]

31   Fair values for the investments in equity securities are Packard, $84,000; AT&T, $48,000; and Apple, $45,000.

31   For preparing financial statements, note the following post-closing account balances: Common Stock, $500,000, and Retained Earnings, $350,000.

2020

Jan. 1   Sold all of the Packard shares for $108,000 cash.

May 30   Received $3,100 cash dividend from AT&T.

June 15   Received $1,600 cash dividend from Apple.

Aug. 17   Sold all of the AT&T stock for $52,000 cash.

19   Purchased 2,000 shares of Coca-Cola common stock for $50,000 cash as a long-term investment. The stock represents less than a 5% ownership in Coca-Cola.

Dec. 15   Received $1,800 cash dividend from Apple.

31   Fair values of the investments in equity securities are Apple, $39,000, and Coca-Cola, $48,000.

31   For preparing financial statements, note the following post-closing account balances: Common Stock, $500,000, and Retained Earnings, $410,000.

PLANNING THE SOLUTION

- Account for the investment in Packard under the equity method.
- Account for the investments in AT&T, Apple, and Coca-Cola as stock investments with insignificant influence.
- Prepare the information for the two years' balance sheets by including the relevant asset and equity accounts, and the two years' income statements by identifying the relevant revenues, earnings, gains, and losses.

SOLUTION

1. Journal entries for 2019.

Sep. 9	Equity Method Investments	80,000	
	Cash...		80,000
	Acquired 1,000 shares, a 30% equity in Packard.		
Oct. 2	Stock Investments	60,000	
	Cash...		60,000
	Acquired 2,000 shares of AT&T.		
Oct. 17	Stock Investments	40,000	
	Cash...		40,000
	Acquired 1,000 shares of Apple.		
Nov. 1	Cash	5,000	
	Equity Method Investments		5,000
	Received dividend from Packard.		
Nov. 30	Cash	3,000	
	Dividend Revenue...............................		3,000
	Received dividend from AT&T.		
Dec. 15	Cash	1,400	
	Dividend Revenue...............................		1,400
	Received dividend from Apple.		
Dec. 31	Equity Method Investments	21,000	
	Earnings from Equity Method Investments		21,000
	Record 30% share of Packard's earnings of $70,000.		
Dec. 31	Unrealized Loss—Income	7,000	
	Fair Value Adjustment—Stock*....................		7,000
	Record change in fair value of stock investments.		

Stock Investments

12/31/2018	0
10/2/2019	60,000
10/17/2019	40,000
12/31/2019	100,000

Fair Value Adj.–Stock

12/31/2018	0
Adj.	**7,000**
12/31/2019	7,000

*Fair value adjustment computations.

	Cost	Fair Value	Unrealized Gain (Loss)
AT&T	$ 60,000	$48,000	$(12,000)
Apple	40,000	45,000	5,000
Total	$100,000	$93,000	$ (7,000)

Required balance of the Fair Value Adjustment—Stock account (credit)	$(7,000)
Existing balance..................	0
Necessary adjustment (credit)	$(7,000)

2. The December 31, 2019, selected balance sheet items follow.

Assets—Long-term investments	
Stock investments (at fair value; cost is $100,000)...	$ 93,000
Equity method investments.....................	96,000
Total long-term investments	$189,000

The relevant income statement items for the year ended December 31, 2019, follow.

Dividend revenue	$ 4,400
Unrealized loss—Income	(7,000)
Earnings from equity method investments	21,000

1. Journal entries for 2020.

Jan. 1	Cash	108,000	
	Equity Method Investments		96,000
	Gain on Sale of Stock Investments		12,000
	Sold 1,000 shares of Packard for cash.		
May 30	Cash	3,100	
	Dividend Revenue.........................		3,100
	Received dividend from AT&T.		
June 15	Cash	1,600	
	Dividend Revenue.........................		1,600
	Received dividend from Apple.		
Aug. 17	Cash	52,000	
	Loss on Sale of Stock Investments	8,000	
	Stock Investments		60,000
	Sold 2,000 shares of AT&T for cash.		
Aug. 19	Stock Investments	50,000	
	Cash...		50,000
	Acquired 2,000 shares of Coca-Cola.		
Dec. 15	Cash	1,800	
	Dividend Revenue.........................		1,800
	Received dividend from Apple.		
Dec. 31	Fair Value Adjustment—Stock*	4,000	
	Unrealized Gain—Income.....................		4,000
	Record change in fair value of stock investments.		

Packard cost at Jan. 1 is $80,000
− $5,000 + $21,000 = $96,000.

Stock Investments

12/31/2019	100,000		
		8/17/2020	60,000
8/19/2020	50,000		
12/31/2020	90,000		

Fair Value Adj.—Stock

		12/31/2019	7,000
Adj.	4,000		
		12/31/2020	3,000

*Fair value adjustment computations.

	Cost	Fair Value	Unrealized Gain (Loss)
Apple	$40,000	$39,000	$(1,000)
Coca-Cola	50,000	48,000	(2,000)
Total	$90,000	$87,000	$(3,000)

Required balance of the Fair Value Adjustment—Stock account (credit)	$(3,000)
Existing balance (credit)	(7,000)
Necessary adjustment (debit)........	$ 4,000

2. The December 31, 2020, balance sheet items follow.

Assets—Long-term investments	
Stock investments (at fair value; cost is $90,000)	$87,000

The relevant income statement items for the year ended December 31, 2020, follow.

Dividend revenue	$ 6,500
Unrealized gain—Income	4,000
Gain on sale of stock investments	12,000
Loss on sale of stock investments	(8,000)

Summary: Cheat Sheet

BASICS OF INVESTMENTS

Short-term investments: Investments that (1) management intends to convert to cash within one year and (2) are readily convertible to cash. Short-term investments are current assets.

Long-term investments: Investments that are not going to be converted into cash in the short term. Long-term investments are noncurrent assets.

Debt securities: Reflect a creditor relation and include notes and bonds.

Equity securities: Reflect an owner relation and include stock.

DEBT INVESTMENTS

Acquiring debt investments:

Debt Investments	30,000	
Cash		30,000

Interest earned and received:

Cash	1,050	
Interest Revenue		1,050

Unrealized gain (or loss): A gain (or loss) not yet confirmed by actual sales of securities.

TRADING SECURITIES:

Debt investments that are actively bought and sold for profit. Trading securities are *always* current assets.

Fair value adjustment—Trading securities: Reflects gain (shown here) or loss.

Fair Value Adjustment—Trading.	1,500	
Unrealized Gain—Income.		1,500

Reporting fair value—Trading securities: An unrealized gain (or loss) from a change in the fair value of the portfolio of trading securities is reported on the income statement under Other Revenues and Gains (or Expenses and Losses). Fair Value Adjustment—Trading is an asset account that adjusts the trading securities portfolio to fair value.

Current Assets		
Debt investments—Trading (at cost)	$11,500	
Fair value adjustment—Trading.	1,500	
Debt investments—Trading (at fair value)		$13,000

Selling trading securities: When sale price > cost, record a gain (shown here). When sale price < cost, record a loss. A gain (or loss) is reported in Other Revenues and Gains (or Expenses and Losses) section on the income statement.

Cash	120	
Debt Investments—Trading.		100
Gain on Sale of Debt Investments		20

HELD-TO-MATURITY (HTM) SECURITIES:

Debt investments that are held until maturity. They are current assets if their maturity is *within* one year and are long-term investments if their maturity is *over* one year. They are *not* reported at fair value.

Receipt of principal and interest—HTM:

Cash	102	
Debt Investments—HTM		100
Interest Revenue		2

AVAILABLE-FOR-SALE (AFS) SECURITIES:

Debt investments not classified as trading or held-to-maturity. They are current assets if they are to be sold *within* one year and long-term investments if they are to be sold *beyond* one year.

Fair value adjustment—AFS securities: Reflects gain (shown here) or loss.

Fair Value Adjustment—Available-for-Sale	1,550	
Unrealized Gain—Equity		1,550

Reporting fair value—AFS securities: An unrealized gain (or loss) from a change in the fair value of the portfolio of AFS securities is reported in the equity section of the balance sheet (as part of comprehensive income). Fair Value Adjustment—AFS is an asset account that adjusts the AFS securities portfolio to fair value.

Assets		
Debt investments—Available-for-sale (at cost)	$73,000	
Fair value adjustment—Available-for-sale.	1,550	
Debt investments—Available-for-sale (at fair value). . . .		$74,550

Selling AFS securities: Identical to selling trading securities.

EQUITY INVESTMENTS

Stock investments (insignificant influence): When a company owns less than 20% of voting stock of another company, it has insignificant influence. Can be classified as short or long term.

Acquiring stock investments (insignificant influence):

Stock Investments	7,000	
Cash		7,000

Dividends received from stock investment (insignificant influence):

Cash	10	
Dividend Revenue		10

Fair value adjustment—Stock (insignificant influence): Reflects gain (shown here) or loss.

Fair Value Adjustment—Stock	2,000	
Unrealized Gain—Income		2,000

Reporting fair value adjustment from stock (insignificant influence): An unrealized gain (or loss) from a change in the fair value of the portfolio of stock investments is reported on the income statement under Other Revenues and Gains (or Expenses and Losses). Fair Value Adjustment—Stock is an asset account that adjusts the stock investments portfolio to fair value.

Assets		
Stock investments (at cost)	$7,000	
Fair value adjustment—Stock	2,000	
Stock investments (at fair value)		$9,000

Selling stock investments: When sale price > cost, record a gain (shown here). When sale price < cost, record a loss. A gain (or loss) is reported in Other Revenues and Gains (or Expenses and Losses) section on the income statement.

Cash	800	
Stock Investments		500
Gain on Sale of Stock Investments		300

Equity method investments: When a company owns between 20% and 50% of voting stock of another company, it has significant influence. Classified as long term.

Acquiring equity method investments:

Equity Method Investments	70,000	
Cash		70,000

Recording share of earnings (equity method): Calculated as percentage of ownership times net income of investee.

Equity Method Investments	6,000	
Earnings from Equity Method Investments		6,000

Recording share of dividends (equity method): Calculated as percentage of ownership times total dividends paid by investee.

Cash	3,000	
Equity Method Investments		3,000

Reporting equity method investments: Equity method investments are not adjusted to fair value. Instead, the account is increased by investee net income and decreased by investee dividends.

Equity Method Investments			
1/1/2019 Investment acquisition	70,000		
12/31/2019 Share of earnings	6,000		
12/31/2019 Balance	76,000		
		1/9/2020 Share of dividend	3,000
1/9/2020 Balance	73,000		

Selling equity method investments: When sale price > book value, record a gain (shown here). When sale price < book value, record a loss.

Cash	80,000	
Equity Method Investments		73,000
Gain on Sale of Stock Investments		7,000

Equity securities with controlling influence: When an investor owns more than 50% of a company's voting stock, it has control over the investee and the *consolidation method* is used. The controlling investor is called the **parent,** and the investee is called the **subsidiary.**

REPORTING AND ANALYSIS

Classification	Investments Account Reported at
Short-Term Investment in Securities	
Debt Investments—Held-to-Maturity	Cost (without any discount or premium amortization)
Debt Investments—Trading	Fair value (with fair value adjustment to income)
Debt Investments—Available-for-Sale	Fair value (with fair value adjustment to equity)
Stock Investments—insignificant influence	Fair value (with fair value adjustment to income)
Long-Term Investment in Securities	
Debt Investments—Held-to-Maturity	Cost (with any discount or premium amortized)
Debt Investments—Available-for-Sale	Fair value (with fair value adjustment to equity)
Stock Investments—insignificant influence	Fair value (with fair value adjustment to income)
Equity Method Investments—significant influence	Equity method (no fair value adjustment)
Consolidated Investments—controlling influence	Consolidation method (no fair value adjustment)

Key Terms

Available-for-sale (AFS) securities (C-5)
Comprehensive income (C-12)
Consolidated financial statements (C-12)
Equity method (C-9)
Equity securities with controlling influence (C-11)
Equity securities with significant influence (C-9)

Fair Value Adjustment (C-2)
Held-to-maturity (HTM) securities (C-4)
Long-term investments (C-1)
Other comprehensive income (C-12)
Parent (C-12)
Profit margin (C-13)
Return on total assets (C-13)

Short-term investments (C-1)
Subsidiary (C-12)
Total asset turnover (C-13)
Trading securities (C-2)
Unrealized gain (loss) (C-3, C-8)

Multiple Choice Quiz

1. A company purchased $30,000 of 5% bonds for investment purposes on May 1. The bonds pay interest on February 1 and August 1. The amount of interest revenue accrued at December 31 (the company's year-end) is

  a. $1,500.   **c.** $1,000.   **e.** $300.

  b. $1,375.   **d.** $625.

2. This period, Amadeus Co. purchased its only available-for-sale investment in the notes of Bach Co. for $83,000. The period-end fair value of these notes is $84,500. Amadeus records a

  a. Credit to Unrealized Gain—Equity for $1,500.

  b. Debit to Unrealized Loss—Equity for $1,500.

  c. Debit to Investment Revenue for $1,500.

  d. Credit to Fair Value Adjustment—Available-for-Sale for $3,500.

  e. Credit to Cash for $1,500.

3. Mozart Co. owns 35% of Melody Inc. Melody pays $50,000 in cash dividends to its shareholders for the period. Mozart's entry to record the Melody dividend includes a

  a. Credit to Investment Revenue for $50,000.

  b. Credit to Equity Method Investments for $17,500.

  c. Credit to Cash for $17,500.

  d. Debit to Equity Method Investments for $17,500.

  e. Debit to Cash for $50,000.

4. A company has net income of $300,000, net sales of $2,500,000, and total assets of $2,000,000. Its return on total assets equals

	Profit Margin	Total Asset Turnover
a.	1.5%	13.3
b.	13.3%	1.5
c.	13.3%	0.7
d.	7.0%	13.3
e.	10.0%	26.7

  a. 6.7%.   **c.** 8.3%.   **e.** 15.0%.
  b. 12.0%.   **d.** 80.0%.

5. A company had net income of $80,000, net sales of $600,000, and total assets of $400,000. Its profit margin and total asset turnover are

ANSWERS TO MULTIPLE CHOICE QUIZ

1. d; $30,000 \times 5\% \times 5/12 = \$625$

2. a; Unrealized gain = $84,500 - \$83,000 = \$1,500$

3. b; $50,000 \times 35\% = \$17,500$

4. e; $300,000/\$2,000,000 = 15\%$

5. b; Profit margin = $80,000/\$600,000 = 13.3\%$
    Total asset turnover = $600,000/\$400,000 = 1.5$

🔲 Icon denotes assignments that involve decision making.

Discussion Questions

1. Under what two conditions should investments be classified as current assets?

2. 🔲 On a balance sheet, what valuation must be reported for short-term debt investments in trading securities?

3. If a stock investment with insignificant influence costs $10,000 and is sold for $12,000, how should the difference between these two amounts be recorded?

4. Identify the three classes of debt investments and the three classes of equity investments.

5. Under what conditions should investments be classified as current assets? As long-term assets?

6. For investments in available-for-sale debt securities, how are unrealized (holding) gains and losses reported?

7. If a company purchases its only long-term investments in available-for-sale debt securities this period and their fair value is below cost at the balance sheet date, what entry is required to recognize this unrealized loss?

8. On a balance sheet, what valuation must be reported for debt securities classified as available-for-sale?

9. Under what circumstances are long-term investments in debt securities reported at cost and adjusted for amortization of any difference between cost and maturity value?

10. In accounting for investments in equity securities, when should the equity method be used?

11. Under what circumstances does a company prepare consolidated financial statements?

12. 🔲 Refer to **Apple**'s statement of comprehensive income in Appendix A. What is the amount **APPLE** of *change in foreign currency translation, net of tax effects,* for the year ended September 30, 2017? Is this change an unrealized gain or an unrealized loss?

13. Refer to **Google**'s statement of comprehensive income in Appendix A. What was the **GOOGLE** amount of its 2017 *change in net unrealized gains (losses)* for its AFS investments?

14. 🔲 Refer to the income statement of **Samsung** in Appendix A. How can you **Samsung** tell that it uses the consolidated method of accounting?

🔳 **connect**

QUICK STUDY

QS C-1

Distinguishing between short- and long-term investments

C1

Which of the following statements are true of long-term investments?

_____ **a.** They can be considered cash equivalents.

_____ **b.** They can include assets not used in operations, such as investments in land.

_____ **c.** They generally include investments that will mature in 3 to 12 months.

_____ **d.** They are reported with noncurrent assets on the balance sheet.

_____ **e.** They are always easily sold and therefore qualify as being marketable.

_____ **f.** They can include bonds and stocks not intended to be sold in the near future.

QS C-2

Distinguishing between debt and equity securities

C1

Identify investments as an investment in either debt (D) securities or equity (E) securities.

_____ **a.** U.S. Treasury bonds   _____ **e.** IBM corporate notes   _____ **i.** Chicago municipal bonds

_____ **b.** Google stock   _____ **f.** German government bonds   _____ **j.** Apple stock

_____ **c.** Certificate of deposit   _____ **g.** Amazon stock   _____ **k.** David Bowie bonds

_____ **d.** Apple bonds   _____ **h.** Costco corporate notes   _____ **l.** Facebook stock

Prepare Hertog Company's journal entries to record the following transactions for the current year.

May 7   Purchases Kraft bonds as a short-term investment in trading securities at a cost of $10,300.
June 6   Sells its entire investment in Kraft bonds for $11,050 cash.

QS C-3
Accounting for debt investments classified as trading **P1**

Kitty Company began operations in the current year and acquired short-term debt investments in trading securities. The year-end cost and fair values for its portfolio of these debt investments follow. Prepare the journal entry to record the December 31 year-end fair value adjustment for these debt securities.

QS C-4
Fair value adjustment to a portfolio of trading securities

P1

Trading Securities	Cost	Fair Value
Tesla bonds	$12,000	$ 9,000
Nike bonds	20,000	21,000
Ford bonds	5,000	4,000

Refer to the information in QS C-4. (1) After the fair value adjustment is made, prepare the assets section of Kitty Company's December 31 classified balance sheet. (2) In which income statement section is the unrealized gain (or loss) on the portfolio of trading securities reported?

QS C-5
Reporting trading securities on financial statements **P1**

Prepare Garzon Company's journal entries to record the following transactions for the current year.

Jan. 1   Purchases 6% bonds (as a held-to-maturity investment) issued by PBS at a cost of $40,000, which is the par value.
July 1   Receives first semiannual payment of interest from PBS bonds.
Dec. 31   Receives a check from PBS in payment of principal ($40,000) and the second semiannual payment of interest.

QS C-6
Accounting for debt investments classified as held-to-maturity

P2

Journ Co. purchased short-term investments in available-for-sale debt securities at a cost of $50,000 cash on November 25. At December 31, these securities had a fair value of $47,000. This is the first and only time the company has purchased such securities.

1. Prepare the November 25 entry to record the purchase of debt securities.
2. Prepare the December 31 year-end adjusting entry for the securities' portfolio.
3. Prepare the April 6 entry when Journ sells 10% of these securities ($5,000 cost) for $6,000 cash.

QS C-7
Accounting for available-for-sale debt securities

P3

During the current year, Reed Consulting acquired long-term available-for-sale debt securities on July 1 at a $70,000 cost. At its December 31 year-end, these securities had a fair value of $58,000. This is the first and only time the company purchased such securities.

1. Prepare the July 1 entry to record the purchase of these debt securities.
2. Prepare the year-end adjusting entry related to these securities.

QS C-8
Recording fair value adjustment for available-for-sale debt securities

P3

On December 31, Reggit Company held the following short-term investments in its portfolio of available-for-sale debt securities. Reggit had no short-term investments in its prior accounting periods. Prepare the December 31 adjusting entry to report these investments at fair value.

QS C-9
Adjusting available-for-sale debt securities to fair value

P3

Available-for-Sale Securities	Cost	Fair Value
Verrizano Corporation bonds	$89,600	$91,600
Preble Corporation notes	70,600	62,900
Lucerne Company bonds	86,500	83,100

Check Unrealized loss, $9,100

Refer to the information in QS C-9. (1) After the fair value adjustment is made, prepare the assets section of Reggit Company's December 31 classified balance sheet. (2) Is the unrealized gain (or loss) on the portfolio of available-for-sale securities reported on the income statement?

QS C-10
Reporting available-for-sale securities on financial statements **P3**

Prepare Riley Company's journal entries to record the following transactions for the current year.

Apr. 18   Purchases 300 common shares of XLT Co. as a short-term investment at a cost of $42 per share. With this stock investment, Riley has an insignificant influence over XLT.
May 30   Receives $1 per share from XLT in dividends.

QS C-11
Accounting for stock investments **P4**

QS C-12
Adjusting stock
investments to fair value
P4

Prepare Tiker Company's journal entries to record the following transactions and the adjusting entry to record the fair value of the stock investments portfolio. This is the first and only time the company purchased such securities.

May 9   Purchases 200 shares of Higo stock as a short-term investment at a cost of $30 per share. Tiker has insignificant influence over Higo.

June 2   Sells 20 shares of its investment in Higo stock ($600 cost) at $33 per share.

Dec. 31   The closing market price (fair value) of the Higo stock is $23 per share.

QS C-13
Reporting stock
investments with
insignificant influence   **P4**

On May 20, Montero Co. paid $150,000 to acquire 30 shares (4%) of ORD Corp. as a long-term investment. On August 5, Montero sold one-tenth of the ORD shares for $18,000.

1. Prepare entries to record both (*a*) the acquisition and (*b*) the sale of these shares.

2. Should this stock investment be reported at fair value or at cost on the balance sheet?

QS C-14
Financial statement
presentation of investments
C1   P1   P2   P3   P4

Indicate where each of the following items is reported on financial statements. Choose from the following categories: (*a*) current assets, (*b*) long-term investments, (*c*) current liabilities, (*d*) long-term liabilities, (*e*) other revenues and gains, (*f*) other expenses and losses, and (*g*) equity.

_____ **1.** Trading securities

_____ **2.** Unrealized gain on available-for-sale securities

_____ **3.** Held-to-maturity securities (due in 15 years)

_____ **4.** Unrealized gain on trading securities

_____ **5.** Fair value adjustment—Trading

QS C-15
Equity method transactions
P5

Rowan Co. purchases 100 common shares (40%) of JBI Corp. as a long-term investment for $500,000 cash on July 1. JBI paid $5,000 in total cash dividends on November 1 and reported net income of $100,000 for the year. Prepare Rowan's entries to record (1) the purchase of JBI shares, (2) the receipt of its share of JBI dividends, and (3) the December 31 year-end adjustment for its share of JBI net income.

QS C-16
Equity securities with
controlling influence   **C2**

Accenture purchases 55% of the voting common stock of JBL. After the purchase, Accenture has a controlling influence over JBL. (1) Which method does Accenture use to account for its investment in JBL? (2) What type of financial statements does Accenture prepare after the acquisition?

QS C-17
Return on total assets
A1

Fivio Co. reports the following information. (1) Compute return on total assets for the current year and for 1 year ago. (2) Is Fivio more efficient or less efficient in using total assets to produce income in the current year versus 1 year ago?

	A	B	C	D
1		**Current Year**	**1 Year Ago**	**2 Years Ago**
2	Total assets, December 31	$770,000	$340,000	$210,000
3	Net income	55,500	38,400	30,200

QS C-18
Component return on
total assets   **A1**

The return on total assets is the focus of analysts, creditors, and other users of financial statements.

1. How is the return on total assets computed?

2. What does this important ratio reflect?

3. Return on total assets can be separated into two important components. Write the formula to separate the return on total assets into its two basic components.

4. Explain how these components of the return on total assets are helpful to financial statement users for business decisions.

connect

EXERCISES

Exercise C-1
Debt and equity securities
and short- and long-term
investments
C1

Complete the following descriptions by filling in the blanks using the terms or phrases *a* through *g*.

a. not intended   **b.** not readily   **c.** cash   **d.** operating cycle   **e.** one year   **f.** owner   **g.** creditor

1. Debt securities reflect a(n) _____ relation such as with investments in notes and bonds.

2. Equity securities reflect a(n) _____ relation such as with investments in shares of stock.

3. Short-term investments are securities that (1) management intends to convert to cash within _____ _____ or the _____ _____, whichever is longer, and (2) are readily convertible to _____.

4. Long-term investments in securities are defined as those securities that are _____ _____ convertible to cash or arc _____ _____ to be converted into cash in the short term.

Brooks Co. purchases debt investments as trading securities at a cost of $66,000 on December 27. This is its first and only purchase of such securities. At December 31, these securities had a fair value of $72,000.

1. Prepare the December 27 entry for the purchase of debt investments.

2. Prepare the December 31 year-end fair value adjusting entry for the trading securities' portfolio.

3. Prepare the January 3 entry when Brooks sells a portion of its trading securities (costing $3,000) for $4,000 cash.

Exercise C-2
Accounting for debt investments classified as trading   **P1**

Check   (3) Gain, $1,000

Prepare Natura Co.'s journal entries to record the following transactions involving its short-term investments in held-to-maturity debt securities, all of which occurred during the current year.

a. On June 15, paid $1,000 cash to purchase Remed's 90-day short-term debt securities ($1,000 principal), dated June 15, that pay 10% interest.

b. On September 16, received a check from Remed in payment of the principal and 90 days' interest on the debt securities purchased in part *a*.

Exercise C-3
Accounting for held-to-maturity debt securities   **P2**

Prepare Krum Co.'s journal entries to record the following transactions involving its short-term investments in available-for-sale debt securities, all of which occurred during the current year.

a. On August 1, paid $50,000 cash to purchase Houtte's 9%, six-month debt securities ($50,000 principal), dated August 1.

b. On October 30, received a check from Houtte for 90 days' interest on the debt securities in part *a*.

Exercise C-4
Accounting for available-for-sale debt securities   **P3**

On December 31, Lujack Co. held the following short-term available-for-sale securities. Lujack had no short-term investments prior to the current period. Prepare the December 31 year-end adjusting entry to record the fair value adjustment for these debt securities.

Available-for-Sale Securities	Cost	Fair Value
Nintendo Co. notes	$44,450	$48,900
Atlantic bonds	49,000	47,000
Kellogg Co. notes	25,000	23,200
McDonald's Corp. bonds	46,300	44,800

Exercise C-5
Fair value adjustment to available-for-sale debt securities   **P3**

Ticker Services began operations in Year 1 and holds long-term investments in available-for-sale debt securities. The year-end cost and fair values for its portfolio of these investments follow. Prepare journal entries to record each year-end fair value adjustment for these securities.

Portfolio of Available-for-Sale Securities	Cost	Fair Value
December 31, Year 1	$13,000	$15,000
December 31, Year 2	20,000	25,000
December 31, Year 3	23,000	29,000
December 31, Year 4	16,500	19,000

Exercise C-6
Multiyear fair value adjustments to available-for-sale debt securities   **P3**

Prepare journal entries to record the following transactions involving the short-term stock investments of Duke Co., all of which occurred during the current year.

a. On March 22, purchased 1,000 shares of RPI Company stock at $10 per share. Duke's stock investment results in it having an insignificant influence over RPI.

b. On July 1, received a $1 per share cash dividend on the RPI stock purchased in part *a*.

c. On October 8, sold 50 shares of RPI stock for $15 per share.

Exercise C-7
Accounting for stock investments with insignificant influence   **P4**

Check   (c) Dr. Cash $750

On December 31, Mars Co. had the following portfolio of stock investments with insignificant influence. Mars had no stock investments in prior periods. Prepare the December 31 adjusting entry to report these investments at fair value.

Stock Investments	Cost	Fair Value
Apple stock	$ 6,000	$ 8,000
Chipotle stock	4,000	1,500
Under Armour stock	12,000	14,000

Exercise C-8
Fair value adjustment to stock investments with insignificant influence   **P4**

Exercise C-9
Reporting stock
investments on financial
statements   **P4**

Refer to the information in Exercise C-8. (1) After the fair value adjustment is made, prepare the assets section of Mars Co.'s December 31 classified balance sheet. Assume Mars plans to sell its trading securities within the next six months. (2) In which income statement section is the unrealized gain (or loss) on the portfolio of stock investments reported?

Exercise C-10
Transactions and fair value
adjustments for stock
investments with
insignificant influence
P4

Carlsville Company began operations in the current year and had no prior stock investments. The following transactions are from its short-term stock investments with insignificant influence. Prepare journal entries to record these transactions. On December 31, prepare the adjusting entry to record the fair value adjustment for the portfolio of stock investments.

July 22   Purchased 1,600 shares of Hunt Corp. at $30 per share.
Sep. 5   Received a $2 cash dividend for each share of Hunt Corp.
Sep. 27   Purchased 3,400 shares of HCA at $34 per share.
Oct. 3   Sold 1,600 shares of Hunt at $25 per share.
Oct. 30   Purchased 1,200 shares of Black & Decker at $50 per share.
Dec. 17   Received a $3 cash dividend for each share of Black & Decker.
Dec. 31   Fair value of the short-term stock investments is $180,000.

Check   Dec. 31: Dr. Fair
Value Adjustment—Stock,
$4,400

Exercise C-11
Transactions in held-to-
maturity, trading, and stock
investments
P1   P2   P4

Prepare journal entries to record the following transactions involving both the short-term and long-term investments of Cancun Corp., all of which occurred during the current year.

a. On February 15, paid $160,000 cash to purchase GMI's 90-day short-term notes at par, which are dated February 15 and pay 10% interest (classified as held-to-maturity).

b. On March 22, bought 700 shares of Fran Inc. common stock at $51 cash per share. Cancun's stock investment results in it having an insignificant influence over Fran.

c. On May 15, received a check from GMI in payment of the principal *and* 90 days' interest on the notes purchased in part *a*.

d. On July 30, paid $100,000 cash to purchase MP Inc.'s 8%, six-month notes at par, dated July 30 (classified as trading securities).

e. On September 1, received a $1 per share cash dividend on the Fran Inc. common stock purchased in part *b*.

f. On October 8, sold 30 shares of Fran Inc. common stock for $54 cash per share.

g. On October 30, received a check from MP Inc. for three months' interest on the notes purchased in part *d*.

Exercise C-12
Accounting for equity
method investments
P5

Prepare journal entries to record the following transactions and events of Kodax Company.

Year 1

Jan. 2   Purchased 30,000 shares of Grecco Co. common stock for $411,000 cash. Grecco has 90,000 shares of common stock outstanding, and its activities will be significantly influenced by Kodax.
Sep. 1   Grecco declared and paid a cash dividend of $1.50 per share.
Dec. 31   Grecco announced that net income for the year is $486,900.

Year 2

June 1   Grecco declared and paid a cash dividend of $2.10 per share.
Dec. 31   Grecco announced that net income for the year is $702,750.
Dec. 31   Kodax sold 3,000 shares of Grecco for $71,000 cash.

Exercise C-13
Classifying investments in
securities; recording fair
values
C1   P2   P3   P4   P5

The following information shows Carperk Company's individual investments in securities during its current year, along with the December 31 fair values.

a. Investment in Brava Company bonds: $420,500 cost; $457,000 fair value. Carperk intends to hold these bonds until they mature in 5 years.

b. Investment in Baybridge common stock: 29,500 shares; $362,450 cost; $391,375 fair value. Carperk owns 32% of Baybridge's voting stock and has a significant influence over Baybridge.

c. Investment in Duffa bonds: $165,500 cost; $178,000 fair value. This investment is not readily marketable and is not classified as held-to-maturity or trading.

d. Investment in Newton notes: $90,300 cost; $88,625 fair value. Newton notes are not readily market-able and are not classified as held-to-maturity or trading.

e. Investment in Farmers common stock: 16,300 shares; $100,860 cost; $111,210 fair value. This stock is marketable, and Carperk intends to sell it within the year. This stock investment results in Carperk having an insignificant influence over Farmers.

Required

1. Identify whether each investment *a* through *e* should be classified as a short-term or long-term invest-ment. For each investment, indicate in which of the six investment classifications listed in Exhibit C.2 it should be placed.

2. Prepare a journal entry dated December 31 to record the fair value adjustment for the portfolio of available-for-sale debt securities. Carperk had no available-for-sale debt securities prior to this year.

Check (2) Unrealized gain, $10,825

Selected accounts from GermX Co.'s adjusted trial balance for the year ended December 31 follow. Prepare the assets section of a classified balance sheet. *Hint:* Fair Value Adjustment—Trading *increases* trading securities; Fair Value Adjustment—Stock *decreases* stock investments.

Exercise C-14
Prepare assets section of balance sheet

C1 P1 P2 P3 P4 P5

Trading securities (at cost).................	$ 5,000	Cash	$10,000	
Short-term stock investments (at cost)	23,000	Fair value adjustment—Stock	(1,000)	
Equity method investments	70,000	Accounts receivable.......................	2,000	
Held-to-maturity securities (long-term)........	13,000	Fair value adjustment—Trading..............	500	

Wixi Co. has the following equity investments in FSN, DELL, and ATI. (1) Which of these companies are subsidiaries of Wixi? (2) How are individual assets and liabilities of a parent and its subsidiary(ies) re-ported on a balance sheet?

Exercise C-15
Equity securities with controlling influence

C2

FSN stock: Wixi owns 70% of the voting common stock and has controlling influence.

DELL stock: Wixi owns 5% of the voting common stock and has insignificant influence.

ATI stock: Wixi owns 30% of the voting common stock and has significant influence.

Use the following information of Prescrip Co. to prepare a calendar year-end statement of comprehensive income.

Exercise C-16
Preparing a statement of comprehensive income

C2

Total comprehensive income (final total)............	$ 9,400	Other comprehensive income (subtotal).....	$ (600)
Net income	10,000	Change in foreign currency translation......	1,400
Change in value of available-for-sale securities......	(2,000)		

Following are financial data for **Nike** and **Under Armour**. (1) Compute return on total assets for the current year for (*a*) Nike and (*b*) Under Armour. (2) Compute both profit margin and total asset turnover for the current year for (*a*) Nike and (*b*) Under Armour. (3) Which company more efficiently used its assets in the current year?

Exercise C-17
Return on total assets

A1

	Nike		Under Armour	
$ millions	Current Year	1 Year Prior	Current Year	1 Year Prior
Net income	$ 3,760	$ 3,273	$ 257	$ 233
Net sales..................	32,376	30,601	4,825	3,963
Total assets...............	21,396	21,597	3,644	2,866

---

connect

Kirkland Company had no trading debt securities prior to this year. It had the following transactions this year involving trading debt securities.

PROBLEM SET A

Problem C-1A
Recording and adjusting trading debt securities

P1

Aug. 2   Purchased Verizon bonds for $10,000.
Sep. 7   Purchased Apple bonds for $35,000.
        12   Purchased Mastercard bonds for $20,000.
Oct. 21   Sold some of its Verizon bonds that had cost $2,000 for $2,100 cash.
        23   Sold some of its Apple bonds that had cost $15,000 for $15,400 cash.
Nov. 1   Purchased Walmart bonds for $40,000.
Dec. 10   Sold all of its Mastercard bonds for $18,000 cash.

Required

1. Prepare journal entries to record these transactions.

2. Prepare a table to compare the year-end cost and fair values of its trading debt securities. Year-end fair values: Verizon, $8,500; Apple, $22,000; and Walmart, $39,000.

3. Prepare the adjusting entry to record the year-end fair value adjustment for the portfolio of trading debt securities.

Problem C-2A

Recording, adjusting, and reporting available-for-sale debt securities

P3

Mead Inc. began operations in Year 1. Following is a series of transactions and events involving its long-term debt investments in available-for-sale securities.

Year 1

Jan. 20	Purchased Johnson & Johnson bonds for $20,500.
Feb. 9	Purchased Sony notes for $55,440.
June 12	Purchased Mattel bonds for $40,500.
Dec. 31	Fair values for debt in the portfolio are Johnson & Johnson, $21,500; Sony, $52,500; and Mattel, $46,350.

Year 2

Apr. 15	Sold all of the Johnson & Johnson bonds for $23,500.
July 5	Sold all of the Mattel bonds for $35,850.
July 22	Purchased Sara Lee notes for $13,500.
Aug. 19	Purchased Kodak bonds for $15,300.
Dec. 31	Fair values for debt in the portfolio are Kodak, $17,325; Sara Lee, $12,000; and Sony, $60,000.

Year 3

Feb. 27	Purchased Microsoft bonds for $160,800.
June 21	Sold all of the Sony notes for $57,600.
June 30	Purchased Black & Decker bonds for $50,400.
Aug. 3	Sold all of the Sara Lee notes for $9,750.
Nov. 1	Sold all of the Kodak bonds for $20,475.
Dec. 31	Fair values for debt in the portfolio are Black & Decker, $54,600, and Microsoft, $158,600.

Required

1. Prepare journal entries to record these transactions and the year-end fair value adjustments to the portfolio of long-term available-for-sale debt securities.

2. Prepare a table that summarizes the (a) total cost, (b) total fair value adjustment, and (c) total fair value of the portfolio of long-term available-for-sale debt securities at each year-end.

3. Prepare a table that summarizes (a) the realized gains and losses and (b) the unrealized gains or losses for the portfolio of long-term available-for-sale debt securities at each year-end.

Check (2b) Fair Value Adj. bal.: 12/31/Year 1, $3,910 Dr.; 12/31/Year 2, $5,085 Dr.
(3b) Unrealized Gain at 12/31/Year 3, $2,000

Problem C-3A

Debt investments in available-for-sale securities; unrealized and realized gains and losses

P3

Stoll Co.'s long-term available-for-sale portfolio at the *start* of this year consists of the following.

Available-for-Sale Securities	Cost	Fair Value
Company A bonds	$535,300	$490,000
Company B notes	159,380	154,000
Company C bonds	662,750	640,940

Stoll enters into the following transactions involving its available-for-sale debt securities this year.

Jan. 29	Sold one-half of the Company B notes for $79,200.
July 6	Purchased Company X bonds for $126,600.
Nov. 13	Purchased Company Z notes for $267,900.
Dec. 9	Sold all of the Company A bonds for $515,000.

The fair values at December 31 are B, $81,000; C, $610,000; X, $118,000; and Z, $278,000.

Required

1. Prepare journal entries to record these transactions, including the December 31 adjusting entry to record the fair value adjustment for the long-term investments in available-for-sale securities.

2. Determine the amount Stoll reports on its December 31 balance sheet for its long-term investments in available-for-sale securities.

3. What amount of gains or losses on transactions relating to long-term investments in available-for-sale debt securities does Stoll report on its income statement for this year?

Check (1) Dec 31:
Cr. Unrealized Loss—
Equity, $22,550

Rose Company had no short-term investments prior to this year. It had the following transactions this year involving short-term stock investments with insignificant influence.

Apr.	16	Purchased 3,500 shares of Gem Co. stock at $24 per share.
July	7	Purchased 2,000 shares of PepsiCo stock at $49 per share.
	20	Purchased 1,000 shares of Xerox stock at $16 per share.
Aug.	15	Received a $1.00 per share cash dividend on the Gem Co. stock.
	28	Sold 2,000 shares of Gem Co. stock at $30 per share.
Oct.	1	Received a $2.50 per share cash dividend on the PepsiCo shares.
Dec.	15	Received a $1.00 per share cash dividend on the remaining Gem Co. shares.
	31	Received a $1.50 per share cash dividend on the PepsiCo shares.

Problem C-4A
Recording, adjusting, and reporting stock investments with insignificant influence

P4

Required

1. Prepare journal entries to record the preceding transactions and events.

2. Prepare a table to compare the year-end cost and fair values of Rose's short-term stock investments. The year-end fair values per share are Gem Co., $26; PepsiCo, $46; and Xerox, $13.

3. Prepare an adjusting entry to record the year-end fair value adjustment for the portfolio of short-term stock investments.

Check (2) Cost = $150,000

(3) Dr. Unrealized Loss—
Income, $6,000

Analysis Component

4. Explain the balance sheet presentation of the fair value adjustment for Rose's short-term investments.

5. How do these short-term stock investments affect Rose's (*a*) income statement for this year and (*b*) the equity section of its balance sheet at this year-end?

Selk Steel Co., which began operations in Year 1, had the following transactions and events in its long-term investments.

Year 1

Jan.	5	Selk purchased 60,000 shares (20% of total) of Kildaire's common stock for $1,560,000.
Oct.	23	Kildaire declared and paid a cash dividend of $3.20 per share.
Dec.	31	Kildaire's net income for the year is $1,164,000, and the fair value of its stock at December 31 is $30.00 per share.

Year 2

Oct.	15	Kildaire declared and paid a cash dividend of $2.60 per share.
Dec.	31	Kildaire's net income for the year is $1,476,000, and the fair value of its stock at December 31 is $32.00 per share.

Year 3

Jan.	2	Selk sold 3% (equal to 1,800 shares) of its investment in Kildaire for $54,200 cash.

Problem C-5A
Accounting for long-term investments in stock with significant influence

P5

Required

Prepare journal entries to record these transactions and events for Selk. Assume that Selk has a significant influence over Kildaire with its 20% share of stock.

Refer to the transactions in Problem C-5A. Assume that although Selk owns 20% of Kildaire's outstanding stock, circumstances indicate that it does *not* have a significant influence over the investee.

Required

Prepare journal entries to record the preceding transactions and events for Selk.

Problem C-6A
Accounting for long-term investments in stock without significant influence

P4

PROBLEM SET B

Problem C-1B
Recording and adjusting trading debt securities

P1

Ancore Company had no trading debt securities prior to this year. It had the following transactions this year involving trading debt securities.

July	28	Purchased Target bonds for $30,000.
Aug.	17	Purchased Kroger bonds for $105,000.
	26	Purchased Ford bonds for $60,000.
Sep.	5	Sold some of its Target bonds that had cost $6,000 for $6,300 cash.
	8	Sold some of its Kroger bonds that had cost $45,000 for $46,200 cash.
Oct.	12	Purchased Marshall bonds for $120,000.
Nov.	28	Sold all of its Ford bonds for $54,000 cash.

Required

1. Prepare journal entries to record these transactions.

2. Prepare a table to compare the year-end cost and fair values of Ancore's trading debt securities. Year-end fair values: Target, $25,500; Kroger, $66,000; and Marshall, $117,000.

3. Prepare the adjusting entry to record the year-end fair value adjustment for the portfolio of trading debt securities.

Problem C-2B
Recording, adjusting, and reporting available-for-sale debt securities

P3

Paris Inc. began operations in Year 1. Following is a series of transactions and events involving its long-term debt investments in available-for-sale securities.

Year 1

Mar.	10	Purchased Apple bonds for $30,600.
Apr.	7	Purchased Ford notes for $56,250.
Sep.	1	Purchased Polaroid bonds for $28,200.
Dec.	31	Fair values for debt in the portfolio are Apple, $33,000; Ford, $54,600; and Polaroid, $29,400.

Year 2

Apr.	26	Sold all of the Ford notes for $51,250.
June	2	Purchased Duracell bonds for $34,650.
June	14	Purchased Sears notes for $25,200.
Nov.	27	Sold all of the Polaroid bonds for $30,600.
Dec.	31	Fair values for debt in the portfolio are Apple, $31,000; Duracell, $32,400; and Sears, $27,600.

Year 3

Jan.	28	Purchased Coca-Cola bonds for $40,000.
Aug.	22	Sold all of the Apple bonds for $25,800.
Sep.	3	Purchased Motorola notes for $84,000.
Oct.	9	Sold all of the Sears notes for $28,800.
Oct.	31	Sold all of the Duracell bonds for $27,000.
Dec.	31	Fair values for debt in the portfolio are Coca-Cola, $48,000, and Motorola, $82,000.

Required

1. Prepare journal entries to record these transactions and events and any year-end fair value adjustments to the portfolio of long-term available-for-sale debt securities.

Check (2b) Fair Value Adj. bal.: 12/31/Year 1, $1,950 Dr.; 12/31/Year 2, $550 Dr.
(3b) Unrealized Gain at 12/31/Year 3, $6,000

2. Prepare a table that summarizes the (a) total cost, (b) total fair value adjustment, and (c) total fair value for the portfolio of long-term available-for-sale debt securities at each year-end.

3. Prepare a table that summarizes (a) the realized gains and losses and (b) the unrealized gains or losses for the portfolio of long-term available-for-sale debt securities at each year-end.

Problem C-3B
Debt investments in available-for-sale securities; unrealized and realized gains and losses

P3

Troy's long-term available-for-sale portfolio at the *start* of this year consists of the following.

Available-for-Sale Securities	Cost	Fair Value
Company R bonds	$559,125	$580,440
Company S notes	308,380	293,250
Company T bonds...................................	147,295	151,800

Troy enters into the following transactions involving its available-for-sale debt securities this year.

Jan. 13   Sold one-fourth of the Company S notes for $72,250.
Apr. 5   Purchased Company V bonds for $133,875.
Sep. 2   Sold all of the Company T bonds for $156,750.
Oct. 30   Purchased Company X notes for $48,750.

The fair values at December 31 are R, $568,125; S, $234,345; V, $134,940; and X, $45,625.

Required

1. Prepare journal entries to record these transactions, including any necessary December 31 adjusting entry to record the fair value adjustment of the long-term investments in available-for-sale securities.

Check   (1) Dec. 31: Cr. Fair Value Adj—AFS, $690

2. Determine the amount Troy reports on its December 31 balance sheet for its long-term investments in available-for-sale securities.

3. What amount of gains or losses on transactions relating to long-term investments in available-for-sale securities does Troy report on its income statement for this year?

Slip Systems had no short-term investments prior to this year. It had the following transactions this year involving short-term stock investments with insignificant influence.

Problem C-4B
Recording, adjusting, and reporting stock investments with insignificant influence

P4

Feb. 6   Purchased 3,400 shares of Nokia stock at $41 per share.
Apr. 7   Purchased 1,200 shares of Dell stock at $39 per share.
June 2   Purchased 2,500 shares of Merck stock at $72 per share.
      30   Received a $1.00 per share cash dividend on the Nokia shares.
Aug. 11   Sold 850 shares of Nokia stock at $46 per share.
      24   Received a $0.10 per share cash dividend on the Dell shares.
Nov. 9   Received a $1.50 per share cash dividend on the remaining Nokia shares.
Dec. 18   Received a $0.15 per share cash dividend on the Dell shares.

Required

1. Prepare journal entries to record the preceding transactions and events.

2. Prepare a table to compare the year-end cost and fair values of the short-term stock investments. The year-end fair values per share are Nokia, $40; Dell, $41; and Merck, $59.

Check   (2) Cost = $331,350

3. Prepare an adjusting entry, if necessary, to record the year-end fair value adjustment for the portfolio of short-term stock investments.

(3) Dr. Unrealized Loss—Income, $32,650

Analysis Component

4. Explain the balance sheet presentation of the fair value adjustment to Slip's short-term investments.

5. How do these short-term stock investments affect (*a*) its income statement this year and (*b*) the equity section of its balance sheet at this year-end?

Brinkley Company, which began operations in Year 1, had the following transactions and events in its long-term investments.

Problem C-5B
Accounting for long-term investments in stock with significant influence

P5

Year 1

Jan. 5   Brinkley purchased 20,000 shares (25% of total) of Bloch's common stock for $200,500.
Aug. 1   Bloch declared and paid a cash dividend of $1.05 per share.
Dec. 31   Bloch's net income for the year is $82,000, and the fair value of its stock is $11.90 per share.

Year 2

Aug. 1   Bloch declared and paid a cash dividend of $1.35 per share.
Dec. 31   Bloch's net income for the year is $78,000, and the fair value of its stock is $13.65 per share.

Year 3

Jan. 8   Brinkley sold 5% (equal to 1,000 shares) of its investment in Bloch for $12,025 cash.

Required

Prepare journal entries to record these transactions and events for Brinkley. Assume that Brinkley has a significant influence over Bloch with its 25% share.

Problem C-6B

Accounting for long-term investments in stock without significant influence

P4

Refer to the transactions in Problem C-5B. Assume that although Brinkley owns 25% of Bloch's outstanding stock, circumstances indicate that it does *not* have a significant influence over the investee.

Required

Prepare journal entries to record these transactions and events for Brinkley.

SERIAL PROBLEM

Business Solutions

P1

©Alexander Image/Shutterstock

This serial problem began in Chapter 1 and continues through most of the book. If previous chapter segments were not completed, the serial problem can begin at this point.

SP C   While reviewing the March 31, 2020, balance sheet of **Business Solutions,** Santana Rey notes that the business has built a large cash balance of $68,057. Its most recent bank money market statement shows that the funds are earning an annualized return of 0.75%. S. Rey decides to make several investments with the desire to earn a higher return on the idle cash balance. Accordingly, in April 2020, Business Solutions makes the following investments in trading securities.

Apr. 16   Purchases Johnson & Johnson bonds for $10,000.
Apr. 30   Purchases Starbucks notes for $4,400.

On June 30, 2020, the fair value of the Johnson & Johnson bonds is $12,000 and the Starbucks notes is $3,800.

Required

1. Prepare journal entries to record the April purchases of trading securities by Business Solutions.
2. On June 30, 2020, prepare the adjusting entry to record any necessary fair value adjustment to its portfolio of trading securities.

GENERAL LEDGER PROBLEM

The following **General Ledger** assignments focus on the account for investments in available-for-sale securities and equity method investments.

GL C-1   General Ledger assignment C-1 is adapted from Problem C-4A. Prepare journal entries related to short-term investments in available-for-sale securities, including the adjustment to fair value, if necessary.

GL C-2   General Ledger assignment C-2 is adapted from Problem C-3A. Prepare journal entries related to long-term investments transactions and the related realized and unrealized gains.

Accounting Analysis

COMPANY ANALYSIS

A1 **APPLE**

AA C-1   Use **Apple**'s financial statements in Appendix A to answer the following.

1. Compute Apple's return on total assets for the years ended September 30, 2017, and September 24, 2016.
2. Is the change in Apple's return on total assets from part 1 favorable or unfavorable?
3. Recently, Apple acquired 100% of Beats Electronics (Beats by Dre) for $3 billion. Will Apple account for Beats using the equity method or consolidation?

AA C-2   Key figures for **Apple** and **Google** follow.

$ millions	Apple			Google		
	Current Year	1 Year Prior	2 Years Prior	Current Year	1 Year Prior	2 Years Prior
Net income	$ 48,351	$ 45,687	$ 53,394	$ 12,662	$ 19,478	$ 16,348
Net sales	229,234	215,639	233,715	110,855	90,272	74,989
Total assets	375,319	321,686	290,345	197,295	167,497	147,461

Required

1. Compute return on total assets for Apple and Google for the two most recent years.
2. Which of these two companies has the better return on total assets for the current year?
3. Compute both profit margin and total asset turnover for Apple and Google for the most recent year.

AA C-3   Following are selected data from **Samsung, Apple,** and **Google**.

In millions	Samsung			Apple		Google	
	Current Year	One Year Prior	Two Years Prior	Current Year	Prior Year	Current Year	Prior Year
Net income	₩ 42,186,747	₩ 22,726,092	₩ 19,060,144	$ 48,351	$ 45,687	$ 12,662	$ 19,478
Net sales	239,575,376	201,866,745	200,653,482	229,234	215,639	110,855	90,272
Total assets	301,752,090	262,174,324	242,179,521	375,319	321,686	197,295	167,497

Required

1. Compute Samsung's return on total assets for the two most recent years.
2. For the current year, is Samsung's return on total assets better or worse than (*a*) Apple's and (*b*) Google's?
3. For the current year, compute Samsung's profit margin.
4. For the current year, compute Samsung's total asset turnover.

Beyond the Numbers

BTN C-1   Kasey Hartman is the controller for Wholemart Company, which has numerous long-term investments in debt securities. Wholemart's investments are mainly in five-year bonds. Hartman is preparing its year-end financial statements. In accounting for long-term debt securities, she knows that each long-term investment must be designated as a held-to-maturity or an available-for-sale security. Interest rates rose sharply this past year, causing the portfolio's fair value to substantially decline. The company does not intend to hold the bonds for the entire five years. Hartman also earns a bonus each year, which is computed as a percent of net income.

Required

1. Will Hartman's bonus depend in any way on the classification of the debt securities? Explain.
2. What criteria must Hartman use to classify the securities as held-to-maturity or available-for-sale?
3. Is there likely any company oversight of Hartman's classification of the securities? Explain.

BTN C-2   Assume that you are Jolee Company's accountant. Company owner Mary Jolee has reviewed the 2019 financial statements you prepared and questions the $6,000 loss reported on the sale of its investment in Kemper Co. common stock. Jolee acquired 50,000 shares of Kemper's common stock on December 31, 2017, at a cost of $500,000. This stock purchase represented a 40% interest in Kemper. The 2018 income statement reported that earnings from all investments were $126,000. On January 3, 2019, Jolee Company sold the Kemper stock for $575,000. Kemper did not pay any dividends during 2018 but reported a net income of $202,500 for that year. Mary Jolee believes that because the Kemper stock purchase price was $500,000 and was sold for $575,000, the 2019 income statement should report a $75,000 gain on the sale.

Required

Draft a half-page memorandum to Mary Jolee explaining why the $6,000 loss on sale of Kemper stock is correctly reported.

TAKING IT TO THE NET

P1 P2 P3 P4

BTN C-3 Access the July 28, 2016, 10-K filing (for year-end June 30, 2016) of **Microsoft** (ticker: MSFT) at **SEC.gov**. Review its note 4, "Investments."

Required

1. How does the "cost-basis" total amount for its investments as of June 30, 2016, compare to the prior year-end amount?
2. Identify at least eight types of investments held by Microsoft as of June 30, 2016.
3. What were Microsoft's unrealized gains and its unrealized losses from its investments for 2016?
4. Was the cost or fair value ("recorded basis") of the investments higher as of June 30, 2016?

TEAMWORK IN ACTION

C2 P1 P2 P3 P4

BTN C-4 Each team member is to become an expert on a specific classification of long-term investments. This expertise will be used to facilitate other teammates' understanding of the concepts and procedures relevant to the classification chosen.

1. Each team member must select an area for expertise by choosing one of the following classifications of long-term investments.
   a. Held-to-maturity debt securities
   b. Available-for-sale debt securities
   c. Equity securities with significant influence
   d. Equity securities with controlling influence
2. Learning teams are to disperse and expert teams are to be formed. Expert teams are made up of those who select the same area of expertise. The instructor will identify the location where each expert team will meet.
3. Expert teams will collaborate to develop a presentation based on the following requirements. Students must write the presentation in a format they can show to their learning teams in part 4.

   Requirements for Expert Presentation

   a. Write a transaction for the acquisition of this type of investment security. The transaction description is to include all necessary data to reflect the chosen classification.
   b. Prepare the journal entry to record the acquisition.

   [*Note:* The expert team on equity securities with controlling influence will substitute requirements (*d*) and (*e*) with a discussion of the reporting of these investments.]

   c. Identify information necessary to complete the end-of-period adjustment for this investment.
   d. Assuming that this is the only investment owned, prepare any necessary year-end entries.
   e. Present the relevant balance sheet section(s).
4. Re-form learning teams. In rotation, experts are to present to their teams the presentations they developed in part 3. Experts are to encourage and respond to questions.

ENTREPRENEURIAL DECISION

P4

BTN C-5 Assume that **Echoing Green** makes an investment in **Sustain Inc.**, a sustainability consulting firm. The company purchases 200 shares of Sustain stock for $15,000 cash plus a broker's fee of $500 cash. Sustain has 500 shares of common stock outstanding, and Echoing Green will be able to significantly influence its policies.

Required

1. Prepare the journal entry to record the investment in Sustain on January 1.
2. Sustain declares and pays a dividend of $1,000. Prepare the journal entry to record Echoing Green's receipt of its share of the dividend on July 1.
3. Sustain reports net income of $5,000. Prepare the journal entry to record Echoing Green's share of those earnings on December 31.

HITTING THE ROAD

C2

BTN C-6 Review financial news sources such as **Yahoo! Finance** (**finance.yahoo.com**) and **Google Finance** (**google.com/finance**). Identify a company that has recently purchased 50% or more of another company's outstanding shares and will report consolidated financial statements.

Required

1. Identify whether the acquired company is a supplier, customer, competitor, or unrelated company relative to the purchasing company.
2. What does the purchasing company hope to accomplish with the investment? What is its strategy?

Index

Note: page numbers followed by *n* indicate information found in footnotes. **Bold** entries indicate defined terms.

Chart of Accounts

Following is a typical chart of accounts, which is used in several assignments. Each company has its own unique set of accounts and numbering system.
*An asterisk denotes a contra account.

Assets

Current Assets

101 Cash
102 Petty cash
103 Cash equivalents
104 Short-term investments
105 Fair value adjustment–_____ (ST)
106 Accounts receivable
107 Allowance for doubtful accounts*
108 Allowance for sales discounts*
109 Interest receivable
110 Rent receivable
111 Notes receivable
112 Legal fees receivable
119 Merchandise inventory (or Inventory)
120 _____ inventory
121 Inventory returns estimated
124 Office supplies
125 Store supplies
126 _____ supplies
128 Prepaid insurance
129 Prepaid interest
131 Prepaid rent
132 Raw materials inventory
133 Work in process inventory, _____
134 Work in process inventory, _____
135 Finished goods inventory
136 Debt investments–Trading (ST)
137 Debt investments–Held-to-maturity (ST)
138 Debt investments–Available-for-sale (ST)
139 Stock investments (ST)

Long-Term Investments

141 Long-term investments
142 Fair value adjustment–_____ (LT)
144 Investment in _____
145 Bond sinking fund
146 Debt investments–Held-to-maturity (LT)
147 Debt investments–Available-for-sale (LT)
148 Stock investments (LT)
149 Equity method investments

Plant Assets

151 Automobiles
152 Accumulated depreciation–Automobiles*
153 Trucks
154 Accumulated depreciation–Trucks*
155 Boats
156 Accumulated depreciation–Boats*
157 Professional library
158 Accumulated depreciation–Professional library*
159 Law library
160 Accumulated depreciation–Law library*

161 Furniture
162 Accumulated depreciation–Furniture*
163 Office equipment
164 Accumulated depreciation–Office equipment*
165 Store equipment
166 Accumulated depreciation–Store equipment*
167 _____ equipment
168 Accumulated depreciation–_____ equipment*
169 Machinery
170 Accumulated depreciation–Machinery*
173 Building _____
174 Accumulated depreciation–Building _____*
175 Building _____
176 Accumulated depreciation–Building _____*
179 Land improvements _____
180 Accumulated depreciation–Land improvements _____*
181 Land improvements _____
182 Accumulated depreciation–Land improvements _____*
183 Land

Natural Resources

185 Mineral deposit
186 Accumulated depletion–Mineral deposit*

Intangible Assets

191 Patents
192 Leasehold
193 Franchise
194 Copyrights
195 Leasehold improvements
196 Licenses
197 Right-of-use asset
198 Accumulated amortization–_____*
199 Goodwill

Liabilities

Current Liabilities

201 Accounts payable
202 Insurance payable
203 Interest payable
204 Legal fees payable
207 Office salaries payable
208 Rent payable
209 Salaries payable
210 Wages payable
211 Accrued payroll payable
212 Factory wages payable

214 Estimated warranty liability
215 Income taxes payable
216 Common dividend payable
217 Preferred dividend payable
218 State unemployment taxes payable
219 Employee federal income taxes payable
221 Employee medical insurance payable
222 Employee retirement program payable
223 Employee union dues payable
224 Federal unemployment taxes payable
225 FICA taxes payable
226 Estimated vacation pay liability
227 Sales refund payable
229 Current portion of long-term debt

Unearned Revenues

230 Unearned consulting fees
231 Unearned legal fees
232 Unearned property management fees
233 Unearned _____ fees
234 Unearned _____ fees
235 Unearned janitorial revenue
236 Unearned _____ revenue
238 Unearned rent

Notes Payable

240 Short-term notes payable
241 Discount on short-term notes payable*
244 Current portion of long-term notes payable
245 Notes payable
251 Long-term notes payable
252 Discount on long-term notes payable*

Long-Term Liabilities

253 Lease liability
255 Bonds payable
256 Discount on bonds payable*
257 Premium on bonds payable
258 Deferred income tax liability

Equity

Owner's Equity

301 _____, Capital
302 _____, Withdrawals
303 _____, Capital
304 _____, Withdrawals
305 _____, Capital
306 _____, Withdrawals

Paid-In Capital

307 Common stock, $ _____ par value
308 Common stock, no-par value
309 Common stock, $ _____ stated value
310 Common stock dividend distributable

311 Paid-in capital in excess of par value, Common stock
312 Paid-in capital in excess of stated value, No-par common stock
313 Paid-in capital from retirement of common stock
314 Paid-in capital, Treasury stock
315 Preferred stock
316 Paid-in capital in excess of par value, Preferred stock

Retained Earnings
318 Retained earnings
319 Cash dividends (or Dividends)
320 Stock dividends

Other Equity Accounts
321 Treasury stock, Common*
322 Unrealized gain–Equity
323 Unrealized loss–Equity

Revenues
401 _____ fees earned
402 _____ fees earned
403 _____ revenues
404 Revenues
405 Commissions earned
406 Rent revenue (or Rent earned)
407 Dividends revenue (or Dividends earned)
408 Earnings from investment in _____
409 Interest revenue (or Interest earned)
410 Sinking fund earnings
413 Sales
414 Sales returns and allowances*
415 Sales discounts*
420 Earnings from equity method investments

Cost of Sales
Cost of Goods Sold
502 Cost of goods sold
505 Purchases
506 Purchases returns and allowances*
507 Purchases discounts*
508 Transportation-in

Manufacturing
520 Raw materials purchases
521 Freight-in on raw materials
530 Direct labor
540 Factory overhead
541 Indirect materials
542 Indirect labor
543 Factory insurance expired
544 Factory supervision
545 Factory supplies used
546 Factory utilities
547 Miscellaneous production costs
548 Property taxes on factory building
549 Property taxes on factory equipment
550 Rent on factory building
551 Repairs, factory equipment
552 Small tools written off
560 Depreciation of factory equipment

561 Depreciation of factory building
570 Conversion costs

Standard Cost Variances
580 Direct material quantity variance
581 Direct material price variance
582 Direct labor quantity variance
583 Direct labor price variance
584 Factory overhead volume variance
585 Factory overhead controllable variance

Expenses
Amortization, Depletion, and Depreciation
601 Amortization expense–_____
602 Amortization expense–_____
603 Depletion expense–_____
604 Depreciation expense–Boats
605 Depreciation expense–Automobiles
606 Depreciation expense–Building _____
607 Depreciation expense–Building _____
608 Depreciation expense–Land improvements _____
609 Depreciation expense–Land improvements _____
610 Depreciation expense–Law library
611 Depreciation expense–Trucks
612 Depreciation expense–_____ equipment
613 Depreciation expense–_____ equipment
614 Depreciation expense–_____
615 Depreciation expense–_____

Employee-Related Expenses
620 Office salaries expense
621 Sales salaries expense
622 Salaries expense
623 _____ wages expense
624 Employee benefits expense
625 Payroll taxes expense

Financial Expenses
630 Cash over and short
631 Discounts lost
632 Factoring fee expense
633 Interest expense

Insurance Expenses
635 Insurance expense–Delivery equipment
636 Insurance expense–Office equipment
637 Insurance expense–_____

Rental Expenses
640 Rent (or Rental) expense
641 Rent expense–Office space
642 Rent expense–Selling space
643 Press rental expense
644 Truck rental expense
645 _____ rental expense

Supplies Expenses
650 Office supplies expense
651 Store supplies expense

652 _____ supplies expense
653 _____ supplies expense

Miscellaneous Expenses
655 Advertising expense
656 Bad debts expense
657 Blueprinting expense
658 Boat expense
659 Collection expense
661 Concessions expense
662 Credit card expense
663 Delivery expense
664 Dumping expense
667 Equipment expense
668 Food and drinks expense
671 Gas and oil expense
672 General and administrative expense
673 Janitorial expense
674 Legal fees expense
676 Mileage expense
677 Miscellaneous expenses
678 Mower and tools expense
679 Operating expense
680 Organization expense
681 Permits expense
682 Postage expense
683 Property taxes expense
684 Repairs expense–_____
685 Repairs expense–_____
687 Selling expense
688 Telephone expense
689 Travel and entertainment expense
690 Utilities expense
691 Warranty expense
692 _____ expense
695 Income tax expense

Gains and Losses
701 Gain on retirement of bonds
702 Gain on sale of machinery
703 Gain on sale of investments
704 Gain on sale of trucks
705 Gain on _____
706 Foreign exchange gain or loss
801 Loss on disposal of machinery
802 Loss on exchange of equipment
803 Loss on exchange of _____
804 Loss on sale of notes
805 Loss on retirement of bonds
806 Loss on sale of investments
807 Loss on sale of machinery
808 Loss on _____
809 Unrealized gain–Income
810 Unrealized loss–Income
811 Impairment gain
812 Impairment loss
815 Gain on sale of debt investments
816 Loss on sale of debt investments
817 Gain on sale of stock investments
818 Loss on sale of stock investments

Clearing Accounts
901 Income summary
902 Manufacturing summary

BRIEF REVIEW: FINANCIAL REPORTS AND TABLES

Income Statement*
For *period* Ended *date*

Net sales (revenues)		$ #
Cost of goods sold (cost of sales)		#
Gross margin (gross profit)		#
Operating expenses		
Examples: depreciation, salaries, wages, rent, utilities,	$ #	
interest, amortization, advertising, insurance,	#	
taxes, selling, general and administrative	#	
Total operating expenses		#
Nonoperating gains and losses (unusual and/or infrequent)		#
Net income (net profit or earnings)		$ #

*A typical chart of accounts is at the end of the book and classifies all accounts by financial statement categories.

Balance Sheet
Date

ASSETS

Current assets		
Examples: cash, cash equivalents, short-term investments,	$ #	
accounts receivable, current portion of notes receivable,	#	
inventory, inventory returns estimated, prepaid expenses	#	
Total current assets		$ #
Long-term investments		
Examples: investment in stock, investment in bonds,	#	
land for expansion	#	
Total long-term investments		#
Plant assets		
Examples: equipment, machinery, buildings, land	#	
Total plant assets, net of depreciation		#
Intangible assets		
Examples: patent, trademark, copyright, license, right-of-use, goodwill	#	
Total intangible assets, net of amortization		#
Total assets		$ #

LIABILITIES AND EQUITY

Current liabilities		
Examples: accounts payable, wages payable, salaries payable,	$ #	
current notes payable, taxes payable, interest payable,	#	
unearned revenues, current portion of debt, sales refund payable	#	
Total current liabilities		$ #
Long-term liabilities		
Examples: notes payable, bonds payable, lease liability	#	
Total long-term liabilities		#
Total liabilities		#
Equity		
Common stock		#
Paid-in capital in excess of par (or stated value)		#
Retained earnings		#
Less treasury stock		(#)
Total equity		#
Total liabilities and equity		$ #

Statement of Cash Flows
For *period* Ended *date*

Cash flows from operating activities		
[Prepared using the indirect (see below)† or direct method]		
Net cash provided (used) by operating activities		$ #
Cash flows from investing activities		
[List of individual investing inflows and outflows]		
Net cash provided (used) by investing activities		#
Cash flows from financing activities		
[List of individual financing inflows and outflows]		
Net cash provided (used) by financing activities		#
Net increase (decrease) in cash		$ #
Cash (and equivalents) balance at beginning of period		#
Cash (and equivalents) balance at end of period		$ #

Attach separate schedule or note disclosure of "Noncash investing and financing transactions."

†Indirect Method: Cash Flows from Operating Activities

Cash flows from operating activities		
Net income		$ #
Adjustments for operating items not providing or using cash		
+Noncash expenses and losses	$ #	
Examples: Expenses for depreciation, depletion, and amortization; losses from disposal of long-term assets and from retirement of debt		
−Noncash revenues and gains	#	
Examples: Gains from disposal of long-term assets and from retirement of debt		
Adjustments for changes in current assets and current liabilities		
+Decrease in noncash current operating asset	#	
−Increase in noncash current operating asset	#	
+Increase in current operating liability	#	
−Decrease in current operating liability	#	
Net cash provided (used) by operating activities		$ #

Statement of Retained Earnings
For *period* Ended *date*

Retained earnings, beginning	$ #
Add: Net income	#
	#
Less: Dividends declared	#
Net loss (if exists)	#
Retained earnings, ending	$ #

Statement of Stockholders' Equity†
For *period* Ended *date*

	Common Stock	Capital in Excess of Par	Retained Earnings	Treasury Stock	Total
Balances, beginning	$ #	$ #	$ #	$ #	$ #
Net income	⋮	⋮	⋮	⋮	⋮
Cash dividends					
Stock issuance					
Treasury stock purchase					
Treasury stock reissuance					
Other					
Balances, ending	$ #	$ #	$ #	$ #	$ #

† Additional columns and account titles commonly include number of shares, preferred stock, unrealized gains and losses on available-for-sale securities, foreign currency translation, and comprehensive income.

Premium Bond Amortization (Straight-Line) Table*

Semiannual Period-End	Unamortized Bond Premium†	Bond Carrying Value‡
Bond life-start	$ #	$ #
....	⋮	⋮
....		
Bond life-end	0	par

*Bond carrying value is adjusted downward to par and its amortized premium downward to zero over the bond life (note: carrying value less unamortized bond premium equals par).
†Equals total bond premium less its accumulated amortization.
‡Equals bond par value plus its unamortized bond premium.

Discount Bond Amortization (Straight-Line) Table*

Semiannual Period-End	Unamortized Bond Discount†	Bond Carrying Value‡
Bond life-start	$ #	$ #
....	⋮	⋮
....		
Bond life-end	0	par

*Bond carrying value is adjusted upward to par and its amortized discount downward to zero over the bond life (note: unamortized bond discount plus carrying value equals par).
†Equals total bond discount less its accumulated amortization.
‡Equals bond par value less its unamortized bond discount.

Effective Interest Amortization Table for Bonds with Semiannual Interest Payment

Semiannual Interest Period-End	Cash Interest Paid[A]	Bond Interest Expense[B]	Discount or Premium Amortization[C]	Unamortized Discount or Premium[D]	Carrying Value[E]
#	#	#	#	#	#
⋮	⋮	⋮	⋮	⋮	⋮

[A]Par value multiplied by the semiannual contract rate.
[B]Prior period's carrying value multiplied by the semiannual market rate.
[C]The difference between interest paid and bond interest expense.
[D]Prior period's unamortized discount or premium less the current period's discount or premium amortization.
[E]Par value less unamortized discount or plus unamortized premium.

Installment Notes Payment Table

Period Ending Date	Beginning Balance	Payments: *Debit* Interest Expense	+	Payments: *Debit* Notes Payable	=	Payments: *Credit* Cash	Ending Balance
#	#	#		#		#	#
⋮	⋮	⋮		⋮		⋮	⋮

Bank Reconciliation
Date

Bank statement balance	$#	Book balance	$#
Add: Deposits in transit	#	Add: Interest earned & unrecorded cash receipts	#
Bank errors understating the balance	#	Book errors understating the balance	#
	#		#
Less: Outstanding checks	#	Less: Bank fees & NSF checks	#
Bank errors overstating the balance	#	Book errors overstating the balance	#
Adjusted bank balance	$#	**Adjusted book balance**	$#

Balances are equal (reconciled)

FUNDAMENTALS

① Accounting Equation

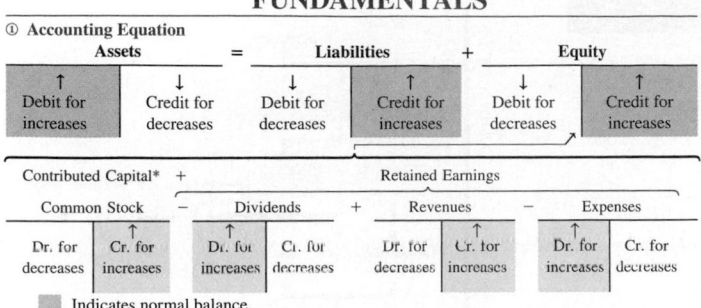

| Assets | = | Liabilities | + | Equity |

| ↑ Debit for increases | ↓ Credit for decreases | ↓ Debit for decreases | ↑ Credit for increases | ↓ Debit for decreases | ↑ Credit for increases |

Contributed Capital* + ⎴⎴ Retained Earnings ⎴⎴

Common Stock — Dividends + Revenues — Expenses

| Dr. for decreases | Cr. for increases | Dr. for increases | Cr. for decreases | Dr. for decreases | Cr. for increases | Dr. for increases | Cr. for decreases |

☐ Indicates normal balance.
*Includes common stock and any preferred stock.

② Accounting Cycle

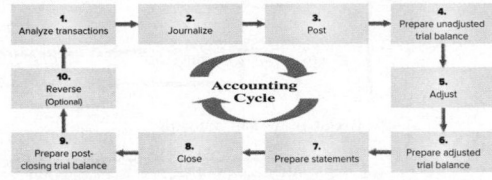

1. Analyze transactions
2. Journalize
3. Post
4. Prepare unadjusted trial balance
5. Adjust
6. Prepare adjusted trial balance
7. Prepare statements
8. Close
9. Prepare post-closing trial balance
10. Reverse (Optional)

Accounting Cycle

③ Adjustments and Entries

Type	Adjusting Entry	
Prepaid Expenses	Dr. Expense	Cr. Asset*
Unearned Revenues	Dr. Liability	Cr. Revenue
Accrued Expenses	Dr. Expense	Cr. Liability
Accrued Revenues	Dr. Asset	Cr. Revenue

*For depreciation, credit Accumulated Depreciation (contra asset).

④ Four-Step Closing Process
1. Transfer revenue and gain account balances to Income Summary.
2. Transfer expense and loss account balances to Income Summary.
3. Transfer Income Summary balance to Retained Earnings.
4. Transfer Dividends balance to Retained Earnings.

⑤ Accounting Concepts

Characteristics	Assumptions	Principles	Constraints
Relevance	Business entity	Measurement	Cost-benefit
Faithful representation	Going concern	Revenue recognition	*Materiality*
	Monetary unit	Expense recognition	*Industry practice*
	Time period	Full disclosure	*Conservatism*

⑥ Ownership of Inventory

Shipping Terms	Ownership Transfers at	Goods in Transit Owned by	Transportation Costs Paid by
FOB shipping point	Shipping point	Buyer	**Buyer** Merchandise Inventory... # Cash............ #
FOB destination	Destination	Seller	**Seller** Delivery Expense........ # Cash............ #

⑦ Inventory Costing Methods
- Specific identification (SI)
- First-in, first-out (FIFO)
- Weighted-average (WA)
- Last-in, first-out (LIFO)

⑧ Depreciation and Depletion

Straight-line:
$$\frac{\text{Cost} - \text{Salvage value}}{\text{Useful life in periods}}$$

Units-of-production:
$$\frac{\text{Cost} - \text{Salvage value}}{\text{Useful life in units}} \times \text{Units produced in current period}$$

Declining-balance: Rate* × Beginning-of-period book value
*Rate is often double the straight-line rate, or 2 × (1/Useful life)

Depletion:
$$\frac{\text{Cost} - \text{Salvage value}}{\text{Total capacity in units}} \times \text{Units extracted in current period}$$

⑨ Interest Computation
Interest = Principal (face) × Rate × Time

⑩ Accounting for Investment Securities

Classification	Investments Account Reported at
Short-Term Investment in Securities	
Debt Investments—Held-to-Maturity	Cost (without any discount or premium amortization)
Debt Investments—Trading	Fair value (with fair value adjustment to income)
Debt Investments—Available-for-Sale	Fair value (with fair value adjustment to equity)
Stock Investments—insignificant influence	Fair value (with fair value adjustment to income)
Long-Term Investment in Securities	
Debt Investments—Held-to-Maturity	Cost (with any discount or premium amortization)
Debt Investments—Available-for-Sale	Fair value (with fair value adjustment to equity)
Stock Investments—insignificant influence	Fair value (with fair value adjustment to income)
Equity Method Investments—significant influence	Equity method (no fair value adjustment)
Consolidated Investments—controlling influence	Consolidation method (no fair value adjustment)

ANALYSES

① Liquidity and Efficiency

Current ratio $= \dfrac{\text{Current assets}}{\text{Current liabilities}}$ pp. 108 & 506

Working capital = Current assets − Current liabilities   p. 506

Acid-test ratio $= \dfrac{\text{Cash} + \text{Short-term investments} + \text{Current receivables}}{\text{Current liabilities}}$ pp. 159 & 507

Accounts receivable turnover $= \dfrac{\text{Net sales}}{\text{Average accounts receivable, net}}$ pp. 285 & 507

Inventory turnover $= \dfrac{\text{Cost of goods sold}}{\text{Average inventory}}$ pp. 203 & 507

Days' sales uncollected $= \dfrac{\text{Accounts receivable, net}}{\text{Net sales}} \times 365*$ pp. 250 & 508

Days' sales in inventory $= \dfrac{\text{Ending inventory}}{\text{Cost of goods sold}} \times 365*$ pp. 203 & 508

Days' payable outstanding (or Days' sales in payables) $= \dfrac{\text{Accounts payable}}{\text{Cost of goods sold}} \times 365*$

Cash conversion cycle $= \dfrac{\text{Days' sales}}{\text{uncollected}} + \dfrac{\text{Days' sales}}{\text{in inventory}} - \dfrac{\text{Days' payable}}{\text{outstanding}}$

Total asset turnover $= \dfrac{\text{Net sales}}{\text{Average total assets}}$ pp. 320 & 508

Plant asset useful life $= \dfrac{\text{Plant asset cost}}{\text{Depreciation expense}}$

Plant asset age $= \dfrac{\text{Accumulated depreciation}}{\text{Depreciation expense}}$

*360 days is also commonly used.

② Solvency

Debt ratio $= \dfrac{\text{Total liabilities}}{\text{Total assets}}$ Equity ratio $= \dfrac{\text{Total equity}}{\text{Total assets}}$ p. 62

Debt-to-equity $= \dfrac{\text{Total liabilities}}{\text{Total equity}}$ pp. 392 & 509

Times interest earned $= \dfrac{\text{Income before interest expense and income taxes}}{\text{Interest expense}}$ pp. 354 & 509

③ Profitability

Profit margin ratio $= \dfrac{\text{Net income}}{\text{Net sales}}$ pp. 108 & 509

Gross margin ratio $= \dfrac{\text{Net sales} - \text{Cost of goods sold}}{\text{Net sales}}$ p. 159

Return on total assets $= \dfrac{\text{Net income}}{\text{Average total assets}}$ pp. 18 & 509

$= \text{Profit margin ratio} \times \text{Total asset turnover}$ p. C-13

Return on common stockholders' equity $= \dfrac{\text{Net income} - \text{Preferred dividends}}{\text{Average common stockholders' equity}}$ p. 510

Book value per common share $= \dfrac{\text{Stockholders' equity applicable to common shares}}{\text{Number of common shares outstanding}}$ p. 433

Basic earnings per share $= \dfrac{\text{Net income} - \text{Preferred dividends}}{\text{Weighted-average common shares outstanding}}$ p. 432

Cash flow on total assets $= \dfrac{\text{Cash flow from operations}}{\text{Average total assets}}$ p. 467

Payout ratio $= \dfrac{\text{Cash dividends declared on common stock}}{\text{Net income}}$ p. 433

④ Market

Price-earnings ratio $= \dfrac{\text{Market price per share}}{\text{Earnings per share}}$ pp. 432 & 510

Dividend yield $= \dfrac{\text{Annual cash dividends per share}}{\text{Market price per share}}$ pp. 433 & 510

Residual income = Net income − Target net income

BRIEF REVIEW: SELECTED TRANSACTIONS AND RELATIONS

① Merchandising Transactions Summary—Perpetual Inventory System

	Merchandising Transactions	Merchandising Entries	Dr.	Cr.
Purchases	Purchasing merchandise for resale.	Merchandise Inventory	#	
		Cash or Accounts Payable		#
	Paying freight costs on purchases; FOB shipping point.	Merchandise Inventory	#	
		Cash		#
	Paying within discount period.	Accounts Payable	#	
		Merchandise Inventory.		#
		Cash		#
	Paying outside discount period.	Accounts Payable	#	
		Cash		#
	Recording purchases returns or allowances.	Cash or Accounts Payable.	#	
		Merchandise Inventory		#
Sales	Selling merchandise.	Cash or Accounts Receivable	#	
		Sales		#
		Cost of Goods Sold	#	
		Merchandise Inventory.		#
	Receiving payment within discount period.	Cash	#	
		Sales Discounts	#	
		Accounts Receivable		#
	Receiving payment outside discount period.	Cash	#	
		Accounts Receivable		#
	Receiving sales returns of nondefective inventory.	Sales Returns and Allowances	#	
		Cash or Accounts Receivable		#
		Merchandise Inventory	#	
		Cost of Goods Sold		#
	Recognizing sales allowances.	Sales Returns and Allowances	#	
		Cash or Accounts Receivable		#
	Paying freight costs on sales; FOB destination.	Delivery Expense	#	
		Cash		#

	Merchandising Events	Adjusting and Closing Entries	Dr.	Cr.
Adjusting	Adjustment for shrinkage (occurs when recorded amount larger than physical inventory).	Cost of Goods Sold	#	
		Merchandise Inventory.		#
	Period-end adjustment for expected sales discounts.*	Sales Discounts	#	
		Allowance for Sales Discounts.		#
	Period-end adjustment for expected returns—both revenue side and cost side.*	Sales Returns and Allowances	#	
		Sales Refund Payable.		#
		Inventory Returns Estimated.	#	
		Cost of Goods Sold.		#
Closing	Closing temporary accounts with credit balances.	Sales	#	
		Income Summary		#
	Closing temporary accounts with debit balances.	Income Summary	#	
		Sales Returns and Allowances.		#
		Sales Discounts		#
		Cost of Goods Sold		#
		Delivery Expense		#
		"Other Expenses"		#

*Period-end adjustments depend on unadjusted balances, which can reverse the debit and credit in the adjusting entries shown; the entries in gray are covered in Appendix 4B.

⑥ Stock Transactions Summary

	Stock Transactions	Stock Entries	Dr.	Cr.
Issue Common Stock	Issue par value common stock at par (par stock recorded at par).	Cash.	#	
		Common Stock.		#
	Issue par value common stock at premium (par stock recorded at par).	Cash.	#	
		Common Stock.		#
		Paid-In Capital in Excess of Par Value, Common Stock		#
	Issue no-par value common stock (no-par stock recorded at amount received).	Cash.	#	
		Common Stock.		#
	Issue stated value common stock at stated value (stated stock recorded at stated value).	Cash.	#	
		Common Stock		#
	Issue stated value common stock at premium (stated stock recorded at stated value).	Cash.	#	
		Common Stock		#
		Paid-In Capital in Excess of Stated Value, Common Stock		#
Issue Preferred Stock	Issue par value preferred stock at par (par stock recorded at par).	Cash.	#	
		Preferred Stock		#
	Issue par value preferred stock at premium (par stock recorded at par).	Cash.	#	
		Preferred Stock		#
		Paid-In Capital in Excess of Par Value, Preferred Stock		#
Reacquire Common Stock	Reacquire its own common stock (treasury stock recorded at cost).	Treasury Stock, Common	#	
		Cash		#
Reissue Common Stock	Reissue its treasury stock at cost (treasury stock removed at cost).	Cash.	#	
		Treasury Stock, Common		#
	Reissue its treasury stock above cost (treasury stock removed at cost).	Cash.	#	
		Treasury Stock, Common		#
		Paid-In Capital, Treasury		#
	Reissue its treasury stock below cost (treasury stock removed at cost; if paid-in capital is insufficient to cover amount below cost, retained earnings is debited for remainder).	Cash.	#	
		Paid-In Capital, Treasury.	#	
		Retained Earnings (if necessary)	#	
		Treasury Stock, Common		#

② Merchandising Cash Flows

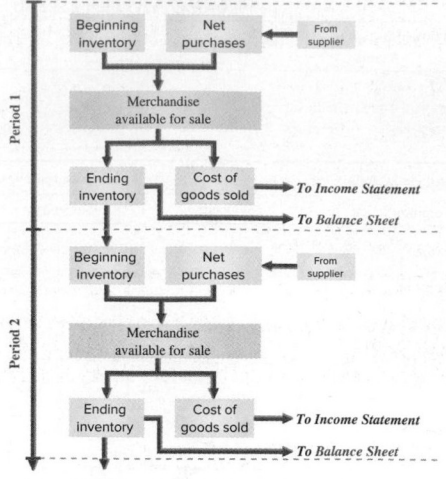

③ Credit Terms and Amounts

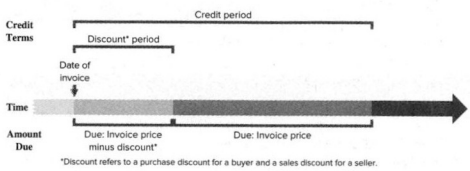

*Discount refers to a purchase discount for a buyer and a sales discount for a seller.

④ Bad Debts Estimation

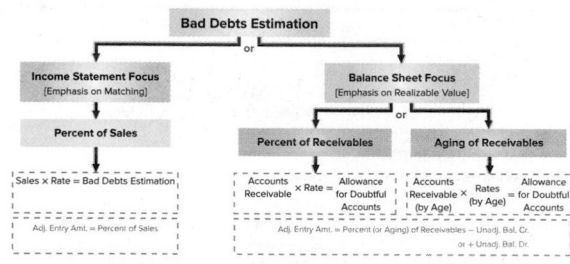

⑤ Bond Valuation

Bond Sets	Market Sets	Bond Price Determined
Contract rate	Market rate	Contract rate > Market rate → Bond sells at premium
		Contract rate = Market rate → Bond sells at par
		Contract rate < Market rate → Bond sells at discount

⑦ Financial Statement Effects of Dividends and Splits

	Cash Dividend	Small Stock Dividend	Large Stock Dividend	Stock Split
Total assets	**Decrease**	No change	No change	No change
Total liabilities	No change	No change	No change	No change
Total stockholders' equity	**Decrease**	No change	No change	No change
Common stock	No change	Increase	Increase	No change
Paid-in capital in excess of par	No change	Increase	No change	No change
Retained earnings	**Decrease**	Decrease	Decrease	No change

⑧ A Rose by Any Other Name

The same financial statement sometimes receives different titles. Following are some of the more common aliases.*

Balance Sheet	Statement of Financial Position
	Statement of Financial Condition
Income Statement	Statement of Income
	Operating Statement
	Statement of Operations
	Statement of Operating Activity
	Earnings Statement
	Statement of Earnings
	Profit and Loss (P&L) Statement
Statement of Cash Flows	Statement of Cash Flow
	Cash Flows Statement
	Statement of Changes in Cash Position
	Statement of Changes in Financial Position
Statement of Stockholders' Equity	Statement of Shareholders' Equity
	Statement of Changes in Shareholders' Equity
	Statement of Stockholders' Equity and Comprehensive Income
	Statement of Changes in Owner's Equity
	Statement of Changes in Owner's Capital
	Statement of Changes in Capital Accounts

*The term **Consolidated** often precedes or follows these statement titles to reflect the combination of different entities, such as a parent company and its subsidiaries.